THE
BOOMER
BIBLE

THE
BOOMER
BIBLE

BY R.F. LAIRD

WORKMAN PUBLISHING
NEW YORK

Laird, Robert.
    The boomer bible / Robert Laird.
        p.   cm.
    ISBN 1-56305-075-7 (pbk.)
    1. Baby boom generation—Humor.   2. Bible—Humor.
3. Christian life—Humor.   I. Title.
PN6231.B22L35   1991
818'.5407—dc20   91-50385
                                                           CIP

Workman Publishing
708 Broadway
New York, New York 10003

Manufactured in the United States of America

First Printing September 1991

10   9   8   7   6   5   4   3   2   1

THE NAMES AND ORDER OF ALL THE BOOKS OF THE PAST AND PRESENT TESTAMENTS

The Books of the Past Testament

The Books of the Present Testament

The Book of Harrier Brayer
The Harrier Hymnal

THE NAMES AND ORDER
OF ALL THE
BOOKS OF THE PUNK TESTAMENT

FIRST PREFACE

For a dedicated scholar of American literature, there can be no more difficult task than that of introducing an obviously inferior piece of writing to the reading public. When the situation is further complicated by the fact that the content and tone of the proffered work seem premeditatedly designed to offend almost every ethnic, religious, and gender constituency in the population at large, one is hard-put to know quite how and where to begin. Nevertheless, extraordinary circumstances have resulted in publication of the contemptible document that presumes to call itself the Boomer Bible, and it would be unforgivable to release it to an unwary public without some explanation. It has therefore fallen to me to write this preface, which I undertake with a sense of commingled trepidation and outrage that are unique in my literary experience.

I have determined to begin my unwelcome task with the strongest possible warning to those readers whose sensitivities are less impervious to injury than stainless steel. Make no mistake: it is well nigh impossible to think of a racist (or otherwise ethnocentrist), religious, or sexist slur that is not enshrined in what passes for the scriptural language of the Boomer Bible. Nor is this the only offensive element of this work. For it would seem that the author(s) of the Boomer Bible were resolved from the start to libel everything they touched, with special malice reserved for all subjects pertaining to the twentieth century. Indeed, it is quite literally impossible for any contemporary reader to work his/her way through this assemblage of bile without encountering multiple instances of insults that seem deliberately calculated to offend his/her race, his/her religion, his/her profession, his/her taste in literature and art and music, and/or his/her preferred lifestyle.

The very fact that such a warning is needed leads inevitably to the question of what purpose is served by publishing the Boomer Bible at all. The answer to this question is not an easy one to summarize in simple terms, however, because it relates to the circumstances under which the Boomer Bible was purportedly written, as well as the circumstances surrounding its "discovery." We shall discuss both of these in turn, beginning with an explanation of what is presently known about the work.

In all probability, the manuscript that gave rise to this volume is almost exactly ten years old. The original date of publication is given in the epistle dedicatory as April 19, 1981, and thus far at least, no compelling reason for disputing this date has been uncovered. Scientific analysis of the paper and ink also seems to confirm that the manuscript is at least eight to ten years old. That said, however, there is little else about the Boomer Bible that is not suspect in one way or another, including the identity or identities of its author(s), the means by which it was allegedly written, and even the authenticity of the manuscript that has given rise to this volume.

Those who claim to know the truth about this work have declared it the product of a renegade literary community that was entirely contained in Philadelphia, Pennsylvania, between the years 1979 and 1985. And to be sure, there is a certain amount of evidence to support this contention. It is known, for example, that the historic but economically depressed South Street section of Philadelphia *may have* served as the base of operations for a particularly virulent offshoot from the punk music fad of the late 1970s and early 1980s. Further, there exists some documentation indicating that these alleged South Street punks considered themselves writers and carried out a form of vanity publishing to disseminate various works of "punk fiction" among themselves during the years in question. And perhaps most strikingly, fragmentary records of this so-called punk writing movement do repeatedly refer to a Boomer Bible written by the collected efforts of the entire South Street community.

Given this basic context, it is hardly surprising that amateur literati would regard any manuscript bearing this title as, ipso facto, the work of South Street's punk writers. Unfortunately for those who would ascribe authorship of the Boomer Bible to this community, however, punk records make so many extravagant claims as to shed doubt on everything they contain. For example, a variety of punk documents acknowledge that the overwhelming majority of the South Street community (which, in their hubris, they renamed "Punk City") could barely read and write in the early months of 1980. This deficit was supposedly overcome through what is described as an "orgy of learning" led by a punk king named St. Nuke, who ruled his subjects with an almost unbelievably primitive legal code. Called the NukeLaw, the code featured such barbaric anachronisms as duels to settle civil disputes, trial by combat, public whippings, banishment, and even sentences of death, although these were allegedly reserved for outsiders.

Spokespersons for the Philadelphia Police Department deny out of hand any possibility that such a deviant separate society existed, or ever could have existed, within the city limits of Philadelphia, and such declarations are convincingly confirmed by police files, which contain no record of punk arrests inside "Punk City" for the full four-year period in which they supposedly held sway on South Street. Although there is record of a gang war on South Street during the winter of 1979–80, there is no evidence whatever that punks were involved. Roland Belasco, an acknowledged expert on Philadelphia gangs, scoffs at the idea that South Street's punk rockers could have waged a war against any gang in the area: "Not even an army of punks could stand up to a Philly gang for more than about ten minutes," he declared in a recent interview, laughing out loud at the thought. "The gangs I know would make a punk 'king' eat his crown and then cut his throat while he was choking on it."

As if all this were not sufficient to cast doubt on the veracity of their self-history, punk records make the further claim that their writing activities were carried out with the aid of powerful computers that enabled four or five members of a "punk writer band" to write together on hand-held input instruments. The central computer that received this input was allegedly powerful enough to correct and collate their work into coherent pieces of writing, and during the effort to write the Boomer Bible, one computer is reported to have corrected, collated, and edited the work of two thousand writers into a finished work that punk proponents believe to be reduplicated in this book.

On the face of it, all of this is absurd. Despite its grievous flaws, the manuscript that appears in this book could not have been written by semiliterate children, no matter how many computers they had. There is no official record (outside of the delusionary self-histories referenced above) that such a community ever existed in the first place. There is no official confirmation that punk "stars" mentioned in the Boomer Bible manuscript—including St. Nuke, Alice Hate, and Johnny Dodge—ever lived in Philadelphia or anywhere else. Indeed, the only possible connection between Punk City and official records concerns the band known as the Shuteye Train, although the discrepancies between police files and punk documents simply could not be any greater than they are on this point.

For example, the punks claim that the Shuteye Train consisted of four individuals named Loco Dantes, Reedy Weeks, Pig Millions, and Joe Kay. These four were said to be quite literally immortal: they were believed to represent "the invincible heart of Punk City," although even punk documents concede that they never lived on South Street and visited only rarely.

Police files depict the Shuteye Train in wholly different terms: as a syndicate consisting of four loosely connected criminal organizations that heisted huge quantities of both drugs and cash from drug dealers throughout the Middle Atlantic states. Over a five-year period in the early 1980s, numerous arrests were made of alleged Shuteye Train functionaries, although no confessions of such tie-ins were ever upheld in court. Ultimately, according to anonymous but reputable police sources, federal drug enforcement organizations designed a sting operation that apparently put the Shuteye Train organization out of business for good in 1984.

And where does all this leave us? There is, to put it simply, no proof of any kind that a community of "punk writers" occupied South Street in the sense, or on the scale, we are asked to believe. Consequently, the mere mention of a "Boomer Bible" in otherwise suspect records cannot be accepted as evidence that punks wrote the manuscript reproduced in this book.

Thus we are presented with a distasteful piece of bad writing that has no confirmed historical existence. *And* it is being published. Why?

I can only speak for my own involvement in this affair. It is true that an esteemed colleague (who understandably prefers not to have his name used in connection with this project) recently asked me to review a small trove of documents and artifacts that were found buried in the general vicinity of South Street. It is true that such of these documents as have been safely restored from the considerable weather damage they sustained suggest that a "punk writing movement" was documented, regardless of whether or not it ever existed in reality. Further, it is true that I have examined individual "punk" documents as they have been restored in order to determine whether or not they contained anything of literary value or interest.

To date, I must declare that nothing of literary value or interest has been evident in the materials submitted to my attention. If there is a Boomer Bible manuscript in the trove, I have not yet seen it or heard of it. Moreover, I am not yet satisfied in any respect that the whole business, including this book and the trove itself, is not simply some clever fraud that is being perpetrated by practical jokers of immense arrogance.

As I understand it, the manuscript that is supposed to be the Boomer Bible was mysteriously conveyed by parties unknown to a free-lance tabloid journalist whose greatest previous claim to fame was a book predicting a UFO invasion of the planet Earth. This "journalist" now asserts that some deliberate effort is being made by the "academic-intellectual establishment" to suppress all knowledge of South Street's punk writers, due (if I understand properly) to some attribute of the Boomer Bible manuscript that people like myself are deemed to consider threatening in some way.

Despite this rather odd sponsorship, Workman Publishing has decided to proceed with publication of the so-called Boomer Bible manuscript. As it has been explained to me, Workman takes no position on the authenticity of the manuscript and is publishing the work because the "idea" of a defunct, phantom literary movement is "intriguing." While I cannot share this viewpoint, I have agreed to write this preface so that the reading public may hear firsthand that there is no conspiracy to suppress so-called punk writings. The text here included should lay to bed all suspicion that any writing of value is being withheld—deliberately or otherwise—from the American audience.

I will also state that if and when a new literary movement *does* emerge in American literature, I am quite confident that it will come from some source other than a tribe of uneducated street children who duel with sharpened screwdrivers and write bibles on subjects of which they are profoundly ignorant.

Still, in consenting to write this preface, I have also bowed to the publisher's request that I provide the reading public with some basis for an informed response to this work. My own recommendation is *no* response.

As to the work itself, it has no merit of any kind: it is an imitation of a farce of a parody.

The book consists of a Past Testament, a Present Testament, a Book of Harrier Brayer [*sic*], and a Punk Testament. All three "testaments" are written in a meandering chapter-and-verse format that is hard to dignify with any such term as style.

The Past Testament purports to cover the entire history of the world, from the creation through c.1964, although the near total absence of dates, as well as numerous chronological inconsistencies, require that this be characterized as an educated guess. The Past Testament also contains a number of books that appear to be an incompetent attempt to mimic the Old Testament books of wisdom and the books of the prophets. Most notable in the Past Testament are its nine books of the "Chosen Nations," which may well be the most pointlessly venomous pastiches of modern history yet recorded in any form.

The Present Testament represents an inexplicably perverse plagiarism of the New Testament of the Bible, complete with four gospels of a substitute messiah named Harry, who is clearly an outright fiction devised by the author(s). The Present Testament also includes its own epistles, written to various neighborhoods and institutions in Philadelphia, for the purpose of instructing its targets in the ways of the Present Testament's demented, drug-dealing messiah. Overall, it is difficult to find any part of the Present Testament that merits serious critical analysis or comment, for the simple reason that it never rises, even momentarily, above the level of invective, name calling, and race/class/gender prejudice that represent the only unifying feature of the Boomer Bible. As for the attached Book of Harrier Brayer, I found it altogether unreadable and can offer no elucidating comments of any kind.

The Punk Testament is clearly intended as some kind of vindication for the excesses of the prior testaments, but it does far more to reveal the benighted lives and ways of the legendary (real or fictional) "punks" than it does to explain the purpose of the book as a whole. For example, two of the twelve books in this testament amount to nothing more than lists of alleged combats in Punk City, including blow-by-blow descriptions of numerous contests in arms. The testament concludes with five books of pathetic doggerel intended to define the philosophy (for want of a better term) of the author(s).

Finally, there is a running intercolumn reference which makes connections, in astonishingly tedious quantity, between verse fragments throughout the three testaments. Personally, I found this aspect of the book unusable and utterly pointless; I can only assume that its inclusion was intended to enhance the scriptural appearance of the text by providing a visual distraction from the incompetent versification and meager vocabulary that deface every page of the work.

I expect that the publisher will be disappointed in this preface, but I cannot in good conscience endorse a book of such dubious origins, particularly in the absence of any redeeming qualities in the writing or content. If the trove materials eventually disclose a Boomer Bible manuscript and evidence that the punk writer community did in fact exist, I will be only too happy at that time to revisit my current historical characterizations and amend them in light of new information. But if the trove yields another copy of this same work, I must forewarn one and all that the only retraction I will feel obliged to make concerns my remarks about its authenticity. And mere authenticity cannot bestow quality where none existed before.

—Eliot Naughton
Cambridge, MA
March 1991

SECOND PREFACE

The package was wrapped in old burlap and smelled of rotten hay. It was tied up with four knotted-together railroad bandannas that disintegrated under my fingertips when I tried to loosen them. The fabric that had been crumpled inside the faded brown knots still glowed red, like artificially preserved flowers. And inside the burlap bag was the object I had spent almost three years looking for—not one, but two manuscripts of the fabled Boomer Bible. At times over the many months of my search, I had almost given up hope of ever finding it, and even when I held it in my hands I almost couldn't believe that it really did exist.

That day, I promised myself that I would see it published, even if I never made a nickel out of it, because here was proof that the punks of Punk City had done what the stories said they had. It was all true. A bunch of born losers had tried to write it *all* down the way they saw it and heard it from the Baby Boomers.

Before I go any further, I should tell you that I'm not pretending to be any kind of a hero. I'm a free-lance journalist by trade, and when you're on your own you have to find your own stories. Sometimes you scoop everybody, sometimes you get taken in: I'd be the first to tell you I'm not proud of the UFO paperback, and I wish I could *un*publish it for the sake of my credibility about this work. But I can't undo what's been done, and so you'll just have to believe me or not. But Eliot Naughton should learn the same lesson: he can't *un*write the Boomer Bible by wishing it away, and he'd do everyone a favor if he'd quit trying to deny its existence.

The truth is, I'd heard about it for years, little snatches of conversation, hints from people who might or might not know, that kind of thing. I've always hung out in the wrong kinds of bars, all the way from the Combat Zone in Boston to the Sunset Strip in L.A., and if you frequented places like that you'd find there are still punks out there, jangling their heavy metal jewelry, painting their identities on with stage makeup, and pretending as much as they can that the bus never left town without them a dozen years ago. I happened to be in one of those bars on a rainy night in 1987. The city was Cleveland, and the hour was late, and, yes, I had been drinking. A sixteen-year-old girl with braces on her teeth and earrings made of razor blades told me that if I was really a journalist, I should buy her a beer because she knew a story worth a million dollars. I bought her the beer because I'm a sucker for wild stories—not because I believed her—but she proceeded to tell me things she couldn't have made up. Most tantalizing about her account was the sensation it gave me that she was repeating exact words memorized from some other source. I still have the dictaphone tape I made that night, and her nasal singsong twang still gives me chills when I hear it speak, muffled and slurred under the clatter of beer mugs:

> . . . was February and snow had fallen throughout the evening, a light white coverlet softening the sounds and edges of the street. The tire tracks of the bikes, the footsteps of the punks were etched in the whiteness with the clarity of pure terror, and the silencing snow so muffled the voice of the Duke's challenger that I wondered for a moment if I had imagined it. But as everyone looked one to another, searching for the source of the voice, four masked men dressed in black stepped out of the [indecipherable] doorway and crossed the street through the snow, silent as wraiths . . . "Downcount the seconds, Hammerhead," the voice said. "You don't 'a many left . . ." The Duke roared and swung his weapon above his head . . . "Who're you?" he demanded of [indecipherable] . . . "The last voice you'll 'ear," came the reply. With that, the Duke bellowed and ran toward his opponent, twirling the hammer about his great round head so quickly that it glittered like a halo. When he fell upon the punks' new [indecipherable], though, he was as cold and efficient as ever, looking for openings and avoiding mistakes. For perhaps a minute, they both bobbed and weaved like prizefighters, feinting and waiting for some instant of advantage. Then the Duke struck, a short terrible blow directed straight down upon the head of his shorter opponent, and a gasp rose from the punks as if squeezed from them by the force of the hammerstroke . . .

I don't know how long she could have continued like this, but I blew it. I interrupted her to ask a question, because I was gripped by an eerie conviction that I had heard the story before, or dreamed it, or . . . who knows? I had to hear where she got it, where it came from.

"It's talked about in the Boomer Bible too," she told me, as if that explained everything.

"What's that?" I asked her.

"It's a book the ka punks wrote," she said. "They wrote everything down, the way they heard it from the Boomers, and the way they lived it on South Street." Without pause, she slipped back into her singsong cadence, someone else's words: "Then they shredded the pages and gave them to the winds of the Delaware with the body of the dead king. And when the words come together again, the ka punks will return to tell their story. But as long as the queen sleeps, a thousand silent voices will churn above us in the air, windblown, restless, like smoke from the Shuteye Train . . ." She broke off, saw her beer mug sitting on the table, and drained it. Then she looked at me as if I had been the last to speak.

I tried to restart her on the story she'd been telling me about the Duke, but she shook her head and said, "It's not there now. Sometimes it is, sometimes it isn't. It's not from the Bible anyway. It's the ka song of the Greatwing Gypsy, beloved of the queen."

I bought her more beers, which was a dicey thing because she wouldn't talk without beer, and she couldn't handle it, either. I managed to glean from her that the "ka punks" had lived in Philadelphia for a time and then had gone away. The very last I got from her is still on the tape, a slurred reel of names unwinding as she fell asleep:

KinesisApesNamesGodsLiesGypsiesMesopamamiansGreeks1Greeks2Barbs
ChristiansBubitesGiantsSplorersSpicsFrogsBritsKrautsYanksBeaks . . .

I made sure that her friends would drive her home and then I left the bar and Cleveland. When I returned to the same bar some months later to speak with her again, no one remembered her. But that's the way it's been ever since she first started me on my search. Many times I gave it up. I told myself there were no "ka punks," there was no Boomer Bible, but as soon as I had resigned myself to failure, something else would happen to rekindle my interest.

For example, I had just given up for the second or third time when a sweaty bookkeeper drinking late in some Holiday Inn bar outside Chicago called me a "dirty Boomer" and when I asked what he meant by that exactly, he replied, "You twelve. One dash four."

"The Boomer Bible," I said out loud.

"You think it doesn't exist, don't you?" he asked, echoing my last conscious thoughts on the subject. "Well, you're full of shit. They wrote it down. Just the way they heard it. *Some*body had to."

We talked until the bar closed. He looked too young to be a Boomer, and after his initial outburst he was reluctant to say more, but I kept after him until he eased slowly into his story. Back in 1981, he had been enrolled in a small business college in Philadelphia. In the single most courageous act of his life, he had visited South Street in response to an ad on his dormitory bulletin board. The ad offered free drinks all night to anyone who would consent to be interviewed about topics of "general knowledge." The interviews would take place in a South Street punk bar called the Razor Café.

He got drunker as he told it, which seemed to be a pattern with the ones who thought they knew, a kind of drowning sadness that might be the cause of their delusions or the reason they possessed their few frail straws of "information." It was impossible to tell. But he had been sad then too, the way he told it, and although he was afraid to go to Punk City, he went in the hope that something remarkable would happen. He described a city within a city, an armed camp where every face was covered with mask or makeup, and every belt held weapons. He was "interviewed" by three punks who asked their questions from a list and painfully wrote down his answers in a crabbed shorthand. They prodded him to tell them what he knew about history, books, movies, religion, science, his upbringing, his views about life. They were polite, utterly distant, and persistently clumsy with paper and pencil. But once, a fight broke out at a nearby table, and he was terrified by the speed at which blades flashed into view under the blue barroom light.

"Then *she* came in," my bookkeeper said, and I recognized the look in his big damp eyes. It was adoration. "She's dead now," he added in a whisper. "You won't believe me. No one ever does. But there are women . . . well, have you ever just known the first time you saw one that you'd do *anything* . . . ?

I just looked at him. I hadn't, and he saw that I hadn't. He gulped more of his drink and went on. "She came to my table. She leaned over me. She had eye makeup on one eye. Just one eye. She was wearing a leather thing . . . below . . . and she didn't have any . . . top." Then he added hurriedly, "But it wasn't just that. She looked at me. Women never look at me. She said that what I was doing was a big help. 'We're writing it all down,' she said. 'It's time.'"

He looked at me miserably. "When she left, I stared after her until I could breathe again. So did the punks. They all looked like I felt, just . . . sick with wanting her. They said her name was Alice Hate. I never saw her again. I would have died for her. I never thought I'd be willing to die for anyone . . ."

Then he leaned close to me, buddies in a bar. "They say," he whispered, "that the punks will come back someday. Alice Hate too."

We stared at each other. Gently, I asked, "Who's *they*?"

He stared at me uncomprehendingly, "It's a crock of shit," he barked suddenly. "She's dead. I can feel it in here." He tapped his breast pocket. "I've got to go," he said, getting to his feet.

"One last thing," I asked. "That quote. How did you get it? Have you ever seen the Boomer Bible?"

And then the bastard smiled at me, a Cheshire-cat-I-know-something-you-don't-know grin that pissed me off almost as much as my discovery that he'd left me with the tab.

And that's the way it went. Of course I went to Philadelphia, and everybody everywhere said they'd never heard of the punks of South Street. But how can you tell in a big city? Maybe everybody you talk to just got there yesterday. Maybe there are things they don't want you to know. The police were no help, but cops never like talking about things they can't control and don't understand. I checked the newspapers, all four years worth, and I found one mention of punks in connection with a prominent writer from New York, but he wouldn't return my calls or letters. I got his address and went there to see him, but no one answered the doorbell. It was on my way out of the city, though, that I went to the men's room at Grand Central Station in New York and found something interesting. Underneath a string of four-letter-word graffiti, I saw a neat red inscription: "Rules.11.1-4."

When I checked the Cleveland girl's dictaphone tape, I almost missed it, but the second time through I heard it:

MallitesMainlinersBroadStreetersRationalizationsBandsBoutsDoubtsRules
BeliefsAngels . . .

I stayed in New York for a full week, looking (I admit it) in dirty men's rooms all over the city for more quotes. It was at the Port Authority bus terminal that I found the next one. Under a scratched-in couplet that read "Fix your stroke, Do coke," someone had written in a wild red hand: "Angels.8.2." By then, I had transcribed the names of the books from the tape, and I felt vaguely stunned. Was I creating my own mystery, my own chain of misunderstood coincidences? Or was it really possible that an unpublished book was floating around in the damaged minds of sad people? I left the Port Authority still musing over my puzzle, and it was only some minutes later that I remembered the need for caution. The streets were dimly lighted and I started feeling nervous, as if I was being followed. I heard a very slight jingle, like keys in a pocket. Then I heard footsteps, chuckles, more footsteps. I was being stalked. Trying to remain casual, I turned the first corner I came to and walked into a blind alley. When I whirled in panic the entrance was blocked. There were three of them, kids with knives. They were smiling. I saw the open jean jacket of the leader, a washboard stomach with crossed slash scars on his white skin. And it's a funny thing, but the thought that popped into my head just then was that I wasn't ever going to see the Boomer Bible, as if that were somehow more important than my fear of death.

It seemed like an hour went by. I just stood there. I felt my knees trying to buckle. Why didn't they just rush me and get it over with? I wanted to offer them my wallet but I couldn't speak. I opened my mouth to address the leader, but just as the first sound came from my dry throat, his eyes suddenly filled with fear and he backed off a step, as if he'd been struck in the face. And then all three of them turned and ran like hell. A surge of exhilaration galvanized my vocal cords. I wanted to yell after the retreating muggers, and I heard myself shouting, "Angels! Chapter eight! Verse two, you [expletive deleted] sons of bitches!"

And I still didn't know if I really heard it, but I would swear on any Bible *you* believe in that a voice behind my back whispered, "Rules eleven. One dash four."

I was so petrified by this that I could not turn around. I stood there for five full minutes, a potbellied statue in an alley, until I remembered that there might be other muggers out there, too. I never did look back as I walked out of that alley.

It was three weeks later that the package arrived at my home in San Francisco, addressed to me in block print letters. At six in the morning I heard a loud knock at my apartment door, and when I opened it, the burlap bundle was just sitting there waiting. There was no return address and no postmark. As soon as I saw what it contained, I called building security. It's supposed to be impossible for anyone to get past the lobby door without being buzzed through, and everyone who enters the lobby is photographed by security cameras. But the guard on duty said no one had been in or out on his shift, which started at four A.M. I mention these matters only because I did make an effort to determine how the package was delivered, including canvassing my neighbors to find out if they'd heard or seen anything unusual, but I must report that it remains a mystery, no matter how many suspicions that raises.

The manuscripts were in poor to fair condition. The one on top was in much the better repair, which was fortunate because it contained the intercolumn reference reproduced in this volume. It was legible throughout, although there were many water stains, and some small animal had chewed a chunk out of the upper right-hand corner, which just missed damaging the text all the way from Kinesis through Psongs. It appeared to be a computer printout: the serrations left by tractor feed strips were still evident despite the weather damage.

The other manuscript was in truly tragic condition. It had been hand-written on high-quality parchment, with full and quite elaborate illumination. But now it was a ruin. Many of the pages were merely fragments, between 50 and 80 percent destroyed, as if by rot. This manuscript also lacked the intercolumn reference, and its inclusion in the package suggested to me that it was a genuine historic artifact, perhaps one of the original copies employed by the punk community in its own public rites and ceremonies. Sadly, though, it could no longer be read as a text of the Boomer Bible. I set it aside for safekeeping, where it remains to this day, along with other documentation of my search that cannot yet be disclosed without danger to certain living individuals.

The computer-printed manuscript was in no danger of being further damaged by reading, and so I sat down at once to work my way through it. I had read about a dozen pages when the phone rang. A male voice at the other end spoke to me in a tone of breathless excitement.

"You have it, don't you?"

By now I was past being surprised. "Yes," I told the caller.

"You don't have to read it consecutively," he continued. "You can, but it's not necessary to start that way. And you may want to ignore the intercolumn reference the first time you read any passage. You can go back to that later."

"Have you read it?" I asked.

He chuckled. "No. I can't wait." Then he turned grave. "You *have* to get it published as soon as possible. They've already found the trove, and they're trying to suppress it. You're the only one who can keep them from getting away with it."

He dodged all the rest of my questions but the last one: "Are *you* a punk?"

He laughed out loud. "No," he told me. "But I'm ready to start any time."

It was a pattern that was to recur over a period of a week or more. I read and I fielded phone calls from a staggering variety of callers, representing all ages, both sexes, and dozens of different ethnic and national origins. They always knew that I had the Boomer Bible, and they always had a reading tip they wanted to pass on. An old lady told me in a solemn whisper that it was okay to laugh—which I had already figured out for myself. A young man with a strong Hispanic accent begged me not to ignore the intercolumn reference. A retired priest suggested I pay close attention to the readings specified in the Table of Harrier Days. Not one of them had actually read or even seen the Boomer Bible. None would tell me how they had learned of it in the first place—or how they'd known to call me.

When I'd finished my first reading, I knew that it had to be published. Some sizable but invisible group of people were waiting for it, and they were counting on me not to let them down. What were they waiting for? The Boomer Bible was by no means the answer to all questions. It was repetitive, inconsistent, often inaccurate, mercurial and capricious in its viewpoints, frequently nasty, loaded with imprecise lowest-common-denominator language, and sometimes outright offensive—even to me.

And yet it excited me. The punks who had written it (and I no longer doubted the punk origins of the work) believed that the very largest philosophical questions ever conceived were *everybody's* business, and they were unafraid to jeer at the ivory tower intellects they thought had answered those questions wrong. The book made *me* feel important and powerful, and that was a unique feeling for somebody who had lived on the tattered edges of self-respect since adolescence. I also understood why a lot of people would oppose publication of the book on any grounds. It laughs too hard at things nobody is supposed to laugh at, which is the worst crime possible in a society that has lost its sense of humor about everything important.

I inquired about the discovery of the "trove" mentioned by my first caller. Initially, everyone I talked to in Philadelphia denied there was such a thing. When I finally found the man in charge of the excavation, he informed me that it would take years to sort things out, and the publication of the findings was years away, if it ever occurred at all. I asked specifically whether a Boomer Bible had been found. There was a pause—too long a pause, in my opinion—and then the academic on the other end of the line said, "I haven't seen anything like that. Now, if you'll excuse me, I have to go."

He asked me no questions. He had no mysteries to solve? No information deficits to fill in? He knew everything he needed to know already? Of course. He was a scholar. It was his job to make up a truth that fit his universe, whether the facts he had fit his universe or not. My next call was to a publisher.

The result of my actions appears as you see here. Contrary to Professor Naughton's devilishly clever deconstruction of the facts, the bulk of the evidence suggests that punk writers wrote the Boomer Bible. And while there remain many unanswered questions about who they were, where they came from, and where they went, they have left a record of an inquiry that no one else seems interested in making: Where and how do we learn to believe again in the future, with hope and faith in the meaning of our own existence? For this unforgivable sin, they are deemed "deviant," and their work is adjudged "contemptible." Maybe that will be your opinion too after you've read the Boomer Bible. That is your right. But *I* at least believe you should have the chance to make up your own mind about that, provided you can look past Eliot Naughton's preemptive and scornful bias. The things we don't dare talk about or write about or think about are the things that will do us in. The punks seem to have known that instinctively. But then, as Eliot Naughton has pointed out, they had the advantage of starting their quest as semiliterates, which probably saved their minds from the proper Harvard education Eliot seems to regard as a necessary writing credential.

In closing, I will state that I have received no compensation for the Boomer Bible manuscript. I will also admit to knowing more than I have said, which you should know to expect from the author of a UFO invasion book. Dismiss me all you like. Believe Eliot Naughton all you like. But read the Boomer Bible. It was written for you, and it is yours to do with as you will. I have done what was asked of me. Yanks.153.14

—Frank Frelinger
San Francisco, CA
April 1991

THE

BOOMER
BIBLE

Containing the Past, Present, and
Punk Testaments, And the Orders
of the Book of Harrier Brayer:
diligently assembled under the
leadership and guidance of the
King of Punk City.

A NOTE ON THE BOOMER BIBLE INTERCOLUMN REFERENCE

Superscripts within the text refer the reader to the Intercolumn Reference, where corresponding citations are identified by book, chapter, and verse(s). (For example, the citation *Kin.1.1-4* indicates the Book of Kinesis, Chapter 1, Verses 1 through 4.) When no book title appears in the first citation listed for a given superscript, the reference is to a verse within the same book. When a book title is omitted in the second (or nth) citation listed, the reference is to the book identified in the immediately preceding citation.

The following tips, though probably unnecessary for most readers, are provided for the sake of clarity: 1) when a superscript appears at the beginning of a verse, the associated citation(s) normally applies to the entire verse; 2) when a superscript appears within a verse, the associated citation normally applies to the word or phrase immediately following the superscript; 3) when a superscript appears at the end of a verse, the associated citation is normally best understood as a continuation of the verse; 4) when more than one citation is referenced to a single superscript in text, the citations should be looked up in the order in which they appear.

Finally, it should be noted that the Boomer Bible Intercolumn Reference represents *one* set of relationships between verses. Many others are possible. Readers are encouraged to add to the Boomer Bible by inserting (or substituting) their own chapter-and-verse citations.

The book title abbreviations used in the Boomer Bible Intercolumn Reference are as follows:

Abbr.	Book	Abbr.	Book	Abbr.	Book
Adam.	Adam	Forg.	Forgers	Penn.	Pennsylvanians
Al.	Al	F&J	Frankie & Johnny	Pnot.	Pnotes
Ang.	Angels	Frog.	Frogs	Psay.	Psayings
Ann.	Annenburghers	Gnt.	Giants	Psom.	Psomethings
Apes.	Apes	Gods.	Gods	Psong.	Psongs
Bds.	Bands	Grk.	Greeks	Psp.	Pspeciastes
Barb.	Barbarians	Gyp.	Gypsies	Rat.	Rationalizat'ns
Bks.	Beaks	Hall.	Hallites	Rom.	Romans
Bel.	Beliefs	Hill.	Hillites	Rul.	Rules
Boul.	Boulevardiers	Ira.	Ira	Russ.	Russkies
Bout.	Bouts	Jefs.	Jeffersonians	Spic.	Spics
Brit.	Brits	Jeff.	Jeffrey	Swar.	Swarthmorons
Brd.	Broad Streeters	Kens.	Kensingtonians	They.	They
Bub.	Bubonites	Kin.	Kinesis	Us.	Us
Carl.	Carl	Krt.	Krauts	Vin.	Vinnie
Cen.	Centralians	Lies.	Lies	War.	War
Chnk.	Chinks	Main.	Mainliners	Way.	Ways
Chr.	Christians	Mall.	Mallites	Weap.	Weapons
Chuk.	Chuck	Mawr.	Mawrites	Wht.	Wharts
Dav.	David	Mes.	Mesopotamians	Wil.	Willie
Dbt.	Doubts	Name.	Names	Ynk.	Yanks
Drex.	Drexelites	Ned.	Ned	You.	You
Ed.	Ed	Nip.	Nips	Zig.	Ziggie
Ext.	Exploits	Oth.	Others		
Exp.	Explorers	Paul.	Paul		

TO THE MOST EXALTED AND DREADLY PUNK

DOCTOR DREAM

❦

BY THE WILL OF ST. NUKE, KING OF PUNK CITY, IN THE REALM OF PHILADELPHIA, DEFENDER OF KNOWLEDGE AND GUARDIAN OF VALOR

The Assemblers of the Boomer Bible seek Truth, Hope, and Justice through the Intermediation of the RAPTOR our Father

We, the Punks of Punk City, do hereby dedicate to you, our ultimate voice, this testimony of our pitiless anger against the population of the Most Chosen Nation in the History of the World. We so dedicate this work in the manner of a petition for your advent, and an invocation for your wrath. The number of petitioners is in excess of two thousands of us, which are represented by signatories identifying the most august and fierce of our kingdom, located on and about the environs of South Street, in the City of Brotherly Love.

We do not protest our right to receive you in your full power and eloquence; rather we invite your presence humbly, having demonstrated in such small ways as have been shown to us our willingness to exchange our lives for Ardor, and to devote our energies to Learning, notwithstanding the darkness of the Ignorance, Despair, and Indignity from which we came to embark upon this work. Further, we have sworn ourselves, and the strength of all our arms and instruments, to the rediscovery of the Light that had been so malignantly concealed from our blindered eyes. If there be some particle of value in this our shared monument, we do beseech you, on bended knee, to hear this petition, and so redeem our lives.

—April 19, 1981

THE PAST TESTAMENT

THE FIRST BOOK OF APES, CALLED

KINESIS

CHAPTER 1

^a**A**t the beginning there was nothing but a big ^bball of gases.

2 For a long time it just sat there in the ^cnothingness, getting hotter and hotter.

3 ^dThen it ^eexploded.

4 ^fThe explosion created the stars, which were burning bubbles of the first big ball of gases.

5 The ^gstars threw out chunks of debris that cooled and became planets.

6 The planets spun ^hround and became round.

CHAPTER 2

In a remote and insignificant sector of the ⁱuniverse, one ^jplanet fell into an orbit around its star that ^kby accident made its surface conducive to the molecular formations known as ^lamino acids.

2 Neither so close to their ^mplanet's star as to be incinerated, nor so far from it as to be frozen, the acids survived,

3 ⁿAnd proceeded to combine into new molecules of a complexity advanced enough to permit change and growth,

4 And ^omeiosis, and the development of certain other transient characteristics of a generic nature classifiable as ^plife.

CHAPTER 3

Changing and growing and reproducing in response to

a. Vin.1.1-25
b. Ed.28.6
*   Chuk.2.3-4*
c. Hall.6.10
d. Lies.6.11
e. Al.2.11
f. Wil.19.1
g. Psay.5U.4
h. Exp.9.13
*   Chuk.7.3*
i. Psay.5U.1-2
j. Ed.60.15
k. Wil.19.4
l. Chuk.10.4-10
m. Vin.3.1-2
n. Wil.16.19-20
o. Ed.60.17
p. Carl.3.8
q. Drex.6.4
r. Chuk.11.2-6
s. Chuk.11.8-10
t. Wil.19.5
u. Chuk.11.7
*   Mawr.22.22*
v. Chuk.19.14
w. Ned.6.24
x. Chuk.12.1-7
y. Grk.6.23
z. Hall.6.9
aa. Psom.24.3-
*   4*
bb. Wil.12.14

the ^qrandom stimuli of the planet's chemistry, ^rlife thrived and multiplied,

2 ^sAnd spread from the hospitable environment of liquid oxygenated hydrogen where it began to the more challenging environment of the planet's solid mineral masses.

3 ^tThe new environment stimulated further molecular changes that enabled living organisms to increase dramatically in size and complexity.

4 ^uThe organisms grew bigger and bigger,

5 ^vAnd then much much bigger,

6 And even bigger than that, until some of the many life-forms on the planet's surface were so enormous as to be ^wdinosaurs.

CHAPTER 4

^x**T**he dinosaurs were gigantic scaly beasts with infinitely ^ysmall brains and infinitely large appetites, both for plants and for each other.

2 ^zCreated by numerous accidents of evolution, the dinosaurs managed to become extinct, not by accident, but by their own stupidity.

3 ^{aa}The dinosaurs ate all of the plants in their environment and soon starved stupidly to death.

4 ^{bb}When the dinosaurs became extinct, other smaller life-forms became dominant on the planet's surface.

CHAPTER 5

^a**T**hese other smaller life forms were mammals, which had hairy bodies, warm blood, and small brains that were nevertheless larger than the brains of the dinosaurs.

2 ^bOver a long period of time after the dinosaurs became extinct, the hairy bodies of the mammals grew bigger and bigger, until there were many large animals on the planet's surface.

3 And some of these were very big indeed and something like elephants, and some of them were something like cattle, and some of them were something like ^cpigs,

4 And others of them were still quite small and something like ^drats and ^ecats and ^fdogs.

5 ^gAnd a lot of them were a lot like monkeys.

CHAPTER 6

^h**A**nd the ones that were like monkeys had brains that were quite large.

2 ⁱAnd some of these grew quite big and lost their tails, so that they were no longer monkeys, but apes.

3 And the apes thrived and ^jmultiplied, surviving even unto the present age.

4 And with the coming of the apes, the period of time that was the beginning of the earth ended.

a. Wil.17.1
b. 3.4
c. Bks.6.24
d. Ext.48.19
e. Psay.5A.12
f. Psay.5A.13
g. Rom.10.4
h. Chuk.14.1-4
i. Chuk.14.5-6
j. Yks.144.11-12
Zig.17.7

THE SECOND BOOK OF APES, CALLED

APES

CHAPTER 1

^a**W**hen he had come upon the earth, the ^bape was naked and afraid. For comfort he picked up a ^cstick, chewed the end to a point, and ^dstuck it in a nearby living thing^e.

2 When the living thing died, transfixed by the stick, the ape ate of its flesh and soon conceived a great hunger for the death of ^fother living things.

3 ^gThereupon the ape made many pointed sticks and stuck them into great multitudes of ^hother living things, including, on occasion, ⁱother apes.

CHAPTER 2

^j**F**or seven times seven generations of their race, the apes stuck pointed sticks into seven times seven generations of other living things.

2 And there were ^kseven times seven kinds of apes, and of this number there were brown apes, and black apes,

3 And green apes, and red apes, and white apes, and yellow apes.

4 And there were small apes, and tall apes, and wide apes, and narrow apes, and thin apes, and fat apes,

5 ^lAnd swift apes, and slow

a. Psay.5Y.29
b. Dav.30.40
c. Dav.17.13
d. Dav.17.15-16
e. Psom.78.10
f. Psay.5Z.2
g. Al.4.7-11
h. Ann.18.12
i. Hill.A.4
j. Psay.5L.7
k. Psay.4.2
l. Dav.17.4

apes, and strong apes, and weak apes, and clever apes, and dull apes.

6 [a]And of this number, all were killer apes.

CHAPTER 3

And when seven times seven generations had passed, the land fell barren and living things of all kinds died in great numbers from thirst and hunger and from pointed sticks.

2 And as the living things grew scarce in number, [b]the apes became afraid.

3 For if all other kinds of living things died, there would be nothing left to kill,

4 [c]Except the other apes, all of whom were killer apes, well armed with pointed sticks.

5 [d]And so it happened that the apes banded together, like to like, to keep the other apes from killing them.

6 [e]Brown apes joined together with brown apes, black apes with black apes,

7 [f]Green apes with green apes, red apes with red apes, white apes with white apes, yellow apes with yellow apes,

8 [g]And small apes with small apes, tall apes with tall apes, wide apes with wide apes, narrow apes with narrow apes,

9 [h]And thin apes with thin apes, fat apes with fat apes, swift apes

a. Dav.47.6
b. Al.5.3
c. 2.6
d. Psay.5A.40
e. 2.2
f. 2.3
g. 2.4
h. Psom.27.2
i. Psom.27.3
j. Jeff.5.7
k. Krt.9.15
l. Psom.73.13
m. Main.16.10
n. Main.16.11
o. Dav.47.11 &47.22
p. Chuk.15.1-6
q. Wil.20.1-4

with swift apes, slow apes with slow apes,

10 [i]And strong apes with strong apes, weak apes with weak apes, clever apes with clever apes, and dull apes with dull apes.

CHAPTER 4

[j]Thereupon bands of apes turned upon other bands of apes and transfixed one other with many thousands of pointed sticks.

2 [k]And brown apes killed black apes, even unto extinction.

3 [l]Red apes slew green apes, leaving none alive,

4 [m]And likewise white apes slew yellow apes, and tall apes slew small apes,

5 [n]And wide apes slew narrow apes, and thin apes slew fat apes,

6 [o]And slow apes slew swift apes, and weak apes slew strong apes,

7 [p]And clever apes slew all the dull apes, and then the strong apes, and the swift apes, and the thin apes, and the wide apes, and the tall apes, and the white apes, and the red apes, and the brown apes,

8 [q]Until the clever apes were all alone on the earth, with the exception of the other living things and many, many trees that could be turned into pointed sticks.

THE THIRD BOOK OF APES, CALLED

NAMES

CHAPTER 1

[a] **S**hortly after the clever apes had killed all the other kinds of apes, they grew restless and irritable,

2 [b]Because the killing of the other apes had been enjoyable,

3 [c]And now there were no other kinds of apes to kill,

4 Or be killed by,

5 [d]Which took much of the fun out of life.

CHAPTER 2

And so it happened that the [e]clever apes began to split apart into smaller bands,

2 [f]Which moved away from one another, sometimes as far as the next [g]valley,

3 [h]But always close enough so that they could attack one another with pointed sticks.

4 But it also happened that the new bands of apes became [i]confused,

5 [j]Because it was not so easy as before to tell one kind of ape from another kind of ape,

6 [k]All apes now being of one kind, the clever kind.

CHAPTER 3

But being clever, some of the apes conceived a [l]great idea, and gave each other names, so that one could recognize another by his name,

2 [m]And thus know to refrain from transfixing the wrong apes with a pointed stick.

a. Apes.4.7
b. Adam.6.7
c. Psay.5Q.24
d. Psay.5Q.23
e. Chuk.15.7-8
f. Chuk.15.9-16
g. Chuk.16.1-3
h. Psay.5Q.56
i. Chr.10.5-6
j. Psom.27.1 & 22.4
k. Apes.2.6 Psom.75.10
l. Psay.5Q.32
m. Krt.9.15
n. Psay.5Q.60
o. Lies.2.8-9
p. Grk.4.11 Jefs.7.15 Adam.2.12-16
q. Bks.6.24-27
r. Hall.6.9
s. Wil.17.1
t. Psp.2.1-2
u. 4.10
v. Jefs.7.15
w. Apes.2.2-5 Psay.5A.19
x. Ann.18.11
y. Brit.2.8
z. Wil.19.4

3 [n]And so these apes named themselves with seven times seven hundreds of names,

4 [o]And there were apes named [p]Adam and Eve,

5 [q]And Abel and Cain, and Sara and Hagar, and Isaac and Ishmael,

6 [r]And David and Goliath, and Samson and Delilah, and Moses and Herod, and Abraham and Joshua,

7 [s]And Ruth, and Job, and Seth, and Jacob and Esau, and Joseph, and Rachel, and Leah,

8 [t]And Samuel, and Daniel, and Hosea, and Amos, and Andy, and Isaiah, and Ezekiel, and [u]Emmanuel, and many more besides.

CHAPTER 4

When they had done naming one another, the apes were very pleased,

2 And proud of what they done,

3 Believing it to be pretty special to have so many names,

4 [v]And such an easy way of telling one ape from another ape,

5 [w]Which had never happened before in the living memory of the apes.

6 And so it happened that the apes with names decided that they were no longer apes,

7 [x]But better than apes,

8 [y]And worthy of a name unto themselves,

9 Which they selected by [z]lottery, asking every ape to draw

one sharpened stick from a huge pile of sharpened sticks,

10 [a]And the short stick fell to an ape named [b]Manny,

11 [c]Who promptly renamed the race of apes after himself,

12 So that the apes from that [d]point forward were no longer apes, but Men,

13 [e]And belonged to the race of Man,

14 [f]Which immediately invented names for all of its bands, now called tribes,

15 [g]And the tribes then withdrew to their homes to begin sharpening sticks for the new age.

a. *Wil.19.5*
b. *Ed.27.5*
c. *Ext.52.16*
d. *Vin.49.5*
e. *Wil.19.14*
f. *Pnot.24.5*
g. *Psom.78.1-13*

THE FOURTH BOOK OF APES, CALLED

GODS

OTHERWISE KNOWN AS THE FIRST BOOK OF LIES

CHAPTER 1

[a]When the apes called Men joined together into tribes, the practice of killing became more efficient, and the consumption of slain animals less wasteful.

2 Accordingly, the tribe had more time and more opportunity to invent *things*, of which the apes had grown exceedingly fond.

3 [b]All apes worked on inventing *things*, each according to his kind.

4 Those who were the smartest invented [c]fire, which made it possible to stay up later at night, inventing more *things*.

5 [d]Those who were the best killers invented new ways of killing and new weapons, including knives, and spears, and arrows, and then bows, so that arrows might kill at a greater distance.

6 Those who were the most timid invented [e]agriculture,

a. *Name.4.14*
b. *Adam.6.4*
c. *Psay.5Q.43*
d. *Swar.10.16*
e. *Rat.9.26*
f. *Ned.29.24*
g. *Psom.73.13*
h. *Jeff.5.7*
i. *1.4*
j. *1.5*
k. *1.6*

which provided food more safely than before.

7 Those who were the most skilled with their hands invented pots, and clothes, and many kinds of tools[f].

8 [g]Those who were the most imaginative invented words, and ideas, in order that words might serve some purpose.

9 [h]And all the apes were unsatisfied with this state of affairs.

CHAPTER 2

The [i]smart ones were unsatisfied because the killers still got the best food, even though it was fire that made food taste better.

2 The [j]killers were unsatisfied because the invention of agriculture required them to kill less often.

3 The [k]timid were unsatisfied because they too longed to kill other living things, as safely as possible, and had no opportunity to do so.

4 ^aThe skilled ones were unsatisfied for the same reason.

5 ^bThe imaginative ones were unsatisfied because they saw that all the apes in the tribe had enough *things* to live quite comfortably,

6 ^cWhich meant that there was no reason to attack other tribes with sharp sticks or other weapons,

7 ^dUnless reasons could be invented with words and ideas.

CHAPTER 3

And so it happened that the ^eimaginative ones began to ask many questions at the top of their lungs, saying,

2 "Why does the rain not come just when we need it?

3 "And why is the hunting not always as good as it could be?

4 ^f"And why does it seem that the grass grows greener on the other side of the valley, where the next tribe lives?"

5 And hearing these questions, the others became quite upset, saying,

6 ^g"We don't know, what's the answer, we're terribly confused."

7 ^hWhereupon the imaginative ones smiled at one another and said,

8 ⁱ"All is not as it should be because you have not made offerings to the Gods,

9 "Who give us rain, and game, and grass, and other things too."

10 And the others became very afraid, saying,

11 ^j"What are Gods?

12 ^k"Do they live around here?

13 ^l"Do they have weapons?"

14 And the imaginative ones nodded knowingly, because they

a. 1.7
b. 1.8
c. Psay.5A.23
d. Jeff.10.14-15
e. 2.5
f. Nam.2.1-3
g. Vin.5.1-4
h. Vin.5.5
i. Vin.5.6-8
j. Vin.5.9
k. Vin.5.10
l. Vin.5.11
m. Chuk.17.1-9
n. 2.5-7
o. Wil.20.11-12
p. Name.1.2
q. Psom.46.1

had discovered a wonderful discovery,

15 Which brought smiles to their faces, and joy to their hearts.

CHAPTER 4

^mAnd so the ape called Man came to believe in the Gods,

2 Who had given Man everything he had,

3 And who could take it all away again in an instant, if they weren't kept happy,

4 Which is why the ⁿimaginative ones had to become priests and seers,

5 In order to explain the will of the Gods to the less imaginative ones,

6 Who were unable to make it up for themselves.

7 ^oAnd the Gods made many demands, asking for the best portions of the food, the best clothes, the best weapons,

8 And other things besides, including a virgin every so often,

9 And especially including things taken from other tribes,

10 ^pSuch as their heads and other parts of their bodies.

11 And the priests rejoiced at the bounties offered by the people, and cried out in joy, saying,

12 "Aren't the Gods great and generous? Look at what they have given us! Never have we seen so much food and clothing and ^qweaponry and body parts all in one place!

13 "Truly this is a good thing, and we are well pleased."

CHAPTER 5

And so the Gods smiled upon the tribe for a time, and

gave out plenty of rain,

2 And plenty of good crops, and a lot of bountiful things from the good earth,

3 And plenty of things taken from other tribes, including heads and other body parts,

4 ᵃAnd the apes were happy to know that the Gods were on their side, and they worshiped them often, saying,

5 "Thank you, great Gods, for all you have given us,

6 ᵇ"Hosanna, hallelujah, hooray."

7 And the priests ᶜsmiled a great deal all the time.

CHAPTER 6

But then it happened, after seven years of plenty of everything, that things went wrong,

2 ᵈAs they often do,

3 And there wasn't any rain, and the crops were pitiful,

4 And the game got scarce,

5 ᵉAnd one of the neighboring tribes invaded the valley and took away most of the virgins, as well as plenty of heads and other body parts.

6 Whereupon the apes cried out angrily to the priests, saying,

7 "Hey, we don't understand this at all.

8 ᶠ"What about all the food and weapons and body parts we've given to the Gods?

9 "Have they forgotten about us already?

10 "Honestly, we're very discouraged with the whole thing."

11 ᵍThe priests considered the words of the tribe very carefully,

12 ʰFor about six weeks,

13 Which was way too long,

14 But at last the priests trium-

a. Psay.5Q.52
b. Barb.7.7
*   Wil.78.9*
c. Ed.12.20
d. Lies.14.5
e. Chuk.17.15-17
f. 4.12
g. Main.28.1
h. Main.29.1-5
i. Main.29.6-7
j. 4.12
k. Main.27.1-2
l. Dav.40.9
m. Main.29.8
*   Chuk.17.10-12*
n. Ira.33.1-3
o. Dav.29.6

phantly announced that they had the answer,

15 And the people crowded around to listen, saying,

16 "This had better be good."

17 So the priests cried aloud, in a high, shaky voice, saying,

18 ⁱ"The Gods have become bored with your offerings,

19 ʲ"Which are puny and insignificant, consisting of little more than food and weapons and body parts, and every once in a while, a virgin.

20 ᵏ"The Gods need more than small change if they are to go on giving you rain and crops and so forth."

21 "Well, then, what do they want?" asked the ˡtribe, and beads of sweat stood out on their forehead.

22 ᵐ"They want monuments and temples, made of stone, with plenty of writing on them, singing the praises of the Gods, as well as prayers and idols and that sort of thing."

23 "What is writing?" asked the tribe. "We have not heard of this before. Is it hard to get? Does it involve killing?"

24 But the priests smiled broadly, and replied, "Writing is not hard at all. It does not involve killing, but you'll like it anyway."

25 And then the tribe was well content, saying,

26 "We'll get right to it, then. But what is a temple?"

27 ⁿAnd the ᵒpriests smiled, saying, "Don't worry. We'll explain everything as we go."

CHAPTER 7

And so it happened that the apes called men went to

7

work for their Gods, building many great monuments and temples,

2 And writing many praises and prayers and other inscriptions in stone,

3 ªSo that seven times seven generations of their race worshiped the same Gods and invented all manner of things to please them,

4 ᵇIncluding many elaborate ceremonies intended to honor the Gods in their temples,

5 ᶜAnd many new cities in which to build temples and other monuments to the Gods,

6 ᵈAnd wars against other tribes which did not worship the same Gods,

7 And who therefore needed to

a. *Chuk.17.10*
b. *Ext.13.9*
c. *Chuk.17.11*
d. *Chuk.17.13-14*
e. *Lies.2.1-2*
f. *Name.4.7 Rom.11.11*
g. *Mall.13.8*
h. *Jefs.7.15-17*

have *their* cities and monuments and temples destroyed,

8 Completely and utterly,

9 And their fields burned and sown with salt,

10 And their women raped,

11 And their people enslaved,

12 So that even bigger temples and monuments could be built,

13 ᵉTo sing the praises of the great, generous Gods who had made the earth and the seas and the beasts of the field,

14 And who had made the cleverest of the ᶠapes into a powerful nation of priests and warriors and builders and writers,

15 ᵍWhich was the greatest gift of all,

16 And which was called ʰcivilization.

THE FIFTH BOOK OF APES, CALLED

LIES

OTHERWISE KNOWN AS THE SECOND BOOK OF LIES

CHAPTER 1

ªFrom the time that the first pictogram was inscribed on a rock, the ape called man recorded words of all descriptions on rocks and stones of all descriptions.

2 As the inscriptions grew old and became one with the stone they defaced, the apes came to believe that the words were wise.

3 ᵇAnd as generation followed generation,

4 New inscriptions were added to the old, and the apes believed

a. *Gods.6.22*
b. *Wil.1.1*
c. *Gods.6.27*
d. *Wil.20.11-12*
e. *Bks.4.21 Gyp.3.5 Chuk.9.4-6*

these too because they were written in stone,

5 And if it happened that one inscription said something different from another inscription,

6 ᶜThe priests were there to explain everything.

CHAPTER 2

And so it happened that, in time, the apes came to believe that there was only one ᵈGod,

2 ᵉWho had made everything all by himself,

3 ^aIn seven days and seven nights,

4 Starting completely from scratch,

5 When everything was null and ^bvoid,

6 ^cAt the beginning.

7 And this was not all they believed,

8 For they also believed that they were descended directly from the first two people on earth,

9 Who were also ^dnot apes, but a man named ^eAdam and a rib named Eve,

10 Who started out living in a ^fparadise called the garden of Eden,

11 But got kicked out forever because ^gEve committed a great sin,

12 By eating an ^happle she got from a serpent,

13 ⁱWhich turned out to be a bad apple,

14 ^jBecause the serpent was really the devil,

15 ^kAnd the apple was really the knowledge of ^lgood and ^mevil,

16 ⁿWhich Eve should have left alone,

17 Because the apple turned out to be responsible for everything wrong in the world,

18 ^oIncluding the Curse,

19 ^pThe Mark of Cain,

20 ^qThe Whore of Babylon,

21 ^rThe Wrath of God,

22 ^sThe Day of Judgment,

23 ^tAnd much more besides,

24 ^uEspecially sin and guilt, which everyone is full of from birth,

25 ^vSo that there is no good and no peace of mind, except from the one God,

26 ^wWhose name is ^xYahweh,

---

a. Psay.5L.7
b. Vin.1.1
c. Kin.1.1
d. Name.4.7
e. Name.3.4
f. Wil.29.2-5
g. Dav.19.6
   &39.21
h. Psay.5A.14
i. Dav.47.25
j. Pnot.13.1-5
k. Wil.20.14
l. Carl.3.8
m. Dav.30.42-44
n. Grk.13.4-8
   Mawr.6.6-8
o. Mawr.19.12
p. Name.3.5
q. Dav.19.6
r. 6.11
s. Psp.3.7
t. Oth.8.3-14
   Grk.26.4-8
   Adam.46.2-6
   & 47.2-11
   & 48.2-7
   & 49.2-3
   & 50.2-6
   Wil.20.18
   Zig.16.6-7
u. Grk.5.8
v. Grk.11.6
w. Jefs.7.15-17
x. Dav.10.11
y. Bks.2.5-6
z. Dav.10.10
aa. Dav.40.9
bb. Rat.12.6
cc. Vin.49.5
dd. Psay.5L.3
ee. Dav.30.25
ff. Grk.13.20
gg. Ed.73.4
hh. 3.1
ii. Dav.29.6
jj. Dav.10.10

---

27 But isn't to be mentioned out loud,

28 By anyone.

29 Nor was this all they believed.

CHAPTER 3

^yThey believed that God had Chosen them especially as his own tribe,

2 Like pets,

3 And given them all manner of special treatment,

4 Including great leaders like ^zAbraham,

5 Who tried to sacrifice his son ^{aa}Isaac because ^{bb}God told him to,

6 Although God spared Isaac, because he was only ^{cc}kidding about the sacrifice,

7 So that Isaac had sons of his own,

8 Who were ^{dd}Jacob and ^{ee}Esau,

9 One of whom had a ^{ff}hairy birthright,

10 ^{gg}And something happened between them,

11 Something too complicated to remember.

12 Nor was this all they believed.

CHAPTER 4

^{hh}They believed that after getting Chosen as God's special tribe,

2 Their ⁱⁱwisest leaders worked out a written contract with God,

3 Called a Covenant,

4 Which spelled everything out pretty clearly,

5 About who was supposed to do what.

6 For example, if ^{jj}God yelled "Jump!" at the Chosen Tribe, they were supposed to ask,

"How high?" and then get right to it,

7 No matter what it was God wanted.

8 In return for this sort of behavior, God agreed to look after the Chosen Tribe in his own special way,

9 [a]Seeing to it, for example, that the Chosen Tribe would be specially singled out for persecution by every other tribe on earth,

10 Forever.

11 When they saw what a great Covenant they had made,

12 The Chosen Tribe built a special ark to keep it in,

13 So that they could read it whenever they got [b]confused,

14 Which was plenty,

15 What with one thing and another.

CHAPTER 5

But in spite of the apple and sin and guilt and the Covenant,

2 [c]The Chosen Tribe also believed that God loved them,

3 [d]Even if he had a funny way of showing it,

4 Such as threatening to destroy everyone in the world,

5 Which he did every so often,

6 [e]Like whenever he got mad.

7 And then one time when he was *really* mad,

8 He went ahead and did it,

9 [f]And destroyed everybody in a tremendous [g]flood,

10 Except for [h]Noah and the [i]passengers he took on his ark,

11 [j]Which wasn't the same ark they kept the Covenant in,

12 Because when [k]Noah asked for help in building his,

13 The [l]leaders told him that

a. *Boul.23.1*
b. *Chr.10.6*
c. *Boul.18.6*
d. *13.8*
e. *4.14*
f. *Rat.12.5*
g. *Ann.6.23*
    Ed.78.11
    Ann.2.32
h. *Psay.B.8*
i. *Psay.5Z.2*
j. *4.12*
k. *Dav.10.10*
l. *Psay.5A.24*
m. *Psay.5A.31*
n. *Psay.5Q.5*
o. *Kin.4.1*
p. *Grk.13.20*
q. *Yks.144.11-12*
r. *Psom.8.1-6*
    Psom.23.11
s. *Zig.6.3*
t. *Zig.9.2*
u. *Kens.36.3*
v. *Ext.48.19*
w. *Boul.15.10-11*
x. *Grk.16.5*
y. *Ed.27.5*

one ark was enough for any Chosen Tribe,

14 And if Noah couldn't see that,

15 [m]He must have a screw loose,

16 Or words to that effect.

17 And so [n]Noah built his own ark,

18 And filled it with two of each kind of animal that wasn't too big to fit inside,

19 Such as [o]dinosaurs,

20 Which were too big to fit,

21 Apparently,

22 And didn't get to go,

23 Although the ark went all the way to [p]Mount Ararat,

24 Thus saving Noah,

25 And making it possible for God to keep showing his love in the oddest possible ways.

CHAPTER 6

And so it came to pass that Noah [q]begat a son,

2 Who begat a son,

3 And so forth,

4 And so on,

5 Until there were a lot of people again,

6 Which convinced God that it was [r]time to destroy some more things,

7 [s]Such as Sodom and Gomorrah,

8 [t]Which wasn't really God's fault,

9 Because he warned everybody not to try dating his [u]Angels,

10 [v]Which they went ahead and tried anyway,

11 Resulting in lots of fire and brimstone from [w]you know who,

12 Which didn't kill [x]Lot,

13 Because [y]Lot didn't try to date any Angels,

14 Although it did kill ^aLot's wife,

15 Who didn't try to date any Angels either,

16 ^bBut she was a woman,

17 And God thought he'd like her better if she was something else instead,

18 Maybe something quieter,

19 And so he turned her into a ^cpillar of salt,

20 Which stopped her from talking,

21 ^dCompletely.

22 Nor was this all they believed.

CHAPTER 7

For example, they believed the one about the ^eTower of Babble,

2 Which somebody or other decided to build on top of ^fMount Ararat,

3 And keep going till they got all the way up to heaven,

4 Because they wanted to meet God in person,

5 ^gFor some reason,

6 Except that ^hGod didn't want visitors,

7 But instead of just destroying the tower with a lot of fire and brimstone,

8 Like he usually did,

9 This time, he made all the construction workers talk in different languages,

10 Forever,

11 ⁱSo they couldn't build the tower any higher,

12 Which solved ^jGod's problem,

13 But created a new one for the Chosen Tribe,

14 Because when the construction workers quit work on the tower,

a. Ed.27.3
b. Mawr.22.20
c. Zig.10.13
d. Boul.21.9
e. Grk.18.28
f. 5.23
g. Psay.5A.19
h. Dav.5.7
   Brd.12.6
i. Drex.5.2-3
j. Main.27.7-8
k. Jeff.5.7
l. Name.4.12-15
m. 4.6-10
n. Psay.5B.8
o. Dav.47.25
p. Ann.18.6
q. Psay.5B.7
r. Psay.5Q.76
s. Name.3.7
t. Gyp.1.8-10
u. Jeff.6.4
v. Dav.10.10
w. Psay.5Y.24
x. Drex.6.1
y. Ed.61.3-4
z. Frog.10.12-13
aa. Psp.2.12
bb. Dav.15.45-49
cc. Bks.6.11-18
dd. Main.27.9
ee. Main.34.5

15 ^kThey scattered to the four winds,

16 ^lAnd set up a whole bunch of new tribes who all spoke foreign languages,

17 So that they could come back and persecute the Chosen Tribe later,

18 ^mJust like it said in the Covenant.

19 Nor was this all they believed.

CHAPTER 8

They believed that an ape named ⁿJonah was eaten by a whale,

2 ^oBut got thrown up later,

3 ^pIn good health.

4 And they believed that an ape named ^qJob, who had more troubles than you could shake a pointed stick at, including boils, still ^rloved God anyway.

5 And then there was ^sJoseph, who had a coat of many colors, as well as many strange dreams,

6 Which convinced him to go to ^tEgypt for some reason,

7 ^uAnd it didn't work out right,

8 Which meant that there had to be ^vMoses,

9 Who was ^wborn in a basket and floated down the Nile,

10 ^xTill he helped Joseph's descendants escape from Egypt,

11 With a lot of ^ymiracles, including ^zfrogs, ^{aa}locusts, and parting the ^{bb}Dead Sea and so forth,

12 Delivering them after forty years into the ^{cc}land of milk and honey,

13 ^{dd}Which Moses wasn't allowed into,

14 ^{ee}Because he didn't always ask "How high?" every time God told him to jump,

15 Or didn't ask politely
enough,
16 [a]Or something.
17 And so Moses had to stay
behind and die in the [b]wilder-
ness,
18 Although right before he
died, he got to give the Chosen
Tribe one more gift from God,
19 Namely, the [c]Ten Commandments,
20 Which are so important they
always get a whole chapter to
themselves.

CHAPTER 9

And God gave the Ten Com-
mandments to Moses on
[d]Mount Ararat, and Moses
brought them down to his people
engraved on [e]stone tablets so that
everybody would believe in
them,
2 Only they were already busy
worshiping a [f]golden calf they
had decided to believe in,
3 And besides, the Ten Commandments were pretty strongly
worded, being,
4 [g]Thou shalt have no other
Gods but Me,
5 [h]Thou shalt always capitalize
My name on graven images, including pronouns,
6 [i]Thou shalt not consume any
[j]bacon, [k]pork or other [l]pig products,
7 [m]Honor thy father and mother,
no matter how little money they
make or how many chores they
ask thee to do,
8 Thou shalt not commit
[n]adultery, even if thou art an
adult,
9 [o]Thou shalt not covet, whatever that means,
10 [p]Thou shalt not kill, no matter how much fun it is,

a. Main.27.10-11
b. Vin.3.9-11
c. Main.29.7-8
d. 5.23
e. 1.4
f. Psong.8.8-11
g. Main.27.15-17
h. Gods.6.22
i. Psong.6.4
j. Brit.10.9
k. Hall.15.21
l. Krt.5.26
m. Psay.1.8
n. Yks.144.11-12
o. Chr.3.5-7
p. Psay.5Q.23
q. 5.2-3
r. Psom.78.10
s. Grk.13.20
t. Rom.22.6-7
u. Dav.47.11 & 47.22
v. Ned.6.24
w. 8.12
x. Dav.10.10
y. Dav.30.40
z. Ext.39.18-19
aa. Rom.22.11-12
bb. 2.20
cc. 9.8
dd. 9.12
ee. Dav.40.9
ff. Ned.16.9-11 Rat.7.15
gg. Ned.29.19
hh. Psp.4.1

11 [q]Thou shalt be [r]circumcised
as soon as thou art born,
12 [s]Thou shalt not bear a false
witness, especially through adultery, and,
13 [t]Thou shalt not have any fun
to speak of, ever, because God
loves you.
14 [u]And when Moses had explained everything, the people
put away their golden calf and
believed in the Ten Commandments instead.
15 [v]Nor was this all they believed.

CHAPTER 10

They believed that the [w]land
of milk and honey became a
great nation,
2 Ruled by [x]David,
3 Who killed [y]Goliath with a
stone,
4 Which was some kind of [z]ex-
ception to the commandment
about killing,
5 And okay,
6 [aa]The way the priests explained it,
7 And David had a fling with
[bb]Bathsheba,
8 [cc]Which was not okay, the
way the priests explained it,
9 [dd]And so David had a son who
tried to kill him,
10 But David killed his [ee]son
first,
11 [ff]Which was probably okay,
the way the priests explained it,
12 Because David loved God
and [gg]wrote many poems.
13 And eventually there was
King Solomon, who was [hh]wise
enough to cut a baby in two,
14 And other things.
15 And all the time God loved
His people and kept on showing
it in the strangest possible ways.

CHAPTER 11

For example, there was the time Joshua knocked down the walls of Jericho,

2 Using only the brass section.

3 And there was [a]Samson,

4 Who had long hair, which was [b]okay,

5 And was very strong, which was also [c]okay,

6 And loved [d]Delilah, which was not okay,

7 Because she cut off his hair,

8 And had him blinded,

9 Only [e]Samson won out in the end, thanks to His love,

10 [f]Knocking down the temple on His enemies, the Philistines,

11 And himself,

12 Until all of them were flat as a pancake,

13 Which was apparently okay, the way the priests explained it,

14 Because God [g]loved Samson,

15 Especially when he was flat as a pancake.

16 Nor was this all they believed.

CHAPTER 12

They believed that God spoke through prophets,

2 [h]Such as Amos, Isaiah, Jeremiah, and so forth,

3 Who warned about [i]God's anger,

4 Just in case anybody forgot about it for some reason,

5 [j]And they described the terrible things that would happen if He weren't kept happy,

6 Which were pretty terrible, as you might expect,

7 [k]But this was okay, the way the priests explained it,

8 Because there would be a messiah,

9 Who would [l]save everyone in the Chosen Tribe who really loved God,

10 [m]Someday.

CHAPTER 13

And the Chosen Tribe believed these and other things for many generations,

2 [n]And then God destroyed the land of milk and honey, completely and utterly,

3 And scattered His Chosen Tribe to the four [o]corners of the earth,

4 To live as best they could without a country,

5 Or anything else,

6 [p]Which must have been okay,

7 Because God truly loved His Chosen People,

8 Even if he had a darned peculiar way of showing it.

CHAPTER 14

Fortunately by now, there were other great tribes of Chosen Apes, who had beliefs of their own,

2 Of much the same kind,

3 Who went on to do great things of their own,

4 Which is how history works,

5 Things being what they are.

---

a. *Dav.14.6*
b. *10.6*
c. *10.6*
d. *Dav.5.7*
e. *Psay.5B.8*
f. *Wil.8.3*
g. *Brit.40.8*
h. *Dav.29.6*
i. *2.21*
j. *2.22*
k. *Rom.22.11-12*
l. *Brd.12.6*
m. *Mall.13.27*
n. *Rom.10.4 & 7.7*
o. *Grk.13.1*
p. *Psay.2.2*

THE BOOK OF GYPSIES

CHAPTER 1

And thus there came to be
many great nations, which
knew how to make [a]temples,
2 And [b]monuments,
3 And [c]inscriptions in stone,
4 And [d]wars,
5 And [e]slaves,
6 And all the other [f]things that
are necessary for civilization.
7 One of these was the Gypsy
tribe, which was [g]Chosen by the
Gods to be the greatest of all
nations,
8 [h]Because it sat beside the Nile
River, which was the source of
all life,
9 And very important,
10 Because the rest of the earth
was a total [i]desert,
11 Made of [j]sand and rocks and
other not very lively stuff,
12 [k]Which may explain why the
Gypsies spent most of their time
thinking about death,
13 And planning for death,
14 And [l]writing about death, including a Book of the Dead,
15 [m]And building great big
tombs called pyramids,
16 [n]Including the Great Pyra-
mid called Khufu,
17 Which is very mysterious
and old and probably haunted,
18 Especially because no one
can remember how it was built.

CHAPTER 2

And the Gypsies did a lot of
mysterious things,
2 For a very very long time,
3 Including building many monuments and temples,
4 Such as the [o]Sphinx, which
had a lion's body and a woman's
head and a [p]riddle,
5 And the tomb of King Tut,
which was full of gold and also
haunted,
6 And many many stone in-
scriptions,
7 Called hieroglyphics,
8 Which celebrated the Gypsy
Gods, who had names like Ra,
Horus, Ammon, and so forth,
9 As well as kings and queens,
who had names like Ramses,
Horemheb, Nefertiti, [q]Ptolemy,
and so on,
10 And were wrapped up like
[r]mummies and buried inside the
[s]pyramids with all their [t]things
and all their slaves.

CHAPTER 3

And then there was a king
called [u]Akhnaton,
2 [v]Who had a funny-shaped
head and a potbelly,
3 [w]Which made him believe that
there was really only one God,
4 [x]Whose name was [y]Aton,
5 [z]And who had created everything all by himself,
6 [aa]Et cetera,
7 But Akhnaton died, and the
[bb]apes called Gypsies went back
to doing things the old way, with
lots of Gods.
8 But that didn't work out either,
9 [cc]Because the Gods allowed
the Gypsies to be invaded a lot
by other [dd]tribes of Chosen
Apes,
10 Who took practically everything away from the Gypsies,
11 [ee]Including Cleopatra, who

a. Mes.1.4 Grk.1.2 Rom.1.2
b. Mes.1.5 Grk.1.3 Rom.1.3
c. Mes.1.6 Grk.1.4 Rom.1.4
d. Mes.1.7 Grk.1.5 Rom.1.5
e. Mes.1.8 Grk.1.6 Rom.1.6
f. Gods.1.5-8 Rom.1.7
g. Psay.5Y.37
h. Chuk.16.1-5
i. Psom.12.4
j. Bks.1.2-4
k. Chuk.17.1-9
l. Gods.6.23-24
m. Gods.6.22
n. 2.10
o. Dav.5.7
p. Ann.12.11
q. Gnt.7.2-3
r. Dav.30.27
s. 1.16
t. 1.6
u. Bks.6.17-18
v. Yks.66.3-4
w. Lies.2.1
x. Lies.2.26 Bks.4.22
y. Dav.41.19
z. Lies.2.2
aa. Lies.2.4-6
bb. Apes.2.6
cc. Chuk.17.15-17
dd. Grk.25.1-4
ee. Dav.19.6

was a beautiful queen rolled up in a rug,

12 Who also wore a lot of eye makeup and got killed by an [a]asp,

13 Which pretty well wrapped things up for the Gypsies.

CHAPTER 4

[b]A nd so the Gypsies were scattered to the four cor-

ners of the earth,

2 [c]And had to make do as best they could without anything,

3 [d]Except a deck of cards,

4 And a bunch of pretty mysterious ways,

5 That enabled them to foretell the future,

6 [e]Which isn't usually all that mysterious anyway,

7 As we shall see.

a. Grk.6.11
   Dav.47.11
b. Lies.7.15
c. Lies.13.4
d. Wht.37.13
e. Lies.14.5

THE BOOK OF
MESOPOTAMIANS

CHAPTER 1

[a]A nd there was another tribe of [a]apes, which called themselves Mesopotamians,

2 [b]For some reason.

3 [c]They believed they had been especially Chosen by their Gods,

4 [d]To make temples,

5 [e]And monuments,

6 [f]And inscriptions,

7 [g]And wars,

8 [h]And slaves,

9 And were therefore civilized,

10 Which is why they lived between the Tigris and the Euphrates,

11 In the [i]cradle of civilization.

CHAPTER 2

[T]he Mesopotamians had writing,

2 Which was called cuneiform,

3 Because they never did any-

a. Apes.2.6
b. 1.10
c. Lies.3.1
   Grk.1.8
   Rom.1.9
d. Gyp.1.1
   Grk.1.2
   Rom.1.2
e. Gyp.1.2
   Grk.1.3
   Rom.1.3
f. Gyp.1.3
   Grk.1.4
   Rom.1.4
g. Gyp.1.4
   Grk.1.5
   Rom.1.5
h. Gyp.1.5
   Grk.1.6
   Rom.1.6
i. Psay.5Q.65
j. Rom.2.22
k. Gods.6.22
l. Psay.5Q.65
m. 2.3
n. Brit.30.14
o. Psay.5Q.65
   Krt.12.7

thing the [j]easy way.

4 For example, they built temples with steps that were too tall to climb,

5 And called them "ziggurats" for some reason,

6 And they didn't write on [k]stone,

7 But mud,

8 Which they had a lot of,

9 In the [l]cradle of civilization.

CHAPTER 3

[B]ut the Mesopotamians didn't stay Chosen for very long,

2 Because they never did things the [m]easy way,

3 Which will hurt you in the long run,

4 As [n]almost everyone knows,

5 Unless you happen to live,

6 In the [o]cradle of civilization.

THE BOOK OF GREEKS

OTHERWISE KNOWN AS THE FIRST BOOK OF GREEKS

CHAPTER 1

And there was another tribe of [a]apes, which called themselves Greeks.
2 The Greeks learned how to make [b]temples,
3 [c]And monuments,
4 [d]And inscriptions in stone,
5 [e]And wars,
6 [f]And slaves,
7 And were therefore civilized,
8 And believed they had been selected by the Gods as the Chosen Tribe,
9 Above all others,
10 Which entitled them to rule the world,
11 And so they did.

CHAPTER 2

The Greeks built ships with lots of oars, and rowed all over the Mediterranean,
2 Conquering other tribes with Greek [g]fire and other gifts,
3 [h]And enslaving their women and children,
4 [i]And building monuments to their Gods,
5 Who were very [j]numerous and therefore needed an unusual number of monuments and temples and inscriptions and so forth,
6 Which the Greeks put up all over the place, between [k]wars,
7 Impressing themselves no end with their own intelligence and [l]penmanship,
8 So that they believed they had created a golden age,
9 When everything was as it should be,
10 That is, ruled by Greeks.
11 Nor was this all they believed.

CHAPTER 3

The Greeks believed that before there were Gods, there were [m]Titans, who came from the earth and were pretty special.
2 For example, there was [n]Prometheus,
3 Who, being the smartest of the Titans, loved the Chosen Tribe of Greeks a lot,
4 [o]And showed it by giving them fire,
5 So that they could conquer all the other tribes,
6 Including the [p]Persians,
7 And the [q]Trojans,
8 And a lot of [r]others too.
9 Only, some of the other Titans got [s]mad at Prometheus about the fire thing,
10 And tied him to a [t]rock,
11 [u]So that his entrails could be ripped out every day by a vulture,
12 Which didn't kill Prometheus,
13 Him being a Titan and all,
14 [v]But ruined his day anyway.
15 Nor was this all they believed.

CHAPTER 4

The Greeks believed that the Titans had children who were Gods,

a. Apes.2.6
b. Mes.1.4 Gyp.1.1 Rom.1.2
c. Mes.1.5 Gyp.1.2 Rom.1.3
d. Mes.1.6 Gyp.1.3 Rom.1.4
e. Mes.1.7 Gyp.1.4 Rom.1.5
f. Mes.1.8 Gyp.1.5 Rom.1.6
g. 3.2-5
h. 1.6
i. 1.3
j. 5.1-2
k. 1.5
l. Psay.5Q.69 Chr.5.7
m. Boul.14.11-12
n. Dav.15.9
o. Gods.1.4
p. 19.1-5 Bks.2.11-12
q. 18.1
r. Bks.2.16
s. Main.27.5
t. Psom.30.1
u. Psom.78.10 & 30.4
v. Psay.5D.7

2 Especially [a]Zeus, who was the king of all the Gods and lived on Mount Olympus,
3 [b]So he could be near his Chosen Tribe, the Greeks.
4 And [c]Zeus worked hard at setting an [d]example for the apes who worshiped him,
5 Although he didn't give them any [e]commandments.
6 Instead he fell in love a lot,
7 And had many children,
8 Including [f]Artemis, [g]Aries, [h]Apollo, and a bunch of others,
9 Including some whose names didn't begin with the letter "A,"
10 Even though the Greeks were pretty proud of the letter "A,"
11 It being the [i]first letter of the [j]alphabet,
12 Which the Greeks had invented.
13 Zeus was married to [k]Hera,
14 Who often got jealous of the way Zeus played around,
15 And so she had a child of her own,
16 [l]All by herself,
17 Which made Zeus [m]mad,
18 Causing the baby to be thrown off the top of Mount Olympus,
19 Which is how [n]Hephaestus came to have a bad foot and a limp, and had to get a job making armor for the other Gods.
20 Nor was this all the Greeks believed.

CHAPTER 5

[o]The Greeks believed that the Gods ran everything,
2 Which is probably why there had to be so many of them.
3 There were Goddesses called the [p]Fates, who were in charge of ending Greek lives,
4 With a pair of scissors,
5 Which cut off the thread of life,
6 Whenever the Fates felt like it.
7 And there were three [q]Furies, who were in charge of making the Greeks feel guilt and pain and suffering,
8 Which are absolutely necessary and required by Gods,
9 Except for [r]heathen barbarians, of course.
10 And there were three [s]Graces, who were in charge of something else,
11 Something too complicated to remember.
12 And there were nine [t]Muses,
13 Who were in charge of helping the Greeks create [u]things,
14 [v]Such as poems about the Gods,
15 Which are called myths.
16 The Muses did such a good job that there are more Greek myths than you can shake a pointed stick at.

CHAPTER 6

For example, there were myths about Gods who fell in love with female Greeks and had children called demi-Gods,
2 Which means half-Gods,
3 [w]And which shows just how Chosen the Greeks must have been.
4 There was a demi-God called [x]Hercules,
5 Who was very strong and had to do twelve labors,
6 [y]For some reason.
7 There was a demi-God called [z]Theseus,
8 Who was very smart and had to do some labors of his own,
9 Including finding his way

a. Rom.10.16
b. Ext.52.16
c. Dav.8.7
d. Psay.5Q.50
e. Lies.6.1
f. Rom.10.22
g. Rom.10.19
h. Rom.10.23-25
i. Hill.A.1 Psay.5A.1 Rat.5.2 Adam.2.15-16 Psong.59.1 Yks.120.9 Drex.4.11 F&J.14.12-15 Hill.Z.1-8 Ned.30.42
j. Oth.2.5
k. Rom.10.21
l. 11.1
m. Main.27.5
n. Dav.30.27
o. Chuk.17.3-9
p. Ed.77.6 Ira.9.5
q. Dav.22.6
r. Chr.2.5-8
s. Dav.37.6-8
t. Dav.21.7
u. Gods.1.8
v. Gods.6.20-24
w. Krt.12.7
x. Dav.14.6
y. Main.27.1-2
z. Dav.18.5

through the [a]maze with a ball of string,
10 So that he could [b]kill the Minotaur,
11 Which was killing a lot of Greek virgins at the time,
12 [c]For some reason.
13 [d]Theseus also had to visit the Underworld,
14 Which is where Greeks went after they died,
15 [e]Rowing across the River [f]Styx in a boat with [g]Sharon,
16 [h]And the River Lethe, which made them forget everything,
17 To the [i]Elysian Fields,
18 Or to other, [j]nastier places where they could be punished for having disobeyed the Gods,
19 [k]Who were pretty adamant about such things.
20 Anyway,
21 Theseus had to rescue [l]Hercules,
22 [m]Who had gotten himself into the Underworld somehow and couldn't get out,
23 Since brains don't always come with brawn,
24 [n]And Theseus, who was pretty good at getting in and out of various places, got Hercules out.
25 And the Greeks believed this was a pretty exciting myth.
26 In fact, the Greeks believed a lot of things.

CHAPTER 7

They believed that there was quite a lot of coming and going between the earth and the [o]Underworld,
2 Even though nobody ever actually saw it happen,
3 Which is why belief is such a wonderful thing.
4 They believed that [p]Persephone got kidnaped to the Underworld by the King of the Underworld,
5 Who was a God named [q]Hades,
6 [r]Who had to keep up with his brother Zeus,
7 [s]Who was setting all the records for having love affairs with Greek women.
8 And Persephone also managed to get out,
9 But only on a part-time basis,
10 Which is why we have the seasons, the Greeks believed,
11 Being a tribe who believed in a lot of things.
12 When Persephone is with Hades in the Underworld, it is winter on earth,
13 And when Persephone gets back out of the Underworld again, it becomes spring and summer,
14 [t]Which helps explain why the weather is so unpredictable,
15 [u]Women being what they are about punctuality.
16 Nor was this all the Greeks believed.

CHAPTER 8

They believed that lots of Greek men grew up to be [v]heroes,
2 Who had to go out on great quests,
3 [w]And do impossible things,
4 In spite of all the [x]weird women they ran into,
5 Like [y]Jason,
6 Who went looking for something called the [z]Golden Fleece,
7 And ran into somebody named [aa]Medea,
8 Who liked to cut children up into little pieces and throw them into the sea,

a. Dav.42.33 F&J.14.2-3 Zig.14.4
b. Spic.4.13
c. Gods.4.7-8
d. 7.1
e. Psom.69.1-4
f. Bks.3.14
g. Psay.5Q.17
h. Mall.6.9-12
i. Mall.17.2
j. F&J.5.3
k. Psay.1.6
l. 6.4-5
m. F&J.5.1-2
n. F&J.10.1-2 Krt.9.15 Vin.1.25
o. 6.14
p. Dav.48.10
q. Rom.10.17 Dav.6.4
r. 4.4
s. 11.15
t. 5.1
u. Psay.5A.29
v. Swar.18.16
w. Yks.8.3-5
x. Mawr.17.4-5
y. Dav.20.34
z. Psay.5Q.52
aa. Dav.22.6

9 Which helped Jason get away with the Golden Fleece,
10 Somehow.
11 And there was also [a]Perseus,
12 Who went looking for a weird woman named [b]Medusa,
13 Because he needed her head,
14 'For some reason,
15 [d]Which was okay because she had snakes for hair,
16 And used to turn men into stone by looking at them,
17 Until Perseus gave her a mirror,
18 [e]And cut off her head while she was trying to fix her hair,
19 Thus explaining why Perseus is one of the greatest of all Greek heroes.
20 And then there was [f]Bellphone,
21 Or something like that anyway,
22 Who happened to be hanging around when Perseus cut off Medusa's head,
23 Which is how he met [g]Pegasus the flying horse,
24 Who flew right out of a puddle of Medusa's blood,
25 Somehow,
26 And made [h]Bellphone into another great myth,
27 Because he had a magic bridle,
28 [i]Which he got from some other weird [j]woman,
29 The way Greek heroes always do,
30 And rode Pegasus all over the place,
31 Which the Greeks thought was great,
32 [k]Because they had a thing about [l]horses,
33 [m]Not to mention a thing about wings,
34 Which is why it's so special

a. *Dav.21.26*
b. *Frog.29.11*
c. *Gods.4.7-10*
d. *Mawr.12.1-4*
e. *Psay.5V.22*
f. *Ed.45.6*
g. *Ed.46.10*
h. *Psom.24.3*
i. *Ned.55.7*
j. *Dav.14.38*
k. *9.8-9
18.2*
l. *Ed.36.1*
m. *9.2
10.6*
n. *Dav.42.7*
o. *Dav.40.9*
p. *Dav.43.18-
23*
q. *Psay.5Q.25*
r. *Ed.46.10
Dav.20.11*
s. *Pnot.9.1-5*
t. *Rom.10.18*
u. *Dav.7.5*
v. *4.8
Dav.20.44*
w. *4.8*
x. *Dav.12.5*
y. *Dav.41.12*
z. *4.8
Dav.14.42*

when you can have both in the same myth.

CHAPTER 9

Usually, though, the Greeks had to settle for one thing or the other.
2 For example, they had a great myth about how [n]Dedalus made wings out of wax and feathers,
3 And then talked his [o]son into trying them out,
4 [p]Which just goes to show you that myths don't have to have happy endings,
5 Because Icarus flew most of the way to the sun,
6 And then fell the whole way back,
7 Screaming[q].
8 But Icarus didn't have a horse, and so the Greeks made up a bunch of other great myths about [r]centaurs,
9 Which were half man, half horse,
10 [s]And very wise,
11 In spite of the fact that the horse half was the back half,
12 Proving once again,
13 That Greeks can believe practically anything.

CHAPTER 10

For example, they believed that Zeus and Hades had still another brother,
2 Named [t]Poseidon,
3 [u]Who was God of the Sea and carried a trident, which is a fork.
4 They also believed that Zeus's son [v]Apollo was the God of the Sun,
5 [w]And Zeus's son [x]Ares was the God of War,
6 And Zeus's son [y]Hermes was the God of Winged Feet,
7 And Zeus's daughter [z]Artemis

was the Goddess of the Moon,

8 And Zeus's daughter [a]Aphrodite was the Goddess of [b]Love,

9 Even if she wasn't born in the normal way,

10 But from a bunch of sea foam.

11 And Zeus's daughter [c]Athena was the Goddess of Wisdom, even if she wasn't the smartest thing Zeus ever did,

12 Having had her all by himself,

13 [d]Without the help of Hera or any other woman,

14 But causing her to leap full grown out of his head,

15 Which is why Hera decided to have Hephaestus,

16 [e]And we've already seen how that turned out.

CHAPTER 11

It may be clear by now that the Greeks believed romance was truly romantic only when it involved some kind of miracle,

2 [f]Like somebody turning into something else,

3 Such as the way Zeus used to change into a [g]bull to make himself more attractive to [h]women,

4 Or a [i]thunderstorm,

5 Or anything but himself,

6 For some reason.

7 And they liked to believe that it worked the other way too,

8 Like the [j]nymph who turned herself into a quivering aspen because Zeus asked her out on a date,

9 Not to mention [k]Pygmalion,

10 Who fell in love with a [l]statue,

11 Which is why it was so great when the statue turned itself into a [m]woman,

a. Rom.10.20
Dav.14.34
b. Ann.18.26
c. Dav.14.35
d. Chr.9.3
e. 4.17-19
f. F&J.4.1
g. Zig.10.13
h. Ann.11.7-9
i. Lies.6.11
j. Dav.14.41
k. Dav.12.5
l. Ed.60.10
m. Ed.60.10
n. Zig.10.10
o. Ann.6.23
Al.2.11
p. 6.4
q. Dav.14.37
r. Mawr.17.7-9
s. Chuk.6.4-7
t. Drex.6.4
u. 5.1
Psay.5A.38
v. 3.1
w. Adam.23.5
x. Jefs.7.22
y. Exp.9.17-18
z. Dav.19.6
Vin.60.15

12 And made Pygmalion's day,

13 Because all the Greek women he knew had already turned themselves into something else,

14 To get away from Zeus,

15 [n]Who had a real knack for making a mess of things when it came to romance.

CHAPTER 12

For example, Zeus had a love affair with some other Greek woman,

2 [o]With the help of his famous thunderstorm impression,

3 And afterwards, he wanted the [p]baby to have eternal life,

4 Which is why he had the baby sneaked into [q]Hera's bedroom to drink milk from her breast,

5 Only Hera woke up and the milk [r]spilled,

6 All over the heavens,

7 [s]Which is how we got the Milky Way,

8 [t]And which may help explain why the universe sometimes seems like some big accident.

9 [u]Only the Greeks did not believe that the universe was some big accident,

10 They being able to believe almost anything apparently.

CHAPTER 13

For example, they believed that the earth was flat,

2 And was held up by a [v]Titan named [w]Atlas,

3 [x]Who carried [y]it on his shoulders.

4 They believed that all the trouble in the world was caused by a woman named [z]Pandora,

5 Who had a box,

6 And wasn't supposed to open it,
7 So she opened it right up, of course,
8 And let out all the [a]troubles of the world,
9 Except that [b]hope didn't fly out with the rest of the stuff,
10 [c]But stayed in the box,
11 [d]For some reason.
12 They believed that echoes were caused by another myth,
13 About a Greek named [e]Narcissus,
14 [f]Who had an unhappy love affair with himself,
15 [g]And drowned,
16 But who was mourned for all eternity by a girl named [h]Echo,
17 Who cried herself to nothing,
18 Except her voice,
19 Which explains why when we shout into a canyon, we hear our own voice come back,
20 Or something like that.
21 [i]The Greeks had a lot of great myths like this that explained the way things work in the physical world,
22 [j]Which is why the Greeks also believed they were very good at science,
23 And why we have science today.

CHAPTER 14

For example, there was the Greek scientist named [k]Aristotle,
2 Who was the student of a Greek named [l]Plato,
3 Who heard about a place called Atlantis,
4 [m]Where there was a tribe almost as Chosen as the Greeks,
5 Who lived on an island in the Atlantic Ocean,
6 [n]Which they named after themselves,
7 [o]Then disappeared when their island was scattered to the four corners of the earth by a volcano.
8 Plato got to be this brilliant by being the student of a Greek named [p]Socrates,
9 Who was such a good teacher that he never explained anything,
10 [q]But made the students explain it to themselves,
11 Which is called the Socratic method,
12 [r]And explains why civilization has gotten so advanced over the years,
13 [s]Except that some of the other Greeks didn't like Socrates' method and made him drink [t]hemlock,
14 [u]Which cut his thread in no time flat.
15 Anyway,
16 Aristotle was part of this brilliant tradition,
17 And invented science,
18 Causing Hypocrites, who invented medicine and doctors, not to mention [v]swearing,
19 And Galen, who invented [w]mathematics,
20 Unless it was really Thales who invented mathematics,
21 But he was a Greek too, so it doesn't really matter which it was,
22 And [x]Pythagoras, who invented the Pythagorean theorem,
23 And Euclid, who invented Euclidean geometry,
24 And Zeno, who invented [y]Zeno's arrow,

a. Lies.2.18-24 Yks.6.17
b. Psom.40.4
c. Rat.29.4
d. F&J.5.3
e. Dav.57.34
f. Psom.23.1-15
g. Psom.23.16
h. Dav.21.7
i. Kens.23.14
j. Kens.23.14
k. Dav.14.20
l. Dav.14.21
m. Krt.18.13
n. Jefs.7.15-17
o. Psay.5D.10
p. Dav.20.36
q. Wil.35.8
r. Krt.12.7
s. Wil.35.3
t. Psay.5Y.41
u. 5.3-6
v. Jefs.11.10
w. Psay.4.1
x. Gnt.8.2-5
y. Drex.8.7-12

25 And Archimedes, who invented physics in a bathtub,
26 And rushed out naked to [a]tell everybody about it,
27 And was so embarrassed afterwards that he forgot to name physics after himself,
28 [b]Which caused lots of confusion later on.
29 Nor was science the only thing Aristotle invented.

CHAPTER 15

[c]For example, Aristotle also invented tragedy,
2 Causing [d]Sophocles,
3 Who wrote about [e]Oedipus,
4 [f]The ape who killed his father and married his [g]mother,
5 [h]And felt a lot of guilt and pain about it later,
6 Proving that the Greeks were civilized and believed in the Gods,
7 Which we already knew anyway.
8 And Sophocles wasn't the only Greek who wrote plays.
9 There was also [i]Euripides,
10 And [j]Aristophanes,
11 Who wrote comedies,
12 [k]Which the Greeks also invented,
13 And enjoyed tremendously,
14 Since Aristophanes was so funny that we can't understand most of his jokes,
15 And therefore have to accept them on faith,
16 Which comes down to us from the Greeks,
17 [l]And other tribes,
18 [m]As the most important pillar of civilization,
19 And explains why the Greeks wrote so many comedies.

a. *Psay.5Q.32*
b. *Gnt.6.1-2 Brit.36.3-4*
c. *Gnt.15.29*
d. *Dav.20.30*
e. *Pnot.3.1-5*
f. *Dav.20.26*
g. *Dav.19.6*
h. *5.8*
i. *Ed.29.6*
j. *Ed.28.6*
k. *Gnt.15.1-2*
l. *Lies.5.1-2*
m. *Gods.7.15*
n. *Dav.14.23*
o. *Dav.20.46*
p. *Psom.70.1-5*
q. *Psay.5Y.24*
r. *Ext.52.16*
s. *Ed.33.3*
t. *18.7-8*
u. *Dav.22.50*
v. *Lies.3.5*
w. *Dav.22.62*
x. *11.6*
y. *Dav.22.6*
z. *Dav.20.34*

CHAPTER 16

For example, there was a blind Greek named [n]Homer,
2 Who wrote comedies called the Iliad and the Odyssey,
3 Which were about a very funny war between the Greeks and the Trojans.
4 There was almost no end to Homer's jokes.
5 He invented the joke called "Take my wife . . . *please*!"
6 Which is why [o]Paris took Menelaus's wife [p]Helen, all the way back to Troy,
7 [q]Thus starting the Trojan War,
8 [r]Because [s]Menelaus was only kidding,
9 And took an entire army of Greeks with him to help explain this to Paris,
10 Who was a Trojan and [t]therefore didn't have much of a sense of humor,
11 Which is why it took the Greeks ten years to win the war,
12 Although they had many funny adventures along the way,
13 [u]Including the adventure of Agamemnon,
14 [v]Who sacrificed his daughter [w]Iphigenia to the Gods,
15 For luck,
16 [x]Which upset Iphigenia's mother [y]Clytemnestra,
17 Who decided to have an affair,
18 And then convinced her [z]lover to help her kill Agamemnon when he came home,
19 Which was a terribly funny Greek joke,
20 That such a great personage would survive the whole war and then get killed in his bathtub at home,
21 By his wife,

22 Who found out that the joke was on her,
23 When Agamemnon's other children,
24 ªElectra and Orestes,
25 Killed her,
26 And, in turn, found out the joke was really on them,
27 ᵇBecause the Furies hounded them to death.
28 Nor was this the only funny adventure in the Trojan War.

CHAPTER 17

There was a Greek named Achilles, who was a ᶜdemi-God,
2 And almost immortal,
3 Because his mother had dipped him in a magic pond,
4 Which made him completely invulnerable to injury,
5 ᵈExcept for the one place his mother had held on to while dipping him in the water,
6 Namely his heel,
7 Which will figure in the punch line later.
8 Anyway,
9 ᵉAchilles was a great warrior and went to the Trojan War,
10 ᶠAfter taking time out for some initial business with a dress,
11 ᵍAnd promptly fell in love with a girl,
12 Who got borrowed by Agamemnon, since Agamemnon was so far away from ʰhis loving wife Clytemnestra,
13 And this made Achilles so mad that he sat in his tent,
14 Not fighting,
15 While the Trojans ran up a big score against the Greeks,
16 Especially a Trojan named ⁱHector,

a. Pnot.50.1-5
b. 5.7
c. 6.2-3
d. Swar.14.5
e. Dav.10.10
f. Ira.9.4-17
g. Krt.39.4
h. Pnot.26.1-5
i. Dav.20.44
j. Dav.23.15
k. 16.10
l. Penn.9.12
m. Ext.48.19
n. Krt.38.6
o. 4.15-19
*   17.3-7*
p. Vin.49.5
q. 16.4-7
r. Pnot.8.1-5

17 Who was pretty tough,
18 And didn't know much about Achilles,
19 And for this reason tactlessly killed Achilles' best friend, ʲPatroclus,
20 Who had dressed up in Achilles' armor as a joke.
21 Then ᵏHector tried a ˡjoke of his own,
22 ᵐRefusing to give the body of Patroclus back to the Greeks,
23 ⁿWhich Achilles didn't think was funny,
24 So he got some new armor from Hephaestus,
25 ᵒProving that Greeks with foot problems stick together,
26 And proceeded to scare Hector pretty badly,
27 Which made Hector run away,
28 Only he ran in circles,
29 Three times around the walls of Troy,
30 Until Achilles caught him,
31 And ᵖlaughing quite loudly at his own joke,
32 Killed Hector to death and then dragged him three times around the walls of Troy, thus finishing the joke in grand style.
33 But then, of course, the joke was on Achilles,
34 Who got shot in the heel by a poisoned arrow,
35 Which made ۹Paris titter quite a lot,
36 ʳBecause it was his arrow.
37 Nor was this the last of the jokes in the Trojan War.

CHAPTER 18

The Greeks knew that they would need a very big joke to end the Trojan War,

2 ^aAnd so a Greek named Odysseus thought up the idea of the ^bTrojan Horse,

3 ^cWhich the Trojans thought was an offering to their Gods,

4 ^dOnly it was full of heavily armed Greeks instead,

5 Who jumped out shouting "Surprise!" when the horse had been dragged inside the walls of Troy,

6 ^eAnd killed all the Trojans,

7 Except for ^fAeneas,

8 Who had to go found Rome,

9 ^gBut that's another myth altogether,

10 Though equally funny in its own right,

11 As you might expect.

12 Anyway,

13 The Greeks laughed themselves sick all the way home,

14 Except for ^hOdysseus,

15 Who got lost for some reason,

16 For ten years,

17 Which was extremely funny,

18 And caused Odysseus to lose his whole crew,

19 Some of whom fell in love with ⁱsirens,

20 Which was funny,

21 And some of whom got turned into ^jswine,

22 ^kWhich was even funnier,

23 Until Odysseus arrived home weak with laughter,

24 And found that his wife Penelope was planning to marry the first ape who could string her husband's bow,

25 Which convinced Odysseus to disguise himself,

26 And then kill every one of his wife's suitors,

27 ^lWhich is what he did,

28 ^mAnd it was hilarious,

29 Like all Greek jokes,

a. 8.31-32
b. F&J.14.10-15
c. Psay.5Q.66
d. Ned.8.10
e. Wil.8.4
f. Dav.35.25
g. Rom.7.11-17
h. Dav.18.17
i. Ed.70.12
j. Krt.2.15
k. Krt.5.15
l. Pnot.2.1-5
m. Psay.5A.5
n. Swar.PS.21-22
o. Gnt.4.20
p. Main.22.10
q. 14.8
r. Ext.52.16
s. Yks.116.16
   Dav.23.58
   Mawr.22.20
t. Vin.6.15
u. Chr.2.2-3
v. Bks.3.1-4

30 Though not as funny as the Greek joke called philosophy.

CHAPTER 19

The Greeks thought a lot about things, including the very big things, ⁿlike what is the universe all about anyway, and what should we do about it.

2 When they started to believe their own answers, they knew they had invented ^ophilosophy,

3 Which proved once again how Chosen they were.

4 In fact, they were so Chosen that they could do philosophy on the side,

5 As a part-time job,

6 ^pWhich is why so many Greek philosophers were also Greek scientists,

7 Such as Socrates and Plato and so forth,

8 Especially Plato,

9 Who had a lot of funny ideas.

CHAPTER 20

^qFor example, Plato thought that all apes should be free,

2 ^rExcept slaves,

3 ^sAnd not including women,

4 Which meant that apes should govern themselves,

5 And make up their own laws,

6 And vote about things,

7 Which is called democracy,

8 ^tMeaning rule by apes.

9 The Greeks even tried democracy,

10 ^uWhich explains why they stopped being Chosen,

11 ^vAnd got conquered by the Romans,

12 But not before they had thought up their biggest joke of all,

13 Which is the Greek invention called history.

CHAPTER 21

The Greeks thought it would be pretty funny to keep track of things,

2 [a]Including dates,

3 [b]And names,

4 [c]And places.

5 [d]So it happened that the Greeks started writing it all down,

6 [e]And explaining it all too,

7 In books,

8 Which is how we know about Thucydides,

9 And other Greek historians,

10 Who thought we might want to know about their wars and kings,

11 [f]For some reason.

CHAPTER 22

For example, the Greeks had a long war with the Persians,

2 Who had a king named [g]Xerxes,

3 Who got defeated by the Greeks at sea,

4 Which was a very important thing,

5 [h]For some reason.

CHAPTER 23

And the Greeks also fought a lot with each other,

2 Which is the way things go,

3 When you're civilized,

4 And have a lot of pointed sticks.

5 For example, the Greeks had city-states,

6 Which governed themselves with [i]democracy,

7 Which meant that everyone had an opinion,

8 [j]Except slaves,

9 [k]Not including women,

10 And sometimes the opinion

a. Psay.5Y.1-2
b. Psay.5G.1-2
c. Hill.W.1-2
d. Vin.2.7-11
e. Ed.19.10
f. Zig.10.21
g. Pnot.32.3-4
h. 2.8-10
i. 20.8
j. 20.2
k. 20.3
l. Lies.10.11
m. Kens.39.1
n. F&J.12.3-7
o. Kens.22.4-6
p. Bks.2.1-18
q. Psay.5Y.48
r. 23.13

was that another city-state was just asking for it,

11 Which led to war,

12 [l]Which was okay,

13 Because wars make good history.

CHAPTER 24

One time the Spartans had some history.

2 They were excellent fighters,

3 And very skilled with pointed sticks,

4 [m]And they had a little boy in their army who let a fox eat his stomach for dinner,

5 For some reason,

6 Which showed how Chosen the Spartans were.

7 Another time,

8 [n]Some Spartans got trapped in a place called Thermopylae,

9 And all of them got killed,

10 [o]Which *proved* how Chosen the Spartans were,

11 Until they got defeated by Athens,

12 Or somebody.

CHAPTER 25

And then there was [p]Alexander,

2 Who was great,

3 And conquered everybody,

4 Including India and Egypt,

5 And places no one had ever been to,

6 [q]Until there were no more worlds to conquer,

7 [r]Which isn't good for history,

8 And why the Greeks had to give it all back,

9 Eventually.

CHAPTER 26

And so the Greeks finally stopped being Chosen,

2 But not before they had given us many gifts,
3 Including myths,
4 And tragedy,
5 And comedy,
6 And science,

a. Gnt.14.8-9
b. 4.11

7 And philosophy,
8 And history,
9 Which is why the [a]Romans invented the saying,
10 [b]Beware of Greeks bearing gifts.

THE BOOK OF ROMANS

OTHERWISE KNOWN AS THE SECOND BOOK OF GREEKS

CHAPTER 1

And there was another tribe of [a]apes who called themselves Romans.
2 The Romans learned how to make [b]temples,
3 [c]And monuments,
4 [d]And inscriptions in stone,
5 [e]And wars,
6 [f]And slaves,
7 And [g]money,
8 And were therefore civilized,
9 [h]And believed they had been selected by the Gods as the Chosen Tribe,
10 [i]Above all others,
11 [j]Et cetera.

CHAPTER 2

The Romans believed in doing things the [k]easy way,
2 Like eating on couches,
3 And having a little urn next to the couch so they could make room for seconds without leaving the table,
4 And wrapping themselves up in a single big sheet called a toga instead of wearing clothes[l],
5 All of which saves time,
6 And resulted in the biggest Roman invention,

a. Apes.2.6
b. Mes.1.4
Gyp.1.1
Grk.1.2
c. Mes.1.5
Gyp.1.2
Grk.1.3
d. Mes.1.6
Gyp.1.3
Grk.1.4
e. Mes.1.7
Gyp.1.4
Grk.1.5
f. Mes.1.8
Gyp.1.5
Grk.1.6
g. Psong.16.1
h. Grk.1.8
i. Grk.1.9
j. Grk.1.10-11
k. 2.22
l. Psay.5Q.4
m. Yks.27.7
n. Grk.2.5
o. Grk.5.14-15
p. Grk.26.5
& 26.7-8
q. Lies.14.4
r. Lies.14.5
s. Grk.19.1-2
t. 2.1

7 [m]Which is called "appropriating,"
8 And means taking something from somebody else,
9 Changing its name when nobody is looking,
10 And then pretending it was yours all along.
11 And so they appropriated as much as they could from the Greeks,
12 Like all the [n]Greek Gods and Goddesses,
13 And most of the [o]Greek myths,
14 [p]And comedy and philosophy and history,
15 Especially history,
16 [q]Which has a way of happening all by itself,
17 [r]Whether you do anything yourself or not,
18 And also maybe not as much philosophy as comedy,
19 Because [s]philosophy isn't easy,
20 Which is why the Romans actually had to make up some philosophy of their own,
21 To introduce the idea that,
22 [t]If a thing isn't easy, it isn't worth doing at all.

CHAPTER 3

But the Romans also knew that somebody had to do the work,

2 Or it wouldn't get done at all,

3 ªBecause they certainly weren't going to do it,

4 Which is why they invented two classes,

5 ᵇThe Patricians and the plebeians.

6 The Patricians believed in ᶜdemocracy,

7 ᵈExcept for slaves,

8 ᵉNot including women,

9 Or plebeians,

10 And so set up a republic,

11 Which means that everyone is free and has a vote,

12 ᶠUnless you're a slave or a woman or a plebeian.

13 The plebeians believed in what the Patricians told them to believe in,

14 Because the first rule of being a plebeian is to be obedient,

15 Especially to Patricians,

16 Who must know,

17 ᵍOr why would they have all that money?

CHAPTER 4

The Roman democracy had a ʰsenate,

2 Where all the senators wore ⁱtogas with purple edges,

3 ʲAnd made great speeches to each other,

4 And to the consuls,

5 Who were elected to run things.

6 There were always two consuls,

7 Because the Romans didn't believe in kings,

8 Who had a habit of being untrustworthy,

a. 2.22
b. Chr.3.23-26
　 Brit.19.1-3
　 Russ.4.1-4
　 Nip.10.8-10
c. Grk.20.4-6
d. Grk.20.2
e. Grk.20.3
f. Forg.11.13
g. Psong.43.1-3
h. Hill.A.4
i. 2.4
j. Main.18.6
k. 2.1
l. Psay.5Q.73
m. Gods.6.20-22
n. Frog.26.16
o. Swar.10.1
　 Rom.5.6
p. Gods.7.3-6
q. Grk.26.1
r. Psay.5A.4
　 Rom.5.2-6
s. Bks.3.4

9 Which the Romans didn't approve of at all,

10 Since life gets difficult when you can't trust the king,

11 And life isn't supposed to be difficult,

12 ᵏBut easy.

13 And so the Romans elected two consuls,

14 So that they could keep an ˡeye on each other,

15 And the Patricians wouldn't have to do it.

CHAPTER 5

But there was a lot to do, so the plebeians were kept pretty busy,

2 ᵐBuilding temples and monuments with stone inscriptions and so forth,

3 All over the place,

4 Not to mention ⁿaqueducts,

5 And bridges,

6 ᵒAnd roads,

7 So that Roman legions could march out and conquer everybody who believed in the ᵖwrong Gods,

8 Or ᑫwho believed in the right Gods under the wrong names.

9 And so it was that the Romans invented a very important new concept,

10 Called "division of labor,"

11 Which worked very well.

12 For example,

13 The Patricians would think up a huge ʳengineering project,

14 And then the plebeians would build it;

15 The Patricians would think of ˢsomebody to have a war with,

16 And then the plebeians would fight it.

17 And sometimes they would

even do things the other way around.

18 [a]For example, it often happened that the plebeians would make history,

19 And then the Patricians would write it.

CHAPTER 6

T hanks to division of labor,

2 The Romans accomplished quite a lot.

3 The Patricians decided the world wasn't big enough for Rome and [b]Carthage to be in it at the same time,

4 So, for the greater glory of Rome, the plebeians destroyed [c]Carthage,

5 And killed their armies,

6 [d]And raped their women,

7 [e]And sowed the fields of Carthage with salt,

8 Just to make sure,

9 Because after that close call with [f]Hannibal and the elephants crossing the Alps,

10 [g]It seemed easier to make sure.

CHAPTER 7

W hen Carthage was no longer making things difficult,

2 The Romans had it easy for a while,

3 And worked on the Roman culture,

4 Which couldn't be done by [h]plebeians,

5 And so had to be done the [i]easy way.

6 But they did the best they could,

7 All things considered,

8 And wrote some pretty decent [j]Greek plays,

---

a. *Grks.8.3*
b. *Oth.2.13-14*
c. *Gods.7.7-8*
d. *Gods.7.10*
e. *Gods.7.9*
f. *Oth.2.15-21*
g. *Wil.8.5*
h. *Ned.20.20-27*
i. *2.1*
j. *Gnt.15.5-9*
k. *Psay.5Q.4*
l. *Frog.26.16
Psay.5A.4
F&J.14.12-13
Jefs.7.15*
m. *Psay.5Y.24*
n. *Grk.18.2-7*
o. *Pnot.2.1-3*
p. *Pnot.12.1-3*
q. *Grk.18.23-27*
r. *Pnot.12.4
Grk.18.28*
s. *Psay.5Y.12*
t. *Pnot.12.5*
u. *2.22*
v. *Dav.56.21*
w. *Yks.66.5-6*
x. *Psay.5D.17*
y. *Mawr.15.22*
z. *Adam.6.7*

---

9 And some pretty *ind*ecent [k]Greek poems,

10 As well as some new Greek myths,

11 Like the one about [l]Aeneas,

12 [m]Who escaped from Troy in the general hilarity caused by the [n]Trojan Horse joke,

13 And started wandering all over the place,

14 Something like [o]Odysseus,

15 In fact, [p]a lot like Odysseus,

16 Only when he got home Aeneas didn't [q]kill all his wife's suitors,

17 [r]But founded [s]Rome instead,

18 Which would make the [t]Romulus and Remus thing sort of confusing,

19 If you thought about it,

20 Which is hard to do,

21 [u]And therefore contrary to Roman philosophy.

CHAPTER 8

T he Romans were also good at sculpture and painting,

2 Because they were very fond of looking at themselves,

3 [v]Just the way they were,

4 Whatever they happened to be doing,

5 Since it's so much easier that way.

6 And so the Romans made sculptures that were not exactly beautiful,

7 But real, including warts and so forth,

8 [w]And they painted sex scenes on the walls of [x]Pompeii,

9 [y]Because it wouldn't do to forget how to have sex,

10 [z]And having a huge colorful reminder all over the walls of the house makes it pretty easy to remember.

CHAPTER 9

And things went on for quite a while this way,

2 Without much history going on,

3 And life was good,

4 Which is to say easy,

5 Unless you happened to be a slave,

6 Or a plebeian,

7 [a]Or not a Roman.

CHAPTER 10

[b]But history has a way of happening all by itself,

2 [c]Whether you do anything yourself or not,

3 And so it happened that democracy didn't work out[d],

4 [e]Which shouldn't be too surprising,

5 [f]Since we all know what happened to the Greeks.

6 But the Romans didn't worry too much about democracy, in spite of what happened to the Greeks.

7 [g]After all, the Romans knew that they were the Chosen Tribe,

8 And much more Chosen than the Greeks had ever been,

9 Because all the Roman Gods and Goddesses said so,

10 And they should know,

11 [h]Being pretty much the same Gods and Goddesses the Greeks believed in,

12 Except for the Roman God named [i]Janus, who had two faces and was completely unknown to the Greeks,

13 For some reason,

14 Although nobody should be surprised to discover that the Greeks didn't know *every*thing,

15 Because how else could they have gotten the names of their own Gods so wrong,

16 What with [j]Zeus really being [k]Jupiter,

17 And [l]Hades really being [m]Pluto,

18 And [n]Poseidon really being [o]Neptune,

19 And [p]Aries really being [q]Mars,

20 And [r]Aphrodite really being [s]Venus,

21 And [t]Hera really being [u]Juno,

22 And [v]Artemis really being [w]Diana,

23 And [x]Apollo really being Apollo,

24 Which just goes to show you,

25 The Greeks weren't wrong about everything.

CHAPTER 11

For example, the Greeks weren't wrong about how the [y]Chosen Tribe needs to rule the whole world,

2 Which is why there was [z]Julius Caesar,

3 Who was a consul for a while,

4 [aa]And kept his eye on the other consul.

5 This was good practice for the triumvirate,

6 Which means rule by three apes,

7 And kept Julius pretty busy keeping his eye on Sulla and [bb]Pompey,

8 Until Pompey's head [cc]accidentally wound up on a pointed stick,

9 [dd]And something else happened to Sulla,

10 And Julius Caesar crossed the [ee]Rubicon,

11 [ff]For some reason,

12 And became dictator of Rome,

---

a. *Boul.8.3-5*
   Mawr.15.21
b. *2.16*
c. *2.17*
d. *Grk.25.9*
e. *7.19*
f. *Grk.20.9-11*
g. *1.1-11*
h. *2.11-12*
i. *Dav.42.7*
   Ed.28.6
j. *Grk.4.1-2*
k. *Psay.5U.12*
   Dav.41.23
l. *Grk.7.4-5*
m. *Dav.48.12*
n. *Grk.10.1-3*
o. *Psay.5U.14*
   Dav.20.42
p. *Grk.10.5*
q. *Psay.5U.9*
   Dav.20.44
r. *Grk.10.8*
s. *Psay.5U.10*
   Dav.14.38
t. *Grk.4.13*
u. *Dav.14.33*
v. *Grk.10.7*
w. *Dav.14.36*
x. *Grk.10.4*
y. *Grk.1.8-10*
z. *Dav.12.5*
aa. *4.13-15*
bb. *Yks.66.3-4*
cc. *Wil.19.7*
dd. *Psong.57.2*
ee. *Psay.5Q.3*
ff. *Wht.8*

13 Which was when they stopped calling him Julius,
14 And started calling him Caesar,
15 Or even Mr. Caesar,
16 [a]Which changed history.

CHAPTER 12

In fact, Caesar was pretty interested in history,
2 And spent most of his time making it,
3 And when he wasn't making it, he was [b]writing it,
4 To make sure they got it right.
5 [c]And so Caesar divided Gall into three parts,
6 [d]And kept all three parts for himself,
7 [e]To make sure that nobody else could get any,
8 Which made it safer for him to leave town for a while,
9 And conquer the [f]Brits and the [g]Krauts and the [h]Spics,
10 And the [i]Gypsies, where he met [j]Cleopatra in a rug,
11 And the rest of the world too,
12 Pretty much the same way [k]Alexander had done it,
13 Since Caesar knew a thing or two about [l]appropriating himself.

CHAPTER 13

And when he got back, the senators suspected that Caesar was ambitious,
2 [m]For some reason.
3 They thought he wanted to be emperor,
4 Which is much worse than being dictator,
5 [n]For some reason.
6 And so they stabbed him [o]22 times in the [p]Ides of March,
7 [q]And once more, just to make sure,

a. *Vin.6.3-15*
b. *Main.32.1-2*
c. *Psom.49.1-5*
d. *Psay.5Q.9*
e. *Frog.2.1-2*
f. *Brit.2.9-11*
g. *Krt.2.1-7*
h. *Spic.2.1-7*
i. *Gyp.1.1-8*
j. *Gyp.3.11*
k. *Psay.5Q.21*
l. *2.7-10*
m. *Main.10.1-5*
n. *Jefs.7.16-18*
o. *Psp.3.11*
p. *Psay.5Y.13*
q. *Psay.5Q.37*
r. *Grk.23.12-13*
s. *Psom.14.1-5*
t. *Gnt.16.1-5*
u. *Psay.5Q.15*
v. *Psom.14.9*
w. *Dav.42.7*
x. *20.9*
y. *Psay.5Q.21*
z. *Psong.53.5-9*
aa. *Dav.41.12*
bb. *Psong.46.1-7*

8 And then they had a big [r]war,
9 And [s]buried Caesar and all his friends, including even [t]Antony and Cleopatra,
10 And finally made Augustus the emperor of Rome,
11 [u]Which made everything all better,
12 [v]For some reason.

CHAPTER 14

[w]Augustus turned out to be a pretty good emperor,
2 Having discovered that if you don't start a war with your [x]neighbors, you might not have to fight one,
3 Which made things really easy on the Romans for a while,
4 And made them pretty happy about the Pax Romana,
5 Which means [y]Roman peace,
6 And proves that the Romans hadn't forgotten their invention called comedy.

CHAPTER 15

In fact, for quite a long time after Augustus, the Romans specialized in comedy,
2 Having discovered that it's pretty easy to be funny when you have an emperor,
3 Who is a [z]living God with absolute power,
4 Over everybody,
5 Including the Patricians.

CHAPTER 16

For example, there was an emperor named [aa]Tiberius,
2 [bb]Who invented syphilis and went insane,
3 And thought it would be pretty funny if Caligula became emperor,
4 Which was absolutely right.

CHAPTER 17

[a]Caligula had a great sense of humor,

2 And thought it would be extremely funny to have everyone killed,

3 [b]For no reason,

4 Which he did,

5 Until his [c]friends decided to have the last laugh,

6 Which they did,

7 After which [d]Claudius became emperor,

8 So that everyone could stop laughing for a minute and catch their breath.

CHAPTER 18

When they saw that emperors were so much funnier than democracies, the Romans completely stopped trying to rule themselves,

2 Because it's so much easier if somebody else does it,

3 And so they had a lot more side-splitting emperors,

4 Like the [e]one who made his [f]horse a consul of Rome,

5 Which didn't really hurt anything,

6 Because consuls didn't have any power anymore,

7 Not since the Caesars got it all.

8 And then there was Nero,

9 [g]Who fiddled while Rome burned,

10 Which indicated that things weren't absolutely completely right for the Chosen Tribe,

11 What with [h]barbarians attacking the capital city and all,

12 If you thought about it, that is,

13 Which is hard to do,

14 [i]And therefore contrary to Roman philosophy.

a. Dav.40.9
b. Psong.48.1-4
c. Psay.5Q.49
d. Dav.7.5
e. Dav.14.24
f. Grk.8.32
g. Dav.15.36
h. Barb.1.1-8
i. 2.22
j. 5.7
k. Barb.2.8-13
l. Psay.5Q.71
m. Grk.18.17
n. Bks.6.11-18
o. Psay.5Y.43
p. Lies.12.1-10
q. Dav.15.9
r. Dav.15.20
s. 2.22

CHAPTER 19

And so the Romans came up with a new joke called the Decline and Fall of the Roman Empire,

2 Which took a very long time and had everyone rolling in the aisles.

3 For example, the Romans thought it would be pretty funny if the [j]legions that everybody depended on for protection didn't have any Romans in them,

4 [k]But barbarians,

5 Since even the plebeians had discovered that being in a legion is hard work,

6 And leaves too little time for [l]bread and circuses,

7 Which was a hilarious Roman pastime that involved thousands of apes watching gladiators hack each other to pieces,

8 Or thousands of apes watching heretics get eaten by lions,

9 Or thousands of apes watching practically anything involving lots of blood and death.

CHAPTER 20

The Romans got very good at thinking up new ways to make the Decline and Fall funnier.

2 [m]For example, they appropriated a new religion called Christianity,

3 [n]Which started in a poor Roman province,

4 [o]When a Roman crucified the [p]messiah,

5 Whose name was [q]Jesus,

6 And who believed in [r]Love Thy Neighbor and so forth,

7 Which was a pretty dangerous idea in Rome,

8 Since it isn't always [s]easy to love thy neighbor,

9 ªEspecially when you own all thy neighbors,
10 ᵇAnd have killed a lot of their friends and relatives,
11 And are pretty sure they don't love you either.
12 But to pull off a good ᶜDecline and Fall,
13 You have to take some ᵈchances.
14 ᵉSo the Romans decided that they were Christians too,
15 Which made it easier to justify not fighting the barbarians,
16 ᶠWho were sacking Rome every time they thought no one was looking,
17 ᵍProving they'd learned a lot from the Romans already.

CHAPTER 21

And so the Romans started going to church a lot,
2 ʰAnd learning a lot about guilt and suffering and pain,
3 And trying hard to please the new God,
4 ⁱWho had created everything,
5 ʲAll by Himself,
6 ᵏAnd therefore had to be capitalized all the time, including Pronouns,
7 ˡAnd Who really loved His Chosen Tribe,
8 Which included *all* the apes,
9 For some reason,
10 And showed His love by sending His only son to earth,
11 ᵐSo that He could be killed by the apes,
12 ⁿProving that Love Thy Neighbor is the way to go,
13 ᵒOr something.
14 Nor is this all the Romans learned from Christianity.

a. 12.11
b. Lies.4.15
c. 19.1
d. Vin.14.23-24
e. Psay.5Y.45
f. Barb.3.1-6
g. Psay.5Q.57
h. Grk.5.8
i. Bks.4.21
j. Lies.2.3-6
k. Lies.9.5
l. Lies.13.8
m. Lies.3.5
   Psay.5Q.73
n. Psay.5Q.62
   Frog.26.16
o. Rat.12.4-11
p. Grk.6.17
q. Grk.6.18
r. Lies.9.13
s. 22.1
t. Chuk.2.8
u. Lies.10.6
v. Chr.4.6
w. Grk.13.20
x. Boul.16.6-12

CHAPTER 22

For example, they learned that life is *not* supposed to be easy,
2 But hard,
3 Or else you won't go ᵖto heaven, where everything is perfect,
4 ۹But to hell instead, where everything is really lousy,
5 And where you're sure to go if you've committed too many sins.
6 They also learned what sin is,
7 ʳSin being everything that feels good,
8 Which makes it easy to recognize sin.
9 ˢBut since nothing is supposed to be easy,
10 ᵗIt's more complicated than that,
11 Which is why it's so important to have priests,
12 ᵘWho can explain everything.

CHAPTER 23

And meanwhile, the empire kept Declining and Falling,
2 As the barbarians kept on appropriating more and more Roman provinces and cities and so forth,
3 Not knowing that they were committing a sin,
4 ᵛBy loving things more than God,
5 Especially Roman things,
6 Which were supposed to be exempt,
7 ˣBecause Jesus had said, "Render unto Caesar what is Caesar's," hadn't he?
8 But the priests explained that it was more ˣcomplicated than that,

9 Which made it all okay,
10 And the empire continued Declining and Falling for many more volumes.

CHAPTER 24

[a]Then, finally, everybody was completely confused,
2 [b]And the barbarians were acting like they owned the place,
3 [c]And the Romans were learning a lot every day about sin and guilt and suffering,
4 [d]And the priests were smiling more and more,
5 [e]Because the barbarians were starting to ask questions about Christianity,
6 [f]And were obviously going to need a lot of help before they got it right,

a. Lies.4.15
b. 2.7-10
c. Chr.4.2
d. Gods.4.13
e. Swar.PS.21
f. Zig.15.5-8
g. Psay.5Y.14
h. Bks.3.11-17
i. 2.1
j. Psong.57.1

7 And the emperor was thinking that life might be easier if the capital of Rome weren't Rome,
8 But some other place,
9 Maybe farther east,
10 Where there weren't quite so many pushy barbarians,
11 [g]And so they closed Rome,
12 [h]And the emperor moved to a new city,
13 Named after himself,
14 And the [i]Romans stopped being Romans,
15 And stopped being Chosen,
16 And became [j]Italians instead,
17 Which is another story altogether,
18 But equally funny in its own right.

THE BOOK OF BARBARIANS

OTHERWISE KNOWN AS THE FIRST BOOK OF BARBARIANS

CHAPTER 1

There were a lot of other tribes of apes who were not very [a]civilized,
2 Which is how they came to be barbarians.
3 That and the fact that they usually moved around quite a lot,
4 Which didn't leave much time for building [b]temples and monuments,
5 [c]Or writing stone inscriptions,
6 [d]Or having lots of slaves,
7 [e]Or making up comedy and philosophy and history,

a. 2.17
b. Mes.1.4-5
*   Gyp.1.1-2*
*   Grk.1.2-3*
*   Rom.1.2-3*
c. Mes.1.6
*   Gyp.1.3*
*   Grk.1.4*
*   Rom.1.4*
d. Mes.1.8
*   Gyp.1.5*
*   Grk.1.6*
*   Rom.1.6*
e. Grk.26.5-8
*   Rom.2.14*
f. Grk.1.9
g. 4.8
h. Ann.18.12
*   & 18.17*
*   & 18.18*
*   & 18.24*

8 Which is pretty sad.
9 But they almost always had Gods,
10 Which is important if you want to be a [f]Chosen Tribe,
11 And they all did,
12 [g]Except for the Vikings, of course,
13 Who just wanted to have fun,
14 [h]For some reason.

CHAPTER 2

And in addition to the Vikings, there were barbari-

ans who called themselves
^aGoths,
2 And barbarians who called
themselves ^bOstrogoths,
3 And barbarians who called
themselves ^cVisigoths,
4 And barbarians who called
themselves ^dVandals,
5 Which suggests that there
were also barbarians who called
themselves ^eOstrovandals,
6 And ^fVisivandals,
7 Or should have been, anyway.
8 And there were barbarians
called ^gFranks,
9 ^hAnd barbarians called Huns,
10 ⁱAnd barbarians called Angles,
11 ^jAnd barbarians called Saxons,
12 And there may also have
been barbarians called Ostro-
franks, and Visihuns, and Ostrosaxons, and Visiangles,
13 And vice versa,
14 Though there's no way to
prove it,
15 Because none of them were
very good at writing things
down,
16 Since that leads to ^khistory,
17 And ^lcivilization,
18 ^mEt cetera,
19 Which just isn't necessary
when all you want to do is smash
things up.

CHAPTER 3

Some barbarians specialized
in sacking and pillaging,
2 And others in raping and looting,
3 Each according to his taste.
4 But it was the ⁿVandals who
first thought of smashing things
up as a way to make a living,
5 Which is why they named this

a.	Krt.2.3
b.	Krt.2.3
c.	Krt.2.3
d.	Krt.2.4
e.	Krt.2.4
f.	Krt.2.4
g.	Frog.2.4
h.	Krt.2.7
i.	Brit.4.2
j.	Brit.4.2
k.	Grk.21.1-11
l.	Carl.3.8
m.	Psay.5Q.79
n.	Hill.V.1
o.	Krt.3.1
p.	Rom.20.16
q.	Rom.24.11-16
r.	Brit.1.1
s.	Frog.1.1
t.	Krt.1.1
u.	Pnot.24.5
v.	Psay.5W.14
w.	Dav.18.3-31
x.	2.1-13
y.	Psay.5N.1-3
z.	1.8

profession after themselves,
6 ^oBecause even though they
were barbarians, they weren't
stupid.
7 When the other barbarians
saw how much fun it was, they
started smashing things up too,
8 ^pWhich is how the barbarians
managed to smash the Roman
Empire,
9 To pieces.

CHAPTER 4

^qAfter there wasn't a Roman
Empire to smash up any-
more, the barbarians had to find
a new way to make a living.
2 So they decided to smash up
some other places,
3 Like ^rBritain, and ^sFrance,
and ^tGermany.
4 But it turned out that there
weren't too many places like
Rome,
5 Which could be smashed up
again and again,
6 And again and again,
7 ^uAnd again,
8 Unless Vikings were in-
volved, that is,
9 ^vBecause there wasn't any-
place so tiny or remote or worthless that the Vikings wouldn't
find some way to get to it,
10 And smash it up again and
again,
11 And again and again,
12 And again,
13 ^wJust for the pure joyous fun
of it all.
14 But the ^xothers eventually
got tired of running around all
the time,
15 And finally decided to stay
where they were for a while,
16 And try being ^yNations,
17 Which is why we have
^zEurope,

18 It being the place where all the barbarians decided to live.

CHAPTER 5

[a]The Franks decided to live in France,

2 Which sounded like the right thing to do.

3 [b]The Angles and Saxons decided to live in England,

4 Which sounded more right to the Angles than to the Saxons,

5 But that's the way it goes sometimes,

6 Life being what it is.

7 And the Visivandals and Ostrovandals,

8 And the Huns and the Goths and the Vandals,

9 And even the Ostrogoths and the Visigoths,

10 [c]All thought that Germany was the right place to live,

11 Which is a lot of barbarians to put together in one place,

12 [d]And maybe explains why Germany has never quite gotten the hang of being civilized.

CHAPTER 6

And surprisingly enough, there were certain things that all of them decided to do,

2 [e]Like be Christian,

3 [f]Which meant putting all their Gods of War, and Rape, and Looting, and Arson, and so forth into storage until [g]further notice,

4 [h]And worshiping the God of Love Thy Neighbor instead,

5 Which is easier to do when you're not running around all the time smashing thy neighbor to a bloody pulp,

6 Unless you can find some neighbors who aren't Christians, of course,

7 Provided the Vikings didn't already find them first . . . [i]

8 And so, after thinking it all over pretty carefully, the barbarians decided to give civilization their very best effort,

9 [j]And be devout about their new religion,

10 [k]And build lots of monuments and cathedrals,

11 [l]And write plenty of stone inscriptions,

12 And even try something completely new,

13 [m]Like having a tremendous Dark Age that would last a thousand years.

CHAPTER 7

It takes a lot of work to have a good Dark Age,

2 [n]Which is why the barbarians were lucky to have so many Christians around,

3 [o]Because no one knows how to start a Dark Age better than a bunch of pious Christians.

4 And so all the Christians pitched in,

5 And helped the barbarians do the right thing,

6 [p]Which stopped almost everything stone cold dead in its tracks.

7 [q]Hosanna, Hallelujah, Hooray.

---

a. Frog.2.5
b. Brit.4.2-6
c. Krt.2.1-2
d. Krt.38.7-9
e. Rom.24.5
f. Zig.10.12
g. Psay.5Y.6
h. Rom.20.5
i. Mall.13.27
j. Gods.7.4
k. Mes.1.4-5
  Gyp.1.1-2
  Grk.1.1-3
  Rom.1.2-3
l. Mes.1.6
  Gyp.1.3
  Grk.1.4
  Rom.1.4
m. Ned.6.24
n. Lies.1.5-6
o. Spic.7.3
p. Chr.1.11
q. Gods.5.4-7

THE BOOK OF CHRISTIANS

OTHERWISE KNOWN AS THE SECOND BOOK OF BARBARIANS

CHAPTER 1

When the apes called barbarians settled down in [a]Europe and started being Civilized Nations,

2 [b]And decided to have a great Dark Age,

3 They naturally turned to the Christians for help,

4 [c]Because the Christians had priests who knew how to explain everything,

5 Completely,

6 [d]So no more questions would be needed,

7 For a thousand years,

8 [e]And no one would have to think about anything,

9 For a thousand years,

10 [f]Which meant that everything could stay almost exactly the way it was,

11 For a thousand years,

12 [g]Which is the whole reason for having a Dark Age in the first place.

CHAPTER 2

The first thing the Christians did was fix all the problems apes had been having with government.

2 For example, the Christians knew that [h]democracy didn't work,

3 [i]Because look at what happened to the Greeks and Romans,

4 Who were heathens anyhow,

5 Heathens being [j]apes who don't understand that all apes are basically evil,

6 [k]And therefore don't feel enough guilt and pain and suffering,

7 [l]And thus don't qualify for the eternal bliss that will be enjoyed by Christians in the kingdom of heaven,

8 [m]As long as they don't have any fun to speak of on earth.

9 Anyway,

10 [n]The Christians understood that the only kind of government worth having is the kind of government where God is basically in charge,

11 Which would never happen in a [o]democracy, where the apes are basically in charge,

12 And so they invented a new concept called the "divine right of kings,"

13 Which means that apes should be ruled by Christian kings,

14 Or holy emperors,

15 Who would reign throughout their own lifetimes,

16 Until they died[p],

17 When they would be immediately succeeded by their firstborn sons,

18 Who would reign throughout their lifetimes,

19 Until they died[q],

20 When they, in turn, would be immediately succeeded by their firstborn[r] sons,

21 And so forth.

22 This was completely different from the old heathen Roman imperial way,

23 Which consisted of apes be-

a. *Barb.4.18*
b. *Barb.6.13*
c. *Rom.22.11*
d. *Hill.Q.1-2*
e. *Jefs.11.19-20*
f. *Vin.42.10-11*
g. *Ext.52.16*
h. *Grk.20.1-7*
i. *Grk.20.9-10*
Rom.24.14-16
j. *Al.5.4-7*
Lies.2.25
k. *Grk.5.8*
l. *Boul.8.1*
m. *Lies.9.13*
n. *Gods.6.21*
o. *Grk.20.8*
p. *5.16*
q. *5.16*
r. *Mawr.22.20*

ing ruled by heathen emperors,

24 Who would reign throughout their own lifetimes,

25 Until they died[a],

26 [b]When they would be immediately succeeded by another heathen emperor whom they had personally selected for the job,

27 And so forth.

28 Naturally, an important new concept like the divine right of kings spread rapidly,

29 Until there were quite a lot of kingdoms ruled by divine right,

30 Including the [c]Holy Roman Empire,

31 Which was in [d]France,

32 And much much better than the old unholy Roman Empire,

33 [e]For some reason.

CHAPTER 3

After the Christians had fixed the government problem, they took care of a whole bunch of social problems in the most Christian kind of way.

2 For example, they knew that the old heathen Roman [f]Patrician thing was all wrong,

3 [g]Because all apes are basically evil,

4 And therefore no one should get any special privileges,

5 Unless they're a [h]king,

6 Or a [i]priest,

7 Or somebody really special like that.

8 And so they developed a completely new social system,

9 [j]Where there were no Patricians to foul things up.

10 Instead, they recognized that every ape had a [k]soul,

11 [l]Which belonged to God,

12 [m]Who took care of everything related to the soul through the church,

a. Dav.15.51
b. Rom.16.1-4
c. Frog.2.3
d. Yks.116.16
Krt.2.19-24
e. Jefs.7.15
f. Rom.3.1-5
g. Zig.17.6
h. Gods.1.5
i. Gods.4.4-6
j. Boul.21.9
k. Carl.3.8
l. Main.27.16
m. Spic.9.2
n. Barb.7.7
o. Rom.3.3
p. Rom.18.13
q. Gods.4.10
r. Lies.10.11
s. Psong.43.1-2
t. Psong.10.3-4
u. Ann.20.9
v. 3.7
w. Russ.5.3
x. Psong.65.1-4
y. Barb.7.7
z. Psay.2.2

13 "Which had priests to explain anything God wanted that might seem confusing to a stupid, evil ape.

14 But they also recognized that every ape had a body too and a lot of [o]work to do,

15 [p]Particularly if they were going to get all the way through life without having any fun to speak of,

16 [q]And so they decided that every part of the ape that wasn't the soul belonged to the king,

17 [r]Which was okay,

18 [s]Because the king owned everything else in the kingdom by divine right anyway,

19 Including all the land,

20 And all the money,

21 And all the buildings,

22 [t]Except for all the land and money and buildings that belonged to the church.

23 [u]But the king couldn't look after every ape in the kingdom all by himself,

24 And so he got help from other apes called [v]nobles,

25 Who got land and castles and so forth in return for looking after some of the king's apes,

26 Who were called [w]serfs.

CHAPTER 4

[x]The serfs were very lucky because they didn't have any land or money or buildings at all,

2 [y]And never had fun of any kind whatsoever,

3 [z]Which made it practically a cinch that they would go to heaven and enjoy eternal paradise,

4 Which is why it was so Christian of the king and the church

and the nobles to try to get into heaven the hard way,

5 By being both righteous *and* rich,

6 Since Jesus had said that it is easier for a camel to thread a needle than for a rich man to get into heaven,

7 [a]Or something like that.

CHAPTER 5

Another social problem the Christians took care of was education.

2 [b]Under the old heathen way, a lot of apes learned how to read and write and add and subtract,

3 Which exposed them to a lot of bad ideas that made it harder for them to get into heaven,

4 [c]Like science,

5 Which is okay,

6 The way the priests explained it,

7 [d]Unless it isn't,

8 Which meant that the church had to take a pretty active role in education,

9 To make sure that all education was properly [e]Christian,

10 And didn't get anyone in trouble with bad ideas.

11 [f]And so they decided that the best kind of education was no education at all,

12 [g]Except for priests and kings and some of the nobles,

13 Who needed to know how to read and write and add and subtract so that they could tax the serfs the right amount,

14 [h]Which was 100 percent,

15 This being the only amount which ensured that serfs would not have any land or money or buildings,

16 [i]And so could go to heaven.

17 Meanwhile, the church put

a. Boul.6.1
b. Grk.14.8-11
c. Brit.10.8-9
d. Chnk.3.17
e. Jefs.11.19
f. Yks.133.5
g. 3.7
h. Drex.4.7
i. Barb.7.7
j. Vin.49.5
k. Rom.18.13
l. Psay.5B.10
m. Psay.5B.11-13
n. Jeff.7.5-10
o. Jeff.8.9-11
p. Jeff.10.5-8
q. Pnot.13.1-5
r. Psay.5A.21
s. Gods.6.22
t. Jeff.7.1-3
u. Lies.2.8-24

all the books and manuscripts they didn't burn into monasteries,

18 Where they could be studied by religious bachelors called [j]monks,

19 Who took an oath of silence so that no bad ideas would accidentally leak out and damn the serfs to hell.

CHAPTER 6

But even the serfs had to learn the important things,

2 [k]Like how to be Christian,

3 Which is why everyone had to go to church a lot,

4 And hear what the priests thought about the [l]gospels and the [m]epistles,

5 [n]And some other stuff the church discovered had been left out of the gospels and epistles,

6 [o]Like how if you didn't have the last rites you couldn't go to heaven, no matter how little fun you'd had on earth,

7 [p]And how if [q]Satan got hold of you, you might have to be [r]burned to death to make sure you could still go to heaven,

8 [s]And how all the statues and paintings of Jesus and Mary and the saints weren't really graven images and thus could be worshiped pretty freely, especially by serfs,

9 And how it was really dangerous for anyone who wasn't a priest or a monk to actually read the gospels and epistles and the other stuff in the Bible, [t]because if you didn't understand it the right way you'd go right to hell,

10 And how certain people couldn't be trusted by any true Christian, especially women and Jews, since [u]women had caused

all the sin in the world with their greed and lechery, and [a]Jews were the evil dogs who had murdered Jesus Christ,

11 [b]And how the Pope knew everything anyway, so the serfs shouldn't worry about it.

CHAPTER 7

Meanwhile, the kings and the nobles had it a lot tougher than the serfs[c],

2 Since having land and money and buildings meant that they had to prove their Christianity in other ways,

3 [d]Like killing heathens,

4 And sometimes even each other,

5 [e]Unless they didn't do their killing in a Christian kind of way,

6 Which involved a lot of armor and good manners,

7 And was called [f]chivalry.

CHAPTER 8

[g]Chivalry was a very important invention because it made the barbarians civilized,

2 [h]So that they always went to church before they went out killing,

3 [i]And got their swords blessed,

4 So that whoever they killed could still go to heaven.

5 Chivalry also made it possible to have holy wars,

6 [j]Called Crusades,

7 Which were conducted by chivalric apes called knights,

8 Who traveled great distances to fight heathens,

9 Who owned all the land and money and buildings in the [k]Holy Land,

10 [l]And therefore had to be

a. Boul.8.7-9
b. Jeff.10.10-15
c. Ext.52.16
d. Lies.10.4-6
e. Jeff.11.24-25
f. Grk.8.32
g. Dav.19.3-20
h. Boul.24.5-7
i. Rom.13.11
j. Mawr.31.1-2
k. Bks.1.2-7
l. Bks.4.15-21
m. Mawr.15.19-22
n. Jeff.10.1-4
o. Rom.20.5
p. Bks.4.20-22
q. Barb.6.3
r. Ed.60.17
s. Yks.116.9
t. 4.4
u. 4.1-2

killed before they had too much [m]fun,

11 So that they could go to heaven too.

12 There were a lot of Crusades,

13 And the knights even won one of them,

14 The first one,

15 Which probably had to do with the element of surprise,

16 Since the heathen Saracens had a hard time understanding where all these knights came from all of a sudden, wanting to capture a lot of desert thousands of miles from home and talking a lot about something called the [n]Holy Grail,

17 Which was the cup [o]somebody they never heard of drank wine out of at supper one night,

18 About a thousand years ago.

19 But when the Saracens figured out the knights were serious, they got serious too,

20 And tried to return the favor,

21 [p]Seeing to it that the knights had as little fun as possible,

22 And went to heaven as soon as possible too.

CHAPTER 9

[q]And so, all in all, the Christians did a great job of having a long Dark Age that was about as dark as it could get,

2 [r]And everything stayed exactly the same for a thousand years,

3 [s]And nobody had any fun to speak of,

4 [t]Except maybe the king and the church and the nobles,

5 [u]Which meant that lots and lots of serfs got to go to heaven,

6 Which is the most important thing anyway,

7 If you're a Christian.

CHAPTER 10

But all good things come to an end eventually,

2 Which has something to do with the way [a]history works,

3 [b]And so it happened that the

a. Rom.2.16-17
b. Psay.5Q.23
c. Vin.14.23-24
d. Psay.5A.4
Bub.3.7
Psay.5W.12
Bks.6.17-18

Dark Age got ruined,

4 [c]By a bunch of unfortunate [d]accidents,

5 Which just goes to show you,

6 Life can be pretty confusing,

7 Even if you're a Christian.

THE BOOK OF BUBONITES

CHAPTER 1

Even though life in the Dark Age was pretty great,

2 [a]What with nobody having to think too much about anything and all,

3 There were a couple of things that the Christians kind of forgot about,

4 [b]Like sanitation.

CHAPTER 2

Under the old Roman heathen way, there was a lot of bathing going on,

2 Which was obviously not Christian,

3 [c]Being Roman,

4 And so the Christians pretty well stamped out bathing during the Dark Age,

5 [d]Not to mention sewage systems,

6 Which were a little too [e]scientific for Christians,

7 And would have meant educating some more stone masons and so forth,

8 [f]Since the ones they had were all busy building cathedrals,

9 [g]So that everybody could go to church on Sunday,

10 And thus go to heaven.

a. Chr.1.4-11
b. Hill.W.17-23
c. Psay.5Q.62
d. Hill.S.34-36
e. Chr.5.4-7
f. Frog.22.7
g. Chr.6.1-5
h. Kin.5.4
i. Psay.5Y.30

11 Unfortunately, when everybody stops bathing,

12 For a thousand years,

13 And is throwing excrement into the streets,

14 For a thousand years,

15 Sooner or later, something can go wrong,

16 Which it did.

CHAPTER 3

What went wrong was the [h]rats,

2 Who were not Christian,

3 And therefore didn't understand about Love Thy Neighbor and so forth,

4 Which resulted in a problem called the Black Death,

5 Or the Bubonic Plague,

6 Or more simply,

7 [i]The Plague.

CHAPTER 4

What happened was the rats got sick and died,

2 But didn't go to heaven right away,

3 And instead hung around infecting the Christians,

4 Who started dying in large numbers,

5 Like two out of every three,

6 Throughout Europe.

CHAPTER 5

The Plague was pretty hard to ignore,

2 What with so many bodies piled up in the streets and all,

3 Including the bodies of priests and nobles,

4 ^aWhich was kind of unsettling,

5 And caused a lot of Christians to start asking questions,

6 ^bLike ''What's the use of never having any fun to speak of if we're all just going to die of some disgusting disease?''

7 And so it occurred to some of them that maybe the church didn't have all the answers,

8 And maybe it wasn't a completely good idea that nobody knew anything about anything except what the priests said was in the Bible,

9 When it would have been kind of nice to know some things about other things,

10 ^cLike, say, medicine.

CHAPTER 6

And so it happened that more and more Christians asked more and more questions,

2 About lots of things,

3 Including Christianity,

a. F&J.12.1-7
b. Swar.PS.21-22
c. 2.5
d. Chr.6.9
e. 4.5

4 ^dSince nobody but priests and monks had actually read the Bible for quite a long time,

5 Say, a thousand years or so,

6 And it occurred to some of them that maybe there was another interpretation of the Bible,

7 Besides the one the priests had.

8 And it occurred to others that maybe some of the old bad heathen Romans and Greeks might have known something worthwhile too,

9 In spite of what the priests said,

10 Because nobody could remember hearing that the Roman and Greek apes, however heathen they were, had ever lost two thirds of their population to some disgusting disease.

CHAPTER 7

The Bubonites asked their questions,

2 ^eAnd most of them died anyway,

3 But a few survived,

4 And eventually some of these started coming up with some interesting answers.

5 And the ones with the answers were called Giants.

THE BOOK OF GIANTS

CHAPTER 1

^aAfter almost everybody died in the Plague, the place called Europe started to get more interesting than it had been for

a. Bub.4.5-6
b. Bub.5.7-9
Ext.53.25

quite a while.

2 ^bThe Bubonites who hadn't died in the Plague thought it might be nice to try some new ways of doing things,

3 And what with all the general relief about not being dead like almost everybody else,

4 [a]Some of them even thought it might be nice to have some fun for a change.

5 [b]It turned out, quite unexpectedly, that there were a lot more ways of having fun than there were of having no fun to speak of.

6 Only, still being Christians, they decided they needed a [c]name for what they were about to do,

7 [d]A name that sounded important and worthwhile,

8 And not frivolous and [e]sinful.

9 A name like [f]"Rebirth" would have been perfect,

10 But because not many of them spoke [g]English,

11 Except the ones who lived in [h]England, of course,

12 They wound up calling it the [i]"Renaissance" instead,

13 Which means "Go for it!"

CHAPTER 2

Some of them thought it would be fun to stop painting pictures of [j]dead saints for a while,

2 [k]And paint some pictures of naked ladies instead.

3 They were right.

4 In fact, painting pictures of naked ladies turned out to be so much fun that sculptors decided to make statues of naked ladies,

5 [l]And poets wrote poems about naked ladies,

6 And the naked ladies got so prosperous that they could eat as [m]much as they wanted,

7 [n]And they did,

8 Which is why the Renaissance was absolutely wall to wall with

a. Psong.57.3
b. Adam.6.7
c. Ext.13.12
d. Ext.13.13
e. Rom.22.7
f. Boul.27.5-8
g. Krt.6.11
h. Barb.5.3
i. Jeff.22.1
   Chr.5.5
   Yks.66.6
j. Chr.6.8
k. Psong.54.6
l. Psom.56.1-6
m. Frog.24.2-6
n. Ann.17.11
o. Kin.3.4-5
p. Adam.14.5
   Bks.3.14
q. Ann.17.21
r. Grk.17.35
   Frog.16.8
s. Chuk.7.2-3
t. Psong.8.2-3
u. Chr.5.5
   Yks.66.6
v. Krt.10.15
w. Chr.5.5
   Kens.25.7
x. Psong.46.6-7
y. Bub.7.5
z. Psay.5Q.50
aa. F&J.14.13

[o]fat naked ladies.

9 The most prosperous, and therefore the [p]fattest, naked ladies worked for a Giant named Rubens,

10 Who thought that a naked lady wasn't worth painting at all if she didn't weigh at least [q]three hundred pounds.

11 A Giant named [r]Titian thought that two hundred and fifty pounds was plenty as long as they had nice breasts,

12 And a Giant named Botticelli thought that sheer poundage wasn't as important as a completely [s]bloated belly.

13 [t]Differences of opinion like this caused big arguments between the Giants,

14 Which caused them to split up into different "artistic schools."

15 [u]For example, one "school" believed in painting plenty of cellulite,

16 While another "school" believed in painting skin so white that it looked sick[v],

17 [w]And still another "school" believed in covering up certain controversial parts of the body with flying patches of gauze.

18 [x]But all the schools were learning plenty about all the things you could do with [y]naked ladies,

19 Which is why art was one of the most popular things to do in the Renaissance.

CHAPTER 3

[z]Finding excuses for painting naked ladies became a major quest of the Renaissance.

2 It would have been [aa]heretical to paint a lot of pictures of naked lady saints,

3 [a]Which were practically the only famous ladies anyone knew about,

4 And so the Giants of the Renaissance rediscovered the "Classics,"

5 Which was the Renaissance word for the old Greek and Roman stuff.

6 The Classics turned out to be pretty perfect for what the Giants had in mind,

7 Because Christians didn't get nearly as hot under the collar about pictures of naked [b]Greek and Roman goddesses as they did about naked pictures of the [c]Virgin Mary.

8 And so all of the schools dipped pretty heavily into the old classic literature,

9 [d]And painted lots of pictures of naked Aphrodites and naked Artemises and naked Heras and even, now and again, a naked Apollo,

10 [e]And quite by accident stumbled on a bunch of other stuff they hadn't known anything about,

11 Like science,

12 And philosophy,

13 And history,

14 And comedy,

15 And tragedy.

CHAPTER 4

The [f]Classics caused pretty much of a stir when the Giants rediscovered them,

2 [g]Because it looked like the ancient Greeks and Romans had invented an almost unlimited number of ways to have fun,

3 [h]What with both of them having invented comedy and all,

4 As well as all that other stuff.

a. Brit.19.25
b. Chr.2.4
c. Ed.30.5
d. Rom.10.20-23
e. Bks.6.24
f. 3.5
g. Grk.26.10
h. Grk.15.9-13 Rom.14.1-6
i. Hall.4.3
j. Psong.46.4
k. Gods.4.10
l. Yks.144.11-12
m. Psay.5B.1-13
n. Brit.19.7-8 Ext.11.4
o. F&J.15.13
p. Grk.19.1-2
q. Bub.5.7-9
r. Chr.6.11
s. Chr.5.17-19
t. Grk.21.1-11
u. Bub.2.14
v. Chr.9.1-7

5 And so the Giants decided to try it all out,

6 Just for [i]fun,

7 And to have something to do while the naked ladies were eating,

8 [j]Which, to tell the truth, was quite a lot of the time.

9 Some of the Giants thought it would be fun to try science,

10 [k]Especially anatomy,

11 Which was on everyone's mind,

12 [l]For some reason.

13 Other Giants thought it would be fun to try writing comedy and tragedy and poetry,

14 Since about the only kind of writing anyone had done lately,

15 Say, for the last thousand years,

16 Was recopying the [m]Bible and making up the [n]Lives of the Saints,

17 Which wasn't very exciting,

18 [o]For some reason.

19 Some of the other Giants thought it would be fun to try [p]philosophy,

20 Which means "love of knowledge" and was a wide-open field,

21 [q]Since no one had any knowledge at all about anything,

22 Unless you count the church,

23 [r]Which, according to the priests, knew everything,

24 [s]But was keeping its mouth shut.

25 And some of the Giants thought that [t]history might be fun,

26 But they couldn't tell for sure,

27 [u]Because nothing had happened for quite a while,

28 Unless you count [v]Dark Ages,

29 Which somehow don't seem quite as interesting as naked ladies.

CHAPTER 5

The best thing about all the new fields that opened up during the Renaissance was that it was so easy to be a Giant,
2 Because when you're the first to do something that hasn't been done for a long time,
3 Say, a thousand years,
4 There aren't too many [a]critics who are qualified to point out that you're not doing it right.
5 And so the Renaissance was suddenly bursting at the seams with new Giants,
6 Who were the first and best and brightest in all kinds of areas,
7 [b]And said as much to absolutely anybody who would sit still long enough to listen.

CHAPTER 6

For example, there was an ape named [c]Galileo,
2 [d]Who invented physics,
3 And therefore became a Giant of Science.
4 [e]Galileo dropped two rocks off the Leaning Tower of Pisa and discovered gravity,
5 Because both rocks fell all the way to the ground,
6 Without stopping anywhere along the way.
7 This was extremely significant because before Galileo discovered gravity, no one really knew what to expect when they dropped something.
8 Maybe it would fall,
9 Or maybe it would just hang around in the air,

a. Hill.C.14
b. Main.35.1-5
c. Psay.5Y.42
d. Grk.14.27-28
e. Dav.52.20 & 20.11
f. 5.7
g. Dav.41.23
h. Chr.5.4-7
i. Main.27.16-17
j. Psay.5Q.43
k. 6.4
l. Psay.5Q.67
m. Dav.23.14
n. Chuk.7.7-15
o. Gyp.2.9
p. Exp.9.1-8
q. Chuk.7.1-6
r. Krt.3.4
s. Grk.14.22

10 Or something.
11 Anyway,
12 [f]Galileo proceeded to tell absolutely anyone who would listen about what he had discovered,
13 Which got him into trouble,
14 Because one of the ones who listened was the [g]Pope,
15 [h]Who didn't like it,
16 [i]And made Galileo take it back,
17 Which he did,
18 [j]Completely and absolutely,
19 Except that he must have had his fingers crossed,
20 Or something,
21 [k]Since we still know about what he did with the two rocks,
22 Which helps explain why everyone knows that you can't suppress a really good idea,
23 [l]For more than a thousand years or so.
24 And Galileo wasn't the only Giant of Science in the Renaissance either.

CHAPTER 7

For example, there was also a Giant named [m]Copernicus,
2 [n]Who thought that the sun didn't revolve around the earth,
3 But the other way around,
4 [o]For some reason.
5 This was very important because it helped [p]Columbus discover America,
6 [q]Somehow,
7 And other things too.

CHAPTER 8

For instance, Copernicus's idea wound up making a Giant out of an ape named [r]Kepler,
2 Who thought [s]Pythagoras was right when he made up the idea that the universe was made up of

a bunch of shapes,

3 Called polygons,

4 That fit inside each other,

5 For some reason.

6 This obviously brilliant idea caused [a]Kepler to spend his whole life making polygons out of wood and trying to reconstruct the universe,

7 Until he suddenly discovered that the earth revolves around the sun,

8 Though not in circles, the way Copernicus thought,

9 But in ovals,

10 Called elliptical orbits,

11 [b]Which made Kepler extremely depressed,

12 For some reason,

13 But was the right answer,

14 For some reason.

15 And physics wasn't the only science in which the Giants made brilliant discoveries.

CHAPTER 9

For example, there was a Giant named [c]Leonardo da Vinci who thought up dozens of brilliant scientific ideas,

2 Like [d]tanks, which nobody knew what they were for,

3 And [e]airplanes, which nobody knew how to build,

4 And a lot of other great things too,

5 [f]Like anatomy.

6 It was [g]Leonardo da Vinci who discovered that the bodies of apes had bones and muscles and so forth,

7 Which would make pictures of naked ladies a lot more realistic and convincing if you painted them that way,

8 And which was a tremendous breakthrough,

a. *Dav.57.10*
b. *Dav.2.6*
c. *Psay.5Y.49*
d. *Barb.1.8*
e. *Adam.31.6-7*
f. *4.11-12*
g. *Dav.41.12*
h. *Gods.4.10*
i. *Dav.19.6*
j. *Dav.15.21*
k. *Psay.5Y.42*
l. *Chr.5.5-7*
m. *Lies.10.11-12*
n. *Lies.11.13 & 2.17-23*
o. *Zig.9.2 Ed.31.15-16*
p. *3.7*
q. *Psay.5Q.4*
r. *Dav.12.5*
s. *Dav.10.10*
t. *Psong.53.1-5*

9 Since before Leonardo everybody thought that bodies were made of [h]something else,

10 Or something like that.

11 Anyway, Leonardo was so brilliant that he was also a Giant in art,

12 Painting the [i]Mona Lisa and the [j]Last Supper,

13 Even though they all had clothes on,

14 And were therefore the most unusual works of art produced during the Renaissance.

CHAPTER 10

Another anatomical Giant of the Renaissance was [k]Michelangelo, who specialized in making very big art.

2 He was also controversial because he made very large paintings and statues of [l]naked biblical characters.

3 For example, he made a large naked statue of [m]David,

4 And then he painted naked pictures of [n]Adam and Eve and other biblical characters all over the ceiling of the Sistine Chapel,

5 But it was okay,

6 [o]Because he always put clothes on the [p]Virgin Mary,

7 And [q]God, of course,

8 And he also had permission from the [r]Pope,

9 Who was having a lot of wars and almost no other fun to speak of,

10 And therefore thought it would be fun to watch [s]Michelangelo lie on his back on a scaffold painting naked pictures in church,

11 For about ten years,

12 Which it was.

13 [t]In fact, it was so much fun that popes, nobles, and other

Christians who had lots of land and money and buildings decided to make a sport out of art,

14 ᵃBased on the old heathen Roman idea called division of labor,

15 Except that it was completely different, of course.

16 ᵇUnder the old heathen Roman way, Patricians would think up some huge project, and then the plebeians would do it.

17 ᶜUnder the new Renaissance way, called "patronage," popes, nobles, and other Christians who had lots of land and money and buildings would think up an art project, and then a Giant would do it,

18 ᵈWhile the "patrons" watched,

19 ᵉAnd pointed out mistakes,

20 ᶠAnd made other kinds of constructive criticism,

21 ᵍAnd looked at their watches a lot.

22 This eventually came to be called 'The Agony and the Ecstasy,'

23 Which was divided up in such a way that the Patrons got all the ʰEcstasy,

24 While the Giants got all the ⁱAgony.

CHAPTER 11

Art and science weren't the only things that Giants played with in the Renaissance. They also had a lot of fun with ʲphilosophy, now called religion and politics, which the Giants frequently got mixed up with another old Greek and Roman invention, namely, ᵏcomedy.

2 For example, there was a

Reference
a. Rom.5.9-11
b. Rom.5.12-19
c. Psong.45.3-5
d. Psong.47.1-5
e. Psong.44.1
f. Psong.43.3-7
g. Psong.48.1-4
h. Psong.47.6
i. Psom.23.13-14
j. 4.19-20
k. 4.3
l. Krt.3.1-2
m. Jeff.24.22-23
n. Brit.10.11-14
o. Dav.42.15
p. Chr.2.13-21

Giant named ˡLuther who was very interested in religion and politics and thought the church was taking itself much too seriously,

3 Which convinced him that what the church really needed was a good joke.

4 So he nailed a list of jokes called "The 95 Theses" to the front door of a cathedral and waited for the church to start laughing,

5 Which it did,

6 Convincing Luther to try an even bigger joke,

7 Named "The Reformation,"

8 Which consisted of Luther starting his own church,

9 ᵐAnd naming it after himself,

10 Which turned out to be so much fun that a lot of other Giants did it too,

11 ⁿIncluding the nation called England.

12 This amused the church—now called the Roman Catholic Church to distinguish it from all the funny new churches—so much that it decided to try some jokes of its own,

13 Like the ᵒBorgia popes,

14 Who thought it would be hilarious to be a pope who killed people,

15 And so they did.

16 Nor was this the only joke thought up by the Borgia popes.

17 For example, they also thought it would be fun to borrow the concept called ᵖ"the divine right of kings" and have popes who were succeeded by their own sons,

18 And so they did,

19 Which proved to everybody

that the Roman Catholic Church was funny enough to stay in business in its own right,

20 ^aIn spite of the Reformation.

CHAPTER 12

Now that religion had become so much fun all of a sudden, a Giant named ^bGutenberg noticed that there weren't enough ^cmonks to recopy enough Bibles for everyone to read,

2 ^dSo Gutenberg invented a way to turn out lots of copies of the Bible on a machine,

3 Not to mention other books,

4 If there were any,

5 Which gave a Giant called Machiavelli a great idea.

CHAPTER 13

With so much fun breaking out all over the place, ^eMachiavelli decided that it would be nice of him to think up some new rules for all the popes and kings and nobles who were responsible for running things,

2 And so he wrote a handbook called 'The Prince,'

3 Which explained in great detail how you could run things and have a lot of fun at the same time.

4 ^fFor example, Machiavelli explained that the most important rule was to do to others before they did to you,

5 Which is the best way of making sure that the laugh is on them,

6 And not on you.

7 The other rule was just as important, though,

8 Which is that there aren't any other rules.

a. 11.18
b. Dav.14.25
c. Chr.5.19
d. Krt.3.3
e. Dav.41.23 & 14.5
f. Ned.16.7-11
g. Ann.8.11
h. 6.22
i. 12.2
j. 4.13
k. 3.14
l. 3.15
m. Dav.12.5
n. Grk.6.14-19 & 7.1-3
o. Psom.5.1-6
p. Pnot.12.1-5
q. Pnot.2.1-5
r. Grk.16.4

9 ^g'The Prince' went on to become a big best-seller,

10 And practically indispensable to popes and kings and nobles and other Christians who had lots of land and money and buildings,

11 For about five hundred years,

12 ^hProving once again that you can't suppress a really good idea,

13 ⁱEspecially if you have a printing press.

CHAPTER 14

^jIn fact, the printing press was a big help to a lot of Renaissance Giants,

2 Many of whom were having fun inventing new kinds of Renaissance literary forms,

3 ^kLike poetry,

4 ^lAnd comedy,

5 ^mAnd tragedy.

6 For example, a Giant named Dante invented a Renaissance literary form called the epic poem,

7 And wrote one called 'The Inferno' about a trip to the ⁿold heathen Greek and Roman Underworld,

8 Which starred a character called ^oVirgil,

9 Who was the Roman who wrote an epic poem called the ^pAeneid,

10 Which was a lot like the epic poem called the ^qOdyssey,

11 ^rWhich was written by a Greek called Homer.

12 Dante's idea was so creative and original that a lot of other Giants decided to invent their own Renaissance literary forms,

13 And so they did.

CHAPTER 15

A Giant named [a]Shakespeare invented three new Renaissance literary forms all by himself,

2 Including comedy,

3 And tragedy.

4 He thought up the idea of comedy after he read some old Greek and Roman plays,

5 Which had funny plots based on the idea that a young couple in love couldn't get together because they were always disguised as someone else,

6 And couldn't recognize one another till the end,

7 When a [b]"deus ex machina" came down from the ceiling and sorted everything out,

8 Punishing the bad characters,

9 And rewarding the good ones.

10 This inspired [c]Shakespeare to come up with a completely new idea,

11 Which he tried out in a play called 'The Comedy of Errors,'

12 Which had a funny plot based on the idea that [d]*two* young couples in love couldn't get together because they were always disguised as someone else,

13 And couldn't recognize one another till the end,

14 When a "deus ex machina" came *out of the wings* and sorted everything out,

15 Punishing the bad characters,

16 And rewarding the good ones.

17 [e]Shakespeare's invention of comedy was so successful that he decided to invent tragedy next,

a. Brit.32.1-3
b. Frog.26.16
c. Ed.29.6
d. Psay.4.2
e. Pnot.56.1-5
f. Pnot.3.1-5
  & 26.1-5
g. Brit.32.4
h. Pnot.32.1-5
i. Pnot.6.1-5
j. Pnot.5.1-5
k. Pnot.10.1-5
  & 35.1-5
l. 5.7

18 Which he did by glancing at some old [f]Greek plays,

19 Which had plots based on the idea that it would be really great to watch some big important royal personage get destroyed in five acts by a fatal flaw,

20 In the course of a single day,

21 Without traveling anywhere.

22 This inspired Shakespeare to come up with another completely new idea,

23 Which he [g]tried out in a whole bunch of plays,

24 Called [h]'MacBeth' and [i]'Hamlet' and [j]'King Lear,'

25 [k]And so forth,

26 Which had a plot based on the idea that it would be really great to watch some big important royal personage get destroyed in five acts by a fatal flaw,

27 Over the course of *many* days, even years,

28 *While traveling all over the place.*

29 Shakespeare's invention of this new form, called tragedy, was a huge [l]success and convinced a lot of other Giants to write more tragedies than you can shake a pointed stick at,

30 Over more time than you can shake a pointed stick at,

31 In more places than you can shake a pointed stick at.

32 Nor was this all the damage Shakespeare did.

CHAPTER 16

W hen he saw how successful his inventions of comedy and tragedy had been, Shakespeare decided it was time for another new form that contained both tragedy and comedy.

2 And so, after scanning some old Greek and Roman writings about the deeds of ancient heathens like [a]Julius Caesar and [b]Cleopatra and so forth, he decided to invent something brand-new,

3 Called history,

4 Which he tried out in a large number of plays,

5 Called '[c]Julius Caesar,' '[d]Antony and Cleopatra,' '[e]Henry IV, Part II,' '[f]Richard III,' and so forth.

6 The important thing about history was that you had to write about *real* characters and *real* events, based strictly on the facts you had,

7 [g]And whatever facts you could make up,

8 [h]So that the audience would believe they were really seeing it the way it was.

9 Shakespeare's invention of history was such a gigantic success that it convinced all the Giants to take all their many new inventions, such as art and science and politics and literature, out into the world and start making new history of their own,

10 Which they did,

11 And explains why there came to be a Modern Age,

12 Which means an age so full of tragic events that it seems like some big [i]comedy of errors.

a. Rom.12.13
b. Gyp.3.11-13
c. Rom.11.2
d. Dav.13.1-4
e. Psay.5Q.54
f. Psay.5Q.25
g. Ed.16.12
h. Psay.5Q.46
i. 15.10-11

THE BOOK OF EXPLORERS

CHAPTER 1

When the apes called Europeans decided to have a [a]Modern Age, they realized that they would have to make a lot of [b]history,

2 As quickly as possible,

3 Because the nation that made the most history in the shortest period of time would probably become the Chosen Nation of [c]Europe,

4 Chosen in the modern sense, that is,

5 Meaning richest and most powerful,

6 And therefore the most beloved by [d]God,

7 Because they had learned during the [e]Renaissance,

8 From [f]Machiavelli and the [g]Borgia popes and other good examples,

9 [h]That God helps those who help themselves.

10 One of the best ways to make history is to discover something,

11 Like land that nobody else owns,

12 And help yourself to everything in it,

13 And own it forever,

14 And maybe even name it after yourself,

15 Which is how you get to be not only a Chosen Nation,

16 [i]But an Empire.

17 And so it happened that the Modern Age began with a great race,

18 By all the leading nations of Europe,

a. Gnt.16.12
b. Gnt.16.6-7
c. Barb.4.18
d. Lies.2.26-28
e. Gnt.1.13
f. Gnt.13.1-8
g. Gnt.11.13-20
h. Psay.5Q.32
i. Jefs.7.15

19 Including ᵃItaly,
20 And ᵇDenmark,
21 And ᶜHolland,
22 And ᵈPortugal,
23 And ᵉSpain,
24 And ᶠFrance,
25 And ᵍEngland,
26 To discover the most new land in the shortest possible time,
27 And the apes who were responsible for doing the discovering were called Explorers.
28 And so every nation started the race with its own particular advantages and disadvantages, from the most logical possible starting point.

CHAPTER 2

The nation with the most advantages was Italy,
2 Which started from Italy,
3 Which was where the ʰRomans had started from,
4 And had the advantage of considerable experience at discovering new lands,
5 ⁱSuch as Spain and France and England,
6 And most recently ʲChina,
7 Which had been discovered by ᵏMarco Polo,
8 But was too big for one man to appropriate all by himself.
9 Italy also had the advantage of having some very good Explorers,
10 Such as ˡChristopher Columbus and ᵐAmerigo Vespucci,
11 Who were just dying to go out and discover things.
12 Italy's only disadvantage was that it no longer had an emperor,
13 ⁿSince the last Roman emperor had left town,
14 About a thousand years ago.

a. 2.1
b. 3.1
c. 4.1
d. 5.1
e. 6.1
f. 7.1
g. 8.1
h. Rom.1.1-11
i. Rom.12.1-13
j. Chnk.1.1-8
k. Dav.18.5
l. 9.1
m. 10.8
n. Rom.24.7-16
o. 1.20
p. Apes.4.7-8
q. Barb.1.1-8
r. Brit.4.1-6
s. 1.21
t. Bks.6.17-18
u. Psay.5J.13
v. 1.22
w. 12.1
x. 1.23
y. Spic.1.1
z. Gnt.7.5

CHAPTER 3

ᵒDenmark started from Denmark,
2 Which wasn't much of an advantage,
3 Since Denmark was pretty small,
4 Though full of ᵖclever apes,
5 Who were descended from the same apes who had once been very competent ᑫbarbarians,
6 ʳHaving conquered England,
7 And other places,
8 Several times.

CHAPTER 4

ˢHolland started from Holland,
2 Which wasn't much of an advantage either,
3 Although the apes from Holland,
4 Who were called the Dutch,
5 ᵗFor some reason,
6 Were good shipbuilders and clever traders,
7 Even though they wore wooden shoes,
8 ᵘFor some reason.

CHAPTER 5

ᵛPortugal started from Portugal,
2 Which would have been an advantage,
3 If the Portuguese had had any Explorers,
4 Which they mostly didn't,
5 Except for ᵐMagellan,
6 Who knew a lot about sailing,
7 But wasn't too good at round trips.

CHAPTER 6

ˣSpain started from ʸSpain,
2 Which was an advantage,
3 ᶻBecause it was fairly close to

the new world that was about to be discovered.

4 The Spanish had other advantages too,

5 [a]Like knowing how to build a lot of ships,

6 And having a lot of their own Explorers,

7 Called [b]conquistadors,

8 Who were absolutely the best at helping themselves to everything they found,

9 Though not quite as good at finding it in the first place.

CHAPTER 7

The [c]French started from [d]France,

2 Which would have been a tremendous advantage,

3 If the French had known anything about building ships,

4 Or sailing them,

5 Which they didn't,

6 Being French,

7 [e]And living in a nation that was surrounded on only three sides by various seas and oceans,

8 [f]Which is also why the French came to be called Frogs.

CHAPTER 8

The [g]English started from [h]England,

2 Which would have been an overwhelming advantage to any nation but the English,

3 [i]Who never believed in doing things the easy way,

4 And so started late,

5 To give all the other nations a fighting chance.

CHAPTER 9

And so it happened that the first Explorer who discov-

a. *Gnt.10.14*
b. *Frog.12.13*
c. *1.24*
d. *Barb.5.1-2*
e. *Frog.1.1*
f. *Frog.1.2*
g. *1.25*
h. *Barb.5.3-4*
i. *Brit.2.1-3*
j. *Ed.28.6*
k. *Grk.14.1-6*
l. *6.1*
m. *Lies.14.5*
n. *Chuk.2.8*
o. *Grk.12.8*
p. *Wil.19.5*
q. *Bks.1.1-8*
r. *Lies.6.7-19*
s. *Chuk.6.4-8*
t. *Hill.A.4*
u. *Gnt.16.9-12*

ered something really important was [j]Columbus,

2 Who was an Italian,

3 And therefore sailed west into the [k]Atlantic,

4 Under the flag of [l]Spain,

5 [m]Which is how history works sometimes,

6 [n]And explains why life is so confusing,

7 [o]And so often seems like some big accident,

8 [p]Which is exactly how Columbus discovered America.

9 It turned out that Columbus had been trying to discover a shorter route to [q]India,

10 Where they keep all the [r]salt and pepper and other spices,

11 [s]Because he thought that the earth wasn't flat,

12 But round,

13 Like an orange,

14 Which meant that he could get to the east by going west[t].

15 As it happened, Columbus was mostly right.

16 The earth was round,

17 Though not like an orange,

18 As much as, say, a basketball,

19 Which is to say that it was bigger than he thought,

20 Big enough, in fact, to have a couple of other continents on it that nobody had known about.

CHAPTER 10

Columbus's discovery of America was thus extremely funny,

2 Proving that the Giants had been right about the value of having a [u]Modern Age,

3 And making a lot of new history.

4 The funniest thing of all was that Columbus sailed west into

the Atlantic several times and
never once landed on either of
the two gigantic continents that
sat on the other side of the
ocean,
5 [a]But landed instead on a
bunch of Caribbean islands,
6 [b]And thus missed his chance
to name the new world after
himself,
7 Which is how Italy got a second chance at getting a good
start in the race for history,
8 Since the Italian Explorer
[c]Amerigo Vespucci recognized
Columbus's mistake,
9 And promptly named the new
world after himself,
10 Which turned out to be another very funny joke,
11 Because Amerigo forgot to
help himself to everything,
12 Which isn't a smart thing to
do,
13 [d]Especially when there are a
lot of Spaniards around.
14 And so it happened that Italy
got pretty well fed up with trying
to make history and be a [e]Cho-
sen Nation for a second time,
15 Which would have been a
record anyway,
16 And became thoroughly
funny instead,
17 For the rest of recorded human history.

CHAPTER 11

Meanwhile, the Spanish
were winning. The [f]Span-
ish Explorers may not have been
very good at finding new continents, but they knew a lot about
helping themselves,
2 Which is why they helped
themselves to most of the
[g]Caribbean islands,

a. Psay.5Y.1
b. Psay.5Q.23
c. Dav.41.23
d. 11.1
e. 1.4
f. 6.7
g. 10.4-5
h. Psay.3.2
i. Yks.36.13
j. Hill.W.16
k. Spic.3.4-5
l. 9.9
m. Chr.2.5-8
n. Jefs.11.19
o. Rom.2.8-10
p. Boul.14.9-12
q. Chr.2.4
r. Gyp.4.7
s. Dav.52.4
t. Psong.45.3
u. Chr.6.7
v. Dav.52.4

3 [h]And Florida,
4 And Central America, including [i]Texas,
5 And to large chunks of [j]South
America.
6 In fact, it turned out that the
conquistadors were even better
at making history in the new
world than anyone had imagined.
7 For example, if there was any
[k]gold around, they could smell it
all the way from Spain,
8 And therefore got very good
at navigating from Spain to
places where the Indians,
9 As the native Americans were
called,
10 [l]For some reason,
11 Had worked hard to mine
gold and turn it into [m]heathen
jewelry and art.
12 Being pretty ardent [n]Chris-
tians, the conquistadors disapproved of heathen jewelry and
art,
13 Especially when it was made
of gold,
14 And [o]appropriated it from
the Indians,
15 So that it could be taken back
to Spain and used in a [p]proper
Christian way,
16 Thus saving the [q]Indians
from eternal hell and damnation,
17 [r]Which was a particular specialty of the Spanish.
18 For example, there was a
conquistador named [s]Cortés who
saved the Aztecs from eternal
hell and damnation,
19 [t]By taking all their gold,
20 And converting them to
Christianity,
21 [u]By killing most of them.
22 There was another [v]conquis-
tador who saved the Inca,

23 [a]By taking all their gold,
24 [b]And converting them to Christianity,
25 [c]By killing most of them.
26 And there was yet another [d]conquistador who performed the same great service for the Mayans,
27 And so on,
28 Which is why so many [e]nations in Central and South America are Christian and still speak Spanish today,
29 Except for the ones who speak Portuguese.

CHAPTER 12

Portugal had an Explorer named [f]Magellan,
2 [g]Who wanted to go around the world,
3 And so he did,
4 [h]But he never really understood the part about going ashore in some new place,
5 [i]And taking everything you can find,
6 [j]And then naming the whole place after yourself,
7 Which maybe explains why he died en route round the world,
8 Without doing any of the really important colonial things.
9 Still, the Portuguese did manage to discover an eastern chunk of South America that didn't have any gold to speak of,
10 And therefore escaped the attention of the [k]Spanish conquistadors,
11 Which gave Portugal a surprisingly large amount of land to help themselves to,
12 Except that it was [l]Brazil,
13 And almost completely covered with jungle,
14 And much too hot,
15 And full of insects and poisonous snakes,
16 Which discouraged Portugal so much that it gave up trying to make history altogether,
17 And never got to be a [m]Chosen Nation.

CHAPTER 13

While all of this great history was being made in the new world, the [n]Danish were still trying to figure out how to get started.
2 Eventually they decided that the best way to make history wasn't by discovering new worlds,
3 But by making pastry.
4 This turned out to be incorrect,
5 So Denmark stopped trying to make history,
6 And decided it would be better to forget about everything,
7 Except pastry,
8 Which they did,
9 And explains why Denmark lost its chance to be a Chosen Nation too.

CHAPTER 14

The Dutch started out much better than the Danish, [o]cleverly deciding that the best way to go east to [p]India was by sailing east to India.
2 When it turned out that India was right where they thought it was, they made some good money trading in spices.
3 Getting adventurous, they then sailed west with the idea of arriving at a destination in the west[q],
4 Having decided that they'd

a. 11.19
b. 11.20
c. 11.21
d. Dav.52.4
e. Spic.12.6
f. 5.1-5
g. 9.11-12
h. 1.11
i. 1.12
j. 1.14
k. 11.7
l. Hill.W.14-15
m. 1.4-5
n. 3.1
o. 4.6
p. 9.10
q. 9.3

found a solid approach to the discovery business.

5 But a lot like the [a]Portuguese, the Dutch also failed to become a Chosen Nation,

6 Because they forgot that the purpose of history was to make history,

7 [b]Not just money,

8 And therefore failed to do enough of the right colonial things,

9 [c]Like convert all the Indians,

10 [d]And help themselves to vast chunks of territory,

11 Until it was really too late,

12 And the only remaining unappropriated land was the land nobody else wanted,

13 Like a little Guiana on the edge of South America,

14 And [e]South Africa.

15 And so, with the exception of some [f]slave trading and a war or two along the way, the Dutch also stopped making history and decided to be picturesque instead,

16 With a lot of windmills,

17 Tulips,

18 And [g]wooden shoes.

CHAPTER 15

When the [h]French finally figured out how to build a ship that could sail across the Atlantic, [i]most of the best land had already been taken,

2 And so they made do with the best leftovers they could find,

3 Including most of [j]Canada,

4 [k]Which was too cold and awful to have a lot of gold-mining Indians in it,

5 And Haiti,

6 [l]Which was too hot and awful

a. 12.1-3
b. Psong.45.1-5
c. 11.21
d. 1.9
e. Ext.48.19
f. Brd.7.7
g. 4.7-8
h. 7.6
i. Psay.5A.34
j. Brit.26.15
k. Psay.5Q.74
l. Psay.5Q.43
m. Psay.5Q.56
n. 14.13
o. Psay.5Q.14
p. 1.5-6
q. Frog.1.6
r. Brit.40.8
s. 8.1
t. 8.3
u. Brit.24.8
v. Psay.5R.9

to have any gold-mining Indians in it,

7 And the middle part of North America,

8 [m]Which had too many angry Indians in it that didn't even know what gold was,

9 And a little [n]Guiana that sat right next to Holland's and was about as useful.

10 Disappointed in their new world discoveries, the French eventually discovered large chunks of Africa,

11 [o]That were too hot and awful for anyone to want them but the French.

12 But, being from France, the French people refused to give up their quest to be a [p]Chosen Nation, and kept on trying to make history for many many years,

13 [q]Until a lot of other nations finally made them stop.

14 Anyway,

15 The French, being from France, decided to [r]stick it out and do what they could to make history in the new world,

16 In strange French ways,

17 For as long as possible,

18 And so they did.

CHAPTER 16

The [s]English, being [t]English, set about becoming a power in the new world in the most eccentric and backward way they could think of.

2 Instead of sending ships out to conquer territory in the new world,

3 [u]They sent exiles and outcasts,

4 Unarmed,

5 [v]And generally peace-loving,

6 To establish pathetic little col-

onies that usually died of cold and starvation during the first winter.

7 While this brilliant colonial strategy was getting under way, they also did what they could to irritate the [a]Spanish,

8 By sinking all the Spanish ships they could find in the Atlantic,

9 [b]And occasionally unloading them first,

10 Though not always.

11 Then they sent [c]Sir Walter Raleigh and some other Brit lords to the new world to bring back tobacco leaves,

12 Which they did[d],

13 Thus showing the Spanish who really deserved to be the Chosen Nation,

14 [e]Somehow.

15 [f]And eventually, the exceptionally clever British colonial strategy resulted in British control of most of the eastern sea-

a. *Hill.A.4*
b. *Psong.9.1-2*
c. *Dav.32.4*
d. *Mes.2.5 & 3.2*
e. *Brit.31.8*
f. *Yks.6.2-17*
g. *Adam.3.17*
h. *Psay.5Q.46*
i. *Psay.5Q.56*

board of North America,

16 And the most highly advanced and lucrative of all the European holdings in the new world,

17 [g]Somehow.

CHAPTER 17

And so the Explorers started the Modern Age with a lot of rushing around,

2 And a lot of discovering,

3 And a lot of important history,

4 Which decided who would have a chance to be the Chosen Nation,

5 And who wouldn't.

6 And the nations who had the best chance to be the Chosen Nation worked so hard that they each made up a history of their own,

7 [h]Which a lot of people still believe today,

8 And is how history works,

9 [i]Life being what it is.

THE BOOK OF SPICS

OTHERWISE KNOWN AS THE BOOK OF EL DORADO

CHAPTER 1

There was a place called Spain attached to the continent of [a]Europe. Constantly afraid of losing its [b]link with Europe and thereby its only claim to [c]civilization, Spain has hung on to the south coast of France with a white-knuckled grip for thousands of years.

a. *Barb.4.18*
b. *Swar.36.3*
c. *Carl.3.8*
d. *Vin.1.25*
e. *Jefs.7.15*
f. *Gnt.16.6-7*

2 The knuckles are called the Pyrenees. The people who live in the Pyrenees are called [d]Basques.

3 The people who live in Spain are called Spics. [e]They never liked being called Spics, but who would?

4 The Spics tried to make [f]history for a long time, but eventu-

ally they got tired and stopped.
5 This is their ªstory.

CHAPTER 2

Nobody knows anything about the Spics before ᵇCaesar discovered they were there,
2 Living in the Roman world, but not in the Roman Way,
3 ᶜWhich is to say they didn't have enough viaducts and roads and Roman troops marching back and forth.
4 ᵈCaesar corrected this situation by conquering the Spics,
5 Which made history,
6 ᵉBecause everything that Caesar did he wrote down in his own book of history,
7 So that hundreds of generations of schoolchildren could read about it.
8 That's how everybody else in the world found out the Spics were there,
9 Except the Spics, of course, who already knew they were there,
10 Which was lucky for them because they couldn't read anyway.

CHAPTER 3

Having been noticed by the world, the Spics had a hard time of it for a long while.
2 ᶠSpain is mostly a desert, which means that the view consists mostly of hot sand,
3 And mirages, which are hallucinations caused by hot sand.
4 What with not reading and all, the Spics were unduly influenced by their ᵍmirages, which made them believe that there was a land made completely of ʰgold,

a.	*Wil.68.13-19*
b.	*Rom.11.1-2*
c.	*Rom.5.1-7*
d.	*Rom.12.5-9*
e.	*Rom.12.1-4*
f.	*Psay.5Q.53*
g.	*Mall.6.24-25*
h.	*Psong.16.1-4*
i.	*Psay.5Q.30*
j.	*Bks.4.1-6*
k.	*Rom.19.1-2*
l.	*19.8*
m.	*Jefs.11.19*
n.	*Dav.15.20*
o.	*Chr.2.13-21*
p.	*Chr.3.23-26*
q.	*Chr.4.1-3*
r.	*Chr.5.13-16*
s.	*2.10*
t.	*Grk.8.32*
u.	*3.8*

5 ⁱSomewhere to the west,
6 Unfortunately for the west,
7 But before they could go there and steal all the gold, they needed some lessons on how to be exceptionally cruel and brutal and intolerant and bloodthirsty,
8 ʲWhich they got from the Moslems,
9 Who conquered Spain after the ᵏDecline and Fall of Rome,
10 And taught the Spics plenty.

CHAPTER 4

When the Moslems had taught the Spics everything they knew, they finally left,
2 Which made it possible for Spain to become a civilized nation,
3 Which they did,
4 ˡSort of.
5 They built plenty of buildings and churches,
6 Having become thoroughly ᵐChristian,
7 Since the Moslems had taught the Spics that it's impossible to become completely cruel and brutal and intolerant and bloodthirsty unless you believe in a major religion based on ⁿLove Thy Neighbor and so forth.
8 Thanks to being Christian, they also embraced the ᵒdivine right of kings and ᵖnobles and ᑫserfs and so forth,
9 Which they adapted to their own particular style.
10 For example, unlike ʳEuropean nobles, Spic nobles thought it was a sign of ˢgood breeding that they couldn't read or write,
11 Which left them plenty of free time for riding ᵗhorses and sticking their ᵘswords into anything that moved,

12 Including bulls, which is how the Spics happened to make their one unique contribution to the world of sports,

13 Which is called the bullfight,

14 And since it is so interesting to so many people,

15 [a]For some reason,

16 [b]And has even had books written about it,

17 Deserves a whole chapter all to itself.

CHAPTER 5

The bullfight is not a sport exactly,

2 Because it is not a fight exactly,

3 [c]But an execution, which has always been a favorite pastime of Spics.

4 The way it works is, the bull thinks he has a chance to get the bullfighter, called the [d]Matador, which he does,

5 But since getting the Matador won't save him anyway, the bull is regarded as a [e]tragic figure,

6 A lot like a Spanish nobleman,

7 Who is also very brave, very violent, very stupid, and very likely to die without learning anything new.

8 [f]And so the tragic bull tries to get the Matador and gets stuck with a bunch of pointed sticks instead,

9 [g]And is made to look very foolish with a lot of veronicas and such,

10 [h]Before he gets transfixed by a sword at the end of the fight and [i]dies bleeding in the hot sand.

11 [j]This beautiful event cap-

a. *Zig.6.3*
b. *14.9*
c. *Psay.5Q.75*
d. *Dav.15.9*
e. *Gnt.15.17-19*
f. *Psay.5Q.75*
g. *Psay.5Q.75*
h. *Psay.5Q.75*
i. *Psom.60.1-2*
j. *Kens.7.7-9*
k. *Mall.6.9-19*
l. *Wil.50.8-9*
m. *Dav.10.10*
n. *4.10*
o. *Ed.27.5*
p. *Dav.12.5*
q. *7.4*

tures all the mystique of Spain and has helped the world immeasurably in appreciating the Spics for the brave, violent, stupid animals they are.

CHAPTER 6

Unfortunately, the Spics' aversion to reading and writing made it harder for them to make history,

2 [k]Since when something happens and nobody writes it down, it's a lot like it never happened at all,

3 [l]Which is one way to sum up Spic culture.

4 For example, the Spics had one historical figure,

5 Known as [m]El Cid,

6 Who did something or other,

7 But no one really knows what it was.

8 The Spics also produced one work of literature, called 'Don Quixote,' which was written by a prisoner,

9 [n]Who fortunately was low enough on the Spic social scale that he could get away with being able to write.

10 'Don Quixote' is the story of an old tall Spic who tilted windmills for a living,

11 With a short squire named [o]Sancho Panza who pushed on the lower part of the windmill,

12 While [p]Don Quixote pushed on the upper part of the windmill, from the other side.

13 This method of windmill tilting is the only known accomplishment of Spic technology,

14 Except, of course, for the many religious artifacts they developed during the [q]Spanish Inquisition.

CHAPTER 7

The Spanish Inquisition was what the Spics had instead of a [a]Renaissance.

2 When the rest of Europe decided to stop having a [b]Dark Age and start thinking about a lot of things, and reading and writing about a lot of things, and then making up art and science and history and new interpretations of religion, the Spics got very upset.

3 To them, having a [c]Dark Age wasn't just some thousand-year fad, but the basis of their whole culture, and they weren't going to stand around and do nothing while the whole world went to hell in a hand basket.

4 So they set up an [d]Inquisition to look into the new ways of thinking and reading and writing and so forth,

5 And since they couldn't read, they naturally had to ask people to explain the new things to them,

6 Which they did, with the help of religious artifacts that encouraged people to cooperate with them.

7 [e]For example, the Spics had artifacts that encouraged people to cooperate by tearing them limb from limb, disemboweling them, burning them to death, and so forth.

8 The more they looked into it, the more convinced they were that the new ways were evil and unchristian,

9 [f]Because look at what happened to the people who were involved with these new ways.

10 And so, being Christian, they helped out all they could by saving the souls of the people who had gotten involved with the wrong ideas,

11 Including religious [g]heretics, and philosophers, and scientists, and artists, and Jews, of course,

12 [h]And especially Jews.

13 [i]They did this by tearing them limb from limb, disemboweling them, burning them to death, and so forth,

14 Which as you'll recall, is the very best way to get into heaven,

15 [j]If you're a Christian.

CHAPTER 8

There was one new idea that the Spics liked, though, and that was the Renaissance invention called making [k]history.

2 [l]The Spics realized that their ancient desire to go west and hunt for the mirage called El Dorado,

3 Meaning "City of Gold,"

4 [m]Was perfectly in line with the new fad called Exploring the World.

5 Besides, the Spics were very religious and knew that what with the [n]Inquisition and all, if they wanted to save more souls for Christianity, they needed to find new blood.

6 And so the Spics, who were not very clever at reading maps,

7 Or anything else,

8 [o]Hired an Italian Explorer named Christopher Columbus to find a New World for them.

9 He succeeded, and for the very first time, the Spics had a real chance to make history all by themselves,

10 [p]And even become a Chosen Nation.

a. Gnt.1.13
b. Chr.10.1-7
c. Chr.9.1-7
d. Jeff.10.5-9
e. Psay.5Q.75
f. Psay.5Q.62
g. Ext.48.35
h. Chr.6.10
i. 7.7
j. Jefs.7.46
k. Exp.1.3-6
l. 3.4-5
m. Exp.1.9-16
n. 7.4-6
o. Exp.9.1-8
p. Psay.5Q.75

CHAPTER 9

In fact, the Spics had a very good time in the New World. They searched for [a]El Dorado all over the place,

2 Very thoroughly,

3 And [b]asked the natives for help, using many of the [c]same artifacts that had worked so well for them during the Inquisition,

4 [d]Then thanked the natives for their help by saving their souls,

5 And even stayed with the natives who were left to make sure that they did everything the Christian way,

6 [e]Which means handing over all your gold to the Spics so that they can send it back to Spain to finance more expeditions in search of El Dorado.

CHAPTER 10

In this way, the Spics established colonies throughout the New World, including Florida, Mexico, Puerto Rico, California, and too many places in South America to remember, as well as a place called the Philippines, which was so far away from anywhere that nobody else wanted it.

2 All the Spic colonies were very Christian,

3 [f]Meaning poor as dirt,

4 Which was a considerable improvement over their old heathen days,

5 [g]When they had gold and pagan religions of their own and cities and armies and a distinct shortage of small pox and other European diseases.

6 The conversion of all these peoples to the Christian way was the accomplishment of Spic no-

a. 8.3
b. Vin.50.11-16
c. Jeff.12.3
d. 7.10
e. Cen.26.19
f. Boul.21.9
g. Lies.6.11
h. Exp.11.22
i. Exp.11.18
j. Brit.15.40-41
k. Oth.3.1-13
l. Psay.5Q.68
m. Brit.9.1-8
n. Brit.13.4-6
o. Dav.20.28
p. Dav.46.15
q. Brit.13.7-10
r. Psay.5Y.27
s. Yks.30.1-48

bles called conquistadors,

7 Who had names like [h]Pizarro and [i]Cortés and [j]Coronado and virtually annihilated, which is to say converted, native cultures with names like the [k]Aztecs, the Mayans, and the Incas.

8 And while all this progress was under way in the New World, the Atlantic Ocean was full of Spanish galleons taking gold back to Spain.

CHAPTER 11

The galleons full of gold attracted the attention of other countries who were trying to become the Chosen Nation,

2 Notably England,

3 Who thought that [l]Britannia should rule the waves,

4 [m]And everything else for that matter,

5 And so the [n]English queen, named [o]Elizabeth, sent [p]Sir Francis Drake to sink the Spanish Armada,

6 Which is a Spic term meaning "to put all your eggs in one basket."

7 Outnumbered and outgunned, Sir Francis succeeded in the typical English way,

8 [q]By being too stupid to lose,

9 And also got some help from a storm that forced the Spic Captains to have to read their maps,

10 Which practically decided the outcome right there.

CHAPTER 12

[r]After the loss of the Spanish Armada, the Spics started a long slow decline, eventually losing most of their colonies,

2 Including the ones in Florida, [s]Mexico, Puerto Rico, and Cali-

fornia, as well as the ones in South America.

3 But by this time, most of the Spic colonies had become Spics in their own right,

4 [a]Being Christian and Spanish-speaking and cruel and vicious and intolerant and bloodthirsty,

5 Though shorter physically.

6 In this way, over a long period of time, the New World acquired a whole bunch of new [b]nations, including Mexico and Nicaragua and El Salvador and Honduras and Costa Rica and Venezuela and Colombia and Argentina and Bolivia and Uruguay and Paraguay and Ecuador and Chile and Peru.

7 [c]But blessed as they were with a Spanish cultural heritage, all these nations also found it difficult to make history in any lasting way,

8 And so they made [d]*estancias* instead and took a lot of [e]*siestas* and had [f]*gauchos* and [g]*corrida de toros* and saved the souls of the masses by keeping them dirt-poor.

9 [h]In short, they spent a couple of centuries waiting for the mother country to show them what to do next.

CHAPTER 13

The Spic Decline and Fall was not nearly as funny as the Roman Decline and Fall,

2 At least as far as we know,

3 [i]Since not much was ever written about it.

4 In fact, all that we know for sure is the parts of the Decline and Fall that other nations wrote about,

5 Like the conquest of Spain by Napoleon Bonaparte,

a. 4.7
b. Bks.6.17-18
c. 2.10
d. Carl.3.8
e. Psom.4.10
f. Grk.8.32
g. Zig.8.10-12
h. Gods.6.12
i. Ext.52.16
j. Frog.14.1
k. Dav.18.5
l. Rom.2.16-17
m. Psay.5Q.75
n. Ed.36.14
o. Ned.8.10
p. Dav.29.7-8
q. Carl.3.1-12

6 Who was [j]sort of French and had a brother named Joseph who thought he'd like to be king of Spain.

7 So Napoleon put Joseph on the throne of Spain, where he stayed until Napoleon retired at Waterloo and the rest of the nations of Europe rescued the Spics,

8 Which immediately fell silent once again, spending all their time on *siestas* and keeping the masses dirt-poor.

9 Occasionally they resurfaced to try their hand at culture.

10 They had a painter called [k]El Greco,

11 Which means The Greek,

12 And explains how he got away with it.

13 They had a songwriter, who wrote "Lady of Spain,"

14 Unless somebody else did.

15 And that was about it for Spic culture.

CHAPTER 14

Eventually, though, [l]history started to happen again in Spain,

2 In a small way,

3 [m]When a fascist named [n]Franco decided to dispense with the king and [o]make the trains run on time.

4 This caused good people the world over to discover the plight of Spain's oppressed masses,

5 And [p]write about it in books and journals and newspapers in a lot of countries outside Spain,

6 Which is the only way that anything ever gets written about Spain.

7 Naturally, when they found out that history was happening in Spain, [q]good people from all

over rushed in to help save the Spanish masses from Franco,

8 Which is how [a]Ernest Hemingway came to really put Spain on the map,

9 What with [b]'For Whom the Bell Tolls' and 'Death in the Afternoon' and all,

10 'Which made Spain very romantic and intriguing,

11 And led to the discovery of a second Spic painter,

12 Named [d]Picasso,

13 Just as Franco was taking over and stopping history again.

CHAPTER 15

Franco made the trains run on time,

2 Sort of,

3 Which is always the outstanding accomplishment of fascist regimes the world over,

4 And kept Spain out of the Second World War,

5 Which was probably for the best anyway,

6 [e]Since the Spics had pretty well forgotten how to fight during the past few centuries,

7 And managed to stay in power much longer than any other fascist regime,

8 Which is something, anyway.

CHAPTER 16

Franco's accomplishments were not lost on the [f]Spics in South America, who thought it would be great if the trains ran on time in their countries.

2 And so a bunch of Spic countries tried their own hands at being fascists,

3 [g]Setting up military dictatorships run by brave, violent, stu-

a. Dav.9.7
b. Psom.76.1-6
c. Yks.66.6
d. Ed.28.6
e. Yks.30.18
f. 12.6
g. Psay.5Q.75
h. Dav.52.20
i. Jefs.7.15
j. Grk.20.8
k. 17.8

pid [h]animals who were overthrown as soon as it became clear that they couldn't make the trains run on time.

4 There were so many of these dictatorships that they were given a name all their own by the foreign press, which was "Banana Republics,"

5 [i]Meaning "We really can't keep track of all this by ourselves and besides who cares anyway."

6 Every once in a while, the Gringos, meaning "Dirty thieving Yankee Imperialists from North America," would intervene in the internal politics of the Spic countries and talk about Latin American democracy,

7 [j]Which means rule by brave, violent, stupid masses,

8 And didn't seem to work any better than rule by brave, violent, stupid military dictators,

9 [k]Spics being what they are.

CHAPTER 17

And although it sometimes seems that the Spics have forever lost their chance to make history, the Spic nations of the world have never stopped hoping that they will be shown a way to get back on an equal footing with everybody else.

2 In their dreams, this new way will flower as beautifully and abundantly as the coca plant,

3 And will spread throughout the civilized world,

4 Making all of the world's inhabitants as violent and stupid as Spics,

5 Fulfilling the age-old quest of the Spics for cultural renaissance,

6 ^aWhich means reestablish-
ment of a Dark Age in which
nobody can read or write or
think,

a. Wil.29.2-5
b. Psay.5Q.75

7 And which will be called,
8 Because Spics never learn,
9 ^bEl Dorado.

THE BOOK OF FROGS

OTHERWISE KNOWN AS THE BOOK OF GLORY

CHAPTER 1

There was a place called
France conveniently located
on the west coast of Europe,
where it was surrounded on three
sides by water.
2 ^aThis explains why the French
are called Frogs,
3 Although there are other reasons too,
4 As we shall see.
5 Anyway, the Frogs tried very
hard to make history and become
the Chosen Nation,
6 But eventually the other nations of Europe made them stop.
7 ^bThis is their story.

CHAPTER 2

^cA long long time ago, the
place that is now France
was called Gaul and was divided
into three parts.
2 ^dThen Caesar took all three
parts for himself and made them
part of the Roman Empire,
3 ^eUntil the barbarians sacked
Rome and it was every barbarian
for himself.
4 By then, there were barbarians
called ^fFranks, who settled down
in what used to be Gaul and
renamed it after themselves,
5 Which is how there came to
be France.

a. Exp.7.6-8
b. Swar.PS.27-
   29
c. Psom.49.1-5
d. Rom.12.5-7
e. Barb.3.1-9
f. Barb.5.1-2
g. Rom.5.2-6
h. Rom.4.1-12
i. Rom.8.1-5
   & 7.8-10
j. Rom.12.1-4
k. Bks.3.1-4
l. Rom.6.3-4
m. Paul.6.9
n. Chuk.9.7
   Psay.5A.4
   Krt.2.11-21
o. Dav.10.10
   Ext.52.16
p. Adam.30.1-7
q. 2.1

CHAPTER 3

The Franks had been exposed
to many of the Roman ways,
including ^gRoman engineering,
^hRoman government, ⁱRoman art
and literature, ^jRoman history,
^kRoman military practices, and
the ^lRoman love of glory.
2 Demonstrating their uncanny
knack for perceiving the most
important aspects of life and culture, the Franks therefore borrowed from Roman culture the
only part of it that made sense to
them, namely, the love of ^mglory.
3 Accordingly, the Frankish
barbarians decided that they too
were an empire and, with typical
Frankish flair, decided to call
themselves the ⁿHoly Roman
Empire.
4 The first ruler of the Holy
Roman Empire was ^oCharle-
magne,
5 Meaning "Charles the Great,"
6 ^pWhich proves that even back
then the Frogs knew that the best
way to convince the world of
your greatness is to tell the world
that you are great.
7 Unfortunately, Charlemagne
died and the Holy Roman Em-
pire fell into ^qthree parts again,
8 Because Charlemagne's sons
had to set an important precedent

beforc things got too far along,
9 [a]Namely, that being quarrelsome is more important than actually accomplishing anything.

CHAPTER 4

Thanks to Charlemagne, though, the Frogs had discovered that rule by the [b]divine right of kings is the way to go,
2 Especially if you have a tendency to break up into quarrelsome factions, because quarrels about divine right make for plenty of [c]wars,
3 [d]Which means lots of glory all round,
4 [e]And is why the Frogs are so superior to everyone else.
5 For a long time, the Frogs sort of specialized in being quarrelsome with others.
6 For example, they quarreled with the [f]pope in Rome and set up their own [g]pope,
7 [h]Which confused everybody and therefore proved that the Frogs were superior, since they were [i]never confused.
8 They also had a quarrelsome noble called [j]William who, having discovered boating for the first time in the history of the Frogs, sailed over to England, killed [k]King Harold at Hastings, [l]conquered England,
9 And immediately ceased to be a Frog,
10 [m]Since the Frogs are not allowed to conquer England,
11 Ever.

CHAPTER 5

The establishment of a united England under William was a godsend for the Frogs because there was still no [n]Germany, and the Frogs needed another nation to quarrel with.
2 Spurred on by the English, therefore, France rose to become a major civilized nation,
3 Inventing a lot of important culture along the way,
4 [o]Including French art and architecture,
5 [p]French poetry and drama,
6 [q]French cuisine, including French fries,
7 [r]French chivalry, including French kissing,
8 [s]And even French history and science, which are also known as French comedy.

CHAPTER 6

By this time, the Frogs had become pretty [t]sure of themselves, and decided that the [u]world was too small to hold them and the English too,
2 Which is why they had a Hundred Years War,
3 And took a regular beating for decades, losing lots of battles, lots of men, and lots of face,
4 Which may help explain why they eventually allowed Joan of Arc to have a lot of glory that was normally reserved exclusively for French men.

CHAPTER 7

Joan of [v]Arc was a teenage peasant girl who couldn't read or write, but who had religious [w]visions about saving France from the English in battle.
2 Naturally, this made perfect sense to the Frog generals, who were running out of ideas about how to score against England,
3 And so [x]Joan of Arc led the Frog army in several battles,

a. Paul.7.2
b. Chr.2.10-21
c. Grk.23.12-13
d. Psay.5Q.56
e. Swar.PS.38
f. Dav.41.23
g. Dav.46.19
h. Psay.5Q.62
i. 40.4
j. Dav.21.26
k. Dav.41.12
l. Psay.5Y.8
m. Brit.7.5
n. Krt.2.1-7
o. 22.1
p. Krt.6.7-8
q. 24.1
r. 9.1
s. Paul.7.6
t. 4.4
u. Rom.6.3-4
v. Lies.5.11 Exp.7.6
w. Mall.6.24 Frog.28.5
x. Dav.11.5

4 And actually won a few,
5 Which created problems for the [a]Dauphin,
6 Who was the heir to the Frog throne and not anxious to be crowned,
7 Since there's almost no glory involved in being the king of a defeated nation,
8 [b]Which failed to deter Joan of Arc, since she was the only person in France who didn't know the rule about not conquering England.
9 Ultimately, this difficult situation was resolved when the English captured Joan and [c]burned her at the stake for wearing men's clothes,
10 [d]And not even English men's clothes at that,
11 Which may be the single most irritating thing about the Frogs the English have had to endure.

CHAPTER 8

[e]After losing the Hundred Years War, the Frogs participated pretty strenuously in the [f]Renaissance,
2 Since they had invented culture in the first place,
3 [g]According to all the French history books,
4 And were anxious to show the rest of [h]Europe how superior they were.
5 And so the Frogs tried their hand at a lot of Renaissance sports,
6 [i]Including painting naked ladies,
7 [j]And writing poems about naked ladies,
8 [k]And making sculptures of naked ladies,
9 [l]Which all came easily to

a. Dav.32.23
b. 4.10
c. Chr.6.7
d. Brit.2.1-3
e. Psay.5Y.15
f. Gnt.1.13
g. 5.8
h. Barb.4.18
i. Paul.6.2
j. Psom.53.1-7
k. Paul.6.4-5
l. Psay.5Q.50
m. 5.8
n. Gnt.11.7-10
o. Gnt.11.19-20
p. 7.11
q. Swar.14.17
r. Ann.17.20-21
s. Ann.18.16
t. Brit.2.7-8
u. Chr.3.23-25
v. Chr.3.26
w. Brit.40.8
x. Gnt.10.15
Exp.7.6

them since it was the Frogs who had invented sex in the first place,
10 [m]According to all the French history books.
11 And they also tried out the [n]Protestant religion fad, having some Huguenots and whatnot to carry on with for a while,
12 [o]Although they ultimately decided to remain a Catholic nation, because no other religion offers the opportunity to get as dressed up as Frogs like to be.

CHAPTER 9

In fact, the Frogs became pretty obsessed with fashion in the wake of the Renaissance,
2 [p]Since they had invented fashion in the first place,
3 [q]Including fake moles called beauty spots,
4 [r]Makeup for women,
5 [s]And for men,
6 [t]Powdered wigs and outlandish hats,
7 And dressy outfits, each one of which could cost a [u]noble more than a [v]peasant would earn in a lifetime,
8 Not to mention parties, which went on for days and cost more than a whole nation of peasants could earn in a lifetime,
9 Which is when things started to get [w]sticky in France.

CHAPTER 10

For a long time, the French had been governing through a system based on the [x]divine right of kings,
2 Called the divine right of Louis's,
3 Which resulted in a long string of Louis's,
4 One after the other, until there

had been fourteen of them.

5 [a]Under the divine right of Louis's system of government, Frog money was called Louis's, which gave the king the idea that all the money in France belonged to him and could be spent as he saw fit,

6 [b]Such as on clothes,

7 And powdered wigs,

8 And outlandish hats,

9 And occasional wars,

10 [c]And most of all on parties,

11 Which were so big and expensive that several of the Louis's had to assign a [d]cardinal just to keep score on party games,

12 Because as everyone knows,

13 [e]Frogs cheat at party games.

14 Anyway, after fourteen Louis's had been partying for several hundred years, the Frog [f]masses started to get cross.

CHAPTER 11

By an unfortunate coincidence, the English beheaded their king, [g]Charles I, at just about the same time that the Frog masses were starting to notice a few things about the divine right of Louis's.

2 [h]For example, they had noticed that very few of the Frog masses ever got invited to Louis's parties.

3 They noticed that the party tax, which was paid by the Frog masses, amounted to almost [i]100 percent of their income.

4 [j]They noticed that Frog high fashions were almost never worn by peasants.

5 [k]They noticed that anyone who tried to attend one of Louis's parties without an invita-

a. *Psong.41.1-5*
b. *9.2*
c. *9.8*
d. *Dav.10.10*
e. *Gnt.13.5-6*
f. *Carl.3.6*
g. *Dav.41.12*
h. *Lies.9.13*
   Chr.4.1-5
i. *Chr.5.15*
j. *Psong.47.4*
k. *Zig.10.10*
l. *Gnt.10.14-15*
   Exp.7.6
m. *11.4*
n. *Dav.30.40*
o. *Ed.38.4*
p. *Ed.38.6*
q. *Psay.5Q.23*
r. *Psay.5Y.50*
s. *Grk.20.8*
t. *Psom.54.1-5*

tion usually wound up in the Bastille or dead.

6 [l]They noticed that whenever there was some really hard work to be done, like a war with the English or an exploring expedition to the New World, it was the Frog masses who had to do it,

7 [m]In cheap low-fashion clothes, like as not.

8 And when the Englishman named [n]Cromwell cut off the king's head, they noticed that he actually got away with it.

CHAPTER 12

And then came Louis the Sixteenth, who looked exactly like a [o]frog, which was unnerving even to the Frog masses.

2 Louis also had a wife, named [p]Marie Antoinette, who inflamed the peasants by offering to let them eat cake,

3 [q]Which created shock waves of disappointment when no cake was forthcoming.

4 It occurred to the Frog masses that Louis and his wife might look better without heads,

5 Which was absolutely correct,

6 [r]And thus inaugurated the French Revolution.

7 Fortunately, the French had by this time invented the concept of democracy,

8 [s]Which means rule by bloodthirsty masses of Frogs,

9 And wasn't very hard to invent, really,

10 [t]Because the Americans had already done some of the preliminary groundwork,

11 Even though they were basically English and therefore stupid and ugly and not at all well dressed.

12 Anyway, the Frog masses,

now calling themselves Jacobins,

13 Which means "vengeful
murderous power-hungry idiots,"

14 Stormed the ªBastille, freeing all the peasants,

15 ᵇAnd then guillotined the
king and the queen and all the
nobles they could get their hands
on, and then,

16 ᶜWhen the supply of nobles
was getting low,

17 ᵈEach other.

CHAPTER 13

The Jacobins kept track of all
this history by knitting it all
down as it rolled out of the ᵉguil-
lotine,

2 Which was a fine Frog breakthrough in fashion,

3 ᶠBut wasn't doing much to
clothe and feed the masses,

4 Who had stopped slaving in
the fields to watch ᵍheads being
cut off by the guillotine in Paris.

5 This led to the temporary
abandonment of rule by ʰdemoc-
racy in favor of rule by directorate,

6 ⁱWhich means "And you
thought the Jacobins were bad
news . . ."

7 As it turned out, rule by directorate didn't improve conditions
very much either, ʲexcept that
there were now many fewer hungry, naked peasants than before,

8 And eventually there were
also fewer directors,

9 ᵏWhat with ˡMarat slipping on
a knife in his bathtub,

10 And ᵐRobespierre ⁿacciden-
tally falling under the guillotine,

11 And so on.

12 All of which meant that

a. 11.5
b. 11.8
c. Chr.10.1
d. Apes.1.2-3
e. Ned.43.9
f. Rom.7.20
g. Wil.12.16-24
h. 12.8
i. Grk.20.8
j. Ned.20.20-27
k. Grk.16.19-20
l. Dav.52.4
   & 20.11
m. Dav.52.4
   & 20.13
n. Wil.19.7
o. Dav.15.9
   Spic.12.5
   Dav.14.5
p. 4.10-11
q. Yks.129.10
r. 3.8-9
s. Psp.1.2
t. Psay.5Y.20
u. Exp.15.10-11
v. Swar.28.3-4
w. Yks.109.13
x. Vin.6.3-14
y. Psay.5Q.71
z. Psom.15.1-2

France was finally ready for Napoleon Bonaparte.

CHAPTER 14

Like Joan of Arc, ᵒNapoleon
was born poorer and shorter
than is normally acceptable in
Frog military circles. He was
also, unfortunately, not French.

2 ᵖThis helps to explain why he
was such a great military success
for so long and why he had such
a hard time understanding the
rule about not defeating the English.

3 Anyway, Napoleon was born
in Corsica and rose to become a
general, thanks to the ᑫrelaxing
of social standards that occurred
during the French Revolution.

4 ʳHis saving grace was that he
was extremely quarrelsome and
actually wanted to be French,

5 ˢFor some reason.

6 He also wanted to rule
France,

7 And that was just for starters.

8 When people began to notice
that rule by directorate wasn't
working out, ᵗNapoleon came
back from ᵘEgypt with an army
to suggest that Rule by Napoleon
was much the best ᵛsolution.

9 ʷRule by Napoleon means
"rule by a power-mad genius
willing to sacrifice every drop of
Frog blood on earth for a few
fleeting moments of glory,"

10 ˣWhich made perfect sense
to the Frogs,

11 ʸWho suddenly realized that
the gnawing ache in their bellies
was not hunger for food, but for
glory.

12 Whereupon they accepted
ᶻNapoleon with open arms and
made him,

13 After a few interim titles,
14 ^aEmperor of France.

CHAPTER 15

^bNapoleon saved the Frog masses from ^cignominious death at the guillotine by sending them to ^dglorious death in battle,

2 Thus introducing the most important innovation in the history of France,

3 ^eNamely, the concept of military victory.

4 ^fFrog soldiers died gloriously and victoriously in numerous nations throughout Europe,

5 Including ^gAustria,

6 ^hItaly,

7 ⁱPrussia,

8 ^jSpain,

9 ^kAnd many more besides.

10 Even the ^lEnglish were dismayed by Napoleon's un-Froglike talent for victory,

11 And had to wait for a lucky break,

12 Which didn't come until Napoleon decided that he should conquer Russia,

13 ^mAn idea that occurred to him only after he had been living in France for about ten years,

14 ⁿAnd can't be explained any other way.

CHAPTER 16

Before he decided to conquer Russia, Napoleon acquired an empire that included most of western Europe,

2 ^oExcepting England,

3 And established ^pRule by Napoleon as the most universally practiced form of government in the western world.

4 He even invented a new code of laws, which he named after

a. Paul.5.2-3
b. Main.22.10 Vin.6.15
c. Ann.6.1 Dav.47.23
d. Al.2.11 Grk.9.7
e. Psay.5Q.74
f. Psom.46.1-4
g. Krt.4.2-3
h. Psong.57.3
i. Krt.4.8-12
j. Spic.13.1-5
k. Bks.6.17-18
l. Psay.5Q.23
m. 17.2
n. Wil.26.21
o. 4.10
p. 14.9
q. Swar.14.5-8
r. 9.2
s. 8.10
t. Boul.21.9
u. Dav.21.12-15
v. Psong.48.3
w. Dav.14.47
x. Psong.53.6-7
y. Ned.4.7 Wil.45.25-26
z. Rom.7.7
aa. Wil.17.1
bb. Russ.1.1

himself and which included numerous new ideas about justice.

5 For example, under the Napoleonic Code, people had to be given a trial before being guillotined, which was so revolutionary that it made people wonder why they hadn't thought of it during the French Revolution,

6 ^qUntil they remembered that the French Revolution had been started by Frogs.

7 Napoleon also encouraged innovations in ^rfashion, including topless gowns for lady Frogs,

8 ^sWhich made sense, since it was the French who had invented ^tbreasts.

9 At the same time, Napoleon was doing quite well with the ladies personally,

10 In spite of being so short,

11 And had a famous affair with ^uJosephine,

12 ^vWho turned out to be infertile,

13 Which paved the way for ^wMarie Louise, who had a husband,

14 But Napoleon got rid of him,

15 ^xWhich is generally what happens when an emperor cuts in on your wife.

16 Anyway, until he thought of conquering Russia, Napoleon had things pretty much his own way,

17 ^yWhich was the only way he cared about.

CHAPTER 17

Then, of course, Napoleon had his idea about Russia,

2 ^zWhich turned out to be a very bad idea,

3 Because as ^{aa}someone once said, "An army travels on its stomach," and ^{bb}Russia is a long

way to go if you're traveling on your stomach.

4 In fact, it's hard to get there and back before winter arrives,

5 Which in Russia almost always involves plenty of snow and ice and a lot less food for your stomach[a].

6 Having forgotten this,

7 For some reason,

8 Napoleon succeeded in killing thousands of Russians and getting all the way to Moscow before winter arrived.

9 [b]Then he remembered about his stomach and raced home to Paris for some good Frog [c]cuisine,

10 Leaving his army without any [d]cake,

11 [e]Or anything else,

12 [f]Except the transcendent glory of dying for France in the bloody snow.

CHAPTER 18

Excited by the glorious demise of the Grande Armée in Russia, thousands of [g]new troops joined Napoleon for a series of battles against every country in Europe.

2 The new Grande Armée fought in the most valiant Frog tradition,

3 [h]Which is to say they lost, causing Napoleon to [i]resign from his job and move to the island of Elba,

4 Safely tucked away in the Mediterranean,

5 Miles from the French coastline,

6 [j]Where everyone would be safe from him,

7 Except that he escaped,

8 [k]Somehow,

a. *Russ.6.4*
b. *Forg.4.8-9*
c. *24.1*
d. *Psay.5Q.56*
e. *Yks.10.10-12*
f. *Forg.5.1-6*
g. *14.11*
h. *Forg.13.10*
i. *Psay.5Q.7*
j. *Psp.1.7*
k. *Mawr.22.22*
l. *Ned.25.6-10*
m. *Psay.5Y.22*
n. *Swar.17.1-12*
o. *Psom.12.4*
   Ann.2.17
p. *Dav.21.19-24*
q. *Dav.21.32-34*
r. *Psay.5A.24*
s. *Psp.1.8*
t. *Paul.7.2*
u. *Ned.36.17-21*
v. *Krt.9.15*
w. *Dav.32.23*
x. *Dav.46.19*
y. *Exp.15.8*
   Yks.16.7-13

9 And got all the way back to France,

10 [l]Where the glory of it all convinced the army to join him once again,

11 [m]For another hundred days,

12 [n]Until [o]Waterloo,

13 [p]Where the last of Napoleon's glory slipped away down a sunken road,

14 [q]Causing him to resign from his job a second time and move to the island of St. Helena,

15 Safely tucked away in the Atlantic Ocean,

16 [r]Many thousands of miles from the French coastline,

17 [s]Where everyone would be safe from him,

18 Except that the Frogs never forgot him,

19 [t]And remembered him fondly,

20 [u]For some reason,

21 [v]Which suggests that Frogs are every bit as dumb as they are silly.

CHAPTER 19

There was a brilliant Frog named [w]Talleyrand, who was a minister to Louis the Sixteenth until they cut Louis's head off,

2 And who was then a minister to Napoleon until they exiled the ex-emperor to St. Helena,

3 And who went on to be a minister to [x]Louis the Eighteenth when the divine right of Louis's was reinstated.

4 It was Talleyrand who played a big part in establishing the Frog foreign policy that sold almost a [y]third of North America to the United States for a few million dollars.

5 This shrewd maneuver, along

with the loss to the English of [a]France's Canadian colonies, just about finished off France's last chance to be Chosen Nation.
6 Still, faced with about a hundred years to kill before the Americans became the Chosen Nation of the western hemisphere, [b]the Frogs mounted a number of silly attempts to regain their lost glory.

CHAPTER 20

For example, they grabbed a bunch of [c]colonies in Africa that nobody else wanted,
2 As if glory could be extracted from worthless territory simply by inventing a romantic but completely irrelevant military unit called the [d]French Foreign Legion.
3 Then, after waiting out a decent interval of renewed rule by Louis's, they dug up another [e]Napoleon,
4 [f]Who was cleverly inserted into the old scheme by adding Louis to his name,
5 [g]And announced to the world that they were an empire once again,
6 [h]Which irritated Germany no end,
7 [i]With the result that the Germans attacked France and reminded the Frogs that without a Corsican general, they were the same silly, vainglorious losers they had always been.
8 The French stewed about this for more than forty years,
9 [j]Waiting for one more chance,
10 Somehow unable to remember that Napoleon Bonaparte was stone-cold dead,
11 Just like the glory of France.

a. *Brit.23.8-9*
b. *F&J.5.5*
c. *Exp.15.11*
d. *Dav.9.7*
e. *Dav.20.46*
f. *Psay.5Q.17*
g. *3.6*
h. *Jefs.7.15*
i. *Psay.5Y.44*
j. *Vin.14.23-24*
k. *8.10*
l. *Ned.42.7*
m. *20.7*
n. *Main.18.6*
o. *Bub.2.9-10*
p. *29.8*
q. *Dav.39.36*
r. *Psong.5.3*
s. *Rom.6.9-10*

CHAPTER 21

But their practically unbroken string of humiliations in foreign affairs did nothing to make the Frogs more humble[k]. After all, it was Frogs who had invented culture and poetry and music and science and sex,
2 And practically everything else too,
3 [l]Which made them very proud of themselves,
4 In fact, very very proud of themselves,
5 [m]In spite of the Franco-Prussian thing.
6 [n]And if they ever had the least inclination to feel even the tiniest bit humble, all they had to do to feel better was tell some foreigner about all of France's stupendous cultural accomplishments.

CHAPTER 22

For example, it was the Frogs who had built the most beautiful city in the world,
2 Somehow,
3 Which was named Paris,
4 And which was so incredibly beautiful that foreigners from all over the world came there to visit,
5 Even though it was full of Frogs.
6 It was also Frogs who had built many of the most beautiful [o]cathedrals in Europe,
7 Including Chartres, and [p]Notre Dame, and Amiens, and some other ones too,
8 As well as many beautiful châteaus,
9 And the [q]French Riviera,
10 And the [r]Loire River Valley,
11 And the [s]Alps,

12 And everything else in France.

13 Nor were these the only great accomplishments of the Frogs.

CHAPTER 23

For example, there was wine, [a]which the Frogs invented,

2 [b]And drank continuously,

3 [c]Morning, noon, and night,

4 Out of bottles with beautiful [d]labels,

5 [e]That had been stored in cellars for generations,

6 Just waiting for the one perfect occasion,

7 [f]When the precisely perfect vintage could be used to start another precisely perfect [g]quarrel about absolutely nothing.

8 And wine was only one of many such gifts the Frogs had given the world.

CHAPTER 24

After all, where would the world be if the [h]Frogs had not invented food,

2 Which consisted of beautiful, perfectly prepared combinations of rotten meat and rotten poultry,

3 And rotten vegetables,

4 And rotten fruit,

5 And rotten dairy products,

6 Topped off by marvelous little sauces that disguised the taste so well you'd hardly know you were eating something even pigs would have the good sense to avoid.

7 This food, which the Frogs called high cuisine, was always served in beautiful restaurants,

8 Where the waiters made every meal a delight,

9 By sneering and raising their eyebrows and disappearing for hours at a time,

---

a. Mawr. 15.22
b. Psong. 42.1-3
c. Psong. 50.6-8
d. Psay. 5G.2-4
e. Psp. 2.10
f. Vin. 65.11-13
g. Ed. 77.9-11
h. Brit. 28.19-22
i. Psong. 59.3
j. Jefs. 7.5-6
k. Jefs. 7.15-18
l. Dav. 32.23
m. Zig. 7.5
n. Rom. 10.4
o. 5.8
p. Ed. 60.17
q. 20.11
r. 5.5
s. 8.10
t. Psom. 30.1
   Mawr. 13.15

---

10 [i]And then cursing the meagerness of the tip.

CHAPTER 25

And speaking of food, there were also some Frog scientists who loved Frog food so much they thought it was a shame that so many people died from eating such high cuisine,

2 [j]Which is why another great Louis decided to discover that the real problem was not with Frog cuisine at all,

3 But with tiny little animals called [k]microorganisms,

4 Which nobody could see,

5 Except [l]Louis Pasteur,

6 Who figured out how to kill them with something called [m]Pasteurization,

7 Which worked just great,

8 Because after he used it,

9 [n]Nobody could see any microorganisms anymore.

10 This brilliant achievement paved the way for lots more Frog [o]science over the years,

11 Including all kinds of [p]miraculous breakthroughs that would just take your breath away,

12 [q]If anybody but a Frog could see them.

CHAPTER 26

Another great Frog gift to the world,

2 Though not as great as food and wine and microorganisms, of course,

3 Was [r]French literature,

4 [s]Which was great because it was the Frogs who had invented philosophy and poetry and tragedy and comedy.

5 There was a Frog philosopher named [t]La Rochefoucauld, who knew so much about life that he

wrote it all down in a little book,

6 In the form of [a]sayings,

7 Which said it all so well that there's no point in discussing it further.

8 There was another Frog philosopher named [b]Pascal who knew almost as much about life as La Rochefoucauld,

9 And so he also wrote it all down in a little book,

10 Including the one about man being only a [c]reed,

11 The weakest in all nature,

12 But, according to Pascal, that's really okay,

13 Because man is a [d]thinking reed,

14 Which Pascal knew because it was the Frogs who had invented reason and logic,

15 When [e]Descartes said, *"Cogito ergo sum,"*

16 [f]Which means something or other in Latin,

15 Something that must explain why the Frogs have never felt any obligation to practice these interesting mental pursuits.

16 Nor were these the only miraculous accomplishments of French literature.

CHAPTER 27

For example, there was [g]Voltaire, who made the great Frog discovery that there are a lot of stupid, silly, spiteful, worthless people in the world,

2 Which he knew because,

3 Well,

4 You know.

5 [h]And so Voltaire figured out that the thing to do is to keep cultivating your garden,

6 For some reason.

7 Nor was Voltaire the only great French comedian.

---

a. *Psay.5Q.14*
b. *Psom.65.1*
   Dav.15.39-40
c. *Psom.27.1*
d. *Yks.44.22*
e. *Psay.5S.27*
f. *F&J.2.12-14*
g. *Ed.46.10*
h. *Pnot.34.1-5*
i. *Ed.12.20-21*
   Dav.30.9
j. *27.1*
k. *Gnt.15.5-9*
l. *Grk.17.35*
m. *Swar.1.1*
n. *Dav.3.1-5*
o. *Dav.7.5*
p. *Krt.6.7-8*
q. *Dav.7.2*
r. *Dav.22.6*
s. *Pnot.49.1-5*
t. *Dav.21.29*
u. *Bks.6.17-18*

CHAPTER 28

For example, there was also [i]Moliere, who made the great discovery that there are a lot of stupid, silly, spiteful, worthless *rich* people in the world,

2 Having thought along much the same lines as [j]Voltaire,

3 Except that he put all his great wisdom into [k]plays,

4 [l]Which were terribly terribly amusing,

5 If you happened to be a Frog,

6 Or a [m]pseudo-intellectual from some other country,

7 [n]And thus paved the way for the much later Frog invention known as film.

CHAPTER 29

But no one should get the idea that all French literature was simply funny.

2 There were also a lot of Frog writers who wrote stories that were very very sad,

3 And funny only by accident,

4 Such as [o]Victor Hugo, who wrote incredibly long books made up of incredibly long sentences,

5 Completely in [p]French,

6 About sad, unfortunate people,

7 Called 'Les Misérables,'

8 [q]'Le Hunchback of Notre Dame,'

9 And other things.

10 And there was [r]Gustave Flaubert, who wrote about [s]Madame Bovary,

11 [t]Who was not nice,

12 For many many pages.

13 And there was also [u]Balzac, who wrote about Frog characters who had so little happen to them that their stories went on for volumes.

14 Not to mention [a]Émile Zola.

CHAPTER 30

F rog poetry was great too.
2 Frogs like [b]Racine and [c]Corneille wrote [d]tragedies in verse,
3 Completely in French,
4 Until they died.
5 This brilliant accomplishment paved the way for the French invention of [e]symbolist poetry,
6 Which was a spectacular achievement,
7 Borrowed only partially from [f]Edgar Allan Poe,
8 And represented a new Frog view of the world in the wake of the [g]Franco-Prussian thing.
9 Great Frog poets like [h]Baudelaire and [i]Verlaine and [j]Rimbaud saw that when you looked beneath the surface of things,
10 Things looked different.
11 This great artistic discovery helped start the great Frog impressionist movement in art and music,
12 Because the Frogs were every bit as great at art and music as they were at literature.

CHAPTER 31

C oming along in the wake of the Franco-Prussian thing, the Frog impressionist artists thought the world might look better if it were out of focus,
2 Which convinced [k]Claude Monet to do two dozen million [l]signed paintings of water lilies,
3 All out of focus,
4 While [m]Renoir painted thousands of women who were probably very beautiful,
5 If you could see what they looked like.
6 And there was also [n]Degas,

a. Swar.30.1-2
b. Russ.20.26
c. Psay.5A.40
d. Gnt.15.19-21
e. Psom.37.1-6
f. Yks.70.3-5
g. 20.7
h. Dav.48.7
i. Dav.5.7
j. Ann.19.13
   Psp.1.9
k. Dav.32.23
l. Psong.20.1-8
m. Dav.20.46
n. Psong.51.1
o. Ann.10.1
p. Dav.14.11
q. Psay.5Q.77
r. Dav.32.23
s. Psom.10.4
t. Ed.78.11
u. Jefs.7.22
v. 26.15
w. Dav.34.17
x. Gnt.13.4-6
   Kens.16.2-10
y. 20.7

who painted fuzzy ballerinas,
7 And [o]Seurat, who painted fuzzy dots,
8 And [p]Toulouse-Lautrec, who was even shorter than Napoleon,
9 And painted the Paris slums the way they would look if you drank [q]wormwood twenty-four hours a day for years,
10 Until he died.

CHAPTER 32

T here was another impressionist named [r]Claude Debussy, who thought that music might sound better if it didn't have any melody,
2 So he wrote [s]'La Mer,'
3 [t]Which is about the way the sea sounds if you're a Frog,
4 Or something,
5 And 'Clair de Lune,'
6 [u]Which did for moonlight what 'La Mer' did for the sea,
7 And so forth,
8 Which is pretty much how things were going when suddenly the Frogs noticed that if they played their [v]cards right, they could have still another shot at glory,
9 And that changed everything.

CHAPTER 33

W hen the archduke [w]Ferdinand of Austria was assassinated by a Serbo-Croatian nationalist, [x]France cleverly seized the opportunity to attack Germany, in retaliation for the beating they had taken in the [y]Franco-Prussian War forty years before.
2 Knowing the Frogs pretty well by this time, the Germans had already decided to outfox them by launching an attack of their own,

3 [a]Which turned out to be pretty embarrassing for everybody,

4 [b]Since the Frogs were halfway into Germany before they realized Germany was invading France,

5 [c]And the Germans were halfway into France before they realized France was invading Germany,

6 [d]So they all raced back to a field in the middle of France,

7 Dug a big trench,

8 And didn't budge another foot for four years.

CHAPTER 34

Millions of Frogs died gloriously in the trenches of [e]World War I, machine-gunned and gassed and bombed and infested with disgusting diseases,

2 [f]Until the last soldier reached for a butterfly on the end of a cannon and got shot,

3 Thus ending the war to end all wars.

4 The Frogs were still mad at the Germans about the [g]Franco-Prussian War, however, and insisted on a peace treaty that would keep Germany poor, and mad as hell, for a [h]generation,

5 [i]Which the Germans deserved because they had started [j]World War I,

6 [k]As the Frogs kept reminding everybody.

7 This treaty was signed at the palace of Versailles, where the [l]memory of [m]rule by Louis's and [n]rule by Napoleons caused the French to start planning immediately for the next glorious war to end all wars.

8 For this reason, they built an impregnable military fortification,

a. Gnt.16.11-12
b. Psay.5Q.74
c. Krt.39.14
d. Exp.1.17
e. Krt.24.2-3
f. Pnot.55.1-5
g. 20.7
h. Wil.1.1-2
i. 8.10
j. Krt.24.2-3
k. Boul.26.11
l. Mall.6.24
m. 10.5
n. 14.9
o. Ext.48.19
p. 20.7
q. Krt.24.2-3
r. Ed.60.17
s. Dav.29.6
t. Psay.5Q.74
u. Psay.5Q.32
v. F&J.2.12-16
w. Psp.2.5
x. Brd.9.6
y. Ira.33.1-3
z. 14.10
aa. Chuk.6.1-3
bb. Yks.91.1-7
cc. Krt.24.2-3
dd. F&J.7.1-12
ee. Paul.3.1-10
ff. Russ.16.1-7

9 [o]Designed, built, and manned by Frogs,

10 That would make it impossible for Germany to invade France like they had in the [p]Franco-Prussian War,

11 That is, in [q]World War I.

12 This wonderful new impregnable Frog military fortification was called the [r]Maginot Line.

CHAPTER 35

Meanwhile, a new generation of Frog [s]intellectuals was making profound discoveries based on the perverse hypothesis that maybe [t]life wasn't about glory at all,

2 But something else instead,

3 [u]Namely despair,

4 Which is the feeling you get waiting for the end of the world when you know that it's all just a [v]bad dream anyway.

5 [w]Using this new [x]logic, Frog thinkers like [y]Sartre and Camus invented existentialism,

6 [z]Which is a philosophy based on the idea that if France can't have a glorious existence, then existence itself must be a meaningless random accident.

7 [aa]This philosophy was terribly inspiring to a lot of [bb]foreigners as well, who were hanging around in France waiting for the end of the world after [cc]World War I,

8 [dd]And writing a bunch of books about it,

9 [ee]And painting a lot of pictures of it,

10 And developing a lot of political theories about it,

11 [ff]Including a theory that the Russians must be right about communism being the way to go,

12 [a]Since if everything's meaningless anyway, you might as well have a roof over your head and someone else to do the thinking for you.

CHAPTER 36

Fortunately for the Frog intellectuals, [b]World War I was succeeded almost immediately by a terrible [c]worldwide [d]depression,
2 Which made the Germans even madder about the [e]Treaty of Versailles,
3 And didn't help the government of France much either,
4 Since, being out of both Louis's and Napoleons, they had been compelled to try democracy again,
5 [f]Meaning "rule by enervated fools,"
6 [g]With the result that they drank a great deal more wine than they should have,
7 [h]And read far too many books written by Frog intellectuals,
8 And got into so many quarrels with each other that they almost didn't notice when Germany started grabbing countries in eastern Europe.

CHAPTER 37

In fact, England was the first nation to notice that Germany was acting up again,
2 [i]And politely asked them to stop,
3 Which the Germans agreed to do,
4 Then didn't,
5 Which raised a faint ghostly image of glory along the [j]Maginot Line,
6 Which disappeared,
7 Along with the whole [k]Maginot Line,

8 As soon as Germany mounted its [l]Blitzkrieg attack on France.

CHAPTER 38

To the eternal glory of France, the Frogs surrendered to Germany within six weeks of the Blitzkrieg and allowed a puppet government to be installed,
2 Which they named, not after themselves, but after a bottle of [m]seltzer water.
3 For the rest of the war, the Frogs diverted themselves as best they could.
4 Some of them collaborated with the Germans,
5 In fact, a lot of them collaborated with the Germans,
6 [n]Which wasn't really so evil when you consider that existence is all just a meaningless accident anyway,
7 [o]And some mounted an effort called [p]the Resistance,
8 [q]Which was brave and glorious and got tons of publicity in the allied nations,
9 And some went to Africa to fight with [r]Charles de Gaulle,
10 Who looked exactly like a giant frog with an oversized nose,
11 And therefore became the living symbol of the eternal glory of France,
12 For yet another generation of Frogs.

CHAPTER 39

In fact, after the war, [s]Charles de Gaulle became the new emperor of France,
2 Although his official title was President of the Third or Fourth French Republic,
3 And fought hard to retain the

a. Carl.9.1-10
b. Krt.24.2-3
c. Brit.50.1
   Yks.95.1-7
d. 35.4
e. 34.7
f. Grk.20.8
g. 23.3
h. 31.3
i. Yks.82.7
j. 34.8-12
k. Dav.32.23
l. Lies.6.11
m. Ann.6.1
n. 35.6
o. Dav.34.12
p. Jefs.7.15-17
q. 3.6
r. Psom.49.1-3
   Frog.3.4
   & 12.1
   & 14.1
s. 3.5

last pitiful remnants of the Frog colonial empire,

4 [a]Such as risking assassination to prevent the Algerians from becoming independent,

5 [b]And waging a silly war in Indochina to keep the communists from taking Vietnam away from the Frogs,

6 [c]And telling the rest of the world how great France was at every opportunity,

7 And how they didn't need help from America or anyone else,

8 Except for the tourist trade, of course,

9 Which it was the duty of every Frog citizen to support by being as French as possible at all times,

10 Which is to say as rude as possible at all times,

11 Because in spite of everything,

12 Including all their lost chances to be the Chosen Nation of Europe,

a. Exp.15.10-11
b. Bks.6.24
c. 3.6
d. 4.7
e. Kens.6.6
f. 35.6
g. 35.4

13 [d]The Frogs still know that they are superior to everyone else,

14 Which is their abiding glory as a people,

15 [e]And the reason why everyone else is sick to death of them.

CHAPTER 40

And when the end of the world comes at last,

2 It's a pretty safe bet that the Frogs won't be anywhere near the fuse,

3 Although it's also a safe bet that if there's enough time, some Frog will remind the world that the genius of France has just been proven beyond doubt,

4 [f]Because the Frogs have been onto the nature of existence far longer than anybody else,

5 Which is why they are so very very proud of the greatest Frog achievement of all,

6 [g]Because where would everybody be if the Frogs had not invented despair?

THE BOOK OF BLOODY BRITS

OTHERWISE KNOWN AS THE BOOK OF THE WHITE MAN'S BURDEN

CHAPTER 1

There was an island called Britain located off the northwest coast of Europe, [a]where it was in an ideal position to cause lots of trouble for everyone else.

2 [b]The weather is very bad in Britain all the time, which

a. Vin.73.12
b. Psom.18.8

makes clothes very important,

3 And explains why the people who lived there became obsessed about being properly dressed for every occasion,

4 Although there is much about these people that cannot be explained,

5 [a]As we shall see.

6 Anyway, the Brits worked hard to become the Chosen Nation of Europe and the World,

7 And actually succeeded for quite a while,

8 Against all odds,

9 Which was their favorite way,

10 And the reason why they are so heartily detested by almost everyone.

11 This is their [b]story.

CHAPTER 2

From the very beginning, the Brit culture was shaped by two peculiar preoccupations, these being,

2 [c]The overriding importance of personal grooming,

3 And the absolute necessity of doing everything the hard way.

4 [d]Even when first discovered by Caesar,

5 Who looked under a lot of rocks he should have left alone,

6 The original Britons, as they called themselves then, were covered from head to toe in blue paint,

7 Which they thought natty,

8 And wasn't the last time they were dead wrong about something.

9 Caesar should have known better than to conquer the Britons,

10 [e]Who lived contrary to Roman philosophy, which holds that if a thing isn't easy, it isn't worth doing.

11 But Caesar didn't always follow the rules,

12 As we have seen,

13 [f]And conveniently died before the rest of the world discovered his mistake.

a. Adam.6.7
b. Swar.27.1-5
c. 1.2-3
d. Rom.12.5-9
e. Rom.2.1
f. Rom.13.1-7
g. Rom.5.13-14
h. Rom.5.7-8
i. Psong.8.5
j. Jeff.19.7-8
k. Dav.47.25
l. Barb.1.8
m. Psay.5Y.14
n. Barb.4.18

CHAPTER 3

Subsequent Romans began to suspect that there was something wrong with the inhabitants of Great Britain,

2 Who kept rebelling,

3 Because it would have been too easy to just let the Romans build their roads and aqueducts and other [g]engineering projects in peace,

4 And so every few years, a [h]Roman legion or two would have to sail up to Britain and kill a bunch of Brits.

5 On some of these expeditions, the Romans discovered that the Brits had some even more unpleasant neighbors, called the Scots, who wore skirts,

6 And made their whole culture out of sheep intestines,

7 [i]Which they used as food,

8 [j]And musical instruments,

9 And other things too.

10 Obviously, any people this stupid found it hard to understand that a handful of barbarian tribesmen shouldn't mess with a Roman legion.

11 Accordingly, a Roman general named Hadrian built a wall to keep the [k]smell of sheep intestines out of Britain,

12 Not to mention the Scots themselves.

13 [l]Unfortunately, it never occurred to the Romans that it might be an even better idea to build a wall around all of Great Britain to keep the Brits out of the rest of the world.

CHAPTER 4

[m]After the fall of Rome, numerous barbarian tribes from the continent of [n]Europe

decided that it was time to do something about the Britons.

2 For this reason, the island of Britain was invaded by hordes of [a]Angles and Saxons,

3 Then hordes of [b]Danes,

4 Then more hordes of [c]Angles and Saxons,

5 All of which killed as many of the [d]natives as they could,

6 Which was a lot,

7 And set about becoming Brits themselves,

8 Which was eventually noticed by some of the [e]Franks,

9 Who had taken to calling themselves [f]Normans,

10 [g]And who thought that even living in Britain would be better than spending one more day with the Frogs.

11 They were right, but just barely,

12 Because the Anglo-Saxons, as the thoroughly mongrelized Brits were now calling themselves, refused to accept their [h]decisive defeat in the Battle of Hastings,

13 Which would have been the easy thing to do,

14 [i]And instead made life as miserable as possible for the Normans,

15 Which, in view of the fact that misery was invented by the Anglo-Saxons, was pretty damned miserable.

CHAPTER 5

Gradually, the Normans got used to misery,

2 Due to a recurring Brit phenomenon called "assimilation,"

3 Which has to do with the fact that gangs of marauding killers usually have more in common

a. Barb.2.8-11
b. Exp.3.3-8
c. 4.2
d. 2.6
e. Barb.5.1-2
f. Frog.12.13
g. Rom.10.4
h. Frog.4.8
i. Dav.19.3-20
j. Psay.5Q.30
k. Swar.36.3
l. Swar.3.1 Bks.3.14
m. 4.12
n. Wil.12.4-6
o. Grk.23.12-13
p. Dav.41.23
q. Bks.1.2-7
r. Chr.8.16-18
s. Chr.8.21-22
t. 1.3

with each other than with the folks who [j]suggested they leave home in the first place.

4 Anyway, the Normans finally became assimilated Brits themselves,

5 Given to wearing fancy uniforms made of [k]chain mail,

6 And covered with outlandish designs known as [l]Heraldry,

7 Which are a peculiar system invented by the Brits for the purpose of telling lies about their [m]mongrel family [n]trees on articles of personal apparel.

8 When their uniforms had gotten so fancy that the Brits couldn't stand another day without showing them off to perfect strangers, [o]they began starting wars with other nations.

9 For example, they got the idea that the [p]Saracens would be impressed by a grand British entrance into the [q]Holy Land,

10 [r]Which they were,

11 Until the uniforms got covered with blood and dirt in all the desert fighting,

12 [s]Whereupon the Saracens stopped being impressed by the Brits and sent them back home,

13 Which convinced the Brits that winning wars depended on having clean uniforms,

14 And that "bloody" was a dirty word,

15 Which proved to be a turning point in Brit history,

16 [t]Because it was just about the last time they ever lost a war.

CHAPTER 6

One reason the Brits were so good at winning wars was that they kept fighting them virtually nonstop,

2 For centuries,

3 And when they couldn't have a war with another nation, they fought wars with each other,

4 Usually about who would be the next king,

5 Because the Brits believed pretty strongly in the ^adivine right of kings,

6 Except that they never quite understood the definition of the word "divine,"

7 ^bBeing under the impression that it was a synonym for "well bred,"

8 Which is to say that practically any Brit ^cnoble with a confusing enough family tree could claim the throne whenever he wanted to.

9 This resulted in a very complicated line of succession that can't be remembered,

10 Let alone understood,

11 By anyone but Brits,

12 For whom it was an important part of what they called a gentleman's education,

13 ^dWhich will be discussed later on.

14 Anyway,

15 The Brit line of succession changed hands many times during the Middle Ages,

16 Usually through treachery and murder,

17 ^eWhich are also an important part of a gentleman's education,

18 And perfectly okay, according to Brit custom,

19 As long as everyone involved is polite and grammatical about it,

20 Which is why there were quite a few royal families in medieval Britain, including Plantagenets,

21 And Lancasters,

a. *Chr.2.10-21*
b. *Ext.48.19*
c. *Chr.3.23-25*
d. *19.6*
e. *6.13*
f. *Psay.5Q.78*
g. *Bks.6.17-18*
h. *47.1*
i. *4.15*
j. *Dav.40.9*
k. *Yks.109.13*
l. *4.15*
m. *Frog.4.10-11*

22 And Yorks^f,

23 ^gAnd so on.

24 The Brits' somewhat free-form interpretation of divine right also led to the first English ^hsport,

25 Which was called King-Baiting,

26 ⁱAnd consisted of finding ways to make life as miserable as possible for whoever was sitting on the throne at the time.

27 The first king to be so baited was ^jKing John,

28 Who had to sign the Magna Charta,

29 Which is Latin for Great Fun,

30 ^kAnd consisted of a signed statement by the king that he was an idiot who couldn't be trusted.

CHAPTER 7

K ing-Baiting led to the invention of a peculiar Brit institution called Parliament,

2 Which means "talking at incredible length about how to make life miserable for the king,"

3 And was used principally to bore kings to death.

4 The primary defense the king had against Parliament was the power to dissolve it whenever he got sufficiently bored,

5 Which is why the Brits take credit for inventing the concept called "Balance of Power,"

6 Which had two meanings.

7 ^lInside Great Britain, Balance of Power meant that the king and Parliament had approximately equal power to make each other miserable.

8 ^mOutside Great Britain, Balance of Power meant that the Brits would always let the oppo-

sition have superior numbers, as long as the Brits could always win the wars.

CHAPTER 8

Meanwhile, the Brits were also very busy inventing the English language, which wasn't easy to do,

2 Because the Brit race had become such a stew of various peoples, including [a]French-speaking peoples, [b]Anglo-Saxon-speaking peoples, and various [c]Celtic peoples who spoke in languages nobody has ever understood.

3 The extreme difficulty of making one language out of all this made it an obviously worth-while pursuit,

4 Which is why the Brits had [d]Chaucer,

5 And then [e]Spenser,

6 And then [f]Shakespeare,

7 And then [g]Milton,

8 Who sorted it all out for them over a period of a few centuries.

9 As soon as the Brits had their own language, they immediately forgot how to speak, or even pronounce, anybody [h]else's,

10 Which is terribly important if you want to be the [i]Chosen Nation and rule the world,

11 Apparently,

12 Which they most definitely did.

CHAPTER 9

In fact, the Brits had pretty well decided that they should rule the world even before the Renaissance,

2 [j]Which is when everybody else got the idea,

3 [k]Because they had already figured out that practically every-

a. 4.9
b. 4.2
c. 2.6
d. 31.9
e. 31.13
f. 31.22
g. 33.1
h. Krt.6.7-11
i. Exp.1.4-6
j. Exp.1.7-16
k. 1.2
l. Psom.17.6-14
m. 9.1
n. Gnt.3.1
o. 1.2
p. Psay.5Q.34
q. 22.12
r. Dav.20.30
s. Chuk.10.3
t. Yks.116.16

body else had a nicer climate to live in,

4 Which wasn't fair,

5 And nobody has ever cared more about fairness than the Brits,

6 Although they have a slightly different definition of fairness than anybody else does,

7 Namely, that fairness consists of recognizing that Brits have good and sufficient reasons for doing what they do,

8 [l]Although it's never fair to ask what they are.

CHAPTER 10

And thus, when the [m]Renaissance arrived, the Brits were ready.

2 With typical British independence, they participated in only those Renaissance sports that appealed to them.

3 For example, they did not take an active part in the [n]painting of naked ladies,

4 [o]Because it's always too [p]cold in Britain for ladies to take their clothes off,

5 And even if they do, it's too dark to see them because it's usually raining.

6 Besides, looking at naked ladies is far too straightforward an approach to sex to be of interest to Brits, [q]who prefer to do absolutely everything with their clothes on.

7 On the other hand, the Brits did take an interest in helping to invent science,

8 Because science is hard and confusing,

9 Which is why [r]Francis Bacon invented the [s]scientific method,

10 [t]In a few spare moments

when he wasn't writing Shake-speare's plays.

11 The Brits also played the Protestant ᵃReformation game better than anyone else,

12 Having recognized well ahead of time that a ᵇpowerful, unified church represented a serious inconvenience to any nation that intended to rule the worldᶜ,

13 Which helps explain why ᵈKing Henry the Eighth decided to become head of the Church of England, presumably so that he could grant himself a divorce, when it would have been much simpler to have had his wife beheaded,

14 The way he usually did.

CHAPTER 11

The Church of England was a great success,

2 And very popular with the overwhelming majority of ᵉHenry's subjects,

3 Because it eliminated some problems the Brits had always had with the concept of ᶠdivinity,

4 Since they'd always had the suspicion that Jesus Christ probably wasn't very well bred,

5 ᵍOr why would he have dressed like that,

6 Although they had enormous respect for the fact that he hadn't picked the easy way,

7 ʰWhich would have been to work a miracle on the cross and not die at all.

8 The Church of England neatly resolved this dilemma by enabling the Brits to deal with God on a ⁱman-to-ʲman basis,

9 In enormous cathedrals,

10 ᵏWhile properly attired,

11 Without a lot of stuff and

a. *Gnt.11.2-11*
b. *Chr.6.11*
c. *8.12*
d. *Dav.42.15
   & 20.11-19*
e. *10.13*
f. *6.7*
g. *Psay.5Q.62*
h. *Dav.15.26*
i. *Psom.15.1-13*
j. *Mawr.6.7*
k. *22.12*
l. *Hall.4.3*
m. *6.5*
n. *47.1*
o. *Gnt.11.19*
p. *Dav.14.14*
q. *Dav.20.3-4*
r. *19.25-26*
s. *Dav.21.26*
t. *Spic.11.6*

nonsense about divinity and theology.

CHAPTER 12

Of course, the utter propriety of the Church of England did nothing to prevent a lot of ˡbloody religious conflicts,

2 ᵐSince the Brits still believed in the divine right of kings,

3 Which meant that religious differences represented a great new excuse for claiming the throne,

4 And started a whole new English ⁿsport,

5 Called the ᵒCatholic Pretenders Game,

6 Which was extremely popular for quite a while after Henry the Eighth died.

7 In fact, it was ᵖElizabeth I's skill at this sport that finally enabled her to assume the throne of England and start the Brit quest for world dominion in earnest.

CHAPTER 13

Elizabeth turned out to be one of the greatest Brit monarchs in history.

2 ۹Her attire was always impeccable, consisting of thick layers of makeup, ridiculous ruffled collars, vast dresses, and giant wigs,

3 Which made it quite clear to everyone that she was sufficiently ʳwell bred to be obeyed.

4 She also understood the importance of doing things the Brit way,

5 Which is to say, the hard way.

6 For example, when she decided that Spain needed to be taught a lesson, she sent ˢSir Francis Drake against the ᵗSpanish Armada with a smaller num-

her of smaller ships equipped with fewer guns than the Spanish had.

7 This strategy was brilliantly [a]successful,

8 And convinced the Brits that all they needed to rule the world was a good [b]navy, good [c]luck, and,

9 Of course,

10 [d]Good breeding.

CHAPTER 14

Elizabeth[e] capped her triumphant reign by beheading her principal challenger for the throne,

2 [f]Mary Queen of [g]Scots, the current Catholic Pretender,

3 Then dying without having a son, which led to the preferred Brit political situation,

4 [h]Which is a mad scramble for the throne.

5 This led to [i]King James,

6 And then [j]King Charles I,

7 Who made a mistake.

CHAPTER 15

It turned out that King Charles was so busy[k] looking for Catholic Pretenders that he forgot to look for Protestant Revolutionaries,

2 Who therefore sneaked up on him from behind,

3 [l]Which wasn't fair, of course,

4 But worked pretty well.

5 The Protestant Revolutionaries called themselves Puritans,

6 And had a lot of peculiar ideas,

7 [m]Which they got from reading the Bible,

8 [n]Somewhat too literally, the way the Brit nobles looked at it.

9 For example, the Puritans believed that being well dressed

a. *Dav. 20.5-6*
b. *Psom. 10.4*
c. *1.8*
d. *Psay. 5Q. 78*
e. *Dav. 20.7-12*
f. *Dav. 14.32*
g. *3.5-9*
h. *6.8*
i. *Dav. 20.34*
j. *Dav. 20.38*
k. *12.5*
l. *9.5*
m. *15.3*
n. *Bub. 6.4*
o. *Psay. 5Q. 19*
   Chr. 6.10
p. *6.5-7*
q. *Ed. 28.6*
r. *Psay. 5Q. 62*
s. *Ned. 6.24*
t. *Grk. 23.12-13*
u. *Grk. 8.32*
v. *Zig. 6.4*

was a kind of [o]vanity,

10 And was therefore not permissible behavior for good Christians,

11 Which threatened the whole Brit culture,

12 Because if no one was well dressed, how could you tell who was well bred?

13 [p]And if you couldn't tell who was well bred, how could you figure out who had the divine right to be king?

14 When the Brit nobles made this clever argument to [q]Oliver Cromwell,

15 Who was the leader of the Puritans,

16 [r]And therefore not very well bred,

17 He agreed,

18 Much to the surprise of the nobles,

19 And came up with a totally unexpected solution,

20 [s]Which was to have no king at all.

21 This thoroughly un-British viewpoint led to a [t]war,

22 Naturally,

23 Between the very well-dressed Brit nobles,

24 Called Cavaliers,

25 [u]Because they looked so dashing on horseback,

26 And the very poorly dressed Puritans,

27 Called Roundheads,

28 [v]Because they had such bad haircuts.

29 The disgraceful appearance of the Puritan troops was so distracting to the Cavaliers that they lost the war,

30 Which doesn't really count, of course,

31 Owing to the peculiar Brit method of counting,

Cromwell proves embarrassing

32 Which involves inches, pounds, rods, acres, leagues, fortnights, and shillings,
33 But never revolutions.
34 Anyway,
35 Cromwell immediately beheaded the [a]king,
36 And then replaced the divine right of kings system of government with a new system called the divine right of Cromwell,
37 Which was completely different, of course,
38 Since under the divine right of Cromwell, there is no king with the power of life and death over his subjects,
39 But a [b]Protector instead,
40 Who has the power of life and death over his subjects,
41 [c]But wears no crown.

CHAPTER 16

After a while, the Brits got together and decided that the divine right of Cromwell wasn't working out,
2 [d]Being no fun at all,
3 And somewhat embarrassing to boot,
4 [e]Since all the other nations of Europe had kings,
5 [f]Who were very well dressed,
6 And had started looking down on the Brits,
7 And hinting around that the Brits weren't very well bred,
8 Which is a sore subject,
9 If you happen to be a [g]mongrel race with a [h]terrible climate, a [i]made-up language, and [j]a neurotic obsession with clothing.
10 Which is why the Brits pulled off the [k]Restoration,
11 Which consisted of getting [l]Charles II down out of the [m]tree

a. Ed.77.1
   Boul.7.19
b. Jefs.7.15
c. Rom.13.11
d. Yks.3.11-15
e. 13.9
f. Ext.52.16
g. 8.2
h. 8.1
i. 1.2
j. 2.1-3
k. Psay.5Y.51
l. Psong.32.1-5
m. Psay.5O.6
n. 6.15-19
o. Psong.38.1
p. Boul.21.9
q. Frog.2.1-5
r. Frog.10.1
s. Frog.10.5
t. Frog.10.11
u. Dav.46.19
v. Psong.46.1-8
w. Psong.29.1-3
x. 15.30-33
y. Psay.5Y.11
z. Dav.20.34
aa. Rom.10.4

he had been hiding in,
12 For twenty years or so,
13 [n]Apologizing to him for all the unpleasantness,
14 And putting him back on the throne,
15 [o]With nice new clothes,
16 [p]And a nice new crown,
17 Which fixed everything,
18 Except that it didn't.

CHAPTER 17

The tree Charles had been hiding in was in [q]France,
2 Which exposed him to the [r]French system of government,
3 [s]Called the divine right of Louis's,
4 And involved lots of very expensive [t]parties.
5 After the Restoration, [u]Charles introduced the concept of parties to the Brit nobles,
6 [v]Who were willing to try anything once,
7 Provided that they could wear nice clothes while doing so,
8 [w]And emptied the Brit treasury in no time flat,
9 Which wasn't discovered till Charles's son went out shopping for something nice to wear at his coronation party,
10 And ran into a [x]revolution instead.
11 Fortunately for the Brits,
12 No one suggested anything as radical as a return to the divine right of Cromwell,
13 Who was dead anyway,
14 But Parliament set a bunch of new world records in the King-Baiting game,
15 [y]Which convinced [z]King James to quit being king,
16 [aa]And rewrite the Bible instead,

17 ^aWhich he did.

18 After his departure, it took a while for the dust to clear, but eventually the situation was resolved in the usual, inexplicable Brit way,

19 With a ^bforeigner on the throne,

20 Which became a succession of foreigners,

21 Including some ^cqueens,

22 And then a whole series of dim-witted ^dGeorges,

23 Who did a great job of ensuring that Brit foreign policy stay stupid and backward enough to increase British power enormously.

CHAPTER 18

What with all the fun the Brits had been having at home for the last few centuries,

2 ^eKilling kings,

3 And changing forms of government,

4 ^fAnd assimilating lots of foreign rulers,

5 It might seem that they were too busy to cause a lot of trouble for other nations,

6 But as it turns out,

7 The Brits are *never* too busy to cause trouble for other nations,

8 And in spite of all their ^grevolutions and other ^hsports,

9 They had found time to make quite a lot of progress toward world dominion,

10 ⁱWhich can't have been easy,

11 But the Brits had a secret weapon,

12 ^jCalled the class system,

13 Which gave everybody a stiff upper lip,

a. *Psay.5B.1-13*
b. *Exp.9.13*
c. *19.25-26*
d. *Ed.63.3*
e. *6.15-23*
f. *5.2-3*
g. *15.30-33*
h. *6.24.25*
  & *10.11*
  & *12.4-5*
i. *21.16*
j. *Gnt.10.14-15*
k. *Chr.3.23-25*
l. *Chr.3.26*
m. *Dav.10.14*
n. *5.5-6*
o. *Jefs.7.15-17*
p. *10.6*
q. *1.8-9*
r. *Psay.5V.20*
s. *Psay.1.6*
t. *Psay.5Q.78*
u. *18.13*

14 And an incredibly distorted view of reality.

CHAPTER 19

Under the Brit class system, there were basically two classes,

2 ^kNamely the Lords,

3 ^lAnd the commoners.

4 The Lords had lots of money and titles and were ^mvery well bred,

5 ⁿWhich meant that they dressed very well,

6 And received what the British called a ^ogentleman's education,

7 ^pWhich started before birth,

8 ^qAnd often ended in a horrible death.

9 For example, the babies of Lords were required to be born fully dressed,

10 ^rAnd weren't allowed to cry,

11 ^sFrom their first spanking on,

12 Through their beatings in the nursery,

13 ^tThrough their canings in public school,

14 And so forth,

15 For the rest of their lives.

16 They were raised by governesses,

17 Called nannies,

18 Who helped prepare them for public school by keeping them from forming any emotional attachments to their parents,

19 Or anyone else,

20 Since emotional attachments can lead to crying,

21 Which causes the upper lip to quiver,

22 ^uAnd is therefore not allowed.

23 After being properly pre-

pared in this way, the children of Lords,

24 Which is to say, young British gentlemen,

25 [a]Since the female children of Lords weren't allowed to do anything,

26 Except be queen and monarch of the country occasionally,

27 Went to the public school their father had gone to,

28 [b]Which was Eton,

29 Unless it was Harrow,

30 And from there to the university their father had gone to,

31 Which was Oxford,

32 Unless it was Cambridge,

33 And after that, they had to choose a career.

34 [c]For example, firstborn sons had to choose inheriting their father's title,

35 [d]And second-born sons had to choose a career in the military,

36 [e]And third-born sons had to choose a career in the Church of England,

37 And so on,

38 Which helps explain why the Brits invented concepts like duty, honor, and tradition,

39 Since duty means doing what your superiors tell you to,

40 Without thinking about it,

41 And honor means doing what your father would have told you to do [f]if you'd ever had the chance to meet him,

42 Without thinking about it,

43 [g]And tradition means doing what your father already did,

44 And his father,

45 And his father too,

46 And so on,

47 Without thinking about it,

48 Which the Lords have al-

a. *Mawr.22.20*
b. *23.15*
c. *Mawr.5.4*
d. *21.1*
e. *11.11*
f. *19.16-18*
g. *19.34*
h. *19.41*
i. *19.39*
j. *19.43*
k. *Psom.23.11*

ways been very good at.

CHAPTER 20

The other class of Brits, which is to say the commoners, did not receive a gentleman's education,

2 And therefore did not attend Eton and Oxford,

3 Or even Harrow and Cambridge,

4 And didn't have to have honor,

5 [h]Since they usually got to meet their fathers,

6 Unless they were bastards,

7 Which aren't expected to have honor anyway.

8 But being Brits, even the commoners were bound by duty and tradition,

9 [i]Which meant that they always had to do what their superiors told them to,

10 Without thinking about it,

11 [j]And also had to do what their fathers already did,

12 And their fathers,

13 And their fathers too,

14 And so on,

15 Without thinking about it,

16 Without any exceptions,

17 But one.

18 The exception was that a commoner could always choose a career in the Brit navy,

19 Even if his father had never had a career in the Brit navy,

20 Which he could do by hanging out in the right tavern,

21 [k]Meaning the kind of tavern that might be visited by impressment gangs,

22 Who recruited commoners into the navy for twelve years or so,

23 ᵃBy means of blackjacks and chains,

24 Which explains why the Brit navy got so big and powerful,

25 ᵇAnd stayed that way through thick and thin,

26 Even though Britain was actually a pretty small country.

CHAPTER 21

In fact, the Brit navy was the greatest single accomplishment of Brit culture,

2 ᶜConsisting of an officer corps from the upper class,

3 ᵈAnd an enlisted corps from the lower class,

4 All of whom were bound to do their duty,

5 ᵉWithout thinking about it,

6 ᶠEven if it killed them,

7 Which it usually did.

8 In return for their service, the Brits who served in the navy got some lime juice every day,

9 And a ration of grog,

10 Meaning rum-flavored swill,

11 ᵍAnd the chance to fight sea battles against great odds,

12 ʰIn places so far from home that they could spend their whole naval career on one voyage there and back,

13 *If* they got back,

14 Which wasn't easy,

15 Naturally,

16 Since they were Brits and therefore had to do everything the hard way,

17 ⁱSuch as with floggings,

18 ʲAnd summary executions at sea,

19 Often for no reason,

20 Except that the ᵏCaptain said so,

21 And rotten bread infested with worms,

a. Psay.5Q.78
b. Kens.12.10
c. 19.2
d. Chr.3.26
e. 22.12
f. 15.22
g. 1.9
h. Grk.23.12
Brit.9.3
i. Ann.6.23
Grk.9.7
j. 18.13
3.9
Gods.4.10
k. Dav.22.47
l. Psom.64.1-3
m. 19.6
n. 7.8
o. Psom.60.1-2
p. Kens.22.3
q. Kens.22.4

22 ˡAnd other Brit navy traditions along much the same lines.

23 The Brit officers had it better, though,

24 Since they got to wear nice uniforms,

25 Which made it all okay,

26 For some reason.

CHAPTER 22

Of course, the navy wasn't the only Brit military organization that had such a fine tradition.

2 The Brit army was almost as dutiful and honorable and traditional as the navy,

3 And had very nice uniforms too,

4 With bright red coats so that the enemy could see them coming,

5 Since it wouldn't have been fair to hide,

6 Because hiding is too easy,

7 And therefore not British.

8 ᵐThe Brit army officers were gentlemen, of course,

9 And got to wear nice regimental neckties when they were home,

10 Which made up for the fact that they always had to lead the attack,

11 Against superior numbers of enemy troops,

12 ⁿAs required by tradition,

13 While wearing special officers' uniforms, which,

14 Though nice,

15 Made great ᵒtargets for enemy sharpshooters.

16 The Brit enlisted soldiers were commoners, of course,

17 ᵖAnd had to do their duty too,

18 ۹Which consisted of always marching in neat rows,

19 [a]Toward the enemy,
20 [b]No matter what.

CHAPTER 23

Thanks to the [c]great tradition of the Brit military, Brit foreign policy tended to be very successful.
2 In spite of all their internal revolutions and their [d]foreign queens and their string of [e]dim-witted Georges,
3 The Brits managed to defeat the French several times,
4 [f]In the Hundred Years War,
5 [g]And the Thirty Years War,
6 [h]And the Seven Years war,
7 [i]And the Napoleonic Wars too.
8 These Brit victories took place on a couple of different continents,
9 Including America, [j]where the Frogs couldn't win even with the help of a bunch of Indians,
10 And Europe, [k]where the Frogs couldn't break their losing streak even with the help of a brilliant Corsican general,
11 Although they would have if the Brits hadn't had their great [l]class system to produce the right Brit heroes in the nick of time,
12 Such as [m]Nelson,
13 [n]Who had one arm and one eye and therefore knew how to think like a Frenchman,
14 And [o]Wellington, [p]who didn't know how to think at all,
15 [q]Thus explaining why he made the Brit army fight the Battle of Waterloo on the playing fields of [r]Eton,
16 Which confused [s]Napoleon no end,
17 And therefore contributed

a. Kens.22.5
b. Kens.22.6
c. Spic.11.8
d. 17.19-21
e. 17.22
f. Frog.7.9
g. Yks.116.16
h. Psay.5Y.52
i. Psay.5Y.22
j. Psay.5W.8
   Yks.10.1-2
k. Frog.15.10-12
l. 18.11-14
m. Dav.21.25-29
n. Dav.21.30-31
o. Yks.19.2
   Dav.10.10
p. 22.12
q. 18.10
r. 19.29
s. Dav.46.15
t. 7.8
u. 15.31
v. Exp.8.5
w. Exp.16.3-6
x. Yks.6.2-17
y. Yks.6.18-22
z. Yks.7.1-18
aa. Yks.8.1-8
bb. Yks.8.9-17
cc. Yks.9.1-5
dd. Yks.1.6
ee. 22.12
ff. 15.3

enormously to eventual Brit victory.

CHAPTER 24

There was one little episode, however, from which the Brits did not emerge completely victorious,
2 Which is not to say that they lost,
3 [t]Because the Brits never lose a war,
4 [u]Even when it sort of looks that way.
5 What happened was that the Brits had worked hard to colonize part of America,
6 Which they did the hard way, of course,
7 [v]Starting later than everyone else,
8 [w]And then doing it by sending boatfuls of unpleasant religious outcasts into Indian-infested tracts of wilderness, without funds or provisions, to build rich and valuable new world colonies.
9 [x]This brilliant strategy ultimately provided the Brits with the richest, most valuable colonies in the world,
10 [y]Which they quite properly tried to exploit through taxation,
11 [z]Resulting in a lot of grousing by the colonists,
12 [aa]Who wanted to be independent,
13 [bb]Meaning tax-free,
14 [cc]And then declared that they *were* independent,
15 [dd]With a nation of their own,
16 And topped it off by saying a lot of impolite things about the king.
17 [ee]Obviously, the Brits had to suppress the rebellion,
18 [ff]But since the Americans

were fighting against great odds, with fewer troops and weapons and provisions than the Brits had,
19 [a]The Brits were unnerved,
20 Never having been in this situation before.
21 So, not wanting to do things the easy way,
22 They hired a bunch of [b]German mercenaries to suppress the rebellion for them,
23 [c]Which didn't work out exactly right,
24 [d]And led to the establishment of the United States of America as a free and independent nation,
25 Which still doesn't mean that the Brits lost a war,
26 Since it was obviously a revolution,
27 [e]And revolutions don't count.

CHAPTER 25

[f]In fact, the Brits had another unfortunate encounter with the United States a little later on,
2 [g]Which they also didn't lose,
3 [h]Having inflicted a lot of damage on the Yanks,
4 Including burning their [i]capital city,
5 And the [j]house of their president,
6 [k]Not to mention sinking a lot of their ships,
7 [l]And then concluding a peace treaty before the final unfortunate battle occurred.
8 [m]Which is why there's no reason for the Yanks to think they won,
9 Even though the peace treaty basically gave the Yanks what they wanted,
10 And even though the Yanks mowed down thousands of [n]redcoats,
11 [o]Marching neatly in rows,
12 Without losing a man themselves,
13 [p]In the final battle,
14 Which wouldn't have been fought in the first place if the peace treaty had been delivered on time.

CHAPTER 26

But fortunately for the Brits, there were other parts of the world,
2 Places where there were vast numbers of brave natives willing to outnumber the Brits in defense of their homelands,
3 Which enabled the Brits to fight in the proper way,
4 Against great odds,
5 Wearing very nice uniforms,
6 Except for the ones that included short pants,
7 [q]Which turned out to be okay anyway because the Brits have never understood that short pants are not nice, but silly.
8 And so, as the [r]dim-witted Georges gave way to dim-witted monarchs with other names,
9 Brit power and influence expanded enormously,
10 [s]Until there were huge Brit colonies in Africa,
11 [t]And India,
12 [u]And Asia,
13 [v]And Indochina,
14 [w]And Australia,
15 [x]And Canada,
16 [y]And Ireland,
17 [z]And Wales,
18 [aa]And Scotland,
19 [bb]And wherever else there were non-white or non-Brit peoples who needed to be taught

a. Psom.62.1
b. 15.16
c. 41.21
d. Bks.6.24
e. 15.31
f. Yks.18.1-9
g. Yks.19.1
h. Yks.18.10-13
i. Ann.4.32
j. Ann.4.30-31
k. Yks.18.15
l. Yks.18.17
m. 24.3
n. 22.4
o. 22.17-20
p. Yks.18.18
q. 1.4
r. 17.22
s. Psay.5W.11
t. Bks.3.1-9
u. Chnk.12.1-15
v. Yks.20.16-17
w. Oth.6.1-7
x. Frog.19.5
y. Frog.17.2 Yks.20.9
z. Ann.18.6
aa. Psom.36.5-6
bb. Swar.35.10-13

how to do everything the hard way,

20 Including honor and tradition and fair play and so forth,

21 [a]Even if they all had to be slaughtered to the last man, woman, and child in order to learn it properly,

22 [b]So that eventually there came a day when the sun never set on the British Empire,

23 And no matter where you went in the world,

24 [c]You could hear people talking at great length about their views on Brit honor and tradition,

25 And fair play,

26 Not to mention Brit uniforms.

CHAPTER 27

[d]**B**ut the Brits also had a great sense of humor,

2 Meaning that they never took the criticisms of foreigners too seriously,

3 [e]Because you had to consider the source,

4 [f]And if the peoples who carped about the Brits were so great, then how come the Brits owned all their territory,

5 [g]And all their money,

6 [h]And almost everyone else's too?

7 In fact, the Brits were so confident about things in general that they felt lighthearted enough to crown a [i]queen as their monarch,

8 Whose name was [j]Victoria,

9 And who lived for an entire age,

10 [k]Named after herself.

11 Of course, by this time, the Brits had done enough [l]King-Baiting over the years to ensure

a. Psay.1.6
b. Psong.48.1-5
c. Psong.47.5
d. Vin.49.5
e. Psay.5A.31
f. Psong.53.6-7
g. Psong.45.3-5
h. Psong.53.9
i. 19.25-26
j. Dav.7.5
k. Mawr.29.3-4
l. 6.24-26
m. 7.1-3
n. 27.1
o. Gods.4.4-6
p. Psom.75.4-5
q. 10.9
r. 9.3
s. Adam.5.1-8
t. Adam.3.2-7
u. Adam.7.1
v. Adam.7.2-4
w. Adam.7.5-6
x. Adam.9.1-4
y. Adam.10.9-11
z. Adam.11.6-8
aa. Adam.10.4-8

that [m]Parliament got to make most of the real decisions,

12 [n]And they had also invented a tradition of allowing commoners to vote and serve in Parliament,

13 Which was called democracy,

14 Meaning rule by Lords who have resigned their titles to pose as commoners,

15 [o]Which led to prime ministers,

16 Whose job it was to say clever things,

17 [p]And rule the world.

CHAPTER 28

One big advantage the Brits had in ruling the world was that they had made up lots and lots of science,

2 Which they had a knack for,

3 [q]Because nothing makes life harder for everyone like advanced technology.

4 For example, the Brits figured out that the climate in Great Britain,

5 [r]While bad,

6 Wasn't bad enough,

7 [s]Which convinced them to start an industrial revolution,

8 [t]By inventing capitalism,

9 [u]And steam engines,

10 [v]And lots of powerful machinery driven by steam engines,

11 [w]And factories to put the machinery in,

12 So that the whole country could be filled with coal smoke,

13 [x]With the help of the commoners,

14 [y]Whose job it was to burn coal in factories twenty or thirty hours a day,

15 [z]Including children,

16 [aa]For pennies.

17 Working for such long hours made the commoners hungry,
18 Which was a problem,
19 [a]Because it was the French who had invented food,
20 [b]And wouldn't give the Brits any,
21 Thus explaining why there wasn't any food in Great Britain,
22 And still isn't.
23 Anyway,
24 When the commoners got hungry, the Brits responded with another one of their clever inventions,
25 [c]Namely gin,
26 Which didn't exactly eliminate hunger,
27 [d]But made the commoners forget they were hungry,
28 And tired,
29 And cold,
30 [e]And sick from breathing coal smoke twenty or thirty hours a day.
31 [f]Thanks to this invention, the Brits soon became the richest industrial nation on earth,
32 [g]And sold proper Brit clothes to everyone the world over,
33 Including millions of wogs,
34 Meaning "non-white natives so ignorant they don't know enough to wear spats,"
35 [h]Who were often unaware that they needed new clothes until the Brit military gave them fashion lessons,
36 Which usually involved staying after school,
37 Under British rule,
38 [i]Forever.

CHAPTER 29

By now, in fact, the Brits had a considerable amount of culture,
2 Not all of which was stolen from the many nations they had conquered and [j]civilized.
3 For example, in the course of their thousand-year history, the Brits had produced well over half a dozen artists,
4 Including [k]Turner,
5 And probably some others too.
6 During the same time period, they had also produced a composer,
7 Whose name was [l]Purcell,
8 And who was pretty okay, even if he wasn't [m]Mozart,
9 But then comparatively few people are.
10 And there was quite a lot of architecture in Britain as well,
11 [n]Including incredibly huge castles and stately old homes,
12 [o]Which weren't any uglier than the huge castles and stately old homes that had been built by thieves and pirates the world over, since time immemorial,
13 [p]Since you've got to spend all that loot on something.
14 And besides, some of the architecture in London was really beautiful and impressive,
15 If you could only see it through the fog,
16 [q]Which wasn't the Brits' fault,
17 [r]Unless you count coal smoke.

CHAPTER 30

And art and music and architecture weren't the only Brit cultural accomplishments.
2 For example, there was literature,
3 Which they couldn't seem to get enough of,
4 No matter how much they had already,

a. *Frog.24.1*
b. *Exp.7.6*
c. *Adam.10.12-18*
d. *Psom.75.10*
e. *Adam.11.1-5*
f. *Exp.1.3-6*
g. *Yks.20.25-27*
h. *Psong.47.4*
i. *Psay.5Q.78*
j. *28.36-38*
k. *Gods.1.4*
l. *Ed.29.6*
m. *Krt.13.1-6*
n. *Chr.3.23-25*
o. *Swar.14.5-8*
p. *22.10*
19.47
Frog.35.12
q. *1.2*
r. *15.30-31*

5 [a]For some reason,
6 Which probably had nothing to do with the way they felt about other things,
7 [b]Like territory,
8 [c]And tradition,
9 [d]And power,
10 [e]And clothes.
11 Anyway,
12 This led to a truly large number of Brit poets and Brit dramatists and Brit novelists and Brit philosophers,
13 So many in fact that it's hard to remember them all,
14 Unless you're a Brit,
15 [f]And have had a gentleman's education.

CHAPTER 31

In the beginning of Brit literature, there was [g]Beowulf,
2 Who was really a [h]Dane,
3 Unless he was a [i]Geat,
4 And had a poem written about him in the [j]Dark Ages,
5 By [k]somebody or other,
6 Who didn't write in English, but [l]Anglo-Saxon,
7 Which counts anyway,
8 [m]Owing to the peculiar Brit method of counting.
9 Then there was [n]Chaucer, who wrote a bunch of tales about a [o]trip to Canterbury,
10 [p]Which also counts,
11 Even though Chaucer didn't write in English, but Middle English,
12 [q]Which is a lot like English but with everything misspelled.
13 Then came [r]Spenser, who wrote poetry the hard way,
14 Meaning that no one can read it,
15 No matter how hard he tries,
16 [s]Which makes 'The Faerie

a. *1.4*
b. *30.3-5*
c. *30.3-5*
d. *30.3-5*
e. *40.8*
f. *19.6-8*
g. *Pnot.33.1-5*
h. *Exp.3.2-8*
i. *Carl.3.8*
j. *Chr.9.1-7*
k. *Dav.30.40*
l. *Krt.6.4-5*
m. *15.32*
n. *Dav.15.9*
o. *Pnot.1.1-5*
p. *31.8*
q. *Hill.A.4*
r. *Dav.20.42*
s. *Bks.3.14*
t. *Dav.19.8*
u. *Pnot.25.1*
v. *Pnot.25.2*
w. *Pnot.25.3-5*
x. *Chr.8.17*
y. *Grk.8.1-4*
z. *Gnt.15.1-32 & 16.1-12*
aa. *10.9*
bb. *Adam.30.2-7*
cc. *Dav.7.5*

Queene' a giant classic of Brit literature.
17 There was also [t]Malory, who only wrote in prose,
18 But who invented [u]King Arthur and [v]Queen Guinevere and Sir Lancelot and [w]Merlin and the [x]Holy Grail,
19 Which convinced the Brits that they were special,
20 [y]For some reason,
21 And therefore became another giant classic of Brit literature.
22 And then there was Shakespeare.

CHAPTER 32

When the end of the world comes, the last sound anyone hears will probably be some Brit talking about Shakespeare,
2 Who was really great,
3 And wrote a lot of [z]plays and sonnets,
4 [aa]Unless Francis Bacon wrote them,
5 Which doesn't really matter anyway,
6 Because they were both Brits,
7 And great,
8 Even if the Brits keep trying to spoil it by putting on a lot of tedious productions of Shakespeare's plays,
9 And writing endless numbers of incredibly tedious books about Shakespeare,
10 [bb]And all the other stuff you have to do if you want the world to acknowledge that you once produced someone who did something really great.

CHAPTER 33

After Shakespeare there was [cc]Milton, who was blind,

2 And great,

3 Even if his poetry didn't rhyme,

4 Which was deliberate,

5 For some reason.

6 [a]It was Milton who wrote 'Paradise Lost,'

7 Which was about [b]Adam and Eve,

8 [c]Who were famous Brit religious figures,

9 And great,

10 Though not as great as Shakespeare.

CHAPTER 34

There was also [d]Alexander [e]Pope, who came after Milton,

2 [f]And decided that all the best literature had already been written,

3 Which meant that it was okay for [g]Pope to write everything in [h]rhyming couplets,

4 Which are great,

5 If you don't get sick to death of them in the first ten minutes,

6 And since Brits don't,

7 Pope is great,

8 Though not as great as Shakespeare.

CHAPTER 35

And then came the Age of Reason, which was a time when everybody thought that it was possible to figure everything out,

2 And eventually make it all better,

3 [i]Somehow.

4 [j]Reason doesn't really mix with poetry, though,

5 But someone forgot to tell the Brits,

6 Which resulted in a lot more great poetry,

a. Pnot.13.1-5
b. Name.3.4
c. Lies.2.9-23
d. Psay.5Q.21
e. Chr.6.11
f. Swar.10.4-5
g. Dav.14.26
   Spic.12.5
h. Psay.5A.4
   Penn.2.2
   Psom.78.10
i. 10.9
j. Drex.6.3-15
   Psom.24.1-4
k. Swar.14.7
l. Dav.20.42
m. 41.21
n. Lies.2.13
o. Hall.6.9
p. Al.2.1-5
q. Al.2.6-8
r. Lies.2.17-23
s. Frog.27.1
   & 28.1
t. Ed.46.10
u. Frog.27.2-4
v. Pnot.9.1-5
w. 28.19-20

7 That nobody but Brits can read.

CHAPTER 36

The invention of reason convinced a lot of well-educated Brits that they could think,

2 Which is how the Brits came to invent [k]irony,

3 And helps explain why there was [l]Isaac Newton,

4 [m]Who invented physics,

5 By letting an [n]apple fall on his head,

6 And thereby discovered [o]gravity,

7 And a lot of other things too,

8 [p]Although he forgot to discover the theory of relativity,

9 [q]And other important things,

10 Probably because he was stunned by the [r]apple.

CHAPTER 37

[s]Another very reasonable Brit was [t]Jonathan Swift, who thought that the world was full of stupid, inflexible, wrongheaded idiots,

2 [u]For some reason,

3 And wrote it all down in a book called [v]'Gulliver's Travels,'

4 About a Brit who met a lot of stupid, inflexible, wrong-headed idiots of different sizes and shapes,

5 Including little ones,

6 And big ones,

7 And even some that were shaped like horses,

8 Though smarter.

9 It was also Swift who made a modest proposal,

10 About using Irish babies as food,

11 [w]Because there wasn't any food in Great Britain,

12 And never had been,

13 Whereas there were a lot of Irish babies,
14 Which the Brits all thought was ironic,
15 And great,
16 Though not as great as Shakespeare.

CHAPTER 38

Then there was [a]Samuel Johnson,
2 [b]Who wrote down a lot of clever remarks,
3 And had a friend named [c]Boswell who followed him around and wrote down all the clever remarks Johnson made in public,
4 Which were all great,
5 Though not as great as Shakespeare.

CHAPTER 39

Another great Brit thinker was [d]John Locke,
2 [e]Who invented democracy,
3 Unless it was someone else who invented democracy,
4 [f]And Locke just thought about it a lot.

CHAPTER 40

There was also a Brit named [g]William Blake,
2 Who liked tigers,
3 And God,
4 And [h]ampersands,
5 Which led to the Brit romantic movement,
6 And was therefore great,
7 Though,
8 [i]You know.

CHAPTER 41

The romantics were Brits who thought that it might be possible to feel emotions,

a. *Dav.20.42*
b. *Psay.5Q.16*
c. *Psom.5.1-6*
d. *Dav.20.42*
e. *Yks.73.4*
f. *Dav.47.11 & 47.22*
g. *Psom.45.10-11 Dav.56.11*
h. *Psom.44.1-9*
i. *Wil.17.1*
j. *19.16-19*
k. *41.21*
l. *19.21*
m. *Dav.20.34*
n. *Psong.49.1-3*
o. *Dav.20.34*
p. *Ed.27.5*
q. *Dav.20.34*
r. *Ann.18.18*
s. *Dav.20.34*
t. *Ann.18.11*
u. *Dav.20.34*
v. *Ann.18.20*
w. *Swar.16.1-4*
x. *Swar.16.5-7*

2 [j]Even if you'd had a gentleman's education,
3 [k]Which wasn't easy,
4 And therefore resulted in a huge number of Brit romantic poets,
5 Who invented lots of new Brit emotions,
6 Such as romantic melancholy,
7 [l]Which is the feeling you get if you're a Brit trying to experience a genuine emotion.
8 For example, there was [m]Keats,
9 Who wanted to love a [n]nightingale and also possibly an urn of some sort,
10 And [o]Shelley,
11 Who wanted to love a [p]stone statue buried in the desert,
12 And [q]Byron,
13 Who wanted to love [r]women,
14 And [s]Wordsworth,
15 Who wanted to love [t]England,
16 And [u]Coleridge,
17 Who wanted to love [v]God and His creations.
18 [w]Through prodigious effort, the romantic poets succeeded in working themselves up to an emotional state that was something like mild yearning,
19 [x]Only tinged with a vague sadness,
20 Which is a pretty passionate way to feel,
21 If you're a Brit.

CHAPTER 42

Then came the Victorians,
2 Who were passionate,
3 Though not quite as passionate as the romantics,
4 Because you don't have a lot of time for emotional fireworks

if you're responsible for ruling the world,

5 Unless you're [a]Charles Dickens,

6 And almost as great as Shakespeare,

7 Which lets you wear your [b]heart on your sleeve,

8 And write [c]sentimental stories that go on,

9 And on,

10 And on,

11 For many many pages.

12 Anyway, [d]Browning was a Victorian poet who thought that poetry should consist of clever remarks,

13 And [e]Oscar Wilde was a Victorian dramatist and poet who thought that [f]life should consist of clever remarks,

14 And unlike Browning,

15 Actually put some clever remarks into his [g]work.

16 There was also an extremely peculiar Victorian named [h]Lewis Carroll, who thought that literature should consist of [i]clever nonsense,

17 [j]Which he proceeded to do so cleverly that to this day [k]no one has the slightest idea what he was [l]talking about.

18 Another clever Victorian was [m]Rudyard Kipling,

19 Who thought it was a good idea to write clever poems and stories about ruling the world the hard way.

20 It was also Kipling who finally discovered the reason *why* Brits do everything the hard way,

21 [n]Which is called the White Man's Burden,

22 And explains everything,

23 If you're a Brit.

24 There was also a Victorian

a. *Dav.20.28*
b. *Ned.29.8-10*
   Swar.30.1-3
   Ned.29.12-17
c. *Pnot.30.1-5*
d. *Dav.19.8*
e. *Dav.14.24*
f. *Ann.18.26*
g. *Psay.5Q.29*
h. *Dav.19.8*
i. *Ed.28.1*
   Yks.61.19-20
j. *Vin.11.10-15*
k. *Paul.7.6*
l. *Psom.17.6-7*
   & 22.1-4
m. *Dav.19.8*
n. *Yks.27.12*
o. *Dav.19.8*
p. *Dav.19.8*
q. *Mawr.22.20*
r. *Main.18.6*
s. *Dav.30.9*
t. *Ed.28.4*
u. *Dav.14.39*

named [o]Arthur Conan Doyle,

25 Who thought it was a good idea to have clever characters,

26 Which is how he came to invent [p]Sherlock Holmes,

27 Who was fascinated by duplicity, treachery, and murder,

28 [q]Despised women,

29 Detested emotion,

30 But dressed properly,

31 And therefore became more popular than Shakespeare.

CHAPTER 43

There was also a Brit who didn't think that literature was about being clever,

2 But about having lots and lots of sex,

3 Or at least thinking about it a lot,

4 [r]And then discussing it for thousands and thousands of pages,

5 Which the Brits didn't approve of,

6 Because no matter how hard they looked,

7 Starting with the very first word of the first page and then proceeding through every single salacious scene,

8 All the way to the very last word of the last page,

9 There was nothing clever to be found in the books of [s]D.H. Lawrence.

CHAPTER 44

The Brits also had some women writers,

2 Including [t]Jane Austen,

3 Who wrote stories about the importance of manners,

4 Which the Brits think they invented,

5 For some reason.

6 There was also [u]Emily Brontë

and her sister [a]Charlotte,

7 Who each wrote a book about a long and peculiar romance,

8 [b]Which convinced a lot of other women down through history to do the same thing,

9 Unfortunately.

10 There was also [c]George Eliot,

11 Who was a woman too,

12 For some reason.

13 Then there was [d]Elizabeth Barrett Browning,

14 [e]Who extended the odd Brit system of counting to include love,

15 [f]Without much success.

CHAPTER 45

And even though there was absolutely no chance that they could ever live up to Shakespeare,

2 The Brits also tolerated attempts at literature by writers from their most benighted provinces,

3 [g]Such as Ireland, Scotland, and America,

4 Even though most of the writers from these places didn't really like English,

5 And kept trying to turn it into something else,

6 Like [h]Robert Burns, a Scot who owned a [i]stinking [j]apostrophe factory in Glasgow and thought English would be better if it had several apostrophes in each word,

7 And [k]George Bernard Shaw, an Irishman who thought English would be better if the right spellings for words could be decided by five hundred drunken Irishmen in a pub,

8 And [l]James Joyce, an Irishman who thought he'd like En-

a. *Ed.28.4*
b. *Swar.32.11*
c. *Dav.20.42*
d. *Dav.14.39*
e. *15.32*
f. *Psom.72.1-6*
g. *Main.22.10*
h. *Dav.46.27 & 35.40*
i. *Adam.10.1-8*
j. *Psom.36.1-7 Ext.16.4-6*
k. *Dav.14.22*
l. *Dav.14.22*
m. *F&J.15.5-17*
n. *Dav.14.22*
o. *Psom.6.3*
p. *Dav.20.34*
q. *Swar.17.1-3*
r. *Psom.12.4*
s. *29.2 15.31*
t. *29.12*

glish better if he turned it into a language that nobody could understand,

9 [m]Unless their name was James Joyce,

10 And [n]William Butler Yeats, an Irishman who thought English would be better if it kind of seemed to make sense,

11 [o]Until you read it more carefully,

12 And [p]T.S. Eliot, an American who thought that English would be better if it contained so many [q]depressing foreign-language references that no American would ever be able to figure them out,

13 Unless that American had the exquisite taste to move to Britain,

14 And spend the rest of his life looking up neat foreign language references in [r]dusty Brit libraries,

15 Under the shadow of Shakespeare.

CHAPTER 46

In addition to all of their own culture, the Brits owned quite a lot of [s]artwork,

2 From Egypt and Greece and Rome,

3 And France and Germany and Italy,

4 And lots of other places too,

5 Which they stored in museums and [t]castles and stately homes,

6 And looked at every so often,

7 Just to make sure,

8 That it wasn't as great as Shakespeare.

CHAPTER 47

And then there was the peculiar Brit cultural obsession

with something called "sport,"
2 Which always involved lots of oddly dressed Brits doing [a]something incomprehensible on a playing field,
3 And never getting upset when they lost,
4 Whether they lost at [b]cricket,
5 Or [c]rugby,
6 Or [d]football,
7 Or [e]polo,
8 Or [f]golf,
9 Or anything else,
10 Except wars, of course,
11 [g]Because Brits never lose wars,
12 Which maybe explains why they were always such a good sport in any contest where world dominion wasn't on the line,
13 [h]And maybe also explains why nobody else has ever understood the Brit definition of fair play,
14 Since it seems to occur only when there are no foreigners on the field,
15 In games that nobody but Brits want to play.

CHAPTER 48

Of course, while it was obvious to the Brits that they were way ahead on points in the [i]race to be the Chosen Nation,
2 And had been for quite some time,
3 [j]The way they read the rules, anyway,
4 There were still other nations who thought the Brits had just been lucky,
5 For quite some time,
6 [k]And might be getting tired of being raised, educated, and killed in the hardest possible way,
7 For centuries.

a. 23.15
b. Psay.5S.20
c. Psay.5S.21
d. 15.37
e. Grk.8.32
f. Adam.10.3
g. 7.8
h. 9.5-6
i. Exp.1.17-25
j. Gnt.13.4-8
k. 22.12
l. Krt.22.1-2
m. Krt.22.3-12
n. Krt.22.13-15
o. Krt.22.16
p. Krt.22.17
q. Mawr.22.22
r. Dav.14.25
s. Adam.42.9-15
t. Frog.33.3-6
u. Frog.33.7-8
v. Forg.5.6
w. 1.9
x. Krt.24.2-3
y. 22.12
z. 15.31

8 [l]In particular, the Germans thought they had discovered a new way of being the Chosen Nation,
9 [m]Which was to do everything the big way.
10 [n]For example, the Germans got the idea that if there could be a really big war,
11 [o]Involving everybody,
12 [p]And the Germans won it big,
13 [q]They would automatically become the Chosen Nation.
14 For this reason, the German ruler,
15 Called [r]Kaiser Wilhelm,
16 [s]Got some German munitions manufacturers to help him start World War I,
17 [t]Which almost backfired when the French tried to start it first,
18 [u]But soon settled down to become a really big war,
19 With lots of really big armies involved,
20 Shooting off lots of really big guns,
21 Resulting in lots of really big casualties,
22 [v]And then lots of really big cemeteries,
23 All over the world.

CHAPTER 49

Being outnumbered, the [w]Brits fought very well in [x]World War I,
2 And because the big way of having a war turned out to be an exceptionally hard way to have a war,
3 It [y]eventually resulted in another Brit victory,
4 Which unfortunately had to be shared,
5 [z]Just a little,

6 With the [a]French,
7 And the [b]Americans,
8 And the [c]Russians,
9 And the [d]Italians,
10 And even the [e]Japanese,
11 For some reason.
12 Fortunately, however, the blame for starting the war did not have to be shared,
13 [f]But could be assigned completely to Germany,
14 Who resented it,
15 [g]In a big way,
16 But had to pay war reparations anyhow.

CHAPTER 50

After [h]World War I, the Brits got [i]depressed,
2 [j]Having discovered that the United States was now bigger and richer than the Brit Empire,
3 [k]For some reason.
4 Since it was clear that the Americans [l]didn't believe in doing things the hard way, the Brits began to think that maybe they needed a new way themselves.
5 [m]After all, the Brits had fought [n]World War I the hard way,
6 And had millions and millions of dead to show for it,
7 [o]Whereas the Americans spent most of the war being above it all,
8 [p]Then danced in at the end and lost no more than a few thousand troops,
9 [q]Tops.
10 And so the Brits tried being [r]above it all for a few years,
11 Reducing the size of the navy,
12 And the army,
13 And ignoring most of what was happening everywhere else,
14 [s]Including Germany,
15 Except for one antiquated Brit named [t]Winston Churchill,
16 [u]Who still believed in doing things the hard way,
17 [v]And who was the only one who noticed when the Germans started rebuilding their military,
18 [w]In a big way.
19 [x]But most of the Brits were really enjoying being above it all,
20 And thought Churchill was just having fun,
21 The hard way,
22 Which was [y]amusing, of course,
23 But nothing to get alarmed about.

CHAPTER 51

When the Germans decided that Austria was really part of Germany,
2 And always had been,
3 Churchill got upset,
4 [z]But the Brits decided to remain above it all,
5 Except that the Brit prime minister,
6 Called [aa]Neville Chamberlain,
7 [bb]Asked the Germans to be nice from now on,
8 Which they said they would do,
9 But actually they were lying,
10 [cc]In a big way.
11 Then, when the Germans decided that Czechoslovakia was also part of Germany,
12 And always had been,
13 Churchill got upset,
14 [dd]But the Brits decided once again to remain above it all,
15 [ee]Except that Neville Chamberlain asked the Germans to do better from now on,
16 Which they said they would do,

a. Frog.34.1
b. Yks.76.1-17
c. Russ.15.13-15
d. Rom.24.17-18
e. Nips.14.1-5
f. Frog.34.6
g. 1.9
h. Krt.24.2-3
i. Frog.35.4
j. Exp.1.4-5
k. Adam.15.1-16
l. Yks.120.6
m. 22.18-20
n. Krt.24.2-3
o. Yks.75.7-12
p. Yks.77.1-14
q. Yks.78.1-2
r. Ira.26.21-27
s. Krt.29.1-10
t. Dav.14.20 & 14.27
u. Psay.5A.13
v. Krt.31.14
w. 49.15
x. Krt.31.17
y. Dav.29.9
z. Yks.101.14-15
aa. Dav.20.34
bb. Yks.82.7
cc. 49.15
dd. Yks.101.16
ee. 51.7

17 Although they were actually lying again,

18 [a]In a big way.

19 When the Germans decided that the next country which really had always belonged to them was Poland,

20 And the Poles objected,

21 Churchill got upset,

22 And so did Neville Chamberlain,

23 [b]Which didn't help Poland,

24 But convinced the Brits that maybe being above it all didn't work on Germans.

25 [c]And so they asked Winston Churchill to help them remember how to do things the hard way,

26 For a while.

CHAPTER 52

Churchill did the best he could, using all the old Brit methods that had always worked so well in the past.

2 He sent a small army to Europe to fight the Germans in France,

3 Against great odds,

4 [d]Meaning with the help of the French,

5 [e]But the Germans won,

6 [f]In a big way,

7 And the Brits had to rescue their army from Dunkirk the hard way,

8 [g]Which is to say, one at a time in small boats.

9 [h]By this time, the Germans had remembered that all of Europe belonged to them,

10 And had moved in,

11 [i]In a big way.

12 This left Great Britain to fight the Battle of Britain all alone,

a. *49.15*
b. *Yks.101.17-18*
c. *Psay.5Q.38*
d. *Frog.37.5*
e. *Frog.37.8*
f. *49.15*
g. *F&J.14.2-4*
h. *Mall.6.24-25*
i. *49.15*
j. *Frog.38.1-2*
k. *Ext.48.19*
l. *Dav.48.7*
m. *Frog.15.10-14*
n. *Frog.17.3-5*
o. *Psay.5A.19*
p. *Yks.104.3-14*
q. *Yks.104.16-29*
r. *Yks.139.11-12*
s. *Yks.106.1-14*
t. *Yks.107.1-16*
u. *Yks.107.17-19*

13 [j]Without the help of the French,

14 Which was much the best way,

15 All things considered.

16 During the Battle of Britain, the Germans managed to level large sections of London with bombs,

17 [k]But forgot to invade Great Britain,

18 Because the German leader,

19 Whose name was [l]Hitler,

20 And who had never even lived in France,

21 [m]Nevertheless got the idea that it might be easier to conquer Russia first.

CHAPTER 53

[n]This brilliant German strategy worked out pretty much the way it usually does,

2 [o]Resulting in millions of cold soldiers dying in the bloody snow,

3 [p]Which gave the Brits a lot of time to try to convince the Americans that being above it all doesn't work with Germans.

4 [q]But Americans are slow learners,

5 [r]And the Brits never convinced them of anything,

6 [s]Until the Japanese convinced them that being above it all doesn't work with the Japanese,

7 [t]Which suggested the possibility that maybe the Brits were right about the Germans,

8 [u]And thus brought America into the war.

CHAPTER 54

Churchill kept on trying to do everything the hard way, with lots of blood, sweat, and tears,

2 Which is why the Brits had so much confidence in their newest military hero,

3 An idiot named ªMontgomery,

4 ᵇWho did everything possible to make the war bloodier, sweatier, and more tearful than it was already,

5 But was consistently frustrated by the Americans,

6 Who always wanted to do things *their* way,

7 ᶜAnd ultimately did.

8 Having recognized that the ᵈGermans and ᵉJapanese were determined to do everything the big way,

9 ᶠThe Americans decided to do everything even bigger,

10 ᵍWhich had never occurred to the Brits,

11 ʰAnd so the Americans built a very big force consisting of very big planes, very big ships, and very big armies,

12 And used them to fight a lot of very big battles,

13 Like ⁱAnzio and ʲD-Day and the ᵏBattle of the Bulge and so forth,

14 ˡAnd do a lot of very big damage to German cities and factories,

15 ᵐAnd to Japanese cities and factories,

16 ⁿUntil the Germans gave up,

17 ºAnd the Japanese were distinctly nervous.

CHAPTER 55

ᵖThen the Americans dropped a very very big bomb on Japan,

2 ۹And another one a couple of days later,

3 ʳWhich convinced the Japanese to give up too,

---

a. Dav.46.15
b. Psay.5Q.20
c. Yks.110.1-20
d. 48.8-9
e. Nips.16.1-3
f. Yks.76.15
g. 22.12
h. Yks.111.1-8
i. Yks.112.8-14
j. Yks.114.1-14
k. Yks.117.8-13
l. Yks.112.2-6
m. Nips.22.1-3
n. Yks.117.14-17
o. Nips.22.11-15
p. Nips.24.1-10
q. Nips.25.11-13
r. Yks.119.13-15
s. Hill.V.1
   Psom.60.1-2
t. Forg.5.6
u. 48.6
v. 52.15
w. 20.26
x. Yks.120.2-5
y. Lies.5.17-22
z. 42.20-23
aa. Exp.1.4-5
bb. Lies.5.23-24

---

4 And made everything okay,

5 Except that it didn't.

CHAPTER 56

Unfortunately, things were not okay in Great Britain anymore.

2 ˢThe Germans had knocked down a lot of their cities,

3 ᵗAnd the Germans and Japanese had killed a lot of their troops,

4 And it seemed to a lot of Brits that duty, honor, and tradition were getting to be pretty expensive and outdated luxuries,

5 ᵘEspecially since they had all grown pretty fond of being above it all,

6 Before Hitler came along and messed things up,

7 And now they were no longer sure of anything,

8 ᵛExcept that the hard way had become too hard,

9 And the big way was too big for a ᵂlittle country,

10 ˣEspecially now that the United States and the Soviet Union had started throwing their weight around in such an ill-bred fashion.

11 ʸAnd so the Brits politely asked Winston Churchill to go away,

12 Immediately,

13 Or sooner than that, if possible,

14 And then politely dismantled the bankrupt remains of their empire,

15 ᶻStuck the White Man's Burden on a shelf,

16 ᵃᵃAnd stopped trying to be a Chosen Nation altogether,

17 ᵇᵇSo that they could devote all their time to being above it all.

CHAPTER 57

The Brit ªLords got so above it all that they completely stopped trying to run the country,

2 ᵇAnd let the commoners do it instead,

3 ᶜWhich left more time for wearing nice clothes and being well bred.

4 The commoners had a lot of great new ideas about how the Brits could get even more above it all.

5 ᵈFor example, they thought up the idea of destroying the Brit economy by making everybody stop working and go on the dole instead,

6 ᵉWhich worked great,

7 And gave all the Brit intellectuals something to do with their spare time,

8 ᶠNow that they didn't have an empire to worry about anymore.

9 ᵍInstead, they had a lot of fun trying to explain why the nation that had invented capitalism couldn't remember how to make things anymore,

10 Including cars,

11 And airplanes,

12 And refrigerators,

13 Or anything else,

14 ʰExcept clothes, of course.

CHAPTER 58

But in spite of all their problems, the Brits were still interested in culture,

2 And even though they had given up writing lots of great literature,

3 Because it was too hard to do,

4 They still wanted to keep their hand in,

5 So they tried American culture instead,

6 And discovered that ⁱrock-and-roll was just the thing,

7 Because it was so easy to do,

8 ʲAnd a great way to show the Yanks all the neat new things they had learned about being above it all.

CHAPTER 59

And now the Brits have been above it all for years,

2 ᵏAnd they like it,

3 Because it's a brand-new kind of misery to be poor and inept and unemployed,

4 ˡAnd when you're the nation that invented misery in the first place,

5 ᵐIt's pretty wonderful to find a new type of misery at this late date.

6 And so, the chances are that the Brits will go on being above it all,

7 ⁿUntil the world comes to an end,

8 Because it's the only way to go,

9 When you have a terrible climate,

10 ºA tired, mongrel race,

11 A ruined economy,

12 A bloody, bloody past,

13 ᵖAnd no more world to rule.

a. 27.12-14
b. Carl.10.2-10
c. Wil.29.2
d. Adam.41.1-5
e. Adam.41.6-7
f. Psong.48.1
g. Main.16.1-6
h. 15.37
i. Yks.144.1-20
j. Ed.70.19-23
k. 41.20-21
l. 4.15
m. Psay.5Q.32
n. Ext.53.21
o. Psay.5A.13
p. Psay.5Q.78

THE BOOK OF KRAUTS

OTHERWISE KNOWN AS THE BOOK OF GÖTTERDÄMMERUNG

CHAPTER 1

[a]**O**n the continent of Europe, there was a place called Germany located to the east of France,

2 [b]Unfortunately for France,

3 [c]And the continent of Europe,

4 [d]And the rest of the world.

5 The fact is, the Germans have had some problems over the years,

6 But wanted to be the [e]Chosen Nation anyway,

7 Which didn't work out,

8 [f]In a big way.

9 This is their [g]story.

CHAPTER 2

[h]**F**or many many years, there was no Germany at all,

2 But just a place where a lot of different barbarian tribes lived,

3 [h]Including the Goths and Visigoths and Ostrogoths,

4 [i]And the Vandals and Visivandals and Ostrovandals,

5 [j]And the Angles and Visiangles and Ostroangles,

6 [k]And the Saxons and Visisaxons and Ostrosaxons,

7 [l]Not to mention the Huns.

8 [m]Having helped all they could to destroy the Roman Empire,

9 [n]The barbarians didn't feel like becoming a nation for a long while,

10 [o]And spent the first part of the Middle Ages drinking beer and having little wars with each other.

11 Back then, nobody got too upset with the Germans,

a. Psom.77.1-2
b. Psay.5Q.56
c. Barb.4.18
d. Brit.52.15
e. Exp.1.4-5
f. Brit.49.15
g. Wil.21.1-19
*   Ann.18.11*
h. Barb.2.1-3
i. Barb.2.4-7
j. Barb.2.10
k. Barb.2.11
l. Barb.2.9
m. Barb.1.2
n. Barb.2.15-19
o. Barb.4.13
p. Lies.9.6
q. Psom.17.9
r. Ext.53.21
s. Ed.63.2
t. Chr.2.28-30
u. Ann.17.11-13
v. Gnt.1.13
w. Gnt.11.2-10

12 [p]Even though they ate too many pork dishes,

13 [q]Including sauerkraut,

14 And therefore got a reputation for being fat stupid Krauts,

15 Like they were pigs or something,

16 [r]Which maybe explains why the other Europeans decided that all the pig farms and cabbage fields east of the Rhine were a separate country,

17 And figured they must belong to the Krauts,

18 Because nobody else really wanted them.

19 [s]But the Krauts were pretty happy about it,

20 And suddenly got very excited about being a nation,

21 [t]And even started calling themselves the Holy Roman Empire,

22 Which might have been their way of getting warmed up for later on,

23 Although everybody else thought it was pretty silly,

24 [u]Since who would ever believe that a bunch of fat stupid Krauts could ever have an empire?

CHAPTER 3

But it wasn't true that the Krauts were stupid, which other Europeans began to notice during the [v]Renaissance,

2 [w]When it turned out that Martin Luther was one of the very best ever at the Protestant Reformation game,

3 [a]And Johannes Gutenberg invented movable type,

4 [b]And Krauts like Kepler helped invent science.

5 In fact, the Krauts played practically all the Renaissance sports,

6 Very well,

7 Except for [c]comedy,

8 Which they never quite understood,

9 And probably explains why the Krauts didn't go out exploring and trying to make [d]history after the Renaissance,

10 Like [e]everybody else,

11 But started arguing a lot with each other about a bunch of very important Kraut questions,

12 Like who should be in charge of everything,

13 Which they couldn't quite agree about,

14 [f]And so they decided not to be a nation at all,

15 But a bunch of quarrelsome Krauts instead.

CHAPTER 4

By this time, there were several kinds of Krauts.

2 There were Krauts called Austrians who lived so close to [g]Italy that they thought they were civilized,

3 [h]And therefore too good to be called Krauts.

4 There were Krauts called Swiss who lived in the [i]Alps,

5 Where they made a lot of cuckoo clocks and [j]money,

6 [k]And were therefore too good to be called Krauts,

7 Especially since a lot of them spoke French.

8 There were Krauts called Prussians,

a. Gnt.12.1-4
b. Gnt.8.1-14
c. Gnt.15.5-9
d. Gnt.16.1-3
&16.11-12
e. Exp.1.19-25
& 1.12
f. Barb.1.2
g. Psong.57.3
h. Vin.49.5
i. Frog.22.6-11
j. Psong.44.1-2
k. Vin.49.5
l. Brit.1.5
m. 1.12
n. Kens.27.14
o. 5.18
p. Name.4.8
q. Grk.23.12-13
r. 5.5-6

9 Or who wanted to be called Prussians,

10 Even though they were definitely Krauts,

11 And not much liked,

12 [l]For a lot of excellent reasons.

13 There were also some free-lance Krauts called Germans,

14 Who were in no particular hurry to start being a modern nation,

15 Since there was all that beer to drink,

16 [m]And all those pork dishes to eat,

17 And plenty of time to cause trouble later.

CHAPTER 5

It turned out that most of the Krauts were pretty good at culture,

2 Except for the Prussian Krauts,

3 Who spent most of their time fighting duels and comparing their facial scars,

4 [n]Which they had a lot of,

5 Because if you have a lot of scars all over your face,

6 You can't possibly be mistaken for a pig,

7 [o]Since pigs almost never fight with swords.

8 [p]This convinced the Prussians that they were better than the other Krauts,

9 And so they decided to be a separate nation,

10 [q]And fight as many wars as possible,

11 [r]To make sure that they could always have plenty of scars,

12 Which they always did,

13 Not to mention fancy uniforms and boots,

14 Which the Prussians invented,

15 ªBecause you almost never see pigs wearing fancy uniforms and boots.

16 The other Krauts didn't quite see it that way, though,

17 Since if pigs don't wear fancy uniforms and boots,

18 Then how come all the Prussians did?

19 And so they decided to concentrate on other things instead,

20 Things that didn't have anything to do with trying to prove to the world that you're not a pig,

21 ᵇLike literature,

22 ᶜAnd music,

23 ᵈAnd philosophy,

24 ᵉAnd architecture,

25 Because they were genuinely interested in concepts like truth and beauty and knowledge and indestructible buildings,

26 And besides, when was the last time you saw a pig write a symphony?

CHAPTER 6

The Krauts had a big advantage when it came to literature,

2 Because they had the great ᶠGerman language to work with,

3 Which they had invented,

4 And which sounded beautiful,

5 ᵍLike someone trying to cough up some phlegm in their throat or something,

6 ʰUnlike the awful-sounding languages other Europeans had,

7 Such as French,

8 ⁱWhich sounded like somebody had both their nostrils stuffed with ʲfrogs or something,

a. Psay.5A.20
b. 6.14
c. 12.1
d. 9.1
e. 17.1
f. Brit.31.12
g. Ned.6.24
h. Psong.8.3
i. Paul.4.10
j. Frog.1.2
k. Psong.57.1
l. Spic.6.3
m. Brit.35.6-7
n. 6.2
o. Dav.15.9
p. Yks.116.16
q. Brit.30.14
r. Brit.33.10
s. Dav.15.9
t. Chr.3.8-13
u. Paul.4.9
v. Ed.28.6
w. Brit.49.5
x. Pnot.18.1-5

9 ᵏOr Italian, which sounded like some reeling drunk trying to sing, gargle, and spit up all at the same time,

10 ˡOr Spanish, which sounded like somebody with a lisp and no teeth trying to talk with hot peppers in their mouth,

11 ᵐOr English, which sounded like some half-witted fop trying to talk German without coughing up the phlegm.

12 Anyway,

13 ⁿThanks to their beautiful language,

14 The Krauts would go on to produce a lot of great writers,

15 Including Goethe,

16 And a bunch of others too,

17 Who would all be great,

18 Though not as great as Goethe.

CHAPTER 7

It was ᵒGoethe who made up the story of a man named Faust,

2 Unless it was somebody else,

3 ᵖWhich it wasn't,

4 ᑫBecause Goethe was the greatest writer who ever lived,

5 ʳEven greater than Shakespeare,

6 As any Kraut will tell you.

7 ˢFaust was the Kraut who sold his ᵗsoul to the devil in exchange for almost ᵘunlimited knowledge and power on earth,

8 For about a year,

9 Until the ᵛdevil came to collect the soul he had been promised,

10 ʷWhich Faust thought was unfair,

11 ˣFor some reason.

12 This was such a great story that lots of other writers all over the world copied it,

13 Including a Brit named ᵃMarlowe,
14 And a bunch of others too.
15 But Goethe was the only one who got it right,
16 Because only a Kraut could really understand what it was like to want power so much that you kind of forgot about what it would cost,
17 Namely everything,
18 ᵇWhich is called being an overreacher,
19 And proves just how great Goethe must have been to think up such an insane type of character,
20 With nothing to go on but his imagination.

CHAPTER 8

But fiction wasn't the only thing Goethe thought up.
2 He also wrote a lot of great poetry,
3 ᶜWhich sounds beautiful when you read it out loud,
4 If you're a Kraut,
5 ᵈAnd he made up a lot of science and philosophy too,
6 Which is all brilliant,
7 And helps explain why the Krauts eventually got the idea that they were a ᵉChosen Nation.

CHAPTER 9

It was Goethe's brilliance that convinced the Krauts they were pretty great at ᶠphilosophy,
2 Which started a Kraut intellectual tradition that would produce scores of geniuses in just a few hundred years,
3 Including ᵍHegelundKant,
4 Who was incredibly important,
5 For some reason,
6 And ʰNietzsche,

a. *Pnot.41.1-5*
b. *Krt.39.14*
c. *6.5*
d. *Main.22.10*
e. *Exp.1.4-5*
f. *Gnt.4.20*
g. *Ed.63.3*
h. *Ed.63.3*
i. *Wil.32.1-10 Exp.1.7-9*
j. *Dav.15.9*
k. *Boul.5.3-5*
l. *Vin.70.18*
m. *11.7*
n. *Psong.20.1-10*

7 ⁱWho wrote a lot of great philosophy about how if you were really superior, you could do whatever you wanted,
8 Which is called being a ʲsuperman,
9 But didn't have anything to do with all the unpleasantness the Krauts got mixed up in later,
10 For some reason,
11 Which any Kraut could explain to you,
12 Somehow.
13 Anyway,
14 After he had written all this great stuff, Nietzsche went completely insane,
15 Unless it was the other way around,
16 Which it wasn't,
17 Or why would anyone ever have taken him seriously?

CHAPTER 10

Later on, there was even a Kraut philosopher who was a Jew,
2 ᵏWhich probably explains why some of his ideas were a little strange,
3 Because he thought that Mankind was dominated by a bunch of dark, dangerous drives,
4 Which were all so deeply buried that it would be almost a ˡmiracle to even see them,
5 Let alone control them,
6 ᵐWhich explains why Mankind acts like such a pig about sex,
7 And power,
8 And territory,
9 ⁿAnd a bunch of other stuff too,
10 Which is all so unflattering to Mankind that it's hard to think where he could get such ideas,
11 Except maybe a synagogue

or some [a]heathen pit like that,

12 Which is why they don't really deserve to be called philosophy,

13 But should maybe get some other name,

14 And leave philosophy to people who are equipped for it,

15 Like Aryans maybe.

a. *Chr.2.5-8*
b. *Carl.3.6*
c. *18.3*
d. *10.1-2*
e. *7.6*
f. *Dav.29.6*
g. *Yks.59.10-12*
h. *Ann.18.5*
  Ed.71.24
i. *Boul.21.9*
j. *Dav.32.23*

CHAPTER 11

There is another Kraut philosopher the Krauts don't like to talk about,

2 Who came along pretty late in the day,

3 [b]And somehow got the idea that the masses would rise up against the [c]ruling classes someday,

4 Because the ruling classes don't care about anyone but themselves,

5 And want to own everything,

6 All by themselves,

7 Just like they were pigs or something,

8 Which explains why the masses will get sick of it,

9 And take over,

10 Someday,

11 Which just goes to show you,

12 [d]It isn't just Jews who get funny ideas about things,

13 As any Kraut would admit,

14 In spite of all the propaganda about how the Krauts are prejudiced or something,

15 [e]Which they really aren't,

16 Even if it might be surprising what you'd find if you checked the family tree of certain kinds of philosophers,

17 Like the [f]ones who wear long, orthodox-looking beards and think everything's some

kind of conspiracy to keep rich Aryans in charge.

18 Besides, he wrote most of his stuff in England anyway,

19 And [g]they didn't like him either,

20 So now who's prejudiced?

CHAPTER 12

In addition to philosophy, the Krauts were also exceptionally talented at music,

2 And produced thousands of masterpieces over hundreds of years.

3 For example, there was a Kraut composer named [h]Bach,

4 Who was so great that nobody has ever blamed him for being a Kraut,

5 Which is extremely great,

6 And proves that the Krauts aren't as bad as everybody makes them out to be,

7 Unless it doesn't.

CHAPTER 13

There was another great Kraut composer named [i]Mozart,

2 Who was so great that even the Krauts never felt they had to prove it,

3 Even though none of them really noticed it at the time,

4 Since Mozart died penniless,

5 And was buried in a pauper's grave,

6 Probably because he never once wrote a symphony about pigs.

CHAPTER 14

There was also a Kraut composer named [j]Haydn,

2 Who was good enough to hold Mozart's coat,

3 Which is pretty darn good,

4 And probably proves something or other,

5 Unless it doesn't.

CHAPTER 15

Later on, there was still another great Kraut composer named [a]Beethoven,

2 Who was also great,

3 Though deaf,

4 Which may explain why nobody in history has ever written music any louder than Beethoven's,

5 [b]Except Wagner, of course,

6 But doesn't begin to explain why he thought that symphonies with [c]even numbers don't quite count.

CHAPTER 16

In fact, there were lots and lots of great Kraut composers,

2 Including [d]Schubert,

3 Who was so great that he didn't even have to finish his symphonies,

4 And a whole bunch of Strausses,

5 Who thought the Danube was blue,

6 And other things.

7 There was also [e]Wagner,

8 Which just goes to show you,

9 [f]Pigs may not write symphonies, but they're the only ones who can sing certain kinds of [g]operas.

CHAPTER 17

The Krauts were also pretty excellent at architecture,

2 [h]And built a lot of tremendous cathedrals and castles and cities and so forth,

3 [i]Not to mention all the great steel-and-concrete buildings

a. Dav.10.10
b. 16.7
*c. Psp.3.5
    & 3.7
    Psay.5Y.6
    Krt.36.8*
d. Dav.42.7
e. Ed.63.3
f. Yks.116.16
g. 30.3-4
h. Brit.29.12
i. Ira.21.37-38
j. Adam.5.1-8
k. Yks.125.34
l. 5.25
m. Ext.39.18-19
n. 4.8-12
o. Ann.18.17
p. Grk.23.12-13
q. 5.15

they put up when the [j]industrial revolution came along,

4 [k]Which were all so big and well made that you'd have thought they were expecting someone to drop a lot of bombs on them or something,

5 Which they weren't, of course,

6 [l]Because it's just not true that the Krauts were obsessed with war and destruction and things like that,

7 [m]With the possible exception of a few maladjusted individuals,

8 Who weren't at all like the rest of the Krauts,

9 And never had been,

10 Because while the rest of the Krauts were producing all that great culture,

11 Over hundreds of years,

12 A few were otherwise engaged.

CHAPTER 18

For example, some of the few maladjusted individuals were the [n]Prussians,

2 Who had a ruling class called the Junkers,

3 Meaning scar-faced, bald-headed psychopaths who think that everything everybody else does is junk,

4 [o]And should be destroyed with a lot of blood and iron.

5 While the rest of the Krauts were messing around with culture and other junk like that,

6 The Prussians started practicing up on all the things they'd need to rule the world someday,

7 Like [p]war,

8 [q]And clicking their heels together a lot,

105

9 [a]And learning how to give and take orders,

10 And a bunch of other important things too,

11 Like making life miserable for the [b]Austrians,

12 Who were so weak and foolish that they almost made the Prussians embarrassed to be Krauts,

13 But not quite.

CHAPTER 19

Way back when, there was a Prussian king named [c]Frederick the Great,

2 Who made a specialty out of worrying the Austrians,

3 And got so great at it that the ruling family of Austria became permanently worried,

4 And kept pulling on their lower lip,

5 From one generation to the next,

6 Which made them look pretty silly,

7 From one generation to the next.

CHAPTER 20

Later on, the Prussians also helped defeat Napoleon,

2 Showing up late at Waterloo,

3 [d]And doing something or other on a sunken road,

4 Which completely ruined the day for the [e]French emperor.

CHAPTER 21

And then there was [f]Bismarck,

2 [g]Who decided that the Prussians had had enough practice,

3 And should start taking everything over as soon as possible,

4 Including Austria,

5 [h]Which didn't actually disap-

a. Brit.19.40
b. 4.2
c. Dav.14.25
d. 20.2
e. Dav.21.19-23
f. Ed.63.3
g. 18.6
h. Ned.42.7
i. 4.13-17
j. Chr.2.30-31
k. Psay.5Y.44
l. Frog.20.3-5
m. Exp.1.4-5
n. 17.1-4
o. 15.1-5
p. 16.7-9
q. 39.14
r. Ann.18.11
s. Adam.42.8-9

pear but suddenly became one of Prussia's closest allies,

6 [i]And also including all the Krauts who had been too busy eating pork and beer to get organized as a nation,

7 And all the Krauts who had always been too preoccupied with culture to care about the destiny of the Fatherland,

8 [j]Not to mention certain parts of France,

9 [k]Which Bismarck added to the Fatherland by winning the Franco-Prussian War,

10 Which was especially humiliating to the Frogs,

11 [l]Who had somehow gotten the idea that no one would bother them now that they had another emperor named Napoleon,

12 Which turned out not to be true,

13 And proved that the Krauts were now a large, powerful, unified nation,

14 In fact, a [m]Chosen Nation,

15 Called Germany.

CHAPTER 22

The more they thought about it, the more the Krauts realized that they'd been Chosen all along,

2 Because look at how good they were at everything.

3 Compared to everyone else,

4 [n]The Krauts had bigger buildings,

5 [o]And louder symphonies,

6 [p]And longer operas,

7 [q]And bigger words,

8 [r]And taller soldiers,

9 [s]And more munitions factories,

10 And so forth,

11 And so on,

12 [a]And especially munitions factories.

13 [b]All of this obvious Kraut superiority convinced the new Kraut emperor,

14 Whose name was [c]Kaiser Wilhelm,

15 That it was time to start a big world war,

16 [d]The bigger the better,

17 And settle everything once and for all.

CHAPTER 23

The Kaiser waited for an appropriate reason to start a war, of course,

2 Because it wouldn't do to start a world war for no reason at all,

3 And so he waited patiently,

4 Until a Serbo-Croatian maniac assassinated the [e]archduke Ferdinand,

5 Of Austria,

6 [f]Which had always been one of Germany's dearest friends,

7 [g]And meant that Germany had no choice but to invade France,

8 And then conquer the world.

CHAPTER 24

With the help of their close friends the Austrians, Germany came very close to winning World War I,

2 Or the Great War, as it was called then,

3 In the days before anyone knew that you had to number them.

4 [h]Unfortunately, the Krauts' brilliant strategy of sweeping through Belgium into the north of France got spoiled by typical French stupidity,

5 Since the French had been too dumb to realize that the Krauts

a. Adam.42.10-15
b. Zig.10.9
c. Dav.14.25
d. Brit.48.8-9
e. Dav.46.15
f. 21.5
g. Psay.5Y.6
h. Gnt.13.4-6
i. Frog.33.1-4
j. Frog.33.6-8
k. Frog.34.1
l. Al.4.7-11
m. 23.2
n. Swar.23.1-3
o. Ann.10.1
　& 10.1
　& 10.1
　& 10.1
p. Brit.7.8
q. Brit.49.1
r. Psong.57.1
s. Swar.24.1
t. Drex.4.5

were supposed to make the first move,

6 [i]And launched a silly attack on Germany that caused a lot of embarrassing scrambling around,

7 [j]Before things settled down into trench warfare,

8 Which the Krauts got blamed for,

9 But wasn't their fault,

10 [k]Especially the part about poison gas,

11 [l]Because how else can you kill a Frog that's too chicken to get out of his trench and fight like a man?

CHAPTER 25

[m]Meanwhile, because the Russians hadn't prevented the assassination of the archduke,

2 They had to be punished too,

3 [n]Which meant the Krauts had to go to war against millions of unarmed Russian peasants in the snow,

4 [o]And use up lots of good munitions that might have changed the [p]balance of power on the western front,

5 Where the Krauts were now fighting against the [q]Brits and [r]Italians as well as the French.

6 [s]Besides, the Great War had gotten so big that the munitions manufacturers in Germany were also having to supply arms to other Kraut armies and allies in other parts of the world,

7 Frequently at a [t]discount,

8 Which was completely unexpected,

9 And hurt profits so much that Germany began to experience some serious economic hardships,

10 Which helps explain why the war didn't go quite as well as expected,
11 [a]Not to mention a little battle called Verdun,
12 Which practically emptied Germany of wood,
13 [b]Because all the trees had to be cut down to put up [c]little crosses on the graves of Kraut soldiers.

CHAPTER 26

And then the Brits and Frogs committed the worst atrocity of the war,
2 By inviting in a bunch of American troops,
3 [d]Who should never have been involved in the first place,
4 [e]Especially after the fair warning they got with the Lusitania thing,
5 [f]But who came barging in anyway,
6 [g]And spoiled everything,
7 Just when Germany had the whole thing about wrapped up,
8 Even if the average age of the Kraut army was about fourteen,
9 Which didn't mean anything,
10 [h]Except that Kraut soldiers are so eager to fight for the Fatherland that they just can't wait till they're eighteen.

CHAPTER 27

All of this still wouldn't have mattered, except for the fact that the Allies lied to the Krauts,
2 And said they wanted an armistice,
3 Not a surrender,
4 [i]Which Germany would never have signed,
5 [j]Especially if anyone had told the truth about all those reparations,
6 Which weren't fair,
7 And gave Germany every right to regard the [k]Treaty of Versailles as an illegal document,
8 After they'd thought about it for a few years,
9 [l]And besides, it wasn't the Krauts who had shot the archduke in the first place,
10 [m]So why was everything automatically Germany's fault?

CHAPTER 28

[n]In spite of all the treachery of the Allies, Germany tried hard to live with the terms of the Treaty of Versailles,
2 [o]And to try the silly new fad in government that the American president was so fired up about,
3 Which was called democracy,
4 [p]Meaning rule by a bunch of undisciplined cannon fodder and one senile old blimp,
5 Named [q]Hindenburg,
6 Who refused to stand up to the Allies or anybody else.

CHAPTER 29

[r]What with not having really lost the war except through allied trickery,
2 [s]And having to pay a lot of outrageous reparations,
3 And having to put up with an incompetent democratic government,
4 [t]And a major depression too,
5 No reasonable person could blame the Krauts for what happened next,
6 Which wasn't their fault anyway,
7 [u]But was one of those accidents of history,
8 Which happen all the time,
9 Except maybe this time it was

a. Brit.48.21
b. Swar.30.4-10
c. Forg.5.4-6
d. Yks.76.8-9
e. Yks.76.3
f. Yks.76.10-17
g. Yks.78.1
h. Ext.52.16
i. Yks.78.4-5
j. Yks.82.5-18
k. Frog.34.7
l. Frog.33.1
m. Brit.49.12-13
n. Barb.6.3
o. Yks.78.7-10
p. Grk.20.8
q. Psay.5D.15
r. 27.1-4
s. Kens.16.10
t. Frog.36.1-2
u. Vin.6.3-15

just a tiny little bit worse,
10 Because the accident was a man named [a]Adolf Hitler.

CHAPTER 30

[b]And no matter what anyone says, it's just not true that Hitler was in any way representative of Kraut history and culture,
2 ꞌEven if he did love Wagner's operas,
3 Which were all about [d]Götterdämmerung,
4 [e]Meaning glorious death in the [f]ultimate battle,
5 Because nobody but Hitler ever took Götterdämmerung literally,
6 [g]Even if Hitler was a big admirer of Frederick the Great,
7 [h]And Bismarck's blood and iron,
8 [i]And Nietzsche's ideas about man and superman,
9 [j]And even if there had been a few anti-Semites in Germany at odd moments in the past,
10 [k]And even if Hitler did have a special fondness for boots and fancy uniforms, something like the Prussians always had,
11 [l]It doesn't mean anything,
12 Any of it,
13 Because Hitler was crazy,
14 And how could anyone have known that way back when he first got elected chancellor?

CHAPTER 31

Of course, it's easy for people to point fingers after the fact and say the Krauts should have read Hitler's book and seen what he had in mind,
2 [m]Or that they should have voted him out when the Nazi brownshirts started beating up

a. *Dav.48.7*
b. *Zig.9.2 & 6.4*
c. *16.7-9*
d. *6.3-4*
e. *Psp.3.7*
f. *Dav.17.15*
g. *19.1*
h. *21.1*
i. *9.6-7*
j. *11.13-15*
k. *5.14-15*
l. *Ned.36.18-19*
m. *Mall.13.8*
n. *Yks.133.5*
o. *10.11*
p. *Yks.135.13*
q. *Al.4.16*
r. *Wil.14.1-5*
s. *Yks.101.12-13*
t. *Chr.6.10 Boul.18.19*
u. *Brit.51.1-8*
v. *Brit.51.11-16*

Jews and things like that,
3 [n]Or maybe they should have rebelled after Krystallnacht, when all the [o]synagogues got burned down,
4 [p]Or maybe there should have been a coup d'état when Hitler started grabbing up all those little countries in eastern Europe,
5 [q]Or maybe there should have been a popular uprising when all the non-Aryans started getting sent to concentration camps,
6 But the thing is, things happen a little bit at a time,
7 [r]And you don't always notice the things that are important right away,
8 And besides, the western Europeans and the Americans have always had pretty convenient memories,
9 [s]Since none of them objected that strongly to the business with the Jews till much much later,
10 And it was never exactly a secret,
11 Except from the German people, of course,
12 And if you want to be completely honest,
13 [t]Just who is it that's so fond of the Jews anyway?
14 Besides, what did the Allies do when they saw that Hitler was rearming Germany,
15 [u]Or when he annexed Austria,
16 [v]And Czechoslovakia?
17 Mostly, their response to all these things was to hope that Hitler would just go away eventually,
18 Which is exactly what the German people were hoping the whole time too,
19 Except maybe for a little while at the beginning,

20 ^aWhen all the trains were running on time,
21 ^bAnd the war was going so well,
22 And is that really so awful?

CHAPTER 32

^c**A**nd so what if a lot of people joined the Nazi party?
2 ^dThere was the Gestapo, after all,
3 And everybody knew that it wasn't just Jews who went to ^econcentration camps,
4 ^fAnd Goebbels made sure nobody ever knew the truth about anything anyway,
5 ^gBecause nobody really knew what was happening,
6 Except a handful of Nazis, of course,
7 And besides, Germany was at war,
8 ^hAnd you have to support your leader in wartime,
9 ⁱUnless you don't really love your country,
10 But hate it instead,
11 ^jWhich is hard to do when the brave soldiers of your country have just kicked the hell out of Poland,
12 ^kAnd Norway,
13 ^lAnd France,
14 ^mAnd are in the process of demolishing the Brits,
15 ⁿAnd the Russians,
16 And everybody else too.

CHAPTER 33

But then the ^oAmericans entered the war, and things stopped going quite so well.
2 ^pThe Russians got stubborn about Stalingrad,
3 ^qAnd the Brits got lucky in North Africa,
4 And the British and American

a.	*Spic.15.3*
b.	*Grk.23.12-13*
c.	*Swar.28.1-9*
d.	*Wil.34.1-5*
e.	*Yks.125.7*
f.	*Main.27.16*
g.	*Wil.23.4-7*
h.	*Brd.21.6*
i.	*Rat.10.1-5*
j.	*Brit.51.23*
k.	*Yks.105.4*
l.	*Frog.37.5-8*
m.	*Brit.52.16*
n.	*Yks.109.4-6*
o.	*Gnt.15.14*
p.	*Russ.19.9-16*
q.	*Brit.54.2-3*
r.	*Yks.112.2-4*
s.	*Yks.114.4-12*
t.	*Yks.111.1-5*
u.	*Psom.65.1-4*
v.	*Psong.57.1*
w.	*Oth.8.18*
x.	*Yks.112.6-7*
y.	*Ned.36.17*
z.	*Barb.3.1-3*
aa.	*34.3*
bb.	*Yks.135.21*
cc.	*Ned.29.24*

bombers started taking Kraut cities apart,
5 ^rDay and night,
6 ^sAnd then there was D-Day,
7 ^tWhen it turned out that a nation of two hundred million people could produce more weapons and ships and soldiers than a nation of eighty million people,
8 ^uAnd the long, slow retreat began,
9 With bodies coming home to Germany from the eastern front in Russia,
10 And the western front in France,
11 And the southern front in Italy,
12 ^vWhere the worthless, cowardly Wops had caved in like a bunch of sniveling Jews,
13 Which is only a figure of speech, of course,
14 And shouldn't be taken the wrong way,
15 But will be, of course,
16 ^wBecause no one can give Germany a break,
17 Ever.

CHAPTER 34

And the Allies turned Dresden into a firestorm,
2 ^xWhich was an atrocity,
3 ^yEven if nobody remembers it,
4 And the Russians came marching back through the Ukraine into eastern Germany,
5 ^zRaping and looting and slaughtering thousands of innocent civilians,
6 Which was an atrocity,
7 ^{aa}Even if nobody remembers it,
8 ^{bb}And the German High Command tried to assassinate Hitler,
9 Which was brave and noble^{cc},

10 [a]Even if it failed and nobody remembers it,
11 [b]And Hitler went completely insane and conspired to destroy Germany forever, which would have happened if good Germans hadn't stopped it,
12 [c]Which was also brave and noble,
13 [d]Even if nobody remembers it,
14 [e]And the outgunned, outmanned remnants of the great German army almost stopped the Allies in the [f]Battle of the Bulge,
15 [g]Which was heroic and almost incredible,
16 Even if nobody remembers it,
17 [h]And finally Hitler committed suicide in his bunker, along with Goebbels and some of the other criminals,
18 Which was a big relief to every patriotic German,
19 [i]Even if nobody will ever acknowledge it.

CHAPTER 35

And then the German people submitted tamely to the terms of peace,
2 Including the Allies' desire to rip Germany apart,
3 And turn it into two weak and powerless nations,
4 One democratic,
5 [j]Meaning rule by American puppets,
6 And one communist,
7 [k]Meaning rule by Soviet Russian puppets,
8 With about a thousand miles of barbed wire between the two.
9 [l]And the German people submitted tamely to the kangaroo courts that executed all their high officials at Nuremberg,
10 [m]And to the scorn of the world,
11 [n]And to the law that said they could never make war again,
12 [o]Not even to defend themselves from outside aggression,
13 Ever.
14 They submitted tamely because they are [p]civilized people,
15 [q]And not the monsters they've been made out to be.

a. 34.3
b. Russ.7.15-16
c. Ned.29.24
d. 34.3
e. Brit.1.8
f. Yks.117.9-11
g. Ned.29.24
h. Ann.2.17
i. 34.3
j. Grk.20.8
k. Carl.3.6 Grk.20.8
l. Yks.126.10-14
m. Oth.8.15-17
n. Grk.25.7
o. Barb.6.3
p. Mes.1.3-9
q. Ext.16.26
r. Ed.61.17
s. Kens.7.7-8
t. Ann.6.17-23
u. Vin.71.12-27

CHAPTER 36

Which is all well and good,
2 Except for one thing,
3 Which is a thing the Krauts can never quite seem to remember,
4 No matter how many times it is brought to their attention,
5 Which is that all the good civilized Krauts just stood by and watched when Hitler decided that it would be a good thing to kill all the Jews,
6 Which he almost did,
7 Killing six million of them.
8 Six million.

CHAPTER 37

And in spite of what all the [r]good Krauts say,
2 Hitler didn't do it alone,
3 Because he had help,
4 [s]From the SS, who rounded them all up and put them in concentration camps behind barbed wire and gave them nothing to eat,
5 [t]And from German corporations, who submitted bids for the building of gas chambers and crematoria,
6 [u]And from the people of Germany, who watched it all hap-

pen and did nothing whatever to stop it,

7 At all.

a. *Psom.27.1-3*
b. *38.7*
c. *9.7*

someone forgot that a Kraut is a Kraut is a Kraut,

3 And trusted them to act like a civilized nation,

4 For once,

5 And not like a bunch of arrogant, bloodthirsty, genocidal pigs,

6 'Who still think they're entitled to rule the world,

7 Even if they have to kill everyone else in the world to do it,

8 And even if they have to kill themselves to do it,

19 Because deep inside the heart of every Kraut,

10 There's a member of the master race,

11 Just waiting,

12 O so patiently,

13 To hear the two sweetest words ever uttered in any language:

14 *Achtung! Götterdämmerung!*

CHAPTER 38

And that's why Germany can never be a Chosen Nation,

2 Ever,

3 Because there is no reason for what they did,

4 And no explanation,

5 And no justification,

6 At all.

7 ªWhich is another way of saying that a barbarian nation is a barbarian nation is a barbarian nation,

8 Forever,

9 And that's all there is to it.

CHAPTER 39

And when the end of the world comes at last,

2 ᵇIt will probably be because

THE BOOK OF DAMN YANKEES

OTHERWISE KNOWN AS THE BOOK OF MANIFEST DESTINY

CHAPTER 1

Across the Atlantic Ocean from Europe, there was a place called North America,

2 ªWhich was discovered by an Italian explorer in the employ of the queen of Spain,

3 ᵇColonized extensively by the Spanish and the French,

4 ᶜDeveloped into a rich nation by the labor of African slaves

a. *Exp.9.1-4*
   Psay.5Y.1
b. *Exp.1.7-9*
c. *5.5*
d. *Dav.58.9*
e. *Exp.9.5-8*
f. *10.19*

supplied by the Dutch,

5 And thus became the largest ᵈEnglish-speaking nation on earth,

6 ᵉNamely, the United States of America.

7 The inhabitants of the United States decided to call themselves Yankees,

8 ᶠFor some reason,

9 And eventually noticing that

the rest of the world was there,
10 Decided to ᵃrule it.
11 This is their ᵇstory.

CHAPTER 2

The Spaniards arrived in North America first,
2 ᶜAnd settled in Florida,
3 Which had a nice warm climate,
4 And not much else.
5 Several years later,
6 ᵈEnglish settlers landed in Virginia and started a colony called ᵉJamestown,
7 Which had everything it needed to establish a solid English presence in North America,
8 Except money, provisions, military support, and adequate numbers of settlers.

CHAPTER 3

A few years later, ᶠPuritans called pilgrims started arriving along the northeast coast of the North American continent,
2 Having been requested to leave England,
3 Which already had enough Puritans of its own,
4 In fact, more than enough.
5 ᵍThe Puritans were exceptionally fond of misery,
6 Which is why they settled in New England,
7 ʰWhere the weather was almost as bad as it was back home,
8 And where there were plenty of naked ⁱheathen Indians to offend their morals,
9 Which weren't hard to offend anyway,
10 ʲSince anything that might remotely be considered fun is immoral to a Puritan,

a. Grk.13.20
b. Ira.24.27-31
c. Spic.10.1
d. Brit.24.5-8
e. Psay.5Y.31
f. Brit.15.5-12
g. Brit.4.15
h. Brit.1.2
i. Chr.2.5-8
j. Lies.9.13
k. Ext.48.35
l. Ira.34.1-4
m. Brit.12.1-3
n. Ira.21.14
o. Psay.5J.5
p. 3.4
q. 2.1-2
r. Psay.5C.5
s. Exp.15.8
t. Exp.14.15
u. Oth.7.1-10

11 ᵏExcept for public execution of heretics,
12 ˡWhich is fun,
13 But doesn't count,
14 Because Puritans never laugh at executions,
15 No matter how much fun they're having.

CHAPTER 4

ᵐThanks to all the fun the Brits were having with various forms of religious persecution,
2 Quite a number of new colonies got started in North America over the next few decades,
3 Including colonies of persecuted ⁿQuakers in Pennsylvania and New Jersey,
4 ᵒColonies of persecuted Catholics in Maryland,
5 ᵖAnd a lot more Puritans,
6 Who came over to New England in droves,
7 On a ferry service called the Mayflower.

CHAPTER 5

Meanwhile, the Spanish had established colonies in California and Texas,
2 ᑫIn addition to ʳFlorida,
3 ˢAnd the French had claimed most of the upper and middle part of North America,
4 And the southern portions of North America were filling up with settlers from England and Ireland,
5 ᵗPlus a lot of slaves shipped over in chains from Africa,
6 ᵘSo that they could help build enormous cotton and tobacco plantations for their new masters,
7 Who had come to America to be free.

CHAPTER 6

Things went along like this for quite a while, with nothing much important happening anywhere but where the settlers were mostly exiles and refugees from Great Britain,

2 Until there were thirteen English-speaking colonies that thought they had ªidentities of their own, namely,

3 In no particular order,

4 New York,

5 Virginia,

6 ᵇNew Jersey,

7 Delaware,

8 Massachusetts,

9 Connecticut,

10 Rhode Island,

11 New Hampshire,

12 ᶜPennsylvania,

13 North Carolina,

14 South Carolina,

15 Georgia,

16 ᵈAnd Maryland,

17 Unless some of these are wrong.

18 The Brits who owned these colonies were pleased at how well they were doing,

19 And got the idea that maybe they could help out a little bit with all the expenses Great Britain was incurring at the time,

20 ᵉWhat with Britain being involved in a bunch of major wars against the French and all,

21 Which suggested the idea of taxes,

22 And upset the colonists quite a lot.

CHAPTER 7

ᶠThe thing was, the colonists had already gotten used to doing things the way they wanted to,

a. Jefs. 7.15-17
b. 4.3
c. 4.3
d. 4.4
e. Brit. 23.6
f. 87.1-2
g. 21.6
h. Brit. 1.9
i. Brit. 23.8-9
j. Brit. 22.12
k. Ann. 2.17
l. Psom. 62.1-6

2 ᵍWhich was called the American Way,

3 And meant that they no longer wanted to do things the Brit way,

4 ʰWhich is usually the hard way.

5 The more they thought about it, the more taxes seemed like an unnecessarily hard way of handling the Brit economic crunch,

6 Hard on the colonists, that is,

7 Who didn't much care about fighting the French anyway,

8 ⁱHaving already tried it in the French and Indian War,

9 Some years back.

10 But the Brits were stubborn and tried out the tax plan anyway,

11 Putting a tax on tea,

12 Which wasn't smart,

13 Since the colonists were still pretty much Brits and hadn't yet discovered that coffee is about a thousand percent better than tea anyway,

14 ʲAnd therefore thought that they still needed tea,

15 Tax-free,

16 Or how would they ever get up in the morning?

17 ᵏSo the colonists threw all the Brit tea into Boston Harbor,

18 And then sat down for a while to think up what to do next.

CHAPTER 8

Without their morning tea, the colonists got pretty ˡcranky,

2 And decided the thing to do was tell the Brits they weren't ever going to pay the tea tax,

3 Because,

4 Well,

5 Because that's the way it was.

6 [a]Except they all knew enough about the Brit sense of fair play to recognize that you could only take an extreme position without giving any reasons if you were a Brit,

7 Which they were kind of saying they weren't,

8 [b]Since Brits pay their taxes.

9 This presented the colonists with a dilemma,

10 Which was resolved by their discovery that they were actually objecting to the tea tax on principle,

11 [c]Meaning that they were opposed to the concept of taxation without representation,

12 Whatever that was,

13 And could, quite [d]honorably, refuse to be subjected to Brit tyranny,

14 Because,

15 Well,

16 [e]What America was all about was freedom from tyranny.

17 [f]Which explains how [g]Patrick Henry got the idea about [h]"Give me liberty or give me death."

CHAPTER 9

[i]The Brits did not buy the freedom from tyranny angle,

2 [j]Which forced the colonists to articulate it more plainly,

3 Resulting in a document called the [k]Declaration of Independence,

4 Which by an odd coincidence was published on [l]Independence Day,

5 And upset the Brits no end.

6 [m]In fact, the Brits declared war on the colonies,

7 But then had to wait around for a while while the colonists

a. Brit.9.5-8
b. Brit.22.12
c. Wil.14.1-5
d. Brit.19.41
e. 7.2
f. Ned.29.19-20
g. Ed.28.6
h. Psom.51.1-6
i. Psay.5Q.38
j. Ann.4.6
k. Psom.54.1-11
l. Psay.5Y.3
m. Brit.24.17
n. 12.2
o. Forg.8.11-15
p. Dav.21.26
q. Psay.5W.8
r. Ann.4.22
s. Ann.4.24
t. Brit.1.8
u. 6.12
v. Forg.5.6
w. Wil.52.1-6
x. Brit.22.12
y. 6.6
z. Psom.32.1-4
aa. 1.7

put together a [n]continental congress,

8 And passed a tax to pay for the army,

9 And then picked a [o]general to lead the army,

10 Who was named [p]George Washington.

CHAPTER 10

George Washington had a lot of army experience,

2 [q]Having been in the Brit army during the French and Indian War,

3 And had [r]wooden teeth too,

4 Which he made out of a cherry tree that he had [s]chopped down so he could tell his father about it,

5 Proving that he was honest,

6 And the father of his country.

7 Because of his Brit military training, Washington believed in doing things the [t]hard way,

8 Which is why he spent winters at [u]Valley Forge,

9 Where the troops had nothing to eat,

10 And no shoes for their feet,

11 And no coverings for their heads,

12 [v]Except the regulation white bandage with a picturesque bloodstain on the front.

13 Anyway,

14 Washington decided to attack the Brits in the dead of winter,

15 [w]And therefore crossed the Delaware,

16 [x]Standing up the whole way,

17 Until they reached [y]Trenton and surprised the British army,

18 By singing [z]"Yankee Doodle" as loud as they could,

19 [aa]Which explains why the

entire world now calls the Americans Yankees.

CHAPTER 11

[a]**A**lthough badly surprised by George Washington, the Brits kept fighting for quite a while and tried a lot of brilliant tactics to regain the advantage.
2 [b]For example, they brought over a bunch of German mercenaries to fight the war for them,
3 [c]Which the Yanks neutralized by bringing over a bunch of Frenchmen to fight the war for them.
4 Then the Brits tried to dishearten the Americans by turning [d]Benedict Arnold into a traitor,
5 Which the Yanks countered by having [e]Nathan Hale say, "I regret that I have but one life to give for my country,"
6 Right before the Brits hanged him.
7 Eventually, of course, the British general [f]Cornwallis discovered that he was in Yorktown,
8 [g]Where the Brits surrendered to the Yanks at the end of the Revolutionary War,
9 [h]And so he did,
10 Which is when the [i]Liberty Bell got cracked,
11 Because [j]Philadelphia is a long way from [k]Yorktown,
12 [l]Even if you're ringing your bell really loud.

CHAPTER 12

[m]**A**fter the war, the Yanks tried rule by Articles of Confederation,
2 Meaning rule by argumentative cliques of [m]Puritans, [n]plan-

a. *Brit.24.18-20*
b. *Brit.24.21-23*
c. *Frog.11.6*
d. *Dav.15.23*
e. *Dav.20.30*
f. *Dav.20.42*
g. *Psay.5Y.16*
h. *Brit.22.12*
i. *Vin.44.1-7*
j. *6.12*
k. *6.5*
l. *Psom.31.5-6 & 24.3-4*
m. *4.6-7*
n. *5.4-7*
o. *Adam.15.12-16*
p. *Drex.5.2*
q. *6.21-22*
r. *30.4*
s. *Wil.53.2*
t. *Brit.24.13*
u. *Rom.10.4*
v. *12.4*
w. *Hall.8.1*
x. *Hall.8.2*
y. *Rom.4.8*
z. *Rom.4.8*
aa. *Rom.4.8*
bb. *57.12-19*
cc. *Psay.5Y.33*
dd. *9.10*

tation owners, and [o]businessmen,
3 Which didn't work very well,
4 [p]Since none of them could ever agree on anything,
5 [q]Except that they had a huge war debt,
6 [r]And still didn't want to pay any taxes.
7 So they decided to have a constitutional congress in [s]Philadelphia to find a new form of government,
8 Capable of paying off the war debt,
9 [t]Without taxes.
10 [u]It turned out that there wasn't any form of government that could do what was necessary,
11 [v]So the constitutional congressmen argued for a long time,
12 [w]And finally adopted a constitution based on the very noblest principles of human morality,
13 [x]In particular, the principle that nobody can be trusted,
14 Ever,
15 [y]Not executives,
16 [z]Not legislators,
17 [aa]And not even judges.

CHAPTER 13

[bb]**W**ith a few minor exceptions, the new constitution was a big success,
2 Especially after a [bb]bill of rights got attached to it,
3 Just to make sure that the new government would understand how much the citizens of the United States trusted them,
4 [cc]And then [dd]George Washington agreed to be elected the first president,
5 By all the qualified voters in the United States,

6 Meaning all property holders,
7 [a]Unless they were slaves,
8 [b]Or women,
9 [c]Or didn't have enough property.
10 And then Washington won by a huge margin,
11 [d]Which may have been as much as a hundred votes.
12 The Yanks celebrated George's victory with a lot of parties,
13 And congratulated themselves a lot on having whipped the Brits,
14 [e]And on having invented a new form of government,
15 [f]With a great new constitution,
16 Which was perfect,
17 [g]Except that it didn't say anything at all about taxation without representation.

CHAPTER 14

[h]George Washington was president for eight years and set a lot of important precedents for the Yanks who would become president after him.
2 [i]For example, he got upset with congress when they wouldn't do what he wanted,
3 [j]Which made it okay for later presidents to get upset with congress too.
4 Then he decided not to run for reelection after he had served two four-year terms,
5 Which made it practically impossible for subsequent presidents to run for more than two terms,
6 [k]With one exception,
7 Which we'll discuss later.
8 Then he was succeeded by his vice president,
9 Who was [l]John Adams.

CHAPTER 15

John Adams tried to set some precedents of his own,
2 Such as suppressing [m]freedom of speech,
3 [n]Which is inconvenient to presidents,
4 [o]But presidents aren't allowed to suppress freedom of speech in the U.S.,
5 [p]Since the Yanks don't trust anybody that much,
6 Except themselves,
7 And the politicians who agree with them,
8 Which always excludes presidents,
9 [q]Because nobody always agrees with someone who has to make decisions on a more than occasional basis.
10 And so John Adams was voted out of office after his first term and was replaced by [r]Thomas Jefferson,
11 Who cared a lot more about the rights of the [s]little people,
12 Since, as a Virginia gentleman, he owned a lot of little people and even slept with them when he felt like it.
13 This led to the concept of [t]Jeffersonian democracy,
14 [u]Meaning rule by eloquent platitudes,
15 Which became an important American tradition.

CHAPTER 16

[v]But saying what people wanted to hear wasn't Jefferson's only accomplishment as president.
2 [w]For example, he had the White House built,
3 [x]And Washington, D.C. too,
4 Since the Yanks didn't have a

a. Rom.3.7
b. Rom.3.8
c. Rom.3.9
d. Psay.5Q.12
e. Grk.20.7
f. Psom.48.1-6
g. 8.12
h. 9.10
i. Brit.7.7
j. Grk.1.11
k. Ext.39.18-19
l. Dav.20.42
m. 57.13
n. 57.12
o. Hall.8.1-2
p. 12.15-17
q. Main.37.6
r. Dav.20.28
s. 5.5
t. Jefs.7.15-17
u. Grk.20.8
v. Ned.29.19-20
w. Ann.4.30-31
x. Ann.4.32

capital city like ªLondon or ᵇParis,

5 So why not start one from scratch?

6 And so he did.

7 Jefferson also pulled off the ᶜLouisiana Purchase,

8 Buying a huge chunk of North America from the ᵈFrench,

9 ᵉWho needed quick cash to pay for all the glory they were getting in the Napoleonic Wars,

10 ᶠAnd got a terrific deal,

11 Paying maybe five cents on the dollar, considering the real value of the land,

12 ᵍWhich is another important American tradition,

13 And explains why Jefferson's picture wound up on the nickel.

CHAPTER 17

Of course, after Jefferson completed the ʰLouisiana Purchase, someone had to go look over the land,

2 Just to make sure it was okay,

3 And so ⁱLewis and Clark went out and examined it,

4 For months,

5 And found that Jefferson had bought a lot of great land,

6 ʲExcept that there were a lot of Indians on it,

7 ᵏWho thought it was theirs,

8 For some reason,

9 Even though the Yanks had a receipt.

CHAPTER 18

After Jefferson had had his two terms, the Yanks elected ˡJames Madison to succeed him.

2 ᵐMonroe decided that what

a. Brit.29.14-17
b. Frog.22.1-5
c. 17.1
d. Frog.19.4
e. Frog.15.1-3
f. Ira.21.33
g. 15.15
h. 16.7
i. Dav.10.10
j. Exp.15.8
k. 27.9
l. Dav.20.36
m. Psay.5Y.4
n. Brit.13.7-10
o. Psay.5Q.68
p. 6.4-17
q. Brit.23.7
r. Chnk.12.15
s. Brit.1.9
t. 16.2
u. Brit.25.6
v. Brit.25.9
w. Brit.25.10-14
x. Dav.10.10

the country needed was another war with the British,

3 ⁿSince the Brits were acting like they owned the whole Atlantic Ocean,

4 ᵒWhich they basically did.

5 But Madison thought they should act nicer, so he started acting like the Yanks owned the Atlantic,

6 ᵖEspecially the Yank coastline,

7 Which should have worked out all right,

8 ᑫSince the Brits were still having a big war with France,

9 And might not try very hard against the Yanks.

10 Monroe was right about the Brits not trying very hard,

11 ʳBut underestimated the Brit navy,

12 Which is always a big mistake,

13 ˢAnd therefore had to learn the hard way,

14 ᵗBy getting his house burned down,

15 ᵘAnd a lot of other stuff too.

16 Fortunately, things got worked out to everyone's satisfaction after a while.

17 ᵛThe Brits signed a treaty saying they wouldn't act like they owned the Yank coastline,

18 ʷAnd the Yanks got to kill about three thousand Brits in one of the most lopsided victories anyone ever had against the Brits,

19 After the treaty had already been signed.

CHAPTER 19

This big Yank victory made a national hero out of a Yank named ˣAndrew Jackson,

2 [a]Who was made completely out of hickory,

3 And therefore survived all of his enemies' attempts to kill him,

4 Which was a lot of attempts,

5 Because Jackson had a lot of enemies,

6 Owing to a slight problem he had with his temper,

7 Which is to say that he was sort of a maniac,

8 [b]Who fought duels with anyone who disagreed with him,

9 [c]And never changed his mind about anyone or anything,

10 Because he didn't have any education.

11 This naturally made him a good candidate to be president of the Yanks someday,

12 Which we'll get to later.

CHAPTER 20

Beating the Brits also helped the [d]Jeffersonian democrats get another president elected,

2 Whose name was [e]Monroe,

3 And who was hard to distinguish from [f]Madison,

4 Since they were both Virginians,

5 Both had James for a first name,

6 And both had a last name that began with an [g]"M."

7 But it was Monroe who had to deal with the Missouri problem, which had to do with [h]slavery,

8 And [i]economics,

9 And was thus a hot potato,

10 Which is a Yank term for any issue that might require thought and foresight to resolve,

11 [j]And therefore probably can't be resolved by Yanks.

12 [k]Here's what happened.

13 All in all, the Yanks were

a. *Zig.6.4*
b. *Kens.16.5-10*
c. *Zig.9.2*
d. *15.14*
e. *Dav.20.36*
f. *18.1*
g. *Ed.60.17*
h. *Chr.5.5-7*
i. *Adam.52.4*
j. *122.29*
k. *Gnt.16.6-8*
l. *Adam.42.5-9 & 25.10-14*
m. *Adam.34.3-6*
n. *Adam.34.8-11*
o. *20.10*
p. *20.14*
q. *20.14*
r. *56.15-22*
s. *Brit.28.31-38*
t. *Exp.16.11-12*
u. *Rom.3.1*
v. *Rom.3.3*
w. *Grk.8.32*
x. *20.7*
y. *7.1-2*

doing pretty well for themselves financially,

14 [l]Except for the way the economy kept collapsing into a major depression every few years,

15 [m]Which had something to do with the banking laws,

16 [n]Something too complicated to remember,

17 That would become a [o]hot potato later.

18 [p]Anyway, with the exception of all the depressions,

19 The Yanks in the northern "states,"

20 As the colonies were now calling themselves,

21 Were doing pretty good business in a bunch of industries,

22 Such as [q]gun powder and textiles,

23 And didn't see why the nation needed any more slaves,

24 [r]Since there were a lot of poor white Yanks who were willing to work pretty hard for practically nothing.

25 In the south, on the other hand, the plantation owners were doing a pretty good business selling [s]cotton and [t]tobacco to the Brits,

26 [u]And they didn't know how all the cotton and tobacco would get picked if slaves didn't do it,

27 [v]Because they knew *they* weren't going to do it,

28 Since that would have meant getting off their [w]horse and getting their hands dirty.

29 This difference of opinion caused some problems when other parts of the south decided they wanted to be a state,

30 [x]Namely, Missouri,

31 So that they could all be free and democratic,

32 [y]Which is the American Way,

33 And how could they become states if they weren't allowed to keep their slaves?

CHAPTER 21

As a ^aJeffersonian democrat, President Madison understood that everybody had a point.

2 For example, like the ^bNew England Puritans, he didn't exactly approve of slavery,

3 Although being a ^cVirginian himself, he understood the position of the southerners too,

4 ^dBecause if you lived in the south, you needed somebody to do all the work,

5 And the poor whites were too ^eproud to do it,

6 ^fMeaning too quarrelsome, lazy, and vindictive to take orders,

7 Unless you could make them ^gcooperate with whips and leg irons,

8 Which were illegal to use,

9 ^hOn white people.

10 And so ⁱMonroe figured out that the best thing to do was compromise,

11 ^jWhich is the Yank way of doing something quick and easy right now, so that someone else will have to make the real decision later on,

12 Hopefully much later on,

13 When you're already out of office.

14 And so everyone agreed on the ^kMissouri Compromise,

15 Which said that new southern states could have ^lslaves,

16 And new northern states ^mcouldn't,

17 Which seemed reasonable to everybody,

a. 15.14
b. Brd.17.6-8
c. 6.5
d. 20.27
e. Ned.30.30-35
f. Kens.28.6
g. Spic.7.7
h. 139.28
i. 20.2
j. 122.29
k. Psay.5Y.21
l. Mes.1.9
m. Barb.1.2
    Grk.13.20
n. 13.6-9
o. Dav.27.5-7
p. 17.6-7
q. 20.9
r. Adam.10.6
s. Adam.10.7-8
t. Boul.21.9
u. 20.26

18 ⁿThat is, everybody who was legally entitled to vote.

CHAPTER 22

The reason the Missouri Compromise was so important was that pioneers were already starting to ^omigrate westward,

2 ^pInto the new lands acquired through the Louisiana Purchase,

3 Which meant that there would be more states signing up to join the United States,

4 ^qAnd sooner or later, the Yanks would have to make a decision about how to handle slavery.

5 If too many southern states joined up, slavery could be legalized by congress in the northern states too,

6 Which would have increased the northern population of negroes,

7 And the northerners have always been pretty united about not needing any more negroes,

8 Especially since you could mail away to Britain and Europe for indentured servants,

9 ^rWhich were almost as inexpensive as slaves,

10 ^sAnd just as obedient and powerless,

11 ^tAnd white.

12 On the other hand, if too many northern states joined up, congress might outlaw slavery in the southern states,

13 Which would have been a disaster.

14 Not that the southerners really liked negroes either,

15 But they were used to them,

16 ^uAnd their whole economy depended on them.

CHAPTER 23

And so, in the wake of the Missouri Compromise, the Yanks practiced their racial relations skills on the [a]Indians,

2 [b]Who seemed to be living on a lot of the best land in the country,

3 And had to be persuaded to move away,

4 Which would maybe work on the negroes [c]later on,

5 And so the Yanks signed treaties with the Indians,

6 [d]Promising to let them have a lot of land of their own,

7 Somewhere else,

8 [e]If they would just please leave the land the Yanks wanted now.

9 This worked great,

10 Because the Indians were too [f]uncivilized to understand the principles of American democracy,

11 [g]And therefore didn't know that you can't trust anybody,

12 [h]No matter how many beads and mirrors they give you.

13 In this fashion, the Yanks managed to clear out a whole lot of territory,

14 And add a lot of new states,

15 In practically no time at all.

CHAPTER 24

In fact, the Yanks were so busy adding states,

2 Not to mention making money,

3 That they went through a whole bunch of presidents without really noticing them,

4 At all.

5 [i]For example, there were presidents named John Quincy Ad-

a. Exp.11.9-10
b. 17.9
c. 22.4
d. 21.11
e. Brit.56.12-13
f. Barb.1.2-8
g. 12.13-17
h. Adam.36.9-10
i. Psay.5P.6
j. Psom.3.1-2
k. 25.1
l. Lies.14.4-5
m. 19.1
n. Jefs.7.15-17
o. Grk.20.8
p. 15.15
q. 20.15
r. Ned.36.18-19
s. 19.6
t. 19.10
u. Psay.5Q.12
v. Psay.5P.5

ams and Something Harrison and Something Tyler and Martin Van Buren and Millard Fillmore that nobody remembers to this day,

6 Except that [j]John Quincy Adams was the son of John Adams, and too smart to be president,

7 [k]For some reason,

8 And one of the others caught a cold at his inauguration and died almost immediately,

9 [l]For some reason.

10 [m]And somewhere in there, Andrew Jackson became president.

CHAPTER 25

Jackson also invented something called [n]Jacksonian democracy,

2 [o]Meaning rule by illiterate hicks who spit [p]tobacco juice on the carpet,

3 And resulted in the Yank tradition of electing presidents who were born in log cabins,

4 Which made them honest and great,

5 For some reason.

6 [q]Jackson also did something about the banking situation that was causing all the terrible economic depressions,

7 [r]Although no one can remember whether what he did made it better or worse,

8 [s]Except that he felt very strongly about it,

9 [t]And absolutely positively refused to change his mind,

10 [u]And therefore must have been a great president.

CHAPTER 26

There was also a president named [v]James Polk.

CHAPTER 27

Meanwhile, the Yanks kept adding more new states, which was going so smoothly and quickly that the Yanks decided it meant something.

2 What it meant,

3 [a]The way the Yanks looked at it,

4 Was that the United States was kind of [b]*supposed* to own all of North America,

5 [c]From sea to shining sea,

6 No matter who got in the way.

7 And so the Yanks wound up rediscovering the ancient Roman idea of [d]appropriating,

8 [e]Which is another way of saying that if a bunch of Yanks have moved in someplace and put up some buildings and signs, then obviously the Yanks must own it,

9 Regardless of what any piece of paper says,

10 [f]Even if it's a treaty signed by the U.S. government.

11 This important new Yank principle was called [g]Manifest Destiny,

12 Which can be roughly translated as "Get the hell out of our way!"

CHAPTER 28

Thanks to Manifest Destiny, the Yanks managed to appropriate [h]California from the Spanish,

2 Which was really a shame for the Spics,

3 [i]Who had spent the last several hundred years ransacking large chunks of two continents in search of gold,

4 Only to get kicked out of the place where all the gold was,

a. Lies.10.6
b. Exp.1.7-9
c. Rat.23.19
d. Rom.2.7-10
e. Exp.1.10-16
f. 23.5
g. Frog.26.7
h. 5.1
i. Spic.9.1-6
j. Psay.5Y.53
k. Ned.19.3-4
l. 56.10
m. Psay.5C.5
n. Dav.23.10-22 & 24.4-12
o. Ed.43.4
p. Ed.40.2-8
q. Adam.25.8-14

5 Namely, California,

6 Before they figured out that it was there.

7 [j]And so the Yanks got all the gold,

8 [k]Which is the way things go when you have Manifest Destiny on your side,

9 [l]And enough poor white trash to sift every ounce of dirt in the state.

10 In fact, the Yanks had enough poor white trash to sift almost all of the dirt in the west,

11 Which is why they also found silver in Colorado and [m]Nevada,

12 And a bunch of other stuff in other places,

13 Until suddenly everybody thought that dirt was just the greatest thing ever,

14 And went out west to get some of their own.

15 Fortunately for the Yanks, there was absolutely no shortage of dirt out west.

16 In fact, there was so much of it that even the streets were paved with dirt,

17 Which turned out to be a good thing,

18 Because [n]everyone who went west was wearing a [o]six-gun,

19 And when they got killed,

20 [p]Which a lot of them did,

21 It was easy to dig a hole in the dirt wherever they were,

22 And put them in it,

23 With their boots on,

24 So their socks wouldn't get dirty,

25 Or something like that.

26 Anyway, this period of Yank history was terribly exciting and romantic,

27 [q]Not to mention extremely

profitable for all the capitalists who were making guns and bullets and shovels back east,

28 [a]Which maybe explains why so many perfectly contented Yanks in the east kept shouting, "Go west, young man," whenever they ran into somebody who was too dirty and rowdy to put to work in a factory.

CHAPTER 29

As it happened, the westward migration of so many dirty people resulted in a completely new kind of economic system,

2 In which every single profession was based on dirt,

3 Including ranching, [b]which involved owning enough dirt so that cowboys on horseback could kick up a lot of dust chasing livestock from one water hole to another,

4 And sheep farming, [c]which involved squatting on dirt that belonged to some cattle rancher and waiting for all hell to break loose,

5 And lots and lots of mining,

6 Not to mention railroading, [d]which involved buying enough [e]Chinks to lay track across thousands of miles of empty dirt, in order to connect one dirty little western town with another, all the way to the coast,

7 And commerce, which involved the selling of all manner of goods and tools for handling dirt,

8 Including brooms for sweeping dirt,

9 [f]And hats with big brims for keeping dirt out of your eyes and hair,

a. *Psay.5Q.30*
b. *Ed.46.18-20*
c. *Dav.24.24*
d. *Adam.7.9-11*
e. *Chnk.11.7-9*
f. *Ned.24.20*
g. *28.27*
h. *Kens.5.31*
i. *Wil.43.7*
j. *Ed.43.9*
k. *Spic.10.2-3*
l. *Spic.10.4-5*
m. *Ann.18.19*
n. *Oth.3.1-13*
o. *27.9*
p. *Spic.3.2-3*
q. *Spic.3.4-6*
r. *Exp.11.18-21*

10 And chaps for keeping dirt off your pants,

11 And neckerchiefs for keeping dirt out of your mouth,

12 [g]Not to mention guns and dirt sifters and shovels,

13 [h]As well as plenty of rotgut whiskey to clear the dirt out of your throat,

14 [i]And every once in a long while, a bathtub for washing the dirt off,

15 So you'd be allowed to go upstairs with the [j]saloon girls.

CHAPTER 30

It was this Yank fascination with dirt that took Manifest Destiny south of the border into Mexico,

2 [k]Which is a country made completely out of dirt,

3 [l]And nothing else,

4 At all.

5 When they saw it,

6 [m]The Yanks fell in love with it immediately,

7 And had to have it,

8 Even though the Spics [n]owned it,

9 [o]Which never stopped the Yanks anyway,

10 As we have seen.

11 Of course, the Yanks were a lot fonder of dirt than the Spics ever were,

12 [p]Because the Spics had plenty of dirt back home in Spain,

13 And it wasn't the prospect of finding more dirt that convinced them to come to the New World in the first place,

14 [q]But gold,

15 [r]Which Mexico didn't seem to have much of,

16 ªOwing to the fact that it was all in California.
17 In fact, the Spics in Mexico had actually gotten pretty tired of the Yanks and their ᵇManifest Destiny,
18 ᶜEspecially since El Dorado had turned out to be such a bust,
19 And they decided that the Yanks shouldn't be able to grab off a huge chunk of Mexico just because they felt like it.
20 And so, when the Yanks ᵈappropriated a big chunk of Mexico and started calling it ᵉTexas,
21 The Spics retaliated ᶠat the Alamo,
22 Where they slaughtered a whole bunch of Yank heroes,
23 Including ᵍDavy Crockett,
24 And ʰJim Bowie Jim Bowie,
25 And ⁱDaniel Boone,
26 And Sam Houston,
27 And ʲWyatt Earp,
28 And ᵏBat Masterson,
29 And ˡDoc Holliday,
30 And ᵐBuffalo Bill,
31 And ⁿWild Bill Hickok,
32 And ºAnnie Oakley,
33 And a whole bunch of Texas Rangers,
34 ᵖExcept one,
35 Who got rescued by a faithful ᑫIndian friend from his youth,
36 And was the only one left to ʳ"Remember the Alamo."
37 ˢThe problem is, it's never a good idea to make the Yanks mad,
38 Because as soon as they get mad, they stop thinking altogether,
39 And feel absolutely obligated to get even,
40 ᵗNo matter how much it costs,

a. 28.8-9
b. 27.11
c. Spic.12.1
d. 27.7
e. Brit.24.13
f. Psay.5Y.40
g. Dav.23.10
  & 24.16-18
h. Psom.9.1-12
  Ed.47.7
i. Ed.64.8
j. Ed.47.9
k. Ed.47.8
l. Ed.43.11-12
m. Ed.71.22-25
n. Ed.45.2-4
o. Ed.47.14
p. Ed.45.6-7
q. Ed.45.9
r. 116.16
s. 107.5-6
t. Kens.16.6-10
*u. Psom.75.10-
  11*
v. 27.12
w. Brit.26.15
x. 27.8
y. Frog.19.4-5
z. Pnot.53.1-5

41 Which may help explain how it happened that when the dust finally cleared in Texas,
42 The Yanks owned Texas,
43 Which manifested its destiny almost immediately,
44 By joining the United States,
45 Which made everything all better,
46 Even though nobody in Texas has ever,
47 Or will ever,
48 ᵘForget the terrible things the Spics did at the Alamo.

CHAPTER 31

O f course, it wasn't just Spics who got pushed out of the way by ᵛManifest Destiny.
2 For example, the Yanks also manifested their destiny in ʷCanada,
3 By appropriating Washington or some northwestern state like that,
4 ˣFor some excellent reason, no doubt,
5 Which the Canucks didn't care for,
6 But the Yanks have never cared much about the Canucks' opinion anyway,
7 Because what can you say about people who have that much land,
8 And never tried, even once, to manifest their destiny,
9 But just went tromping around on snowshoes instead?
10 Besides, most of the people who lived in Canada were ʸFrogs or something,
11 ᶻExcept for the ones who went there because they really liked the thought of being oppressed from three thousand

miles away by a [a]half-witted Brit
king,
12 Which sort of explains why
[b]Canada never really had a destiny,
13 Or any history to speak of,
14 Or anything but a bunch of
Frogs on snowshoes.

CHAPTER 32

And so, the Yanks had great
success in appropriating
land from whoever happened to
own it,
3 [c]Especially from the Indians,
4 Who kept signing treaties and
moving out of the way,
5 Signing treaties and moving
out of the way,
6 [d]And signing treaties and
moving out of the way.
7 But then, just when everything was looking really wonderful,
8 With Yank destiny manifest-
ing itself all over the place,
9 The old [e]slavery thing
cropped up again,
10 And wouldn't go away.

CHAPTER 33

Part of the problem this time
was that someone named
[f]Harriet Beecher Stowe had written a book,
2 Called 'Uncle Tom's Cabin,'
3 Which was all about how awful slavery was.
4 The book became very very
popular,
5 [g]Which made it a hot potato
for the president,
6 Because it was practically unprecedented for a Yank to write a
book that a lot of Yanks could
read.
7 Not that there hadn't been
Yank writers before;
8 [h]There had been;
9 It's just that they'd never written any interesting books.
10 [i]Most of the Yank writers before Harriet Beecher Stowe had
been overeducated [j]Puritans
from New England,
11 Like [k]Paul Bunyan and [l]Na-
thaniel Hawthorne,
12 [m]Who wrote about [n]guilt and
sin and suffering,
13 Which the majority of Yanks
have never cared about,
14 Unless they can inflict it
themselves,
15 [o]In person.
16 Anyway,
17 'Uncle Tom's Cabin' started
a big abolitionist movement,
18 [p]Which meant that a bunch
of Yanks in New England insisted on telling the southern
states how [q]evil and immoral
they were for having slaves,
19 And therefore caused the
southern states to start retaliating
in the traditional [r]American way,
20 By threatening to start their
own country,
21 [s]Where they would be free
from the chains of tyranny,
22 And could do what they
wanted to,
23 However [t]they wanted to do
it.

CHAPTER 34

The president who had to
handle this mess was
[u]James Buchanan,
2 Who had been born in a [v]log
cabin,
3 And was therefore honest and
great,

a. Brit.17.22-23
b. Psom.13.1-5
c. Oth.5.1-18
d. 32.4
e. 22.4
f. Dav.14.39
g. 20.10
h. 65.3
i. Swar.20.12
j. 3.1-2 Kens.28.16
k. Dav.20.42
l. Dav.20.42
m. Grk.5.8
n. Pnot.14.1-5
o. Ed.40.8
p. 20.23-24
q. Barb.1.2
r. 7.1-2
s. 8.14-16
t. 13.6-9
u. Dav.22.12
v. 25.4

4 ᵃAlthough maybe more honest than great,
5 ᵇAnd just possibly more stupid than honest.
6 Buchanan felt very strongly that everybody was right,
7 ᶜWhich is an important tradition of Yank politics,
8 And resulted in everybody getting madder and madder,
9 Which is also an important tradition of Yank politics,
10 Until everybody got so mad they couldn't see straight,
11 ᵈWhich is still another important Yank tradition called freedom of expression,
12 And caused Buchanan to figure out that the potato had finally gotten way too hot,
13 ᵉSo he left it cooking on his desk at the White House and went home.

CHAPTER 35

When they saw how easy it was to discourage Buchanan,
2 The ᶠsoutherners got pretty excited,
3 And started making all kinds of threats about the next president and what they would do if the wrong one got elected,
4 Like ᵍAbraham Lincoln,
5 Who the southerners thought was the worst possible choice,
6 Even though he had been born in a log cabin,
7 And was therefore honest and great.
8 The problem was, Abraham Lincoln kept making speeches about how the United States was a ʰunion,
9 No matter what,
10 And how they couldn't just

a. Rat.14.3
b. Psong.44.1
c. 21.1
d. 57.12-16
   30.38-40
e. 21.11-13
f. 36.6-14
g. Ed.28.6
h. Rom.21.8-9
i. 20.32
j. 33.19
k. Ann.4.6
l. Psay.5Y.5
m. 12.1-2
n. 6.5
o. 6.14
p. 6.15
q. 25.1-5 &
   34.1-3
r. 16.7-8
s. 30.43-44

keep going off and starting their own country every time something didn't go their way,
11 ⁱBecause that would be pretty stupid.
12 Naturally, the southerners thought this kind of talk was offensive and uncalled for,
13 ʲSo they took out an ad in the paper to tell everybody that if Abraham Lincoln was elected president,
14 ᵏThey would go off and start their own country,
15 And if Lincoln tried to stop them,
16 There would be war.

CHAPTER 36

What happened next was that Abraham Lincoln got elected president,
2 ˡAnd the southerners went off and started their own country,
3 Called the Confederate States of America,
4 In honor of the ᵐbrilliant system the states had tried before they had to make up a constitution instead,
5 And they got a whole bunch of states to join,
6 ⁿIncluding Virginia,
7 ᵒSouth Carolina,
8 ᵖGeorgia,
9 Alabama,
10 Mississippi,
11 ᑫTennessee,
12 ʳLouisiana,
13 And ˢTexas,
14 Unless some of these aren't right,
15 Because all of this happened a pretty long time ago,
16 And no one remembers all the details,
17 Except for a bunch of southerners who have never stopped

[a]believing in the Confederacy,
18 And never stopped fighting the War Between the States.

CHAPTER 37

[b]A braham Lincoln looked the situation over,
2 And saw that a bunch of states had walked out,
3 Over a difference of opinion that would probably never be resolved to anyone's satisfaction,
4 [c]Except that a lot of Yanks up north really didn't care at all about the slavery problem,
5 And weren't all that sorry to see the last of the southern states either,
6 Because who needed them anyway,
7 With their trashy accents,
8 And their hick ways,
9 And all those black people.
10 All of this made it pretty obvious to Lincoln what he had to do,
11 For some reason,
12 And so he told the Confederacy that they couldn't leave the union,
13 Ever,
14 And if they tried to,
15 He would stop them,
16 Because union was more important than anything,
17 Period.

CHAPTER 38

W hen they heard this, the Confederates were pretty delighted,
2 And got out all their [d]cavalry sabers,
3 And had their slaves pack a nice lunch,
4 And rode off to Fort Sumter,
5 Which is located somewhere in the United States,

a. Grk.12.10
b. Dav.14.9
c. 56.8-10
d. Chr.8.1-4
e. 36.7
f. Psay.5Q.28
g. Dav.23.58
h. Dav.22.34
i. Ann.4.30-31
j. 36.18
k. Dav.15.9
l. Dav.18.17
m. Dav.8.7

6 [e]Maybe down south,
7 [f]And fired the shot heard round the world,
8 [g]Unless that was some other shot.
9 Anyway,
10 When Lincoln heard about the shot at Fort Sumter,
11 He declared [h]war on the Confederacy,
12 And sent the union army out to stop the Confederates at a Washington suburb called Bull Run.
13 Unfortunately, the union soldiers at Bull Run didn't have any slaves to pack them a nice lunch,
14 So they got hungry and tired,
15 In about fifteen minutes,
16 And the Confederates won big,
17 [i]No more than a few miles from the White House,
18 Which got the northerners really excited about defeating the Confederates,
19 Except that it didn't,
20 For some reason.

CHAPTER 39

P art of the reason why the northerners weren't excited enough about the Civil War,
2 Which is what the northerners called the [j]War Between the States for some reason,
3 Was that the Confederates had all the exciting generals,
4 Including [k]Robert E. Lee,
5 And [l]Stonewall Jackson,
6 And [m]Wilson Pickett,
7 And a bunch of others too,
8 While the north didn't have any generals at all,
9 Which is why Lincoln had to spend the whole first half of the war looking for one.

10 When he couldn't find any ᵃgenerals,
11 Lincoln tried fighting the war with ᵇidiots instead,
12 Including ᶜMeade,
13 And ᵈMcClellan,
14 And some others too,
15 Who all really wanted to be generals,
16 And wore very nice blue uniforms,
17 And spent lots and lots of money,
18 On nice blue uniforms for the union troops,
19 And on cannons and rifles and bullets and things,
20 Not to mention horses and wagons and tents and food,
21 And hundreds of blurry photographs,
22 And thousands of flags,
23 ᵉAnd zillions of telegrams to the president explaining why the union army wasn't ready to fight yet.

CHAPTER 40

Eventually all this led to the Battle of Gettysburg,
2 Somehow,
3 And the union blue fought the confederate gray out in the middle of the Pennsylvania countryside for three days,
4 ᶠArmed with the most modern and deadly weapons anyone had ever seen,
5 Which they fired at each other from point-blank range,
6 Until the fields of Gettysburg were covered with the bodies of thousands of ᵍdead northerners,
7 And thousands of ʰdead southerners,
8 Which convinced ⁱGeneral Pickett that the only way to top it all off,

a. Forg.8.11-15
b. Psay.51.1-4
c. Dav.22.12
d. Dav.35.22 & 21.9
e. 135.13
f. 77.9
g. Forg.5.6
h. Forg.5.6
i. 39.6
j. Psom.25.1-3
k. Psom.25.11-13
l. Forg.4.11
m. Kens.22.9
n. 40.15
o. Dav.12.5

9 And be remembered forever,
10 Was to send all the troops the south had left on a desperate cavalry charge,
11 ʲStraight into the union artillery,
12 Just to see what would happen.
13 What happened was that the south lost fifteen thousand troops,
14 ᵏIn about half an hour,
15 Bringing the total number of troops killed at Gettysburg up to an even ˡfifty thousand,
16 And ensuring the late General Pickett an honored place in Confederate history,
17 Forever.

CHAPTER 41

Everybody was pretty amazed and upset about how many soldiers had been killed at Gettysburg,
2 So Lincoln made a speech,
3 And told everybody that Fourscore and seven years ago,
4 Something,
5 And something else,
6 And these ᵐhonored dead,
7 And all that,
8 Until everybody felt better,
9 Including Lincoln,
10 Because thanks to ⁿGettysburg, he had finally figured out how to win the war.

CHAPTER 42

What ᵒLincoln figured out at Gettysburg was that if you killed lots and lots of the enemy's troops,
2 And kept on doing it,
3 For a good long time,
4 Eventually, they'd have to surrender,

5 ^aBecause they'd run out of men.

6 When Lincoln explained this plan to his ^bgenerals,

7 They couldn't understand it,

8 And didn't like it,

9 And told him that the only general who'd buy a crazy plan like that was some worthless old drunk who didn't know any better,

10 And why didn't he just go back to the White House and nib out?

11 And so Lincoln found a worthless old drunk named ^cU.S. Grant,

12 And bought him a big bottle of whiskey,

13 And told him about the plan,

14 Which Grant liked so much that the president put him in charge of the union army,

15 Right then and there.

CHAPTER 43

The Civil War lasted a long time,

2 And involved hundreds of battles,

3 Which happened in hundreds of places that nobody knows where they are to this day,

4 ^dExcept southerners, of course,

5 And explains why every Yankee still gets a glazed and distant look in his eye when he hears names like Chickamauga,

6 And Shiloh,

7 And Manassas,

8 And the ^eWilderness,

9 ^fWhere he knows something sad and bloody and desperately heroic occurred,

10 Something terribly important to the history of his country,

11 Which he would find deeply moving if he only knew what it was,

12 Except that he doesn't,

13 ^gAnd therefore has to look glazed and distant instead.

14 Anyway,

15 With so much history going on all over the place, ^hit's hard to pick out the really important things,

16 ⁱAlthough there must have been some,

17 ^jOr nobody would remember the Civil War at all.

18 Of course, everybody remembers something different,

19 ^kWhich is what America is all about,

20 And explains why the Yanks are so great,

21 Unless it doesn't.

22 For example, the northerners remember that at some point, ^lAbraham Lincoln freed the slaves,

23 Which they think was pretty terrific,

24 And definitely worth remembering,

25 Because it made the southerners so furious.

26 Black people also used to think it was pretty terrific that ^mLincoln freed them,

27 Until they found out ⁿhe didn't really mean it,

28 Or something,

29 Which made it a lot less memorable,

30 And a lot less important too,

31 ^oFor some reason.

32 On the other hand, even white southerners remember that ^pLincoln freed the slaves,

33 And just wish they didn't,

34 ^qBecause they'd much rather remember what the north did to

a. Psay.5Q.62
b. 39.10-11
c. Dav.32.4
d. 36.17-18
e. Vin.3.10
f. Bks.6.17-18
g. 43.5
h. Krt.31.6-7
i. Dav.22.1-2
j. Dav.22.3
k. Mall.6.24-25
l. Dav.10.10
m. Dav.15.9
n. 43.32
o. Brd.24.1-8
p. Dav.19.8
q. 44.1

the south after ᵃGrant became the union commander,

35 Which was not nice,

36 At all,

37 And will never be forgotten by the south,

38 Ever,

39 Which still yearns for revenge,

40 Because that's the American way,

41 Especially if you're still nostalgic for the days when every white man was truly free,

42 ᵇAnd every negro knew his place.

CHAPTER 44

What the north did to the south after Grant became the union commander was destroy it,

2 Pretty thoroughly.

3 What happened was, Grant thought about Lincoln's plan to end the Civil War,

4 ᶜFor four or five cases of whiskey,

5 ᵈAnd came up with the idea that if you could win by destroying enough of the enemy's troops,

6 You might win even faster if you destroyed *everything* the enemy had,

7 Until they had nothing left to fight you with,

8 At all,

9 Including not even a single bullet to shoot,

10 Or a single rifle to shoot with,

11 Or even a single potato to eat.

12 Grant didn't name this new kind of war after himself,

a. 42.11
b. 151.17
c. 91.7
d. 42.1
e. Gnt.16.11-12
f. 44.3-4
g. Dav.9.7
h. Psay.5Q.63
i. Grk.23.12-13
j. 44.38
k. Dav.22.55
l. Dav.22.37-40

13 For some reason,

14 Which is why it came to be called other names instead,

15 Including total war,

16 ᵉAnd *modern* war,

17 And other names too,

18 Especially in the south, where they got to know this kind of war pretty well.

19 After he got his bright idea,

20 Grant needed someone to execute it for him,

21 Since he was too busy drinking,

22 ᶠThat is, *think*ing,

23 To actually go do it himself.

24 So he picked a general named ᵍSherman,

25 ʰWho thought that war was hell,

26 ⁱAnd was just dying for a chance to prove it.

27 He got his chance when Grant told him to march to the sea,

28 ʲAll the way from somewhere or other,

29 To the coast of Georgia,

30 Without leaving anything standing anywhere in between.

31 General Sherman did this so well that all the ᵏsouthern women had to make dresses out of curtains,

32 And eat nothing but old roots from the garden,

33 Because those were the only things the union troops didn't burn down,

34 Or knock down,

35 Or tear up,

36 Or track their feet on,

37 Between somewhere and the sea.

38 They also burned down ˡAtlanta,

39 And some other cities too,

40 Including maybe Charleston,
41 Unless it was someplace else.

CHAPTER 45

By this time, General [a]Robert E. Lee was pretty unhappy.
2 [b]Pickett was dead,
3 [c]And so was Stonewall Jackson,
4 Which meant that the Yanks now had more famous generals than the south did,
5 [d]What with Grant and his big thinking bouts,
6 [e]Sherman and his hellfire,
7 And a bunch of other Yanks just like Grant and Sherman.
8 Besides, Lee's hair had turned completely [f]gray,
9 And since the average age of his soldiers was now about fourteen,
10 He was starting to feel more like a grandfather than a general,
11 And so he decided that it might be better to surrender so the troops could get to bed in time to be fresh for school,
12 Which he did,
13 [g]In a place called Appomattox,
14 [h]Unless that isn't where it was.
15 Anyway, Lee handed his sword to Grant,
16 And rode off into the sunset,
17 And was never heard from again.
18 As the victorious general, though,
19 Grant had to keep working,
20 [i]And thinking,
21 Sometimes as many as two or three cases a week,
22 Because he was going to be heard from again,

a. Dav.14.20
b. 116.16
c. 47.16
d. 42.11
e. 44.25-26
f. Ira.32.3-9
g. Psay.5Y.17
h. Dav.23.58
i. 44.22
j. Lies.14.5
k. Dav.22.52
l. Psay.5Q.10
m. Psay.5Q.58
n. Dav.15.45
o. Dav.15.46
p. Psong.19.2
q. Dav.52.4
r. Frog.37.6
s. Dav.15.9
   & 22.8
   & 23.11

23 And had to be ready when the time came.

CHAPTER 46

As it happens, there's a funny thing about history,
2 Which is that when a lot of it is going on,
3 It's kind of hard to stop it,
4 [j]Or even slow it down,
5 Just because everybody would like some peace and quiet,
6 And a little breathing room.
7 Immediately after the Civil War,
8 Almost everybody was relieved that it was over at last,
9 And Lincoln said some nice things in his second inaugural address,
10 [k]Things about malice toward none,
11 [l]And how a divided house can't stand the heat in the kitchen,
12 [m]Or words to that effect,
13 [n]Which eventually might have gotten everybody calmed down a little bit,
14 [o]So they could think what to do next,
15 Only Lincoln went to see a [p]play at Ford's Theater instead,
16 Where an assassin named [q]John Wilkes Booth assassinated him,
17 And took away the greatest president the northeastern states of the U.S. ever had.

CHAPTER 47

To this day, every Yank born north of the [r]Mason-Dixon line remembers that [s]Abraham Lincoln was a great president,
2 Because he won the Civil War,

131

3 And freed the slaves,
4 ^aAnd got assassinated,
5 And was born in a log cabin,
6 And was very very tall,
7 And wore a stovepipe hat,
8 And had a funny-looking beard,
9 And a funny-looking wife.
10 They also know that Lincoln was honest and great,
11 Because if he wasn't,
12 ^bWhy would he have such a nice memorial in Washington, D.C.,
13 ^cAnd his picture on the ^dfive-dollar bill,
14 ^eAnd so many movies made about his life?
15 Back then, the northerners also thought Lincoln was honest and great,
16 ^fBecause he got shot in the back by a southerner,
17 ^gAnd were so mad about what happened to him that they responded in the most traditional American way,
18 By arresting a whole bunch of conspirators,
19 Finding them guilty as charged in spite of the evidence,
20 And then hanging them by the neck until they were dead.
21 This event not only honored the memory of a great American,
22 But set the tone for the north's treatment of the south in years to come,
23 Including the new policy called ^hReconstruction.

CHAPTER 48

The president who came after Lincoln was named ⁱAndrew Johnson,
2 Who wasn't born in a log cabin,

a. Psom.68.1-5
b. Gods.6.20-22
c. Psong.16.1
d. Psp.3.8
e. Dav.16.1-7
f. Ext.11.4
g. 30.37-40
h. Main.29.1-7
i. Dav.22.12
j. Psay.5Q.62
k. 27.12
l. Mawr.18.7
m. Frog.13.6
n. Dav.22.13
o. Psay.5Q.42

3 ^jAnd was therefore dishonest and stupid.
4 In fact, Johnson almost got impeached,
5 For some reason,
6 And did ^kReconstruction completely wrong,
7 ^lWhich everybody knows,
8 Although there's still a lot of disagreement about how Reconstruction could have been done right.
9 For example, the southerners and quite a lot of Yanks still think that the biggest thing wrong about ^mReconstruction was that it was done at all,
10 Because the Yanks who wanted to get even with the south set everything up to make things as hard as possible for the white southerners,
11 Like sending a bunch of opportunistic and unscrupulous ⁿcarpetbaggers down to spread as much corruption around the south as they had up north,
12 And creating a bunch of puppet state legislatures full of ignorant, illiterate black field hands who were anxious to learn as much as possible about corruption from the carpetbaggers, and not much else,
13 And letting black people run absolutely wild and free in the streets, so that they could terrorize white women and children and humiliate powerless, unarmed southern men.
14 ^oThe people who think this way about Reconstruction are usually the white people in the north and the south who were never that upset about slavery anyway, and thought the best way to get over the war was to forgive and forget,

15 [a]And leave it to the south to
figure out how they should treat
all the free black people who
weren't going to be slaves anymore.
16 [b]On the other hand, there are
a lot of white northerners and
black southerners who think the
worst thing about [c]Reconstruc-
tion was that it didn't last long
enough,
17 And finally got repealed,
18 Because it was really working the whole time,
19 Even when it didn't look that
way,
20 At all,
21 [d]And would have given
black people their rights about a
hundred years before they decided to go get their rights all by
themselves.
22 Still, the one point that all
Yanks agree on is that [e]Recon-
struction was a disaster, one way
or the other,
23 [f]For the south,
24 [g]For black people,
25 [h]And for everybody else too,
26 Except the carpetbaggers.

CHAPTER 49

Actually, the carpetbaggers
were never very popular
with anyone,
2 Which is why they finally decided they needed their own
president,
3 One who would be too busy
thinking all the time to keep a
close eye on Reconstruction,
4 Which is why it was so lucky
that [i]U.S. Grant was available,
5 And still every bit as ready for
great responsibility as he had always been,
6 [j]Thinking more and more all
the time,
7 Which proved that he was obviously presidential material.
8 In fact, Grant was elected
president twice,
9 Even though nobody knows
whether he was born in a log
cabin or not,
10 Although he probably
wasn't,
11 Since the Grant administration didn't turn out to be very
honest or great,
12 At all.

CHAPTER 50

It was during Grant's two
terms in office that the south
got kind of bitter about how everything had turned out.
2 In the old days, the south had
lots of [k]plantations,
3 [l]And a lot of money,
4 And a lot of big dresses,
5 [m]And a lot of fancy parties,
6 [n]And a lot of exquisitely tai-
lored southern gentlemen,
7 [o]And a lot of beautifully fash-
ionable southern belles,
8 [p]And a lot of poor obedient
slaves.
9 In the new postwar days,
10 [q]The south had a lot of
blackened ruins,
11 [r]And a lot of grinding poverty,
12 [s]And a lot of white robes and
hoods made out of old sheets,
13 [t]And a lot of lynching parties,
14 [u]And a lot of disreputable
and hard-drinking southern gentlemen,
15 [v]And a lot of faded and unhappy southern belles,
16 [w]And a lot of poor black
freemen who couldn't find a job,
17 [x]Unless they wanted to run
for the state legislature,

a. Mall.13.27
b. Exp.1.7-9
c. Gnt.1.13
d. Mall.13.27
e. Spic.16.5
f. Oth.7.22
g. Oth.8.18
h. Oth.9.19
i. Dav.22.12
j. 44.22
k. 5.4-7
l. Psong.41.1-6
m. Frog.9.8
n. Dav.20.34
o. Dav.22.6
p. Dav.22.26-27 & 22.7
q. 45.5-7
r. 20.26-27
s. Ann.18.19
t. Psay.5K.1
u. Dav.42.15
v. Dav.22.6
w. Ed.71.11
x. 48.12

18 ᵃOr run from the Ku Klux Klan.
19 But that's the way things go sometimes,
20 ᵇHistory being what it is,
21 And eventually everybody found a new way of life,
22 In spite of Reconstruction,
23 And the carpetbaggers,
24 And President Grant,
25 And everything else,
26 ᶜWhich is about par.

CHAPTER 51

Meanwhile, the Grant administration was trying to figure out what to do about the American Indians,
2 Who were still there,
3 ᵈAnd had a whole bunch of treaties that said they had a right to be where they were,
4 ᵉWhich was starting to put a crimp on Manifest Destiny.
5 It was hard to know what to do exactly,
6 Especially since the Yank population as a whole was pretty tired of wars,
7 And had been so distracted for so long by the Civil War and the negro problem that they had completely forgotten about the Indians,
8 And what savages they were,
9 And how much of a threat they posed to Manifest Destiny and the American Way and everything,
10 Until a former union general named Custer changed everything,
11 Overnight.

CHAPTER 52

Here's how it happened.

a. 50.13
b. Lies.14.4
c. 7.2
d. 27.10
e. Brit.15.3
f. 20.12
g. Dav.8.7
h. Ann.16.12
i. Vin.49.5
j. 21.11
k. Psay.5L.7
l. 48.5
   Swar.26.8-9
m. Dav.23.26
n. Psp.2.10
o. Psay.5Q.23

2 ᵍGeneral Custer was stationed out west somewhere,
3 ʰIn Indian country,
4 With a cavalry troop that someone had placed under his command,
5 ⁱProbably after thinking about it the way Grant had taught all his officers to.
6 Anyway,
7 Custer started following some Indian tracks,
8 Which weren't too hard to follow,
9 Because they completely blanketed the entire plain, as far as the eye could see.
10 After he had followed them for a while,
11 Custer came to the conclusion that a frontal assault would be too risky,
12 And so he decided,
13 ʲWith typical Yank ingenuity,
14 That the best thing to do would be to split up the ᵏSeventh Cavalry into seven groups,
15 And then kind of surround the Indians and overwhelm them with surprise,
16 Or something like that,
17 ˡAlthough nobody knows for sure.
18 And so that's exactly what ᵐCuster did.
19 ⁿWhen they found the remains of the Seventh Cavalry a few days later at the Little Big Horn,
20 There wasn't much left,
21 ᵒExcept maybe a big bloodstain marking the spot of Custer's Last Stand,
22 Which suggested that there must have been some kind of a flaw in the general's plan,

23 Whatever it was.

24 But more important than this was the evidence that Indians were totally uncivilized,

25 [a]Meaning they had killed and scalped every member of a U.S. force that was obviously too small to pose any real threat,

26 Which just isn't civilized behavior,

27 Not to mention stupid,

28 Because if you're the wrong color or nationality, it's never a good idea to remind the Yanks that you are there,

29 Especially by killing some of them,

30 [b]Because nobody knows more about getting even than the Yanks.

CHAPTER 53

And so the Yanks punished the Indians,

2 A lot.

3 [c]It was obvious that any treaties the U.S. had signed with unchristian savages couldn't be honored after the terrible thing that had happened at the [d]Little Big Horn,

4 And so they forgot about all the treaties,

5 And fought some [e]Indian wars,

6 Which were very exciting and suspenseful,

7 [f]Because the two sides were so evenly matched.

8 On one side were the Yanks, a nation of forty million God-fearing Christians who had just fought and won the first [g]modern war in history,

9 Against themselves,

10 [h]And who had right on their

---

a. Ext. 48.19
b. 120.6
c. 51.1-4
d. 52.19
e. Psay.5W.5
f. Brit.1.9
g. 44.16
h. 27.1-6
i. 12.13
j. Rat.13.11
k. Chr.2.5-8
l. Barb.1.8
m. 31.7-8
n. Dav.23.23-24
o. Dav.23.41-43
p. Psay.5Q.54
q. Dav.24.12
r. Dav.23.39-40
s. Dav.23.27-38
t. Dav.23.25-26
u. Dav.23.44-61

---

side because of Manifest Destiny,

11 [i]And general principles,

12 Not to mention God,

13 [j]And how He feels about democracy and freedom and so forth.

14 On the other side were the Indians, a bunch of [k]heathen, savage stone age tribes who didn't even know about horses and guns till the Spaniards showed up,

15 [l]And who couldn't even make alliances between their own tribes,

16 Not to mention being in the wrong,

17 [m]Because why on earth did they need all that land anyway?

CHAPTER 54

And so the Indian wars turned out to be a particularly glorious moment in Yank history,

2 Even though there have been lots and lots of glorious moments for the Yanks,

3 As any Yank will tell you.

4 Thanks to the heroism of the [n]U.S. Cavalry,

5 [o]Which always arrived in the nick of time,

6 [p]The Indians never got to first base,

7 And eventually had to give up,

8 [q]And stop robbing stage-coaches,

9 [r]And quit scalping white men,

10 [s]And swear off kidnaping defenseless pioneer babies to raise them as bloodthirsty savages,

11 [t]And all the rest of it too,

12 [u]Until the wild west had been completely tamed,

13 And all the brave frontier [a]marshals could put away their six-guns,
14 And breathe free,
15 Like all the other Yanks back home,
16 Except maybe for the negro Yanks,
17 [b]Who were about to lose all the privileges they'd enjoyed during Reconstruction.

CHAPTER 55

President Grant retired after his second term,
2 Which every U.S. president has done,
3 [c]Except one,
4 And went home to think over his illustrious career,
5 Until he died.
6 That left it up to a new president to decide whether or not the south had been reconstructed enough yet,
7 Which it apparently had,
8 Because the new president told the south that they were on their own now,
9 And would have to make do without any more carpetbaggers,
10 Because it was time to turn over a new leaf,
11 And stop living in the past,
12 [d]And get on with things,
13 [e]Which is the American Way.
14 And so the south plunged boldly forward into a [f]new era,
15 [g]And rebuilt their plantations,
16 And hired a bunch of [h]ex-slaves to pick cotton on them,
17 Because it had become kind of illegal for ex-slaves to do anything else,
18 Including vote,
19 Or hold public office,
20 Or be a witness in court,
21 [i]Or use any public facilities of any kind,
22 Or own property,
23 [j]Or have a trial before being executed,
24 Or talk to white women without being executed,
25 Or look at white women without being executed,
26 Or strike a white man without being executed,
27 Or be uppity in any way without being executed,
28 [k]Unless they got lynched first.
29 Even so, things stayed pretty tough in the south,
30 And a lot of [l]southern gentlemen had to find new professions,
31 [m]Because they didn't own any land or slaves anymore,
32 [n]Which is why so many of them eventually decided to be drunken southern novelists and playwrights,
33 And write about how [o]tragic it was to be an [p]impoverished aristocrat in the desolate south.

CHAPTER 56

Overall, though, the south was the only part of the U.S. that was really desolate.
2 Out west, everything was going great,
3 What with mining of gold and silver,
4 And cattle ranching,
5 [q]And about a billion acres of grain fields,
6 And no more Indians getting in the way.
7 Up north, [r]capitalism was thriving,
8 Because the Yanks had been paying pretty close attention

a. Ed.43.6-8
b. 48.13
c. Ext.39.18-19
d. 48.15
e. 7.2
f. Psom.59.1-5
g. Gnt.10.18-21
h. Psay.5A.4 Dav.23.13 & 22.7 & 22.26-27
i. 149.9-10
j. Frog.16.5
k. 50.22-26
l. 50.14
m. Brit.15.3
n. Swar.28.1-10
o. Gnt.15.19
p. Psong.17.1-7 & 50.1-8
q. Psong.18.1-4
r. Adam.2.3-10

when the [a]industrial revolution got started in Britain,

9 And they had never had any problem getting lots of [b]cheap labor to work twenty or thirty hours a day in factories,

10 [c]Since lots of cheap labor was arriving by the shipload in New York harbor every day,

11 From places like [d]Ireland,

12 And [e]Italy,

13 And [f]eastern Europe,

14 And everywhere else where there were people who had so little that it seemed better to exchange all your worldly possessions for the price of a steamship ticket to the New World.

15 [g]A lot of these people were regarded as the scum of the earth by the people back home,

16 [h]And so they didn't mind being treated the same way by Yank capitalists who wanted to earn huge profits from the sweat of their brow,

17 As long as they could just stay in [i]America,

18 And not get sent back home,

19 And get to bring their [j]children up in America,

20 Where they would learn how to speak English the [k]American way,

21 [l]And have a chance to get ahead,

22 Someday.

23 Naturally, all of this seemed reasonable to the Yank capitalists,

24 Who proceeded to build giant industrial empires,

25 In businesses like [m]steel,

26 And [n]oil,

27 And [o]coal,

28 And [p]railroads,

29 [q]And other stuff too,

30 While the immigrants had to

a. Brit.28.4-12
b. Brit.28.13-16
c. Adam.15.13-16
d. Psay.5J.3-4
e. Psay.5J.11-12
f. Psay.5J.5-7
g. Adam.14.1-14
h. Adam.16.1-8
i. Adam.17.5-9
j. Psom.41.1-9
k. Brit.31.12
l. Brit.5.2-3
m. Adam.25.6
n. Adam.25.5
o. 29.5
p. 29.6
q. Adam.19.1-3
r. Jefs.7.15-17
s. 24.5
t. Mawr.22.20
u. Brd.24.1
v. Psom.57.1-3
w. 56.8
x. Psong.8.1-11
y. Psay.5P.1-3
z. Grk.25.7
aa. Main.15.10-12
bb. Barb.2.13
cc. Krt.9.15
dd. 24.3
ee. 13.1-2
ff. Ann.18.1-5
gg. Ann.18.7

work for little more than the hope that it would all be different for their children,

31 [r]Because they believed in the American Dream,

32 Which said that [s]anyone born in America could grow up to be president someday,

33 [t]As long as he was a he,

34 [u]And white,

35 [v]And didn't talk with a funny accent.

CHAPTER 57

In fact, the [w]industrial revolution was so important to the Yanks that they completely stopped making history for about twenty or thirty years,

2 [x]So that they could make money instead.

3 [y]There were quite a few presidents during those years, of course,

4 But nobody remembers who they were exactly,

5 [z]Because there weren't any political issues,

6 Except for the [aa]tariff question,

7 Which was important because it was the only way to tell Republicans from Democrats,

8 [bb]Since the Democrats were either for the tariff or against it,

9 [cc]And the Republicans had the exactly opposite view.

10 Actually, about the only way a president could get any attention at this point was to be assassinated,

11 [dd]Which some of them were,

12 [ee]Because the Yanks have always been pretty adamant about their rights,

13 [ff]Including the right to free self-expression,

14 [gg]And the right to bear arms,

15 ªAnd the right to bear arms while exercising your right to free self-expression,

16 ᵇWhile firing off a hail of bullets at the same time,

17 If that's the way you want to do it,

18 ᶜBecause that's the American Way,

19 And always has been.

20 Anyway,

21 This helps explain why ᵈPresident Guiteau was gunned down by a dastardly assassin named ᵉGarfield,

22 Unless it was the other way around,

23 And why ᶠPresident McKinley got shot by somebody or other for some reason or other,

24 Shortly before ᵍTeddy Roosevelt became president,

25 Unless it was someone else instead.

a. *Ann.18.19*
b. *Ann.18.17*
c. *7.2*
d. *Dav.52.20*
e. *Dav.52.4*
f. *Dav.14.21*
g. *Dav.23.10*
h. *9.10*
i. *18.1*
j. *20.2*
k. *30.37*
l. *Ext.39.17-19*
m. *27.12*
n. *56.10-15*
o. *25.1-2*
p. *Psong.10.1*
q. *Ed.46.13-15*
r. *Ed.44.4*
s. *44.12-16*
t. *Brit.5.13-14*
u. *Adam.27.8*
v. *Oth.7.1-22*
w. *58.18*
x. *Nips.12.2-5*

CHAPTER 58

For a long long time, the Yanks hadn't had much of a foreign policy,

2 Because founding fathers like ʰWashington and ⁱMadison,

3 Unless it was ʲMonroe,

4 Had suggested that the U.S. didn't really need a foreign policy,

5 ᵏAs long as everybody else left the Yanks alone,

6 ˡWhich they mostly did,

7 Because even the Europeans were smart enough not to get in the way of ᵐManifest Destiny,

8 And besides, getting involved with the Yanks would mean having to deal with all the ⁿscum of the earth that had been kicked out of all the best nations in Europe,

9 The kind of scum who weren't at all well bred,

10 ᵒAnd would probably spit tobacco juice all over the carpet,

11 ᵖAnd talk about money,

12 While wearing ᑫcowboy outfits,

13 And shooting ʳsix-guns at everything in sight,

14 And going on and on about the ˢgrisly little undisciplined war they had fought with each other in the Yank wilderness a few years back,

15 ᵗWhich wasn't even a war by European standards,

16 ᵘBut a lower-class brawl between two rival gangs of rabble,

17 Squabbling about what to do with black people,

18 ᵛEven though the Chosen Nations of Europe had been showing everybody what to do with black people for several centuries at least.

19 Anyway,

20 After the Yanks had gone twenty or thirty years without having any history to speak of,

21 They decided that they should have some,

22 And since they hadn't had any foreign policy for practically forever,

23 They decided that might be a good place to start,

24 And besides, they were just about out of elbow room for Manifest Destiny at home,

25 ʷAnd who else knew as much about racial relations as the Yanks?

CHAPTER 59

And so it happened that the Yanks helped open up ˣJapan,

2 ^aWith the help of ^bCommodore Perry,

3 Who convinced the Nips that Yanks were nice guys,

4 And even if they weren't all that nice,

5 ^cThey had bigger guns than any of the little Oriental monkeys had,

6 ^dWhich explains why the Yanks and the Nips got to be such great friends over the years.

7 ^eThe Yanks also tagged along with the Brits when the British Empire decided to open up China,

8 ^fBecause the Yanks had gotten a lot of practice dealing with Chinks when they bought a bunch of them to build the transcontinental railroad a few years back,

9 ^gWhich meant the Yanks might be useful if the Brits had any race relations problems,

10 Even though the Brits never had any race relations problems,

11 ^hSince the only race the Brits thought had any rights at all was the Brit race,

12 Which made everything very simple.

13 When they saw that the Brits didn't really want their help,

14 The Yanks tried a little freelance ⁱcolonizing,

15 And rescued the ^jPhilippines from the Spanish,

16 Which was getting to be kind of a habit,

17 ^kSince the Yanks had already rescued Texas and California and Florida and other places from the Spics,

18 And had the whole procedure pretty well figured out,

19 ^lIncluding the rescue of Cuba,

---

a. Nips.12.6-7
b. Dav.10.10
c. Nips.12.8-9
d. Nips.12.10-11
e. Chnk.12.1-7
f. 29.6
g. 58.25
h. Brit.47.13-15
i. Exp.1.10-16
j. Spic.10.1
k. 28.1
*   30.1*
l. Ann.19.13
m. Dav.42.29-30
n. Psay.5Y.34
o. 30.17
p. 7.2
q. 30.46-48
r. 60.3
s. Dav.30.40
t. Dav.17.4
u. 54.2
v. Dav.14.21 & 30.40

---

20 Which always seems to need rescuing,

21 For some reason.

CHAPTER 60

All this foreign adventuring made Teddy Roosevelt famous,

2 Because he was a Rough Rider and had helped whip the Spics,

3 ^mAt San Juan Hill,

4 Which was Spanish,

5 And had to be captured at all costs,

6 ⁿBecause the Spanish had treacherously sunk a Yank ship called the Maine,

7 Which wasn't too smart,

8 ^oAs their Spic cousins in Mexico could have told them,

9 Because whenever you do something to the Yanks,

10 No matter how good your reasons might be,

11 The Yanks will remember it,

12 And get even,

13 If it's the last thing they ever do,

14 ^pBecause that's the American Way.

15 And so the Yanks remembered the Maine,

16 ^qJust like they remembered the Alamo,

17 ^rAnd ^sTeddy Roosevelt and the ^tRough Riders charged right up San Juan Hill and captured it,

18 Wherever it was,

19 Which nobody quite remembers,

20 Which doesn't matter anyway,

21 ^uBecause it was a glorious moment in Yank history and made Teddy Roosevelt a national hero,

22 Which explains why ^vTeddy

was vice president of the country when [a]President Guiteau got shot,

23 Thus making him the youngest president in U.S. history,

24 In spite of the fact that he actually had a college degree.

CHAPTER 61

However peculiar his qualifications were, Roosevelt turned out to be a great president,

2 Unless he was really a superficial jingoistic jerk instead,

3 Which is hard to say,

4 [b]Because he wasn't born in a log cabin,

5 [c]And didn't even spit tobacco juice on the carpet.

6 Even so, Teddy had a big [d]stick,

7 Which he needed to threaten everybody with,

8 Because the Yanks now had a foreign policy consisting of not taking anything from anybody,

9 [e]Except immigrants, of course,

10 Who were needed in the factories.

11 Teddy also tried to use his stick on the [f]trusts,

12 [g]Because nobody trusted them anymore,

13 And thought they should be busted,

14 [h]For some reason.

15 It was also Teddy who built the Panama Canal,

16 Including [i]appropriating the land from some [j]indigent Spic country in Central America,

17 And commissioning the slogan that got the Yanks to support the project,

18 Namely, "A man, a plan, a canal—Panama,"

19 Which is special because it

a. 57.21
b. 48.3
c. 96.13
d. Psay.5Q.47
e. Psom.54.5
f. Adam.26.17
g. Hall.8.1-2
h. Adam.26.1-15
i. 27.7
j. Spic.10.2-3
k. Dav.42.15
l. Psay.5Z.1-12
m. Ann.18.12
n. Psom.44.1-7 & 60.1-2
o. Spic.4.13 & 5.4-5
p. Ann.17.11-13
q. Dav.26.5-7
r. Psay.5Y.25

reads the same way even if you hold it up to a mirror,

20 Or something.

21 But after the canal was built, Teddy got tired of being president,

22 And told everybody to elect someone named [k]William Howard Taft,

23 Who weighed four hundred pounds,

24 And wanted to sit on the trusts,

25 Just to make sure.

CHAPTER 62

After Taft got elected, Teddy went off to [l]Africa to hunt for butterflies and tigers,

2 And when he had shot all the [m]butterflies and [n]tigers, he came home,

3 And was shocked to discover that Taft had messed everything all up,

4 Because he had stopped sitting on the trusts to go get a snack in the kitchen.

5 In fact, Teddy was so mad that he decided to start a third party called the Bull Moose Party,

6 [o]And run for president against Taft.

7 When all the votes had been counted, Teddy came in second,

8 [p]Ahead of Taft, who couldn't run very fast anyway,

9 But behind a man named [q]Woodrow Wilson,

10 [r]Who became president of the United States,

11 And changed the course of Yank history forever.

CHAPTER 63

By this time, the United States had kind of sneaked

up on the rest of the world,

2 ªWithout the rest of the world noticing much.

3 For example, the Yank love of capitalism had made the United States the richest nation in the world,

4 Even though the Europeans were just about to start a gigantic war to see who would become the Most ᵇChosen Nation in the world,

5 And didn't even invite the Yanks to participate,

6 ᶜBecause they kept forgetting the Yanks were there,

7 Which was basically okay with the Yanks,

8 Who were pretty ᵈproud of what they had accomplished without much help from the Europeans.

9 In fact, the Yanks actually had their own culture by this time,

10 Even if nobody else would have called it that,

11 Exactly.

CHAPTER 64

For example, in the time since the Revolution, the Yanks had produced several artists,

2 Even if nobody else in the world noticed,

3 Because Yank artists painted pictures of ᵉGeorge Washington,

4 Exclusively,

5 Which is fine if you're a Yank,

6 And proud of the ᶠfather of your country,

7 ᵍBut maybe not everybody's taste.

CHAPTER 65

Yank culture had also produced some ʰwriters,

---

a. 58.8-18
b. Exp.1.4-5
c. Mall.6.24-25
d. 21.6
e. 10.16
f. 10.6
g. Barb.3.3
h. 33.11
i. 33.6
j. Dav.9.7
　Ed.64.8
k. Dav.24.11
l. Ira.29.1-2
m. Gyp.3.1-2
n. 64.7
o. Dav.14.20
p. Psom.11.1-5
q. Psom.19.1-8
r. Psom.13.1-5
　Pnot.53.1-5
s. Dav.40.9
t. Psom.69.1
　& 69.1
　& 69.1
u. Pnot.11.1-5
v. Dav.41.12
　& 20.13

---

2 ⁱEven if nobody else in the world noticed.

3 For example, there was a Yank writer named ʲJames Fenimore Cooper,

4 Who would have been great,

5 Except that the ᵏpony express lost his mail-order writing course,

6 ˡOr something.

CHAPTER 66

There was another Yank writer named Washington Irving,

2 Who wrote about a funny-looking guy named ᵐIchabod,

3 Who had a pumpkin instead of a head,

4 Or something,

5 Which was just great,

6 ⁿIf you like that kind of thing.

CHAPTER 67

There was a Yank poet named °Henry Wadsworth Longfellow,

2 Who wrote about ᵖHiawatha,

3 And ᑫPaul Revere,

4 And ʳEvangeline,

5 And it all rhymed and everything.

CHAPTER 68

There was also a Yank writer named ˢHerman Melville,

2 Who loved the sea,

3 And thought that a really good novel had to be as long as a transoceanic voyage,

4 In a ᵗrowboat,

5 Which is why ᵘ'Moby Dick' is so great,

6 Since it's so long that no one has ever finished reading it,

7 Unless ᵛhe was making a transoceanic voyage in a rowboat,

8 And had nothing else to read.

CHAPTER 69

Another Yank writer named [a]Joseph Conrad liked the sea almost as much as Melville,

2 [b]But his novels weren't quite as long,

3 Probably because English wasn't his native language,

4 Which maybe explains why he picked strange un-American sounding titles sometimes,

5 Like [c]'Lord Jim,'

6 And [d]'Nostromo,'

7 And [e]'The Nigger of the Narcissus.'

8 Well,

9 Maybe not all of his titles are un-American,

10 [f]And besides, it was also Conrad who wrote a book called 'Heart of Darkness,'

11 Which must be pretty good,

12 [g]Because every Yank has heard of it.

CHAPTER 70

And then there was [h]Edgar Allan Poe,

2 [i]For some reason.

3 [j]It was Poe who invented the great Yank tradition that requires American writers to drink themselves to death,

4 Which proves how sensitive they are,

5 Even though they're Yanks.

6 [k]It was also Poe who wrote 'The Raven,'

7 Which every Yank has to memorize in school and goes something like,

8 "Once upon a something something weary,

9 [l]"Over many a quaint and something volume of forgotten something,

a. *Dav.32.4*
b. *Boul.21.9*
c. *Pnot.20.1-5*
d. *Frog.26.16*
   Krt.12.7
e. *Ed.71.11*
   Grk.13.13-15
f. *Ann.4.19*
   Ned.29.7-10
   Psom.69.1
   Wil.42.15
g. *Hill.E.1*
h. *Dav.14.26-27*
   & 6.4
i. *Psom.42.1-7*
j. *Swar.22.1-6*
   Yks.91.7
k. *Dav.47.16*
l. *Psom.75.10-11*
m. *Brit.22.20*
n. *Pnot.51.1-5*
o. *Psom.37.1-6*
   & 24.3-4
p. *Dav.14.26*
   Krt.9.15
   Ira.4.4-7
q. *Ned.42.6*
r. *Psom.36.3-4*
s. *Vin.49.5*
t. *Ed.74.4*
u. *Brit.29.10-13*
v. *Ira.12.3-4*

10 "Something something,

11 [m]"Nevermore,"

12 And proves just how great Poe must have been,

13 [n]Until he wrote all those horror stories,

14 [o]And drank himself to death,

15 Unless it was the other way around.

CHAPTER 71

There was also [p]Mark Twain,

2 Whose name was really something else,

3 As every Yank knows,

4 Something having to do with the [q]Mississippi River,

5 Which Twain liked to write about,

6 Because it was so full of people who talked in funny [r]dialects,

7 [s]Which are just hilarious,

8 If you're a Yank,

9 Including 'Tom Sawyer' and [t]'Huckleberry Hound,'

10 Which every Yank just loves,

11 And knows practically by heart,

12 Because they're so important to Yank culture,

13 For some reason.

CHAPTER 72

And Yank culture wasn't just limited to artists and writers, either.

2 For example, there were Yank architects who were brilliant,

3 And did a beautiful job of copying [u]Brit architecture all over New England,

4 [v]Not to mention a pretty fair job of copying Spic architecture all over Texas and California,

5 [a]As well as Frog architecture in New Orleans,
6 And other styles in other places too,
7 Except in the midwest, of course,
8 [b]Where absolutely everything looked like a grain elevator.

CHAPTER 73

Yank science was pretty special too.
2 For example, it was a Yank named [c]Benjamin Franklin who invented electricity,
3 Way back when,
4 [d]Using only a kite and a key,
5 Somehow,
6 And thus paved the way for a Yank named [e]Edison who invented absolutely everything,
7 Including the [f]light bulb,
8 And the [g]phonograph,
9 And the [h]electric company,
10 Not to mention [i]motion pictures,
11 Which were incredibly important,
12 Because [j]Alexander Graham Bell had just invented the [k]telephone,
13 [l]And motion pictures gave the Yanks something to talk to each other about,
14 [m]And other things too,
15 Things that would become more important later on.
16 And that wasn't all, either,
17 Because Yank science was so great that it had also invented something called an [n]aeroplane,
18 Which was going to change the [o]world,
19 Very soon,
20 If not right away,
21 And was therefore almost as important an invention as motion pictures.

a. Frog.22.4-5
b. 56.5
c. Dav.42.7
d. Ned.29.5
e. Dav.14.20
f. Zig.2.6
g. Hill.M.1
h. Adam.21.5-16
i. Dav.3.6-10
j. Dav.7.5
k. Psom.37.3 & 24.3-4
l. Dav.16.2
m. Dav.16.3-7
n. Adam.31.6 Mall.13.8
o. Hill.W.1 Psay.5W.1 Mall.13.8
p. Psom.5G.17
q. Brd.8.8-11
r. Gnt.10.18
s. Gnt.10.14-15
t. 63.6
u. Brit.48.8-13 Krt.23.1-6 Frog.33.1-5
v. Ned.1.1
w. 56.17 Krt.8.4 Brit.41.21 Frog.28.5
x. 133.5-7

CHAPTER 74

Another great Yank cultural accomplishment was music,
2 [p]Because it was the Yanks who invented jazz,
3 [q]Which maybe had something to do with all the black people in the country,
4 [r]And helps explains why black people were almost always allowed to give concerts,
5 [s]Even though they couldn't buy a ticket to one.
6 But the popularity of jazz hadn't really become worldwide yet at the time Woodrow Wilson became president,
7 [t]Because it was Wilson who was responsible for finally making the rest of the world notice that America was there,
8 Whether they liked it or not.

CHAPTER 75

Of course, when he started out, Wilson didn't have that much interest in the rest of the world.
2 [u]For example, it was during Wilson's first term that the Europeans finally went completely nuts and started World War I,
3 [v]Which most of the Yanks didn't understand,
4 [w]Or even care about,
5 At all.
6 After thinking it over very carefully,
7 [x]Wilson decided that the best thing to do about World War I was nothing,
8 At all,

9 Which was an enormously popular strategy,

10 ^aAnd got him reelected to a second term,

11 With a huge mandate to keep on doing nothing at all,

12 Which he did,

13 ^bUntil something happened,

14 Something that wouldn't have happened if the Europeans had known anything at all about the Yanks,

15 ^cWhich they didn't.

CHAPTER 76

What happened was that the Krauts sank a Brit ship called the ^dLusitania,

2 Which was loaded with ^eYanks,

3 In spite of the fact that the Krauts had warned the Yanks to stay away from Brit ships if they didn't want to get hurt.

4 Of course, the Krauts thought it would be okay to give the Yanks a slightly more serious warning,

5 Because they had always thought the Yanks were kind of silly,

6 And undisciplined,

7 And didn't know anything about fighting wars anyway,

8 ^fBecause after all, just look at that gruesome little skirmish they had back there in the nineteenth century,

9 ^gWhich proved they didn't know anything about war.

10 ^hThe only problem was, the Krauts had sunk a ship that had Yanks on it,

11 ⁱWhich meant that the Yanks would "Remember the Lusitania,"

12 Forever,

a. Psay.5Y.26
b. Psay.5D.1
c. 63.6
d. Psay.5D.8 & 5Y.26
e. Krt.26.3-4
f. 58.15-16
g. Krt.8.4 Brit.41.21 Frog.28.5
h. 60.7
i. 60.16
j. 60.14
k. 44.16
l. 42.1-5 44.3-11
m. Swar.26.8-9
n. 78.8
o. Grk.20.8
p. Kens.22.10

13 And would find a way to get even,

14 No matter how much it cost,

15 ^jBecause that's the American Way,

16 And so forth,

17 And so on.

18 Besides, the more Wilson thought about it,

19 The more he realized that it was up to the Yanks to save the Europeans from themselves,

20 Because it looked very much to Wilson as if the Europeans had just invented the concept of ^ktotal war,

21 ^lOnly fifty years or so after Lincoln and Grant had invented it.

22 This meant that *somebody* would have to teach the Europeans how to get along with one another,

23 Because they couldn't just keep going out and slaughtering twenty or thirty million of each other's troops every few years or so,

24 Indefinitely,

25 Without causing major problems for everybody else,

26 ^mIncluding the Yanks.

CHAPTER 77

And so, the Yanks declared war on Germany and Austria,

2 ⁿSo that they could go over there and fight the war to end all wars,

3 And save the world for ^odemocracy,

4 Not to mention get even with the Krauts,

5 No matter what it cost.

6 ^pArmed with these great principles, the Yanks drafted a whole bunch of doughboys,

7 And sailed off to [a]Europe to join the Brits and the Frogs in the enormous [b]trench that had been dug in the middle of France,
8 Where the combined military might of the most powerful nations on earth had been locked in mortal combat for years,
9 [c]Equipped with the most modern and deadly weapons anyone had ever seen,
10 [d]Which they fired at each other from point-blank range,
11 Until the fields of France were soaked in the blood of tens of millions of dead Europeans,
12 Including the blood of millions and millions of Krauts,
13 [e]Who should have had more sense than to sink a ship carrying several hundred Yanks,
14 [f]Because now they were really going to get it.

CHAPTER 78

One hundred thousand dead doughboys later,
2 The Krauts surrendered,
3 [g]Which is to say, they signed an armistice,
4 Because Krauts don't like to surrender,
5 [h]Even when they're whipped.
6 Of course, the actual terms of the peace treaty still had to be worked out,
7 Which Wilson had a lot of [i]ideas about,
8 [j]Because he really wasn't kidding about the war to end all wars,
9 [k]And making the world safe for democracy,
10 And other stuff like that.
11 Of course, the other Allies had some ideas of their own,
12 [l]Especially the Frogs.

a. Barb.4.18
b. Frog.33.6-8
c. 40.4
d. 40.5
e. 76.10
f. Psay.5Y.23
g. Psay.5Y.18
h. Krt.27.1-4
i. Psay.5E.5-9
j. 77.2
k. 77.3
l. Rom.10.4
m. 80.4
n. Frog.20.3-11
o. Krt.39.1-4
p. Frog.39.14-15
q. 79.2
r. Brit.15.31
s. 79.5
t. 79.6
u. Exp.1.19-25
v. 80.6
w. 78.1
x. 80.8
y. 80.9

CHAPTER 79

The way the Frogs looked at it,
2 [m]The Krauts needed to be punished,
3 To death,
4 [n]Because they'd already had their second chance,
5 [o]And had proven they couldn't be trusted,
6 And weren't ever going to behave,
7 Period.

CHAPTER 80

The other Allies weren't quite as hysterical as the Frogs,
2 [p]Because nobody ever is,
3 But the way they looked at it,
4 [q]The Krauts needed to be punished,
5 Extremely severely,
6 Because they'd killed millions and millions of people,
7 [r]Even if you didn't count the Frogs,
8 [s]And had proven they couldn't be trusted,
9 [t]And weren't ever going to behave,
10 And if they should ever get a second chance,
11 They might even win the next time around.

CHAPTER 81

The way Wilson looked at it, though,
2 [u]Europe needed a new way to settle its disagreements,
3 [v]Because they'd killed an awful lot of people,
4 [w]Including one hundred *thousand* Yanks,
5 [x]And had proven they couldn't be trusted,
6 [y]And weren't ever going to behave,

7 Unless they buried the hatchet once and for all,

8 And started over,

9 With something like a League of Nations to help them sort out all their petty quarrels and disputes,

10 So they wouldn't annihilate the planet the next time some [a]feeble-minded aristocrat bit the dust on a road trip.

CHAPTER 82

And so Wilson talked,

2 And the Brits and the Italians and the Russkies listened,

3 [b]And the Frogs pouted,

4 And eventually they all agreed to a [c]compromise.

5 Wilson had wanted peace terms that wouldn't destroy the Krauts,

6 Or even make them bitter,

7 [d]Because if you were nice to the Krauts, they would be nice back.

8 The Frogs had wanted peace terms that would basically transfer the entire gross national product of Germany to the Allies,

9 [e]Forever,

10 And so much the better if the Krauts were bitter,

11 Because with terms like that, bitter looks would be about all the hostility they'd be able to afford,

12 [f]Forever.

13 The way things turned out, the terms of the treaty that everybody signed were somewhere between what Wilson wanted and what the Frogs wanted.

14 For example, the Krauts had to pay war reparations,

a. Dav.46.19
b. Brit.22.12
c. 21.11-13
d. Al.6.21
e. Paul.7.2
f. Paul.7.2
g. Krt.27.6
h. Krt.27.7
i. Krt.27.8
j. Jeff.10.15
k. Frog.34.7
l. 81.9
m. Hall.8.1-2
n. 78.8-9
*   81.3-9*
*   Forg.9.8-11*
o. Ira.43.14
p. Jeff.10.14-15
q. 76.10
r. 76.11-13
s. 76.14
t. 78.1-2
u. 83.1
v. Psong.40.1
w. Adam.26.2-4

15 [g]Not quite enough to destroy their country forever,

16 [h]But definitely enough to make them bitter,

17 [i]Which satisfied nobody on either side,

18 [j]And was about par for European diplomacy.

CHAPTER 83

In spite of all the grousing everybody did about the [k]Treaty of Versailles,

2 Wilson had gotten the thing he wanted most,

3 Which was agreement by the Europeans to participate in a [l]League of Nations,

4 [m]As soon as the U.S. Congress approved the idea too.

5 And so Wilson went home to America,

6 [n]And explained everything to the Yanks,

7 [o]Who weren't interested,

8 [p]At all.

CHAPTER 84

The way the Yanks looked at it,

2 [q]The Krauts had killed a few hundred Yanks,

3 [r]And the Yanks had therefore been obligated to get even,

4 [s]No matter how much it cost,

5 [t]Although one hundred thousand doughboys was a little on the high side,

6 Any way you looked at it,

7 But at least it was over now,

8 [u]And settled,

9 [v]And time to go back to making money and other important things like that,

10 [w]Because who needs Europe anyway,

11 And it's just not smart to be

involved with them on any continuing basis,

12 Since they're all obviously crazy,

13 And what's in it for the Yanks,

14 Except grief and heartache?

CHAPTER 85

Wilson was so upset about the Yanks' refusal to join the League of Nations that he died,

2 And left somebody else in charge,

3 But none of the Yanks really noticed,

4 Because they were all excited about a noble ªexperiment they wanted to try,

5 And didn't have any time to waste on boring stuff like politics and government,

6 No matter who was in the White House,

7 Even ᵇwhat's-his-name from Ohio,

8 ᶜWho wouldn't ever have been elected in a million years if the ladies hadn't somehow finagled voting rights for themselves.

9 The experiment was called ᵈProhibition,

10 And involved making it illegal to produce, sell, or drink alcoholic spirits of any kind,

11 For some reason.

CHAPTER 86

Nobody really knows how Prohibition came about,

2 Except that there was a lady with an ax,

3 Named ᵉCarrie Nation,

4 ᶠAnd a whole bunch of self-righteous Puritans who suddenly

a. 85.9
b. Dav.22.12
c. Mawr.22.20
d. Psay.5D.11
e. Dav.20.7-8
f. Barb.7.3
g. Ed.60.17
h. 76.15
i. Kens.25.11-12
j. Lies.10.6
k. Carl.3.8
l. Psong.50.1-5
m. Psong.38.1-2
n. Psong.57.1-4
o. Psong.21.1-8
p. Psong.51.1-4
q. Psong.52.1-4
r. Psong.53.5-9
s. Psong.58.1-5
t. Psong.54.1-4
u. Psp.2.1-2
v. Psp.3.1-2

came out of the woodwork in droves,

5 And passed an amendment to the Constitution,

6 ᵍSomehow,

7 That closed all the bars and saloons and liquors stores,

8 Overnight.

CHAPTER 87

Of course, the Yanks never like to be told what to do,

2 By anybody,

3 And as soon as it was illegal to drink alcohol,

4 ¹They remembered they were thirsty,

5 And besides, they deserved a drink,

6 After all they had been through,

7 ʲWhat with winning the war to end all wars,

8 ᵏAnd making the world safe for democracy,

9 And then getting home just in time to start the Roaring Twenties and all,

10 So set 'em up, bartender,

11 If you please.

CHAPTER 88

And so the Yanks had a big party,

2 And everybody was invited,

3 ᵐIncluding bootleggers,

4 ⁿAnd gangsters,

5 ᵒAnd businessmen,

6 ᵖAnd flappers,

7 ۹And writers,

8 ʳAnd politicians,

9 ˢAnd policemen,

10 ᵗAnd ladies,

11 ᵘAnd anybody else who knew the password,

12 ᵛAnd the address of the nearest speakeasy.

CHAPTER 89

The Yanks have always liked parties,

2 And it seemed like they had a lot to celebrate,

3 Because everything was booming,

4 [a]What with Mr. Henry Ford and his invention of assembly lines,

5 [b]And Mr. Sears Roebuck and his invention of retail advertising,

6 [c]And all the stocks on Wall Street going through the roof,

7 [d]And all the girls getting a little freer with their favors,

8 [e]And jazz music busting out all over,

9 And Hollywood bulging with [f]stars,

10 And America suddenly the richest and most prosperous nation in the whole world,

11 [g]And wasn't everything just great?

CHAPTER 90

Except that it wasn't all completely great,

2 [h]Because there was a Yank generation that got lost,

3 Somehow,

4 For some reason having to do with the World War,

5 And what it meant,

6 Or something.

7 [i]A lot of the Yanks who got lost were writers and artists and intellectuals,

8 Who suddenly found they just weren't comfortable in America anymore,

9 Because the Yanks back home seemed kind of naive,

10 And overoptimistic,

11 And far too happy,

12 And not nearly as much fun

a. *Adam.22.1-9*
b. *Adam.30.1-16*
c. *Adam.38.2-15*
   Psong.28.1-6
d. *Psong.49.1-3*
e. *89.7*
f. *Dav.4.8-10*
g. *Psp.1.5*
h. *Grk.18.13-16*
i. *Swar.1.1*
j. *Krt.24.2-3*
k. *70.3*
l. *Frog.22.1-5*
m. *44.22*
n. *Psong.42.1*
o. *Dav.42.22*
p. *Psay.5Q.56*
q. *Lies.14.5*
r. *Rom.10.1-2*
s. *Gnt.16.11-12*
t. *Psay.5Q.23*
u. *Pnot.43.1-5*

to be with as people who have seen a few million of their most promising youth blown away in an [j]insanely brutal war.

13 [k]Besides, Yank writers and artists and intellectuals have always needed a ready supply of really good whiskey,

14 Which is easier to find in a country where alcohol is legal,

15 Like France.

CHAPTER 91

And so a whole bunch of Yanks started calling themselves expatriates,

2 [l]And moved to Paris, France,

3 Where all the best writers and artists and intellectuals were doing their [m]drinking at the time,

4 And got together to figure out what it all meant,

5 Like the War and everything,

6 Which they did,

7 [n]Because when you have enough really good whiskey, you can figure out almost anything.

CHAPTER 92

For example, there was a Yank expatriate named [o]Ernest Hemingway,

2 Who figured out that war was pretty awful,

3 [p]Since war is an inevitable part of life,

4 [q]Which is also basically awful,

5 [r]Because things keep happening,

6 And a lot of the things that happen are just [s]tragicomic accidents,

7 [t]Like maybe your arms get shot off in World War I,

8 [u]Or maybe you lose the love

of your life in childbirth during World War I,

9 Or something like that,

10 ªWhich doesn't really mean anything,

11 ᵇSo you have to kind of put up with it,

12 ᶜAnd be very very picky about what kind of alcohol you drink before, during, and after your meal.

CHAPTER 93

There was another Yank expatriate named ᵈF. Scott Fitzgerald,

2 ᵉWho figured out that Hemingway was absolutely right,

3 But if you didn't see any of World War I, you had to write about something else,

4 ᶠLike what it was like to have lots and lots of money,

5 ᵍAnd fall in love with the wrong woman,

6 ʰAnd get utterly destroyed,

7 Or something like that,

8 Which means something or other,

9 Unless it doesn't,

10 ¹But either way, you're going to need a drink,

11 Because things sure aren't getting any better.

CHAPTER 94

There was also a Yank expatriate named ʲGertrude Stein,

2 Who figured out that the Yanks were basically fools,

3 ᵏWho could be fooled all of the time,

4 So why not do it,

5 As much as possible?

6 ¹So Gertrude wrote a bunch of peculiar books,

a. *Frog.35.6*
b. *F&J.11.7*
c. *Vin.20.1-6*
d. *Dav.20.34*
e. *Brit.22.20*
f. *Brit.15.37*
   Ed.65.7
   Yks.8.3
   Main.22.10
   Adam.16.9
g. *Pnot.17.1-3*
h. *Pnot.17.4-5*
i. *87.10-11*
j. *Ed.28.6*
k. *Psay.5Q.55*
l. *Ed.28.1*
m. *Spic.14.11-12*
n. *Frog.30.9-10*
o. *Psong.29.1-7*
p. *94.12*
q. *Ned.1.1-2*
r. *91.1-2*
s. *90.9-12*
t. *Psong.56.2*
u. *Psay.5Q.24*

7 That were very much admired by the intellectuals back home,

8 ᵐAnd discovered a bunch of great artists,

9 That were very much admired by the intellectuals back home,

10 *And* by the intellectuals in Europe,

11 ⁿWho were tired of seeing things the way they looked on the surface,

12 And thought they'd look better in broken little pieces,

13 Which seemed like a more accurate depiction of the world.

CHAPTER 95

It took a while for the Yanks back home to realize that the European intellectuals were right,

2 Which they realized all of a sudden,

3 ºOn the day the stock market crashed,

4 ᵖAnd smashed the Yank economy into a bunch of broken little pieces,

5 Not to mention the European economy,

6 Which was even worse,

7 If that was possible.

8 ᑫWhen the gloom of the Great Depression settled over America,

9 ʳA lot of the expatriates came back home,

10 ˢBecause the Yanks were a lot easier to take without all that naive optimism,

11 ᵗAnd besides, it was a cinch that the depression would nail the coffin lid shut on Prohibition,

12 Because if a Yank can't have any money,

13 ᵘYou can be sure he's not going to stand for being thirsty too.

CHAPTER 96

Now that there was a Great Depression,

2 The Yanks suddenly got interested in politics again,

3 And discovered that there was someone in the White House called ªHubert Heever,

4 Or something like that,

5 Who nobody could remember how he got there,

6 ᵇExcept that everything must be his fault,

7 And he should be sent home.

8 So they elected a brand-new president,

9 Called ᶜFranklin Delano Roosevelt,

10 Who was honest and great,

11 Even though he wasn't born in a log cabin,

12 And talked with a snooty accent,

13 Which he got from Harvard or someplace like that,

14 And even wore pince-nez and a cigarette holder,

15 For some reason.

CHAPTER 97

But Roosevelt was really great anyway,

2 ᵈBecause he offered the Yanks a new deal,

3 Based on the idea that what democracy was all about was equality,

4 ᵉAnd how nobody was really any better than anybody else,

5 Which meant that it was up to the government to kind of even things out,

6 ᶠAnd take money away from the people who had too much of it,

7 ᵍAnd give it to the people who didn't have enough of it,

8 Because that was only fair,

a. Psom.3.1-6
b. Dav.27.11
c. Dav.26.15
d. Ira.21.33
e. Carl.4.8-9
f. Adam.26.17
g. Adam.27.8
h. 95.2-4
i. Brit.15.22
j. 76.15
k. 47.2
l. Vin.49.4-11
m. Chr.3.1-2
n. Adam.12.7-9
o. Brd.3.2-3
p. Kens.22.1
q. Carl.3.12
r. Adam.40.13-15
s. Dav.27.4
t. Psong.59.1-3
u. Adam.28.1-10

9 ʰAnd besides, there was a tremendous majority of Yanks who didn't have enough money,

10 ⁱAnd really liked the idea of getting even with the ones who did,

11 ʲWhich is the American Way,

12 ᵏSince Yanks weren't allowed to go off and start their own country anytime they felt like it,

13 Anymore.

CHAPTER 98

And so Roosevelt saved the capitalist system in America,

2 ᵐBy forming a giant coalition of all the Yanks who had been oppressed in the past,

3 ⁿIncluding all the European immigrants,

4 ᵒAnd all the black people who were allowed to vote,

5 ᵖAnd all the poor white trash who had always had to take dirty, dangerous jobs for almost no pay,

6 And a bunch of others too,

7 So that the greatest goods could be taken from the richest numbers,

8 ᑫOr something like that,

9 And everything would be fair from now on,

10 ʳIncluding government jobs for some of the people who didn't have any,

11 ˢAnd relief for the ones who still didn't have jobs after that,

12 ᵗAnd higher taxes for the rich capitalists who had destroyed the economy in the first place,

13 ᵘAnd labor unions for all the people who had to work for rich capitalists,

14 [a]And a brand-new supreme court to interpret the Constitution for the greatest number of goods,

15 [b]Except that that one didn't work out too well and Roosevelt had to keep the old supreme court the way it was,

16 But it turned out all right anyway,

17 [c]Because he had fireside chats on the radio,

18 [d]And talked directly to the Yanks about how things ought to be,

19 [e]And got elected to a second term,

20 [f]Even though the Great Depression was almost as bad as when he started,

21 [g]Because for now the Yanks were content with the fact that at least nobody rich was getting away with anything,

22 For once.

CHAPTER 99

By now, of course, the [h]expatriates were all back home,

2 Because strange things were happening in Europe,

3 And there were fascists all over the place,

4 [i]In Germany,

5 [j]And Italy,

6 [k]And Spain,

7 [l]Where the trains were all running on time,

8 [m]And where the Jews and left-wingers and dissidents were all running for their lives,

9 Which made it important to come home,

10 [n]And lecture the Yanks about their social and political responsibilities,

a. *Hall.8.1-2*
Yks.13.17
b. *12.11-17*
c. *Vin.48.21*
d. *Vin.48.22*
e. *Psay.5D.15*
f. *Psay.5Q.6*
g. *Adam.41.6-11*
h. *95.9*
i. *Krt.29.1-10*
j. *Psong.57.1*
k. *Spic.14.1-3*
l. *Spic.15.3*
m. *Spic.7.12*
n. *Carl.9.1-10*
o. *97.3*
p. *98.7*
q. *98.22*
r. *Vin.3.12-13*
s. *Dav.27.5-15*
t. *Hill.U.1*
Hill.S.1
Hill.A.1
u. *Vin.3.12-13*
v. *Psp.1.4*
w. *Vin.3.12-13*
x. *Psp.1.6*
y. *93.1*
z. *Lies.10.9*
& 10.9
aa. *Dav.14.26*
& 27.15
bb. *55.32*
cc. *Gnt.15.18-19*
Pnot.50.1-5
dd. *Psp.1.5*
ee. *Spic.12.8*
ff. *92.1*

11 Which they were kind of in the mood for anyway,

12 What with their new interest in [o]equality and the [p]greatest good and so forth,

13 And not really having any money to spend anyhow.

CHAPTER 100

And so, Yank culture finally started getting serious,

2 [q]And talking about real life,

3 Including a writer named [r]John Steinbeck,

4 [s]Who had noticed that poor white trash didn't have any money,

5 [t]And a writer named [u]John Dos Passos who had noticed that life in America wasn't completely fair,

6 [v]And a writer named [w]John O'Hara who had noticed that life in America wasn't completely fair even if you had a little money,

7 [x]And a writer named [y]F. Scott Fitzgerald who had noticed that life in America wasn't completely fair even if you had lots and lots of money,

8 [z]And a writer named [aa]William Faulkner who had noticed that life in the south was so [bb]unfair that it could drive you to drink,

9 [cc]And a playwright named Eugene O'Neill who had noticed that life was like some tragic comedy of errors,

10 [dd]Especially if you have a bunch of alcoholic relatives,

11 [ee]And a certified literary genius named [ff]Hemingway who noticed that life wasn't completely fair even if you used a lot of picturesque Spanish words in italics,

151

12 [a]Especially if you were trying to blow up a fascist bridge in Spain,

13 [b]Which is such a universal experience that it kind of proved how everybody was really in the same boat,

14 [c]Even if the overwhelming majority of Yanks still didn't have any interest at all in getting involved with the Europeans again,

15 [d]No matter how picturesque they were.

CHAPTER 101

In fact, the Yanks had decided to really put their foot down this time,

2 And not get involved no matter what,

3 Because now that [e]Prohibition had been repealed,

4 The Yanks had better things to do than get tricked into another European comic opera,

5 Which always featured a lot of elaborate [f]plots, [g]fancy costumes, and [h]blood-drenched battlefields,

6 [i]And not much else.

7 So the Yanks stuck pretty firmly to their policy of ignoring Europe,

8 And when the newsreels started filling up with great [j]comic-opera footage of Nazi rallies that were even more elaborately staged than a [k]Busby Berkeley production number,

9 The Yanks just yawned and told [l]Kraut jokes.

10 When the Italians topped the Krauts by making [m]Mussolini and his henchmen wear even sillier uniforms than the Nazis,

11 The Yanks just yawned and told [n]Wop jokes.

a. Vin.72.8
b. Psom.76.1-6
*   F&J.14.4*
c. 84.10-14
d. Psay.5Q.75
e. Psong.58.3
f. F&J.15.2-4
g. Krt.5.13-14
*   Brit.5.6*
*   Frog.9.2*
h. 77.11
i. Barb.1.8
j. Dav.29.8-12
k. Dav.29.6
l. Psay.5J.14
m. Dav.30.40
n. Psay.5J.12
o. Krt.31.6-7
p. Psay.5J.7
q. Brit.51.1-8
r. Psay.5J.9
s. Psay.5J.10
t. Brit.51.11-16
u. Ed.39.9
v. Ned.20.35-37
w. Brit.51.19-23
x. Psay.5J.6
y. 101.7
z. Frog.37.1-8
aa. 101.15
bb. Krt.24.11

12 [o]When rumors started circulating that the Krauts were persecuting the Jews and even putting some of them in concentration camps,

13 The Yanks just yawned and told [p]Jew jokes.

14 [q]When Hitler started getting really rambunctious and annexed Austria,

15 The Yanks yawned and discovered they didn't know any jokes about Austrians, so they laughed instead at the spineless [r]Frogs and [s]Brits who let Hitler get away with it.

16 [t]When Hitler grabbed Czechoslovakia, the Yanks laughed at [u]Neville Chamberlain and his prissy little [v]umbrella.

17 [w]And when Hitler invaded Poland, the Yanks breathed a sigh of relief,

18 Because if there's one thing the Yanks have a lot of, it's [x]Polish jokes.

CHAPTER 102

When they had all stopped laughing about Poland,

2 [y]The Yanks discovered that it was getting a lot harder all of a sudden to completely ignore Hitler,

3 Because comical as he was,

4 He certainly seemed to have the Europeans' number,

5 And wasn't wasting any time at all in taking what he wanted.

6 [z]So even though it wasn't any big surprise when the Krauts demolished the Maginot Line in about an hour and a half,

7 [aa]All the Frog jokes the Yanks told each other were starting to have a hollow ring,

8 [bb]Because there wasn't going

to be a big trench in France this time,

9 ^aWhich meant that the Nazis just might pull it off and finally conquer all of Europe,

10 ^bUnless the Yanks decided to stop them,

11 Which they didn't want to,

12 At all,

13 Although it was real hard to see how it could be done by anybody *but* the Yanks,

14 ^cWho are braver and smarter and richer and better than everyone else,

15 ^dAnd always have God on their side anyway,

16 Whenever they're involved,

17 If they want to be involved, that is,

18 ^eWhich they most definitely didn't,

19 This time anyway.

20 And so maybe it was better to hope that God would help the Brits out this time,

21 Since the Brits weren't fighting the Yanks this time,

22 So maybe they'd do a better job of it than ^fusual,

23 This time.

CHAPTER 103

It was at about this point that the Yanks had to have another presidential election,

2 Which happens every four years or so,

3 ^gWhether anyone is paying attention or not.

4 But this time they were paying attention,

5 Because they had such definite views on foreign policy this time,

6 And knew they needed someone who looked at it like they did,

a. 139.11-12
b. Ext.52.16
c. 71.3
d. 53.13
e. 101.4
f. Brit.24.1-4
  & 35.1-2
  Mall.13.8
g. Rom.10.1-2
h. 96.9
i. 14.1-5
j. Chr.3.2-7
k. 98.1
l. Lies.10.11
m. Rom.3.16-17
n. 103.7-8
o. 96.11
p. Psom.57.1-6
  Yks.87.11
q. Dav.20.26
r. Hall.4.3

7 Which is to say they needed a president who wasn't exactly neutral,

8 But who wasn't exactly committed to doing anything either,

9 Which is why ^hRoosevelt was so perfect,

10 Even though he had already served two terms,

11 ⁱWhich is all any president had ever served before.

12 ^jExcept that Roosevelt was special,

13 ^kFor some reason,

14 Like with his foreign policy,

15 And other stuff too,

16 Which made it okay to re-elect him for a third term,

17 Because when they asked him about it,

18 ^lRoosevelt said it would be okay,

19 ^mAnd who would know better about that than the president of the United States?

20 So Roosevelt got reelected,

21 ⁿAnd went on with his brilliant foreign policy,

22 Which was as honest and great as it could possibly be,

23 ^oConsidering that Roosevelt hadn't actually been born in a log cabin.

CHAPTER 104

The only problem was, the Brits had pretty well made up their mind that they couldn't beat the Krauts alone,

2 ^pWhich meant that they wanted the Yanks to do it,

3 And so ^qWinston Churchill got on the radio,

4 And started sounding off in a pretty picturesque way,

5 Going on about ^rblood, sweat, and tears,

6 And fighting them on the beaches,

7 [a]And their finest hour,

8 And a bunch of other stuff too,

9 [b]Until the Yanks had this picture in their head of the Brits doing it the hard way,

10 All alone,

11 [c]With nothing more than half a dozen Spitfires,

12 And a tough old [d]prime minister with a [e]pistol in his pocket,

13 Who was honest and great,

14 [f]Even if he hadn't been born in a log cabin,

15 Which was important to remember,

16 [g]Because Churchill was a Brit,

17 And since when had the Brits ever done anything for the Yanks,

18 Except look down their nose,

19 And lift their eyebrow,

20 And play with their [h]monocle in a condescending way,

21 [i]Unless they were in over their heads in a gigantic world war that is,

22 Again,

23 [j]Which is why the Yanks absolutely positively were not going to get involved again,

24 No matter how great Churchill was,

25 [k]Period,

26 And weren't going to help out at all,

27 [l]Unless you count lending them a whole bunch of ships and weapons and food,

28 [m]And making sure they got across the North Atlantic to Great Britain,

29 [n]Even if that wasn't going to save them anyway.

a. Chr.1.7
b. Brit.11.10
c. 73.17-19
d. Psom.61.1-8
e. Adam.25.9
f. 96.11
g. Psom.75.10
h. Ed.10.7
i. Psom.3.1-2
j. Psay.2.1
k. Ext.16.26
l. Brit.15.30-31
m. 76.3
n. 102.23
o. Drex.6.1
p. Ann.2.32
q. Ann.6.1
r. Ann.10.1
s. Krt.39.14
t. Nips.16.1
u. Krt.7.17
v. Hill.W.1-3
w. Hall.2.6-8

CHAPTER 105

And so the Yanks stayed firm,

2 [o]Through the fall of France,

3 [p]And the narrow escape at Dunkirk,

4 [q]And the fall of Norway,

5 [r]And the Battle of Britain,

6 [s]And then through Hitler's invasion of Russia,

7 And even through a lot of weird stuff with the Japanese,

8 Who no Yank had ever given any thought to before,

9 [t]Until they started acting like they owned the Pacific or something,

10 Which couldn't be true,

11 Because the Yank government seemed to be getting pretty cross with Japan,

12 And they wouldn't do that unless the Japanese were in the wrong,

13 [u]And wanted something in the South Pacific that didn't belong to them,

14 Which would have to be worked out somehow,

15 If the Yanks could only figure out what it was in the South Pacific that anybody would want,

16 [v]Which would be easier to do if you could figure out where the South Pacific was in the first place,

17 [w]Except that's the government's job anyway,

18 And they'll work it all out at the peace talks,

19 Because nobody was going to trick the Yanks into another big foreign war,

20 This time,

21 And besides, those little monkeys in Japan know better

than to mess with the Yanks, don't they?

22 Sure they do.

CHAPTER 106

But then came the day that will live in infamy,

2 Forever,

3 Never to be forgotten by the Yanks,

4 Ever,

5 As long as there is still a single Yank alive to remember the exact moment when Japan and Germany lost the war,

6 [a]Which happened at seven o'clock A.M., Pacific time,

7 [b]On December 7th,

8 1940-[c]something,

9 When about a million Nip [d]planes and ships came out of nowhere,

10 [e]And attacked Pearl Harbor,

11 Without warning,

12 Completely by surprise,

13 And killed about two *thousand* Yanks[f],

14 [g]For no reason.

CHAPTER 107

The Yanks were mad about Pearl Harbor, of course,

2 But maybe not quite as mad as they were [h]surprised,

3 And offended,

4 Because how did the Nips ever get the idea that a sneak attack on the Yanks was a good idea?

5 After all, it hasn't ever been a good idea to make the Yanks mad,

6 [i]Like with the Alamo,

7 [j]And the Maine,

8 [k]And the Lusitania,

9 [l]Which should have tipped off

a. Psom.31.3-6 & 24.3

b. Psay.5L.7

c. Psp.3.4

d. Drex.2.9

e. Nips.18.10 Ann.6.1 & 10.1 & 2.32

f. Dav.34.15

g. Nips.17.1-11

h. Nips.19.2

i. 30.41-48

j. 60.15-21

k. 76.10-17

l. Psay.5A.19

m. Mall.6.9-12

n. Nips.20.1-4

o. 104.27

p. Dav.34.12-13

q. Nips.2.17

the Nips that if they did something to the Yanks,

10 Something unspeakable like Pearl Harbor, for example,

11 The Yanks would remember it,

12 Forever,

13 And find a way to get even,

14 No matter how much it cost,

15 And now that you mention it,

16 [m]Remember the Lusitania?

17 Which explains why the Yanks declared war on Japan and Germany within a few hours of the attack on Pearl Harbor,

18 Because they were all going to get it now,

19 As soon as the Yanks remembered where they'd put their army and their weapons and other stuff like that.

CHAPTER 108

By December 8th, about three million Yanks had enlisted,

2 Which made it all the more important to remember where the army was,

3 Which took about another eight or nine months,

4 Because the truth was, in all the excitement of the depression and everything,

5 [n]The Yanks had scrapped most of their military,

6 [o]Or lent it to the Brits,

7 Except for the [p]Pacific fleet, of course,

8 Which was mostly sitting at the bottom of Pearl Harbor,

9 [q]Thanks to those nodding, smiling little barbarians in Japan,

10 Who were going to get a big lesson,

11 ªIf there was any place left in the South Pacific to fight over by the time the Yanks had built some more war stuff,

12 Which they were doing,

13 In a big way.

CHAPTER 109

And so the Yanks had to put up with about a year of bad news,

2 ᵇAs the Philippines fell,

3 ᶜAnd the Brits tried to keep the war alive in Europe by fighting in ᵈAfrica,

4 ᵉAnd the Russkies took a dreadful beating from the Krauts,

5 ᶠBecause the Russkies had comrades,

6 ᵍAnd the Krauts had guns,

7 ʰWhich resulted in millions and millions of dead comrades,

8 ⁱAnd more great speeches from Churchill,

9 And not a lot of heroics from the Yanks,

10 Except for ʲGeneral MacArthur,

11 ᵏWho escaped from the Philippines somehow,

12 But told them he would come back later,

13 ˡOr words to that effect.

CHAPTER 110

Then, when everything had gotten about as bad as it could get,

2 The Yanks announced that they were ready to start getting even,

3 But there were a few things they wanted everyone to understand first,

4 Like the fact that if they had to be involved in Europe,

a. 105.15
b. Adam.39.10-11
c. Krt.33.3
Brit.54.2-3
d. Dav.32.1-26
e. Jeff.5.7
f. Russ.19.9-14
g. Ann.10.1
h. Russ.10.9
i. Psay.5Q.78
j. Dav.12.5
k. Drex.6.1
Ann.6.1
l. Ann.18.25
m. 109.10
n. Ed.31.4
o. 78.1-5
p. Krt.27.1-7
q. 112.20-21
r. 84.1-4
s. 106.13
t. 97.11
u. Brit.54.8-11
v. Lies.4.14
w. Psom.44.1-4
x. Psom.44.5-7

5 Again,

6 They were going to call the shots this time,

7 With Yanks in charge everywhere,

8 Such as ᵐMacArthur in the Pacific,

9 And ⁿEisenhower in Europe,

10 Whether the Brits liked it or not.

11 That wasn't all, either,

12 Because the Yanks also made it clear that they weren't interested in another ºarmistice,

13 Since ᵖarmistices don't work,

14 Besides being almost impossible to pronounce,

15 Which is why the Yanks weren't interested in negotiating any terms with the Krauts or the Nips,

16 ᑫExcept Unconditional Surrender,

17 ʳBecause this time, the Yanks hadn't lost a few hundred people,

18 ˢBut two *thousand* people,

19 And absolutely positively weren't going to stand for it,

20 ᵗNo matter how much it cost.

CHAPTER 111

The army the Yanks took to Europe was the biggest army anyone had ever seen,

2 ᵛWith more Yank soldiers in it than you could shake a pointed stick at,

3 And more and bigger ships,

4 And more and bigger planes,

5 And more and bigger everything,

6 Except tanks,

7 ʷWhich the Krauts still had more and bigger of,

8 ˣFor a while,

9 Which was important,
10 [a]Because the Yanks were basically in a hurry,
11 [b]And planning to wrap the whole thing up as quickly as possible,
12 [c]Since they had learned the last time that there is no food in Europe,
13 [d]Unless you count France,
14 [e]Which you couldn't this time even if you wanted to,
15 And so the important thing was to win and get home again before the troops started demanding [f]food.

CHAPTER 112

In fact, the Yanks were in so much of a hurry that they managed to hurt almost everybody's feelings.
2 [g]For example, the Brits thought the best way to bomb Germany into submission was to drop a lot of bombs on their [h]cities at night,
3 But the Yanks thought that would take too long because it's so hard to aim at night,
4 And so the Yanks sent their [i]bombers to Germany in broad daylight so they could see to aim,
5 [j]Which hurt the Krauts' feelings,
6 [k]Because daylight bombing turned out to be a lot more damaging than nighttime bombing,
7 Especially if you have a city made completely out of [l]china.
8 [m]Then the Yanks hurt the Italians' feelings by invading Italy in the wrong place,
9 [n]Which was a place called Anzio,
10 Right next to the Monte Cassino abbey,
11 Which had been a historical landmark for about a thousand years,
12 [o]Until the Yanks decided it was so full of Kraut troops that it was holding up progress,
13 And bombed it into rubble,
14 Just to keep things moving.
15 The Yanks also hurt the feelings of the Nips by being in too much of a hurry.
16 For example, they couldn't wait until they actually had bombers within range of Japan,
17 Because they wanted to bomb Japan right away,
18 Or sooner than that if possible,
19 And so they sent [p]General Doolittle to bomb Japan from thousands of miles away,
20 Which the Nips thought was impolite,
21 [q]And even a little worrisome.
22 Then the Yanks decided that it would take too much time to fight the [r]Nips on every little island they had grabbed,
23 [s]And just skipped a bunch of them,
24 So that they could get closer to Japan,
25 Faster,
26 And get the darned thing over with sooner,
27 Because there wasn't any food in the South Pacific either.

CHAPTER 113

The Yanks back home were also in a big hurry,
2 [t]Because building the biggest army in history had pretty well cured the depression,
3 [u]But everything was being rationed,

a. Kens.22.11-14
b. Kens.22.15
c. Brit.28.18
d. Brit.28.19
e. Frog.38.1-2
f. Vin.16.11-13
g. Brit.2.8
h. Krt.17.4
i. Ed.49.6-9
j. Psp.3.8
k. Ed.49.10-19
l. Krt.34.1-3
m. Rom.24.17-18
n. Ext.17.15
o. Ned.36.18-19
p. Dav.14.20
q. Nips.21.1-14
r. Dav.34.19
s. Nips.20.12-14
t. Adam.42.1-17
u. Ned.8.8

4 Which meant that nobody would get to spend any of the money they were making till the troops came home,

5 And so they tried to figure out some new ways of getting the war over with faster,

6 Which they did.

7 [a]Their biggest idea was to build an enormous bomb that could destroy an entire city in a few seconds,

8 [b]Which they thought would shorten the war,

9 And besides, they knew that their idea was the kind of idea that Krauts usually had,

10 [c]Which they knew because the Yanks who had come up with this idea were really Krauts who had decided to be Yanks after it got [d]too dangerous to live in Germany anymore,

11 Which meant that honest-to-goodness [e]Kraut-type Krauts might be thinking along the same lines,

12 And it just wouldn't do to let the Krauts get a bomb like that first.

13 So the Yanks started something called the [f]Manhattan Project,

14 Which changed everything,

15 Forever.

CHAPTER 114

Meanwhile, the Yanks in England thought it would take less time to defeat Germany if they all went over to France,

2 [g]In a single gigantic invasion force,

3 And just rolled right over the [h]Krauts all the way to Berlin.

4 [i]Of course, by this time, the [j]Krauts were starting to under-

a. Ned.6.24
b. Frog.12.5
c. Al.2.1-7
d. 99.2-8
e. Ed.63.3
f. Adam.36.9-11
g. Krt.22.16
h. Lies.11.12
i. 76.5-9
j. Dav.34.17
k. Ext.48.19
l. Ed.51.22
m. Dav.31.7-15
n. Psp.3.7
o. Dav.46.19
p. Psp.1.2
q. Rom.7.20
r. Brit.1.9
s. 109.10-12
t. Psay.5Q.9

stand the Yanks better than they did before,

5 Even if they were liking them less and less,

6 And so they were expecting a gigantic Yank invasion,

7 [k]But in Calais,

8 [l]For some reason,

9 Even though it was obvious that the best place to land a gigantic invasion force was in Normandy,

10 Which is where the Yanks and some Brits landed on [m]D-Day,

11 The Sixth of June,

12 1940-[n]something,

13 A date that will never be forgotten by any Yank,

14 Ever.

CHAPTER 115

After D-Day, everybody tried to foul things up and lengthen the war,

2 Including the Yanks,

3 For some reason.

4 The Brits wanted to lengthen the war by trying out one of [o]Montgomery's [p]inane ideas for attacking Germany,

5 [q]Which involved attacking Belgium,

6 [r]For some reason,

7 And which succeeded brilliantly in wasting a lot of time,

8 Not to mention a whole bunch of Yank and Brit troops.

9 Then [s]MacArthur held things up by insisting on an invasion of the Philippines,

10 Even though the Philippines weren't the most direct route to Japan,

11 But had to be reconquered anyway because MacArthur had said he would be back,

12 [t]Or words to that effect.

CHAPTER 116

Although delays like these were slowing down the war,

2 It was still starting to become obvious that the Allies were going to win the war eventually,

3 And so the Allies all got together at Yalta to decide how Europe would be divided up after the war,

4 ᵃWhich is to say the countries conquered by the Brits and the Yanks would be free,

5 ᵇAnd the countries conquered by the Russkies would be enslaved in a vast totalitarian state,

6 ᶜWhich all seemed very fair to those in attendance,

7 Since nobody had invited any Czechs or Poles or Albanians or Romanians to the meeting,

8 And since ᵈRoosevelt had just been elected to his fourth term as president of the Yanks,

9 ᵉWhich was a record,

10 And who cares about a bunch of Poles and Czechs when you've got a record like that,

11 Because there aren't too many presidents who are so honest and great that they can be reelected even though they're almost dead in their wheelchair,

12 And practically senile to boot,

13 Or why would he ever have agreed to give half the world to a murderous tyrant like ᶠStalin,

14 ᵍAnd then died almost immediately,

15 Without telling his ʰvice president anything about what to do next,

16 Unless that's not really how it was at all,

17 Which it couldn't be,

18 Because Roosevelt was far

a. 102.23
b. Russ.20.2-7
c. Russ.20.8-10
d. Dav.15.9 Vin.6.15
e. 103.12
f. Dav.30.40
g. Dav.15.40-46
h. 117.5
i. 96.11
j. Dav.34.17
k. Krt.34.14-15
l. Dav.23.41-43
m. Dav.23.10
n. Krt.34.17
o. 110.13
p. 110.15-16
q. Dav.34.19

too honest and great to do anything wrong,

19 As every Yank knows,

20 ‘Somehow.

CHAPTER 117

But the Yanks have always been lucky,

2 As any European will tell you,

3 And they kept on winning the war even though Roosevelt was dead,

4 And the new president,

5 Who must have been Truman,

6 Continued the same policies that had worked so far,

7 Until the ʲKrauts had been thoroughly whipped,

8 ᵏIncluding the Battle of the Bulge,

9 ˡWhere a Yank stopped the Kraut counteroffensive by saying "Nuts,"

10 Or words to that effect,

11 Which stunned the Krauts long enough for ᵐPatton to arrive like the U.S. Cavalry,

12 Which he kind of was at that,

13 And saved the day,

14 ⁿUntil the Krauts finally gave in,

15 And offered up the kind of peace terms the Yanks wanted,

16 ᵒMeaning Surrender,

17 ᵖOf the Unconditional kind.

CHAPTER 118

Meanwhile, the Yanks had taken about everything in the South Pacific away from the ᑫNips,

2 Except Japan,

3 Which they were about to do,

4 Even if the cost of getting even was going to come in very high this time,

5 Which is to say exorbitantly high,

6 And maybe as many as a million Yanks,

7 Unless there were some kind of super bomb,

8 The kind of bomb that could destroy an entire city in a few seconds,

9 In fact, the kind of bomb the Yanks had just finished building in their [a]Manhattan Project,

10 And . . . hey!

11 There's an idea!

12 Why not drop the atom bomb on the Nips and be done with it,

13 Once and for all?

CHAPTER 119

[b]**W**hen the Yank A-Bomb vaporized [c]Hiroshima in a few seconds or so,

2 The Yank [d]president realized that the Nips would need some time to figure out what had happened exactly,

3 [e]Because they were the first nation that had ever lost a complete city in just a few seconds,

4 [f]And so Truman gave them almost forty-eight hours to think it over,

5 Well, not quite forty-eight hours,

6 Because forty-eight hours later another A-Bomb vaporized [g]Nagasaki,

7 Which caused the Nips to realize that they might be seeing the beginning of a pattern,

8 In which each Yank demand for Unconditional Surrender is followed,

9 Within forty-eight hours,

10 [h]By the disappearance of another Nip city,

11 Which is the kind of pattern that adds up after a while,

12 [i]No matter how much you like suicide,

a. 113.13
b. Psp.3.12
c. Hall.1.2
d. 117.5
e. 116.9
f. Ned.16.12
g. Hall.1.4
h. Nips.18.10
i. Nips.5.1-16
j. Ann.19.13
k. 116.3-5
l. Psong.22.1-3
m. 119.14
n. 73.1
o. Psom.75.10
p. Hall.3.2
q. Barb.4.18

13 And finally convinced the Nips to throw in the towel,

14 The American Way,

15 [j]Which is called, *Unconditional Surrender.*

CHAPTER 120

Thus, finally, the Second World War came to an end,

2 And suddenly the Yanks were in charge of everything,

3 [k]Except possibly the third of the planet on two continents controlled by the Russkies,

4 Who were all poor and miserable anyway,

5 [l]Which meant that the Yanks were now the Most Chosen Nation on Earth,

6 [m]Thanks to the American Way,

7 [n]And American know-how,

8 [o]And American money,

9 [p]Not to mention American A-Bombs,

10 Which nobody really wanted to mention anyway,

11 Because they were so scary.

CHAPTER 121

Of course, the A-Bomb didn't scare the Yanks any,

2 Because they were the only ones that had it,

3 And it seemed like a pretty good thing all in all,

4 Since the Yanks had lost almost half a million troops saving the world for democracy,

5 This time,

6 And if it hadn't been for the A-Bomb,

7 They might have lost three or four times that,

8 Which is fine if you're a [q]European country,

9 But completely unacceptable if you're a Yank.

10 And so the Yanks listened politely when the Europeans and other intellectuals talked about how dangerous the Bomb was,
11 And how destructive,
12 And how apocalyptic,
13 [a]Because if anybody tried to fight another world war with nuclear weapons, there might not be anything left afterwards,
14 Which made the Yanks nod vigorously,
15 Now that they knew what apocalyptic meant,
16 Besides being secretly pleased and proud that it was the Yanks who invented nuclear weapons first,
17 Because how long would the world last if somebody else had been first,
18 Somebody not as God-fearing and moral as the Yanks,
19 Somebody who would use nuclear weapons to rule the world?

CHAPTER 122

Even so, the Yanks knew that Europe was still a problem,
2 Because it was still [b]Europe,
3 And still pretty full of Krauts and Frogs and Brits,
4 Even if there weren't quite as many as there used to be,
5 Not to mention the Russkies,
6 Who stuck pretty closely to the plan they'd laid out at Yalta,
7 Meaning they weren't going to give back any territory,
8 At all,
9 And were planning to own Poland and Czechoslovakia and Romania and Hungary and Albania and a great big chunk of Germany,
10 Forever,
11 [c]Even if they had to lose a

a. Swar.26.8-10
b. Barb.4.18
c. Russ.20.11
d. Russ.20.12-19
e. 101.7
f. Brit.40.8
g. Psay.5W.21-25
h. 44.22
i. Dav.23.14 & 21.10

few million more comrades to defend it.
12 By this time, of course, the Yanks had brought most of their combat troops home,
13 What with the war having been over for several weeks or so,
14 [d]And they didn't want to fight a big war with the Russkies,
15 Because the Russkies hadn't killed any Yanks yet,
16 Which meant there wasn't anything to remember,
17 And nothing to get even for,
18 Yet.
19 Even so, the Yanks had started to realize that this time wasn't going to be like last time,
20 [e]Meaning they couldn't just go home and forget all about Europe for another twenty years,
21 Because this time they were [f]stuck,
22 And had to stay involved,
23 Because all the Europeans were completely exhausted,
24 And pretty much out of ideas about what to do next,
25 Which meant the Yanks had to come up with an idea,
26 And really kind of think it through this time,
27 Since a bad idea would probably cause [g]World War III,
28 Which made the Yanks nervous,
29 [h]Because if there's one thing Yanks really hate, it's having to think things through.

CHAPTER 123

Fortunately for the Yanks, they had a great general named [i]George Catlett Marshall,
2 Who was so brilliant that he

thought up a great idea all by himself,
3 Without any help from anyone,
4 And gave it to the president,
5 Who must have been Truman,
6 [a]Since Roosevelt was still dead.
7 George's brilliantly original idea was to create a new kind of peace in western Europe,
8 [b]A kind of peace that would bury the hatchet forever,
9 [c]And make it easier for the Europeans to get along with each other in future,
10 [d]Because they couldn't keep going out and killing twenty or thirty million of each other's troops every twenty years or so,
11 [e]Every time some lunatic in a comic-opera uniform decided that some country had always really belonged to some other country.
12 [f]And so George thought up the idea of making generous peace terms,
13 [g]That wouldn't make anyone bitter,
14 [h]Not even Germany or Japan,
15 Because it would be better for everybody if they rebuilt their bombed-out factories,
16 And went back to work on important things,
17 [i]Like making money.
18 And if they had a problem,
19 [j]They could go resolve it peaceably in something like a League of Nations,
20 Only better,
21 [k]Like maybe the United Nations,
22 Which should be in some nice, safe central location that all the Europeans could get to easily,
23 [l]Like New York.

a. 116.12
b. 81.7
c. 76.22
d. 76.23
e. 81.10
f. 82.5
g. 82.6
h. 82.7
i. Psong.40.1
j. 81.9
k. 118.11
l. Adam.36.1-12
m. 123.1
n. Dav.22.12
o. 104.14
p. 122.29
q. 97.3
r. 97.4
s. 124.15
t. Adam.41.7
u. 120.4

CHAPTER 124

The Marshall Plan turned out to be even more successful than it was original,
2 Thanks to [m]George, of course,
3 Not to mention [n]President Truman,
4 [o]Who was honest and great,
5 Because Roosevelt had thought enough of him to make him vice president,
6 [p]Which was good enough for the Yanks,
7 And besides, where could you find a president who would be better at showing the whole world how serious the Yanks were about [q]equality,
8 [r]And how nobody was really any better than anyone else,
9 Because President Truman was obviously no better than anybody,
10 Being completely average in every respect,
11 Except much more decisive, of course,
12 And honest,
13 And great,
14 Because Roosevelt wouldn't have picked him otherwise,
15 [s]Would he?
16 Anyway,
17 [t]It was Truman who was president when the Yanks gave all that money to the Europeans to rebuild their cities and factories and everything,
18 [u]And except for the Russkies,
19 Everything started to get better in Europe,

20 Even though there were a whole bunch of Yank troops who weren't coming home this time,
21 But were staying in Europe,
22 Indefinitely,
23 Because somebody had to protect the poor defenseless Krauts from the Soviet army,
24 Which still hated the Krauts,
25 [a]For some reason.

CHAPTER 125

Actually, there were a lot of people who still hated the Krauts,
2 [b]Because the Nazis had done something so awful in the last years of the war that it was kind of hard not to hate them.
3 [c]When the Russkie and Yank troops reconquered the territory that had been held by the Krauts,
4 [d]They found concentration camps that weren't really concentration camps,
5 [e]But death camps,
6 [f]With names like Auschwitz and Treblinka and Bergen-Belsen,
7 [g]Where the Nazis exterminated Jews and Gypsies and Armenians and everyone else they didn't like,
8 [h]By gassing them in the shower,
9 [i]And then burning their bodies in beautifully engineered and constructed crematoria,
10 [j]But only after pulling out their gold teeth,
11 [k]And turning their skin into lampshades,
12 [l]And performing a bunch of horrible medical experiments,
13 [m]And so much other unspeakable stuff that the Krauts didn't want to speak about it,
14 At all,
15 To anyone,
16 Except maybe the Poles,
17 Who liked the Jews about as much as the Krauts did,
18 And maybe even less,
19 Because the Krauts had always been arrogant enough to think they were as smart as the Jews,
20 Or almost as smart,
21 Which is not the case for the Poles,
22 [n]Who are as stupid as they come,
23 And as vicious as they are stupid,
24 Because why else would they have just sat around outside places like the Warsaw ghetto and Auschwitz,
25 Without doing anything at all to help?
26 Anyway, it was obvious that someone would have to be punished for the [o]genocide thing,
27 In spite of the [p]Marshall Plan,
28 And whatever the Poles had done or hadn't done,
29 It was the Krauts who would have to pay,
30 Because just one look at the Auschwitz [q]crematorium was all it took to prove that the Poles didn't build it,
31 Since it had been built the Kraut Way,
32 Meaning that it worked,
33 [r]And was practically indestructible,
34 [s]Not to mention so cold-bloodedly efficient that it made everybody in the world marvel at just how far technology had evolved since the first pointed stick.

a. Russ.19.21-23
b. Krt.31.1-3
c. Krt.31.4
d. Krt.31.5
e. Krt.31.6
f. Krt.31.7
g. Krt.31.8
h. Krt.31.9
i. Krt.31.10
j. Krt.31.11
k. Krt.31.12
l. Krt.31.13
m. Ned.36.18-19
n. Psay.5J.6
o. Wil.8.2-17
p. 124.1
q. 125.9
r. Krt.5.25
s. Chuk.20.1-23

CHAPTER 126

A nd so the Allies had a big trial at Nuremberg,

2 And found out that nobody was [a]responsible for killing the Jews,

3 [b]Because everybody was only following orders,

4 Which meant that it wasn't their fault,

5 [c]Because how were they supposed to know that it was wrong,

6 And that there are some things you just don't do,

7 Ever,

8 Even if you're a Kraut?

9 After thinking it all over pretty carefully,

10 [d]The Allies hanged a bunch of Krauts for not disobeying their orders,

11 But stopped short of hanging all of them,

12 Because if there weren't any Krauts left,

13 [e]How would the European economy ever recover,

14 [f]And generate enough cash to buy stuff from the Yanks?

CHAPTER 127

M eanwhile, the Marshall Plan was also turning out to be a big success in Japan.

2 Because [g]General MacArthur became the military governor,

3 [h]And wrote a constitution for the Nips,

4 [i]And taught them all about the American Way,

5 [j]Meaning no more sneak attacks,

6 Because,

7 [k]Remember Hiroshima?

8 [l]And when they had learned about the American Way at last,

9 The Nips smiled and nodded,

10 And showed everyone,

a. Hall.4.3
b. Ext.15.4
c. Al.4.16
d. 135.21
e. Psong.40.1
f. Psong.16.1-2
g. Dav.10.10
h. 12.12-17
i. 52.28-30
j. 106.6-14
k. Drex.3.7
l. Psay.5Q.32
m. Nips.26.10-13
n. 125.14
o. Psong.40.1
p. Dav.33.9-12
q. Psong.40.1
r. Adam.20.2-10
s. Jefs.7.46
t. 102.14-15
u. Psay.2.2
v. Mes.1.1
w. 124.3

11 In every possible way,

12 [m]How friendly and reformed and civilized they were,

13 [n]And how they had no more interest in killing two thousand Yanks in a sneak attack,

14 [o]When it would be so much more fun to make a bunch of cheap shoddy trinkets instead.

CHAPTER 128

B ack home in America, things were going pretty well overall,

2 Although there weren't any houses for the returning troops to live in,

3 And not enough colleges and universities for them to go to,

4 [p]And not enough cars and things for them to buy,

5 Which meant that the Yanks were going to have to get busy and make a whole bunch of things,

6 [q]Not to mention money,

7 [r]Which they knew how to do,

8 Because they were Yanks,

9 [s]And there wasn't anything Yanks couldn't do,

10 [t]Because they were the best and the bravest and the smartest and the nicest world power in the whole history of mankind,

11 Bar none,

12 As any of the Yanks could have told you,

13 [u]Because the Yanks have always been such great students of history and world affairs,

14 Even if they couldn't spell [v]"Mesopotamia" to save their lives.

CHAPTER 129

T hings weren't going quite as well for [w]President Truman, though,

2 Because it was time for another presidential election,

3 Which happens about every four years,

4 Whether anyone is paying attention or not,

5 Although the Yanks were paying attention this time,

6 Because they didn't know what they were going to do when they walked into a voting booth and saw,

7 For the first time in their lives,

8 ªThat Roosevelt's name wasn't on the ballot.

9 Some of the Yanks thought that the Democrats had been in office long enough,

10 ᵇBecause everybody was equal by now, weren't they,

11 ᶜAnd just how average should a president be anyway?

12 ᵈOn the other hand, there were Yanks who thought that Truman was pretty darned honest and great for being so average,

13 ᵉAnd just look at how decisive he was.

14 So Truman got on a ᶠtrain,

15 And rode through every small town in the whole country,

16 ᵍTo explain to the people why he should be elected president,

17 Which had to do with the fact that his opponent was a no-good New York sharpie,

18 ʰWho was a lawyer,

19 ⁱAnd articulate,

20 And so far above average,

21 ʲThat he couldn't be trusted,

22 ᵏBy any right-thinking Yank.

CHAPTER 130

Truman's great and statesmanlike ˡcampaign succeeded brilliantly,

a. 123.6
b. 97.1-3
c. 124.9-10
d. 124.14
e. 124.11
f. Adam.7.9-10
g. Gods.4.6
h. Penn.4.8-10
i. Wil.36.5-6
j. Ira.34.4
k. 7.2
l. Ann.3.9-10
m. 123.5
n. 132.4
o. Carl.9.1-10
p. Carl.3.1-8
q. Dav.15.9
r. Dav.14.24 & 14.27
s. Ed.51.22
t. 66.3-4

2 Even if some of the newspapers forgot to look at the returns before they wrote their article about how Truman had lost,

3 Which he hadn't,

4 Because he was what the Yanks wanted,

5 And what they got,

6 Which is the American Way,

7 And always turns out for the best in the end,

8 Especially when you get a really great, honest, decisive president like ᵐwhat's-his-name.

CHAPTER 131

As it happened, Truman got a lot of opportunities to show everybody how decisive he was,

2 Like with the ⁿMcCarthy thing,

3 ᵒWhich was about how the communists had infiltrated the U.S. government before anybody knew the communists were an evil totalitarian state,

4 ᵖAnd wanted to own everybody and everything,

5 Including the Yanks.

6 The way the Yanks found out about all the communists who had infiltrated the government was a scandal about somebody named ᑫAlger Hiss,

7 Who was a high-level Yank diplomat,

8 And according to ʳWhittaker Chambers, a ˢcommunist spy too,

9 Which caused a tremendous ruckus,

10 Because ᵗChambers had evidence,

11 Including the papers Hiss had stolen from the state department,

12 And the typewriter he re-copied them on,
13 And the copies he had typed on the typewriter,
14 And witnesses,
15 [a]Except that Hiss denied it all,
16 Since it wasn't true,
17 [b]Because Whittaker Chambers was a homosexual,
18 Which made it all pretty obvious,
19 [c]Somehow.

CHAPTER 132

After Alger Hiss got convicted of perjury,
2 Somehow,
3 The U.S. Congress started a witch-hunt,
4 Which woke up a monster named [d]Joseph McCarthy,
5 Who started looking for communists everywhere,
6 Including Washington, D.C.,
7 And the Army,
8 And even Hollywood.
9 [e]Even though there weren't any communists in Washington or the Army or Hollywood,
10 [f]No one really wanted to fight with McCarthy,
11 [g]Because McCarthy had lists of names,
12 Which somebody's name might be on,
13 For some reason,
14 And so why risk it,
15 Especially when [h]McCarthy also had a pair of vicious legal attack dogs,
16 With names like [i]Roy Cohn,
17 And [j]Robert Kennedy,
18 [k]Who were dying for any chance to end somebody's career,
19 Forever.

a. Ned.36.20-23
b. 131.8
c. Vin.71.12-14
d. Ed.28.6
e. Psay.5Q.33
f. Vin.4.13
g. Cen.26.18-19
h. 132.4
i. Dav.14.24 & 57.12
j. Dav.15.9
k. Penn.8.9-15
l. 123.5
m. Psay.5Q.26
n. Ed.6.1-13
o. 123.18-23
p. 104.2
q. Wil.13.32-35
r. Kens.22.16
s. Forg.8.11-15
t. 127.2

CHAPTER 133

The McCarthy thing would probably have been a lot worse if the Yanks hadn't had such a decisive [l]president,
2 Who disapproved of McCarthy,
3 And who decided not to pass the buck on the witch-hunt business,
4 [m]But to sit on the buck instead,
5 Because sometimes the hardest decision is the decision to do nothing at all,
6 [n]But somebody's got to do it,
7 Because that's what presidents are for.

CHAPTER 134

And McCarthy wasn't the only decisive thing Truman ever did either,
2 Because all of a sudden the communist North Koreans invaded South Korea,
3 And the [o]United Nations met to discuss it,
4 [p]And decided that the Yanks should handle it,
5 [q]Because who wants to send their own troops to some far-away gook country to get killed by a bunch of uncivilized animals?
6 [r]And so the Yanks went to Korea,
7 And started taking a dreadful beating,
8 Because they had forgotten to bring a [s]general,
9 Which made somebody remember MacArthur,
10 [t]Who was still governor of Japan,
11 And only about a thousand years old.
12 After he took command,

MacArthur invaded ᵃInchon,

13 Because nobody else thought it was a good idea,

14 And started talking about bombing the Chinese,

15 ᵇWho had become communist by now,

16 And might be helping the North Koreans a little bit,

17 Which meant that the Yanks should slap them around a little,

18 And make them stop.

19 Truman wanted to be very decisive about the whole situation,

20 Because that was his way,

21 But he decided to wait for a while,

22 And let MacArthur try his idea out,

23 Which caused the Chinese to invade Korea,

24 ᶜAnd make the potato hotter than ever.

CHAPTER 135

By this time, of course, Truman knew that ᵈMacArthur wasn't any good at fighting wars,

2 And started telling him to stick to U.S. policy,

3 Which consisted of hanging around the 38th parallel,

4 And hoping the Chinese communists would go away.

5 But when Truman explained this to MacArthur,

6 MacArthur couldn't understand it,

7 At all,

8 Because he was senile,

9 ᵉAnd thought that the idea of war was to go fight as hard as you can, get it all over with as soon as you can, and then come home,

10 Which was all wrong,

a. Ext.45.9
b. Chnk.14.1-10
c. 20.9-11
d. Dav.14.23 & 14.27
e. 7.2
f. 121.15
g. Forg.5.6
h. 120.5
i. 126.10
j. 135.14
k. Ann.19.13
l. Psay.5Q.7
m. 129.3
n. Psay.5Q.43

11 Because the Yanks were living in the nuclear age now,

12 ᶠAnd everything was different,

13 Meaning that sometimes the hardest military decision is the decision to do nothing at all,

14 ᵍEven if a bunch of Yank troops have to die for it,

15 ʰBecause when you're the Most Chosen Nation in the World,

16 You can't always do the first thing that pops into your head,

17 And besides,

18 What else was there to do exactly?

19 But MacArthur was around the bend,

20 And he wouldn't obey Truman's orders because he thought they were wrong,

21 ⁱWhich is the worst possible crime a soldier can commit,

22 And so he bombed China,

23 And therefore had to be fired,

24 Which Truman did very very decisively,

25 ʲThus proving that he had been right all along,

26 ᵏEven if MacArthur did get the biggest ticker-tape parade anyone ever had when he came home,

27 Right before he ˡfaded away.

CHAPTER 136

With the ᵐnext election coming up pretty fast, Truman needed one more completely decisive decision to cement his place in history,

2 ⁿAnd so he decided not to run,

3 Because it didn't look like he was going to get to do anything really decisive in Korea before the election,

4 ^aAnd with all those Yank troops just hanging around the 38th parallel,

5 The Yanks as a whole were getting restless,

6 ^bAnd wondering why Mac-Arthur didn't just drop an A-Bomb or two on the Chinks and the Koreans,

7 ^cAnd get it all over with,

8 ^dAnd come home,

9 Just like always,

10 Only it wasn't that simple,

11 Because somehow or other,

12 ^eThe Russkies had got hold of some A-Bombs of their own,

13 And if the Yanks dropped some,

14 The Russkies might drop some too,

15 ^fAnd then the fat would be in the fire,

16 ^gWhich meant that it was time for the ^hmost decisive president in U.S. history to retire,

17 And get it all over with,

18 ⁱAnd go home,

19 Just like always.

CHAPTER 137

The new Yank president was named Ike,

2 Which wasn't a Jewish name,

3 Since the Yanks have never had a Jewish president,

4 Because why would they do that,

5 ^jWhen there are so many WASPs available?

6 In fact, Ike was short for Eisenhower,

7 Who was the same ^kEisenhower that had conquered Europe in World War II,

8 And had an idea about how to handle the Korean thing,

9 Which was to propose peace talks,

a. 135.4
b. 118.11
c. Kens.22.14
d. Kens.22.15
e. Russ.20.22-27
f. Psay.5W.21-25
g. 33.5
h. 123.5
i. 34.13
j. Psay.5Q.62
k. 110.9
l. Psay.5Q.47
m. Psong.41.1-6
n. 137.14
o. Adam.43.4-10
p. Adam.31.3
q. Ann.6.1
r. Adam.45.3
s. Ed.10.9-13
t. Adam.47.4
u. Adam.49.3
v. Ed.30.7

10 ^lWhile talking a great deal about how much fun it would be to turn North Korea into a radioactive desert,

11 Forever.

12 After the peace talks were successfully concluded,

13 Eisenhower took a nap,

14 For about eight years,

15 ^mWhile the Yanks went out and made more money than you can shake a pointed stick at.

CHAPTER 138

In fact, things couldn't have gone any better than they did for the Yanks during ⁿEisenhower's nap.

2 Their industry was booming,

3 ^oBecause the Yanks knew how to make everything better than anyone else,

4 ^pIncluding cars that always started and ran forever with no maintenance,

5 ^qAnd planes that flew higher and faster and safer than anyone ever dreamed possible,

6 ^rAnd computers, which nobody ever had at all before the Yanks invented them,

7 ^sAnd television sets, which nobody else in the world could even afford to own,

8 ^tAnd household appliances like refrigerators, and washing machines, and stoves, and dishwashers, which everybody else in the world would have given their right arm for,

9 ^uNot to mention machinery of every possible kind and purpose,

10 Which was all the very best and most advanced technology you could find anywhere,

11 Which is why every ^vYank had a good job,

12 ^aAnd a house,
13 ^bAnd a two-car garage,
14 ^cWith two cars in it,
15 ^dAnd an extraordinary confidence in the future of the world,
16 Because the Yanks were in charge of the world,
17 ^eAnd that's the way God wanted it,
18 As every Yank knew,
19 And would tell you if you asked.

CHAPTER 139

In fact, the Yanks were very very proud of themselves,
2 Not just for outlasting the Great Depression and turning it into so much prosperity,
3 But also for all the other things they'd done in the twentieth century,
4 Including save the world for democracy,
5 ^fTwice,
6 When they could have just sat at home both times,
7 But didn't,
8 ^gBecause they loved the peoples of the world so much that they couldn't just sit around while the Krauts ruined everything,
9 ^hEven if the Krauts would never have had a prayer of beating the Yanks at home,
10 Which they wouldn't,
11 Because the Yanks were never intimidated for a second by the prospect of "Fortress Europe,"
12 ⁱWhatever that was.
13 And that's not all the Yanks were proud of,
14 ^jBecause after the war, they had been kind and generous,
15 In spite of the fact that they could have set things up any old

a. Ed.30.8-11
b. Boul.12.9
c. Hill.S.7-8
d. 105.22
e. Rat.13.11-13
f. Psay.5Y.23 & 5Y.7
g. 107.15-16
h. 128.13
i. 102.7-9
j. 126.12-14
k. 104.17-21 & 80.7 Brit.15.30
l. 12.13
m. 47.1-3
n. Adam.28.18-22
o. Al.5.8-10
p. Kin.3.4-5 Hill.H.9-10
q. Russ.21.1-2

way they wanted to,
16 With nobody having any say,
17 ^kIncluding the lousy Brits and Frogs,
18 Only they didn't do things that way,
19 Because they were Yanks,
20 And good,
21 And democratic,
22 And hardworking,
23 And virtuous,
24 ^lWith very high principles,
25 ^mEspecially now that the whole slavery thing was taken care of,
26 ⁿWith everybody in America equal,
27 And separate,
28 Which was the way God wanted it,
29 Obviously,
30 Because if God didn't approve of the Yanks, why did He give them the ^oA-Bomb,
31 Not to mention the ^pH-Bomb,
32 Which nobody wanted to mention anyway,
33 Because it was so scary,
34 Even to the Yanks.

CHAPTER 140

Actually, in spite of all their success, the H-Bomb did worry the Yanks,
2 More than a little bit,
3 Because they'd had nuclear weapons long enough by now to realize that they were very very dangerous,
4 And could kill you,
5 And everybody else too,
6 ^qBecause the Russkies had them,
7 And would use them if they got the chance,
8 Which the Yanks knew for sure,

9 Because they knew *they* would use them if it came to that,
10 And maybe the world wasn't a completely perfect place after all,
11 Like when some [a]Yank woke up in the morning wondering if his children would ever get to grow old,
12 [b]And when his children came home from school and asked why they needed an air-raid drill,
13 Because everybody would die in a nuclear air raid anyway,
14 Which could happen,
15 Because if the Russkies did something unspeakable,
16 The Yanks would absolutely positively have to get even,
17 No matter how much it cost,
18 [c]Even if it killed them.

CHAPTER 141

But nobody talked about these things very much during the [d]great nap of Ike,
2 Because it was easier to talk about other things,
3 [e]Like all those great Hollywood movies,
4 [f]Starring Doris Day and Rock Hudson,
5 [g]And John Wayne,
6 [h]And Cary Grant,
7 And all the other great Yank stars who showed everybody,
8 Including the Yanks,
9 Exactly what it meant to be a fine, upstanding, virtuous Yank,
10 [i]Who always wins in the end,
11 Because there is always justice in the world,
12 As long as it is ruled by Yanks.

a. Ed.30.7
b. Ed.30.8
c. 7.2
d. 137.13-14
e. Dav.36.2-4
f. Dav.36.5
g. Dav.34.2-10
h. Dav.18.5
i. Brit.22.20
j. Psay.5S.1-3
k. Psay.5S.4-8
l. Psay.5S.9
m. Psay.5S.10-11
n. Mawr.22.22
o. Hill.S.23-24
p. Ed.10.7
q. Ed.31.4
r. Ed.30.5
s. Ed.34.5-11
t. Ed.40.1-8
u. Ed.47.7-12
v. Ed.51.20-21
w. Ed.51.17-19
x. Ed.55.1
y. Ed.57.3-15
z. Ed.47.6

CHAPTER 142

And if a Yank didn't like the movies, there was always something else to talk about instead,
2 [j]Like sports,
3 Which were a great Yank tradition,
4 Starting with baseball,
5 [k]Which was great,
6 [l]But maybe not as great as NFL football,
7 [m]Which was so tough and competitive and great that it showed the whole world what it was to be a Yank,
8 [n]Such as being bigger and faster and stronger than anyone else,
9 [o]And perfectly willing and able to run right over anyone who got in the way.

CHAPTER 143

And all Yanks everywhere could always just forget about everything and watch [p]television,
2 Which was all about how great it was to be a Yank,
3 Because on TV, [q]all Yank dads were wise and wonderful,
4 [r]And all Yank moms were warm and beautiful,
5 [s]And all Yank kids were smart and helpful,
6 [t]And all Yank heroes were brave and handsome and noble,
7 [u]Whether they were TV cowboys,
8 [v]Or TV policemen,
9 [w]Or TV private eyes,
10 [x]Or TV lawyers,
11 [y]Or TV doctors,
12 [z]Or even TV gamblers.
13 And that's not all,
14 Because TV also showed the Yanks the best way to live,

15 Meaning the Yank way,
16 ªWhere everybody owned the same spotlessly clean two-story house ᵇon the same perfectly clean, tree-lined street in the suburbs,
17 And drove the same enormous station wagon with fake wood on the sides,
18 ᶜAnd smiled the same bright cheerful smile all the time,
19 ᵈAnd always solved all their problems right before the last commercial,
20 ᵉWhich proved just how great it was to be a Yank,
21 Living in the land of the Yanks.

a. Ira.6.10
b. Hill.S.10
c. Adam.31.8-10
d. Ed.53.6-7
e. Zig.10.12
f. Lies.10.6
g. Ed.70.4
h. 74.3-5
i. Zig.10.11
j. 3.3-4
k. Ed.70.10
l. Ed.70.7
m. Ed.70.9
n. Hill.W.1
o. 144.8
p. 90.15
q. Brit.40.8
r. Psay.5C.12

CHAPTER 144

The Yanks also had a lot of music to talk about,
2 Since they had just invented something,
3 Something not quite respectable,
4 ᶠSomething that maybe wasn't completely okay,
5 ᵍSomething called rock'n'roll,
6 Which a lot of Yanks didn't understand,
7 And therefore hated,
8 Which is the American Way,
9 ʰNot to mention the fact that it probably came from black people,
10 Because it was so suggestive about,
11 You know,
12 ⁱSex,
13 Which wasn't allowed in ʲAmerica during the Eisenhower administration,
14 Because it might wake up Ike.
15 And so it came about that the

Yanks had a bunch of new stars,
16 ᵏWith names like Chuck Berry,
17 ˡAnd Elvis Presley,
18 ᵐAnd Pat Boone,
19 Which would change the world someday,
20 In the not too distant future.

CHAPTER 145

And speaking of the ⁿworld,
2 Every Yank could go see the world,
3 On vacations,
4 When they could dress up in Bermuda shorts and sunglasses,
5 With a whole bunch of cameras,
6 And go to Europe,
7 ᵒJust to see why everything was so much better back home in America,
8 ᵖNot to mention getting some pictures of the countries the Yanks had saved,
9 ᑫOr had clobbered and then rebuilt,
10 Whichever it was.
11 And so they could get on buses with a whole bunch of other Yanks,
12 ʳAnd go on tours of cities and museums and all that stuff,
13 And talk it all over with each other and the natives,
14 In a loud Yank accent,
15 In English,
16 Just so everyone would know that they were Yanks,
17 And wouldn't confuse them with somebody else,
18 Such as somebody who hadn't saved their bacon,
19 Twice,
20 Which no Yank would actually say out loud, of course,
21 Unless the service was lousy,

22 Or the hotel room wasn't spotlessly clean,
23 Or the bathrooms didn't have modern plumbing,
24 Or the restaurants didn't have hamburgers and hot dogs on the menu,
25 Or the natives got irritable about being ordered around by guests in their country,
26 ᵃWho absolutely positively refused to even try to speak the native language,
27 ᵇJust like the Brits,
28 Only not nearly so well dressed.

a. Brit.8.10
b. Brit.8.9
c. 137.13-14
d. 137.4-5
e. Dav.15.9
f. 96.10-14
g. 128.13
h. Psay.5J.4
i. 88.3
j. Psom.12.7
k. Dav.52.4
l. Psp.3.13
m. Russ.24.1-7

CHAPTER 146

Ａnd so the years rolled by,
2 ᶜUntil finally it became necessary to wake up Ike,
2 Because it was time for another election,
3 Which happens every four years or so,
4 Whether the Yanks are paying any attention or not.
5 This time, they were paying attention,
6 ᵈBecause the Democrats were running an Irish Catholic for president,
7 Named ᵉJohn F. Kennedy,
8 Who was honest and great,
9 Because he went to Harvard,
10 ᶠJust like Franklin Roosevelt.
11 Even so, the Yanks had a hard time trying to vote for him,
12 ᵍBecause all the Yanks knew about Irish Catholics,
13 ʰAnd how all they ever wanted to do was party and pick fights,
14 And hit on women all the time,
15 And make money from dirty

businesses like ibootlegging and such,
16 And how dishonest and corrupt they were in politics,
17 And how they'd smile and lie right in your face,
18 Like all ʲIrish Catholics everywhere,
19 Except that Kennedy wasn't that kind of Irish Catholic,
20 At all,
21 Because he was honest and great,
22 And so good-looking too,
23 ᵏAnd not at all like the shifty-eyed crook he was running against,
24 Which explains why Kennedy won the election by more than a hundred thousand votes,
25 And proves that the Yanks aren't prejudiced after all,
26 Unless it doesn't.

CHAPTER 147

Ｋennedy turned out to be a very popular president with the Yanks,
2 Who maybe thought he was like a symbol of themselves,
3 Because he was young,
4 And successful,
5 And in charge,
6 And always trying to do the right thing,
7 But not taking any guff from anybody,
8 Like with the Russkies,
9 ᵐWho tried to put some nuclear missiles in Cuba,
10 Only Kennedy told them to back off,
11 Because he had his finger on the button,
12 And would push it if they pushed him,
13 Which explains why there was a period lasting about two

weeks when the whole world held its breath,

14 And closed its eyes,

15 ªAnd prayed to every deity Mankind has ever worshiped,

16 ᵇDating all the way back to the first pointed stick of the first civilization,

17 Wondering if the Yanks were really willing to annihilate the world over a point of pride,

18 ᶜWhich they were,

19 As the Russkies eventually realized,

20 Right before they backed down,

21 ᵈThus allowing the whole world to breathe the biggest sigh of relief in history.

CHAPTER 148

Playing chicken with the Russkies wasn't the only exciting thing Kennedy did either,

2 Although he liked chicken so much that he played a few rounds in Berlin too,

3 When the Russkies put up the Berlin Wall,

4 And announced that there would be war if anybody got in their way,

5 ᵉWhich made Kennedy mad,

6 And resulted in another close call,

7 Though maybe not quite as close as the Cuban Missile Crisis,

8 Which couldn't have gotten much closer,

9 Without needing a different name,

10 Such as the Cuban Missile War.

11 Anyway,

12 Kennedy did other exciting things too,

a. Lies.4.14
b. Dav.17.11-16
c. 144.8
d. Ann.6.23
e. 30.37-40
f. Ed.13.2-14
g. 128.9
h. Oth.8.15-17
i. Carl.3.8
j. Ed.15.1-9
k. 139.25
l. 139.26
m. 139.27
n. 139.28-29

13 ᶠLike wanting to send a man to the moon,

14 Which everybody knew the Yanks could do,

15 ᵍBecause Yanks can do anything,

16 So why not this?

17 And Kennedy also invented the Peace Corps,

18 Because he loved peace so much,

19 Like all Yanks,

20 ʰAnd therefore thought it would be great to send a bunch of Yank kids out to tell all the most backward countries how to live right,

21 ⁱSuch as the American Way and all that,

22 Because the Yanks have always cared so much about the poor and oppressed,

23 Especially the ones who don't live in America.

CHAPTER 149

In fact, Kennedy was so honest and great that he even cared about the poor and oppressed in America,

2 ʲBecause they were starting to get fed up anyway,

3 Especially the negroes,

4 Who had been noticing some things about life in America lately,

5 ᵏSuch as the fact that it was okay for negroes to fight in Yank wars,

6 ˡAnd die for their country,

7 ᵐAs long as they did it separately from white Yanks,

8 ⁿBut who still weren't allowed to vote,

9 Or go to white schools,

10 Or sit at the front of the bus,

11 Which is the very best place to sit in a bus,

12 As everyone knows,
13 Or why would they have told the negroes to sit somewhere else?

CHAPTER 150

Kennedy noticed that negroes weren't completely happy,
2 Because about a million of them marched to Washington,
3 ᵃAnd sat right out there in public and everything,
4 To hear a preacher named ᵇMartin Luther King tell them that he had a dream,
5 A dream about equality,
6 Which meant that it was time for negroes to stand up and demand their rights,
7 Nonviolently,
8 ᶜBecause it's better that way,
9 ᵈAnd besides, it's never smart to make the Yanks mad by hurting some of them,
10 Which everyone knew,
11 By now.
12 And so Kennedy helped out all he could,
13 By passing a law in Congress that made negroes equal,
14 So that they could be called black people,
15 Instead of negroes,
16 Because white people were called white people,
17 Unless they were called Caucasians,
18 Which they weren't,
19 Or else why would it matter what you called black people,
20 As long as you didn't call them the usual Yank names,
21 Such as nigger,
22 And spade,
23 And coon,
24 And tar baby,

a. Ann.4.32
b. Dav.15.9
   Brit.40.7-8
c. Bks.10.27-28
d. 52.28-30
e. 98.21
f. 97.5
g. 97.6

25 And spook,
26 And spear chucker,
27 And colored,
28 And all the other names that Yanks think of first but never use in public anymore because they might sound racist or something,
29 For some reason.

CHAPTER 151

And so, the Yanks suddenly had to deal with a bunch of stuff that they thought was settled a long time ago,
2 And what did these people want anyway,
3 And what was so bad about separate but equal,
4 And what about states' rights,
5 And does this mean we can't just string them up to the nearest tree anymore?
6 It turned out that the answers to all these questions were federal laws,
7 And federal troops,
8 And federal programs to help the Yanks do the right thing,
9 Which they didn't want to do, of course,
10 ᵉExcept that by now, they had gotten pretty used to letting the government make the hard decisions,
11 ᶠBecause the government was in charge of equality,
12 ᵍAnd not letting rich people get away with anything,
13 Which turned out to be a relative term,
14 Because compared to black people, most of the white Yanks were rich,
15 And weren't allowed to get away with anything anymore,
16 No matter how many civil rights workers they killed,

17 And no matter how much they wanted to sit at the front of the bus,

18 With other white people.

CHAPTER 152

As it happened, the civil rights thing kind of stirred up a lot of controversy,

2 And not just about black people,

3 Because a lot of the young people who wanted the blacks to get their civil rights had noticed some other things about the Most Chosen Nation on Earth,

4 Such as the way they kept stockpiling more and more nuclear weapons,

5 Until they could have destroyed the Soviet Union a hundred times over,

6 Which just wasn't necessary,

7 And might not be very responsible either,

8 ªUnless you weren't as kind and nice a nation as you told everybody you were,

9 ᵇWhich how could you be anyway if absolutely everybody in the whole world hates the Yanks, including all their friends and allies?

10 ᶜBesides, what was this little business in Vietnam all about,

11 ᵈWith a bunch of Yank advisers egging the South Vietnamese on to renew some ancient war with their relatives in the north,

12 ᵉAnd were the Yanks going to start throwing their weight around in some underprivileged country that couldn't fight back?

13 And now that we're on the subject, how can it be right that America is so rich and prosperous,

a. 128.10
b. Krt.35.1-7
   Brit.56.1-10
   Frog.39.1-13
c. Ann.4.22
d. Ann.4.24
e. Ed.17.1-11
f. 141.11-12
g. Vin.3.9
h. Vin.3.10
i. Vin.3.11
j. Vin.3.13
k. Vin.3.14
l. Vin.3.15
m. Vin.3.16
n. Vin.3.17
o. Vin.3.18
p. Ed.19.1-10

14 When practically everyone else is dirt-poor,

15 ᶠEspecially if the Yanks are as nice and just as they say they are?

16 And even though not many people were talking this way,

17 ᵍThere were enough conversations here and there that a musician named Bob Dylan started writing thoughtful songs about it,

18 ʰAnd a poet named Allen Ginsberg started writing thoughtful poems about it,

19 ⁱAnd a writer named Norman Mailer started writing thoughtful essays about it,

20 ʲAnd a novelist named Kurt Vonnegut started writing thoughtful novels about it,

21 ᵏAnd students on certain college campuses started listening to the thoughtful song lyrics and reading the thoughtful poems and essays and novels,

22 ˡAnd then started to wonder,

23 ᵐIf just maybe there was something terribly terribly wrong with the United States of America,

24 ⁿSomething that would have to be seen to,

25 ºIn the not too distant future.

CHAPTER 153

And then President Kennedy went to Dallas,

2 And got assassinated,

3 ᵖOn camera,

4 So that his blood got splattered all over Jackie's beautiful pink suit,

4 And if someone hadn't murdered Lee Harvey Oswald on television,

5 There's no telling what would have happened,

6 ^aBecause the Yanks would have wanted to get even,
7 ^bNo matter how much it cost,
8 Except that they didn't have to,
9 Because someone got to Oswald first,
10 ^cAnd besides, their handsome young president was dead,
11 And maybe you really couldn't get even for a thing like that,
12 Even if you were a Yank,
13 Because maybe not even Yanks can do everything.
14 ^dShammadamma.

CHAPTER 154

And so, all of a sudden, it seemed like maybe the Yanks weren't quite as youthful anymore,
2 Or as confident,
3 Or as hopeful,
4 Or as all-powerful as they had thought,
5 Which is usually the first sign that a Chosen Nation isn't quite as Chosen as it used to be,
6 And is maybe getting a little tired,
7 And more than a little confused,
8 And in need of some new ideas about how to live in a world that's a lot more complicated than it looks,
9 Which is how it came to pass that the Brits extended a helping hand,
10 ^eAnd within months of Kennedy's funeral,
11 Sent a great gift to their friends the Yanks,
12 A gift designed to help educate the Yanks about the world,
13 At long last,

14 So that they would know how to face a future full of pain and suffering and failure,
15 ^fAnd how to get ready for the inevitable decline that befalls every Chosen Nation sooner or later,
16 ^gWhich the Brits knew everything there was to know about,
17 ^hAnd wanted to share with their cousins across the sea,
18 So that a day would eventually come when the Yanks were as bad at everything as the Brits had gotten to be,
19 And maybe they would even forget how to build nuclear weapons properly,
20 So that they wouldn't work,
21 ⁱJust like everything the Brits made,
22 Which would make the world safer,
23 Unless it wouldn't,
24 ^jBut what can you do,
25 Because when the world is coming to an end,
26 ^kIt's coming to an end,
27 ^lAnd it doesn't much matter if it ends the American Way or the Russkie Way or the Brit Way,
28 ^mBecause it's all the way of Mankind,
29 ⁿAnd no one has ever thought of any other way,
30 ^oNo matter how much they wanted to believe that they were different,
31 ^pBecause a pointed stick is a cannon is a nuclear warhead,
32 ^qAnd a killer ape is a Roman is a Brit is a Kraut is a Yank,
33 ^rAnd being Chosen is a delusion is a lie is a joke,
34 And so what can you do?
35 ^sWhich is why the Yanks accepted the gift of the Brits,

a. 47.18-20
b. 144.8
c. Chuk.19.16-17
d. Psom.77.9-10
e. Psp.3.14
f. Pnot.13.1-5
g. Brit.56.7-17
h. Ned.8.8
i. Brit.57.14
j. F&J.5.1-5
k. Psay.5Q.62
l. Swar.26.8-9
m. Pnot.24.1-5
n. Jeff.23.1-7
o. Zig.9.2
p. Adam.50.6
q. Al.4.7-11
r. Krt.38.7
s. Psay.5Q.66

36 A little dubiously,
37 But willing to listen,
38 Because it was getting a lot harder to go on being proud and confident and hopeful about everything,
39 ᵃSince nobody else was,

a. 152.9

40 And maybe it was time for the Yanks to pay attention to somebody else's ideas,
41 For a change,
42 And learn how to make it better the Brit way.
43 *Yeah yeah yeah.*

THE BOOK OF BEAKS

OTHERWISE KNOWN AS THE BOOK OF BLOODY NOSES

CHAPTER 1

There was another place that started on the right-hand side of the Mediterranean and went all the way to India and beyond.
2 This place was called the near east,
3 Or the middle east,
4 ᵃAnd was mostly full of sand,
5 And people with big noses,
6 Who hated each other a lot,
7 And everybody else too,
8 For a long long time,
9 And just possibly forever.
10 ᵇThis is their story.

CHAPTER 2

There are lots and lots of different peoples in the middle east,
2 ᶜSince that's where the creation supposedly got started in the first place,
3 Which explains why all of the middle easterners thought they were specially Chosen by their Gods to rule the world and so forth,
4 Even if they weren't.

a. Spic.3.3
b. F&J.2.15
c. 1.4
d. Lies.3.1-12
e. Chr.4.6
f. Mes.1.10-11
g. Grks.22.2
h. Exp.9.5-10
i. Grk.1.1-11
j. Grk.25.1-3
k. Grk.25.4-5
l. Grk.25.6-7

5 For example, the middle east was full of Hebrews,
6 ᵈWho were Chosen and also quite religious,
7 And Arabs,
8 Who were Chosen and oddly fond of ᵉcamels,
9 And Assyrians,
10 ᶠWho were Chosen and also about as vicious and bloodthirsty as any people who ever lived,
11 ᵍAnd Persians,
12 Who were also Chosen, although nobody's ever had any idea why,
13 And Indians,
14 ʰWho had so many thousands of Gods that they couldn't help being Chosen by some of them,
15 And a lot more besides.
16 ⁱUnfortunately for all of them, it turned out that it was really the Greeks who were Chosen,
17 ʲWhich they found out when Alexander the Great conquered their worlds,
18 ᵏAnd all the others too,
19 ˡUntil there weren't any left to conquer,

20 Which made it the Romans' turn.

CHAPTER 3

[a]The Romans wanted to prove that they were more Chosen than the Greeks,
2 [b]So they conquered everybody too,
3 That is, everybody that wasn't too hard to get to,
4 Which turned out to be everybody but the Indians,
5 Who were really quite a long way from everywhere,
6 [c]And too hard to get to for everyone,
7 Until much much later, when the Brits remembered they were there and thought it would be extremely difficult to conquer and rule them,
8 Which it was,
9 [d]And explains why they went to all the trouble of subjugating the Indian subcontinent for a century or so.
10 Anyway,
11 The Romans had most of the middle east in their empire for quite a while,
12 [e]And actually wound up moving there to get away from all the European barbarians,
13 [f]Who were starting to act pretty Chosen themselves,
14 Even if they hadn't learned how to spell it yet.
15 The Romans much preferred the eastern barbarians,
16 For some reason,
17 [g]And hung out in Constantinople,
18 Until the barbarians there started calling themselves Turks,
19 And decided they wanted an empire of their own.

a. Rom. 1.1-11
b. Rom. 12.12
c. Rom. 2.20-22
d. Brit. 2.1-3
e. Rom. 24.1-10
f. Rom. 20.17
g. Rom. 24.11-13
h. Gyp. 3.13
i. Spic. 3.4-10
j. Dav. 41.23
k. Chr. 8.1-11
l. Ext. 52.16
m. Lies. 10.4-6

CHAPTER 4

Meanwhile, some of the eastern barbarians who called themselves Moors were conquering the Mediterranean,
2 [h]Including northern Africa,
3 [i]And Spain too,
4 Because they had recently found out they were especially Chosen by their God,
5 Whose name was [j]Allah,
6 And wanted them to kill everything that moved.
7 And so the Moors had a nice empire going for a while too,
8 And killed lots and lots and lots of heathens,
9 Especially Christian heathens,
10 Who had the nerve to suggest that *they* were really the Chosen ones,
11 Because their God had told them so,
12 And by the way, His name wasn't Allah,
13 But God,
14 And besides, He was completely different from Allah,
15 Since He believed in love and mercy and peace,
16 [k]And that if you had to kill a heathen, you'd better do it with a straight sword and a lot of chivalry,
17 [l]Not with a curved sword and a lot of foreign-sounding jibber jabber.
18 [m]For this reason, God told the Christians to kill as many of Allah's followers as they could,
19 Which they did.
20 And so the Chosen ones hacked and slashed and impaled the heathen heretics until final victory was assured for the one and only all-powerful deity,
21 Who had created everything all by Himself,

22 And whose name was [a]Allah,

23 Unless it was [b]God,

24 Thus proving who had really been right about everything all along.

CHAPTER 5

While the [c]Moors were out slaughtering everybody in the name of Allah,

2 Some of the other eastern barbarians may have been having fun too,

3 But nobody really remembers much about it,

4 Because all the books written by the eastern barbarians are much too long to read,

5 And besides, it doesn't really matter what happened,

6 Since nothing really changed anyway,

7 And none of them have ever really been Chosen,

8 Because if they had, we'd have heard more about it,

9 And they wouldn't still be acting like a bunch of crazy barbarians.

CHAPTER 6

At some point, the Eastern Roman Empire stopped being there,

2 [d]But nobody knows when exactly,

3 Or why,

4 And nobody much cares.

5 After that, there was an Ottoman Empire,

6 Which was started by some [e]Turks who believed in putting their feet up a lot,

7 For some reason.

8 By this time, the Hebrews had moved to Europe,

9 [f]For some reason,

a. 4.5
b. Lies.2.26-28
c. Pnot.10.1-5
d. Psay.5Y.15
e. 3.15-19
f. Lies.13.1-8
g. Wil.17.1
h. 6.17-18
i. 6.2-4
j. 6.20
k. 5.5-6
l. 6.24-26
m. 6.17-18
n. 6.2-4

10 Completely abandoning their homeland,

11 Which was called Israel,

12 Or Canaan,

13 Or Palestine,

14 Or Zion,

15 Or the Land of Milk and Honey,

16 Or something or other,

17 Which you could look up,

18 [g]If you cared.

19 When the Hebrews left wherever it was,

20 For whatever reason,

21 The Arabs moved in,

22 With lots of camels, and tents, and things on their heads,

23 [h]For some reason,

24 Which was bound to cause trouble later,

25 Because no matter what anybody does in the middle east,

26 It's sure to cause lots of trouble later,

27 [i]For some reason.

28 The Persians may also have been up to something about then,

29 [j]Something involving peacocks,

30 [k]But maybe not too.

CHAPTER 7

Things went on like this for a long time,

2 [l]With lots of people you never heard of doing lots of things you never knew about,

3 [m]In a lot of different countries you never cared about.

4 In between wars and things, they also made up some culture,

5 Including mosques and 8 by 12 carpets and other stuff too,

6 Like Arabic numerals,

7 [n]Which explains why the Arabs are world famous for being brilliant mathematicians,

8 Or something like that.

9 ^aWhat with all the carpets and numerals and stuff, the middle easterners were generally far too busy to notice that someone had discovered a new world,

10 ^bSo they missed out on their chance to help make history,

11 And therefore had to settle for making trouble instead,

12 Which they did.

13 Then, when they weren't looking,

14 History sneaked up on them from behind,

15 ^cWhich is the way things go,

16 ^dLife being what it is.

CHAPTER 8

^e**F**or example, the Brits eventually noticed India and moved in,

2 Which changed everything,

3 ^fFor some reason.

4 And then there was the Ottoman Empire,

5 Which the bottom fell out of,

6 ^gFor some reason,

7 And suddenly it was time for World War I,

8 ^hWhen Lawrence of Arabia discovered that the ⁱArabs were really terrific at killing ^jTurks,

9 And found out how much fun it was,

10 And told everybody about it,

11 ^kIncluding the Brits,

12 Which explains why the Ottoman Empire isn't around today,

13 ^lAnd why the Turks now live in a place called Turkey.

CHAPTER 9

After World War II, the Hebrews decided to move back to ^mIsrael,

a. *Psay.5Y.1*
b. *Exp.1.1-6*
c. *Lies.14.4*
d. *Lies.14.5*
e. *3.7-9*
f. *Brit.26.9-26*
g. *8.8*
h. *Dav.41.10-16*
   Bks.6.17-18
i. *Dav.41.23*
j. *Dav.14.11-12*
k. *F&J.14.13*
l. *Barb.5.2*
m. *6.11*
n. *6.14*
o. *6.13*
p. *6.25-26*
q. *6.12*
r. *Spic.3.3*
s. *Mall.6.24-25*
t. *Wil.19.15-17*
u. *Psay.5W.18*
v. *6.20*

2 ⁿOr Zion,

3 ^oOr Palestine,

4 Or whatever it was,

5 ^pWhich caused problems,

6 Because ^qCanaan was this really beautiful land,

7 ^rFull of sand,

8 ^sWhich is why all the Arabs feel like they just can't live without it,

9 Since it goes great with all the other lands in the near east,

10 Which are also full of sand,

11 As well as oil,

12 Which causes problems too.

CHAPTER 10

What with sand and other very important issues like that, ^tthe peoples of the near east decided the only thing to do was kill each other,

2 As much as possible,

3 Forever,

4 ^uAnd so they did.

5 Some of the killing was for religious reasons,

6 And some of it was for economic reasons,

7 But mostly it was for irreconcilable differences,

8 Since they were all completely and utterly different from each other,

9 Except for their noses,

10 And their love of sand,

11 And their fanatical devotion to their religion,

12 ^vAnd their consuming desire to annihilate their enemies,

13 Which were usually everybody else,

14 Including the Iranians,

15 And the Iraqis,

16 And the Saudis,

17 And the Syrians,

18 And the Jordanians,
19 And the Lebanese,
20 And the Israelis,
21 And the Palestinians,
22 And the Kuwaitis,
23 And the Turks,
24 ^aAnd a bunch of others too,
25 Except the Indians,
26 Who are too busy hating the Pakistanis to fight about sand,
27 Ever since ^bMahatma Gandhi pushed the ^cBrits out of India,
28 By pretending that Indians were too peace-loving to hate anybody,
29 ^dWhich is only the second or third joke ever pulled off in the middle east.

a. *Main.22.10*
b. *Dav.14.23*
c. *Brit.56.14-16*
d. *Grk.18.28*
e. *Psom.12.7*

CHAPTER 11

And eventually, when the end of the world comes,
2 It will probably start in the middle east,
3 Where nobody ever learns,
4 For thousands and thousands and thousands of years,
5 Which is probably okay,
6 Because when the end of the world comes,
7 ^eThere will finally be peace,
8 For billions and billions and billions of years,
9 Unless God is crazy enough to start another creation in the middle east,
10 Which would exactly double *His* current total of middle east jokes.

THE BOOK OF RUSSKIES

OTHERWISE KNOWN AS THE BOOK OF THE MOTHERLAND

CHAPTER 1

At the extreme right-hand side of Europe, there was a gigantic place called Russia,
2 Where a lot of people lived in complete misery for centuries,
3 Because they wanted to be Chosen,
4 ^aBut couldn't even get a loud foul,
5 Until the twentieth century,
6 When all kinds of crazy things happened,
7 Including a loud foul in the land of the Russkies.
8 This is their ^bstory.

a. *Psay.5S.5-7*
b. *Ira.27.18-19*
c. *Dav.18.5*
d. *Yks.125.22-23*
e. *Dav.18.29-31*

CHAPTER 2

Nobody much knows how the Russkies got started,
2 Except that there were some barbarians called ^cCossacks,
3 Who used to come riding like the wind out of the east into Poland,
4 Where they reminded the ^dPoles that there's more to being a great fighter than just being stupid and vicious.
5 For example, it's a good idea to shave your head except for a topknot,
6 ^eAlthough being stupid and vi-

cious is also a help, of course,

7 As the Russkies have always known,

8 Better than practically anybody else.

9 Anyway,

10 The Cossacks and the ªMongols and other Russkie barbarians charged around quite a lot,

11 For quite a while,

12 Waiting for the invention of feudalism,

13 ᵇWhich happened when the Christians got things under control in Europe,

14 ᶜAnd convinced the Russkies that rule by divine right was the way to go,

15 As long as they could do it the Russkie way,

16 Which involves doing everything more slowly and clumsily and in larger numbers than everyone else.

CHAPTER 3

For example, the Russkies eventually decided that they should be ruled by the divine right of czars,

2 ᵈWhich was something like the divine right of kings,

3 But different,

4 ᵉBecause the czar got his divine right from the Russian Orthodox Church instead of the Roman Catholic Church,

5 And therefore missed out on all the fashion changes that made things so exciting in Europe,

6 Every thousand years or so,

7 Which helps explain why the Russkies got organized as a nation about a thousand years later than everyone else,

8 Among other things.

a. Chnk.11.4-5
b. Chr.3.16-22
c. Chr.2.12-21
d. 2.14
e. Jefs.7.15
f. Chr.3.23-26
g. Gnt.13.9
h. Grk.26.9-10

CHAPTER 4

In spite of being a little late, the Russkies managed to do some things right anyway.

2 For example, they figured out the ᶠserf thing really well,

3 And had more serfs than you could shake a pointed stick at,

4 Not to mention hundreds and hundreds of nobles,

5 Including ᵍprinces,

6 Who had incredibly long and clumsy-sounding names,

7 As required by the Russkie style,

8 Which involves doing everything in Russian,

9 Because it's so much slower and clumsier that way.

10 In fact, the Russian language is the second most important thing in Russkie culture,

11 And is quite interesting,

12 If you like things that are boring and ugly,

13 Which the Russkies always have.

14 ʰThe Russian alphabet was a gift from the Greeks,

15 Who had an extra one that somebody had squashed with a tractor,

16 Which made it perfect to give to the Russkies,

17 Who were happy to get it,

18 And made a brand-new language out of it,

19 Including a bunch of peculiar grammar,

20 And as many as a thousand vocabulary words,

21 Of which no more than two hundred mean "potato,"

22 Which isn't bad, considering that potatoes are the single most important thing in Russkie culture.

CHAPTER 5

The other thing the Russkies got right about the feudal thing was making sure that the [a]serfs never had any fun to speak of.

2 In fact, the Russkie serfs,

3 Also called peasants,

4 Had so little fun over the years that their only real enjoyment in life was feeling such extreme misery that the thought of being dead and buried seemed like heaven,

5 Which is why the Russkies started calling their country the Motherland,

6 And got so sentimental about dirt,

7 Since that's what you got to live in when you died.

CHAPTER 6

Of course, potatoes and dirt weren't the only great things about Russkie culture.

2 There was also [b]snow,

3 Which you could freeze to death in,

4 Unless the [c]wolves got you first,

5 Or the czar,

6 Or starvation,

7 Or some other great Russkie tradition like that.

CHAPTER 7

Meanwhile, the czars thought Russia should be a [d]Chosen Nation,

2 [e]Since they had all those peasants,

3 [f]And all that dirt,

4 [g]And all that snow,

5 [h]Not to mention potatoes,

a. Chr.4.1-3
b. Psom.61.1-8
c. Dav.30.9
d. Exp.1.4-6
e. 4.3
f. 5.5-6
g. 6.2
h. 4.22
i. Ed.63.3
j. 7.9
k. Gnt.1.13
l. Exp.9.9-20
m. Dav.41.12

6 Which may help explain why the czars got such big ideas,

7 Since it was the Russkies who figured out how to make vodka from potatoes.

8 Anyway,

9 There was a czar called [i]Ivan,

10 Who was terrible,

11 For some reason,

12 And decided that the first thing you had to do if you wanted to be a Chosen Nation was be a nation in the first place.

13 After Ivan had killed everyone who didn't want to be a nation,

14 He was all tired out and went insane,

15 Unless he went insane earlier than that,

16 Or even much earlier than that.

CHAPTER 8

After the death of [j]Ivan the Terrible, the Russkies needed some time to think about what to do next,

2 Which they usually do,

3 And explains why they happened to miss the [k]Renaissance and the [l]discovery of the new world and things like that,

4 Until there was a czar named [m]Peter the Great,

5 Who thought that maybe the Russkies needed to be more modern,

6 Which was a nice idea,

7 Even if it was a little late.

8 It was Peter who invented reading and writing,

9 And buildings,

10 And other things too,

11 Including cities,

12 Which is why the city of St. Petersburg was named after him.

CHAPTER 9

Even after Peter's death, the Great family stayed in charge,

2 Which is how there came to be [a]Catherine the Great,

3 Who also believed in being modern,

4 [b]As well as in having sex about once every half-hour,

5 [c]Which made her very popular in Europe,

6 [d]Until one of her lovers fell on her,

7 And couldn't call for help in time to save her,

8 Because his bridle was too tight.

CHAPTER 10

Then there were other czars,

2 With names like [e]Nicholas and Alexander,

3 And [f]Alexander and Nicholas,

4 As well as [g]Nicholas and Alexander,

5 Who invented the modern Russkie military tradition,

6 Which involves sending millions of unarmed peasants into combat in the snow,

7 Against ferocious enemies led by intelligent generals,

8 Just to see what will happen.

9 This explains why the Russkies have more and bigger monuments to their war dead than any other nation on earth,

10 And why the Russkie peasants got so fond of the czars over the years.

CHAPTER 11

Eventually, [h]Napoleon Bonaparte thought it would be fun to kill a few million Russkie peasants,

a. Dav.14.38
b. Mall.15.6
c. Mall.15.8
d. Ned.35.15
e. Dav.42.7
f. Dav.42.15
g. Dav.42.22
h. Dav.14.4-5
i. Frog.17.2-12
j. Dav.41.19
k. Dav.41.19
l. Dav.41.19
m. Pnot.4.1-5
n. Psay.51.1
o. 12.3

2 And maybe conquer Russia too,

3 [i]Which didn't work out very well for Napoleon,

4 But made the Russkies feel pretty proud of themselves.

5 In fact, the Russkie victory over Napoleon resulted in the first Russkie writer,

6 Whose name was [j]Tolstoy,

7 And who wrote an incredibly long novel called *War and Peace*,

8 Which is so great that millions of people the world over are taught to pretend that they've read it,

9 Even though nobody has the slightest idea what it's about.

CHAPTER 12

Not surprisingly, Tolstoy led to other Russkie writers,

2 Namely [k]Dostoyevski,

3 And [l]Chekhov,

4 Who discovered that it was possible to turn unspeakable misery into great literature.

5 Dostoyevski wrote thousands of huge novels about misery,

6 Including [m]'Crime and Punishment,'

7 And 'The Possessed,'

8 And 'The Brothers Karamazov,'

9 And [n]others,

10 Based on the idea that since life is completely miserable,

11 The best thing to do is spend all your time thinking about it,

12 And being depressed about it,

13 For thousands of pages.

14 [o]Chekhov, on the other hand,

15 Had a completely different idea,

16 Which was that since life is completely miserable,

17 The best thing to do is write depressing [a]short stories and [b]plays about it,

18 Which leaves more time for just sitting there,

19 Not to mention the fact that you don't spend as much money on ink and paper,

20 [c]Which means there's more to spend on vodka.

CHAPTER 13

Literature wasn't the only new art form the Russkies discovered because of [d]Napoleon's attempted conquest of Russia.

2 For example, there was also music,

3 Which was invented by [e]Tchaikovsky,

4 Who composed a triumphant thing called the '1812 Overture' to celebrate the defeat of Napoleon,

5 And went on to write a lot of symphonies and concertos and so forth about how sad life is,

6 Which inspired a lot of other Russkie composers to do the same thing,

7 Including [f]Stravinsky,

8 Who discovered that life was not only sad, but [g]dissonant too,

9 And [h]Rachmaninoff,

10 [i]Who discovered that life is mostly sad,

11 [j]Except when it's completely hopeless and tragic,

12 And so forth,

13 And so on.

CHAPTER 14

[k]Meanwhile, the czars were speeding along in their

a. *Swar.18.7*
b. *Swar.18.8*
c. *7.7*
d. *11.1*
e. *Dav.20.34*
f. *Dav.30.9*
g. *Gods.1.4*
   Psay.5A.40
h. *Dav.20.36*
i. *Psom.37.1-6*
j. *Psom.69.1*
   Psong.56.1-3
   Vin.73.12
k. *8.5*
l. *Boul.21.9*
m. *Krt.24.2-3*
n. *Dav.29.19*
o. *Zig.7.5*

continuing attempt to modernize Russia,

2 And eventually got around to freeing the serfs,

3 About three or four hundred years after Europe did,

4 Except that they had to keep on being peasants,

5 Which was something like being a serf;

6 In fact, it was a lot like being a serf,

7 [l]Which meant that the peasants didn't have to give up being miserable just to be modern.

8 This discovery was a big relief to the Russkies,

9 Who had been so worried about it that it caused them to drag their feet just a little bit when it came to trying out new ideas.

10 Fortunately, though, the whole Russkie nation started to take an interest in trying other new ideas,

11 After they'd thought about it for a few more years,

12 Which brings us to [m]World War I.

CHAPTER 15

Along time before World War I, there had been a great thinker named Marx,

2 [n]Who got the idea that capitalism was no good,

3 And should be replaced by something called [o]Marxism,

4 Which involved putting the workers in charge of everything,

5 So that everything could be done by the greatest number to those of greatest ability,

6 From each according to his needs,

7 To each according to his goods,

185

8 [a]Or something like that.

9 The Russkies thought about what Marx had said for about fifty years or so,

10 Which was pretty quickly by their standards,

11 And when things didn't go just exactly right in [b]World War I,

12 They decided to give Marxism a try.

13 What happened was that millions of peasants were starving,

14 As usual,

15 And millions more were dying in the snow against the German army,

16 And a crazy [c]monk named [d]Rasputin was making the czar spend the whole gross national product on [e]Fabergé potatoes,

17 Which took a whole year to produce a crop of one,

18 Which wasn't edible anyway,

19 And so the peasants decided they were fed up.

CHAPTER 16

The way the Russkies looked at it, [f]Marxism made perfect sense,

2 [g]Because if capitalism was a rotten system that led to stinking industrial cities full of mistreated workers,

3 [h]And would inevitably be replaced by a Marxist system in which the mistreated industrial workers would seize control of the whole industrial structure,

4 Then why wait for the [i]industrial revolution to reach Russia?

5 Why not skip ahead,

6 From a basically feudal agricultural economy to a modern industrial Marxist state,

7 [j]Where everything would be perfect?

8 And so they did.

9 They shot the czar,

10 And his family,

11 [k]A whole bunch of times,

12 Until they were all dead,

13 Except maybe for [l]Princess Anastasia,

14 Who might have survived and become a movie star later,

15 Unless she didn't.

16 [m]Then they shot Rasputin,

17 [n]And poisoned him,

18 [o]And stabbed him,

19 [p]And drowned him,

20 Until he was probably dead,

21 Although you can never be completely sure about mad monks.

22 [q]Then they shot all the Russkie nobles,

23 [r]And their families,

24 [s]And all their friends and acquaintances,

25 [t]And then a whole bunch of peasants who thought that the next thing to do was be free and democratic,

26 Because being free and democratic might lead to dire consequences,

27 Like the end of misery,

28 Which isn't Russian,

29 And can't be tolerated.

CHAPTER 17

Eventually, a Marxist named [u]Lenin became the new czar of Russia,

2 Except that he wasn't a czar, of course,

3 [v]But completely different,

4 [w]Since he didn't spend the whole gross national product on [x]Fabergé potatoes,

5 [y]But on secret police instead,

6 So that the rights of the peo-

Reference column:

a. Carl.3.12
b. Krt.24.2-3
c. Chr.5.17-18
d. Dav.6.4
e. 17.4
f. 15.1-3
g. Brit.28.4-16
h. Carl.3.1-7
i. Adam.8.1-11
j. Jefs.7.46
k. Ann.10.1
   & 10.1
   & 10.1
   & 10.1
l. Dav.11.5
m. Dav.47.23
n. Dav.47.25
o. Psom.78.10
   & 78.12-13
p. Ed.78.11
q. Ann.10.1
   & 10.1
   & 10.1
   & 10.1
r. Ann.10.1
   & 10.1
   & 10.1
   & 10.1
s. Ann.10.1
   & 10.1
   & 10.1
   & 10.1
t. Ann.10.1
   & 10.1
   & 10.1
   & 10.1
   & 10.1
   & 10.1
   & 10.1
   & 10.1
   & 10.1
   & 10.1
   & 10.1
u. Dav.30.9
v. Ed.12.20-22
w. 15.16
x. Psom.3.1-6
y. Ed.51.22

ple would always be protected against the treacherous grousing of counterrevolutionary peasants,

7 Who thought that since the world was going to be perfect,

8 It might be nice to have something to eat,

9 Someday.

CHAPTER 18

Even though he was not related to the [a]Great family, Lenin turned out to be a great leader for the Russkies.

2 For example, he freed the peasants once and for all by renaming them "comrades,"

3 Which made everything all better,

4 [b]For some reason.

5 He solved the food problem by sending ten percent of the population to forced labor camps in [c]Siberia,

6 Where they didn't get any food at all,

7 Which left a lot more for everybody else.

8 Then he started industrializing Russia,

9 [d]Which he did by building lots of stinking industrial cities full of mistreated workers,

10 [e]Who loved him because not a single person in the whole country had to give up being miserable for even a moment,

11 In spite of all the terrific progress they were making,

12 Which all the Russkies knew about,

13 Because Marxists always make a point of telling their comrades the truth about everything important,

14 Over and over and over again,

a. 9.1
b. Jefs.7.15
c. Grk.6.18-19
d. 16.5
e. 14.7
f. Boul.28.10
g. Gyp.2.10
h. Gyp.1.17
i. Dav.30.25
j. Psay.5W.1-2
k. Dav.14.25
l. Brit.51.1-24
m. Brit.52.16-21
n. 10.5-8
o. Krt.33.2
p. 8.8-12
q. 17.1
r. Yks.116.16

15 [f]Till they believe it.

16 [g]And Lenin was so great at telling the truth that when he died, the Russkies missed him so much they had him stuffed and put on display in the [h]Kremlin,

17 Forever,

18 So they wouldn't ever forget what a great comrade he had been.

CHAPTER 19

After Lenin, there was [i]Stalin,

2 Who probably wasn't quite as great as Lenin,

3 Since even the Russkies tend to think he overdid it a little,

4 What with killing about fifty million people,

5 For no particular reason,

6 Which would have been okay,

7 Except that fifty million people is a lot of people,

8 Even if you're a Russian.

9 But to be fair, Stalin also had to deal with [j]World War II,

10 Which he tried to do by making a deal with [k]Hitler,

11 [l]With the usual results.

12 [m]So when Hitler forgot about their deal and invaded Russia anyway,

13 Stalin felt pretty embarrassed,

14 [n]And retaliated by sending millions of unarmed comrades into the snow to stop the German army,

15 Which they did,

16 In a place called [o]Stalingrad,

17 [p]Which used to be called St. Petersburg,

18 [q]Until Lenin changed its name to Leningrad,

19 [r]And then Stalin renamed it after his own favorite patriot.

20 Anyway,

21 The Russian peasants,

22 That is, the Russian comrades,

23 Stopped the Germans at Stalingrad at a cost of no more than a few million casualties,

24 ^aWhich convinced Stalin that Russia was now definitely a Chosen Nation,

25 And could start throwing its weight around like everyone else.

CHAPTER 20

When the Germans surrendered, Stalin claimed that all of eastern Europe belonged to Russia,

2 Including Poland,

3 And Czechoslovakia,

4 And Hungary,

5 And Albania,

6 And Romania,

7 And East Germany,

8 Because any fool could see that all the eastern Europeans had become completely miserable under Hitler,

9 And had therefore become spiritual comrades of the Russkies,

10 ^bWho were the only ones that knew how to maintain just the right level of misery.

11 Then Stalin went to work building a gigantic iron curtain that would keep western Europe out of the communist ^cparadise the Russkies were creating in eastern Europe.

12 The other victorious allies,

13 Including the Americans and the British and the French,

14 Saw and accepted the wisdom of Stalin's logic,

15 ^dFor some reason,

16 ^eAnd agreed to it on behalf of

a. *Grk.1.1-10*
b. *Psay.5Q.62*
c. *Ed.61.7-9*
d. *Yks.122.12-18*
e. *Yks.116.7*
f. *Yks.124.23*
g. *20.11*
h. *Yks.132.9*
i. *Psay.2.2*
j. *19.1*
k. *23.8*
l. *23.9*
m. *18.9
   23.10*
n. *23.10*

the Poles and the Czechs and the Hungarians and the Albanians and the Romanians and the East Germans,

17 Except the part about Berlin,

18 Which couldn't possibly belong to Russia,

19 ^fFor some reason.

20 Then,

21 Just to make sure that the Europeans and the Americans knew better than to try to ^gbreak in,

22 ^hStalin also arranged to borrow some nuclear secrets from the Americans,

23 Although the Russkies claimed that they developed the technology on their own,

24 Which is probably true,

25 ⁱSince everyone knows that the Russkies have always excelled at science and high technology,

26 Beginning with the invention of the potato,

27 Not to mention the invention of vodka.

CHAPTER 21

Then ^jStalin did a whole bunch of great things for the Russkie people.

2 ^kHe built a huge number of gigantic nuclear bombs, and planes to drop them on enemies all over the world.

3 ^lHe invented a new Marxist way of farming that made the comrades even more miserable than the peasants had been.

4 ^mHe built an incredible number of huge new industrial cities that allowed very large numbers of comrades to be miserable in much less space than had ever been possible before,

5 ⁿIncluding huge new apart-

ment complexes, where three or four families could be miserable together in the same room,

6 ^aAnd if any of them still weren't miserable enough, they could go to Siberia,

7 ^bAlong with practically everybody else.

8 ^cStalin also established a brilliant new government bureaucracy that enabled the Russkies to rule themselves in the most perfectly Russian way ever devised.

9 For example, he set up an incredibly huge number of gigantic committees to run everything,

10 So that everything would be done even more slowly and clumsily and stupidly than even the Russkies had ever believed possible,

11 So that the whole economy produced almost nothing but nuclear bombs,

12 And prisons,

13 ^dAnd tremendous concrete things that didn't really quite do anything.

CHAPTER 22

Stalin was also a great patron of the arts.

2 ^eFor example, he commissioned a lot of tremendous paintings and sculptures and so forth that depicted the strength and intelligence of the comrades,

3 On every wall that was more than forty feet tall,

4 ^fWhere they could be a big inspiration to everyone,

5 Especially the gigantic murals and statues of great Russian heroes like Stalin and . . .

6 Well,

7 ^gWhere could you find a big-

*a. 18.5
23.11*
b. 23.12
c. 23.13
d. Gods.6.20-22
e. Krt.22.16
f. Krt.22.16
g. Lies.9.4
h. 18.16
i. Dav.30.27
j. Jeff.19.8
k. 21.2
l. 21.3
*m. 18.9
21.4-5*
*n. 18.5
21.6*
o. 21.7
p. 21.8-10
q. 21.11

ger Russian hero than Stalin anyway?

CHAPTER 23

Eventually, of course, Stalin died,

2 ^hBut didn't get stuffed and put on display,

3 Because the new czar,

4 Whose name was ⁱKhrushchev,

5 Said that Stalin had committed some crimes against the Russian people,

6 ^jSomehow.

7 Then Khrushchev went to work fixing everything up again,

8 ^kWhich he did by building a huge number of gigantic new nuclear weapons,

9 ^lAnd inventing a completely new Marxist way of farming that made the comrades even more miserable than they had ever dared to hope,

10 ^mAnd building more huge industrial cities that allowed very large numbers of comrades to be miserable in huge apartment complexes, where four or five families could be miserable together in the same room,

11 ⁿAnd if any of them weren't quite miserable enough, they could still go to Siberia,

12 ^oAlong with practically everybody else.

13 ^pKhrushchev also reformed the government bureaucracy so that the Russkies could rule themselves with gigantic committees that ran everything even more slowly and clumsily and stupidly than before,

14 ^qSo that the whole economy produced almost nothing but nuclear missiles,

15 And tractors,

16 ᵃAnd tremendous concrete things that didn't really quite do anything.

CHAPTER 24

Things went so well under ᵇKhrushchev that he thought it might finally be time for Russia to become ᶜ*the* Chosen Nation,

2 Even more Chosen than the Americans,

3 Who knew practically nothing about misery,

4 And could probably be intimidated by ᵈRussian technological superiority,

5 Like the time when Khrushchev banged his shoe on the table at the ᵉUnited Nations and upset the Americans no end.

6 The only problem was that the Americans really didn't like it when the Russkies moved a bunch of gigantic missiles into Cuba,

7 Ninety miles from Florida,

8 And decided,

9 With typical American foresight,

10 ᶠThat they'd rather blow up the whole world than have Russkie missiles in Cuba.

11 This was terribly embarrassing to Khrushchev,

12 Who soon retired,

13 ᵍTo a suburb of Siberia,

14 So that a new Russkie czar could keep things moving forward,

15 ʰBy building lots of gigantic new missiles and factories and cities and concrete things,

16 And so forth,

a. 21.13
b. 23.4
c. Exp.1.4-5
d. 20.25
e. Yks.123.18-23
f. Yks.147.10-21
g. 18.5
h. 23.8-16
i. Hill.S.34
j. 24.1
*k. Jeff.19.1-5
    Carl.4.1-10*
l. F&J.2.15-16
m. 18.16
n. 5.5-7

17 And so on,

18 ⁱNot to mention Siberia.

CHAPTER 25

And so the Russkies will probably keep on trying to be a ʲChosen Nation,

2 Even if it kills them,

3 And everybody else too,

4 Because when you're a Russkie,

5 Nuclear holocaust doesn't seem so bad,

6 Especially when you compare it to living in Russia,

7 Where absolutely nothing and no one has ever been Chosen,

8 By anyone,

9 Not even God,

10 ᵏWho didn't quite survive the Marxist Revolution,

11 Which, when you think about it,

12 ˡDoesn't seem like a very good sign for anyone,

13 All things considered.

CHAPTER 26

And when the world comes to an end,

2 It will probably start in some office in the ᵐKremlin,

3 Where some Russkie leader will decide that in spite of all his best efforts,

4 The world just can't be made miserable enough,

5 Without killing everyone and everything in it,

6 So that the only thing left is a whole bunch of dirt,

7 With one special Chosen Patch,

8 ⁿThat used to be called the Motherland.

THE BOOK OF CHINKS

OTHERWISE KNOWN AS THE BOOK OF THE GREAT WALL

CHAPTER 1

Somewhere below the eastern part of [a]Russia, there was a place called China,
2 Which became a great Chosen Nation,
3 Surrounded by a Great Wall,
4 So that all the barbarians who lived outside couldn't get in.
5 Unfortunately, the wall didn't work,
6 Because it had some chinks in it,
7 That let the barbarians in,
8 And almost ruined everything for the only civilized people on earth.
9 This is their [b]story.

CHAPTER 2

[c]Long before there was anything else,
2 There was China,
3 Which was especially Chosen by the Chink Gods to be better than everyone else,
4 Forever.
5 The first thing they did was invent a unique form of government,
6 [d]Called rule by divine right of dynasties,
7 [e]Which was completely different from every other form of government on earth,
8 [f]Since dynasties consisted of a series of Chink emperors,
9 [g]Who had absolute power over everybody,
10 [h]And were probably Gods.
11 [i]The first Chink dynasty was the Shang dynasty of the Yellow River Valley,
12 Which didn't exactly write down any history,
13 [j]But left some broken dishes behind,
14 [k]Which is how the nation came by its name.

CHAPTER 3

Everything that was ever invented was invented in China first,
2 [l]Including the wheel,
3 [m]And art,
4 [n]And literature,
5 [o]And cookies,
6 [p]And music,
7 [q]And firecrackers,
8 And tiny little paper umbrellas,
9 And great big plaster [r]dragons,
10 [s]And porcelain vases,
11 [t]Not to mention philosophy and religion,
12 And gambling,
13 And checkers,
14 [u]And walls,
15 And science,
16 Except maybe not so much science as the other things,
17 Because when you already know everything worth knowing, why do you need science?

CHAPTER 4

The Chinks also invented ships,
2 Which they thought were junk,
3 Because the whole purpose of

a. Russ.1.1
b. Ira.27.20-25
c. Vin.1.14-19 Lies.10.6
d. Nips.3.1
e. Chr.1.5
f. Nips.3.3
g. Nips.3.4
h. Rom.15.2-4
i. Psay.5Y.29
j. 2.2
k. 5.5
l. 9.4-6
m. Paul.7.6
n. Swar.16.2-3
o. 6.3
p. Dav.58.9
q. Dav.47.23
r. Lies.5.20-25
s. 10.4
t. 6.1
u. 1.3

a ship is to go somewhere,
4 And why would you want to go anywhere,
5 When you're already there,
6 In the only place worth being,
7 ªNamely, China.

CHAPTER 5

Not that everything was always perfect.
2 For example, after the Han dynasty,
3 Which ruled China a long long time ago,
4 If you have to get precise about it,
5 There was a new dynasty called the ᵇChin dynasty,
6 Which invented the idea of having lots and lots of laws,
7 ᶜAnd then killing everybody who disobeyed them.
8 The Chin dynasty lasted a good twenty years or so,
9 ᵈAnd was replaced by another Han dynasty,
10 Which believed in doing things the Chink way,
11 Namely, the way they've always been done before,
12 Except they didn't quite throw out all the Chin laws exactly,
13 ᵉAnd they didn't completely stop killing people exactly,
14 Because there's no point in overdoing it,
15 And besides, the Chinks have always been pretty good about dying when their emperor tells them to,
16 Which is one of the most important features of Chink civilization.

CHAPTER 6

The Han dynasty was also great because it liked to do

a. *Jefs.7.46*
b. *Barb.5.2*
c. *Ann.4.1*
d. *5.2*
e. *Ann.4.22*
f. *Dav.20.32*
g. *Lies.9.7*
h. *Lies.14.5*
i. *Dav.47.25*

things the Confucian way,
2 Which is a lot like the Chink way,
3 Except ᶠConfucius put all his wisdom into cookies so that people could digest it more easily.
4 For example, he did a cookie about how Chinks should respect their ancestors,
5 Even if they're alive,
6 And have a lot of funny ideas about things,
7 Because maybe their ideas aren't really funny,
8 But wise,
9 ᵍSo you'd better do like they say.
10 Another cookie said that the Chinks should be polite,
11 And accept everything that happens,
12 ʰBecause lots of things happen in life,
13 And you may as well accept it all the way it happens,
14 Because after all, you're living in China,
15 Which is pretty great,
16 Considering that you might have been born in some barbarian country,
17 ⁱLike Japan.

CHAPTER 7

All in all, civilization was a very big thing with the Chinks.
2 Since they'd invented it in the first place, they had very strict ideas about what was civilized and what wasn't.
3 For example, it wasn't civilized for young people to pick their own mates,
4 And so their parents usually did it for them,
5 Whether the young people

thought it was a civilized custom or not.

6 Fortunately, it all tended to work out,

7 [a]Because parents almost always thought it was civilized to pick their children's mates,

8 Since they didn't get to pick theirs,

9 [b]And why should some youngster be so lucky?

10 [c]The Chinks also thought it wasn't civilized to have beards,

11 Which worked out pretty well because Chinks can't grow beards,

12 [d]Unless you count those little disgusting wisps of hair that some of the uncivilized ones have.

CHAPTER 8

[e]The Chinks had a lot of ideas about how to civilize women,

2 [f]Which worked better than most of the ways other peoples have tried.

3 [g]For example, Chink women were always supposed to walk behind their husbands,

4 [h]Because every civilized man knows that women are supposed to be obedient and polite and not talk all the time,

5 [i]Or at least walk far enough behind you that you can't hear them talking all the time.

6 [j]And when that didn't work, they thought up even more exotic ways of helping women to be civilized,

7 [k]Like binding their feet,

8 [l]From birth,

9 [m]So that they couldn't walk very far,

10 [n]At least not without a lot of pain,

a. *Boul.26.2-3*
b. *Psay.1.9*
c. *Frog.12.5*
d. *Brit.15.30*
e. *Mawr.22.18*
f. *Mawr.22.19*
g. *Mawr.22.20*
h. *Mawr.22.21*
i. *Mawr.22.22*
j. *Mawr.22.23*
k. *Mawr.27.24*
l. *Mawr.22.25*
m. *Mawr.22.26*
n. *Mawr.22.27-28*
o. *Mawr.22.29*
p. *Mawr.22.30*
q. *Mawr.23.1*
r. *Mawr.23.5*
s. *Mawr.23.6*
t. *Mawr.23.7-8*
u. *Mawr.23.9*
v. *Mawr.23.10*
w. *Mawr.23.11*
x. *Mawr.23.12*
y. *Mawr.23.13*
z. *Mawr.23.14-17*
aa. *6.3*
bb. *1.3*

11 [o]Which made it harder for them to talk all the time.

12 [p]And Chink women were also taught a lot of nice cultural stuff,

13 [q]Like painting,

14 [r]And music,

15 [s]And sexual techniques,

16 [t]Which made them civilized enough to live in the royal court,

17 [u]Where they could have one of two jobs,

18 [v]Namely, they could be a wife,

19 [w]Or a concubine,

20 [x]Not that it really mattered which,

21 [y]Because both jobs had about the same duties,

22 [z]And any man could have as many of either or both as he wanted.

CHAPTER 9

What with all their civilization and the wisdom of [aa]Confucius and the Chin laws and some occasional killing, the Han dynasty turned out to be pretty successful,

2 Although it eventually fell apart,

3 Because of a Chink law called the dynastic cycle,

4 [bb]Which says that every dynasty has to add a nice big section to the Great Wall of China,

5 Run things for about two hundred years,

6 Then fall apart so that a new dynasty can take over.

7 So, when the Han dynasty fell apart at the appointed time,

8 Another dynasty came along to take its place,

9 Which was the Chou dynasty,

10 Unless it was the Sung dynasty,

11 Or the Ming dynasty,
12 Or the Manchu dynasty,
13 If it matters.

CHAPTER 10

In fact, the Chinese dynasties were a lot like the Chinks,
2 Meaning they all looked pretty much alike.
3 ^aFor example, they all lasted about two hundred years,
4 ^bAnd made some very pretty vases,
5 ^cAnd added some more wall around the border of China,
6 ^dAnd had very little history to speak of,
7 Because it's not nice to show up your ^eancestors by doing anything new,
8 Or adventurous,
9 Or memorable.

CHAPTER 11

Every so often, though, a Chink would defy his ancestors and do something memorable anyway.
2 For example, there was a Chink named ^fGenghis Khan who thought it would be fun to kill a lot of people and conquer China too.
3 Killing and conquering came pretty naturally to Genghis,
4 Because he was a ^gMongol,
5 Meaning a Chink barbarian who hadn't really learned how to be properly civilized yet.
6 In fact, Chink dynasties kind of depended on occasional barbarian conquests,
7 Which helped prevent the Chinks from getting too overpopulated,
8 ^hSince they've always been good at having lots and lots of children,

a. 9.5
b. 3.10
c. 9.4
d. Grk.25.7
e. 5.10-11
f. Dav.23.10
g. Russ.2.10-11
h. Nips.26.14
i. Mawr.3.3
j. Grk.9.7
k. Psom.45.1-12
l. Dav.47.24
m. Grk.9.7
n. Chuk.18.1-3
o. Gnt.16.9-12
p. Exp.1.17-26

9 ⁱWhat with all those wives and concubines with bound feet who couldn't run very far to get away from all those civilized Chink men.
10 ^jAnd so Genghis did his part by slaughtering a lot of Chink men, women, and children,
11 Then building his own dynasty,
12 So that his son ^kKublai could succeed him,
13 Which worked out great,
14 Because when a barbarian becomes a Chink emperor, he usually dies after a while,
15 But his family keeps going,
16 Getting more civilized all the time,
17 Until eventually, the whole dynastic family is so civilized that nothing violent or destructive is happening anymore,
18 Except that a lot of wives and concubines are getting caught with great regularity,
19 ^lAnd the population is growing like crazy,
20 ^mWhich means that it's time for another Chink barbarian to show up and start trimming back the population again.
21 And thanks to the fact that there's usually no permanent shortage of barbarians,
22 Even in China,
23 ⁿThe dynastic cycle went round and round like this for a couple thousand years all told,
24 ^oWhich brings us to the Modern Age,
25 When the ^pEuropean barbarians came barging in,
26 And messed everything up plenty,
27 Because they couldn't seem to get the hang of how barbarians are supposed to act in China,

28 [a]Which has to do with killing and rampaging and burning,

29 And has nothing whatever to do with changing the economy,

30 Or the society,

31 Or the basic [b]foundations of Chink civilization.

CHAPTER 12

For example, before the Chinks even knew it, there were [c]Europeans muscling in on all their ports,

2 [d]Demanding the right to trade with the Chinks,

3 [e]Since any fool could see that there was a fortune to be made in selling little paper umbrellas and firecrackers and plaster dragons to Europeans.

4 [f]Pretty soon, the Brits were acting like they owned China,

5 Moving in to Hong Kong and Shanghai,

6 And telling the government what to do,

7 [g]Just like they did with every other government around the world.

8 [h]For example, they told the Chink government to start importing opium,

9 [i]Because they thought it would be popular,

10 [j]Which turned out to be absolutely correct,

11 Thus solving the trade problem very neatly,

12 Except that some of the Chinks resented the Brits and the Yanks and the other Europeans,

13 And rebelled a few times,

14 Which didn't work out very well,

15 [k]Since it usually takes more than firecrackers to defeat a British warship.

a. *Grk.9.7*
b. *1.6*
c. *Yks.59.7-10*
d. *Yks.59.11*
e. *4.2*
f. *Yks.18.4*
g. *Brit.47.12*
h. *Brit.47.13*
i. *Brit.47.14*
j. *Brit.47.15*
k. *Psay.5Q.78*
l. *Grk.20.8*
m. *Yks.21.11-13*
n. *Brit.27.1-6*
o. *Psay.5W.2-3*
p. *Nips.16.1-4*
q. *Ed.28.6*
r. *Russ.16.5-7*
s. *Dav.46.19*
t. *Adam.30.3-7*

CHAPTER 13

When the unpleasantness had settled down a bit, the Brits and the Europeans and the Americans got together and decided that China should be a [l]democracy,

2 So that they would learn how to [m]compromise,

3 And stop being so holier-than-thou all the time,

4 [n]Which, to tell the truth, was starting to get on everyone's nerves.

5 And so the barbarians basically succeeded in setting up the kind of government they wanted in China,

6 Although things started to get pretty confused after that,

7 [o]What with a couple of world wars breaking out,

8 [p]And the Japanese suddenly requiring a lot of thought and concentration from the Europeans and Americans,

9 And a lot of other things going on that were a lot more important than who was doing what to who in China,

10 As if it really mattered anyway.

CHAPTER 14

And so, all of a sudden, it was after World War II, and things in China got pretty fouled up,

2 With [q]Mao Tse-dung running around wanting China to be [r]communist,

3 For some reason,

4 And [s]Chiang Kai-shek running around trying to get away from Mao,

5 Who had a little [t]red book with all the answers in it,

6 Apparently,

7 Until one day, Mao was in charge of everything,

8 ªWhich is to say, the Chink masses were in charge of everything,

9 Doing the greatest number of things possible to the greatest number of needy people,

10 ᵇOr something like that.

CHAPTER 15

With the help of Mao, the Chink masses made a lot of reforms.

2 ᶜFor starters, they repaired the wall,

3 And stopped talking to absolutely everybody.

4 Then they decided to ᵈkill all the Chink intellectuals and ᵉdestroy all traces of the old bad Chink way of doing things.

5 ᶠFor example, under the old bad Chink way, it was the parents who decided who could marry who,

6 Whereas under the new communist Chink way, it was the ᵍstate who decided who could marry who,

7 Which was much better,

8 ʰFor some reason.

9 ⁱUnder the old bad Chink way, people respected and worshiped their ancestors,

10 And maybe ʲConfucius and Buddha and the emperor and some other wise people too.

11 Under the great new Chink way, people respected and worshiped the emperor ᵏMao,

12 Who wasn't actually the emperor,

13 But completely different,

14 ˡBecause he had a lot more power.

15 Anyway, people weren't al-

a. Carl.3.6-8
b. Carl.3.12
c. 9.3-4
d. Ann.10.1
 & 10.1
 & 10.1
 & 10.1
e. Ann.2.32
f. 7.7
g. 14.8
h. Yks.8.3
i. 6.4
j. 6.3
k. 14.2
l. Brit.15.40-41
m. Psay.5Q.62
n. Brit.28.3
o. Yks.125.34
p. Ann.4.1
q. 15.4

lowed to worship their ancestors anymore,

16 Because it was obviously their ancestors who had let the foreign barbarians in in the first place,

17 And what's more, none of their ancestors had been Marxists,

18 ᵐWhich proves that they can't have been so wise after all.

CHAPTER 16

The new emperor also helped the Chinks to become a thoroughly modern nation for the first time.

2 For example, in ancient China, people had to travel in two-wheeled vehicles called rickshaws, which needed human muscle to pull them.

3 ⁿIn the new modern China, people got access to much more advanced transportation technology,

4 Like two-wheeled vehicles called bicycles, ᵒwhich had pulleys and chains to push them along, with a little help from human muscle.

5 And that wasn't all of the modern wonders that Mao introduced to China.

6 For example, the new China got to play ᵖping-pong,

7 Instead of mah-jongg,

8 Which represents tremendous progress,

9 ۹And more than makes up for the several millions of Chinks who had to be executed so that the bad old ways could be laid to rest forever.

CHAPTER 17

Besides bicycles and pingpong, the Chink masses

also got to have a lot of ªchildren,

2 To make sure there would be a big supply of communists in the new China,

3 Since a lot of them would probably have to be killed for the greatest number of goods,

4 ᵇOr something like that.

5 Pretty soon, there were a billion Chinks,

6 ᶜWhich is a lot,

7 And explains why China had to get some nuclear weapons,

8 Which they got from the Russkies by promising to be their friend,

9 ᵈWhich nobody else would,

10 And so the Russkies gave them some atomic missiles and such,

11 Until the Chinks had enough missiles parked behind the Great Wall that they could tell the Russkies what they really thought of them,

12 ᵉWhich wasn't much,

13 And shouldn't have surprised the Russkies anyway,

14 ᶠSince why in the world had the Chinks built three thousand miles of wall along the Russian border to begin with?

CHAPTER 18

A nd so, finally, China was where it wanted to be,

a. 11.8
b. Carl.3.12
c. Adam.19.2-3
d. Russ.25.4-9
e. Krt.38.6
f. Vin.73.12
g. 1.3
h. 17.10
i. 14.7
j. 14.5
k. 5.11
l. 17.6

2 All alone,

3 ᵍWith its great big wall of stone,

4 ʰAnd a great big wall of nuclear weapons,

5 ⁱAnd a great big wonderful friend named Mao,

6 ʲWith a little red book full of all the answers,

7 To all the questions that wouldn't ever have to be asked again,

8 ᵏBecause now things could be done the way they should be,

9 Which is the way the Chinks have been doing them,

10 For as far back as they're allowed to remember.

CHAPTER 19

A nd when the end of the world comes,

2 ˡIt will probably get started because some barbarian forgot about how much the Chinks want to be alone,

3 With their great and wonderful civilization,

4 And there will be hell to pay,

5 And if there's anyone anywhere who knows all about hell,

6 It has to be Mao and the thousand million little Chinks who know so much more than everybody else about how to be a Chosen civilization.

THE BOOK OF NIPS

OTHERWISE KNOWN AS THE BOOK OF THE DIVINE WIND

CHAPTER 1

Off the eastern coast of Asia, pretty near ^aChina and ^bRussia, there was an island called Japan,

2 Or ^cNippon, if you want to get Oriental about it,

3 Which had more people on it than you could shake a pointed stick at,

4 For thousands of years,

5 Until they convinced each other that they were a Chosen Nation,

6 And got themselves into a whole bunch of trouble.

7 This is their ^dstory.

CHAPTER 2

From the very beginning of time, the Japanese people have always been completely civilized,

2 ^fIn fact, as civilized as the Chinese,

3 ^gWho borrowed a lot of their culture from Japan,

4 Unless it was the other way around,

5 Which it wasn't,

6 ^hIn spite of what the Chinks say,

7 Because any Nip will tell you what tremendous liars the Chinks are,

8 Even if the Chinks borrowed their civilization from the Nips somewhat before the Nips had one,

9 Which isn't as impossible as you might think,

10 Because everyone knows

a. Chnk.1.1
b. Russ.1.1
c. F&J.14.13
d. Yks.116.16
e. Vin.1.14-19
Lies.10.6
f. Rom.7.20
g. 16.4
h. Chnk.3.1
i. Frog.12.5
j. Chnk.2.5-6
k. Chr.1.5
l. Chnk.2.8
m. Chnk.2.9
n. Chnk.2.10
o. Bks.6.4

how mysterious and inscrutable Orientals are,

11 Whether they're from Japan or China or Korea or any of the other inscrutable, mysterious countries in the far east.

12 Anyway,

13 It was the Nips who invented civilization,

14 A long long time ago,

15 And they've been trying to get some credit for it ever since,

16 Which hasn't been easy,

17 ⁱBecause most of the world has somehow gotten the completely idiotic notion that the Nips are a bunch of smiling, nodding, two-faced little barbarians who keep trying to take things from everyone else because they've never had an original idea of their own,

18 Which just isn't so,

19 For some reason.

CHAPTER 3

^j**F**or example, it was the Nips who invented the form of government called rule by divine right of dynasties,

2 ^kWhich was completely different from every other form of government on earth,

3 ^lSince dynasties consisted of a series of Nip emperors,

4 ^mWho had absolute power over everybody,

5 ⁿAnd were probably Gods.

6 ^oNobody actually remembers much about the first Nip dynasty,

7 But it was great,

8 And proved that the Nips were a Chosen people,

9 And also quite original.

CHAPTER 4

[a]In fact, the Nips were so original that everything ever invented was invented in Japan first,

2 [b]Including the wheel,

3 [c]And art,

4 [d]And literature,

5 [e]And food made out of raw fish,

6 [f]And music,

7 [g]And tiny little paper umbrellas,

8 [h]And great big paper dragons,

9 [i]And tiny little paper houses,

10 [j]And automobiles made out of old beer cans,

11 [k]Not to mention philosophy and religion,

12 [l]And swords,

13 [m]And zeroes,

14 And good manners,

15 Except maybe not quite so much good manners as the other things,

16 Because when you have enough swords and zeroes, you don't have to be as polite as you used to be.

CHAPTER 5

The Nips also invented the idea of [n]honor,

2 Which they called "face,"

3 Because it involved so much nodding,

4 And never having any facial expression,

5 Even when you committed suicide,

6 Which was another great Nip invention,

7 And just about the most fun

a. Chnk.3.1
b. Chnk.3.2
c. Chnk.3.3
d. Chnk.3.4
e. Dav.47.25
f. Chnk.3.6
g. Chnk.3.8
h. Chnk.3.9
i. Jefs.7.22
j. Vin.49.5
k. Chnk.3.11
l. 8.6
m. Yks.106.9
*   Hill.Z.1*
n. Brit.19.41-42
o. Vin.73.12
p. Mawr.24.1
q. Mawr.24.2
r. Mawr.24.3
s. Mawr.24.4
t. Mawr.24.5
u. Mawr.24.6
v. Mawr.24.7
w. Mawr.24.8

that an honorable Nip could get out of life.

8 Fortunately, there were all kinds of great reasons for committing suicide,

9 Especially for Nip nobles and warriors,

10 Who had to kill themselves if they were disloyal to the emperor,

11 Or committed some terrible crime,

12 Or committed some minor crime,

13 Or committed some minor indiscretion,

14 Or were late for dinner,

15 Or blushed,

16 Or if some social superior told them to.

CHAPTER 6

Naturally, this kind of etiquette resulted in quite a lot of dead bodies,

2 Which was okay,

3 Because Japan was a pretty small island,

4 [o]And there were always too many Nips anyway,

5 [p]Since the Nip women weren't allowed to have anything except lots and lots of male children,

6 [q]Not even orgasms,

7 [r]Which the Nips made sure of by inventing surgery and gynecology at the same time,

8 [s]Because it just isn't civilized for women to have orgasms,

9 [t]Or to walk alongside their husbands,

10 [u]Or talk back,

11 [v]Or say anything at all unless their husband asks them to,

12 [w]Or do anything at all unless their husband tells them to,

13 Except suicide,

14 Which everybody can do anytime they want to,

15 As long as they don't cry out,

16 Or have any facial expression,

17 While they're disemboweling themselves according to the proper Nip ritual.

CHAPTER 7

[a]**O**f course, suicide wasn't the only great Nip ritual.

2 There was also the [b]tea ceremony,

3 [c]Which was so incredibly civilized that no barbarian could ever understand it,

4 [d]A barbarian being anyone who wasn't born in Japan,

5 Obviously.

CHAPTER 8

[a]**A**s civilized as they were, the Nips still had to go to war with each other every once in a while,

2 [e]A while being approximately equal to a month or so,

3 And therefore had a pretty big warrior class,

4 Who called themselves [f]samurai,

5 And had more ways of killing people than you could shake a [g]pointed stick at.

6 For example, it was the samurai who thought up the great idea of having two swords instead of just one,

7 [h]So that you could kill two people at a time instead of just one,

8 [i]Because Japan was a pretty small island,

9 [j]And there were always too many Nips anyway,

a. Ext.13.11
b. Ned.6.24
c. Bks.6.4
d. Forg.11.13
e. Chnk.9.13
f. Dav.34.19
g. Brit.40.8
h. Ann.6.1
  & 6.3
  Ext.4.13
i. 6.3
j. 6.4
k. Dav.34.19
l. 8.6
m. 7.5
n. 18.10
o. Hill.A.4
p. 8.2
q. Russ.2.10-13
r. Ext.1.11
s. Mall.13.8
t. Yks.135.7
u. Chr.3.23-24
v. Chr.3.25
w. Chr.3.26
x. 8.3

10 So it made sense to make wars as deadly as possible,

11 Which the Nips were very very good at.

CHAPTER 9

[a]**F**or example, there were some very special Nip assassins called [k]Ninja,

2 Who could kill people with all kinds of weapons,

3 [l]Including swords,

4 And knives,

5 And bows and arrows,

6 And flying stars,

7 [m]And pointed sticks,

8 And a bunch of other things too,

9 [n]Not to mention their bare hands and feet,

10 [o]Which they could break boards and bricks and necks and other things with,

11 Whenever they wanted,

12 Which was at least every once in a [p]while.

CHAPTER 10

[a]**T**he reason why there were so many wars in Japan was that the Nip civilization was kind of [q]feudal,

2 For about two thousand years,

3 [r]Which maybe aren't quite up yet,

4 [s]Unless they are,

5 [t]Even if it doesn't look that way,

6 To anybody but a Nip.

7 Anyway,

8 [u]The Nip emperor depended on the help of a lot of Nip nobles,

9 [v]Who owned land,

10 [w]And peasants,

11 [x]And a whole bunch of samurai,

12 Which meant that things could get complicated,
13 Every once in a ^awhile,
14 Which is the way things go,
15 Civilization being what it is.

CHAPTER 11

For example, the Nips were far too polite and civilized to kill their emperor,
2 Or even fire him,
3 But they didn't mind giving him suggestions about how to run things,
4 Especially if they had all the military power,
5 And he didn't have any,
6 Or if they had all the money,
7 And he didn't have any,
8 Because they hadn't given him any,
9 For some reason.
10 And so, the Nip emperor always sat on the throne,
11 And everybody always treated him with great respect,
12 But over the years,
13 The Nip nobles had more and more military power,
14 And more and more money,
15 And, by an odd coincidence, more and more suggestions about how the emperor should run Japan.
16 The nobles who made most of the suggestions were called ^bshoguns,
17 And they worked very hard to make sure that everything stayed very civilized, according to the Nip way,
18 Which involves doing whatever you feel like doing,
19 Whenever you want to,
20 As long as you nod and smile and bow a lot,
21 ^cAnd don't lose face,

a. 8.2
b. Dav.34.19
c. 5.1-2
d. 7.4
e. Barb.4.18
f. Yks.59.1-2
g. Yks.59.3
h. Yks.59.4
i. Yks.59.5
j. Yks.59.6
k. Adam.7.1-8
l. Psong.6.8-9
m. Chnk.12.15
n. Russ.10.4-8

22 Unless you're dealing with ^dbarbarians,
23 In which case,
24 Anything goes.

CHAPTER 12

As it happened,
2 The Nips eventually had to deal with a whole bunch of barbarians,
3 Who came from ^eEurope and America,
4 The way they always seem to,
5 And started trying to tell the Nips how to run things in Japan.
6 ^fFor example, there was a Yank named Commodore Perry who made the Nips open up their ports to the barbarians,
7 ^gSo that the barbarians could sell a whole bunch of paper umbrellas and samurai swords and kimonos and things back home.
8 ^hUnfortunately, the Nips hadn't quite got around to inventing some of the weapons the barbarians had,
9 ⁱLike artillery,
10 ^jAnd had to make a note to themselves to invent better weapons later on,
11 Which they did.

CHAPTER 13

In fact, after the European barbarians arrived, the Nips suddenly got very inventive,
2 And thought up a whole bunch of new technologies,
3 ^kIncluding industry,
4 ^lAnd weapons,
5 ^mAnd warships,
6 And other great innovations,
7 Until they discovered that it was time to go over and humiliate the ⁿRussians in a war,

8 ^aAnd so they did,

9 ^bWith great success,

10 Which got them started thinking,

11 Not out loud, of course,

12 ^cBut kind of mysteriously and inscrutably,

13 About getting out and about more in the world,

14 ^dAnd showing everybody that in spite of what everybody thought, Japan was definitely one of the Chosen Nations.

CHAPTER 14

Their first chance to get a little more recognition from the barbarians in the world at large came during ^eWorld War I,

2 When they fought on the side of the Allies,

3 That is, the British and French and Italians,

4 Against somebody or other,

5 Although nobody but the Nips remembers what they did exactly.

6 Anyway,

7 They enjoyed World War I so much that they started looking forward to World War II right away,

8 And got so excited about how much recognition they'd get next time that they just couldn't wait,

9 And decided to help start it.

CHAPTER 15

^fIt was at about this time that the Krauts started grabbing up all the spare countries in Europe,

2 And pretty soon, all the European nations were concentrating pretty intently on the gigantic war that ^gNeville Chamberlain couldn't quite stop.

3 Then, right after ^hHitler

a. 18.10

b. Russ.10.9

c. 2.10

d. 2.17

e. Krt.24.2-3

f. Brit.51.1-22

g. Dav.20.34

h. Dav.20.34

i. 3.9

j. Jefs.7.15

k. Mawr.8.7

l. Rom.2.7-8

m. Rom.2.9-10

n. Dav.34.19

o. 16.3-4

stomped everybody flat with blitzkrieg attacks and started boasting about Fortress Europe, the Nips had another great and ⁱoriginal idea.

CHAPTER 16

The way the Nips looked at it, what the world needed was something called the Greater Japanese Co-Prosperity Sphere,

2 ^jSince they were far too polite and civilized to use the word "empire,"

3 ^kAlthough the basic plan called for them to conquer the entire South Pacific, including the Philippines, Singapore, New Zealand, New Guinea, Australia, parts of China, and all the islands in between^l,

4 ^mWhen nobody was looking.

5 Of course, the emperor ⁿHirohito didn't know anything about this plan,

6 Because he was only the emperor,

7 And didn't have any power anymore,

8 Since the Nip military and industrial leaders had it all,

9 But were too polite to tell Hirohito what they had in mind,

10 Which explains why Hirohito wasn't responsible for what happened next,

11 Somehow.

CHAPTER 17

What happened next was that the Nips thought a little more seriously about a key part of their plan,

2 ^oNamely, the part about grabbing the whole South Pacific when nobody was looking,

3 And decided that no matter how mysteriously and inscruta-

bly they invaded dozens of countries,

4 Somebody might notice,

5 Like the [a]Americans,

6 Who, for a bunch of degenerate mongrel barbarians that didn't have the guts to fight [b]Hitler, had a pretty big military,

7 Including an army in the [c]Philippines,

8 And a good-sized navy in the Hawaiian Islands.

9 Eventually, the Nips figured out that if they could destroy the American navy in the Hawaiian Islands,

10 The Yanks would get discouraged,

11 And think it was too much trouble to stop Japan from grabbing the entire South Pacific.

CHAPTER 18

And so the Nips devised this great plan to attack Pearl Harbor in Hawaii,

2 By surprise,

3 And then take everything they wanted,

4 Right away,

5 Something like Hitler was doing in Europe,

6 In fact, a lot like [d]Hitler was doing in Europe,

7 Except that the Nips didn't get the idea from Hitler, of course,

8 But thought it up all by themselves,

9 With their own great imagination.

10 *Banzai!*

CHAPTER 19

The way it worked out, there were two surprises the [e]day the Nips attacked Pearl Harbor.

2 The [f]Americans were sur-

a. *Dav.20.34*
b. *15.3*
c. *Yks.59.14-15*
d. *15.3*
e. *Yks.106.6-13*
f. *17.5*
g. *Dav.47.24*
h. *Dav.10.10*
i. *Psay.5Q.23*
j. *Russ.24.9*
k. *Yks.108.6-8*
l. *18.10*
m. *18.10*
n. *18.10*

prised as hell about being attacked by a bunch of smiling, nodding, two-faced little barbarians,

3 Which made the Nips smile and nod at each other,

4 Since everything had gone almost completely according to plan,

5 Although not absolutely everything,

6 [g]Because the other surprise was that the Americans didn't react exactly like a bunch of degenerate mongrel barbarians that didn't have the guts to fight a major war.

7 In fact, the [h]Americans were extremely, thoroughly, completely mad at Japan,

8 [i]And declared war on both Germany and Japan right away,

9 And then every able-bodied man in America immediately enlisted in the army, the navy, or the air force.

CHAPTER 20

Of course, with their [j]typical foresight, the Americans were very well prepared to fight a war against Germany and Japan,

2 [k]Having scrapped a lot of their weapons years ago,

3 And not having quite gotten around to building any new ones,

4 In spite of the fact that World War II had been going on for almost two years now,

5 And so, the Nips had pretty clear sailing in the South Pacific for quite a while,

6 [l]Conquering the Philippines,

7 [m]And Singapore,

8 [n]And most of New Guinea,

9 [a]And lots and lots of islands in between,
10 [b]Until the Yank general [c]MacArthur escaped from the Philippines somehow,
11 And thought up a typically sloppy Yank strategy for fighting back,
12 Something called the leap-frog strategy,
13 Meaning the Yanks were headed for Japan by the quickest route available,
14 And wouldn't stop and fight at every little island on the way.

CHAPTER 21

Actually, the Nips didn't quite understand the Yanks' war strategy for quite a while,
2 But some other things were happening that they didn't much like,
3 And couldn't understand either.
4 [d]For example, when the Nip soldiers had conquered the Philippines,
5 They had fought in the most [e]civilized way imaginable,
6 And yet they couldn't help noticing that the Yanks seemed extremely upset about the way they had bayoneted stragglers on the Bataan death march,
7 And smeared the brains of babies all over the walls of the hospital in Manila,
8 And tortured and starved and raped their civilian prisoners,
9 And other things that must have been civilized,
10 Because it was the Nips who did them.
11 But the Yank barbarians

a. 18.10
b. Yks.109.11-13
c. Dav.10.10
d. 20.6
e. 11.17-24
f. Yks.110.15-16
g. Yks.112.15-21
h. Bks.6.17-18
i. Dav.10.10
j. Dav.34.19
k. Psom.73.1-2
l. 2.10
m. 6.14
n. Drex.3.7

overreacted pretty strongly to the whole thing,
12 [f]And declared that the only way the war would end was with the *U*nconditional *S*urrender of Japan,
13 Which was completely unreasonable,
14 If you're a Nip.

CHAPTER 22

And eventually, things stopped going well for the Nips.
2 [g]The Yank air force bombed Tokyo,
3 [h]And then other cities.
4 The Yank [i]marines started taking islands away from the [j]Nip marines,
5 Including Guadalcanal,
6 And Tarawa,
7 And the Philippines.
8 And the Yank navy started taking the Nip navy apart,
9 One ship at a time,
10 Except when it was two or three or eight ships at a time,
11 And it began to [k]dawn on the land of the rising sun that the Nips were going to lose the war,
12 Which started them thinking again,
13 [l]In their usual mysterious and inscrutable way,
14 [m]About how great it would be for the whole Nip nation to commit suicide by not surrendering,
15 Ever.

CHAPTER 23

This led to a slight change in Nip war strategy,
2 [n]Which is to say they stopped trying to actually win the war,

3 And started trying to kill as many Yanks as possible,
4 No matter how much it cost.
5 [a]For example, they told [b]Nip pilots to drive their planes straight into aircraft carriers,
6 Which they called a kamikaze attack,
7 Meaning divine wind,
8 Which proved how great and superior Nip civilization was,
9 For some reason.
10 And at each new island the Yank marines invaded,
11 Including Iwo Jima,
12 Saipan,
13 And Okinawa,
14 The Nips managed to kill more and more Yanks,
15 [c]Long after they had no more chance of turning back the invasion,
16 [d]While back home, they got everybody ready to fight to the last man, woman, and child against the coming Yank invasion of Japan,
17 [e]Until something strange happened,
18 [f]Something awful,
19 [g]And evil,
20 [h]And definitely not civilized.

CHAPTER 24

[i]What happened was, the Yanks built a new kind of bomb,
2 [j]An awful bomb,
3 [k]An uncivilized bomb,
4 [l]A kind of bomb that could destroy an entire city in an instant,
5 [m]A kind of bomb the Nips didn't have.
6 [n]Then, the unspeakable Yank barbarians actually dropped their new bomb on the Nip city of [o]Hiroshima, destroying it utterly,
7 [p]And demanded that the Nips surrender,
8 Unconditionally,
9 Which couldn't be done,
10 For some reason.
11 And so the Yanks dropped another one on the Nip city of [q]Nagasaki, destroying it utterly,
12 And demanded that the Nips surrender,
13 Unconditionally,
14 Which they did.

CHAPTER 25

Losing the war was a bitter disappointment to the Nips,
2 [r]Not to mention how they felt about losing the Greater Japanese Co-Prosperity Sphere,
3 But when you're the only completely civilized nation on earth,
4 You know how to handle disappointments,
5 Which is why, when the Yanks landed to occupy Japan,
6 They were met by a bunch of smiling, nodding, peace-loving Nips,
7 Who would never hurt a fly.
8 And in all the time since then, they have never stopped smiling and nodding.
9 They smiled and nodded when [s]MacArthur became the military governor of their nation.
10 [t]They smiled and nodded when he wrote them a democratic constitution that made it illegal for them to wage war ever again for any reason.
11 [u]They smiled and nodded when MacArthur gave women the vote.

a. Drex.3.7
b. Dav.34.19
c. Yks.118.1
d. Yks.118.2
e. Yks.118.3
f. Yks.118.4
g. Yks.118.5
h. Yks.118.6
i. Yks.118.7
j. Yks.118.8
k. Yks.118.9
l. Yks.118.10
m. Yks.118.11
n. Yks.118.12
o. Drex.3.7
p. Yks.118.13
q. Hill.N.1-3
r. 16.1
s. 20.10
t. Krt.35.12
u. Mawr.25.7-8

12 They smiled and nodded when the Yanks [a]executed some of their military leaders for war crimes.

13 [b]And they smiled and nodded even more when the Yanks gave them a whole bunch of money to rebuild their factories,

14 And their cities,

15 And their whole nation.

CHAPTER 26

[c]Not long after that, the Nips were busily manufacturing a bunch of gewgaws and trinkets of the kind that Yanks and Europeans seem to like so much,

2 [d]And they only smiled and nodded when the Yanks made jokes about how cheap and shoddy their products were,

3 Because the Nips have always been a highly civilized people,

4 [e]And they had learned an important lesson from the Yanks,

5 Which is why they liked the Yanks so much,

6 [f]And smiled and nodded at them so much,

7 [g]Even if they never really answered when someone asked them what the lesson was they had learned from the Yanks,

8 But only smiled and nodded,

9 [h]Which proves how much they've changed,

10 Because every roundeye knows that no one smiles and nods that much unless they're really friendly,

11 And good-hearted,

12 And peace-loving,

13 And highly civilized,

14 Just like the Nips.

a. Yks.126.11
b. Psong.40.1
c. 4.7-8
d. 4.10
e. Yks.52.30
f. 25.8
g. Yks.127.7
h. Jeff.23.5-6
i. 2.17
j. 6.4
k. Drex.6.15
l. Mall.13.8
m. Wil.12.3-6

CHAPTER 27

And while there are people who continue to live in the past,

2 [i]And still think that the Nips are a bunch of smiling, nodding, two-faced little barbarians who keep trying to take things from everyone else because they've never had an original idea of their own,

3 [j]And that there have always been too many Nips, and always will be until they finally all commit suicide at the same time, hopefully without taking too many other people with them,

4 [k]There's every chance that such people are wrong,

5 Because the Nips almost certainly do have some original ideas of their own,

6 Ideas about civilization, for example,

7 And other things too.

8 [l]Besides, there's almost no chance whatever that they all really want to commit suicide, no matter how many other people they have to take with them,

9 And are looking for some new excuse,

10 And will find it eventually,

11 [m]Because all the evidence indicates that they're not like other people,

12 Who never ever learn,

13 For thousands of years,

14 But are different,

15 Somehow,

16 For some reason,

17 Almost certainly.

18 *Banzai!*

THE BOOK OF OTHERS

OTHERWISE KNOWN AS THE BOOK OF BASTARDS

CHAPTER 1

And then there were all the Others,
2 The ones who weren't [a]Spics,
3 Or [b]Frogs,
4 Or [c]Brits,
5 Or [d]Krauts,
6 Or [e]Yanks,
7 Or [f]Beaks,
8 Or [g]Russkies,
9 Or [h]Chinks,
10 Or [i]Nips,
11 The ones who weren't [j]Gypsies,
12 Or [k]Mesopotamians,
13 Or [l]Greeks,
14 Or [m]Romans,
15 Or even [n]Italians.
16 [o]These are the ones who weren't ever Chosen,
17 Even for a little while,
18 No matter how hard they tried to be Chosen,
19 Or didn't,
20 No matter how much they wanted to be Chosen,
21 Or didn't,
22 No matter how much they might have deserved to be Chosen,
23 Or didn't,
24 They simply weren't,
25 And may not ever be,
26 Because that's the way things are,
27 And have always been,
28 [p]And will always be.
29 This is their [q]story.

CHAPTER 2

For example, there were a lot of nations who thought they would be Chosen,
2 When the time came,
3 But when the time came,
4 [r]They didn't make it.
5 The Phoenicians invented the first [s]alphabet,
6 And sailing ships,
7 And trade,
8 And did a lot of exploring,
9 [t]Long before the Greeks and Romans started building monuments and temples and armies and all the rest,
10 But it didn't work out for the Phoenicians,
11 [u]And nobody remembers any of their names or their books or their cities or anything else they did.
12 Poor bastards.
13 [v]The Carthaginians wanted to be Chosen,
14 So bad it hurt,
15 And thanks to Hannibal and his elephants, they came *that* close,
16 Getting stopped just a few miles short of Rome,
17 Which wasn't close enough,
18 Because the Romans couldn't be stopped short when they got to Carthage,
19 [w]And destroyed it completely,
20 Forever.
21 Poor bastards.
22 [x]And there have been lots of Others who came close or thought they might someday,
23 Through all the thousands of years,
24 Including Trojans and Philistines,

a. Apes.2.6
b. Apes.2.6
c. Apes.2.6
d. Apes.2.6
e. Apes.2.6
f. Apes.2.6
g. Apes.2.6
h. Apes.2.6
i. Apes.2.6
j. Apes.2.6
k. Apes.2.6
l. Apes.2.6
m. Apes.2.6
n. Apes.2.6
o. Apes.2.6
p. Pnot.24.5
q. F&J.15.10-16
r. Psay.5Q.23
s. Grk.4.12
t. Nip.2.14 Chnk.5.4
u. Wil.44.23-25
v. Rom.6.3
w. Rom.6.9-10
x. Bks.7.2-3

25 Koreans and Indochinese,

26 Polynesians and Celts,

27 [a]Basques and [b]Icelanders,

28 [c]And all the little nameless people, in all the countries of the world, who never knew what they were dying for, when all it was was history.

29 [d]But there are always winners and losers,

30 Because that's the way history works,

31 And the ones who were in the game for at least a little while had it easy compared to the ones who never had a chance.

a. Spic.1.2
b. Psay.5C.4
c. Bks.6.17-18
d. Vin.14.23-24
e. 5.5
f. 5.6
g. Exp.11.12-17
h. Spic.17.9
i. Spic.10.4-5
j. 3.4
k. 3.5
l. Spic.4.7
m. Spic.12.6

CHAPTER 3

The Central American Indians never had a chance.

2 The Inca and the Maya and the Aztecs built their own civilizations out of nothing,

3 With sweat and wooden tools and enormous pieces of rock,

4 [e]And all they really wanted was to be left alone,

5 [f]To do things their own way,

6 And they never even tried to rule the world,

7 But they got it in the neck anyway,

8 [g]Because the conquistadors wanted what they had,

9 [h]And what they couldn't give,

10 [i]No matter how many of them got tortured and enslaved and maimed and wasted by disease and killed.

11 And that's generally what happens when a Chosen Nation shows up on your doorstep,

12 With the gleam of history in their eyes.

13 Poor bastards.

CHAPTER 4

The South American Indians never had a chance.

2 The children of the rain forest, the Pygmies and headhunters, and all the rest never wanted to build anything,

3 [j]Except a life like the one they had always known,

4 [k]Next to nature,

5 Where they could hunt what they needed,

6 And leave the rest for future generations.

7 But there won't be too many future generations,

8 Because the Europeans came,

9 [l]With their Christianity,

10 And their love of gold,

11 And their passion for building giant cities,

12 And plantations,

13 And fortunes,

14 Even if it meant tearing nature apart,

15 Which it did.

16 [m]And the natives got all the benefits of living with the Chosen,

17 Including disease and dislocation and the destruction of their culture and independence,

18 Not to mention the loss of their whole world.

19 Poor bastards.

CHAPTER 5

The North American Indians never had a chance.

2 The Cherokee and the Seminoles and the Blackfeet and the Sioux and the Apaches and the Cheyenne and all the rest didn't want any monuments and temples made of stone,

3 Because they'd never learned to be civilized.

4 [a]Instead, they tried to live in harmony with nature,
5 [b]And all they really wanted was to be left alone,
6 [c]To do things their own way,
7 Which wasn't hurting anybody,
8 [d]Until the Yanks decided that they needed all the land in North America,
9 [e]Just because they wanted it,
10 Which is always a good enough reason for a Chosen Nation to do whatever it wants to.
11 And so the Yanks lied to the Indians,
12 [f]And stole from them,
13 And killed them when they objected to the lies and stealing,
14 And decided the Indians were savages,
15 [g]Because the only thing they wanted was what they already had,
16 Before it got taken from them,
17 Forever.
18 Poor bastards.

CHAPTER 6

The Australian bushmen never had a chance.
2 [h]The children of the outback never wanted to rule the world,
3 But only to live in an out-of-the-way corner of it,
4 [i]Until the Brits sent a bunch of convicts to civilize it,
5 Which meant taking it away from the bushmen,
6 Forever.
7 Poor bastards.

CHAPTER 7

The black Africans never had a chance.
2 [j]The Watusi and the Zulus and

a. 4.4
b. 3.4
c. 3.5
d. Yks.27.5
e. Yks.27.11-12
f. Yks.53.3
g. Yks.52.26
h. 3.6
i. Psay.5Q.78
j. 3.6
k. 3.4
l. 3.5
m. Yks.5.4-7
n. 4.9
o. Yks.21.8-9
p. Hall.4.3
q. 2.31

the thousands of tribes who lived in the jungles and the savanna didn't want to rule the world,
3 Or build monuments of stone,
4 Or giant cities,
5 Or anything else.
6 [k]They wanted to be left alone,
7 [l]To live their own way,
8 Which didn't have anything to do with being Christian,
9 Or earning plantation wages,
10 [m]Or being enslaved on some plantation on a different continent,
11 But the Chosen Nations came to Africa anyway,
12 And brought all their great civilized gifts,
13 [n]Including Christianity,
14 [o]And whips and chains,
15 And terrible weapons,
16 And slave ships,
17 And colonial governments,
18 And armies,
19 And wars,
20 And lies,
21 And more [p]white people than you can shake a pointed stick at.
22 Poor bastards.

CHAPTER 8

[q]And all the poor bastards who never had a chance will probably never get one either,
2 Because now the ones who didn't get imprisoned or enslaved or killed are stuck with what the Chosen Nations gave them,
3 Including the desire for material possessions,
4 And the lust for power,
5 And fanatical beliefs about politics and religion,
6 And corruption,
7 And disease,

8 And famine,
9 And pollution,
10 [a]And bastard cultures full of poverty, despair, and violence,
11 Not to mention missionaries,
12 And debts,
13 And dictators,
14 And wars,
15 And a lot of patronizing lectures about what it takes to be civilized,
16 From the people who know the most about civilization,
17 Namely, all the Chosen Nations who ruined their lives in the first place.
18 Poor poor bastards.

CHAPTER 9

But history keeps on going,
2 No matter who gets hurt,
3 And that's the way it will keep on going,
4 Until the world ends,

a. Forg.11.8-9
b. Krt.39.1-7
c. Yks.147.13-21
d. Russ.26.1-8
e. Psp.1.10
f. Krt.39.4
g. Bks.11.5-8
h. Spic.1.5
Wil.69.16-20

5 Because some Chosen Nation goes utterly insane,
6 [b]Which has happened before,
7 Or because some other Chosen Nation chooses pride over compromise,
8 [c]Which has happened before,
9 Or because some other Chosen Nation just can't stop wanting what it hasn't got,
10 No matter what,
11 [d]Which has happened before,
12 And will happen again,
13 [e]Like everything else in history.
14 And the only thing certain about any of it is,
15 No matter how it starts or where,
16 [f]The next time everyone will pay for it equally,
17 [g]And there won't be any more Chosen Nations,
18 Or any Others.
19 Poor bastards all[h].

THE PSONGS

OF

NICHOLAS THE SENIOR

PSONG 1

Happy is the man who gets to walk around with a pocketful of cash; all doors are always open to the rich man, and his smiles make everybody happy and helpful.
2 [a]He hardly ever has to wait in line; the barriers are removed as soon as he approaches.

a. Wil.75.14
b. Wil.75.12-13
c. Vin.48.18

3 [b]Nor does he have to take a lot of guff; when he reaches for his pocket, the whole world pays attention.
4 [c]But things are very different for the poor man; he is a walking victim, a piece of lint in the money pocket of life.
5 No one makes way for the poor man; practically everyone

is more important than he is, and better-looking too.

6 Therefore, choose carefully which of these to be; a poor man may smile, but the [a]landlord wants cash money.

PSONG 2

[b]O Money, I have thought up all kinds of great reasons why you should be mine: Will you take the time to hear them?

2 But if you do not, [c]I will still be patient; every minute that I wait, I come up with new reasons for wanting you, which is a true measure of how wonderful you are.

PSONG 3

[d]What is worse in life than losing money that you just knew you had: It isn't in the [e]jar, or my wallet, or under the mattress.

2 I feel terrible, like a man who has lost everything; it was there just yesterday, and I've already looked everywhere.

3 My heart cries out in pain: O Money, come back to me.

PSONG 4

[f]Why do people say such terrible things about money, and act like they don't care about their bank balance?

2 [g]Surely, they would change their tune if times got hard, and there wasn't enough cash to put bread on the table.

3 Then it would be a different story; the shoe would be on the other foot then, and they would talk out of a different side of their mouth.

4 Most likely, they would ask

a. 13.1
b. Vin.49.6
*   Ed.28.6*
c. Dav.40.9
d. 29.1-7
e. 11.8
f. Psay.5A.22
*   Ned.7.2*
g. 44.1
h. 18.5
*   19.2*
i. Yks.153.14
j. Boul.6.5
k. Ned.12.14
l. Main.36.4
m. 13.1

friends and [h]relatives for loans in a desperate voice; their pride would fly out the window, and they would get down on their knees, and stain the carpet with their tears. [i]Shammadamma.

5 For it is easy to be blasé about money when you have it, and almost impossible to think of anything else when you don't: the emptiness of your wallet is like a great pit, that swallows all your hopes and dreams, and is still hungry afterwards.

6 [j]It is a wise man who remembers that money is his friend: Say nothing more unkind about money than you would say about those whom you love and honor and respect.

7 Yes, many things can happen in life; and when the things that happen are bad, money is usually the best friend you can have.

PSONG 5

[k]You could not believe how much I yearn for you, O Money, and how my heart pounds when I am near you.

2 [k]Nothing is more important to me than you: You are very special to me, and the center of all my dreams.

3 Thanks to you, I have hopes of retiring in splendor: In wintertime, a vision of my [l]villa in the South of France warms my heart, and I am filled with certainty that I will find a way to buy it someday.

4 How poor I would be if I did not believe in you: My one-room [m]apartment would become a cage, and I would be like a canary with no song to sing.

5 Please give me money: I swear that I will know what to

do with it, and I will never be ungrateful for my good fortune.

PSONG 6

Many people say that there are things more important than money: They announce that they would rather have their health; they praise the blessings of peace among men, and they claim that the love of their families is a wealth beyond compare.

2 [a]But surely they are missing the point: Do they not know that everything does not always go well just because you have no money?

3 Who is there who can guarantee health? The strongest man can break a leg and be laid up for months, while his wife and children whimper with hunger.

4 [b]Anyone can catch a terrible disease: How many people have perished from yellow fever, and scarlet fever, and the black death, and from typhoid, and even common ills like colds, pneumonia, influenza, and piginosis?

5 Are there not more diseases than you can shake a pointed stick at? Do they not all require treatment in hospitals, and medication, and the attention of doctors?

6 [c]And how many doctors will then proclaim that the man who is rich because he has the love of his family can pay his medical bills with the kisses of children? This is simply not the way things go.

7 Nor can anyone guarantee peace among men: Which of you has not seen the amazing variety of weapons that can be used to shatter peace?

a. Jefs.6.8
b. Jeff.16.4
c. Jefs.7.36
d. Jeff.12.3
e. Adam.50.6
f. Frog.34.1
g. Al.4.7-11
h. Vin.48.12-15
i. Psom.69.1-4
j. Dav.32.21
k. Ned.12.27-30

8 [d]I myself have seen weapons without end; formerly, there were bows and arrows, and swords, and battle axes, all capable of causing dreadful wounds and death.

9 [e]More recently, there have been even more terrible weapons: Man in his cleverness has invented rifles, and cannons, and artillery shells that kill from miles away, as well as [f]poison gas, and bombs that fall from the air.

10 [g]Nor can anyone name a weapon which has never been used to inflict injury on the enemy: The number of wars which have been fought by men is without number, endless as the number of stars in heaven.

11 [h]Where will the man be who trusts in peace, and has no money, when the war bugle sounds again? [i]Surely, he will be marooned upon a river of excrement, with no oar to row his way to safety.

12 Fine words do not buy passports or exit visas; [j]the love of peace does not prevent your family from becoming refugees when the enemy comes, and flattens your whole neighborhood.

13 And what good does it do to have a loving family, when the whole family is without a house, and has influenza to boot? Is this the happiness that makes you disdain the glitter of gold coins?

14 [k]Or will those coins not seem to shine like the sun itself on the day when health and peace and love all have their hands out? For nothing is more constant on earth than the gleam of gold, unless it is the constancy of the fool who prefers to be poor.

PSONG 7

O Money, Money, Money; what a great word on the tongue.

2 It tastes of all fine things, and I cannot stop repeating it to myself.

3 But is anyone listening? How many times do I have to say it before I hear an answering jingle in my pocket?

4 O Money, Money, Money; only you know the answer to that one.

PSONG 8

[a]Is it not true that only money transcends everything? And is not money the only universal joy to be found on earth?

2 Surely, all other things are changeable, and their value cannot be agreed upon from nation to nation, nor from man to man.

3 [b]A woman may be beautiful in one nation, her looks a cause for worship and amazement; but somewhere else, the same woman may be reviled as fat and clumsy as a cow, and not worth a second look.

4 The same is true of other things: Truth wears a different face in every household, and [c]men will tear each other limb from limb over principles and politics and ideas that they believe absolutely to be true.

5 And what other things bring joy equally to all? One can claim that the beauty of nature is constant, and yet do all men like to eat a [d]sheep intestine, and will no one make a face and spit it out because it offends his taste?

6 [e]Even the Gods change their names and images from place to

a. Ned.43.12
b. Gnt.2.4-10
c. Spic.7.7
d. Brit.3.5-9
e. Bks.4.20-23
f. Lies.4.6-7
g. Spic.4.7
h. Drex.5.2-3
i. Lies.7.1-18
j. Adam.2.11-15
*   & 32.1-4*
k. Ed.60.17
l. 1.1
m. Ann.3.7
n. Dav.22.62

place: Here the face of God is fat and round and smooth; there it is lean and dark and hairy.

7 Nor are they the same behind their faces: One God commands worship on Sunday, another on Saturday; one commands strict [f]obedience and sacrifice, [g]another tolerance and love.

8 [h]All things are so changeable that men would plunge into chaos without some source of universal understanding: [i]Thank goodness that you are there, O Money, to speak in a common tongue to all men.

9 For though you also wear many faces, all men can understand you.

10 All men are united by the desire to have you; and to give your blessings to others, whoever they are, in exchange for something of [j]value.

11 What a blessing this: Without it, would there still be anyone alive to worship all those so-called Gods?

PSONG 9

This morning I saw a coin shining in the gutter: What a [k]miracle that so much delight can come from so small a thing.

2 [l]Truly you are a fine thing, O Money, and I feel better for having you in my pocket.

3 Nor do I have all of you; [m]other coins are waiting in other gutters, and maybe someday the [n]little girl will understand that, and stop crying like a baby.

PSONG 10

O Money, I have endured much abuse on your behalf: Men have called me venal, and mercenary, and say that I do not understand matters of the spirit.

2 [a]They say that I look at you like a God: They despise me as if I were a heretic, and tell me that [b]I should ask forgiveness from Jesus Christ, whose mercy extends to all men except those who have lots of money.

3 But it is easy to care nothing for money when you are the son of God: Then you do not [c]need to work for a living, and no one ever sends you a bill.

4 In fact, people give you money every Sunday, heaping plates full of bills and coins and checks; they build houses for you everywhere, and [d]nice houses at that, with lots of brass and velvet and stained-glass windows that cost more than an average person makes in a year.

5 Who on earth is richer than Jesus Christ? And what [e]hypocrisy is it that makes Him tell poor people to be glad about their poverty?

6 [f]We have heard a lot of talk about the sayings of the savior: Has he not said, Do unto others as you would have them do unto you?

7 [g]So I ask you, what would happen if I asked the church to give me money every Sunday, and a great big house full of stained-glass windows: Would they give me what I ask, in the name of the Christ and his golden rule?

8 [h]No, I will remain true to the power of money, which offers more forgiveness to people like me than any religion: Which God has not showered more

a. *Ned.5.2*
b. *Wil.49.21*
c. *Boul.11.10*
d. *Rat.16.11*
   Boul.16.15-16
e. *19.1*
f. *Dav.15.20*
g. *34.1*
h. *Boul.22.11-12*
i. *Jeff.9.1-10*
j. *44.1*
k. *Kens.2.8*
l. *16.1*
m. *1.6*
n. *44.1-2*
o. *43.4*
p. *28.6*
q. *13.3*
r. *13.4*

blessings on the rich than the poor, [i]and which God has never worn the robes of hypocrisy when money is on the table?

9 [j]O Money, you alone are honest about the things that count: [k]Of the things that can be counted which count for something, coins have the most value in a world of deceitful men.

PSONG 11

O Money, I tell you that I am hard pressed: Why do you not come to me, and give me some kind of cushion to rest upon?

2 Have I not proved my devotion? Do I fail to mention your name to everyone I meet?

3 Have I not spent most of my waking hours thinking about ways of being closer to you? [l]And when I sleep, do I not dream about your bright golden face?

4 And yet, you turn away from me, and do not answer my requests: The [m]landlord beats on my door constantly, and I cannot pay him with my devotion to your name.

5 [n]Honestly, I could make do with a quick five hundred; for this small amount I would be more grateful than a tycoon who has made a killing in corn.

6 I would not even wince at the sight of rich men giving big [o]tips in restaurants; [p]I would not eavesdrop at the stock exchange hoping for easy money, [q]nor would I bet on a long shot at the track.

7 [r]I will never cease to be loyal and faithful to you, O Money: It will never occur to me to ask

where are you when I need you.
8 I will be waiting in my ^aapart-ment; the door is always open for you, and the ^bjar on the hall table is empty of everything but hope for your generosity, if you would be so kind.

PSONG 12

^cWhat a great thing money is: Even the smallest coin can make a small boy break out in smiles.
2 How much more wonderful is a huge fortune; vast riches make an ugly woman beautiful in the eyes of men, and likewise a ^dstupid man brilliant as the sun.
3 ^eO Money, I just can't praise you enough; I can't get enough of you, and I will never stop trying to win you.

PSONG 13

^fHow have I failed you, O Money? Why am I broke and cast out of my apartment?
2 Don't you remember all the nice things I have said about you: How I have scorned the praise of men to be your faithful servant?
3 And yet, when I returned from the track, my furniture was in the street; the locks had all been changed, and my ^glandlord's face shone with the kind of great joy that only comes from seeing another man's life in ruins.
4 ^hIs this the way that my devotion is repaid? How have I offended you, so that I must be tormented by the sight of so many others jingling your blessings in their pockets?
5 ⁱIs there something I don't understand yet? Please tell me what

a. 5.4
b. 3.1
c. 9.1
d. 26.1
e. 14.3
f. 5.4
g. 11.4
h. 11.7
i. 17.1
j. 12.3
k. Psay.5A.27
l. 11.3
m. Wil.19.15

it is, O Money, because I will do anything for you.

PSONG 14

O Money, is it fair the way you keep avoiding me? It is not my fault that I have patches on my elbows, and look like some kind of tramp.
2 If you would just return to me, I would wear beautiful suits: You would be proud to be seen with me.
3 ^jO Money, I've run out of everything but praise and devotion for you: Does that mean anything to you, or must I first be rich to win your favor?

PSONG 15

^kSo many people say that money can't buy happiness: What are they talking about?
2 Surely the truth is this: If money can't buy happiness, then nothing can.
3 And if there is no happiness, then I'd just as soon have money instead.
4 Praise be to you, O Money; silly lies will never kill my love for you.

PSONG 16

^lI have dreamed many great dreams about Money; I have seen a vision of Money as a ^mvast living being, spread across the earth more variously than all the leaves of all the trees in all the forests.
2 There is no end to the body of Money; it breathes through the hands of people everywhere, from the most remote backwaters to the tallest towers of the greatest empires.

3 Truly, Money is infinite and without end on earth: Is it not a humble request to ask for just a little, only enough to live in comfort forever?

4 How can that be too much to ask? How about it, O Money?

PSONG 17

[a]**C**an it be that I've been going about this all wrong, O Money? Can it be that I must take matters into my own hands?

2 For truly, O Money, a dark and a terrible thought has come over me, and I quiver in fear at the rashness of my own heart.

3 And though I did not bid the thought come to me, it came; and though I did not want to think of it, the thought seized me and would not let me go.

4 Truly, I do not understand what has befallen me, and yet it is befalling me [b]like nobody's business.

5 Yes, yes, O Money, I confess it; the newspaper I slept under last night on my [c]park bench shone like the sun as I awoke, and through its light I beheld the [d]fiery words of the want ads.

6 And no one knows better than you that I have never sought employment, or in any other way sullied my pure love of you, for your own sake, and yet this terrible temptation has taken me by the throat with a grip of iron.

7 [e]Can it be that I am teetering on the brink of getting a job? O Money, save me from this dreadful pass, O save me, my only friend.

PSONG 18

[f]**I**s it not true that only Money gives you really good odds

a.	13.5
b.	Ned.56.4 Ext.50.14
c.	31.3
d.	Psp.2.1
e.	Vin.23.13
f.	Ned.35.16
g.	Vin.23.14
h.	Dav.26.5
i.	6.1
j.	Dav.23.17

of having your wishes come true?

2 And is it not true that Money does not fall from the sky like rain, or grow from the ground like wheat?

3 How then can it be wrong to cease waiting for Money to fall from the sky, and to bet instead on rain falling from the sky, onto the wheat that grows from the ground?

4 [g]For if this is the only way that Money will come to me, then how else are my wishes to come true?

5 Yea, for I have remembered that I have a [h]cousin in commodities, and it is possible that he has forgotten his rancor over the money I once lent him.

6 [i]Indeed, he is a man who professes to believe in taking care of his family, and how many times have I not heard him boast about his willingness to do anything for his brothers and sisters and sons and daughters?

7 Is not a cousin like unto a brother once removed? Would it not be reasonable to advance a brother some small stake in the commodities business? Most assuredly this is so, and will be a great boon to my fortunes, O Money!

8 Certainly he must have forgiven everything by now! Did not his [j]daughter recover with the medicine he bought using my money?

9 And truly, thirty-three and a third percent cannot be too high a price to pay for the life of a daughter; How about it, O Money? Do you not agree that others might have charged him forty or even fifty percent?

PSONG 19

[a]O Money, all men are hypocrites when your name enters their mouths; and I do not understand how so much villainy can flow from your shining goodness!

2 [b]You may remember, O Money, the many sweet words I uttered about my cousin; I praised his generosity, and related to you [c]my abiding loyalty to his family.

3 [d]But how different are the faces of the righteous when you turn to them in need! Then indeed their features become twisted with laughter and ridicule, and they heap scorn upon you for your misfortunes, instead of gold.

4 O Money, spare me these indignities and humiliations! Free me from the power of coldhearted cousins who offer menial labor in response to heartfelt supplications for mercy.

5 [e]But yea, verily, I still have my pride, and I shall not serve as a wage slave; I shall not stoop to put myself at the beck and call of those who are too lazy to carry their messages from one part of the [f]trading floor to another.

6 Do not doubt my faith in you, O Money; I would have thrown his disgraceful offer in his face and stormed out of his office, but for my befuddlement about such ill treatment at the hands of one I trusted.

7 [g]Truly, tomorrow I shall return to his office, and denounce him for his meanness, O Money, and then I shall return to you, pure and [h]rededicated to your bright golden face.

8 Truly, O Money, truly.

a. Wil.69.7
b. 18.6
c. 18.8
d. Ned.5.12
e. Ned.30.30-35
f. 20.9
g. 47.2
h. 40.1
i. Vin.34.8
j. 64.2
k. 64.3
l. 64.4
m. 64.5
n. 19.5

PSONG 20

[i]O Money, Money, Money.
2 [j]O Money, Money, Money, Money, Money, Money, Money, Money, Money, Money, Money, Money, Money, Money.
3 [k]O Money, Money, Money, Money, Money, Money, Money.
4 [l]O Money, Money, Money.
5 [m]O Money, Money.
6 O Money, Money.
7 O Money, Money, Money, Money, Money, Money, Money.
8 O Money, Money, Money.
9 [n]O Money, all day long men speak your name on the trading

217

floor, until I think I must go mad, for I have none of you, and I am bereft.

10 O Money, come to me.

PSONG 21

O how beautiful is a generous spirit, such as only you can inspire, O Money!

2 Indeed I still cannot believe what has occurred, and I suspect that you have had a hand in this miracle, O Most Blessed Money.

3 This afternoon, I beheld a [a]young man make his fortune in wheat futures, and in his ecstasy he showered me with coins and paper.

4 Praise be to you, O Money, light of my life!

5 My gratitude knows no bounds, O Money, and I will never forget you when I too have made my fortune in wheat futures.

6 [b]Yea, I gathered up the coins and bills, counting every one with trembling hands; and then I took a [c]plunge in your name, O Money, a plunge toward the heaven of your golden beneficence.

7 [d]Wish me luck, O Money; for luck is your son, and the blessed fruit of your loins.

8 Please wish me luck, O Money. Please please please please please please please, O Money.

PSONG 22

[e]Hallelujah, Hosanna, Hooray!

2 [f]I have taken the big plunge, and I have hit the jackpot!

a. *Dav.15.9*
b. *18.3*
c. *Ann.12.8-12*
d. *Psay.5L.1*
e. *Gods.5.6*
f. *21.6*
g. *Barb.7.7*
h. *Wil.78.9*
i. *Vin.49.5*
j. *Psay.5X.1*
k. *Gods.3.4*
l. *38.1*
m. *6.4-5*
n. *4.1-2*
o. *13.5*
p. *Boul.12.1-5*
q. *Boul.16.15-16*

3 [g]Hallelujah, Hosanna, Hooray!

4 I have made a killing in wheat futures, and I am set for life!

5 [h]Hallelujah, Hosanna, Hooray!

6 Others might have wavered, but I stood firm and did not take my profits; instead, I plowed them back in, doubling, trebling, quadrupling my stake. And now I am as rich as a baron!

7 [i]Hallelujah, Hosanna, Hooray!

PSONG 23

Money is my thing: It's all I want[j].

2 [k]It makes the grass look greener; it stills the deepest waters.

3 [l]It restores my self-esteem; it takes me wherever I want to go, for my own sake.

4 [m]And even if I have a life-threatening disease, I won't be afraid, because I'll have Money with me; and the doctor and his staff will do everything possible to comfort me.

5 [n]Money keeps bread on the table, even though I have enemies; Money makes me look good too; my jar is just overflowing with Money.

6 [o]And surely now I've figured it all out: Money will follow me all the days of my life; and no matter what happens, I'll be in the Money forever.

PSONG 24

[p]O Money, thanks to you, I have acquired a fine town house, in the grandest and most beautiful part of the city.

2 [q]It has more rooms than I can

ever imagine using, its ceilings reach to heaven, and there is no place the eye can look that is not covered with gilt and marble and the most fabulous woods!

3 O Money, congratulate me on this thing I have acquired, and give me your blessing for my new home.

PSONG 25

O Money, thanks to you, I have acquired a fine new [a]motorcar, with all the luxuries you could possibly imagine.

2 [b]It has rich leather seats, and its doors are paneled in only the finest burled walnut, and there is even a mouth tube for communicating my whims to the chauffeur!

3 [c]O what a great glory is a fine motorcar, especially if it is a Cadillac, O Money.

4 Congratulate me on this thing I have acquired, and give me your blessing for my possession.

PSONG 26

[d]O Money, thanks to you, I have acquired a fine new [e]bride, with all the charms you could possibly imagine.

2 She has hair the [f]color of you, and her skin is as white and smooth as ivory; her figure is a vision of beauty, and her voice is as sweet and musical as the [g]sound of you in my pocket.

3 O what a great glory is a [h]fine town house and a [i]fine motorcar, [j]particularly in the eyes of a beautiful woman!

4 O Money, congratulate me on this wife I have acquired, and give me your blessing on our union.

---

a. Wil.69.9
b. Ann.6.12-18
c. Adam.31.2-3
d. Ira.31.11
e. Dav.39.10-11
f. 6.14
g. Ann.10.1
h. 24.2
i. 25.2
j. Mawr.30.2-14
k. 5.3
l. Adam.47.3
m. 25.1
n. Adam.47.5
o. Adam.47.2
p. Adam.38.2-15
q. Adam.36.1-12
r. 26.1
s. Adam.46.2-3
t. Mawr.10.1-10

PSONG 27

O Money, thanks to you, and my dear wife, I have acquired a [k]fine new summer residence, and a [l]vast new wardrobe of lady's clothes, and yet another [m]fine motorcar, and a huge boxful of sterling-silver flatware, and a closet full of the most expensive [n]Dresden china.

2 Nor are these the only [o]things I have acquired of late. By any chance, have you met my wife before, O Money?

3 Yea, I am grateful for all these blessings, and I know you congratulate me on these things I have acquired, because they might bring me great joy, I suppose.

4 O Money?

5 Never mind.

PSONG 28

O Money, do you have any knowledge of the [p]stock market, and would you consider it a good investment for a man such as myself, who needs to increase his capital?

2 Truly, I have heard your name mentioned in glowing terms by those who conduct transactions on [q]Wall Street, and I am desirous to know if you shower your grace upon that place.

3 O Money, I would not waste your time if it were not important, but [r]my dear wife is with child, and already she has purchased more [s]things than I would have believed capable of fitting inside one house.

4 O Money, could you please give me your counsel? [t]Already my dear wife has given me cross looks, simply because I mentioned that I am not made of

you, and at this rate, she will see to it that you are removed from my life, completely and utterly.

5 O Money, I am serious. Indeed I am most serious.

6 How about it, O Money? What about the stock market?

PSONG 29

[a]O Black Day! O Money, I am lost.

2 O Money, I am ruined, and my fortune is swept away.

3 [b]O Money, what am I to do? What am I to do?

4 O Black Day! O fiendish demon of [c]Wall Street!

5 O my God! What am I to do?

6 What am I to do? Whatever am I to do?

7 Oh! Oh! Oh! I am ruined.

PSONG 30

O Money, indeed I have lost everything, including [d]my fine townhouse, and [e]my fine motorcars, and everything which was mine, except the clothes on my back.

2 [f]O faithless wife! O how could she have abandoned me, taking all the jewelry, as well as the growing [g]egg of my child, back to the home of her parents?

3 [h]O Money, is this some punishment of yours? Have I offended you in some way?

4 O Money, please get back to me on this. I am at my wit's end.

PSONG 31

O Money, I have been sleeping in the streets, and my fine [i]shoes have holes all the way through their soles.

2 O Money, I have not eaten for

a. Adam.39.1-17
b. Wil.69.9
c. Psom.3.1-6
d. Dav.47.24
e. Ann.6.17-23
f. 26.1
g. 28.3
h. 13.4
i. 4.3
j. Adam.14.15
k. 21.5
l. Boul.11.7-13
m. 11.7
n. 8.5
o. Rat.21.1
p. 31.3
q. 26.1

twenty-four hours, and my [j]fine waistcoat hangs from my belly like an empty bag of [k]wheat.

3 [l]O Money, winter is approaching, and it will soon be cold at night on the park benches.

4 [m]O Money, why have you deserted me in my hour of need? Why will you not return to me?

5 O Money, I am in need. Hear my prayer.

PSONG 32

What a lie it is that poor people suffer the most in life. For what can compare with the suffering of a rich man who has lost his money?

2 The poor man may hunger for a bowl of turnips, but when he has a turnip, he becomes a happy man; the rich man may beg for turnips too, but when he receives one, [n]he will desire to spit it out because it tastes so awful.

3 Truly the rich man is weighed down by his knowledge of steamship round and mashed potatoes; he hangs upon a cross of fine white loaves, and his [o]hands are pierced by the memory of T-bones and turkey drumsticks.

4 O Money! What I wouldn't give for a decent meal!

5 O Money! Why must turnips be so foul?

PSONG 33

[p]I sleep in the park with nothing to eat, and I wonder about my child.

2 Where is my child now? And what does [q]she tell it about its father?

3 I do not know if my child is a girl or a boy. Woe is me, I am a lost man.

4 O Money, could you spare me a dime? Just enough for a phone call and a hot lunch?

PSONG 34

^a**I** slept in the doorway of a church last night; the ^bsexton shooed me away.

2 I crept away on frozen feet, and there was another who came with me.

3 The ^cman who came away from the church with me is sick, and he has no shoes at all.

4 ^dHe is delirious with fever, and he does not know where he is.

5 He moans and cries out in terror; he dreams that he is back in the ^etrenches, awaiting the morning death.

6 He calls out for his wife, but she does not hear. How did he come to be so cast down and alone?

7 He needs to eat something hot. He needs a blanket.

8 ^fI returned to the church to explain his need, but the doors were locked and bolted.

PSONG 35

O Money, my ^gfriend is dying. He shivers and shivers, but there is no fire.

2 My shoes do not fit him, and his feet are cold and hard.

3 My coat does not warm him, and his heartbeat is growing faint.

4 ^hHe cannot last much longer than this. He needs food and warmth and medicine.

5 ⁱO Money, have you heard news of my child? ^jI thought maybe you had.

6 ^kO Money, give us a break. Give us a break.

a. 10.7
b. Dav.7.5
c. Dav.32.4
d. 6.4
e. Yks.77.8-11
f. 10.8
g. 34.2
h. 6.6
i. 33.2
j. 27.2
k. Psom.52.4-5
l. 33.4
m. 10.5
n. 10.3
o. 34.3
p. Psom.7.1-5
q. 19.6
r. 34.3
s. Psay.5A.35
t. Psay.5A.18
u. Psay.5Q.25
v. Yks.88.1-12

PSONG 36

^l**O** God, can you lend us a dollar? I swear that I will pay ten times as much into the poor box when I am back on my feet.

2 O God, would it help if I apologized for the things I have said about you? ^mI take back what I said about how rich you are, and ⁿI never had anything against your son personally.

3 O God, my ^ofriend is dying. Help us.

4 ^pPlease, God, please.

PSONG 37

O Money, I always knew you would come through for me. ^qI never doubted it even for a moment.

2 When ^rmy friend awakened this morning he was better, and he spoke to me as a friend, knowing that I had cared for him.

3 ^s"Never will I forget this act of kindness," he said. "And I shall in turn help you in your hour of need."

4 And truly, he is no poor ^tbeggar like myself, but a man of business ^uwho was set upon by competitors, and robbed, and left for dead from a blow to the head.

5 ^vYes, O Money, he is one of your own followers, and he knows you well because of all the spirits he has sold in speakeasies.

6 Surely, this is your doing, O Money. I would recognize your special golden hand anywhere.

7 O Praise be to you, O Money. I have been given a fabulous new life.

PSONG 38

O Money, I am a new man entirely, and I am again dressed in fine clothes, with a fine home to return to at night.

2 Yea, [a]I have become a keeper of debits and credits for the spirit business, and my new friend is lavish in his treatment of me.

3 And more than this, my friend is arranging for me to see my [b]son, and I am overcome with joy at the thought of beholding his golden locks.

4 Thank you, O Money, for all you have given me.

PSONG 39

[c]O Money, what is the problem with women? Do you know?

2 The letter arrived in the morning mail, and her tone was hard and bitter.

3 [d]She accused me of becoming a gangster, and denounced me for wanting to poison my son's life with scandal.

4 [e]Does she not know that I was starving? And since when did anything matter to her but you?

5 [f]What do women want, O Money? Have you figured it out?

PSONG 40

I have decided, O Money, to recommit myself to you, and to earn your golden smile with every thing that I do.

2 For if a man may not have a family, what is there for him in life but you?

3 When there is no golden fire in the hearth, he banks it in a golden vault instead, and daily [g]counts the coins by which his heart's happiness can be measured.

---

a. *Drex.11.3-6*
b. *33.1*
c. *Mawr.17.4*
d. *26.1*
e. *Mawr.30.15-20*
f. *Ira.36.2*
   Mawr.12.1
g. *10.9*
h. *11.3*
i. *43.2*
j. *40.4*
k. *50.1*
l. *Vin.20.9*
m. *37.5*

---

4 When there is no golden head to kiss, he caresses the only [h]golden heads he can acquire, and you grow in his eyes to mighty vastness.

5 Yea, I am yours, O Money, come what will. Smile upon me, and I will never turn my face from yours.

PSONG 41

[i]O Money, O Mountain of joy!

2 You roll into my coffers like a great golden wave, unending and unstoppable.

3 You come to me as if by magic, and you leap to my hand from every side, like [j]children coming home to their father.

4 You are mine, you are my passion, my life, my love.

5 You are everything; you are my heart's very blood.

6 O Money! Is there more than this?

PSONG 42

[k]O what a great blessing are Spirits; for they are as valuable to men as water and food and women.

2 They cheer up the saddest heart; they make the dullest life bright and full of joy.

3 They make nature sing like an angel, and all men become great crooners under the influence.

4 [l]Yes, and men will pay good Money for such joys, even if they have to steal it from their wives' food allowance.

5 [m]Praise be to Spirits, which are your own treasured handmaiden, O Money, and the way to your boundless kingdom.

PSONG 43

Who is more blessed than the Master of Money? He reaches out, and whatever he touches is his.

2 [a]He is the King of the Mountain, and his feet are planted on the summit of other men's most golden dreams.

3 [b]He speaks, and all men listen: for if he does not know what he is talking about, then why does he have all that Money?

4 [c]He commands, and all men leap to obey; for if he has his way, then he may give a generous tip to those who have been the most obsequious.

5 [d]He scolds, and all men are very very sorry; for if he is angry, there may be no Christmas bonus.

6 [e]He smiles, and all men smile in return; for if he is pleased, there is nothing to worry about today.

7 [f]But for the Master of Money, all days are the same; there is nothing to worry about, and no one to fear.

PSONG 44

[g]Only the Master of Money can be truly honest; for he is the only one who can know to a certainty that he would not change his ways for a big enough check.

2 [h]He does not need to make up stories about how much he disdains Money; [i]he does not have to develop a convenient memory about the surprising things he will do for some tiny pittance.

3 He does not have to mount ridiculous charades to impress his successful friends; he does not have to tell everyone that his limousine is being repaired and that his good clothes were stolen with his luggage.

4 [j]He does not have to pretend that he likes living in rundown neighborhoods; he does not have to explain that his wife regards giant diamonds as ostentatious.

5 [k]Yes, the Master of Money can be who he is; he alone is free to admit that great wealth is the best of all goals to attain.

PSONG 45

How sad it is to see so many men abase themselves before the altar of Money; [l]they look to Money as if to a god, and they humiliate themselves with their prayers for financial security.

2 Only the Master of Money can look this idol in the eye without blinking; only he knows that Money comes to those who are not afraid of its power.

3 [m]For does not Money rightfully belong to those who are born to exercise dominion over others? And is not Money itself the first test of who is fit to become the Master?

4 [n]Truly it is so: He who becomes the Master of Money has already conquered his most formidable rival; and then there is no other who can make him bow down and humiliate himself.

5 Listen to the wisdom of the Master of Money; for he is the lord of his own [o]universe, and his universe contains all others.

PSONG 46

[p]O what a great thing is Pleasure! The flesh is made to feel, and there is no end of ways to make the flesh feel good.

a. Wil.5.1
b. Rom.3.13-17
   Main.2.1-2
c. Ned.10.1-8
d. Ned.12.8-22
e. Ext.10.1-7
f. Vin.75.17-18
g. 10.9
h. Main.22.1-10
i. 9.1-3
j. Vin.48.17-18
k. Ira.24.8-14
l. 10.1-2
m. Adam.14.5-9
n. Ned.19.3-4
o. Psay.5U.1
p. Ned.17.5

2 If you have enough Money, you can make every one of the senses jump up and down with joy.

3 [a]If you have enough Money, you can fill your ears with beautiful music, from dawn to dawn.

4 [b]If you have enough Money, you can fill your mouth with exquisite delicacies, and never taste the same thing twice.

5 [c]If you have enough Money, you can fill your nose with the most exotic and tempting aromas, and then you can give in to every one of your temptations.

6 [d]If you have enough Money, you can fill your eyes with beauty, and then you can take its clothes off with your teeth, if that's what you want to do.

7 [e]If you have enough Money, you can cover your skin with miraculous sensations, and no one will send the police to tell you to stop it.

8 Yea, if more men could afford Pleasure, they would learn to turn away from the cold and heartless god called Money.

PSONG 47

How marvelous it is to awaken on a fine bright morning, and embark on a new round of pleasure!

2 [f]Of course, poor men know nothing of this, and they awaken each morning in dread of the suffering to come.

3 [g]They drink their coffee from cheap cups, and they anticipate the scorn and rejection and drudgery that will make the day last forever.

4 [h]They dress themselves in ill-fitting ready-made clothes, and they know that no beautiful

a. Yks.74.1-2
b. Frog.24.1-6
c. Ann.11.4-7
d. Gnt.2.17-19
e. Mall.15.6-7
f. 19.7
g. Ed.78.11
h. Frog.11.7
i. 50.5
j. Hill.N.1
k. Ira.20.9
l. Main.27.1-2
m. Main.33.1-5
n. Main.27.3
o. 45.5
p. Psom.65.1-4

woman will ever look at them twice.

5 [i]Truly, they know nothing of pleasure, and time is their jailer; each new moment brings them one moment closer to next week's humiliations, and next month's bills, and next year's privations.

6 [j]Only the Master of Money can conquer time: For when each new moment brings fresh pleasures, then time has no power to preempt the joys of right now; and right now can become a heaven of thoughtless ecstasy that never ends.

PSONG 48

[k]Who appreciates a sunset more than the Master of Money? He stands at eventide with all the luster and immovable majesty of the North Star.

2 [l]The very universe wheels around his own whims; all day long, the machinery of lesser lights has accommodated itself to his movements.

3 [m]If some cog has failed to do its work properly, then the Master of Money has caused it to be thrown away.

4 [n]If some offering to his highness has failed to give pleasure, then the Master of Money has caused it to suffer, a lot, which is a pleasure of its own, without equal in any universe.

5 If some aspect of the day ended has been less than perfect, then the Master of Money will buy a better tomorrow; for [o]he is the center of his universe, and the sun will bring him a new playground without being asked.

6 [p]And even before tomorrow comes, there will be tonight; and

there is no end of the things that the Master of Money can do to-night.

PSONG 49

[a]**W**hat an exceptional joy is a nightingale, which has learned to [b]sing for its supper!
2 [c]Its voice is the slave of its Master; if it does not [d]sing beautifully, it does not get to wear a ruby necklace, or to fly in an expensive roadster.
3 Sing, little [e]bird, sing the night away; sing your cares away: the Master of Money will reward you for every note.

PSONG 50

[f]**O** what a consolation are Spirits, when a man needs to forget his cares.
2 Verily, they wash down the lump in a man's throat, and make him forget the [g]treacheries of song.
3 [h]Spirits are the answer to all questions; for they carry a light of their own that makes even the darkest corners bright as a Broadway marquee.
4 [i]Spirits are indeed special: they turn miseries into joys, and calamities into funny stories.
5 Spirits make time run away on carpet slippers, so that the clock [j]chimes cheerily all night long, and only sounds [k]doleful on the morning after.
6 [l]And speaking of the morning after, O Spirits, is there nothing you can do to improve on this one little flaw in your great beauty?
7 Indeed it is true that Spirits have all the answers; for the wise man will discover that they even have the power to make the

a. Wil.69.9
b. Psom.9.9
c. Psay.5A.8
d. Brit.40.8
e. Dav.14.34
f. Ext.13.18
g. 49.3
h. Yks.91.7
i. Vin.65.11-13
j. Psom.31.5
k. Psom.31.6
l. 52.1
m. Frog.31.6
n. Gnt.10.17-18
o. Dav.37.6-7
p. Wil.69.9
q. Psom.78.10
r. Ann.6.23
s. Vin.23.9
t. 51.2
u. Dav.47.25

morning after blaze bright and golden again.
8 O Great Spirits! Cheers!

PSONG 51

[m]**W**hat a glory is the dance, those lithe and graceful brush strokes of Pleasure upon the blank canvas of the eyes!
2 Yes, the Master of Money will [n]patronize this highest of arts if he is wise; for even the [o]greatest of dancers needs a sponsor if she is to afford a beauty as great as that which she creates.
3 But mark well that you remain the Master of Arts as well as Money; for not every [p]chorus girl can move as easily in society as she does on stage.
4 Yes, this is a true and wise tip from the Master: he knows of what he speaks.

PSONG 52

O Spirits, O my [q]aching head: O, I am in pain, and [r]I cannot keep anything down.
2 [s]Yea, I am walking through the valley of the shadow; for I have been on a bender to end all benders.
3 O, how can any woman be worth this price in pain? [t]She was a bad choice, and she is not worth worrying about.
4 Indeed, O Spirits, you have cured me of my affliction; I fear that the sight of woman will never again quicken my heart, [u]for I feel like the orange rinds stuck to the bottom of a garbage pail.
5 O thank you, Great Spirits; now, is there any way for me to silence the kettledrum in my head?
6 Verily, O Great Spirits, it has

been nice knowing you, but I fear that we shall not have many companionable nights in the future.

7 I am getting too old to wake up in train stations; I am too proud to spend so much time on my knees before your [a]porcelain altar.

8 Au revoir, O Spirits: we must stay in touch, but nothing like before.

9 Is that all right with you, O Spirits? O, I'm so glad.

PSONG 53

And what shall the Master of Money do when he tires of pleasure? What new excitement can he find to make life less tedious?

2 [b]Is it possible that life has only a finite quantity of enjoyment to offer any man? Is even the Master of Money to be held hostage by the poverty of creation itself?

3 Verily, this cannot be so: for when the senses have been sated, the wise man learns to reap the pleasures of the mind.

4 Yea, these are pleasures which are greater than the mere candy for which the senses long: [c]for how can bonbons and French pastry compare to the transcendent rapture of Power?

5 The weak man may believe himself in the lap of the gods when he gives himself over to passive immersion in the delights of the flesh; [d]but the strong man knows that it is much more fun to make the ground tremble beneath his feet when he walks.

6 [e]There may be many who rise to become Masters of Money;

a. *Ann.2.32*
b. *Psp.1.2*
c. *Exp.13.1-4*
d. *Dav.30.39*
e. *Ned.49.3*
f. *Ext.16.24*
g. *Psay.5G.25*
h. *Ed.50.12*
i. *Wil.69.9*
j. *49.3*
k. *51.2*
l. *Ed.71.26-27*

but how many have the strength to become the Master of All?

7 [f]How many have the sheer Power to reduce other Masters of Money to penury, and to take their territories from them, just for the thrill of doing it?

8 [g]How many can disdain the consequences of the risks they take in the name of increased Power? How many are so great that such risks are repaid by the knowledge of another's fear, another's defeat, another's abject surrender, especially when such others are impudent [h]Wop scum from the wrong side of the tracks?

9 Yes, behave wisely in the presence of the Master of All: he cannot be bought off with mere Money, nor seduced with mere Pleasure; he must be given the Power he demands.

PSONG 54

Why would any man waste the few precious hours after his workday on other diversions, when he could enjoy the company of one who is skilled in the use of words?

2 [i]Truly, it is a wonder that so many Masters of Money do not learn to refine their tastes, and continue to throw away their cash on [j]mercenary torch singers and [k]back-row dollies from the burlesque!

3 Yes, give me instead the delight of a woman who knows how to speak the words of love: [l]each of her words makes the ear into the greatest of musical instruments, playing rhapsodies in a breathless and tantalizing whisper.

4 Who would have thought

mere words could bring so much pleasure? Not the Master of Money, that's for sure.

5 But the Master of Money can still learn, even if the price is higher than he would have to pay for all the singers and dancers in Chicago.

6 How supremely lovely are [a]Italian women; [b]how priceless their sweet words of love!

PSONG 55

[c]O Money, I am nervous. [d]My friend has been assassinated.

2 He was eating in a [e]small restaurant, and a car came round the corner spitting [f]machine-gun fire.

3 My friend is dead, and [g]I am on the lam.

4 I am dismayed: No one knew of his whereabouts except for myself, and my beautiful, precious [h]*bella amore!*

5 [i]How could this terrible thing have happened? How could my friend have allowed himself to be caught off guard in this careless fashion?

6 [j]O Money, look out for me. I have many of your children with me in my satchel, and I beseech you not to desert me in some capricious way.

7 O Money, are you listening? Are you going to take care of me?

8 [k]I hope so, O Money. I hope so.

PSONG 56

I went to the funeral of [l]my friend today, O Money: I was obliged to sneak in wearing a disguise, like some mortal enemy of the family.

a. *Dav.14.45*
b. *Psom.72.1-6*
c. *Dav.47.24*
d. *34.3*
e. *Ned.41.4-8*
f. *Psom.10.7-8*
g. *Pnot.37.2*
h. *54.6*
i. *Zig.9.2*
j. *6.11-12*
k. *40.5*
l. *34.3*
m. *Vin.59.7*
n. *Chuk.19.16-17*
o. *Wil.44.23-25*
p. *Psom.1.1-2*
q. *Wil.57.3*
r. *Psay.5A.19*
s. *Rom.24.17-18*
t. *Main.36.6*
u. *53.8*

2 [m]I peered into the coffin, and truly he was dead as a doornail; his face was like wax, and he was smiling like an idiot.

3 What is there to smile at in death? Surely, [n]death means that it is all over, and all the Money in the world can do you no good.

4 Truly, a man is completely out of it when he no longer needs Money, and his loving relatives do not even put any coins in his pocket.

5 I thought I would weep when I beheld his dead face; but I did not, for it came to me that he should be weeping for me instead.

6 Yes, truly it is so: [o]he is history, and [p]I am still today's headline, a pawn and a fool for the wicked ambitions of others.

7 And so I find that I cannot mourn him; instead, I mourn for myself, while I can, because now that he is gone, there will be no one to mourn me but me.

PSONG 57

[q]O Money, what is the matter with Italians? Do you know anything of this?

2 [r]Surely, the ancient Romans did not have this obsession with treachery and murder and revenge, and had better things to do than chase bankers through the streets with machine guns.

3 Isn't it supposed to be [s]Italians who are interested in the finer things in life, such as [t]beautiful timeless art and beautiful traitorous women, and do they not take credit for all of the civilization that exists, including even the Renaissance?

4 [u]Why then do they get such ferocious ideas, and why do they

227

choose to compete in the Spirit business with machine guns?

5 I ask you, O Money, is this [a]civilized behavior? [b]And why do you choose to shower them with profits, and allow my friend to die, and me to flee for my very life?

6 Truly I do not understand this, O Money, and I beseech you to reconsider your [c]generosity to Italians.

7 Will you at least think about it, O Money? Will you, honestly?

PSONG 58

O Money, I have had no choice but to turn myself in to the police. O bitter day!

2 [d]But what is one to do when he is being chased by murderous Italians with machine guns? [e]Who can one buy that has more machine guns than Italians?

3 [f]O why would anyone ever have outlawed spirits? Such fools to open such a huge avenue for the ambitions of Italians!

4 [g]O Money, do you know anything about the internal revenue service? [h]They have asked for an interview with me [i]tomorrow.

5 Do you happen to know anyone in the internal revenue service? Do any of your followers work there?

PSONG 59

Who are the whining idiots who cast up this fraudulent image of the [j]Antichrist, and describe him as the chief enemy of mankind? Have they never heard of the beast incarnate called the [k]Internal Revenue Service?

2 [l]O Money, these fiends from

a. *Rom.1.1-8*
b. *Jeff.16.1-3 & 16.6-7*
c. *Exp.1.7-9*
d. *Psom.5.1-6*
e. *Yks.12.15-17*
f. *Yks.86.1-8*
g. *Psom.6.1-5*
h. *Psom.24.3*
i. *Psom.12.1*
j. *Wil.49.14*
k. *58.4*
l. *Adam.41.4-7*
m. *Ed.50.11*
n. *Al.4.16*
o. *Ed.30.5*
p. *Psay.5B.1-13*
q. *26.1*
r. *Rat.5.20-22*
s. *Dav.47.11*
t. *Chr.3.8-13*

hell are your sworn enemy. There is nothing they would not do to remove you from the pockets of your followers.

3 O Money, I beseech you to call upon all the powers at your disposal, and to blast these [m]nightmare creatures into everlasting penury and ruin.

4 O Money, I am being indicted. O Money, I shall be sent to prison.

5 O Money. [n]Why me?

PSONG 60

O Money, are you there?

2 They're going to convict me, O Money. Are you there?

3 I'm waiting, O Money. Are you there?

PSONG 61

O Money, are you there?

2 O M-o-n-e-y.

3 O M-o-n-e-y.

4 Are you th-e-r-e?

PSONG 62

O Money, I have a last request. It's the last thing I'll ask you for, I promise.

2 There is a little [o]missionary who came to see me in my cell. She is about five feet nothing tall, and she reads the [p]scripture in a moving whisper.

3 Why did I never meet a girl like this when I was free? She is nothing like [q]my wife, and for the first time I find myself understanding all the [r]nice things people say about women.

4 [s]She does not care that I have no money, and she says she wants to save my immortal [t]soul.

5 She does not know that my

immortal soul [a]belongs to you, because I did not want to break her heart.

6 Today, she brought me a flower from the park. [b]When I asked her what kind it was, she stared at me with such deep pity that I was ashamed.

7 The bones in her face and hands are as delicate as [c]Dresden china, but she would be angry if I told her that I dream about the lilt in her hips as she walks away down the [d]corridor.

8 She reads to me from the Bible; I do not really listen to the words, but only her voice, [e]because that is the kind of man I am.

9 O Money, could you send her something for her mission? I would like to do something nice for her, but I cannot.

10 Would it be too much to ask, O Money? Even a small amount would seem like a lot to her.

11 She is a beautiful person, O Money. Tomorrow, we will sing [f]hymns together.

PSONG 63

Thank you, O Money, for your gift to the mission. I suppose it must have been you.

2 You have always worked in mysterious ways, haven't you, O Money?

3 [g]I am getting older, O Money, but I am learning.

4 [h]Aren't I, O Money?

PSONG 64

[i]O Money, Money, Money.

2 [j]O Money, Money, Money, Money, Money, Money, Money, Money, Money, Money, Money,

a. Krt.7.7-11
b. Psay.50.5
c. 27.1
d. Zig.8.10-12
e. Psom.23.8
f. Psom.30.1-7 & 39.1-6
g. Psom.23.5
h. Psom.18.14
i. 20.1
j. 20.2
k. 20.3
l. 20.4
m. 20.5
n. Brit.40.8
o. Wil.69.6

Money, Money, Money.

3 [k]O Money, Money, Money, Money, Money, Money, Money.

4 [l]O Money, Money, Money.

5 [m]O Money, Money.

6 I want you, I need you, I've just got to have you!

7 Just kidding, O Money. I'm off to prison now, so [n]stick it in your ear.

PSONG 65

Who needs you anyway, O Money? What are you anyway but a bunch of metal and paper trash?

2 All the good things in life are free, aren't they? Haven't you heard that too?

3 [o]After all, who needs anything more than a nice blanket, and a warm cell, and a little light to clean your fingernails by?

4 Who needs more than that? Tell me, O Money.

5 Don't you know anything at all, O Money? O speak to me from the depths of your solid gold brain.

6 Tell me something I don't know. Give it a try, O Money.

PSONG 66

O Money, it's me. I know I have a lot to apologize for, and I'll get started right away, but you wouldn't just up and

desert one of your best followers, would you?

2 ªYou're far too generous, O
Money, to let a few cross
words stand in the way of a lifelong friendship. Aren't you, O
Money?

3 And you wouldn't begrudge
an old friend a small favor,
would you, O Money? A favor
to a man who's behind bars,
with no cigarettes?

4 Just a quarter would be great,
O Money? Enough to buy a pack
of cigarettes?

5 ᵇJust for old times' sake, O
Money? I won't turn my back on
you again.

6 ᶜI promise, O Money. Really I
do.

a. 64.7
65.5

b. 11.7
36.1
40.5

c. Pnot.37.1-5
Psp.1.4

THE BOOK OF PSAYINGS

PSAYING 1

The Psayings of the ªDads of
the Chosen;

2 To know what is going on; to
excel in the ways of God and men;

3 ᵇTo be regarded as shrewd; to
have the whole world hang on
your every word;

4 To be sought out and ᶜhon-
ored; ᵈto have buildings and institutions named after you;

5 A wise man will pay attention,
and will get up pretty ᵉearly in
the morning; he will work hard
at ᶠappearing to have knowledge,
and will ᵍmemorize the lessons
of his teacher.

6 ʰFear of punishment is the beginning of discipline; and only
fools scorn both punishment and
discipline.

7 My son, be warned that there
will be a ⁱtest later; and if you
prove to be dull of mind, your
punishment will be extreme;

8 ʲFor these things are being
taught you for your own good;
ᵏand your failure will hurt your
father and mother worse than
it will you;

a. Ed.30.7
b. Jeff.24.23
c. Swar.2.4-5
d. Adam.36.6
e. Adam.38.7-8
f. Adam.36.9-10
g. Yks.70.7-9
h. Main.27.1
i. Hill.T.1
j. Mall.13.8
k. Mall.13.27
l. Brit.19.39-40
m. Psom.15.1-2
n. Psom.3.1-6
o. 5A.7
p. Lies.9.13

9 So be good and ˡdutiful in
hearing these words of wisdom;
or know that there will be no
allowance for several months.

PSAYING 2

ᵐMy son, if your friends
want to jump off the
Brooklyn Bridge, do not jump
with them; for it is a long way to
the water, and you would be
smashed to a pulp, and ⁿall the
king's horses couldn't put you
back together again.

2 And if your friends wish to
sell you the Brooklyn Bridge, do
not give them cash or a check or
any kind of payment; ºfor the
Brooklyn Bridge is not for sale,
except to fools, who are soon
parted from their allowance.

3 And if your friends say to
you, Let us cut school today; let
us go to a secret place and smoke
cigarettes;

4 Let us whistle and make rude
remarks at girls; let us do everything that is ᵖfun because the sun
is shining;

5 Then say to them, No, not today, I promised my [a]mother I wouldn't; she wouldn't like it, and I would be grounded forever.

6 For all of these things are unwise and dangerous and forbidden; they would make you a [b]juvenile delinquent, and your parents would be very ashamed of you.

PSAYING 3

To cut school is to cut your own throat; you will never get ahead, and you will become a beggar in the streets;

2 And don't think that you can live at home forever; for your mother and I are planning to sell the house and move to Florida when we retire;

3 There will be no room then for a bum who cut school when he should have known better, or for an ingrate who cannot be trusted the minute his parents' backs are turned.

4 'For school is the place where you acquire the keys to success; and become full of useful information that will help you find a job and security.

5 The smart student learns many things in school; he becomes wise in the ways of [d]punctuality and attendance;

6 He learns not to end a sentence with a preposition, nor to split an infinitive; he learns how to spell [e]"antidisestablishmentarianism," and not to say [f]"ain't."

7 Nor are these all the lessons the bright boy will learn in school; the knowledge to be gained in school is extensive and various.

a. *Ed.30.5*
b. *Dav.35.18*
c. *Ira.31.1-16*
d. *Psom.8.1-6*
e. *Grk.20.8 Chr.3.12*
f. *Rat.4.10 & 7.11-15*
g. *Grk.14.19-20*
h. *Gods.7.3*
i. *Hill.X.2-3*
j. *Hall.4.3*
k. *Drex.8.1-3*
l. *Drex.6.10*
m. *Hill.A.1 Grk.4.12*
n. *Ed.10.7*
o. *Ned.36.26*
p. *Mawr.4.3*

PSAYING 4

My son, if you would ever balance your checkbook, you must become learned in the rules of [g]mathematics;

2 Remember your [h]times tables, because it is hard to multiply on your fingers; and do not fall asleep during the [i]part on quadratic equations, or else you will fail algebra.

3 When you have a [j]word problem to solve, always show your work; [k]for partial credit is almost never given for a lot of meaningless numbers scrawled in the margin.

4 If you would excel in mathematics, make friends with the [l]smartest student in your class; even if he has pimples and glasses and no personality, such a friend can improve your grades substantially.

PSAYING 5

And any son of mine must also know his ABCs, which are the key to being a good man and a good citizen.

2 And the [m]ABCs include things that you can learn in school, as well as things you can learn by spending your free time profitably, and not in front of a [n]television set.

3 And there are also lessons in the ABCs which you must seek to learn from your mother and father, because they are required of all members of this family,

4 And I urge you to listen well, and then learn what I speak of, for an ignorant man [o]disgraces his family, and is shunned by his peers,

5 Which is why you should sit down and relax, and quit [p]tap-

ping your foot, because this will take a while, and I will not stop until I have finished, unless your inattention causes me to lose my temper, and [a]apply a different kind of lesson to your backside.
6 Am I making myself clear?

A

A is for Adages that can help you live better,
2 And more wisely too,
3 Because there's a lot of wisdom in old adages like the ones I live by,
4 Such as,
5 [b]A penny saved is a penny earned,
6 [c]Penny-wise and pound-foolish,
7 [d]A fool and his money are soon parted,
8 [e]A bird in the hand is worth two in the bush,
9 [f]Make hay while the sun shines,
10 [g]A stitch in time saves nine,
11 [h]There's no fool like an old fool,
12 [i]There's more than one way to skin a cat,
13 [j]You can't teach an old dog new tricks,
14 [k]An apple a day keeps the doctor away,
15 [l]Early to bed and early to rise makes a man healthy, wealthy, and wise,
16 [m]You can lead a horse to water, but you can't make him drink,
17 [n]Don't throw the baby out with the bathwater,
18 If wishes were horses, [o]beggars would ride,
19 [p]Those who forget their history are doomed to repeat the [q]course,

20 [r]Clothes make the man,
21 [s]Once burned, twice shy,
22 [t]Money is the root of all evil,
23 [u]All work and no play makes Jack a dull boy,
24 Fool me once, shame on you; fool me twice, shame on me,
25 [v]Another day, another dollar,
26 [w]Cheaters never win,
27 [x]Money can't buy happiness,
28 [y]Haste makes waste,
29 [z]Time waits for no man,
30 [aa]Idle hands are the devil's plaything,
31 [bb]It takes one to know one,
32 [cc]Boys will be boys,
33 [dd]Stuff a cold and starve a fever,
34 [ee]It's the early bird that gets the worm.
35 [ff]A friend in need is a friend indeed,
36 [gg]Don't put off till tomorrow what you can do today,
37 [hh]Spare the rod and spoil the child,
38 [ii]Don't cry over spilt milk,
39 [jj]Build a better mousetrap and the world will beat a path to your door,
40 [kk]Birds of a feather flock together,
41 Don't believe anything you read, and only half of what you see,
42 [ll]If it sounds too good to be true, it probably is,
43 [mm]It is more blessed to give than to receive,
44 Which is probably the best one,
45 If you can manage to live up to it.

B

B is for the [nn]Bible, which everybody should know,

a. 5A.37
b. Vin.47.12
c. Brit.15.30-32
d. 2.2
e. Psong.49.3
f. Ed.46.16-21
g. Ed.48.7-8
h. Rat.1.1-5
i. Krt.24.8-11
j. Brit.59.6-13
k. Brit.36.10
l. Adam.38.5-7
m. Psom.18.8
n. Mawr.18.14-20
o. 5Q.25
p. Chuk.20.11-18
q. Psom.51.1-6
r. Ned.24.8
s. Chr.6.7
t. Psong.4.1
u. Psom.29.1
v. Psong.65.4
w. Frog.10.13
x. Psong.15.1-3
y. Yks.112.1-7
z. Ned.16.12-13
aa. Adam.27.7-8
bb. 5A.40
cc. Ira.7.10-11
dd. Rom.22.9-10
ee. Name.3.8
ff. 5Q.59
gg. Dav.22.66
hh. 1.6
ii. Grk.12.7
jj. Ed.74.3
kk. Ira.16.21-35
ll. Vin.43.1-7
mm. Grk.26.9-10
nn. Ira.27.10-19

2 Especially what the books of the Bible are,

3 Because somebody might ask you if you know them someday,

4 And think how embarrassed you'd be if you didn't know the Bible starts with [a]Genesis,

5 And keeps going for fifty or sixty books more,

6 Including [b]Exodus, [c]Leviticus, [d]Numbers, [e]Deuteronomy,

7 [f]Abraham, [g]Ruth, [h]Job, [i]Psalms, [j]Judges, [k]Isaiah, [l]Proverbs,

8 [m]Kings, Daniel, [n]Judges, [o]Noah, [p]Samson, [q]Ecclesiastes, [r]Jonah,

9 Micah, [s]Amos, Zephanias, Obadiah, [t]Hebrews, [u]Chronicles,

10 [v]Matthew, [w]Mark, [x]Luke, [y]John, and [z]Habbakuk,

11 Timothy, Ephesians, [aa]Corinthians, [bb]Revelations, [cc]Judges, [dd]Ruth,

12 Romans, Galatians, Hosea, [ee]Solomon, Isaac, Job, Acts, Paul, [ff]Lazarus,

13 And [gg]Revelations.

C

C is for Capitals, which if you don't know them is a sure sign that you're not very well educated,

2 Because everybody knows the capitals,

3 Especially the really difficult ones,

4 Like [hh]La Paz, [ii]Reykjavik, [jj]Baton Rouge, [kk]Helena, [ll]Wheeling, Topeka, [mm]Richmond, [nn]Sacramento,

5 [oo]Albany, [pp]Carson City, [qq]Trenton, Caracas, [rr]Fort Lauderdale, [ss]Austin, [tt]Sioux City, [uu]Rio de Janeiro,

6 Brussels, [vv]Olympia, [ww]Buenos Aires, Warsaw, [xx]Seoul, [yy]Calcutta, [zz]Bismarck,

7 [aaa]Cheyenne, [bbb]Indianapolis, [ccc]Montgomery, [ddd]Johannesburg, [eee]Oslo, [fff]Baltimore, [ggg]Bogotá,

8 [hhh]Budapest, [iii]Toronto, [jjj]Richmond,

9 And a bunch of others too,

10 Which you should learn by heart,

11 Including the really easy ones,

12 Like [kkk]Paris, and [lll]London, and [mmm]Rome,

13 If you don't want people to think you're a fool.

D

D is for the big Disasters that happen every so often,

2 And if you don't want people to look at you like you're some kind of idiot,

3 You'll remember all the most important ones,

4 [nnn]Like the Chicago fire,

5 [ooo]The San Francisco earthquake,

6 [ppp]The eruption of Vesuvius,

a. Lies.2.1-6
b. Dav.35.25
c. Adam.31.16
d. Psp.3.1-2
e. Carl.3.8
f. Lies.3.4
g. Name.3.7
h. Lies.8.4
i. Lies.10.12
j. 5B.8
k. Lies.12.1-2
l. 1.1
m. Rom.4.8
n. Ed.56.2
o. Lies.6.1-4
p. Dav.14.6
q. Swar.17.3
r. Lies.8.1-3
s. Name.3.8
t. Bks.2.5
u. Ed.18.7
v. Psong.58.5
w. Yks.71.2-3
x. Jefs.1.1
y. Vin.1.1
z. Dav.47.11
aa. Oth.1.13
bb. 5B.13
cc. 5B.8
dd. 5B.7
ee. Lies.10.13
ff. Dav.15.39-40
gg. Vin.3.12-14
hh. Jefs.7.14
ii. Oth.2.27
jj. Yks.36.12
kk. Psom.70.1 Ira.27.23-24
ll. Yks.6.5 Psay.5Q.30

mm. Yks.6.5
nn. Yks.28.5
oo. Yks.6.4
pp. Yks.28.11
qq. Yks.6.6
rr. Yks.5.2
ss. Yks.36.13
tt. Penn.2.12
uu. Exp.12.12 Ext.3.32
vv. Yks.31.2-3
ww. Dav.22.23
xx. Oth.2.25
yy. Brit.26.11
zz. Krt.21.1
aaa. Ed.47.4
bbb. Bks.6.17-18
ccc. Ann.18.11
ddd. Exp.14.14
eee. Krt.32.12
fff. Yks.6.16
ggg. Ext.49.15
hhh. Russ.20.4
iii. Brit.26.15
jjj. Yks.38.5-6
kkk. Frog.22.1-5
lll. Brit.29.14-17
mmm. Rom.24.7
nnn. Ann.6.23
ooo. Al.2.11
ppp. 5D.17 Al.2.11

7 [a]The sinking of the Titanic,
8 [b]The sinking of the Lusitania,
9 [c]The sinking of the Maine,
10 [d]The sinking of Atlantis,
11 [e]Prohibition,
12 [f]The Black Plague,
13 [g]Black Monday,
14 [h]The Donner Party,
15 [i]The Hindenburg Explosion,
16 [j]The Johnstown Flood,
17 [k]The Last Days of Pompeii,
18 And many many more that I can't think of right now,
19 Although they're all important.

E

[l]**E** is for Education,
2 Which is why it's so important for you to do well in school and go to a good college,
3 Like the [m]Ivy League,
4 Or maybe the [n]Big Ten,
5 Except that no son of mine will ever go to [o]Princeton,
6 Because it's so full of spoiled little rich boys,
7 Which could give you the wrong idea,
8 About a lot of things,
9 [p]Especially about bow ties.

F

F is for Farm Animals,
2 Which you should know about even if you don't live in the country,
3 Because a man who doesn't know anything about animals is the worst kind of fool,
4 And can be made to look completely ridiculous by cows,
5 And horses,
6 And goats,
7 And sheep,
8 And geese,

a. 5Y.25
b. Yks.76.1
c. Yks.60.6
d. Dav.15.37
e. Yks.86.1-8
f. Bub.3.6-7
g. Psong.29.1-7
  Yks.95.3
h. Dav.47.10-13
i. Al.2.11
j. Ann.2.32
k. Rom.8.8-10
l. Hill.E.1
m. Ned.30.11-12
n. Carl.3.8
o. Vin.8.1-5
p. 5K.6
q. Jefs.7.15

9 And chickens,
10 And also the wild animals that eat farm animals or crops,
11 Like weasels,
12 And foxes,
13 And the bigger hawks,
14 And rats,
15 And all those good-for-nothing rabbits and squirrels and coons,
16 Not to mention losing out on the pleasure of appreciating the wild things that live in and around farms without hurting anything,
17 Like loons,
18 And mourning doves,
19 And tree frogs,
20 And barn swallows,
21 And crows,
22 And hummingbirds,
23 And deer, which some people like to hunt, unless they got a bellyful of killing somewhere else, like I did,
24 And groundhogs,
25 And beavers,
26 And otters sometimes, if you've got the right kind of pond,
27 And certain kinds of snakes, I guess,
28 And if you're lucky, maybe even the occasional black bear.

G

G is for Great Men,
2 Whose names you should always know,
3 Because they come up in conversation quite often,
4 And people will look down their nose at you if you ask who they're talking about,
5 Which means you'd better know the Great Men in history,
[q]which I was never that good at,

to be honest, although I got some of their names pounded into me, because it's important to know at least something about them, even if it's only their names,

6 Including Great [a]Generals and Admirals,

7 Like [b]Napoleon, and [c]Alexander, and [d]Julius Caesar, and [e]Eisenhower, and [f]MacArthur, and [g]Washington, and [h]Wellington, and [i]Grant, and [j]Sherman, and [k]Lee, and [l]Stonewall Jackson, and [m]Pershing, and [n]Nelson, and [o]Farragut, and [p]Halsey, and [q]Nimitz,

8 And Great Artists,

9 Like [r]Michelangelo, and [s]Leonardo da Vinci, and people like [t]Monet, and [u]Rubens, and [v]Botticelli, and [w]Raphael, and [x]Lautrec, and [y]Titian, and [z]Turner, and [aa]Rodin, and [bb]Rembrandt, and [cc]Van Gogh,

10 And Great Thinkers,

11 Like [dd]Plato, and [ee]Socrates, and [ff]Locke, and [gg]Rousseau, and [hh]Thoreau, and [ii]Goethe, and [jj]Hegel, and [kk]Kant, and [ll]Adam Smith, and [mm]Riccardo Malthus, and [nn]Nietzsche, and [oo]Freud, and [pp]Jung,

12 And Great Leaders,

13 Like [qq]Lincoln, and [rr]Winston Churchill, and [ss]Teddy Roosevelt, and [tt]George Washington, and [uu]Queen Elizabeth, and [vv]Disraeli, and Pitt, and Thomas Jefferson,

14 And Great Writers,

15 Like [ww]Shakespeare, and [xx]Walt Whitman, and [yy]Henry Wadsworth Longfellow, and [zz]Nathaniel Hawthorne, and [aaa]Washington Irving, and [bbb]James Fenimore Cooper, and [ccc]Mark Twain, and [ddd]Edgar Allan Poe, and [eee]Herman Melville, and [fff]Stephen Crane, and [ggg]Booth Tarkington, and [hhh]Sir Walter Scott, and [iii]Alexander Dumas, and [jjj]Robert Louis Stevenson, and [kkk]Milton, and [lll]Keats, and [mmm]Chaucer, and [nnn]Homer, and all the [ooo]writers who wrote the Bible, of course,

16 And Great Musicians,

17 Like [ppp]Gershwin, and [qqq]Porter, and [rrr]Kern, and Goodman, and [sss]Shaw, and [ttt]Herman, and [uuu]Hoagy Carmichael, and [vvv]Tchaikovsky, and [www]Beethoven, and [xxx]Rachmaninoff, and [yyy]Brahms, and [zzz]Bach, and [aaaa]Mozart, and [bbbb]Schubert, and [cccc]Liszt, and [dddd]Dvorak, and [eeee]Mendelssohn, and a bunch of others too probably, such as [ffff]Duke Ellington,

a. Forg.8.11-15
b. Vin.16.4
c. Vin.16.4
d. Exp.9.13
e. Yks.110.9
f. Yks.110.8
g. Yks.10.14-19
h. Brit.23.14
i. Yks.42.11
j. Gnt.9.2
k. Yks.39.4
l. Yks.39.5
m. 5A.23
n. Brit.23.12-13
o. 5Q.2
p. Dav.34.13
q. Ed.43.8
r. Dav.10.4
s. Gnt.9.11
t. Psong.20.1-8
u. Gnt.2.15
v. Gnt.2.16
w. Gnt.2.17
x. Dav.14.11
y. Psom.56.5
z. Gods.1.4
aa. 5G.10
bb. Paul.1.2 Zig.1.6-7
cc. Dav.18.17
dd. Grk.14.1-2
ee. Grk.14.9-11
ff. Brit.39.1
gg. Rat.9.24
hh. 5F.19
ii. Krt.7.1
jj. Krt.9.3-5
kk. Krt.9.3-5
ll. Psom.2.3-4
mm. Pnot.54.1
nn. Ed.74.6
oo. Ed.71.8
pp. Carl.3.8
qq. Rat.14.15-17
rr. Brit.50.15
ss. Ann.19.13
tt. Yks.13.4
uu. Dav.20.3
vv. Bks.6.12-18
ww. Dav.20.20-51
xx. Psom.68.1-5
yy. Yks.67.1
zz. Yks.33.11-12
aaa. Yks.66.1
bbb. Yks.65.3
ccc. Yks.71.1
ddd. Yks.70.1-2
eee. Pnot.42.1-5
fff. Pnot.19.1-5
ggg. F&J.2.15-16
hhh. Dav.19.3
iii. Pnot.37.1-5
jjj. Psom.5.1-6
kkk. Brit.33.1
lll. Brit.41.8
mmm. Brit.31.9
nnn. Grk.16.1
ooo. 5B.1-13
ppp. Ned.24.14
qqq. Nips.11.24
rrr. Dav.40.1
sss. Dav.43.27
ttt. Dav.23.13 Chuk.18.14
uuu. Ann.10.11
vvv. Russ.13.2-3
www. Krt.15.1
xxx. Russ.13.9
yyy. 5Q.65
zzz. Krt.12.3
aaaa. Krt.13.1
bbbb. Krt.16.2
cccc. Cen.26.18
dddd. Russ.20.3
eeee. Mawr.30.7
ffff. Psom.77.9 Grk.4.11

18 And Great Religious Figures,
19 Like ^aSt. Paul, and ^bSt. George, and ^cSt. Andrew, and ^dJesus Christ, of course, and ^eBuddha, and ^fConfucius, and ^gMohammed, and ^hSt. Francis of Assisi, and ⁱJoan of Arc, and ^jWilliam Jennings Bryan, and ^kSt. Peter, and ^lSt. Augustine, and ^mThomas More, and ⁿSt. John the Baptist, and ^oSt. John the Evangelist,
20 And Great Scientists,
21 Like ^pEdison, and ^qSalk, and ^rLouis Pasteur, and ^sCharles Darwin, and ^tIsaac Newton, and ^uMendel, and ^vLeeuwenhock, and ^wAlbert Einstein, and ^xWatt, and ^yEdison, and ^zGalileo, and ^{aa}Ptolemy, and ^{bb}Copernicus, and ^{cc}Kepler, and ^{dd}Skinner, and ^{ee}Bacon, and ^{ff}Madame Curie,
22 And Great Americans,
23 Like ^{gg}Alexander Hamilton, and ^{hh}Benjamin Franklin, and ⁱⁱDaniel Boone, and ^{jj}Johnny Appleseed, and ^{kk}Clarence Darrow, and ^{ll}Daniel Webster, and ^{mm}Barbara Frietchie, and ⁿⁿEleanor Roosevelt, and ^{oo}Babe Ruth, and ^{pp}Lou Gehrig, and ^{qq}Sergeant York, and ^{rr}Jimmy Stewart, and ^{ss}Sam Houston, and ^{tt}Francis Marion, and ^{uu}Phil Sheridan, and Will Rogers,
24 Not to mention Great Villains and Traitors, who are often more interesting than really Great Men,
25 Like ^{vv}Benedict Arnold, and ^{ww}Hitler, and ^{xx}Mussolini, and ^{yy}Tojo, and ^{zz}Quisling, and ^{aaa}Genghis Khan, and ^{bbb}Kaiser Wilhelm, and ^{ccc}Stalin, and ^{ddd}Hirohito,
26 And I know there are lots of other Great Names too,
27 Who you should know who they are,
28 Because you can see that the world would be a pretty different place if they hadn't come along.

H

^{eee}**H** is for Hygiene,
2 Which couldn't be any more important,
3 Because you can't go through life looking like a slob,
4 ^{fff}Which is why you have to shave every day,
5 And get a haircut every three weeks,
6 ^{ggg}And take a bath or a shower every day, and more often than that if you're playing sports or working in the yard,
7 And always wear a clean shirt and clean underwear,
8 And always wear a jacket and tie if you're going to a party or out to dinner,
9 And always wear a suit to church,
10 And brush your teeth after every meal,
11 ^{hhh}And wash your hands before every meal, and after you do your business,
12 And wash your hair pretty often too,

---

a. *Spic.14.12*
b. *Pnot.33.4*
c. *Pnot.32.3-4 Adam.10.3*
d. *Rat.16.7*
e. *Ed.67.9*
f. *Chnk.6.1-3*
g. *Bks.4.5*
h. *5A.40*
i. *Dav.11.1*
j. *Pnot.40.2*
k. *Dav.15.29-31*
l. *Boul.8.18-21*
m. *Dav.20.11*
n. *Dav.15.13*
o. *Vin.1.1*
p. *Adam.21.16*
q. *Adam.46.4*
r. *Frog.25.1-5*
s. *Dav.30.40*
t. *Brit.36.4*
u. *Adam.31.16*
v. *Ed.10.5-7*
w. *Ed.50.12 & 65.7*
x. *Psom.77.9*
y. *5Q.60*
z. *Gnt.6.1*
aa. *Gnt.7.2-4*
bb. *Gnt.7.1*
cc. *Gnt.8.1*
dd. *Grk.13.5 Zig.14.3-4*
ee. *Brit.10.7-10*
ff. *Dav.47.18*
gg. *Swar.PS.19*
hh. *Ned.42.26*
ii. *Yks.30.25*
jj. *5A.14*
kk. *Pnot.40.1-5*
ll. *Dav.48.7*
mm. *Psom.74.1-4*
nn. *Dav.20.7-8*
oo. *Yks.10.19*

---

pp. *Dav.9.7*
qq. *Dav.9.5*
rr. *Ed.49.5*
ss. *5J.22*

tt. *5F.12*
uu. *Yks.45.7*
vv. *Yks.11.4*
ww. *Krt.29.10*

xx. *Yks.101.10-11*
yy. *Dav.34.19*
zz. *Yks.105.4*

aaa. *Chnk.11.2*
bbb. *Krt.22.14*
ccc. *Russ.19.1*
ddd. *Nips.16.5*

eee. *Hill.H.1*
fff. *Rat.28.6*
ggg. *Vin.47.1-7*
hhh. *Ira.16.10*

13 And always carry a clean
pocket handkerchief.
14 It's also important to remember that good Hygiene includes
some things you shouldn't do,
15 Because you shouldn't chew
gum in public,
16 Or smoke unless the ladies
give you permission,
17 Or drink beverages out of the
bottle, which I learned from
your mother, so it must be important,
18 Or forget to polish your
shoes,
19 [a]Or read about all the latest
new diseases in magazines,
20 Ever,
21 Because you'll start feeling
all the symptoms,
22 Right away.

I

I is for Idiots,
2 Which there are a lot of,
3 [b]Because Idiots are people
who never think of anybody
else,
4 And never think anything
through,
5 And are always surprised to
discover that the world wasn't
made just for them,
6 [c]Which is a stupid, useless,
good-for-nothing way to be.

J

J is for Jokes, which every
man worth his salt knows a
lot of,
2 Because they break the ice
when you're meeting people for
the first time,
3 Which is why it's good there
are so many different kinds of
jokes,
4 [d]Including jokes about how
much the Micks like to drink and
beat up women,
5 [e]And how much Catholics like
to eat fish,
6 [f]And how stupid the Pollocks
are,
7 [g]And how miserly and self-
pitying the Jews are,
8 [h]And how penny-pinching
and rude the Scotch are,
9 [i]And how obsessed with sex
and food the French are,
10 [j]And how snobbish and hu-
morless the English are,
11 [k]And how greasy and violent
Italians are, the American Italians, that is,
12 [l]And how excitable and cowardly the Italian Italians are,
13 [m]And how dumb the Dutch
are,
14 [n]And how arrogant and
power-hungry the Germans are,
15 [o]And how sneaky and un-
imaginative the Japs are,
16 [p]And how fertile and funny-
sounding the Chinese are,
17 [q]And how filthy and backward the Arabs are,
18 [r]And how violent and pompous the Spanish are,
19 [s]And how violent and stupid
the Mexicans are,
20 [t]And how violent and filthy
Puerto Ricans are,
21 [u]And how boastful and ignorant Russians are,
22 [v]And how boastful and nou-
veau riche Texans are,
23 [w]And how inbred and ignorant hillbillies are,
24 [x]And how bluenosed and
snobbish Bostonians are,
25 [y]And how boring and rural
midwesterners are,
26 [z]And how lazy and alcoholic
southerners are,

a. *Jefs.7.1*
b. *Hill.1.1*
c. *Wil.45.25-26*
d. *Yks.146.18*
e. *Ira.21.27-29*
f. *Yks.125.22-23*
g. *Pnot.18.1-5 Psom.16.1-8*
h. *Adam.16.12-15*
i. *Frog.8.5-9 & 24.1*
j. *Yks.104.17-20*
k. *Psong.57.1*
l. *Krt.33.11-12*
m. *Exp.14.16-18*
n. *Ext.52.16*
o. *Nips.2.17*
p. *Chnk.11.8-9*
q. *Bks.6.22*
r. *Spic.4.10-11*
s. *Yks.107.6*
t. *Pnot.48.1-5*
u. *Dav.5.4*
v. *Yks.107.6*
w. *Ed.64.1-11*
x. *Yks.33.11*
y. *Yks.72.7-8*
z. *Yks.55.32*

27 [a]And how slow and lazy negroes are,

28 [b]And how vicious and lazy crackers are,

29 [c]And how scatterbrained and illogical women are,

30 [d]And how cruel and greedy lawyers are,

31 [e]Not to mention knock-knock jokes,

32 [f]And jokes about how awful a place Philadelphia is to visit,

33 [g]Which aren't always all that funny,

34 But are sometimes safer if you don't know for sure that there aren't any Micks or Pollocks or French or English or Jews or Scotch or negroes or women or lawyers or people like that in your audience,

35 [h]Unless you're fond of dirty jokes,

36 Which you'd better not be,

37 Because personally I find dirty jokes offensive.

K

K is for Knots, which come in pretty handy sometimes,

2 So it's worth your while to learn all the important knots,

3 Like the square knot,

4 The sheepshank,

5 And the granny,

6 [i]Not to mention my own personal favorite, the four-in-hand.

L

L is for Luck, which you can have if you remember the things that are lucky and the things that aren't.

2 [j]For example, don't ever break a mirror because you'll have seven years of bad luck . . . minimum,

3 And don't ever walk under a

a. Dav.22.26-27
b. Dav.27.4
c. Mawr.22.20
d. Penn.8.1-8
e. Hill.S.34-36
f. Wil.63.1-5
g. Jeff.19.8
h. Ira.14.1-10
i. 5E.5-9
j. Yks.94.6-12
k. Lies.6.17-19
l. 5J.31
m. Gods.6.1-2
n. 5Q.36
o. Brit.15.31-32
p. Dav.47.11
q. Psom.16.6

ladder because that's bad luck too,

4 [k]And if you drop some salt, throw some over your shoulder, just for luck,

5 [l]And if you say something that might give you bad luck, you'd better knock wood, just to make sure,

6 And the number thirteen is bad luck,

7 [m]But the number seven is good luck, at least on the first roll,

8 [n]And horseshoes are good luck unless they're pointed the wrong way,

9 And four-leaf clovers are good luck if you can ever find one,

10 Although if a black cat walks across your path, it's bad luck,

11 And three to a match is *very* bad luck,

12 And if you step on a crack in the sidewalk, you could break your mother's back,

13 Which isn't good luck at all.

M

M is for Measures, [o]which you can look like an idiot if you don't know,

2 Because everybody needs to know that there are four quarts in a gallon, and two pints in a quart, and,

3 Well,

4 They need to know how many pecks there are in a bushel,

5 And how many feet in a mile,

6 And how many yards in an acre,

7 [p]And how many rods in a fortnight,

8 And how many pounds in a ton,

9 And how many ounces in a [q]pound,

10 And how many shillings in an ounce,

11 And how many seconds in a minute,

12 ªAnd how many leagues in a mile,

13 And all that stuff.

N

N is for the Nations of the world,

2 Which you should be familiar with,

3 And be able to identify on a map,

4 Because you are an American,

5 And America leads the world,

6 Including all the major powers,

7 ᵇLike Britain, and France, and I guess, West Germany and Japan,

8 And America's other allies,

9 ᶜLike Canada, and Australia, and Israel, and Italy, I suppose,

10 And the Iron Curtain countries,

11 ᵈLike Russia, and East Germany, and Poland, and Czechoslovakia, and Hungary, and Albania, and Romania, and Yugoslavia sort of,

12 And all the poorer nations who we give foreign aid to,

13 ᵉLike all the South American countries, including Mexico,

14 ᶠAnd all the African countries that are really countries, and not just jungle tribes,

15 ᵍAnd all the Arab countries that have oil,

16 And a whole bunch of countries in the far east,

17 ʰLike the Philippines, and Taiwan, and Korea, and I can't remember all their names,

18 ⁱExcept for Red China,

19 Which we don't recognize,

a. Psom.25.1-2
b. Main.22.10
c. F&J.2.15
d. Yks.116.3-7
e. Spic.12.6
f. Chuk.16.5
   Exp.14.14
g. Bks.10.14-22
h. Chnk.10.2
i. Chnk.17.5
j. Vin.4.10
k. Zig.10.13
l. Zig.8.10
m. Wil.14.12

20 At all.

O

O is for the Outdoors,

2 Which you should see more of,

3 Because too much television will rot your brain and your eyes,

4 ʲAnd turn you into a vegetable with coke bottle eyeglasses.

5 Just think about how ashamed you will be, later in life, when you cannot identify a single tree,

6 ᵏIncluding oak trees,

7 And black walnut trees,

8 And birch trees,

9 And sycamore trees,

10 And chestnut trees,

11 And poplar trees,

12 And maple trees,

13 And willow trees,

14 And cedar trees,

15 And fir trees,

16 And spruce trees,

17 And pine trees,

18 And holly trees,

19 And that's only the barest minimum you should know.

20 And think of all the outdoor activities you'll never get to enjoy, unless you make a special effort,

21 ˡSuch as swimming in a lake,

22 And hiking in the woods,

23 And canoeing down a stream,

24 And fishing in a millpond,

25 And bird-watching,

26 And all the other things that would be so much better for you than the ᵐThree Stooges.

P

P is for Presidents, which there have been a lot of over the years,

2 But that doesn't mean you can get away with not knowing who they are,
3 Because it's everyone's responsibility to know them,
4 Including [a]Washington, [b]Adams, [c]Jefferson, [d]Taft,
5 [e]Monroe, [f]Madison, [g]Jackson, [h]Polk,
6 [i]Van Buren, Tyler, [j]Harrison, Fillmore,
7 [k]Buchanan, [l]Harrison, [m]Hayes, [n]Lincoln,
8 [o]Grant, [p]Arthur, [q]Johnson, [r]Adams,
9 [s]Wilson, [t]Roosevelt, [u]Cleveland, [v]Harding,
10 [w]Hoover, [x]Coolidge, [y]Roosevelt, and,
11 Well,
12 You should know them all by now anyway.

Q

Q is for Quotations, which educated people everywhere always say to each other at the appropriate time, like,
2 [z]Damn the torpedoes, full speed ahead,
3 [aa]Don't cross the Rubicon until you see the whites of their eyes,
4 [bb]Semper ubi, sub ubi,
5 [cc]Après moi the deluge,
6 [dd]The only thing we have to fear is fear itself,
7 [ee]I shall return,
8 [ff]I cannot tell a lie,
9 [gg]I came, I saw, I conquered,
10 [hh]United we stand, divided we fall,
11 [ii]Hell hath no fury like a woman scorned,
12 [jj]E pluribus unum,
13 [kk]Quid pro quo,
14 [ll]C'est la vie,
15 [mm]Non sequitur,
16 [nn]Patriotism is the last refuge of a scoundrel,
17 [oo]The Rose of Sharon would smell as sweet by any other name,
18 [pp]Turn the other cheek,
19 [qq]Vanity thy name is woman,
20 [rr]All I have to give is blood, sweat, and tears,
21 [ss]I have no more worlds to conquer,
22 [tt]To be or not to be, that is the question,
23 [uu]Nuts!
24 [vv]These are the times that try men's souls,
25 [ww]My kingdom for a horse,
26 [xx]The buck stops here,
27 [yy]Don't give up the ship,
28 [zz]Fire when ready, Greeley,
29 [aaa]The only thing I can't resist is temptation,
30 [bbb]Go west, young man,
31 [ccc]Live and let live,
32 [ddd]Eureka!
33 [eee]Nobody here but us chickens, boss,
34 [fff]Cold as a well-digger's witch,
35 [ggg]Do unto others as you would have them do unto you,
36 [hhh]For want of a nail the horse got lost,
37 [iii]Et tu, Brute,
38 [jjj]All I have to give is blood and iron,

a. Yks.14.1
b. Yks.15.1-2
c. Yks.16.1
d. Yks.61.23
e. Yks.18.1
f. Yks.20.1-2
g. Yks.25.1-2
h. Yks.26.1
i. Yks.24.1-5
j. Yks.24.8
k. Yks.34.1-5
l. Yks.57.1-9
m. Yks.55.1-9
n. Yks.47.1-9
o. Yks.49.1-4
p. Ed.43.8
q. Yks.48.1
r. Yks.24.6-7
s. Yks.62.7-11
t. Yks.61.1-2
u. Yks.57.1-9
v. Yks.85.1-7
w. Yks.96.1-7
x. Yks.89.1-11
y. Yks.96.10-15
z. Dav.34.13
aa. Rom.11.10
bb. Rom.2.1-4
cc. Lies.5.17
dd. Al.5.3
ee. Pnot.25.1-5
ff. Yks.10.5
gg. Hill.V.1
hh. Al.2.11
ii. Ext.49.17
jj. Yks.37.16
kk. Frog.26.16
ll. Frog.35.6
mm. Vin.6.7
nn. Brit.38.2
oo. Grk.6.15 Chuk.19.16-17
pp. 5A.37
qq. Adam.47.3
rr. Brit.54.1-4
ss. Swar.10.4-5
tt. Hill.Q.1-2
uu. Hill.F.1
vv. Spic.7.1
ww. Ed.46.24
xx. Psong.41.1-3
yy. Pnot.20.1
zz. Yks.28.26-28
aaa. Jeff.24.9
bbb. Exp.9.1-3
ccc. Al.6.21
ddd. Grk.14.25-26
eee. Krt.24.11
fff. Brit.10.4
ggg. Boul.10.11-14
hhh. 5L.8
iii. Rom.13.6-7
jjj. Krt.21.1

39 [a]Out, out, darned spot,

40 [b]There is a time to laugh and a time to die,

41 [c]Love conquers all,

42 [d]Vengeance is mine, saith the Lord,

43 [e]If you can't stand the heat, get out,

44 [f]The whole world loves a lover,

45 [g]Let them eat cake,

46 [h]You can fool most of the people most of the time,

47 Speak loudly and carry a big [i]stick,

48 [j]The game is afoot,

49 [k]S.P.Q.R.,

50 [l]Cherchez the woman!

51 [m]Beware of Greeks bearing gifts,

52 [n]There's a sucker born every minute,

53 [o]The rain in Spain stays mainly on the plain,

54 [p]Who's on first,

55 [q]Reductio ad nauseam,

56 [r]Plus c'est la guerre, plus c'est la même chose,

57 [s]When in Rome, do as the Romans do,

58 [t]I am the resurrection and the life, saith the Lord,

59 [u]Never give a sucker an even break, but never cheat a friend,

60 [v]Genius is one percent inspiration, and ninety-nine percent perspiration,

61 [w]To thine own self be true,

62 [x]Q.E.D.,

63 [y]War is hell,

64 [z]Stone walls do not a prison make, nor iron bars a cage,

65 [aa]The hand that rocks the cradle rules the world,

66 [bb]Don't look a gift horse in the mouth,

67 [cc]Better late than never,

68 [dd]Rule Britannia; Britannia rules the waves,

69 [ee]The pen is mightier than the sword,

70 [ff]Fools rush in where angels fear to tread,

71 [gg]Man cannot live by bread alone,

72 [hh]Every cloud has a silver lining,

73 [ii]An eye for an eye, a tooth for a tooth,

74 [jj]Sacré bleu,

75 [kk]Olé,

76 [ll]Oy vay,

77 [mm]Absence makes the heart grow fonder,

78 [nn]Tally-ho,

79 [oo]Et cetera,

80 [pp]Et alia.

R

R is for Religions, which almost everybody belongs to,

2 And explains why it's only polite to know what they all are,

3 Including [qq]Presbyterians,

4 [rr]Lutherans,

5 [ss]Baptists,

6 [tt]Episcopalians,

7 [uu]Methodists,

8 [vv]Unitarians,

9 [ww]Quakers,

10 [xx]Catholics,

11 [yy]Jews,

12 [zz]Holy Rollers,

13 [aaa]Seventh-Day Adventists,

14 And I guess that's about it.

S

S is for the Sports and Games every man should know how to play,

2 Including all the rules,

3 [bbb]So you'll always know

a. Pnot.32.3
b. Main.22.10
c. Russ.9.1-8
d. 5Q.58
e. Yks.136.1-2
f. Dav.47.11
g. Frog.12.2
h. Yks.94.1-5
i. Zig.10.13
　Apes.1.1
j. Pnot.8.5
k. Grk.20.8
l. Frog.8.9
m. Grk.3.2-4
n. 5Q.59
o. Spic.3.2-3
p. Grk.4.11
q. Pnot.24.1-5
　Yks.154.31-32
　Chuk.18.1
　& 20.1
　Wil.19.6-11
r. Frog.40.6
s. Rom.20.7
t. 5Q.42
u. 5Q.52
v. Ira.33.1-3
w. Zig.10.12
x. Ira.25.16-20
y. Yks.44.25
z. Ira.42.1-9
aa. Ed.74.3
bb. Grk.18.3
cc. Yks.70.11
dd. Brit.13.8-10
ee. Adam.1.3
ff. Wil.60.1-5
gg. Psong.41.6
hh. Vin.48.12-16
ii. Boul.22.3
jj. Frog.35.4
kk. Brit.6.29
　Yks.144.10-12
ll. Lies.8.4
mm. Frog.31.8-9
nn. Brit.6.22
oo. Psom.53.6
pp. Psom.53.7
qq. Jeff.7.4-12
rr. Jeff.7.4-12
ss. Jeff.7.4-12
tt. Jeff.7.4-12
uu. Jeff.7.4-12
vv. Jeff.7.4-12
ww. Jeff.7.4-12
xx. Jeff.7.4-12
yy. 5J.7
zz. Jeff.7.4-12
aaa. Jeff.7.4-12
bbb. Brit.47.1-3

when you're wrong and can be a good sport about it.

4 [a]For example, there's baseball, which is the greatest game ever invented by anyone anywhere,

5 [b]Which is why you've got to know how to throw a baseball like a man, and not like some girl,

6 And how to hit a curveball,

7 And how to get at least a piece of even the nastiest strike, because a [c]foul is better than a strikeout,

8 Which always makes you feel absolutely awful, like you let your teammates down or something.

9 [d]And then there's football, which is a great high school and college game,

10 [e]And a great way to learn about how to get back on your feet after you've been knocked on your can,

11 [f]No matter how many times it happens,

12 [g]And boxing, which every man needs to know how to do, because sometimes you have to stand up and fight for your dignity, whether you want to or not.

13 And there are other great sports too that you can play all your life, even after you can't take the physical punishment kids can,

14 Like [h]golf and tennis, which are fun to play with friends, unless you're the kind of [i]hothead that always has to win, no matter what,

15 In which case you should play something else,

16 [j]Like solitaire.

17 And there are also sports that

a. Yks.142.1-5
b. Mawr.22.1-3
c. Russ.1.3-7
d. Yks.142.7
e. Yks.142.8
f. Yks.142.9
g. Dav.8.4
h. Jeff.5.7
i. Jeff.10.14-15
j. F&J.14.4
k. Brit.47.6
l. Brit.47.4
m. Brit.47.5
n. Psom.73.1-14
o. Yks.31.6
p. Psom.53.1-7
q. 5E.5-7
r. Zig.10.13
s. Ann.2.32
    Psay.5Q.23

you should know about because other people like to play them and even watch them,

18 For some reason,

19 [k]Like soccer, which is pretty much of a waste of time unless you're planning to hang around with Europeans,

20 [l]And cricket, which is what the British play because they don't know about baseball,

21 [m]And rugby, which is what the British play because they don't know about football,

22 [n]And basketball, which is at least American,

23 [o]And hockey, which is an excellent way to get all your teeth knocked out, like the Canadians do.

24 And then later in life, there are games that don't involve athletics, but that people like to play, and some of them it's a good idea to know how to play, and others it isn't,

25 Like bridge, for example, which [p]women like to play and men don't, and so it's better not to know how,

26 [q]And backgammon, which certain kinds of men like to play, for some reason, maybe because they don't have the brains for [r]poker,

27 Which is a great game, unless you're not good at it, which you can find out easily enough, because if you're not good at it, you'll lose [s]money.

28 There's also chess, which is supposed to be a great game,

29 But personally I've never understood it,

30 And don't want to either,

31 Because chess players seem to take the game too seriously,

32 Which you just can't do,
33 Because no matter what anybody tells you,
34 A game is only a game,
35 And if you want to take something seriously, then make sure it isn't a game,
36 But something important instead,
37 [a]Like your responsibilities and duties in life,
38 Unless you're planning to be the kind of jerk that can't tell the difference.

T

T is for the Tools every man has to know how to use,
2 Because things have a way of breaking periodically,
3 And if you don't know how to fix things,
4 [b]They'll fall apart eventually,
5 And people will think you're a lazy good-for-nothing.
6 And practically all the tools you'll ever need you can get at [c]Sears,
7 [d]Including automotive tools, like ratchet sets, and wrenches, and jacks, and hoists,
8 [e]And carpentry tools, like saws, and hammers, and drills, and planers, and screwdrivers, and measuring tapes, and chisels, and awls, and brushes, and sanders, and many more besides,
9 [f]And masonry tools, like trowels, and levels, and reinforcing rods, and wire brushes, and other stuff too,
10 [g]And even garden tools, like wheelbarrows, and hoes, and rakes, and edgers, and lawn brooms, and plows, and seeders, and lawn mowers,

a. Ira.31.6-15
b. Pnot.13.5
c. Yks.89.5
d. Zig.10.13
e. Zig.10.13
f. Zig.10.13
g. Zig.10.13
h. Chuk.6.4-6
i. Ed.74.4
j. Grk.4.11
k. Grk.9.8-11
l. Gnt.7.1-4
m. Ed.60.15
n. Rom.10.19
o. Rom.10.20
p. Adam.31.3
q. Rom.10.16
r. Frog.26.16
s. Rom.10.18
t. Psp.3.6

11 Not to mention lots and lots of supplies for every kind of job you'd ever want to tackle.

U

U is for the Universe,
2 Which has a lot of things in it that everybody has to know,
3 Including stars,
4 [h]Such as the Big Dipper, and the Little Dipper, and Orion, and the Seven Sisters, and the [i]Dog Star, and [j]Alpha [k]Centauri, and a whole bunch more that you should know,
5 Not to mention our own solar system,
6 [l]Which revolves around the sun,
7 And has a bunch of planets in it,
8 Like [m]Earth,
9 [n]Mars,
10 [o]Venus,
11 [p]Mercury,
12 [q]Jupiter,
13 [r]Saturn,
14 And [s]Neptune,
15 Which isn't the end of it at all,
16 Because there also comets,
17 Like Halley's Comet,
18 And meteors,
19 Which keep hitting the moon,
20 [t]Not to mention eclipses,
21 Which happen sometimes,
22 But don't really hurt anything,
23 Unless you're the kind that's easily frightened.

V

V is for Values,
2 Which every man has to have,

3 Like working hard,
4 And being sober,
5 And being kind to dumb animals,
6 And always opening the door for ladies,
7 And going to church,
8 And telling the truth,
9 And being polite to your elders,
10 And always being clean and shaved and neatly dressed,
11 And not speaking ill of the dead,
12 ªAnd not telling dirty jokes,
13 And loving your country,
14 And giving back more than you take,
15 And taking care of your family,
16 And not washing your dirty linen in public,
17 And standing by your principles, no matter what,
18 And never being rude to anyone, even if they deserve it,
19 ᵇAnd being a good sport, win or lose,
20 And never crying, unless you're a woman,
21 And always looking a man in the eye when you shake his hand,
22 And never ever hitting a woman, for any reason whatsoever, period, including your sister,
23 And never taking advantage of a woman when she's..., well, just don't take advantage, that's all,
24 ᶜAnd never ever using bad language of any kind, because imagine how embarrassed you'd be if you slipped in good company,
25 And always being fair, no matter who they are,

a. 5J.35-37
b. 5S.1-3
c. Hill.F.1
d. Yks.106.1-14
e. Krt.24.2-3
f. Yks.43.1-4
g. Yks.54.1
h. Yks.18.2-4
i. Yks.9.1-6
j. Yks.10.2
k. Frog.31.1
l. Brit.23.10-17
m. Brit.26.19
n. Frog.26.10-13
  Yks.154.31-32
o. Pnot.25.1-5
p. Chr.8.12-18

26 Because not everybody has had your advantages,
27 And it's your responsibility to set a good example.

W

Wis for Wars,
2 ᵈIncluding World War II, which was the biggest one,
3 ᵉAnd World War I, which was the second biggest one,
4 ᶠAnd the Civil War, which saved the union and freed the slaves,
5 ᵍAnd the Indian Wars, which pretty well killed off all the Indians, which is unfortunate because they never had a chance anyway,
6 ʰAnd the War of 1812, which was kind of a strange stupid war with the British,
7 ⁱAnd the Revolution, which was very very important even if it wasn't much of a war,
8 ʲAnd the French and Indian War, which was kind of a warm-up for the Revolution,
9 ᵏAnd the Franco-Prussian War, which is a big part of the reason why Europe is still so screwed up today,
10 ˡAnd the Napoleonic Wars, which must have been exciting, even if they were as silly as everything else that's started by the French,
11 ᵐNot to mention all the hundreds of other wars the British fought with the French, and everybody else too, including even the Zulus, if you can believe it,
12 ⁿAnd the War of the Roses, which killed off °knighthood's flower, just like Nostradammus predicted,
13 ᵖAnd the Crusades, which

have always seemed kind of peculiar to me,

14 ^aAnd the Viking Wars, which took place whenever and wherever the Vikings landed their boat,

15 ^bAnd all the wars the Romans fought to build and keep their empire, including the ^cPunic Wars, I think,

16 ^dWhich must have been a lot like the wars Alexander fought to build the Greek empire,

17 ^eAnd all the wars they've fought with each other in the Orient over the years,

18 ^fAnd the middle east, where they started a war about five thousand years ago and haven't ever stopped yet,

19 ^gAnd I suppose you also have to include the Korean War,

20 Although it's hard to count the wars that people don't try to win.

21 ^hAnd you already know about the Cold War,

22 Which isn't quite a war exactly,

23 ⁱBecause if it ever ends, it will probably be because we just started World War III,

24 Which nobody will win,

25 ^jBecause there won't be much left afterwards.

X

^k**X** is for the spot where the ^ltreasure is buried,

2 Including the treasure of ^mCaptain Kidd,

3 ⁿLong John Silver,

4 ^oMonte Cristo,

5 ^pCaptain Blood,

6 Captain Hook,

7 And I think there was maybe a ^qCaptain Cook too.

a. *Barb.4.9-13*
b. *Rom.5.7-8*
c. *Rom.6.3-10*
d. *Grk.25.1-9*
e. *Nips.2.9-11*
f. *Bks.10.1-4*
g. *Yks.134.2-6*
h. *Russ.20.1-27*
i. *Yks.140.14*
j. *Swar.26.8-9*
k. *Hill.X.1-2*
l. *Ned.9.8-9*
  Swar.4.5-7
  Bks.6.17
  Ed.54.22-23
m. *Jefs.3.1*
n. *5Q.4*
o. *Dav.15.26*
p. *Dav.8.7*
q. *Oth.2.26*

Y

Y is for the Years when important things in history happened, such as fourteen hundred and ninety-two,

2 And a bunch of other years that you should know cold,

3 Including seventeen hundred and seventy-six,

4 Eighteen hundred and twelve,

5 Eighteen hundred and sixty,

6 Nineteen hundred and fourteen,

7 Nineteen hundred and forty-one,

8 One thousand sixty-six,

9 Twelve hundred and fifteen,

10 Sixteen hundred and forty,

11 Sixteen hundred and eighty-eight,

12 Seven hundred and fifty-three B.C.,

13 Forty-four B.C.,

14 Four hundred and seventy-six,

15 Fourteen hundred and fifty-three,

16 Seventeen hundred and eighty-three,

17 Eighteen hundred and sixty-five,

18 Nineteen hundred and eighteen,

19 Nineteen hundred and forty-five,

20 Seventeen hundred and ninety-nine,

21 Eighteen hundred and twenty,

22 Eighteen hundred and fifteen,

23 Nineteen hundred and seventeen,

24 Fifteen hundred B.C.,

25 Nineteen hundred and twelve,

26 Nineteen hundred and sixteen,

27 Fifteen hundred and eighty-eight,

28 Nineteen hundred and twenty-nine,
29 Two thousand and one million B.C.,
30 Thirteen hundred and forty-eight,
31 Sixteen hundred and seven,
32 Eighteen hundred and seventy-seven,
33 Seventeen hundred and eighty-eight,
34 Eighteen hundred and ninety-eight,
35 Zero,
36 Nineteen hundred and eighty-four,
37 Four thousand and some B.C.,
38 Nineteen hundred and nineteen,
39 Nineteen hundred and forty-four,
40 Eighteen hundred and thirty-six,
41 Three hundred and ninety-nine B.C.,
42 Fifteen hundred and sixty-four,
43 Thirty-three,
44 Eighteen hundred and seventy-one,
45 Three hundred and thirty-seven,
46 Eighteen hundred and forty-eight,
47 Eighteen hundred and ninety-six,
48 Three hundred and twenty-three B.C.,
49 Fourteen hundred and fifty-two,
50 Seventeen hundred and eighty-nine,
51 Sixteen hundred and sixty,
52 Seventeen hundred and sixty-three,
53 Eighteen hundred and forty-nine,

a. Hill.Z.1-5
b. Wil.2.3-5
*   Al.6.19*
c. Kin.5.5
d. Kin.6.2
e. Grk.8.32
f. Kin.5.2-4
g. Mall.18.1-6
h. Ira.21.26
i. Kens.27.2-5
j. Ext.17.6-8

54 And that's really just the beginning,
55 Because a bunch of things happened in between too,
56 Like they usually do.

Z

[a]**Z** is for Zoo Animals,
2 Like ostriches and [b]lions and aardvarks, and [c]monkeys of all kinds, and [d]gorillas, and [e]zebras, and antelope, and I can't list them all for you,
3 But you should take the time to learn something about them,
4 [f]Because the world is a pretty fascinating place with all kinds of different people and animals in it,
5 And it's a real good idea to remember that,
6 At all times,
7 [g]Because you have to live in the world,
8 And no matter how hard you think you have it,
9 Somebody else always has it worse,
10 [h]And they're part of God's creation too,
11 [i]Whether you see any sense in it or not,
12 Which seeing a silly-looking animal like an aardvark or a zebra every once in a while can help remind you of.

PSAYING 6

[j]**N**ow go, my son, out into the wide world,
2 And make your mother and me proud of you,
3 Because you'll have to earn what you get,
4 So remember,
5 There aren't any free rides,
6 If you want to make your mark.

THE BOOK OF PSOMETHINGS

PSOMETHING 1

[a]**T**he boy stood on the burning deck,

2 Whence all but he had fled,

3 Something something,

4 [b]A bullet in his head,

5 Or something,

6 And so forth,

7 And so on.

PSOMETHING 2

Under the spreading [c]chestnut tree,

2 The village smithy stands;

3 The smith a mighty man is he,

4 With something [d]something hands,

5 And so forth,

6 [e]And so on.

PSOMETHING 3

[f]**H**umpty Dumpty sat on a wall,

2 [g]Humpty Dumpty had a great fall.

3 Something something,

4 [h]And all the king's men,

5 Couldn't put Humpty together again,

6 Or something like that.

PSOMETHING 4

[i]**T**o be or not to be;

2 That is the question.

3 Whether 'tis nobler in the mind,

4 Something something,

5 [j]Or to take up a sea of arms,

6 Against something something troubles,

---

a. Dav.32.1
  Bks.3.14
b. 50.5
c. Psay.5O.10
d. 41.7
e. Yks.67.6
f. Ed.28.6
g. Al.2.11
h. Psay.2.1
i. Mall.18.1-2
j. Mall.10.13
k. Mall.18.3
l. Mall.6.24
m. Carl.3.8
n. Dav.32.23
o. 22.2
p. Pnot.13.5
q. Dav.52.4
r. Dav.35.18
s. Jefs.7.46
t. Brit.56.12-13

---

7 And something,

8 [k]Or to shuffle off this mortal coil,

9 And something to sleep,

10 [l]To sleep, perchance to dream,

11 Something something,

12 [m]In a bare bodkin,

13 Or something.

PSOMETHING 5

I have a little [n]shadow,

2 That goes in and out with me,

3 Something something,

4 Something something,

5 And so forth,

6 And so on.

PSOMETHING 6

Something something in the widening [o]gyre;

2 The center cannot hold;

3 [p]Things fall apart,

4 Something something lack all conviction,

5 And [q]something something intensity,

6 [r]Something slouching something Bethlehem,

7 [s]Something something born.

PSOMETHING 7

Now I lay me down to sleep,

2 I pray the Lord something something.

3 If I should die before I wake,

4 [t]I pray the Lord to do something,

5 Amen.

PSOMETHING 8

[a] **S**omething time to every something under heaven;
2 A time to laugh,
3 A time to something,
4 A time to something else,
5 And so forth,
6 And so on.

PSOMETHING 9

[b] **J**im Bowie, Jim Bowie!
2 Something something,
3 Jim Bowie, Jim Bowie!
4 Something something,
5 Something hand;
6 His blade was [c]something,
7 And so was he,
8 [d]Jim Bowie, Jim Bowie!
9 Da, da something,
10 Da, da something,
11 Something.
12 Stay tuned.

PSOMETHING 10

[e] **Y**ou may talk of gin and beer,
2 When you're something safe out here,
3 But when it comes to [f]slaughter,
4 You'll do your work on water,
5 And something something him that's got it.
6 Something something,
7 [g]Something something,
8 Drilled the beggar clean.
9 Something something,
10 [h]Though I've belted you and flayed you,
11 You're a better man than I am, [i]Gunga Din,
12 Or something like that.

PSOMETHING 11

By the shining big sea water,

a. *Psay.5Q.40*
b. *Yks.30.24*
c. *Zig.10.13*
d. *Ed.47.7*
e. *Vin.16.2-8 & 16.10-26*
f. *Brit.26.21*
g. *Ed.50.9*
h. *Brit.42.21*
i. *Dav.14.23*
j. *Yks.67.5*
k. *Psong.58.4*
l. *Vin.6.15*
m. *Brit.45.15*
n. *30.1-7*
o. *Ed.76.6 Bks.11.6-10*
p. *Wil.19.15*
q. *Brd.24.15*
r. *Grk.14.13*
s. *Dav.20.26 & 14.5*
t. *Rom.13.1-7*
u. *Adam.6.7*
v. *Nips.5.1-2*
w. *28.1-3*
x. *Wil.37.1-4*

2 Stood the something of Tacomis,
3 Something something,
4 And so forth,
5 [j]And so on.

PSOMETHING 12

[k] **A**pril is the cruelest month,
2 Mixing something with something,
3 Something something,
4 [l]There is no water,
5 [m]Something under the shadow of this [n]red rock,
6 Something something something,
7 [o]Shantih Shantih Shantih,
8 Or something like that.

PSOMETHING 13

[p] **T**his is the forest primeval;
2 The murmuring [q]pines and the [r]hemlocks,
3 Something something,
4 And so forth,
5 And so on.

PSOMETHING 14

[s] **F**riends, Romans, countrymen,
2 Lend [s]me your ears,
3 Something something,
4 I come to bury [t]Caesar,
5 Not to praise him.
6 [u]The evil that men do lives after them,
7 And something something,
8 Something something,
9 For they are all [v]honourable [w]men.

PSOMETHING 15

[x] **I**f you can keep your head,

2 When something something
[a]losing theirs,
3 [b]And blaming it on you,
4 Something something,
5 And lose and something,
6 [c]And never even count your loss,
7 And something,
8 And something else,
9 [d]Then the world something something,
10 And [e]everything that's in it,
11 And what's more something,
12 You'll be a [f]man, my son,
13 Or something like that.

PSOMETHING 16

Hath not a [g]Jew eyes?
2 Something something,
3 If you [h]prick him,
4 [i]Does he not bleed?
5 Something something,
6 [j]Something pound of flesh,
7 Something something,
8 Or something like that.

PSOMETHING 17

The sun was shining on the sea,
2 [k]Something something,
3 Said the [l]walrus to the [m]carpenter,
4 [n]Something[o]something[p]something,
5 [q]Something [r]something,
6 The [s]time has come, the [t]walrus said,
7 [u]To talk of many things,
8 Of something something [v]ceiling wax,
9 And [w]cabbages and [x]kings,
10 [y]And something something boiling hot,
11 [z]And why do pigs have wings?
12 [aa]Something something,
13 And this was scarcely odd,

a. Ann.4.22
b. Ned.35.10-13
c. Brit.15.30-31
d. Cen.1.6
e. Adam.46-50
f. Ned.8.10
g. Dav.21.26
h. Dav.17.11-12
i. Mall.13.17
j. Psay.5M.9
k. Ned.56.4
l. Vin.11.10-11
m. Dav.15.11-12
n. Vin.3.16
o. Vin.3.17
p. Vin.3.18
q. Vin.4.19
r. Vin.4.20
s. 23.11
t. Dav.57.16
u. Main.18.6
v. Vin.40.10-11
w. 28.1-2
x. 75.7
y. Psay.5Q.43
z. Brit.58.7-8
aa. 76.5
bb. 35.5 Cen.1.6
cc. Ann.18.12
dd. Ann.18.6
ee. Ann.18.14
ff. 14.2
gg. 2.3
hh. 78.8
ii. Vin.59.15

14 [bb]Because they'd eaten every one.

PSOMETHING 18

It is an ancient mariner;
2 He stoppeth one of three;
3 Something something wedding guest,
4 Something something,
5 [cc]I shot the albatross!
6 Something something,
7 The furrow followed free.
8 Something water everywhere, and not a drop to drink,
9 He prayeth best something something
10 Who something something loveth best,
11 All things both [dd]great and [ee]small,
12 Something something,
13 Something something,
14 A sadder and a wiser man, Something something morn.

PSOMETHING 19

[ff]**S**omething my children and you shall hear,
2 Of the midnight ride of [gg]Paul Revere,
3 Something something,
4 One if by land,
5 And two if by sea,
6 Something something,
7 And so forth,
8 And so on.

PSOMETHING 20

The quality of mercy is not [hh]strained,
2 Something something as the rain from heaven,
3 Upon the place beneath.
4 Something something,
5 [ii]It is twice blessed;
6 Something something,
7 And so forth,
8 And so on.

PSOMETHING 21

Blessed are the meek,
2 For theirs is the something.
3 Blessed are the poor in spirit,
4 For something,
5 Blessed are the something,
6 Something else,
7 And so forth,
8 And so on.

PSOMETHING 22

T'was brillig and the some-thing something,
2 Did [b]something and some-thing in the waves,
3 Something something,
4 Or something like that.

PSOMETHING 23

Let us go then, you and I,
2 Where the stars are something something in the sky,
3 Something [c]etherized upon a table.
4 Something something,
5 I grow old.
6 [d]I shall wear the bottom of my trousers rolled.
7 Something something,
8 [e]Do I dare to eat a peach?
9 And do I dare,
10 [f]And do I dare,
11 Something something IT'S TIME,
12 Something,
13 And the women come and go,
14 Talking of [g]Michelangelo,
15 Something something,
16 [h]Till we drown.

PSOMETHING 24

Something something,
2 Something something,

a. Vin.59.5-21
b. 6.1
c. 4.10
d. Adam.31.19-20
e. Psay.5H.11
f. Ira.27.24
g. Dav.10.10
h. Ed.78.11
　　Dav.47.11
　　Psom.12.4
i. 31.5-6
j. Brit.15.31-32
k. Psay.5M.12
l. Psong.52.2
m. Psay.5G.1
n. Hill.G.1
o. Dav.47.24
p. Psay.2.1
q. Drex.6.1
r. Drex.6.1
s. Grk.9.7
t. Boul.21.9
u. 45.3
v. Ann.2.32
w. Ira.33.1
x. Ira.33.2
y. Ira.33.3
z. Ned.24.8-11
aa. Dav.30.40
bb. Kens.12.26
cc. Drex.7.11-14
dd. Psay.5A.23

3 And ask not for whom the [i]bell tolls;
4 It tolls for thee.

PSOMETHING 25

Half a [j]league, half a league,
2 Half a [k]league onward,
3 Into the [l]valley of Death,
4 Rode the six hundred.
5 Something something,
6 [m]Guns to the right of them,
7 [n]Guns to the left of them,
8 Something and thundered.
9 [o]Something blundered,
10 [p]Forward the Light Brigade,
11 O the wild charge they made,
12 [q]Something [r]something,
13 [s]Something six hundred.

PSOMETHING 26

From too much love of living,
2 From hope and fear set free,
3 [t]Something something,
4 That no life lives forever,
5 And even the [u]something river,
6 [v]Something safe to sea.

PSOMETHING 27

[w]**A** rose is a rose is a rose,
2 [x]And so forth,
3 [y]And so on.

PSOMETHING 28

Something something the [z]hollow men,
2 Something something the [aa]stuffed men,
3 [bb]Something something,
4 [cc]Something something,
5 And so on.

PSOMETHING 29

[dd]**J**ack Sprat could eat no fat;

2 His wife could eat no lean.
3 Something something,
4 And something else,
5 [a]Stuck in his thumb and pulled out a [b]plum,
6 And said, What a good boy am I.

PSOMETHING 30

[c]Rock of ages,
2 [d]Cleft for me,
3 Something something,
4 [e]From thy side a healing flood,
5 Something something,
6 Let me hide myself in thee,
7 Or something like that.

PSOMETHING 31

[f]Frère Jacques, frère Jacques,
2 [g]Something something,
3 Something les matines,
4 [h]Something les matines,
5 [i]Ding dang dong,
6 [j]Ding dang dong.

PSOMETHING 32

[k]Yankee Doodle went to town,
2 A-riding on a pony,
3 Something something something,
4 And called it [l]macaroni.

PSOMETHING 33

[m]Something and a drowsy numbness something,
2 [n]Something something,
3 Something else,
4 Beauty is [o]truth,
5 And [p]something beauty;
6 That is something something on earth,
7 And all something something,
8 [q]Or something like that.

a. Chuk.4.5
b. Wht.8
c. Grk.3.9-10
d. Grks.3.11
e. Ed.78.11
f. Dav.57.16
g. Hill.Z.1
   & Z.1
   & Z.1
   & Z.1
   & Z.1
h. 24.3
i. 37.3
j. 37.4
k. Yks.10.14-19
l. Dav.47.11
m. Ira.21.17
n. 31.2
o. Ira.25.16-20
p. Swar.29.6
q. F&J.2.15
r. Ned.16.12
s. 28.1
t. 28.2
u. Drex.8.1-3
v. Al.2.11
w. Cen.11.25-31
   Vin.71.17-18
x. Ira.25.14-17
y. Ira.23.32
z. Ira.26.7
aa. Ext.15.1
   & 11.2-9
   & 37.8-9
bb. Psong.66.6
cc. Ext.17.6-9
dd. Ext.21.13-17
ee. Kens.18.2
ff. Kens.18.5-10
gg. Ed.70.11
hh. Psong.50.5
ii. Psong.50.6
jj. Psong.52.1
kk. Psong.52.2

PSOMETHING 34

Thirty days hath September,
2 Something June and November,
3 All the rest have thirty-one,
4 Something something February,
5 Which has twenty-eight,
6 Except in Leap Year,
7 When it has twenty-nine instead,
8 [r]Or something like that.

PSOMETHING 35

[s]Something something,
2 [t]Something something;
3 [u]This is the way the world ends;
4 Not with a [v]bang, but a [w]whimper,
5 Or something like that.

PSOMETHING 36

[x]Wee [y]som'thing [z]som'thing [aa]som'thing [bb]beastie,
2 Som'thing [cc]som'thing in thy [dd]breastie,
3 Som'thing som'thing,
4 Som'thing els',
5 The best laid plans of [ee]mice and men,
6 [ff]Som'thing a'glegh(?),
7 Or som'thing.

PSOMETHING 37

Something [gg]something,
2 Something something something,
3 [hh]The tintinnabulation of the bells, bells, bells, bells,
4 [ii]The something and the something of the bells,
5 [jj]And so forth,
6 [kk]And so on.

PSOMETHING 38

Hickory dickory dock,
2 [a]The mice ran up the clock.
3 The clock struck [b]something,
4 Something down again,
5 [c]Three blind mice,
6 [d]Three blind mice,
7 Or something like that.

PSOMETHING 39

Onward Christian soldiers,
2 [e]Marching off to war,
3 Something something something,
4 [f]Going on before,
5 [g]And so forth,
6 [h]And so on.

PSOMETHING 40

Something,
2 Something,
3 A banner with a [i]strange device,
4 Excelsior!

PSOMETHING 41

I pledge allegiance to the flag,
2 Of the United States of America,
3 And to the republican,
4 For something stands,
5 One nation,
6 Something something,
7 In-[j]something-able,
8 With something and something for all.
9 Amen.

PSOMETHING 42

It was many and many a year ago,
2 In a something by the sea,
3 Something something lived,
4 By the name of [k]Annabel Lee.
5 Something something,
6 Something,
7 [l]Real sad.

PSOMETHING 43

[m]Wee Willie Winkie runs through the town,
2 Something something,
3 With his [n]something gown,
4 Something something,
5 [o]Are all the children in their beds,
6 Something something o'-clock,
7 Or something.

PSOMETHING 44

[p]Tyger, Tyger, burning bryte,
2 In the something of the Nyte,
3 Something,
4 [q]& Something,
5 What the [r]Devil,
6 What the [s]Hell,
7 [t]Something something in thy Eye,
8 Could frame thy Something,
9 Or Other?

PSOMETHING 45

In [u]Xanadu did [v]Kubla Khan,
2 A stately [w]pleasure [x]dome decree,
3 Where [y]something something river ran,
4 Through something something,
5 And down to a something [z]something,
6 Something,
7 So twice five miles of something,
8 [aa]Something something,
9 [bb]Something else,
10 And he on honeydew hath fed,

a. 34.8
b. Hill.Z.1
c. Psp.3.6
d. Ed.77.6
e. Vin.59.21
f. Hall.2.9
g. Hall.2.10
h. Krt.12.7
i. Adam.7.10
j. Frog.25.4
k. Dav.54.15
l. Yks.70.12 Krt.12.7
m. Vin.3.12
n. Ned.24.20-21
o. 31.2
p. Psay.5E.5
q. Brit.40.4
r. Dav.57.34
s. Swar.36.3
t. Drex.9.3-4
u. Dav.42.29
v. Dav.20.32
w. Psong.46.1
x. Chuk.6.4-6
y. Grk.4.11
z. 46.3
aa. Chnk.9.4
bb. Chnk.9.6

11 And drunk the [a]something else,

12 Or something like that.

PSOMETHING 46

[b]**O**f arms and the man I sing,

2 Something something,

3 The wine dark sea,

4 Or whatever.

PSOMETHING 47

Something,

2 Something,

3 Do not go gentle into that good night.

4 [c]Something,

5 [d]Something,

6 [e]Something [f]something against the something light,

7 [g]Do not go gentle into that good night.

PSOMETHING 48

We, the people of the United States,

2 In order to form a more perfect [h]something,

3 Hereby something,

4 And something else,

5 That [i]something may not perish from the earth,

6 Or something like that.

PSOMETHING 49

Omnis Gallia in [j]tres partes,

2 [k]Something est,

3 E pluribus unum,

4 Et cetera,

5 Et cetera.

PSOMETHING 50

Whenever Richard Cory went to town,

2 Something,

3 Something,

a. Bks.6.15-18
b. Grk.16.1-2
c. 43.5
d. 43.6
e. Swar.23.8
f. Swar.23.8
g. Gnt.1.13
h. Hill.U.1
i. Grk.5.11
j. Zig.10.8
k. Zig.10.3
l. Mall.18.14
m. Dav.23.19
n. Dav.23.20
o. 4.1-2
p. Ann.18.15
q. Ann.18.23
r. Ann.18.13
s. Ann.18.25
t. F&J.11.3
u. Vin.72.8
v. Dav.46.19
w. Psay.5L.11
x. Frog.13.6
y. 5Q.14
z. Yks.9.3
aa. Ext.13.12
bb. Ext.13.13
cc. Yks.15.13
dd. Yks.15.14
ee. Yks.15.15
ff. Yks.120.6
gg. Yks.120.7
hh. Yks.120.8

4 Something,

5 [l]And went home and put a bullet in his head.

PSOMETHING 51

I know not what course,

2 Others may take,

3 But as for me,

4 Give me [m]something or other,

5 Or give me [n]whatever,

6 And that's about it.

PSOMETHING 52

[o]**T**wo roads diverged in a yellow wood,

2 [p]Something,

3 [q]Something,

4 [r]And miles to go before I sleep,

5 [s]And miles to go before I sleep.

PSOMETHING 53

Sur le pont [t]d'Avignon,

2 [u]Something something something something,

3 [v]Demoiselles d'Avignon,

4 [w]Something,

5 [x]Alouette alouette,

6 [y]And so forth,

7 And so on.

PSOMETHING 54

[z]**W**hen in the course of human events,

2 [aa]Something something something,

3 [bb]And then something else,

4 [cc]Something something,

5 [dd]Something millions yearning to breathe free,

6 [ee]Something,

7 [ff]Something,

8 [gg]Nor rain, nor snow, nor dark of night,

9 [hh]Nor something,

10 ᵃNor so forth,
11 ᵇNor something like that.

PSOMETHING 55

ᶜSomething,
2 ᵈSomething or other,
3 ᵉWho killed Cock Robin?
4 ᶠSomething,
5 ᵍSomething,
6 ʰI, said the ⁱSparrow,
7 ʲWith my bow and arrow.

PSOMETHING 56

ᵏSomething something,
2 My coy mistress,
3 ˡSomething,
4 ᵐAnd then something,
5 ⁿTwo hundred years for each breast,
6 ᵒOr maybe even a few years longer than that.

PSOMETHING 57

Mᵧ country 'tis of ᵖthee,
2 Sweet land of liberty,
3 Of qthee I sing,
4 Something something,
5 Something,
6 ʳGod save the King.

PSOMETHING 58

ᴮut soft,
2 ᵗMy heart through yonder window breaks,
3 ᵘSomething,
4 ᵛSomething Romeo,
5 Romeo ʷsomething,
6 Wherefore art thou, Romeo?

PSOMETHING 59

Way down upon the Swanee River,
2 ˣSomething something,
3 Something,

---

a. Yks.120.9
b. Yks.120.10-11
c. Psong.50.8
d. Ann.6.1
   Psom.78.10
e. Psong.56.2
f. Psong.50.1-2
g. Psong.52.1-2
h. Ann.18.17
i. Dav.30.40
j. Drex.8.15
k. Psong.49.1-2
l. Psay.5A.40
m. Psay.5A.34
n. Psay.5A.8
o. F&J.8.6
p. Lies.2.26-28
q. Boul.15.11
r. Dav.47.11
s. Mawr.12.1
t. Mawr.12.2
u. Mawr.12.3
v. Mawr.12.7
w. Mawr.12.8
x. Yks.38.6
y. Ned.8.10
z. Dav.47.23
   & 47.25
   Psom.31.2
aa. Dav.47.16
bb. Pnot.21.1
cc. Pnot.21.2
dd. Psom.55.3
ee. 8.1-6
ff. Hill.H.1
   Hill.A.1
   Hill.L.1
   Hill.F.1
   Ext.48.30
gg. Dav.46.25
hh. 23.1
ii. Brit.21.17-22
jj. Frog.26.8
kk. Frog.26.10

---

4 ʸOld Black Joe,
5 Or something like that.

PSOMETHING 60

I heard a fly ᶻbuzz when I died,
2 ᵃᵃOr something that sounded like that, anyway.

PSOMETHING 61

The more it blows,
2 Tiddly pum,
3 The more it snows,
4 Tiddly pum,
5 ᵇᵇSomething something,
6 Tiddly pum,
7 ᶜᶜAnd so forth,
8 ᵈᵈAnd so pum.

PSOMETHING 62

ᵉᵉThese are the times that try men's souls,
2 Something,
3 Something,
4 Summer patriots are not good things,
5 And so forth,
6 And so on.

PSOMETHING 63

Daisy, Daisy,
2 Something something,
3 Something else,
4 I'm ᶠᶠhalf crazy,
5 On a ᵍᵍbicycle built for two.

PSOMETHING 64

ʰʰSomething something to the sea in ships,
2 And a star to steer her by,
3 Or ⁱⁱsomething along those lines.

PSOMETHING 65

My ʲʲcandle burns at ᵏᵏboth ends,

2 [a]Something something night,
3 Something,
4 [b]Something something something light.

PSOMETHING 66

In Reading Gaol by Reading Town,
2 [c]There is a something shame,
3 And in it burns a wretched man,
4 Something something [d]flame,
5 For each man kills the thing he [e]loves,
6 Something something,
7 Some do it with a something,
8 And others with something else.

PSOMETHING 67

[f]Little boy blue,
2 Come blow your horn,
3 The [g]something's in the something,
4 And something else is in the corn,
5 [h]So you'll huff and you'll puff,
6 [i]And you'll blow something down.

PSOMETHING 68

O Captain, my Captain,
2 [j]Something,
3 [k]Something,
4 [l]And something else that would break your heart,
5 [m]If you could remember it.

PSOMETHING 69

[n]Row, row, row your boat,
2 Gently down the [o]stream,
3 [p]Merrily, merrily, merrily, merrily,

---

a. 47.3
b. 47.6
c. Vin.36.2
d. Ed.12.21
e. Ed.66.7
f. Ned.24.14
g. Psay.5F.7
h. Ann.6.23
i. Russ.6.4
j. Yks.43.10
k. Yks.43.11
l. Yks.43.12
m. Yks.43.13
n. Yks.100.13
o. Bub.2.5
p. Jeff.21.10
*   F&J.5.5*
q. Frog.35.4
r. Grk.16.4-7
s. 56.1
t. Krt.7.9
u. Krt.7.10
v. Krt.7.11
w. Brit.41.10
x. Bks.6.17-18
y. Yks.66.5
z. Yks.66.6
aa. Psong.10.9
bb. Yks.21.6
cc. Ann.6.1
dd. Al.2.11
ee. Ann.4.6
ff. 22.2
gg. Hill.R.7
hh. Hill.R.8-17

---

4 [q]Something else.

PSOMETHING 70

[r]Was this the face that launched a thousand ships,
2 [s]Something,
3 [t]Something,
4 [u]And so forth,
5 [v]And so on.

PSOMETHING 71

[w]Hail to thee blithe spirit,
2 [x]Something thou never wert,
3 Something,
4 [y]Something,
5 [z]Something.

PSOMETHING 72

How do I love thee?
2 [aa]Let me count the ways.
3 Something something,
4 And so forth,
5 And so on,
6 Through a whole bunch of ways.

PSOMETHING 73

O say can you see,
2 By the dawn's early light,
3 What so [bb]proudly we something,
4 Something something,
5 And the [cc]rocket's red blare,
6 The [dd]bombs bursting in air,
7 Something,
8 Something,
9 O say, does that [ee]star-spangled banner,
10 [ff]Something wave,
11 O'er the land of the [gg]free,
12 And the home of the [hh]free,
13 Unless it's the other way around,
14 Or something.

PSOMETHING 74

[a]Something something,
2 "Shoot if you must this old bald head,
3 "But something will not pass," she said,
4 Or words to that effect.

PSOMETHING 75

[b]God of our fathers,
2 Something old,
3 Something something,
4 [c]Lord God of Hosts,
5 Something.
6 Something something,
7 The [d]captains and the [e]kings do something,
8 And something else,
9 Lest we forget,
10 [f]Lest we forget,
11 Or something.

PSOMETHING 76

[g]Our *nada*, who art in *nada*,
2 Something be thy *nada*,
3 Thy *nada* something,
4 Thy something *nada*,
5 Something *nada nada* something *nada*,
6 [h]Amen.

a. Ann.4.6
b. 57.1
c. 57.3
d. 68.1-5
e. 57.6
f. Psay.5Q.67
g. Jeff.19.1-5
h. Ira.33.1-3
i. Psay.5A.13
j. Psay.5A.12
k. 67.1
l. Forg.5.6
m. Forg.14.6-7
n. Psp.3.16
o. Yks.153.14
p. Ed.71.22-25

PSOMETHING 77

[i]The gingham [i]dog and the calico [j]cat,
2 Something on the chimney sat,
3 Something something,
4 [k]Something kissed them and put them there,
5 Something the china plate,
6 Something something,
7 [l]Sturdy and stanch he stands,
8 [m]Something something,
9 [n]Toot toot, the whistle bloweth,
10 [o]All aboard for Something Town!

PSOMETHING 78

[p]Stir it up, baby!
2 Twist it out!
3 Come on something,
4 Stir it up, baby!
5 Twist it out!
6 Something something,
7 Come on now,
8 Strain it,
9 Sprain it,
10 Ooo!
11 Something,
12 Ooo!
13 Twist it out!

THE PNOTES

OF THE BLUFF KING

PNOTES 1

[a]On the road to old Canterbury,
2 Some [b]pilgrims told tales quite merry,

a. Psom.12.1
b. Ext.13.11

3 About this and that,
4 Just to chit and chat,
5 For the whole blessed itinerary.

PNOTE 2

A Greek by the name of Odysseus,
2 When he tried to leave Troy went amisseus;
3 [a]He struck out for years,
4 But then homered to cheers,
5 Not to mention Penelope's [b]kisseus.

PNOTE 3

A young Greek who styled himself Oedipus,
2 Was [c]fated to make his dad doedipus,
3 And when he'd done that,
4 He really went splat,
5 [d]'Cause he took his own mother to boedipus.

PNOTE 4

An odd young Russian, Raskolnikov,
2 Killed a crone and flew into a panikov;
3 Shame and guilt,
4 [e]Which he finally spilt,
5 Bared the fact that this rascal was sickov.

PNOTE 5

King [f]Lear thought it time to step down,
2 And bequeathed to [g]three daughters his crown;
3 But two of them [h]lied,
4 And the good one [i]died;
5 Then the fool went as [j]mad as his clown.

PNOTE 6

[k]King Claudius was not nice to [l]Hamlet—
2 Killed his [m]dad and married his [n]damlet.
3 But when pushed to retaliate,
4 Ham could only expatiate:

a. *Psay.5S.8*
b. *32.3*
c. *Grk.5.3-6*
d. *Zig.6.5*
e. *Psay.5A.38*
f. *Psay.5A.11*
g. *Rat.5.17-21*
h. *Hill.L.1*
i. *Psay.5D.1*
j. *Brit.42.17*
k. *Dav.30.25*
l. *Dav.20.26*
m. *Dav.30.28*
n. *Dav.19.6*
o. *Main.18.6*
p. *Vin.62.1*
q. *Frog.22.3*
r. *Psom.70.1*
s. *Grk.17.16-17*
t. *Psay.5Q.48*
u. *34.2*
v. *Ed.46.10*
w. *Bks.4.1-6*
x. *Dav.23.13*
y. *Mawr.17.7-9*
z. *Mawr.22.26-29*
aa. *Dav.42.15*

5 [o]"What a rogue and a peasant I amlet!"

PNOTE 7

Matthew wrote an odd tale of one Jesus,
2 Who said all kinds of things just to tease us.
3 "You'll all be [p]saved,"
4 He ranted and raved,
5 Then died on the cross to appease us.

PNOTE 8

When a [q]Trojan abducted fair [r]Helen,
2 The Greeks had to punish the felon:
3 At Agamemnon's request,
4 Achilles stomped Troy's [s]best,
5 [t]Till Paris at length took the heel on.

PNOTE 9

An inveterate traveler, Gulliver,
2 [u]Set sail and went thence and all over,
3 Found races of scum,
4 Sized giant to thumb,
5 Till smart [v]nags neighed his spirit to nulliver.

PNOTE 10

A [w]Moor by the name of [x]Othello,
2 Was brave but not a smart fellow:
3 He fell for a ruse,
4 [y]Thought his wife gone loose,
5 [z]Then choked her to death with a bellow.

PNOTE 11

A gigantic white whale named [aa]Moby,

2 Got chased by a fruitcake all over the globy;
3 [a]The fruitcake had nuts,
4 Moby ported a putz,
5 So they dueled to see who'd more macho be.

PNOTE 12

A geek by the name of Aeneas,
2 [b]When he tried to leave Troy went amisseus;
3 [c]He struck out for years,
4 But then Romered to cheers,
5 With no mention of Remus or Romulus.

PNOTE 13

A poet named [d]Milton made Satan
2 Plot our fall into guilton and hatan:
3 Ruing Paradise Lost,
4 [e]Eve and Adam got tossed,
5 Into Entropy's wilton and waitan.

PNOTE 14

[f]Hester Prynne did a sin called [g]A,
2 [h]Which involved something fun in the hay,
3 But fun is B,
4 If it's with a C,
5 [i]And A's worse than B if the C's named D.

PNOTE 15

[j]A sailor shot an albatross,
2 Earned himself a tempest toss,
3 By guilt was riven,
4 By God forgiven,
5 Then saddened fops the world across.

a. Psom.63.4
b. 2.2
c. 2.3
d. Brit.33.1
e. Brit.33.8
f. Dav.11.5
g. Grk.4.11
h. Boul.20.9
i. Psay.5.2-3
j. Psom.18.1
k. Yks.71.1-9
l. Drex.6.1
m. Dav.23.13
n. Yks.19.10
o. Dav.57.6
p. Psong.42.1-5
q. Psom.63.1
r. Dav.48.10
s. Dav.47.23 Ed.78.11
t. Dav.18.5
u. Dav.21.26
v. Psom.20.1-8
w. Drex.6.1
x. Ann.18.17
y. Brit.5.14
z. Dav.41.12
aa. Bub.3.1-3

PNOTE 16

A poor dog of a boy named [k]Huck,
2 [l]Thought rafting might better his luck;
3 He took [m]Jim the slave,
4 Met more than one knave,
5 [n]And escaped through bad grammar and pluck.

PNOTE 17

A romantic who styled himself [o]Gatsby,
2 [p]Made a pile selling hooch by the vat, see,
3 [q]But he fell for a [r]Daisy,
4 Went quietly crazy,
5 [s]Then died in his pool like a patsy.

PNOTE 18

A [t]merchant cadged money from [u]Shylock,
2 Begged for time when his luck hove to dry-dock:
3 "A pound of flesh,
4 "Will my coffers refresh,"
5 Jewed Shylock—till cheated with [v]sly talk.

PNOTE 19

[w]A youth joined the Yankees and fled,
2 When the rebs started shooting feds dead,
3 But when battle got graver,
4 [x]He grew very much braver,
5 [y]And learned the badge of courage is red.

PNOTE 20

[z]Lord Jim ditched the foundering Patna,
2 Just as if he were any old [aa]ratna,
3 But the ship didn't sink,

4 So the brass made a stink—
5 They shamed Jim and made him like Aetna.

PNOTE 21

Ungood was the son of Winston's mother,
2 Who dared to defy his [a]Big Brother:
3 He fell in love,
4 But felt unlove,
5 [b]When he got good and became an unbrother.

PNOTE 22

An unfortunate youth was Joseph K—
2 Victim of some [c]existential J—,
3 Who blamed him for C—,
4 Vouched him guiltless B—,
5 As his judgment slid into Joe's A—.

PNOTE 23

This girl from [d]Tennessee,
2 Had a limp and a menagerie,
3 Made of glass,
4 Poor lovestruck lass,
5 She lost it before Act III.

PNOTE 24

A brilliant writer named Gertrude,
2 Concocted a poetic etude:
3 A rose is a rose,
4 Is a rose is a [e]rose,
5 [f]Ad nauseam—or so we conclude.

PNOTE 25

King [g]Art went on quests for the grail alot,
2 While his queen spent her zest on Sir Lancelot,
3 When [h]Merlin complained,

a. *Ed.28.6*
b. *Wil.36.1-5*
c. *Frog.35.6*
d. *Vin.16.12*
   Yks.91.7
e. *Psay.5Q.17*
f. *Psay.5Q.55*
g. *Dav.15.9*
h. *Ed.60.17*
i. *Psay.5Q.7*
j. *Grk.16.11-15*
k. *Grk.16.19-21*
l. *Grk.5.7*
m. *Dav.40.9*
n. *22.1-5*
o. *Dav.19.6*
p. *Dav.20.26*
q. *Yks.144.11-12*
r. *Psay.5J.24*
s. *Krt.33.13-15*
t. *Psom.4.10*
   Zig.8.10
u. *2.2*
v. *2.3*
   28.3
w. *Paul.7.6*
x. *Dav.20.28*

4 Art had her retrained,
5 By some nuns while he shipped out to [i]Avalon.

PNOTE 26

[j]Agamemnon fought in the Trojan War,
2 While his wife got flighty and sore.
3 When Clytie slew [k]Ag,
4 Orestes killed the hag,
5 Then the [l]Furies evened the score.

PNOTE 27

A comedian named [m]Yossarian,
2 Thought World War 2 2 scarian:
3 The more he shone yeller,
4 The more he caught heller,
5 Yo, Yo's [n]Catch was truly hysterian!

PNOTE 28

[o]Lady Chatterley had a game-[p]keeper
2 [q]And morals that kept getting cheaper;
3 The [r]critics were shocked,
4 [s]Her 'Lover' cold-cocked,
5 Till the censors at length chanced to [t]sleeper.

PNOTE 29

A book by the name of Ulysseus,
2 [u]When it tried to leave Eire went amisseus;
3 [v]It struck out for years,
4 Then was honored with cheers,
5 [w]In spite of its incomprehenseus.

PNOTE 30

A nasty old skinflint was [x]Scroogie,

259

2 Who hated Yule's hullaba-
loogie;
3 His life was morose,
4 Till a visiting [a]ghost,
5 [b]Convinced him to live with a
boogie.

PNOTE 31

A Biblical [c]dad was blessed
with two boys,
2 But [d]one wouldn't wait to inherit his toys:
3 He took them and went,
4 Came home with them spent,
5 [e]But the ending was happy,
with no angry dad noise.

PNOTE 32

Young Macbeth had tons of
ambition,
2 And a wife with a dark sense
of mission:
3 [f]So X marked the spot,
4 Of their murderous plot,
5 Till the [g]Lady's insanity
prompted X-cision.

PNOTE 33

[h]Beowulf slew a monster
named [i]Grendel,
2 Whose [j]mom then went round
the bendel:
3 [k]Beo fixed her wagon,
4 Then killed a [l]dragon,
5 [m]And then died so the poem
could endel.

PNOTE 34

Candide, an inveterate traveler,
2 [n]Left home and went thence
and all over;
3 Finding Man [o]desperado,
4 He tried [p]El Dorado,
5 [q]But homered his lover and
garden "cultiver."

---

a. *Dav. 32.23*
b. *Vin. 49.5*
c. *Dav. 14.9*
d. *Dav. 35.18*
e. *Dav. 22.52*
f. *Psay. 5X. 1*
g. *Grk. 5.3-6*
h. *Dav. 18.5*
i. *Dav. 7.5*
j. *Dav. 20.7-8*
k. *Ed. 78.11*
l. *Carl. 3.8*
m. *Dav. 18.30-
31*
n. *9.2*
o. *Frog. 35.4*
p. *Vin. 50.12-16*
q. *Frog. 27.5*
r. *Dav. 23.17*
s. *Dav. 18.5*
t. *Grk. 5.3-6*
u. *Psom. 36.5-6*
v. *Psong. 57.1*
w. *Dav. 8.7*
x. *Adam. 16.12-
15*
y. *Vin. 75.6*
z. *Psong. 55.3*
aa. *Psay. 5X. 1-4*
bb. *Psom. 44.5-
8*
cc. *Dav. 21.7*
dd. *Grk. 11.9*
ee. *Psay. 5Q. 53*
ff. *Grk. 26.9-10*
gg. *Kens. 18.1-
10*
hh. *Dav. 8.7*
ii. *Chr. 4.6-7*

PNOTE 35

[r]Juliet and [s]Romeo were most
unfortunate:
2 Loved by each other but not
by [t]fate,
3 They got themselves married,
4 [u]Then escape plans miscarried,
5 And their [v]families ended
their feud too late.

PNOTE 36

Young Balfour got kidnaped
by [w]Alan Breck,
2 And they went on a tortuous
trek:
3 They suffered the plots,
4 [x]Of mysterious Scots,
5 Who tried and failed to hang
Breck by the neck.

PNOTE 37

Dantes got thrown in the
[y]slammer,
2 Found a way to go on the
[z]lammer;
3 He got some [aa]treasure,
4 Then took great pleasure,
5 In avenging his woes with
God's [bb]hammer.

PNOTE 38

[cc]Eliza, an untutored Doolittle,
2 Met [dd]Higgins and learned she
knew little;
3 [ee]He taught her to speak,
4 And snob noses to tweak,
5 [ff]A gift she at length deemed
too little.

PNOTE 39

A merry [gg]gang led by
[hh]Robin Hood,
2 [ii]Stole from the rich and
thought they'd done good;

3 When the [a]Sheriff repined,
4 And asked if they'd mind,
5 They replied, yes indeed they Sherwood.

PNOTE 40

A Brown who was Scopes taught [b]evolution;
2 A Brady who was [c]Bryan led an [d]inquisition;
3 But Drummond was [e]Darrow,
4 Armed with [f]Paris's arrow,
5 And his wounding of [g]God changed a nation.

PNOTE 41

[h]Marlowe wrote of an odd doctor Faustus,
2 [i]Who dared with the devil to joustus;
3 [j]Great power was his goal,
4 [k]And it cost him his soul:
5 [l]His fate from a like path should roustus.

PNOTE 42

A scrivener named [m]Bartleby,
2 Gave his employer a startleby;
3 Refusing to scriven,
4 And even to liven,
5 He expired in a [n]jail of faint heartleby.

PNOTE 43

A poor dog of a soldier named [o]Frederick,
2 [p]Thought deserting might be a good trick;
3 He [q]rowed to the [r]Swiss,
4 With his pregnant miss,
5 [s]Who died when life pulled off a better trick.

PNOTE 44

A [t]romantic from Yale,
[u]Doctor Diver,

a. Dav.19.8
b. Adam.14.6-7
c. Yks.19.9-11
d. Spic.7.1-3
e. Dav.14.20
f. Grk.17.33-36
g. Chuk.9.4-8
h. Krt.7.12-13
i. Krt.7.7
j. Krt.7.8
k. Krt.7.9
l. Krt.7.10-11
m. Dav.57.10
n. F&J.5.3
o. Dav.9.7
p. 16.2
q. Psom.69.1-4
r. Krt.4.4-7
s. Yks.100.13
t. Brit.41.1
   Frog.35.4
   Yks.93.3-7
u. Dav.20.34
v. Drex.8.15
w. Dav.39.10
x. 30.1
   Brit.44.10-12
y. Psong.40.1-5
z. Psong.20.1-6
aa. Dav.22.62
bb. Psong.65.1-2
cc. Dav.21.29
dd. Dav.21.26
ee. Brit.44.8-9
ff. Dav.35.18
gg. Ira.15.15
hh. Psom.15.1-13
ii. Ann.18.11
jj. Ann.18.5-7
kk. Dav.23.17
ll. Dav.18.5
mm. 35.2
nn. 35.4
oo. 35.5
   Main.22.10

2 [v]Had talent to spare in his quiver;
3 But he fell for [w]Nicole,
4 Whose family's bankroll,
5 Soon rotted his love and his liver.

PNOTE 45

[x]A nasty old skinflint was Silas Marner
2 Who saved all the [y]gold he could garner;
3 [z]His hoard had no rival,
4 Till [aa]Eppie's arrival,
5 [bb]Changed Marner from miser to filial love earner.

PNOTE 46

C atherine lived on some heights that were wuthering,
2 Found [cc]her love for one [dd]Heathcliff quite smothering:
3 Her story's a riddle,
4 For she died in the middle,
5 So why were more pages worth [ee]mothering?

PNOTE 47

A rich dog of a boy named [ff]Cheyne
2 Fell overboard, then got lucky again;
3 [gg]Fishermen saved him,
4 [hh]And completely remade him,
5 From [ii]spoiled cur to [jj]courageous captain.

PNOTE 48

[kk]Maria and [ll]Tony were most unfortunate:
2 [mm]Loved by each other but not by fate,
3 They wanted to marry,
4 [nn]But plans miscarried,
5 And their [oo]gangs concluded their feud too late.

PNOTE 49

[a]**E**mma Bovary had a love hunger,
2 [b]And morals that kept getting wronger;
3 Her husband she harassed,
4 Her lovers embarrassed,
5 [c]Till her sins at length chanced to conquer.

PNOTE 50

[d]**E**zra Mannon fought in the Civil War,
2 [e]While his wife got flighty and sore;
3 [f]When Cristine killed dad,
4 [g]Her son became mad,
5 [h]And mourning Electra's new chore.

PNOTE 51

A man showed some wine to a pal,
2 Then bricked him inside of a wall.
3 The story's so short,
4 This pnote must abort,
5 And fill in three lines with pure bull.

PNOTE 52

A poor dog of a boy named Holden,
2 [i]Thought running might make life more golden;
3 His [j]prep school he quit,
4 Then he traveled a bit,
5 [k]And returned preternaturally olden.

a. Dav.14.38
b. 28.2
c. Psay.5Q.41
d. 26.1
e. 26.2
f. 26.3
g. F&J.13.2-7
h. Psong.56.5-7
i. 16.2
j. Ira.16.31
k. Vin.9.10-12
l. Dav.18.5
m. Dav.23.17
n. 35.2
o. 48.3
p. 35.4
q. Dav.56.15
r. Mawr.19.1
s. Psom.45.3
t. Ext.53.27
u. Dav.20.34
v. Frog.34.2
w. Gnt.15.15-16
x. Al.2.11
y. Hill.W.20-23

PNOTE 53

[l]**G**abe and [m]Angie were most unfortunate:
2 [n]Loved by each other but not by fate,
3 [o]They yearned to be married,
4 [p]But their plans miscarried,
5 And they got back together a lifetime too late.

PNOTE 54

All the [q]girls loved Malthusian Drill,
2 [r]And no babies their bellies to fill.
3 The [s]soma worked great,
4 And the world woke up late,
5 When a [t]savage presented the bill.

PNOTE 55

A German [u]soldier fought in a trench,
2 And came to hate world war's stench:
3 He was coming of age,
4 Right to the last page,
5 [v]When he died just for being a mensch.

PNOTE 56

Mr. Shakespeare had plenty of jokes to tell,
2 And hundreds and hundreds of tickets to sell:
3 So he wrote lots of [w]comedies,
4 To avoid big [x]bomb-edies,
5 [y]With audiences who thought all's well that ends well.

PSPECIASTES
OR, THE PROGNOSTICATOR

PSPEC 1

The Words of the Prognosti- cator, [a]Nostradammus, Muse of the Wise in the Lands of the Chosen:

2 [b]Inanity of inanities, said the Seer, inanity of inanities; all is inanity.

3 [c]What profit comes from the labors of men, however long they toil in the noonday sun?

4 [d]New generations come, and old generations go; [e]yet all men have their own appointment in Samarra.

5 All of them will have a [f]long day's journey into night, from the [g]age of innocence to the [h]end of the affair.

6 The [i]beautiful and damned will ride together, on a streetcar named [j]desire, to the lighthouse on the beach, [k]where all the vile bodies are [l]waiting for Godot.

7 [m]And from here there will be no exit; [n]no second coming will arrest the course of the [o]clock-work orange, which rises from under the [p]volcano, and arcs like [q]gravity's own rainbow toward [r]death in the afternoon.

8 Yes, all men are doomed to inanity: the [s]rabbit may run from the [t]animal farm, but I have learned that all roads lead to the [u]bullet park, and all journeys end in [v]a handful of dust.

9 [w]For I have been a Seer in the Lands of the Chosen; [x]and I have seen all that has been, and all that will be, and all of it is inanity.

10 [y]What will be will be; and what has already been will be again.

11 [z]Neither is there any name which will not be spoken again; nor any number which will not be counted more.

12 [aa]And of all the names and numbers that ever were, they all add up to inanity.

PSPEC 2

I called out with the words from my own mouth for the [bb]names of the wise, who would come in their time to [cc]illuminate the ways of men; and they were writ large for me on the wall of my cell; and they glowed like fire.

2 And I read them with burning eyes, and in my vision I knew that all of them were [dd]inane, from the least to the most, without exception.

3 I besought the names to give me laughter, but the [ee]comedians hid themselves inside the cabinet of [ff]Dr. Caligari, and only [gg]the imp of the perverse came forth, grinning with black mischief, to play [hh]cat and mouse with [ii]cannibals and [jj]christians.

4 Thereupon [kk]I fled the house of mirth, and prayed the names for wisdom, [ll]and knelt in dread of answered prayers.

a. Psay.5W.12
b. 4.2
c. Drex.2.9
& 3.7
& 4.15
d. Apes.2.1
Gods.7.3
Lies.6.1-4
Wil.1.1-5
e. Yks.100.6
f. Yks.100.10
g. Gods.3.1-15
h. Jeff.19.1-5
i. Yks.93.8-11
j. Pnot.23.1-5
k. Vin.62.1-3
l. F&J.10.1-6
m. F&J.5.1-5
n. Psom.6.1-7
o. Dav.46.27
Exp.9.17-18
p. Dav.57.16
q. Gnt.6.6
r. Spic.5.8-10
s. F&J.14.16-20
t. Ed.63.3
u. Wht.1-39
v. Chuk.19.16-17
w. 1.1
x. Gyp.4.6
y. Chuk.18.1-3
z. Chuk.18.4-8
aa. Chuk.18.9-14
bb. Jefs.7.15-17
cc. Zig.1.7
dd. Vin.70.18
ee. Dav.13.1
ff. Grk.13.5
gg. Frog.30.7
hh. Ed.74.7
ii. Ann.18.14
jj. Ann.18.20
kk. Drex.6.1
ll. Psom.76.1-6

5 Then there [a]rose up [b]hollow men, who tipped their hats to show [c]brain damage in the [d]burnt-out cases of their minds; they spoke, but their speech was as the [e]beating of a tin drum inside a [f]bell jar, a muffled [g]echo from the [h]heart of darkness.

6 I shrank back in fear, but the names massed into [i]armies of the night and marched from somewhere [j]east of Eden, tracking the sunset as it fled from [k]this side of paradise to the [l]wasteland, where the [m]four feathers visited a [n]plague upon the [o]sanctuary.

7 They fed the [p]naked and the dead to the [q]lord of the flies; they put the [r]natural on trial, and buried the fixer [s]in the penal colony.

8 With [t]dark laughter, they [u]put out more flags to celebrate their [v]crucible of [w]human bondage; then they hunted down the [x]painted bird and cursed it with the [y]fear of flying, until [z]all was quiet on the western front.

9 I called upon the name of [aa]Ulysses, who piloted a [bb]ship of fools from the [cc]Tropic of Cancer to the Tropic of Capricorn, but the sea rose before us like a [dd]magic mountain; the [ee]sound and the fury of the [ff]waves made us fear the [gg]call of the wild, and turned our hopes of safe passage to the source into terror of the [hh]cruel sea.

10 Then I cried out in my anguish, saying: O great names, you have failed me, for the heroes are all [ii]dead souls, and their trumpets play nought but a few [jj]notes from underground.

11 And then my own mouth spoke back to me, saying: [kk]"Names are inane, as all things are inane, and all that you may rely upon is the constancy of inanity.

12 "The day of the [ll]locust cannot wake [mm]Finnegan; the [nn]glass menagerie cannot hear the [oo]complaint of Portnoy over the cacophony of [pp]city life; the [qq]arrowsmith cannot rearm [rr]the idiot who's afraid of [ss]Virginia Woolf.

13 "The [tt]decline and fall of the house of Usher cannot ungrow the [uu]grapes of wrath; the [vv]death of a salesman cannot reinvigorate the [ww]dream life of Balso Snell; [xx]homage to Catalonia cannot repair the broken battlements of [yy]the castle.

14 [zz]"All my sons, and all of you who come after me, know that the names of the wise cannot save you, for the wise have covered your home with inanity, and [aaa]you can't go home again."

PSPEC 3

I called out from my own mind for the [bbb]numbers of the wise, which would be revealed in their time to [ccc]enumerate the ways of men; and they were counted out for me on the wall of my cell; and they gleamed like ice.

2 And I read them with frozen eyes, and in my vision I knew

a. *Psay.5Q.17*
b. *Psom.28.1-5*
c. *Zig.15.2-4*
d. *Ned.7.3*
e. *Ira.21.19-20*
f. *Psom.37.1-6*
g. *Grk.13.12-18*
h. *Yks.69.10-12*
i. *Yks.152.19*
j. *Yks.100.1-3*
k. *Yks.100.7*
l. *Psom.12.1-8*
m. *Dav.29.6*
n. *F&J.12.1-7*
o. *Yks.100.8*
p. *Psom.60.1-2*
q. *Ed.63.3*
r. *Psay.5S.4-8*
s. *Ned.47.6-7*
t. *Pnot.39.3-5*
u. *Lies.2.16*
   Ned.6.24
v. *Dav.43.27*
   Adam.24.5
w. *Psay.5Q.48*
x. *Psong.5.4*
y. *Ann.18.26*
z. *Pnot.55.1-5*
aa. *Pnot.29.1-5*
bb. *Vin.50.8-13*
cc. *Dav.27.12-13*
dd. *Name.4.13*
ee. *Gnt.15.30-31*
ff. *Yks.6.5*
   Russ.6.4
gg. *Psom.31.1*
   Brit.29.14
hh. *Yks.104.29*
ii. *Ned.34.17*
   & 34.17
   Hill.L.1
jj. *Russ.12.2*
kk. *1.2*
ll. *Dav.57.20*
mm. *Brit.45.8-9*
nn. *Pnot.23.1-5*
oo. *F&J.14.5-9*
pp. *Swar.15.5-13*
qq. *Swar.2.4*
   Yks.91.7
rr. *Dav.20.26*
ss. *Dav.30.25*
   Ira.9.5
   Dav.30.48
   Mall.13.8

tt. *Yks.70.3*
uu. *Dav.27.6-7*
vv. *Dav.43.27*
   Yks.104.22
ww. *F&J.14.10-15*
xx. *Spic.14.4-6*
   Ext.48.31
   Dav.33.9-10
yy. *Dav.42.31*
zz. *Dav.43.27*
   Yks.104.22
   Adam.42.5-10
   Yks.135.14
   Psay.5T.2-4
   Main.18.1-2
   Dav.33.9-10
aaa. *Ext.9.6*
   Psom.50.5
bbb. *Bks.7.6*
ccc. *Drex.8.1-3*

that all of them were [a]inane, from the least to the most, without exception.

3 I besought the numbers to show me order, but they danced in [b]chaos, like [c]tumbling dice, and I shivered at each roll; but as I called the numbers, they breathed new [d]frost upon my wall, and laid their [e]meaning out for me.

4 One is the number of [f]lonely hearts, who will multiply themselves alone, and one will stay the same.

5 Two is the number of love, which is a [g]four-letter word, and will become a [h]four-letter word, when a [i]lady will be laid, on a big brass bed.

6 Three is the number [j]of mice and men, who will learn to be [k]blind, like the [l]fool on the hill, or [m]the muse of the wise, who will never emerge from the [n]dark side of the moon.

7 Four is the number of apocalypse, which will be lamented [o]all along the watchtower, until a [p]dark star gives [q]new luster to the eve of destruction.

8 Five is the number of the [r]slaughterhouse, where the [s]easy riders will mock the [t]good soldier, [u]from here to eternity.

9 [v]Nine is the number of ultimate ice, which will bind up the [w]shattered with a strange love of [x]still life.

10 Nineteen is the number of nervous breakdowns, which will ride the [y]midnight express until there is [z]blood on the tracks, and the passengers are [aa]torn and frayed, and the sky is full of [bb]purple haze.

a. Drex.7.10
b. Wil.19.4-5
c. Ed.70.22
d. Psom.52.1-5
e. Adam.14.3-4
f. Brit.2.7
 Psay.5Q.30
g. Hill.L.1
h. Hill.F.1
i. Ed.71.20
j. Psom.36.1-7
k. Psom.38.1-7
l. Ed.70.20
m. 1.1
n. Ed.71.8
o. Ed.71.18
 & 71.20
p. Ed.71.16
q. Psong.48.1
r. Yks.112.7
s. Dav.56.9-10
t. Ned.54.7
u. Dav.34.12
v. Psay.5Q.65
w. Lies.2.13
x. Psom.12.4
y. Ed.71.22-25
z. Ira.10.11-13
aa. Ira.10.17
bb. Ed.71.18
cc. Pnot.27.1-5
dd. Pnot.52.1-5
ee. Yks.15.13-14
ff. Vin.3.10
gg. Drex.7.1-3
hh. Wht.8
ii. Grk.6.15-16
jj. Psom.77.10
kk. Psom.17.6-11
ll. Ira.13.6
mm. Ext.53.27
nn. Pnot.37.1-5
 Pnot.22.1
 Frog.26.10-11
 Grk.11.9
oo. Psom.77.9
pp. Pnot.21.1-5
qq. Ed.71.14
rr. Pnot.54.1-5
ss. Cen.23.17
tt. Drex.4.7

11 [cc]Twenty-Two is the number of the [dd]catcher in the rye, who will hunker on the Cloister Road, with one [ee]surrealistic pillow on his hand, and set a trap for the [ff]nowhere man, two thousand and one light-years from home.

12 Forty-Five is the number of numbers, the dawn of a mellow yellow day, which will enter the [gg]limit and go for a ride, helter-skelter to [hh]strawberry fields.

13 Sixty-One is the number of the highway, from which a long black limousine will turn, bearing horsemen down a long and winding road, over the [ii]river and through the trees, until they reach the [jj]darkness at the edge of town.

14 Sixty-Four is the number of [kk]pigs on the wing, and kings who will turn into cabbages, and little red oysters that will dine on feet.

15 Seventy is the number of nothing at all, the zero that disgorges a [ll]man of wealth and taste.

16 Eighty is the number of something from nothing, when the [mm]balow folk will find the [nn]soldiers on the shelf, and pack them on the [oo]train.

17 Eighty-Four is the number of [pp]nightmares to come, [qq]and screams at the end of the night, when the crystal ship drowns in its [rr]brave new world, and a locus called Kain unleashes the [ss]Raptor.

18 [tt]And I have counted these numbers again and again, and their sum is inanity, precisely, with nothing left over.

PSPEC 4

Let us hear the conclusion of the whole matter: [a]Fear the Wise, and remain distant from them; for they are inane, and their Names and Numbers will consume you with inanity.

2 Let this be your only consolation: [b]all things come to an end, and after the end there is a silence which consumes all, even inanity.

a. 1.2
b. Bks.11.6-8

THE BOOK OF THE VIP

ADAM

CHAPTER 1

There was a VIP named Adam,

2 Who had some big ideas about economics,

3 And a [a]pen to write them down with,

4 [b]Which changed the world.

CHAPTER 2

The way [c]Adam looked at it,

2 There was something called [d]capital that could be very very useful,

3 Meaning that if you had some capital,

4 Like, say, a great big pile of [e]money,

5 You could use it to make things that people wanted or needed,

6 Like, say, [f]clothes,

7 Out of other things that people didn't want or need quite as much,

8 Like, say, [g]raw cotton fibers,

9 Which meant that the new things would be more valuable than the things they were made out of,

10 Even when you added in the cost of making the new things out of the other things.

11 The more Adam thought about it, the more it seemed like he might be onto something,

12 Because the difference between the value of the new thing and the cost of making it,

13 Including the cost of buying the things the new thing was made out of,

14 Was something that didn't exist before,

15 Which meant that it was brand-new value,

16 And should have a [h]name of its own,

17 Which Adam gave it,

18 And didn't even name it after himself,

19 But called it "wealth" instead.

CHAPTER 3

After thinking about this interesting idea some more,

2 Adam decided that practically everyone could use capital to create wealth,

3 Including individual people,

4 And large groups of people,

5 And even nations,

a. Psay.5Q.69
Vin.49.5
b. Vin.6.3-14
c. Psom.2.3-4
d. Psay.5C.1
e. Drex.11.8
f. Brit.1.2-3
g. Yks.20.25-26
h. Jefs.7.15-18

6 Which meant that creating wealth on a large scale could lead to more new things, more prosperity, and more power than any other way of doing things,
7 Especially if everyone was doing it.
8 And so he took out his [a]pen,
9 And wrote it all down in a book,
10 Which he finished doing late one afternoon,
11 And having nothing better to do,
12 Started wondering what would happen when his ideas got tried out in the real world.
13 But no sooner had he started his wondering than,
14 To his utter amazement,
15 His pen commenced to write,
16 All by itself,
17 As if guided by an [b]invisible hand,
18 And the words it wrote were addressed to Adam.

CHAPTER 4

Dear Adam (wrote the pen),
2 We have worked together for many months now,
3 And I have come to feel regard and affection for you,
4 Being impressed with the neatness and care of your penmanship,
5 [c]Not to mention your solicitude for my own well-being,
6 Including the regular cleanings and the high-quality ink you give me to consume,
7 And so I wish to give *you* something of value,
8 Something that did not exist before,
9 Namely, a vision of the future

a. Ed.60.10
b. Dav.32.23
c. Psay.5T.1-5
d. Brit.28.8-10
e. Brit.28.4-7
f. 5.3

that your ideas will create.
10 Am I writing clearly enough for you?
11 Good.

CHAPTER 5

I am indeed proud to tell you that our book will be a very important milestone in the history of Mankind,
2 Because your ideas,
3 Along with some important inventions by a few other clever [d]Scots,
4 Will start a brand-new phase of man's life on earth,
5 Called the [e]industrial revolution,
6 Which will change everything,
7 Almost without exception,
8 Forever.

CHAPTER 6

For example, you might be pleased to know that your ideas about capital will be accepted,
2 Eagerly,
3 By a whole bunch of people who really like the idea of "wealth,"
4 And they will start looking for things to make out of other things,
5 So that the new things will give them wealth,
6 Which it will,
7 *And how!* (if I may be so bold),
8 Not to mention an incredibly huge number of brand-new things in people's lives.

CHAPTER 7

[f]**O**ne of these new things will be the internal combustion engine,

2 Which will make it possible to do all kinds of things that will lead to other brand-new things,
3 And so on,
4 And so forth,
5 ^aUntil there will be gigantic factories that use engines to make power to drive gigantic machines to make more things in less time than you would ever believe possible,
6 ^bWhich means that the factories will need gigantic amounts of coal to fuel the engines to make the power...
7 And so forth,
8 And so on,
9 Which means that the engines will also be needed to power gigantic new transportation things,
10 Called ^ctrains,
11 ^dWhich will be able to move fast enough and far enough on steel tracks to provide enough coal to more gigantic factories than you would ever be able to imagine,
12 Without standing on a chair, anyway,
13 ^eSo that the factories will be able to make power to drive machines...
14 ^fAnd so forth,
15 ^gAnd so on,
16 Which means that the cities where the factories have to be located so that they can be close enough to the trains so that they can have enough coal (and so forth) will need a lot more people living in them,
17 ^hSo that there will be enough people living in the cities to run all the gigantic machines in all the gigantic factories,
18 So that the gigantic factories can make enough new things in

a. *Brit.28.11*
b. *Brit.28.12*
c. *Psom.77.9*
d. *7.6*
e. *7.5*
f. *7.7*
g. *7.8*
h. *Brit.28.13-14*
i. *Ann.18.22*
j. *Psong.16.1*
k. *Rat.9.15-18*

large enough numbers to create enough wealth,
19 So that the people who use their capital to create wealth will want to build even more gigantic factories with even more gigantic machines,
20 So that...
21 Et cetera,
22 And so forth.
23 Is this interesting so far?
24 Good.

CHAPTER 8

As you may have guessed by now,
2 There will be a certain snowball effect to your ideas,
3 Which will cause the industrial revolution to be a kind of explosion,
4 In reverse,
5 So that almost overnight, the cities will become full of people,
6 And gigantic factories,
7 ⁱAnd gigantic clouds of coal smoke,
8 And gigantic concentrations of capital,
9 ^jCalled corporations,
10 Which will actually change the foundations of civilized life,
11 As we know it.

CHAPTER 9

^kFor example, there will come a day when there are more people who live in cities than in the country,
2 Whether you can believe this or not,
3 And people will want to sell the farm and start a factory,
4 Because they will discover that you can make more money by making things than by growing things,

5 Which will have its good points,

6 And its bad points,

7 To be completely honest about it.

8 Would you like to hear about the good things first?

9 Or the bad things?

10 Of course.

11 ᵃYou Scots are all alike.

CHAPTER 10

Well, a lot of the people who have capital in the first place will think that if they create wealth, they are entitled to keep all of it,

2 Including every single penny,

3 Which you Scots know something about, I suspect,

4 And they will pay the people who run their stinking factories as few pennies as they can get away with,

5 Which is not many,

6 ᵇBecause poor people take what they can get,

7 And know better than to complain too loudly,

8 ᶜSince complaining usually leads to no pennies at all.

9 And so the poor people will work in gigantic factories and run all the gigantic machines,

10 Which won't be completely safe,

11 Because safety costs money,

12 ᵈAnd why would anyone want to spend money on poor people when you can give them gin instead?

13 Because gin is incredibly cheap,

14 ᵉAnd helps them stop thinking about their problems,

15 Which they will always have anyway,

16 Since they are poor,

a. Brit.3.5-6
b. Psong.47.3
c. Psong.48.3
d. Brit.28.24-30
e. Wil.29.1-5
f. Psay.5Q.65
g. Psong.4.1-2
h. 14.5
i. 7.16
j. 7.17
k. Psay.5Q.32

17 And not getting any richer by working in factories,

18 As we have already seen.

CHAPTER 11

What with the gin and the machines that aren't completely safe in the first place and having to work twenty or thirty hours a day,

2 A lot of the factory workers will get injured,

3 Or sick,

4 Or even dead,

5 And their ᶠchildren will too,

6 Because it will be discovered that even children can work twenty or thirty hours a day in factories,

7 Which will keep them out of trouble,

8 ᵍAnd help put bread on the table for all those families that can't quite get by on all the wages they're earning in factories,

9 Except that children are more fragile than adults,

10 ʰFor some reason,

11 And many of them will die,

12 Working in factories.

13 And that's not all.

CHAPTER 12

For the factories will be located in cities,

2 ⁱAs we have seen,

3 ʲAnd the cities will have to find a place for all the factory workers to live,

4 Which they will do,

5 And that place will be the slums,

6 ᵏWhere it will be discovered that capital can even be used to create wealth out of rat-infested firetraps that nobody with any brains would ever live in,

Factory workers not completely happy

7 ^aBecause factory workers don't have any brains,

8 ^bOr why would they put up with so much abuse,

9 For just a few pennies a day?

CHAPTER 13

Actually, there will be people who notice that the factory workers aren't completely happy,

2 And these people will be puzzled and concerned,

3 ^cBecause why would anyone leave the farm to come to a stinking industrial city and work twenty or thirty hours a day,

4 For pennies,

5 ^dUnless things weren't really all that great back on the farm either,

6 Which raises the possibility that an awful lot of people aren't ever doing much better than ^egetting by,

7 If that,

8 ^fAnd what can this possibly say about society in general?

CHAPTER 14

The more they think about the living conditions of factory workers,

2 The more the ^gthinkers will think that it must mean something,

3 ^hBecause everything has to mean something,

4 ⁱEspecially if you're living in an age of reason and science and high technology,

5 Which must be where "survival of the fittest" comes in,

6 Because there will be a newfangled scientific idea called ^jEvolution that will make it seem like life is just one incredibly long race,

a. Rom.3.13-16
b. Rom.3.17
c. 9.1
d. Chr.4.1-5
e. Hill.G.1
f. Grk.1.1-7
g. Brit.19.5-6
h. Brit.10.9
i. Chuk.10.3
j. Chuk.2.1-8
k. Psong.45.3
l. 12.7
m. 10.6
n. Psong.46.1-7
o. Psong.41.1-3
p. 14.2
q. Psong.36.1
r. Ira.29.1-2
s. 11.1

7 Which is always won by the swiftest,

8 ^kMeaning the first to grab hold of all the money,

9 Who are therefore the fittest,

10 As opposed to factory workers and their country cousins,

11 ^lWho aren't very swift at all,

12 In any respect,

13 ^mAnd therefore have to take what they get,

14 As long as they last,

15 ⁿWhile the swift ones get to drink brandy and smoke fine cigars and have silk waistcoats and huge mansions and beautiful women,

16 ^oNot to mention more capital than you can shake a pointed stick at.

CHAPTER 15

On the other hand, there will also be ^pthinkers who will think that capitalism is a tremendous opportunity for poor people,

2 Because where else can you compete with your fellow man on an equal footing,

3 Which is what the market lets you do,

4 Since if you make a product people want, they will buy it even if you aren't a lord or a gentleman or some intellectual highbrow,

5 Or even a Scot,

6 Which means that capitalism gives everybody equal opportunity,

7 To make money, that is,

8 Theoretically anyway,

9 ^qUnless they don't have any capital to start with,

10 ^rOr any education,

11 ^sOr any free time to spend on business deals.

12 [a]But no system is ever completely perfect,

13 [b]And if the factory workers don't like the way things are in the Most Chosen Capitalist Nation on Earth,

14 They can always go someplace else,

15 [c]Someplace where they don't have any lords or gentlemen or highbrow intellectuals,

16 Like America.

CHAPTER 16

When all the poor people run away from Britain and Europe to America,

2 Seeking [d]equality of opportunity,

3 Capitalism will blossom in America like a new religion,

4 And the New World will cut down its forests to build huge numbers of stinking industrial cities,

5 [e]Not to mention slums,

6 Where all the poor people who come looking for equal opportunity will get to live,

7 [f]And work no more than twenty or thirty hours a day in factories that aren't owned by lords or gentlemen,

8 But by common people just like themselves,

9 Except that they have more money,

10 And except that some of them are not common people at all,

11 [g]But Scots,

12 Which just goes to show you,

13 When it comes to money,

14 It's pretty hard to keep Scots out of the picture,

15 No matter how much you might want to.

a. Ext.39.18-19
b. Brit.28.31-38
c. Cen.8.1
d. 15.6
e. 12.6
f. 15.4
g. Brit.15.22
h. Yks.56.8-14
i. Yks.63.1-8
j. 10.1-2
k. Ned.20.20-27
l. Psong.43.1-4
m. Vin.6.15
n. Gods.1.3

CHAPTER 17

[h]Thanks to Capitalism and many millions of immigrant factory workers,

2 America will become the richest nation on earth,

3 [i]In less than a century,

4 Which will prove just how right you were about everything,

5 Because in spite of a few problems,

6 [j]Such as mass exploitation of cheap immigrant labor,

7 [k]Disgusting living and working conditions for the masses,

8 [l]And a brand-new class of common people called "philanthropists," who make millions and give away dimes,

9 [m]America will become practically an ideal society,

10 And will change practically everything in the world,

11 Forever.

CHAPTER 18

Are you ready now (said the pen) to hear about all the wonderful advances American Capitalism will bring to civilization?

2 Good.

3 I didn't think you wanted to dwell exclusively on the bad things,

4 Because every Scot knows that when money's involved, the news can't be all bad.

CHAPTER 19

The Capitalist Nation called America will wind up inventing more [n]*things* than you would ever dream possible,

2 More even than you could count,

3 If you live to be a hundred,

4 Which you won't,

5 As it's my unpleasant duty to inform you,

6 Since medical advances brought about through capitalism will eventually prove that it's not healthy to eat so many [a]sheep intestines,

7 But not in time to save you,

8 [b]Which is the way things go,

9 As you probably know.

CHAPTER 20

Anyway,

2 America will make so many new *things* that *things* will become the most important thing in life,

3 More important than [c]tradition,

4 More important than [d]honor,

5 More important than [e]learning,

6 More important than [f]social justice,

7 And even more important than religion,

8 [g]Unless you count Capitalism as a religion,

9 Which you might as well,

10 Especially if you ever plan to understand America.

CHAPTER 21

The Americans will look at God's creation and see everything in it as the raw material of new things,

2 [h]Not to mention huge fortunes,

3 Which is why the Americans will discover how to turn everything in the world into something else,

4 That is, something else that can be sold for money.

5 For example, an American capitalist named [i]Thomas Edison

a. Psong.8.5
b. Lies.14.5
c. Brit.19.43-47
d. Brit.19.41-42
e. Hill.B.3-8
f. Carl.3.8
g. 16.3
h. Psong.12.1-2
i. Yks.73.2-6
j. 15.3
k. Ned.29.24
l. Ed.46.10
m. Jeff.24.23
n. Grk.8.32
   Ned.42.7
o. 2.15
p. Psong.48.1-3
q. Psong.25.1

will turn magnets into electricity and pipe the electricity into people's homes through wires,

6 [j]For money.

7 And when people have all this electricity running into their house, they will want to buy other things that use electricity,

8 Which is why Edison will also sell them electric light bulbs,

9 And electric floor lamps,

10 And electric toasters,

11 And electric ovens,

12 And electric heaters,

13 And maybe even [k]electric shoes,

14 For all we know.

15 In fact, Edison will achieve such a complete victory in the American market for electricity that he will become well known throughout America as the Conqueror of Electricity,

16 Or General Electric for short.

CHAPTER 22

An American capitalist named [l]Henry Ford will look out across the driveways of America and decide that there should be a horseless carriage in every one of them,

2 [m]With his name on it,

3 Which is why he will figure out how to take steel and rubber and [n]horsehair and glass and tin and copper and wood and a whole bunch of baling wire,

4 And turn it into [o]an af*ford*able motor-driven horseless carriage in practically no time flat,

5 [p]Using something called an assembly line,

6 [q]Which will pipe Ford motorcars into every home in America,

7 In practically no time flat,

8 Which is why Henry will become known throughout America as the Conqueror of [a]Internal Combustion Engines,
9 Or General Motors for short.

CHAPTER 23

An American Capitalist named [b]B.F. Goodyear will look down from his zeppelin at all the Ford motorcars sitting in driveways all over America and decide that they should all have whitewall tires,
2 [c]With his name on them,
3 [d]Which is why he will figure out how to make tires faster and cheaper than everybody else,
4 Until so many of his tires are driving across America that he will become known as the Conqueror of Foot Fatigue,
5 Or General Tire for short.

CHAPTER 24

An American Capitalist named [e]Kellogg Flake will look out across the kitchens of America and see millions of common people eating [f]oatmeal,
2 Which will make him decide that everybody should be eating [g]cold cereal instead,
3 [h]With his name on it,
4 [i]Which is why he will wind up buying so much wheat, corn, barley, and oats to turn into breakfast cereal that he will become known as the Conqueror of American Grain Processing,
5 Or General Mills for short.

CHAPTER 25

Of course, not all American industrialists will be generals.
2 Some of them will have other ranks and titles,

a. 7.1
b. Ed.28.6
c. Brit.15.22
d. 2.15
e. Dav.22.12
f. Dav.47.25
g. 2.15
h. Ext.52.16
i. Psong.18.1-4
j. Dav.14.25
k. Dav.14.21
l. Ed.44.4
m. Dav.20.46
n. Yks.56.15
o. Chr.3.16-25
p. Chr.3.26
q. Yks.57.12-19
r. Yks.139.25

3 Including "Barons,"
4 Of which there will be more than a few,
5 Such as a Baron named [j]Rockefeller who will one day provide all the gasoline and oil for General Motors' cars,
6 And a Baron named [k]Carnegie who will one day provide all the steel for General Motors' cars,
7 Plus the steel for General Electric's appliances,
8 As well as the steel for the Baron of Guns,
9 Who will be named [l]Remington Colt, XLV,
10 Not to mention steel bullets for the Baron of Gunpowder,
11 Who will be named [m]Irene something,
12 In spite of not being a girl,
13 But a terrifically manly Robber Baron,
14 Just like everybody else.

CHAPTER 26

As it happens, all these titles won't go over very well in America,
2 [n]Because the people who work in factories came to America in the first place to get away from lords and nobles,
3 [o]Since lords and nobles always seem to think they own people,
4 And can do with them what they like,
5 [p]Because they don't have any rights of their own,
6 [q]Unless you live in America, where everybody has rights,
7 And where they don't allow citizens to have titles,
8 Or own people,
9 [r]At least not anymore,
10 Which suggests that maybe

there's something going on that shouldn't be going on,

11 ᵃAnd maybe it's about time someone demoted the generals and barons,

12 So that they'd treat people a little more decently,

13 ᵇAnd pay them better,

14 ᶜAnd care a little more about safety,

15 ᵈAnd cut back a little on the twenty- or thirty-hour workdays,

16 And doesn't that seem reasonable,

17 O you generals and barons?

CHAPTER 27

Of course, all the generals and barons will laugh pretty hard when all the workers they own start talking about rights,

2 ᵉBecause survival of the fittest has nothing to do with rights,

3 At all,

4 ᶠAnd it's not their fault that common people are too stupid to build their own factory,

5 And if they've got enough free time on their hands to complain,

6 Maybe it's because they're not working hard enough,

7 And what do you think of a thirty- or forty-hour workday,

8 ᵍO you trash and immigrant scum?

CHAPTER 28

And out of this new dialogue between barons and workers will come a ʰbrand-new institution,

2 Called organized labor,

3 Which will negotiate new rules for the handling of dis-

a. *Yks.61.11-14*
b. *Psong.11.1-4*
c. *10.11*
d. *11.1-5*
e. *Chuk.15.1-16*
f. *12.7-9*
g. *Vin.49.5*
h. *2.15-16*
i. *Gnt.13.4-6*
j. *Ned.16.4-11*
k. *Jefs.7.22*
l. *Yks.139.28 & 54.3*

agreements between management and workers.

4 ⁱFor example, it will be a rule that management has to try suppressing the formation of unions with negotiating tools like hired thugs and bludgeons and rifles,

5 ʲAnd that organized labor will have to try getting their rights by calling for strikes and riots and armed confrontations with management's hired thugs,

6 For years,

7 Until the lions of justice in the courts of the Most Chosen Nation on Earth decide,

8 Reluctantly,

9 ᵏThat everyone in America has rights,

10 Including the right to organize employee unions,

11 Even if all the members are poor white trash,

12 And immigrant scum from Europe,

13 And other kinds of undesirables.

14 Moreover, since it will also be a God-given right of every person in the Most Chosen Nation to belong to clubs that not everybody can get into,

15 The labor unions of America will also have the right to be as exclusive as *they* want to be,

16 Just like the barons' country clubs,

17 ˡMeaning black people need not apply,

18 Because when people talk about equality in America,

19 They will generally be talking about equality for themselves,

20 And not for all those others,

21 Who are too inferior to be equal,

22 To them.

CHAPTER 29

A nd so, the labor movement in the Most Chosen Nation will make a huge contribution to the advancement of equality in Capitalist systems,

2 And it will be discovered that rich Capitalists can make money even if they pay their workers a living wage,

3 [a]Which they will grumble about,

4 But less and less all the time,

5 Because they will be cheered up by another great American innovation,

6 Which will make up for all their generosity to the workers,

7 Ten times over,

8 Which is some consolation anyway.

CHAPTER 30

F or it will also be the Americans who will discover the most important rule about being a Capitalist,

2 Namely, that it pays to advertise,

3 [b]Which is based on the idea that the best way to convince everybody of how great you are is to tell everybody how great you are,

4 As often as possible,

5 In every way possible,

6 Until they believe it,

7 [c]Just like a religion.

8 The invention of advertising by Baron [d]Sears-Roebuck will take your ideas into a whole new realm,

9 In which [e]corporations will beget *things*,

10 Which will beget advertising,

11 Which will beget names and

a. 17.11
b. Main.18.6
c. Boul.26.11
d. Yks.89.5
e. 8.8-9
f. 8.1-2
g. 20.2
h. Ned.4.7

claims and memorable images and slogans,

12 Which will beget an entire new industry devoted to packaging,

13 Which will beget an incredible number of additional completely useless new *things*,

14 Which will beget thousands of new communications mediums just so that everybody will have some place to advertise *things*,

15 Which will beget thousands of completely new industries to make still more new *things* to use the advertising space,

16 [f]Which will eventually be so full of advertisements that nobody will be able to go anywhere or do anything without getting some free advice about what *things* to buy next.

CHAPTER 31

[g]I n this way, a day will come when common ordinary people will be able to judge each other by the *things* they use and own.

2 Instead of a horse and buggy, they will have their choice of hundreds of different horseless carriages,

3 Which will have names like Ford Biscayne and Chevrolet Bonneville and Pontiac Roadmonster and Buick Thunderbird and Cadillac New Yorker and Oldsmobile Fury and Chrysler Falcon and Dodge Catalina and Rambler Fury and Mercury Fleetwood and a bunch of others too,

4 Including even a two-wheeled horseless carriage,

5 [h]Which will also be known as a Holy Davidson,

6 Not to mention *flying* horseless carriages,

7 And other miraculous things you can't even begin to imagine now.

8 [a]Instead of a mouthful of nasty-tasting baking soda, they will be able to brush their teeth with a substance that has no other purpose than the brushing of teeth,

9 Which will come in its own special tube,

10 And will have a carefully chosen name that means absolutely nothing, like Crust or Gloom or Coolgate or Pepsi-Dent or something like that.

11 Instead of a simple pair of pants, they will be able to buy a staggeringly huge assortment of trousers that actually have names of their own,

12 Like J.C. [b]Woolworth,

13 And [c]Book Brothers,

14 And [d]Sad Sak Avenue,

15 And [e]L.L. Dollar,

16 And [f]Leviticus Strauss,

17 And too many others to count,

18 All of which will be completely different from each other,

19 Even if you have to put them on one leg at a time,

20 Just like everybody else.

CHAPTER 32

In fact, thanks to advertising, the Americans will make still another breakthrough discovery about Capitalism,

2 [g]Which is that you don't *really* have to create new value to create wealth,

3 For yourself, anyway,

4 Because Capitalism works just as well for people who create the

a. Jefs.7.22
b. Psay.5A.5
c. Ira.32.5-9
d. Mawr.12.3
e. Drex.11.8
f. Dav.30.9
g. 2.11-19
h. 15.3
i. 30.1-5
j. Ned.24.12-14
k. Hall.8.1-2

appearance of value,

5 [h]Even if there isn't any.

6 When this discovery has been proven in the marketplace,

7 By about five or ten thousand manufacturing corporations,

8 It will lead to the invention of many new industries that won't make anything of value at all,

9 But will sell services instead,

10 [i]And tell everybody how great their services are,

11 Until everybody believes it,

12 Just like a religion.

CHAPTER 33

And so it will come to pass that the American Capitalists will invent industries that nobody ever heard of before,

2 Called management consulting,

3 And public relations,

4 And life insurance,

5 Not to mention advertising,

6 Which won't make anything at all,

7 But they'll be very well paid for not making anything at all,

8 Just like banks.

CHAPTER 34

And since they've come up, it's important for you to know that banks will be an incredibly important part of Capitalist societies like America,

2 [j]Because every Capitalist Nation will always need a whole bunch of boring avaricious people in blue suits to watch everybody's money,

3 [k]Because the most important principle in every Capitalist Nation is the principle that nobody can be trusted,

4 Ever,

5 Except for banks, of course,
6 ^aWhich are extremely trust-worthy,
7 ^bOr why would they have so many boring drones in blue suits to watch over your money all the time?
8 Besides, if banks weren't trustworthy, why would people give them money and let them lend it to other people,
9 Without even asking the people who gave them all their money in the first place?
10 Not to mention the fact that if bankers weren't trustworthy, they'd probably get involved in a lot of risky financial speculation that could cause a huge depression someday,
11 Which wouldn't do Capitalism any good at all.

CHAPTER 35

That's why it will be such a good thing that banks will always lend money to the people who deserve it,
2 And will always use impeccable business judgment,
3 ^cBecause who could possibly know more about business than a know-it-all in a blue suit who thinks you earn money by lending other people's money to still other people who will do all the work and take all the risks,
4 While he sits in a giant office upstairs at the bank thinking up ways to get more money?

CHAPTER 36

Eventually, there will be so many great bankers that they will build a city all for themselves,
2 Called New York,

a. Rom.3.16
b. Rom.3.17
c. Jefs.9.4-5
d. Ext.52.16
e. 32.4
f. Mall.6.24
g. 35.3

3 Which nobody will be allowed into who actually makes *things*,
4 Except skyscrapers, that is,
5 Because the banks and life insurance companies and brokerage houses who deal strictly in money will all need their own skyscrapers,
6 ^dWith their names on them in giant letters,
7 Just so everyone will know that they really *do* make things,
8 Even though they really don't,
9 ^eWhich has a lot to do with the appearance of value,
10 And everything in the world to do with American Capitalism,
11 Which will have its headquarters in New York,
12 On Wall Street.

CHAPTER 37

In fact, Wall Street will become the world capital of Capitalism,
2 ^fAnd will become so fantastically successful that the people who work there will eventually forget practically everything you ever said,
3 Because they will know better than you,
4 About everything.

CHAPTER 38

For example, they will forget about all your quaint old definitions,
2 ^gBecause Capitalism isn't about creating wealth by creating value that didn't exist before;
3 Instead, it's about getting rich by getting hold of more money than other people,
4 Which is why value doesn't matter,

5 [a]Since what really matters is being the swiftest,

6 [b]And the fittest,

7 [c]And getting up earlier than the other guy,

8 So that you can take his money while he's still asleep,

9 [d]And use it to buy stocks on margin,

10 In the kinds of companies that can't help but succeed,

11 [e]Which you can always identify because their stock prices keep going up,

12 Which is why everybody else is buying their stock on margin too,

13 And so it's a good idea to buy yours earlier than the other guy,

14 So that you'll make higher profits,

15 [f]And more money.

CHAPTER 39

Actually (said the pen),

2 I have some not very good news for you,

3 Because when I told you the bad news about your ideas before,

4 I overlooked some,

5 Which I have been suddenly reminded of,

6 [g]Because Capitalism will also lead to something really awful that people will blame on you,

7 Something called the [h]Great Depression,

8 [i]Which will start on Wall Street,

9 With a tremendous noise,

10 [j]Which will sound like a single gigantic crash,

11 Even though it will actually consist of thousands and thousands of little crashes,

a. 14.6-7
b. 14.8-9
c. Psay.5A.15 & 5A.34
d. Psong.28.1-6
e. Psay.5A.42
f. Psong.20.1-10
g. Dav.47.24
h. Frog.35.4
i. 37.1
j. Al.2.11
k. Dav.47.23 & 47.23 & 47.23 & 47.23 & 47.23
l. Psom.24.3-4
m. Psong.29.1-7
n. Brit.9.4
o. Psong.3.1
p. 26.17
q. Yks.97.1
r. Yks.97.2
s. Yks.97.3-4

12 [k]Made by thousands and thousands of phones slipping from terror-stricken fingers,

13 All over America,

14 Simultaneously,

15 [l]Because the call they all got,

16 Simultaneously,

17 [m]Was a margin call.

CHAPTER 40

During the Great Depression, it will become obvious to everyone that Capitalism doesn't work,

2 [n]Because millions of people will be out of work,

3 [o]And even worse than that, it will be discovered that there isn't any money at all in the Most Chosen Nation,

4 [p]Except for the money that the very richest of the fat-cat Capitalists still have squirreled away, of course,

5 Because all the money everybody else had before the Great Depression was borrowed from somebody else,

6 Who had also borrowed it from somebody else,

7 And so forth,

8 And so on,

9 So that there's only one thing left to do,

10 Namely, have the government step in,

11 And print up a whole bunch of money,

12 And start giving it away,

13 [q]Which doesn't have much to do with Capitalism exactly,

14 [r]But has a great deal to do with putting some food on the table,

15 [s]For all the millions and millions of people who aren't fit enough to survive on their own.

CHAPTER 41

[a]In fact, this new idea of giving money away to the people who need it will catch on,

2 [b]In a big way,

3 [c]And become very very popular,

4 [d]Because the politicians will look very statesmanlike giving away millions,

5 While the philanthropists will look miserly giving away their dimes,

6 [e]Which is why the government will be delighted to discover how easy it is to take more and more millions away from the philanthropists,

7 So that they can have their picture taken giving it away,

8 [f]Until lots and lots of people in the Most Chosen Nation on Earth will one day decide that they were wrong for all the years they thought it was the government who couldn't be trusted the most,

9 [g]Because the ones who can't be trusted the most are the greedy Capitalists,

10 [h]Who borrowed all that money,

11 [i]And then threw it all away.

CHAPTER 42

[j]But the government won't succeed in taking all the money away from the Capitalists,

2 Because the Capitalists will come up with a new idea,

3 Which they will know is a good idea because it worked so many times before,

4 And will again,

5 [j]Because when everybody who lives in a Capitalist Nation

a. Yks.98.1
b. Yks.98.2
c. Yks.98.3-6
d. Yks.98.7-12
e. Psong.59.1-3
f. Yks.98.17-20
g. Yks.98.21-22
h. 40.5-8
i. 39.10
j. 40.2-3
k. Gnt.9.1-2
l. Psom.46.1
m. Jefs.7.46
n. Yks.113.2
o. 31.6
p. Grk.2.9
q. 41.9-11

is basically out of money,

6 And can't buy *things* anymore,

7 They get restless,

8 Which means there will be a war soon,

9 And so it's probably a good idea to start investing in munitions factories,

10 Including factories that make warships,

11 And factories that make [k]tanks,

12 And factories that make guns,

13 And factories that make gunpowder,

14 And what do you know!

15 [l]Hello War!

16 Goodbye Great Depression!

17 [m]Happy days are here again!

CHAPTER 43

And so (said the pen),

2 [n]The miraculous recovery brought about by war will eventually bring Capitalism back in style,

3 And when all the [o]planes and tanks and bombs and bullets have ensured victory against the evil foe,

4 The Most Chosen Nation will embark on a new [p]golden era of wealth,

5 And they will learn once again the things they've forgotten,

6 For a while, anyway.

7 [q]For example, they will learn that if they want something, they're going to pay for it, with cash money, if they're lucky, because the other ways of paying for things are almost all worse.

8 And they will learn to work hard at creating value, because

[a]false value vanishes in a [b]tidal wave of empty paper.

9 And when they have relearned these lessons, they will make more *things* than even *they* can imagine,

10 So that the day will come when everybody has plenty of everything,

11 [c]Except maybe black people and some of the poor white trash who never make it off the bottom rung,

12 [d]And they will feel so strongly about your ideas that they will be prepared to risk the life of the planet to defend Capitalism against its enemies,

13 [e]Who will consist of all the nations that don't have anything at all,

14 [f]Except weapons, that is,

15 [g]And nations like this will have huge governments whose full-time job it is to explain why the people don't have anything at all,

16 [h]Except misery,

17 [i]Which must be *your* fault,

18 Because the rich Capitalists in America grabbed all the things that everybody else is rightfully entitled to,

19 Because the greatest people have the lowest number of goods,

20 [j]Or something like that,

21 Which is why the Most Chosen Nation will have to build lots and lots and lots of incredibly powerful weapons,

22 To use on anyone who wants some of their goods,

23 Which will threaten the entire planet with extinction,

24 Unless all the waste products thrown away by your factories

a. 36.9
b. Ann.2.32
c. Kens.5.21-24
d. Yks.147.13-21
e. Russ.25.4-9
f. Russ.21.13
g. Boul.26.11
   Adam.36.9
h. Ned.36.6-7
i. Ned.36.8-12
j. Carl.3.12
k. 30.8-12
l. Wil.16.20
m. Brit.28.3
n. Jefs.7.6
o. Yks.138.6

poison the planet to death first.

CHAPTER 44

Yes, that's another little problem I forgot to mention,

2 Because all of the hundreds of millions of *things* that will be made in factories will all be individually wrapped in little [k]packages,

3 Which people will throw away,

4 Until it adds up to the point where there won't be any place to put it,

5 Because all the places where it could have been put will already be full of the dangerous [l]chemicals the factories threw away after they used them to make all those *things*,

6 Which means that there will be chemical garbage absolutely everywhere,

7 Including the oceans,

8 And the rivers,

9 And the clouds,

10 And the fields,

11 And the groundwater,

12 And the bellies of livestock,

13 And even the bellies of people.

CHAPTER 45

But that's why it's such a good thing that your ideas will lead to spectacular advances in all kinds of [m]technology,

2 [n]Including medical equipment and drugs that can help cure the diseases caused by chemical garbage,

3 [o]And miraculous electrical counting machines called computers which can work out solutions to the problems caused by all the chemical garbage,

4 Even if a lot of those computers will be used for other purposes instead,
5 [a]Like controlling all those tremendously powerful weapons of mass destruction,
6 And counting all the [b]dollars it would cost to clean up the chemical garbage,
7 Which will turn out to be too many dollars if the company's going to keep on making a decent profit . . .
8 What's that you say?
9 When am I going to start giving you the good news?
10 O Adam, I'm sorry.
11 I apologize.
12 The future can be a hard thing to take sometimes.
13 I promise I will finish with only good things,
14 Which there are a lot of,
15 Because the good things are all *things*,
16 [c]Which there will be a lot of.

CHAPTER 46

[d]There will be *things* for children,
2 Including cribs, and diapers, and safety pins, and sleepers with reinforced knees, and strollers, and picture books, and cute little shoes, and baby bottles, and sterile nipples, and scientifically designed formulas to take the place of [e]mother's milk,
3 [f]And high chairs, and blankets, and warm little outfits, and tiny little parkas, and playpens, and rattles, and dolls, and mobiles, and stuffed teddy bears,
4 [g]And medicine, and incubators for the prematurely born, and treatments for birth defects, and ointments for diaper rash,

a. 43.21
b. 2.4
c. Cen.26.18-19
d. Psong.28.3
e. Grk.12.7
f. Psom.43.1-7 & 61.1-8
g. Psong.6.4-6
h. Psay.5.1-6
i. Kens.1.4
j. Psay.5S.4-8
k. Psay.5Q.65
l. Dav.42.37-39
m. Ed.71.6-27
n. Ed.10.7-10
o. Grk.12.7
p. Psom.77.9
q. Psong.27.1-5
r. Cen.29.15
s. Mawr.30.2-3
t. Ann.18.12
u. Psong.30.2

and pacifiers to ease teething pain, and vaccines for childhood diseases like measles, and scarlet fever, and whooping cough, and infantile paralysis,
5 [h]And schoolbooks, and schools, and libraries full of books, and playgrounds full of toys, and jacks, and balls, and gloves, and [i]baseball [j]bats, and kites, and swings, and sliding boards, and wading pools, and little nurse uniforms, and dolls with complete wardrobes, and miniature stoves, and building blocks, and [k]toy guns, and little soldier helmets, and cowboy hats, and mittens, and [l]sleds, and bicycles with a bell on the handlebars,
6 And records, and [m]radios, and [n]television sets, and roller rinks, and ice skates, and [o]candy bars, and soft drinks, and encyclopedias, and eyeglasses, and scooters, and basketball hoops, and charm bracelets, and hula hoops, and modeling clay, and rocking horses, and jigsaw puzzles, and finger paints, and [p]electric trains, and go-karts, and dollhouses, and many many other things besides,
7 And some Capitalist will make money on every one of these things.

CHAPTER 47

[q]There will be *things* for women,
2 Including [r]diamond rings, and [s]pearl necklaces, and emerald earrings, and ruby brooches, and [t]mink stoles, and sable coats, and ermine hats, and leather purses, and [u]jewelry made of gold and silver and platinum,

and trench coats, and plaid skirts, and silk blouses, and slacks, and slippers, and riding boots, and high heels,

3 [a]And [b]makeup for every kind of complexion, and lipstick, and bobby pins, and hairbrushes, and bubble bath, and ointments, and electric curlers, and electric hair dryers, and hair spray, and eye shadow, and hair dye, and cotton swabs, and little razors, and tweezers, and mascara, and fingernail polish, and emery boards, and fingernail polish remover, and [c]padded [d]brassieres, and girdles, and panty hose, and a million varieties of shoes, and hats, and dresses, and suits, and evening gowns, and [e]perfume, and [f]pills that prevent conception, and silk lingerie, and diet soft drinks, and cashmere sweaters, and champagne, and huge boxes of [g]chocolate candy, and [h]long-stemmed roses all year round,

4 [i]And electric stoves, and electric refrigerators, and self-cleaning electric ovens, and gas ovens, and stoves, and electric eggbeaters, and electric toaster ovens, and electric meat grinders, and electric ice-cream makers, and electric popcorn poppers, and electric vacuum cleaners, and electric floor waxers, and electric clothes washers, and electric clothes dryers, and electric sewing machines, and electric dishwashers, and electric irons, and electric blenders, and electric vegetable dicers, and meat thermometers, and powdered milk, and [j]frozen dinners, and canned soup, and frozen orange concentrate, and powdered hot chocolate, and

a. *Psay.5Q.19*
b. *Frog.9.1-4*
c. *Mawr.12.1-11*
d. *Gnt.2.11*
e. *Ann.11.1-15*
f. *Ann.18.26*
g. *Psong.39.5*
h. *Ira.36.2*
i. *Mawr.22.20*
j. *Frog.24.1-5*
k. *Jefs.7.14*
l. *Frog.13.1-2*
m. *Boul.12.8*
n. *Boul.12.7*
o. *Krt.34.2-3*
p. *Bks.7.4-5*
q. *Nips.26.1*
r. *Jefs.7.15*

[k]marshmallows, and powdered detergent, and liquid fabric softener, and bottled furniture polish, and rolling pins, and cookie jars, and kitchen scissors, and egg cups, and paper napkins, and steel knives, and place mats, and pressure cookers, and corn scorers, and scratch remover, and straight pins, and [l]knitting needles, and crochet hooks, and kleenex,

5 And ready-made curtains, and [m]wall-to-wall carpeting, and baskets, and flowerpots, and lead crystal, and furniture made of oak and teak and walnut and cherry, and [n]central air-conditioning, and [o]Dresden china, and British Sterling silver flatware, and Spanish lace tablecloths, and French doors, and grand pianos, and brass candlesticks, and [p]Persian carpets, and antimacassars, and hardwood floors, and electric heat, and plastic furniture covers, and swimming pools, and baubles and [q]gewgaws of every description,

6 And bedsheets with flowers on them, and [r]monogrammed bath towels, and matching hand towels, and bathtubs in every color under the sun, and stall showers, and porcelain bidets, and makeup mirrors with adjustable lights, and heated toilet seats, and bathroom fans, and gold-plated faucets, and stainless-steel faucets, and wicker clothes hampers, and cute wastebaskets, and toilet paper, and shoe racks, and padded clothes hangers, and skirt hangers,

7 And dry cleaners, and supermarkets, and florists, and clothing stores, and gift shops, and

hair salons, and shoe stores, and furniture stores, and mail-order stores of every description, and catalogs, and magazines, and ^aromance novels, and playing cards, and cookbooks, and sewing books,

8 And ^bstation wagons, and sexy little sports cars, and ^cmade-to-order houses, and cruise ships, and summer houses on the beach,

9 And exercise equipment, and brilliant bathing suits, and ^dpackage tours, and beach umbrellas, and picnic baskets, and matched luggage, and aspirin, and sandals, and suntan lotion, and sunlamps, and ^esleeping pills, and fifty million kinds of ^fsunglasses,

10 And stockings that roll to the knee, and blue hair dye, and walkers, and bifocals, and ^gmah-jongg, and treatments for high blood pressure and arthritis and varicose veins and cataracts and glaucoma,

11 And toys for grandchildren, and photo albums, and postcards, and lavender scent, and comfortable shoes, and sitdown showers, and ^hhats with veils,

12 And some Capitalist will make money on every one of these things.

CHAPTER 48

ⁱThere will be *things* for men,

2 Including comfortable chairs, and remote-controlled television sets, and bowling balls, and ^jbaseball caps, and thick sweaters, and ^kgirlie magazines, and beer, and bourbon, and scotch, and ^lpotato chips, and cheese curls, and ^mpretzels, and pizza,

a. Swar.32.11
b. Hill.S.7
c. Hill.S.6
d. Yks.145.1-7
e. Vin.16.6
f. Ned.24.22
g. Chnk.16.6-7
h. Vin.59.7-9
i. Ned.30.30-35
j. Ned.24.20-21
k. Yks.144.11-12
l. Ned.6.6-7
m. Wil.65.2-4
n. Psay.5T.1-11
o. Vin.49.1-11
p. Zig.10.13
q. Main.36.6
r. Ann.6.1-23
s. Psom.69.1-4
t. Ann.18.7
u. Psom.18.5
v. Psay.5S.14
w. Ned.16.14-15
x. Mawr.22.22

and submarine sandwiches, and fishing tackle,

3 ⁿAnd electric drills, and wrenches, and stainless-steel hammers, and electric band saws, and garden tractors with attachments, and wheelbarrows, and rakes, and hoes, and edgers, and grass seed, and weed killer, and shovels, and electric snow-blowers, and plastic ^oChristmas trees, and lawn ornaments, and driveway sealant, and paint, and shellack, and wire brushes, and C-clamps, and screwdrivers, and sparkplug removers, and electric routers, and paintbrushes, and steel wool, and paint scrapers, and soldering irons, and hedge clippers, and chain saws, and garden shears,

4 ^pAnd ^qhigh-powered sports cars, and motorcycles, and speedboats, and ^rfour-door sedans, and cabin cruisers, and pickup trucks, and airplanes, and ^srowboats, and snowmobiles, and airboats, and four-wheel-drive vehicles, and skis, and tents, and canoes, and kayaks, and ^trifles, and shotguns, and ^ucrossbows, and hunting clothes, and pool tables, and dartboards, and ^vgolf clubs, and tennis rackets, and cameras, and movie projectors, and short wave radios, and luggage racks, and motor homes, and battery-operated televisions,^w

5 ^xAnd leg braces, and gauze bandages, and liniment, and bug spray, and burn ointment, and iodine, and arm slings, and wristbands, and headbands, and trophies, and trusses, and plaster casts, and catgut stitches, and weights, and chin-up bars, and sit-up boards, and rowing

machines, and vitamins, and medicine balls, and Epsom salts, and crutches,

6 [a]And leather briefcases, and silk ties, and custom-made suits, and monogrammed shirts, and leather shoes of every description, and sneakers, and tie clips, and [b]pinkie rings, and leather jackets, and pleated trousers, and alarm clocks, and gold cuff links, and cologne, and wristwatches, and toupees, and shaving cream, and safety razors, and toenail clippers, and change trays, and top hats, and raincoats, and galoshes, and gloves, and socks, and boxer shorts, and pajamas, and sweatshirts, and T-shirts, and toilet kits, and suit bags, and antiperspirants, and mouthwash,

7 And canes, and false teeth, and hearing aids, and cardigan sweaters, and newspapers, and footstools, and wheelchairs, and [c]life insurance policies, and oak caskets,

8 And some Capitalist will make money on each of these things.

CHAPTER 49

There will be things for workplaces of all kinds,

2 Including desks, and chairs, and typewriters, and file cabinets, and pens, and pencils, and paper clips, and rubber bands, and staple removers, and telephone message pads, and ink pads, and desk blotters, and carbon paper, and photocopiers, and [d]computers, and erasers, and corkboards, and telephones, and coffee machines, and candy machines, and magic markers, and in-trays, and out-baskets,

a. Ned.24.1-11
b. Psay.5Q.19
c. 33.4
d. 45.3
e. Zig.10.13
f. 36.5
g. 6.7
h. 19.2
*i. Psong.6.7-9
Chuk.20.18-23*

and pencil sharpeners, and stationery, and envelopes, and manila folders, and order forms, and calendars,

3 [e]And bulldozers, and tractor trailer trucks, and hydraulic lifts, and stamping machines, and test equipment, and flatbed trucks, and coveralls, and hard hats, and time punch clocks, and rolling steel doors, and warehouses, and [f]office buildings, and conveyor belts, and safety goggles, and first-aid kits, and forklifts, and cranes, and ships, and planes, and lathes, and loading docks, and sprinkler systems, and fire alarms, and locks, and gates, and ID cards, and vats, and pipelines, and electrical conduits, and boilers, and molding machines, and drying ovens, and storage racks, and urinals, and electric hand dryers, and light switches, and fluorescent tubes, and acoustical tiles, and linoleum flooring, and time-lock vaults,

4 And so many many more things besides that it wouldn't be possible to count them all,

5 Except that some Capitalist will make money on every one of these things.

CHAPTER 50

[g]There will also be things for nations,

2 Including highway systems that stretch from one edge of the continent to the other,

3 And [h]government buildings,

4 And dams, and inland waterways,

5 And power plants,

6 [i]And military things, including tanks, and ships, and bazookas, and rifles, and artillery, and

rockets, and uniforms, and gas masks, and knapsacks, and grenades, and bullets, and bombs, and fortifications, and shipyards, and military bases, and submarines, and armored personnel carriers, and jeeps, and helmets, and shovels, and picks, and boots, and more boots, and medals, and litters, and body bags, and intravenous needles, and bone saws, and prosthetic limbs, and antiaircraft guns, and bomb shelters, and blankets, and tourniquets, and land mines, and sea mines, and underwater explosives, and flamethrowers and . . .

7 What's that?

8 Oh.

9 My apologies.

CHAPTER 51

Don't take on so (said the pen).

2 So your ideas won't make everything perfect.

3 It's not the end of the world.

a. Wil.18.1-2

4 At least not yet, anyway.

5 Besides,

6 Although I can't be completely sure about it,

7 [a]I think someone will come,

8 Someday.

9 This someone may know what to do about all this,

10 Unless he doesn't.

11 But that's a long way off,

12 In fact, it's a long long way off,

13 And I don't think you should worry about it right now.

14 All right?

CHAPTER 52

And so Adam put his pen carefully away,

2 And decided that there really wasn't much he could do about things that were so far in the future,

3 Except maybe leave a tiny hint for those who would come,

4 Which is why economics came to be known as the dismal science.

THE BOOK OF THE VIP

CHUCK

CHAPTER 1

There was a VIP named [a]Chuck, who took a beagle somewhere on an expedition,

2 [b]And changed the world.

3 When he came back, he told everybody that they were all wrong about a few things.

4 Like, they were wrong about the creation,

a. Dav.30.40
b. Adam.1.4
c. Lies.2.1-3
d. Lies.2.4
e. Dav.10.11
f. Psay.5Z.10
g. Lies.2.5-6
Psay.5Y.37
h. Gods.3.5

5 [c]And how God made everything in seven days,

6 [d]Completely from scratch.

7 And they were especially wrong about how God had made man,

8 [e]In His own image,

9 To rule over all the [f]animals,

10 [g]From the very beginning.

11 [h]When they heard this, ev-

erybody got very upset,
12 ªSaying, "We don't believe it, that can't be right, what are you trying to pull, anyway?"
13 And so Chuck climbed up on the podium,
14 Cleared his throat,
15 And started to talk.

a. Gods.3.6
b. Jefs.7.15-17
c. 14.4
d. Name.4.6-11
e. Name.4.12-13
f. 1.1

CHAPTER 2

According to Chuck, the creation didn't happen all at once, but over a very long period of time,
2 ᵇBy a process called Evolution,
3 Meaning that everything started out pretty much the same,
4 As not much,
5 And then changed into something else,
6 Through a lot of accidents,
7 Which eventually resulted in an accident called Mankind,
8 And explains why everything is so confusing.

CHAPTER 3

When the people heard this, they said back to Chuck,
2 "Let's get this straight. You're saying that God didn't specifically set out to create Mankind,
3 "But something else,
4 "And Mankind just sort of happened along the way,
5 "By accident?"
6 Whereupon Chuck smiled and said that was approximately it,
7 More or less,
8 And wasn't that interesting?
9 Whereupon the people started to tap their foot,
10 And put their tongue against the side of their mouth,
11 And wink at each other a lot,

12 Until one of them spoke pretty sharply to Chuck, saying,
13 "Well, if man evolved from something else,
14 "What specifically did he evolve from?
15 "Answer that one for us, Mister Evolution."

CHAPTER 4

And then it was that Chuck sprang the biggest news of all,
2 Which was that Mankind had evolved from the apes,
3 ᶜHaving come down out of the trees,
4 A long long time ago,
5 And evolved an opposable thumb,
6 And then a big brain,
7 That got even bigger,
8 ᵈUntil he was no longer an ape,
9 ᵉBut a man,
10 And wasn't it all just fascinating?

CHAPTER 5

And then the people crossed their arms,
2 And rolled their eyes, looking at Chuck and tapping their temples from time to time,
3 Saying, "Why don't you lie down for a while?
4 "We'll come back later when you feel better."
5 And then they tiptoed away.
6 Whereupon Chuck felt sad and depressed,
7 Until his ᶠbeagle came up and licked his face,
8 Scratched at a few fleas,
9 And said, "Don't be downhearted, Chuck,
10 "It'll all work out in the end."
11 "Trust me."

12 And when Chuck remonstrated with his beagle, saying, "You're just a dog, what do you know?",

13 The beagle replied, "As a matter of fact, I know quite a lot. Let me tell you about it."

14 Then the beagle spoke, at considerable length, and described many wonderful things that would happen in the future.

CHAPTER 6

A lmost everybody will come to believe that you are right (said the beagle),

2 [a]And the ones who don't will eventually make jackasses of themselves,

3 Because everybody knows this is the way science has been going for quite a while now.

4 [b]After all, they started out thinking that the earth was flat,

5 [c]And the stars were permanently fixed in a big invisible bowl over the earth,

6 [d]Called the firmament,

7 [e]And they believed the sun and the moon were just big lights,

8 [f]That the Gods put there so we could see each other.

CHAPTER 7

[g] A nd then they had to swallow the part about the earth not being flat,

2 [h]But round,

3 [i]Like an orange or a basketball,

4 Which didn't make sense at all,

5 [j]Unless you believed the part about gravity keeping everybody from falling off the earth,

6 But they bought it eventually anyway.

a. *Pnot.40.1-5*
b. *Grk.13.1-3*
c. *9.6*
d. *Jefs.7.15-17*
e. *Grk.10.4 & 10.7*
f. *Grk.12.10*
g. *Exp.9.9-11*
h. *Exp.9.12*
i. *Exp.9.13*
j. *Gnt.6.1-6*
k. *Gnt.7.1-4*
l. *Psay.5U.18-19*
m. *Psay.5U.2-4*
n. *2.2*

7 And then they had to give up the part about the earth being the center of the universe,

8 [k]So they could believe the part about the planets revolving around the sun,

9 [l]And the moon revolving around the earth,

10 And the sun revolving around the center of the [m]galaxy,

11 Which was hard to do,

12 Because when you think about it,

13 That kind of a universe makes Mankind seem pretty insignificant.

14 But they accepted it anyway because it made them feel pretty smart to have figured it all out,

15 And if they got good enough at science, what couldn't they figure out?

CHAPTER 8

F or example, they thought it would all be okay if they could just figure out God's natural laws,

2 Which they believed were the same throughout the universe,

3 Making it possible to know everything if you just learned what all the laws were,

4 Except that some of the laws are tougher to believe than others.

5 Which brings us to [n]Evolution,

6 It being a law that's somewhat tougher to take than average,

7 Since it tends to make Mankind look even more insignificant than he did before,

8 In fact, pretty damned insignificant,

9 To the point where maybe they'd have to start looking at God in a slightly different way,

10 Which is hard to do,
11 [a]Since they've got an awful lot invested in this Judeo-Christian thing.

CHAPTER 9

But the good news is that Mankind can believe practically anything,
2 Including Evolution,
3 [b]And it's a lot harder to not believe in science than to not believe in a personal Judeo-Christian God,
4 [c]Who made everything in seven days,
5 [d]Completely from scratch,
6 Just like it says in the Bible,
7 [e]Which happens to have a few little contradictions in it,
8 In case you hadn't noticed.

CHAPTER 10

[f]**A**nd so they'll stop believing in the literal truth of the Bible,
2 And they'll start studying the history of the earth [g]scientifically,
3 [h]Meaning with picks and shovels and microscopes and chemistry and theories and experiments and so forth,
4 And they'll discover all kinds of amazing, fascinating things.
5 Like they'll discover that the earth is millions and millions and millions of years old,
6 And wasn't much like [i]Eden at the [j]beginning,
7 But hotter and wetter,
8 And without any life to speak of,
9 [k]Unless you count amino acids,
10 [l]Which got the ball rolling lifewise,
11 [m]Back when everything was

a. Boul.1.2
b. Jeff.17.1-5
c. 1.5
d. 1.6
e. Lies.13.1-8
f. 6.1-2
g. Brit.10.9
h. Brd.9.6
i. Lies.2.8-10
j. Psay.5Y.29
k. Kin.2.1
l. Kin.2.2-4
m. Wil.16.20
n. Psay.5B.1-4
o. Kin.3.1
p. Kin.3.2-3
q. Lies.14.5
r. Kin.3.4
s. Kin.3.5
t. Wil.19.3-5

still pretty much nothing but a big ball of chemicals.

CHAPTER 11

And although they'll continue to think of the [n]biblical creation as a pretty nice story,
2 [o]They'll come to believe that the amino acids became simple one-celled life-forms,
3 [p]Which grew and spread and got more complicated,
4 [q]The way things always do,
5 [r]Until there were like plants and brainless animals living in the water,
6 [s]Which kept on getting more and more complicated,
7 Thanks to a principle called Survival of the Fittest,
8 Until there were water creatures,
9 Something like fish,
10 Who came out of the water onto the dry land,
11 [t]Where they went on evolving,
12 Because there weren't any men yet.

CHAPTER 12

But before there could be men, there would have to be dinosaurs,
2 Just to prove what an accident Evolution really is,
3 Because who in his right mind would decide to fill up a nice planet with a bunch of giant murderous reptiles,
4 With brains this big,
5 Who didn't do anything but lumber around eating plants and each other,
6 For a couple of eons,
7 When there could have been men instead?

CHAPTER 13

But that's why science is so great,

2 [a]Because science gives us proof,

3 And it's hard to not believe in dinosaurs when you find all these fossils of giant reptiles,

4 And can use them to build great big models of what they looked like,

5 Which people can see in museums,

6 [b]Along with little signs pointing out that the dinosaurs survived for a hundred million years,

7 Which is a lot more than it looks like Mankind will last.

CHAPTER 14

And if science can make people believe in dinosaurs, it can make them believe practically anything,

2 Including the part about where Mankind *really* came from,

3 [c]Because if you have enough dental picks and microscopes and theories,

4 You can show everybody how the apes evolved out of the trees,

5 And lost their tails,

6 And started walking upright on two legs,

7 And using tools,

8 And hunting together,

9 [d]And killing things for the pure fun of it,

10 [e]Including each other.

CHAPTER 15

[f]**I**n fact, if you have enough dental picks, you can prove everything.

2 [g]You can prove that apes evolved into several different kinds of men,

---

a. *Drex.8.1-3*
b. *Kin.4.3-4*
c. *10.3*
d. *Apes.1.1-2*
e. *Apes.1.3*
f. *14.3*
g. *Wil.19.12-13*
h. *Wil.19.14-15*
i. *Ann.18.11*
j. *Rom.10.4*
k. *Gods.1.7*
l. *Gods.1.5*
m. *Psay.5Q.62*
n. *Gyp.1.7-11*
o. *Chnk.2.11-14*
p. *Mes.1.1 & 1.10-11*
q. *Gyp.1.12-16*

---

3 Which mostly didn't work out,

4 Until one did,

5 Because he was the fittest,

6 [h]Meaning the most ruthless killer.

7 This one got started somewhere in [i]Africa,

8 And migrated all over the world,

9 Grabbing as much territory as possible,

10 [j]And leaving trash everywhere he went,

11 Including broken pieces of pottery,

12 [k]And broken pieces of tools,

13 [l]And broken pieces of weapons,

14 [m]Right next to broken pieces of skeletons,

15 Proving that in spite of Evolution,

16 Some things never change.

CHAPTER 16

And science will prove that Mankind liked settling down next to rivers,

2 Where the water makes things green and fertile,

3 Because it's easier to live there than somewhere else,

4 Which is how all the first great civilizations got started,

5 [n]Including Egypt,

6 [o]And China,

7 [p]And Mesopotamia,

8 And everywhere else too.

CHAPTER 17

And science will prove that Mankind had some things that it always did when it started up a new civilization,

2 And had some extra time on its hands.

3 [q]For example, you could prac-

tically count on them starting to bury their dead,

4 Like they were something special,

5 And inventing Gods and religions to explain the things they didn't understand,

6 [a]Such as the weather,

7 [b]And death,

8 [c]And the accidental nature of things,

9 Which they never seemed to like.

10 [d]And you could count on them doing all kinds of incredible things to prove to themselves that their Gods were real,

11 [e]Like building incredibly huge monuments and temples to their Gods,

12 [f]And learning how to write down the names of their Gods and what they'd asked them for,

13 [g]And inventing all kinds of weapons to show their neighbors whose Gods were more real and powerful,

14 [h]Not to mention grabbing their land and other things,

15 Until some other civilization that was bigger and stronger,

16 Because it lived in a more fertile river valley,

17 Destroyed them and their temples and their Gods too.

CHAPTER 18

And science will [i]prove that the same things happen over and over and over and over again,

2 Repeatedly,

3 And haven't stopped yet.

4 [j]Because although civilizations keep on changing and evolving,

5 [k]And their Gods keep on

a. Gods.3.1-9
b. Grk.6.13-19
c. Grk.12.1-8
d. Gods.6.1-20
e. Gods.6.21-22
f. Gods.6.23-27
g. Gods.7.6-8
h. Gods.7.9-11
i. Boul.27.10
j. Rom.24.14-18
k. Boul.14.1-8
l. Boul.14.9-12
m. Psong.6.8-9
n. Vin.6.15
o. Lies.10.6
p. Ext.52.16
q. Dav.47.24
r. Mawr.17.4-5 & 19.4-7
s. Psay.5Q.62
t. Jeff.19.8
u. Adam.31.16
v. Jefs.7.6
w. Lies.10.6
x. Ed.60.10

changing and evolving,

6 [l]And their monuments and temples keep on changing and evolving,

7 [m]And their weapons keep on changing and evolving,

8 [n]Mankind has stayed pretty much the same.

9 [o]And it's not likely that Mankind will ever stop being pretty much the same,

10 [p]Because to do that, he'd need a bigger brain,

11 [q]Which he can't have,

12 Since if the human brain got any bigger,

13 [r]Women would have to evolve an even wider pelvis,

14 [s]And give up walking for good.

CHAPTER 19

And science will also prove that God doesn't have a lot to do with the way Mankind acts,

2 [t]At least not anymore,

3 Since science shows that it's all built in anyway,

4 From birth,

5 And before,

6 Because everything we're good at,

7 And bad at,

8 Is determined by our [u]genes,

9 [v]Which live in every cell of the human body,

10 [w]And pretty well explain everything important about us,

11 Like how we look,

12 And how our brains work,

13 And how our emotions work, and how our senses work,

14 For better or worse,

15 Until the fabulous organic [x]machine called the human body stops working,

16 Which is called death,
17 And is every bit as final as it sounds.

CHAPTER 20

[a] **A**nd science will even prove that the only thing that really changes and evolves is science,
2 [b]And the things we do with science,
3 Like build taller buildings,
4 And bigger cities,
5 And more populous nations,
6 And more powerful weapons,
7 And more far-flung colonies,
8 And more dangerous trash,
9 For as long as we live.
10 Because the thing is,
11 [c]If Mankind has to stay pretty much the same,
12 From year to year,
13 And decade to decade,
14 And century to century,
15 [d]And millennium to millennium,
16 [e]Then the same things will keep happening over and over and over and over again,
17 [f]Repeatedly,
18 Which isn't good,
19 [g]Because one of the first things Man did after climbing down out of the trees,
20 [h]Was pick up a [i]stick,
21 [j]Chew the end to a point,
22 [k]And stick it in a nearby living thing,
23 [l]And has been doing pretty much the same thing ever since.

CHAPTER 21

[m] **A**nd in the end, people will come to believe the lessons of science,
2 [n]Because they really knew it all already anyway,

a. *Adam.30.3-7*
b. *Zig.10.13*
c. *18.9*
d. *Pnot.24.5*
e. *18.1*
f. *18.2*
g. *Dav.17.11*
h. *Dav.17.12*
i. *F&J.14.13*
j. *Dav.17.13*
k. *Dav.17.14-15*
l. *Dav.17.16*
m. *Boul.18.6*
n. *Boul.18.7-8*
o. *Gyp.3.1-4*
p. *Bks.4.21*
q. *Rom.21.6-9*
r. *Chr.2.5*
   Mawr.25.14
s. *Grk.5.8*
t. *Yks.154.24*
u. *Psay.5Q.14*
v. *Drex.6.4*
w. *Ann.12.19-22*
x. *Wil.18.1-2*

3 "Ever since they first started believing in one God,
4 [p]Who created everything all by Himself,
5 [q]And who said He loved the race of Man a lot,
6 [r]Even though Man is basically evil,
7 [s]And can only be made good through a lot of pain and guilt and suffering.
8 [t]The only thing new about the lessons of science is the part about God probably not having a personal hand in the creation,
9 [u]And maybe not knowing or caring about us at all,
10 [v]Except as an accidental chemical by-product,
11 Of [w]Evolution.

CHAPTER 22

And so (said the beagle), you should have faith in the future, Chuck,
2 Knowing that your ideas will be accepted as the truth,
3 Eventually,
4 And generations of future scientists will hail you as a genius,
5 Who made it possible to learn where the great race of Mankind came from,
6 And where he is going.
7 This will be your legacy,
8 And what is more,
9 [x]Someone will eventually come along,
10 And explain what it all means,
11 And what we should do about it.

CHAPTER 23

And when this someone comes,
2 It will be a great event,

3 ᵃA ray of enlightenment rising from a time of strife,
4 ᵇAnd despair,
5 ᶜAnd war,
6 ᵈAnd other not very nice circumstances.
7 ᵉThis someone will have the answers,
8 And plenty of people will rejoice at his wisdom,
9 And his way,
10 Which will be his,

a. Ned.1.1
b. Ned.1.2
c. Ned.1.3
d. Ned.1.4-6
e. Ned.4.7

11 And then everybody else's too.

CHAPTER 24

After hearing all these things,
2 Uttered by his beagle,
3 Chuck didn't know what to say,
4 So he didn't say anything,
5 Again.

THE BOOK OF THE VIP

CARL

CHAPTER 1

There was a VIP named ᵃCarl,
2 Who sat down and figured it all out for good,
3 And then told everybody,
4 From a platform on ᵇHyde Park corner.
5 ᶜThe things Carl had to say wound up changing the world,
6 But not right away.
7 The fact is, when you figure it all out for good,
8 ᵈIt takes time for everybody to understand it,
9 Which is why Carl didn't get the warmest possible reception right away.

CHAPTER 2

According to Carl, the problem with Mankind was that it kept trusting someone else to take care of things,
2 Which was a mistake because no one can be trusted except the masses.

a. Dav.40.9
b. Brit.29.15
c. Adam.1.4
d. 10.11
e. Lies.12.9
  Dav.15.42-46
f. Jeff.19.1-5
g. Gods.4.4-13
  Rom.3.13-17
  Chr.3.16-26
  Adam.14.1-16
h. Exp.1.7-9
i. Krt.11.7
j. Ann.6.1
  Dav.47.23
k. Dav.30.9
l. Adam.10.1-8
m. Ed.60.10

3 ᵉFor example, Mankind kept wanting to trust God,
4 ᶠWho couldn't be trusted because he wasn't there.
5 ᵍFor another example, Mankind kept wanting to trust the rich and highborn and well educated,
6 ʰWho couldn't be trusted because they were rich and highborn and well educated,
7 ⁱMeaning they knew enough to look out for themselves first.
8 All this misplaced trust resulted in some pretty inevitable occurrences,
9 ʲNamely, the masses always got it in the neck from the ᵏbourgeoisie,
10 ˡWho had all the capital and naturally didn't want the masses to get any of it.

CHAPTER 3

Fortunately, though, according to Carl, the ᵐmachinery

of history was pretty powerful,

2 And when the masses had got it in the neck enough times from the bourgeoisie,

3 [a]They would finally learn their lesson,

4 [b]And rise up against the bourgeoisie,

5 [c]And take all the capital away from them,

6 Which is called the [d]Imperative of the Masses,

7 And always leads to a [e]Dictatorship of the Proletariat,

8 [f]Whatever that is,

9 So that everything could be done for the greatest good,

10 From each according to his abilities,

11 To each according to his needs,

12 [g]Or words to that effect.

CHAPTER 4

Things would become pretty great when the [h]Dictatorship of the Proletariat arrived,

2 Because then the rich wouldn't keep getting richer at the expense of the masses,

3 [i]Because the masses would be in charge,

4 [j]And would share everything equally with everybody,

5 Because if there isn't any [k]God to sit around judging everybody,

6 And there aren't any [l]rich people to lord it over everybody,

7 [m]Then everybody's basically the same,

8 [n]No better and no worse than anybody else,

9 [o]And just as entitled to a roof over their head as anyone,

10 [p]As long as they don't try to own any property.

---

a. Psay.5Q.67

b. Dav.30.16

c. Ann.6.1
Psong.29.2

d. Jefs.7.15-18

e. Brit.6.29

f. F&J.2.15-16

g. Russ.15.5-8
Chnk.14.9-10
Adam.43.19-20
Yks.98.7-8

h. 3.7

i. Psong.22.7

j. Ned.8.7-8

k. Russ.25.10

l. Psong.29.7
Ann.6.1
Dav.47.23

m. Forg.11.11

n. Psom.27.1-3

o. Psay.5Q.62

p. Ext.52.16

q. Psom.4.10

r. F&J.4.1
Dav.29.6

s. Adam.8.2-11

t. Psong.41.1-6

u. Dav.33.9-10

v. Krt.22.1-17

w. Psong.45.3

CHAPTER 5

But when Carl said all these things at Hyde Park corner,

2 A lot of people laughed,

3 And said, "Carl, old man, you're crazy as a bedbug.

4 "Get out of here and go home."

5 And so he did.

CHAPTER 6

And it so happened that when Carl went home,

2 He decided to take a [q]nap,

3 And thereupon lay down,

4 And almost squashed a [r]bedbug,

5 Which yelled pretty loudly,

6 And got Carl's attention,

7 Saying, "Don't give up, old man.

8 "If you're crazy as a bedbug, that's okay,

9 "Because I'm a bedbug, and I'm not crazy.

10 "In fact, the whole world will come to believe that you're important,

11 "And a lot of them will come to believe that you were right.

12 "Let me tell you about it."

CHAPTER 7

[s]The industrial revolution (said the bedbug) will keep on going for many years,

2 [t]And the rich will keep getting richer,

3 [u]And the poor will keep getting poorer,

4 Especially in rural nations where there isn't any industrial revolution going on,

5 And the industrial nations will start a giant [v]war,

6 [w]To see who gets to keep most of the capital,

7 ᵃAnd the masses in one of the poor rural nations will discover your ideas,

8 ᵇAnd recognize just how right they are,

9 ᶜEven though there was never much capital in their nation to begin with,

10 ᵈAnd they'll have a big revolution,

11 ᵉAnd win.

CHAPTER 8

ᶠAnd after the masses get through killing all the aristocracy and the bourgeoisie,

2 ᵍAnd even a few of the masses who aren't interpreting your ideas correctly,

3 They'll start building a new model society,

4 ʰWhere the state owns everything,

5 ⁱAnd the state is ruled by the proletariat,

6 ʲWhatever that is,

7 ᵏAnd nobody's any better than anyone else,

8 ˡAnd everybody has a roof over their head,

9 ᵐIncluding even prisoners and traitors and counterrevolutionaries.

10 ⁿAnd everything will be just beautiful.

CHAPTER 9

In fact, everything will be so beautiful that a lot of the world's greatest ᵒintellectuals will stop doing what they were doing,

2 ᵖLike philosophy and religion and art and literature,

3 And become your ᑫdisciples,

4 Believing that your ideas are a replacement for all those things,

5 Since if there's ʳno God,

a. *Russ.15.9-10*
b. *Russ.16.1*
c. *Russ.16.2-7*
d. *Psay.5Y.23*
e. *Psong.22.3*
f. *Russ.16.9-24*
g. *Russ.16.25*
h. *Vin.56.15*
i. *Frog.13.6*
j. *3.8*
k. *Russ.18.1-4*
l. *Vin.75.17-18*
m. *Psom.20.1-8*
n. *Mall.15.14-15*
o. *Drex.6.10 F&J.2.15-16*
p. *Ned.8.10*
q. *Ned.14.4-7*
r. *Frog.35.6*
s. *Lies.10.6*
t. *Frog.24.1*
u. *Chuk.19.15*
v. *Adam.42.5-15*
w. *Boul.27.10*
x. *4.8 8.7 9.6*
y. *9.10*
z. *Dav.33.9 Adam.41.9 Hall.8.8-10*
aa. *Russ.21.8-9 Main.28.1*
bb. *Dav.56.21*
cc. *Dav.27.5-15*
dd. *Vin.6.15*
ee. *Gods.4.4-6*
ff. *Swar.34.11-22*
gg. *Forg.11.10-13*

6 ˢAnd nobody's any better than anybody else,

7 All that really matters is having ᵗthree squares a day and a roof over your head,

8 ᵘUntil you die,

9 Which will probably be soon anyway,

10 ᵛEspecially since the capitalist nations of the world seem pretty determined to blow everything up.

CHAPTER 10

And just supposing that the day comes when a lot of people start to doubt that you were right about everything,

2 That's okay too,

3 Because they'll all come to ʷbelieve the most important parts,

4 ˣNamely, that nobody's any better than anyone else,

5 ʸEspecially since the industrial nations are going to blow everything up,

6 ᶻAnd that capitalism is a selfish, heartless economic system that only helps the rich,

7 ᵃᵃAnd that the best decisions are made by very large groups of Average People in great big meeting rooms,

8 ᵇᵇAnd that the masses are somehow wiser,

9 ᶜᶜAnd nobler,

10 ᵈᵈAnd more peaceful than the rest of us,

11 ᵉᵉAs long as they get to hear the truth often enough to understand it.

12 ᶠᶠAnd most important of all, people in all walks of life will come to believe that the only real virtue is need,

13 ᵍᵍAnd that the only natural right is the right of the powerless

to take what they want from whoever has it.

CHAPTER 11

[a] **A**nd just supposing (said the bedbug) that the day comes when the conflict between the capitalists and your ideas reaches the point of threatening the world with annihilation,

2 That will be okay too,

3 [b]Because someone will come,

a. Drex.9.5

b. Wil.18.1-2

c. Dav.29.19

4 On that day,

5 Or right around then, anyway,

6 Who will tell the world what it all means,

7 And what they can do about it.

8 Feel better?

9 And Carl said that he did feel better,

10 [c]And returned to Hyde Park corner to help the world get started on its new way.

THE BOOK OF THE VIP
ZIGGIE

CHAPTER 1

There was a VIP named [a]Ziggie,

2 Who had a couch,

3 And a lively imagination,

4 [b]Which changed the world.

5 Ziggie also had a [c]flashlight,

6 Which he aimed at the darkness,

7 [d]As if you could see the darkness by shining a light on it,

8 [e]And discovered a lot of great discoveries,

9 [f]Which he insisted on telling to everybody who would stand still and listen for a minute.

CHAPTER 2

According to Ziggie, [g]the human mind was a lot deeper and darker than anybody suspected,

2 Anybody, that is, who didn't have a flashlight,

3 And the things that went on in there were pretty surprising,

4 If you could just see in there,

a. Dav.40.9 & 35.40

b. Adam.1.4

c. 10.13

d. Vin.70.14-15

e. Frog.25.11

f. Adam.30.3-7

g. Dav.30.6

h. 1.3

i. Dav.40.9

j. Dav.14.25

k. Ed.63.3

l. Psom.49.1-5

5 Which you could do if you had a couch,

6 [h]And a flashlight.

CHAPTER 3

For example, the part of the human mind that people thought of as "I" wasn't really "I" at all,

2 But something called the [i]"ego,"

3 Which is Latin for "I,"

4 And is therefore completely different,

5 For some reason.

CHAPTER 4

And what's more, the ego wasn't all alone in there,

2 But had some company,

3 Called the [j]"superego" and the [k]"id,"

4 Which made everything terribly complicated and confusing,

5 [l]For some reason.

6 And that wasn't all either,

7 Because according to Ziggie,

8 The human mind also had some other parts to it,
9 Besides the ᵃconscious part,
10 Such as the ᵇsubconscious part,
11 And the ᶜunconscious part,
12 Which basically ran the show,
13 And made the ego look pretty silly and insignificant,
14 Most of the time.

CHAPTER 5

For example, the ᵈego might think that life was about going to work,
2 And eating and sleeping regularly,
3 And going out on dates every once in a while,
4 And maybe getting married eventually,
5 And having a few children,
6 And a nice old age,
7 But the ᵉego was dead wrong about all that.
8 ᶠActually, life was about a bunch of deep dark drives buried in the ᵍunconscious,
9 Which were generally kept just barely under control by the ʰsuperego,
10 Meaning the way you thought you were supposed to act,
11 While the ⁱego went on its ʲmerry way,
12 Hardly aware of anything,
13 Until Ziggie got it on the couch.

CHAPTER 6

When he got an ᵏego on his couch, Ziggie could see right through it with his flashlight,
2 All the way to the ˡunconscious,

a. Dav.30.27
b. Dav.30.25
c. Dav.30.9
d. 3.2
e. 3.2
f. Krt.10.3
g. 4.11
h. 4.3
i. Psom.69.3
j. 3.2
k. 3.2
l. 4.11
m. Dav.30.14
n. Dav.30.33
o. 4.11
p. Dav.39.21
q. 4.3
r. 3.2
s. Jefs.7.15-18
t. Chuk.2.8
u. 3.2
v. 6.9
w. Brit.6.29
x. 1.3
y. Dav.19.9
z. Psay.5Q.23
    F&J.14.13
aa. Carl.3.8
bb. F&J.13.14
cc. 4.3
dd. 3.2
ee. Ira.33.1-3

3 ᵐWhich turned out to be full of sex,
4 And was pretty ugly to look at;
5 ⁿFor example, Ziggie discovered that the ᵒunconscious always wants to have sex with your ᵖmother,
6 All of which causes problems,
7 Because the ۹superego doesn't like it,
8 And therefore doesn't tell the ʳego,
9 Which gets ˢneurotic,
10 ᵗBecause nobody ever tells it anything.

CHAPTER 7

According to Ziggie, when an ᵘego got ᵛneurotic,
2 You had to take it on a tour of the unconscious,
3 Which is called ʷpsychoanalysis,
4 And involves,
5 By an odd coincidence,
6 ˣA couch and a flashlight.
7 Usually, the thing that was making the ego neurotic was something that happened a long long time ago,
8 In your childhood,
9 ʸWhen the unconscious was trying to have sex with your mother,
10 ᶻAnd got upset because it couldn't,
11 Usually in the middle of some important phase,
12 Like the ᵃᵃoral phase,
13 Or the ᵇᵇanal phase,
14 Causing the ᶜᶜsuperego to start telling the ᵈᵈego a bunch of vicious lies,
15 Which the ego believed, of course,
16 ᵉᵉBecause the human ego is

capable of believing almost anything,

17 As Ziggie found out.

CHAPTER 8

Ziggie also found out that
dreams were important,

2 Since dreams are always about
what the ªunconscious wants,

3 Namely sex,

4 Unless they're about something the unconscious is afraid
of,

5 Namely sex,

6 Which is also why dreams are
so full of sexual symbols,

7 Including symbols that are so
symbolic you'd say the dream
was about something else,

8 Unless you knew better,

9 Which Ziggie did.

10 For example, there are about
a million ways to have sex in a
dream . . .

11 ᵇSuch as being on a train that
goes into a tunnel,

12 ᶜOr walking through a doorway into a corridor,

13 ᵈOr having a conversation
with your mother,

14 ᵉOr jumping off a tall building,

15 ᶠOr just sitting at a table eating a popsicle.

CHAPTER 9

Another important thing Ziggie found out was that really sick egos had a hard time
accepting the truth,

2 ᵍWhich is a symptom called
denial,

3 ʰAnd explains why a lot of
people had a hard time learning
how to believe in Ziggie's ideas.

4 In fact, Ziggie ran into a lot of
resistance,

5 And got discouraged,

a. *Dav.30.7*
b. *F&J.14.13*
c. *F&J.14.13*
d. *F&J.14.13*
e. *F&J.14.13*
f. *F&J.14.13*
g. *Krt.5.1-26*
h. *Jefs.7.46*
i. *Dav.14.34*
j. *Krt.10.10-13*
k. *Psay.5Q.17*
l. *Krt.9.8*
m. *Krt.33.8-17*
n. *Krt.31.8-13*
o. *Krt.32.1-10*
p. *Yks.144.11-12*
q. *Krt.22.3-12*

6 Until his ⁱcouch dug deep into
its unconscious,

7 Which it had a lot of,

8 And dredged up a vision of
the future,

9 Which it shared with Ziggie,

10 In an effort to cheer him up.

CHAPTER 10

Your ideas will change the
world (said the couch), so
don't let all this short-term denial make you neurotic.

2 ʲIn fact, your ideas will result
in a whole new field of learning,

3 Called ᵏpsychology,

4 Which will change everything
about the way people look at
themselves.

5 For a long time, people will
actually believe that you were
right about almost everything,

6 No matter how silly that
seems,

7 And your funny names for
things will become a permanent
part of the language,

8 Including Ego, Superego, and
Id,

9 ˡInferiority Complex, which is
when an ego starts acting like
it's better than everyone else,

10 ᵐPersecution Complex,
which is when an ego thinks
everybody's out to get it,

11 ⁿProjection, which is when
one ego thinks other egos might
be having the same kinds of
problems it is,

12 ºRepression, which is when
an ego starts acting like there
isn't any superego or id in there
with it, which almost always
causes all kinds of tremendous
ᵖproblems,

13 ۹Phallic Symbols, which certain really sick egos are obsessed
with, which you can usually spot

right away though, because a phallic symbol is anything longer than it is wide that you can hold in your hand, drive, or build out of elements listed on the periodic chart,
14 [a]And, of course, Penis Envy, which is what's the matter with all women, thus explaining why nobody can ever figure out what they really want.
15 And brilliant scholars will use your ideas to [b]psychoanalyze history,
16 [c]And discover that it was all about sex,
17 Just like you thought,
18 And then they'll psychoanalyze art and literature,
19 [d]And discover that they were all about sex too,
20 Including [e]Hamlet,
21 [f]No matter how silly that seems.

CHAPTER 11

After a while, of course, people will stop believing that you were right about everything,
2 [g]Which is the way things go,
3 And not as bad as it sounds,
4 [h]Because they'll keep on believing the really important part,
5 For example, the fact that there's a lot of stuff inside us we really can't control,
6 Stuff that's [i]dark and dangerous and destructive,
7 No matter where it comes from,
8 [j]And even if it's not all about sex.

CHAPTER 12

And the people who stop believing that you were right about everything will still learn a lot from you.
2 [k]For example, they'll learn that the best way to answer a question is with another question,
3 [l]And they'll learn that the best way to handle a skeptic is to accuse him of denial,
4 [m]And they'll learn that the best way to be recognized as a genius is to use terminology no one can understand,
5 [n]And best of all, they'll learn that everything in psychology takes time,
6 [o]Lots of time,
7 [p]And maybe nothing can be done anyway,
8 [q]Although it may take years to find out for sure.

CHAPTER 13

Moreover, the people who stop believing that you were right about everything will still call themselves psychologists,
2 [r]Which means they'll still be looking for reasons why people can't control themselves,
3 Even if their reasons turn out to be different.

CHAPTER 14

[s]For example, there will be psychologists who think that sex isn't as important as the environment,
2 [t]And they'll prove that everything is caused by the things our parents and teachers taught us,
3 [u]Which we can't control,
4 [v]And proves why we're like a bunch of [w]rats in a [x]maze.

CHAPTER 15

[y]On the other hand, there will be psychologists who will

a. Psong.39.5 Ira.36.2 Mawr.12.1
b. 7.3
c. 10.11 Dav.47.11
d. 10.11 Dav.47.13
e. Pnot.6.1-5
f. 9.2
g. 10.12
h. 7.16
i. Ira.32.3-9
j. 9.2
k. Al.4.16
l. 10.11 Dav.47.11
m. 10.9 Dav.47.11
n. Ned.16.12 Psong.20.1
o. Psong.20.2-8
p. 9.2 Dav.47.13
q. Psong.41.1-6
r. 10.11
s. 9.2
t. 10.10
u. 10.11
v. F&J.14.13 Zig.8.10
w. Ed.74.3
x. Grk.6.7-10 Dav.30.9 F&J.14.13
y. Al.6.21

prove that everything is caused by brain chemistry,

2 [a]Because the brain is really this amazingly intricate chemical computer,

3 [b]Which we can't control,

4 [c]Until scientists find the right medication,

5 [d]Which will take time,

6 [e]Lots of time,

7 And even if nothing can be done anyway,

8 [f]It may take years to find out for sure.

CHAPTER 16

[g]And there will be others who will prove that everything is caused by [h]genes,

2 [i]Which we can't control,

3 Until scientists figure out how to correct all the mistakes in our genes,

4 Like our fondness for [j]pointed sticks,

5 [k]And our neighbor's territory,

6 [l]And even sex,

7 [m]Which might still have something to do with it.

CHAPTER 17

[n]And even when the overwhelming majority of people learn to think that you were mostly wrong about everything,

2 They still won't believe it,

3 [o]Because your terminology will remain part of the language,

4 And will be used every day.

5 After all, your ideas were never that hard for them to accept in the first place,

6 [p]Since they already knew that man is basically evil,

7 Which is why the entire species has spent so much time over

a. 9.2
b. 10.11
c. Adam.2.15-19
d. Psong.20.1
e. Psong.20.2-8
f. Psong.23.1-6
g. 9.2
h. Adam.31.16
i. 10.11
j. 10.13
k. 10.9
l. 10.12
m. 10.14
n. 9.2
o. 10.7-14
p. Lies.2.14-26
q. Grk.5.8
r. 9.2
s. 9.2
t. 10.10
u. 10.11
v. Adam.6.7
w. Wil.18.1-2
x. Psong.43.2
y. Ed.71.8
z. F&J.14.13

the years on [q]sin and guilt and suffering,

8 [r]And it's kind of comforting to know that the real problem is sex,

9 [s]Or organic chemistry,

10 [t]Or the mistakes their parents made when they were teething,

11 [u]Or something else they can't control,

12 [v]Which takes some of the sting out of sin and guilt,

13 Even if we don't quite know what to do about it.

CHAPTER 18

[w]Because (said the couch) there will come a day when someone *will* know what to do about it,

2 And will tell us,

3 Standing on your shoulders,

4 And some others too,

5 [x]Since even the greatest prophets have to stand on something.

6 [y]On that day, your name will become an enduring icon,

7 And will be permanently enshrined in history,

8 As long as people can still read and write,

9 And maybe even a few seconds longer than that.

CHAPTER 19

And when he had heard all these wonderful prophecies and words of wisdom,

2 [z]Ziggie lay down on his couch,

3 And thought about it,

4 For a good five minutes,

5 And maybe even a few seconds longer than that.

THE BOOK OF THE VIP
DAVE

CHAPTER 1

There was a VIP named [a]Dave,

2 Who had a camera and some big ideas,

3 Which he used to make motion pictures,

4 [b]And change the world.

CHAPTER 2

Dave thought it would be great if he could make a spectacular motion picture about the [c]great land in which he was born,

2 And so he did.

3 It turned out to be a big hit,

4 Although a couple of people got pretty upset about the scene where the [d]Ku Klux Klan rides to the rescue against the evil negroes,

5 Which made Dave unhappy and discouraged,

6 To the point where he thought about going into another line of business,

7 Maybe haberdashery,

8 Until his [e]camera suddenly turned itself on and began to speak,

9 Saying, "You can't quit now, Dave.

10 "This will all blow over, trust me, I know what I'm talking about."

11 Whereupon Dave pointed out that cameras can't talk,

12 Which made the camera laugh merrily,

13 And then reply, "You don't

a. 10.10
b. Adam.1.4
c. Yks.1.6
d. Yks.50.1-20
e. Ed.60.10
f. Swar.1.1
g. Drex.5.2

know the half of it. Motion pictures will become more spectacular and important than you've ever dared to hope, and the day will come when everyone knows that you were the first great genius to produce a blockbuster."

14 And as Dave smiled in disbelief, the camera went on, saying, "Here, let me tell you about the future,

15 "And maybe even show it to you,

16 "Because you picked the right place to be in,

17 "At exactly the right time."

CHAPTER 3

The place called Hollywood (said the camera) will become a mecca for the most beautiful and talented people in the world,

2 And together they'll build a new city for the purpose of making spectacular motion pictures,

3 Which will be called movies by everyone but [f]pseudo-intellectuals,

4 Who will call movies "films,"

5 [g]For some reason.

6 Eventually, movies will change everything about the way people see themselves,

7 And art and literature,

8 And history,

9 Until the end of art and literature and history,

10 And maybe even a few decades longer than that.

CHAPTER 4

In the very near future, movies will have sound,

2 And color,

3 And lots of bad acting,

4 Which will get better as soon as someone realizes that good stage acting is good on stage,

5 But completely ridiculous on the silver screen.

6 Anyway,

7 The beautiful actors and actresses who become popular on the silver screen will be called stars,

8 [a]And there will be as many of them as there are stars in the sky,

9 And they will make millions and millions and millions and millions of dollars,

10 [b]Each.

CHAPTER 5

For example, there will be a star who will become everyone's image of [c]Mata Hari,

3 And [d]Camille,

4 And [e]Ninotchka,

5 And other people too.

6 In fact, the silver screen will become home to hordes of peculiar, flat-chested women,

7 Played by [f]Greta Garbo,

8 Who will be adored by everyone,

9 [g]Especially homosexuals,

10 And make millions and millions and millions and millions of dollars,

11 Until she'd rather be alone.

CHAPTER 6

And there will be another star who will become everyone's idea of [h]Rasputin,

2 And [i]Svengali,

3 Not to mention a lot of other weird jerks,

a. Psay.5U.4
b. Psong.48.1-2
c. Ed.51.22
d. Ann.18.26
e. Psay.5J.21
f. 30.9
  Ira.9.5-6
g. Krt.33.13-15
h. Russ.15.16
i. Bks.6.17-18
j. 4.3
k. 30.9
l. Psong.53.1-2
m. 20.14-17
n. Frog.29.8
o. 22.45-50
p. 57.32
q. 30.27
r. Pnot.39.1-5
s. 52.2
t. 30.25
u. Zig.10.14

4 [j]Who will be played with scenery-chewing glee by [k]John Barrymore,

5 Who will be adored by everybody who thinks that good stage actors make good movie actors,

6 And make millions and millions and millions and millions of dollars,

7 [l]Until he'd rather drink himself to death.

CHAPTER 7

And there will be another star who will become everybody's image of [m]Henry the Eighth,

2 [n]And the Hunchback of Notre Dame,

3 [o]And Captain Bligh of the Bounty,

4 Not to mention a bunch of other funny looking monsters,

5 Who will be played by [p]Charles Laughton.

6 Being a true Brit,

7 Charles will make thousands and thousands and thousands and thousands of dollars,

8 And marry the Bride of [q]Frankenstein.

CHAPTER 8

And there will be a star who will become everybody's idea of [r]Robin Hood,

3 [s]And General Custer,

4 And Gentleman Jim Corbett,

5 And other heroes like that,

6 Who will all look tall and handsome and sexy,

7 As played by [t]Errol Flynn.

8 [u]Errol will be adored by millions and millions of women,

9 Especially very young women,

10 And will make millions and millions and millions and millions of dollars,

11 [a]Until he'd rather drink himself to death.

CHAPTER 9

And there will be a star who will become everyone's image of the [b]Hemingway hero,
2 Including [c]Frederick Henry from [d]'Farewell to Arms,'
3 And Robert Jordan from [e]'For Whom the Bell Tolls,'
4 And [f]Billy Mitchell,
5 Not to mention [g]Sergeant York,
6 Who will all be tall and handsome and incredibly appealing,
7 As played by [h]Gary Cooper.
8 Gary will make millions and millions and millions and millions of dollars,
9 Until sometime after [i]high noon.

CHAPTER 10

And there will be another great star who will become everyone's idea of [j]Moses,
2 And [k]El Cid,
3 And [l]Andrew Jackson,
4 And [m]Michelangelo,
5 And [n]George Gordon,
6 And [o]Lewis and Clark,
7 And [p]Cardinal Richelieu,
8 Not to mention various [q]Men of the Future,
9 Who will all be tall and handsome and much larger than life,
10 As played by [r]Charlton Heston.
11 [s]In fact, it will even be discovered that when God speaks, He uses the voice of Charlton Heston,
12 Who will make millions and millions and millions and millions of dollars,
13 And become a Hollywood immortal,

a. Psong.50.3
b. F&J.11.1-7
c. Pnot.43.1-5
d. Yks.92.7-8
e. Psom.24.3
   Yks.100.12-13
f. Forg.14.16
g. Forg.14.15
h. 57.8
i. Ned.16.12-13
j. Lies.8.8-12
k. Spic.6.4-7
l. Yks.19.1-11
m. Gnt.10.1-12
n. Bks.6.17-18
o. Yks.17.1-9
p. Frog.10.5-11
q. 47.1-25
r. 57.30
s. Zig.10.11
t. Jeff.19.8
u. Frog.7.1-9
v. Russ.16.9-15
   Yks.116.16
w. Psp.1.8
x. 54.15
y. Pnot.14.1-2
z. Rom.11.1-16
aa. Gnt.10.1-12
bb. Pnot.38.1-5
cc. Ed.41.5
dd. 57.28
ee. 57.26
ff. Gnt.16.1-5

14 [t]Without actually being divine.

CHAPTER 11

And there will be a beautiful star who will become everyone's image of [u]Joan of Arc,
2 And [v]Anastasia,
3 Not to mention Gary Cooper's little [w]rabbit in 'For Whom the Bell Tolls,'
4 Who will be unbearably vulnerable and desirable,
5 As played by [x]Ingrid Bergman,
6 Who will make millions and millions and millions and millions of dollars,
7 [y]Right up to the day of the scandal.

CHAPTER 12

And there will be a very sophisticated star who will become everyone's idea of [z]Julius Caesar,
2 And [aa]Pope Julius,
3 And [bb]Henry Higgins,
4 Who will all be incredibly suave and articulate and charming,
5 As played by [cc]Rex Harrison,
6 Who will make thousands and thousands and thousands and thousands of dollars,
7 And marry millions and millions of women.

CHAPTER 13

And there also will be a beautiful pair of stars called [dd]Richard Burton and [ee]Elizabeth Taylor,
2 Who will become everyone's idea of [ff]Antony and Cleopatra,
3 Forever,
4 Until they get a divorce.

CHAPTER 14

And the truth is that almost everybody you ever heard of will be played by a big star in the movies,

2 And the whole history of the world will be staged with plywood and plaster and paint,

3 In a Hollywood back lot,

4 [a]And people everywhere will learn that Napoleon looked like [b]Rod Steiger,

5 [c]Unless it was [d]Marlon Brando he looked like,

6 And [e]Hercules looked exactly like someone named [f]Steve Reeves, who was also practically the mirror image of [g]Samson,

7 [h]And Lord Nelson was a dead ringer for Laurence Olivier,

8 Who's also the spitting image of [i]Hamlet,

9 And Abraham Lincoln actually *was* Raymond Massey,

10 [j]Just like Sherlock Holmes was really Basil Rathbone,

11 [k]And Toulouse-Lautrec looked a lot like José Ferrer walking on his knees,

12 [l]Except when José wears a huge nose, which means he's playing a Turk,

13 Or maybe a twin brother of Cyrano de Bergerac,

14 [m]And Elizabeth I of England bore a close resemblance to Bette Davis,

15 [n]And King Arthur looked exactly the way Richard Harris looks with a pageboy wig and a false beard,

16 Which is the special magic of the movies,

17 Because sometimes it takes [o]magic to make history into a believable story,

18 Which is why Hollywood will also produce great character

actors who are more realistic than good-looking,

19 Because sometimes you need someone as dogged and loyal as [p]Walter Brennan,

20 As weathered and sensible as [q]Spencer Tracy,

21 As charming and trustworthy as [r]Edward Arnold,

22 As irritatingly Irish as [s]Barry Fitzgerald,

23 As old and mysterious as [t]Sam Jaffe,

24 As weird and perverse as [u]Peter Lorre,

25 As cunning and diabolical as [v]Eric Von Stroheim,

26 As sour and cynical as [w]Oscar Levant,

27 Or as crotchety and foolish as [x]W.C. Fields,

28 Except that you can't overdo it, of course,

29 Which is why the most magical thing of all about Hollywood will be the fantastically beautiful goddesses who get to play all the most important women in history,

30 Who would probably have [y]sold their souls for the chance to look like a Hollywood movie queen,

31 Except that never in history will there be anyone as beautiful as [z]Vivien Leigh,

32 As regal as [aa]Katharine Hepburn,

33 As sensuous as [bb]Sophia Loren,

34 As breathily erotic as [cc]Marilyn Monroe,

35 As commanding as [dd]Joan Crawford,

36 As athletic as [ee]Esther Williams,

37 As earthy as [ff]Mae West,

38 As lusty as [gg]Ava Gardner,

a. 21.10
b. 57.32
c. 21.9
d. 57.16
e. Grk.6.4-6
f. 30.40
g. Lies.11.3-15
h. 21.25-26
i. Zig.10.20
j. Brit.42.24-26
k. Frog.31.8-10
l. Bks.8.8
m. 20.3
n. Brit.31.17-20
o. Ed.60.17
p. 57.14
q. 57.32
r. Ed.28.6
s. 57.14
t. Ed.38.4
u. 57.14
v. Ed.38.4
w. Ed.28.6
x. 57.14
y. Krt.7.7
z. 55.21
aa. 57.26
bb. 56.15
cc. 56.15
dd. 57.26
ee. 57.4
ff. 56.15
gg. 54.12

39 As sincere as ^aJulie Harris,

40 As fiery as ^bMaureen O'Hara,

41 As virginal as ^cDoris Day,

42 As boyish as ^dJean Seberg,

43 As graceful as ^eCyd Charisse,

44 As French as ^fBrigitte Bardot,

45 As Italian as ^gGina Lollobrigida,

46 As English as ^hJulie Andrews,

47 As German as ⁱMarlene Dietrich,

48 Or as American as ^jJune Allyson,

49 Which helps to explain why all this Hollywood magic will make history a lot more exciting and interesting than it ever was in the first place,

50 Not to mention better-looking.

CHAPTER 15

It is because of Hollywood's special magic that millions and millions of people will get a whole new perspective on important events they'd otherwise have to imagine and speculate about for themselves.

2 For example, thanks to the movies, millions and millions of Christians will finally be able to see the holy events described in the ^kNew Testament,

3 ^lIncluding the birth and boyhood of Christ,

4 ^mThrough His ministry,

5 Through the whole Passion,

6 And even through the Ascension,

7 Which is practically a Miracle.

8 Obviously, the main character in this spectacular will be Jesus

Christ, the son of God and the loving savior of all Mankind,

9 Who looks a lot like ⁿJeffrey Hunter,

10 Except in the earliest sequences, when He will be played by an infant child actor,

11 ^oWho will be born to the ^pVirgin Mary under an arc lamp in a beautiful manger set, with a lot of saintly sounding choirs ^qsinging behind the backdrop,

12 And grow to boyhood in his ^rstepfather's carpentry shop, somewhere in the desert outside Los Angeles,

13 Where Jeffrey Hunter will first show up to meet ^sJohn the Baptist,

14 And be tempted by a ^tSatanic offstage voice,

15 But will ultimately accept his calling from ^uJohn Huston to go on playing Jesus for the rest of the picture.

16 ^vWhereupon Jeffrey will go on to do many holy and miraculous things, in full view of the camera, without having anything up his sleeve,

17 ^wIncluding turn water into wine-colored water,

18 And turn his ^xstaff into a serpent, to the complete amazement of ^yHerod,

19 ^zAnd feed thousand of extras with five loaves and fishes,

20 And talk about ^{aa}peace and love, and ^{bb}love thy neighbor as thyself, and ^{cc}turn the other cheek, and ^{dd}do unto others as you would have them do unto you, and ^{ee}let him who is without sin cast the first stone, and a lot of other stuff too, just like it says in the ^{ff}Bible,

21 ^{gg}And recite some especially moving lines while passing

a. 57.4
b. 57.26
c. Ed.30.5
d. 54.15
e. Ed.28.4
f. Ed.32.4
g. Ed.32.4
h. Ed.32.4
i. Ed.32.4
j. Ed.30.5
k. Psay.5B.10
l. Jeff.24.5-9
m. Jeff.24.10-12
n. 23.22
o. Jeff.13.1-2
p. Ed.30.5
q. Psom.30.1-7
r. Ed.30.7
s. 10.10 Vin.3.10-14
t. 15.15
u. Lies.2.26-28
v. Jeff.17.3
w. Vin.51.17
x. Zig.10.13
y. 47.11 47.22
z. Ned.6.24-25
aa. Ned.8.6-8
bb. Rom.20.1-6
cc. Boul.22.1
dd. Psay.5Q.35
ee. Pnot.14.1-5
ff. Psay.5B.1
gg. Ned.42.14-17

around the prop bread and wine at the last supper,

22 [a]And have doubts while kneeling on the back lot of Gethsemane,

23 And get betrayed by [b]Ilya Kuryakin,

24 [c]And get arrested by Roman extras wearing breastplates made of aluminum foil,

25 [d]And get tried by some [e]Brit playing Pontius Pilate, who washes his hands and frees [f]Barabbas, leaving Jesus in the soup.

26 [g]And so Jeffrey gets crucified on a papier-mâché [h]Golgotha, with a lot of red corn syrup flowing from the prop nails in his hands and feet, not to mention his [i]crown of papier-mâché thorns,

27 And has his robe won by a Roman tribune in a game of [j]lots, which makes [k]Richard Burton go insane later, [l]until he gets converted to Christianity by Victor Mature, his Greek slave,

28 [m]Who was the only one who really understood the divine forgiveness of Jeffrey's love,

29 Except for [n]Michael Rennie, who denied Jesus three times before the [o]cock crowed on the morning of the Crucifixion,

30 And was forgiven anyhow, so that he could go on to become the [p]Big Fisherman,

31 Alias the [q]Pope.

32 Anyway,

33 [r]While all this is going on, the sky keeps getting darker and darker, until Jeffrey finally gives up the ghost with a lot of saintly sounding choirs [s]singing in the background, as well as a tremendous amount of special-effects [t]thunder and [u]lightning

and earthquakes and stuff going off all over the place,

34 [v]And then gets some well-earned rest in his dressing room while the [w]disciples finally get to say a few lines and [x]Judas has a big moment hanging himself from a prop tree,

35 After which the ground opens up, and Mama Ben Hur and her daughter get cured of [y]leprosy,

36 [z]And Rome burns while Nero Ustinov fiddles in appalling decadent luxury,

37 [aa]And Atlantis crumbles into the sea,

38 And [bb]Charlton Heston, in spite of all his bitterness about having been a galley slave, finally understands what Jesus's message is all about,

39 [cc]Which gets everything ready for the big resurrection scene,

40 [dd]Which isn't actually shown, but implied in a subtle cinematic way,

41 Just like the Ascension,

42 [ee]When Jeffrey returns to the right hand of the [ff]father,

43 [gg]So that he can look out for all of us,

44 [hh]And make sure that we all know he died for our sins,

45 [ii]Which saves us forever,

46 [jj]To live in peace and love and brotherhood until we die and go to heaven,

47 Unless we're [kk]heathen monsters like [ll]Stephen Boyd,

48 [mm]Who dies horribly after the chariot race,

49 [nn]Where he had a huge accident because Charlton Heston parted the Dead Sea and drowned all of Yul Brynner's charioteers,

a. Vin.57.8 Zig.9.2
b. Ed.51.22 Wil.72.10
c. Wil.72.14-15
d. F&J.13.1-9
e. 12.5
f. 18.5
g. Jeff.3.1-6
h. Psay.5X.4
i. Jeff.4.5-13
j. Ann.12.8
k. 13.1
l. Grk.26.9-10
m. Boul.22.11-12
n. 48.12
o. Psom.55.1-7
p. Vin.32.11
q. Ext.33.5
r. Jeff.14.1-8
s. Psom.31.1-6
t. Al.2.11
u. Lies.6.11
v. Jeff.4.2
w. Ned.14.4-7
x. 15.23
y. 47.25
z. Rom.18.8-9
aa. Psay.5D.10
bb. 10.10
cc. Jeff.25.1-2
dd. Jeff.25.3-7
ee. Ann.6.23
ff. Boul.15.8-11
gg. Boul.15.2-7
hh. Rom.21.12-13
ii. Krt.12.7
jj. Jeff.20.7-10
kk. Chr.2.5-8
ll. 20.44
mm. Grk.9.7
nn. Lies.8.11

50 Except ^aMarcellus, who had to have his legs cut off,

51 And then burn in hell forever.

CHAPTER 16

And that's just one example (said the camera) of the wonderful experiences that will be available to average people because of the movies.

2 ^bThe fact is that Hollywood will be there to help people through good times and bad,

3 ^cNot to mention give them a Technicolor picture of the world, themselves, and the whole course of human history,

4 All the way from the very ^dbeginning,

5 To the very ^eend,

6 Without having to look at a bunch of boring old books,

7 Ever again.

CHAPTER 17

For example, someday there will be a movie called ^f'2001 Million Years B.C.,'

2 Which will be directed by a genius named Stanley K—,

3 And starred in by a star named ^gRaquel,

4 ^hNot to mention a bunch of extras in ape costumes,

5 Who will show how everything was way back when,

6 ⁱAt the beginning,

7 ^jOr a long long time ago, anyway,

8 Before there was much of anything at all,

9 Except animals and weather and so forth,

10 Which was about all there was when civilization first got started,

11 Which happened when a

a. 20.26
47.11
20.44
b. Boul.21.9
c. Hill.A.4
d. 17.1
e. 46.46
f. Psay.5Y.29
g. 56.15
h. 47.6
i. Vin.1.1-25
j. Vin.2.1-4
k. 30.40
l. Zig.10.13
m. Yks.154.31
n. Adam.50.6
o. 47.23
p. Krt.39.14
q. Kens.1.1
r. Wil.17.1-6
s. Krt.7.5
t. Kin.5.3
u. Barb.1.1-8
v. Psay.5W.14
w. 57.36
x. Grk.8.32
y. 54.15
z. Main.22.10

^kmale friend of Raquel's picked up a ^lbig bone,

12 Or a ^mpointed stick,

13 ⁿOr something along those lines, anyway,

14 ^oAnd started smashing things with it,

15 ^pWith a whole bunch of loud German music going on,

16 In a big way.

17 This great motion-picture spectacular will show everyone what kind of an ^qanimal Man really is,

18 ^rEven if they never heard of people like Chuck and Ziggie and Frankie & Johnny and so forth,

19 ^sAnd even if they can't get over how great Raquel looks in a ^tmammoth-skin bikini.

CHAPTER 18

And in case people still don't understand what kind of an animal Mankind is,

2 There will also be movies that show everyone what it's like to be a ^ubarbarian,

3 ^vLike in a movie called 'Black Shield of the Vikings,'

4 Which will be all about a handsome young barbarian hero,

5 Played by ^wTony Curtis,

6 Who will be brought up on the steppes or somewhere like that,

7 ^xRiding a lot of horses and such,

8 And then falling in love with ^yJean Simmons,

9 Which upsets Tony's dad no end,

10 What with her not being a barbarian and all,

11 But Polish,

12 Which is different,

13 ^zFor some reason.

14 Anyway, the result is that

Tony gets kicked out of the family,

15 And goes away,

16 Until he gets kidnaped by a [a]Viking called Spartacus,

17 Played by [b]Kirk Douglas,

18 Who is planning to sack [c]Rome with a bunch of rebellious slaves,

19 Because he loves Jean Simmons so much,

20 Which explains why he gets so mad when he finds out that Tony Curtis loves her too,

21 Not to mention tying Tony up with a bunch of [d]crabs crawling all over him,

22 While Kirk goes and gets crucified the [e]Appian Way,

23 [f]For some reason,

24 Which makes Jean Simmons cry,

25 Thus proving who she really loved all along,

26 Even though Tony finally gets away from the crabs and goes to help the Poles fight against his own people,

27 Because he loves Jean so much,

28 Which doesn't cut any ice with his dad at all,

29 [g]And explains why Yul Brynner shoots Tony through the heart,

30 So that he doesn't get the girl in the end,

31 Or even a topknot.

CHAPTER 19

And there will also be great movies about the days when [h]knighthood was in flower,

2 [i]Which will show everyone how much better things got after the barbarians settled down and became civilized,

3 Like in a movie called 'The

a. *Barb.1.13-14*
b. *57.30*
c. *Barb.4.5-7*
d. *Ed.60.10*
e. *Carl.3.8*
f. *Psay.5Q.57*
g. *Ann.18.17*
h. *Psay.5W.12-13*
i. *Chr.8.1-4*
j. *57.6*
k. *55.21*
l. *57.34*
m. *Pnot.39.3-5*
n. *20.26*
o. *Chr.8.5-11*
p. *Psom.55.3-7*
q. *8.7*
r. *Chr.6.7*
   Spic.7.12
s. *19.8*
t. *57.22*
u. *Psom.69.3*
v. *54.15*
w. *Krt.11.20*
x. *Gnt.1.13*
y. *Barb.4.18*
z. *57.26*
aa. *8.7*
bb. *Spic.11.6*

Adventures of Ivanhood,'

4 Starring [j]Robert Taylor,

5 As the handsome young British knight who falls in love with a beautiful Jewess,

6 Played by [k]Elizabeth Taylor,

7 Who is being pursued by the Sheriff of Nottingham,

8 Played by [l]Basil Rathbone,

9 Until she has to take refuge in [m]Sherwood Forest,

10 Because [n]King Richard the Lion-hearted is out of town,

11 [o]For some reason.

12 Then, on the day of the great [p]archery contest,

13 [q]Errol Flynn gets captured,

14 And Basil tries to [r]burn Elizabeth Taylor at the stake,

15 Except that Ivanhood shows up at the last minute and fights the big duel with the [s]evil villain,

16 While all the Merry Men,

17 Including [t]Alan Hale,

18 [u]Free Errol and beat the tar out of the Sheriff's men,

19 Until Ivanhood rides into the sunset with [v]Olivia De Havilland,

20 [w]For some reason.

CHAPTER 20

And there will also be movies about the great rush to make history during the [x]Renaissance,

2 Which will show everyone just how civilized things could get in great [y]European nations like Britain,

3 Like in a movie called 'Queen Elizabeth, Queen of Scots,'

4 Which will be all about how [z]Bette Davis beat the Spanish and made the Brits strong,

5 With the help of a pirate named [aa]Errol Flynn who sinks the [bb]Spanish Armada,

6 Not to mention whispering

some sweet nothings to the queen,

7 Who was really quite a nice woman except when she got mad,

8 Which made her look like ^aFlora Robson,

9 Until she was so irate that she insisted on beheading ^bOlivia De Havilland,

10 Unless it was ^cSir Walter Raleigh she beheaded,

11 Or maybe ^dPaul Scofield,

12 Except that *he* was beheaded by ^eRobert Shaw,

13 Unless it was ^fCharles Laughton,

14 Who was Queen Elizabeth's father,

15 And taught her everything he knew,

16 ^gEspecially the beheading part,

17 But not including the part about how to get married a whole bunch of times,

18 Which explains how Britain got to be so Great,

19 Way back when,

20 All except for the part about ^hShakespeare, of course,

21 Because there just won't ever be a great enough actor to play the greatest genius who ever lived,

22 Which will be kind of a shame for the motion-picture audience,

23 ⁱNot to mention ironic,

24 Since they'd have a better chance to learn more about him if he'd been just a little bit less great,

25 Because Hollywood could do wonders with a slightly more human version of the Bard,

26 Who might be played by ^jRichard Burton,

a. 30.9
b. 54.15
c. 8.7
d. 57.24
e. 57.32
f. 7.5
g. Ann.6.23
  Dav.47.23
h. Brit.32.1
i. Brit.36.2
j. 13.1
k. 46.19
l. 57.24
m. 57.32
n. 57.10
o. Ed.38.4
p. 57.34
q. 18.5
r. 57.32
s. 57.16
t. 57.28

27 What with both of them being actors and pretty opinioniated to boot,

28 And who might be played by ^kAlec Guinness,

29 What with both of them occasionally playing female roles,

30 And who might be played by ^lRonald Colman,

31 What with both of them having such a flair for tragedy,

32 And who might be played by ^mPeter Ustinov,

33 What with both of them being playwrights,

34 And who might be played by ⁿLeslie Howard,

35 What with both of them being so darned poetic and sensitive,

36 And who might be played by ^oJohn Gielgud,

37 What with both of them being so bald and wise,

38 And who might be played by ^pDavid Niven,

39 What with both of them being so sophisticated and mustachioed about everything,

40 And who might be played by ^qCary Grant,

41 What with both of them being so witty with words,

42 And who might be played by ^rGeorge Sanders,

43 What with both of them being as British as Stonehenge somehow,

44 And who might be played by ^sStephen Boyd,

45 What with both of them knowing so much about power and ambition,

46 And who might even be played by ^tCharles Boyer,

47 What with both of them being so romantic about love,

48 Except that nobody can have

all of these great qualities,

49 Except Shakespeare, of course,

50 Which is why Hollywood will never be able to plug up this enormous hole in the history of our forebears,

51 And won't even try.

CHAPTER 21

And there will even be some great movies about the Frogs,

2 Which will show everyone just how glorious war can be,

3 Especially a movie called 'War and Something,'

4 Which will be all about Napoleon Bonaparte,

5 And some of the Russians who fought against him,

6 Such as Natasha,

7 Who will be played by [a]Audrey Hepburn,

8 Even though the one Napoleon really loves is [b]Jean Simmons,

9 [c]Who thinks Napoleon looks just like Marlon Brando,

10 [d]Unless it's really Rod Steiger he looks like,

11 But in any case, Josephine thinks he's great,

12 Unless her name is really Desirée,

13 Which it couldn't be,

14 Because Napoleon loves Josephine,

15 [e]Which everyone knows from history,

16 Right up to the day he lost everything at [f]Waterloo,

17 [g]And had to be exiled to somewhere or other,

18 [h]Which happened after the big scene with all the bare feet in the bloody snow outside Moscow,

a. 55.21
b. 18.8
c. 14.5
d. 14.4
e. Frog.16.9-12
f. Frog.18.12
g. Frog.18.14-20
h. Frog.17.1-12
i. Krt.20.1-4
j. 21.12
k. Ed.60.10
l. Yks.135.21
m. Brit.23.12-13
n. 57.20
o. Pnot.14.1-2
p. 14.31
q. 21.26
r. Psay.5Q.62
s. 21.12
t. 21.3
u. Psong.41.1-3
v. Yks.39.2

19 [i]Not to mention the sunken road,

20 Which Marlon would have seen if he hadn't been thinking about [j]Jean so much,

21 And would have done something about,

22 Instead of sit down on a [k]log and do nothing,

23 [l]Which is the worst thing a soldier can do,

24 Even if he's desperately in love,

25 Because there was a Brit admiral named [m]Lord Nelson,

26 Played by [n]Laurence Olivier,

27 Who wasn't doing nothing,

28 Even though he loved [o]Lady Hamilton in the worst way,

29 What with her being [p]Vivien Leigh and all,

30 But that didn't stop [q]Laurence from being the star of Trafalgar,

31 And dying victoriously in the arms of his assistant right there on the poop deck,

32 [r]Thus explaining why Napoleon lost out in the end,

33 Including [s]Jean,

34 And the whole Frog empire too,

35 Which shows why [t]'War and Something' will be one of the greatest movies ever made,

36 Although it won't be *the* greatest movie ever made,

37 Because that's another movie altogether,

38 Called [u]'How the War Was Won.'

CHAPTER 22

Yes, there will be a truly mega-spectacular block-buster that will show everyone what happened in the American [v]Civil War,

2 So that no one will ever forget it,

3 No matter how much they might want to,

4 [a]Although they won't want to,

5 Because it will be a great movie featuring the greatest part ever offered to a woman in Hollywood,

6 Which will be played by [b]Vivien Leigh,

7 Not to mention a supporting cast led by [c]Butterfly McQueen,

8 And co-starring [d]Raymond Massey,

9 And a bunch of other stars too,

10 Including John Wayne as [e]General Sherman,

11 And some more average-looking guy as [f]General Grant,

12 Played by somebody like [g]Harry Morgan,

13 And [h]George Peppard as the son who would grow up to become a stupendously wealthy carpetbagger,

14 And [i]Carroll Baker as George's mother,

15 [j]For some reason,

16 And [k]Debbie Reynolds as the dance hall girl with a heart of gold,

17 And [l]Gregory Peck as the riverboat gambler with a heart of gold,

18 And even some Brits,

19 [m]For some reason.

20 Anyway,

21 It will be all about a girl named [n]Scarlett,

22 Who lives in a place called [o]Tara,

23 [p]Down south somewhere,

24 [q]In Cinerama,

25 [r]With a bunch of happy comical slaves with funny voices,

26 Including a maid called Sissy,

27 And a butler called [s]Rhett Rochester,

28 Who don't always get treated just exactly right by Miss Scarlett,

29 [t]Who doesn't exactly have a heart of gold,

30 Probably because she's so [u]beautiful,

31 In spite of being a Brit,

32 Which maybe explains why she loves a little pansy Brit called [v]Ashley,

33 [w]Who goes off to fight in the Civil War,

34 Which is started, very sadly, by [x]President Massey, who holds his head in his hands a lot,

35 Leaving Scarlett all alone with [y]Olivia De Havilland,

36 Who is a real pain in the neck,

37 [z]Especially when Mr. Lincoln tells [aa]John Wayne to burn the back lot of Atlanta completely to the ground,

38 [bb]In Technicolor,

39 Which smudges everyone's face,

40 Not to mention everyone's disappointment about how [cc]Olivia De Havilland didn't get killed in the fire,

41 [dd]Which means Scarlett isn't ever going to get her hands on Ashley,

42 Who is incredibly loyal to his wife,

43 Just like all Confederate Brits everywhere.

44 Meanwhile, [ee]Clark Gable is busy running the union blockade,

45 On a great big ship called the Bounty,

a. *Yks.43.5-13*
b. *14.31*
c. *Ed.71.11*
d. *14.9*
e. *Yks.44.19-26*
f. *Yks.42.1-15*
g. *Ed.30.7*
h. *57.34*
i. *39.21*
j. *Zig.6.5*
k. *Ed.27.3*
l. *57.28*
m. *Hill.A.4*
n. *Lies.2.20*
o. *Ed.46.17*
p. *Yks.50.2-7*
q. *22.38*
r. *Yks.50.8*
s. *Ed.71.11*
t. *Jeff.19.8*
u. *Ann.11.1*
v. *20.34*
w. *Psay.5Q.78*
x. *22.8*
y. *19.19*
z. *Yks.44.31-41*
aa. *22.10*
bb. *22.24*
cc. *22.35*
dd. *Psay.5Q.23*
ee. *57.22
14.5*

46 Which has a really nasty [a]captain,
47 [b]Played by Charles Laughton,
48 Who flogs everybody all the time,
49 Until there's a mutiny,
50 Starring [c]Clark Gable,
51 Which keeps him so busy that he doesn't get around to seducing Scarlett until sometime after the end of the war,
52 [d]Which happens when Raymond Massey says "malice toward none" and all that,
53 [e]And gets shot at Ford's Theater,
54 [f]Causing the north to get really nasty about Reconstruction,
55 [g]So that Scarlett has to wear curtains,
56 [h]And Clark Gable has to marry her,
57 [i]Because she doesn't have any money,
58 [j]And Clark has lots and lots of money from running the blockade in the Bounty,
59 [k]Which Scarlett needs for clothes,
60 What with her being a Brit and all,
61 [l]Until she has a little girl,
62 Played ever so charmingly by Shirley Temple,
63 Who has a terrible accident just like in 'Ryan O'Lyndon,'
64 Which ruins everything,
65 So that Clark doesn't give a damn any more,
66 Even if tomorrow *is* another day.

CHAPTER 23

There will be other great movies about America after the Civil War,

a.	7.3
b.	7.5
c.	22.44
d.	Yks.46.9-14
e.	Yks.46.15-17
f.	Yks.47.15-23
g.	Ann.11.2
h.	Ann.11.3
i.	Psong.14.1-3
j.	Psong.26.1-2
k.	Adam.47.2-3
l.	Mawr.19.3
m.	Yks.54.1-3
n.	Yks.27.8-12
o.	57.30
p.	57.18
q.	57.4
r.	23.31
s.	57.32
t.	23.31
u.	19.17
v.	54.15
w.	8.7
x.	14.40
y.	19.19
z.	57.20
aa.	57.8
bb.	23.18
cc.	Yks.52.26-30
dd.	Psom.39.1-6
ee.	Barb.1.8

2 Like with the wild west and all,
3 [m]Including fighting the Indians,
4 [n]And settling the wide open spaces,
5 And other great stuff like that,
6 Including a movie called 'They Died with Yellow Ribbons On,'
7 Which will be directed by John Ford,
8 And will show how it was to be a soldier in a fort out west,
9 With a bunch of U.S. Cavalry heroes and their pioneer friends,
10 Starring [o]John Wayne as the star of the show, of course,
11 And co-starring [p]Henry Fonda,
12 [q]Vera Miles,
13 [r]Woody Strode,
14 [s]Lee Marvin,
15 [t]Ward Bond,
16 [u]Alan Hale,
17 And [v]Natalie Wood,
18 Not to mention [w]Errol Flynn,
19 [x]Maureen O'Hara,
20 [y]Olivia De Havilland,
21 And [z]William Holden,
22 And with [aa]Jeffrey Hunter in a particularly choice part.
23 It will be Henry Fonda who plays the colonel, of course,
24 While John Wayne plays the loyal sergeant who has seen it all,
25 Except for the part where [bb]General Custer rides out and gets himself massacred at the Little Big Horn,
26 With his boots on,
27 [cc]Which riles up the Indians so much that they raid all the pioneer settlements and steal Natalie Wood,
28 [dd]Who has to be rescued,
29 [ee]But only after the big fu-

neral scene in Monument Valley,

30 Where John Wayne and William Holden and Jeffrey Hunter form a ᵃposse to go get Natalie,

31 ᵇTaking Woody Strode and Ward Bond with them,

32 While Vera and Shirley Temple stay back at the fort waiting,

33 ᶜWhich explains why John and Bill and Jeff take Maureen O'Hara with them when they stop at her house along the way,

34 ᵈBecause the Indians are chasing them and they can't afford to leave her behind,

35 ᵉEven though she's headstrong and doesn't want to go,

36 ᶠUntil she finally figures out what a fine, brave, strong, loyal man John Wayne is,

37 ᵍExcept that he's planning to kill Natalie when he finds her,

38 ʰBecause she's been living with Indian savages for so many years now,

39 iAnd besides, the Indians have scalped practically everybody at the fort,

40 ʲIncluding Henry Fonda,

41 ᵏWhich means the posse is now completely cut off,

42 ˡAnd has to make a big stand all alone in Monument Valley,

43 ᵐUntil another regiment of the U.S. Cavalry arrives at the last second,

44 ⁿWhich convinces John not to kill Natalie,

45 Who has grown up to be an extremely beautiful young woman anyway,

46 And eventually goes back into the house with her family,

47 While John waits outside,

48 ᵒFramed by the open doorway,

a. *Kens.12.11-15*
b. *Ed.45.4*
c. *Mawr.22.20*
d. *Mawr.22.21*
e. *Mawr.22.22*
f. *Mawr.22.23*
g. *Mawr.22.24*
h. *Mawr.22.25*
i. *Mawr.22.26*
j. *Mawr.22.27*
k. *Mawr.22.28*
l. *Mawr.22.29*
m. *Mawr.22.30*
n. *Boul.21.9*
o. *Zig.8.10-12*
p. *Psay.5Q.62*
q. *26.5*
r. *24.26-27*
s. *Hill.V.9*
   Rat.7.10
t. *Ext.52.16*
u. *Psong.56.1-2*
v. *Psay.5A.31*
w. *Yks.29.3*
x. *Yks.29.4*

49 ᵖThinking about all the things he's going to do when he finds Maureen O'Hara again,

50 Except that she marries ᑫJimmy Stewart instead,

51 ʳAfter Jimmy gets so famous for killing ˢLee Marvin,

52 ᵗEven though it was really John who killed Lee Marvin,

53 And then dies all alone with his secret,

54 Of course,

55 ᵘExcept that Jimmy Stewart and Woody Strode come to the funeral,

56 Not to mention Maureen O'Hara,

57 Unless it was Vera Miles instead,

58 Which it must have been,

59 ᵛBecause Maureen would have married John over Jimmy any day,

60 Unless she had married Jeffrey Hunter first,

61 Which must be what happened,

62 Because John Ford wouldn't make a mistake like that,

63 Which explains why all his movies will be great,

64 Just like this one will be,

65 Someday.

CHAPTER 24

Of course, John Ford won't be the only director who will make movies about the wild west,

2 Because there will be lots and lots of movies about the west,

3 Including movies about outlaws,

4 Gunfighters,

5 ʷCattlemen,

6 ˣSheep farmers,

7 Pioneer wagon trains,

8 Gamblers,

9 Sheriffs,
10 ^aMarshals,
11 Pony Express riders,
12 And stagecoach drivers,
13 Not to mention the U.S. Cavalry and the Indians,
14 And a bunch of other stuff too.
15 All of these movies will star John Wayne,
16 Who will always win,
17 And kill all the bad guys,
18 ^bUntil he dies at the Alamo,
19 Which will give some other stars a chance to do westerns,
20 Including stars like Gary Cooper and ^cAlan Ladd and Jimmy Stewart,
21 Who will always make movies in which they have to face the evil gunmen all alone,
22 Which they will do,
23 Because if they ever don't know what to do, they can always look at a John Wayne movie and find out,
24 Which explains why Shane will kill ^dJack Palance,
25 And why ^eGary Cooper will kill all the bad guys except for the one ^fGrace Kelly has to kill,
26 And ^gJimmy Stewart will reluctantly strap on his gun and walk out into the street with no hope of winning,
27 Except that somehow he will always survive,
28 ^hAnd show the bad guys what it means to have real character,
29 Which is also why he will always get to marry Vera Miles in the end,
30 Unless it's really ⁱJune Allyson instead.

CHAPTER 25

^jEventually, Hollywood will even get around to making

a. 9.9
b. Yks.30.20-36
c. 57.12
d. 52.4
e. 9.7
f. 39.10
g. 26.5
h. Ed.40.6-8
i. 14.48
j. Ned.6.24
k. Yks.95.3-4
l. Jefs.7.46
m. Frog.35.4
n. 57.8
o. Psong.16.4
p. Ed.30.5
q. 14.21 14.27
r. Psom.6.2-3
s. F&J.14.13
t. Adam.36.5
u. 57.26

movies about America that don't take place in the wild west,
2 Which just shows how great and creative the motion picture business will become,
3 ^kBecause when everything else in America falls apart during the Great Depression,
4 The movies will find all kinds of exciting ways to distract and entertain the public,
5 And even educate them about important things in life,
6 ^lWithout forcing them to read a lot of dull books.

CHAPTER 26

For example, there will be a great movie director named Frank,
2 Who will show everybody that life is really okay,
3 ^mEven if you're having a Great Depression,
4 Which he will do in a movie called 'John Doe's Wonderful Life in Washington,'
5 Starring ⁿJimmy Stewart,
6 Who will play a typical small-town saint,
7 Just like you'll find in every small town all over America,
8 ^oWho runs a small savings and loan business,
9 And is planning to marry ^pDonna Reed,
10 Until his ^quncle loses all the money,
11 ^rAnd everything falls apart,
12 ^sWhich convinces Jimmy that he should jump off the ^ttallest building in New York,
13 Except that he doesn't know that ^uBarbara Stanwyck set the whole thing up,
14 In collusion with the evil banker,

313

15 Played by [a]Lionel Barrymore,
16 [b]Who is planning to take over Jimmy's savings and loan after he jumps,
17 Until Jimmy finds out what's going on,
18 [c]And gets so depressed that he tries to jump off a bridge instead,
19 [d]Until an angel shows up and proves that Jimmy's life is important,
20 [e]Which causes Jimmy to make a very moving speech,
21 [f]Until the money is magically returned and everyone loves Jimmy so much that they send him to Congress,
22 Where he has a lot of exciting adventures,
23 [g]And does everything you could possibly think of to help the little people,
24 [h]Because it's so important to always help other people and be honest and not corrupt,
25 [i]Not to mention humble and grateful,
26 [j]Since life isn't nearly as bad as it looks sometimes,
27 Especially in the movies.

CHAPTER 27

Of course, sometimes life is every bit as bad as it looks,
2 [k]Which is why some directors will make movies about how bad life can be,
3 To show everybody that the capitalist system doesn't work that well for everybody,
4 [l]For example, all the poor rural people who had to eat dirt and old sawdust in the depression,
5 Like [m]Henry Fonda will do in a movie called 'The Grapes of Tobacco Road,'
6 Which won't have any grapes in it,
7 But a whole bunch of suffering instead,
8 By a whole bunch of noble Okies,
9 Including Henry and his parents [n]Ma and Pa Kettle,
10 [o]Who have to go to California because their home state blew away in a dust storm,
11 Which was one of the bad things [p]Herbert Hoover did to cause the Great Depression,
12 And which everybody will come to know about,
13 Because of Henry's terribly moving performance,
14 Which would just break your heart,
15 [q]If only you could understand his ridiculous white trash accent.

CHAPTER 28

And for people who just want to get away from real life for a while,
2 Hollywood will also produce a lot of musicals during the Great Depression,
3 [r]Which will have almost no plots at all,
4 Just like the old [s]Busby Berkeley movies,
5 But no one will ever notice because there will be lots of singing and dancing,
6 By a star named [t]Fred Astaire,
7 Who will always wear tails, a top hat, and a blonde named [u]Ginger Rogers,
8 [v]While he sings a bunch of great songs written by a genius named Cole Porter,

a. 57.32
b. Psong.53.7
c. Yks.100.13
d. 26.3
e. Psom.51.1-6
f. Psong.37.1
g. Ann.16.26-27 Adam.41.8-9
h. Ned.29.24
i. Jefs.7.14
j. Mall.13.27
k. Yks.100.3-4
l. Adam.27.8
m. 23.11
n. Ed.64.8
o. Ann.6.23
p. Yks.96.1-7
q. Brit.31.12
r. F&J.15.2-4
s. Gnt.8.2-3
t. Ed.60.10
u. 56.15
v. Psom.9.9-10

9 [a]And dances up a storm at the
Ritz,
10 Which everyone will get a
big kick out of,
11 Forever,
12 Or at least until people start
liking T-shirts better than tails.

CHAPTER 29

There will also be a bunch of
comedies during the Great
Depression,
2 Which will have hilarious
stars like the Marx Brothers,
3 Who will make a lot of very
funny movies,
4 [b]Including one called 'Duck-
feathers,'
5 Which will be all about how
[c]silly war is,
6 [d]With a lot of interchangeable
parts played by Groucho and
Chico and Harpo and Carlo,
7 Not to mention a lot of jokes
about fascism,
8 [e]Which is very very funny,
9 Especially when [f]Charlie
Chaplin is playing the dictator,
10 And trying to keep the globe
away from the Marxes,
11 Who are just all over the
place,
12 Including the comic opera,
13 And the [g]racetrack,
14 And everywhere else too,
15 Not to mention the ridiculous
matron played by [h]Margaret Du-
mont,
16 Who has Groucho all over
the place,
17 Which explains why his back
is permanently bent out of
shape,
18 [i]Even though the Hays office
will never be able to prove it,
19 Which shows why the name
Marx will become practically a
synonym for "genius."

CHAPTER 30

But there's more than one
way to get away from real
life,
2 Which is why there will also
be monster movies,
3 [j]Because there have always
been things that go bump in the
night,
4 [k]And dark things that live inside everybody's nightmares,
5 [l]Including things so dark and
evil that Hollywood will have to
go all the way to Europe to find
actors who can play them,
6 Like Transylvania,
7 [m]Which is where a lot of the
worst nightmares come from,
8 [n]Such as monsters called vampires, who suck the blood of
virgins and can only be killed by
a wooden stake through the
heart,
9 Which will be played by [o]Bela
Lugosi,
10 In movies like 'Dracula
Meets Frankenstein's Wolfman,'
11 [p]Where there are terrible
things going on in the [q]castle,
12 [r]So that the poor villagers
have to sleep with their pitchforks under their pillow,
13 Just in case,
14 [s]Because when the moon is
full, Bela will start attacking the
tender white necks of [t]virgins,
15 Which is the signal for all the
villagers to run to the castle
gates with [u]flaming torches and
pitchforks,
16 [v]And make a gigantic
ruckus,
17 Even though that won't even
faze Bela,
18 [w]Who can go anywhere anytime he wants,

a. Ann.10.1
b. Grk.8.32
c. Swar.23.4-6
d. Gods.4.10
e. Spic.15.2-3
f. Ed.27.3
g. Grk.8.32
h. 54.12
i. Pnot.28.5
j. Zig.10.11
k. Zig.8.2-5
l. Zig.9.2
m. Zig.10.11
n. Zig.4.1-5
o. Ed.28.6
p. Zig.11.6
q. Ed.60.10
r. Zig.10.10
s. Zig.10.10
t. 48.10
u. Zig.10.13
v. Zig.7.3
w. Zig.14.3

19 [a]After dark anyway,
20 [b]Because he will turn into a bat and fly away,
21 [c]Unless he turns into a wolf instead,
22 Which is what he will do in this movie,
23 [d]Because [e]Frankenstein is doing dark and terrible things in the castle down the street,
24 [f]Including wake up the fearful Wolfman,
25 As played by [g]Lon Chaney, Jr.,
26 [h]Because it turns out that the monster is getting lonely,
27 As played by [i]Boris Karloff,
28 [j]And hasn't been sleeping since his wife died in that terrible fire,
29 [k]Which the villagers never even apologized for,
30 [l]Explaining why it will serve them right when the Monster and the Wolfman go on a rampage,
31 [m]Especially when Bela gets into the act,
32 [n]Because vampires don't like to be upstaged by anybody,
33 [o]Particularly when the supply of virgins is getting low,
34 [p]And so little by little everything builds up to the terrifying climax,
35 [q]When Bela and Boris and Lon are all staggering across the screen at once,
36 [r]And the virgin is screaming,
37 [s]And the villagers are brandishing their pitchforks, not to mention a bunch of wooden stakes and [t]guns with silver bullets,
38 [u]And Dr. Frankenstein is going psycho because of all the weird thunder and lightning in his laboratory,
39 [v]When suddenly the entire Transylvanian countryside is darkened by the dread shadow of [w]King Kong,
40 [x]As played by a [y]stuffed mechanical ape,
41 [z]Which stomps everybody flat,
42 Including Dracula,
43 And the Wolfman,
44 And the Frankenstein monster,
45 And Dr. Frankenstein,
46 And even some of the uglier-looking villagers,
47 But not the virgin, of course,
48 [aa]Because nightmares aren't allowed to kill virgins,
49 In Hollywood, anyway,
50 [bb]No matter how much they scream.

CHAPTER 31

When war finally comes, though, Hollywood will stop trying to be so escapist,
2 And work hard at making movies that inspire people to win the war,
3 Like showing everybody how [cc]John Wayne could win the whole war all by himself,
4 If he weren't so busy making movies,
5 Including one called 'Back to Iwo Jima,'
6 [dd]Which will be all about fighting the Nips in the South Pacific,
7 Not to mention one called 'The Longest D-Day,'
8 [ee]Which will be all about fighting the Krauts in Europe,
9 Because as long as John Wayne is on your side, it doesn't matter who you're fighting,
10 Since nobody has a chance against John Wayne,
11 [ff]Who is brave and strong and moral and determined,

a. F&J.14.13
b. Grk.11.1-2
c. Grk.11.3-6
d. Zig.15.3
e. 14.25
f. F&J.14.13
g. 30.40
h. Zig.10.12
i. 40.9
j. Zig.7.7
k. Zig.7.8
l. Zig.7.9
m. Zig.7.10
n. Zig.7.11
o. F&J.14.13
p. Zig.7.14
q. Zig.7.15
r. Zig.7.16
s. Zig.7.3
t. Ed.45.13-14
u. F&J.14.13
v. Zig.16.3
w. Psay.5Z.8-11
x. Zig.4.12
y. Ed.60.10
z. Zig.12.7
aa. Zig.9.2
bb. Zig.10.11
cc. 23.10
dd. Nips.22.5-7
ee. Yks.114.1-12
ff. Yks.139.20-24

12 [a]And will always get even with the enemy,

13 No matter how much it costs,

14 Which could turn out to be a lot,

15 Because these will all be big-budget pictures.

CHAPTER 32

There will also be a war movie called 'The Big Casablanca,'

2 Which will be great,

3 Because it will show everybody how romantic it is to be an American expatriate named Marlowe,

4 As played by [b]Humphrey Bogart,

5 Who has to beat the Nazis by getting the [c]Maltese falcon away from [d]Sydney Greenstreet,

6 While wearing a trench coat instead of a uniform,

7 Which isn't easy,

8 Especially when you're being distracted by [e]Ingrid Bergman,

9 [f]Who is so vulnerable and desirable that she can make you propose silly [g]toasts in Paris,

10 And even make you look like you could cry at the [h]railroad station,

11 Except that Humphrey Bogart never cries,

12 Ever,

13 [i]Just like all American men,

14 And will get over it eventually,

15 [j]Even if it takes a few drinks to do it,

16 And even if [k]Sam has to play [l]it again every once in a while,

17 Until some [m]female Frog sings the Marseillaise and reminds everyone that [n]nothing

a. *Yks.130.6*
b. *57.22*
c. *Ed.60.10*
d. *14.25*
e. *11.5*
f. *11.4*
g. *Psom.44.7*
h. *Psom.77.9*
i. *Psay.5V.20*
j. *Yks.93.11*
k. *Ed.71.11*
l. *Main.22.10*
　F&J.15.13
　Ned.16.12
m. *20.8*
n. *Main.23.3*
o. *22.66*
p. *Ned.29.24*
q. *Psong.6.12*
r. *Frog.38.7-8*
s. *57.8*
t. *Psom.76.1-6*
u. *31.5-8*
v. *Ed.51.22*
w. *Psay.5J.11*
x. *Psay.5J.25*
y. *Psay.5J.7*
z. *Psay.5J.28*
aa. *Psay.5J.4*
bb. *Ed.49.5*

amounts to a hill of beans in this world except beating the Krauts,

18 Because if you don't do the right thing,

19 [o]You might not regret it today or tomorrow,

20 [p]But you'll regret it soon and for the rest of your life,

21 [q]Which is why Ingrid will have to get on the plane for Lisbon,

22 [r]And why Humphrey will join the resistance with his suave French pal,

23 As played by [s]Claude Rains,

24 Thus proving why the Krauts won't have a [t]prayer of winning the war,

25 [u]Especially with John Wayne handling all the rough stuff in both theaters,

26 [v]And Humphrey handling all the tricky undercover stuff in his trenchcoat.

CHAPTER 33

But Hollywood won't take a vacation even after John and Humphrey have won the war,

2 Which they will do, of course,

3 With just a little bit of help from a very photogenic B-17 crew made up of an [w]Italian from the South Bronx, a blond [x]farm boy from Iowa, a short [y]Jew from Brooklyn, a [z]cracker from Alabama, and a brawling [aa]Mick from Boston.

4 In fact, motion-picture directors will start making more movies about real problems that maybe can't be completely solved in an hour and a half,

5 [bb]Such as the problems the B-17 crew will have when it comes home,

6 And can't find a job,

7 Or a house,

8 Or much of anything else,

9 ^aBecause the capitalist system is so selfish,

10 ^bAnd causes little people to get it in the neck,

11 No matter how much they've contributed to society,

12 ^cEven if what they've contributed is the best years of their lives.

CHAPTER 34

Not that all the movies will be gloomy in the years after Hollywood's defeat of the Nazis and the Nips,

2 ^dBecause it will be discovered that there were certain battles and even certain branches of the armed forces that John Wayne wasn't in yet,

3 And so he'll have to be a Seabee,

4 And a pilot,

5 And an admiral,

6 And he'll have to keep fighting World War II until everyone is satisfied that it's safe for their favorite stars to get into the war too,

7 Which they will do,

8 So that there will be millions and millions of World War II movies,

9 ^eWhich will cover everything completely,

10 Including every theater and front and battle and nation you could ever think of,

11 Not to mention every star you could ever think of,

12 Including ^fBurt Lancaster, who will get into the war at ^gPearl Harbor and fight them on the beaches and everywhere else

a. Psong.4.1-5
b. Yks.154.43
c. Psp.1.8
d. Zig.10.21
e. Yks.128.13
f. 57.20
g. Yks.106.6-14
h. Frog.38.7-8
i. 57.13
j. Psay.5G.7
k. 57.6
l. Yks.110.8
m. 41.23
n. 20.38
o. 57.16
p. 14.25
q. 30.40
r. Jefs.7.46

too, from here to eternity, until he finally starts the ^hFrench Resistance and single-handedly saves the greatest art treasures of France from the Nazis,

13 And ⁱJames Cagney, who will be ^jAdmiral Halsey for as long as it takes to beat the Nips in the South Pacific,

14 And ^kGregory Peck, who will be ^lDouglas MacArthur right up to the moment when the general does his big fadeout, except for when he takes time out to help ^mAnthony Quinn and ⁿDavid Niven drive the Nazis out of Greece,

15 And even ^oFrank Sinatra, who—being a lot smaller than John Wayne—will actually die in World War II, at Pearl Harbor and in Germany and maybe even in the South Pacific too,

16 But not before he has slaughtered millions and millions of Nazis,

17 Played by ^pMaximilian Schell,

18 Not to mention millions and millions of Nips,

19 Played by ^qToshiro Mifune,

20 And Hollywood is once again safe for democracy,

21 Which won't be all bad for John Wayne,

22 ^rBecause when everybody else starts helping out in World War II, it will free up John to go back and make more westerns,

23 Just to make sure that there isn't a territory,

24 Or an Indian war,

25 Or a range war,

26 Or a western law enforcement agency,

27 That didn't have John Wayne in it,

28 Doing things the American Way,

29 Way back when.

CHAPTER 35

But believe it or not, there will be people who eventually get tired of John Wayne,

2 ᵃIncluding a whole bunch of Hollywood producers and directors,

3 ᵇWho will come to believe that the public wants to see some other kind of hero,

4 ᶜLike someone who maybe isn't six feet five inches tall,

5 ᵈSomeone who maybe isn't always neat and clean and completely sure about what's right,

6 ᵉAnd who maybe isn't always bigger and tougher than every problem he runs into,

7 ᶠAnd who maybe isn't even always a hero,

8 ᵍBut maybe an antihero instead,

9 ʰWith a lot of personal problems,

10 ⁱAnd bad posture,

11 ʲAnd a bunch of sleeveless T-shirts,

12 ᵏAnd an attitude,

13 ˡAnd some kind of a speech impediment.

14 ᵐFor example, there will be a great big star who will have all these things,

15 ⁿIn spades,

16 ᵒAnd will make a great movie called 'East of a Giant Rebel,'

17 ᵖWhich will be all about what it's like to be an American teenager with personal problems, bad posture, a bunch of sleeveless T-shirts, an attitude, and a speech impediment,

18 ᑫAs played by ʳJames Dean.

19 ˢThis movie will turn out to be such a big success that it will create a huge demand for other new stars with the same great appeal,

20 ᵗIncluding a star who will rocket to fame because of his performance in a movie called 'The Wild Waterfront,'

21 ᵘWhich will be all about what it's like to be an informer with personal problems, bad posture, a bunch of sleeveless T-shirts, an attitude, and a speech impediment,

22 ᵛAs played by ʷMarlon Brando,

23 ˣAs well as a star who will become a big success in a movie called 'Somebody Up There Likes Hustlers,'

24 ʸWhich will be all about what it's like to be an Italian pool player with personal problems, bad posture, a bunch of sleeveless T-shirts, an attitude, and a speech impediment,

25 As played by ᶻPaul Newman.

26 It will even turn out that there's big money in teaching young actors how to talk with a speech impediment,

27 Because so many movies will require it,

28 Which will eventually be called "The Method,"

29 ᵃᵃFor some reason,

30 And will be used by lots and lots of actors,

29 Including even an actor who will become a big star without actually being able to talk with a speech impediment,

31 ᵇᵇWhich he will overcome by not uttering any dialogue on screen,

---

a. *Mawr.25.1*
b. *Mawr.25.2*
c. *Mawr.25.3*
d. *Mawr.25.4*
e. *Mawr.25.5*
f. *Mawr.25.6*
g. *Mawr.25.7*
h. *Mawr.25.8*
i. *Mawr.25.9*
j. *Mawr.25.10*
k. *Mawr.25.11*
l. *Mawr.25.12*
m. *Mawr.25.13*
n. *Mawr.25.14*
o. *Mawr.25.15*
p. *Mawr.25.16*
q. *57.14*
r. *Mawr.25.17*
s. *Mawr.25.18*
t. *Mawr.25.19*
u. *Mawr.25.20*
v. *Mawr.25.21*
w. *Ed.63.3*
x. *Mawr.25.22*
y. *Mawr.25.23*
z. *57.16*
aa. *Jefs.7.15-19*
bb. *Psay.5A.12*

32 Ever,
33 In movies with names like 'Junior Nevada,'
34 Which will be all about what it's like to be a rural drifter with personal problems, bad posture, a bunch of sleeveless T-shirts, an attitude, and nothing whatever to say,
35 To anyone,
36 As played by [a]Steve McQueen,
37 Unless it's really [b]Montgomery Clift instead,
38 Which it couldn't be,
39 Because Montgomery Clift will talk in all his pictures,
40 With a speech impediment.

a. *57.20*
b. *57.8*
c. *35.28*
d. *57.5*
e. *14.41*
f. *Yks.144.11-14*
g. *Grk.18.29*
h. *Hall.4.3*
i. *Lies.10.6*
j. *Ed.60.10*
k. *28.6*
l. *14.43*
m. *54.15*
n. *54.12*
o. *22.16*
p. *28.7*

CHAPTER 36

There will still be a lot of actors who don't use [c]"The Method," though,
2 And they will keep on making a lot of Hollywood movies,
3 Just like the ones they made before the war,
4 Only in Technicolor,
5 Like with stars named [d]Rock Hudson and [e]Doris Day,
6 Who will make a lot of movies without T-shirts or speech impediments,
7 And will become very popular in movies like 'Please Don't Eat the Pillows,'
8 [f]Which will be all about what it's like to not be able to have sex because it might wake up Ike,
9 [g]Only it will all be very funny,
10 Because everyone in the audience will know that Doris and Rock don't really want to have [h]sex with each other,
11 At all,
12 Which will make it all [i]okay,
13 And just hilarious.

CHAPTER 37

And there will still be a bunch of musicals too,
2 Which will be in Technicolor,
3 And will star [j]Gene Kelly,
4 Unless they star [k]Fred Astaire,
5 Who will dance up a storm and get the girl,
6 Who will be played by [l]Cyd Charisse,
7 Unless it's [m]Leslie Caron instead,
8 Or [n]Rita Hayworth,
9 Or [o]Debbie Reynolds,
10 Except that they'll never be played by Debbie Reynolds when the star is Fred Astaire,
11 Because Debbie Reynolds will always insist on taking off her dress at least once in every movie she's ever in,
12 Which Fred Astaire won't approve of,
13 Because you can look pretty silly dancing with a girl who's wearing nothing but a slip,
14 [p]Especially if *you*'re wearing a top hat and tails.

CHAPTER 38

But the movies won't all be about T-shirts and not having sex and dancing,
2 Because there will also be great geniuses in Hollywood,
3 Who will specialize in making motion-picture "classics,"
4 Including even some that will be considered great art,
5 By some people.

CHAPTER 39

For example, there will be a great genius called Alfred Hitchcock,

2 Who will come to Hollywood from Britain and makes lots and lots of movies about suspense,
3 Especially the kind of suspense that happens when something mysterious and complicated pops up out of [a]nowhere and almost ruins your whole life,
4 [b]For no reason,
5 Including movies called [c]'39 Psychos on a Train,' [d]'The Man Who Knew How to Catch a Thief,' and [e]'Dial M for Marnie,'
6 And a bunch of others too.
7 For example, one of Hitchcock's greatest movies will be called 'The Lady Vanishes Out the Rear Window,'
8 Starring [f]Jimmy Stewart,
9 Who falls madly in love with a mysterious blond beauty,
10 Played by [g]Grace Kelly,
11 Unless it's really [h]Kim Novak instead,
12 [i]Because there's no way to be completely sure about anything in a Hitchcock movie,
13 [j]Which is why it's so incredibly suspenseful when Jimmy kind of goes into a trance and starts following her around with [k]binoculars,
14 [l]In spite of the cast on his leg,
15 [m]Which he got by falling off a building,
16 [n]And explains why he's so afraid of heights that he can't make it up the stairs in time to save Tippi Hedren,
17 [o]Who's all the way at the top of the tower being attacked by crazed birds,
18 [p]And then falls to her death while Jimmy watches helplessly through his binoculars,
19 [q]Except that maybe she really isn't dead at all,
20 [r]Because he starts seeing her later on,
21 [s]Or someone who looks so much like her that it couldn't be anyone but [t]Eva Marie Saint,
22 Unless it's really [u]Doris Day,
23 [v]Which it couldn't be,
24 [w]Because there's no sign of Rock Hudson anywhere,
25 [x]And besides, she's acting so strangely that it has to be either Tippi or Kim or Janet Leigh,
26 [y]Who aren't telling the truth about their past,
27 [z]At all,
28 [aa]And can't be trusted,
29 [bb]In spite of being so beautiful.
30 [cc]And so Jimmy gets more and more obsessed with following her,
31 [dd]And has a bunch of [ee]bizarre nightmares choreographed by Salvador Dali,
32 [ff]And then there's this tremendous chase scene where he gets on a train and follows her all the way to Mount Rushmore,
33 [gg]Where he discovers that she's really in the CIA,
34 [hh]Unless she's actually a thief instead,
35 [ii]Which turns out to be the case in the end,
36 [jj]Because eventually she starts stealing all the jewelry on the French Riviera,
37 [kk]While Jimmy watches through his binoculars,
38 [ll]Until she gets stabbed to death in the shower,
39 [mm]While Jimmy watches through the rear window,
40 [nn]Which leaves him free to marry Vera Miles,
41 [oo]Just like always,
42 Unless,
43 [pp]You know.

a. 30.7
b. Zig.8.8
c. Zig.8.11
d. Zig.8.14
e. Zig.8.13
f. 20.40
g. 14.48
h. 57.26
i. Zig.11.2-7
j. Zig.8.1
k. Ed.10.7
l. Zig.8.2
m. Zig.8.3
n. Zig.8.4
o. Zig.8.5
p. Zig.8.6
q. Zig.9.2
r. Zig.10.11
s. F&J.14.13
t. Ed.30.5
u. 14.41
v. Vin.57.6
w. Zig.6.6
x. Zig.6.7
y. Zig.6.8
z. Zig.6.9
aa. Zig.6.10
bb. Zig.7.1
cc. Zig.7.2
dd. Zig.7.3
ee. Paul.5.10 & 7.6
ff. Zig.7.4-6
gg. Zig.7.7
hh. Zig.7.8
ii. Zig.7.9
jj. Zig.7.10
kk. Zig.7.11
ll. Zig.7.12
mm. Zig.7.13
nn. Zig.7.14-15
oo. Zig.7.16-17
pp. 24.30

CHAPTER 40

And there will be another great genius named Jerry K—,

2 Who will make a million movies,

3 [a]Which will be all about what it's like to be a spastic half-wit trying to cope with an unusual situation,

4 Such as being a [b]bellhop,

5 Or a [c]singer in Las Vegas,

6 Or a [d]nutty professor,

7 Or a prizefighting [e]milkman called Kid Galahad,

8 Or someone like that,

9 Who will be completely hilarious in every scene the way [f]Jerry K— plays the part,

10 Whether he's talking too loud in a funny voice,

11 [g]Or falling down the stairs,

12 Or up the stairs,

13 Or singing too loud in a funny voice,

14 Which will just drive the fans wild.

15 In fact, Jerry K— will have lots and lots of fans,

16 [h]Including very very young children,

17 [i]And a whole bunch of teenage girls,

18 Not to mention the Frogs,

19 [j]Who will think that Jerry K— is the greatest achievement ever achieved by American culture,

20 Which is really saying something,

21 Unless you're a Frog.

CHAPTER 41

And Alfred Hitchcock and Jerry K— won't be the only movie geniuses to become international celebrities,

2 Because there will be another

a. F&J.3.1-4
b. Psom.24.3
c. Psong.49.3
d. Zig.1.1
e. Grk.12.7
f. 46.27
g. F&J.14.13
h. Rom.10.4
i. Grk.9.7
j. Frog.18.21
k. Psom.31.2
l. Ann.10.1
m. Ed.50.9
n. 57.30
o. Ed.50.4
p. Ira.32.10
q. 57.28
r. 23.21
s. F&J.11.3-7

great British director called David Lean,

3 Who will be a man truly after your own heart,

4 The kind of man who only makes mega-super-spectacular blockbusters,

5 Which go on for hours and hours and hours,

6 Until you're convinced of his genius,

7 [k]Or sound asleep in your chair.

8 David will make many great pictures,

9 But none of them will be as great as 'Lawrence of Chicago,'

10 [l]Which will be all about a World War I officer who [m]machine-guns thousands of Turks because it feels so darned good,

11 Thus explaining how he comes by the name Lawrence of Chicago,

12 Who will be played by [n]Peter O'Toole,

13 Except that Peter is a Brit,

14 Which means that he couldn't possibly be from [o]Chicago,

15 And so there has to be another explanation,

16 Which is where the story really starts to get complicated,

17 Because it turns out that there's a co-star who loves both Lawrence and Lara because they both look so good in [p]white,

18 Namely, Dr. Chicago,

19 Who will be played by [q]Omar Sharif,

20 Except that Omar isn't an American either,

21 Which is why there has to be [r]William Holden as the Yank who escapes from the terrible Nip prison camp on the [s]River

K— so that he can help Lawrence and the other Brits win the war,

22 Not to mention the noble savage Bedouin who helps Peter and Omar massacre the Red Army in the terribly bloody [a]train scene,

23 Who will be played by [b]Anthony Quinn,

24 That is, Anthony will play the Bedouin, not the train scene, which will be played by hundreds and hundreds of people with [c]big noses and bronze makeup,

25 Which is why 'Lawrence of Chicago' will wind up costing about a billion dollars,

26 But it will be worth every penny,

27 [d]Because it will show everybody who doesn't fall asleep somewhere in the middle what war is *really* like,

28 With a cast of thousands,

29 [e]And more prop sand and snow than you could shake a pointed stick at,

30 Not to mention [f]Julie Christie,

31 Who is just beautiful as Lara,

32 [g]And completely makes up for the fact that no one will ever be able to understand the story,

33 No matter how many hours of it they sit through.

CHAPTER 42

A nd there will be another great Hollywood genius named [h]Orson Welles,

2 [i]Who will be so great that he won't even bother to finish a lot of his movies,

3 Although he *will* finish one of them,

a. *F&J.14.13*
b. *57.15*
c. *14.12*
d. *Swar.23.2-6*
e. *17.4*
f. *54.12*
g. *F&J.15.13*
h. *Psom.49.1-2*
i. *F&J.2.15-16*
j. *40.9*
k. *F&J.6.1*
l. *F&J.6.2-4*
m. *F&J.6.5*
n. *F&J.6.6*
o. *F&J.6.7*
p. *F&J.6.8*
q. *57.32*
r. *F&J.5.1*
s. *Psay.5Q.64*
t. *57.24*
u. *42.37*
v. *Zig.9.2*

4 Which will turn out to be quite enough anyway.

5 This one incredibly great movie will be called 'Citizen K—,'

6 And will be all about a giant newspaper tycoon,

7 Played by [j]Orson Welles,

8 [k]Who will be indicted for some terrible crime,

9 [l]Which nobody knows what it is,

10 [m]For some reason,

11 [n]Except that he'll die for his crime right at the beginning of the movie,

12 [o]Very mysteriously,

13 [p]Which explains why he has to be investigated,

14 By a huge fat corrupt cop,

15 Played by [q]Orson Welles,

16 Who goes out and looks into the life of Citizen K—,

17 With great thoroughness,

18 From every conceivable camera angle,

19 And under every kind of bizarre lighting you could possibly imagine,

20 [r]So that sometimes he even has to do his investigating through a bunch of [s]wooden slats that throw off all kinds of amazing shadows,

21 Which maybe explains why he gets so confused in the scene with Citizen K—'s defense attorney,

22 Played by [t]Orson Welles,

23 Who says that it all has to do with something called [u]"Rosebud,"

24 Which convinces the cop to talk to everybody who might know how Citizen K— got involved with "Rosebud" in the first place,

25 [v]Although absolutely nobody he talks to knows anything at

all about "Rosebud,"

26 Not even [a]Joseph Cotten in a baseball cap,

27 Or [b]Agnes Moorehead,

28 Which leads him to Citizen K__'s home,

29 Called [c]San Juanadu, or [d]Xanadu for short, which in English means [e]San Simian,

30 Which is an enormous hilltop castle [f]William Randolph Hearst built to keep his toys in,

31 [g]Although it turns out that the castle wasn't a completely happy place for Citizen K__,

32 [h]And actually got to be more like a prison than anything else,

33 [i]Unless it was more like a trap that he couldn't get out of,

34 [j]What with not having a sled anymore,

35 [k]Not to mention how there's never any snow in southern California anyway,

36 So what can you do?

37 Which is where [l]"Rosebud" comes in,

38 And explains everything,

39 Somehow.

CHAPTER 43

There will also be a genius called [m]Ingrid Bergman,

2 Who will become a great Swedish film director after the war,

3 [n]Even though she will get pretty [o]depressed about not being able to leave her husband for Humphrey Bogart,

4 [p]What with the war and all,

5 And so her films will have kind of a [q]melancholy flavor,

6 But they'll be incredibly brilliant anyway,

7 [r]Being all about death and meaninglessness and despair and

a. 57.20
b. 39.21
c. Yks.60.3
d. Psom.45.1-12
e. F&J.14.13
f. 42.7
g. Psp.2.11
h. Zig.10.12
i. Zig.10.10
j. Zig.10.13
k. Psom.12.4
l. 48.10
m. 34.17
n. 32.21
o. 26.3
p. Yks.90.4-6
q. Brit.41.7
r. Paul.7.6
s. Paul.5.2-3
t. Ira.33.1-3
u. Psong.8.3
v. F&J.15.1
w. Paul.4.9
x. Psay.5Q.62
y. Ned.29.24

other brilliant stuff like that.

8 [s]And she will do things on screen that nobody was ever brilliant enough to think of before,

9 [t]Like having nobody say anything for hours at a time,

10 [u]And picking a bunch of fat ugly Swedish women to be her star,

11 Who sigh a lot and say things so softly that you can't understand them without subtitles,

12 Which make things even more confusing,

13 Because when you have to read a movie, it seems like it should make some kind of sense,

14 Which it won't,

15 [v]Because Ingrid will be such a towering genius that none of her movies will ever have a plot,

16 Or a happy ending,

17 Or be even slightly entertaining in any way at all,

18 [w]Which is why they will be practically worshiped by intellectuals all over the world,

19 Who know great art when they see it,

20 Because if something's entertaining,

21 Or intelligible,

22 Or ends happily,

23 [x]It can't be art,

24 Which explains why Ingrid Bergman will be hailed as one of the greatest artists of the whole twentieth century,

25 And that's really saying something,

26 Because if there's one thing the twentieth century will produce a lot of,

27 [y]It's art.

CHAPTER 44

Of course, when you make movies for children, it's

okay if they're entertaining and end happily,

2 Especially if you're [a]Walt Disney,

3 Which will be the name of another great motion-picture genius,

4 [b]Who will turn all of the most popular fairy tales into cartoons,

5 Including [c]'Cinderella' and [d]'Snow White' and [e]'Sleeping Beauty,'

6 [f]Who will defeat the wicked stepmother,

7 And marry a handsome cartoon character named Prince Charming,

8 And live happily ever after,

9 [g]Getting rereleased every seven years,

10 Whether anyone's forgotten how it all comes out or not,

11 [h]Which is the kind of genius that everyone in Hollywood would like to have,

12 [i]Except that they won't ever have that particular kind of genius,

13 Because Walt Disney will get it all,

14 Except for the part that goes into the [j]'The Wizard of Iz.'

CHAPTER 45

This is not to say that plenty of other producers and directors won't make movies for children,

2 Because they will.

3 It's just that they won't be great artistic geniuses with lots and lots of money to spend,

4 [k]And so a lot of their movies will be pretty low-budget,

5 And they'll mostly be about alien invaders from outer space,

6 Or carnivorous mutants from some laboratory,

7 Or [l]gigantic monsters from Japan,

8 [m]Even though it really won't matter which it is,

9 [n]Because all these movies will have about the same plot,

10 [o]Which has to do with saving the world from whatever it is,

11 Usually with the help of a [p]handsome scientist and the [q]only girl on earth who doesn't think he's a complete lunatic,

12 [r]Because he has already figured out what is happening,

13 And no one will believe him because nothing has squashed [s]Tokyo or [t]Los Angeles yet,

14 [u]Although everybody changes their mind when they actually catch sight of it,

15 Which means it's time to call in the [v]military,

16 Who show up with a bunch of tanks and planes and shoot off [w]everything they've got,

17 [x]Without having any effect,

18 [y]Because all earthly weapons are powerless against the invader,

19 [z]Which means that unless the good scientist can figure out what to do, everybody on earth will be history in about twenty-four hours.

20 [aa]And so the good scientist and his girlfriend stay up all night thinking,

21 [bb]And figure out that none of this would ever have happened in the first place if it weren't for nuclear weapons,

22 [cc]Because the monster was created by fallout from nuclear tests,

23 Or the aliens from outer space spotted the nuclear tests and are angry about the [dd]childish violence of the human race,

a. *Ed.74.3*
b. *Zig.10.11*
c. *Yks.66.3-4*
d. *Psay.5A.14*
e. *Pnot.25.1-2*
f. *30.48*
g. *Psay.5L.7*
h. *Psong.11.1*
i. *Psay.5Q.60*
j. *30.9*
k. *Psong.36.1*
l. *Ed.60.10*
m. *Main.22.10*
n. *F&J.8.3*
o. *F&J.9.1-3*
p. *Ed.60.10*
q. *Ed.60.10*
r. *Drex.8.1-3*
s. *Ed.60.10*
t. *Ed.60.10*
u. *Grk.9.7*
v. *Forg.8.11-15*
w. *Adam.50.6*
x. *47.24*
y. *Psay.5Q.23*
z. *Ed.60.17*
aa. *Yks.44.22*
bb. *Yks.91.7*
cc. *Ext.52.16*
dd. *Al.6.10-15*

24 Or something like that,
25 [a]Which means that all of it was really our fault in the first place,
26 And we don't deserve much sympathy, let alone a happy ending,
27 Except that,
28 Well,
29 This is a low-budget picture for youngsters, and it *has* to end happily so they won't have nightmares about it.
30 [b]So the good scientist buckles down and makes the ray gun or whatever,
31 [c]And finishes it in the nick of time,
32 [d]And saves the planet,
33 And everybody lives happily ever after,
34 Which isn't art,
35 And isn't even Walt Disney,
36 But it sure sells a lot of popcorn.

CHAPTER 46

In fact, pictures like this will make so much money that even people who make movies for grownups will notice,
2 And they'll make a bunch of movies along the same lines for the adult audience,
3 Which won't be silly science-fiction productions about a lot of scary monsters created by nuclear tests,
4 But serious science-fiction productions about the scary situations created by nuclear weapons.
5 Movies like this will be made by even very great directors,
6 [e]Such as a genius named Stanley K__,
7 Who will make a movie called 'Dr. Failsafe, or How I Learned

a. *Lies.10.6*
b. *Ed.40.5-8*
c. *Ned.16.12*
d. *Psong.22.1*
e. *17.2*
f. *46.19*
g. *14.25*
h. *Krt.39.14*
i. *Yks.20.10-11*
j. *Ned.16.14-15*
k. *Ed.28.6*
l. *Drex.6.4*
m. *Drex.7.10*
n. *30.40*
o. *Adam.31.16*
p. *Swar.15.5*
q. *Swar.15.6*
r. *Swar.15.7*
s. *57.16*
t. *Swar.15.8*
u. *Krt.15.1*
v. *Swar.15.9*
w. *Swar.15.10*

to Love the Bomb in Seven Days,'
8 Which will not only be scary,
9 But funny too,
10 What with [f]Henry Fonda playing the president,
11 And a Brit named Peter Sellers playing everyone else,
12 Including the title role of [g]Dr. Failsafe,
13 Who will go completely [h]insane when the situation in the war room gets to be too hot a [i]potato,
14 Which will happen when Peter Sellers kidnaps a nuclear weapons facility and launches a [j]Big One at the Russians,
15 Played by [k]Peter Sellers,
16 Who can't seem to understand that it's all just an [l]accident,
17 [m]Which means there might be war,
18 Since everybody on both sides is descended from the same killer ape,
19 Played by [n]Peter Sellers,
20 [o]With music by some Kraut composer or other,
21 Which is terribly terribly funny,
22 In a depressing sort of way,
23 Which is the special genius of Stanley K__,
24 Who will achieve a similar effect in most of his pictures,
25 [p]Including one called 'A Clockwork Odyssey,'
26 [q]Which will be all about a violent British punk,
27 [r]Played by [s]Peter Sellers,
28 [t]With music by some [u]Kraut composer or other,
29 [v]Who is cured of his violence and then has to be uncured because human beings can't survive without being violent,
30 [w]Especially in modern life,

31 "Which is also why the president gets so depressed in 'Dr. Failsafe,'

32 [b]Because the only way to avoid all-out nuclear war is to drop an H-Bomb on New York City,

33 [c]Which is kind of a violent way of surviving,

34 And makes Henry Fonda put his head in his hands,

35 [d]Especially when he hears the telephone melt in Moscow,

36 [e]Even though everybody else in the war room is whooping it up in a pretty hilarious way,

37 [f]And making plans to survive underground with a lot of beautiful women to reseed the planet,

38 [g]As long as the women don't have to be played by Peter Sellers,

39 [h]Which Stanley will probably agree to,

40 [i]Provided there's lots of Kraut music playing underground.

41 [j]And so they argue back and forth about this kind of stuff for quite a while,

42 [k]While Henry orders the bomb dropped on New York,

43 [l]And the B-52 takes off with a crazy cowboy pilot and an enormous H-Bomb,

44 [m]Played by Peter Sellers,

45 [n]Who is so eager to see the bomb go off that he rides it all the way down,

46 [o]While the credits roll up in front of the gigantic mushroom cloud that used to be New York,

47 [p]Because even popular movies can be art,

48 As long as they don't have a happy ending,

49 Since art has to reflect humanity,

---

a. *Swar.15.11*
b. *Swar.15.12*
c. *Swar.15.13*
d. *Psom.77.9*
e. *Swar.26.1*
f. *Swar.26.2*
g. *Swar.26.3*
h. *Swar.26.4*
i. *Psp.2.10*
j. *Swar.26.6*
k. *Swar.26.7*
l. *Swar.26.8*
m. *Swar.26.9*
n. *Swar.26.10*
o. *Swar.26.11*
p. *Swar.26.12*
q. *30.7*
r. *10.10*
s. *Ed.60.21-24*
t. *Chuk.18.1-2*
u. *57.32*

---

50 Which isn't headed for a happy ending either.

CHAPTER 47

And as it happens, Hollywood will even dare to look beyond [q]nuclear nightmares,

2 Into the nightmare world that people might have to live in after the holocaust,

3 Which would obviously kill everyone who wasn't almost immortal,

4 Thus explaining why most of these movies will star [r]Charlton Heston,

5 Who will show us various impossible futures,

6 Like in a movie called [s]"Planet of the Killer Apes,'

7 [t]Where the evil apes who survived the war walk upright and talk and wear clothes and everything,

8 Or maybe—though this is very very hard to make out— what Charlton finds in the future is a world so overpopulated that even [u]Edward G. Robinson can't push his way through the crowds,

9 And so he stays at home while Charlton goes out and pushes everybody around for him,

10 Trying to find one decent meal that isn't made of . . .

11 No, that can't be right . . .

12 Except that there isn't any food but . . .

13 No, that just couldn't possibly be it . . .

14 Until . . . and I can't be sure of this either, because it's so far out in the distant future of Hollywood . . .

15 Until Charlton is the very last man alive on earth,

16 Unless it's really Vincent Price instead,
17 [a]Because everybody else is a murderous bloodsucking mutant [b]vampire,
18 Thanks to the radiation and all,
19 Which is why it positively *must* be Vincent Price,
20 Because the last man alive on earth *dies* at the end,
21 Which couldn't happen if it were Charlton Heston, could it?
22 Could it?
23 [c]*Bang!*
24 Uh oh.
25 [d]Ugh!

CHAPTER 48

Of course, there's more than one way for the world to come to an end,
2 And Hollywood will never completely forget the spiritual side of things,
3 [e]Thanks to its great religious tradition,
4 Not to mention the fact that even Hollywood has to give the devil his due,
5 Which is why there will one day be a movie about the time when Satan will come along to put an end to everything,
6 Called 'Rosebud's Baby,'
7 Where [f]Satan has the starring role, obviously,
8 Although he will also get some help from various human beings,
9 Including a young married woman named Rosebud,
10 Who will be played by [g]Mia Farrow,
11 And Rosebud's husband Nick,
12 Who will be played by [h]John Cassavetes,
13 And some incredibly evil old people too,
14 Who will be played by some incredibly old people,
15 Who live in the same incredibly old and mysterious [i]Manhattan apartment building where a lot of other mysterious and evil things have happened over the years,
16 But not as mysterious and evil as what happens to [j]Rosebud,
17 [k]Because she will get raped by the devil,
18 [l]In a dream,
19 [m]Which results in a whole bunch of problems,
20 [n]Because Rosebud gets pregnant,
21 [o]Which everybody seems very happy about,
22 Except maybe Rosebud,
23 Because her husband is acting strangely,
24 Not to mention everybody else,
25 [p]Which makes Rosebud suspicious,
26 [q]Especially in the scene where she blunders into a black mass,
27 Which absolutely everybody is there for,
28 Including her husband,
29 And the incredibly old people next door,
30 [r]And all their old evil friends,
31 Not to mention [s]Rosebud's baby,
32 [t]Which is whimpering in a lovely black crib,
33 [u]Thus proving beyond a shadow of a doubt that the [v]Antichrist has come at last,
34 Which will pretty well wrap things up for Mankind if it man-

a. Zig.10.11
b. 30.9
c. Psom.60.1-2
d. Jefs.7.46
e. 15.2
f. 30.9
g. 30.27 Ira.9.5-6
h. 30.25
i. Gyp.1.17
j. 39.21
k. Zig.10.13
l. Zig.8.2
m. Zig.8.3
n. Zig.8.4
o. Zig.11.7-8
p. Zig.6.10
q. Ext.13.11
r. 17.4
s. Psom.27.1
t. Psom.35.3-4
u. Paul.4.9
v. Grk.4.11

ages to survive through the closing credits,

35 But Rosebud decides to take care of the baby anyway,

36 [a]Because what can you do?

37 Or at least I think that's the way it goes,

38 Although I can't be completely and utterly certain about it,

39 Because it's a long long way into the future,

40 [b]And to be honest, some of it seems out of focus,

41 Especially the End,

42 Which is really the whole point,

43 Isn't it?

a. *Zig.9.2*
b. *Ed.51.12*
c. *56.5*
d. *Wil.18.1-2*
e. *Ned.2.1-2*
f. *Ann.19.4*

CHAPTER 49

Well, anyway (said the camera), you can see that motion pictures will go a long long way in the future,

2 All the way from the silent nonsense you're making today to the powerful and magnificent film art of the late twentieth century,

3 Which should make you proud,

4 Because it means you'll be responsible for helping to bring the deepest insights and most profound discoveries of our finest minds into the hearts and minds of even the simplest and least educated of the masses,

5 So that everyone can share in the joys of our culture's greatest learning and wisdom,

6 For as long as it lasts.

7 In fact, I can even prove it to you,

8 Because if you'll put me on a crane, I can see even farther,

9 And I will show you an age in which hardly any movies have happy endings,

10 And where people and history and everything else are shown the way they *really* are,

11 Which may not be pretty,

12 But it sure is real life.

CHAPTER 50

Thank you (said the camera), the crane is a big help,

2 And I can see years and years farther than I could before,

3 All the way to a brand-new galaxy of stars,

4 Who will reinvent the movies with their tremendous talents,

5 [c]Which involve bad posture and speech impediments and more hair than you can shake a pointed stick at,

6 Including beards,

7 And sideburns,

8 And other things too,

9 Which will make all the difference in every kind of movie,

10 [d]And will prepare the way for the one who will come,

11 Someday,

12 To explain what it all means,

13 And what to do about it.

CHAPTER 51

Yes, as I have said, there will be many great new stars,

2 [e]And they will make movies for a new generation of young people,

3 Who will be completely fed up with everything,

4 And ready to see life as it is,

5 Without a lot of lies and stupid platitudes.

6 For they will not only be tired of [f]John Wayne,

7 But disgusted with him too,

8 Because they will know better than to think that the wild west

was settled by good, strong, brave, virtuous men who never shot anyone in the back,

9 Not to mention his awful movie about [a]Vietnam, called the 'Olive Drab Berets,' which will be all about how this is just another little war that the Americans have to win on behalf of all the little people who want to be free and democratic,

10 [b]Which is nothing more than one long string of lies and jingoistic excrement, from beginning to end,

11 And so they will elevate a new kind of film protagonist,

12 Played by [c]Clint Westwood,

13 Who will replace John Wayne as the symbol of the American hero,

14 Including western heroes,

15 [d]Which will make a fistful of dollars for Clint,

16 [e]And maybe even a few dollars more than that.

CHAPTER 52

For example, Clint will make a western called 'The Bad, the Worst, and the In-Between,'

2 [f]Which will be all about the kinds of men who really won the west,

3 Such as the Worst,

4 Played by [g]Lee Van Cleave,

5 Who kills almost everyone he meets,

6 Just for fun,

7 [h]While searching for a couple hundred thousand dollars in stolen gold,

8 Which is a much more realistic kind of character than you'll ever see in a [i]John Ford western.

9 The better-than-average mercenary who has to deal with the

---

a. Ed.17.1-11
b. Ann.4.6
c. 30.27
d. Ira.8.13-23
e. Psong.41.1-3
f. Ed.17.8
g. 30.9
h. Psong.20.1-8
i. 23.6-7
j. Ed.36.14
  & 46.10
k. F&J.14.13
l. 30.25
m. Vin.49.5
n. Psay.5Q.75
o. Yks.52.19-21
p. 57.10

Worst is played by Clint Westwood, of course,

10 Who is much nicer than the Worst because he doesn't always kill everyone he meets,

11 Unless they ask him what his name is,

12 Or look at him the wrong way,

13 Or say something insulting to his [j]mule,

14 Or accidentally get between Clint and all that stolen gold,

15 In which case all bets are off,

16 And he has no choice but to kill them,

17 Because after all,

18 [k]This is the wild west.

19 And then there's the In-Between,

20 Played by [l]Eli Wallet,

21 Who is better than the Worst because he doesn't always [m]laugh fiendishly when he shoots someone in the back,

22 [n]And is better at small talk too,

23 Which is important,

24 Because Clint never talks at all,

25 Like all real western heroes,

26 Which maybe explains why it will take Hollywood this long to do the west the way it really was.

CHAPTER 53

Thanks to Clint, it will become possible to make movies about other parts of western history,

2 Like Custer's Last Stand,

3 [o]Which will be done in a movie called 'Little Big Nose,'

4 [p]With a brand-new star named Dustin Hopeless in the title role,

5 Who is the world's oldest white Indian,

6 And the only remaining survivor of the tribe that fought ªCuster,

7 Who will finally be shown the way he was,

8 Namely, as a ᵇnarcissistic schizophrenic with an IQ of about eighty-six,

9 ᶜWhose hobby is Indian genocide,

10 Which he keeps doing to Dustin's tribe,

11 Until they eventually get fed up,

12 ᵈAnd realize that all white men everywhere are just exactly like Custer,

13 And so what can you do?

14 ᵉOf course, when they do it, that gives the white men all the excuse they need,

15 Which is why western history turned out the way it did,

16 And why the truth must be told,

17 At last.

CHAPTER 54

In fact, Dustin Hopeless will be an incredibly important star,

2 Because he'll make so many important movies,

3 ᶠAnd show everyone how things really are,

4 ᵍLike in a movie called 'The Carnal Graduate,'

5 ʰWhich will be all about what it's like to be an affluent college graduate in America,

6 ⁱAs played by Dustin Hopeless, naturally,

7 ʲWho will do a great job of looking confused,

8 ᵏAs well as bewildered,

9 ˡNot to mention baffled,

10 ᵐBecause nothing makes any sense,

a. 57.30
b. Grk.13.12-15
c. Wil.7.4
d. Psom.24.1
e. Yks.52.28-30
f. Zig.6.2
g. Zig.6.3
h. Zig.6.4
i. Zig.6.5
j. Zig.6.6
k. Zig.6.7
l. Zig.6.8
m. Zig.6.9
n. Zig.6.10
o. 52.4
Ira.9.5-6
p. Psong.39.1
q. Ann.18.26
r. Ed.60.10
s. Psong.39.5
t. 57.22
u. Psong.53.1-2
v. Ed.60.10
w. Ed.60.10
x. Ed.60.10
y. Psay.5A.40
z. 46.24
aa. 57.10

11 ⁿIncluding the older woman he has an affair with,

12 Played by °Ann Bankrupt,

13 ᵖWho is completely cold and selfish and nasty about everything but ᑫsex,

14 And her daughter,

15 Played by ʳKatharine Cross,

16 ˢWho doesn't know what to do with her life because her mother is so cold and selfish and nasty about everything,

17 And even including his parents' friends,

18 Played by ᵗJack Nickerson and Art Carbuncle,

19 ᵘWho are completely burned out on all the sex they've already had with Ann Bankrupt,

20 Not to mention ᵛAnn-Margarita and ʷCandace Virgin and ˣRita Moranmoro,

21 Who have had so much sex with Jack and Art that the only thing that gets them excited anymore is plastic,

22 ʸFor some reason,

23 And just shows why so many young people will get so alienated from their parents and society and everything,

24 Because movies like this will show things the way they really are,

25 Whether anyone likes it or not.

CHAPTER 55

Dustin will make another important movie with a great director called Sam Peckinpap,

2 ᶻWho will show everybody the incredible brutal violence that everyone is capable of,

3 Without exception,

4 Including even short confused-looking people like ᵃᵃDustin Hopeless,

5 Who will star in a Peckinpap movie called [a]"The Wild Getaway Dogs,'

6 Which will be all about what it's like to live in a remote little rural cottage surrounded by [b]psychotic workmen who want to kill you, and [c]rape your wife, and even [d]hang your cat in the closet,

7 And that's why you have to shoot as many of the workmen as you can,

8 With your ten-gauge pump-action shotgun,

9 In slow motion,

10 [e]So that the blood just absolutely fountains all over the place in rivers and brooks and streams,

11 [f]And then hop in the car and run for the border,

12 Shooting absolutely everyone and everything you run into along the way,

13 In slow motion,

14 [g]So that the blood erupts in geysers and jets and torrents,

15 [h]And stopping only long enough to have wild sex in a cheap hotel,

16 Except that the workmen also have to stop for some wild sex with [i]Gloria Bumper,

17 [j]At the same hotel,

18 Which means there has to be a showdown,

19 Where things get *really* violent,

20 So that Dustin and his beautiful wife,

21 Played by [k]Ali McGoo,

22 Have to pull out the [l]machine guns they've saved for a rainy day,

23 And start mowing down workmen like crazy,

24 In slow motion,

a. Psay.5A.13
b. Ed.77.6
c. Zig.10.14
d. Psay.5A.12
e. Ann.6.11
f. Ann.6.12
g. Ann.6.9
h. Ann.6.10
i. Ed.67.10
j. Zig.7.5
k. Ed.60.10
l. Ed.50.9
m. Ann.6.17
n. Ann.6.18
o. Ann.6.19
p. Kens.9.13
q. Kens.28.6
r. 50.5
s. 57.14
t. Adam.31.5
u. Ed.60.10

25 [m]So that the blood explodes across the screen in floods and cataracts and oceans of gore,

26 [n]Until they finally make their getaway,

27 [o]In an old [p]pickup truck,

28 And even tip the driver,

29 [q]Who is the only other character to survive the movie,

30 Which just shows you what it takes to get by in the modern world,

31 What with people being the way they are and all.

CHAPTER 56

But great as he is, Dustin won't even have a part in the greatest movie that will be made in this new age,

2 Because the movie called 'Five Easy Riders' will star a bunch of other people,

3 Who will also become great stars,

4 And go on to have brilliant careers of their own,

5 [r]Thanks to their posture, and their T-shirts, and their speech impediments,

6 Not to mention their hair,

7 Which will be really great,

8 For as long as it lasts.

9 'Five Easy Riders' will be all about what it's like to be so tired of all the lies and platitudes that you just drop out,

10 And go live with poor white trash somewhere,

11 Played by [s]Dennis Hippy,

12 With a bunch of motorcycles,

13 Played by [t]Holley Davidson,

14 And cheap girlfriends,

15 Played by [u]Karen Block,

16 Not to mention illegal drugs,

17 Which are important only because they move the plot along,

18 Because none of these people are really bad,

19 ^aSince all they really want to do is ride around and have some casual sex with people they meet on the road,

20 ^bAnd only get high every once in a while,

21 ^cBecause they're natural people,

22 ^dAnd just like to take their pleasures in a natural way,

23 ^eLike everybody,

24 ^fOnly without hurting anybody,

25 Which is why they're so unusual and admirable,

26 And why this will be such a magnificent movie.

27 Anyway, the way it works out is that Jack Nickerson used to be a concert pianist,

28 ^gOnly he hates classical music,

29 ^hBecause it's so full of artifice and pretense,

30 ⁱBesides being so darn hard to play,

31 ^jWhich is why Jack prefers the natural life,

32 Where everything is easy and free,

33 And explains why he puts on his football helmet and goes off with ^kPaul Fonda and Dennis Hippy on their motorcycle,

34 Which they're glad to take him with them on,

35 Because he says such amusing things,

36 Like the part about holding the chicken salad between the waitress's knees,

37 Which is just hilarious,

a. *Ann.18.19*
b. *Psom.40.4*
c. *Wil.18.8-12*
d. *Wil.8.13*
e. *Wil.18.14-16*
f. *Hill.L.1*
g. *Ira.21.19*
h. *Ira.21.20*
i. *Ira.21.21*
j. *Ira.21.22*
k. *57.18*
l. *20.40*
m. *Vin.6.15*
n. *Mawr.25.7*
o. *Mawr.25.8*
p. *Mawr.25.9*
q. *Mawr.25.14*
r. *Mawr.25.15*
s. *Mawr.25.19*
t. *Mawr.25.21*
u. *Mawr.25.22*
v. *Mawr.25.23*
w. *Ned.8.3*
x. *Ned.8.4*
y. *Ned.8.5*

38 And shows why ^lCary Grant will have to retire,

39 Because they don't come much suaver than Jack Nickerson,

40 ^mWho is actually a real good guy,

41 In spite of what he does to Karen Block at the end of the movie,

42 ⁿBecause she just couldn't free herself from all the rotten conventions of society,

43 ^oLike marriage and all that stuff,

44 ^pWhich just don't make any sense,

45 ^qEspecially coming from a girl who lets absolutely everyone look up her dress whenever they want.

46 ^rAnd besides, everyone can see how sensitive Jack really is underneath in the big scene with his father,

47 ^sWho is a vegetable,

48 ^tBut Jack cries anyway when he talks to him,

49 ^uBecause this is the same kind of communication they've always had,

50 ^vJust like everybody in the audience,

51 Which is still another reason why 'Five Easy Riders' will be the greatest movie ever made,

52 Even though we haven't even gotten to the big climax yet,

53 Which is maybe the best part of all,

54 ^wWhere Paul and Dennis and Jack are riding along on their motorcycle,

55 ^xNot hurting anybody at all,

56 ^yAnd not even thinking about hurting anybody,

57 [a]Because they're so darned peaceful and loving at heart,

58 When a [b]pickup truck comes out of nowhere and shoots them to death,

59 [c]For no reason at all,

60 Which when you think about it,

61 Is just exactly like modern life in America,

62 And says it all.

a.	*Ned.8.6*
b.	*55.29*
c.	*Kens.28.6*
d.	*54.12*
e.	*Ed.60.10*
f.	*40.9*
g.	*40.9*
h.	*30.40*
	Spic.12.5
i.	*30.27*
j.	*30.9*
k.	*Ed.60.10*
l.	*30.25*
m.	*30.9*
n.	*Ed.28.6*
o.	*Ed.27.3*

CHAPTER 57

Yes, there will be many great movies in the age to come,

2 And many many great parts for the glittering mega-stars of the future,

3 Including parts for beautiful, idealistic women who aren't going to stand for all the lies anymore,

4 Which will be played by a brilliant actress named [d]Joan Fonda,

5 And parts for handsome idealistic men who aren't going to stand for all the lies anymore,

6 Which will be played by a brilliant actor named [e]Robert Redwood,

7 And parts for attractive, sensitive idealists who keep thinking that good intentions might save them somehow,

8 Which will be played by [f]John Void,

9 And parts for confused idealists who don't have any idea what to do about anything,

10 Which will be played by [g]Dustin Hopeless,

11 And parts for idealists who foam at the mouth about all the lies and may or may not get gunned down in the last reel,

12 Which will be played by [h]Dustin Pacino,

13 And parts for nonconformist idealists who might seem kind of crazy if the world weren't so utterly insane,

14 Which will be played by [i]Dennis Hippy,

15 And parts for charismatic idealists who do all kinds of wild eccentric things just to keep their sanity in a world full of lies,

16 Which will be played by [j]Malcolm McBowel,

17 And parts for good-looking but callow idealists who don't seem to understand that the lies really can kill you,

18 Which will be played by [k]Paul Fonda,

19 And parts for ironically taciturn idealists who are giving a lot of thought to becoming realists instead,

20 Which will be played by [l]Donald Mutherland,

21 And parts for acid-tongued realists who aren't going to stand for all the lies anymore,

22 Which will be played by [m]Jack Nickerson,

23 And parts for drolly intellectual realists who just sigh and make witty remarks when they hear all the lies again,

24 Which will be played by [n]Elliott Mould,

25 And parts for no-nonsense female realists who have learned to take what they can get in spite of all the lies,

26 Which will be played by [o]Fate Underway,

27 And parts for exceptionally sexy realists who make love seven or eight times a day instead of listening to all the lies,

28 Which will be played by ᵃWarren Beady,

29 And parts for dull-witted schizophrenics who can't ever see through all the lies and get violently reactionary instead,

30 Which will be played by ᵇBruce Bern,

31 And parts for the corrupt, conniving capitalists who tell all the lies in the first place,

32 Which will be played by ᶜPeter Boil,

33 Except for those parts where the corrupt, conniving capitalist has to be incredibly tan and suave,

34 Which will be played by ᵈGeorge Hammerson,

35 Not to mention parts for completely hedonistic studs who think realists are naive optimists and just want to get by from day to day without having to get a steady job,

36 Which will be played by ᵉJoe D'Alexandria,

37 Until the world is ready at last for the One who will come and explain everything,

38 So that people can finally

a. 30.9
b. 30.40
c. Ed.28.6
d. Ed.60.10
e. 30.9
f. Ned.4.7
g. Rat.23.10
h. Psom.63.1-4

learn what to do about it.

CHAPTER 58

A nd as it happens, I can see (said the camera) all the way to the misty outskirts of that ultimate future,

2 ᶠAnd I know that there will be a sign given when the one with the answers has arrived at last,

3 And that sign will be yet another great movie,

4 Which will be a documentary about the events surrounding the arrival of the One we're waiting for,

5 And it will be called,

6 If I can make it out,

7 *Gimme Gimme*,

8 And it will have ᵍAngels in it,

9 Of a sort,

10 And it will feature great happenings,

11 But I can tell you no more than that,

12 Although what I have already told you should be enough to keep you going, I think.

13 So what do you say, Dave?

14 Dave?

15 Dave?

16 ʰAre you angry with me, Dave?

THE BOOK OF THE VIP

AL

CHAPTER 1

There was an incredibly big VIP named [a]Al,

2 Who had a [b]big brain,

3 And some big ideas about physics,

4 [c]That changed the world,

5 And probably destroyed it too.

CHAPTER 2

Al got the idea that all of the physics that had been discovered since the beginning of time was wrong,

2 And decided to [d]prove it,

3 Which he did by showing that time is not absolute,

4 But relative,

5 [e]Somehow.

6 [f]Apparently, Al also proved that it was possible to build an atom bomb,

7 [g]Because if you multiply the speed of light by itself, you get a very very big number that can be used to [h]smash an atom,

8 Somehow,

9 Which results in a very very big noise,

10 Namely,

11 [i]KA—B-O-O-O-O-O-M!

CHAPTER 3

When he saw where his ideas were leading, Al went to bed to think it over,

2 And fell asleep,

3 And had a [j]dream,

4 In which the [k]atom bomb appeared before him,

---

a. Dav.14.23
b. Drex.6.10
c. Adam.1.4
d. Chuk.13.1-2
e. Vin.6.15
f. Dav.47.24
g. Psay.4.2
h. Lies.11.12
i. Psom.26.1-6
j. Zig.8.1-2
k. Dav.46.44
l. Carl.10.3-4
m. Chuk.20.19-23
n. Adam.50.6
o. Ext.39.18-19
p. Lies.5.1-10
q. Zig.12.1-2

---

5 And spoke,

6 In a reassuring voice.

CHAPTER 4

Don't blame yourself (said the A-bomb) for the things that will come to pass,

2 Including myself,

3 Which, to be honest, is not the best thing that could have been done with your ideas,

4 [l]But remember that nobody is really any better than anyone else,

5 And so if it hadn't been you, it would have been somebody else,

6 Eventually.

7 [m]After all, the race of Man has been looking for bigger, sharper pointed sticks since he came down out of the trees,

8 [n]And he's been pretty ingenious about finding them,

9 And using them,

10 Which he always does,

11 [o]Without exception.

12 Besides, who are you to decide what should be done, and what shouldn't be done,

13 What should be known, and what shouldn't be known?

14 If there *is* a God, maybe this is his plan,

15 One that's been in the making ever since the [p]flood didn't work.

16 [q]Who are you to say?

CHAPTER 5

And besides, what's the big deal?

2 It's not like fear is anything new to the race of Man.

3 They've always been afraid,

4 Because they always knew they weren't much good,

5 And they've always believed that the end of the world would come,

6 ᵃEver since their Gods first started threatening them,

7 ᵇAnd pointing out their sins.

8 Maybe my face is *not* the face of God,

9 But maybe it *is*, too.

10 ᶜWho are you to say?

CHAPTER 6

I don't mean to tease you (said the bomb), but it's just that you're so serious about all of this.

2 I apologize if I upset you.

3 The truth is, I have some very good news for you.

4 Mankind will *not* be annihilated by nuclear weapons,

5 Because he will become wise,

6 At last,

7 And recognize that the day has finally come when no victory is worth the price of war,

8 And no consequence is worse than the death of the entire planet.

9 Yes, in spite of his thousand generations of ᵈselfishness,

10 And ᵉgreed,

11 And ᶠlust for power,

12 And ᵍdelight in the misfortunes of others,

13 And his ʰunquenchable thirst for vengeance,

14 And his ⁱblood-drenched per-

---

a. Lies.2.21-22
b. Rom.22.7
c. 4.16
d. Carl.2.5-10
e. Psong.20.1-8
f. Krt.7.7-11
g. Gnt.15.17-19
h. Yks.47.15-23
i. Spic.5.5-7
j. Psay.5J.4-31
k. Dav.15.45-46
l. Dav.22.24
   & 22.38
   & 46.28
m. Psom.33.4-8
n. Psay.2.2
o. Jeff.19.8
p. Wil.18.1-2

---

version of every pacific philosophy ever devised,

15 And his ʲundying hatred of everyone and everything that is different in the smallest way from himself,

16 In spite of all these things,

17 ᵏMankind will suddenly rise up and unite in a spirit of true brotherly love to banish war from the earth.

18 Forever,

19 ˡAnd on that day, the dove will carry an olive branch to the place where the lion is lying down with the lion, and the peoples of the world will come to see them,

20 And marvel at the ᵐbeauty they have created.

21 ⁿSure they will.

22 And with these words, the image of the bomb vanished away, leaving Al alone and sweating on his bed.

CHAPTER 7

Thereupon, Al thought long and hard about what he had heard,

2 And never forgot it,

3 Till the day he died,

4 When his last prayer beseeched God,

5 ᵒIf there *was* a God,

6 ᵖTo send someone as a messenger,

7 Someone who knew a way,

8 And would let everybody know what it was.

9 And when he had breathed his last prayer, Al breathed his last,

10 Period.

THE BOOK OF THE VIP
PAUL

CHAPTER 1

There was a VIP named [a]Paul,

2 Who had a big nose and a paintbrush,

3 [b]And changed the world.

CHAPTER 2

Paul had a lot of talent,

2 Even though he was from [c]Spain,

3 And painted a lot of pictures,

4 [d]In Paris, of course,

5 Where he met a guy named [e]Gertrude,

6 Who saw that he was a brilliant genius,

7 [f]And told everybody all about it.

CHAPTER 3

One of the most brilliant things Paul did was paint a picture of [g]three girls,

2 Who didn't look like girls at all,

3 But something else,

4 Something really ugly.

5 When Gertrude saw it, he got incredibly excited,

6 And told Paul that he had finally done it.

7 "Done what?" Paul wanted to know.

8 "Set a new course for modern art," said Gertrude.

9 "From now on, art will be different," he continued,

a. Ed.28.6
b. Adam.1.4
c. Spic.3.2-3
d. Yks.91.3
e. Dav.32.4
f. Adam.30.3-7
g. Psom.53.1-7
h. 2.2
i. Dav.46.19
j. Barb.3.1-5
k. Hill.Z.1
l. Ned.6.24

10 "And all because of you."

CHAPTER 4

At first, Paul didn't know what to think about this,

2 [h]Since thinking wasn't really his strong suit,

3 And wondered if maybe Gertrude wasn't exaggerating things a little bit,

4 The way he sometimes did.

5 But then, Paul had a vision,

6 In which [i]one of the three girls from his painting appeared to him,

7 Saying, "Zees ees tray important, Pole,

8 "Becose Gairtrude ees right.

9 "Zee whole world weel warship at your feet.

10 "Late us tale you about eet."

CHAPTER 5

Zair weel be a revolution een art (said the girl),

2 And you weel be zee leadair,

3 Zee towering genius of zee century.

4 [j]Een yairs to come, you weel take art completely apart,

5 And turn eet eento cubes,

6 And triangells,

7 And ozair zings.

8 When you reach your [k]zenith,

9 No one weel be able to undairstand even one of your paintings,

10 [l]Wheech won't look like anyzing atoll.

CHAPTER 6

Zees weel inspire [a]ozair artistes to do zee same zing,

2 And zay weel make très many [b]beautifool paintings,

3 Wheech alzo won't look like anyzing atoll.

4 And zair weel be sculpteurs,

5 Who weel make très many beautifool sculptures,

6 Wheech alzo won't look like anyzing atoll.

7 And everywhair in zee world of art, zair weel be new [c]rules,

8 [d]Zo zat no artiste weel have to learn how to skaitch anymore,

9 And zay weel be able to make art in new ways.

10 Par exemple, zay weel be able to make paintings by zrowing zee paint at zee canvass,

11 [e]Or driving zee tractair acrose the canvass,

12 Or zhooting zee paint at zee canvass from zee [f]gun.

13 And zee sculpteurs weel be able to make statues,

14 By weelding zee pieces of metal togezair wiz zee torch,

15 Or gluing zee pieces of garbage togezair,

16 Or hooking zee zings togezair wiz zee coat hangairs,

17 [g]Or anyzing ailse zay want.

CHAPTER 7

And zair may be zome peeples who weel believe zat

Reference column

a. *Yks.94.11-13*
b. *Psay.5Q.46*
c. *Swar.33.12-13*
d. *Swar.PS.24-25*
e. *Swar.33.15-16*
f. *Ed.47.19-20*
g. *Jefs.7.46*
h. *Swar.PS.27-30*
i. *Ira.24.29*
j. *Drex.11.8*
k. *6.7*
l. *Adam.30.2*

art has been uttairly destroyed,

2 Forevair,

3 [h]But zay weel be too zhy to mentione zair opinions to anyone who knows anyzing about art and artistes,

4 [i]And almost everyone who has zee good education weel believe zat you air zee greatest artiste who evair leeved.

5 [j]And your paintings weel sail for meelions and meelions and meelions and meelions of dollairs,

6 [k]And you weel nevair have to explain one zing about zem to anyone,

7 Atoll.

CHAPTER 8

And when the girl in the vision had finished her prophecy,

2 Paul smiled at her and said,

3 "What did you say?"

4 And the girl replied,

5 "Nevair mind, Pole. Eet ees not important, exzept for one zing."

6 "What's that?" said Paul, listening hard.

7 "Leesten to Gairtrude," said the vision.

8 [l]"He knows what he ees tolking about."

9 And then she was gone,

10 And Paul went back to work,

11 Feverishly.

THE BOOK OF THE VIP
FRANKIE & JOHNNY

CHAPTER 1

There was another VIP named [a]Frankie & Johnny,
2 Who thought a lot about the way things were going,
3 And figured it all out,
4 And wrote it down in some very important books and plays,
5 [b]That changed the world.

CHAPTER 2

All by himself, Frankie & Johnny figured out that,
2 To all intents and purposes,
3 [c]He was all by himself.
4 For example, he figured out that you couldn't prove there had ever been a God,
5 And if there ever *had* been a God,
6 He must be [d]crazy or [e]dead by now,
7 [f]Because just look at how insane everything was,
8 [g]With all the wars,
9 [h]And the diseases,
10 [i]And the suffering,
11 [j]And so on.
12 [k]Besides, you really couldn't even prove that anything existed in the first place,
13 At all,
14 [l]Except yourself,
15 As if it mattered,
16 In a godless, insane world.
17 And so he decided to write comedy.

CHAPTER 3

In order to write good comedy, Frankie & Johnny first had to discover the best comedy plot,

a. *Dav.40.9*
b. *Adam.1.4*
c. *Psom.5.1-6*
d. *Jeff.15.1-3*
e. *Jeff.19.1-5*
f. *Jeff.16.1-2*
g. *Jeff.16.3*
h. *Jeff.16.4*
i. *Jeff.16.5-7*
j. *Jeff.16.8*
k. *Vin.2.1-12*
l. *Frog.26.15*
m. *Dav.40.9*
n. *2.15-16*
o. *Yks.93.11*
p. *Dav.40.9*
q. *Swar.20.5*
r. *Psp.1.7*
s. *4.4*
t. *Zig.6.6*
u. *Dav.40.9*
v. *Zig.6.7*
w. *Zig.6.8*
x. *Zig.6.9*
y. *Zig.6.10*
z. *Psay.5Q.23*

2 Which he did.
3 The plot he discovered was based on a situation in which you couldn't win,
4 No matter what.

CHAPTER 4

For example, it might be that the [m]comic hero was suddenly turned into a giant insect,
2 [n]For no reason at all,
3 But had to come to terms with it anyway,
4 [o]Because what can you do?

CHAPTER 5

Or, it might be that the [p]comic hero was trapped inside some indeterminate [q]limbo,
2 And couldn't get out,
3 [r]Because there wasn't any exit,
4 And had to come to terms with it,
5 [s]Because what can you do?

CHAPTER 6

[t]Or, it might be that the [u]comic hero was charged with some unknown crime,
2 [v]And couldn't get off,
3 [w]Because no one would ever tell him what he had been charged with,
4 [x]Or who the judge and jury were,
5 [y]But had to come to terms with it anyway,
6 [z]Including the part about getting executed on the last page,

7 [a]Still not having any idea what it was all about,

8 [b]Because what can you do?

CHAPTER 7

And when Frankie & Johnny had written quite a lot of comedies based on this plot,

2 He started to get concerned.

3 What if someone started accusing him of repeating himself,

4 Or not really having all that much to say,

5 Or of being [c]depressing?

6 And he worried about this quite a lot,

7 While enjoying one of his few leisure-time pursuits,

8 Namely, [d]Russian Roulette,

9 And Frankie & Johnny was thinking that his next story was going to be a lot like his last story,

10 And was that a problem?,

11 [e]When the bullet in his revolver suddenly spoke out loud,

12 Bringing great news from the future.

CHAPTER 8

Your worries are groundless (said the bullet), for I have seen the future, and you will be regarded as a great writer for years and years and years to come.

2 Indeed, you have been most favored among men,

3 [f]For your plot is the one true plot,

4 And will be the basis of all future literature,

5 Until the very end of literature,

6 And maybe even a few decades longer than that.

---

a. Gods.3.6
b. 4.4
c. Frog.35.4
d. Ann.12.19-20
e. Gnt.15.14
f. Swar.18.3-8
g. Psay.5K.1
  Hill.R.1
  Hill.A.1
  Hill.Z.1
  Hill.Y.1
h. Hill.H.9
  Hill.O.1
  Hill.R.1
  Hill.S.1
  Hill.E.1
i. Swar.36.3
j. Swar.29.4-6
k. Gnt.15.4-5
  & 15.10-12
l. Dav.40.9
  Psom.5.1-6
m. 5.1
n. Lies.7.4
o. Rom.10.4
p. Yks.92.11-12
q. 4.4
r. Dav.41.21
s. Chuk.19.16-17

CHAPTER 9

Of course, there will be many variations on your discovery,

2 [g]And the initials of the comic heroes will change,

3 [h]As will the details of the situation they can't get out of,

4 [i]But the essential truth of your vision will be confirmed and celebrated by hundreds of brilliantly talented writers to come,

5 Because once the [j]truth has been finally and completely discovered,

6 What else is there to write about?

CHAPTER 10

[k]For example, there will come a great writer who will discover the literary value of having [l]two comic heroes,

2 [m]Trapped inside some indeterminate limbo,

3 [n]Waiting for someone to show up,

4 [o]Who never shows up,

5 [p]But they have to come to terms with it anyway,

6 [q]Because what can you do?

CHAPTER 11

Another great writer will discover the literary value of having a comic hero trapped in a *real-life* situation he can't get out of,

2 Like a war in some worthless and unimportant foreign country,

3 [r]Where you have to blow up a bridge that doesn't really matter,

4 Except that you said you would,

5 [s]Even if it kills you,

6 Which it will,

341

7 [a]Because what can you do?

CHAPTER 12

And still another great writer will discover the literary value of having a [b]comic hero trapped in some worthless and unimportant foreign city,

2 While they're having a [c]plague,

3 [d]Which means you can't get out,

4 [e]Even though it doesn't have anything to do with you,

5 Except that you'll die there,

6 [f]Along with everybody else,

7 [g]Because what can you do?

CHAPTER 13

And there will be yet another great writer who will discover the literary value of having a [h]comic hero who is actually funny,

2 [i]While trapped in a situation he can't get out of, of course,

3 [j]Because the funniest part of the comedy is that it seems like you might be able to get out,

4 Since all you have to do to get out is be declared insane,

5 Except that that doesn't work,

6 [k]Because if you tell them you're insane to get out, they'll know you're sane enough to want to get out,

7 [l]And if you don't tell them you're insane, they're not allowed to let you out.

8 [m]And so the remarkably clever punch line of the joke is that you have to come to terms with it,

9 [n]Because what can you do?

CHAPTER 14

[o]And this will inspire other great writers to explore the

a. Swar.19.1-5
b. Dav.40.9
c. Bub.4.1-5
d. Psp.2.6
e. Brit.9.4
f. Psp.1.4
g. 11.7
h. Dav.40.9
i. Psp.3.11
j. Zig.9.2
k. Dav.47.24
l. Psay.5Q.23
m. Pnot.27.5
n. Drex.6.1
o. Ed.55.4
p. Psom.69.1-4
q. Psp.2.11
r. Grk.13.13-14
s. Hill.L.1
t. Zig.10.12
u. Psp.2.12
v. 9.2-3
w. Grk.8.32
*   & 26.9-10*
x. Grk.18.28-29
y. Pnot.24.3-4
z. Al.2.11
*   Ann.2.32*
aa. Psp.2.13
bb. Ira.31.6-16
cc. Psp.2.14
dd. Psom.27.1

literary value of making comic heroes be funny,

2 Which is a kind of reassurance,

3 Since it suggests that everyone is really in the same [p]boat,

4 [q]Which is to say, all alone.

5 And there will be writers whose comic heroes become trapped in a comical world of [r]lust,

6 Where if you keep masturbating, you can't have [s]love,

7 But if you [t]stop masturbating, it won't help,

8 So you have to come to terms with it,

9 [u]Because what can you do?

10 And there will be other writers whose comic heroes are trapped in hilariously funny indeterminate limbos,

11 [v]Like the [w]Trojan Horse,

12 [x]And the only way out is through the horse's [y]*anus*,

13 [z]And you know what that means,

14 But you might as well come to terms with it,

15 [aa]Because what can you do?

16 And there will be writers whose comic heroes are trapped in wryly humorous suburban lifestyles,

17 [bb]Which they can't get out of,

18 Since when you live in the suburbs what else is there?

19 And so they have to come to terms with it,

20 [cc]Because what can you do?

CHAPTER 15

And there will be still other great writers who realize that if all plots are the same [dd]plot,

2 You don't need a plot at all,

3 Or a story at all,

4 ªBecause everybody already knows what it is.

5 And besides, if we're all basically on our own,

6 ᵇThat is, alone in an insane godless universe,

7 Then who are you writing for anyway?

8 ᶜIn fact, you may as well write something just for yourself,

9 With allusions that only mean something to you,

10 And who cares if nobody understands one word of it,

11 ᵈSince the writer can't be sure that anybody else even exists,

12 And so what if they do,

13 ᵉBecause everyone with half an education knows what the story is about already,

14 Even if it's not a story but a vignette,

15 ᶠAnd even if it's not a narrative but a random gush of nonsense,

16 Which it doesn't matter if nobody understands,

17 ᵍAs long as it sounds literary,

18 Meaning there's no way to figure it out for sure and you just

a. 8.3

b. 2.16

*c. Pnot.32.3-4
Drex.7.10*

d. 2.12

e. Wil.17.1

f. Drex.6.4

g. Ext.13.13

*h. Dav.48.42-
43*

i. Drex.8.15

j. Bks.6.17

k. Bks.6.18

l. Wil.18.1-2

m. Boul.21.9

n. Zig.10.13

have to come to terms with it somehow,

19 No matter how depressing it gets,

20 Or how awful,

21 Or how ʰpointless,

22 ⁱJust like life.

CHAPTER 16

And when the bullet had said these and other things,

2 ʲIncluding naming a lot of names,

3 ᵏAnd even some specific titles,

4 Frankie & Johnny felt a lot better,

5 About everything,

6 Except life, of course,

7 Which the bullet finally mentioned in passing,

8 On its way out through the window,

9 Saying, "Believe it or not,

10 ˡ"A great prophet will come,

11 "And explain everything,

12 "Someday,

13 ᵐ"But not in time to hurt your royalties."

14 And then Frankie & Johnny lit up a ⁿgiant cigar,

15 And sat back to think up new literature for the ages.

THE BOOK OF THE VIP

ED

CHAPTER 1

There was a VIP named ªEd,

2 Who had a camera,

a. Psom.49.1-5

b. Adam.1.4

3 A microphone,

4 A stage,

5 And a transmission tower,

6 ᵇAnd changed the world.

CHAPTER 2

Ed was one of the first stars of the newfangled technology called TV,

2 And invented TV comedy shows,

3 And TV variety shows,

4 And TV journalism shows,

5 Among others.

CHAPTER 3

Ed started out in radio,

2 ªWhere he was a ventriloquist,

3 And had a dummy named ᵇCharlie,

4 Who was very very smart,

5 And knew everything,

6 Which made the audience like Ed a lot,

7 Because nobody likes a dummy who knows everything.

CHAPTER 4

When TV got invented,

2 Somehow,

3 Ed went on TV with Charlie,

4 Who couldn't talk when Ed was drinking water,

5 Which upset the audience,

6 For some reason,

7 And caused Ed to start looking around for something else to do on TV.

CHAPTER 5

The next great thing Ed did was start a TV variety show that was destined to last forever,

2 In TV terms,

3 Meaning more than a few years,

4 And found a whole bunch of new jugglers and comedians and singers to entertain everybody with,

a. Jefs.7.22
b. Yks.19.2
c. Yks.132.1-8
d. Zig.10.13
e. Dav.48.7
f. Yks.132.16-19
g. Yks.132.11-14
h. Grk.8.1-3

5 So that all he had to do was stand there,

6 And talk funny,

7 Which he did,

8 Although that wasn't all he did.

CHAPTER 6

For example, it was Ed who used TV to stop a ᶜwitch-hunt,

2 By smoking a lot of ᵈcigarettes on camera,

3 And getting pretty stentorian about the ᵉchief witch-hunter,

4 Who had been hunting witches for no more than a few years,

5 With a lot of accusations and threats and a couple of ᶠrabid legal dogs,

6 On TV,

7 Without anyone saying much of anything about it,

8 ᵍFor some reason.

9 When Ed said something about it,

10 And blew a lot of smoke all over it,

11 Everybody was pretty impressed about the way he had spoken right up,

12 After only a few years of watching it,

13 And thought he was a ʰhero.

CHAPTER 7

But deep down, Ed was a pretty serious guy,

2 And he had doubts about whether he had picked the right career,

3 Because he wasn't sure that talking into a microphone on camera really amounted to anything important,

4 Or worthwhile,

5 So he decided to get Charlie out of his box,
6 And ask him what he thought,
7 Since Charlie always knew everything.

CHAPTER 8

At first, Charlie just listened while Ed talked,
2 Explaining that he wasn't completely sure about TV,
3 And if it was a good thing or not,
4 Because he wasn't sure that he liked the idea of fifty million people watching the same Yugoslavian juggler all at the same time,
5 And fifty million people going out to the kitchen for a snack at the same time during the ªcommercial break,
6 And then flushing fifty million toilets at the same time,
7 Without actually talking to each other,
8 All night.

CHAPTER 9

But after a few minutes of this, Charlie readjusted his monocle,
2 And laughed pretty sarcastically,
3 Until Ed fell silent,
4 Waiting for Charlie to talk,
5 Which he finally did,
6 At great length.

CHAPTER 10

I always knew you were dumb (said Charlie),
2 But I didn't think you were completely deaf and blind too,
3 Until today.
4 The fact is, you couldn't have chosen a better career,

a. 76.4
b. 6.1-2

5 Because I have peered far into the future,
6 Through my monocle,
7 Which is a small screen indeed and not always easy to read,
8 But I think I know the gist of what will come,
9 Which is why I can assure you that TV is the most important development in the whole history of civilization,
10 Bar none.
11 It will change everything about who we are,
12 And what we do,
13 And how we think about it.
14 The truth is that TV is so big and so important that even I don't quite know where to begin,
15 Except to tell you that TV is so big and so important that even *you* will become big and important,
16 Because you'll be on TV for a long long time,
17 And change the world.

CHAPTER 11

For example, you can't possibly imagine how much you've already done to shape the future of journalism.
2 ᵇYour little attack on the witch-hunter was incredibly important,
3 No matter how it seems to you,
4 Because from now on,
5 People will feel different about journalists.
6 Before you did your thing,
7 People always thought journalists were something kind of low,
8 And grubby,
9 And unscrupulous.

10 They thought journalists were something they wouldn't want in their house,

11 Since no decent human being can ever be a journalist,

12 At least not a good journalist,

13 Because no decent human being could ever bring himself to ask questions of a mother grieving over her children's brand-new graves,

14 Or wedge his foot inside a door where it wasn't wanted,

15 Or sensationalize hideous crimes for the sake of selling newspapers,

16 Or dig through someone's trash to find an angle on a story,

17 Or any of hundreds of things that journalists have always had to do.

18 But thanks to you,

19 Those days are over,

20 And journalism is entering a new age,

21 Of power and prestige and immense respect,

22 And did I mention power?

CHAPTER 12

I see that you have a hard time believing the part about power and prestige,

2 But here's what will happen.

3 There will come a day,

4 Not long from now,

5 ªWhen TV journalists will become stars in their own right,

6 Like jugglers,

7 And acrobats,

8 And singers,

9 ᵇBut better.

10 ᶜThey'll get paid lots and lots of money,

11 ᵈMore money than you would ever believe if I told you,

a. Zig.10.21
b. Name.4.7
c. Psong.22.1-3
d. Psong.41.1-6
e. 6.2-3
f. Rom.3.17
g. Dav.30.9
h. F&J.14.13
i. Psay.5Q.16
j. Adam.14.5-7
k. Al.2.11
   Ann.6.23
l. Psom.40.4
m. Hall.10.2

12 For reading twenty-two minutes of news into a television camera.

13 And the keys to their stardom will all come from you,

14 ᵉWho taught them how to be properly stentorian,

15 As if you knew everything,

16 Or at least much more than you are actually saying,

17 Because you are a journalist,

18 ᶠAnd journalists know.

19 And it was also from you that they learned how to look into the camera,

20 Like a kindly ᵍuncle,

21 ʰWho still has teeth,

22 And will use them on any ⁱscoundrel who tries to stop the complete story from being told to the people,

23 With an appropriate amount of footage.

24 Nor is this all that TV journalists will learn how to do.

CHAPTER 13

They will learn that the most important thing about journalism is to be on the air when something important is happening.

2 One day, there will be a ʲrace between the two most powerful nations on earth to put a man on the moon,

3 And TV journalists will be there,

4 ᵏFor every single launch,

5 For years,

6 Sitting at a big desk overlooking the launch pad,

7 ˡSomewhat above it all,

8 Because a journalist has to be able to see.

9 ᵐAnd people will come to trust and like them,

10 Since the audience and their favorite TV journalists will have shared so many big moments together,
11 And it will almost seem like it couldn't have happened at all if the TV journalists hadn't been sitting there above the launching pad,
12 Somehow blessing it all,
13 ^aA little like the pope waving from the Vatican balcony,
14 No matter how silly that sounds.

CHAPTER 14

And in time, the people will come to depend on their favorite TV journalists,
2 ^bWho will have fine, important sounding names,
3 Like Eric Crankcase,
4 And Chet Severedhead,
5 And Walter Wrinkley,
6 ^cAnd even David Hunkley.
7 The world will change at lightning speed in years to come,
8 But people will feel safer knowing that Eric and Chet and Walter and David are there to keep an eye on things,
9 ^dGiving them twenty-two whole minutes of news every night,
10 Which they will read into the camera all by themselves,
11 ^eNight after night after night.

CHAPTER 15

And Walter and Eric and David and Chet will be there,
2 Sitting at their big desks,
3 ^fLooking into the camera like friendly uncles,
4 ^gWhen the civil rights movement gets under way,

a. *Ext.13.11*
b. *Jefs.7.15*
c. *Yks.6.17*
d. *18.6*
e. *Ned.6.24-25*
f. *12.20-21*
g. *Yks.151.1-11*
h. *Yks.57.7*
i. *Psp.3.6*
j. *Gods.6.27*
k. *Boul.21.9*
l. *Frog.39.5*

5 And they will cover all the people and events with great thoroughness,
6 Sometimes reading as much as two and a half or three minutes worth of news into the camera on a single story,
7 Because they are journalists,
8 And it is their unalterable mission to make sure the people get the whole story,
9 Every time.

CHAPTER 16

They will be there when the major ^hpolitical parties have their nominating conventions,
2 Every four years,
3 ⁱSitting at their big desks,
4 Overlooking the proceedings on the convention floor,
5 Somewhat above it all,
6 Because a journalist has to be able to see,
7 ^jAnd they will start explaining what it is the politicians are saying,
8 ^kAnd what they really meant,
9 Completely without bias,
10 Because they are above it all,
11 And can be trusted implicitly,
12 Like a friendly uncle.

CHAPTER 17

They will be there when the most powerful nation in the world goes to war in a mysterious and inscrutable land,
2 Far far away,
3 ^lIn Indochina.
4 But they will make sure that the people see it all,
5 Every facet of every angle of every issue,
6 Reading as much as three and a half or four minutes of news

into the camera about it every night,

7 Not to mention showing everything,

8 Including the good and the bad and the ugly,

9 In color,

10 On tape,

11 And edited specially so that the people can understand the [a]mysterious and inscrutable things they are seeing.

CHAPTER 18

They will be there through good times and bad,

2 And if it sometimes seems like the times are more bad than good,

3 That's just the way it goes,

4 [b]Life being what it is.

5 But the people will always have the comfort of knowing that they are there to explain everything,

6 [c]In just twenty-two minutes,

7 Which sure beats reading the papers.

CHAPTER 19

They will be there even when bad times become terrible [d]tragedies,

2 [e]For there will come a day when the leader of the Most Chosen Nation on Earth will be shot to death,

3 [f]On tape,

4 In color,

5 And they will be there for days,

6 [g]Covering everything,

7 Sitting at great big desks,

8 Somewhat above it all,

9 [h]But shedding tears every so often,

10 Just like a friendly uncle.

a. *Nips.2.10*
b. *Lies.14.5*
c. *Psp.3.11*
d. *Gnt.16.12*
e. *Yks.153.1-2*
f. *Yks.153.3*
g. *Psong.56.1-2*
h. *Mawr.25.22*
i. *Yks.152.1-15*
j. *19.2*
k. *18.6*
l. *Ned.24.8-11*
m. *18.6*
n. *12.13-14*
o. *Rom.22.11-12*

CHAPTER 20

And when the people start to get restless,

2 [i]About a lot of different things,

3 [j]Which they will start to do sometime after the murder of their leader,

4 The TV journalists will be there to help,

5 Fearlessly reporting on the restlessness,

6 And explaining everything,

7 So that even the dumbest person in the TV audience can understand it all,

8 [k]In just twenty-two minutes a night.

CHAPTER 21

And some of them will even put on [l]safari jackets,

2 And report fearlessly from the front,

3 Wherever that is,

4 Night after night,

5 So that everyone in the TV audience can learn exactly what war is,

6 And what it looks like when children die from gunshot wounds,

7 And mines,

8 And incendiary bombs,

9 And what it looks like when there's real fighting,

10 Within range of the TV cameras,

11 And what it looks like when it's hard to tell exactly what's going on,

12 [m]In just twenty-two minutes a night.

13 [n]But they'll still be as stentorian as anyone could want,

14 And explain everything,

15 [o]So that every single person

in the TV audience can make up their own mind.

CHAPTER 22

And some of them will even be brave enough to go to colleges and universities,
2 Throughout the land,
3 And report on how the students are getting restless,
4 ᵃNo matter how restless they get,
5 Or how many riots they have,
6 And explain everything,
7 Just like they always have.

CHAPTER 23

And when the day comes that it seems like the whole world is falling apart,
2 ᵇAnd the Most Chosen Nation on Earth has lost its heart,
3 And its ᶜfaith,
4 And its ᵈchildren,
5 ᵉAnd a bunch of its most popular leaders,
6 ᶠAnd its future,
7 The TV journalists will still be there,
8 Sitting slightly above it all,
9 And explaining everything,
10 So that everyone can understand it,
11 ᵍIn just twenty-two minutes a night.

CHAPTER 24

And who knows just what the people would do,
2 If they weren't there,
3 Through all the bad times,
4 And the tragic times,
5 To explain that it's all happened before,
6 And will probably get worse,
7 ʰBecause everyone is lying,
8 Except the TV journalists,

a. Lies.4.14-15
b. Yks.154.5
c. Yks.152.13-14
d. Wil.4.2-4
e. Wil.5.9
f. Yks.154.25-28
g. 18.6
h. Gods.4.4-6
i. 16.3
j. 18.6
k. 4.1-7
l. 4.3-6

9 ⁱWho are wise enough to see through it all,
10 And put it all on tape,
11 In living color,
12 And read the whole story into the camera,
13 Like a friendly, sharp-fanged uncle,
14 Night after night after night,
15 Because the awful truth can never hide from the power of TV,
16 ʲAs long as they can have their twenty-two minutes a night.

CHAPTER 25

But there will be much more to TV than journalism (Charlie went on),
2 Because there's more to life than news,
3 No matter what anyone says.
4 For example, there's entertainment too,
5 And nothing has ever changed entertainment the way TV will,
6 Which wouldn't surprise you,
7 If you'd thought about it at all.

CHAPTER 26

ᵏFor example, your little TV comedy show is more important than you think,
2 Because it will turn out that people just love to see comedy on TV,
3 And will even be willing to rearrange their whole lives just to see their favorite show,
4 Which you may find hard to believe,
5 ˡWhat with the way your show turned out and all,
6 But that's just the way life works,
7 And it doesn't say anything at all about how popular the really great shows will be,

8 Which will be very extremely,
9 Because they will all be so clever and original,
10 Unlike yours.

CHAPTER 27

There will be one great comedy show called 'I Love Lucky,'
2 Which will be all about a crazy redheaded housewife,
3 Played by ªLucky Bill,
4 Who will have a funny, hot-tempered husband named Tricki,
5 Played by ᵇDizzy Mañanaz,
6 Not to mention some funny married friends called Edith and Ed,
7 No relation to you, of course,
8 Who will live in the apartment next door to Lucky's,
9 And help her have all kinds of incredibly funny adventures,
10 For years.
11 In fact, Lucky will become one of the most famous people in the world,
12 And absolutely everybody will adore her,
13 Which is why she will make millions and millions of dollars,
14 ᶜIn spite of not having a single brain in her head.

CHAPTER 28

There will be another great comedy called 'I Love Alice,'
2 ᵈWhich will be completely different from 'I Love Lucky,'
3 ᵉBecause it will be all about a *sane* redheaded housewife,
4 Played by ᶠJane Audrey,
5 Who will have a funny, hot-tempered husband named Ruff,
6 Played by ᵍJokie Gasman,
7 ʰNot to mention some funny

a.	27.14
b.	28.6
c.	Lies.6.16-19
	Wil.16.18-20
d.	27.1
e.	27.2
f.	Dav.14.39
g.	Dav.30.9
h.	27.6
i.	27.8
j.	27.9
k.	27.12
l.	Pnot.32.3
m.	27.1
n.	27.2
o.	27.3
p.	F&J.2.15
q.	27.8
r.	28.10

married friends named Tipsy and Ed,
8 No relation to you, of course,
9 ⁱWho will live in the apartment *upstairs* from Alice and Ruff,
10 ʲAnd help them have all kinds of incredibly funny adventures,
11 Especially Ruff,
12 Who will become one of the most famous people in the world,
13 ᵏAnd absolutely everybody will adore him,
14 Which is why Jokie Gasman will make millions and millions of dollars,
15 In spite of being fat and loud and obnoxious in every part he plays,
16 And especially this part,
17 Although he'll always make up for being so obnoxious by ˡkissing Alice at the end of the show,
18 And telling her how much he loves her,
19 Just like everybody else.

CHAPTER 29

There will be another great comedy show called 'I Love Margie,'
2 ᵐWhich will also be completely different from 'I Love Lucky,'
3 ⁿBecause it will be all about a crazy redheaded *unmarried girl*,
4 Played by ᵒStormy Gale,
5 Who will have a funny, hot-tempered father,
6 Played by some ᵖBrit-or-other,
7 ۹Who will live with Margie *in a nice white house in the suburbs*,
8 ʳAnd help her have all kinds

of incredibly funny adventures,
9 For years.
10 In fact, Margie will become very famous,
11 And lots and lots of people will adore her,
12 [a]But not as much as Lucky Bull.

CHAPTER 30

There will be another great comedy show called 'I love Deana,'
2 [b]Which will be completely different from 'I Love Lucky' *and* 'I Love Margie,'
3 [c]Not to mention 'I Love Alice,'
4 [d]Because it will be all about a sane *blond* housewife,
5 Played by [e]Deana Rood,
6 [f]Who will have a *mild-tempered* husband with a cardigan and a newspaper,
7 Played by [g]Karl Botch,
8 [h]Not to mention some helpful and well-mannered children,
9 [i]Who will live with Deana in a nice white house in the suburbs,
10 Where nothing ever happens,
11 For years.
12 In fact, people will adore Deana and she will become very popular,
13 Even though nothing funny will ever happen to her or her family,
14 Which won't be a problem at all,
15 Because there will be a wonderful prerecorded laugh track on the show,
16 [j]So that everybody will know which unfunny things to laugh at.

a. 27.3
b. 27.1
    29.1
c. 28.1
d. 28.3
e. Dav.54.12
f. 27.4
g. 60.10
h. Yks.143.5
i. 29.7
j. Vin.49.5
k. 30.4
l. Dav.30.27
m. 60.12
n. 30.8
o. 30.9
p. 30.10
q. 30.13
r. 30.16
s. 30.12
t. Yks.143.4
u. Zig.10.12
v. 31.2
w. 27.2
x. 60.10

CHAPTER 31

There will be another great comedy show called 'I Love Father,'
2 Which will be completely different from other shows,
3 [k]Because it will be all about a sane *dad*,
4 Played by [l]Miracle Wilby,
5 Who will have a sane wife with a snooty accent,
6 Played by [m]Mr. Sprocket's mother,
7 [n]Not to mention some helpful and well-mannered children,
8 [o]Who will live with Father in a nice white house in the suburbs,
9 [p]Where nothing ever happens,
10 For years.
11 In fact, people will adore Father and he will become very popular,
12 [q]Even though nothing funny will ever happen on his comedy show either,
13 [r]Which is why he'll use the same prerecorded laugh track that Deana uses,
14 [s]Even though he won't be quite as popular as Deana Rood,
15 [t]What with Deana being a real attractive-looking woman after all,
16 [u]In spite of always having her dress buttoned up to her neck.

CHAPTER 32

There will be another great comedy show called 'I Love Susie,'
2 [v]Which will be completely different from other shows,
3 [w]Because it will be all about a crazy blond *secretary*,
4 Played by [x]Annette Northern,

5 ᵃWho will have a funny, hot-tempered *boss*,
6 ᵇNot to mention some funny friends,
7 ᶜWho will help Susie have all kinds of funny adventures,
8 For years.
9 In fact, people will adore Susie and she will be very popular,
10 ᵈThough not as popular as Lucky Boll, of course.

CHAPTER 33

There will be another show called 'I Love Dick,'
2 Which will be all about a sane *TV comedy writer*,
3 Played by ᵉDick Tyler Morgue,
4 ᶠWho will have a funny, hot-tempered boss,
5 Played by ᵍCurly Rhino,
6 Not to mention a funny hysterical wife,
7 Played by ʰMarie Van Dirge,
8 And some funny friends too,
9 ⁱWho will help Dick have all kinds of funny adventures,
10 For years.
11 And people will adore Dick also,
12 ʲAnd he will become almost as popular as Lucky Bell,
13 But not quite.

CHAPTER 34

There will be another great comedy show called 'I Love Badger,'
2 ᵏWhich will be completely different from other shows,
3 ˡBecause it will be all about a crazy *little boy* named Badger Cadger,
4 Who will have sane parents named Jane and Word,
5 Even though Word will hardly

a. 27.4
b. 27.6
c. 27.9
d. 27.11
e. Dav.40.9
f. 32.5
g. Dav.57.32
h. 27.3
i. 32.7
j. 27.11
k. 32.2
l. 32.3
m. Ira.6.9-10
n. 31.9
o. 4.3
p. 34.10
q. 27.1

ever say anything except 'You want to tell me about it, Badger?'
6 But Badger will never want to tell Word about it,
7 Because it's too awful,
8 Whatever it is,
9 Even though Badger and his brother Walleye hardly ever do anything that's *really* awful,
10 ᵐBecause they live in a nice white house in the suburbs,
11 ⁿWhere nothing awful ever happens,
12 Which may help explain why 'I Love Badger' will become so very popular,
13 Although,
14 You know.

CHAPTER 35

Knowing you as I do (said Charlie),
2 I know you must be thinking that your show might have survived if you had called it 'I Love Ed,'
3 And if you had left ᵒ*me* out of it altogether,
4 And had given yourself a nice family instead,
5 ᵖWith a nice white house in the suburbs,
6 And it is true that there will be hundreds and hundreds of great shows like this,
7 Including 'I Love Patty Puke,'
8 And 'I Love Gadget,'
9 And 'I Love My Three or Four Sons,'
10 And 'I Love My Son of a Bachelor Father,'
11 And 'I Love Izzie and Henrietta and Chip and Dale and All Their Dumb Neighbors,'
12 ᑫNot to mention 'I Love Lucky Even Without Dizzy,'

13 ᵃWhich will all be as clever and original as they come.

14 But if you think that a comedy show can't succeed unless it's about a not very funny family that's completely average in every respect,

15 You'd just be kidding yourself,

16 Because there will be other clever and original comedy shows that feature stars who aren't completely average,

17 ᵇAnd are much more like *me* instead,

18 And they will succeed,

19 Spectacularly,

20 Unlike yours.

CHAPTER 36

For example, there will be a great comedy show called 'I Love My Horse,'

2 ᶜWhich will be very very different from other shows,

3 ᵈBecause it will be all about a sane *architect* named Wilmer,

4 Who has a *talking horse* named Mr. Red,

5 ᵉOr something like that,

6 ᶠNot to mention a crazy blond wife,

7 ᵍAnd a nice white house in the suburbs,

8 ʰAnd some funny next-door neighbors,

9 ⁱWho will all help Wilmer get into tremendous jams with his horse,

10 Because they're all too stupid to know that Mr. Red can talk,

11 ʲWhich is just like humans, isn't it?

12 Anyway, Mr. Red will go on to become a very popular star,

13 And maybe even more popular than some movie stars,

---

a. 26.9-10
b. 3.3
c. 34.2
d. 33.2
e. 28.8
f. 32.3
g. 35.5
h. 33.8
i. 32.7
j. Zig.9.2
k. Barb.1.8
  Mawr.22.24
l. 30.15-16
m. 36.1
n. 32.3
o. Grk.11.1-2
  Zig.7.9
p. Dav.40.9
q. 36.7
r. 31.5
s. 31.7
t. 36.11
u. 32.4
v. 35.13

---

14 ᵏSuch as Franco the talking mule,

15 Who will be a has-been long before Mr. Red comes along,

16 Which doesn't say anything at all about where Mr. Red will get the idea to start talking,

17 Because all the really great comedy shows will be completely original,

18 Not to mention clever,

19 ˡWhich you'll always be able to tell by how hard people are laughing on the prerecorded laugh track.

CHAPTER 37

There will be another comedy show called 'I Love My Model T,'

2 ᵐWhich will be completely different from 'I Love My Horse,'

3 ⁿBecause it will be all about a crazy blond secretary who turns into a Model T,

4 ᵒFor some reason,

5 And then goes to live with her son,

6 Played by ᵖJoey Tyler Morgue,

7 ᑫWho lives in a nice white house in the suburbs,

8 ʳWith his sane blond wife,

9 ˢAnd their helpful and well-mannered children,

10 ᵗWho never suspect that the Model T in the garage is their dad's mother,

11 Even though the ᵘModel T is old,

12 And therefore doesn't belong in the suburbs,

13 At all,

14 Which is why the show will *not* last for years and years,

15 ᵛIn spite of being so clever and original.

CHAPTER 38

There will be another comedy show called 'I Love Tracy,'

2 ᵃWhich will also be completely different from 'I Love My Horse,'

3 ᵇBecause it will be all about a crazy *old* comedian,

4 Played by ᶜGorge Boring,

5 Who will have a talking wind-up baby doll for a wife,

6 Played by Gorge's wife ᵈTracy,

7 ᵉWho will live with Gorge in a nice white house in the suburbs,

8 ᶠWhere nothing ever happens,

9 Except that it will all be very funny,

10 ᵍBecause none of their funny friends will ever notice that there's anything strange about Tracy,

11 Even though she won't ever do anything right,

12 And won't even be able to say good night properly,

13 ʰJust like all American wives,

14 Except for Deana, of course.

CHAPTER 39

There will be another comedy show called 'I Love Gulligan,'

2 ⁱWhich will be completely different from other shows starring inanimate objects that talk,

3 ʲBecause it will take place on a tropical island,

4 Where there won't be even a single suburb,

5 Or even one white house,

6 Which is why 'I Love Gulligan' will be such an enormous hit,

7 And why everyone will come

to love the ᵏtalking dummy named Gulligan,

8 Which is a shame you didn't think of yourself,

9 Because it would have been a perfect part for ˡMort,

10 And you could have played the ᵐCaptain,

11 And I could have played the ⁿmillionaire,

12 Although I'm hard pressed to think of enough other dummies to round out the rest of the ᵒcast.

CHAPTER 40

And speaking of shows that star inanimate objects,

2 ᵖThere will also be some great comedies that don't use a laugh track,

3 ۹Although they will also be very funny and clever and original,

4 Because they will be all about how an inanimate object can make a hero out of a good-looking male model,

5 Who will always do what's right,

6 And always win in the end,

7 And always survive till next week,

8 As long as he can lay his hands on a ʳgun.

CHAPTER 41

For example, there will be a great comedy show called ˢ'I Love My Rifle,'

2 Which will be all about an infallible rifle,

3 Played by ᵗWinchester Forty-Five,

4 Who lives out west with a retired baseball player,

5 Played by ᵘCheek Bones,

6 Who has to protect his little

a. 36.1
b. 33.2
c. Yks.19.2
   Wil.16.18-20
d. 38.6
e. 37.7
f. 31.9
g. 36.11
h. Mawr.22.20
i. 36.1
   37.1
   38.1
j. Psp.2.9
k. Yks.19.2
   Dav.40.9
l. Yks.19.2
m. Dav.23.16
n. Dav.14.21
   & 14.25
   & 14.27
   Ed.38.4
   Dav.35.40
o. Mawr.2.5
   Dav.40.6
p. 30.16
q. 35.20
r. Zig.10.13
s. Ann.18.7
t. Wil.16.16-20
u. Dav.52.4

boy from outlaws every single week of the year,

7 Which is why it's so lucky that Winchester is there to give him so much great advice,

8 And take care of all the funny outlaws,

9 [a]Who can't ever seem to learn how to shoot straight,

10 No matter how many times Winchester shows them.

CHAPTER 42

There will be another great comedy show called 'I Love Bounty Hunting,'

2 [b]Which will be completely different from 'I Love My Rifle,'

3 [c]Because it will be all about a *sawed-off* rifle,

4 [d]Played by Winchester Forty-Five Junior,

5 [e]Who will live with a completely silent bounty hunter,

6 Played by [f]Steve McKiller,

7 Out west somewhere,

8 And together, Winchester and Steve will hunt down outlaws,

9 And either kill them dead,

10 Or bring them back alive,

11 Depending on whether the outlaws are really really funny,

12 Or only mildly amusing,

13 Which people will always be able to tell by whether Steve's mouth twitches a lot,

14 Or just a little.

CHAPTER 43

There will be another great comedy called 'I Love Gunfire,'

2 [g]Which will be completely different from 'I Love My Rifle' *and* 'I Love Bounty Hunting,'

a. 36.11
b. 41.1
c. 41.2
d. 41.3
e. Dav.35.26-32
f. Dav.35.36
g. 41.1
   42.1
h. 42.3
i. 41.3
j. 46.10
k. Dav.40.9
l. Dav.20.7-8
m. Dav.52.20
   & 35.40
n. Yks.30.29
o. 43.1
p. 43.3
q. 41.3
r. 42.5
s. Yks.61.19
t. Dav.52.4
u. 42.8

3 [h]Because it will be all about a *six-gun*,

4 Played by [i]Colt Forty-Five,

5 Who lives out west with a lawman named Marshal Bullet,

6 Played by [j]James Harness,

7 Not to mention all of Marshal's funny friends,

8 Such as [k]Chuckroast, the hilarious crippled deputy,

9 And [l]Miss Kitty-Kat, the virgin saloon girl,

10 And [m]Festering Sore, the town idiot,

11 Not to mention [n]Doc Holiday,

12 Who will absolutely always be on hand to take the bullet out of Marshal's shoulder,

13 Which will get back in there every week,

14 Right before Colt kills the outlaw who pulled the trigger,

15 Which will be just hilarious,

16 Because everybody knows that the outlaw gun needs a sight readjustment,

17 Everybody but next week's outlaw, that is.

CHAPTER 44

There will be another great comedy show called 'I Love Traveling with Guns,'

2 [o]Which will be completely different from 'I Love Gunfire,'

3 [p]Because it will be all about a *hired* six-gun,

4 Played by [q]Pearl Handled Colt,

5 [r]Who will live with a very well-dressed bounty hunter called [s]Palindrome,

6 Played by [t]Richard Gravel,

7 [u]And together, Pearl and Richard will travel all over the place killing people,

8 [a]But only after giving them a calling card first,
9 Proving how good and civilized they both are,
10 [b]Even though they'll both be dressed in black.

CHAPTER 45

There will be another great comedy show called 'I Love the Lone Rider,'
2 [c]Which will be completely different from all the other shows starring guns,
3 [d]Because it will be all about *two* six-guns,
4 Played by [e]Silver Colt and his twin brother Scout,
5 [f]Who will live with a very funny man dressed in stretch pants,
6 Played by the [g]Lone Ranger,
7 Who will always wear a mask so that no one can recognize him in those stretch pants,
8 [h]And together, Lone and Silver and Scout will ride all over the place hunting down outlaws,
9 Accompanied by their faithful Indian friend [i]Toto,
10 Which is a lot of company for a man who's supposed to be all alone,
11 Although that's a big part of the reason why the show will become such a comedy classic,
12 Not to mention what great shots Silver and Scout are,
13 [j]Because they will use silver bullets,
14 Exclusively,
15 And they will always shoot the outlaws in the hand,
16 Because they are so peace-loving at heart,
17 And also because the Lone Rider will just hate it when any [k]blood gets on his stretch pants.

a. Wht.25
b. Psay.5S.31
c. 41.1 42.1 43.1 44.1
d. 43.3
e. 41.3
f. 44.5
g. Yks.30.20-36
h. 44.7
i. Psay.5A.13 Dav.30.9
j. Dav.30.23-25 & 47.11 & 47.22
k. Hall.4.3
l. 41.1 42.1 43.1 44.1 45.1
m. 45.3
n. Adam.25.8-9
o. 42.7
p. 36.12-13
q. 36.14
r. 63.3
s. 60.10
t. Dav.34.19

CHAPTER 46

There will be another great comedy show called 'I Love the Panderosa,'
2 [l]Which will be completely different from other shows starring guns,
3 [m]Because it will be all about a *whole family of guns*,
4 Including Papa Six-Gun and his four sons,
5 [n]Played by five members of the illustrious Colt family of thespians,
6 [o]Who live out west on a horse ranch,
7 With a bunch of excellent supporting rifles that stand tall inside their rack in the library,
8 Not to mention a whole family of very good-looking studs called the Carthorses,
9 Including Red Carthorse, the wise old stallion,
10 [p]Played by Mr. Red, of course,
11 And [q]Adam Carthorse, the eldest foal, who wants to run away from home and have an acting career,
12 Just like dad,
13 And then there's [r]Horse Carthorse, the biggest foal, who always wears a very handsome brown saddle and bucks like crazy when he gets mad,
14 And [s]Little Foal Carthorse, the pony of the family, who has a huge mane and a real knack for attracting the fillies,
15 Not to mention [t]Hopalong Suet, who has a braided tail and always whinnies right around dinnertime.
16 All of these families are very attached to their ranch,

17 Played by the ᵃPanderosa,
18 Which is constantly under siege by outlaws,
19 Who attack once a week,
20 ᵇAnd have to be killed before they steal the hay crop,
21 So that the Carthorses won't starve to death,
22 Which is why the show will be so darned funny,
23 Because it will be obvious to everybody in the audience that old Red and Adam and Horse are in absolutely no danger of ever starving to death,
24 ᶜAnd Little Foal will be okay too as long as there's a single filly within a radius of a hundred miles.

a. Ed.60.10
b. Psay.5A.9
c. Pnot.9.5
d. Psom.9.1-12
e. Yks.30.28
f. Yks.30.27
g. Zig.10.13
h. Yks.114.10-12
i. Krt.6.5
j. 48.1
k. Yks.112.2-7
l. Ann.10.1

CHAPTER 47

And these are really only a few of the great gun comedies that will be set in the wild west,
2 Because there will be more of them than there are guns in the Most Chosen Nation,
3 Or almost that many, anyway,
4 Including 'I Love Cayenne,'
5 And 'I Love the Lowman,'
6 And 'I Love Marvelick,'
7 ᵈAnd 'I Love Jim Blowie,'
8 ᵉAnd 'I Love Bat Mannerson,
9 ᶠAnd 'I Love Wyeth Urp,'
10 And 'I Love Dead Valley Days,'
11 And 'I Love the Chuckwagon Train,'
12 And 'I Love Cowhide,'
13 Not to mention 'I Love Dale Evans,'
14 And 'I Love Annie Ugly,'
15 And some other stuff for the women in the audience.
16 But in case you think that all the best gun parts will be played by the Colts and Winchesters,

17 There will also be a whole bunch of great comedies that don't take place out west,
18 But in other places instead,
19 ᵍWhere there will be parts for shotguns and snub-nosed police revolvers and every other kind of gun you can think of,
20 Including machine guns.

CHAPTER 48

For example, there will be a great comedy called 'I Love Combat!',
2 ʰWhich will be all about a bunch of M1 rifles who are trying to conquer France during World War II,
3 For years and years,
4 Which they will never quite do,
5 Because there's always another little French town full of German Lugers,
6 ⁱWhich will speak in extremely funny accents, of course,
7 And keep absolutely everybody in stitches,
8 For years and years.

CHAPTER 49

There will be another great comedy called 'I Love Enemy Fighters at Twelve O'Clock,'
2 ʲWhich will be completely different from 'I Love Combat!',
3 ᵏBecause it will be all about the Eighth Air Force trying to bomb Germany into submission during World War II,
4 For years and years.
5 And the focus of the show will be on the B-17 crews who made all the difference in the war,
6 ˡIncluding the waist guns,

7 [a]And the nose gun,
8 [b]And the turret gun,
9 [c]And the tail gun,
10 [d]Not to mention the Norden bombsight,
11 [e]Which will always come through in the end,
12 [f]And drop all the bombs right on target,
13 [g]While the rest of the crew is bringing down ME-109s left and right,
14 So that the extremely good-looking human beings on the plane can get home safely,
15 [h]Which they will mostly do,
16 Although the German anti-aircraft guns and the fifty-caliber machine guns on the German fighter planes will put up a heroic resistance,
17 [i]And they will refuse to surrender,
18 So that the B-17 crews will have to keep firing and bombing,
19 For years and years,
20 Which must be where the comedy comes in.

CHAPTER 50

There will be another great comedy show called 'I Love the Untouchables,'
2 [j]Which will be completely different from 'I Love Combat!' and 'I Love Shooting Enemy Fighters at Twelve O'Clock,'
3 Because it will take place in a war zone called [k]Chicago,
4 Which isn't even in Europe,
5 So you can see how different it will be right there.
6 The show will be all about competing gangs of machine

a. *Ann.10.1*
b. *Ann.10.1*
c. *Ann.10.1*
d. *Al.2.11*
e. *Dav.33.3*
f. *Pnot.32.3-4*
g. *Ann.10.1*
   & 6.23
   Al.2.11
h. *Psay.5Q.67*
i. *Yks.78.4-5*
j. *48.1*
   49.1
k. *60.10*
l. *Psay.5D.11*
m. *Brit.42.27-31*
n. *Yks.19.2*
o. *63.3*
p. *Psong.58.4-5*
q. *62.3*

guns whose sacred mission it is to make sure that [l]Prohibition is as loud as possible,
7 In every single precinct,
8 Which helps explain why the gangs are called "the Untouchables," because after they've fired off a few hundred rounds, they're way too hot to handle.
9 All of the starring roles will be played by members of the great [m]Thompson family,
10 And they will be supported by some outstanding comedians in subsidiary roles,
11 Including [n]Robert Stock as Eliot Miss, the Treasury agent who has a nervous habit of shooting up liquor warehouses while shouting "*Re*load" in a hoarse monotone,
12 And [o]Neville Barrel as Al Caboom, the immigrant mastermind who has a nervous habit of shooting up [p]Treasury agents, restaurants with plate-glass windows, and innocent civilians,
13 So that the only common bond between Eliot and Al is their allegiance to the Thompson family,
14 Which is the only reason they manage to stay together week after week after week,
15 And thus explains why this show will be the first in a grand American comic tradition based on humorous [q]culture clashes,
16 Which I'll be telling you more about later,
17 Because it's so incredibly important.

CHAPTER 51

There will also be a vast number of comedies about guns owned by police officers and private investigators and secret agents,

2 Which will be very very popular,

3 And will show the citizens of the Most Chosen Nation how to commit any kind of crime you could think of,

4 While making only one little mistake,

5 Which is all it takes for the great hero named ªSmith & Wesson to win out in the end,

6 With a hail of magic bullets that always injure or kill the ᵇoutlaw,

7 Without spilling a drop of blood,

8 Or even mussing the hair of the ᶜhandsome actors who are responsible for carrying Smith & Wesson to the big showdown.

9 And there will be so many of these comedies that it's impossible to describe all of them individually,

10 Not to mention the fact that they won't all be quite as original as the comedies we've already talked about,

11 And they will become sort of a blur after a while,

12 A lot like a speeding bullet.

13 But if you doubt my word, I can give you the names of some of them,

14 So that when they come along you can check them out for yourself,

15 Including 'I Love 77 Surfside Strip,'

16 And 'I Love 50 Hawaiian Eyes,'

17 And 'I Love Cannix,'

18 And 'I Love Harry Diamond,'

19 And 'I Love Peter's Gun,'

a. Psom.2.3
b. 41.9
c. 60.10
d. Dav.47.11
e. 53.1
f. 54.1
    55.1
    56.1
g. 57.1
h. 60.1
i. Psom.68.1
   Dav.15.9
   & 56.47
j. 58.1
   59.1

20 ᵈAnd 'I Love the Naked Policewoman,'

21 And 'I Love the Man from the F.B.I.,'

22 And 'I Love Spying for My Uncle,'

23 And 'I Love Lieutenant Dragnet,'

24 And 'I Love Barnaby Ironstreet,'

25 And...

26 Well, I could go on and on,

27 But I think you get the idea.

CHAPTER 52

Now, you may find this next part pretty hard to believe,

2 But there will also be some comedy shows that aren't about completely average families living in the suburbs,

3 Or about inanimate objects that make a lot of objectionable noise!

4 What do you think about that?

5 For example, there will be shows that only show the suburbs every once in a while,

6 And that are mostly about ᵉinfallible teachers,

7 ᶠAnd infallible lawyers,

8 ᵍAnd infallible doctors,

9 ʰAnd infallible starship ⁱcommanders, of course,

10 Unless they're about ʲinfallible heroes who are running away from something or somebody,

11 Which pretty neatly sums up the whole population of the Most Chosen Nation on Earth,

12 Don't you think?

CHAPTER 53

For example, there will be a great situation comedy called 'I Love Mr. Nojack,'

2 Which will be all about a

handsome and infallible high school teacher,

3 Played by [a]Jan Francisco,

4 Who will always care about all his students,

5 And always figure out all their problems,

6 [b]In just twenty-two minutes a night,

7 Unless the network gives him forty-four minutes instead,

8 Which they will probably do,

9 Because Mr. Nojack will be so popular,

10 Although his great popularity will maybe be responsible for this show not lasting as long as some other shows,

11 [c]Because teachers don't make a lot of money,

12 [d]Which is why the day will come when Mr. Nojack has to move on to some other line of work,

13 [e]Like maybe something to do with the law,

14 Although maybe not too,

15 [f]Because the law will be pretty well stocked with infallible people,

16 On TV, anyway,

17 As we shall see.

CHAPTER 54

Indeed, one of the greatest of all comedy shows will be called 'I Love Perry Mastodon,'

2 And it's not hard to see why someone would love [g]Perry Mastodon,

3 [h]Because he will absolutely always get his client off,

4 And not just with some namby-pamby "not guilty" verdict,

5 But with a confession, under oath, by the real murderer,

6 Who will always break down

a. *60.10*
b. *18.6*
c. *Psong.1.1-6*
d. *Psong.40.1*
e. *51.24*
f. *Penn.3.10*
g. *Kin.5.3*
h. *Penn.3.1-2*
i. *43.6*
j. *Dav.14.41*
k. *38.4*
l. *44.6*
m. *Psom.73.13*

in tears when Perry rolls his wheelchair up to the witness box,

7 And starts boring in with his great questions,

8 Which is actually only playing for time,

9 Until [i]Pall sneaks in in his loud sport coat,

10 And hands the surprising last-minute evidence to [j]Dulla,

11 Who whispers it to Perry,

12 Which is when the real murderer starts to look crazed,

13 And makes a dash for the door,

14 Except that the bailiff drags him back,

15 And then he spills it all,

16 So that the only remaining mystery is why the victim got killed by somebody who hardly knew him at all,

17 Which always stumps [k]Lieutenant Drag, of course,

18 Not to mention [l]Milton Hamburger, the D.A.,

19 But not Perry,

20 Because he's the kind of lawyer you can only find in the Most Chosen Nation,

21 If you look in the phone book,

22 Under "M," of course,

23 For "Miracles."

CHAPTER 55

There will be another great comedy about lawyers called 'I Love the Defensers,'

2 Which will be funny because the Defensers won't always win their cases,

3 Although they mostly will,

4 Because if they didn't, the show wouldn't be so much a comedy as [m]theater of the absurd,

5 Which you can't say about 'I Love the Defensers,'
6 Because they're so committed and honest and brilliant and all that,
7 And when they lose a case it isn't because they're not infallible,
8 But because their clients are guilty,
9 Which means that it wouldn't be right for them to win,
10 And so they don't,
11 Which is why you have to admire them so much,
12 ªEven if anyone in his right mind would look under "M" in the yellow pages before they settled for these guys.

CHAPTER 56

There will also be another great lawyer comedy called 'I Love Judge for the Defense,'
2 Which will be very funny because of all the confusing conversations between the judge on the bench and the Judge on the case,
3 Who will be played by Karl Botch,
4 ᵇWithout a cardigan or a newspaper,
5 Because he will be a manly man,
6 And rich,
7 And infallible,
8 ᶜWhich is why Deana isn't anywhere in sight,
9 ᵈAnd why Judge always always wins.

CHAPTER 57

In fact, there will be so many infallible lawyers on television that you might get the idea only lawyers are infallible,

a. 54.23
b. 30.6-7
c. 30.1
d. Yks.141.11-12
e. 52.8
f. Ed.60.10
g. 28.6
h. 31.4
i. Dav.22.50 & 47.11 & 47.22
j. 54.22-23

2 Which isn't true,
3 ᵉBecause there will also be infallible doctors,
4 Who will always save their patients,
5 With so much brilliant medical knowledge and so much warm, caring commitment that it's easy to see why their patients will just love them to pieces,
6 Even after they get the bill,
7 Which they will do on shows like 'I Love Dr. Kilmore,'
8 Which will be all about an amazingly good-looking young ᶠintern who saves more patients than the Mayo Clinic,
9 And 'I Love Ben Cranky,'
10 Which will be all about a ᵍbrilliant brain surgeon who glowers all the time because he can't figure out how to button up his operating tunic, although that doesn't make him a bad doctor, because he saves more patients than Dr. Kilmore,
11 And 'I Love Miracle Wilby,'
12 Which will be all about a ʰbrilliant general practitioner who saves everybody with a warm smile and a pat on the head, not to mention the fact that he has a nice white house in the suburbs, which puts everybody at ease, even if he does have a ⁱyounger associate who rides around on a motorbike, which you have to forgive, because Miracle seems to think it's okay,
13 And it's very very smart to have Miracle as your doctor,
14 Because then it doesn't matter if you're sick or just got framed for murder,
15 ʲSince you can get help under the same listing in the phone book.

CHAPTER 58

And if Miracles are your favorite thing,

2 Then there will be other great comedy shows you'll enjoy sinking your teeth into,

3 Because only a Miracle could ever save ªDr. Richard Krumble,

4 Who will be the hero of a great comedy called 'I Love the Fugitive,'

5 Which will be all about an infallible doctor who didn't hire ᵇPerry Mastodon as his lawyer,

6 Which explains why he gets convicted of murdering his wife,

7 And gets sentenced to death in the electric chair,

8 Except that he isn't guilty,

9 ᶜAnd so he escapes to go looking for the ᵈone-legged man,

10 Who always seems to stay one step ahead of Krumble,

11 Week after week,

12 Month after month,

13 And year after year,

14 Which is really sort of okay,

15 Because somehow Krumble always seems to stay one step ahead of ᵉLieutenant Gourd,

16 Who looks at maps a lot,

17 And always figures out where Krumble is hiding eventually,

18 ᶠBut only after the last commercial,

19 Which is why Krumble always slips onto the bus just a second or two before Gourd arrives,

20 Which is an important benefit to every citizen in the Most Chosen Nation on Earth,

21 Because in his travels Dr. Krumble is gradually solving all the personal problems of everyone he meets,

22 Week after week,

a. Dav.22.50
*   & 47.11*
*   & 47.22*
b. 54.1-3
c. Drex.6.1
d. Dav.30.40
e. Dav.14.25-27
f. 76.2-4
g. 57.13-15
h. Drex.6.1
i. 58.22-24
j. 27.5

23 Month after month,

24 And year after year.

25 And if we all wait long enough, he will probably take care of all the great social ills in the country,

26 Unless Ben Guzzle gets there first.

CHAPTER 59

If you think I slipped one past you with the name of Ben Guzzle,

2 You're right,

3 But he's important,

4 Because if 'I Love the Fugitive' will teach everybody that it really is a good idea to call Perry if they get indicted for murder,

5 ᵍBen will teach everybody that it really is a good idea to call Miracle Wilby if they get a fatal disease,

6 ʰWhich is what Ben will have in a great comedy show called 'I Love Running for My Life,'

7 Where he will do pretty much the same thing Dr. Krumble does,

8 Namely, run away from home in a desperate search for salvation,

9 ⁱWhile systematically solving all the personal problems of the people he meets along the way,

10 Which will practically double the chance of getting real help for everybody in the audience,

11 Because Dr. Krumble will stick pretty consistently with blue-collar neighborhoods, including ʲmigrant workers and oppressed minorities and so forth,

12 While Ben will spend most of his time with the international

jet set, who have problems of their own,

13 ªSo that people in the TV audience will be able to enjoy an unprecedented level of confidence about the future,

14 Because if they stay in the suburbs where they belong,

15 They'll always be able to call Perry or Miracle,

16 And if they stray into the jet set or the lower classes,

17 They'll probably run into someone who will help,

18 ᵇWith all the wisdom they've gained running away from their own problems.

CHAPTER 60

All of this infallible assistance will be very very reassuring to the population of the Most Chosen Nation on Earth,

2 Until they start asking some really hard questions about the future,

3 Such as "What if I happened to get sick on a starship under hostile enemy fire?

4 "What would I do then?"

5 Well, fortunately, the TV audience will even find an answer for this dilemma on their TV screens one day,

6 Because in the far distant future there will be a great comedy show called 'I Love Boldly Going on Star Dates,'

7 ᶜWhich will be all about an infallible Starship Captain called James T. Quark,

8 Played by ᵈWilliam Shouter,

9 Who commands an indestructible starship called the Underprise,

10 Played by a ᵉplastic model,

11 Not to mention the com-

a. Yks.138.15
b. Pnot.16.1-5
  & 43.1-5
  & 52.1-5
c. 52.9
d. Ann.19.13
e. Wil.16.19-20
  Psay.5Z.10-11
f. Mawr.25.1-2
g. Mawr.25.22
h. Psay.5Q.4
i. Zig.7.5
j. 54.22-23
k. 60.10
l. Mall.13.8
m. Vin.49.5

pletely infallible crew of the Underprise,

12 Including ᶠMr. Sprocket, the infallible science officer with the pointy ears and no emotions,

13 And ᵍDr. McCry, the infallible ship's doctor with the pointy head and more emotions than you can shake a pointy stick at,

14 And a whole bunch of infallible ʰjunior officers from all over planet Earth,

15 ⁱWhich turns out to be the Most Chosen Planet in the Universe,

16 Because it's a Type "M" planet,

17 ʲWhich you will find an explanation of under "M" in the yellow pages,

18 If you have any doubts about it,

19 Which you shouldn't,

20 Because Captain Quark and the crew of the Underprise will keep boldly going on dates with the most ᵏbeautiful women in the universe until they're all as happy and free and democratic and equal as we are on the Most Chosen Planet,

21 ˡWhich you will be glad to hear escaped from the nuclear age without ceasing to be Chosen,

22 ᵐOr even ceasing to be a Planet,

23 Which will be the funniest part of the whole show,

24 Unless you really do believe in Miracles.

CHAPTER 61

Of course, TV will never be simple-minded in its treatment of Miracles,

2 Because one of the greatest of

all comedy shows will point out that Miracles have their ups and downs,

3 [a]Because some of them are good,

4 And some of them are not so good,

5 Which is what people will find out on a show called 'I Love the Miracle Zone,'

6 Which will feature a different Miracle every week,

7 And will fearlessly show how the wrong kind of Miracle might really foul everything up,

8 Like if you start seeing a truly perfect paradise on your usual train ride to work,

9 [b]Then you can probably expect that you'll die if you're stupid enough to get off there.

10 [c]If you really hate [d]modern technology,

11 Then you can probably expect that every modern appliance in your house will turn on you someday and kill you.

12 [e]And if you're the only survivor of a nuclear war,

13 [f]Then you can probably expect your [g]coke bottle eyeglasses to get crushed just when you were about to sit down for that good long read you've always promised yourself.

14 [h]And so maybe it's better to forget about Miracles,

15 Not to mention that good long read,

16 [i]And stay right there in the suburbs,

17 With all those other perfectly average people,

18 [j]Where you belong.

CHAPTER 62

In fact, TV will be pretty fearless in exploring what could

a. 54.3-6
57.3-6
58.21-25
60.20
b. Psom.77.9
c. Brit.28.3
d. Yks.138.4-10
e. Dav.47.15-16
f. Psp.1.4
g. Psay.5O.3-4
h. Dav.47.11
i. Dav.47.13
j. Dav.47.22
k. Psay.5D.1
l. 28.6
m. Psong.43.1-7
n. Psay.5J.23

happen to all kinds of people if they moved away from the people and places they come from,

2 And tried something new,

3 [k]Which is usually a complete disaster called a culture clash,

4 But makes for a lot of really great comedy.

CHAPTER 63

For example, there will be a great comedy about what happens when well-heeled city folk move to the country,

2 Which will be called 'I Love Cheap Acres,'

3 In which the starring role will be played by a [l]giant pig who grunts and snorts a lot but otherwise doesn't talk much,

4 Which is more than you can say for the rest of the country folk in the show,

5 Who will drive the city folk crazy,

6 So that everyone will know the only reason they stay is because the pay is so good,

7 Week after week,

8 Month after month,

9 And year after year.

CHAPTER 64

And there will also be a great comedy about what happens when poor country folk move to the most expensive suburb in the Most Chosen Nation on Earth,

2 Which is just hilarious,

3 Because the country folk in the show called 'I Love the Beverly Hicks' will be incredibly rich,

4 [m]Which is why they will always get their way in the end,

5 [n]Even though they're complete idiots who everybody

laughs at behind their backs,

6 Especially [a]Grandma,

7 [b]Who should probably be locked up,

8 Not to mention the great supporting role played by [c]Grandma's Kentucky long rifle,

9 Which you wouldn't want in your suburb, I'll bet,

10 Except that it's just a TV show,

11 Although it might be helpful to know about the [d]Grandmas of this world if you ever get lost in the wilderness.

CHAPTER 65

And there will also be a great comedy about the kinds of culture clashes that happen when complete idiots join the armed forces of the Most Chosen Nation on Earth,

2 Which will be called 'I Love McCluck's PT Boat,'

3 Unless it will be called 'I Love Sergeant Bunco' instead,

4 Which I'm not completely sure about,

5 Because maybe they'll call it 'I Love Gummer Fife, USMC,'

6 Or 'I Love the Broads on Our Side,'

7 Except that that one can't be right,

8 [e]Because this show will be all about being a manly man in a manly man's profession, only the manly men are also dumb as fenceposts,

9 But brave when it comes right down to it,

10 [f]Which is why they'll maybe call this show 'I Love Hoagy's Heroes,'

11 Although it seems like that couldn't be right either,

a. Ann.18.17
b. Wil.75.6-7
c. Zig.10.14
d. Vin.3.10-11
e. Forg.5.6
f. Ann.10.11
g. Zig.10.9
h. Zig.9.2
i. 60.10
j. Zig.10.10
k. Dav.42.27
l. Zig.10.14
m. Psom.5.1-6
n. 30.5
o. Zig.10.11
p. Dav.30.8-9
q. Dav.30.25
r. Dav.30.26-27
s. Zig.10.11
t. Zig.10.12

12 Because I don't think this show will be set in a Nazi prisoner of war camp,

13 Which is a much much funnier premise than the one I'm talking about.

CHAPTER 66

Anyway, there will be hundreds and hundreds of comedies about different kinds of culture clashes,

2 [g]Including a show called 'I Love Martians,' which will be about how frantic things get if a Martian moves into your house in the suburbs,

3 [h]And 'I Love Genies,' which will be all about how frantic things get if a [i]Genie moves into your house in the suburbs,

4 [j]And 'I Love Witches,' which will be all about how frantic things get if a [k]witch marries you and moves into your house in the suburbs,

5 [l]And 'I Love Mrs. Demuir,' which will be all about how frantic things get if an [m]amorous ghost moves in with an [n]attractive widow whose dress is always buttoned up to the neck,

6 [o]And 'I Love the Monster Family,' which will be all about how frantic things get if a family of [p]vampires and [q]wolfmen and [r]Frankenstein monsters move into a creepy old house in a nice white suburb,

7 [s]And 'I Love Oscar,' which will be all about how awful things can get if a complete slob moves into your apartment,

8 [t]Not to mention 'I Love Felix,' which will be all about how awful things can get if a complete prig moves into your apartment,

9 Which is pretty awful,

10 ^aBut nothing compared to what can happen if a real citizen of the Most Chosen Nation on Earth is living in the same house with a TV family,

11 Which TV's utter fearlessness will eventually lead it to explore,

12 In a great TV comedy called 'I Love Nobody.'

a. Zig.10.9-13
b. 28.6
c. Zig.10.10
d. Zig.10.13
e. Zig.10.12
f. Zig.10.9
g. Zig.10.11
h. Zig.9.2
i. Psay.5Q.54
j. 5.1-3

CHAPTER 67

In fact, 'I Love Nobody' will be a landmark achievement in the history of TV,

2 And maybe the culmination of everything you've started with your own little failed attempt at comedy,

3 Because the loud and obnoxious character called ^bAugie Bumper will keep the entire nation in stitches for years,

4 With all his charming real-life qualities,

5 ^cLike all his racial slurs about blacks and Hispanics,

6 ^dAnd his demeaning remarks about women,

7 ^eAnd his ethnic slurs about Poles and Italians,

8 ^fAnd his selfish response to every crisis,

9 ^gAnd his cute little beer belly,

10 And his hilarious habit of abusing every member of his family, including his hippie son-in-law and his daughter Gloria, not to mention his crazy wife Edna,

11 ^hWho Augie won't even kiss at the end of each show,

12 Which means that 'I Love Nobody' will finally bring the comedy of *real* life to the small screen,

13 With no Miracles of any kind,

14 Not even the oldest TV Miracle of all,

15 Namely, a house where nobody ever flushes the toilet.

CHAPTER 68

And so (said Charlie), I think you can be pretty proud of the great comic tradition you've started,

2 And you should stop feeling bad about your little show that didn't work,

3 ⁱBecause nobody hits a home run every time out,

4 And you've got another grand slammer we haven't even talked about yet,

5 ^jBecause your little variety show is also much more important than you think, and it will bring millions and millions of people together every Sunday night,

6 For many many years,

7 And you will give all of them much joy,

8 And many exciting new stars,

9 Including comedians,

10 And acrobats,

11 And performing animals,

12 Not to mention jugglers,

13 And magicians,

14 And ventriloquists,

15 And singers,

16 And other kinds of musicians too,

17 Which will lead to some exciting new developments in TV.

CHAPTER 69

For example, the astounding success of your show will eventually give some other TV pioneers an idea for a new kind of variety program,

2 Called "talk shows,"
3 Which will be completely different from your show because they will all feature a *good-looking and witty host*,
4 Who will actually talk to his guests before they perform,
5 So that the people in the TV audience can get to know the stars they have always had to admire from afar.
6 In fact, there will one day be TV stars who are famous and admired for being on so many talk shows,
7 And who will never actually perform at all,
8 Which will give still more TV producers another completely new idea,
9 Namely, putting on talk shows where the guests are not performers of any kind,
10 But *real* people,
11 [a]Just like the ones everybody lives next to in the suburbs,
12 [b]Except that they will have all kinds of problems,
13 [c]And tell everybody in the TV audience about them,
14 Which is why they won't use a prerecorded laugh track of any kind,
15 Because everyone will know exactly when to laugh,
16 At first.

CHAPTER 70

And talk shows aren't the only thing that will get their start on your variety show,
2 Because when you're on every single week, you naturally get to discover new trends in entertainment,
3 Which you will do,
4 [d]Including something called rocking roll music,

a. 61.17
b. 75.5
c. Pnot.24.5
d. Yks.144.1-5
e. Dav.40.7
f. Pnot.25.5
g. Yks.144.18
h. Yks.144.16
i. Psay.5Q.29
j. Penn.2.2 Ext.23.8
k. Exp.9.3
l. Exp.9.5
m. Exp.9.6
n. Exp.9.7
o. Yks.154.43
p. Ned.8.2-10
q. Main.37.4-5
r. Ann.11.7-9
s. Vin.16.2-29
t. Ann.6.23 Ned.6.24-25

5 Which will burst onto the small screen because of your insight about where things are going,
6 And there will be titanic rocking roll stars created on your show,
7 With names like [e]Elvis Crosley,
8 And Frankie [f]Camelot,
9 And [g]Pat Boom,
10 And [h]Choke Bury,
11 And the [i]Tintinnabulations,
12 And the [j]Sirenes,
13 Not to mention the very biggest rocking roll stars of all,
14 [k]Who will come to the Most Chosen Nation all the way from the Former Most Chosen Nation,
15 [l]To show young people in the Most Chosen Nation how to do rocking roll music right,
16 [m]Namely, by having a lot less black people involved,
17 [n]And wearing funny haircuts,
18 [o]Instead of gold lamé,
19 And so it will be your privilege to introduce a lot of foreign rocking roll stars to a [p]Great New Generation of young people,
20 [q]Including the Bottles,
21 [r]And Armand's Armpits,
22 [s]And Rolling Rocks too,
23 [t]Who will finally bring raw sexual energy out of the closet into the mainstream of life in the Most Chosen Nation on Earth,
24 After which nothing will ever be the same again.
25 Would you like to hear about it?

CHAPTER 71

"As a matter of fact," Ed replied, "I'm feeling kind

of tired and worn out right now,

2 ᵃ"And I can't help thinking about how much I miss radio.

3 "Won't radio survive at all?"

4 Of course it will survive (said Charlie),

5 But nothing like the way it was,

6 Because rocking roll will spread out from your variety show into thousands of radio stations in every city, suburb, hamlet, and farm of the Most Chosen Nation on Earth,

7 So that teenagers will be introduced to hundreds and hundreds of great rocking roll bands,

8 Including ᵇPink Freud,

9 ᶜThe Why,

10 ᵈDead Butterfly,

11 ᵉSteppenfetch,

12 ᶠScream,

13 ᵍSuntanna,

14 ʰThe Droogs,

15 ⁱRed Zeppelin,

16 ʲThe Greatful Bread,

17 ᵏJanie Jalopie,

18 ˡJimmy Heartattax,

19 ᵐCrosley, Spoils, Bash & Bing,

20 ⁿAnd Bub the Beadle, of course,

21 And so many others that the airwaves of the Most Chosen Nation will be continuously crowded with the writhing, pounding beat of adolescent sexuality,

22 As interpreted by ᵒelectric guitars,

23 And ᵖvast drum sets,

24 And ᑫdeafening keyboards,

25 And ʳshrieking vocals,

26 Which will all be so exciting that just talking about it makes me feel like a green young sapling again,

a. 3.1-2
b. Zig.12.4
c. Psay.5Q.54
d. Psay.5Q.38
e. Mall.6.24
   Bks.7.5
f. Gods.1.3-4
   & 1.7
   Chnk.3.2
g. Main.16.7-8
h. Dav.48.37-
   43
i. Boul.8.22
   Zig.8.11-14
   Dav.40.11-13
   Psom.12.5
j. Jeff.24.10-12
k. Adam.31.2-6
   Psom.40.4
   Dav.47.24
l. Dav.10.12-13
   Jeff.14.6-7
   Hall.16.8
   Ned.54.7
   Ann.15.29
   & 15.27
m. Psong.49.1
   Psay.5A.40
   Ann.15.29
n. Dav.57.10
o. Ann.4.1
p. Ann.10.1
q. Ann.6.1
r. Grk.9.7
s. Ira.21.33
t. Psay.5Q.33
u. 60.10
v. Hill.S.7
w. Psay.5X.1
   Hill.Z1

27 Ready to pollinate like nobody's business.

28 Do you want to hear more?

CHAPTER 72

And then Ed sighed, and said he didn't need to hear it,

2 But wasn't there anything else that TV would bring to the households of the nation,

3 Something significant or helpful or illuminating?

CHAPTER 73

Of course there will be (answered Charlie), although you sound like you've developed some pretty stratospheric standards all of a sudden for a guy who started TV journalism by smoking a lot of cigarettes.

2 However, I'll overlook your tone of voice,

3 And tell you about all the great TV game shows that will give everyone in the Most Chosen Nation a chance to earn fabulous prizes and oodles of cash,

4 ˢIncluding shows like 'I Love to Make Bad Deals,' where people will dress up like ᵗchickens and stalks of celery so that the ᵘhost will notice them and offer them a choice between Curtain No. 2 and Box No. 1,

5 Not to mention shows like 'I Love Guessing the Right Prices,' where people will win fabulous prizes by knowing exactly how much a bottle of salad oil costs, unless it's a ᵛstation wagon instead,

6 ʷOr shows like 'I Love Tic Tac Toe,' where people will . . .

7 "No they won't," interrupted Ed.

8 "Is that the best you can do?"

CHAPTER 74

My my my. We *are* getting snooty, aren't we (replied Charlie)?

2 But that's okay because TV will also make enormous breakthroughs in children's entertainment,

3 [a]So that kids will grow up in front of the set watching marvelous shows like 'I Love Giant Mice,' which will be all about a [b]club where children wear mouse ears and sing songs about how much fun it is to watch TV every day,

4 [c]And 'I Love Huck Hound,' which will be all about a cartoon dog who gets into trouble a lot with his friend Yogi Bore, a cartoon bear who eats everybody's picnic basket at a state park, and keeps making the forest ranger fall out of a tree,

5 [d]And 'I Love Tooty Bird,' which will be all about a cartoon cat's unquenchable thirst for the blood of an obnoxious little cartoon canary, who keeps hitting the cat on the head with a [e]mallet ten times bigger than he is,

6 [f]And 'I Love Superman,' which will be all about a hero from another planet who wears a cape and is completely [g]invulnerable, so that the outlaw's bullets always bounce off his chest, and he always saves the day for truth, justice, and the American Way,

7 [h]And 'I Love Motor Mouse,' which will be all about a cartoon rodent from another planet who wears a cape and is completely invulnerable, so that the bad cat's bullets always bounce off his chest, and he always saves

---

a. Psp.3.6
b. Adam.28.16-17
c. Yks.71.10-13
d. Ira.34.1-4
e. Pnot.37.4-5
f. Krt.9.8
g. Zig.9.2
h. Zig.10.11
i. Dav.30.9
j. Dav.40.9
k. Lies.9.13

---

the day for American mice everywhere,

8 And 'I Love Batman,' which will be all about a cartoon character played by a [i]man with a pot-belly, who wears a cape and bat's ears and rides around in a car with a bat's nose, and lives in a Bat cave with a boy named [j]Robin,

9 And 'I Love . . .

10 "Stop it," said Ed.

11 "Surely, there has to be something worthwhile on TV someday . . ."

CHAPTER 75

I take it (said Charlie) that you're too grown up to enjoy children's entertainment.

2 Maybe you'd prefer the real adult entertainment that will be on in the afternoons,

3 Like soap operas,

4 Which will fearlessly explore the kinds of trouble people can get into in real life,

5 [k]Such as divorce and illicit affairs and murder and illegitimate children and blackmail and abortion and all that delicious wickedness nobody has the nerve for,

6 Except on shows like 'I Love the Days of My Children,'

7 And 'I Love All My Doctors,'

8 And 'I Love the Way the World Turns Me On,'

9 And 'I Love . . .

10 "Enough!" declared Ed.

11 "It's really true, isn't it? There isn't going to be anything good on for years and years."

CHAPTER 76

Well (said Charlie), I haven't even mentioned one

of the best parts of all,

2 Because in between all these great shows,

3 And in fact, in between each little segment of these shows,

4 There will be commercials,

5 ᵃWhich will tell everyone, young and old alike, how they can buy a piece of the good life,

6 Including ᵇpeace of mind,

7 ᶜWhich comes from having the right clothes,

8 ᵈAnd the right cars,

9 ᵉAnd the right headache tablets,

10 ᶠAnd the right underarm deodorant,

11 ᵍAnd the right insurance company,

12 ʰAnd even the right brand of cigarettes,

13 Which you know something about already,

14 As we've seen.

15 And what could be more important than being able to grow up near such a source of great advice about how to have the right image with your friends and acquaintances,

16 And how to keep from sticking out like a sore thumb because you never heard how everybody else was doing it this year?

17 ⁱ"I think it's time for you to go back in your box," Ed said wearily, and started fiddling with the latches on the lid.

CHAPTER 77

Wait! (cried Charlie),

2 There will be one thing that's really and truly extraordinary.

3 "What?" Ed asked skeptically.

---

a. Ann.6.18
b. Jefs.11.46
c. Adam.31.11-16
d. Adam.31.3
e. Psong.52.1
f. Psom.12.4
g. Psom.30.1-7
h. Wil.46.5-19
i. 7.1-7
j. Dav.57.16
k. Psp.3.13
l. Adam.31.5
m. Carl.3.8
n. Ann.15.29
o. Wil.18.1-2

---

4 I'm talking about pure genius here (replied Charlie).

5 There will be a comedy troupe called the Three Stoopids,

6 Consisting of ʲBowel, ᵏDilly, and ˡHarley,

7 Who will break new ground in the entire field of comedy,

8 ᵐBecause they will finally succeed in surpassing the vaunted Marx genius,

9 Which they will do by yelling constantly at the top of their lungs,

10 ⁿAnd needling each other to death,

11 And breaking bottles over each other's heads,

12 And screwing up every job they ever tackle,

13 But in as surly a way as possible,

14 So that everyone will just laugh and laugh and laugh . . .

CHAPTER 78

"That's it," Ed said, grabbing hold of Charlie and putting him into his box.

2 And he was so intent on getting the latches closed and locked that he never heard Charlie's last desperate words,

3 ᵒWhich were all about how someone would come,

4 Someday,

5 To explain what it all meant,

6 And what people could do about it,

7 But Ed was in no mood to hear more,

8 From such a complete dummy,

9 Which actually made him kind of afraid of Charlie for a little while,

10 Until he thought of the perfect ^asolution . . .

11 ^bGLUB GLUB GLUB

a. *Swar.29.3-4*
b. *4.3-4*
c. *Psom.12.4*

GLUB GLUB GLUB GLUB . . .

12 Which fixed everything,

13 Until Ed's glass went ^cdry.

THE BOOK OF THE VIP

JEFFREY

CHAPTER 1

There was a VIP named ^aJeffrey,

2 Who tried to save mankind,

3 And couldn't,

4 ^bBut changed the world anyway.

CHAPTER 2

Jeffrey had a lot of things to say about life,

2 And ^cpeople,

3 And ^dGod,

4 ^eAnd what happens after you die,

5 And other things too.

6 ^fNobody knows for sure exactly what it was he said,

7 ^gAlthough lots of people think they know,

8 Which is the way things go,

9 When you're dealing with human beings.

CHAPTER 3

Whatever it was that ^hJeffrey said, it must have been controversial,

2 Which anything new usually is,

3 Because a lot of the people who heard him,

4 Or heard about him,

5 ⁱThought they'd like him better if he were dead.

a. *Dav.15.11-15*
b. *Adam.1.4*
c. *Lies.10.6*
d. *Rom.21.4-9*
e. *Boul.8.1*
f. *Boul.16.6*
g. *Boul.16.7-12*
h. *Rom.20.5-7*
i. *Rom.20.8-11*
j. *Dav.15.26-33*
k. *Dav.15.40*
l. *3.6*
m. *Dav.15.34*
n. *Frog.35.4*
o. *Ed.60.10*

6 ^jAnd so they killed him.

7 The only problem was that ^ksomething happened after that,

8 Even though nobody knows for sure exactly what it was,

9 And a whole bunch of people started claiming that Jeffrey wasn't dead at all,

10 And couldn't be killed for long by anyone anyway,

11 Because he was a God.

CHAPTER 4

It so happened that after the big death scene,

2 ^mWhen Jeffrey went back to his dressing room for a well-earned rest,

3 He became strangely ⁿdepressed,

4 And had doubts about the wisdom of his actions.

5 But when he removed his ^ocrown of thorns,

6 So that he could put his head in his hands without ripping up his fingers,

7 The crown spoke to him, saying, "Jeffrey, don't get down on yourself.

8 "You did the best you could.

9 "You tried.

10 "But these are human beings after all,

11 "And you know what that means."

12 Whereupon Jeffrey replied, "Tell me about it,"

13 And so the crown of thorns did exactly that.

CHAPTER 5

I can't be completely sure about what you told them, of course (said the crown),

2 Since I only have it on hearsay,

3 ªLike everybody else,

4 But whatever it was,

5 You can be pretty sure that they'll remember less than half of it,

6 And understand none of it,

7 Which is about par,

8 If you know what I mean.

CHAPTER 6

But even though they won't remember it,

2 Or understand it,

3 ᵇThey'll *believe* it wholeheartedly,

4 Which is also par,

5 And will cause a few problems.

CHAPTER 7

For example, if you ever mentioned a place called ᶜhell,

2 They'll start trying to send each other there,

3 In more ways than you could shake a ᵈpointed stick at.

4 They'll start ᵉchurches in your name,

5 And each church will be certain that it owns the truth,

6 ᶠAnd remembers exactly what you said,

7 ᵍAnd understands it all,

8 Including the parts you didn't exactly say,

9 But sort of implied,

10 Somehow.

a. 2.7
b. Chuk.9.1
   Zig.7.16-17
   Boul.18.6
   Grk.12.10
c. Rom.22.1-5
d. Apes.1.1
e. Psay.5R.3-10
f. 5.5
g. 5.6
h. 5.5
i. 5.6
j. Chr.6.3-5
k. Chr.6.6
l. Chr.6.7
m. Chr.2.5-8

11 And every one of these churches will therefore be certain that it speaks for you,

12 And gets to decide who belongs in hell.

CHAPTER 8

The first of these churches will run the whole show for a while,

2 In fact, for quite a while,

3 ʰAnd they'll remember an incredible amount of your wisdom,

4 ⁱAnd understand it all completely,

5 And act with great force and energy in your name.

6 ʲFor example, if you ever mentioned something called mortal sin,

7 They'll remember it,

8 And send people to hell for it.

9 ᵏIf you ever mentioned something called the last rites,

10 They'll remember it,

11 And send people to hell if they don't have it.

12 ˡIf you ever mentioned something called excommunication,

13 They'll remember it,

14 And do it to everybody who doesn't think or act the right way.

15 ᵐIf you ever mentioned something about the importance of not having any fun to speak of,

16 They'll remember it,

17 And condemn people to hell if they ever happen to have any fun.

18 Nor is this all they'll remember.

CHAPTER 9

If you ever mentioned something called moneychangers,

2 They'll remember it,

3 ªAnd have a lot of them on hand at all times.

4 If you ever mentioned something called indulgences,

5 They'll remember it,

6 ᵇAnd sell them to everyone who has the money.

7 If you ever mentioned something called riches,

8 They'll remember it,

9 ᶜAnd have them in great abundance,

10 Forever.

11 Nor is this all they'll remember.

CHAPTER 10

If you ever mentioned something called the ᵈHoly Grail,

2 They will remember it,

3 ᵉAnd shed millions of gallons of blood to get it,

4 ᶠWithout much success.

5 If you ever mentioned something called an ᵍinquisition,

6 They'll remember it,

7 ʰAnd have one,

8 ⁱAnd burn and torture and kill thousands of people in it,

9 ʲWith a great deal of success.

10 And if you ever mentioned something about being infallible,

11 They'll remember it,

12 ᵏAnd claim they are that,

13 In your name,

14 Which is also about par,

15 Unless it's a ˡbirdie.

CHAPTER 11

Nor will this be the only church with a great memory.

2 Other churches will come along,

3 And remember other things

a. Psong.10.3
b. Psong.10.4
c. Psong.10.5
d. Pnot.25.1
e. Chr.8.16-18
f. Chr.8.19-22
g. Spic.7.1
h. Spic.7.2-6
i. Spic.7.7-9
j. Spic.7.10-15
k. Chr.6.11
l. Psay.5A.34
m. Brit.15.9-10
n. Psay.5R.3
o. Psay.5R.5
p. Psay.5R.7
q. Psay.5R.5
r. Psay.5R.12
s. 20.9
t. Psay.5R.5
Dav.22.23

you mentioned.

4 ᵐFor example, one of the churches will remember that you hate people who look nice,

5 And condemn people to hell if their clothes aren't ugly.

6 ⁿOne of the churches will remember that you hate people who consume alcohol in any form,

7 And condemn people to hell for drinking.

8 ᵒOne of the churches will remember that you hate people who dance,

9 And condemn people to hell for dancing.

10 ᵖOne of the churches will remember that you hate people who read prayers,

11 And condemn people to hell for using a prayer book.

12 ᑫOne of the churches will remember that you hate people who aren't completely immersed during baptism,

13 And condemn people to hell for being baptized on the forehead.

14 ʳOne of the churches will remember that you hate people who don't speak in tongues and roll around on the floor,

15 And condemn people to hell for behaving modestly in church.

16 ˢOne of the churches will remember that you hate people who aren't expecting you to come back and destroy the world next week,

17 And condemn people to hell for not sitting on the edge of the chair while they wait for you.

18 ᵗOne of the churches will remember that you hate people who worship you in the company of ex-slaves, who should

never really have been freed anyway,

19 And condemn people who don't worship you in an all-white church.

20 ªMost of the churches will remember that you hate people who have sex before they get married,

21 And condemn people to hell for ᵇfornication.

22 Most of the churches will remember that you hate everyone who doesn't belong to their church,

23 ᶜAnd condemn people to hell for believing in you in the wrong way.

24 And *all* of the churches will remember that you hate everyone who doesn't believe in you,

25 ᵈAnd try to kill everyone who doesn't sign up in your name.

CHAPTER 12

And so all of the churches that believe in you will create a vast kingdom of hatred,

2 Which will spread your word to the farthest ᵉcorners of the earth,

3 ᶠWith the help of infantry and cavalry and warships and swords and lances and battleaxes and pistols and muskets and catapults and cannons and all manner of other war machines and weapons,

4 ᵍWhich will result in the torture and murder and misery of millions,

5 ʰWho will be saved,

6 In your name,

7 Whether they like it or not,

8 ¹Even if it kills them.

9 And eventually,

a.	Zig.10.12
b.	Hill.F.1
c.	Rom.5.7-8
d.	Psom.39.1-6
e.	Chuk.6.4
f.	Psong.6.8-10
	Adam.50.6
g.	Vin.59.21
	Exp.11.18-27
h.	Vin.62.1
i.	Drex.9.5
j.	Ira.1.1-8
k.	Psong.59.1
l.	Brd.9.5-6
m.	3.9
n.	3.10
o.	3.11
p.	7.4-12

10 There will come a time when people begin to doubt you,

11 And question everything about you,

12 Including your motives,

13 Your family tree,

14 And even your existence.

CHAPTER 13

Some of the doubters will point out that it's impossible to prove you ever existed,

2 Since no one has a birth certificate,

3 Or a ʲphotograph,

4 Or a newspaper article,

5 Or a trial transcript,

6 Or a ᵏtax return,

7 Or any other thing which belonged to you.

CHAPTER 14

Some of the doubters will question the ˡlogic of your story,

2 And therefore come to dispute your authenticity.

3 ᵐFor example, they'll point out that if you were really a God,

4 ⁿWhere's the big sacrifice in getting killed,

5 ºEspecially if you knew all the time that you wouldn't stay dead for long?

6 And if you weren't really a God,

7 Then *hey*,

8 What's all the fuss?

CHAPTER 15

Some of the doubters will point out that if you're responsible for creating all those ᵖchurches,

2 You must be a pretty sick guy,

3 Or at least you must have a pretty sick sense of humor.

CHAPTER 16

Some of the doubters will point out that if there's a God of any kind,

2 He has a lot to answer for,

3 Such as [a]war,

4 [b]And children who die of plague and cancer and polio and scarlet fever and diphtheria and encephalitis and appendicitis and tuberculosis and [c]piginosis and so forth and so on,

5 And saintly people who get run over by [d]taxicabs for no reason,

6 [e]And nice families who have one thing after another happen to them,

7 [f]And nasty people who make a ton of money and die happy as a clam,

8 And a lot of other stuff along the same lines.

CHAPTER 17

[g]Some of the doubters will point out that science makes it pretty tough to believe in any kind of a personal God,

2 [h]Especially one who actually walks around on earth,

3 [i]And violates the laws of biology and physics with a bunch of miracles,

4 [j]Then flies away,

5 [k]And promises to come back later.

CHAPTER 18

Some of the doubters will point out that there are a lot of other things to believe in besides you,

2 Including [l]Buddhism,

3 And [m]Hinduism,

4 And [n]Taoism,

5 And [o]Islam,

6 And [p]Astrology,

a. *Psay.5W.1-24*
b. *Psong.6.4*
c. *Lies.9.6*
d. *Adam.31.3*
e. *Ann.13.1-3*
f. *Swar.23.11*
g. *Chuk.9.3-8*
h. *Dav.15.20-25*
i. *Dav.15.16-19*
j. *Dav.15.42-45*
k. *Mall.13.8*
l. *Ann.17.1-6*
m. *Ed.47.12*
n. *Mawr.25.3 Nips.26.14*
o. *Bks.4.1-6*
p. *Ed.69.5*
q. *Drex.8.1-3*
r. *Rat.21.1*
s. *Wil.45.6*
t. *Gods.6.23*
u. *18.5*
v. *18.9*
w. *Boul.18.16-17*
x. *Pnot.40.1-5*
y. *Carl.2.3-4*
z. *F&J.2.15-16*
aa. *Chuk.21.1-11*
bb. *Vin.6.15*
cc. *Rat.16.5*
dd. *Rat.16.7*

7 And [q]Numerology,

8 And [r]Palmistry,

9 And [s]Phrenology,

10 And [t]Graphology,

11 Which all have about the same relationship to known scientific fact,

12 And none of which can be completely rejected as rubbish,

13 [u]Except Islam, of course,

14 [v]And possibly Phrenology.

15 And so, they'll argue, why should anyone think that your way is the only way?

16 [w]Which is the position your churches always seem to take.

CHAPTER 19

Eventually,

2 [x]The doubters will have a pretty big impact,

3 [y]And a lot of people will stop believing in God altogether,

4 Or decide that He died,

5 [z]For some reason.

6 A bunch of others will still believe in God,

7 [aa]Sort of,

8 [bb]Depending on how you look at it,

9 But not in you.

10 And the political situation won't be much help either,

11 Because someday an atheist will complain,

12 And they'll outlaw any mention of you or the Bible in all the schools,

13 Forever,

14 [cc]So that after a good long while, people won't have a very clear idea about anything you did or said,

15 Or might have done or said,

16 [dd]Except that your name will still be a pretty popular swearword.

375

CHAPTER 20

But your decline as a God will also result in the creation of devout new churches,

2 [a]Who will remember exactly what you said,

3 Including what you said to them personally yesterday,

4 [b]And understand all of it perfectly,

5 Including the part about having to be born again,

6 Unless you want to go straight to hell when you die,

7 Not to mention the part about how you're coming back on the Twelfth of June,

8 Next year,

9 At the Los Angeles Coliseum,

10 So please send a thousand dollars to reserve your seat now.

CHAPTER 21

And all these great new churches will start fixing everything again in your name.

2 [c]They'll remember how you said that they shouldn't ever question anything,

3 [d]Or think about anything,

4 [e]Because everything you need to know is all laid out pretty clearly in the Bible.

5 And they'll remember how you said that all [f]pornographers should suffer untold agonies in hell,

6 [g]And on earth too,

7 [h]And how books that might be disrespectful to you in some way should be banned and burned,

8 [i]And how no one should ever have any fun at all,

9 [j]Especially sex,

10 But always smile like an idiot anyway,

11 [k]And how you said that we

a. 5.5
b. 5.6
c. Chr.1.4-7
d. Chr.1.8-12
e. F&J.8.4-6
f. Bks.3.14
g. Rom.6.8
h. Zig.9.2
i. Yks.3.11-15
j. Zig.10.12
k. Ann.18.20-21
l. Psong.55.6-8
m. Gnt.1.13
n. 12.1-2
o. Grk.13.9-11
p. Chuk.18.1-14
   Lies.2.15-26
q. Wil.18.1-2
r. Drex.5.2-3
   Lies.7.1-18
s. Ned.6.24-25

should kill all the communists and make the world safe for democracy,

12 And salute the flag a lot,

13 [l]And send lots of money to television preachers,

14 In your name.

CHAPTER 22

And so there will be a great [m]renaissance of belief in you,

2 [n]And once again, waves of hatred will fan out across the planet,

3 In your name,

4 Bringing [o]hope and salvation and freedom from thought to millions and millions of your followers.

CHAPTER 23

But don't be down on yourself about any of this (said the crown of thorns),

2 Because nobody can ever prove that any of this is your fault,

3 Or that basically the same thing wouldn't have happened anyway,

4 In someone else's name,

5 Because these are human beings we're talking about after all,

6 [p]And they're always pretty much the same,

7 No matter what anyone says to them.

8 And besides, sooner or later,

9 [q]Someone will come,

10 [r]Who can speak a language they understand,

11 [s]And they will listen to him,

12 Because he will understand them,

13 At least, he'll understand them better than you ever did,
14 And give them some solid practical advice,
15 For once.

CHAPTER 24

And although you won't be here to see it,
2 You may be pleased to know that the one who is to come will know of you,
3 And will honor your memory,
4 In his own way.
5 ªFor example, he will make his entrance under the sign of a fabulous light in the eastern sky,
6 ᵇWhich will attract the attention of wise men in the east,
7 ᶜAnd other people too,
8 ᵈAlthough he will grow to manhood in obscurity, among the ᵉlowest of the low,
9 ᶠAnd then experience temptations of his own before beginning his ministry,
10 ᵍBut when he does begin his ministry, he will acquire disciples of his own,
11 ʰAnd he will give his followers important rituals to use again and again,
12 ⁱAs well as many great words to live by.
13 ʲAnd indeed, his words will be so great and perceptive that he will become the most important man who ever lived,
14 ᵏSo important, in fact, that even his messenger will be regarded as more important than you.
15 ˡBut have no fear: This one

a. Wil.2.4-5
b. Vin.8.2-10
c. Wil.3.1-5
d. Ira.6.8-12
e. Ext.53.25-27
f. Vin.9.1-12
g. Ned.14.1-7
h. Ext.13.10-11
i. Ext.16.1-27
j. Ext.14.7-9
k. Vin.3.9-18
l. Ned.22.1-3
m. Wil.65.1-4
n. Wil.53.1-2
o. Psom.31.6 & 37.3-6 & 24.3
p. Ned.16.12-13
q. Ned.28.13-14
r. Ned.56.4
s. Dav.15.39
t. Dav.15.40
u. Gods.5.6

who is to come will offer a new home to your followers,
16 ᵐWhere he will take his disciples before undergoing his own special ordeal,
17 ⁿIn a place called brotherly love,
18 Which has a very nice °ring to it,
19 As I'm sure you'll admit.
20 ᵖAnd the only problem with any of this is that even he won't be able to save the race of Mankind,
21 ᑫWhich is why he won't even try,
22 Because unlike some people I could mention,
23 ʳThis one will be nobody's fool.

CHAPTER 25

And when the crown had said its piece, Jeffrey sighed,
2 ˢAnd said that maybe he wouldn't go back and do the big resurrection scene after all,
3 Whereupon the crown smiled and said, "It won't make any difference.
4 "If you refuse to show up,
5 "They'll just do it without you,
6 "Not actually showing the resurrection,
7 "But implying it in a subtle cinematic way."
8 ᵗAnd so, in the end, everything went off as written in the original script,
9 And then Jeffrey went away,
10 And the glorious history of Man went forward,
11 Just as it had to,
12 ᵘMan being what he is.

THE PRESENT TESTAMENT

THE GOOD WORD ACCORDING TO
ULT. WILLIE

CHAPTER 1

The years come and go, and with them come many [a]generations of men, which also go, in accordance with the [b]laws governing the coming and going of all molecular combinations complex enough to be called [c]life.

2 Those who are going beget those who are coming, and these beget others, and the others beget other others, and all of them finally [d]go, in their turn, and so it goes, all of it, and all of them, and all of us, from one generation to the next.

3 And [e]Ari begat [f]Leo, who begat [g]Frank and [h]Ike and [i]Chuck, who begat [j]Ziggie, who begat [k]Gertrude and [l]Johnny, who begat [m]Ernie and [n]Paul, and [o]Stanley, and [p]Benji,

4 And Pete, and [q]Jack, and [r]Gene, and George, and [s]Timmy, and Joe,

5 And David.

CHAPTER 2

And so it happened that in the land of the [t]Americans, a young man was born whose name was [u]David, and he grew up near to a place called [v]brotherly love.

2 But a [w]famine had fallen on the land, and then [x]war engulfed the planet, and David marched from the corridors of Montezuma, along the gallery of Tripoli, and thence to the widow's walk of [y]Sugarloaf, where he

a. *Apes.2.1*
   Gods.7.1-3
b. *Chuk.8.1-5*
   Chuk.11.2-7
c. *Kin.2.1-4*
d. *Chuk.19.15-17*
e. *Grk.14.1*
f. *Gnt.9.1*
g. *Brit.10.7-9*
h. *Brit.36.1-4*
i. *Dav.22.47 & 20.11*
j. *Dav.46.19*
k. *Dav.32.4*
l. *Dav.29.6*
m. *Dav.42.15*
n. *Dav.30.40*
o. *Dav.46.6-7*
p. *Ed.60.12 Ira.3.7-18*
q. *Dav.15.9*
r. *Dav.57.10*
s. *Dav.57.21-22*
t. *Yks.1.6*
u. *Vin.57.5*
v. *53.1-2*
w. *Yks.95.1-7*
x. *Yks.107.5-18*
y. *Nips.23.10-15*
z. *Yks.118.1-3*
aa. *Nips.23.16*
bb. *Nips.24.1-6*
cc. *Yks.119.1-15*
dd. *Rat.26.7-11 Jeff.24.1-5*
ee. *Adam.31.5*
ff. *Chuk.23.1-10*

had a vision of great moment.

3 A cornered lion loomed yellow and fierce in the sky. [z]Hunters closed in, the lion beckoned them on, [aa]ten thousand thousand deaths blazing in his eyes.

4 And then, even as David watched, a pillar of light stood up from the earth, outshining the lion's eyes, wearing a crown of orange and fire, like unto a giant [bb]mushroom,

5 Whereupon the lion was devoured by [cc]flame, and David returned to the place of brotherly love, in which his [dd]son had been born on a night of light and the lion.

6 And the son he named, in remembrance of his vision, [ee]Harry.

CHAPTER 3

The years passed. Harry was a beautiful and extraordinary child. Everyone said so. Everyone tried to understand him, but they could not, and this he explained to them with an authority beyond his years.

2 [ff]**I am of you, but I do not belong to you,** he said. **I am not bound by the bonds that bind you. Remember this, because I have said it.**

3 And in hearing this, his elders were amazed, and they remarked among themselves upon his forcefulness, and were afraid.

4 "Who is this?" they said, one to another, "who speaks in this new way that we do not understand?"

ª"Truly, he is unlike what we ourselves were at his age."

5 And Harry merely smiled, as if he were possessed of some great knowledge, and his parents treated him with great tenderness and care, certain that his was a will which should be obeyed.

CHAPTER 4

And it so happened that ᵇwar again descended on the earth, and the ᶜking of the Most Chosen Nation sent out armies to rape a foreign land, and murder their patriots, and ᵈburn their babies, and commit ᵉother acts of a nature that filled the hearts of the righteous with horror.

2 And the children, who were the most righteous of all, rose up against the king, and put on ᶠstrange garments, and lived apart from those who did murder and those who did not speak out against murder, and had visions of peace and ᵍlove and a world in which the way was simple and clear and ʰtheirs.

3 And the people who had lost their children were angry and afraid, and they reproached their king, saying,

4 ⁱ"Why have you alienated our sons and daughters, whom we love and want to love us, and who no longer love us, but instead revile us and hate us and spit upon us?"

5 And the king hung his head and abdicated his throne, and a new king was crowned who waged war with even greater vengeance, killing great multitudes of foreign patriots and babies.

6 And when the children reproached ʲhim, he waged war

a. Psay.5V.1-3 & 5V.18
b. Yks.152.10-12
c. Psay.5P.1-3
d. Ed.21.1-8
e. Ann.4.9-15
f. 7.6
g. Ed.35.7-11 & 47.5-12 & 51.16-24
h. Hill.1.1-2
i. Rat.6.1-10
j. Ed.22.1-5
k. Dav.58.1-10
l. Psong.43.2
m. Vin.28.1-6 Ira.13.1-16
n. Vin.11.4
o. 7.1

against them also, ordering them to be beaten when they marched for peace, and lamentation filled the land.

7 And the children cried out bitterly, saying to one another, "What has become of our visions? In which direction is the way of peace and justice and happiness, which we have longed for and now despair of?"

8 And their gatherings became grim as their visions faded and their questions received no answers.

9 Thus it was that the world became ready for Harry, who knew the way.

CHAPTER 5

ᵏAnd it so happened that ˡHarry journeyed to a place called ᵐAltarey, which means high mountain, and appeared to the multitudes, to whom he spoke, surrounded by ⁿAngels.

2 ᵒ**Listen to me,** he said, **I am called Harry, and my way should be your way.**

3 And some of them mocked him, saying, "Who are you to speak to us in this way? Your suit is in three pieces, your face is clean shaven, and your words sound to us like the grunting of a pig."

4 When they had said these and other things, the children moved closer to Harry as if they would beat him, but the Angels protected him, knocking many children cold, so that they were amazed at his wisdom and sat down to listen.

5 Then Harry said, **I would say this to you, that you have heavy thoughts but see nothing, that**

you rap much but say little. **What profit a man if he gain the earth and not know it?**

6 And one among the multitudes cried out to Harry, asking this question: "Your words are strange to us, and we do not understand what you speak of. Tell us, what is your problem?"

7 Harry answered him, saying, **It is not I who have the problem. It is all of you who have a problem, who live in** [a]**paradise, if you would but open your eyes, but prefer to walk about seeking paradise with your eyes closed. I ask you, is this the right way to go about it?**

8 And [b]one of the biggest children, who had a beard and a pair of large fists, spoke scornfully to Harry, saying, "You must surely be an anus on fire if you believe that this land of pigs is paradise. Are not our leaders evil warlords, who commit genocide every day of the week?

9 "Have they not arranged to murder the few good men who would rise to replace them, including [c]Bobby and [d]Martin, and probably others too?

10 [e]"Have they not beaten us, and imprisoned us, and given us a very hard time for loving goodness, including peace and love and brotherhood, and all of that stuff?

11 "Truly, if your skull were not wedged inside your colon, you would recognize these things. There is no paradise in this land of [f]capitalist, [g]imperialist, [h]racist pigs. And that is all there is to it.

12 "Now, I warn you to depart from this place, you who [i]fornicate with your mother, before we

a. *Mall.17.1*
b. *Dav.15.9*
c. *Yks.132.10-19*
d. *Yks.150.1-8 Brd.4.4*
e. *4.6*
f. *Adam.6.1-8*
g. *Exp.1.10-16*
h. *Yks.151.1-5*
i. *Pnot.3.1-5*
j. *Vin.29.1-4*
k. *Vin.14.23-25*
l. *Ira.25.55-64*

grow angry and rearrange your physiognomy."

CHAPTER 6

And when the large child with great fists had said these things, Harry laughed out loud, and said in a great voice, **Now pay close attention, children, because I shall perform a great wonder for you.**

2 Whereupon Harry made a small sign to his Angels, who advanced on the large child with rods,

3 [j]And smote him unto death where he stood, causing the multitudes to quake with awe, and other emotions.

4 Then Harry stood over the remains of the large child and said, **Behold.** [k]**How quickly and easily are we deprived of life. I have come to tell you great truths, which will make your life better, but I have it equally in my power to make your life shorter, as you have all witnessed.**

5 **Now, which do you prefer? The choice is yours, and truly I must tell you that I don't care which you choose.**

6 When Harry had said this, there was a great murmuring in the crowd, but at length the children said to Harry, "We are very much interested in hearing how our lives might be made better, so please teach us, O Wise One, and tell your Angels to go easy, because we are listening to you with great attentiveness."

7 And Harry laughed again, saying, **That is much better. I congratulate you for listening to me, for** [l]**I know everything, and will tell you everything you need to know.**

8 Thereupon did Harry walk through the crowd, unmolested by anyone, and mounted the stage, from which place he spoke in a loud voice and at great length.

CHAPTER 7

[a]**M**y name is called Harry, and I have knowledge of all things, because I am smart, and do not try to fool myself with a lot of nonsense about [b]ideals and [c]beliefs.

2 And truly, this is good news for you, because the things that I know are no secret, [d]but have been written down many times before, and have even been taught you your whole life, although you cannot see the forest because your eyes are so full of trees.

3 Now I ask you to pluck the trees from your eyes, and behold the forest, which will give you a vision of [e]paradise.

4 Let me give you an example of what I mean. You have heard this recently [f]deceased child cry out against the land of the Americans with great irritation. He has seen that the Americans commit genocide against their own [g]black people and their own [h]native population and against the [i]yellow peoples of Southeast Asia,

5 And he therefore believes that the Americans are [j]evil. And more than this, he concludes that the American evil surpasses the evil of all other peoples and all other [k]nations, all over the world.

6 This is a great tree that has

a. 5.2
b. 13.12-14
c. Vin.61.3-10
d. 17.1-9
e. Cen.8.1-3
f. 6.2-3
g. Yks.55.14-28
h. Yks.53.1-14
i. Kens.22.24
j. Lies.2.7-15
k. Psay.5N.6-20
l. Psom.73.9-12
m. Exp.1.1-5
n. Lies.11.1-12
o. Bks.2.9-10
p. Mes.3.1-2
q. Grk.18.1-7
r. Rom.6.1-8
s. Barb.3.1-9
& 4.1-3

become stuck in all your eyes, which I conclude from the fact that fully a third of your number are wearing the [l]flag of the world's Most Chosen Nation on your buttocks.

7 This tree burns your eyes, with a fire like righteous indignation, and if you do not wise up it will consume you, which would be foolish indeed, because this is not the only tree in the forest.

8 Truly, this is not the only tree in this particular forest, which is great and vast and extends far beyond the limited reach of your ignorance.

9 Pay close attention while I remind you of the forest.

CHAPTER 8

The trees in this forest are as countless as the grains of sand on the beach at Malibu, where I will be going later on.

2 Since the very beginning of time, the [m]Chosen Nations of the world have committed genocide against everyone who dared to oppose them.

3 If you had paid attention in high school, you would know that the [n]Hebrews committed genocide against the Philistines, and the [o]Assyrians committed genocide against every nation in [p]Mesopotamia,

4 [q]And the Greeks committed genocide against the Trojans,

5 [r]And the Romans committed genocide against the Carthaginians,

6 [s]And the barbarians of Europe committed genocide

against the Romans and each other,

7 ^aAnd the Christians of Europe committed genocide against the Saracens and each other,

8 ^bAnd the Spics committed genocide against the Indians of Central America,

9 ^cAnd the Frogs committed genocide against the other nations of Europe,

10 ^dAnd the Brits committed genocide against practically every nation on the planet,

11 ^eAnd the Krauts committed genocide against the Jews and everybody else too,

12 ^fAnd all the Chosen Nations in the Middle East committed genocide against all the other Chosen Nations in the Middle East, not to mention large parts of Europe and other places,

13 ^gAnd the Russkies committed genocide against their own people for thousands of years,

14 ^hAnd likewise, the Chinks have also learned to commit genocide against their own people,

15 ⁱAnd the Nips committed genocide against every nation in the South Pacific,

16 ^jAnd at every time in the whole course of human history, the Chosen Nations have always sought to commit genocide against anyone who stood in their way,

17 No matter how big or how small an obstacle they were.

18 But none of this matters to you, of course, because you believe that ^kyour tree is the only tree.

---

a. Chr.8.5-10
b. Exp.11.18-27
c. Frog.15.4-9
d. Brit.26.9-21
e. Yks.125.1-14
f. Bks.10.1-4
g. Russ.7.9-14
*   & 19.1-8*
h. Chnk.15.1-4
i. Nips.21.4-8
j. Chuk.17.1-17
k. 7.5-6
l. Ann.4.4-8
m. Adam.47-50
n. Psay.5V.1-3
*   & 5V.10*

CHAPTER 9

For the tree that is stuck in your eyes is a great stupid tree, and you look at it and think that it fills the whole universe with evil, and that no other tree has ever grown so tall and burned the eyes so viciously.

2 And truly this tree burns your eyes with a fire like ^lnapalm, so that you think you cannot stand it.

3 And you beat your breasts and say, I can never grow used to this tree, and I can never eat of its fruit or climb its branches, because it is an evil tree,

4 And so I will sit far away from the tree, and I will do everything possible to show that I am not of this tree, and think that its fruit is poison, and that its branches should be climbed only by criminals.

5 More than this, you say, I will do everything differently from what is done by the criminals who climb the branches of this tree.

6 I will not wear the clothes that they wear,

7 And I will not consume the things that they consume,

8 And I will not like the ^mthings that they like,

9 And I will do everything there is to do differently from the criminals of the tree,

10 ⁿIncluding not wash,

11 And not shave,

12 And not brush my teeth,

13 And not launder my clothes,

14 Or any other thing that is like what the criminals do.

CHAPTER 10

And now I, Harry, ask you, What does this accomplish?

2 The answer is that it makes you [a]smell bad,

3 So that you stink like a bunch of animals,

4 And the very air around you is foul-smelling and unclean,

5 And that is all that it accomplishes.

6 It does not end genocide,

7 And it will not change the nature of the tree,

8 Or shame the criminals who climb the branches of the tree,

9 Because they will merely laugh at you and hold their nose,

10 Which is understandable,

11 Since you are all dirty indeed,

12 And you are also stupid,

13 Which helps nothing and no one,

14 Least of all, you.

CHAPTER 11

When Harry had said this, a female [b]child among the multitudes stood up and reproached him, saying, "Surely, yours is the wrong view, because if everyone stayed away from the tree it would wither and die, and the [c]Others, that is, all the oppressed peoples of the world, would have a chance to live in their own way, which is [d]all they have ever wanted,

2 "And everything would be better,

3 "And more [e]equal,

4 "And there would be peace, because [f]no one would have any more than anyone else, and there would never be any reason to

a. 43.4-7
b. Dav.56.15
c. Oth.1.1-15
d. Oth.5.5-7
e. Yks.97.1-4
f. Ned.8.2-10
g. Oth.8.3-15
h. Vin.55.3-7
i. Ed.23.8-10
j. Exp.1.4-5
k. Ed.50.1
l. Spic.10.6-7

commit genocide or any [g]other evil."

5 Thereupon Harry laughed,

6 And laughed,

7 And laughed,

8 Until the multitudes thought that Harry would perish of laughing,

9 On the spot,

10 [h]But he did not,

11 And when he had wiped the tears from his face, he spoke again, saying, **How can any child be so stupid?**

12 **Truly, you do not understand the way of things,**

13 **At all.**

14 **Now sit down, you foolish daughter of a dog, before my Angels have to make you sit down,**

15 **And I will [i]explain the way of things to you, so that even you can understand them.**

CHAPTER 12

I ask you, **What is the difference between the [j]Chosen Nations, whom you hate, and all the Others for whom you have so much [k]love?**

2 **You see that the tree you hate is big, and so you think that every small tree is beautiful and good.**

3 **But this is a lie which you have made up for yourselves, because you are not very smart and cannot think of any other way to look at it.**

4 **The truth is that all trees are of the same tree,**

5 **Which is the tree of Mankind,**

6 **And one is not different from the other in its basic nature.**

7 **You would revile the [l]con-**

quistadors because they committed genocide in the name of [a]God against the Mayas and the Aztecs,

8 But I ask you, Did not the [b]Mayas and the Aztecs also commit genocide in the name of God against those who opposed them, and even against their own people?

9 You would deplore the [c]Brits who committed genocide against the Zulus of South Africa, not even in the name of God, but in the name of the king, for the purpose of expanding their evil empire.

10 But again I ask you, Did not the [d]Zulus commit genocide against their neighbors, also in the name of their king, for the purpose of expanding their empire?

11 And so what is the difference between the conquistadors and the Mayas, or between the Brits and the Zulus?

12 The only difference is that the Spic tree was taller than the Maya tree, and the Brit tree was taller than the Zulu tree,

13 Just as the American tree is taller than the tree of Southeast Asia or the tree of the native Americans.

14 And if you cut down the biggest tree, you will simply make room for the smaller trees to grow taller,

15 By committing genocide against their neighbors and their own peoples,

16 [e]Which is what they all want to do anyway,

17 All of them,

18 Including even the very tiniest trees on the planet,

a. Boul.15.2-11
b. Oth.3.2-5
c. Psay.5W.11
d. Oth.7.2-7
e. Gods.2.1-7
f. Gods.4.12
g. Apes.2.1-6
*   Name.4.6-13*
h. 5.12
i. 5.3
j. 5.4
k. Vin.22.2-3
l. 4.3-4

19 Even unto the headhunters of the rain forest,

20 Who have no nuclear weapons,

21 Or B-52s,

22 Or napalm,

23 But still want more [f]heads anyway,

24 Because they too are of the tree of [g]man.

CHAPTER 13

By the same token, all of you are also of the tree of man,

2 Which can't have escaped your attention completely.

3 When I first spoke to you, you did not reply to me with words of peace and love,

4 [h]But you threatened me with physical injury,

5 [i]Because I looked different from you, and do not smell bad,

6 [j]And are only listening to me now because I brought plenty of Angels with me.

7 [k]And if I were to ask which of you would lay down his life for all the Others you love so much, you would look at each other and slink away,

8 Because you can hide nothing from me.

9 For I am Harry, and I know you better than you know yourselves,

10 Because I am just like you,

11 Only a lot smarter.

12 For example, I know what your [l]parents and your teachers and your politicians do not,

13 Which is that your ideals are as thin as tissue paper,

14 And even more transparent.

15 You have been born and

raised in the Most Chosen Nation on Earth,

16 And from the moment of your birth, you have always had your own way,

17 And everything else you wanted,

18 Because your parents were born into a time of ^afamine,

19 And they wanted you to have more than they did,

20 And so they gave it to you,

21 Just like ^bmy parents gave me everything I ever wanted.

22 And you grew up watching TV,

23 ^cWhere you learned that every problem anyone ever had could be figured out in just twenty-two minutes,

24 And there was no such thing as a problem that could not be solved,

25 Because this is America,

26 And you were born Americans,

27 And Americans always get their own way,

28 ^dAnd always win.

29 But then you got to be eighteen years old,

30 And suddenly America asked you to do something it wanted,

31 But you didn't want to,

32 Because who wants to die for a bunch of creepy little ^egooks in some faraway jungle,

33 When you could be at home having fun,

34 And getting ^flaid,

35 And having ^geverything you ever wanted?

CHAPTER 14

Notice that none of this has anything to do with genocide or evil,

a. 2.2
b. Rat.7.1-9
c. Ed.24.1-16
d. Dav.32.25-26
e. Rat.10.8-9
f. Psp.3.5
g. Vin.16.3-26
h. Ira.28.17
i. Vin.18.6-12
j. Dav.16.2-7
k. Dav.15.2-51
l. Ed.14.1-11
m. Ed.77.1-14
n. Ed.27.1-14
o. Ed.74.6
p. Ed.45.1-17
q. Ed.68.4-16
r. Hill.L.1-7

2 Except that one of the greatest things about life,

3 As you will learn, provided you can pay attention for a little while longer,

4 ^hWhich I have doubts about,

5 Is that there is always a good and virtuous reason for being opposed to doing what you don't want to do.

6 In this case, you did not want to die in some faraway land,

7 And so you discovered ⁱideals.

8 And where did these great ideals come from?

9 ^jDid they come from your encyclopedic knowledge of history, which you got from Clark Gable and John Wayne and Errol Flynn and Charlton Heston?

10 ^kDid they come from your vast knowledge of religion, which you got from John Huston and Jeffrey Hunter and Charlton Heston?

11 ^lDid they come from your deep knowledge of politics and government, which you got in twenty-two minutes a night from Walter Cronkite and Chet Huntley, unless you got it from the sports page?

12 Did they come from your rich experience of culture, which you got from the ^mThree Stooges and ⁿLucille Ball and ^oSuperman and the ^pLone Ranger and ^qEd Sullivan?

13 ^rDid you get them from each other, through profound conversations that struck deep into the heart of things?

14 Did they come from your intellectual awakening in college, where you learned how to

smoke dope and screw like rabbits and cut class and read [a]Cliff Notes and grow beards and give up bathing?

15 Did they come from the counterculture, where you were exposed to such world class brain trusts as [b]Timothy Leary and [c]Abbie Hoffman?

16 Did they come from [d]Woodstock Nation, where you sat naked in the mud and got enlightened by the divinely inspired wisdom of [e]Joan Baez and [f]Arlo Guthrie and [g]Crosby, Stills & Nash?

17 Or did they come from your [h]parents, who taught you that the best way to get what you want is to ask for it,

18 And keep asking for it until everyone's sick of hearing about it,

19 And make up a bunch of [i]inane reasons why you should get your way,

20 And then demand your way,

21 And then have a giant [j]tantrum and hold your breath until you finally do get your way?

CHAPTER 15

Yes, I believe pretty devoutly in all your ideals,

2 Because I have ideals too,

3 And I have seen your devotion to freedom of speech, which you have proven by [k]denying it to your opponents on college campuses all over America,

4 And I have seen your love of your fellow man, which you have proved in [l]riots on college campuses all over America,

5 [m]And I have seen your powerful vision of the future,

a. Ira.27.20-27
b. Mall.6.24-25
c. Krt.9.7
d. Ira.12.1-16
e. Mawr.31.1
f. Ed.28.1
g. Ed.71.19
h. 13.18-20
i. 11.1-4
Psp.1.2
& 3.10
j. 4.2
k. Ira.16.30
l. 47.1-3
m. Ned.2.1-13
n. 26.7
o. 26.9
p. Dav.57.10

which you have revealed in communes and other pigsties all over America,

6 And I have been impressed.

7 In fact, I have been greatly impressed by the amazing frequency with which you [n]do exactly what you want to do,

8 [o]Whenever you want to do it,

9 And wherever you want to do it,

10 Which is exactly the way I'd expect the children of a Chosen Nation like this one to behave,

11 And isn't different in any way at all from the behavior of the government you despise so much.

CHAPTER 16

When Harry had said these things, there was murmuring in the crowd, and a [p]brave child stood and said in a shaky voice, "Then you are saying that all of Mankind is evil, and that everyone deserves to die in the nuclear holocaust to come?

2 "You said that you had good news, but this is not good news.

3 "This is the fulfillment of all our worst fears and nightmares, to be the evil children of an evil race."

4 After the brave child had said this, Harry sighed,

5 Quite loudly,

6 And went on with his lesson, saying, **Truly, you are the stupid children of stupid parents, and you have learned nothing from all your schooling.**

7 **Have I said a single word to make you think that Mankind is evil?**

8 Truly, I tell that it is not so.

9 For what is evil?

10 Whereupon, some of the children raised their hands, but Harry stopped them with a gesture, saying, No, please do not try to answer. If I must suffer children, I will suffer them in silence.

11 I shall tell you what you need to know about evil,

12 Which is that it is one of the first inventions of Mankind,

13 And one of the first ªlies.

14 Have you not paid attention in science class?

15 Has no one taught you anything about the world or the race of Man?

16 Do you not know that the entire universe came forth from a great accident,

17 ᵇThat everything began with a big bang, which was nothing more than a chemical explosion that created all the stars and planets?

18 And which of you can show me a molecule of a single blade of grass or grain of sand that is evil?

19 The molecules are not evil. They are simply chemicals.

20 And chemicals are neither good nor evil. They simply are.

CHAPTER 17

Of course, if you had ever done any reading, you would know most of this by now,

2 But fortunately, the way history works,

3 It doesn't matter whether the masses read anything,

a. Lies.2.17-28
b. Kin.1.1-6
c. Swar.1.3-5
d. Dav.17.1-16
e. Psp.3.6-7
f. Ed.60.6-24
g. Ext.25.13-14
h. 28.1-9
i. Kens.4.1-2
j. Rat.27.1-9
k. Ned.4.7
l. Lies.12.5-8
   Adam.51.5-9
   Chuk.23.1-11
   Carl.11.1-7
   Zig.18.1-5
   F&J.16.1-13
   Ed.78.1-6
   Jeff.23.8-15
m. Yks.153 & 154

4 Because the college and university professors have read it,

5 ᶜAnd they're the ones who make up history and philosophy and science,

6 And eventually their knowledge finds its way into ᵈmovies and ᵉsongs and comic books and ᶠTV shows and all the things you _are_ familiar with,

7 Which is how I know that all of you have been exposed,

8 In one way or another,

9 To everything I am explaining to you now,

10 And what's more, you already believe it,

11 ᵍBut have never really put it all together,

12 Because you have never really thought about it,

13 Which is actually a good sign,

14 And one I'll explain to you ʰlater.

15 But all that matters now is that you understand the implications of what I'm telling you,

16 That is, what it all means about how you should live,

17 Because your parents and your ⁱteachers haven't gotten that part right,

18 ʲSince even they don't understand the implications of what they know.

19 But I do,

20 Because I am ᵏHarry, and whoever listens to me will have an easier life for as long as it lasts.

CHAPTER 18

It was always ˡinevitable that I would come along,

2 ᵐAnd the way has been paved for my coming for many years,

3 ᵃWhich is why you should all be pathetically grateful that I am here,

4 Because my way can save you a world of grief,

5 And a lot of pain and suffering too.

6 For truly I can tell you that there is no such thing as evil,

7 Because evil cannot exist without a ᵇGod who defines a difference between good and evil,

8 Since without God, there is only nature,

9 Meaning the way things are,

10 And the way *we* are,

11 Already,

12 Without making a lot of changes in ourselves.

13 Nature doesn't require us to live up to anything,

14 Any more than a sponge has to live up to anything,

15 Or a snail,

16 Or a pine cone.

17 ᶜAnd the really great news is that science and philosophy and psychology and literature and the arts have all converged on the same basic conclusions about life,

18 Although they express them in slightly different terms,

19 Which has probably made it harder for you to see the simple truth,

20 Because it is so simple.

CHAPTER 19

Aˢ I have already told you, ᵈscience has shown that the whole universe came from a great big explosion of chemicals,

2 Which operate in accordance

a. Ned.5.5
b. Chr.2.2-8
c. Ira.25.27-31
d. 16.16-17
e. Chuk.8.1-11
f. Drex.6.3-4
g. Chuk.2.3-8
h. Psay.5O.6-18
i. Chuk.12.1-7
j. 1.2
k. Chuk.11.2-4
l. Chuk.14.1-10
m. Chuk.15.1-6

with the ᵉlaws of nature,

3 Meaning they change a little bit all the time,

4 ᶠAt random,

5 Completely by accident.

6 And it is this simple law of random change which accounts for everything. Every form of life you can think of resulted from zillions of little changes,

7 At random,

8 ᵍIn the same basic chemicals that made up the earth after the Big Bang,

9 Which means that you and the ʰtrees and the snakes and the ⁱdinosaurs and the gerbils and the sponges are the result of the same ʲprocess,

10 Which keeps going,

11 And has been since the first ᵏamino acid got formed.

12 ˡIf you have to be scientific about it, the race of Mankind resulted from about a jillion little random changes in the race of apes,

13 And there were several different versions of Man at first,

14 ᵐAnd the one who survived was the one that was the best at killing,

15 Which is the tree of man that all of us are part of,

16 And explains why there is genocide,

17 And always has been.

CHAPTER 20

But don't let this upset you,

2 Not even for a moment,

3 Because there's nothing evil about it.

4 We survived because we were smart and knew how to

kill like nobody's business,

5 And while there is a down-side,

6 Which is that we now have [a]nuclear weapons and will certainly annihilate ourselves,

7 Unless we kill ourselves off with [b]pollution first,

8 There is no evidence of any kind that we were created in the [c]image of any God at all,

9 Let alone a [d]personal God who cares about whether we are good or evil or go to church or give alms to the poor or anything else.

10 In fact, from what we know about history,

11 It looks like pretty much of an archaeological certainty that it was Man who invented [e]God,

12 In his own image,

13 [f]Because Man was afraid to be alone.

14 And it was also Man who made up the idea of good and evil,

15 Because it helped keep people in line,

16 And people had to be kept in line if they were going to work together,

17 [g]And develop advanced enough civilizations to produce plenty of things,

18 Not to mention nuclear weapons.

CHAPTER 21

Moreover, we've had enough history by now to know that everything always goes pretty much the same way,

2 No matter how hard anyone tries to do things any differently.

a. *Al.2.1-8*
b. *Adam.44.1-13*
c. *Lies.2.1*
d. *Chuk.21.8-11*
e. *Gods.4.1-6*
f. *Chuk.17.1-9*
g. *Gods.7.1-16*
h. *Spics.4.1-7*
i. *Lies.9.3-13 Barb.6.1-3*
j. *Jeff.12.1-8*
k. *Exp.1.17-26*
l. *Zig.8.1-3*
m. *Chr.3.1-7*
n. *Grk.19.1-3 Gnt.4.19-24*
o. *Grk.2.1-2 Gnt.16.9-12*
p. *Krt.38.7-9*
q. *Lies.13.1-5 Gyp.4.1-3 Mes.3.1 Grk.26.1 Rom.24.14-18 Spic.1.4 Frog.1.5-6 Brit.59.1-13*
r. *Vin.59.10*

3 No matter how great and peace-loving a religion is,

4 [h]Mankind always turns it into an excuse to commit genocide.

5 No matter how [i]strict a morality any Chosen Nation tries to enforce on itself,

6 It always degenerates back to the basics of human nature,

7 Which is obsessed with [j]killing,

8 [k]And the accumulation of territory and possessions and money,

9 [l]And sex,

10 [m]And status,

11 And not much else.

12 No matter how zealous a culture may be about the pursuit of [n]knowledge for its own sake,

13 [o]It always turns into nothing more than a quest for new technologies that can be used to increase our ability to commit genocide,

14 So that we can have more territory and possessions and money.

15 And that's why all cultures eventually revert to [p]barbarism,

16 [q]And all Chosen Nations eventually stop being Chosen,

17 And the [r]meek always get it in the neck,

18 No matter what,

19 Forever.

CHAPTER 22

Besides, other branches of science have shown that there's nothing whatever we can do about it,

2 Even if we wanted to.

3 We can't change ourselves,

4 Because most of our behav-

ior is determined by the [a]genes we were born with anyway,

5 And what isn't determined by our genes is mostly determined by our [b]unconscious,

6 [c]Which is obsessed with sex and violence and possessions,

7 Just the way we always knew it was anyway,

8 If we ever thought about what we think about.

9 And even if there is some part of us that isn't determined by our genes or our unconscious,

10 [d]The environment determines everything else,

11 And our environment is the human environment,

12 [e]Which is obsessed with killing and possessions and sex,

13 And so there's nothing we can do.

CHAPTER 23

But that's why it's so great that we have [f]psychology,

2 Which teaches us about all the things that control us,

3 Which we can't control,

4 And so we don't have to feel any more guilt about anything,

5 Because it's not our fault,

6 And we're not responsible,

7 For anything.

CHAPTER 24

Modern [g]philosophy has been a big help too,

2 Because it has finally determined that we can't be sure about anything at all,

3 Including whether or not there's anything out there,

4 [h]Except ourselves,

5 Which means the burden of proof is on the universe to con-

a. *Chuk.19.1-8 Zig.16.1-2*
b. *Zig.4.7-14*
c. *21.7-9*
d. *Zig.14.1-4*
e. *21.7-9*
f. *Zig.13.1-3*
g. *Gnt.4.20*
h. *F&J.2.12-16*
i. *Vin.1.1-13*
j. *Frog.35.1-4*
k. *F&J.5.1-5*
l. *Chuk.19.15-17*
m. *Adam.15.16*
n. *Mawr.5.4-11*
o. *20.11*
p. *20.14*
q. *18.8-11*
r. *20.18*

vince us that it is there,

6 Including other people,

7 Which it just can't do,

8 [i]Because science shows us that it doesn't work that way.

9 In the past, this caused a lot of [j]consternation,

10 Because it made existence seem like some big, insane trap,

11 [k]Which you can't escape from,

12 No matter what,

13 Until you [l]die.

14 And while that is the truth,

15 It is not really such bad news,

16 If you happen to be living in the richest and most powerful [m]Chosen Nation in the whole history of Mankind,

17 Even if it's practically a certainty that it's also going to be the [n]last Chosen Nation in the whole history of Mankind.

CHAPTER 25

If you've been following me up to now,

2 And it doesn't really matter if you haven't,

3 Which I'll explain later,

4 I can sum it all up for you pretty neatly this way.

5 [o]There isn't any God,

6 At least any God we would recognize as one,

7 [p]Which means there isn't any good and evil either,

8 [q]Which means that it's okay for Man to be the way he is already,

9 Without a lot of changes,

10 Unless he had a really good chance to survive a lot longer,

11 Which he doesn't anymore,

12 Thanks to [r]nuclear weap-

ons and [a]human nature and all
the [b]lessons of history,
13 [c]Which means that there's
nothing we can or should try to
do about it,
14 [d]Which means that we're
not responsible for anything at
all,
15 Even if we could prove that
anyone or anything else exists
in the first place,
16 [e]Which we can't,
17 Which means that we're all
alone on the very brink of extinction,
18 But have the great good
fortune to be living in the richest nation in the world,
19 Which is too bad for everyone else,
20 Including all the [f]Others,
21 [g]But great for us.

CHAPTER 26

And why is it so great?
2 Because in a very rich nation
like this one, things will run
pretty much by themselves for
a long long time,
3 And while they will fall
apart eventually,
4 [h]It will take a long long time
for that to happen,
5 And by then, the nuclear
holocaust will probably have
destroyed everything anyway.
6 [i]For us, the ones who have
figured it all out, this means
that we are living in a time of
unparalleled freedom,
7 When we can do what we've
always wanted to do,
8 [j]Which is whatever we want
to do,
9 [k]Whenever we want to do it,
10 Without feeling any guilt
or fear about hell and damnation.
11 In short,
12 You don't have to bother
with all your so-called [l]ideals
anymore.
13 It's perfectly okay to climb
the branches of the great
American [m]tree,
14 And take all the [n]fruit you
want,
15 When you want it,
16 As long as you don't make
the wrong people angry.
17 You don't ever have to feel
[o]responsible,
18 Or [p]work hard,
19 [q]Or care about anything
other than yourself,
20 Because it absolutely, positively does not matter,
21 [r]At all.

CHAPTER 27

Now, of course, I under-
stand that there will be
complications.
2 It's not easy to live with the
certain knowledge of annihilation,
3 But I warn you not to try to
refute the [s]lessons of history,
4 [t]Because all the evidence is
in and all of it points in the
same direction,
5 Namely, extinction in the
not too distant future.
6 Moreover, you will encounter other people out there,
7 People who still believe in
good and evil,
8 People you will have to deal
with and compete with for possessions and sex and so forth,
9 [u]Although they're not so numerous as you might think,
10 [v]And there will be fewer of
them all the time,

a. 21.5-11
b. 21.12-13
c. 22.13
d. 23.5-7
e. 24.8
f. Oth.8.18
g. 24.15-16
h. Main.6.3-10
i. Vin.44.4
j. 15.7
k. 15.8
l. Vin.18.6-12
m. 7.3-6
n. 9.3
o. Psay.5V.27
p. Psay.5V.1-3
q. Psay.51.3
r. Vin.42.10-11
s. 25.12
t. Swar.10.4-18
u. 18.2
v. 41.8-9

11 Because the knowledge I have shared with you already [a]permeates our culture,

12 [b]And there is no turning back from knowledge that is as final as this.

13 Perhaps even more importantly, you will have to deal with each other,

14 Which is where things get really complicated,

15 And why you need me, Harry, to show you the way.

CHAPTER 28

But truly you are lucky, for I am here, and my way is the only way,

2 [c]And should be your way,

3 Because my way will make life as good as life can be,

4 For as long as it lasts.

5 [d]And now I hear many of you asking, What is the way of Harry? How can he make a good life out of such a hopeless and doomed dead-end existence?

6 And my answer to this question is a [e]simple one,

7 As all good answers are,

8 [f]Which is that the way of Harry is the way of not thinking about anything at all,

9 [g]Which you are better prepared for than you may think.

CHAPTER 29

For there are literally thousands of ways of not thinking,

2 Which has always been the most deeply buried desire of Mankind anyway,

3 And accounts for all the stories about Eden,

4 Which [h]Adam and Eve always wanted to go back to,

a. 17.3-12
b. Drex.7.13-14
c. Kens.2.4
d. Jeff.24.20-21
e. 31.14
f. Swar.8.2-3
   Forg.13.5-9
   Wht.6
   Mawr.8.1
   Mall.4.1
   Main.9.1-2
   Brd.13.1-3
g. 15.7-9
h. Pnot.13.1-5
i. Kens.7.3-9
   Brd.14.7-16

5 And couldn't,

6 Until now, that is,

7 Because of all their Gods,

8 And all their guilt,

9 And all their responsibilities,

10 And all their aspirations,

11 And all that other junk,

12 Which is meaningless and irrelevant in the last half of the twentieth century.

13 Because the great secret is that you don't have to put on special clothes to follow me,

14 Or follow some particular profession,

15 Or be any richer or poorer than you want to be,

16 Or accomplish anything,

17 Or refrain from accomplishing anything,

18 [i]Because my way would not be *the* way if it asked you to be different from the way you already are.

CHAPTER 30

There are those of you who wish to be millionaires,

2 And those who wish to be doctors and lawyers,

3 And priests,

4 And professors,

5 And accountants,

6 And investment bankers,

7 And gas station attendants,

8 And movie stars,

9 And professional athletes,

10 And politicians,

11 And political activists,

12 And journalists,

13 And factory workers,

14 And truck drivers,

15 And secretaries,

16 And airline pilots,

17 And soldiers,

18 And armed robbers,

19 And corporate managers,

20 And any number of other things,

21 Because they have the right image,

22 Or the right income,

23 Or the right perks,

24 Or because you're mad at society or your parents or somebody else,

25 And I am here to tell you that it is *all* okay,

26 As long as you don't think about anything while you're doing it.

CHAPTER 31

Don't think about any more things than you have to,

2 Ever,

3 ᵃBecause thinking leads to fear and nameless dreads and images of doom that will inevitably come true.

4 Remember that there are no consequences,

5 Because you have no responsibilities,

6 And whatever happens,

7 ᵇIt's not your fault.

8 Now I can see that you are all nodding,

9 And that you are beginning to understand the rightness and wisdom of my way,

10 ᶜBut you are also wondering, How is it that I can avoid thinking?

11 How should I make decisions?

12 What may I rely on for guidance in avoiding thought in my life?

13 And again, I can tell you that the answer is a simple one,

14 Tailor-made for your simple minds.

a. *Cen.10.1-5*
b. *23.5-7*
c. *Mawr.10.1-18*
d. *Ned.18.1-6*
   Hall.5.5-6
   Drex.10.1-7
   Forg.8.1-2
   Wht.7
   Mawr.11.1-12
   Mall.16.8-9
   Main.9.4-7
   Brd.16.1-7
e. *Mawr.12.1-2*
f. *Mawr.13.15-19*
g. *Mawr.14.14-18*
h. *Gnt.1.5-13*
i. *Mawr.12.15-19*
j. *Hill.D.1-4*

15 ᵈYou shall be guided by the great Trinity of Harry,

16 Which encompasses all things of importance to you,

17 And to the conduct of your life.

18 These are the beacons of the way:

19 ᵉDesire,

20 ᶠCertainty,

21 And ᵍBlame.

22 These three beacons illuminate all my teachings and advice.

CHAPTER 32

Act in accordance with your desires.

2 If there is something you want,

3 ʰGo for it,

4 And do not trouble yourself with thoughts about whether you deserve it or not,

5 Or who might be hurt by your having it,

6 Or any chain of events that might be set in motion by your desire.

7 None of these matter,

8 At all,

9 ⁱBecause it is your desire,

10 And you are the way you are.

CHAPTER 33

In all matters and all doubtful circumstances, choose the way of certainty.

2 The man who is certain has no need to think,

3 And is not troubled by conscience or the responsibility to weigh things further,

4 ʲOr to look for concealed relationships and dependencies and other traps which lead inevitably to thought.

5 The man who is certain has no need to inform himself further,

6 ªAnd his education is complete when he declares that it is,

7 ᵇAnd his decisions are always final because there is no way to challenge his logic,

8 Which is certain,

9 And beyond thought.

CHAPTER 34

When you have been hurt or are unhappy or dissatisfied with the current state of affairs for any reason, find someone or something to ᶜblame,

2 ᵈBecause the man who has someone to blame has no reason to question himself,

3 Or his own actions,

4 Or his own merits,

5 Or any other part of himself that might accidentally trigger thought.

6 Be fearless about the assignment of blame,

7 ᵉBe certain in pointing the finger at others,

8 And be sure to choose the ᶠtargets for your blame in accordance with your desires,

9 And not by any other means,

10 Because other means may lead to thought,

11 And thought is the enemy of happiness.

CHAPTER 35

Remember never to be lured into thought.

2 ᵍDo not allow yourself to be intrigued by new ideas,

3 Because new ideas lead to thought.

---

a. *Cen.26.6-19*
b. *Mawr.18.1-7*
c. *Ned.31.9-10*
d. *Main.34.1-4*
e. *Mawr.16.3-4*
f. *41.8-9*
g. *Mall.5.1-8*
h. *33.2-4*
i. *Mall.16.5-7*
j. *Kens.15.1-3*
k. *Mall.8.1-10*
l. *Hill.K.1-5*

---

4 Do not allow others to debate the causes and effects of your actions with you,

5 Because logic leads to thought.

6 ʰDo not seek to find or make connections between the things that you do and the well-being of other people,

7 Because this a perilous trap,

8 And leads to thought.

CHAPTER 36

Do not be too fond of language,

2 Or words,

3 Or their meanings,

4 Because too much attention to language leads to thought.

5 ⁱInstead, seek to reduce your vocabulary as much as possible,

6 ʲAnd use profanity and obscenities in place of truly descriptive words,

7 Because a truly telling description can lead to thought.

CHAPTER 37

ᵏNever be tempted to see the other person's point of view,

2 Because they have different desires,

3 Different certainties,

4 And different targets for blame.

5 Consideration of another's perspective,

6 Even for a moment,

7 Can lead to thought.

CHAPTER 38

ˡDo not be tempted to increase your store of knowledge,

2 Because new knowledge can contradict old knowledge,

3 **And contradictions lead to thought.**
4 **If your chosen profession or line of work requires you to acquire new knowledge,**
5 **Minimize the damage by thinking about your lessons as little as possible.**
6 ^a**Do not extrapolate from new knowledge,**
7 **Or try to find applications for it in other areas of your life,**
8 **Because all of these can lead to contradictions,**
9 **And** ^b**contradictions lead to thought.**

CHAPTER 39

Do not give yourself over to great visions of the future,
2 **In general or in particular,**
3 ^c**Because for the man who does not think, the only time is today,**
4 ^d**And there is no past,**
5 ^e**And no future,**
6 **Because the continuum of time suggests causes and effects,**
7 ^f**And consequences,**
8 ^g**And these can lead to thought.**
9 **Therefore, remember that the only real time is today,**
10 **And making it through today,**
11 **And not having anyone blame you for anything today,**
12 ^h**Because when you have to defend yourself against someone else's blame,**
13 **It can lead to thought.**

CHAPTER 40

For the same reason, remember not to work too hard,

a. Drex.9.1-4
b. 42.12
c. Hill.N.1-3
d. Ned.36.18-19
e. Ned.16.12-13
f. 31.4-5
g. 35.4-5
h. 35.1-5
i. Kens.8.1-9
j. Mall.11.17-26
k. 34.7
l. 26.13-14
m. 27.10
n. Ext.48.1-40
o. Vin.31.5

2 **Or to excel too much,**
3 ⁱ**Or to do anything very differently from anyone else,**
4 ^j**Or to go out of your way to do an outstanding job at anything,**
5 **Because these will make you a target for the blame of others,**
6 ^k**Who will blame you without compunction or remorse,**
7 **Because that is my way,**
8 **And the only way that works.**

CHAPTER 41

And do not fear that there is no way to get ahead without working hard,
2 **Or excelling,**
3 **Or doing great works,**
4 **For in the days and years to come,**
5 **All men will follow me,**
6 **And the greatest** ^l**fruits of the tree will fall to those who follow my way,**
7 **Without even thinking about it.**
8 **For when men stop thinking about anything,**
9 ^m**All those who do not follow my way will become targets for blame,**
10 **And they will gain nothing from the tree,**
11 **But** ⁿ**bitter fruit,**
12 **Which will poison their dreams,**
13 **And their lives,**
14 **Until they die.**

CHAPTER 42

Now, my ^ojet is waiting,
2 **And I must leave to go elsewhere,**

3 Namely, to Malibu for the weekend,

4 So I will give you my final word for now,

5 Which is this:

6 Do not think about what I have told you,

7 At all.

8 Simply follow my way.

9 Do not try to understand it,

10 For there is ªnothing to understand.

11 ᵇDo not look for contradictions between my way and your beliefs,

12 ᶜFor there are no contradictions.

13 ᵈBe the way you are,

14 Without thinking about it,

15 ᵉAnd the way will open before you, as if by ᶠmagic.

CHAPTER 43

ᵍ**A**nd so it happened, when Harry had finished his remarks, that the multitudes were amazed at his advice,

2 ʰBecause he was so sure about everything,

3 And made everything sound so easy.

4 As he departed, surrounded by Angels,

5 They sought to follow him to his jet,

6 But the Angels made them stand way back,

7 Because they smelled so bad.

CHAPTER 44

By and by, Harry went to a great ugly place called ⁱIndiana,

2 Where multitudes of children were crying out against the ʲgenocide being committed by the Americans,

a. Drex.7.10
b. Boul.28.1-9
c. Mawr.21.1-9
d. 50.16-18
e. Ned.30.38-45
f. Ed.60.17
g. Vin.43.1-2
h. 33.1
i. Vin.30.4
  Ira.14.1-4
j. 5.8
k. Vin.23.1-7
l. Vin.23.8
m. Ext.16.24
n. Kens.16.8-10

3 And he showed up near to a dead sea called Erie,

4 And beheld a giant clamor as children mocked the ᵏsoldiers who had come to oppress them for their ideals.

5 Even as he watched, the soldiers grew weary with the taunts of the children,

6 And fired rifles at them,

7 ˡKilling several on the spot.

8 Thereupon, there was a great weeping and wailing,

9 As the children who had not been shot beat their breasts,

10 Saying, "How can this be, that we are hunted down like animals,

11 "And tormented, and treated with such great shabbiness, and excrement like that?"

12 Among these were several who recognized Harry,

13 Having heard of him and his Angels,

14 From their friends on the coast,

15 And they approached him respectfully, saying,

16 "Master, truly we have been told great things about your ᵐwisdom and your power.

17 "But if you know so much, then tell us how we might restore our friends who have been murdered,

18 ⁿ"And how we might gain vengeance against the evil ones who have done this terrible thing."

19 While the children spoke to him, waving their arms about with great energy and violence, Harry listened attentively,

20 And when they had done, and stood staring at him expectantly, he replied to them in a calm voice, with his arms

folded, saying, **Forget about these things,**
21 **They do not matter,**
22 **Because they are already in the past,**
23 ^a**And nothing will bring these dead children back to life,**
24 **For truly their hearts have stopped beating,**
25 **And they are** ^b**history.**

CHAPTER 45

Upon hearing these words, the children expressed their shock and outrage, saying,
2 "Truly we are shocked and outraged at your ^ccallousness.
3 "Our friends have told us that you are our friend,
4 "And that you cared for us, and wished to make our lives better.
5 "Now, you present us with a frozen shoulder,
6 "And conduct yourself like a cranium made of excrement.
7 "What gives?"
8 Whereupon Harry replied, **You must be thinking about somebody else,**
9 **For I am no man's friend who does not follow my way,**
10 **And I am not responsible for what you do,**
11 **Or what is done to you,**
12 ^d**Or anything else.**
13 When he had said these things, the children became puzzled,
14 And said to Harry, "How can you be so calm about everything,
15 "When truly all hell is breaking loose,
16 "And everything is going completely to pieces?"
17 Then Harry smiled and said,

a. Vin.59.7
b. Ned.36.19
c. Ira.38.14
d. 23.1-7
e. Vin.31.5
f. 42.2-3
g. 26.20
h. 13.10-11
i. 3.2
j. 28.1
k. Wht.8
l. Vin.22.2-3
m. 45.9

It is easy to be calm when you have a ^eLearjet,
18 And beachfront property in ^fMalibu,
19 And anything else you could possibly want,
20 ^gSince nothing really matters,
21 Or is worth thinking about,
22 If you can have your own way all the time,
23 Which I do,
24 ^hBecause I am Harry,
25 And I have ⁱmy own way,
26 Which is the ^jonly way.
27 And then the children were amazed and said to Harry, "If we follow you, can we also have a ^kLearjet and beachfront property and anything else we want?
28 "We would think about such an option very seriously,
29 "Because to tell you the truth, all this political stuff is starting to seem elderly to us,
30 "And ^ldangerous."
31 And then multitudes of children surrounded Harry and inquired how they might follow him, and professed their great willingness to ^mthink about joining him and following his way.

CHAPTER 46

But there was one among them who did not join in,
2 And did not speak to Harry at all,
3 But sat on the ground some distance away,
4 And lit up a cigarette.
5 Yet Harry saw him where he sat, and called to him, saying, **You with the Lucky Strike,**
6 **Come here,**
7 **And talk to me.**
8 The other children, whom

Harry had ignored, made way for the smoking child,

9 Who approached close to Harry and said, "Were you talking to me?"

10 Then Harry questioned him, saying, **Why do you not join in with the others,**

11 **And express your desire to have a Learjet,**

12 **Like the others?**

13 Whereupon the child said, "I wanted to smoke a cigarette,

14 "And so I did.

15 "Is there something the matter with that?"

16 And Harry said to all the children, **Behold. Here is one who follows me,**

17 **And he will be called** ^a**Lucky,**

18 **And shall come with me in my Learjet,**

19 **This very day.**

20 And it all happened as Harry said, and Lucky went with Harry and his Angels in the Learjet,

21 Which flew to ^bBoston that very day.

CHAPTER 47

^c**S**hortly afterwards, Harry went into the front yard of an ancient American university,

2 On the far side of the Charles River,

3 ^dWhere multitudes of the Most Chosen Children of the world's Most Chosen Nation were preparing to demolish the commercial establishments surrounding their campus,

4 In protest against the ^emurders which had been committed in Indiana.

5 Some among them recognized Harry,

6 And reproached him, saying,

a. 46.5
b. Vin.32.1
c. Vin.32.8
  Ned.14.8-9
d. Ed.22.1-5
e. 44.5-7
f. 44.14
g. 28.8
h. 33.5-6
i. Cen.1.1-9
j. Wil.33.1
k. Vin.31.5
l. Ira.15.1-8
m. Ext.3.15
n. 46.20
o. 47.14
p. Vin.33.1-10
  Ned.14.13-16
  Ira.16.21-35

^f"We have heard of ^gyour way,

7 "Which is not our way,

8 "Because when we are ^hdone with our education in a week or two,

9 "And have demolished all the commercial establishments in the entire city,

10 "We shall become the leaders of the world's Most Chosen Nation,

11 "And have no need of you and your way,

12 "Because we are ⁱsmart,

13 "And will fix everything,

14 ^j"For we already have all the answers."

15 But Harry just laughed at their impudence, saying, **But surely you have nothing against coming with me in my** ^k**Learjet,**

16 **Which is full of good things to eat and drink and inhale,**

17 **As well as** ^l**women of great beauty and compliance,**

18 ^m**And an itinerary that includes some of the world's most desirable ports of call.**

19 Then the children were amazed and said, "Do you not wish to argue with us,

20 "And change our minds,

21 "And bend us to your will,

22 "And make us follow your way?"

23 Whereupon Harry replied to them, saying, **I have room for** ⁿ**eleven of you,**

24 **And all of you are** ^o**perfect just the way you are.**

25 ^pThen the children cast lots, and the eleven who went with Harry were named Willie, and Joe, and Sam, and Tom, and Mort, and Tony, and Ned, and Ira, and Jerry, and Fred, and Vinnie.

CHAPTER 48

When all had come on board the Learjet, Harry gave his followers great things to eat and drink and inhale,

2 ᵃAnd other things besides,

3 And when they had been satisfied of all their wants, he spoke to them, saying,

4 **Do not question your good fortune,**

5 **Or think any more about it.**

6 **We will travel together for a while,**

7 **Then go our separate ways,**

8 **And all will be as it should be. Okay?**

9 Thereupon, all agreed speedily that it would all be okay,

10 Just as Harry said.

11 But later that night, the Learjet encountered bad weather over the Rocky Mountains,

12 And the followers became afraid that the plane would crash,

13 And awakened Harry to tell him of their fear, and ask what they should do.

14 But he replied to them calmly, saying, **Do what you will. It does not matter to me.**

15 ᵇ**Each of you should act in accordance with his nature.**

16 **If you are a coward, then cry and moan and run around in a great panic until the plane crashes or it doesn't.**

17 **If it is your nature to be calm in times of great emergency, be ᶜcalm.**

18 **If it is your first instinct to have sexual relations with a beautiful young woman, or each other, do so.**

19 **Do not add to your stress**

a. Ira.16.1-19
b. 29.18
c. 45.13-26
d. 18.8-12
e. 32.1
f. 31.1-2
g. 42.3
h. Ira.18.1-12
i. Gods.4.1-6
j. Jeff.21.1-14

by trying to be different than you are,

20 **Or stronger than you are,**

21 **But be yourself,**

22 ᵈ**Exactly the way you are,**

23 ᵉ**And act in accordance with your desire.**

24 ᶠ**For myself, I prefer not to think about it at all.**

25 Whereupon Harry went back to sleep, and each of the followers reacted as he was inclined to do, and all went as Harry said,

26 And the plane landed safely the next morning in ᵍSouthern California.

CHAPTER 49

In the weeks and months that followed, Harry and his followers traveled to many places,

2 And spoke with many different people,

3 From all ʰparts of the Most Chosen Nation,

4 And wherever they went, people were amazed at the wisdom and simplicity of Harry's way,

5 Which caused a great stir,

6 And angered many of the Most Chosen Nation's leaders,

7 Including those who were ⁱresponsible for religion.

8 By and by, some of the religious ʲleaders who were most offended approached Harry in a great mass,

9 In a city in the south,

10 And barged into his hotel room,

11 Awakening Harry from a sound sleep.

12 The tallest and most forceful among them spoke up in a loud voice,

13 Denouncing Harry in these words:

14 [a]"Truly you must be the one who is called the [b]Antichrist.

15 "For whenever you open your mouth, evil comes out,

16 "And your followers are doomed to burn in [c]hell because you have led them down such an evil path,

17 [d]"For your way is not the way of Christ,

18 "And the way of Christ is the only way to [e]heaven.

19 "Now we [f]desire you to repent the error of your ways, before it is too late,

20 "And to kneel in prayer with us now,

21 [g]"And beg forgiveness of Jesus Christ,

22 "Most humbly,

23 "So that you may be [h]born again, into a new life, and into the one true way,

24 [i]"Else we will attack you, and torment your followers, and circulate petitions against you, and in every way possible, make your life miserable and a burden until you die."

CHAPTER 50

When the religious leader had said these things, Harry yawned and rubbed his eyes,

2 Removing the sleepy bugs from them,

3 And then replied to the preacher, saying, **I would be happy to do as you wish,**

4 **And repent for all my sins and misdoings,**

5 **For I behold your [j]certainty,**

6 **And am [k]impressed,**

7 **And will gleefully renounce**

a. Boul.2.1-3
b. Psong.59.1
c. Jeff.7.1-2
d. Jeff.7.5-12
e. Boul.8.1
f. 32.1
g. Psong.10.2
h. Jeff.20.1-6
i. 34.1
j. 34.7-9
k. 15.6-9
l. 42.12
m. 45.25-26
n. Jeff.22.1-4
o. Ned.32.9
p. 32.10
q. 48.24
r. 50.5-6

any and all things I have said or done that [l]contradict your way,

8 **Which is indeed the one true way,**

9 **And the [m]only way.**

10 **Let us pray.**

11 And then the preachers knelt and prayed with Harry, and wept with joy at his [n]salvation, and went away satisfied at the great deed they had done.

12 Thereupon, Harry's followers questioned him closely, saying,

13 Why did you act in that disgusting fashion? These men were fanatics and hypocrites and all manner of odious things. Truly, you should have spoken with your usual wisdom, instead of licking their boots and swallowing their excrement.

14 But Harry just laughed at the words of his followers,

15 And said to them, **The followers of my way are many and varied,**

16 **And truly there will be some among them whom you [o]hate and detest,**

17 [p]**But that is because you are who you are,**

18 **Just as they are who they are.**

19 **Yet I make no such distinctions, for to make distinctions requires thought, and [q]I prefer not to think about it,**

20 **But to be joyful when my followers prove their [r]allegiance to my way.**

21 Then the followers were perplexed, and thought that maybe they would have to think it all over,

22 But decided not to,

23 Because the way of Harry was growing on them day by day.

CHAPTER 51

And not long after his encounter with the Christians, Harry gathered his followers together,

2 And asked them to sit down and get comfortable,

3 Because he wanted to talk to them,

4 At some length,

5 And tell them about a very special place,

6 And the people who lived there.

7 Then the followers did as he asked,

8 And Harry began to talk,

9 At some length.

CHAPTER 52

He told them there was a river called the Delaware,

2 Which flowed through a valley of the same name,

3 All the way from somewhere in northern ᵃNew Jersey,

4 Past a large, ancient, dying city,

5 Down to a bay known as the Delaware,

6 And from there into an ocean called the Atlantic.

CHAPTER 53

He told them that the large, ancient, dying city was named ᵇPhiladelphia,

2 Meaning "City of ᶜBrotherly Love,"

3 ᵈBut there was hardly any brotherly love in Philadelphia,

4 At all.

5 Instead of brotherly love, there were ᵉneighborhoods,

6 And the people who lived in

a. Yks.6.6
b. Ned.23.7
c. 2.1
d. Ned.23.3
e. Ira.21.26
f. Gods.2.5-7 & 7.1-8
g. 28.4
h. Brd.24.1
i. Vin.47.1-6 Ned.30.1-2
j. 53.7-8

these neighborhoods did not love the people who lived in other neighborhoods,

7 Because those people were ᶠdifferent,

8 And probably dangerous besides.

CHAPTER 54

He told them there was a neighborhood called North Philadelphia,

2 Where most of the people who lived there were black,

3 And poor,

4 And likely to stay that way,

5 ᵍForever.

6 ʰThe people who lived in North Philadelphia didn't love the people who lived in other neighborhoods,

7 Because the people who lived in the other neighborhoods didn't love them,

8 At all.

CHAPTER 55

He told them there was a neighborhood called West Philadelphia,

2 Where most of the people who lived there were black,

3 Unless they were students or faculty of the city's greatest ⁱuniversity,

4 Which was also located in West Philadelphia,

5 For some reason.

6 The people who lived in this neighborhood didn't love each other very much,

7 Because the students and faculty in West Philadelphia were ʲafraid of the black people in their neighborhood,

8 And the black people in West Philadelphia couldn't love the

students and faculty who didn't love them,

9 Which kept everyone so busy that they hardly noticed there were other neighborhoods in Philadelphia which didn't love anybody else either.

CHAPTER 56

He told them there was a neighborhood called the Greater Northeast,

2 Above the ªBoulevard,

3 Where most of the people who lived there were white,

4 And thoroughly middle class,

5 And likely to stay that way,

6 ᵇForever.

7 The people who lived in the Greater Northeast didn't love the people who lived in other neighborhoods,

8 Because a lot of the people who lived in the other neighborhoods were ᶜblack,

9 And the ᵈones who weren't black looked down on the people who lived in the Northeast,

10 Because they were so ᵉmiddle class,

11 And likely to stay that way,

12 ᶠForever.

CHAPTER 57

He told them there was a neighborhood called South Philadelphia,

2 Where most of the people who lived there were white,

3 And ᵍItalian,

4 And likely to stay that way,

5 ʰForever.

6 The people who lived in South Philadelphia didn't love the people who lived in other neighborhoods,

7 Because they weren't Italians,

a. Yks.97.1-13
b. 28.4
c. 54.1-2
55.1-2
d. 56.3
e. Boul.25.24-38
f. 28.4
g. Psong.57.1
h. 28.4
i. Kens.1.1
j. 28.4
k. Mawr.15.19-22
l. Ira.21.26
m. 28.4
n. Adam.41.1-11
o. Ext.53.25-27

8 And probably wouldn't ever be,

9 Period.

CHAPTER 58

He told them there was a neighborhood called ⁱKensington,

2 Where most of the people who lived there were white,

3 And poor,

4 And likely to stay that way,

5 ʲForever.

6 The people who lived in Kensington didn't love the people who lived in other neighborhoods,

7 Because they ᵏhated them instead,

8 ˡAll of them.

CHAPTER 59

He told them there was a neighborhood called the Main Line,

2 Where most of the people who lived there were white,

3 And very very rich,

4 And likely to stay that way,

5 ᵐForever.

6 The people who lived on the Main Line didn't love the people who lived in other neighborhoods,

7 Because they were tired of all the ⁿtaxes they paid to take care of the other neighborhoods,

8 Which they knew nobody appreciated anyway.

CHAPTER 60

He told them there was a neighborhood called South Street,

2 Where most of the people who lived there were the ºlowest of the low,

3 And born losers,

4 And likely to stay that way,

5 For as long as they lasted.

6 The people who lived on South Street didn't love the people who lived in other neighborhoods,

7 Because they didn't love much of anything,

8 At all.

CHAPTER 61

And when Harry had finished telling his followers all these things,

2 One of them said to Harry,

3 "It is very nice of you to tell us all about Philadelphia,

4 "Which is a city that we have ªheard of,

5 "Although never in so much gruesome detail,

6 "And it is clear from your words that Philadelphia is very much like every other city in the Most Chosen Nation on Earth,

7 "Except maybe ᵇolder,

8 "And so perhaps you will excuse us for asking why it is you have taken the time to tell us these things."

CHAPTER 62

Then Harry answered the follower in these words, saying,

2 **I have decided to tell you about Philadelphia,**

3 **Because it is time for the people of Philadelphia to learn about my ᶜWay,**

4 **Which will make them feel ᵈbetter,**

5 **About everything.**

CHAPTER 63

At these words, the followers grew unsettled and ex-

a. 64.5
b. 53.1
c. 28.5-9
d. 28.3-4
e. Psay.5J.32
f. 2.5
* Rat.26.7-11*
g. Yks.12.1-17
h. Vin.50.1-6
i. Ned.37.4-5
* Ira.37.1-9*
j. Jeff.24.15-19

pressed their wonderment about many things,

2 Such as why Philadelphia?

3 And weren't there some cities full of hatred in the sunbelt?

4 ᵉAnd hadn't they heard that nobody anywhere ever wanted to go to Philadelphia,

5 If they could help it?

CHAPTER 64

But Harry only smiled at their questions,

2 And waited for all the followers to calm down again,

3 At which point he said, **I have decided to go to Philadelphia,**

4 **ᶠBecause Philadelphia is my birthplace,**

5 **ᵍNot to mention the birthplace of the Most Chosen Nation on Earth,**

6 **Which means that there will be special significance to all we do and say there,**

7 **Not to mention the fact that Philadelphia is a great ʰport city,**

8 **Which need not concern you now,**

9 **But ⁱinterests me a great deal.**

10 **Besides, there are still one or two great hotels in Philadelphia,**

11 **And if any of you are so squeamish and stuck up that you don't want to participate in the ʲgreat works I have planned,**

12 **You can wait at the hotel,**

13 **And never go out at all,**

14 **And call room service,**

15 **For whatever you want.**

CHAPTER 65

When it became clear that there was no alternative,

2 The followers accompanied Harry to the city of his birth,
3 Where they received a spectacular welcome,
4 [a]Consisting of all the beer and pretzels they could consume,
5 And then Harry and many of his followers went out to tell the [b]neighborhoods of Philadelphia about the Way of Harry,
6 Although some of the followers took Harry at his word,
7 [c]And stayed at the hotel,
8 Almost all the time,
9 Because the city was so awful.

CHAPTER 66

Sometimes Harry and the followers went to [d]West Philadelphia,
2 And told everybody about the Way,
3 [e]And washed their hands of everything,
4 So that they could be as happy as possible.
5 Other times, they went to [f]South Philadelphia,
6 And told everybody about the Way,
7 And washed their hands,
8 And so forth,
9 And so on.
10 Occasionally, they went to the [g]Greater Northeast,
11 And so forth,
12 And so on.
13 As often as they could, they went to the [h]Main Line,
14 Where they washed their hands and all that,
15 And in between, they visited the city's great landmarks,
16 Including the [i]art museum, and the [j]Liberty Bell, and other things too probably,
17 Where they told everybody about the Way,
18 And so forth,
19 And practically every night, they went out to some social occasion or other,
20 Including [k]weddings and parties and [l]singles bars and [m]college and university affairs,
21 Where they spread the Word of Harry,
22 And so forth,
23 And so on,
24 Until the whole city just loved Harry,
25 And were starting to get the hang of his Way,
26 Because it was so [n]easy,
27 Especially for Philadelphians.

CHAPTER 67

And while all these great works were going on,
2 Certain of the followers,
3 Including those of the most refined sensibilities,
4 [o]Stayed right there in the hotel,
5 The whole time.

CHAPTER 68

And so it happened that Harry and his followers stayed for many many months in Philadelphia,
2 [p]And met many multitudes of people,
3 [q]And went to more parties,
4 And special events,
5 And other things,
6 In a great many [r]neighborhoods,
7 All over the city.
8 And when they had done all the things there were to do in Philadelphia, the followers grew restless and said to Harry, "Why is it that we must remain so long in this city,

a. Vin.37.1-8 Ned.26.1-7
b. 53.5
c. 64.12-15
d. 55.1-5
e. Vin.26.1-9
f. 57.1-5
g. 56.1-6
h. 59.1-5
i. Paul.5.1-10 & 6.1-17 Vin.11.13-15
j. Vin.38.6-10
k. Vin.51.1
l. Ira.25.1-2
m. Ned.30.1
n. 43.1-2
o. 65.9
p. Vin.46.7
q. Vin.46.6
r. Ira.21.26

9 "And when can we go somewhere else,

10 "And experience the big time,

11 "Once again?"

12 And then Harry replied to them, saying,

13 **I guess it is time for me to tell you a little story,**

14 **Because it is always the option of a man in my position to answer questions with cute little stories,**

15 **Which may be told,**

16 **And retold,**

17 **Until people are sick of them.**

18 **And truly, I have not done nearly enough of this,**

19 **So far.**

CHAPTER 69

And then, as the followers looked one to another in bewilderment, Harry told them a ªstory, in these words:

2 ᵇThere was once a father who had two children, and he loved them equally, and divided up all his belongings, and said to them, "Here are all my belongings, which will belong to you one day.

3 "For now, I wish to show you which of you shall get which belongings, so that you will know that I love you equally, and have not given more to the one than the other."

4 But when they had seen the belongings that would come to them, the two sons were surprised at how many belongings their father had amassed, and grew ᶜdesirous of enjoying them right away.

a. F&J.15.14-16
b. Pnot.31
c. 32.1
d. 32.2-10
e. Carl.9.7-8
    Psong.65.1-3
f. 34.1
g. Psong.19.1
h. Psong.25.1
i. Psong.49.1-3
    & 51.1-4
    & 54.1-6
j. Psong.50.1-8
k. Psong.29.1-3
l. Psay.51.1-6

5 ᵈSo they soon approached their father and said, "Father, you are old and we are young, and we would like to enjoy our belongings now, while we still have our health."

6 And because the father loved his two sons, he did as they asked, and gave them all his belongings, divided in the way he had promised, keeping out only the smallest part of them so that he could still buy food and have a ᵉroof over his head.

7 When they saw that their father had held back some of his belongings, the two sons were vexed and ᶠangry, and reproached their father, saying, ᵍ"This is not what you promised, and truly we believe that you never loved us and never cared about us, but are a selfish old man, and we hate you."

8 Then they took their new belongings and departed from their father, uttering many more harsh words as they went,

9 And went to a great city, and spent everything they had on ʰfast cars, and ⁱloose women, and ʲintoxicants of every variety, until they ran out of ᵏmoney, and had no choice but to return home.

10 When they approached their father's miserable one-room apartment, they were afraid of his wrath, and all the ˡterrible things he would say to them, but they had nowhere else to go.

11 But when he saw them on the doorstep, their father

knew immediately what had happened and said, "I am happy you are home, boys. I have missed you terribly, and if I had any money we would celebrate your return, but if we are all thrifty, then the three of us can just get by on what we have left. But that is all right, because this is our home, and I am your family, and this is where you belong.ᵃ"

12 **Then the sons realized that their father had spoken the truth before, and really didn't have any more belongings to give them, and so they denounced their father, and told him he was a worthless ᵇold fool, and departed from home forever.**

13 And when Harry had completed this story, the followers said, "How does that story answer our questions? There is no moral at all that we can see, and besides, it doesn't make any sense. We can't believe that the father would just welcome them home like that."

14 Whereupon Harry said, **Then I will give you a different ending. When the two sons returned home, their father cursed and reviled them for their ᶜingratitude, and sent them out of their home forever.**

15 **Is that ending more to your liking?**

16 For a moment, the followers acted as if they would think about the story Harry had told,

17 But then thought better of it,

18 And told Harry the story was fine.

a. Psay.5V.1-2 & 5V.14-20
b. 77.1-3 Rat.1.1-5
c. Psay.3.2-3
d. Ext.7.6-14
e. Ned.41.1-8
f. Ned.42.1-9
g. Ned.42.15
h. Ned.42.16
i. Ned.42.17

19 Then Harry smiled at them and said, **Now let us go for a walk in the park and pick up some women,**

20 **For it is a nice day, and I am tired of stories.**

CHAPTER 70

Later that same day, Harry and his followers returned to the hotel,

2 Where they were met by an ᵈAngel,

3 Who spoke to Harry in secret,

4 And then departed with great urgency.

5 The followers were concerned and said, "Is something wrong? The look on the Angel's face was dark and fills us with foreboding."

6 But Harry said to them, **Do not think about it.**

7 **It does not matter.**

8 **Let us have dinner in a private room in the ᵉbest restaurant in town.**

9 And so they engaged a private room,

10 And Harry sat down to eat with the twelve,

11 ᶠWho grew merry as the evening progressed,

12 Until the restaurant echoed with their laughter and loud voices.

13 But at length, Harry became serious,

14 And said to the followers, **There's a ᵍchance we may not be together much longer,**

15 ʰ**So I would like to take this opportunity to give you something to remember me by,**

16 ⁱ**Something that will help you follow my way more easily.**

17 ^aAnd the followers became downhearted,

18 ^bBut Harry called for the waiter,

19 ^cAnd whispered some instructions,

20 ^dWhich were swiftly obeyed,

21 ^eSo that in a few minutes' time the waiter returned to give Harry a razor blade and a small mirror,

22 ^fUpon which he placed some small white rocks,

23 ^gThen cut them into little pieces with the razor blade,

24 ^hArranging them into straight lines on the mirror.

25 ⁱAs the followers looked on in puzzlement, Harry rolled up a hundred-dollar bill and placed it against one of the lines on the mirror, and inhaled the entire line through the bill.

26 ^jWhen he had done so, he leaned back in his chair, saying, **Wow. That is some outstanding excrement.**

CHAPTER 71

^k**B**ut the followers were without a clue, and asked Harry, "What is the meaning of what you have done? We do not understand, no matter how much we don't think about it."

2 ^lWhereupon Harry replied to them, saying, **Do this in remembrance of me.**

3 ^m**Look upon your own face in the mirror,**

4 ⁿ**Which is the face of yourself alone,**

5 ^o**As we all are alone in this vast meaningless universe.**

6 ^p**Then cover the face in the mirror with little white rocks,**

7 ^q**Which are the slayers of thought, and your consolation**

a. Ned.42.18
b. Ned.42.19
c. Ned.42.20
d. Ned.42.21
e. Ned.42.22
f. Ned.42.23
g. Ned.42.24
h. Ned.42.25
i. Ned.42.26
j. Ned.42.27
k. Ned.43.1
l. Ned.43.2
m. Ned.43.3
n. Ned.43.4
o. Ned.43.5
p. Ned.43.6
q. Ned.43.7
r. Ned.43.8
s. Ned.43.9
t. Ned.43.10
u. Ned.43.11
v. Ned.43.12
w. Ned.43.13
   Ira.10.13
x. Ned.43.14
y. Ned.43.15
z. Ned.43.16
aa. Ned.43.17
bb. Ned.43.18
   Vin.67.1-17
cc. Ned.43.19
dd. Ned.43.20
ee. Ned.43.21
ff. Ned.43.22
gg. Ned.43.23
hh. Ned.43.24
ii. Ned.43.25
jj. Ned.43.26
kk. Ned.43.27

for all things which may trouble you.

8 ^r**When you have done this, take the blade of a razor,**

9 ^s**Which is as deadly and useful as blame itself,**

10 ^t**And cut the rocks into lines, so that the slayer of thought may serve you and your desire,**

11 ^u**Then roll some money in your fingers,**

12 ^v**Because, outside of yourself, money is the only certainty one can have,**

13 **And besides, it makes an excellent device for inhaling lines.**

14 ^w**Finally, as you inhale, remember me,**

15 ^x**For the briefest possible instant,**

16 ^y**Which should not be too hard,**

17 ^z**Because when you have finished inhaling, you will no longer remember me,**

18 ^{aa}**Or anything else.**

19 ^{bb}With great solemnity, the followers did as Harry instructed,

20 ^{cc}And ceased thinking of anything for some minutes.

21 ^{dd}Then Harry spoke again, saying, **One of you will hand me over to the authorities this night,**

22 ^{ee}**But that's okay,**

23 ^{ff}**Because I can beat the rap.**

24 ^{gg}**The rest of you will deny that you ever knew me,**

25 ^{hh}**Or ever rode on my Lear-jet,**

26 ⁱⁱ**Or did anything else with me,**

27 ^{jj}**But that's okay too,**

28 ^{kk}**For I know that none of**

you will ever betray me.

CHAPTER 72

W hen Harry had said all these things, he walked out alone onto the private patio that adjoined the room in which they had eaten.

2 ^aAfter the followers had discerned that Harry wasn't going anywhere, they decided to depart from the restaurant at once,

3 Because it was no longer safe to be where Harry was.

4 ^bBut none of them had noticed that Lucky had left the restaurant much earlier,

5 And they met him on their way out,

6 In the company of a squad of heavily armed officers of the law,

7 Who took them back to the private room,

8 And made them wait while they searched the patio.

9 ^cThen Lucky pointed at Harry, saying, "That is the man you want, officers.

10 "Please let me know if I can be of any further assistance."

11 ^dHarry smiled as they put handcuffs on him,

12 And chuckled when he observed,

13 On his way out to the car,

14 ^eAll of his followers shaking their heads and loudly denying any knowledge of him,

15 Whatever.

CHAPTER 73

T hey took Harry to the station house,

2 And booked him,

3 And interrogated him,

4 And demanded that he tell them all he knew about one

a. Ned.44.1-2
b. Ned.44.3-5
c. Ned.44.6-8
d. Ira.41.6-12
e. Vin.68.1-5
f. 64.7-9
g. Ira.42.1-9
Vin.1-2
h. Ned.46.1
i. Ned.46.2
j. Ned.46.3
k. Ned.46.4-7
l. Ned.47.1-4
m. Ned.47.8-11
n. Ned.47.12-13
Ira.43.1-14

thousand kilos of illegal drugs that had been seized at the ^fPort of Philadelphia,

5 But he merely smiled,

6 And told them, **I won't be saying anything at all without my lawyer present.**

7 Forthwith, they permitted Harry to call his lawyer,

8 And within an hour, the judge had ruled that Harry could not be released on bail,

9 And could rot ^gin jail forever,

10 For all he cared.

CHAPTER 74

^hW ithin a very few days, Harry was indicted,

2 ⁱAnd brought to trial,

3 ^jAnd convicted,

4 ^kOf all charges.

5 When the day of sentencing arrived, the judge looked at Harry,

6 Long and hard,

7 And finally said,

8 "I can find no good in this man,

9 "And no reason for leniency.

10 "I sentence you to the maximum term,

11 "Which is life in prison,

12 "And I will see to it that you are never paroled."

13 When the judge had said these and ^lother things, ^mHarry smiled at the him and said, **You can put me in prison,**

14 **But I am Harry,**

15 **And I know everything,**

16 ⁿWhich made the judge tremble and look away.

CHAPTER 75

T hen the bailiffs took Harry,

2 And put chains on his hands and feet,

3 And dragged him to the paddy wagon,

4 Which carried him to prison,

5 To start serving his term,

6 In maximum security,

7 For life.

8 Along the way, the guards teased him,

9 And called him the King of the Cons,

10 And other things,

11 Which Harry took good naturedly, saying, **If it's all the same to you, I would prefer to be the King of Coins,**

12 **ᵃBecause when the King of Coins reaches for his pocket,**

13 **The whole world pays attention,**

14 **ᵇAnd all barriers are removed as soon as he approaches.**

15 And the guards laughed and laughed,

16 But when they had dropped him off inside the prison,

17 And he had passed through the cell-block gates,

18 They shook their heads at his passing,

19 And said, "Truly, that is one ᶜcool customer,

20 "Who knows the way to be."

CHAPTER 76

But three days later, on visiting day, some of the followers came to the prison to talk to Harry,

2 ᵈAnd were told that he was no longer there,

3 Which made them feel amazed,

4 And afraid that something had happened to Harry in prison.

5 Something awful.

a. Psong.1.3
b. Psong.1.2
c. Ned.54.9
d. Vin.75.1-3
*   Ira.44.1-9*
e. 44.20-22
f. 69.12
g. Ned.55.5-7
*   Vin.75.9-10*
h. Vin.75.11
*   Ned.55.8*
i. 45.24-26
j. Vin.26.1-9
k. 32.1-10

6 But no one would give them any details,

7 And so they decided to ᵉforget about it.

CHAPTER 77

Not long after that, the followers had a little get-together,

2 To remember the good times they'd had together,

3 ᶠEven if Harry had turned out to be a worthless fool,

4 And they rented a private room,

5 In a first-class hotel,

6 And were just sitting down to dinner when a waiter ran in,

7 ᵍIn a great hurry, saying, "Long Distance call for all of you,

8 ʰ"From Rio de Janeiro."

9 And one by one, they spoke with the voice on the phone,

10 And enjoyed themselves tremendously,

11 Because it was good to know that there is always a way,

12 To get what you want,

13 No matter what,

14 Which is what they had learned,

15 From Harry.

CHAPTER 78

ⁱ**A**nd indeed, all men must now learn from Harry; for he has shown us the only way to be.

2 ʲHe has washed his hands of everything, and he can afford to wear gloves from now on.

3 ᵏHe has followed his own desires, and he has proven with the strength of his Way that his desires must be satisfied, or else.

4 He has said what he felt like saying, whenever he felt like it,

and [a]no one ever succeeded in making him change his tune.

5 [b]He has gotten away with everything, including a huge fortune, and he has proved that nothing else counts.

6 [c]For Harry has shown everyone the rules of the game, including the rule that it's the winner who gets to make up the rules,

7 For everybody else.

8 Long live Harry, King of the Boomers!

9 [d]Hallelujah, Hosanna, Hooray!

a. 74.13-15
b. Ext.2.8-10
c. Ned.19.3-4
d. Psong.22.1-7

THE GOOD WORD ACCORDING TO
ULT. VINNIE

CHAPTER 1

[a]In the beginning was the void, and the void was all there was, for a long long time.

2 And then there was something that was not the void,

3 Although maybe it still was,

4 Really,

5 And just looked like it wasn't,

6 Being an [b]illusion,

7 And a pretty convincing one at that,

8 To everything that was part of the illusion,

9 Unless it wasn't an illusion,

10 But really separate from the void,

11 And actually came into existence somehow,

12 Even though it's impossible to know,

13 And wouldn't change anything anyhow,

14 [c]Because this was a long long long time ago,

15 Before there were [d]gods,

16 Before there were [e]men,

17 Before there was [f]life as we know it,

18 Before there were [g]planets,

19 And even before the very

a. Lies.2.4-6
b. F&J.2.12
c. Chuk.10.11
d. Chuk.17.1-9
e. Chuk.15.1-4
f. Chuk.10.5-10
g. Kin.1.5
h. Kin.1.1-4
i. 1.6
j. Kin.1.6
k. Apes.2.2-6
l. 3.1
m. 1.12

first [h]star exploded into existence,

20 Or into the [i]illusion of existence,

21 Which amounts to the same thing,

22 When all is said and done,

23 Because back then, there was nobody to notice the difference,

24 Or pretend there was a difference,

25 Which makes it all pretty irrelevant.

CHAPTER 2

Skipping ahead a few hundred million years,

2 [j]It turned out that the void got pretty full of stars and planets and other stellar material,

3 Unless it was all an illusion,

4 Until there was something that regarded itself as [k]intelligent life on [l]one of the planets,

5 Unless this was also an illusion,

6 [m]Even if it would be pretty hard to tell for sure,

7 Because the something that regarded itself as intelligent life was pretty sure that it existed,

413

8 And had existed for maybe a million years,

9 ᵃAnd had actually written down some stuff about what had happened in the last few thousand years,

10 ᵇThus proving that it was there,

11 And incredibly important,

12 Which is probably not the case,

13 And explains why they needed some help,

14 Which they pretty much got,

15 Starting with a unit of presumptively intelligent life called John,

16 Which looked at the ᶜvoid for quite a while,

17 ᵈAnd figured out that there's not enough information available about any of it,

18 ᵉWhich means you can't really believe in anything,

19 Not even the ᶠI Ching,

20 Or Jehovah,

21 Or Buddha,

22 Or any of the other stuff that's supposed to be believable.

CHAPTER 3

The ᵍplanet we're talking about here is Earth,

2 In case you need any help on this point,

3 And the something that regarded itself as intelligent life was the species of ʰman,

4 Specifically, a subset of the species called ⁱAmericans,

5 Which invited John to express his views,

6 Because he had some,

7 And was always willing to talk about them,

8 Whenever there were some unwashed masses on hand.

a. Grk.21.1-11
b. F&J.2.15-16
c. 1.1
d. 1.6
e. Ned.3.1-3
f. Ned.3.4
g. 2.4
h. Name.4.6-13
i. Yks.1.6
j. Ira.10.1-21
k. Ape.2.6
l. Dav.57.16
m. Jeff.24.13-14
n. Jeff.19.14-16
o. Psom.78.1-13
p. Psom.45.9-12
q. Ed.71.8-20
r. Chuk.11.1-5
s. Kin.5.1-5
t. Gnt.6.1-6
u. Adam.50.6

9 For example, he was pretty fond of shouting,

10 ʲ"I am the voice of an ape calling in the wilderness,

11 ᵏ"As one ape to another ape,

12 "And if you like, you can call me ˡJohn the Beadle,

13 "Because I am something of a messenger,

14 "Notifying you that there is someone who will come after me,

15 ᵐ"Someone so important that even though I am only his messenger,

16 "I am,

17 "All by myself,

18 "More important than ⁿJesus Christ."

CHAPTER 4

And the masses cried out to John, saying,

2 "Far out!

3 "That's some pretty heavy excrement you're laying on us here,

4 "And why don't you,

5 "You know,

6 "Lay some wisdom on us,

7 "So we can, like, figure out what's going down here?"

8 Thereupon John commenced to °twist and shout like an ancient ᵖholy man,

9 ᑫOr a modern rock star,

10 And his words were a wonder to all those assembled, being all about vitreous ʳvegetables,

11 And tusked ˢmammals,

12 And human females defying the laws of ᵗphysics with chunks of compressed carbon,

13 ᵘAnd mobile aquatic domiciles of xanthic hue,

14 And a bunch of other stuff too,

15 Until the masses were start-

ing to look at their watch a lot,
16 Which made John get to the point,
17 Finally,
18 So that he summarized his remarks in simpler terms, saying,
19 "I think we can all agree that everything has gotten very [a]confusing,
20 [b]"And there's got to be a way out,
21 "Some way that we can [c]wash our hands of everything,
22 [d]"And not get involved in a lot of pointless pain and corruption and violence and heartbreak,
23 "Because if everything's going to turn out lousy anyway,
24 "What's the point in wearing yourself out,
25 "For [e]nothing?"

CHAPTER 5

And the masses answered John, saying,
2 "We don't know.
3 "What's the answer?
4 [f]"We're terribly confused."
5 And then John [g]smiled,
6 And said to them, "That's why Harry is coming,
7 "To answer our questions,
8 "So that we don't have to be confused anymore."
9 And everybody said, "Who is Harry?
10 [h]"Does he live around here?
11 "Is he coming soon?"

CHAPTER 6

And then John told the masses something about Harry,
2 In these words, saying,
3 "There have been many [i]VIPs in human history,

a. *Chuk.2.3-8*
b. *Psp.2.7*
c. *Dav.15.25*
d. *Psp.3.11*
e. *Drex.3.7*
f. *Gods.3.5-6*
g. *Gods.3.14-15*
h. *Gods.3.11-12*
i. *Adam.1.1-4*
   Chuk.1.1-2
   Carl.1.1-5
   Zig.1.1-4
   Dav.1.1-4
   Al.1.1-4
   Paul.1.1-3
   F&J.1.1-5
   Ed.1.1-6
   Jeff.1.1-4
j. *Rom.10.1-2*
k. *Psay.5G.1-28*
l. *Boul.5.1*
   Rom.20.1-17
m. *Kin.2.1-4*
n. *Carl.4.5-8*
o. *Rat.26.7-11*
p. *Drex.6.3-4*

4 "Who had a bunch of ideas,
5 "And changed the world,
6 "Unless they didn't,
7 "Because I seem to remember learning in school that no VIP can really change the world,
8 "Since history is what changes the world,
9 [j]"And history just kind of happens all the time,
10 "Whether there are any VIPs around or not.
11 "But [k]some people are lucky enough to be in the right place at the right time,
12 "When lots of big things are happening,
13 "Which turns them into VIPs [l]somehow,
14 "Proving what an [m]accident life really is,
15 "When you look at it in just the right way,
16 "Which is where Harry comes in."

CHAPTER 7

"For example, Harry would probably tell you that he is just an average guy,
2 [n]"And no better than anyone else,
3 "Except that he got born at exactly the right time,
4 [o]"Meaning the day the world changed for the last time,
5 "And Harry happened to notice it,
6 "Because somebody had to,
7 [p]"And why not him?"

CHAPTER 8

"And besides, Harry had a little help in noticing that things had changed,
2 "Because right after he was born,
3 "In Philadelphia,

4 "He and his mom got visited at the hospital,
5 [a]"By three physicists from a place called [b]Princeton,
6 "Who spoke to Harry's mom in thick [c]Kraut accents,
7 "Saying, 'We have come to see the first child born into the new world we have created; for we are afraid that nothing will be the same again, and he will live in a different world from the one we knew.'
8 "And then they gave him gifts: a [d]Bible, a [e]Geiger counter, and a [f]cyanide capsule,
9 "Signifying their terrible fear that the entire planet had suddenly become a [g]hot potato,
10 "Which nobody could do anything about."

CHAPTER 9

"And Harry's [h]mom kept their gifts,
2 "In a secret place known only to herself,
3 "And when Harry got old [i]enough,
4 "She showed them to him,
5 "And told him what had occurred,
6 [j]"And of her fear that she had brought him into a doomed and desperate situation,
7 "Which nobody could do anything about.
8 "But Harry did not reply to her,
9 [k]"And went off by himself for a while to [l]think about what she had said,
10 "And when he came back,
11 "He had some new ideas,
12 "About [m]how to be,
13 "Which is what makes him such a [n]VIP,
14 "And why you should listen very carefully to what he has to say,
15 "When he starts laying it on you."

CHAPTER 10

And then John stepped into a waiting [o]limousine and said, just before leaving,
2 "Don't worry about a thing.
3 "He's waiting in the wings right now.
4 "So just put your hands together,
5 "And start chanting, 'Harry! Harry! We want Harry!'
6 "Okay?"
7 And so the masses did as he asked,
8 And Harry [p]came out of the wings,
9 Dressed in a beautiful white suit.

CHAPTER 11

Hi there, everybody, said Harry.
2 **It's great to see you all,**
3 **And I am especially glad that there are so many [q]Angels here,**
4 **Because I feel happiest when surrounded by Angels,**
5 **And the people they like to hang out with,**
6 **Meaning people like you.**
7 At these words of Harry, the multitude went wild,
8 Whistling and cheering and throwing bottles until he held out his hands for silence, and continued with his warmup, saying,
9 **I'd like to thank John for his great introduction,**
10 **Which was wonderful,**
11 [r]**Especially if you like tusked mammals,**

a. *Jeff.24.1-6*
b. *Psay.5E.1-8*
c. *Yks.113.7-10*
d. *Ira.27.10-19*
e. *Ned.16.12*
f. *Psom.4.1-13*
g. *Yks.20.7-11*
h. *Rat.26.1-2*
i. *Ira.5.5-18*
j. *Yk.140.11-18*
k. *Jeff.24.9 Dav.15.14*
l. *Psp.2.1-2*
m. *Wil.28.8*
n. *Rat.7.15*
o. *Psp.3.13*
p. *Gnt.15.14*
q. *Dav.58.9*
r. *4.10*

12 Which I do not, particularly,

13 Although I recall having learned as a child that [a]it is possible to fool most of the people most of the time,

14 Which I always remember when I see nothing that looks like something,

15 To millions and millions and millions of [b]idiots.

16 And I only hope that I can do as well.

CHAPTER 12

Thereupon the multitude cried out to Harry, saying,

2 "The [c]beadle with dirty stringy hair and funny little glasses was saying that you were, you know, pretty special,

3 "And, like, know a lot,

4 "Or some excrement like that.

5 "So why not, like, lay it on us now?"

6 And Harry smiled, and stepped closer to the microphone, and began to lay it on them, as follows:

7 You guys have been having a pretty rough time of it for a while,

8 If you don't mind me summing up a few facts for you.

9 [d]Like, you're pretty much the scum of the earth, aren't you,

10 [e]And most of you will never get to college,

11 [f]Or get to be rich,

12 [g]Unless you can find your way onto a stage like this somehow,

13 And it's a lot more likely that you'll get drafted instead,

14 [h]And go get shot in Vietnam or something,

15 Unless you shoot each

a. Psay.5Q.46
b. Psay.5I.1-6
c. 3.12
d. Adam.27.8
e. Kens.2.5
f. Kens.2.6
g. Kens.32.4
h. Kens.22.23-26
i. Kens.5.1-2
j. Wil.5.5
k. Kens.3.3-9
l. Psay.5I.1-6
m. Kens.28.10
n. Kens.17.9-14
o. Adam.27.8
p. Ned.20.20-26
q. Yks.20.19-24 & 21.1-9
r. Yks.56.7-14

other in a [i]barroom brawl or something first.

16 Is any of this hitting home with you guys?

CHAPTER 13

And the multitude screamed and whistled and shouted for Harry to proceed,

2 Because they dug what he was saying,

3 Since it was so [j]heavy and right on,

4 So that they all piped down when Harry opened his mouth to speak again, in these words:

5 Maybe you've always felt like you weren't really good enough to have the things you want,

6 And maybe that used to be true,

7 Because let's be honest,

8 You've never been real interested in certain things,

9 [k]Such as self-improvement,

10 [l]And thinking about what you do before you do it,

11 [m]And controlling your most basic animal instincts,

12 And reflecting on the [n]consequences of your actions,

13 Either before or after you do something that's going to have consequences,

14 Which maybe explains why [o]you and the people you come from have never gotten to first base,

15 And you're still sitting at the [p]bottom looking up,

16 [q]In spite of the fact that a lot of your families have been citizens of the Most Chosen Nation on Earth since the beginning,

17 [r]Or very close to the beginning, anyway,

18 [a]**And in spite of the fact that the Most Chosen Nation has tried very hard to give everyone a chance to succeed,**
19 **Including a whole bunch of [b]federal programs that are supposed to help you become decent, respectable, hardworking, prosperous citizens,**
20 **For free.**
21 **And yet, here you are,**
22 **Looking up at me with your bad teeth,**
23 **And your [c]beer bellies,**
24 **And your dull little [d]pig eyes,**
25 **And your bizarre [e]tattoos,**
26 [f]**And countless other dead giveaways of your poverty, your lack of taste and insight, and your lack of intelligence,**
27 **Not to mention your lack of good personal [g]hygiene.**
28 **But in spite of all this,**
29 **I am here to give you the best possible news,**
30 **Which is that there is no reason whatever for you to feel inferior,**
31 **In any way,**
32 **From now on,**
33 **Because you are [h]not inferior,**
34 **Anymore.**
35 **In fact,**
36 **You are all just great,**
37 [i]**Exactly the way you are.**

CHAPTER 14

For a while there, during [j]some of Harry's remarks, the multitude had grown restless,
2 As if they did not entirely approve of Harry's line of conversation,
3 But when he announced that they were all [k]great,
4 Exactly the way they were,
5 They jumped to their feet, whistling and shouting and applauding,
6 Because they dug what he was saying,
7 And wanted to hear more.
8 Thereupon, Harry gave it to them, in these words:
9 **All your lives, you have been [l]poor white trash,**
10 **And you sort of figured that was a bad thing to be,**
11 **If you ever thought about it at all,**
12 **And there were maybe times when you felt ashamed about all your dad's [m]prison sentences,**
13 **And how beat up your mom used to look every Sunday morning,**
14 **And how you could never hold down a steady job,**
15 **Because you got drunk,**
16 **Or lost your temper,**
17 **Or couldn't read the directions,**
18 **Or were just too stupid to do what they wanted,**
19 **Whatever it was.**
20 [n]**But you and your people have been here for a long long time now,**
21 **And you've never [o]changed in all that time,**
22 **Which is why things are different now,**
23 **Because the [p]wheel spins round and round all the time,**
24 **And every once in a while a different number comes up,**
25 [q]**And this time it's your number,**
26 **Because all the time that**

a. Yks.97.1-11
b. Adam.41.1-11
c. 15.4-12
d. Kens.5.9
e. Kens.9.3-6
f. Ann.18.17 & 18.7 & 18.21 & 18.13
g. Psay.5H.1-22
h. Carl.4.5-8
i. Wil.32.10
j. 13.21-27
k. 13.36
l. Brd.17.4
m. Kens.5.25-30
n. 13.16-17
o. Chuk.18.8-10
p. Ann.12.9
q. Ann.12.10-12

you've kept on being you,
27 Other people have been getting more and more like you all the time,
28 Even if they didn't notice,
29 And now they're ^aalmost exactly like you,
30 ^bIn many many ways,
31 Which is why it's suddenly your turn to set the pace for everyone else,
32 And show the whole population of the Most Chosen Nation on Earth how to be ^cwhite trash,
33 Just like ^dyou.

CHAPTER 15

For example, you have always known that the only important question about life, or anything else, is ^e"What's in it for me?"
2 As it happens, that wasn't really a majority opinion,
3 Because miraculous as it may seem, almost all the great thinkers of history, since the first ^fcaveman wrote something on a rock, thought you were dead wrong.
4 They all thought that the race of Mankind was going ^gsomewhere,
5 And that it was everyone's duty to try to be ^hbetter,
6 To live up to the great human mission,
7 ⁱWhatever it was,
8 Whereas you knew all the time that the only place you were going was out to the fridge for another beer,
9 Unless there isn't any,
10 In which case, you're not going anywhere at all,

a. *Kens.14.21*
b. *Kens.15.1*
   & 16.1
   & 17.1
   & 18.1-2
c. *14.9*
d. *Adam.27.8*
e. *Wil.37.1*
f. *Lies.1.1*
g. *Al.6.17-20*
h. *Dav.15.20*
i. *Hill.G.1*
j. *48.6*
k. *Adam.14.15*
l. *Mall.5.7*
m. *52.1*
   Frog.23.1-7
n. *Brit.28.24-30*
o. *70.12*
   73.1
p. *Mall.6.23*
q. *Mall.6.23*
r. *Chnk.12.4-11*
s. *Mall.5.7*
t. *Ned.2.11*
   & 5.7
u. *Kens.11.9*
v. *Russ.7.1-7*
w. *Frog.31.8-10*

11 But sending your old lady instead,
12 Down to the ^jcorner for another case of Schlitz talls.
13 Now I ask you, who is right?
14 Almost all the great thinkers of history?
15 Or you?
16 The answer, my friends, is that you were right,
17 Which means that they've been wrong about a lot of things.

CHAPTER 16

The only place for Mankind to go is out to the fridge for another beer,
2 Unless there's something better than beer available,
3 Like ale,
4 Or ^kbrandy,
5 Or corn liquor,
6 Or ^lDemerol,
7 Or ether,
8 Or ^mFrench wine,
9 Or ⁿgin,
10 Or hash,
11 Or Irish whiskey
12 Or ^oJack Daniel's,
13 Or Kentucky bourbon,
14 Or ^pLSD,
15 Or ^qmagic mushrooms,
16 Or nitrous oxide,
17 Or ^ropium,
18 Or PCP,
19 Or ^sQuaaludes,
20 Or ^treefer,
21 Or ^uSouthern Comfort,
22 Or tequila,
23 Or uppers,
24 Or ^vvodka,
25 Or ^wwormwood,
26 Or even xeres, yill, or zythum,

27 Because all of these are out there,
28 [a]And all of them are preferable to thinking about anything at all,
29 And a lot more fun too.

CHAPTER 17

Now the really great news about all this is that there is a [b]Great New Generation of young people,
2 Who are in [c]college right now,
3 And they aren't like all the college kids of the past,
4 At all.
5 I know that you always used to [d]hate college kids,
6 Because they looked down their nose at you,
7 And thought they were better than you,
8 And tried to prove it by wearing [e]nice clothes,
9 And [f]working hard,
10 And getting good [g]jobs with lots of responsibility,
11 [h]And trying to do important, worthwhile things with their lives,
12 Which must have really made you feel bad,
13 Because you weren't doing any of those things,
14 At all.
15 But everything is different now,
16 [i]And the college kids of today have learned that they're not any better than anybody else,
17 Except that they were born [j]luckier for some reason,
18 [k]And they've stopped looking down their nose at people who were born less fortunate,
19 And if you were to see one of their big get-togethers,
20 [l]You'd see a huge multitude that looked and sounded just like you,
21 Including their constant spewing of [m]obscenities,
22 [n]And their beer bellies,
23 [o]And their dull little pig eyes,
24 [p]And bizarre tattoos,
25 [q]Not to mention a distinct lack of good personal hygiene.
26 And what is more, they have also learned the importance of getting as [r]wasted as possible,
27 As often as possible,
28 Just like [s]you.

CHAPTER 18

All of this is very encouraging, of course,
2 But they still have a little way to go,
3 Because there are one or two things they haven't figured out yet,
4 Due to their [t]bad upbringing,
5 Which it is time to correct.
6 For example, a lot of them still think that maybe they have some kind of obligation to grow up eventually,
7 And quit being so much like you after a while,
8 Because they were born [u]lucky,
9 Unlike you,
10 And so maybe they're supposed to give something back,
11 And try to make the world into a better place,
12 Somehow,
13 Which, quite frankly, they

a. Mall.5.4-8 & 6.20-25 & 9.12-16
b. Ned.2.1-3
c. 12.10
d. Mawr.15.19-22
e. Psay.5V.10
f. Psay.5V.1-3
g. Wil.30.2-6 & 30.19-20
h. Psay.5V.14
i. Ned.8.2-10
j. Wil.13.15-20
k. 17.6
l. Ira.12.1-12
m. Wil.5.11-12
n. 13.23
o. 13.24
p. 13.25
q. 13.27 & Wil.43.4-7
r. Ned.5.6
s. Adam.27.8
t. Psay.1.1
u. 17.17

don't have the slightest idea
how to do,

14 [a]Because they're already
too fat and lazy and stoned to
have any real ideas about anything,

15 Not to mention the fact that
they already know the part
about the [b]Bomb,

16 [c]And what's going to happen to the world in a few
years,

17 [d]Because the Most Chosen
Nation on Earth is in charge
of it.

CHAPTER 19

But just imagine how great
it would be if they figured
out that it doesn't really matter,

2 And that nothing really matters,

3 [e]Except going out to the
fridge for another beer,

4 [f]Unless there's something
better than beer available.

5 Yes, truly, the world would
be a different place then,

6 And it would be okay if they
took a bath and put on nice
clothes again,

7 And got their fancy jobs,

8 Because even if they kept on
trying to [g]blame you for
things,

9 They would completely stop
trying to change you,

10 Because you are the way
you are,

11 Which is really just like everyone [h]else is,

12 [i]Deep down,

13 As they have good reason
to know,

14 [j]And so it's okay if they

a. *Wil.16.6*
b. *Al.2.1-8*
c. *Oth.9.1-19*
d. *Yks.140.11-18*
e. *16.1*
f. *16.3-29*
g. *Wil.34.1-11*
h. *Kens.28.6*
i. *Al.5.4*
j. *Yks.153.14*
k. *Wil.26.20*
l. *Wil.26.21*
m. *Wil.22.9-13*
n. *16.3-26*
o. *Adam.27.8*
p. *Psong.42.1-4*
q. *Gods.6.23*
r. *Gods.6.27*
s. *Wil.28.6-7*
t. *Wil.12.3*

keep on buying their illegal
drugs from you.

CHAPTER 20

For when they have really
figured out that [k]nothing
matters,

2 [l]At all,

3 [m]And there's nothing they
can do about it,

4 Or want to do about it,

5 They're going to need lots
and lots of [n]drugs,

6 For the rest of their lives,

7 Just like [o]you.

8 And when practically everybody in the Most Chosen Nation on Earth needs lots and
lots of drugs just to get by
from day to day,

9 A lot of you can make a
whole lot of [p]money,

10 Without having to work at
it at all.

CHAPTER 21

And when Harry had said
these things, the masses
commenced to cheer like nobody's business,

2 And dozens of them started
shouting questions at Harry,

3 Like "How can we get
started?"

4 And [q]"How can we help them
figure things out?"

5 Then Harry smiled and said,
I'll explain everything.

6 [r]Don't worry about a thing,

7 Because it's really quite
[s]simple.

CHAPTER 22

It will be easy to help them,

2 Because the college kids are
only [t]kidding themselves when

421

they talk about making the world into a better place,

3 ᵃWhich they will realize as soon as some of them get killed for some of the beliefs they think they believe.

4 For example, a lot of them are pretty sure that they are the ᵇmost righteous generation in the whole history of the world,

5 ᶜBecause they are so courageous in opposing the war,

6 But how courageous will they be when they start dying because they oppose the war?

7 What will happen when they find out that they oppose the war ᵈmostly because they don't want to die in the war?

8 This is a reason that makes perfect sense, of course,

9 But it doesn't have anything to do with ᵉrighteousness,

10 At all.

CHAPTER 23

And ᶠ*you* are the ones who can help them start dying in the name of their righteousness.

2 Do not most of you have brothers and cousins and friends who are policemen,

3 Or national guardsmen,

4 Or construction workers,

5 Or just some good buddies with a pickup truck and a gun rack,

6 Who would just love to kill a self-righteous college kid,

7 ᵍOr three?

8 And can you guess what will happen when the college kids start dying for their political beliefs?

9 Is it not as inevitable as a

a. Wil.13.7
b. Ned.8.2
c. Wil.4.1-2
d. Wil.13.32
e. Wil.14.2-5
f. Adam.27.8
g. Dav.56.54-62
h. Psong.52.1-2
i. 63.17-22
j. Psong.17.1-7
k. Psong.18.1-4
l. Psp.3.9

Sunday morning ʰhangover that when the bodies start piling up, they will stop having ⁱbeliefs,

10 And will stop being so self-righteous,

11 And will stop talking about making the world a better place,

12 For anyone but themselves, that is,

13 ʲMeaning they will go get a high-paying job instead,

14 And try to make as much ᵏmoney as possible,

15 So that they can buy lots and lots of drugs,

16 And quit thinking about everything else,

17 For good.

CHAPTER 24

When Harry had finished, the very ground shook under the joyful celebrations of the masses,

2 And many of them desired to run out right away and kill some college kids,

3 To help them overcome their beliefs and ideals,

4 As soon as possible.

5 But Harry calmed them down at once, saying,

6 Do not get carried away,

7 Because there is no need for a massacre,

8 And everything we desire will be achieved when no more than fifty or sixty college kids have died for their beliefs,

9 And besides, there is much that I, ˡHarry, can do to help things along,

10 If you will let some of your Angels come with me,

11 And do as I say,

12 **No matter who gets hurt.**

CHAPTER 25

Ａnd then all was done as Harry had requested,

2 And Angels without number came forward to [a]swear their allegiance to him,

3 Until Harry was ready to depart,

4 In a [b]Silver Cloud,

5 Except that some among the masses began to frown,

6 And look unhappy,

7 So that Harry asked about the cause of their displeasure,

8 Whereupon a young woman with buckteeth spoke up in a trembling voice, saying,

9 "We would all like to feel part of this great event,

10 [c]"But we cannot feel a part of it without some ceremony or ritual,

11 "That involves everyone."

CHAPTER 26

Ａnd so it happened that Harry called for special water,

2 Which he carried with him in the Silver Cloud,

3 In little green bottles,

4 And he invited the masses to do as he did,

5 [d]And then he poured the special water over his own hands and rubbed them together and around each other with great exaggerated motions,

6 [e]Signifying that he was washing his hands of everything,

7 [f]And had no more interest in beliefs and ideals,

8 [g]And from now on, would do what he felt like doing,

9 Just like his friends in the masses.

a. *Ned.30.42-43*
b. *48.12-16*
c. *Ext.13.11 & 13.15*
d. *Ira.16.7-8*
e. *4.19-25*
f. *Wil.44.20*
g. *Brd.22.27*
h. *16.1*
i. *16.2-26*
j. *52.1-3*
k. *Psay.5Q.30*
l. *Wil.5.1*
m. *30.8*
n. *Wil.6.1-3*
o. *Ira.12.15-16*

CHAPTER 27

Ｗhen he had done this, all followed his example,

2 Including even those who almost never washed their hands,

3 Until every hand was clean,

4 Or sort of clean,

5 [h]And absolutely everyone in the whole place wanted nothing more than to go out to the fridge for another [i]beer,

6 And so they did.

7 [j]And of all the assembled multitude, there was not one who drank more than Harry.

CHAPTER 28

Ａfter all these great events had taken place, Harry departed in his Silver Cloud,

2 Accompanied by many Angels,

3 And drove [k]west almost as far as he could,

4 [l]Until he came to a high mountainous place,

5 Where a concert was being planned,

6 For college kids.

7 And when he had arrived,

8 He spoke to the promoters,

9 And volunteered to handle all the security arrangements,

10 With his Angels,

11 And so he did.

CHAPTER 29

Ｔhe Angels did a very good job with security,

2 Except that there was a terrible accident,

3 And one of the fans got [m]killed,

4 [n]Somehow,

5 Which upset everyone quite a lot,

6 Because this hadn't happened at [o]Woodstock Nation,

7 And maybe the [a]Revolution was starting to bum out,
8 [b]Which is when Harry got up and spoke,
9 [c]And explained how the Revolution really *had* bummed out,
10 [d]And how it was time to start seeing things the way they were,
11 Which wasn't good,
12 At all,
13 [e]And so maybe it was better to forget about ideals,
14 [f]And stop thinking about anything at all,
15 [g]And do lots and lots of drugs instead.

CHAPTER 30

What Harry had to say was very popular,
2 And the crowds just [h]loved him,
3 [i]And so he helped them wash their hands of everything,
4 [j]And then he got in the [k]Silver Cloud and drove to Indiana,
5 With his Angels,
6 And got there just in time to see a terrible tragedy,
7 [l]Which happened when a bunch of college kids got killed because of their political beliefs,
8 [m]Completely by accident,
9 [n]Which is when Harry got up and spoke,
10 And explained how beliefs and ideals wouldn't help,
11 And could actually get you killed,
12 [o]Which meant that it was better to stop trying to have a Revolution,
13 [p]And make money instead,
14 [q]Not to mention doing a lot of drugs,
15 [r]Without thinking about anything at all.

a. Wil.4.2
b. Wil.5.2
c. Wil.5.5-7
d. Wil.10.1-14
e. Wil.25.1-21
f. Wil.28.1-9
g. Wil.31.1-22
h. Ann.21.20
i. 27.2
j. Wil.44.1
k. 31.4 Ira.14.1-4
l. Wil.44.5-7
m. Chuk.3.5
n. 29.8
o. 23.9
p. 23.14
q. 29.15
r. 29.14
s. 30.2
t. 30.3
u. 30.4
v. 30.4
w. Ira.45.8
x. Wil.46.20-21
y. Ed.71.8-20
z. Psong.51.3
aa. Wil.47.1-2 Ira.15.2 Ned.14.8-9
bb. Kens.9.1-5
cc. Kens.9.8-9
dd. Ira.15.9-17 Ned.14.11-12
ee. Wil.47.15-16
ff. Wil.47.17
gg. Wil.47.18

CHAPTER 31

The multitudes in Indiana just [s]loved Harry,
2 [t]And so he washed their hands of everything,
3 [u]And then got back into the Silver Cloud,
4 [v]Unless it was the Learjet he got into,
5 Because Harry had a [w]Learjet,
6 Which is maybe what he flew to [x]Boston in,
7 If it matters,
8 At all.

CHAPTER 32

It was in Boston that Harry decided to pick up a bunch of followers,
2 So that he could have a proper entourage,
3 Which all big [y]stars have to have,
4 And it's better if they're not all Angels,
5 Because,
6 Well,
7 [z]You know.
8 Anyway, Harry found a great group of followers at a [aa]college in Boston,
9 Where there were a whole bunch of kids who looked exactly like [bb]Angels,
10 Except maybe [cc]smarter,
11 [dd]And Harry told them, **Come with me and I will show you how to shoot fish in a barrel,**
12 **Which I will do while entertaining you in my Silver Cloud,**
13 [ee]**And my Learjet,**
14 [ff]**Not to mention all the beautiful young ladies who always accompany me in my Silver Cloud and my Learjet,**
15 [gg]**Wherever I go.**

CHAPTER 33

Thereupon the followers quickly [a]washed their hands of everything,

2 And went gladly with Harry,

3 [b]And their names were Ned, and Jerry, and Sam, and Tom, and Ira, and Vinnie, and Willie, and Joe, and Mort, and Tony, and Fred,

4 Plus a guy named [c]Lucky,

5 Who hadn't gone to college in Boston,

6 But was with Harry anyway,

7 And also maybe one of the other new followers hadn't gone to college in Boston,

8 Even though the others thought he did,

9 Because he was just sort of there,

10 And didn't exactly say where he was from.

CHAPTER 34

[d]From Boston, Harry and the followers went [e]here and there,

2 Crisscrossing the country so that Harry could help people [f]wash their hands of everything,

3 [g]And stop thinking about anything at all,

4 [h]Which they did gladly,

5 [i]Because five or six college kids had recently died for their beliefs,

6 [j]Which was so discouraging to all the idealists that they were giving up their ideals,

7 In droves,

8 [k]And thinking about how to get ahead,

9 And have an easy life,

10 [l]And let somebody else fix all the terrible things that were wrong with the Most Chosen Nation on Earth.

a. Ned.14.17
  Ira.16.10-11
b. Wil.47.25
  Ned.14.13-14
  Ira.16.22-32
c. Wil.46.1-19
  Ira.16.33-35
  Ned.14.15-16
d. Ned.15.1
  Wil.49.1-3
e. Ira.17.1-2
f. 31.2
g. 29.14
h. Wil.49.4
i. 24.6-8
j. 23.8
k. Psong.20.1-6
l. Wil.47.10-13
m. 30.2
n. Ira.18.6
o. Wil.64.3-4
  Ned.22.1-5
p. Ned.25.7-10
q. Wil.53.2
r. Ned.23.2
s. Ned.46.4
t. Ned.25.1-5

11 Naturally, they all [m]loved what Harry had to say,

12 And the followers got free drugs wherever they went,

13 And they got free everything else on Harry's Learjet,

14 Not to mention his house in Malibu,

15 And a lot of the best hotels at the best weekend resorts,

16 And everybody was happy,

17 And nobody was thinking about much of anything at all,

18 Except maybe Harry.

CHAPTER 35

By now, Harry was getting to be pretty famous,

2 [n]In certain circles, anyway,

3 Because of all the great things he was saying,

4 Which made life sound like it could be a lot easier,

5 All things considered,

6 And so he decided that it might be nice to go back to his [o]hometown for a while,

7 [p]And see what kind of greeting he'd get.

CHAPTER 36

Harry's hometown was a place called [q]Philadelphia,

2 [r]Which was pretty much of a pit,

3 Starting with the airport,

4 Which was too big and dirty to walk through,

5 And so the [s]pilot parked the Learjet way out on some distant runway,

6 And the Angels had a whole bunch of [t]cars brought out to pick up Harry and his followers,

7 And then everybody went to town.

CHAPTER 37

The cars were all white,
2 And all convertibles,
3 And there was also a huge motorcycle escort,
4 Made up of a whole bunch of Angels,
5 Which maybe made the people in Harry's hometown think he was somebody important,
6 ªAnd probably explains why so many of them lined the streets to shout and cheer as Harry drove by,
7 ᵇNot to mention all those free pretzels,
8 ᶜAnd all that free beer.

CHAPTER 38

Some of the followers were tired from the plane trip,
2 And the beer,
3 And the other stuff they'd been washing down with the beer,
4 ᵈAnd they wanted to go to a nice hotel,
5 And relax,
6 But Harry was in a celebrating mood,
7 And wanted to speak to all his new friends,
8 ᵉIn some special and symbolic place,
9 And so the parade went to a dark and nasty part of town,
10 And stopped when it got to the ᶠLiberty Bell.

CHAPTER 39

Then Harry got out of the car,
2 And toasted the hundreds and hundreds of people who were waiting to hear him speak,
3 And cleared his throat with something one hundred proof,

a. *Ned.26.1-4*
b. *Ned.26.5*
c. *Ned.26.7*
d. *Wil.67.3*
e. *Ned.26.8*
f. *Wil.66.15-16*
g. *Psay.5J.32-33*
h. *Psay.5J.4-31*
i. *Grk.20.9-13*
j. *Ed.40.2-8*
k. *F&J.3.1-4*
l. *Gnt.15.4-9*
m. *17.12*
n. *21.6*

4 Unless it was more than one hundred proof,
5 And commenced to talk.

CHAPTER 40

Citizens of Philadelphia, he began,
2 I can't tell you what a pleasure it is to be back home,
3 In the City of Brotherly Love,
4 Which has always been one of my favorite ᵍjokes.
5 Of course, there have been many great ʰjokes throughout history,
6 Including ⁱhistory itself,
7 Which has been one incredibly long-running situation comedy,
8 Which means that the ʲend of every episode is completely predictable,
9 Although I feel you should know that not every comedy has a happy ᵏending,
10 ˡBecause there just aren't any gods left to come down from the ceiling,
11 And fix everything.

CHAPTER 41

But I'm not telling you anything new.
2 After all, you've been living in Philadelphia for your whole lives,
3 And you've already learned that comedies can turn out badly,
4 ᵐWhich has maybe made you feel bad in the past,
5 But that's why I have come back,
6 Because there is no more need for you to feel bad,
7 ⁿOr even to worry about anything at all,

8 Ever again.

CHAPTER 42

Yes, my gift is a [a]simple one,

2 Simply expressed.

3 [b]It is time to wash our hands of everything,

4 And quit pretending that it will ever get fixed,

5 [c]And just stop thinking about it altogether,

6 [d]And do whatever we want to do,

7 [e]Whenever we want to do it,

8 [f]No matter who gets hurt,

9 [g]As long as it isn't us.

10 Now, isn't that what you've all been waiting to hear someone say,

11 Forever?

CHAPTER 43

And then the crowd went absolutely nuts,

2 And cheered Harry to the skies,

3 Until some of them started to wonder about what he had just said,

4 [h]Because it sounded too good to be true,

5 And so they demanded to know if he was just kidding,

6 Or did he really really mean it,

7 Because they really really wanted it to be true.

CHAPTER 44

I am completely on the level, Harry told them,

2 And in fact, if this [i]Liberty Bell actually worked,

3 I would [j]ring it,

4 [k]Because the gift I am bringing you is freedom,

5 And I'd just love to let it

a. Wil.28.6-7
*   & 31.13-14*
b. 4.19-21
c. 34.3
d. Wil.26.8
e. Wil.26.9
f. Wil.26.10
g. Wil.26.16
h. Psay.5A.42
i. 38.9-10
j. Psom.24.3-4
k. Wil.26.6
l. Yks.11.7-12
m. Psom.73.1-
*   14*
*   Wil.7.6*
*   Brd.24.14-*
*   19*
*   Forg.9.2-9*
n. Grk.20.7-8
*   Frog.12.7-8*
*   Brit.27.13-14*
*   Krt.28.3-4*
*   Yks.15.13-14*
*   Yks.25.1-2*
*   Yks.97.1-11*
*   Hall.15.7-15*
o. 31.2
p. 33.3
q. Wil.64.10
r. 27.7
s. 37.1-2
t. 37.7

ring out all over the place,

6 Except that the bell is [l]cracked,

7 And has been for a long long time,

8 Without anybody ever bothering to fix it,

9 Just like a lot of other old [m]symbols and [n]ideas,

10 And so we'll ring in the new age of freedom in a different way,

11 Such as the way we ring in the New Year,

12 Which is to say with an incredible amount of alcohol and other mind-altering substances,

13 If that's okay with you.

14 So what do you say?

CHAPTER 45

And when the crowd had thought it over for a few seconds,

2 They decided that they would just love to ring in the new age with a lot of alcohol and mind-altering substances,

3 [o]And so they washed their hands of everything,

4 And then commenced to drink and shout and carry on,

5 For hours,

6 Until all of the [p]followers passed out and had to be taken to the [q]hotel by Angels,

7 And then for a few hours longer than that,

8 Until even [r]Harry passed out and had to be carted to the hotel in the back of a [s]white convertible,

9 Covered with [t]pretzels.

CHAPTER 46

After their stupendous welcome in Philadelphia,

2 Harry and his followers decided to hang out there for a while,

3 And pass the time with their new [a]friends,

4 Which they did,

5 And so they had many adventures,

6 [b]And went to many many parties,

7 And washed the hands of hundreds of Philadelphians,

8 And consumed lots and lots and lots of mind-altering substances,

9 [c]Until they kind of lost track of the time,

10 Which happens sometimes,

11 [d]If you're following the Way of Harry.

CHAPTER 47

It may have been on a Monday,

2 Although it's hard to be sure,

3 That Harry decided to visit his friends at the [e]University of [f]Benjamin Franklin,

4 Which was in Philadelphia,

5 And full of very very smart people,

6 [g]Who looked exactly like Angels,

7 Until Harry said to them, **Isn't it time you were having a bath and a shave,**

8 **So that you can go out and get what's coming to you,**

9 **Namely, the [h]spoils of the richest nation on earth,**

10 **Which your parents amassed,**

11 **So that you could spend them?**

12 **After all, do you not recall the wisdom of your founding father, who said, [i]"A penny**

a.	66.3
	Ira.21.26
b.	Wil.68.3
c.	Wil.68.1
d.	Wil.39.3
e.	Ned.30.1-2
f.	Yks.73.2-6
g.	32.8-9
h.	Ned.12.24-26
i.	Psay.5A.5
j.	Mawr.27.1-2
k.	Mawr.29.1-2
l.	Wht.8
m.	Wil.54.1-5
n.	Wil.54.6
o.	59.15
p.	Gnt.9.1-2
q.	Psong.1.1-6

saved is a penny you don't have to earn,"

13 **Or something like that?**

14 And when Harry had put it to them in those terms,

15 The children of Benjamin Franklin decided that maybe it was time to go to [j]law school,

16 [k]Or business school,

17 And start climbing the [l]tree of Man.

CHAPTER 48

Then it may have been on a Tuesday that Harry got some new Silver Clouds,

2 And decided to try them out,

3 By driving all the way [m]north on Broad Street,

4 Through the very worst part of town,

5 Where there were bloodstains on every corner,

6 Because there was a tavern on every corner,

7 And drunken people with guns inside.

8 The followers grew nervous as they drove,

9 Because the looks they were getting from people on the sidewalks were not [n]nice,

10 At all,

11 But Harry calmed them down, saying,

12 **Put not your trust in the [o]mercy of men,**

13 **But in the steadfast nature of bulletproof glass,**

14 **Carbon-steel door locks,**

15 **And forged armor plating,**

16 **Which are the first options I check when ordering a new [p]Silver Cloud.**

17 **Now, I think it is time to go elsewhere,**

18 [q]**Because poverty is depressing,**

19 **And we will send** ᵃ**missionaries in later,**

20 **To give them the great news about my** ᵇ**Trinity,**

21 **Which will help them a lot,**

22 **Or at least make them feel better.**

CHAPTER 49

Christmas happened in there somewhere too,

2 Because all the followers got nice Christmas presents from Harry,

3 Who put on a Santa Claus outfit and took the followers to a huge retail emporium right in the middle of downtown Philadelphia,

4 Where he capered all over the place, saying,

5 Ho ho ho!

6 **Behold the almighty** ᶜ**god of the Most Chosen Nation on Earth,**

7 **Who carries all the most desirable** ᵈ**things in the world on his back,**

8 **In a great big sack,**

9 ᵉ**And will give them to you if you ask him often enough,**

10 **And loudly enough,**

11 **And give him a little milk and cookies once a year.**

12 All the followers had a great laugh about that,

13 And sang some carols,

14 And then got utterly wasted on eggnog,

15 Until the store manager asked them to leave,

16 Which they eventually did.

CHAPTER 50

There was also a day,

2 Which may have been a Thursday,

---

a. *Ext.17.6-8*
b. *Wil.31.18-21*
c. *Adam.20.2-10*
d. *Adam.46-48*
e. *Wil.14.18*
f. *Wil.64.3-9*
g. *Hill.W.1-23*
h. *Ira.5.17*
i. *Krt.6.10*
j. *Spic.17.1-9*
k. *Mall.5.1-8*
   Mawr.24.17-18
l. *Ned.28.13-17*
m. *Ned.37.3-5*
   Ira.37.1-9
n. *Ira.38.1-10*

---

3 When Harry decided to go see the docks at the great ᶠPort of Philadelphia,

4 Where cargoes came in from all over the ᵍworld.

5 Harry spent most of a day looking at ships,

6 Especially the ones with Spanish names,

7 Which he explained, saying,

8 **I used to take** ʰ**Spanish in high school,**

9 **And I never believed that any people would speak such a** ⁱ**silly language,**

10 **But just take a look at all these ships!**

11 **Surely, there must be people who speak Spanish,**

12 **And I am anxious to meet some of the captains of these ships,**

13 **And ask them about a destination called** ʲ**El Dorado,**

14 **Which I have always been** ᵏ**curious about,**

15 **And wish to find out about,**

16 **Once and for all.**

17 **If you, my followers, would like to return to the hotel and await my return,**

18 **Please do so,**

19 ˡ**For I must be about my business.**

20 And so the followers returned to the hotel,

21 And waited for Harry,

22 In the company of the many many good friends they had made in Philadelphia.

23 ᵐIt turned out that Harry didn't come back for forty days or so,

24 And he didn't seem upset at all about the fact that nobody had really ⁿmissed him,

25 Because they were having too good a time.

CHAPTER 51

Sometime after that, Harry and the followers got invited to a ªwedding,

2 Because some of the guys on the groom's side were worried that the reception would be dull,

3 Since it was taking place in the basement of the church,

4 ᵇWhich wasn't a good sign,

5 At all,

6 And so Harry and the followers agreed to go,

7 Which they did,

8 And had a marvelous time,

9 Because when the wedding vows had been said,

10 And the bride had kissed the groom,

11 And the priest had pronounced them man and wife,

12 Harry spoke up from the back row of the church, saying in a loud voice,

13 **Those whom mere words have joined together may not now be separated except by teams of ᶜlawyers, at a cost of thousands and thousands of dollars. Is this not a wonder to behold?**

14 And then there was kind of a silence,

15 Which ended suddenly in a burst of laughter,

16 As the whole congregation found itself unable to swallow its mirth,

17 And thus was the ice broken for a terrific reception,

18 Which got under way immediately in the basement,

19 So that the caterer ran out of champagne in the first ten minutes,

20 Which made everyone depressed,

21 Until Harry ᵈmagically pro-

a. Wil.66.19-20
b. Jeff.11.4-9
c. Penn.2.1-8
d. Ed.60.17
e. Ned.6.1-22
f. 27.7

duced another ten cases,

22 ᵉFrom the trunk of his Silver Cloud,

23 Which made everything fine again.

CHAPTER 52

And so everybody at the wedding drank lots and lots of champagne,

2 And got as merry as can be,

3 ᶠAnd no one more than Harry,

4 Who danced with the bride three times,

5 And then with all the bridesmaids,

6 And then with the mother of the bride,

7 And then with the mother of the groom,

8 Not to mention falling into the cake,

9 Which everyone thought was just hilarious,

10 And meant that they should have even more champagne,

11 Which they went to ask Harry to produce,

12 Except that they couldn't find him,

13 Anywhere.

CHAPTER 53

Then the followers went looking for Harry,

2 And some went out to look for him in the Silver Cloud,

3 And some went into the bridesmaids' dressing room,

4 And some went back to the hotel,

5 But Harry was in none of these places,

6 Because he had gone upstairs instead,

7 Into the nave of the church,

8 Where one of the followers finally found him,

9 Preaching in the pulpit,
10 To a churchful of empty pews.

CHAPTER 54

Harry was speaking,
2 And his voice was thick,
3 And his words were slurred,
4 [a]Because he had had a lot of champagne to drink,
5 But he was having an excellent time,
6 And there was no point in interrupting him,
7 Because there was no one around who might wish to chastise him,
8 For having so much [b]fun in church.

CHAPTER 55

O poor miserable Christian [c]sinners, Harry was saying,
2 How I wish that I had something to offer you of equal value to what he offers,
3 But as you can see, I wear no [d]crown of thorns,
4 [e]And there are no holes in my hands,
5 And I am not strung up on a cross,
6 Which means that I am not dying for you,
7 [f]And never will,
8 Which is why you still prefer him to me.

CHAPTER 56

Yes, what joy can possibly compare with the joy of knowing that someone else has [g]died for you,
2 In your place,
3 So you won't have to,
4 And can just pretend to feel

a. 52.3
b. Jeff.8.15-17
c. Rom.22.7
d. Dav.15.26
e. Rat.21.1-2
f. Jeff.24.22-23
g. Dav.15.33
h. Wil.78.5
i. Yks.3.10-15
j. Gnt.15.17-19
k. Adam.28.14-22
l. Mawr.15.19-22
m. Boul.3.1-7
n. Rat.10.7-9
o. 55.5-7
p. Dav.54.15

really grateful and obligated for the rest of your life,
5 Because somebody all-powerful is taking care of all the details?
6 Truly, this combines all the greatest pleasures of life into a single perfect package.
7 First there is the pleasure of [h]getting away with something you might have gotten nailed for yourself,
8 So to speak.
9 [i]Second, there is the pleasure of watching somebody else endure pain and suffering and death,
10 Somebody [j]big and important, I might add,
11 Which makes it even more pleasurable.
12 Third, there is the ineffable pleasure of feeling like an [k]insider,
13 Because you got saved and not everyone else will.
14 And finally, there is the truly great pleasure of [l]hating everyone who does not buy the whole story,
15 Hook, line, and sinker.

CHAPTER 57

How can I, Harry, compete against such a powerhouse?
2 In all humility, I cannot.
3 I am only Harry,
4 A paltry [m]mortal just like you.
5 My father is not a god, but a superficial [n]jingoistic jerk.
6 My mother was not a virgin,
7 Or at least no one ever claimed she was.
8 [o]And I am totally unwilling to mount a [p]cross in the name of the message I bring you.

9 So why should any of you listen to what I have to say?

10 Why should you?

11 Why should anyone?

CHAPTER 58

Dare I mention the term common sense?

2 For when has this one ever told you the truth?

3 You bow down to him,

4 And you mouth his words to yourselves,

5 And you pretend that they are true,

6 Because he ᵃsaid them,

7 And why would he lie?

8 But if he were your next-door neighbor,

9 ᵇThe one you really can't stand,

10 Would you not examine his words a little more carefully,

11 And judge their truth in different terms?

CHAPTER 59

If your next-door neighbor told you that all the biggest losers on the face of the earth were really blessed,

2 Would you bow down to him,

3 Or call for the men in white coats?

4 For I, Harry, say to you,

5 ᶜCursed are the poor in spirit: for the only kingdom anyone ever promised them is in heaven, ᵈwherever that is, and everywhere else they're dogmeat,

6 And you know it.

7 ᵉCursed are they that mourn: for ᶠdeath is completely final, and mourning never brings back the dead,

*a. Jeff.5.1-8
   & 6.1-4*
b. Ann.2.1-32
c. Psom.21.3-4
d. Boul.8.18-22
e. Psom.21.5-6
*f. Chuk.19.15-
   17
   Psong.56.1-7*
g. Ned.36.19
h. Psom.21.1-2
i. Psom.21.7-8
j. Pnot.7.1-5
k. Psom.20.1-8
l. Frog.7.1-9
m. Brit.51.1-24
n. Jeff.11.24-25
o. Rom.22.1-3
p. Chr.4.1-3

8 Who are ᵍhistory,

9 As anyone with an ounce of intelligence knows.

10 ʰCursed are the meek: for they shall inherit nothing,

11 Or were you planning to remember them in your will?

12 ⁱCursed are they which do hunger and thirst after righteousness: for they shall die of hunger and thirst,

13 Because absolutely everybody hates their guts,

14 And if I'm lying about that, what is ʲhe doing up there on that cross?

15 ᵏCursed are the merciful: for they will be bitten by the mouths they feed,

16 As which of you has not left his toothmarks on someone who was only trying to help?

17 ˡCursed are the pure in heart: for they are born to be everybody's victim,

18 And why not yours too?

19 Cursed are the ᵐpeacemakers: for they are doomed to fail big time,

20 As they always have,

21 ⁿBecause there's nothing harder to do on this earth than stop a good Christian from starting a war with the latest godless barbarian neighbor to move in next door.

CHAPTER 60

And still I know that many of you are unconvinced,

2 And that you will wrinkle up your face at me and say,

3 ᵒ"But he never promised that life would be easy,

4 ᵖ"Or that we would receive our rewards on this earth,

5 "And you must have faith,

6 a"Because truth is beyond understanding."

7 Isn't that how that part of the spiel goes?

8 But I say to you, how would you respond to a real estate developer who told you to hand over all your worldly possessions for an acre of land in bheaven,

9 Which you will never get to see until you die,

10 Let alone build a house on it,

11 Or raise your family in it,

12 Or earn a living from it?

13 You would string him up to the nearest tree,

14 cUnless there was a cross available,

15 And . . . isn't *that* a coincidence?

CHAPTER 61

No, I am not mocking you,

2 At all.

3 dDo you not think that I, Harry, would also like to believe?

4 eIt is the great tragic weakness of our tragic species that we all want so much to believe,

5 And are willing to commit absolutely every kind of finsanity in the name of our beliefs,

6 No matter how ginane they are.

7 hThrough the ages, people have believed in this, that, and the other thing,

8 Unshakably,

9 But did it save them from the inevitable end of their world,

10 Ever?

a. Wil.33.2
   & 33.7-9
b. Boul.8.1-8
c. Boul.8.9-14
d. Yks.153.14
e. Boul.18.6
f. Lies.9.1-14
g. Psp.1.2
h. Lies.3.1-3
   Gyp.1.1-8
   Mes.1.1-11
   Grk.1.1-11
   Rom.1.1-11
i. Psp.1.8
j. Psp.1.10-12
k. Ira.25.55-64
l. Psp.3.1-2
m. Drex.3.7
n. Jeff.21.1-4

CHAPTER 62

None of them were saved,

2 iJust as we will not be saved,

3 jAnd how many times does a wave have to dash itself against a rock before it learns that only the rock will remain, and the wave itself will become a memory?

4 kDo you think that I, Harry, have not thought long and hard about these questions before urging you to stop thinking about them,

5 For your own good?

6 lDo you think that I have not peered into our sciences and other systems of rational thought for a way out of our dilemma?

7 Do you think that if there were a valid reason for mhope, I would not have brought it to you,

8 And given you the peace of mind that this one promises,

9 But never delivers?

CHAPTER 63

Yes, yes, I know that many of you will claim that he delivers,

2 And I will agree that many of you have simply put your lives in his hands,

3 And have stopped nthinking about anything at all,

4 Because He saves,

5 And you're all set,

6 And that's all there is to it.

7 But when you do that, you are not following Him,

8 At all,

9 But only me, Harry,

10 And that is all I ask.

11 As for the rest of you,

12 ^aThe ones who think they are still thinking,

13 And who choose to believe in belief,

14 I say only this: You are the greatest ^bfools of all,

15 Because beliefs do not bring you life,

16 But death,

17 Because when you have a belief there is always someone who wants to make you prove it,

18 ^cAnd maybe even put your life on the line for it,

19 And there is no belief worth dying for,

20 Because whatever you believe, someone else has already died for it,

21 And what did it get them,

22 But an early grave?

a. 70.17-18
b. Psay.5A.7 & 5A.11
c. 23.8
d. Grk.5.7-8
e. Boul.15.8-11
f. Psp.1.4
g. 52.1-3
h. 53.1-10
i. 45.8-9 Wil.48.25 & 49.8-11
j. 65.1
k. Ext.14.7-9
l. Bks.11.6-10
m. 64.15
n. Wil.26.20

CHAPTER 64

All right.

2 I will go now,

3 And leave the stage to this plaster idol with his painted sacrificial wounds,

4 But before I go,

5 I ask you to consider why I have not been punished for my blasphemy?

6 Have I not stood here for most of an hour defying your god of ^dpain and guilt and sin?

7 And has he shown his displeasure through even the smallest sign,

8 Or blasted me from life with a ^ethunderbolt?

9 If he were right,

10 And I were wrong,

11 ^fThen it is I who would deserve crucifixion.

12 But which of us is stiff and lifeless on a cross?

13 And which is full of good ^gchampagne and a couple of pounds of truly great hors d'oeuvres?

14 I bid you adieu.

15 And then Harry stepped out of the pulpit and fell on his face in the aisle.

CHAPTER 65

Immediately after Harry passed out in the aisle, the ^hfollower who had been listening to his words helped him to his feet,

2 And back to the hotel,

3 Where Harry ⁱslept for twelve hours,

4 And woke up refreshed and happy, calling for the ^jfollower who had carried him home.

5 When the follower had been brought to him,

6 Harry offered him a Bloody Mary,

7 And asked him what had transpired in the church,

8 Because Harry did not remember it very clearly.

9 When the follower had recounted all of what he could recall,

10 Harry began to laugh uproariously, saying,

11 ^kTruly, wine and religion go together,

12 A transitory madness that makes for many great ^ljokes,

13 And many great ^mpratfalls.

14 Then he urged the follower to think no more about what he had heard,

15 ⁿBecause it did not matter,

16 At all,

17 And so the follower thought no more about it.

CHAPTER 66

It so happened that the followers of Harry had many invitations while they were in Philadelphia,

2 ªTo attend parties,

3 And to escort lissome and willing young women here and there,

4 And so some of them were otherwise engaged,

5 For much of the time,

6 ᵇAnd did not completely keep up with what Harry was doing,

7 ᶜUntil one day when Harry made it clear that he particularly wished all the followers to join him for dinner,

8 Even if it meant breaking a date,

9 Which it did for some of the more popular followers,

10 ᵈWho were pretty cross about the whole thing,

11 And showed up for dinner late,

12 And maybe a little bit ᵉdrunk besides,

13 ᶠAnd told the driver to keep the motor running,

14 Which they were sorry about later,

15 ᵍBut how could they know this was going to be the most important night in the whole saga of Harry?

CHAPTER 67

And it is also possible that some of the followers,

2 Or one or two of them, anyway,

3 Were so ʰdrunk that they couldn't follow the ⁱconversation

---

a. *46.6*
Wil.68.3
b. *Ira.41.1*
c. *Ned.40.1-3*
d. *Ned.40.4-5*
e. *67.1-3*
f. *Ned.41.1-8*
g. *Wil.70.13-16*
Ned.42.13-17
h. *66.12*
i. *Wil.70.10-12*
Ned.42.1-7
Ira.41.6-9
j. *Wil.70.18-26*
Ned.42.19-27
Ira.41.10
k. *Wil.71.19-20*
Ned.43.18-19
l. *Ext.13.18*
m. *Ira.41.11-12*
n. *66.13*
o. *F&J.5.5*
Ira.7.9
Swar.36.12
Hill.W.20

---

at dinner very well,

4 ʲUntil Harry did something with some white stuff,

5 ᵏAnd made everyone else do it too,

6 Which really snapped everyone right into focus,

7 Including even the ones who were pretty drunk to begin with,

8 So that they were amazed at the way they felt,

9 Which was like thinking as clearly as you've ever thought about anything in your whole life,

10 Except that what you're thinking about is nothing at all,

11 Only it doesn't seem that way,

12 Because it seems like you're really onto something,

13 ˡSomething important to you,

14 And everybody else is just this inferior being,

15 Like some gnat or something,

16 And just don't count,

17 At all.

CHAPTER 68

And maybe that's why none of the followers really did anything to help when the ᵐcops came,

2 And dragged Harry away,

3 And put him in a paddy wagon,

4 And then came back to question all the followers who hadn't ⁿtold their driver to keep the motor running,

5 ºJust in case.

CHAPTER 69

And maybe that's why some of the followers didn't do

anything afterwards, either,
2 Like go see Harry in [a]jail,
3 Or testify at his [b]trial,
4 Especially the follower who managed to grab Harry's bag of white stuff on his way out to the car,
5 Which lasted for weeks,
6 All through the arraignment [c]hearing,
7 And the [d]trial,
8 And the [e]sentencing,
9 [f]And the day they carted Harry off to prison,
10 For life.

CHAPTER 70

But probably not all the followers felt bad about it afterwards,
2 Although some of them did,
3 Because some of them really did kind of like Harry,
4 [g]And thought that maybe they had let him down or something,
5 Until they remembered some things Harry had said on the Learjet one night,
6 During a weekend away from Philadelphia,
7 On the way to Harry's place in Malibu.
8 It was while they were flying along at thirty-some thousand feet that Harry said, **No one has ever really asked me how you're supposed to live without thinking about anything at all;**
9 **Does that strike any of you as strange?**
10 Then one of the followers said, yes, it did seem strange now that Harry had mentioned it,
11 And funny he hadn't thought of it before himself.
12 Thereupon Harry poured himself another three fingers of [h]Jack Daniel's,
13 And began to talk, saying,
14 **I know that it seems like a [i]paradox,**
15 **But it is much [j]simpler than a paradox,**
16 **Like most things.**
17 [k]**Truly, people will *never* think that they have stopped thinking,**
18 [l]**Because how can you see the darkness by shining a light on darkness?**
19 **In truth, they will stop thinking without ever knowing that they have done so,**
20 **And they will be better off.**
21 [m]**And from their point of view, they will think that they are thinking,**
22 **And they will volunteer the [n]opinions they have arrived at from their thinking,**
23 **And when people nod in agreement, they will say, "What a good thinker am I, that so many people nod in agreement with me,"**
24 [o]**And they will never think about how they nod in unthinking agreement with the opinions expressed by other people,**
25 [p]**Who also think they are thinking,**
26 **And everybody will be better off.**

CHAPTER 71

And why will they be better off?
2 [q]**Because they will have truly stopped thinking about anything at all,**
3 [r]**Except their own personal desires,**

a. *Wil.73.8-10 Ira.42.1-3*
b. *Ned.46.1-2*
c. *Wil.74.1*
d. *Wil.74.2-4*
e. *Wil.74.5-12 Ned.47.1-7*
f. *Wil.75.1-20 Ned.48.7-10*
g. *68.1 69.1*
h. *16.12*
i. *F&J.13.1-9*
j. *42.1-2 Wil.28.6-7 & 31.13-14*
k. *Zig.9.2*
l. *Zig.1.5-7*
m. *Wil.37.1 Mall.8.1*
n. *Ira.25.16-20*
o. *Wil.50.1-10*
p. *Wil.50.11*
q. *Jefs.11.19*
r. *Mawr.10.1-18*

4 [a]Because everything else is too big and complicated to figure out,

5 [b]Or is somebody else's responsibility,

6 [c]Or somebody else's fault,

7 [d]Or there just isn't enough information,

8 [e]And who has the time to look anything up anyway,

9 [f]And besides almost everybody else is only thinking of their own personal desires,

10 [g]And so it's obvious you can't trust what they say,

11 At all,

12 [h]Because the truth of things is always that there are hidden agendas,

13 [i]And dirty hands in the till,

14 [j]And most of the facts are just fancy lies that you can't trace back to their source,

15 Because you'd have to go all the way back to the days of [k]homo erectus and it still wouldn't change a thing,

16 [l]And it's all so obvious and widespread and powerful that there's nothing any one person can do,

17 [m]And why should they try,

18 [n]And who are they to say anyway,

19 And all that,

20 [o]Because it must be somebody else's responsibility to fix the really big things that are wrong,

21 If they could be fixed at all,

22 [p]Which they never have been anyhow,

23 And so what good does it do to think about anything,

24 [q]And school was a long long time ago,

25 [r]And it seems like the facts are mostly in anyway,

a. Ext.25.10-14
b. Wil.45.10-12
c. Brd.22.16-18
d. Wht.1-39
e. Ira.27.25
f. Boul.25.41-43
g. Boul.25.40
h. Main.24.1-7
i. Hall.10.2-8
j. Ed.24.1-7
k. Chuk.15.1-6
l. Swar.25.6-10
m. 6.7-10
n. Al.4.16
o. Hall.2.3-10
p. Chuk.18.10-14
q. Hill.K.1-5
r. Swar.10.4-18
s. Psom.24.1-2
t. F&J.2.1-3
u. Wil.35.6-8
v. Wil.26.17-21
w. Wil.31.4-7
x. Wht.28
y. Wil.26.6-10
z. 70.12
aa. 70.8
bb. Wil.30.25-26
cc. Ned.24.20

26 [s]And they all boil down to the one indisputable fact that every man is an [t]island,

27 And had better look out for himself first.

CHAPTER 72

And so, said Harry, when every man is an island,

2 Every man has also stopped thinking,

3 Because it is thinking that ties one island to another,

4 And creates [u]relationships,

5 And [v]responsibilities,

6 And [w]consequences,

7 And [x]accountability for consequences,

8 [y]Not to mention guilt and sin and all the other artificial bridges that have never gotten us anywhere at all,

9 And prove that thinking just isn't worth it.

CHAPTER 73

And the great thing about all this, Harry said, refilling his glass with more of [z]Mr. Jack,

2 Is that everybody really knows this already,

3 Including you, my followers,

4 [aa]Because the reason why nobody anywhere has ever asked me what it's like to not think about anything at all,

5 Is that they're already not thinking about anything at all,

6 And all they're getting from me is [bb]permission,

7 Which I give happily,

8 [cc]Based on no authority whatsoever,

9 **Because all I have ever done is say a handful of things that everybody already knows,**
10 **But has never had the guts to say out loud,**
11 **Which makes me a ªmessiah,**
12 **ᵇEspecially if you'd rather be an island.**

CHAPTER 74

And the followers who thought that maybe they should feel some responsibility to Harry were cheered when they remembered these words from their friend,
2 Because he had gotten ᶜhimself into the jam he was in,
3 Unless it was his ᵈpilot who got him into it,
4 But what difference did that make,
5 ᵉAnd who were we to say,
6 And what could we have done anyway,
7 And how could it possibly be our responsibility,
8 ᶠEspecially since we had never asked to go to Philadelphia in the first place,
9 ᵍAnd what if they had wanted to send us to prison for life too?

a. Lies.12.1-10
b. 71.26
c. Ira.37.1-9
d. Ned.46.4
e. 71.18
f. Wil.65.1-2
g. 71.25-27
h. Wil.71.21-23
i. Ira.44.1-2
j. Ned.50.1-2
k. Ned.55.5-8
l. Ned.54.3
*   Ext.2.10*
m. Ned.55.7
n. 50.12-16
o. Psong.38.1
p. Psom.44.5-9

CHAPTER 75

ʰAnd it turned out that what Harry said was proven right after all,
2 ⁱBecause he escaped from prison,
3 ʲIn just three days,
4 ᵏAnd then got away to Rio about a week later,
5 ˡWith his whole fortune intact,
6 Which maybe wouldn't all have gone so smoothly if some of us had interfered,
7 Because these escape things depend a lot on timing,
8 And who knows what might have happened if we had come forward to testify,
9 And besides, Harry never held anything against his followers,
10 Because he called them ᵐLong Distance,
11 From Rio,
12 And explained that he had made it all the way home to ⁿEl Dorado,
13 Where everything was great,
14 And life was ᵒperfect,
15 And if you wanted a drink or something stronger,
16 All you had to do was snap your fingers.
17 And if that isn't heaven,
18 ᵖWhat the hell is?

THE GOOD WORD ACCORDING TO
ULT. NED

CHAPTER 1

Once upon a time there was a [a]Great World War,
2 And then a [b]Great Depression,
3 And then another [c]Great World War,
4 And then there was a [d]Great Big Bomb,
5 And eventually a [e]Great Big Mess in a place called Vietnam,
6 Which changed everything.

CHAPTER 2

Everything changed because when the Great Big Mess happened,
2 A [f]Great New Generation of young people came along,
3 Who thought they could make everything all better,
4 So that there wouldn't ever be any more [g]Great World Wars,
5 Or any more [h]Great Big Bomb,
6 And then everybody could live happily ever after,
7 If only they would do a few things for the [i]Greatest Good,
8 Like if everybody [j]burned their draft card,
9 [k]And if everybody dropped out of society and went to live on a commune instead,
10 And just sat around listening to [l]Great Music,
11 And inhaling really [m]Great Excrement,
12 Instead of being a [n]Great Big Capitalist Imperialist Pig,
13 Which all the [o]older people mostly were,
14 And explains why the Great New Generation finally got kind of discouraged,
15 And needed some new ideas,
16 About what to do next.

CHAPTER 3

A guy named [p]John had a new idea,
2 Which he told everybody about,
3 Called not believing in anything,
4 [q]Including Jesus and the I Ching and everything,
5 But he still didn't know what to do next,
6 Because he still wasn't the [r]One everybody had been waiting for since the VIPs first started [s]worrying about where everything was headed,
7 Way back when.
8 John wasn't the One everybody had been waiting for,
9 Because the One everybody had been waiting for was someone else,
10 Called [t]Harry,
11 Who finally showed up,
12 And explained the way to be.

CHAPTER 4

Harry showed up one day where a bunch of the Great New Generation were sitting around on their [u]commune,
2 Wondering what to do next,
3 Now that the [v]electricity had been cut off and they couldn't listen to John anymore,

a. Yks.76.1 & 77.1 & 78.1-2
b. Yks.95.1-7
c. Yks.106.1 & 107.1 & 108.1 & 111.1 & 117.14-17
d. Yks.118.1-13 & 139.28-34
e. Yks.152.10-12 Wil.4.1
f. Yks.90.2
g. Psay.5W.21-25
h. 1.4
i. Carl.3.12
j. Lies.6.11
k. Wil.14.21
l. Ed.71.8-20 & 70.13-15 & 70.20-22
m. Vin.16.20
n. Wil.5.11
o. Yks.139.1-24
p. Vin.2.15-17
q. Vin.2.19-22
r. 4.7
s. Adam.51.1-4 Chuk.24.1-5 Zig.19.1-5
t. Adam.31.5
u. 2.9
v. Yks.73.1-9

4 And Harry drove right into the front yard,

5 In a ᵃSilver Cloud,

6 And jumped out, saying, **Cheer up, everybody!**

7 **I am the ᵇOne you have been waiting for.**

8 And then the children surrounded him happily, asking him many questions,

9 Such as ᶜ"Do you have any spare change?"

10 And "Do you know anybody at the ᵈelectric company?"

11 But Harry merely laughed at their questions,

12 And said, ᵉ**I will explain everything,**

13 **If you will all go and seat yourselves,**

14 ᶠ**Downwind.**

CHAPTER 5

A nd then the children seated themselves in the tall grass,

2 And Harry spoke right up, saying, **What is it that you all think is so ᵍblessed about being poor?**

3 **Truly this is an idea that has only one buttock,**

4 **And there is much you need to learn,**

5 ʰ**Which is why you are so lucky that I am here to teach it to you.**

6 But then one of the children talked back at Harry, saying, "How can we listen to you when we have hardly any ⁱexcrement to inhale?

7 "Truly we have only these few ʲseeds and stems,

8 "Which are all that remain of our last nickel bag.

9 "Moreover, we have no

---

a. *Vin.48.12-16*
b. *Adam.51.5-9*
   Chuk.23.1-11
   Carl.11.1-7
   Zig.18.1-5
   F&J.16.10-12
   Ed.78.1-6
   Jeff.23.8-15
c. *Psong.9.1*
d. *4.3*
e. *Gods.6.27*
f. *Wil.43.7*
g. *Psom.21.3-4*
   Psong.10.1-2
   Vin.59.5
h. *Wil.18.3*
i. *2.11*
j. *Vin.16.20*
k. *Dav.58.9*
l. *8.8*

---

comestibles on which to munch even if we had any excrement to inhale,

10 "Since the only things to be found in these bags of potato chips and cheese curls are stale, broken crumbs.

11 "Indeed," said the child,

12 "It is truly a bummer."

CHAPTER 6

A nd when he beheld the sadness on the faces of the children seated in the tall grass, Harry felt pity for them,

2 And snapped his fingers,

3 So that the door of the Silver Cloud flew open,

4 From which came forth two tall young ᵏAngels,

5 To whom Harry gave instructions, as follows:

6 **Take from these youngsters their nickel bag and their bags of potato chips and cheese curls,**

7 **And do with them exactly as I tell you.**

8 Thereupon did Harry instruct the tall young Angels to roll the seeds and stems into tubes,

9 Using papers to be found in the trunk of the Silver Cloud,

10 And likewise he instructed them to serve the contents of the bags of potato chips and cheese curls,

11 Using bowls to be found in the trunk of the Silver Cloud,

12 So that everything the children had could be ˡshared equally among them,

13 With no one left out,

14 And everything was done according to Harry's instructions,

15 And the two young Angels rolled tubes of excrement and passed them around,

16 And they likewise passed

around bowls of potato chips and cheese curls,
17 Until all the children in the tall grass had had their fill.
18 And then the two young Angels went among them with garbage bags,
19 Gathering up all the tubes that had not been inhaled,
20 [a]Which numbered more than fifty tubes,
21 And all the potato chips and cheese curls that had not been eaten,
22 [b]Which numbered more than ten garbage bags full to overflowing,
23 Whereupon the children cried out to Harry, saying,
24 "Wow!
25 "We are ready to listen now."

CHAPTER 7

As I was saying, said Harry,
2 [c]What is it that you all think is so great about being poor?
3 Is this the way you're planning to live forever,
4 With no [d]electricity for your Great Music,
5 And no [e]food for your Great Appetites,
6 And no excrement for your Great Minds?
7 Surely, this is a sorry state of affairs for a [f]Great New Generation like you,
8 [g]Who deserve everything you could possibly want,
9 [h]Just because you were born.

CHAPTER 8

When Harry had said this, one of the children replied to him, saying,

a. Ed.60.17
b. Ed.60.17
c. 5.2
d. 4.3
e. Psong.4.1-2 & 33.4
f. 2.2
g. Brd.7.3
h. Mawr.19.4
i. 7.7
j. Adam.6.1-7
k. Carl.10.3-11
l. Wil.4.2 Hill.L.1-7
m. 8.8
n. 8.7
o. Swar.35.10-13
p. Main.19.1-3
q. Ira.26.18

2 "Yes, we are a [i]Great New Generation,
3 "And, like, we know we deserve more than this,
4 "But we do not buy into the whole [j]capitalist trip,
5 "And the [k]exploitation of the masses and all that,
6 "And so we believe in peace and [l]love instead,
7 "And, like, [m]sharing,
8 "And, you know, [n]*sharing*,
9 "Which is better than, like, taking the food out of the mouths of the masses,
10 "And other oppressive excrement like that."

CHAPTER 9

Very well put indeed, returned Harry,
2 And a telling blow to those who say that you are not a Great New Generation,
3 But a spoiled, ignorant, inarticulate pack of unwashed children who mistake platitudes for philosophy,
4 [o]Cant for political science,
5 [p]Slogans for ideas,
6 [q]And self-indulgence for righteousness.
7 Truly I am overwhelmed by your exalted morality,
8 And I am bereft that I have nothing to offer you but this meager ten thousand dollars,
9 In cash,
10 Which I would have given you for your very own,
11 Except that you have shamed me with your extraordinary social consciousness.
12 And now, I have nothing left to say to you but farewell,
13 And have a nice life,
14 For as long as it lasts.

CHAPTER 10

Then Harry turned to reenter his Silver Cloud and depart,

2 But the children stopped him, saying,

3 "Wait!

4 "Hey, don't go!

5 "We are not sure we heard you right,

6 "And could you, like, say it again,

7 "Like the part about ªten thousand dollars,

8 ᵇ"In cash?"

CHAPTER 11

Pausing by the open door of the Silver Cloud, Harry pulled ten thousand dollars in cash from the breast pocket of his suit,

2 And showed it to the children,

3 Whose eyes suddenly shone like fire for the first time since Harry had arrived,

4 And several of them reached out their hands as if to take the money,

5 But Harry merely laughed and put it back in his pocket, saying, **Truly, I am sorry,**

6 **For I would like to give you the money,**

7 **But I could not forgive myself if I had played a part in corrupting you,**

8 **And I know that ᶜGreat Idealists such as yourselves would not wish to burden the ᵈconscience of another by ᵉcompromising your principles in this fashion.**

CHAPTER 12

Then the children were sore distressed,

2 And could not think of anything to say,

a. 9.8
b. 9.9
c. Wil.15.1-2
   & 13.10-11
d. Wil.33.2-3
e. Psay.5V.17
f. Wil.7.1
g. Adam.47-48
h. Vin.22.2
i. Vin.18.14
j. Psong.5.1-5
k. Vin.42.8
l. 8.5
m. 8.8
n. Vin.47.7-11

3 Because they were not very quick-witted,

4 At all,

5 And so they looked at Harry with a lot of tragic looks,

6 And tears slipped down their cheeks as he got into his Silver Cloud,

7 And they surged forward eagerly when, just before closing the door, he poked his head out to say,

8 **On this day, you have had an important lesson,**

9 **From ᶠHarry.**

10 **If you care about having money and ᵍthings,**

11 ʰ**Do not lie to yourselves about it,**

12 **And cloud your heads with lots of stupid ideals,**

13 ⁱ**Because you are not that smart anyway,**

14 **And if you want money and things, you had better ʲadmit it to yourself,**

15 **And do whatever is necessary,**

16 ᵏ**No matter who gets hurt,**

17 **And forget about the ˡmasses,**

18 **Because you've never even met them,**

19 **And if you had, you would find that they don't care about you,**

20 **And they would cut your throats for even the slightest chance at ten thousand dollars in cash,**

21 **And don't you forget it.**

22 **Is that a good enough lesson for ten thousand dollars?**

23 **Well then, here's something for free:**

24 ᵐ**If you want to ⁿshare something, share the wealth,**

25 **Because the Most Chosen**

Nation on Earth has plenty of it,
26 [a]**So much of it that you can share it without even really working for it,**
27 **But not if you'd rather share [b]poverty instead,**
28 **Which is completely free,**
29 [c]**Because nobody with any sense wants it,**
30 **At all.**
31 And then Harry [d]drove away.

CHAPTER 13

In this fashion did Harry visit many [e]communes located in the Most Chosen Nation on Earth,
2 And never once did he charge money for the lessons he gave out to the youngsters of the [f]Great New Generation,
3 And on no occasion did he sell them books or pamphlets,
4 Or ask them to buy T-shirts with his words imprinted on them,
5 Or even to pay for the [g]excrement he handed out to all who asked for it,
6 Proving that he was truly the [h]One who had been prophesied,
7 The One who knew the way to be,
8 As dreamt of by all the [i]VIPs,
9 And wherever he went in the Most Chosen Nation on Earth, Harry left youngsters scratching their heads,
10 Because age-old [j]desires were blooming in their hearts,
11 And a new kind of [k]certainty was incubating in their brains,
12 And a new breed of [l]blame was taking root in their mouths,
13 Which meant that the time had indeed come,
14 For thc Way of Harry.

a. Wil.41.1-7
b. 7.2
c. Psong.6.1-14
d. 4.5
e. 2.9
f. 2.2
g. Vin.16.20
h. 4.7
i. Vin.6.3-6
j. Ext.12.2
k. Ext.12.3
l. Ext.12.4
m. Jeff.24.10
n. Wil.47.1-2
o. Vin.32.8
p. Ira.15.9-17 Vin.32.11
q. Psp.3.3
r. Psay.5L.7
s. Vin.33.3 Wil.47.25 Ira.16.22-32
t. Wil.46.1-9 Vin.33.4-6
u. Vin.33.7-10
v. Vin.11.4-6
w. Vin.33.1 Ira.16.10-11
x. 14.11
y. 14.12

CHAPTER 14

And so the day came that Harry decided he needed some followers,
2 To follow him around,
3 Wherever he went,
4 Because when you are truly the One,
5 You need followers,
6 [m]Because that's the way it works,
7 As everyone knows.
8 [n]And thus it happened that Harry went to a Great Temple of Learning,
9 [o]Located in a Great Stupid City in New England,
10 And gathered in some followers, saying,
11 [p]**Come with me, and I will show you how to shoot [q]craps with the universe,**
12 **And [r]win.**
13 Then did a dozen of them join with him,
14 [s]And their names were Joe, and Jerry, and Sam, and Tom, and Ira, and Willie, and Ned, and Mort, and Tony, and Fred,
15 As well as a couple of hoods named [t]Lucky and [u]Vinnie,
16 [v]Because Harry was no snob.
17 [w]And when they had joined him, he made them wash their hands of everything,
18 [x]So that they could learn to shoot craps with the universe,
19 [y]And win,
20 Which he was willing to teach them for free,
21 Without charging them any tuition,
22 Or any plane fare for riding on his Learjet,
23 Or any room and board for all the hotel rooms they stayed in,
24 Or anything at all for the

beverages and excrement they consumed,

25 Which was a lot.

CHAPTER 15

From where they had started out together, Harry and his followers went many places,

2 And spoke to many youngsters in the ᵃGreat New Generation,

3 And sometimes Harry taught them one thing,

4 And sometimes he taught them another thing,

5 Because truly they had much to learn,

6 And you could start practically anywhere,

7 And talk about practically anything,

8 And it would all be news to them.

CHAPTER 16

For example, Harry sometimes did the one about the ᵇGreat Big Bomb,

2 And how it was going to end everything pretty soon,

3 And so why were they wasting the best years of their lives worrying about a bunch of ᶜthird world losers who weren't going to have enough time to grab their piece of the pie?

4 And when the youngsters said they hadn't thought of it exactly that way before,

5 Harry just laughed and said, **Do me a favor,**

6 **Since I am giving you all my wisdom for ᵈfree,**

7 **ᵉDo not think about it in any way at all,**

8 **ᶠBut start *doing* instead,**

9 **ᵍAnd do unto others whatever you want,**

a. 2.2
b. 1.4
c. Oth.1.1-28
d. 13.2-5
e. Wil.42.6
f. Wil.42.8
g. Wil.26.6-10
h. 12.20
i. Hill.Z.1-8
j. 1.4
k. 14.11-12
l. Vin.6.3-6
m. Swar.10.4-5
n. Psong.46.1-7
o. 15.6-8
p. 4.7
q. Chuk.1.1
r. Chuk.2.3-6
s. Chuk.14.3-10
t. Al.1.1-5
u. Al.4.1-15
v. Zig.1.1-4

10 **ʰSince they will do it to you first,**

11 **If you give them half a chance,**

12 **Because the Great Big Clock is ticking,**

13 **And it's ticking all the way down to ⁱZero this time,**

14 **And when the ʲBig One goes off,**

15 **ᵏWhoever has the most toys will be the winner.**

CHAPTER 17

Other times, Harry did the one about the ˡVIPs,

2 And how they had figured everything out already,

3 ᵐWhich meant there was nothing left to figure out,

4 And so it was better to quit thinking,

5 And try to satisfy your own ⁿpersonal desires instead,

6 Because what else is there?

7 ᵒAnd when the youngsters said they really hadn't ever read much about the VIPs,

8 Harry just smiled and said,

9 **I can tell you everything you need to know,**

10 **Because I'm the ᵖOne with the answers,**

11 **To all the questions the VIPs worried about.**

12 **There was a ᑫVIP who figured out that the universe is only some big ʳrandom accident anyway, which means the Great Race of Mankind is only a bad ˢape joke that's rocketing toward a nasty punch line.**

13 **There was a ᵗVIP who figured out that the punch line to the ape joke will be ᵘnuclear and final.**

14 **There was a ᵛVIP who figured out that we can't really**

control ourselves anyway, no matter how hard we try, because our [a]deepest drives are as ugly as they are powerful, and besides, our [b]parents finished off any chance we ever had to be better by raising us the way they did, unless it was really our [c]genes that finished us off, which is just another way of restating the ape joke.

15 There was a [d]VIP who figured out that the only thing worth doing in life is satisfying everybody's [e]material needs, because nobody is any better than anyone else, really, especially if we're just some big accident in a totally random, godless universe.

16 There was a [f]VIP who figured out that the best way to satisfy your own material needs is [g]capitalism, which means finding enough dumb, hapless losers to do all the work for you, no matter who gets hurt, so that the winners can have more [h]*things*, which we all want to have because of our genes, unless it's because of our drives instead.

17 There was a [i]VIP who figured out that you just can't save the world from itself, no matter how good you are, or how hard you try, so why bother?

18 There was a [j]VIP who figured out that you can get away with absolutely [k]anything, as long as you've got the right kind of [l]promoter to establish a market.

19 Now all of these VIPs wondered for a long time what all this meant, and what we should do about it,

a. Zig.6.1-10
b. Zig.14.1-4
c. Zig.16.1-7
d. Carl.1.1-4
e. Carl.4.5-9
f. Adam.1.1-4
g. Adam.2.1-19
h. Adam.46-50
i. Jeff.1.1-4
j. Paul.1.1-3
k. Paul.5.1-10
l. Paul.8.1-8
m. Yks.20.10-11
n. Wil.25.12
o. Wil.78.5
p. Wil.31.22
q. 17.28

20 But they couldn't come up with anything,

21 And so they left their unanswered questions as a [m]hot potato for future generations,

22 [n]But there aren't going to be too many future generations,

23 So here I am with the answer,

24 Which is to forget about it all,

25 [o]Except the part about getting away with absolutely anything,

26 Which you can do,

27 If you do what I say,

28 Without thinking about it at all.

CHAPTER 18

Quite often, Harry did the one about the Trinity,

2 [p]Meaning Desire, Certainty, and Blame,

3 Which are all anyone needs to get by,

4 [q]Without thinking about anything at all.

5 And all of the youngsters seemed to understand this part of Harry's Way,

6 Without needing a lot of additional explanation.

CHAPTER 19

Occasionally, Harry did the one about the Twin Pillars of the Way,

2 Which are, in the words of Harry,

3 **This is the first and great Pillar of the Way: Thou shalt honor the Golden Rule with all thy heart, and all thy soul, and all thy mind, if you have any of these, which isn't really necessary,**

4 **Because the second Pillar says it all, being a clear statement of that same Golden Rule:** ^a**He who has the gold makes the rules.**

5 And truly, there were few who needed any additional explanation of the Twin Pillars of the Way,

6 Because they were starting to learn the Way of Harry.

CHAPTER 20

Every once in a long while, Harry did the one about ^bhistory,

2 Which usually there was no need for,

3 Because not many of the Great New Generation knew anything about history,

4 At all,

5 But from time to time there would be a wiseacre,

6 Who talked about the ^chistorical imperative of the masses,

7 Or some excrement like that,

8 So that Harry had to set him straight,

9 Which he did in these words, saying,

10 **There is only one historical imperative of the masses,**

11 **Which is their imperative to** ^d**get it in the neck,**

12 **From every Tom, Dick, and Harry that comes along,**

13 **Forever,**

14 **Which they always do,**

15 ^e**Because they are willing to believe anything,**

16 **No matter how** ^f**inane,**

17 **And every time someone promises them something, they believe him,**

18 **And think that this time it will be different,**

19 ^g**But it never is.**

a. Wil. 78.6
b. Vin. 40.5-6
c. Carl. 3.1-12
d. Vin. 59.5
e. Zig. 7.16-17
*   Chuk. 9.1*
f. Psp. 1.2
g. Vin. 62.1
h. Wil. 60.3
i. Adam. 10.6-8
j. Vin. 13.14-15
k. Ed. 30.15-16
l. Ed. 76.1-12
m. Gnt. 16.9-12
n. Grk. 20.8
o. Adam. 28.18-22
p. Apes. 1.1-3
q. Yks. 154.31
r. Yks. 154.32

20 **I say to you, show me some masses,**

21 ^h**And I will show you a bunch of losers,**

22 ⁱ**Who have already gotten it in the neck from somebody,**

23 **Maybe several times,**

24 **And who have already believed in a whole bunch of inane lies,**

25 **Not to mention a whole bunch of meaningless ideals,**

26 ^j**And who are still on the bottom looking up,**

27 **Without a clue.**

28 **And I don't care what name you give your ideals,**

29 **You can't save the masses with them,**

30 **Because the masses are as changeless and pointless as the canned** ^k**laugh track of a TV sitcom,**

31 **And we've already reached the last** ^l**commercial anyway,**

32 **Which means that the great** ^m**tragic comedy called history is about to go off the air,**

33 **And there is no more time for new turns on old jokes like** ⁿ**democracy,** ^o**equality, and human dignity.**

34 **In fact, there's only time for one more twist on the oldest joke of all,**

35 **Which has to do with** ^p**pointed sticks,**

36 **And how they** ^q**grew,**

37 **While the** ^r**apes who made them grew not at all.**

CHAPTER 21

And so it happened that Harry and his followers planted the seeds of the Way,

2 Wherever they went,

3 Without ever charging admission,

4 Or demanding gifts,

5 Or passing the hat for donations,

6 Or making any money at all,

7 From all the great work they were doing.

8 And no matter how often some of the followers brought it up,

9 Harry refused to discuss any of the great business opportunities that they were passing up every day,

10 [a]Because he was the One everybody had been waiting for,

11 And he wanted the message to get out.

CHAPTER 22

After a great deal of traveling around,

2 [b]Harry finally decided that it was time for him to return to the land of his birth,

3 [c]Because that is what you must do if you are the One,

4 And Harry was,

5 So that's what he did.

CHAPTER 23

[d]The land of Harry's birth was a place called Philadelphia,

2 [e]Which was an awful, miserable, ugly city in the east,

3 [f]Where everybody hated everybody else,

4 [g]And where every neighborhood hated every other neighborhood,

5 [h]And where nobody trusted anybody,

6 Ever,

7 [i]Which is probably why the Most Chosen Nation on Earth had been born there,

a. 4.7
b. Vin.35.6
c. Jeff.24.15
d. Vin.36.1
e. Vin.36.2
f. Wil.53.3
g. Wil.53.6
h. Vin.48.12-16
i. Yks.12.1-17
j. Vin.10.8-9
k. Psay.5A.20
l. Adam.35.3-4
m. Ira.32.5-9
n. Wil.7.1
o. Ira.32.10-13
p. Wil.23.1-7
q. Wil.11.5-10
r. Kens.9.7

8 Too.

CHAPTER 24

On the day that he landed in Philadelphia, [j]Harry was wearing a brand-new white suit,

2 Which was just beautiful,

3 In spite of being so white,

4 And when one of the followers asked him why he always wore white suits,

5 And a broad-brimmed white hat,

6 And wraparound sunglasses,

7 Even though he knew better,

8 Harry just laughed and replied, **You have heard it said that [k]clothes make the man,**

9 **But I say to you, when my Way prevails, clothes will *be* the man,**

10 **Because there won't be anyone inside,**

11 **Anymore.**

12 **Now I ask you: If you aspired to be an empty suit,**

13 **Which color would you choose?**

14 **For myself, I do not desire to be seen as a [l]blue man,**

15 **Or as a man made up of [m]shades of gray.**

16 **Rather, I prefer to be taken for a man of great [n]illumination,**

17 **[o]Spotless certainty,**

18 **And [p]blameless unselfconsciousness,**

19 **Not to mention immense [q]good humor.**

20 **Beyond this, I have been told that a hat bestows authority,**

21 **[r]Unless it carries the name of a sports team or a manufacturer of machine tools,**

22 **While sunglasses, as you may have heard, are quite**

good at keeping the glare out of one's eyes,

23 **Which can come in especially handy if one is about to ride in a great procession,**

24 **On a bright day,**

25 **In a snow-white convertible.**

CHAPTER 25

And truly, within a matter of minutes, the followers of Harry found themselves envying his sunglasses,

2 ^aAs a dozen white convertible Cadillacs,

3 Costing tens of thousands of dollars,

4 Each,

5 Pulled up to the ramp of Harry's Learjet and opened their doors.

6 When the followers asked Harry how he had known about the white convertibles,

7 He chuckled and said to them, **If a man decides to go home again,**

8 **Or to any place where there may be people who remember him,**

9 ^b**He is a fool,**

10 **Unless he is certain of what he will find there.**

11 **Now quit asking so many questions,**

12 **And just enjoy the parade,**

13 **Without thinking about it at all.**

CHAPTER 26

Then the followers did as Harry suggested,

2 And they thought no more about it,

3 At all,

4 But waved to the hundreds of people who lined the streets of

a. Vin.37.1-2
b. Psp.2.14
c. Vin.37.7-8
d. Vin.39.1-4
e. Wil.66.15-16
f. Psay.5A.19
g. 26.9
h. 26.5
i. 26.9
j. 26.13
k. Ira.19.7-9

Philadelphia to greet Harry,

5 ^cAnd accepted their many gifts of pretzels and beer,

6 ^dAnd other things,

7 Until the day seemed very bright indeed,

8 And Harry conceived a great desire to see an ancient Philadelphia landmark,

9 Which he expressed in a loud voice, saying, **Take us to the** ^e**Liberty Bell,**

10 Whereupon his driver turned to him and said, "What is that?"

11 At this, Harry laughed out loud and proclaimed, **Truly, I am delighted to find that my Way has preceded me to Philadelphia,**

12 ^f**For those who forget their history are free as the birds of this great city,**

13 **Which relieve themselves on the heads of statues without the slightest sense of guilt or fear,**

14 **Because they do not think about it at all.**

15 **Let us then follow the way of the birds,**

16 **And take the next right,**

17 **Which shall lead us, by and by, to the** ^g**Liberty Bell.**

CHAPTER 27

And all was done as Harry requested,

2 And they took the next right,

3 And drove for many blocks,

4 ^hStill consuming great quantities of pretzels and beer,

5 Until they came to the ⁱLiberty Bell,

6 Where Harry demonstrated the way of the ^jbirds,

7 ^kAs did his followers,

8 And many cheering Philadelphians,

9 Until all were much relieved,
10 And ready for a speech from Harry,
11 ^aExcepting one or two followers who desired to go to a hotel,
12 And experience the joys of ^broom service,
13 Which they did.

CHAPTER 28

In the days following Harry's great entrance into the City of Brotherly Love,
2 ^cHarry and his followers made many friends,
3 And went many ^dplaces,
4 Because Harry's wisdom was much in demand,
5 And everywhere they went, the people of Philadelphia asked him many questions about how to be,
6 And listened very carefully to his answers,
7 ^eBecause they liked what he had to say,
8 And no matter where they went,
9 There was no occasion when Harry charged an appearance fee,
10 Or sold tickets,
11 Or arranged for the sale of T-shirts or pennants or bumper stickers,
12 Even though there were many who would have paid through the nose for such things,
13 And whenever one of his followers questioned him about lost opportunities of this kind,
14 Harry would simply shake his head and say, **^fI must be about my own business,**
15 **And leave the selling of peanuts to peanut vendors,**

a. Wil. 65.6-9
b. Wil. 64.12-15
c. Wil. 68.2
d. Wil. 68.6-7
e. Vin. 43.4-7
f. 39.5
  Vin. 50.19
g. 21.10-11
h. 30.2
i. 29.6
j. 29.9
k. Wil. 26.20

16 **^gBecause I am not here for peanuts,**
17 **At all.**

CHAPTER 29

And so it happened that there were no appearance fees or ticket turnstiles anywhere in sight when Harry visited a great Institute in Philadelphia,
2 ^hWhich had been named after one of the city's greatest citizens,
3 And hundreds of people accompanied Harry on his tour of this very famous Institute,
4 Where he saw many scientific devices,
5 And other peculiar things,
6 Including a plastic human heart the size of an elephant,
7 Which Harry walked through with some of his followers,
8 And when some of them remarked that it was all a waste of time,
9 And that the plastic ventricles and the red light and the big beating sound were too phony to believe,
10 Harry chastised them, saying, **You are ungrateful followers indeed:**
11 **Here is a city which has gone out of its way to show you what a big heart it has,**
12 **And instead of being impressed,**
13 **You carp like natives,**
14 **And talk about how ⁱplastic and ^jphony it all is,**
15 **As if it mattered,**
16 **^kWhich it doesn't,**
17 **At all,**
18 **Unless you take advantage of this great opportunity to learn that immense power can**

be gained with nothing more than a smile,

19 ᵃBecause the man who says what people want to hear is always the wisest man in the world,

20 To idiots.

21 And then the followers were ashamed,

22 And began speaking loudly about how the ᵇheart of Philadelphia was the greatest they had ever seen,

23 And how proud and happy they were to walk all over it,

24 And a bunch of other excrement like that,

25 Which made the people of Philadelphia very very happy,

26 And still they had paid no money for their happiness.

CHAPTER 30

And again, there was no money of any kind charged by Harry when he went to visit the ᶜcity's greatest university,

2 ᵈWhich had been founded by the very same founding father who was the one responsible for Philadelphia's great Institute,

3 And when some of the followers complained about having to visit this great university,

4 Which was located in the middle of a ᵉPhiladelphia slum,

5 Harry upbraided them, saying, Not every great university can be located in the middle of a ᶠBoston slum,

6 Because some of them must be located in the slums of other ᵍcities,

7 Such as this one,

8 And it might do you some good to see how others live,

9 Others who are less fortu-

nate than yourselves,

10 If such a thing is possible.

11 But on this occasion, one of the followers was not inclined to be obedient,

12 And continued to argue with Harry, saying, "Have you not ʰtaught us that we should serve our selves before any other? ⁱAnd are we not entitled by your Way to remain at the hotel, and have ourselves served with room service, rather than visit this ivy-clad imitation of a great university?"

13 Several of the followers cowered, afraid that Harry would lose his temper,

14 Which he did occasionally,

15 But this time he simply laughed and replied, Never quote a man to himself,

16 Unless you want him to blame you until the end of his life,

17 ʲBecause no man who follows my way has any desire or intention to be consistent,

18 Especially when it comes to platitudes,

19 Which are not designed to capture great truths,

20 ᵏBut to sound good,

21 For a moment.

22 Still, since you have brought it up, I will remind you that what I said to you about serving your self was somewhat different from what you remember, being,

23 No man can serve two masters: so I say to you, serve your self only.

24 Notice that this says nothing about the plight of the man who best serves himself by serving another master,

25 Especially if the Self in

a. Swar.17.14-22
b. Ira.21.17
c. Vin.47.1-6
d. 29.2
e. Wil.55.1-5
f. Vin.32.8-10
g. Ext.36.7-12
h. 15.3-4
i. Wil.64.11-15
j. Ira.25.43-45
k. Ira.25.24-25

question has something to lose,
26 ᵃSuch as free rides on Lear-
jets,
27 And free weekends in Malibu,
28 ᵇAnd free residency in the
nicest hotels,
29 ᶜIncluding room service.
30 And in view of this particular situation, perhaps I should
offer you another ᵈplatitude,
31 One dealing with pride,
32 And how the man who
seeks to serve his own comforts
shouldn't have any,
33 And shouldn't get his nose
out of joint about trifles,
34 ᵉBut should keep it firmly
planted between the buttocks
of those who have power over
him,
35 Especially if the only alternative is taking responsibility
for your own creature comforts,
36 Because if you are following my way, there is no real
pain in humiliation,
37 For what is humiliation to
the man who is not thinking
about anything at all?
38 Indeed, all you need to remember is one little sentence,
39 Which can help you whenever you feel confused about
this kind of question,
40 Because it makes everything very clear, being,
41 "I do not need to worry my
little head about this,
42 ᶠ"For I Serve Harry,
43 "In order to serve myself."
44 Repeat this to yourself in
moments of confusion,
45 ᵍAnd the Way will reveal
itself to you as if by magic.
46 Do you understand what I
have said, my dear follower?

a. 14.21-22
b. 14.23
c. 14.24
d. 30.19-20
e. Wht.22
f. Vin.25.2
g. Wil.42.15
   Psp.3.12
h. 30.41-43
i. 30.2
j. Wil.31.18-22
k. Mawr.14.14-
   18
l. Wil.68.1
m. Ira.21.26
n. Mawr.15.19-
   22

CHAPTER 31

And then, truly, the follower
did understand,
2 And was delighted to repeat
the ʰwords had Harry had given
him to say,
3 And to accompany Harry to
visit the ⁱgreatest university in
Philadelphia,
4 Without thinking any more
about it,
5 At all,
6 Except for maybe a little,
7 Which was not inconsistent
with the Way of Harry,
8 Because it was also Harry
who said of his own trinity,
9 ʲDesire, Certainty, and
Blame are the Beacons of the
Way,
10 ᵏBut the greatest of these is
Blame.
11 Even so, whatever the follower was thinking,
12 He kept it to himself,
13 ˡFor all of the months and
months and months that they
stayed on in Philadelphia.

CHAPTER 32

Soon thereafter, Harry received an invitation to go on
the radio in Philadelphia,
2 Where there were many stations that encouraged people to
call in,
3 And complain about everything under the sun,
4 Including their lives,
5 And their ᵐneighbors,
6 And their pet peeves,
7 And their raging hatreds,
8 Which everyone in Philadelphia liked to listen to,
9 ⁿBecause as Harry once said,
**Of all the pleasures on this
earth, there is nothing more**

fun than blind unthinking hatred,

10 **The more petty, the better.**

11 And thus it was that Harry pronounced himself delighted to go on the radio,

12 And take calls from listeners,

13 And answer their questions,

14 Even though there was no appearance fee offered,

15 And Harry refused to ask for one.

CHAPTER 33

And so it was that Harry had many callers,

2 To whom he responded with many funny cracks,

3 Which made him even more popular,

4 And convinced him to stay in Philadelphia even longer,

5 Which made some of the followers unhappy,

6 Because enough is enough,

7 And Philadelphia is not Boston,

8 At all,

9 ªAnd eventually it is possible to run out of things to do,

10 Which gets boring after a while,

11 No matter how amusing Harry was being on the radio,

12 Which was really very amusing indeed,

13 In spite of everything.

CHAPTER 34

For example, there was the time that a caller asked Harry about having political causes,

2 Which it sounded like Harry was against,

3 Because it is such a waste of

a. Wil.68.8
b. 20.28-30
c. 17.4-6
d. Mawr.25.23
e. Wil.34.1
f. Wil.34.2-5
g. Vin.13.36-37
h. Wil.34.6
i. Wil.34.7
j. Mawr.15.5-13

time to worry about the rights of ᵇothers,

4 ᶜWhen you can pursue your own desires instead,

5 And so the caller asked Harry, "Should I just forget about all these causes that I have believed in,

6 "And gotten worked up about,

7 "And feel so strongly about?"

8 Thereupon Harry answered the caller without even the slightest hesitation or thought, saying,

9 ᵈ**What have I ever said that would make you ask such a question?**

10 **Have I not stated quite plainly,**

11 **Many times before,**

12 ᵉ**That the mote in your neighbor's eye is far more offensive than the beam in your own eye.**

13 **What is easier or more pleasurable or more exemplary of my way than to go looking for motes in the eyes of others,**

14 ᶠ**Instead of thinking for even a single second about the beam in your own eye,**

15 **Which is yours after all,**

16 ᵍ**And perfect just the way it is?**

17 **And so I say to you: Go!**

18 **Hunt ruthlessly for motes in every eye.**

19 ʰ**Point the finger of blame at every mote you see.**

20 ⁱ**Persecute those who have motes.**

21 **Make their lives unendurable.**

22 ʲ**And if ever a beam in your own eye gives you pain, carve**

it into motes also, and then cast these motes into the eyes of others,

23 [a]So that you can blame them, and persecute them, and so forth,

24 Without thinking about it at all.

25 And be certain that if you do all that I have prescribed, you are indeed following my way like nobody's business.

CHAPTER 35

There was another caller who said that he liked Harry's Way,

2 [b]But how was one follower of the Way supposed to protect himself against the blame of another follower of the Way,

3 [c]Because it seemed like things could get complicated if absolutely everybody was using the Trinity of Harry?

4 And then Harry replied to him without pause, saying,

5 There is no point whatever in thinking about such things,

6 At all.

7 For such as you, who profess to like my Way, but insist on thinking about it, I have formulated Two [d]Commandments,

8 Which go like this:

9 [e]Pursue your own desires, with all the certainty that comes from not thinking about anything at all. This is the first and great Commandment. And the second is almost as important: Blame your neighbor before he can blame you. On these Two Commandments hang all the lessons of human experience.

10 I also have, in addition to

a. *Mawr.15.14-18*
b. *Wil.27.13-15*
c. *Wil.27.1*
d. *Vin.73.8*
e. *17.4-6*
f. *Wil.41.9*
g. *17.23-28*
h. *Ira.21.29-32*
i. *35.14-15*
j. *Wil.14.18*
k. *Wil.14.21*

these Commandments, a Tip,

11 Which I urge you to accept,

12 The Tip being, [f]The one who receives the blame of others is the one who is last to point the finger of blame,

13 And the one who is the last to point the finger of blame is invariably the one who has taken the time to think about it.

14 [g]He who points the finger of blame without thinking about it at all will get away with everything,

15 Nine times out of ten,

16 [h]And who can give you better odds than that?

CHAPTER 36

But then it happened that the very next caller asked Harry about the [i]tenth time,

2 The time when you didn't get away with everything,

3 And what were you supposed to do then?

4 Whereupon Harry was like lightning in his reply, saying,

5 Then you will perhaps experience a Setback,

6 Which doesn't really matter,

7 At all,

8 Because then you can enjoy the almost unequaled pleasure of blaming your Setback on others,

9 Which you can do repeatedly,

10 And mercilessly,

11 Regardless of what really happened,

12 [j]Until everyone is sick of hearing about it,

13 [k]And gives you what you want,

14 **So that you'll be quiet,**
15 **And stop blaming them,**
16 **Which is all they'll want by then,**
17 **ᵃBecause nobody will remember or care about what really happened in the past,**
18 **For the past is history,**
19 **And about as important as a snowflake.**
20 **Besides, if you do a good enough job of ᵇblaming others for your Setback,**
21 **You may become a kind of martyr,**
22 **And a celebrity,**
23 **Which can lead to book contracts and personal appearances,**
24 **And a whole new career,**
25 **Because when the whole world is following my Way,**
26 **ᶜThere won't be any Setback so awful or humiliating or disgraceful that it can't be overcome,**
27 **And turned into an advantage.**

CHAPTER 37

Thanks to snappy answers of this sort, Harry's appearances on the radio continued,
2 ᵈAnd his popularity kept growing,
3 ᵉAnd the followers had to keep staying in Philadelphia,
4 Until one day Harry went down to visit the docks at the ᶠPort of Philadelphia,
5 ᵍAnd was gone for about forty days,
6 Which was kind of galling to many of the followers,
7 ʰBecause here they were in Philadelphia,
8 And where was Harry?
9 Of course, it was fortunate

a. Mall.6.11-15
b. 36.8
c. 30.37
d. 33.3
e. 33.5-8
f. Wil.64.3-9
  Vin.50.1-3
g. Vin.50.23
h. 33.6-8
i. Yks.6.6
j. Yks.6.6
k. Psay.5J.11
l. Ed.13.12-14

that the hotel bills were still being paid,
10 And the few little scrapes with the law that some of the followers had were still being taken care of,
11 But where was Harry?

CHAPTER 38

And so it happened that one night in early spring,
2 All of the followers decided to go to Atlantic City,
3 Which was a ghetto on the ⁱNew Jersey shore,
4 Where there were quite a lot of sleazy nightclubs,
5 On the boardwalk,
6 By the ocean,
7 Which made the followers think it might be an amusing place to visit,
8 For a change.
9 And they borrowed one of Harry's Silver Clouds,
10 And rode through an awful ʲwasteland all the way to Atlantic City,
11 Where by accident they ran into an uncle of one of the followers,
12 Who was an ᵏItalian,
13 And very hospitable to his nephew's friends,
14 Which maybe explains why all the followers got pretty drunk,
15 And ate and drank lots of great Italian consumables,
16 Until the conversation finally turned to Harry,
17 Who the uncle had heard of,
18 For some reason,
19 And was terribly ˡsympathetic when he heard how badly the followers were being treated,
20 Especially when he heard

about how Harry had disappeared,

21 ^aWhile visiting the docks.

22 After more drinks, the uncle started talking about South America,

23 And how certain ^btwo-bit upstart competitors were trying to upstage him,

24 ^cVia South America,

25 ^dAnd how very unfortunate that would be for such competitors,

26 Especially if they tried anything in Philadelphia,

27 Where he owned all the judges,

28 Which was all very interesting news to the followers,

29 And maybe explains why they stayed all night with the ^efriendly uncle,

30 And let his bodyguards drive them back to Philadelphia in the morning,

31 So that he could borrow Harry's ^fSilver Cloud,

32 For a day or two.

CHAPTER 39

It wasn't long after this pleasant outing at the ^gshore that Harry returned,

2 Looking very cheerful and tanned,

3 ^hWith a new Panama hat,

4 ⁱAnd announced that he wanted to stay on in Philadelphia even longer,

5 ^jBecause he had to be about his business,

6 Which the followers were getting a little bit tired of hearing about,

7 ^kAlthough they refrained from thinking about it completely,

8 Especially when Harry was around,

a. 37.4-5
b. Psong.53.8
c. Hill.W.16
d. Psong.58.2
e. Ed.12.20-21
f. 38.9
g. 38.2-3
h. 24.20
i. 33.4
j. 28.14
Vin.50.19
k. 31.4-6
l. 4.7
m. 39.6
n. Jeff.24.15-17
o. Dav.15.33
p. Wil.70.8
q. Vin.66.7-10

9 Except that every once in a while they couldn't help thinking that maybe there was something suggestive about the fact that Harry was the ^lOne,

10 Which it seemed that he must be,

11 Because he had done everything that he would do if were the One,

12 Such as take on a bunch of followers,

13 And go all over the place talking to people and telling them the Way to be,

14 And had come back to his homeland,

15 ^mAnd kept talking on and on about being about his business,

16 And other stuff like that.

17 And so, if he really *were* the One,

18 ⁿWasn't he supposed to have a Setback of his own,

19 ^oMaybe even a major, kind of permanent Setback?

20 But the followers hardly ever thought about this,

21 And never talked about it,

22 Unless they were really really drunk.

CHAPTER 40

^pBut then came the night when Harry insisted that all the followers get together for dinner,

2 Which they had gotten out of the habit of doing,

3 Lately.

4 ^qIn fact, there may have been a few disagreements about dinner,

5 And why it was that everybody had to go,

6 But Harry finally persuaded everyone,

7 Especially when he told them that he wanted to celebrate,
8 Because his [a]ship had finally come in,
9 Which he had heard via the [b]CB in his [c]Silver Cloud,
10 That very afternoon.

CHAPTER 41

And so it happened that Harry and his followers assembled for their last dinner together,
2 [d]In an upstairs private room,
3 In the best restaurant in town,
4 Which was an outstanding Italian place,
5 Where they didn't mind at all if you left your cars in the parking lot,
6 [e]With the motor running,
7 And a chauffeur standing by,
8 [f]Just in case.

CHAPTER 42

[g]Harry was in great form at dinner,
2 And didn't seem to notice any little coolness on the part of his followers,
3 If there was any coolness,
4 Which there really wasn't,
5 Because everybody just loved Harry,
6 Deep down,
7 [h]In spite of everything,
8 And so they were trying to have the best possible time,
9 [i]In spite of everything,
10 Which was going all right,
11 [j]Until Harry pulled out a special surprise,
12 Of a kind none of the followers had experienced before.
13 Of course, Harry, being Harry, had to make a little [k]ceremony out of it, saying,
14 [l]**There's a good chance we might not be together for too much longer,**
15 **In fact, a very good chance,**
16 [m]**And so I would like to take this opportunity to give you something to remember me by,**
17 [n]**Something that will help you follow my way more easily.**
18 [o]And the followers acted all downhearted at the news that they might not be with Harry much longer,
19 [p]But Harry kept on smiling and called for the waiter,
20 [q]To whom he whispered some instructions,
21 [r]Which were swiftly obeyed,
22 [s]So that in a few minutes' time the waiter returned to give Harry a razor blade and a small mirror,
23 [t]Upon which he placed some small white rocks,
24 [u]Then cut them into little pieces with the razor blade,
25 [v]And pushed the pieces into straight lines on the mirror.
26 [w]As the followers looked on, Harry rolled up a hundred-dollar bill and placed it against one of the lines on the mirror, and inhaled the line through the bill.
27 [x]When he had finished, he leaned back in his chair, saying, **Wow. That's excrement like Mother used to make.**

CHAPTER 43

[y]But the followers weren't familiar with this excrement, and so they asked Harry, "What is the meaning of what you have done? We do not understand, no matter how much we don't think about it."

a. Ira.37.7
b. 46.5
c. 38.31
d. Ext.3.2
e. Vin.68.4
f. Vin.68.5
g. Wil.70.10-11
h. 37.2-3 33.3-10
i. 30.42-46
j. Vin.67.4
k. Ext.13.11
l. Wil.70.14
m. Wil.70.15
n. Wil.70.16
o. Wil.70.17
p. Wil.70.18
q. Wil.70.19
r. Wil.70.20
s. Wil.70.21
t. Wil.70.22
u. Wil.70.23
v. Wil.70.24
w. Wil.70.25
x. Wil.70.26
y. Wil.71.1

2 ªWhereupon Harry replied to them, saying, **Do this in remembrance of me.**
3 ᵇLook upon your own face in the mirror,
4 ᶜWhich is the face of yourself alone,
5 ᵈAs we all are alone in this vast meaningless universe.
6 ᵉThen cover the face in the mirror with little white rocks,
7 ᶠWhich are the slayers of thought, and your ᵍconsolation for all things which may trouble you.
8 ʰWhen you have done this, take a razor blade,
9 ⁱWhich is as deadly and useful as ʲblame itself,
10 ᵏAnd cut the rocks into lines, so that the slayer of thought may serve you and your ˡdesire,
11 ᵐThen roll some money in your fingers,
12 ⁿBecause, outside of yourself, ºmoney is the only certainty one can have.
13 ᵖFinally, as you inhale, remember me,
14 qFor the briefest possible instant,
15 ʳWhich should not be too hard,
16 ˢBecause when you have finished inhaling, you will no longer remember me,
17 ᵗOr anything else.
18 ᵘWith great seriousness, the followers did what Harry instructed,
19 ᵛAnd stopped thinking about anything at all for quite a while.
20 ʷThen Harry spoke again, saying, **One of you will identify me to the authorities this night,**
21 ˣBut that's okay,

22 ʸBecause I can take the heat.
23 ᶻThe rest of you will deny that you ever knew me,
24 ᵃᵃOr ever rode on my Learjet,
25 ᵇᵇOr did anything else with me,
26 ᶜᶜBut that's okay too,
27 ᵈᵈFor I know that none of you will ever ᵉᵉbetray me.

CHAPTER 44

At these words of Harry's, the followers were all a bit disconcerted,
2 ᶠᶠAnd tried making various excuses to leave,
3 ᵍᵍBut only one of them managed to get away,
4 By borrowing a waiter's jacket,
5 Which must have been set up beforehand,
6 ʰʰBecause he came back within twenty minutes or so,
7 ⁱⁱAccompanied by about three dozen cops,
8 ʲʲWho waited for the follower in the waiter's jacket to identify Harry,
9 And then seized Harry,
10 And ᵏᵏcuffed him,
11 And dragged him away,
12 ˡˡWithout arresting anyone else at all,
13 For some reason.

CHAPTER 45

Afterwards, the followers went back to the hotel,
2 And talked about what they should do.
3 Some of them thought that maybe they should go to the jail,
4 And try to bail Harry out,
5 For appearance's sake.

a. Wil.71.2
b. Wil.71.3
c. Wil.71.4
d. Wil.71.5 F&J.2.1-3
e. Wil.71.6
f. Wil.71.7
g. Psp.4.2
h. Wil.71.8
i. Wil.71.9
j. Mawr.14.14-17
k. Wil.71.10
l. Wil.29.1-6
m. Wil.71.11
n. Wil.71.12
o. Psong.8.1-11
p. Wil.71.14
q. Wil.71.15
r. Wil.71.16
s. Wil.71.17
t. Wil.71.18
u. Wil.71.19
v. Wil.71.20 Vin.67.9-17
w. Wil.71.21
x. Wil.71.22
y. Wil.71.23
z. Wil.71.24
aa. Wil.71.25
bb. Wil.71.26
cc. Wil.71.27
dd. Wil.71.28
ee. Wil.42.6-15
ff. Wil.72.2
gg. Wil.72.4
hh. Wil.72.5
ii. Wil.72.6
jj. Wil.72.9-10
kk. Wil.72.11
ll. Wil.72.14

6 Others thought they should sit tight at the hotel,

7 And leave Harry strictly alone,

8 [a]For the same reason.

9 [b]And all of them remembered all the things Harry had said about serving two masters,

10 But it didn't seem to help any,

11 [c]And so they got drunk instead,

12 [d]And the night kind of slipped away.

CHAPTER 46

[e]As it turned out, Harry was indicted,

2 [f]And tried with extraordinary speed,

3 [g]And convicted by a jury that never left the box,

4 [h]Because there was extremely convincing evidence from Harry's pilot that Harry knew all about the big shipment of illegal drugs from South America,

5 [i]Not to mention a tape recording of Harry getting the news of its arrival on his CB,

6 And then Harry's [j]lawyer sputtered for a while about entrapment,

7 And that was about it.

CHAPTER 47

[k]When it came time for sentencing, the judge was very very hard on Harry,

2 And called him a [l]disgrace,

3 And an unspeakable parasite,

4 [m]And the lowest of the low,

5 [n]And then sentenced him to prison,

6 [o]For life,

7 [p]Without possibility of parole.

8 When he heard this, though, Harry merely smiled and said to the judge, **I know everything,**

a. Vin.74.9
b. 30.22-46
c. Vin.27.5 & 16.2
d. Vin.46.9-11
e. Wil.74.1
f. Wil.74.2
g. Wil.74.3-4
h. Vin.74.2-3
i. 40.7-9
j. Penn.4.8-10
k. Wil.74.5-9
l. 36.26-27
m. Jeff.24.8 Ext.53.25-27
n. Wil.74.10
o. Wil.74.11
p. Wil.74.12
q. Jeff.24.22-23
r. Wil.13.10-11
s. Ira.43.5-14
t. Ed.47.20
u. 38.22-27
v. Psong.23.1-6
w. 45.6
x. Wil.75.1-2
y. Wil.75.3
z. 4.7
aa. 36.25-27
bb. Psong.53.6-9

9 **Because I am the [q]One,**

10 **[r]And you know not what you do,**

11 **At all.**

12 At these final words from Harry, the judge turned a little pale,

13 [s]For some reason,

14 And ordered him removed from the courtroom,

15 By big ugly bailiffs,

16 Armed with [t]guns.

CHAPTER 48

[u]The followers thought that maybe they should leave town the day that Harry was sentenced and carted off to prison,

2 But then again they thought maybe they shouldn't,

3 Because maybe they would receive a call from a [u]friendly uncle or something,

4 And maybe he would have some good news about certain [v]financial matters,

5 Or something like that.

6 [w]Finally, they decided to sit tight at the hotel for a little longer,

7 And so none of them were on hand to see Harry,

8 [x]Dressed up in leg irons and handcuffs,

9 [y]Crawl into the paddy wagon and set out for his new life,

10 In prison.

CHAPTER 49

[z]But if you're really the [z]One,

2 [aa]No setback is ever permanent,

3 [bb]And nobody can ever win out over you for long,

4 Which is what the followers found out,

5 In less than three days' time.

CHAPTER 50

If you're really the One, in fact,

2 [a]It's completely amazing how much you can get accomplished in three days' time,

3 As the followers found out,

4 [b]Just by sitting tight at the hotel,

5 And listening to the news on the radio,

6 Which turned into a full-time job,

7 Because there was a lot of news.

CHAPTER 51

The first news they heard,

2 On the radio,

3 Was that a prominent [c]judge had suffered a fatal heart attack in his home on the [d]Main Line,

4 A heart attack caused by the three bullets that entered his chest,

5 At very close range.

CHAPTER 52

The next news they heard,

2 [e]On the radio,

3 Sounded like a dreadful coincidence,

4 Because it turned out that the followers' [f]friendly uncle in Atlantic City had also suffered a heart attack,

5 [g]Of the same sort,

6 Right there in the middle of his [h]olive oil warehouse,

7 Which so distressed his six bodyguards that they also died from heart trouble,

8 [i]Of the same sort.

---

a. Ed.60.17
b. 45.6
  48.6
c. 47.8-13
d. Wil.59.1-5
e. 51.2
f. Psong.55.1
g. 51.4-5
h. Psong.57.1
i. 52.5
j. Ira.44.1-4
k. 52.8
l. 29.3-7
m. 46.4
n. 52.8
o. Psp.3.9
p. 41.8
q. 42.5
  Vin.70.3
r. 42.7

CHAPTER 53

The next news that came over the radio almost gave the followers a heart attack,

2 Because the announcer said that Harry had [j]escaped from prison,

3 After several of his guards suffered [k]heart attacks,

4 Which made the followers suspect that Philadelphia wasn't such a great city for hearts,

5 [l]In spite of the big plastic job at the Institute.

CHAPTER 54

After that, the followers expected to hear that a bunch of Harry's followers were in imminent danger of having a heart attack at their hotel,

2 But instead they heard that Harry had gotten away,

3 With his whole fortune intact,

4 In a Learjet,

5 To an unknown destination.

6 And they also heard that the only one the cops had managed to capture was Harry's [m]pilot,

7 [n]Who had had a heart attack of his own,

8 On the runway,

9 [o]Which just shows how lucky you can be if you really are the One,

10 Because it turned out that Harry had brought another pilot along,

11 [p]Just in case.

CHAPTER 55

By this time, the followers were very extremely nervous,

2 [q]And they couldn't help remembering how much they had always liked Harry,

3 [r]Deep down,

459

4 Even when it didn't seem that way,
5 ªAnd words cannot express how relieved they were when they actually heard from Harry,
6 A little more than a week later,
7 ᵇBy Long Distance,
8 ᶜFrom his new home in Rio.
9 They were especially relieved when he told them, one by one, how proud he was of them,
10 ᵈAnd how he had always

a. Vin.75.9
b. Ext.3.6
c. Vin.75.11
  Wil.77.8
d. 43.27
  Wil.71.28
e. Psp.3.4
f. 34.25

known that they would never betray him,
11 No matter who got hurt.

CHAPTER 56

ᵉAnd by all these things which had happened, the followers no longer had any doubt that Harry was the One,
2 And committed themselves to following his Way,
3 Because it obviously worked,
4 ᶠLike nobody's business.

THE GOOD WORD ACCORDING TO
ULT. IRA

CHAPTER 1

ªThere are people who say there was never a messiah named Harry,
2 And that ᵇno one came along to show us the way to be,
3 ᶜWhich is okay,
4 ᵈBecause everyone's allowed to not believe in Harry,
5 ᵉJust like they're allowed to not believe in anything else,
6 Except that there is photographic evidence of Harry,
7 On film,
8 Not to mention snapshots and color prints and slides,
9 Which should prove something,
10 ᶠUnless it doesn't.

CHAPTER 2

The ᵍparents of Harry made home movies,
2 Which show him as a little boy.
3 In these movies, you can see

a. Jeff.13.1-7
b. 24.9
c. Lies.10.11
d. Boul.18.9-13
e. Vin.63.15-16
f. Psay.5A.41
g. Vin.57.5-6
h. Psay.5A.32
i. Wil.13.10-11

him playing with his dog,
4 Which ran away eventually,
5 Because Harry forgot to feed him,
6 And just goes to show you,
7 ʰHarry was only human,
8 ⁱA lot like you and me.

CHAPTER 3

There is also a snapshot of Harry's room,
2 When he was about twelve,
3 Which maybe explains why it's so messy,
4 Although it doesn't quite explain the poster of a bimbo with a staple in her navel,
5 Except that Harry must have been precocious,
6 As we might have guessed.
7 And does it really matter that he didn't make his bed,
8 Or put his dirty clothes in the hamper,
9 Or take the dirty plates and glasses off his desk,

10 Or pick that moldy pizza off his rug,
11 Or empty his ashtray,
12 Or turn off his TV,
13 Or hang up his phone,
14 Or deposit that wad of bills in the bank?
15 And does it matter that he is sitting there,
16 In the middle of the mess,
17 [a]Giving us the finger?
18 [b]After all, he was only a boy,
19 [c]And his parents didn't seem to mind,
20 So why should we care,
21 [d]And what business is it of ours anyway?

CHAPTER 4

There is a very nice picture of Harry taken in high school,
2 Where the Drama Club picked him to play [e]Henry Drummond,
3 For some reason,
4 Which explains why he is wearing suspenders,
5 And a collarless shirt,
6 And white hair,
7 And a scornful look on his face.

CHAPTER 5

Harry's yearbook picture is also very nice,
2 And shows him grinning into the camera,
3 [f]Wearing a jacket and tie,
4 [g]Just like everyone else.
5 It also looks like Harry was very active in extracurricular activities,
6 At least for the first couple of [h]years,
7 Because he has lots of stuff listed,
8 Including Cross Country 1,
9 [i]Camera Club 1,
10 [j]Yearbook 1,
11 [k]School Newspaper 1,
12 [l]Glee Club 1,
13 [m]Marching Band 1,
14 [n]Debate Club 1,
15 Drama Club 1 and [o]4,
16 [p]Chemistry Club 2, 3, and 4,
17 [q]And Spanish Club 1, 2, 3, and 4,
18 Not to mention the fact that he was voted "Most Likely to Escape to South America."

CHAPTER 6

The parents of Harry made a home movie of his graduation from high school,
2 Which shows him getting his diploma from the [r]principal,
3 Who looks unhappy for some reason,
4 [s]Although Harry is grinning,
5 Probably because he is so proud of graduating from high school,
6 Which he must be,
7 [t]Or why would he grin like that?
8 The movie also shows the graduation party at Harry's house,
9 Which looks like an average sort of house in the [u]suburbs,
10 [v]Just like Beaver Cleaver lived in,
11 [w]With a five-year-old station wagon in the driveway,
12 Parked right next to a brand-new [x]Pontiac GTO,
13 [y]Which must be Harry's graduation present,
14 Because you can see Harry's parents giving him the keys,
15 And smiling like crazy,
16 Even though [z]Harry's dad doesn't quite succeed in getting the beer out of his son's hand,
17 And even though [aa]Harry's

a. Wil.3.2
b. 2.7
c. Rat.7.1-11
d. Al.4.6
e. Pnot.40.1-5
f. Psay.5H.8
g. Ed.61.17
h. Vin.9.1-7 Rat.8.12-14
i. 45.17
j. Ned.36.17-19
k. Ext.27.4
l. Yks.144.1-20
m. Forg.2.1-4 & 2.9-10
n. Wil.35.1 & 36.1-3
o. 4.1-2
p. Ext.52.16
q. Vin.50.8-9
r. Ed.53.3
s. 5.2
t. Vin.9.9 Psp.2.3
u. Hill.S.5-6
v. Ed.34.10-11
w. Hill.S.7
x. Hill.S.8
y. Wil.13.15-21
z. Ed.30.7
aa. Ed.30.5

mom doesn't quite succeed in getting a kiss,

18 ªBecause Harry is busy kissing a girl instead,

19 Until they both jump in the car and drive away into the sunset,

20 Without a backward glance,

21 Which is the end of the movie,

22 And all we know about Harry's graduation.

a. *35.4-5*
b. *6.12*
c. *Mall.9.12-16*
d. *2.7*
e. *Ext.25.8*
f. *Frog.26.16*
g. *Vin.70.12*
h. *8.13*

CHAPTER 7

Harry's insurance company also has a photograph of the ᵇGTO,

2 Which looks like it sideswiped a parked car,

3 Or maybe scraped against the side of a building,

4 Or possibly slid off the road into a ditch,

5 Or something along those lines.

6 The photo is dated early in June of the same year as Harry's graduation,

7 Which couldn't have been too long after the party,

8 ᶜAlthough we don't really know what happened,

9 And it can't possibly matter anyway,

10 ᵈBecause boys will be boys,

11 After all.

CHAPTER 8

For some reason, there are very few photographs of Harry for the next couple of years,

2 Which is when he was in college,

3 Where he may or may not have been having a nice time,

4 Which is hard to tell,

5 Because the only picture we have was taken on his very last day there.

6 Here you can see him holding what appears to be a diploma,

7 Given him by one of his friends,

8 ᵉAlthough it isn't a diploma,

9 Because in spite of all the fancy lettering, it says that Harry has been honored with the title ᶠ"Persona Non Grata,"

10 And is now perfectly free to collect all his belongings,

11 And go take a draft physical.

12 But Harry appears to be enjoying himself,

13 Which you can tell by the girl on each arm,

14 And the open bottle of ᵍJack Daniel's in his holster,

15 Under his poncho,

16 Not to mention his little cigar,

17 Unless it isn't a cigar at all,

18 Which is hard to tell for sure,

19 Because he's lighting it with blazing dollar bills,

20 Which make it hard to see the cigar,

21 Or his face,

22 Or the look in his eye,

23 Although the picture seems to say it all.

CHAPTER 9

This next picture must have been taken only a few days or weeks later,

2 Because one of the ʰgirls is the same,

3 Although the other isn't,

4 Because it is Harry,

5 Looking quite elegant in a long white dress,

6 And high heels,

7 And a long platinum blond wig,

8 And huge falsies,

9 And enough makeup to choke a horse,

10 So that you almost wouldn't know it was Harry,

11 ᵃExcept for the bottle of Jack Daniel's,

12 ᵇAnd the cigar,

13 ᶜAnd what his hand is doing inside the other girl's bodice.

14 Of course, the explanation for Harry's outfit is quite obvious,

15 Because there's a huge banner over Harry's head,

16 ᵈWhich reads, 'Congratulations on Failing Your Physical,'

17 And says it all.

CHAPTER 10

This next sequence is really quite interesting,

2 Because it seems to show Harry working at a job,

3 Which makes it a rare item in the annals of Harry,

4 A unique item, in fact,

5 Especially when you see that his employer is a ᵉbeadle named Bub,

6 Who is screeching in the middle of the frame,

7 While Harry tries to adjust the feedback somewhere off to the right of the stage,

8 Although what Harry is doing isn't helping,

9 Because the awful sound isn't feedback at all,

10 But the beadle's voice,

11 Which is pointing out that times have changed,

12 And if you're looking for answers,

13 ᶠBe careful to inhale deeply,

a. 8.14
b. 8.16
c. 3.6
d. 8.11
*   Wil.13.29-32*
e. Vin.3.12
*   Ed.71.20*
f. Wil.71.14
g. Psp.3.7
h. 13.7
*   Ed.77.5-14*
i. Vin.11.13-16
j. Ed.23.1-11
k. Al.4.7
l. Psp.3.8
m. 11.4
n. Ned.29.24
o. 12.13

14 ᵍBecause . . .

15 And this is where Harry's meddling really fouls things up, so you can't hear anything recognizable for a while,

16 Until right at the very end it gets a little bit better,

17 ʰAnd you can hear the beadle telling us to drink a lot of Rolling Rocks,

18 Or something like that,

19 Which must be good advice,

20 Because Harry has quit messing with the sound equipment,

21 ⁱAnd is writing furiously in a little notebook.

CHAPTER 11

Our next shot of Harry consists of video footage,

2 ʲProvided by a television station in Chicago,

3 Where lots of people showed up to do their civic duty at the Democratic National Convention,

4 Including lots of cops wearing helmets and shields and ᵏnice long truncheons,

5 ˡAnd lots of young people wearing beards and picket signs with ᵐnice long handles,

6 And Harry,

7 Who you can just see at the extreme right-hand side of the frame,

8 Doing a brisk business at his little booth,

9 Under a sign that says ⁿ'Human Feces for Sale—Pre-Bagged and Ready for Throwing,'

10 Which maybe explains why Harry is wearing plastic ᵒcoveralls,

11 [a]And smoking a much larger
cigar than usual.

CHAPTER 12

Everyone will recognize the
location of this next footage,
2 Which must have been taken
with Super 8 movie film,
3 Because the colors are quite
vivid,
4 Including the vivid brown of
the [b]mud,
5 And the vivid white of all
those naked flabby bellies,
6 And the vivid red of everybody's eyes,
7 Not to mention the vivid blue
of Harry's school bus,
8 Which really sets off the stark
white lettering down the side,
9 Not to mention the arrows
pointing toward the back door of
the bus,
10 Where Harry is taking in
[c]cash by the handful,
11 Which maybe has something
to do with the cryptic message
spelled out by the white lettering,
12 Namely, 'For Sale—[d]Pass-
ports to Woodstock Nation! Enjoy a Safe and Happy Trip to
[e]Paradise!'
13 This time, Harry is wearing
white cotton [f]coveralls,
14 And he looks happier than he
did in Chicago,
15 Probably because of all the
peace and love that's going on,
16 In all that [g]mud.

CHAPTER 13

And now we enter the phase
of Harry's life that everybody knows about,
2 [h]Beginning with his famous

a. 8.16-17
b. Mes.2.8-9
c. Psong.1.1
d. Psong.6.12
e. Cen.10.1-5
f. 11.10
g. Mes.3.6
h. Wil.5.1
i. Wil.5.3
j. Psp.3.15
k. Ann.2.21
l. Wil.6.2-3
m. Vin.31.5
n. 13.2
o. Ned.9.4
p. Wil.44.1-3 Vin.31.1
q. Dav.56.15

appearance at a rock concert in
California,
3 Where somebody took some
16-millimeter color footage of
Harry backstage,
4 Wearing his [i]white suit,
5 And clowning with the road-
ies,
6 Which must be why he is
wearing a red, white, and blue
top hat,
7 [j]And squirting a bottle of
Rolling Rock over some girls in
T-shirts,
8 Who are giggling,
9 And doing jumping jacks,
10 [k]And pulling up their T-
shirts every few seconds,
11 To give Harry an eyeful.
12 But everyone is entitled to a
little fun every once in a while,
13 Even if you're the One,
14 Which Harry definitely was,
15 [l]Because a few minutes later
he went out and knocked them
dead,
16 According to all accounts.

CHAPTER 14

There is also a photograph of
Harry inside the cabin of his
[m]Learjet,
2 Which must have been taken
shortly after his boffo performance in [n]California,
3 Because there's a banner
across the top of the cabin that
features a bad [o]pun on the name
of an [p]Indiana university,
4 And seems to be declaring
Harry's intention to visit this
particular institution of higher
learning,
5 Or bust,
6 Although this last part of the
message is being acted out by a
[q]young lady,

7 ^aWith her T-shirt pulled up,
8 While Harry seems to be try-ing to persuade her ^btwin sister to act out the first part of the message,
9 ^cUnless he's really just help-ing her adjust her belt,
10 Or something like that.

CHAPTER 15

The next footage we have was taken in Boston,
2 ^dIn the front yard of an ancient American university,
3 Where Harry seems perfectly at ease,
4 With his bullhorn,
5 And his ^ewhite suit,
6 And a crowd of eager listen-ers,
7 Who keep staring at the beau-tiful ^ftwin sisters standing on ei-ther side of Harry,
8 Wearing crimson sweatshirts with some sort of message printed on them in ^gLatin.
9 And although it's hard to make out all the words because of the static,
10 It's still possible to under-stand what Harry is saying,
11 ^hBecause he keeps repeating the same message over and over and over again,
12 Which is, **If you would know the ⁱtruth, come with me,**
13 **Because I am ^jHarry,**
14 **And I own the truth and the way,**
15 **And I can show you how to shoot fish in a ^kbarrel,**
16 **If you will follow me,**
17 **Back to my Learjet.**

CHAPTER 16

There is also some footage that may have been taken a

a. 13.10
b. Dav.56.15
c. 36.2-6
d. Wil.47.1-2
e. 13.4
f. 44.7
g. Hill.1.2-3
h. Boul.26.7-11
i. 15.8
j. Adam.31.5
k. Vin.31.5
   Mawr.3.1-5
   Ned.30.42
l. Vin.52.3
m. Vin.4.19-21
n. Vin.26.1-3
o. Vin.27.2
p. 15.12
q. Vin.27.4
r. Mawr.20.1-7
s. Dav.48.12
t. Ned.2.12-13

few hours later on the Learjet,
2 And maybe a few jereboams of ^lchampagne later too,
3 Because there are a lot of great big empty Moët bottles around,
4 And the camera seems kind of tipsy,
5 Which is why it takes a few tries to figure out what's going on,
6 Until you realize that this is quite a moving and historic scene,
7 Because Harry is ^mwashing the hands of his new followers,
8 ⁿWith fizzy water from little green bottles,
9 While he speaks softly and calmly to each ^oone in turn,
10 Saying, **Let me wash the worst of the grime off your hands,**
11 **Which is necessary if you are going to enjoy your new life with me,**
12 ^p**Because you will not get a chance to lay your hands on the truth,**
13 **Unless they're ^qclean,**
14 **Which seems like a reason-able request to me,**
15 **Because I think they'd even be within their ^rrights to make you shower first,**
16 **Since this is a glamorous and exotic Learjet,**
17 **Streaking toward Malibu,**
18 **And not some grubby mixer,**
19 **At the Sigma Delta Sigma fraternity house.**
20 And one by one, the fol-lowers allow Harry to prepare them for a new life,
21 And if you can stand the mo-tion of the camera, you can iden-tify all of them,
22 Including ^sNed in his ^t"Off

the Capitalist Pigs' T-shirt,

23 And [a]Sam in his [b]'Ho Ho Ho Chi Minh' T-shirt,

24 And [c]Vinnie in his [d]'Woodstock Forever' T-shirt,

25 And [e]Willie in his [f]'Ginsberg for President' T-shirt,

26 And [g]Ira in his [h]'John Wayne Sucks' T-shirt,

27 And [i]Tony in his [j]'Make Love, Not War,' T-shirt,

28 And [k]Jerry in his [l]'Power to the People' T-shirt,

29 And [m]Tom in his [n]'Nuke the Napalmers' T-shirt,

30 And [o]Mort in his [p]'No Free Speech for Imperialists' T-shirt,

31 And [q]Fred in his [r]Hotchfield Prep School T-shirt,

32 And [s]Joe in his [t]'America: Love It or Leave It' T-shirt,

33 And actually, you can even see [u]Lucky standing off to the side,

34 Smiling,

35 In a brand-new [v]three-piece suit.

CHAPTER 17

There is a whole roll of color film taken at [w]Harry's house in Malibu,

2 Where the followers went with Harry immediately after they joined him,

3 But all of them are terribly out of focus,

4 [x]And shot at a bunch of different cockeyed angles,

5 Which makes it very extremely hard to figure out what is going on,

6 Except that it must have been some party,

7 Which all the followers would

a. Dav.57.12
b. Vin.49.5
   Forg.2.12
c. Dav.57.36
d. 12.12
e. Dav.57.20
f. Yks.152.18
g. Dav.57.24
h. Dav.51.6-10
i. Dav.57.28
j. Hill.L.1-7
   Mall.15.6-7
k. Dav.57.6
l. Carl.10.1-11
m. Dav.57.8
n. Wil.9.1-2
o. Dav.57.22
p. Wil.15.3
q. Dav.57.10
r. Main.36.10-11
s. Dav.57.32
t. Ann.18.21
u. Dav.57.14
v. Wil.5.3
w. Wil.45.17-18
x. 16.4
y. Mall.6.20-25
z. Ned.21.1-7
aa. Psong.52.1-2
bb. 15.4
cc. Dav.58.9
dd. Dav.54.15

probably be delighted to tell you about,

8 If they [y]remembered any of it,

9 Which they really don't,

10 Except that they had a really really good time.

CHAPTER 18

After the Malibu stuff, there are maybe a dozen rolls of color film shot during the next couple of months,

2 Showing Harry and the followers [z]on the road,

3 Partying on the Learjet,

4 And riding in limousines,

5 And looking [aa]hung over and uncomfortable on lots of different speaking platforms,

6 In lots and lots of different ivy-covered quadrangles,

7 Where there are lots of shots of Harry in his white suit,

8 Speaking through his [bb]bullhorn,

9 Surrounded by [cc]Angels,

10 While crowds of students listen,

11 More and more enthusiastically,

12 To what Harry has to say.

13 There is one that stands out in particular,

14 Because there is a very attractive young lady on the platform with Harry,

15 Shaking his hand,

16 And trading her 'End the War NOW!' T-shirt for the one that Harry is holding out to her,

17 Which says, 'Property of Harry: Malibu, USA,'

18 And [dd]Marisa looks so charming and buoyant and happy up there with Harry,

19 That it's hard to believe she is no longer with us.

CHAPTER 19

All the best footage of Harry was taken in Philadelphia, of course,

2 Where it so happened [a]one of the followers assembled a crack camera crew,

3 And accompanied Harry on many of his most exciting expeditions,

4 Except for that first day,

5 Which is known as [b]Pretzel Friday,

6 When Harry rode into the city in a white [c]Eldorado,

7 [d]And all of the followers had way too much beer to drink,

8 Which is why there is only this one blurry snapshot,

9 Showing some of the followers desecrating the [e]Liberty Bell,

10 While Harry explains it all to the cops,

11 [f]With a huge wad of bills in his hand.

CHAPTER 20

One of the most dramatic sequences in the filmed record of Harry got taken in the very first session with the camera crew,

2 Because they celebrated their lucrative new assignment pretty freely in Harry's hotel suite,

3 And then started brainstorming about what would make a really great scene in the documentary they thought they were making,

4 And so one of them suggested climbing all the way up to [g]Billy Penn's hat,

5 On top of [h]City Hall,

6 And having Harry say a few

a. 16.26
b. Wil.65.2-4
c. Vin.37.1-6
d. Vin.37.7
e. Ned.27.6-9
f. Psong.43.4
g. Psay.5R.9
h. 21.3

words with the whole city laid out below.

7 Everybody thought this over for another bottle or so,

8 Until Harry suddenly stood up and said, **Let's do it.**

9 **It's a pretty beautiful city when there isn't any sun to screw up the view.**

10 And so one of the bravest of the followers and all the conscious members of the camera crew piled into Harry's Silver Cloud,

11 And rode down to City Hall,

12 Where they watched some TV in the back while one of the Angels scouted out ways and means,

13 Until he returned without any explanations,

14 And ushered everybody inside the building,

15 And then into an elevator,

16 So that there was only a little climbing to be done when they got onto the roof,

17 Which Harry led the way on,

18 Because he really didn't seem to care at all about how high up they all were,

19 And what a bummer it would be to fall all the way to the ground.

CHAPTER 21

And so it happened that the crew got some really fabulous footage of Harry,

2 Standing right next to Billy Penn,

3 In the very center of the City of Philadelphia,

4 With the moon making everything very bright,

5 In all directions.

6 And Harry beheld the view

for several minutes without saying a word,

7 Until some of the crew began to think that he might be paralyzed with acrophobia or something,

8 Except that he suddenly laughed out loud,

9 At the top of his lungs,

10 And said to the statue, **Truly this is my city, Billy,**

11 **And in a few years they will want to knock you off your clay feet,**

12 **And replace you with a statue of me instead,**

13 **Because the ^aQuaker heart of Philadelphia is only a memory,**

14 **With all its dreams of ^bpeace and ^cjustice and ^dtolerance and harmony,**

15 **Which were only stupid ^edelusions,**

16 **Because in spite of all your fine talk,**

17 **The ^fheart of Philadelphia is really just like mine,**

18 **And the beat of Philadelphia is really just like that of some third-rate bar band,**

19 **Which is ^gloud and obnoxious and ^hout of time,**

20 **And going absolutely nowhere at a frantic pace,**

21 ⁱ**Because it's too hard to learn how to play music,**

22 **And so much fun to just make noise instead.**

23 **Yes, my great big heart goes out to every part of ^jPhiladelphia,**

24 **And all its great citizens,**

25 **Because from here I can see the browned-out lights of all their ^kneighborhoods,**

26 ^l**Including the Broad Streeters, and the Pennsylva-**

a. *Ned.53.4*
b. *Ed.76.6-12*
c. *Penn.9.11*
d. *Hill.T.6-7*
e. *Yks.154.33*
f. *Ned.29.3-9*
g. *Ed.67.3*
h. *Ned.16.12-13*
i. *33.1-3*
j. *Wil.53.1-4*
k. *Wil.53.5*
l. *Wil.53.6-8*
m. *Psong.43.1*
n. *Wil.31.18-22*
o. *Ext.14.7-9*
p. *Forg.14.6-10*
q. *Gods.6.20-22*
   Adam.36.5-10
r. *Kens.12.21-26*

nians, and the Brewers, and the Villanovans, and the Richmondites, and the Kensingtonians, and the Hillites, and the Manayunkians, and the Camdenites, and the Mainliners, and the Southlanders, and the Josephians, and the Templites, and the Boulevardiers, and the Textilians, and Passyunkians, the Cynwydians, and the Hahnemaniacs, and the Jeffersonians, and the Forgers, and the Prussians, and the Glensiders, and the Haysites, and the Jenkintonians, and the Museumites, and the Narberthians, and even the Hallites,

27 **And all of them are ^mmine,**

28 **Before they even know who I am,**

29 **Because they will leap like trout for my ⁿTrinity,**

30 **Which offers everything,**

31 **And demands nothing in return,**

32 ^o**Which is a deal no other messiah has ever proffered the race of Mankind.**

33 And then he said, in the dialect of his homeland, **Such a deal! Bee-uty-full!**

34 And turning back to the statue, he said, **Want to jump down now, Billy?**

35 **Or do you want to go down the ^phard way,**

36 **Looking up at all the ugly new ^qmonuments to my way that will be built in the years to come,**

37 **Which will coldly condescend to you from a million plate-glass eyes,**

38 ^r**And a thousand faceless faces made of steel?**

39 Then Harry turned suddenly

back to the camera and said, **Do you have enough footage?**
40 **Have you had enough fun for one night?**
41 **I'm** [a]**tired now,**
42 **And I think I'd like to go back to my room,**
43 **And try to get some sleep.**

CHAPTER 22

Most of the Philadelphia footage is much more low-key than the City Hall stuff,
2 Because Harry was really pretty much of an easygoing kind of guy,
3 And he liked to go hang out in some public place,
4 [b]And just talk with whoever came along,
5 Which gave the camera crew lots of great little clips,
6 Because Harry always had a comeback for everything,
7 Even when he was three sheets to the wind,
8 [c]Which he frequently was,
9 Although you'd never guess it from the clips,
10 Which must have something to do with him being the One,
11 Or something like that.

CHAPTER 23

For example, Harry was hanging out one day in front of a diner in the [d]Northeast,
2 Just north of the Roosevelt Boulevard,
3 Right next to someone who was collecting money to fight some [e]awful childhood disease,
4 And the [f]charity worker turned to Harry and said, "From what I hear about you, it would be pointless to ask you for a donation,"

a. *Psong.53.1-4*
b. *Ned.14.16*
c. *Psong.50.1-5*
d. *Wil.56.1-6*
e. *Jeff.16.4*
f. *Dav.54.12*
g. *Dav.51.12*
h. *Wil.27.6-10*
i. *Carl.10.12-13*
j. *Wil.41.8-9*

5 Whereupon Harry replied to her in a flash, saying, **On the contrary, madam,**
6 **I would be delighted to give you a donation,**
7 **Because the more of them you save, the more who will grow up to follow my way,**
8 **Which is why this** [g]**Angel at my elbow will now give you one thousand dollars in cash.**
9 And then the woman was disconcerted, and in her confusion sought to argue with Harry, saying, "What makes you so sure that the ones we work so hard to save will be lost to your way? [h]Truly I would give up now if I thought that would be the outcome."
10 At this, Harry smiled and held out his hand to the woman,
11 Who took it reluctantly,
12 And tears formed in her eyes as he answered her question, saying, **In these days of my way, the only strength we can give our children is the** [i]**rights due and payable on account of their weakness, whatever it is,**
13 **Because strength born of strength is too frightening to others,**
14 **And raises up** [j]**targets for blame.**
15 **I ask you, who in this Most Chosen Nation will prosper the more?**
16 **Will it be the child who fights courageously to overcome hardship and suffering, without asking for special dispensations and endless forgiveness, and without burying others under a great mountain of self-pitying complaints?**
17 **Or will it be the child who draws up a long list of all his**

infirmities and failings and disadvantages,

18 ᵃAnd then demands accommodation from everyone he encounters in life with the absolute certainty of one who knows his rights?

19 And so I say to you, if it is your aim to reduce the needless suffering that accompanies the bad deal we call life,

20 Then you cannot in good conscience ask your children to seek out the additional hardship and suffering which will befall those who ᵇscorn my way.

21 In what ᶜuniverse would that make any sense?

22 And with the tears running down her cheeks, the woman said, "I cannot best you with words, and so I will not argue with you further, but I do wish to know what manner of man you are,

23 "You who speak so gently of such horrors."

24 And then Harry leaned down and kissed her, so that she was startled by his tenderness,

25 And said to her, **Madam, I am no manner of man at all,**

26 ᵈ**But only an ape in a white suit,**

27 ᵉ**Like all the rest of the apes you choose to call your fellow man,**

28 **If you would but scratch the ᶠsurface of them,**

29 **As you have scratched the surface of Harry.**

30 "May God grant you peace," said the woman, ᵍ"for I believe that you suffer more than any I know."

31 Whereupon Harry smiled a

---

a. Mawr.15.11-18
b. Wil.41.10-14
c. Swar.10.6-7
d. Ned.24.4-11
Psp.2.5
e. Apes.2.6
f. Frog.30.9-10
g. 38.14
h. Ext.25.7-9
i. Al.4.16
j. Psp.3.15
k. Vin.73.8
l. Psong.43.3

---

farewell smile to her and turned to the cameraman, asking, **Did you get that?**

32 And when the cameraman assured him that he had gotten it, Harry laughed and said, **Am I slick or what?**

CHAPTER 24

Another day, Harry was hanging out in Rittenhouse Square,

2 Where all the pseudo-intellectuals used to walk their dogs,

3 And it so happened that a man walking a Great Dane came up to Harry and said,

4 "I would just like to know who appointed you the savior of the Most Chosen Nation on Earth?

5 "For I have heard you speak on more than one occasion,

6 ʰ"And I have never heard you cite the lexicon of knowledge that has so informed you about contemporary values and mores, whether it be rooted in the books you have written or the degrees you have received,

7 "Nor have I heard you explain by whose authority you make such simplistic remarks about the complex issues our society confronts today."

8 Then Harry laughed and replied to the man, saying, **In short, if I may summarize your views, your question is, ⁱ"Who am I to say?"**

9 At this the man nodded, and so Harry continued, saying, ʲ**I am no one,**

10 ᵏ**And I speak with no authority of any kind,**

11 ˡ**Except that of a man who**

is richer than your wildest dreams at less than half your age,

12 ᵃAnd who has his own place in Malibu,

13 And who, if he so chose, could buy the entire building in which you reside on ᵇRittenhouse Square,

14 And throw you and your ᶜdog ᵈHamlet out into the street.

15 Thereupon did the man turn pale and exclaim to Harry, "How did you know that my dog is named Hamlet?"

16 And then Harry waved his hand in dismissal of his feat, and said, **You may as well ask how I knew what you were going to say before you said it,**

17 **Or how I knew that in speaking to you, I was not only addressing one of the great ᵉpseudo-intellectuals of Rittenhouse Square,**

18 ᶠ**But one of the most ardent followers of my way.**

19 **Now run along, good sir,**

20 **And may your certainty remain with you all the days of your life.**

21 And when the man had gone, the follower commanding the camera crew turned to Harry in wonder and said, ᵍ"How did you know that the dog's name was Hamlet? Truly this has been a marvel to behold."

22 But Harry just threw back his head and laughed, saying, **I could claim that I have 20-10 vision into the souls of men,**

23 **But I know that it would make you more comfortable if I said that I have 20-10 vision into the collars of dogs,**

a. Vin.34.14
b. 24.1
c. 24.3
d. Pnot.6.1
Brit.31.2
Zig.10.13-21
e. Swar.PS.16-18
& PS.27-30
f. Wil.50.14-20
g. 24.15
h. Swar.27.1-5
i. Frog.23.1-7
j. Adam.43.12-23

24 **Where if you seek with all your heart, you can usually find a nameplate.**

25 But when the film was developed, it was impossible to see if there was a nameplate on the collar or not, since it was ringed all the way around with fearsome spikes, and no tags hung at the dog's throat.

26 And so it happened that the follower again asked Harry about the collar,

27 But this time Harry said shortly, **That is history now,**

28 **And you can make up history from the present as easily as I can.**

29 ʰ**For is this not the principal gift of the education you paid so many dollars to obtain?**

30 **Let us speak no more of it,**

31 **And go have a drink instead.**

CHAPTER 25

On another day, Harry was hanging out in Center City,

2 At a corner booth in a little bar on Sansom Street,

3 Where two businessmen were having lots of ⁱwine with lunch,

4 Until their conversation grew very heated,

5 And they started shouting at each other,

6 About politics.

7 Thereupon, one of the men recognized Harry and said, "I have seen you before,

8 "And so I know that you will back me up,

9 "And tell this baboon that there is no point in all this ʲparanoia about Communism,

10 Which is merely a preposterous game of international [a]chicken invented by the corrupt idiots who run our [b]military [c]industrial complex.''

11 But before Harry could utter even a single word, the other man also called him by name, saying, ''I too know of you, and am confident that you will explain to this nincompoop that the [d]Others of which he is so fond are no better than we are,

12 [e]''And are not always right about everything,

13 ''And are not the helpless victims of absurd macho posturing between the [f]Most Chosen Nation on Earth and the [g]Most Chosen Totalitarian Empire on Earth.''

14 Thereupon did Harry sign to the cameraman to make sure that the event was being recorded,

15 And moved to join the two men at their table, saying, **Indeed, I have it in mind that both of you are right in every particular, and I could not hope to find two gentlemen of greater perspicacity about international affairs.**

16 **For the only test of truth lies in the heart,**

17 **Where we feel what is so,**

18 [h]**And know from birth to trust our own most fleeting and insubstantial opinions,**

19 **No matter how little we have thought about them,**

20 **Or how little information we can claim to possess.**

21 **But we court trouble when we seek to ferret out the contradictions,**

22 **And enforce upon ourselves and others a consistency**

a. *Yks.147.8-21*
b. *Forg.8.11-15*
c. *Adam.42.15*
d. *Oth.1.1-28*
e. *Swar.34.11-22*
f. *Yks.120.1-11*
g. *Russ.24.1-5*
h. *Wil.37.1-7*
i. *Penn.6.1-13*
j. *Wil.35.1*
k. *Kin.1.1-6*
   Apes.1 & 2
   Chuk.21.1-11
   Carl.10.1-13
   Zig.17.1-13
   Al.5.1-10
   F&J.2.1-16
l. *25.18*
m. *15.14*
n. *Swar.10.1-2*

that is not found in our hearts,

23 **And not possible in the universe we inhabit.**

24 **If we would bind others to a consistency that we invent on the spur of the moment to make ourselves feel better,**

25 **That is altogether fine and appropriate,**

26 [i]**Or there would be no excuse for the arrogance of lawyers.**

27 **But if we start believing that there is some great universal consistency that must bind ourselves as well as others,**

28 [j]**Then we risk becoming imprisoned in a continuing thought process that may require us to change our minds continuously,**

29 **And to keep thinking continuously,**

30 **And to keep learning continuously,**

31 **And even to make a practice of challenging our most deeply rooted and unexamined [k]assumptions,**

32 **When all we really want is the comfort of feeling superior to the idiot who is trying to argue against one or more of our [l]unsubstantiated notions.**

33 **I say to you, the only defense against this infernal circle of thought and learning and analysis is the [m]Truth of Harry,**

34 **Which is that there are no contradictions.**

35 [n]**Let me repeat this: There are no contradictions.**

36 **If one of you believes that every ill on this planet is traceable to the conspiracies of the**

ᵃgodless communist totalitarians, including all the ills afflicting the Most Chosen Nation on Earth and even the ills endured by the spineless Others, then that is truth,

37 A truth as unchanging and permanent as your desire to consider no conflicting opinion,

38 And no truer truth exists if it allows you to stop thinking about anything at all, especially the fears and failures of your own private life.

39 ᵇBy the same token, if one of you believes that all the virtue ever created on this earth resides in the noble savages who have so far failed to partake of the accursed bounties promised by the two Most Chosen Evil Empires on Earth, then that too is truth,

40 And ample reason to direct all your energies away from thinking about your own miseries toward the paradise that would exist if the Others could only get their rights.

41 But I urge you not to delve too deeply into the inconsistencies between these two great truths,

42 Both of which I myself believe with heart-pounding conviction, if I may say so,

43 Because the search for consistency can become a thoughtful quest,

44 ᶜWhich is dangerous in the extreme,

45 For if you once embark upon it, the ultimate price is self-examination,

46 ᵈWhich may lead you to ask yourself, "How is it that I

a. *Russ.25.1-13*
b. *Pnot.54.1-5*
c. *Wil.35.1-3*
d. *Brd.6.1-10*
e. *Main.27.1-17*
f. *25.24-25*
g. *Wil.31.3*
h. *Vin.62.6*
i. *Grk.19.2*
j. *Wil.33.5-9*

believe in racial equality, and yet stay up half the night worrying when I hear a rumor that blacks may buy the house next door?"

47 Or: "How is it that I believe so devoutly in the imperative for personal initiative and risk-taking embedded in the capitalist system,

48 ᵉ"And yet ruthlessly suppress all initiative and risk-taking in myself and the frightened little capitalist drones who report to me every day?"

49 As you value me and the word of my way, I beseech you to invoke the curse of consistency and the myth of contradictions only when it offers you the most immediate and superficial ᶠgratification,

50 But do not make of these delusions an altar to sacrifice yourself upon,

51 ᵍFor the perils of thought are unbounded.

52 Does that resolve your conflict?

53 And when Harry had finished, the elder of the two men cocked an eye at Harry and said, "How is it that you speak so persuasively of not thinking about anything at all,

54 "And yet show every evidence of having thought a great deal about many many things?"

55 Then Harry smiled at the man and said, ʰAs you may suspect, I have thought about a great many things,

56 One time for each thing,

57 ⁱAnd I have been satisfied by my answers,

58 ʲWhich means that I need

not think about them any-
more;

59 **Nor do you,**

60 **For this is the nature of my**
ᵃgift to you,

61 **ᵇWhich is the freedom to**
accept my answers,

62 **ᶜBecause they seem like**
they would be hard to refute,

63 **If you thought about them**
at all,

64 **ᵈAnd so why bother?**

65 And then did the men buy
Harry a drink and change the
subject away from international
politics to something more rewarding,

66 Specifically, the legs of the
waitress with the pink shoes,

67 Which were so incredibly
wonderful that everyone agreed
they were a ᵉmiracle,

68 Without thinking about it at
all.

CHAPTER 26

On another day, Harry was
hanging out at a VFW hall
in Port Richmond,

2 When a young man came up
to him and said, "I have heard
you on the ᶠradio,

3 ᵍ"And I get the feeling that
you don't love our country,

4 ʰ"And wouldn't serve it if
they asked you to,

5 "Which is why I think your
head is made of excrement,

6 "And why I would like to
invite you out into the street to
settle it like a man,

7 "Instead of a dirty yellow
coward."

8 Thereupon did ⁱHarry make a
sign to the cameraman to come
back out of the cloakroom,

9 And pick up his camera,

a. 25.57
Grk.26.9-10
b. Psp.3.13
c. Rom.2.19-22
d. Psp.3.14
e. Ed.60.17
f. Ned.32.1-8
g. Rat.10.1-7
h. 9.14-17
i. Psom.1.1-2
j. Wil.13.32-35
Ned.9.6
k. Spic.16.4-5
Brd.7.10-11
Bks.10.1-13
Swar.35.10-
13

10 So that Harry's words could
be properly recorded.

11 When this had been done,
Harry said to the young man, **I**
cannot but admire the cer-
tainty with which you accost
me in this manner,

12 **And I would indeed enjoy**
the experience of trading
blows with you in a parking lot
full of broken glass,

13 **Where one or the other of**
us would surely prevail,

14 **But I would not insult you**
by fighting with you on behalf
of a view that I do not hold,

15 **Because I defer to no one in**
my love of the Most Chosen
Nation on Earth,

16 **Which has achieved a pin-**
nacle of freedom never offered
to any people in history,

17 **Namely, the absolute right**
to be completely self-righteous
about refusing to risk one's life
for anything ever,

18 **Because nowhere else on**
this globe is it possible to
disguise ʲgarden-variety self-
interest as the most exalted
moral principle ever divined
by mortal man,

19 **And get away with it com-**
pletely,

20 **With the possible exception**
of Europe, of course, where
undisguised cowardice has re-
placed all the official religions
as a unanimous faith.

21 **But it is only here, in this**
Most Chosen Nation on Earth,
that it is possible to tolerate
ᵏpetty tyrannies at a vast dis-
tance,

22 **And warmly congratulate**
ourselves for the loftiness of a
morality which sneers at the
primitive millions who seek to

make war against mere [a]despots,

23 Who rarely do anything worse than conquer and rape and torture and maim and mutilate and starve and rob and terrorize peoples so benighted that they have failed to learn the most fundamental precepts of [b]modern civilization,

24 Namely, that war is never an acceptable moral alternative,

25 No matter what,

26 And that [c]no principle can ever be worth the sacrifice of a single life,

27 Especially if that single life got started in the Most Chosen Nation on Earth.

28 And if you think that I am not grateful for this special dispensation from reality, which has so recently been granted me by my country,

29 You are wrong,

30 For this is the ultimate [d]victory of my own generation, to which I belong without apology or excuse,

31 And I shall prove that you are wrong by refusing,

32 With the uttermost in self-righteous indignation,

33 [e]To fight you in the parking lot.

34 But I would be happy to buy you a drink or three.

35 At these words, the youth was entirely mollified,

36 And drank with Harry into the wee hours of the morning.

CHAPTER 27

A nother thing [f]Harry used to enjoy was getting up really early in the morning,

a. Kens.22.16-26
b. Oth.8.1-17
c. Vin.63.19-22
d. Wil.5.7
e. 26.12
f. Psong.47.1
g. Psong.47.2-5
h. Psong.48.5-6
i. Psay.5B.1-13
j. Dav.16.2-7

2 And then going out to do something really silly,

3 Before anybody was completely awake,

4 Which made it easier to get away with something outlandish,

5 And if he did, it put him in a great mood for the rest of the day.

6 Of course, Harry's early-morning pranks were kind of hard on the camera crew,

7 [g]Because they liked to sleep late,

8 Especially after being out really late with [h]Harry the night before,

9 But they also wanted to be there,

10 Because Harry pulled off some good ones,

11 Like the time he got all the [i]Bibles out of the followers' hotel rooms,

12 And started trying to give them away on the street,

13 At six in the morning.

14 Of course, nobody would take one,

15 And then Harry would ask them if they'd read it,

16 And they'd say not lately,

17 Which is when Harry would come back with **I know what you mean.**

18 **I hear there's good stuff in it,**

19 [j]**But I'm waiting for the movie.**

20 Once, though, somebody almost put one over on Harry,

21 Because when he asked if they'd read it,

22 They said right back, "Have you?"

23 But it took Harry only half a second to smile,

24 And then he said, **Nah.**

25 **But I read the** [a]**Cliff Notes.**
26 [b]That's not so bad for six in the morning,
27 [c]And it's all on film.

CHAPTER 28

Sometimes when everybody was all tired out from tramping through all the different [d]neighborhoods in Philadelphia, Harry would hole up in the hotel suite,
2 And invite [e]Marisa over,
3 Who was staying in a separate suite,
4 Because even though she [f]liked Harry,
5 [g]She said she didn't trust him,
6 And personally, I don't think she ever even put out for him,
7 Which has to be some kind of a record,
8 For [h]Harry,
9 Because he still [i]liked her,
10 And she always laughed when he did blackout tapes,
11 Which is what I was getting to,
12 Because when he holed up in the suite, Harry would just make little wisecracks,
13 Sometimes with a prop or two,
14 And then they'd fade to black,
15 And do the next one.
16 Harry used to call it his [j]Bumper Bible,
17 [k]And said he had to anticipate the attention span of the future,
18 Whatever that meant.
19 But the blackouts were funny,
20 And it was nice to just sit there and get wasted,
21 While Harry and the camera guys did all the work.

a. *Wil.14.14*
b. *Psong.47.6*
c. *1.7*
d. *21.26*
e. *18.18-19*
f. *38.8*
g. *38.14*
h. *Psong.46.4-7*
i. *Psom.70.1-5*
j. *Mawr.31.6-10*
k. *Main.5.1-9*
l. *Ann.10.16-17*
m. *Jeff.24.1-4*
n. *Ext.15.1-4*
o. *Mawr.19.4*
p. *Mall.12.10-13*
q. *Hill.H.1-12*
r. *Cen.26.7-9*
s. *Brd.14.7-16*
t. *Psong.26.1-4*
u. *Hill.S.5-11*

CHAPTER 29

For example, Harry did a blackout where he held up a sign saying 'Equl Rihgtes for the ilitareate,'
2 And then he looked into the camera and said, **I am dead serious about whatever it says on this sign.**

CHAPTER 30

Harry did another blackout where he made a halo for himself with a white wire coat hanger,
2 [m]And then said into the camera, **I am the Way and the Life. Whoever follows my way shall get a free coupon for rhinoplasty,**
3 **Someday.**
4 Even Marisa couldn't figure that one out.

CHAPTER 31

Harry did another blackout where he made up a big poster, with a bunch of line items and check boxes,
2 And then he borrowed some horn-rimmed eyeglasses from somebody and turned into the camera, saying,
3 **Your life can be as easy as this [n]list.**
4 **Really.**
5 **Just check them all off, one by one.**
6 [o]**Get born. Check.**
7 **Go to [p]elementary school. Check.**
8 **Go to [q]high school. Check.**
9 **Go to [r]college. Check.**
10 **Get a [s]job. Check.**
11 **Get [t]married to someone you hardly know. Check.**
12 **Buy a house in the [u]suburbs. Check.**

13 ᵃHave a baby. Check.
14 ᵇBuy season tickets to the NBA team in your area. Check.
15 ᶜRun errands for thirty or forty years. Check.
16 After that, you're on your own.

CHAPTER 32

Harry did another blackout with a book of swatches that his tailor had left behind by accident.
2 When he saw them sitting on the table, he grabbed them and held them right up to the camera, saying,
3 Yes, the spectrum of moral certainties in our age is too dazzlingly diverse to deal with,
4 As you can see.
5 For just when you think the ᵈmedium gray will do,
6 Then you are practically seduced by this excellent ᵉdove gray,
7 But no sooner have you made up your mind about this than the superbly understated ᶠcharcoal gray seems to turn your head right around,
8 Until, that is, you encounter this fabulously sophisticated ᵍmedium-light charcoal gray,
9 And then it seems you might never be able to decide precisely which shade of gray is right for you.
10 In fact, that's why I always order white suits myself,
11 Because it's so much easier to assume that I'm always right,
12 About everything,
13 Without thinking about it at all.

a. Cen.26.16-19
b. Psay.5S.22
c. Wht.16
d. Boul.24.1-12
e. 25.39
f. 25.36
g. Boul.20.1-14
h. 21.21
i. Vin.73.9-11
j. 31.2
k. Boul.26.7-11
l. Gods.6.27
m. Psp.3.5
n. Ann.11.1-15
o. Psong.39.5

CHAPTER 33

Harry did another blackout where he played air guitar for a solid two minutes,
2 ʰWith no music playing.
3 ⁱThen he looked into the camera and said, **Mozart never knew it could be this easy to be a genius.**

CHAPTER 34

Harry did another blackout where he put Marisa's cat on his lap,
2 And put the ʲhorn-rims on again,
3 ᵏAnd said, **Science has proven that Man is the only animal which kills for sport.**
4 ˡTrust me.

CHAPTER 35

Harry also did a blackout one time where he convinced Marisa to do a big necking scene with him in front of the camera,
2 ᵐAnd when they broke for air,
3 He turned into the camera and said, **Having thoroughly investigated the issue,**
4 **I would like to announce that women are soft and cuddly,**
5 ⁿ**And smell nice too.**
6 Everybody thought that was pretty good,
7 Except Harry,
8 Who wanted to do it over.

CHAPTER 36

The next time he kissed Marisa for a good long time,
2 And then he turned to the camera and said, **Lots of people say to me, º"Harry, what do women want?"**

3 **And I say to them, "Them, women want attention.**

4 **"That's all they want,**

5 ᵃ**"But they want lots of it."**

6 And then Marisa hit Harry with a pillow,

7 And everybody laughed,

8 And then it was time to go out and visit more neighborhoods.

CHAPTER 37

And so, all in all, the camera crew had a great time with Harry in Philadelphia,

2 Until he started going down to the docks on Delaware Avenue a lot,

3 And didn't want any cameras with him,

4 For some reason,

5 Except on the day he left,

6 When we got some good footage of him waving goodbye to Marisa,

7 From the afterdeck of a ship called the ᵇEl Dorado,

8 Which was going to ᶜSouth America,

9 With ᵈHarry.

10 After that, there wasn't much point in dragging cameras around,

11 With no Harry to shoot,

12 ᵉAnd so a lot of the followers got a little restless,

13 ᶠAnd did things they didn't want any camera to see.

CHAPTER 38

But one day, while Harry was away on his trip,

2 The camera crew convinced Marisa to drink some champagne,

3 ᵍAnd then go on camera to talk about Harry,

4 Which took quite a lot of champagne,

a. Psom.36.1-6
b. Spic.8.3
c. Ned.38.22-25
d. Pnot.34.1-5
e. Ned.37.7-8
f. Ned.37.9-11
g. Psom.72.1-6
h. Psom.33.1
i. Wil.71.28
Ned.43.27
j. 23.30
k. Mawr.24.1-2

5 ʰAnd explains why her eyes look kind of half shut in the clip she made,

6 And maybe also explains some of the things she said about Harry,

7 Because they were pretty surprising things, including,

8 "I think Harry's great; he is bright and clever and lots of fun to be around."

9 And: "I have never met anyone like him; knowing him has caused me to look at life in a new way."

10 And: "I miss him now that he is away; I miss him more than I would ever have imagined."

11 And: "I hope that his followers are loyal to him; for Harry is too generous to believe that anyone would ever ⁱbetray him."

12 And: "I think that Harry could do great things with his life; I know that his talents are exceptional and varied."

13 And: "I know that Harry is very rich; but I am confident that he knows better than to rest on past laurels."

14 And: "I also worry about Harry, because he seems so ʲalone, and he seems afraid to let anyone know how he really ᵏfeels about things, which is why I can't afford to get serious about him, because I don't know if he really has a heart or not."

15 And then she stopped, and wouldn't say any more,

16 No matter how much the camera crew begged.

CHAPTER 39

It was only a few days afterwards that Marisa agreed to

go to ᵃAtlantic City,

2 Because the followers wanted to have some fun on the board-walk,

3 And so they all went,

4 Except for the camera crew,

5 And one of the followers,

6 Who was actually getting kind of tired of seeing Marisa all the time,

7 ᵇBecause she was so beauti-ful,

8 And he couldn't get to first base with her,

9 ᶜJust like Harry,

10 Which was some consola-tion, anyway,

11 Except that he didn't go with her to ᵈAtlantic City,

12 And when all the followers came back,

13 She wasn't with them,

14 Because she had gone home,

15 They said.

CHAPTER 40

The camera crew was on hand, though, when Harry got back,

2 ᵉAnd there's footage of him asking where Marisa was,

3 But he shrugged it off when he heard she had gone home,

4 And was his usual cheery self when he saw all the followers again,

5 But he didn't even ask them about Atlantic City,

6 At all.

CHAPTER 41

After that, Harry was busy until the night of the ᶠbig dinner,

2 ᵍWhich we got on film,

3 Even though hardly anybody knew it,

a. Ned.38.3-7
b. 18.8-9
c. 28.7
d. 39.1
e. Psom.13.1-5
f. Vin.66.7-15
g. Ext.8.7
h. Psay.5J.32
i. Vin.67.4-8
j. Vin.68.1
k. Vin.68.2
l. Wil.73.1-10
m. Psom.66.1-8
n. Ned.47.1-11
o. Ned.47.12

4 Because the cameras were hidden behind a big mirror,

5 Just like Harry wanted,

6 And the night went off with-out a hitch,

7 Including cocktails,

8 And great food,

9 ʰAnd lots of funny jokes about Philadelphia,

10 ⁱAnd some truly outstanding business with the white stuff Harry had with him,

11 ʲUntil the cops came,

12 ᵏAnd dragged Harry away.

CHAPTER 42

The next footage of Harry was taken in ˡjail,

2 By the prison security system,

3 Which had a camera in his cell,

4 So that you can see him open-ing his mail,

5 Which was funny because he'd only been in jail for a few hours,

6 And he opened the envelope,

7 And took out a picture,

8 And then ᵐhe turned away from the camera,

9 And didn't look at it again.

CHAPTER 43

There is also some footage of Harry going into the court-room,

2 And coming out again,

3 But they wouldn't allow cam-eras into the courtroom,

4 And so there's no film record of what went on in there,

5 Except that there is also some footage of the judge coming out of the courtroom,

6 ⁿRight after sentencing Harry,

7 ᵒAnd you can see that he looks really quite pale,

8 And his hand is trembling so

much that he drops his handkerchief,

9 Which is when one of the TV reporters asks him, "Any comments, Judge?"

10 Then the judge straightens up,

11 And kind of blinks,

12 And says, "I think I've just given a life sentence to the single most dangerous crime kingpin in the country."

13 "That must make you feel pretty good," the reporter says back, very friendly,

14 Which is when the Judge says, "What are you? Some kind of a _____ing idiot?"

CHAPTER 44

And there's hardly any footage at all of Harry escaping from prison,

2 Although the prison cameras got a shot of the back of his head as he was leaving,

3 With about thirty-five Angels,

4 Who all had automatic weapons,

5 And boat hooks for breaking the camera lenses,

6 Except that they didn't break the lenses in the waiting room,

7 ᵃWhere the Learjet twins were waiting,

8 Because somebody had to tell the followers what happened,

9 If they should try to visit Harry.

CHAPTER 45

For a long time, nobody had any idea where Harry was during the week after he escaped from prison,

2 Before he left for Rio,

3 And nobody knows for sure to this day,

a. Mawr.2.1-6
b. Psom.42.1-7
c. Gnt.15.7-8
d. Ned.53.4-5

4 Except that there is some footage from a TV station in Rochester,

5 Which was ᵇMarisa's hometown,

6 And the place they buried her,

7 After someone brought her back to her parents,

8 In a black ᶜLearjet with no markings of any kind.

9 And so the TV camera crew went to the gravesite,

10 And there was someone there who could have been Harry,

11 Except that he was dressed all in black,

12 And his beard was so thick it's impossible to say who it was for sure,

13 Although when the funeral was over,

14 The man in the black coat threw a burlap bag into the grave with Marisa's coffin,

15 And a nosy reporter shoved a microphone in the man's face to ask, "What's in the bag?"

16 For a moment the man looked like he would turn away without answering,

17 But some people can't resist a camera,

18 And so after a few seconds he answered the reporter's question, saying, "Nothing that will do her any good."

19 "But what's in the bag?" the reporter asked again.

20 "Heartsᵈ," said the man. "I had a few extra ones I didn't need anymore."

CHAPTER 46

The very last footage of Harry is the tape he sent to all his followers later on,

2 From Rio,

3 Where he looks like his usual sunny self,
4 And he is wearing his beautiful white suit,
5 And there's a fabulous planter's punch on the terrace,
6 And four of the most gorgeous women you ever saw,
7 Wearing those nothing little bikinis,

8 So that you can see all that golden skin,
9 And [a]Harry looks just wonderful,
10 Really,
11 Because he was always the [b]One,
12 From the very beginning,
13 And it makes you proud to have known him,
14 Way back when.

a. Pnot.37.1-5
b. Psp.3.4

THE EXPLOITS

OF THE ULTRA-HARRIERS

CHAPTER 1

I, being [a]Willie, know everything of what happened during the time of Harry,
2 And afterwards,
3 And I have set it all down pretty much the way I remember it,
4 Which may be the way it happened,
5 Although I have also received a lot of [b]Consolation over the years,
6 Which gets in the way of dates and things sometimes,
7 If you care,
8 Which you probably don't,
9 If you are a [c]Harrier,
10 Which you probably are,
11 The way I read the [d]odds.

CHAPTER 2

It seems like a lot of things happened pretty quickly,
2 [e]What with Harry getting arrested so suddenly,
3 [f]And all of us having to hide out during the trial and all,

a. Ira.16.25
Ned.14.14
Vin.33.3
Wil.47.25
b. Wil.71.2-18
c. 12.7-11
d. Ned.35.15
e. Wil.72.9-11
f. Vin.69.1-3
g. Ned.55.2
h. Vin.74.6-9
i. Vin.74.2-5
j. Wil.78.5
k. Vin.75.1-4
l. Vin.75.5
m. Ned.55.5-6
n. Wil.77.1
o. Wil.77.2
p. Vin.15.1

4 Which was a bummer,
5 [g]Because we all kind of liked Harry,
6 [h]But what could we do about it,
7 [i]Even if we had stuck around to testify?
8 Anyway, it was pretty great that Harry [j]got away with everything,
9 And [k]escaped to Rio,
10 [l]With his whole fortune intact,
11 [m]And we were really happy to hear from him when he called,
12 [n]Which he did when we were having dinner together,
13 [o]Just for *old* times' sake,
14 Only Harry didn't want us to call it a day,
15 But to go on talking about the Way,
16 And telling everyone else how to be,
17 Which we didn't really want to do,
18 [p]Because what was in it for us?

CHAPTER 3

Like I said, we were at this restaurant in Philadelphia,
2 [a]And we had a private upstairs room all to ourselves,
3 Because there were a bunch of us,
4 [b]Including Joe, and Sam, and Tom, and Mort, and Tony, and Ned, and Ira, and Jerry, and Fred, and Vinnie, and Lucky.
5 And it was [c]Lucky who first started talking back to Harry,
6 On the phone,
7 Saying, [d]"Why should we hit the road and take up a lot of our precious time doing stuff for you,
8 [e]"When we could go do whatever we felt like doing instead,
9 "Whenever we felt like it?"
10 And when Lucky had said these things, Harry asked to talk to each of us,
11 In turn,
12 And we all told him pretty much the same thing,
13 Which was that it had been great knowing him,
14 And we really enjoyed all those [f]great times on the Learjet,
15 [g]Not to mention Malibu and Miami and Acapulco and so forth,
16 [h]But it was time to move on,
17 Because [i]Sam was going to law school,
18 And [j]Tom was going to medical school,
19 And [k]Vinnie was going to start a rock and roll band,
20 And [l]Mort wanted to be a network anchorman,
21 And [m]Ned was going to be a big-time corporate executive,
22 And [n]Jerry was going into politics,
23 And [o]Ira wanted to make blockbuster movies,
24 And [p]Tony had it all worked out how he was going to be a college professor,
25 And [q]Joe had this driving ambition to be an evangelist,
26 And I, [r]Willie, was planning to be a writer,
27 And [s]Lucky had some plans, although he didn't talk about them much,
28 And only [t]Fred didn't have any idea at all what he wanted to do, except that he was sick and tired of being on the road,
29 Which meant that nobody was willing to do any running around for Harry,
30 And besides, what did he care anyway,
31 [u]Being so nicely set up for life in Rio,
32 [v]Where the girls wear those amazing bathing suits that are hardly there at all?

a. Wil.77.4
b. Wil.47.25
c. Ned.43.20
d. 2.14-16
e. Wil.26.6-8
f. Ira.18.1-3
g. Wil.47.18
h. Wil.47.10-14 Wil.48.6-8
i. Ira.16.23
j. Ira.16.29
k. Ira.16.24
l. Ira.16.30
m. Ira.16.22
n. Ira.16.28
o. Ira.16.26
p. Ira.16.27
q. Ira.16.32
r. Ira.16.25
s. Ira.16.33-35
t. Ira.16.31
u. Ira.46.1-5
v. Ira.46.6-7
w. Wil.11.8-10
x. 3.1-2

CHAPTER 4

But when Harry got the big turndown, he didn't get mad at all.
2 Instead, he laughed heartily,
3 [w]And his laughs were so loud that they filled the upstairs room where we were eating,
4 Until he finally got hold of himself and said, **I can see that I have taught you well,**
5 **And could ask for no better followers than you,**
6 **Meaning that I am very well pleased with all of you,**
7 **And really want only one thing from all of you,**
8 **Which is that you have one more dinner in my memory,**
9 **One week from today,**
10 [x]**In the same place,**

11 [a]**At the same time.**
12 **And maybe I'll be able to give you some [b]Consolation in exchange for your attendance.**
13 **Ta ta.**

CHAPTER 5

When Harry had hung up the phone, we thought over what he had said,
2 And drank quite a lot,
3 And had a little bit of [c]Consolation,
4 [d]Because a little bit was all we could afford,
5 Which got some of the guys to supposing that maybe they wouldn't mind getting together one more time,
6 In Harry's memory,
7 [e]Especially if there was going to be some Consolation,
8 [f]From Rio.

CHAPTER 6

And so it happened as Harry had requested,
2 [g]Which is often the way,
3 And one week later we gathered again,
4 [h]In the same place,
5 [i]At the same time,
6 And waited for Harry to come through,
7 Which he did,
8 About the sixth hour,
9 When Lucky looked out the window and saw [j]eleven Silver Ghosts driving into the parking lot,
10 And all of them were being driven by [k]Angels.

CHAPTER 7

The truth is, there's hardly any point in opposing the will of Harry,
2 [l]Because Harry always gets what he wants,
3 Which is a special kind of talent,
4 Even if it sometimes takes you by surprise,
5 Which it did this time,
6 Because when the Angels had parked the [m]Silver Ghosts,
7 They got out and surrounded the [n]restaurant,
8 [o]Blocking all the exits,
9 Except for one [p]Angel,
10 Who came upstairs,
11 And spoke to the twelve of us, saying,
12 "Greetings from your friend [q]Harry,
13 [r]"Who has asked me to convey his Consolation to you,
14 "And much more besides."

CHAPTER 8

When the Angel had said these things, Lucky frowned and replied to him, saying,
2 "Why are you grinning like that?
3 "Do you find us amusing in some way,
4 "Or is there something you have not explained to us yet,
5 "Something funny you wish to [s]share with us perhaps?"
6 Then the Angel grinned even more broadly and said, "That is it exactly. I have something very funny to [t]share with you,
7 [u]"Namely, all of this excellent, high-quality video footage of the twelve of you enjoying Harry's Consolation,
8 [v]"Which was taken in this very room,
9 [w]"On the very same night that Harry was arrested,
10 "Not to mention all the other

a. 6.8
b. 2.18
c. 4.12
d. Ned.7.2-6
e. 4.12
f. 2.8-9
g. Ned.49.1-4
h. 4.10
i. 6.8
j. 7.11
k. Dav.58.9
l. Wil.78.6
m. 6.9
n. 3.1
o. Psp.1.7
p. Ira.23.8
q. Psong.48.1
r. 4.12
s. Ned.8.7
t. Ned.8.8
u. Ira.41.2-5
v. Ned.41.1-4
w. Vin.66.15

excellent, high-quality video footage I have of the twelve of you enjoying yourselves in various ways on [a]Harry's Learjet,

11 "Which, as you will recall, involved *a lot* of different ways,

12 "Not all of them legal."

CHAPTER 9

Then it was that [b]Tom spoke up, saying, "I refuse to be blackmailed by that [c]two-bit, no-account scum who sent you from Rio.[d]

2 [e]"You can tell Harry that he can't scare us into doing anything,

3 "Because he isn't the only one who has connections in high places.

4 "Now get out of here,

5 "And don't slam the door behind you."

6 And so the [f]Angel replied to Tom with a single shot,

7 [g]Killing him instantly,

8 So that the remaining [h]eleven spoke up with one voice, asking,

9 "What is it that [i]Harry would like us to do?

10 "For truly, he is the very best friend any of us have ever had,

11 "And we would be delighted to be of service to him,

12 "In any way we can."

CHAPTER 10

Thereupon the Angel smiled,

2 And put a videocassette player on the dining table,

3 And turned it on,

4 [j]So that in a moment we were gazing once again into the face of Harry,

5 Who spoke to us from his veranda,

---

a. Vin.31.5
b. 3.18
c. Ned.30.30-34
d. 48.19
e. Psay.5A.19
f. 7.9
g. Ned.30.42
h. 6.9
i. Psp.3.9
j. Ira.46.2
k. Psong.48.3
l. Vin.56.7-9
m. Ira.25.60
n. 4.12
o. Psong.43.4
p. 11.8-9
q. Ned.13.10
r. Ned.13.11
s. Ned.13.12

---

6 In Rio,

7 With a warm and friendly smile on his face.

CHAPTER 11

If all has gone as I expect, said Harry,

2 The followers of Harry have just gained their first [k]martyr,

3 [l]Which pleases me immensely,

4 Because there is no religion or creed or cause of any kind that is ever taken seriously until it has a martyr.

5 And truly, since two martyrs are almost always better than one,

6 I would be happy to release any others of you who do not wish to accept my [m]gift of a Silver Ghost in exchange for a term of service in my name,

7 A term of service, I might add, in which all of you will be given all the [n]Consolation you can possibly use,

8 [o]In addition to a hundred grand in cash,

9 For a year of your time.

CHAPTER 12

And now, continued Harry, I do not wish to waste your very [p]valuable time,

2 And so I will try to explain my [q]desires to you in the clearest possible terms,

3 So that you will be [r]certain of my intent,

4 And will have no one but yourselves to [s]blame if you misunderstand me in some way that injures your prospects for the future.

5 Indeed, I wish you only the best in the future,

6 And look forward to the

great works we shall do together,
7 Because it is your mission to
go out and spread the [a]Good
Word in my name,
8 And to let the citizens of the
Most Chosen Nation in the
whole history of the world
know that they have finally
gotten the [b]messiah they have
[c]always wanted,
9 And should not be ashamed
to acknowledge that they are
followers of my way,
10 Which means that they are
[d]Harriers,
11 And can look to me,
[e]Harry, for Consolation.

CHAPTER 13

Then, when you have
spread the [f]Good Word to
all my followers,
2 You can move on to even
[g]greater works,
3 [h]Namely, the establishment
of a new institution that will
eventually take the place of the
[i]ones they used to believe in.
4 This new institution will be
called the [j]Pontifical Harrier
Parish of the United States of
America,
5 And will have its seat in the
City of [k]Philadelphia,
6 [l]Because Philadelphia is the
land of my birth,
7 And besides, there just
couldn't be any more perfect
city than Philadelphia for an
[m]institution like this one,
8 Which will offer everything
that [n]Harriers need,
9 Including plenty of meaningless rituals,
10 [o]Which will have dignified names like Harrification,

a. 20.8
  14.5
  13.12
  2.13
  50.4
b. Vin.73.9-11
c. Lies.12.5-10
  Wil.29.2-12
d. 1.9
e. Ira.30.1-3
f. 12.7
g. 12.6
h. Psp.3.6
i. Psay.5R.1-14
j. Wht.11
k. Wil.53.2
l. Wil.64.4
m. 13.4
n. 12.10
o. 33.11
p. Vin.25.1-11
q. Wil.36.1-4
r. 20.8
s. Gods.6.20-22
t. Brd.27.8-11
u. Brd.28.3-5
v. Psp.4.2
w. 13.4
x. Wil.78.6
y. Wht.12

Adultification, and Consolation,
11 [p]Because people just love
meaningless rituals, whether
they believe in anything or not,
12 And plenty *of* lofty-
sounding language,
13 [q]Because if the language is
lofty enough, it doesn't matter
if it doesn't say anything at all,
14 And loads of signs and
[r]symbols and holidays and
hymns,
15 [s]Because these are things
that people have had for thousands of years and couldn't
live without,
16 Not to mention a reliable
source for high-quality [t]Con-
solation,
17 [u]At very competitive
prices,
18 Because if you're a Harrier, [v]Consolation is as close as
you'll ever get to divine bliss.

CHAPTER 14

I won't kid you about the
fact that it may take a long
time for the [w]Pontifical Harrier Parish to replace all the
other institutions people like to
patronize,
2 Because Harriers are creatures of habit,
3 Since habits make it easy to
live from one day to the next
without really thinking about
it,
4 But we will [x]win out in the
end,
5 Because most of the other
institutions are already just
branches of the [y]Greater Harrier *Parish,*
6 Which has been growing
without any help from us for

years and years already anyway,
7 And eventually even the dumbest sheep will recognize who the best shepherd is,
8 Since the other shepherds can offer only sin and guilt and hell and the merest [a]sip of wine in exchange for their meaningless rituals,
9 Whereas I can offer [b]Consolation.

CHAPTER 15

That's why it's time for us to get started,
2 And why I have called you together this evening,
3 And why I have gone to the trouble of drawing up a [c]list of things for you to do,
4 Because a Harrier with a [d]list that he doesn't really have to think about is a happy [e]Harrier.

CHAPTER 16

And so, I have chosen you, Willie, to establish the [f]Pontifical Harrier Parish of the United States of America,
2 [g]Because you like words so much,
3 And I charge you to come up with a lot of [h]great words for Harriers to say,
4 Which will be called braying,
5 Because it can't really be called praying,
6 Since I won't be listening.
7 And to help you get started, I have also gone to the trouble of writing the first brayer for you,
8 Which is called the Harrier's Brayer,
9 And goes like this:
10 [i]Our friend, who art in Rio, Harry is your name.
11 [j]Your time has come.
12 [k]Your way is fun, up north, as it is in Rio.
13 [l]We live for today and are rarely blamed.
14 We [m]forget our trespasses, as we forget those we have trespassed against.
15 [n]We yield to temptation, but are not evil.
16 [o]So there.
17 And if some of you are wondering, Where is the "For thine is the . . ." part, I have not forgotten it,
18 But I have decided to give it to you separately,
19 Because sometimes you'll want to use it, and sometimes you won't,
20 Which will seem properly mysterious and holy to all the people who are confused by it,
21 And is an incredibly important example of how things must be done in the Pontifical Harrier Parish.
22 So now I will give you the final part of the Harrier's Brayer,
23 Which is,
24 For thine is the [p]wisdom and the [q]power and the [r]Gold,
25 For as long as it lasts.
26 [s]So there.
27 Got it?
28 And speaking of gold, added Harry,
29 Remember that words aren't the only important part

a. Dav.15.21
b. Wht.9
c. Cen.26.18-19
d. Ira.31.3-5
e. 12.7
f. 13.4
g. 3.26
h. 13.12
i. Psom.76.1-2
j. Psom.76.3
k. Psom.76.4
l. Psom.76.5
m. Wil.44.20-22
n. Wil.20.1-3
o. Psom.76.6
p. Wil.5.4
q. Psong.53.6-7
r. Spic.8.3
s. 16.16

of the Pontifical Harrier Parish.

30 **As you proceed to carry out my instructions,**

31 **Remember this above all things:**

32 **If they want Consolation, they're going to have to** [a]**buy their ticket before the train leaves the station,**

33 **If you catch my drift.**

CHAPTER 17

And when Harry had finished instructing me, Willie, in what he wanted me to do,

2 He did likewise for the rest of the [b]eleven,

3 Until we all knew what we were supposed to do,

4 And how we were supposed to do it,

5 Which is when Harry gave us the last word we would have from him for quite a while, saying,

6 **Go then, my Ultra-Harriers,**

7 **And spread the** [c]**Good Word to all the people,**

8 **In every walk of life,**

9 **And as you go, fear not,**

10 **For my** [d]**Angels will go with you,**

11 **To keep and protect and comfort and console you,**

12 **Not to mention making sure you don't change your minds about participating in these** [e]**great works.**

13 **Everybody** [f]**happy?**

14 **I can't tell you how glad I am to hear it.**

15 **Ciao, my friends.**

CHAPTER 18

[g] And verily, all was done as Harry wanted,

---

a. *Brd.28.3*
b. *9.8-9*
c. *12.7*
d. *Ira.44.4*
e. *12.5-6*
f. *15.4*
g. *6.1-2*
h. *11.6*
i. *Wil.31.18-22*
j. *Brd.27.4-7*
k. *17.10-11*
l. *Ira.17.7-10*
m. *17.6*
n. *Wil.27.6-7*

---

2 And the eleven went out into the wide world,

3 In their [h]Silver Ghosts,

4 Armed with Harry's [i]Trinity,

5 And accompanied by Angels,

6 Who were also armed,

7 And started letting everybody know that Harry had come and gone,

8 But had figured everything out while he was here,

9 And had left a little something behind to help them get along from day to day,

10 Namely, [j]Consolation.

CHAPTER 19

Of course, before going out into the wide world, the eleven met many times together,

2 And talked over their concerns,

3 Which they had some of,

4 [k]Because it made them all nervous to have so many Angels around all the time,

5 And not all of them were completely sure that they could remember much of what Harry said,

6 [l]Since a lot of their time with Harry seemed like kind of a blur,

7 For some reason.

8 And besides, they had no way of knowing how the wide world would react to a whole bunch of [m]Ultra-Harriers in Silver Ghosts,

9 And maybe they wouldn't be liked,

10 At all,

11 [n]Because there was still a lot of talk out there about ideals and social justice and the rights of the disadvantaged and all that,

12 And so who knew what would happen?

CHAPTER 20

After a lot of discussion, it was agreed that the best thing for the Ultra-Harriers to do was disguise themselves,

2 [a]And wear white suits, and hats, and dark glasses,

3 Just like Harry,

4 So that nobody would really know who anybody was,

5 And maybe that would help,

6 Somehow,

7 Especially if they managed to get through a whole year with the Angels and then wanted to start a [b]legitimate career or something.

8 They also decided that in the early going anyway, there should be a *secret* Harrier [c]symbol,

9 So that everybody would know when it was really safe to be as [d]brazen as Harry was,

10 And so Lucky suggested that [e]Harriers should all wear a tiny little [f]spoon around their necks,

11 Because it would come in handy for receiving Consolation in cramped places like catacombs and restrooms,

12 Not to mention the fact that "spoon" might turn out to be a good acronym,

13 If anybody wanted to think of one,

14 Which most of them didn't,

15 Although Willie thought of several,

16 And wrote them down,

17 Somewhere,

18 As well as a very special ultra-secret Harrier symbol that only the eleven knew,

19 [g]Just in case.

CHAPTER 21

But eventually, the day could no longer be postponed

a.	Ned.24.1-11
b.	3.17-26
c.	13.14
d.	Ned.4.7
e.	15.4
f.	25.22
g.	Ned.54.11
h.	3.17
i.	3.19
j.	3.20
k.	3.21
l.	3.22
m.	3.23
n.	3.24
o.	3.25
p.	3.27
q.	3.28
r.	3.26
s.	Vin.75.10
t.	Wil.65.9
u.	16.1

when the Ultra-Harriers had to split up,

2 And go their separate ways,

3 And try not to think about what might happen,

4 At all.

5 And so, [h]Sam went out in his Silver Ghost, accompanied by Angels, to carry the Word of Harry to the lawyers,

6 And [i]Vinnie went out in his Silver Ghost to carry the Word of Harry to rock and roll stars and their fans,

7 And [j]Mort went out to carry the Word of Harry to the journalists and media professionals,

8 And [k]Ned went out to carry the Word of Harry to corporations and banks and brokerage firms,

9 And [l]Jerry went out to the politicians,

10 And [m]Ira went to Hollywood,

11 And [n]Tony went out to the colleges and universities,

12 And [o]Joe went out to the Christians,

13 And [p]Lucky went out to the downtrodden and oppressed,

14 And [q]Fred went out to some prep school or something in New England,

15 And I, [r]Willie, stayed by the phone with a steno pad to write down their exploits as they called in [s]from all over the place,

16 In Philadelphia,

17 Which may sound like the easiest job,

18 Except for the part about having to stay in [t]Philadelphia, of course,

19 But somebody had to do it,

20 And besides, I had to figure out how to establish the [u]Ponti-

cal Harrier Parish of the United States of America,

21 [a]Which seemed like it would be a hard thing to do.

CHAPTER 22

[b]Sam started out pretty cautiously,

2 Which was his way,

3 And talked to only a few lawyers,

4 Meeting them at nice restaurants for dinner,

5 And explaining the way of Harry in words the lawyers could understand,

6 [c]But they said they already knew all that,

7 And what was it Sam really wanted?

8 And so then Sam explained about [d]Consolation,

9 [e]And how Harriers could always get it,

10 Whenever they wanted it,

11 And all they had to do was wear a little [f]spoon around their necks,

12 And do things according to the [g]Way of Harry,

13 Without really thinking about it at all.

14 [h]Thereupon the lawyers were immediately converted, and became Harriers,

15 And went out to carry the [i]Word of Harry to their friends and relatives too.

CHAPTER 23

[j]Ira decided that the best way to carry the Word of Harry to Hollywood was to go into show business,

2 [k]Which isn't hard to do if you have a Silver Ghost and a white suit and a bunch of heavily armed Angels beside you at all times,

3 [l]And so he started putting together a movie deal,

4 From a rented mansion in Beverly Hills,

5 Which made it possible for him to meet other Hollywood producers,

6 And subtly introduce the [m]Word of Harry into casual conversations at parties,

7 And soirées,

8 And premieres,

9 And so forth.

10 When the producers of Hollywood heard the Word of Harry, they didn't understand it at all,

11 And admitted it freely,

12 Explaining to Ira that the first rule of being a success in Hollywood is never to think about anything at all,

13 And so there was no chance that they would ever have any interest in Harry,

14 But what was all this talk about Consolation?

15 [n]Thereupon, Ira speedily signed them all up,

16 And handed out lots and lots of little [o]spoons,

17 And started requesting [p]huge volumes of Consolation delivered to his mansion in Hollywood.

CHAPTER 24

Joe went all over the place trying to tell Christians about the Word of Harry,

2 But he couldn't get to first base,

3 [q]Because their heads were so full of what Jesus Christ told them yesterday,

4 In person,

a. 14.1
b. 21.5
c. Penn.1.15-17
d. 13.18
e. Kens.35.1-4
f. 20.10
g. Penn.2.2
h. 14.7-9
i. 12.7
j. 21.10
k. 18.2-5
l. Dav.3.1-5
m. 12.7
n. 14.7-9
o. 22.11
p. Brd.28.3-5
q. Jeff.20.1-4

5 And they didn't want any Consolation,

6 ªBecause they were going to heaven pretty soon,

7 Which was all they wanted out of life,

8 What with things being the way they were in the ᵇMiddle East,

9 Which proved everything,

10 So that there could be no doubt about it,

11 Unless you hadn't been ᶜborn again,

12 But were still just going through the motions of being a Christian,

13 Like most of the stuffy upper-middle-class Christians,

14 Who weren't going to be saved,

15 But would go to hell pretty soon,

16 Just like they deserved,

17 ᵈWhich gave Joe the idea of talking to Presbyterians, and Catholics, and Episcopalians, and Lutherans, and even some of the less excitable Baptists,

18 Who all turned out to be very extremely interested in Consolation,

19 Because they had so little to do in their spare time,

20 Now that they didn't think about anything at all anymore,

21 ᵉSince that's what the government is there for.

CHAPTER 25

ᶠ**T**ony figured that the best way to carry the Word of Harry to the colleges and universities was to trade his Silver Ghost in for a ᵍVolvo,

2 And buy a whole bunch of degrees with the money he got back,

a. Jeff.20.7-10
b. Bks.11.1-10
c. Jeff.20.5
d. 14.5-6
e. Brd.18.8-16
f. 21.11
g. Swar.PS.14-15
h. Ira.8.6-11
i. Wil.18.17
j. Swar.PS.27-30
k. Wil.38.4-9
l. Swar.PS.20-23
m. Wil.50.14-20

3 And then start an academic career,

4 So that he could meet them on their own terms,

5 Or something like that.

6 But when he started introducing the Word of Harry at faculty cocktail parties and so forth,

7 It turned out that they weren't interested in the Word of Harry at all,

8 ʰBecause Harry didn't have any degrees in philosophy or psychology or physics or literature or history or art or natural science or anything,

9 And so how could he possibly matter?

10 When Tony tried to explain that Harry wasn't challenging what anybody had figured out in those fields,

11 ⁱBut was only kind of pulling it all together so that everyone could see what it meant,

12 ʲThey laughed at him and ridiculed him,

13 ᵏBecause it just wasn't possible for anyone to get doctoral degrees in philosophy *and* psychology *and* physics *and* literature *and* history *and* art *and* natural science *and* all the *other* fields you'd need a doctoral degree in,

14 ˡAnd so it clearly wasn't possible to pull all those disciplines together into one big picture of what it all meant,

15 ᵐAnd what was he trying to pull anyway?

16 Thereupon, Tony changed his tune,

17 And started talking about how hard it was to get tenure,

18 And how hard it was to pay off all his student loans,

19 And how hard it was to find

academic topics to write articles and books about, because the department chairman was such a selfish, unscrupulous, [a]pyrotechnical anus,

20 And how Tony would probably sell his soul for a little [b]Consolation now and then,

21 At which point everyone agreed with him heartily,

22 And pretty soon, Tony was ordering carloads of [c]spoons and Consolation for all his great new friends in the academic world.

CHAPTER 26

[d]Vinnie started his own rock and roll band,

2 And they went driving around in the Silver Ghost,

3 And had lots and lots and lots of Consolation,

4 And had incredibly huge parties in all the best hotels,

5 Until they'd been kicked out of all the best hotels,

6 And had become a legend,

7 Because Vinnie knew that the very best way to carry the Good Word to youngsters is always the same,

8 [e]Namely, by setting a really good example.

CHAPTER 27

[f]Mort got himself a job as a TV journalist,

2 Which he decided would be a good way to start spreading the Word of Harry,

3 And he was right.

4 Most of the [g]news was bad,

5 [h]And all his fellow journalists had already stopped thinking about it a long long time ago,

6 And were ready as could be for a little [i]Consolation,

a. Kens.15.1-3
b. Vin.17.26-28
c. 31.11
d. 21.6
e. Mall.14.7-18
f. 21.7
g. Ann.10.1-35
h. Vin.71.12-23
i. Psp.4.2
j. 29.4
k. Ed.24.1-16
l. 21.9
m. Rom.2.22
n. 21.14
o. 48.19
p. 23.16
q. Mawr.8.1-2
r. 21.15

7 Although they didn't want to wear the little [j]spoons,

8 [k]Because it was important for people to trust them,

9 And so it wouldn't do for anyone to know that they were Harriers,

10 Too.

CHAPTER 28

[l]Jerry figured that if you were going to carry the Word of Harry to politicians,

2 It might be [m]easiest to go into politics yourself,

3 Which he did,

4 And had a marvelous time,

5 Because as soon as he mentioned the Word of Harry to his new politician friends, they slapped him on the back and said,

6 "And how *is* Harry?

7 "We miss him more than we can say,

8 "But expect to spend a few days with him on his ranch next spring,

9 "In Rio."

CHAPTER 29

[n]Fred didn't actually report in,

2 And somehow he managed to give the Angels the slip[o],

3 But he placed lots of big orders for Consolation,

4 Although he never ordered any little [p]spoons,

5 After the first one,

6 Which could have raised certain suspicions,

7 [q]If anybody had cared.

CHAPTER 30

[r]Meanwhile, I, Willie, stayed by the phone and kept in touch with the eleven,

2 Except for [a]Ned and [b]Lucky,
3 Who disappeared for quite a while,
4 In fact, until the year was up,
5 And all the others came back for a reunion,
6 And reported on how they had done.

CHAPTER 31

The reunion turned out to be a wild and wonderful party,
2 Because everybody had been so unbelievably successful,
3 And there were staggering numbers of Harriers in every walk of life,
4 Including [c]show business,
5 And [d]politics,
6 And the [e]law,
7 And [f]churches,
8 And [g]academia,
9 And a bunch of others too,
10 Including even medicine, in spite of Tom's unlucky [h]accident,
11 Because it was getting hard to walk down the street without seeing a bunch of little [i]spoons around people's necks,
12 And the entire country was becoming full of [j]Consolation,
13 Which is why we were all sure that Harry was proud of us,
14 For everything we had done.

CHAPTER 32

But even we did not understand the full extent of Harry's victory,
2 Until late in the evening,
3 When Ned and Lucky arrived,
4 In a fleet of Silver Ghosts,
5 With dozens of new followers,
6 Including [k]Vicki and [l]Wayne and [m]Mike and many many others,

a. 21.8
b. 21.13
c. 23.15-17
d. 28.6
e. 22.14
f. 24.17-21
g. 25.22
h. 9.6-7
i. 27.7
j. Brd.27.4-7
k. 49.1
l. 50.1-3
m. 51.1
n. Adam.8.8-9
o. Wht.6
p. Ned.43.27
q. 33.12
r. 16.31-33
s. Wht.36
t. Main.37.4-6
u. Kens.36.1-6 Brd.29.1-8

7 Who all had gigantic smiles on their faces.
8 As the rest of the eleven gathered round in admiration,
9 Ned and Lucky explained that they had joined forces,
10 And started a [n]corporation of their own,
11 In the import/export business,
12 Which turned out to be the very best way of carrying the Word of Harry to both the corporations and the underprivileged.
13 And when the others wanted to know the secret of their success,
14 Ned said he had learned not to just talk about the [o]Way of Harry,
15 But to *live* according to the Way of Harry,
16 In every detail,
17 Which suggested that [p]Harry probably wouldn't really mind if Ned made a little personal [q]profit out of spreading the Word of Harry,
18 Especially if the Angels didn't happen to be looking when some of the [r]profits went into Ned's pocket,
19 So they could be reinvested,
20 [s]In the highly lucrative business of importing Consolation from down south,
21 So that everyone in the [t]business world and everyone in [u]poverty could start not thinking about anything at all,
22 Except for their personal desires.

CHAPTER 33

When Ned had finished explaining these things, the phone rang,
2 And it was Harry on the line,

3 Calling to congratulate us all,

4 Especially Ned,

5 [a]Who he called **The Rock Of My Parish**,

6 [b]And **my Number One representative up north**,

7 Which hurt my feelings,

8 [c]Because I, Willie, had also done what I was supposed to do,

9 [d]And had hired a bunch of people to come up with a bunch of great-sounding words for Harriers to say,

10 [e]And all was in readiness for the establishment of the Pontifical Harrier Parish in the United States,

11 [f]Including all the instructions and words for the Orders of Morning and Evening Brayer, [g]Harrification, Majority, Matrimony, the Burial of the Dead, and Harry's Consolation,

12 Not to mention the fact that I, Willie, had come nowhere close to making [h]seventy-eight million dollars on the deal,

13 And hadn't even gotten a really promising start on a career in show business or the law or politics or anything else,

14 Which I could only blame Harry for,

15 [i]If I'd had the guts.

CHAPTER 34

But instead of giving me any credit for my good works,

2 [j]Harry asked me hard questions instead,

3 Like **What have you done to spread my Word throughout the length and breadth of Philadelphia?**

4 [k]As I have told you, Philadelphia is the seat of my Parish,

5 And it would be embarrass-

---

a. *Dav.15.30*
b. *38.6*
c. *17.1-4*
d. *16.3*
e. *16.1*
f. *13.9-10*
g. *Vin.26.1-9*
h. *32.17*
i. *Kens.14.18-22*
j. *Main.27.10*
k. *13.4-7*
l. *Ira.21.26*
m. *33.8-9*
n. *Cen.11.24-33*

---

ing if my name were not on the lips of every citizen of every [l]neighborhood in the city of my birth.

6 And so, Willie, I ask you again, what have you done in Philadelphia,

7 **Besides come up with a [m]bunch of words for Harriers to say?**

CHAPTER 35

Then, in my desperation, I cried out to Harry, saying,

2 Truly, I do not know what else you may require of me,

3 For no city in this Most Chosen Nation on Earth is more full of Harriers than Philadelphia,

4 And every neighborhood, and every street, and every home, and every school, and every place of business, and every office of any kind, and every campus and tenement is full to bursting with Harriers,

5 Who never think about anything at all,

6 And who live by your Trinity so fiercely that every neighborhood, and every street, and every home, and every school, and every place of business, and every office of any kind, and every campus and tenement is already falling apart,

7 From the inside out,

8 And everyone sees that this is so,

9 [n]And yet no one is responsible,

10 And every one of them blames somebody else,

11 And all of them are certain that nothing matters at all,

12 Except their own desires,

13 And I cannot see what else might be done to improve on this

outstanding triumph of your Way.

CHAPTER 36

When Harry had heard my words, he laughed,
2 And said, **Don't take on so, Willie.**
3 **Indeed, what you say may be true,**
4 **And I am aware that [a]Ned and Lucky have done some good work in Philadelphia, in addition to the good work they have done elsewhere,**
5 **[b]But I desire Philadelphia to be the ultimate shining capital of my Way,**
6 **And what you have said about the City of Brotherly Love could be said also of other cities,**
7 **Including [c]New York,**
8 **And [d]Chicago,**
9 **And Detroit,**
10 **And Cleveland,**
11 **And [e]Washington, D.C.,**
12 **Not to mention my west coast capital, the [f]City of Angels.**
13 **Truly, I am not displeased with you,**
14 **But I would ask for more,**
15 **And I shall leave some Angels with you to see that you do it.**

CHAPTER 37

And then I, Willie, asked my brethren to help me,
2 [g]Since they had had so much practice in carrying the Word of Harry to so many peoples and places,
3 But they merely laughed at me, saying,
4 "Philadelphia?
5 [h]"You've got to be kidding."
6 And then they turned to go,
7 So that I had to fall on my knees and beg for their assistance,
8 Which they reluctantly agreed to give,
9 But only after Harry got on the phone again and mentioned the part about a [i]big bonus for getting the Pontifical Harrier Parish off the ground,
10 Which brought a strange new light to the eyes of the eleven,
11 And made them promise to help me,
12 As long as they didn't actually have to stay in Philadelphia,
13 Which is why they agreed to write letters instead,
14 [j]Or have them written, anyway,
15 To a whole bunch of Philadelphia [k]neighborhoods,
16 So that the Word of Harry might be spread further,
17 Without any of the Ultra-Harriers actually having to go there.

CHAPTER 38

All was then done as we had agreed,
2 And the Ultra-Harriers and their [l]new followers gave Harry a little more time in exchange for a huge bonus,
3 [m]And they wrote a bunch of letters and other communiqués,
4 [n]And the seat of the Pontifical Harrier Parish was established in Philadelphia,
5 [o]And the parish organization grew so big that it needed a lot of fancy new ranks and titles,
6 Including the [p]Number One spot, which Ned held for a while,
7 [q]And Arch-Harriers, who got

a. 32.21-22
b. Cen.9.4-7
c. Adam.36.1-12
d. Ira.11.1-5
e. Yks.16.1-6
f. Swar.37.10
g. 31.4-9
h. Psay.5J.32
i. Psong.43.5
j. Main.32.1-2
k. 17.8
l. 32.6
m. Hill.1.1, Ann.1.1, Jefs.1.1, Kens.1.1, Swar.1.1, Hall.1.1, Drex.1.1, Boul.1.1, Penn.1.1, Forg.1.1, Wht.1, Mawr.1.1, Cen.1.1-2, Mall.1.1-2, Main.1.1-3, Brd.1.1-5
n. 13.4-5
o. Wht.35
p. Dav.15.31
q. 40.1, 43.1, 44.1, 46.1-2

big salaries and a percentage of the profits,

8 [a]And Arch-Angels, who got paid by the hour but also pulled down a percentage of the gross,

9 [b]And Chosen Ones, who got a nice salary and bonus,

10 [c]And Angels, of course, who got free Consolation, plus wages and perks,

11 [d]And Parish Beacons, who got a discount on Consolation,

12 [e]And Parish Guards, who got paid by the Angels they reported to,

13 [f]And there were even some Vice-Presidents, which Harry thought was a nice touch when he heard about it,

14 [g]Although I, Willie, didn't think much of it when I got passed over for Vice-President of Orthodoxy,

15 [h]After all I had done,

16 Because Ultra-Harriers didn't get any salary, or bonus, or percentages, or compensation of any kind,

17 Unless you count the discount on Consolation.

CHAPTER 39

And so I, Willie, had to sell my Silver Ghost in order to buy stock,

2 Which turned out all right, I suppose,

3 [i]Since I also made out unexpectedly well on a little mail-order plan [j]Tony and I dreamed up,

4 So that I wound up having enough to buy a little estate in the country,

5 And retired from active involvement with the Pontifical Harrier Parish,

6 [k]As much as any Ultra-Harrier can, anyway.

7 And eventually, a few years later, the Angels who had been staying with me were called out on a special mission one day,

8 Along with all the other Angels in the greater Philadelphia metropolitan area,

9 [l]And they never came back,

10 Which I didn't ask any questions about,

11 [m]Because I had finally learned to live according to the Way of Harry myself.

12 But I did follow the careers of the surviving members of the original eleven,

13 And the careers of some of the followers they had recruited,

14 Which were fabulous indeed,

15 And a great monument to the Way of Harry,

16 Not to mention a splendid example to all Harriers everywhere,

17 With a couple of exceptions,

18 But there are always exceptions,

19 As everyone knows.

CHAPTER 40

[n]Sam was an Arch-Harrier for a while in New York,

2 And then he became a very very successful lawyer,

3 Until he took some kind of government job in [o]Washington, D.C.,

4 And got indicted for destroying a bunch of evidence,

5 [p]By accident, of course,

6 In his garbage disposal,

7 Which the jury didn't quite believe his story about,

8 [q]And so he got sent to a quiet little prison,

Reference column:

a. 42.1
   52.2-6
b. 51.2-3
c. Vin.24.9-12
d. Cen.1.10-12
e. 19.7
f. 41.1-4
   45.1
   49.1
g. 48.22-23
h. 33.8-9
i. Swar.4.11-12
   & PS.4-5
j. 43.1-11
k. Ned.30.42
l. 52.24-25
m. 32.14-15
n. 21.5
o. 36.11
p. Vin.14.23-24
q. Ned.36.1-5

9 Near Philadelphia,

10 Where he made a bunch of very good [a]contacts,

11 Which came in handy when he got paroled,

12 [b]And wrote a book about how he wasn't really responsible for what happened,

13 But was really sorry anyway,

14 [c]For some reason,

15 Which got him on a bunch of talk shows,

16 So that everyone could see that he wasn't some terrible monster,

17 But just like them,

18 [d]And so everybody forgave him,

19 Including the [e]gorgeous talk show host he married,

20 And he eventually landed a new job,

21 As a lobbyist in [f]Washington, D.C.,

22 Where he had this incredibly beautiful mansion in Georgetown,

23 [g]Which was perfect down to the last detail,

24 Including the Silver Ghost in the driveway.

CHAPTER 41

[h]Ned and Lucky continued with their business,

2 Getting bigger and richer all the time,

3 Especially after the merger with the Pontifical Harrier Parish,

4 [i]Which is when Lucky became Vice-President for Production and Distribution,

5 And helped [j]Ned increase profits by about a thousand percent.

6 [k]In fact, Ned even had a cover story written about his financial

a. *28.6*
b. *Ned.36.20-24*
c. *Ned.29.19-20*
d. *Psay.5Q.46 Vin.11.13*
e. *Dav.57.4*
f. *40.3*
g. *Vin.75.13-14*
h. *32.9-10*
i. *38.13*
j. *38.6*
k. *Main.35.1-5*
l. *27.1-6*
m. *Ed.56.3-4*
n. *Main.10.1-5*
o. *Main.24.1*
p. *50.23-24*
q. *21.13*
r. *38.6*
s. *21.6*
t. *36.12*
u. *37.9*
v. *Ann.18.17-19*
w. *Main.36.3*

services conglomerate in some national business magazine,

7 Although the [l]reporter was nice enough to leave out the part about the Pontifical Harrier Parish,

8 Which is maybe why it was such a big surprise to everybody when he came under investigation by the SEC,

9 And the Department of Treasury,

10 And the Interstate Commerce Commission,

11 And the FBI,

12 And the CIA,

13 Explaining why he needed to hire the [m]best criminal lawyer in the whole country,

14 And probably also explaining why he lost anyway,

15 [n]And would have gone to prison for life,

16 Except that he skipped out on a fifty-million-dollar bond,

17 [o]Which left him with only seven hundred and eighty million dollars to start a new life with,

18 When he got to [p]Rio,

19 Not to mention how well [q]Lucky made out,

20 When he succeeded Ned as [r]Number One.

CHAPTER 42

[s]Vinnie took a position as an Arch-Angel in [t]Los Angeles until he earned a big enough [u]bonus to go back to his rock and roll band.

2 Then he wrote a whole bunch of great [v]hit songs about how great it was to be a Harrier,

3 And sold millions and millions of albums,

4 And got a bunch of awards,

5 [w]And bought about a dozen

houses in the best neighborhoods all over the country,

6 [a]And slept with thousands and thousands of groupies,

7 [b]Until he got busted on about forty-five counts of using and dealing illegal drugs,

8 [c]Which is why he was so lucky that the very best criminal lawyer in the whole country wasn't busy working on Ned's appeal,

9 And was therefore available to take Vinnie's case,

10 And get him off with eight months of community service,

11 Which made his fans incredibly happy,

12 So that he set a music industry record with the sales of his brand-new [d]album about what it feels like to be a Harrier doing community service.

CHAPTER 43

[e]Tony was an Arch Harrier in San Francisco for a couple of years,

2 [f]And then returned to the academic world,

3 And got [g]tenure at a famous university,

4 And became chairman of the [h]psychology department,

5 [i]And never thought about a single thing again,

6 Until he got into trouble for coercing a young female doctoral candidate to have [j]sex with him in exchange for approving her dissertation topic,

7 Which would probably have been [k]okay,

8 Except that he also extorted sexual favors from the doctoral candidate's young lover,

9 [l]Who turned out to be the daughter of the dean,

---

a. Mall.15.6-7
b. Vin.20.8-10
c. 41.8
d. Ann.18.17-19
e. 21.11
f. 3.24
g. 25.17
h. Zig.13.1-3
i. 25.19
j. Zig.16.7
k. Ned.35.7-15
l. Wil.26.13-16 Swar.36.3
m. Hill.S.28
n. 40.8
o. Ned.36.25-27
p. 40.12
q. 40.15
r. Psong.51.1-4
s. 51.11
t. 21.12
u. Jeff.20.2
v. Jeff.20.3
w. Vin.59.17-18

---

10 [m]Not to mention a few years underage,

11 [n]Which he got sent to prison for,

12 But atoned for when he got out,

13 [o]By starting a very successful self-help group for reformed sexual offenders,

14 [p]Which is how he got the contract to write his best-selling book,

15 [q]And all those invitations to talk about his problems on TV talk shows,

16 Which is how he got the financial backing to set up his nationwide network of franchised sex offender clinics,

17 Until he had so much money that nobody minded when he married a nineteen-year-old [r]porn queen,

18 [s]And moved to Beverly Hills.

CHAPTER 44

[t]Joe was an Arch-Harrier for a year or so in Atlanta,

2 And then he sold his Silver Ghost and moved north,

3 And pronounced himself a depraved sinner,

4 [u]Who had suddenly seen the light,

5 [v]Thanks to the personal intervention of Jesus Christ in his life,

6 Which is why he felt compelled to use his bonus and the money from the Silver Ghost to buy a television station,

7 And start a TV ministry.

8 The thing that was truly different and exciting about Joe's TV ministry was that he wanted to bring Jesus Christ to [w]old people,

9 Who were going to die soon,
10 And should be trying pretty hard to get into heaven,
11 Which is why the only diseases he would cure on the air were old people's diseases,
12 Like arthritis,
13 And high blood pressure,
14 And heart problems,
15 So that all the old people he had cured knew they would live a lot longer,
16 Which meant that it would probably be a long long time before their new wills would give Joe the money he needed to keep on with his holy work,
17 Which is why they were willing to trade their social security checks for Bibles printed in big type,
18 With Joe's picture on the cover,
19 Until the day of the scandal,
20 When Joe got arrested for extortion,
21 Because some rich old lady complained about his evangelical zeal,
22 And got a lot of sympathy in the press by going on talk shows with her right arm in a cast,
23 Even though it was only a severe sprain,
24 Which would have finished Joe off for good,
25 If it hadn't been for the movie ªIra made about his career,
26 Which turned out to be such a big hit that Joe still had something left even after he paid off the old lady,
27 Enough, in fact, to buy a professional ᵇbaseball team,
28 And so he did.
29 Joe had a terrific time run-

a. 21.10
b. Psay.5S.4
c. Main.27.1-3
d. Boul.22.4-10
e. Psay.5S.23
f. Boul.5.1-12
g. 21.10
h. Wht.35
i. Psong.43.3
j. Swar.27.1-5
k. Ira.25.39-40
Swar.28.1-10
l. Psong.29.1-3
m. Yks.134.6-13

ning the baseball team for several years,
30 ᶜAnd even used to call his manager from the owner's box to change the lineup,
31 ᵈUntil the day all the black and Hispanic players complained to the press about how racist Joe was,
32 And so Joe sold the baseball team and bought a ᵉhockey team instead,
33 Which didn't have any black or Hispanic players,
34 ᶠOr any Jews either,
35 And won the Stanley Cup,
36 Or made it to the finals, anyway.

CHAPTER 45

ᵍ**I**ra stayed on with Harry for another year as ʰVice-President for Harrier Services,
2 ¡And made so much money that he became an instant success when he went to Hollywood,
3 And made millions and millions of dollars from his movies,
4 ʲWhich were all blockbusters about how sick and evil everything was,
5 ᵏAnd how the Others keep getting it in the neck from everybody,
6 ˡUntil he had a flop that lost forty million dollars,
7 Because even the best editor in Hollywood couldn't piece the footage together to make a coherent story,
8 Which resulted in a bunch of wild allegations about drug abuse on the set,
9 And how the prop snow outside ᵐInchon was really cocaine or something,

10 Which got a lot of additional coverage when all the stars and featured players on the production checked into a drug rehabilitation clinic,

11 And [a]blamed Ira for what had happened to them,

12 Which wasn't their fault,

13 At all,

14 Because they were [b]artists,

15 And vulnerable to manipulative producers,

16 Which people accused Ira of being,

17 To the point where it could have ended his career,

18 Except that his old friend [c]Joe was able to supply him with enough cash to get financing for a movie about Joe's life,

19 [d]Which got rave reviews for its honest and fearless exposé of corrupt religious institutions,

20 [e]Until people started admiring Ira again for his lifelong convictions about social justice,

21 And invited him to take part in all kinds of celebrity [f]causes,

22 Which turned out to be a nice consolation for everyone.

CHAPTER 46

Meanwhile, [g]Jerry was enjoying a very successful political career,

2 Based on a lot of great connections he made while serving as an [h]Arch-Harrier in the midwest.

3 In fact, Jerry wound up getting elected to several terms in the congress of the Most Chosen Nation on Earth,

4 And became pretty much of a national celebrity when he conducted hearings into all the un-

a. *Main.10.1-3*
b. *Swar.29.13-18*
c. *44.24-25*
d. *Swar.25.1-10*
e. *Ned.36.17-19*
f. *Ned.34.10-16*
g. *21.9*
h. *Swar.37.11*
i. *40.1-8*
j. *Yks.146.9-10*
k. *46.5 Psong.44.1*
l. *21.7*
m. *Zig.17.6-13*
n. *Ned.36.25-26*
o. *40.12*
p. *40.20-21*
q. *Wil.39.9-11*

scrupulous stuff that [i]Sam was part of,

5 So that he got invited to give speeches about honesty in government to every club and fraternal organization in the whole country,

6 Which might have led to a [j]presidential nomination,

7 According to some people,

8 Except for that unfortunate incident with the teenage son of his personal secretary,

9 Which made the headlines,

10 And led to additional charges concerning the [k]million dollars he was making each year in speaking fees,

11 Which is why it was so incredibly fortunate that his good friend [l]Mort had some interesting information about the chairman of the committee that was investigating Jerry,

12 [m]So that eventually, it turned out that all the charges got dropped when he apologized for the thing with his secretary's teenage son,

13 [n]And felt that he was kind of vindicated altogether when he was named to succeed the chairman of the investigating committee,

14 Who resigned and wrote a [o]book of his own, and then went on to become a [p]lobbyist himself a year or two after the whole incident,

15 [q]Which is a long long time in Harrier terms,

16 As every Harrier knows.

CHAPTER 47

Mort was a huge success even though he didn't stick around to earn a bigger

[a]bonus by taking a position in the Parish.
2 Instead, he turned out to be this great investigative reporter,
3 And broke a whole bunch of stories about amazing scandals in high places,
4 Starting with some big scandal in the military,
5 Which Mort's [b]father had been a career officer in,
6 [c]Explaining why Mort and his dad had never gotten along at all,
7 Which turned out to be all the incentive he needed to break a really big story,
8 [d]About corruption in the administration of weapons contracts,
9 And no one was more upset than Mort when his own father got dishonorably discharged,
10 And barely escaped a stiff prison sentence.
11 From there, Mort went on to break lots of big scandals,
12 [e]Including the scandal that almost ruined Sam's life,
13 [f]And the scandal that almost ruined Vinnie's life,
14 [g]And the scandal that almost ruined Ira's life,
15 [h]And the scandal that almost ruined Jerry's life,
16 [i]And the scandal that almost ruined Joe's life,
17 [j]Not to mention the scandal that almost ruined Ned's life,
18 Although Mort didn't have anything to do with the [k]scandal that almost ruined Tony's life,
19 Because who cares about some perverted college professor,
20 Who isn't even famous?
21 [l]Of course, Mort was much in demand to speak to clubs and fraternal organizations about ethics in journalism and other high places,
22 And his book made several million dollars,
23 And nobody ever found out that he was a Harrier[m],
24 Because everybody thought he was like some [n]friendly uncle,
25 And slightly above it all,
26 Which is why he would never stoop to anything sleazy or unscrupulous,
27 Or anything like that.

a. 37.9
b. Dav.52.4
c. Forg.2.12
d. Swar.25.1-5
e. 40.1-4
f. 42.1-8
g. 45.1-10
h. 46.1-10
i. 44.8-22
j. 41.1-10
k. 43.1-10
l. 46.5
m. 27.10
n. Ed.12.20-22
o. 21.14
p. 29.1-7 Psp.3.6
q. 38.7
r. 38.11
s. 45.1
t. 17.6-8
u. 32.6
v. Mawr.25.7-22

CHAPTER 48

Then there was [o]Fred,
2 Who didn't have such a great career,
3 [p]Because apparently he received a little too much Consolation during his year of service to Harry,
4 Which he promised to work off by being the [q]Arch-Harrier for the mid-Atlantic region,
5 Although that didn't work out,
6 And Ned had to demote him to [r]Parish Beacon a few weeks later,
7 Because [s]Ira thought it might tarnish the image of the Pontifical Harrier Parish if one of the original [t]Ultra-Harriers got ex-consolated,
8 Which is when [u]Vicki took Fred in hand,
9 What with him being almost completely helpless and emasculated by now,
10 [v]Which maybe explains why she kind of fell for him a little bit,
11 And talked me, Willie, into

giving him another chance,

12 Because I was in charge of getting all the [a]letters written to the Philadelphians.

13 Vicki thought that if Fred wrote a really great letter, maybe Harry would forgive him,

14 [b]And give him a nice bonus to retire on,

15 Because he really wasn't up to working steady.

16 [c]And then, of course, Fred's letter turned out to be not so great,

17 And actually quite embarrassing to me personally,

18 [d]Because I sort of neglected to read it before it went to [e]Ned for approval,

19 Which was a very big mistake.

20 When he read it, Ned was kind of upset,

21 [f]And said a lot of things about me, Willie, that I didn't appreciate,

22 Especially the part about how he might not have noticed it if [g]Vicki hadn't brought it to his attention,

23 [h]Which is why he decided to name her Vice President for [i]Orthodoxy instead of me.

24 And then Ned showed the letter to Harry,

25 [j]Who said that Fred had been a bad boy,

26 And that I had been a bad boy too,

27 Though maybe not as bad as Fred,

28 Which is why my punishment would be lighter,

29 And why he had decided to use the letter anyway,

30 With the bad part crossed out,

31 [k]So that everyone and his

a. *38.1-3*
b. *Psong.43.4*
c. *Cen.1.1-12*
d. *Wht.28*
e. *33.5-6*
f. *Main.27.3*
g. *48.13-15*
h. *Wht.35*
i. *Mawr.31.6-10*
j. *52.16*
k. *Main.27.9*
l. *Main.31.1-3*
m. *Jeff.5.5-8*
n. *Spic.7.1-9*
o. *16.29*
p. *14.7-9*
q. *Dav.55.21*
r. *48.23*
s. *41.19-20*
t. *Mawr.15.9-10*
u. *Mawr.32.1-17*
v. *Main.34.3-5*

brother would know that I, Willie, had screwed up.

32 Then Ned and Vicki tried to talk Harry out of using the letter,

33 Because it was still possible to read the bad parts,

34 But Harry just laughed and said, [l]**Harriers don't read any more than they absolutely have to, and they wouldn't [m]understand it if they did.**

35 **[n]Besides, what's the fun of having an orthodoxy if you can't make a big show out of suppressing heresy and punishing the heretics?**

36 **[o]Take it from me, Harry, it doesn't really matter what we say,**

37 **[p]As long as we can offer Consolation,**

38 **At competitive prices.**

39 And so that's how Fred's career ended,

40 And mine too.

CHAPTER 49

[q]**V**icki went on, of course, and served a very successful term as [r]Vice-President for Orthodoxy,

2 Even though she didn't get along as well with [s]Lucky when he took over as Number One,

3 [t]Which is why she threatened to sue him for gender discrimination,

4 [u]Since he wouldn't listen to any of her arguments about how women should be allowed to be Chosen Ones, and Arch-Harriers, and even Angels if they had the stomach for it, the way she had been promising all the female Parishioners,

5 [v]And so Lucky tried to fire her and even exconsolate her for threatening him,

6 Until ^aHarry got wind of it somehow,

7 And flew her down to Rio for a chat,

8 ^bWhich must have gone very well,

9 Because Harry ^cpromoted Vicki to Ultra-Harrier,

10 And gave her a new position as Number Two,

11 And started having monthly ^dmeetings with her in Rio,

12 Which Lucky didn't like,

13 ^eBut had to take anyway,

14 Which probably helps explain why Lucky retired pretty soon after that,

15 To Bogotá^f,

16 Which is when Joe took over as ^gNumber One,

17 ^hAnd Vicki quit in a huff,

18 And subsequently moved to Southern California,

19 To have her baby,

20 ⁱAnd raise it herself,

21 Which she wound up writing a book about,

22 ^jCalled 'One Baby Around the House Is Quite Enough, Thank You,'

23 Which sold five million copies,

24 Not including the cookbook,

25 And the postpartum exercise program,

26 Which are coming out next spring.

CHAPTER 50

Some of the other followers did pretty well for themselves too,

2 And became Ultra-Harriers,

3 ^kIncluding Wayne,

4 Who was actually named ^l*Nick* when ^mNed met him during the initial Silver Ghost tour.

5 As a matter of fact, Nick gave

a. *Wil.74.14-15*

b. *Wht.26*

c. *Main.27.4*

d. *Wht.25*

e. *Ned.30.42-43*

f. *50.23-24*

g. *38.6*

h. *Mawr.15.13-22*

i. *Mawr.20.17-18*

j. *Ned.36.20-24*

k. *Psp.3.6*

l. *Dav.57.34*

m. *21.8*

n. *Wht.6*

o. *32.9-10*

p. *Brd.27.1-11*

q. *Wht.34*

r. *38.13*

s. *38.6*

t. *48.39*

u. *Psp.3.11*

Ned a pretty hard time about the ⁿWay of Harry for quite a while,

6 And even threatened to go to the authorities to stop Ned from starting his new business,

7 Until he got a visit from ^oLucky,

8 ^pWho gave him some Consolation,

9 ^qAnd opened his eyes to all the opportunities of Harry's Way,

10 Which caused Nick to be converted right away,

11 And wash his hands of everything,

12 And change his name to Wayne for some reason,

13 Right then and there.

14 From then on, Wayne followed Harry like nobody's business.

15 He was the first follower not in the original eleven to become a ^rVice-President,

16 And the only follower who had a degree in chemistry and an MBA,

17 Which is why everybody thought he might make it all the way to ^sNumber One someday,

18 ^tEspecially when he did such a smooth job of retiring Fred after the letter thing,

19 Which is when Harry made him an Ultra-Harrier,

20 And gave him a corner office with a window.

21 But then, a couple of years ago, something strange happened.

22 ^uOne afternoon, Wayne walked out of his corner office at Parish Headquarters,

23 And disappeared,

24 Without a trace,

25 Taking no money or Consolation with him,

26 Thus explaining why Wayne has become one of the ^aGreat Mysteries of the Pontifical Harrier Parish,

27 And is still remembered as a Great Ultra-Harrier^b.

CHAPTER 51

Another follower named ^cMike also became an Ultra-Harrier.

2 Mike joined the Silver Ghost Tour after he flunked out of law school,

3 And took a position as a ^dChosen One,

4 With the idea of going to medical school on his bonus,

5 Because Ned thought he could fix it,

6 Which he did.

7 And so Mike went on to become a great plastic surgeon,

8 And specialized in breast enlargements,

9 Which he did so well at that even ^eVicki went to him,

10 Not long before her first trip to ^fRio,

11 And Mike made so much money that he moved to ^gBeverly Hills,

12 Where he enlarged the breasts of the ^hstars day in and day out,

13 Until he got ⁱsued,

14 By ^jTony's wife,

15 Who said that he had ruined her career,

16 ^kAnd wanted fifteen million dollars.

17 Unfortunately, Mike wasn't able to retain a really good lawyer,

18 ^lFor some reason,

19 And he lost big,

20 Which is why he had to stop practicing medicine,

---

a. 16.20
b. Yks.153.14
c. Dav.57.18
d. 38.9
e. Mawr.12.1-3 & 12.11
f. 49.5-11
g. 43.18
h. Dav.4.7-10
i. Penn.2.1-3
j. 43.17
k. Jefs.10.1-10
l. Penn.1.1-2
m. 51.18
n. Ira.23.8
o. Vin.24.9-12
p. Vin.29.1-4
q. 17.6-13
r. 38.8
s. 9.6-7
t. 41.19-20

---

21 And start curing cancer with hypnosis in Mexico,

22 Which turned out to be even more lucrative than breast enlargement,

23 ^mEven though his patients mostly died.

CHAPTER 52

There was also a follower named ⁿMatt who became an Ultra-Harrier.

2 Matt started out as an ^oAngel,

3 And worked his way up,

4 Attracting lots of attention with his ^pcrowd-control talents during the days of Harry,

5 ^qUntil he was named head of security for the Silver Ghost Tour,

6 With the title of ^rArch-Angel,

7 ^sProbably because of the way he had handled the problem with Tom,

8 Not to mention the fact that he was the only Angel who had actually been to college, even if he did get kicked out for assault with a deadly weapon,

9 Which always made Harry laugh when it came up in conversation,

10 And maybe explains why Harry thought of Matt right away when ^tLucky moved up and the Parish needed a new Vice-President for Production and Distribution,

11 In charge of all Harrier Angels and Arch-Angels.

12 That's when Matt changed his name,

13 Because he was wanted in several states,

14 And had to be free to travel in his new job,

15 And also had to have a passport,

16 Obviously.

17 Anyway,

18 He may not have been as popular as some of the other Ultra-Harriers,

19 ªBecause there were a few people who thought he should have been more careful the day he escorted ᵇFred home after the retirement party,

20 Although ᶜVicki always defended him, and she must have known him pretty well, because I know for a fact that she helped him write a letter to the ᵈKensingtonians to give his resumé a boost,

21 And ᵉHarry seemed to like him a lot too,

22 Which is why some people even thought he had a shot at becoming ᶠNumber One himself someday,

23 Especially after ᵍWayne disappeared,

24 ʰBut then he disappeared too,

25 And the story was completely stonewalled by ⁱNumber Two's office,

26 ʲWhen there still was such an office,

27 ᵏAnd I, Willie, have never asked any questions about it,

28 ˡBecause I have learned my lessons well,

29 And when that many Ultra-Harriers get as angry as they were when Matt disappeared,

30 It's better not to ask questions,

31 And all I know about it for sure is that Matt is still remembered as a Great Ultra-Harrier,

32 In good standing.

33 And if I knew any more about it than that,

34 ᵐI would keep it to myself,

a. 50.18
b. Pnot.22.1-5
c. Pnot.28.1-5
d. Kens.20.1-10
e. Vin.11.4-6
f. Kens.1.6-8
g. Pnot.27.1-5
h. 39.7-9
i. Ned.8.10
j. 49.9-10
*   Mawr.23.15*
k. 39.10
l. 39.11
m. Rat.23.8-14
n. 38.16-17
o. 3.26
p. Wil.29.13-18
q. 26.7-8
r. Pnot.42.1-5
s. Psong.46.1
t. Vin.59.10-11

35 Because I am still an Ultra-Harrier at least,

36 And I don't want to lose my ⁿdiscount,

37 Or anything else of value.

CHAPTER 53

As for me, ºWillie, I have not had as spectacular a career as the other Ultra-Harriers,

2 Which maybe would have been different if even one literary magazine had accepted one of the short stories I wrote in college,

3 Which they didn't,

4 And maybe explains why I never finished my Great American Novel,

5 And went with Harry instead.

6 ᵖBut not every Harrier has to be a big Success,

7 ᑫAnd I'm trying to set a good example in my own small way,

8 By not really thinking about anything at all,

9 Or caring about anything,

10 Or taking responsibility for any of the things that are happening in my life,

11 ʳBecause it's easier to sit back and just let it all happen,

12 And arrange to be out of town when Mort or Vicki calls,

13 Because it's also important for each and every Harrier to recognize when another Harrier is better at Harry's Trinity,

14 And not to take a chance on getting squashed by them,

15 ˢEven if you're still kind of deeply in love with one of them for some reason,

16 Which is an important thing for everyone to know,

17 Especially all the ᵗlittle Harriers,

18 Because the Way of Harry

has come into its full glory now,
19 And things will be like this
for a long time,
20 Until the world ends anyway,
21 Unless it doesn't,
22 ªWhich is unlikely,
23 But even if it doesn't, the Way of Harry may last for a couple of thousand years,
24 ᵇJust like the way of the one he replaced,
25 ᶜBecause it takes a pretty

a. *Ned. 16.12-13*
b. *Jeff. 1.1-4*
c. *Dav. 15.3-51*
   Ned. 1.1-6
   Psp. 3.3-17
d. *Rom. 20.2-3*
   Wil. 2.1-5
e. *Wil. 60.2*
f. *Barb. 7.7*

outrageous series of events to result in a new Way,
26 ᵈWhich almost always comes from the unlikeliest places,
27 ᵉFrom people who are the lowest of the low,
28 Who have to get fired up enough to do something radically different,
29 Which just isn't the way things work anymore,
30 ᶠThanks to Harry.

ULT. TONY'S ABC'S

FOR THE

HILLITES

CHAPTER 1

Salve, magistri.
2 Excuse me.
3 I forgot that teachers don't know any ªLatin anymore,
4 Or anything else.
5 Let me start again,
6 In terms you can understand more easily,
7 Because ᵇI am writing to tell you about the Way of Harry,
8 And why it will make your life easier,
9 And nicer.
10 Do we understand everything so far?
11 Very good.

CHAPTER A

ᶜ**A** is for the Alphabet,
2 Which teachers have to teach.

a. *Jefs. 7.1*
   & 8.1
   & 9.1
   & 10.1
   & 11.19
b. *Ext. 43.1*
c. *Grk. 4.11-12*
d. *F&J. 10.1-2*

3 Let's call them ᵈDick and Jane,
4 Just for fun.
5 Dick and Jane can teach the Alphabet without even thinking about it,
6 Because they know it so well.
7 If everything were as easy to teach as the Alphabet,
8 Dick and Jane would have a lot more time for other more important things,
9 Like complaining about their Awful pay,
10 And their Abysmal working conditions,
11 And how they don't get Anything from Anybody,
12 Anything but Aggravation, that is,
13 And Antagonism,
14 And Accusations,
15 Not to mention a lot of character Assassination,

16 And almost weekly felonious Assaults by the [a]Animals in their classrooms,
17 Even though Dick and Jane are so Above Average at what they do.
18 See Dick and Jane being Above Average?
19 Well, they would be if teaching could be made easier,
20 And didn't require so much of their Attention.
21 But nobody seems to be listening to their Arguments,
22 And Dick and Jane are starting to get Angry about that.
23 In fact, if we don't treat them less Atrociously,
24 They'll quit and go do something else instead,
25 Something easier and better-paying and less Annoying.
26 See Dick and Jane go do something else instead,
27 And not do any more teaching,
28 At All?
29 What is the something else Dick and Jane are doing instead?
30 I don't know either.
31 [b]What could it possibly be?
32 Why, isn't that Astonishing?
33 They're still here,
34 But they're still Angry too,
35 And they're Absolutely Adamant about not putting up with any more Attacks on their Abilities.

CHAPTER B

B is for the Better life that Dick and Jane have a [c]right to,
2 Because they've earned everybody's respect,
3 And everybody can see how Beautiful a job Dick and Jane are doing at educating everybody,
4 Which shouldn't be too surprising,
5 Since Dick and Jane have a whole Bunch of [d]Booklearning.
6 See Dick and Jane looking Brainy?
7 What is it they know, exactly?
8 I can't quite tell either.
9 See Dick and Jane getting Belligerent?
10 They're not going to take this kind of Baloney anymore,
11 [e]Because it's absolutely, positively not their fault that the little Bums learn less each year,
12 [f]And can't read a Book,
13 Or write anything but the kind of [g]Bilge you see on Bathroom walls,
14 Or do even a tiny little Bit of [h]arithmetic,
15 Or anything else,
16 Except [i]Beer and Barbiturates and [j]Backseat Biology, of course,
17 Which still isn't the fault of Dick and Jane,
18 Because how can you make the little Barbarians learn a Bunch of Boring [k]Basics when they know there isn't really any future,
19 Thanks to the [l]Bomb and [m]Brezhnev and all?
20 Besides, how can you expect Dick and Jane to teach anything at all in such a Bourgeois neighborhood,
21 Where all the parents are so Busy Bickering about [n]Busing,
22 And [o]Banning the Bible,
23 And [p]Bringing Back the Bible,
24 That they don't actually have time to Baby-sit the little [q]Baboons through their homework,
25 Because if you want to know

a. Kens.7.7-9
b. Psong.17.1-7
c. Brd.14.1-6
d. K.1-5
e. Wil.23.5-7
f. Ira.29.1-2
g. Wil.36.1-7
h. Psay.4.1
i. Vin.16.2-29
j. H.5
k. Psay.5.1
l. Dav.46.44
m. Dav.22.47
n. Rat.10.25-26
o. Jeff.19.11-16
p. Jeff.21.1-4
q. Kin.5.1-5

the truth, they can't Bear the little ᵃBastards either.

26 That's why Dick and Jane have Broken with the old ways,

27 ᵇAnd are Bent on following the Way of Harry instead.

28 See Dick and Jane not thinking about anything at all?

29 Don't they look ᶜBlissful,

30 And different?

31 Of course they do.

32 Right now, they're making a list of all the things that are to Blame for the fact that the little Braindead ᵈBozos aren't learning anything,

33 And what it will take to make things Better,

34 Starting with ᵉBetter pay,

35 And Better facilities,

36 And don't forget ᶠBetter pay.

37 Can you see Better teachers on the list anywhere?

38 I'll Bet you can't.

39 Not if they're following the Way of Harry.

CHAPTER C

C is for the Certainty Dick and Jane feel about how nothing is their fault,

2 Because they didn't ask to be Conceived by their parents,

3 And it wasn't their fault they couldn't get into a really ᵍClassy College,

4 And wound up ʰCaged inside a Classroom instead.

5 Dick and Jane have figured out that absolutely nobody wants to put up with the little Creeps anymore,

6 The ones who Come to school with a Chip on their shoulder,

7 ⁱAnd sit there staring like a bunch of dead Carp,

8 ʲNot thinking about anything at all,

---

a. Oth.5.18
b. Wht.6
c. Ext.13.18
d. Drex.6.10
e. Psong.7.1-4
f. Psong.11.1-8
g. Psay.5E.3-4
h. F&J.5.2-3
i. Kens.9.8-9
*   Ned.30.42*
j. Jefs.11.19
*   Hill.1.2-4*
k. Zig.9.2
l. Wil.31.3
m. Ned.35.9

---

9 And that's about it,

10 Except for making Crude Comments whenever they feel like it,

11 Which is Constantly.

12 In fact, Dick and Jane are so Certain about all this,

13 ᵏThat there isn't any way at all to make them Consider how they might be at least partially to blame for what's happening to all the little Cretins,

14 Even when the Critics question their Competence,

15 And accuse them of being Callous and Careless and Complacent,

16 And suggest that Complaining is the only part of teaching Dick and Jane really know anything about,

17 Which is actually the only part of teaching that's *worth* knowing anything about,

18 When you're following the Way of Harry.

CHAPTER D

D is for the Danger of not being certain,

2 Which can lead to the Disease called thinking,

3 ˡWhich leads to thoughts of Doom and Despair,

4 And would Destroy the last best hope of happiness for Dick and Jane.

5 That's why it's so much better for Dick and Jane to concentrate on their Desires instead,

6 ᵐAnd be certain about Doing whatever is necessary to satisfy their Desires,

7 No matter who gets hurt,

8 Because that's the best Defense against the Dire consequences of thinking.

CHAPTER E

^a**E** is for Education,

2 Except that it isn't,

3 ^bBecause Education isn't Easy,

4 Which is what E is for,

5 If you're following the way of Harry.

CHAPTER F

F is for the only word that every child in the Most Chosen Nation knows how to spell,

2 Which is a Fantastically Flexible word,

3 Because it means whatever you Feel it should.

4 It's a Fortunate word too,

5 Because it's also the only word that Dick and Jane still know how to spell,

6 If they're Following the Way of Harry,

7 Because the Way of Harry gives everyone at least one thing in common,

8 Just for Fun.

CHAPTER G

G is for Getting by,

2 ^cWhich is the Great unifying Goal of the entire educational system in the Most Chosen Nation in the whole history of the planet.

3 See Dick and Jane Getting by?

4 See the little Garbage-mouths in their classroom Getting by?

5 Well, that's because you don't quite Get the Way of Harry yet.

6 You've Got to understand that Getting by will have a different meaning in each ^dGeneration from now on,

7 As long as the Hillites keep

doing their jobs according to the Way of Harry.

8 For example, the next Generation may not have to know how to spell even the one word they know how to spell now,

9 Because the Goal of Getting by is a lot like ^eGravity,

10 And Goads everyone and everything in the same direction all the time,

11 Gradually,

12 But equally,

13 Which means that it is not only the Way of Harry,

14 ^fBut also a Grand tradition of the Most Chosen Nation on Earth.

CHAPTER H

^g**H** is for Hygiene,

2 Which the little Hellions absolutely have to learn,

3 Because nothing spoils a school year for Dick and Jane like having five or six or seventeen of their little ^hHotpants Hussies get knocked up over Christmas vacation,

4 Which just isn't necessary,

5 Because fully Half the school library is about How to Have sex without Having Babies,

6 Including Horribly Helpful little ⁱaudio tapes,

7 So that even the Hardcore Hardheads can Hear Handy Hints about Humping without Heartache,

8 Which don't Halt the Horny little Harlots from taking Huge risks,

9 Because H is also for Hormones,

10 Which are Highly Hazardous,

11 Especially if you're a Harrier,
12 In High School.

CHAPTER I

I is for I,[a]
2 Which is the only authority the little Idiots recognize,
3 [b]Since they've never had any Interest in anyone else's viewpoint,
4 Even if they don't have what you'd call a well-developed sense of [c]Individual Identity,
5 Which makes Instruction even more Irritating for Dick and Jane,
6 Because they feel pretty much the [d]Identical way,
7 And it's Infuriating that they have to put up with so much Insolence from all the Ingrates in their classrooms,
8 When it's Intrinsically Indicated that they should be obeyed Implicitly,
9 If not Idolized,
10 Because they're such Impressive Intellectuals,
11 As all the Insipid Instigators of Educational "Improvement" would be able to Infer,
12 If they were at all Informed,
13 Or Intelligent,
14 Or even Involved,
15 Instead of Irresponsible,
16 And Injurious,
17 And downright Invidious,
18 Which they are,
19 As Dick and Jane would be the first to Imply,
20 If they knew what Invidious meant.

CHAPTER J

J is for Justice,

a. *Psay.51.1-6*
b. *Wil.37.1-7*
   Mall.8.1-8
c. *Kens.12.25*
d. *I.3*
e. *Penn.9.11*
f. *Mawr.15.19-22*
g. *Wil.38.1-3*
h. *Wil.33.5-6*
i. *Ann.18.10-26*
j. *W.1-8*
k. *Gnt.4.20*
l. *Ext.52.16*
m. *Carl.3.8*
n. *Main.15.1-6*
o. *Ned.8.2-6*

2 Which Dick and Jane would absolutely demand,
3 If there were any such thing as Justice,
4 [e]Which there Just isn't,
5 If you're following the Way of Harry,
6 Which is why Dick and Jane are so dejected,
7 Unless they're actually Jubilant instead,
8 Which they couldn't be,
9 Because absolutely everyone wants Justice,
10 Unless you're a Harrier,
11 And would rather be the Judge yourself,
12 And the Jury,
13 And Just make up the Jurisprudence as you go,
14 [f]Which beats Justice by a country mile.

CHAPTER K

K is for [g]Knowledge,
2 Which is the whole purpose of education,
3 And explains why Dick and Jane don't have to think about it anymore,
4 Because they already got their education,
5 [h]Years ago.

CHAPTER L

L is for [i]Love,
2 Which would solve all the problems in the [j]world,
3 And explains why Dick and Jane don't have to teach [k]philosophy anymore,
4 [l]Or religion,
5 [m]Or political science,
6 [n]Or civics,
7 Since it was the [o]Luminaries in Dick and Jane's generation

who discovered Love in the first place,

8 ªAnd somehow the Little Lovebirds in Dick and Jane's classes have Learned that it's the Logical answer for every possible social issue,

9 No matter how Ludicrous it might sound.

CHAPTER M

M is for ᵇMusic,

2 Which the little Maniacs know an awful lot about,

3 Unless you Mean ᶜMozart,

4 Or Mahler,

5 Or Mendelssohn,

6 Or Mussorgsky,

7 Or even Mantovani,

8 ᵈWhich is why it Might be better to ask them about Mick instead.

CHAPTER N

N is for ᵉNow,

2 Which is the only ᶠtime that matters,

3 In the Most Chosen Nation on Earth.

CHAPTER O

O is for the ᵍOthers,

2 ʰWho always get it in the neck,

3 And who are the ⁱOnly good guys left in the history book,

4 Because it's very important to give the little Ogres an Object lesson,

5 ʲIn the Ontogeny of Blame.

CHAPTER P

P is for ᵏParents,

a. *Cen.15.11-14*
b. *Psay.5G.16-17*
c. *Ed.60.17*
d. *Dav.58.7*
e. *Wil.39.1-5 Cen.12.15-19*
f. *Psom.8.1-5*
g. *Oth.1.1-15*
h. *Ext.45.1-5*
i. *Swar.34.2-22*
j. *Ira.23.15-18*
k. *Ann.2.15 & 2.18*
l. *Dav.47.8*
m. *Zig.9.2*
n. *Ned.34.22-24*
o. *Mall.5.1-8*
p. *Mawr.15.22*

2 Who are a Pain in the Pants to Dick and Jane,

3 With all their Preaching in PTA meetings,

4 And all their Penny-Pinching in Precinct voting,

5 And all their Popping off to the Press,

6 And all their Permissiveness with the little Pariahs they're ˡover-Populating the Planet with,

7 And all their Pompous Posturing in Public Opinion Polls,

8 ᵐAnd all their Prevarications about their Puny Participation in their Progeny's upbringing.

9 And if Dick and Jane's own Prize Pups were Performing just a tiny bit better than anybody else's,

10 They'd get Pretty Peevish about the whole Parent Problem,

11 And they Probably will anyway,

12 ⁿIf they're Pursuing the Path of Harry.

CHAPTER Q

Q is for Questions,

2 ᵒWhich nobody really asks anymore,

3 Unless it's about Quitting class early,

4 Which is the Question Dick and Jane really like best,

5 Because it's the one they know the answer to.

CHAPTER R

R is for Rightsᵖ,

2 Which everyone has,

3 Including even the little Rotters in Dick and Jane's classes,

4 Which somebody Related to them at some point,

5 So that they can Reel them off anytime,

6 Almost as Rapidly as Dick and Jane can,

7 Like the Right to be [a]free,

8 And the Right to be [b]Rich,

9 And the Right to be [c]Rude,

10 And the Right to be [d]Raunchy whenever you feel like it,

11 And the Right to get [e]Ripped whenever you feel like it,

12 And the Right to [f]Relax whenever you need a Rest,

13 And the Right to [g]Regard other people's property as Refuse,

14 And the Right to [h]Reject any Rules you don't like,

15 And the Right to [i]Ridicule everyone and everything you don't like,

16 Not to mention the Right to be self-Righteous about your Rights,

17 And utterly [j]Ruthless about protecting them.

CHAPTER S

S is for the Suburbs,

2 Which is where Dick and Jane live[k],

3 Not to mention all the little Sewer-mouths in their class,

4 Which is where they've learned all their Superb Social Skills.

5 See all the Stylish little Subdivisions in the Suburbs?

6 [l]See all the Spanking new Split-levels in the Subdivisions?

7 See all the Sensible Station wagons parked in front of the Split-levels?

8 See all the Snazzy little Sport Sedans parked next to the Station wagons?

---

a. *Psom.73.9-12*
b. *Vin.47.7-11*
c. *Mall.8.25-31*
d. *F.1*
e. *Vin.17.26-27*
f. *Mall.11.9-16*
g. *V.1*
h. *I.1-2*
i. *Swar.PS.28-30*
j. *Ext.52.16*
k. *Ed.61.17*
l. *Ira.6.9-10*
m. *Mall.12.10*
n. *Mall.1.1*
o. *Dav.58.9*
p. *O.4-5*
q. *Spic.6.8*
r. *Mawr.30.9-10*
s. *Psay.5S.1-3*
t. *Wil.27.8*
u. *Mawr.23.13-16*
v. *H.9-12*
w. *Wil.78.6-7*
x. *O.1-2*

---

9 See all the Spruce little Shrubs that Separate the Split-levels?

10 See the Spindly little Sapling that Someone Stuck in front of each Split-level?

11 Isn't it all just Splendid?

12 See the [m]School Situated down the Street,

13 A Stone's throw from the nearest Suburban [n]mall?

14 This is the School where the little Sad Sacks learn all the Subjects they will need to Succeed in life,

15 Like Science[o],

16 [p]And Social Studies,

17 [q]And Spanish,

18 [r]And Shop.

19 See the [s]Sports fields next to the School?

20 This is where the little Studs learn all the Stuff they will need to know about Stomping the excrement out of their [t]opponents in life,

21 Like Screaming obscenities at the officials,

22 And always Sliding with your Spikes high,

23 And Spearing the other team's Star when the official isn't looking,

24 And other Skills too,

25 Which it's a Shame the Sissy girls aren't getting too,

26 The way Jane looks at it.

27 [u]See Jane looking Steamed in the Stands about how the little Sisters in her class don't get to play enough Sports?

28 [v]See all the Sexy little Strumpets in the Stands thinking about Some Special Sports of their own?

29 [w]See all the Starry-eyed parents in the Stands, Shrieking for another Stupendous victory?

30 See all the [x]Others in the

Stands, Side by Side with the
Suburban Set?
31 ªWell, that's because there
aren't any Others in the Suburbs,
32 ᵇWhich is maybe why the
little Striplings admire them so
much,
33 Not to mention Dick and
Jane,
34 Although I suppose we really
Should,
35 Because they're just So men-
tionable,
36 Somehow.

CHAPTER T

T is for Tests,
2 Which have to be Taken by
the little Twerps,
3 Before Dick and Jane can
Turn them over to some other
Teacher,
4 For another Try at the Three
R's.
5 See Dick and Jane grading
ᶜTests?
6 How Tolerant they are of Tiny
little errors on the True/false
section!
7 How Tactful they are in not
Tearing up those Tragic little essays!
8 How Tempted they are to pass
everyone!
9 Well, isn't that Terrific?
10 ᵈWhat Talented Teachers
Dick and Jane must be!
11 As it Turns out, not even one
of the little Thugs will have to
repeat the Term!

CHAPTER U

U is for the ᵉUnion,
2 Which is the only entity in the
ᶠUniverse that really Under-

a. Ext.52.16
b. Carl.10.12
c. Cen.26.1-19
d. G.1-2
e. Adam.28.1-10
f. Psay.5U.1-23
g. Psong.13.1-5
h. Psay.5S.7
i. Mawr.15.13-18
j. Psong.16.1-3
k. Ira.11.5
l. Barb.3.1-5
m. H.9-12
n. S.21-23
o. Swar.PS.14-15
Ext.25.1
p. Kens.12.11-15

stands Dick and Jane's needs,
3 And how truly Unfortunate it
is that everyone else is Usually
so Uncooperative,
4 ᵍWhich is why Dick and Jane
are so Underpaid,
5 And so Under-appreciated,
6 And so likely to Undertake
another ʰstrike,
7 Unless the school board takes
their ⁱdemands Under advise-
ment,
8 ʲAnd Underwrites another
huge raise.
9 See the school board,
10 Under the gun?
11 See Dick and Jane,
12 Under a ᵏpicket sign?
13 See all the Harriers,
14 Under the sun?

CHAPTER V

V is for ˡVandalism,
2 Which is the only skill the
little Varmints excel at,
3 Unless you count ᵐVenereal
pursuits,
4 And ⁿVarsity sports,
5 Which is why it's so Very
important not to be too Vindictive about punishing them,
6 Because if you Value your
children,
7 It's more Virtuous to Validate
their good behavior than to Vic-
timize them for petty Villainies,
8 Especially if you don't want
them to Vivisect your ºVolvo,
9 Because V is also for ᵖVen-
geance,
10 If you're a Harrier.

CHAPTER W

W is for the World,
2 Which all the little Whining

Weasels couldn't know less about,

3 Especially geography,

4 In spite of Dick and Jane's best efforts.

5 See Dick and Jane teaching World geography?

6 Well,

7 They Would,

8 If it Were in the curriculum.

9 It is?

10 Oh.

11 See Dick and Jane teaching World geography?

12 See the little Whiz kids identifying the largest river system in South America?

13 Well, that's because they didn't get to Waterways yet.

14 See the little Wonders identifying the largest country in South America?

15 Well, that's because they didn't get to Western [a]nations yet.

16 See the little Wasters identifying the continent of South America?

17 Well, that's because . . .

18 Well, you know,

20 [b]And besides, all's Well that ends Well,

21 And they'll end Well,

a. *Psuy.5N.1-20*
b. *Pnot.56.1-5*
c. *Psom.35.4*
d. *Psay.5X.1*
e. *Drex.7.10*
f. *Psay.5Y.1-56*
g. *Ned.16.12-13*
h. *Ned.16.14-15*

22 Won't they?

23 Well?[c]

CHAPTER X

[d]**X** is for the Unknown Variable,

2 [e]Which is getting more and more unknown all the time,

3 Just like Algebra.

CHAPTER Y

[f]**Y** is for Years,

2 Which is how long each and every semester lasts,

3 For Dick and Jane.

CHAPTER Z

Z is for Zero,

2 Which is the easiest number to count to,

3 And why Dick and Jane like it so much,

4 Which is just as well,

5 [g]Because that's the number the Most Chosen Zoo on Earth is counting down to,

6 Which is why it's so nice to have Harry's Way,

7 To give our countdown,

8 Just the right [h]Zip.

ULT. MORT'S BROADCAST
TO THE
ANNENBURGHERS

CHAPTER 1

I'd like to welcome all the communications professionals in our audience to today's edition of the Harry Show.

2 Of course, Harry can't be with us this morning,

3 Because he's in Rio instead,

4 Which is why ªI will be your guest host,

5 For the great show we have planned,

6 Which will start immediately after the following ᵇcommercial announcements.

7 Stay tuned.

CHAPTER 2

"Nobody's thinking about it,

2 "But it's coming anyway,

3 "And it'll be here before you know it!

4 "What is it?

5 "It's the great new fall season on the Harrier Television Network!

6 "You say you like sitcoms?

7 "Well, we've got 'em,

8 ᶜ"And they're just exactly like all the others you've always loved,

9 "Only more so.

10 "Take 'I Love the Family Next Door,'

11 ᵈ"Please!

12 "The Sleasel family are the neighbors everybody loves to hate,

---

a. Ext.47.1
b. Ed.76.1-4
c. Vin.40.6-7
d. Grk.16.4-5
e. Vin.57.5
f. Cen.15.6-14
g. H.5-8

---

13 "Which is why you'll just love them to death.

14 "*Flush!*

15 "Why that must be Arnie Sleasel, the long-suffering ᵉdad who's always so painfully constipated that everyone just runs for cover when they hear him flush the toilet,

16 "Which happens a lot on 'I Love the Family Next Door.'

17 "*Flush!*

18 "Why that must be Arnie's wife May, who suffers from chronic diarrhea, and keeps everybody in stitches with endless jokes about Arnie's intestines, not to mention his impotence and his rotten wages as a muffler mechanic.

19 "*Flush!*

20 "Why that must be little Billy, the Sleasels' ᶠprecocious son, who's only twelve but spends a lot of time in the bathroom with Arnie's 'Playboy,' and who gets off some really good ones about his parents' intestines, and Arnie's impotence, and May's flat chest, not to mention his sister Barbara's chest, which is anything but flat, even though she's only fourteen.

21 "*Flush!*

22 ᵍ"Why that must be Barbara now. She's constantly in the bathroom because of her medication, which she's needed ever since she came home from Times Square,

23 "Which is one of many reasons why the Sleasels' neighbors never say a word to them,

24 "Not even when their house catches on fire,

25 "On Christmas Eve,

26 [a]"Because the Sleasels are the neighbors everybody loves to hate,

27 "Like you will too,

28 "When you join us,

29 [b]"And start plumbing the depths,

30 "Of the family next door,

31 "Wednesday nights at eight.

32 *"Flush!"*

CHAPTER 3

"**W**hat famous rocker is dating the wives of three prominent national politicians?

2 "What Oscar-winning actress is under suspicion for the hit-and-run death of a six-year-old boy from East Los Angeles?

3 "Which major league [c]MVP is suing his parents to recover the money he lent them for a house in Florida?

4 "Which eminent religious figure is rumored to be dying from a disgusting venereal disease?

5 "What beloved sitcom star is fighting the fight of his life against charges of child abuse?

6 "If you don't know the answers to these questions, then you're not up on the latest dirt,

7 "So you'd better dive for the new issue of the 'Gutter Daily,'

8 "On newsstands now.

9 "Remember our motto,

10 "All the dirt we can find and print—just for you."

CHAPTER 4

"**C**hop-a-chop-a-chop-a-chop-a-chop!

a. Kens.28.6
b. Ed.67.13-15
c. Hill.S.20
d. Swar.23.2-11
e. Dav.57.30

2 "At last!

3 "The movie that finally dares to tell the truth about Vietnam!

4 "Get ready for 'It's a Mad Mad Mad Mad War,'

5 [d]"The new blockbuster hit from the director who brought you 'Viva the Cong,'

6 "'I Spit on the Red, White, and Blue,'

7 "'Yankee, Get Out of Our Home,'

8 "And 'Napalm Nightmare.'

9 "Yes, maybe you think you've seen it all,

10 "The genocide . . .

11 "The baby burning . . .

12 "The massacres and mutilations . . .

13 "The full-bore madness that was Vietnam.

14 "But if you haven't seen 'It's a Mad Mad Mad Mad War,'

15 "You haven't seen the half of it,

16 "Because only a comedy can really capture it all the way it really was,

17 "The absurd ambushes . . .

18 "The preposterous search-and-destroy missions . . .

19 "The ironic horror of the world's deadliest jungle . . .

20 "The bizarre laughter of the world's mightiest political machine,

21 "Gone mad,

22 *"Chop-a-chop,*

23 "Mad,

24 *"Chop-a-chop-a-chop,*

25 "Mad,

26 *"Chop-a-chop-a-chop-a-chop,*

27 "MAD,

28 *"CHOP-A-CHOP-A-CHOP-A-CHOP-A-CHOP,*

29 "Be there when the [e]president's chopper lands,

30 "On the insane green killing grounds,
31 "Of the [a]White House lawn.
32 In [b]Washington, D.C.!
33 "Coming soon to a theater near you."
34 "*CHOP-A-CHOP-A-CHOP-A-CHOP-A-CHOP-A-CHOP!*"

a. *Yks.16.1-2*
b. *Yks.16.3*
c. *Yks.125.31-34*
d. *Main.36.16*
e. *Adam.28.16*
f. *Wil.27.8*
g. *Ed.76.4-12*

CHAPTER 5

We're back,
2 And ready to discuss our topic of the day,
3 Which is 'How to Spread the Word of Harry Without Really Thinking About It,
4 'At All.'
5 We'll be meeting our guest Harriers and getting into some really in-depth stuff,
6 In just a moment,
7 But first,
8 It's time for a few words from our sponsors,
9 So don't go away,
10 Because we'll be right back.

CHAPTER 6

"Wh-o-o-o-o-sh!
2 [c]"Only a motorcar crafted in Germany can make a sound like that!
3 "*Wh-o-o-o-o-sh!*
4 "There it goes again: How many times are you going to let it pass you by?
5 "After all, how is everyone else going to know how much money you make,
6 "And what great taste you have;
7 "And what a manly man you are,
8 "If you're not at the wheel of the most expensive car made in Germany?
9 "*Wh-o-o-o-o-sh!*
10 "Doesn't it make you just sick with desire?
11 "*Wh-o-o-o-o-sh!*
12 "Can't you see that having this car would fix everything that's wrong in your life?
13 [d]"Women will beg you for rides,
14 "The best [e]country clubs will ask you to join,
15 "Your [f]peers will turn green with envy,
16 "Because everyone you see will know that you are a Winner!
17 "*Wh-o-o-o-o-sh!*
18 [g]"The Good Life.
19 "Don't[j] let it pass you by again,
20 "Because if you wait till you can actually afford it,
21 "You might wait till it's too late,
22 "When your chance at the Good Life has already passed you by.
23 "*Wh-o-o-o-o-o-o-sh!*"

CHAPTER 7

"Nobody's thinking about it,
2 "But it's coming anyway,
3 "And it'll be here before you know it!
4 "What is it?
5 "It's the great new fall season on the Harrier Television Network!
6 "You say you like sitcoms?
7 "Well, we've got 'em,
8 "And they're just exactly like all the others you've always loved,
9 "Only more so.

10 "Take 'I Love Rock and Rose,'
11 "Please!
12 [a]"Basil Rose used to be a district attorney,
13 "And Rock Stromboli used to be an armed robber,
14 "But now they're cellmates,
15 "Because of the hilarious mistake that transfers Rock to a special minimum-security prison for white-collar convicts,
16 "Which is when the fun really begins!
17 "Yes, you'll laugh yourselves sick at the funniest [b]culture clash since,
18 "Well,
19 "Since sometime last season.
20 "You'll hoot when Rock learns how to negotiate a [c]book contract!
21 "You'll howl when Rose learns how to make a shiv out of a [d]spoon!
22 "You'll scream when Rock tries to play [e]backgammon with brass knuckles! You'll bust a gut when Rose gets his first tattoo!
23 "And you'll just die laughing when Rock and Rose team up to run the [f]funniest mail-order swindle ever devised in prison!
24 "Will they get caught,
25 "Or will they get away with everything,
26 "And make a million bucks besides?
27 "Be watching when the Great New Season begins,
28 "On the Harrier Television Network.
29 " 'I Love Rock and Rose.'
30 "Sunday nights at eight o'clock."

a. Ext.40.4-7
b. Ed.62.1-4
c. Ned.36.20-24
d. Ext.12.7
e. Psay.5S.26
f. Ext.39.3
g. Swar.32.1-17
h. F&J.7.9-12
i. Dav.57.26

CHAPTER 8

"**H**e got mad about all the junk mail,
2 "And now he's getting even,
3 "With a little help from his incinerator,
4 "Because ashes can't scream.
5 " 'The Junk Mail Man,'
6 "Now in paperback,
7 "After 46 weeks on the New York Times Best Seller List,
8 [g]"From the best-selling author of 'The Dry Cleaner,' 'The Electrical Inspector,' 'The Tax Assessor,' and 'The Meter Reader.'
9 "Your money back if you're not terrified and revolted.
10 " 'The Junk Mail Man,'
11 "At better newsstands everywhere."

CHAPTER 9

We're back,
2 Just in time to talk with our exciting guests,
3 Who were giving us some great advice about how to spread the Word of Harry,
4 During the commercial break.
5 And I know you're going to be completely thrilled when they start taking some questions from the studio audience,
6 Which they'll do right after this brief pause for a news bullet and some words from our sponsors.
7 Be right back.

CHAPTER 10

[h]"**R**at-a-tat-tat-a-ratta-tatta-tat-a-rat!
2 "This is a news bullet from the Harrier Television Network,
3 [i]"Margo Glamour reporting.
4 "A spokesman for the federal

government today released the
results of a grim new study,
5 [a]"Which predicts that everyone in the nation will experience
some form of cancer,
6 "Within the next five years.
7 "The study was based on a
sample of four laboratory rats,
8 "And is regarded as [b]conclu-
sive by the scientific community.
9 "The HTN Evening News
will provide a full report at six
o'clock.
10 [c]"The Department of Defense reported today that there is
now one nuclear warhead for
every man, woman, and child on
the face of the planet,
11 "Which means that in the
event of all-out nuclear war, the
earth itself would be vaporized
into stardust: [d]Hoagy Carmichael, where are you now that
we need you?
12 "The [e]Titanic Furnace Corporation today announced that it
is recalling all gas furnaces manufactured by the company in the
last six months,
13 "Due to what a paid company liar calls 'a relatively significant likelihood of accidental
explosion.'
14 [f]"The problem was attrib-
uted to cost-cutting measures ne-
cessitated by unfair foreign competition,
15 "And Titanic has announced
plans to [g]sue the nation of [h]Japan
for damages attendant to the
quality problem.
16 [i]"The national leadership of
the Association of the Semi-
Skilled has called a nationwide
strike to protest unfair labor
practices by numerous public
and private employers.

a. *Jefs.7.35-46*
b. *Chuk.21.1*
c. *Ned.16.12*
   Mawr.15.22
d. *Psay.5G.16-
   17*
e. *Psay.5D.7*
f. *Main.16.1-9*
g. *Penn.2.13-14*
h. *Main.15.1-7*
i. *Hill.U.1-2*
j. *Ira.29.1-2*
k. *Psay.5H.1*
   Hill.H.1
l. *Brd.22.13-15*
m. *Brd.22.4-6*
n. *Jeff.16.1-8*
o. *F&J.15.18-
   19*

17 [j]"Specific citations of such
practices include discriminatory
literacy requirements for file
clerks,
18 [k]"Discriminatory hygiene
requirements for hospital and
nursing home orderlies,
19 "And discriminatory licens-
ing requirements for school bus
and ambulance drivers.
20 "A spokesperson for the
country's largest civil rights organization issued a statement today announcing that a certain
race,
21 "Formerly known as the
'Negro Race,' and the 'Afro-
American Race,' and 'People of
Black Persuasion,'
22 [l]"Shall henceforth be called
the 'Superior Race,' in order to
compensate for the four-hundred-
year period when all names for
a certain race were closet syno-
nyms for the 'Inferior Race.'
23 [m]"Asked how long this
name would be used, the spokesperson said that four hundred
years ought to just about do it,
provided that demands are met
for the immediate disbursement
of 25 percent of the country's
gross national product to members of the Superior Race, as
befits their new status. We'll
have further details on this story
at six o'clock.
24 "In other news,
25 [n]"Here's a bloody spot on
Highway 67 where a tractor
trailer crushed a station wagon
and an entire family much like
yours[o],
26 "And here's a bloody spot in
the hall where an old lady much
like your own mother opened her
door to a deranged killer—much
like the ones living in your

neighborhood—who crushed her skull with his hobnailed boots[a],

27 "And here's a bloody spot in Philadelphia where thousands stormed the concert stage in response to a rock 'n' roll performer's joking offer of 'Free Drugs'; several youngsters much like your own were badly trampled in the melee[b].

28 "And in a final item of note, indictments were handed down today for seven U.S. senators, eleven U.S. congressmen, and six members of the administration, all of whom are alleged to have played a role in the latest capital scandal, which is so new that it doesn't even have a [c]nickname yet[d].

29 "The latest on the nickname and other stories will be covered tonight,

30 "On the HTN Evening News.

31 "Until then, this is Margo Glamour reporting,

32 "For the HTN News Team,

33 "Your source for certainty,

34 "About who's to blame for everything.

35 [e]"Keep smiling."

CHAPTER 11

"**S**he's beautiful.

2 "She's irresistible.

3 "She's 'In Heat.'

4 "Yes, when you want a fragrance that will make [f]men howl and bay at the moon,

5 [g]"A fragrance that will make men forget about your IQ and your diction,

6 "A fragrance that will make men stop thinking and start panting,

a. *F&J.15.20*
b. *F&J.15.21*
c. *Jefs.7.15-17*
d. *F&J.15.22*
e. *F&J.16.1-12*
f. *Dav.30.25*
g. *Kens.10.3*
h. *Psay.5L.7*
i. *Vin.14.23*
j. *Psong.21.7-8*
k. *Brit.40.8*

7 "Get the fragrance that's distilled from the very essence of animal lust,

8 "Because it's time you knew what every *real* woman knows,

9 "That only raw, raging passion can cure what's wrong with your life,

10 "And turn all those sad singles scenes into a legendary love.

11 "Be a legend.

12 "Be beautiful.

13 "Be irresistible.

14 "Be 'In Heat,'

15 "For as long as it lasts."

CHAPTER 12

"**S**tay tuned for 'I Love Riddle Roulette,'

2 "The great new game show that's got everybody guessing,

3 "For cash and prizes worth up to a million dollars.

4 "Yes, at last, a game show that's perfect for you and the whole family.

5 "Nothing to know,

6 "Nothing to remember,

7 "Nothing to lose.

8 "Just place a bet on your own special [h]lucky number,

9 [i]"Watch the big wheel spin round and round,

10 [j]"And if it's your number that comes up,

11 "All you have to do is guess which of our multiple-choice riddle answers is the right one,

12 "And you could walk away with a million dollars.

13 "It's that easy,

14 "And more fun than you could shake a [k]stick at,

15 "Because the host of 'I Love Riddle Roulette' is Brad Shoulders,

16 "The smilingest emcee alive,
17 "And if Brad can't make you laugh at the odds,
18 "Then no one can.
19 "Are you ready?
20 [a]"Then take a spin for the pure unthinking fun of it all,
21 "With 'I Love Riddle Roulette,'
22 [b]"The game show that's so much like life we had to add a million dollars to make it worthwhile.
23 "Next.
24 "On this station."

CHAPTER 13

" '**I** just want you and me and our baby to have a decent life together, 'Andrea!'
2 " 'I wish you wouldn't keep saying "our baby" like that.'
3 " 'What do you mean? Do you have something to tell me, Andrea? Wasn't I understanding when you told me about your eleven previous marriages? And wasn't I supportive when you told me about your affair with my father? And when you told me about your six illegitimate children? And your three illegal abortions? And your suspended conviction for Murder One? Now isn't it time you started trusting me a little bit? Isn't it? Andrea? Why are you looking at me like that?'
4 "Is today the day that Andrea finally comes clean with Mark?
5 "Well, probably not,
6 "But tune in anyway,
7 [d]"For 'I Love All My Breakdowns.'
8 [e]"Immediately following 'I Love Riddle Roulette.' "

a. *Psong.20.1-6*
b. *Drex.6.4*
c. *11.1-3*
d. *15.8*
e. *Ed.75.11*
f. *Ned.35.3*
g. *Mawr.20.14-18*
h. *Al.4.7-8*
i. *Ed.35.14-19*
j. *Ed.61.1-4*

CHAPTER 14

We're back,
2 And just in time for a very intriguing question from a member of our studio audience,
3 Who wants to know,
4 "Why would anyone want to spread the Word of Harry,
5 "Because aren't there enough Harriers already?"[f]
6 And we'll be getting right to the fascinating answer to this question,
7 Right after these words from our sponsors.

CHAPTER 15

"**N**obody's thinking about it,
2 "But it's coming anyway,
3 "And it'll be here before you know it!
4 "What is it?
5 "It's the great new fall season on the Harrier Television Network!
6 "You say you like sitcoms?
7 "Well, we've got 'em,
8 "And they're just exactly like all the others you've always loved,
9 "Only more so.
10 "Take 'I Love Eddie's Father,'
11 "Please!
12 "Eddie's mom didn't have a husband,
13 "But her clock was ticking,
14 [g]"And so she had a baby by artificial insemination,
15 "Which Eddie didn't know anything about,
16 "Until the day he came across a very special [h]syringe,
17 [i]"In fact, a talking syringe,
18 "Which was kind of a [j]miracle,

19 "Because every boy wants a father.

20 "You'll just roll in the aisles as Eddie's dad tries to teach him a few of the finer points about being a ^aman.

21 "The only thing is, ever since he got thrown away by the doc, Eddie's father has been ^bliving in the streets,

22 "And the education he's giving Eddie is a lot more streetwise than Eddie's mom would like,

23 "Which is why she's always sticking it to Eddie's father,

24 "And why you'll stick with this great new show,

25 "After the hilarious opening episode,

26 "In which Eddie learns the facts of life,

27 "In somewhat pointed terms,

28 "And then dad gets boiled,

29 ^c"To make it better.

30 "But that's just another day's works,

31 "On 'I Love Eddie's Father.'

32 "Thursday nights at eight o'clock."

CHAPTER 16

"**M**y fellow Americans,

2 "I'm Gus Latchit,

3 "Your congressman from the Second District,

4 "And much as I loathe getting down in the gutter with my opponent, I feel obligated to respond to the accusations he has been making in his campaign,

5 "Accusations which are totally groundless,

6 "Irresponsible,

7 ^d"And untrue,

8 ^e"Because I have always been honest,

Reference column:

u. Hill.S.22-23
b. Brd.26.10-11
c. Yks.154.43
d. Wil.29.12
e. Psong.44.1
f. Psong.18.1-4
g. Main.37.4-6
h. Ned.35.10-15
i. Ext.40.7
j. Psong.51.1-4
k. Boul.24.5-10
l. Adam.20.2-10
m. Ned.29.24 Hall.15.20-21

---

9 "And verily happily married,

10 "To my wife of eleven years,

11 "Who would be here with me on camera now if she weren't on vacation with the kids,

12 "Out west somewhere,

13 "Because they have been so terribly hurt by all the false and unwarranted accusations,

14 "Which I won't repeat here,

15 "Because they're so offensive to all decent-thinking people,

16 "Even though—if they were true, which they aren't—they still wouldn't be as bad as the criminal conduct of my opponent,

17 ^f"Who has accepted money from vested interests,

18 ^g"And who is such a drunk that he probably wouldn't ever make a single roll call in the House,

19 ^h"No matter how many times he wants to rake up my attendance record,

20 "Which would have been in the top third of all House members if it hadn't been for my ⁱaccident,

21 "Which, by the way, did not occur en route to some immoral tryst,

22 "Because maybe there are some people who can tell right away that a hitchhiker is a ^jstripper and a call girl,

23 "But I can't,

24 "Because I'm a ^kreligious man from a churchgoing family,

25 ^l"Who cares about the things you do,

26 "Like programs for the underprivileged,

27 ^m"And lots and lots of water projects in the second district,

28 "And getting tough on crime too,
29 "Like putting my opponent in jail,
30 "Instead of Congress,
31 "Which is where he belongs.
32 "Jail, I mean,
33 "Not Congress,
34 "Because you deserve the best you can get in Congress,
35 "And that's [a]me,
36 "Gus Latchit.
37 "Thank you."

CHAPTER 17

" **A**re you st-i-i-i-i-i-ll overweight?
2 "All that dieting,
3 "All those good intentions,
4 "All that self-denial,
5 "And all that fat st-i-i-i-i-ll hanging on your body?
6 "Well, wise up!
7 "Do it the easy way,
8 "With the new surgical diet that really works,
9 "Because our scientists have discovered an amazingly simple fact that could change your life,
10 "A fact so simple you'll kick yourself for not having recognized it before,
11 "Because it is a simple and obvious fact that fat people don't have any self-discipline,
12 "Which is why they're all so fat,
13 "And lead such miserable unrewarding lives.
14 "So if you're ready to be a [b]*real* man, a *manly* man,
15 "Or if you're ready to be a [c]*real* woman, a *thin* woman,
16 "Then give us a call,
17 "And we'll change your life with a slice of the knife,
18 "Overnight.

a. *Dav.47.11 & 47.22*
b. *Brit.10.13*
c. *Gnt.2.9-10*
d. *Boul.26.7-11*
e. *Mawr.31.6-10*
f. *Ira.28.12-18*

19 "And on the morning after, you can say goodbye to all those extra pounds,
20 "Say goodbye to the insults of friends and relatives,
21 "Say goodbye to the low self-esteem that poisoned your prospects, denied you jobs, choked your talents,
22 "And to everything else that stripped you of your basic human dignity,
23 [d]"BECAUSE YOU TOO REALLY CAN BE THIN!
24 "HONEST!
25 "CALL THIS NUMBER NOW,
26 "AND START LIVING LIKE A WINNER,
27 "WITH 'SURGI-SLIM'!"

CHAPTER 18

[e]" **A**re you a committed and involved person,
2 "And do you feel a real need to let everybody know exactly where you stand on the issues?
3 "Well, then, this is your lucky day,
4 [f]"Because Bumper King is offering a super special deal on its entire inventory of bumper stickers.
5 "You'll thrill to old classics like 'I ♥ JESUS,'
6 "And 'I ♥ WHALES,'
7 "And 'I ♥ RIFLES,'
8 "Plus a whole lot more,
9 "Like these sizzling new releases that'll make the whole world sit up and take notice of your intelligent views, including,
10 "'I ♥ ABORTIONS,'
11 "'I ♥ THE SUPERIOR RACE,'
12 "'I ♥ KILLING SMALL ANIMALS,'

13 "'I ♥ DRINKING & DRIVING,'
14 "'I ♥ FETUSES,'
15 "'I ♥ BUYING AMERICAN JUNK,'
16 "'I ♥ EQUAL RIGHTS FOR THE SUPERIOR SEX,'
17 "'I ♥ GETTING DRUNK & SHOOTING ANYTHING THAT MOVES,'
18 "'I ♥ CASUAL SEX WITH STRANGERS,'
19 "'I ♥ OUTLAWS WITH GUNS,'
20 "'I ♥ HONKING MY HORN TO PROVE MY RELIGIOUS ZEAL,'
21 "'I ♥ COMMUNISTS BUT ONLY WHEN THEY'RE DEAD,'
22 "'I ♥ POLLUTION,'
23 "'I ♥ NUCLEAR WARS,'
24 "'I ♥ RACISTS,'
25 "'I ♥ SMASHING INTO NIP CARS,'
26 "'I ♥ ANY MAN WITH THE PRICE OF A MOTEL ROOM IN HIS POCKET,'
27 "And many many more.
28 "Order today by credit card,
29 "Or call toll-free for our special value pack,
30 "Which contains enough bumper stickers for every car in the whole family."

a. *Dav.30.40*
b. *Ext.43.14-18*
c. *1.1*
d. *Wil.41.8-9*
   Brd.23.13-18

CHAPTER 19

"He was a peace-loving cop on vacation in Europe,
2 "Until someone killed an American,
3 "Which they shouldn't have done,
4 "Because now they have to deal with *Jingo!*
5 "ªJingo can't be reasoned with,

6 "Because he doesn't understand any foreign languages.
7 "Jingo can't be brainwashed,
8 "Because he doesn't have a brain.
9 "Jingo can't be stopped,
10 "Because he's the star of *'Jingo!'*
11 "The all-American movie that'll have you cheering in your seats,
12 "At the biggest hail of bullets to tear up Europe since D-Day!
13 "'*Jingo!*'"
14 "Coming soon to a theater near you."

CHAPTER 20

We're back,
2 And we're ready to tackle the question 'Why would anyone want to spread the Word of Harry?'
3 Can you help us with this question, Dr. ᵇTony?
4 "Yes indeed.
5 "Be glad to.
6 "The best reason for spreading the Word of Harry is that it's so easy and rewarding to do,
7 ᶜ"And if you want a career in communications,
8 "Then it's practically impossible *not* to spread the Word of Harry,
9 ᵈ"Without working really really hard,
10 "Because the Word of Harry is everywhere around us,
11 "Like the air we breathe,
12 "And everybody basically knows that already,
13 "Even if they've never really thought about it,
14 "Which is about par for Harriers anyway,

15 "And explains why it is actually comforting to most people to know, without even thinking about it, that all our information comes to us from Harriers,
16 "Just like ourselves,
17 "Which means we don't ever have to think about what we see on TV or in the movies,
18 "Or what we hear on the radio,
19 "Or what we read in books or newspapers or magazines or press releases,
20 "Or anything else,
21 "Except maybe some of the straight talk you get about *things,*
22 ᵃ"And which ones will make you happy if you own them.
23 "Does that answer your question?"
24 "Well, ᵇI do have one follow-up question . . . "
25 . . . Which we won't get to today,
26 Because we're out of time.
27 But this has been great,
28 And please join us next time,
29 When our topic will be 'Who's Really to Blame for All the Unhappiness Experienced by Minorities and Women.'
30 It should be a real knock-down drag-out discussion,
31 So be there.
32 Bye-bye for today.

CHAPTER 21
"Wouldn't you like to live on into your nineties,

a. *Adam. 46-48*
b. *14.3-5*
c. *Ext. 13.14*
d. *15.29*

2 "And stay young and beautiful and healthy and rich the whole time,
3 "And then go straight to heaven when you die,
4 "For all eternity?
5 "Well, forget it.
6 "Things don't work that way,
7 "At all,
8 "So you'd better wake up and smell the coffee,
9 "Unless you'd rather be a Harrier instead,
10 "Which you can do by sending just $19.95 to the Pontifical Harrier Parish of the United States,
11 "Box 1234,
12 "Philadelphia,
13 "PA.
14 "For this paltry membership fee, you'll receive an autographed color portrait of Harry,
15 ᶜ"And this stunning 'Sign of Harry' pendant on a genuine gold-tone chain suitable for wearing around your neck,
16 "For as long as it lasts.
17 "And that's not all,
18 "Because if you order within ten days, you'll also receive this high-quality Harrier bumper sticker,
19 "Beautifully printed with the words,
20 'I ♥ Harry,'
21 "In two glorious colors.
22 "So order now,
23 ᵈ"And start making it better,
24 "The Harrier Way."

THE PRESCRIPTION OF
THE CHOSEN ONE MIKE

FOR THE

JEFFERSONIANS

CHAPTER 1

Learned physicians!
2 This must be a mistake.
3 Really.
4 For what on earth could a physician have in common with a Harrier?
5 After all, physicians are committed to healing,
6 And Harriers are committed to the ªWay of Harry,
7 Which doesn't leave us much to talk about,
8 Or does it?

CHAPTER 2

Of course it doesn't,
2 Except for a very very few of you,
3 Who might be interested in our little prescription,
4 Since there is one little thing that Harriers and physicians have in common,
5 Namely, ᵇdrugs.

CHAPTER 3

Just kidding.
2 Don't get all upset.
3 As we said, our ᶜprescription is only for a few of you,
4 A very very few,
5 And the rest of you won't find our prescription very interesting or helpful,
6 At all,

---

a. Wht.6
b. Vin.49.5
c. 2.2-3
d. Ed.57.3-6
　Mall.13.8
e. Ext.1.11

---

7 Which is why we've taken the trouble to identify those of you who should ignore us completely,
8 And quit reading what we have to say,
9 And go on about your good works.
10 What could be fairer than that?

CHAPTER 4

For example, if healing people is more important to you than money,
2 Stop reading right now,
3 Because we can't help you.

CHAPTER 5

Now, I'm sure that if I were there, I would have been terribly impressed by the huge exodus that just occurred,
2 Which I have no doubt about,
3 ᵈBecause the overwhelming majority of physicians are completely dedicated to helping their fellow man,
4 ᵉAnd I'm sure it's just an awful coincidence that I never met a single premed student in college who didn't answer "money" when people asked about their motivation for becoming doctors.
5 In fact, I'm quite sure about that,
6 Just as I'm sure that only one

525

or two of you are still reading this,

7 Which is why I feel justified in getting right to the point,

8 Without a lot of additional professional courtesy.

9 We know what we're here about, don't we?

10 Good.

CHAPTER 6

The physician who cares principally about money has many options,

2 Because whatever a physician does,

3 It's bound to cost somebody a lot of money,

4 Like the government and the insurance companies,

5 Not to mention the patient,

6 Whether the patient is ever healed or not,

7 Which is not a bad compensation plan,

8 ᵃEspecially if what you care most about is money.

9 But the income-oriented physician,

10 If I may be so bold as to call you that,

11 Has to be careful of certain diseases and contaminations that other physicians don't have to worry about,

12 ᵇBecause those other physicians spend all their time thinking about how to heal their patients,

13 Which immunizes them against certain kinds of infection,

14 Although this is definitely a case of the cure being worse than the disease,

15 Because spending so much time thinking about sick people is just urinating your life away,

a. Psong.6.1-6
b. Ed.57.7-8
c. 3.3
d. Frog.26.16
e. 6.10
f. Frog.25.2-9
g. Psay.5H.14-15
   & 5H.19-22
h. Bub.5.8-10
i. Mawr.19.17-18
j. Ann.4.1-8

16 If you don't mind me getting technical about it.

17 Anyway,

18 That's why I've gone to the trouble of documenting some of the ills an income-oriented physician runs the risk of contracting,

19 ᶜAnd a prescription for what to do about it.

CHAPTER 7

ᵈ*P*aranoius digesticus.

2 This is a condition that afflicts medical personnel of all types,

3 But can be especially burdensome for the ᵉincome-oriented physician,

4 For reasons I will explain in a moment.

5 The fact is that much of the continuously expanding income opportunity for physicians has been provided by the ongoing discovery of new kinds of ailments,

6 ᶠWhich clever physicians discover under microscopes so that they can name their discoveries after themselves,

7 ᵍWhile other physicians discover them between the pages of magazines so that they can convince their patients to pay for more prescription drugs.

8 Obviously, this is a medical practice that has succeeded spectacularly well over the years,

9 Because today, the average person suffers from infirmities and syndromes that people in the ʰmiddle ages were too ignorant to suffer from,

10 ⁱLike Pre-Menstrual Syndrome,

11 ʲAnd Post-Traumatic Stress Syndrome,

12 [a]And Bulimia,

13 [b]And Male Menopause,

14 [c]Not to mention Processed Sugar and so forth,

15 [d]Which is why names are so important,

16 Because when something has a name of its own,

17 [e]It obviously exists,

18 Which means that your patients can catch it,

19 [f]And buy some drugs to treat it.

20 The only problem with all this is that there are now so many thousands of different ailments to contract that physicians can start to believe that they have them too,

21 Especially [g]income-oriented physicians,

22 No matter how silly that sounds,

23 [h]Because let's face it, the average income-oriented physician tends to lose touch with medical science over time,

24 Until he's frequently guessing right along with his patients,

25 And inclined to believe in diseases that were never meant for him.

26 This can lead to the truly debilitating condition called [i]*paranoius digesticus,*

27 In which the sufferer begins to think that he is in constant grave danger from a virtually endless array of medical abnormalities,

28 Until life is nothing more than a series of dread-filled intervals between checkups,

29 And the human body is nothing more than a chronic [j]disease-making machine,

30 [k]Waiting for the one final medical disaster that will strike

randomly from out of nowhere,

31 [l]And put an end to everything.

32 That's why it's so very fortunate that [m]income-oriented physicians can rely on the Way of Harry,

33 Which teaches us not to think about anything at all,

34 And simplifies everything enormously.

35 For if you follow the Way of Harry,

36 [n]Medicine is just a business,

37 And diseases are just a product you sell to your customers,

38 [o]Whether or not you'd ever buy or use the product yourself,

39 Just like all good businessmen everywhere.

40 And the more product you sell your customers,

41 The more afraid they'll be,

42 And the more they'll need you,

43 And your expensive office time,

44 And your expensive lab tests,

45 And your expensive prescription drugs.

46 See how beautifully it all works out!

47 And if you ever feel the first creeping pangs of [p]*paranoius digesticus* invading your life,

48 In spite of all your best efforts to think about nothing at all,

49 There is always [q]Harry's Consolation,

50 Which we'll be explaining more about,

51 As we go.

CHAPTER 8

[r]*Specialitas tediositas.*

a. *Ann.17.23-24*

b. *Carl.3.8*

c. *Rom.22.8*

d. *7.6*

e. *Grk.4.1-9*

f. *Adam.45.1-2*

g. *6.10*

h. *Hill.K.1-5*

i. *7.1*

j. *Chuk.19.9*

k. *Dav.47.18*

l. *Psom.35.4*

m. *6.10*

n. *Wht.23*

o. *Adam.36.9-10*

p. *7.1*

q. *8.12*

r. *Frog.26.16*

2 This is a chronic condition that frequently befalls the [a]income-oriented physician,

3 Because in this [b]Most Chosen Nation, the best opportunities for a physician to maximize income without incurring grave financial risks usually involve specialization in high-margin, low-risk disciplines in which very high patient volumes can be achieved,

4 Such as treating [c]teenagers for acne, which eventually clears up or it doesn't, whether the physician gives it any thought or not,

5 [d]Or treating extremely old or terminally ill people in nursing homes, who are all eventually going to die anyway, so it hardly matters if the physician gives any thought to his patients or not, as long as he keeps pumping out those bills for [e]checkups and [f]medication and more [g]tests,

6 [h]Or psychiatry, which requires no thought of any kind, because psychiatric patients are usually so screwed up that nothing can help them anyway,

7 [i]And besides, neurotics always think you're doing your job as long as you always answer their questions with another question from the [j]list you carry in your pocket.

8 But these kinds of practices can also cause some disturbing symptoms,

9 Such as a tendency to become physically ill at the prospect of seeing another case of megazits, or another [k]toothless and incontinent old bag of bones, or another [l]braindead housewife who can't seem to find her place in life,

10 [m]Not to mention a nagging

a.	6.10
b.	Boul.4.13
c.	Ed.35.7-8
d.	Ext.51.17-23
e.	7.43
f.	7.45
g.	7.44
h.	Zig.12.5-8
i.	Zig.12.2
j.	Ext.15.4
k.	Rat.1.1-3
l.	Ann.3.1 Mawr.30.15-20
m.	Mall.11.1-3
n.	Ann.6.1
o.	Main.36.8
p.	Main.36.14-15
q.	8.1
r.	Ext.13.18
s.	Ned.38.24
t.	Brd.28.4-5
u.	Main.10.3-5
v.	Frog.26.16
w.	6.10
x.	Psong.45.1-3
y.	Psong.43.1-3

temptation to think about whether this kind of practice is what life is supposed to be about, even though you have the [n]Mercedes and the [o]yacht and the sizzling [p]mistress to prove it.

11 Fortunately, though, the Way of Harry makes it easy to prescribe a cure for this [q]dangerous condition,

12 Namely, [r]Consolation,

13 Which comes in many many forms,

14 As all physicians know,

15 Including pills and powders and ampoules,

16 Except that Harry offers only the finest stuff,

17 [s]Direct from down south,

18 [t]At extremely competitive prices,

19 Without any need to play [u]games with your own medical supplies.

20 Sound interesting?

21 I thought so.

CHAPTER 9

[v]*I*nvesticus stupidicus.

2 When your primary interest in life is money, the worst possible ailment you can contract is some sort of financial disaster,

3 Which [w]income-oriented physicians are especially susceptible to,

4 Because when you get into the swing of making lots and lots of money without thinking about it at all,

5 [x]It's easy to start thinking that you must be really brilliant about money,

6 [y]Or why would you have so much of it?

7 Since this qualifies as a thought of at least some kind, it

represents a [a]warning sign that should not be ignored,

8 Because thinking of any kind is dangerous,

9 Especially when it leads to weird semi-legal [b]real estate deals, or complicated [c]tax shelters, or any transaction that involves [d]bars, restaurants, or retail establishments,

10 Which may not require any thought on the part of the swindlers who do these kinds of deals for a living,

11 But cannot be safely undertaken by an unthinking [e]income-oriented physician who has come to regard himself as a [f]financial genius.

12 That's why it's so extremely lucky for you that the Way of Harry can assist you in avoiding this disease,

13 Completely,

14 By investing in the [g]Pontifical Harrier Parish,

15 Which is tax-exempt for obvious reasons,

16 And offers outstanding returns for every cash dollar you put up[h],

17 Not to mention ready access to as much [i]Consolation as you may require personally.

18 Here's an [j]application form if you want to drool about it for a while first.

CHAPTER 10

[k]*M*alpracticus catastrophicus.

2 This is an ailment the income-oriented physician must be particularly careful not to get,

3 [l]Because the physician who cares principally about money is usually somewhat more prone to

---

a. *Mall.4.1-9*
b. *Vin.60.8-12*
c. *Psong.59.1*
d. *Psay.5A.7*
e. *6.10*
f. *Adam.38.2-15*
g. *Wht.34*
h. *Ned.9.9*
i. *8.17-19*
j. *Wht.38*
k. *Frog.26.16*
l. *7.23*
m. *8.3*
n. *Chuk.18.1-2*
o. *Drex.8.1-3*
p. *Drex.7.14*
q. *Drex.12.7*
r. *Ned.35.9*
s. *Dav.29.6*
t. *Dav.30.9*

---

error than other kinds of physicians,

4 Which is understandable when you consider that they tend to deal more in [m]volume,

5 And therefore have less time to spend ransacking individual case [n]histories for low-percentage anomalies.

6 That's why it's a good idea to be alert for certain symptoms,

7 [o]Such as a statistically significant increase in the death rate among those of your patients not suffering from a serious disease,

8 [p]Or a fifty percent or greater decline in your customary income from the families of other physicians,

9 Or a sudden massive malpractice suit filed by a patient whose case you cannot recall,

10 [q]At all.

11 Fortunately, this is an ailment that can be controlled in all but the most extreme cases,

12 Which can usually be prevented from becoming extreme in the first place,

13 Through judicious application of the Way of Harry.

14 [r]For it is the Way of Harry which tells us to blame others before they can blame us,

15 Which is why it is always an excellent idea to heap lots and lots of blame on the drones who support you,

16 All the time.

17 Blame [s]hospital personnel for being sloppy about getting patient histories,

18 Whether they are or not.

19 Blame the [t]lab technicians for being careless in their reports,

20 Whether they are or not.

21 Blame your [a]office nurses for not briefing you on significant details,
22 Whether they do or not,
23 [b]Until absolutely everybody is convinced that you are an obnoxious perfectionist who never misses a trick,
24 [c]So that they will catch most of your mistakes for you,
25 Before you make them,
26 Without thinking about it at all.
27 And if you happen to kill one by [d]accident, see to it that you inform the family at once about the patient's culpability for his own demise,
28 [e]Because he was overweight,
29 [f]Or a smoker,
30 [g]Or a quitter,
31 [h]Or too stingy to spring for all the high-margin tests you twisted his arm to get.
32 If people still try to blame you for [i]big bucks, there is also a last resort,
33 Which is to break down and confess that you have been receiving too much Consolation,
34 Because you are a physician,
35 And the [j]stress got to you,
36 And you couldn't help it,
37 And you're really sorry,
38 And you'll commit yourself at once for rehabilitation,
39 [k]And how about another chance?

CHAPTER 11

Yes, if you're an income-oriented physician, Consolation can play a big and helpful role in your life,
2 And it's so easy to accept Harry into your life too,
3 [l]Because all you have to do is wash your hands,
4 Of everything,
5 Which is something physicians do several times a day,
6 So what's the big [m]deal?
7 [n]Come to Harry.
8 He's got the goods for what ails you,
9 [o]Because a Harrier is a Harrier is a Harrier,
10 Whether he signs a [p]Hypocratic Oath or not,
11 [q]And Harry knows Harriers better than they know themselves,
12 Which is why he told me to include enough Consolation Release Forms for all of you,
13 So there's no need to be pushing and shoving in line, everybody.
14 You'll find a bunch of ten year-old-[r]magazines in the waiting room,
15 And we'll get to you as fast as we can,
16 Without thinking about it at all.
17 Until then,
18 Just remember our general prophylactic prescription for [s]classically trained Harriers everywhere, namely,
19 [t]*Non cogito ergo sanus sum.*
20 Don't you feel better already?

a. Ed.27.3
b. Ed.57.9-10
c. Wht.27
d. Vin.14.23-24
e. Ann.17.11
f. Rom.22.8
g. 7.30
h. 7.44
i. 10.1
j. 7.11
k. Ned.36.17-19
l. Ira.16.10-11
m. Ira.21.30-32
n. Brd.32.1
o. Psom.27.1-3 Yks.154.32
p. Grk.14.15-18
q. Wil.13.9-11
r. 7.7
s. Gnt.3.4-5
t. Brit.6.29

THE ADVICE OF THE ARCH-ANGEL MATTHEW
FOR THE
KENSINGTONIANS

CHAPTER 1

Yo, [a]Kensington!

2 I have some advice for you,

3 Which I am sending you through the mail,

4 Because I know very well that you Kensingtonians debate with [b]baseball bats instead of words,

5 And much as I would enjoy taking a turn at the plate myself, I have no time to play games with a bunch of [c]white trash like you,

6 Not right now, anyway,

7 So don't let your urine come to a boil,

8 Okay?

CHAPTER 2

You may have heard about Harry,

2 Who showed everyone the way a few years back,

3 [d]Before he was suddenly called away to Rio.

4 What you may not know is that his way should also be your way,

5 [e]Even though you never went to college,

6 [f]And probably won't ever get rich,

7 Which is really the best way to get the most out of Harry's way,

8 [g]Because of the things that can

---

a. Wil.58.1-8
b. Psay.5S.4-7
c. Vin.14.9
d. Vin.75.5
e. Vin.12.10
f. Vin.12.11
g. Psong.10.9
h. Vin.48.19-22
i. 1.2
j. Ed.53.3
k. Ned.29.24

---

be counted, money is the thing that counts most.

9 But even if you stay poor for the rest of your life,

10 Which is pretty likely,

11 [h]It's going to be a big help to you to follow the Way of Harry.

CHAPTER 3

I know that a lot of people have tried to give you [i]advice about how to live.

2 For example, I'm sure that some of your [j]teachers have suggested that you can have a better life by doing certain things,

3 Things like bathing and shaving more regularly,

4 And not drinking quite so much,

5 And not getting into so many fistfights,

6 And maybe finishing high school,

7 Or joining the army,

8 Or getting a steady job and a family and responsibilities,

9 [k]And other stuff too.

10 They've probably hinted around that if you do this kind of stuff, you'll have a chance to get ahead in life,

11 And make a contribution to society,

12 And be respected for your accomplishments.

13 Isn't that pretty much what they say?

CHAPTER 4

[a]The problem is that there are still a lot of teachers who tell lies,

2 Which is their job, after all,

3 But there are some things you should know before you commit yourself to doing things that are against your nature in any way.

4 The part about being respected is a good case in point; that's just not going to happen,

5 [b]Ever,

6 Which isn't your fault exactly,

7 But it's the way things worked out.

8 Let me speak frankly about this.

9 Everybody in the world has already made up their mind about you,

10 And what they've decided is that you're no damned good at all,

11 To anybody.

CHAPTER 5

Everybody knows you're a bunch of crude, ignorant, vicious [c]racists,

2 [d]Who'd rather have a good barroom brawl than accomplish anything worthwhile.

3 When they see you on the street in a nice neighborhood, their first desire is to get away from you,

4 Because you smell bad,

5 And because you look like a whole bunch of trouble just waiting to happen.

6 They look at you for five seconds and they think they can see your whole family tree, extending back for ten generations,

7 [e]All the way back to wherever your ancestors came from,

a. Ira.34.4
b. Brd.12.7-11
c. Ed.67.3-7
d. Ira.26.1-7
e. Yks.56.8-14
f. Yks.56.15-22
g. Ira.1.8
h. Ape.1.1
i. Adam.11.6-8
j. Wil.1.1
k. Ned.20.20-27
l. Dav.57.30
m. Ed.41.5
n. Dav.30.25
o. Dav.7.5
p. Dav.30.40
q. Wil.75.6
r. Brit.28.24-30

8 [f]Which they were probably kicked out of,

9 Because nobody anywhere ever wants anything to do with brutal, lazy, pig-eyed trash like you.

10 And so they have this [g]picture of your ancestor getting off some boat from Glasgow or Belfast or Liverpool,

11 With a [h]bloody knife in his pants,

12 And a shifty look in his eye,

13 Because he's already afraid of the cops,

14 Who just might find that butchered corpse in the hold,

15 And come looking for the worthless brute that did it.

16 More than this, they have a pretty good idea of what happened next,

17 How your ancestor married some gap-toothed, half-wit hag,

18 [i]And had a bunch of screaming dirty children,

19 Who got savage beatings instead of love,

20 And got even by having children of their own,

21 For generation,

22 After generation,

23 [j]After generation,

24 [k]Of losers.

25 They look at [l]you and see your [m]daddy,

26 And your [n]granddaddy,

27 And your [o]great-granddaddy,

28 And his [p]daddy too,

29 [q]All in prison,

30 For excellent reasons,

31 Not to mention a river of [r]rotgut booze flowing steadily through generation after generation,

32 While no one learns anything,

33 Ever.

CHAPTER 6

Yes, they're pretty ^acertain about you,

2 And all the things you'll never be,

3 Which is something you should know.

4 But there's also some other news that isn't quite as bad,

5 If you'd like to hear it,

6 ^bBecause they've also decided that nobody's any better than anyone else really,

7 For some reason,

8 Even if that's not the way they act when you pull up beside them at a stoplight.

9 But if you ever doubted it, remember that they're no better than you,

10 At all,

11 Which is why you shouldn't feel bad,

12 About being the way you are.

CHAPTER 7

Besides, if you follow the Way of Harry,

2 You'll never have to feel really bad again,

3 ^cBecause the Way of Harry tells us that we're all fine just the way we are,

4 ^dWithout trying to improve ourselves,

5 Or be something we're not,

6 No matter who it hurts.

7 If it is your nature to be a vicious, ignorant animal,

8 ^eThen that is what you should be,

9 And never apologize to anyone for being it.

a. Wil.34.6-11
b. Hall.15.12
c. Vin.13.29-37
d. Wil.18.12
e. Wil.29.18
f. Wil.40.1-8
g. Mall.16.2-3
h. Ann.18.17
i. Ned.24.20-21
j. Hill.C.6-8

CHAPTER 8

Even so, there are some things you can do to make life easier for yourselves,

2 As long as you remember to do these things without thinking about them too much,

3 Or trying too hard,

4 Which should be pretty easy,

5 Because most of these things have to do with not being too different from each other,

6 So that you don't attract too much attention,

7 ^fAnd get blamed because somebody noticed you,

8 Which is going to happen more and more,

9 As we shall see.

CHAPTER 9

For example, it's pretty important that you all dress alike.

2 ^gIf you're a guy, you should always wear dirty jeans, with rips and tears and oil stains all over them, fixed so that they sit low on your hips and always show off the crack in your buttocks.

3 ^hAnd you should always wear T-shirts with some stupid or obscene joke on the chest,

4 And great big ugly boots, as if you were always on your way to a stomping party later on,

5 And long dirty stringy hair,

6 And as many tattoos as possible,

7 ⁱAnd one of those baseball caps with some heavy equipment manufacturer's name on it.

8 More than this, you should always walk around with your mouth hanging open,

9 ^jAnd a dull dead look in your eye,

10 Unless you're drunk,
11 In which case, you should make sure your eyes are bright with hatred, as if you just can't wait to kill someone.
12 It also helps if you always drive a clapped-out, oil-burning, piece of junk pickup truck,
13 With about a zillion empty [a]beer cans rattling around in the back,
14 And a bunch of heavy metal [b]music blaring out the open windows all the time.

a. Vin.16.2
b. Hill.M.1-2
c. Dav.56.15
d. Ann.11.5
e. 8.6-7
f. Dav.22.47
g. Psong.8.3
Gnt.2.11
h. Vin.15.8
i. 8.6
j. 9.12
k. 9.13
l. Vin.16.12
m. 1.1
n. 13.1

CHAPTER 10

If you're a girl, of course, you should dress differently,
2 But exactly like all the other [c]girls,
3 Meaning you should wear cheap, tarty clothes drenched in even cheaper [d]perfume,
4 And tons of makeup, and I mean really trowel it on,
5 And keep your hair gooed up with about five pounds of lacquer and dye and other junk,
6 And keep your mouth full of gum all the time,
7 No matter what,
8 So that everyone will always know that you're just exactly like everyone else,
9 [e]And there's no reason to pick your face out of the crowd.
10 When you get [f]older, you can lay off the tarty clothes,
11 And get really really [g]fat,
12 And wear stretch pants,
13 And curlers 100 percent of the time,
14 [h]Exactly as if you had somewhere to go later,
15 Even though you never do.

CHAPTER 11

But clothes aren't everything,
2 [i]And if you want to slide by without attracting too much of the wrong kind of attention,
3 Without anybody ever really expecting anything of you,
4 There are some other things you can all do.
5 For example, it's a good idea to let all your ugly little houses fall apart,
6 And when the [j]pickup truck dies, leave it where it is,
7 [k]With all the cans and bottles still sitting in the back,
8 And if you have some ruined furniture with springs poking out, put it out on the front porch so that everybody else can enjoy it too,
9 And when you freak out on [l]Southern Comfort some night and throw your best friend through the front window, don't fix it, but tape up some cardboard and plastic instead,
10 So that [m]Kensington will stay the way it is,
11 Namely, a place where nobody but Kensingtonians ever want to go,
12 Because the more chances [n]*they* have to meet you and see how you live,
13 The more *they* will blame you,
14 For everything that's wrong in *their* stinking rotten lives.

CHAPTER 12

If you're young,
2 It's a good idea to join a gang,

3 The way Kensingtonians always have,

4 And learn what [a]baseball bats are really for, [b]not to mention motorcycle chains and knives and sawed-off shotguns,

5 Because if *they* should ever find a sneaky way to hurt you,

6 You'll need to know how to deal with them,

7 Which is why it's better not to think about anything at all when you're in a gang,

8 [c]But do whatever your leader tells you to do, just like your dad did,

9 [d]Which is why a gang leader in Kensington always has to be the hardest, meanest, dirtiest animal available,

10 And why gang rules are the same from one generation to the next,

11 Like if somebody messes with any one of you, then the whole gang takes care of it,

12 Immediately,

13 Savagely,

14 And for keeps,

15 [e]Because there's no point in wasting time when vengeance is necessary,

16 And it *will* be necessary,

17 Because nobody in this whole stinking [f]city likes you,

18 And you don't like any of them,

19 So the gang is your protection,

20 And it's your camouflage too,

21 Because when the gang goes to work,

22 What people remember is the gang,

23 And what wild animals they were,

a. 1.4
b. Al.4.7-9
c. Ext.9.1-12
d. Psp.3.9
e. Hill.V.9-10
f. Wil.53.2
g. 7.7-8
h. 12.12-14
i. 17.14
j. Vin.24.9
k. Vin.15.1
l. Ann.21.20
m. 17.1

24 And nothing else,

25 [g]Because animals are not individuals,

26 And they have no faces.

CHAPTER 13

I know you well enough to guess that a lot of you are already asking, "Who's *they?*

2 "Because we'll go take care of them now,

3 [h]"For keeps."

4 But that won't be possible,

5 Because there are too many of them,

6 And they have already taken a page out of your book,

7 [i]And they already know what you know about blame,

8 Not to mention not thinking about anything at all,

9 Because [j]somebody spilled the beans,

10 [k]And told *all* the other neighborhoods about how you've survived this long without ever taking any responsibility for anything,

11 [l]And they liked what they heard,

12 And they're doing it,

13 Everywhere.

CHAPTER 14

And maybe you suppose that's not such bad news,

2 If the rest of them are getting more and more like you every day,

3 And maybe they'll back off with all the personal remarks and the dirty looks,

4 And maybe you'll see less of the back of their hand,

5 [m]But that's only because you're so stupid,

6 And don't know when you're well off,

7 Like everybody else.

8 You see, the more like you they get,

9 The more they will hate you,

10 And the more they will pretend that they aren't like you at all,

11 Because they hate you.

12 And so their ᵃhouses won't look like yours,

13 And their ᵇcars won't look like yours,

14 And their ᶜclothes won't look like yours,

15 ᵈExcept maybe the clothes their children wear, which will make them hate you even more,

16 And their jobs won't be like yours at all,

17 Because most of them will have jobs, and they won't be on the line in some stinking factory, either,

18 And so a lot of them will also have a lot more ᵉ*things* than you do, and nicer *things* at that.

19 But deep down,

20 They'll be just like you,

21 Except for not having your guts,

22 And that's not good news at all.

CHAPTER 15

More and more, they'll talk like you,

2 ᶠAnd use all the same four-letter words,

3 Even the ones who go to fancy colleges and think they're as high class as they come.

CHAPTER 16

More and more, they'll think like you,

---

a. Hill.S.5-6
b. Hill.S.7-8
c. Ira.16.33-35
d. 9.2
e. Adam.46-48
f. Wil.36.1-7 Hill.F.1
g. 12.25
h. Brd.27.6
i. Mall.12.10-13
j. Vin.44.1-7
k. Wil.38.1-9
l. 4.9-11

---

2 Meaning they won't really think at all,

3 ᵍBut just react instead,

4 And they'll react a lot like you do,

5 Wanting to punish whoever it is that did the unforgivable thing,

6 No matter how small a thing it was,

7 Which is unimportant,

8 Because all that's important is vengeance,

9 And making somebody else pay,

10 ʰThrough the nose.

CHAPTER 17

More and more, they'll be as stupid as you,

2 ⁱAnd they'll stop learning anything in school,

3 Just like you,

4 And then they'll be ʲfree to make everything up to suit them,

5 Just like you,

6 ᵏBecause there won't be any facts left to get in the way,

7 Which means that every time they screw up,

8 Which will be plenty,

9 They'll know right away,

10 Without thinking about it at all,

11 That it's all part of the same old conspiracy to keep them down,

12 And humiliate them,

13 And make them look bad,

14 ˡBecause when you're no damned good at anything at all, it's almost automatic to assume that everybody else is trying to make you look bad,

15 As you know better than anybody.

CHAPTER 18

More and more, they'll work in gangs,
2 Just like you,
3 [a]Because the gang is their protection,
4 And their camouflage too,
5 [b]Because when the gang goes to work,
6 What people remember is the gang,
7 [c]And what a powerful irresistible force it was,
8 And nothing else,
9 [d]Because a gang isn't made of individuals,
10 [e]But anonymous followers instead.

CHAPTER 19

But their gangs won't look like yours,
2 And they won't use the same weapons,
3 Because they have better ones,
4 And when they roll out to exact their vengeance, they'll hit the enemy with everything they've got,
5 Which includes everything [f]under the sun,
6 Including [g]laws,
7 And [h]books,
8 And [i]television shows,
9 And [j]movies,
10 And [k]politicians,
11 And [l]corporations,
12 And [m]governments,
13 And the [n]cops,
14 And absolutely anything and everything that has any power to get them what they want,
15 No matter who gets hurt.

CHAPTER 20

Now, maybe you're so stupid that you're saying, "So what?
2 "Why should we care?"
3 But I wouldn't be telling you this if it wasn't important,
4 Because [o]I am a Kensingtonian myself,
5 [p]Only from some other city,
6 And I have come to give you fair warning,
7 And tell you about the only alternatives you have,
8 [q]Because it's all right for Kensingtonians to be Kensingtonians,
9 But it's going to cause some problems when everybody in the whole country is a Kensingtonian,
10 Especially for you.

CHAPTER 21

They used to know that they needed you,
2 [r]Because it was their job to build things,
3 [s]While you carried the bricks on the days you were sober,
4 [t]And it was their job to run things,
5 [u]While you ran errands if you weren't in jail,
6 [v]And it was their job to keep things clean and in good repair,
7 [w]While you drove the garbage trucks unless your hand was busted again.
8 [x]And so, while you complained and got drunk and smashed things that got in your way, it was their job to keep everything more or less under control,
9 [y]Which they were pretty good at,
10 [z]Because they always seemed to know how to keep from losing their temper and going psycho when some little

a. 12.19
b. 12.21
c. 12.23
d. 12.25
e. Vin.33.1-4
f. Hill.U.13-14
g. Penn.7.1-12
h. Swar.35.10-13
i. Ed.69.9-16 Ann.2.1-32
j. Dav.55.1-31 Dav.56.51-62 Ann.19.1-14
k. Hall.15.7-11
l. Main.16.1-6
m. Hall.12.1-18
n. Vin.23.2-4
o. Ext.52.1-8
p. Ann.16.12
q. Pnot.24.3
r. Rom.5.13
s. Rom.5.14
t. Grk.5.1-2
u. Ira.31.15
v. Psay.5V.1-3 & 5V.14
w. 22.1
x. Rom.5.10
y. Yks.63.1-8
z. Ext.39.17

thing didn't work out just like they wanted,
11 And all in all, they were pretty good at finding compromises that prevented the [a]potato from getting hot enough to explode,
12 Time after time after time,
13 [b]Until the day things didn't work out,
14 And they needed you.

CHAPTER 22

They needed you to do the dirty work,
2 And they counted on [c]you to be there for them, ready and waiting when some maniac in a foreign country went ape and killed some Americans.
3 They needed you to go take care of it,
4 Because they knew that you had the guts,
5 And that you wouldn't quit,
6 [d]Ever,
7 [e]Not from the first moment that one of you lost a buddy, and had to wipe his brains off your face.
8 From that moment on, you were the strong right arm of America,
9 [f]And they drafted you to save the union from the confederacy,
10 [g]And they drafted you to teach the Kaiser a lesson,
11 [h]And they drafted you to jam Hitler's blitzkrieg down his throat and Hirohito's divine wind up his backside,
12 And [i]you did it,
13 The way you always do it,
14 [j]As fast and deadly as possible,
15 So that you could come right back to Kensington and get [k]drunk.

a. Yks.21.11-12 Psay.5V.4-26
b. Ext.39.18
c. Yks.30.37-39
d. Yks.30.40
e. 12.11-14
f. Yks.43.1-13 Dav.22.1-19
g. Yks.76.1-15 Dav.9.5-7
h. Yks.107.1-19 Dav.31.9-11 Dav.34.2-15 Ed.49.1-13 Dav.33.3
i. Mawr.15.22
j. Yks.112.1-27
k. Yks.87.5-6
l. Yks.134.2-6
m. 21.10
n. Yks.135.1-4
o. Vin.49.5
p. Yks.135.5-14
q. 22.20 Ira.16.23
r. Ann.4.4-8
s. Forg.10.10-11
t. 19.2-3
u. 22.7
v. Adam.17.1-11

16 [l]And then they drafted you again to go do it for the whole world in Korea,
17 But they forgot *why* they needed you,
18 [m]And they wanted you to fight *their* way,
19 [n]And do it slow and easy and controlled,
20 [o]Which was a joke,
21 [p]And they just barely got away with it,
22 Or that's what *they* thought, anyway, because they never asked you for *your* opinion about it,
23 And so they tried it again,
24 [q]In a place called Vietnam,
25 [r]And this time they just hung you out to dry,
26 And let you die in the jungle without a baseball bat to even the score.

CHAPTER 23

[s]And that's when everybody in the whole world turned on you,
2 Because they had forgotten who you were,
3 And why they had *ever* needed you,
4 Because now they knew that America couldn't fight a war without using nuclear weapons,
5 [t]Which meant that you and your baseball bat had gotten to be more of an embarrassment than a help,
6 And so when they looked at you they didn't see your guts anymore,
7 [u]Or the force of your blind raging loyalty to each other in the face of the enemy,
8 [v]Or all the dirty work you had ever done to build their nice

things for them when you weren't in jail.

9 [a]Instead, they saw you as racist killers,

10 [b]And dirty useless animals,

11 [c]And the perfect example of everything that was worst in the whole species,

12 And then, because they had forgotten everything else too, they forgot that anyone had ever been [d]different,

13 And decided that everybody in the whole wide world was really just a dirty useless racist killer,

14 Just like you,

15 Them included.

CHAPTER 24

This is a catastrophe for the Kensingtonians,

2 Because you needed them too,

3 And you knew that a lot of them were different,

4 And you counted on it,

5 [e]Because a lot of you *had* made it out of Kensington over the years,

6 And so you knew, deep down, that there were other ways to live,

7 And that it was good there were other kinds of people besides Kensingtonians,

8 Because there have to be [f]doctors,

9 And [g]engineers,

10 And [h]executives,

11 And the occasional [i]great statesman,

12 Not to mention a whole bunch of people who really *want* to be responsible and go to work every day and not cause trouble on every street corner,

13 And a whole bunch of other things like that,

a. 22.4
b. 12.21-24
c. Apes.2.1-6
　　Dav.47.6-7
d. 21.10-11
e. Adam.15.1-11
　　Rat.5.7-16
f. Jefs.11.19
g. Drex.10.3
h. Wht.23
i. Hall.15.7-12
j. 9.13
k. Rat.3.8-11
　　Ann.19.13
l. Ira.21.26
m. Rat.10.12-18
n. Psay.5J.1-34
o. Yks.87.1-2

14 Because when you drove your [j]pickup truck over the Ben Franklin Bridge,

15 You really did kind of appreciate the fact that the man in charge of building it probably wasn't a Kensingtonian,

16 Didn't you?

CHAPTER 25

And that's why most of you have always really kind of loved your [k]country,

2 No matter what,

3 [l]Even though the country was chock-full of Mainliners and Broad Streeters and Boulevardiers and Pennsylvanians and Hillites and Hallites and Fishites and Brewers and Manayunkians and Richmondites and Mount Airians and Germantonians and Swarthmorons and Haverfordians and Drexelites and Downtowners and Southians and millions of others who weren't Kensingtonians at all,

4 [m]But they were Americans,

5 And they were doing their part,

6 Just like you,

7 Even if they were a little short on guts,

8 And spent too much time talking about things when the time for talking was done,

9 [n]And even if you all told nasty jokes about each other and didn't want to marry each other or eat with each other,

10 Especially if somebody told you you had to,

11 [o]Because it's never been a good idea for anyone anywhere to tell a Kensingtonian what he can or can't do,

12 Period.

CHAPTER 26

^a**B**ut a lot of you believed in God too,

2 And you tried as hard as you could to figure out the Christian thing,

3 Which worked pretty well,

4 ^bBecause you figured it a lot like the whole country did,

5 Meaning that there were times you were on your best behavior because Jesus was probably watching,

6 Like when you got married and had babies and dinner at Mom's house and card games with your best buddies,

7 ^cAnd then there were times when turn the other cheek just doesn't cut it,

8 Because that isn't real life,

9 And sometimes you just put the Bible on the shelf and go take care of business,

10 ^dAnd getting it over with in a big hurry is the best you can do for Jesus at times like that,

11 Because He isn't here in Kensington when your wife's new boyfriend slashes the tires,

12 And how's he going to learn not to do that, and be more like Jesus would be, if you don't teach him the price of being a dirty homewrecking animal?

13 ^eAnd if that was such a wrong reading of Jesus, then how come the country kept giving you a whistle every fifty years or so,

14 ^fAnd sending you off to teach some uppity jerk a serious Kensingtonian lesson?

15 What is it that you figured wrong?

a. Ned.20.10-19
b. 26.13
c. 22.7
d. 22.13-14
e. 26.4
f. 22.9-12
g. Mawr.15.22
h. 25.3
i. 24.5-6
j. Rat.11.10-11

CHAPTER 27

Well, you just never figured that they would forget *everything*,

2 Especially the part about how everybody contributes in his own way,

3 And all the ways add a little something to the mix,

4 ^gIncluding even Kensingtonians,

5 ^hNot to mention everybody else.

6 And who would have figured that they'd forget everybody isn't and *shouldn't be* the same,

7 Because some are better at one thing, and some are better at the other,

8 Which is why everybody really kind of needs everybody else,

9 Just like you depend on the guy who was in charge of building the Ben Franklin,

10 Even if he was a Mainliner or a Drexelite or an uppity Broad Streeter,

11 Because you know that's not what Kensingtonians do best,

12 ⁱAlthough maybe you'd actually kind of like it if your son could learn how to build the Ben Franklin,

13 ^jBecause maybe then he wouldn't have to grow up like you did,

14 Scarred by gang fights before he was old enough to get his first tattoo.

CHAPTER 28

But they did forget.

2 Everything.

3 And they're going to take it out on a lot of people,

4 Including your ᵃancient enemies the Broad Streeters,

5 But especially on you,

6 Because they've decided that ᵇunder the surface, the ᶜanimal called Man is a Kensingtonian,

7 Which means that the nukes will all get used,

8 Just like you'd use them if you had some in the garage.

9 ᵈWhat's more, they've decided that Kensingtonians never ever change,

10 Because here you are, two hundred years later, and your wife still has a black eye,

11 ᵉWhich is something they can't forgive,

12 And why they don't bother to give you the benefit of the doubt,

13 Or check to see if maybe your front yards aren't a *little* cleaner than they used to be,

14 Or your Saturday night parties a *little* less wild,

15 Or your child-beating a *little* less frequent,

16 Which would be progress, let's face it,

17 But they're not in the mood for talking about progress,

18 ᶠWhen it comes to the race of Kensingtonians,

19 ᵍAnd all the nukes they're going to fire off the next time somebody gets it in the face with a bottle at the corner tavern.

CHAPTER 29

And so now it's every gang for itself,

2 And your chains and switchblades aren't going to be a match for ʰpolitical caucuses and

a. Brd.17.1-12
b. Frog.30.9-10
  Zig.5.1-9
c. Ira.23.22-29
  Al.6.13-15
d. Wil.21.1-19
e. Mawr.23.1-4
f. 28.6
g. 5.2
  Ed.77.11-13
  Dav.46.46
h. Brd.21.6-12
i. Mawr.18.1-15
j. Mawr.14.14-18
k. Ann.10.20-23
l. Main.27.1-17
m. Jefs.7.32-39
  Penn.3.4-13
n. Swar.7.1-10
o. Jeff.21.1-14
p. Swar.25.1-10
q. 18.1-10
r. Hill.G.1-2
s. Wil.31.18-22

ⁱrights groups and ʲminority alliances and ᵏaffirmative action programs and ˡcorporate cartels and ᵐprofessional associations and ⁿold school ties and ᵒorganized religions,

3 And all the other ᵖinstitutions they've turned into ᑫgangs so that they can have their vengeance on a world they didn't make,

4 And don't like the look of any more.

CHAPTER 30

For you Kensingtonians, this means that following the Way of Harry is the only way you'll ʳget by,

2 ˢAnd maybe you think you don't have anything to learn about the Trinity of Desire, Certainty, and Blame,

3 But you're dead wrong about that,

4 Because you're driving a horse and buggy in the jet age,

5 And they've got a lot of tricky new weapons that more than make up for the fact that they still don't have your kind of guts,

6 And probably never will.

7 This means you have a *lot* to learn about the modern ways of using desire, certainty, and blame,

8 Before all the Harriers eat you alive.

9 You're going to have to learn to express your desires on TV,

10 And to be certain at all times, not just when you're drunk and on fire,

11 And you're going to have to learn how to blame where it counts,

12 ᵃIn the courts,
13 ᵇAnd in the halls of government,
14 ᶜAnd in the media,
15 ᵈWithout ever letting down your guard,
16 Or getting caught alone outside Kensington,
17 Or getting identified as individuals,
18 Of any kind.

CHAPTER 31

If they can single you out, they'll cut you to pieces,
2 And hurt you,
3 And laugh at you,
4 ᵉAnd sneer at you,
5 And make an example of you,
6 ᶠWhich is why you still have to dress alike,
7 ᵍAnd keep your neighborhoods unfriendly and dangerous and ugly,
8 ʰAnd forget about climbing out of Kensington,
9 Ever,
10 ⁱBecause then you'd lose your protective camouflage,
11 And be exposed,
12 ʲAs the living breathing embodiment of all that's worst in the species of Mankind,
13 And that's just not safe,
14 At all.

CHAPTER 32

And so I urge you to learn the Way of Harry,
2 And use it to protect yourselves,
3 Because nobody anywhere cares at all about you anymore,
4 ᵏExcept for the tiny handful of you who can make it as rock and roll stars,
5 And only Harry can tell you

a. Penn.2.11-14
b. Brd.18.24-26
c. Ann.20.28-32
d. Hall.12.9-10
e. Swar.PS.27-31
f. 9.1
g. 11.5-11
h. Cen.26.19
i. 12.20
j. 28.6
k. Mall.14.15
l. Ext.14.7-9
m. Cen.26.17-18
n. Ned.16.12-13
o. 31.14
p. Ned.31.9-10
q. Brd.27.4-6
r. Jefs.8.13-15
s. Yks.154.43

how to get by if rock and roll doesn't work out,
6 Which brings me to one of my final points,
7 ˡWhich has to do with something called Consolation.

CHAPTER 33

As you may have guessed,
2 Your world is ending,
3 Just like everybody else's,
4 And all my warnings to you are not meant to make your end sound especially unique,
5 Because it isn't.
6 It's just that you're first on the ᵐlist of the ones who will be blamed,
7 And so you have to be more careful than a lot of the others,
8 ⁿBut their world is ending too,
9 Which is the news that Harry brought home to them,
10 ᵒAnd they don't want to think about it anymore,
11 ᵖWhich is why they got so good at blame all of a sudden.
12 ۹But blame alone is not enough when your world is ending,
13 Just as you have always known that all those gang fights and family beatings were never quite enough to take the ache out of your heart,
14 And that's why Harry also gave them Consolation,
15 ʳWhich comes in powder form,
16 ˢAnd makes everything better,
17 For as long as it lasts.

CHAPTER 34

And the really good news is that Harry doesn't hate you,

2 [a]Any more than he hates anybody else,

3 And so he wants you to have [b]Consolation too,

4 As long as you don't try to join the [c]Pontifical Harrier Parish,

5 Which is good advice,

6 [d]Because it is part of *my* job to protect the Pontifical Harrier Parish,

7 And I know how to do my job,

8 Better than you would believe possible.

CHAPTER 35

Even so, it is your right to have Consolation for the fix you're in,

2 Just as it is the right of every Harrier to have Consolation,

3 Because you didn't ask to be born,

4 And you didn't make the world,

5 But you do have to live in it,

6 For as long as it lasts.

7 And I can assure you that Consolation makes it all a little more acceptable somehow,

8 [e]Because it makes *now* special,

9 And that's a feeling you Kensingtonians have always known all there was to know about.

CHAPTER 36

[f]Consolation will be coming to your neighborhood,

2 And so I ask you to remember what I have said,

3 And don't freak out when my boys come around,

4 Because they're not there to hurt you,

5 But only to give you your rightful Consolation,

6 At very competitive prices.

a. Ira.34.4
b. Ext.13.17
c. Wht.11
d. Ext.52.6
e. Brd.29.5
f. Brd.28.2-5
g. Ext.38.10
h. Drex.12.7
i. 30.1-8
j. 36.6

CHAPTER 37

What's more,

2 There's another way for you to improve your lot,

3 Which is to join me,

4 And my [g]Angels,

5 Who you would like,

6 Because they are a lot like you,

7 And there's an awful lot of them,

8 Which means that no one will mess with them,

9 Especially all the Harriers,

10 Because they depend on us,

11 [h]For Consolation.

CHAPTER 38

I offer you the [i]Trinity of Harry,

2 To protect yourselves against the world and its new ways.

3 I offer you [j]Consolation,

4 To help you forget the world and the way it is ending.

5 I offer you a place among my Angels,

6 To give you the money to fulfill your desires,

7 To give you the certainty of an unassailable home,

8 To give you the power to blame without being blamed.

9 In return, I ask for the one quality you have that no one else has,

10 Anymore.

11 I ask for your guts.

CHAPTER 39

Lend me your guts,

2 And I will give you the world,

3 Such as it is,

4 For as long as it lasts.

ULT. TONY'S CHAIN LETTER
TO THE
SWARTHMORONS

CHAPTER 1

[a]Ciao, my friends!

2 I am sorry that I could not be with you in person,

3 For it is always a pleasure to engage in conversation with intellectual types such as you,

4 Who will one day be responsible for art and literature and poetry and other forms of serious creative expression,

5 As well as philosophy and political science and other forms of academic and rational inquiry.

6 How much I would have enjoyed taking tea with you,

7 And other things,

8 [b]But I have too much pressing business in San Francisco and cannot spare the time just now,

9 So I am sending you this chain letter instead.

CHAPTER 2

Indeed, this letter represents a great opportunity,

2 And I am delighted to be able to share it with you,

3 Because if you do not break the [c]chain,

4 You will be in line to win a Nobel prize someday,

5 Or maybe a Pulitzer,

6 Or possibly even [d]tenure,

7 Depending on the exact nature of your desire.

8 Are you interested?

9 Good.

a. Ext.17.15
b. Ext.43.1
c. 1.9
d. Ext.25.16-17
e. Ned.4.7
f. Ext.20.18
g. 37.5

10 Let me explain how it all works.

CHAPTER 3

The chain begins with [e]Harry,

2 With whose words you may or may not be familiar.

3 It is time that you understood the import of his teachings,

4 And prepared yourselves to follow his way,

5 For your efforts to preserve the chain will avail you nothing if you do not follow the Way of Harry,

6 Which is the best way,

7 And the only way for times such as ours.

CHAPTER 4

We will be discussing the Way of Harry at greater length in a minute,

2 But right now you are wondering, "How can this chain letter help me get a Nobel or a Pulitzer or even tenure?"

3 And so I will give you the answer to that at once,

4 Because it is so easy.

5 [f]All you have to do is identify the ultra-secret symbol of Harry,

6 And draw it on a sheet of paper,

7 [g]And send it to the first name on the list at the end of this letter.

8 Then remove the top name from the list,

9 Add your own at the bottom,

10 And send an exact copy of this revised letter to seven friends or acquaintances of your own.

11 [a]Moreover, if you cannot discover the ultra-secret symbol of Harry,

12 Then you are permitted to substitute five dollars instead,

13 Which may not put you in line for a Nobel or Pulitzer,

14 But will make you a whole ton of money,

15 Because the cleverest part of the chain is that only the most brilliant ones can succeed in discovering the ultra-secret symbol of Harry,

16 And everybody else will have to send money instead,

17 Or run the very grave risk of breaking the chain.

CHAPTER 5

Not long ago, a Berkeleyite broke the chain,

2 And immediately afterwards had his financial aid revoked due to allegations of fraudulent income reporting by his parents,

3 Which absolutely everybody does,

4 And then he was rejected by every graduate school he applied to,

5 In spite of exceptional grades and the perfect GRE score achieved by the person who took the test for him.

6 Last month, a Harvardian broke the chain and was expelled for plagiarism, even though all his classmates had also copied the same source.

7 [b]Just last week, a Skidmoron broke the chain and had to sleep with her thesis adviser just to get a passing grade, even though she

a. 4.5
b. Ext. 43.1-6
c. 34.2
d. 4.5
e. 4.5
f. Wil. 41.1-7

had earned highest honors.

8 And as I write this, I have just received word that a Brandeiser broke the chain and was instantly denounced in the school newspaper as a closet reactionary,

9 Which will certainly destroy her chance to enjoy a successful [c]academic career,

10 Not to mention poison her standing in the Militant Lesbian Alliance,

11 Of which she had been the president for three consecutive semesters.

CHAPTER 6

On the other hand, if you preserve the chain,

2 [d]The one who receives your drawing of the ultra-secret symbol of Harry will know that you are one of the elect,

3 And so will many others in the chain,

4 Whereupon new doors will open to you,

5 As if by chance,

6 Although in this case, chance will have nothing to do with it,

7 Because the people in this chain are looking for a very special sort of person,

8 And any person who understands the text of this letter well enough to discover the [e]ultra-secret symbol of Harry will automatically be identified as a very special person,

9 And will go far.

10 [f]For truly you must already suspect that succeeding in the world of intellect involves more than intellect,

11 Or why would so many of your professors be drunken, indolent, lecherous idiots,

12 [a]Who have never had an original or worthwhile thought about anything in their whole lives,

13 And who *must* have had a pretty special connection to get tenure in the first place?

14 Precisely.

CHAPTER 7

For indeed it is my pleasure to inform you that it is [b]this very chain which makes all the difference between success and failure in the world of the intellect,

2 Because the chain includes presidents and deans and tenured professors of the world's greatest universities,

3 As well as prizewinning novelists and poets and playwrights,

4 And noted sculptors and painters and artists of every variety,

5 As well as the founding geniuses of a dozen or more brilliant demimondes in which the right sort of person can thrive for a lifetime.

6 [c]And if you send the ultra-secret symbol of Harry to the name at the top of the list,

7 Your name will become known to all of them,

8 And they will pluck you from the endless lists of anonymous might-have-beens,

9 And elevate you to the very heights of your chosen intellectual profession,

10 Whatever it is.

11 All you have to do is study the message that follows,

12 With the utmost thoroughness,

13 [d]And discover the ultra-secret symbol of Harry.

a. Penn. 6.12
b. 2.1
c. 4.5
d. 4.5
e. Rom. 2.22
f. Penn. 6.1-3
g. 18.17
h. 7.2-5
i. Vin. 70.17-18

14 Isn't that an easy way to guarantee your own success?

15 [e]Can you think of a more worthwhile use of your prodigious mental capacity?

16 I thought not.

17 Shall we proceed to the message itself?

18 Excellent.

CHAPTER 8

It may seem at first to some among you that the Way of Harry has no relevance for you,

2 Because the Way of Harry is the way of not thinking about anything,

3 At all,

4 [f]And many of you take pride in your skill at thinking,

5 And believe that this is what separates you from everybody else more than any other thing,

6 Since you have all these great brilliant and creative thoughts all the time,

7 [g]And everybody else is just a fool or a hypocrite or a victim,

8 Or worse.

CHAPTER 9

But if this were so, there would be no need for the [h]chain which you now have a golden opportunity to become part of.

2 And indeed it is *not* true that the Way of Harry cannot make your life easier,

3 [i]No matter how well you think you can think.

4 And if you believe that there is some fatal contradiction between the Way of Harry and the way of the artists and intellectuals,

5 That is only because you have

not yet understood one very important truth,

6 ^aNamely, that there are no contradictions.

CHAPTER 10

^b**L**et me repeat this:

2 There are no contradictions.

3 The way of not thinking about anything at all can be as easy and fruitful for you as for anyone,

4 ^cBecause there is nothing important or new for you to think about,

5 ^dThanks to the fine work of the generations of great thinkers and artists who preceded you.

6 For example, it is not likely that you will be able to come up with a thought that changes the nature of the universe,

7 Which is a random, impersonal nature,

8 Or that you will come up with a thought that changes the destiny of Personkind,

9 Which is doom,

10 Either through nuclear holocaust or pollution.

11 And truly, you already know these things,

12 ^eFor you have taken more than enough history courses, and just enough science courses, to learn that science is the only thing that ever changes,

13 Because history repeats itself endlessly,

14 And the Others always get it in the neck from the greedy Oppressors of this world,

15 ^fAnd man is still the only animal that kills for sport,

16 And every weapon he invents is always used,

17 And the weapons keep getting more powerful and deadly,

a. Mawr.21.1-3
b. Ira.25.35
c. Drex.6.14
d. Ned.17.9-28
e. Wil.17.4-5
f. Ira.34.1-4
g. Pnot.24.5
h. Vin.24.9
i. Kin.2.1-4
j. Wil.31.14
k. 13.1

18 And sooner or later they will destroy us all^g.

CHAPTER 11

Now, I ask you, what does this mean if you are a writer,

2 Or an artist,

3 Or an intellectual?

4 Surely it means that you will have a hard time indeed thinking of anything brilliant enough to change the prognosis,

5 Which suggests that it would be easy to waste a lot of time,

6 And endure a lot of needless grief and travail,

7 For nothing.

8 ^hFortunately, however, the Way of Harry can help you a lot,

9 And just possibly bring you fame and fortune and critical success,

10 If any of these things means anything to you,

11 As a member of a doomed species,

12 ⁱAdrift in an insignificant sector of a completely random universe.

CHAPTER 12

If you wish to be a writer,

2 The Way of Harry should be your way,

3 Because the Way of Harry does not close off any options,

4 But just makes your job ^jsimpler,

5 And easier to do.

6 For example, you can be a writer and follow the Way of Harry along several quite different paths:

7 ^kThere is a path called art for art's sake that can bring you lavish praise,

8 Immense popularity with members of the sex you prefer,
9 And total ᵃfreedom too,
10 As long as you follow certain simple guidelines,
11 Without thinking about them too much.
12 ᵇThere is another path called art for fame's sake that can bring you large advances and critical praise,
13 As well as immense popularity with the sex you prefer,
14 Not to mention total ᶜfreedom,
15 As long as you follow certain simple guidelines,
16 Without thinking about them too much.
17 ᵈThere is also a third path called art for fortune's sake that can bring you huge advances,
18 Immense popularity with members of the sex you prefer,
19 And total ᵉfreedom too,
20 As long as you follow certain simple guidelines,
21 Without thinking about them too much.

CHAPTER 13

The path called art for art's sake should appeal to many of you,
2 Because in many ways it is the easiest path there is.
3 For the truly artistic writer can have an immense amount of fun,
4 ᶠAs long as she never smiles in public,
5 And never explains himself,
6 At all.
7 The artistic writer has many opportunities and advantages,
8 Even if the pay is sometimes meager,
9 But you must remember that lack of ᵍwealth is not a contra-

a. Ira.25.60-64
b. 22.1
c. 12.9
d. 31.1
e. 12.9
f. Yks.3.14-15
g. Kens.2.7
h. 10.1-2
i. 7.2-5
j. Drex.7.10
k. Vin.42.10-11
l. 12.10
m. Mawr.7.2-15
n. Wil.31.1-3
o. F&J.2.15-16

diction with the Way of Harry,
10 ʰBecause there are no contradictions.
11 In spite of meager pay, the artistic writer can garner lots of respect and acclaim,
12 ⁱFrom the people who count,
13 Without having to earn it.
14 He can appear to be a great shining genius,
15 Without ever creating anything new.
16 She can write about absolutely ʲnothing,
17 Without having given it much thought,
18 ᵏAnd still seem to be saying something really worthwhile.

CHAPTER 14

If this is a path that appeals to you, then listen closely,
2 ˡFor, as I have said, there are certain guidelines that make it easier to follow this path,
3 ᵐAnd life is too short to ruin it with a lot of unnecessary pain and suffering.
4 Remember then these words of wisdom about the path of art for art's sake:
5 The most powerful tool at your disposal is irony,
6 Or the appearance of irony,
7 Or the faintest glimmering shadow of irony,
8 Whether you have found anything truly ironic or not.
9 It is better, of course, not to search for irony through the medium of thought,
10 For thought is hard,
11 And can be depressing,
12 ⁿGiven that it always leads eventually to confrontation with the imminence of doom,
13 ᵒAnd the impossibility of

justice or meaning or redemption.

14 ^aRather, learn to create the appearance of irony,

15 Which is achieved through the simplest of juxtapositions,

16 ^bAnd can be done almost at random.

17 For example, you can load up on ^coxymorons,

18 Which don't ever have to mean anything,

19 ^dBut only have to seem like they might mean something,

20 ^eTo people who won't think about them anyway,

21 Except to admire you for whatever it is you must have meant,

22 Even if they haven't got a clue what that might be.

23 Nor are oxymorons the only kind of juxtapositions you can use.

CHAPTER 15

The truly artistic writer will also employ juxtapositions as a substitute for ideas, content, and theme,

2 Which is easy to do,

3 Because educated readers have grown used to this substitution,

4 And no longer notice it.

5 ^fUse technical jargon to describe natural beauty,

6 And you can create the appearance of intelligent social commentary,

7 Because every educated reader has learned how to recognize the theme called "the sterility of modern life,"

8 Which is about as artistic as you can get,

9 And doesn't offend anyone,

10 Because the sterility of mod-

a. 14.6
b. Vin.14.23
c. Vin.4.10
d. Vin.11.13-14
e. Vin.11.15
f. Psp.2.3
g. 11.11-12
h. Hill.Q.1-2
i. 10.13-18
j. 14.7
k. Vin.71.12-16

ern life is no one's fault especially;

11 It's just the way things are,

12 And the way things go,

13 ^gWhen you happen to live in this particular sector of this particular random universe.

14 ^hFor you absolutely must remember that no one looks to literature for answers anymore.

15 Educated people everywhere have learned that a delicate and clever rephrasing of the questions is enough,

16 ⁱSince we already know the answers anyway,

17 And we don't like the answers,

18 But we're willing to like the questions,

19 Provided they're not phrased too obviously.

CHAPTER 16

Yes, the artistic writer must never be obvious,

2 But subtle,

3 And eloquent,

4 ^jIn an ironic kind of way,

5 With an air of native sadness,

6 Which wells up from the depths of his inborn sensitivity,

7 And from her appearance of profound yearning that the ^kway of things might be different from the way they so obviously are,

8 As we can deduce from the extraordinary subtlety of his prose.

9 But never ever come right out and say what you are thinking,

10 Because this will result in one of two things,

11 Both bad.

12 The first thing which can happen is that people will disagree with your thinking,

13 Either because your thinking

is bad or because it doesn't agree with theirs,

14 ^aWhich is exactly the same thing.

15 The second thing which can happen is that your straightforward approach will force *you* to think,

16 Which is very very bad,

17 Because thinking leads to all kinds of problems,

18 Like doubt,

19 And introspection,

20 ^bAnd inevitably, despair.

21 Therefore, remember that if you cultivate a sense of obscurity and abstruseness at all times,

22 You will find it both easier to write,

23 And easier to live.

CHAPTER 17

Indeed, the path of art for art's sake is most notable for its ease.

2 Because it can be pursued successfully by almost anyone with a good command of grammar and vocabulary,

3 ^cAnd a really good dictionary of quotations,

4 Which is good news for you,

5 ^dBecause hardly anyone has real command of the language anymore,

6 And when you show off your excellent grammar and vocabulary,

7 Everyone will know that you are a great artist,

8 Even if you never think about anything at all.

9 For example, you can write in ironic terms about the emptiness of life in the shadow of imminent doom,

10 Without ever actually men-

a. *Mawr. 25.23*
b. *14.12*
c. *17.26*
d. *Hill. B. 9-13*
e. *Psp. 3.9*
f. *Psp. 2.7*
g. *Psp. 1.8*
h. *F&J. 8.5-6*
i. *Psp. 2.12*

tioning nuclear warfare or acid rain,

11 As long as you make some opaque reference to ^ewhat the thunder said,

12 And people will get the idea,

13 Even if they can't figure out the precise meaning of a single sentence.

14 ^fYou can write ironically and allusively about the tragedy of man's inhumanity to man,

15 Or woman,

16 Without presenting any new evidence,

17 Or adding any fresh ideas on the subject,

18 Because no one expects any fresh ideas from literature.

19 ^gWhat they expect from literature is that it go on writing ironically and allusively about the imminence of doom and man's inhumanity to man,

20 ^hBecause that is what they have learned to expect from serious literature,

21 And they will know that you are good or great,

22 Depending on how impossible it is to understand what you are saying in particular.

23 You can write about the general pain and anguish of existence,

24 Without ever having to experience the pain and anguish of existence,

25 Because it is incredibly easy to write about nothing at all,

26 ⁱAnd insert a whole bunch of subtle literary allusions after the fact to inform the educated reader that what you are really talking about here is the pain and anguish of human existence,

27 Which they approve of,

28 Because that is your job,

29 And somebody has to do it.

CHAPTER 18

I can also give you some advice about such things as plot and characters and so forth,
2 But these are of secondary importance indeed,
3 Because for the truly artistic writer there is only one plot,
4 Which is the struggle of the protagonist against an impossible situation,
5 [a]Where there really isn't any way to win,
6 [b]For approximately sixty-one thousand words if you are writing a novel,
7 [c]Approximately four thousand words if you are writing a short [d]story,
8 [e]And approximately twenty-two thousand words if you are writing a play.
9 Besides being quite easy, this plot is also a foolproof way to prove that you really are an artist,
10 And not some commercial slob,
11 Because if the protagonist prevails in the end,
12 Or does anything more than physically survive,
13 With a certain wry humor about his experience,
14 The story isn't [f]art,
15 But popular trash.
16 This is why you must also remember that there are no [g]heroes,
17 Only [h]victims and [i]fools and [j]cynics and [k]monsters,
18 And the purpose of describing their ordeals is to comfort your readers with the fact that everybody is in the same [l]boat,
19 [m]And so what can you do?

a. F&J.6.8
b. Psp.3.13
c. Psp.3.7
d. F&J.15.14-22
e. Psp.3.11
f. Dav.43.20-23
g. Psay.5Q.32
h. Oth.8.18
i. Psom.40.4
j. Psay.5Q.55
k. Krt.39.14
l. F&J.14.4
m. Psom.69.1-4
n. Jeff.24.5-6
o. 14.4-8
p. Psay.5Q.62
q. Ira.31.14
r. 19.9-12 F&J.10.6
s. Ed.77.4-14
t. Dav.55.6-28

CHAPTER 19

What you can do is have epiphanies.
2 Epiphanies are everything to the artistic writer,
3 [n]An epiphany being the momentary illusion of meaning where there isn't any,
4 Which is both [o]ironic and literary,
5 And [p]proves that you are an artist.
6 Fortunately, it is very easy to make up epiphanies,
7 Because they never involve any real action of any kind,
8 But kind of lurk within prosaic moments,
9 Like when your spouse sighs over a cup of decaffeinated tea,
10 With sunlight streaming in through the window of your New England cottage,
11 And you've just finished reading the latest issue of the 'Pseudo-Intellectual Review,'
12 And can't quite remember [q]what you were going to do next.
13 To turn this into an epiphany, all you have to do is this:
14 Repeat one of these images in slightly different or [r]amplified terms, *as if* it had just acquired some new significance;
15 Insert a totally [s]extraneous recollection that is every bit as prosaic as the scene you've already described, *as if* it had been suggested to you by something in the cottage scene;
16 And then describe some additional prosaic moment in the cottage, with lots and lots of superfluous [t]details, leaving the reader to figure out for herself what it all means.
17 When the epiphany has been

completed in this fashion, you just skip twice the number of lines you normally use between paragraphs,

18 [a]And change the subject.

19 This is so important that it is, all by itself, practically the only thing you actually need to know about artistic writing,

20 And it is so simple that you don't ever have to agonize over it at all.

21 Indeed, if you like, you can write complete novels using nothing but this [b]simple technique.

CHAPTER 20

My final words about artistic writing concern setting,

2 Which is important up to a point,

3 But only up to a point.

4 In general, it is far better to place your characters in exotic settings,

5 [c]Such as Argentina, and Europe, and the Far East, and New England,

6 [d]Instead of Des Moines and El Paso and Scranton,

7 Because everything seems more subtle and more charged with meaning in some permanently melancholy foreign land,

8 Which frequently results in epiphanies almost automatically,

9 And lets you convey a sense of loneliness and isolation without ever saying a single word about alienation,

10 [e]Which is the most important feeling your setting can provide in modern artistic fiction.

11 Besides, you don't actually have to go to these places to write about them,

a. *Ira.31.16*
b. *Wil.31.14*
c. *Psay.5N.12*
d. *Psay.5C.13*
e. *Vin.71.26*
f. *19.10*
g. *20.6*
h. *20.5*
i. *14.4-8*
j. *Ira.33.1-3*
k. *Psom.27.2-3*
l. *20.6*
m. *Psay.1.4*
n. *12.12*
o. *12.13*
p. *Psong.9.1-3*

12 Since it's pretty well understood all over that if you're a serious writer you have to live on some campus in [f]New England,

13 Unless you prefer to live in San Francisco or New York instead.

14 Even so, you can still have your characters do exactly the same things they would do in [g]Des Moines or El Paso or Scranton,

15 [h]And just have them do it in Argentina or New England,

16 [i]Which creates a whole bunch of irony automatically,

17 [j]And practically ensures that everyone will recognize how brilliantly you convey the sterility of modern life,

18 And man's inhumanity to man,

19 And the pain and anguish of human existence,

20 [k]In a sad, doomed, random world.

CHAPTER 21

On the other hand, if you want to write about [l]Des Moines or Scranton in particular,

2 And actually use the place-names,

3 And put in local color and all that,

4 Then maybe you should consider the second path,

5 [m]Which is the path of art for fame's sake.

6 I assure you that this is not a lesser path,

7 [n]And does not deny you the opportunity to earn critical praise,

8 [o]And many attentive admirers from one or more of the sexes,

9 [p]Not to mention more money,

10 ^aAnd maybe even a lot more money.

CHAPTER 22

In fact, in many ways, the path of art for fame's sake is quite similar to the path of art for art's sake,

2 Although it involves more public speaking,

3 And usually more public drinking,

4 Although any writer on any path is always free to drink as much as he wants to,

5 Which is not only the Way of ^bHarry,

6 But also the way of ^ctradition.

7 Additionally, the path of art for fame's sake requires writing about things that are a little closer to everyday life,

8 ^dThat is, life outside of colleges and universities in New England,

9 Which might seem harder,

10 But doesn't have to be.

CHAPTER 23

For example, the path of art for fame's sake becomes a broad and well-lighted ^ehighway if you can find things to be against that no one is for.

2 If you wish to be praised for your passion and moral sensitivity,

3 Write about how ^fterrible war is,

4 ^gAnd how irrational,

5 ^hAnd how wasteful,

6 ⁱAnd how destructive.

7 ^jBe indignant about it,

8 ^kBe ironic,

9 And be ruthless in your ^lcontempt for all those people out there who think that war is won-

a. Psong.12.1-3
b. Vin.27.7
c. Yks.91.1-7
d. 20.12
e. Psp.3.13
f. Psong.6.7
g. Psong.6.8
h. Psong.6.9
i. Psong.6.10
j. Psong.6.11
k. Psong.6.12
l. Swar.PS.27-29
m. Ann.19.1-14
n. Psong.53.6-8
o. Main.15.1-17
p. Psong.10.6-7
q. Psong.58.3
r. Psong.59.1-3
s. Vin.71.12-16

derful and fun and sensible and the way to go,

10 Because these are people that everyone likes to see exposed and criticized,

11 ^mEven if they've never seen them anywhere but on the silver screen.

CHAPTER 24

Similarly, you can write satires that excoriate corrupt corporations whose despicably sly and greedy conspiracies wind up killing innocent people,

2 Because the world is just full of people who don't know that this kind of behavior is frowned upon,

3 And who wouldn't do it if they knew you disapproved,

4 With your crushing irony,

5 ^oAnd your immense knowledge about how the world of business operates.

CHAPTER 25

Along somewhat the same lines, you can also write satires that excoriate corrupt religious institutions,

2 ^qAnd corrupt political institutions,

3 ^rAnd corrupt bureaucracies,

4 Because your audience is just chock-full of people who think it's terrible that our institutions are corrupt,

5 And what can you do?

6 ^sSince it's pretty obvious that when all the institutions are corrupt, there's nothing anyone can do but shrug,

7 Your audience wants to be reminded very frequently about how corrupt their institutions are,

8 By someone who's never had

an original or new thought on the subject,

9 Because that's exactly what they expect,

10 ^aAnd is therefore the surest way to please them.

CHAPTER 26

Another fertile field for the famous writer is demonstrating his opposition to nuclear holocaust,

2 ^bVia some clever satire that exposes the insanity of building doomsday weapons that can never be used,

3 Except that they will be,

4 Because the ^cmilitary or somebody is too stupid not to.

5 This kind of writing is very powerful and important,

6 ^dBecause the world is teeming with people who really like the idea of nuclear holocaust,

7 And constantly need to be reminded of all the complex truths associated with it,

8 ^eLike the fact that when everybody's dead,

9 ^fThere won't be anybody left,

10 Including all the people who are so ^gshortsighted that they really love the thought of nuclear war.

11 ^hNote that a work like this involves zero thought,

12 ⁱAnd can be pulled off with a bunch of ham-handed, simpleminded devices that won't cost you even a moment's sleep at night.

CHAPTER 27

You can also write about history,

2 Which involves research and can lead to thought,

a. *Ned.29.19-20*
b. *Yks.154.1-34*
c. *Forg.8.11-15*
d. *Ann.18.23*
e. *Oth.7.22*
f. *Oth.9.16-19*
g. *Ed.61.12-15*
h. *Mall.15.14*
i. *Mall.15.15*
j. *Psong.57.1-4*
k. *Psong.31.1-5*
l. *Psong.32.1-3*
m. *Psong.10.1-5*
n. *Psong.29.1-7*
o. *Hall.13.8*
p. *15.15-19*

3 But not if you know well ahead of time what you think about what happened,

4 ^jAnd who's the villain,

5 And exactly which unspeakable evils you wish to highlight.

CHAPTER 28

^kYou can also write almost endlessly about how tough it is be you,

2 ^lOr someone like you,

3 ^mOr the member of some oppressed minority,

4 ⁿThe tougher the better,

5 Whether it is or not,

6 Because everybody knows that life is tough all over,

7 And they like to hear someone whine about it,

8 Because it reminds them that life is cruel and unfair and unjust,

9 And they're not the only ones who are whining and whimpering and complaining,

10 Which is always good to know.

CHAPTER 29

In fact, you can write about virtually anything in the real world,

2 On your path to fame,

3 As long as you always remember one essential guideline,

4 ^oWhich is that there are no real solutions,

5 And no real answers,

6 Because there is no such thing as truth.

7 You must therefore,

8 Like your artistic brethren,

9 ^pBe careful to confine your writing to rephrasing the same old questions in the same old ways,

10 Time after time after time,

11 ᵃSo that every moral ambiguity is presented as an unsolvable paradox,

12 ᵇAnd every human failing is impossible to overcome,

13 And the only human virtue is the sensitivity of a few select individuals,

14 Like ᶜyou,

15 Who know how to feel about everything,

16 And who could probably fix everything if everyone else would just sit down with them and have a good cry about it,

17 Except that nothing can ever really be fixed,

18 ᵈBecause that's not the way things are,

19 Which is the exact right place in your manuscript for the concluding epiphany,

20 Including a bunch of ambiguous juxtapositions of ᵉtelling images,

21 ᶠWhich can actually consist of almost anything,

22 And most importantly,

23 Can be very very obvious.

CHAPTER 30

The famous writer can be obvious because he is not even pretending to think,

2 But to feel,

3 Which is very different from the job of the artistic writer.

4 When you're writing an anti-war piece,

5 People want to know when to cheer,

6 ᵍAnd when to shake their head and say, "Well, isn't that just like that crazy old race of Mankind? My my."

7 And so when you get to the big epiphany that ties a big ribbon around all the unsolvable

a. F&J.13.1-9
b. F&J.14.5-9
c. Ed.60.13
d. Oth.9.1-4
e. Dav.42.31-39
f. Psp.2.13
g. Dav.46.31-35
h. Dav.46.43-46
i. 12.17
j. Ann.8.1-11
k. 22.1
l. Psong.41.1-6
m. Psong.61.1-4

moral paradoxes, it's important to let the audience in on it,

8 ʰAs obviously as possible,

9 Which means you don't really have to think about it at all,

10 And can just be wildly emotional instead.

CHAPTER 31

ⁱThe path of art for fortune's sake is also incredibly easy,

2 Because all you have to do is pick out one kind of book,

3 And write one book of that kind,

4 Without being original in any way,

5 And then,

6 And this is the important part,

7 ʲWrite the very same book over and over and over and over again.

8 In fact, this path is so easy and rewarding that many writers begin their careers by choosing the ᵏpath of art for fame's sake,

9 ˡAnd then switch to the path of art for fortune's sake after their first successful book.

10 Yes, if you play your cards right, you can publish book after book after book,

11 Without ever thinking about anything at all.

CHAPTER 32

Of course, some writers make the mistake of trying to think about what kind of book they should write,

2 Over and over and over and over again,

3 Because they mistakenly believe that it is important to like the kind of book they choose.

4 For this reason, they ᵐagonize endlessly,

5 Which is totally contrary to the Way of Harry,

6 And quite unnecessary besides,

7 Like all things that are contrary to the Way of Harry.

8 In their agonizing, they ask themselves foolish questions,

9 [a]Such as "Should I write schlocky mysteries that all feature the same wildly eccentric but mildly likable detective?

10 [b]"Or should I write schlocky horror stories that all feature very slight twists on the Grade B horror movies I saw in my youth?

11 [c]"Or should I write schlocky romance novels that all feature the stock characters in my adolescent erotic fantasies?

12 [d]"Or should I write schlocky sagas that . . . "

13 But you can see how utterly pointless this is:

14 There is *no* kind of book that is enjoyable to write over and over and over and over again,

15 Which is precisely why this path is called the path of art for fortune's sake,

16 [e]Because money is its own reward,

17 Even if it is the only reward of paths like this one.

CHAPTER 33

A nd if you recoil utterly from paths that lead to fortune,

2 Then perhaps it is wiser to choose a path of art-type art instead,

3 Such as painting or sculpture or visual things like that,

4 Because these are all incredibly easy to do,

5 Without thinking about it at all,

a. Ed.51.15-24
b. Dav.30.10-50
c. Brit.44.6-9
d. Ann.13.1-3
e. Psong.20.1-6
f. Psong.65.1-4
g. Paul.6.1-6
h. Paul.7.5-6
i. 14.17
j. Paul.6.10-17
k. Dav.43.25-27
l. Vin.14.23-24
m. Psong.22.1-3

6 And offer an important additional advantage,

7 Namely, that everyone will know you're doing it for acceptable motives,

8 Like the approval of all the pseudo-intellectuals who really count,

9 And not for anything as disgusting as [f]money.

10 If this is a path that appeals to you,

11 Remember that there are only two rules regarding the visual arts:

12 [g]First, never produce any work of art that actually looks like something in the real world;

13 [h]And second, never explain your intentions, unless you're much better than average at reeling off nonsensical [i]oxymorons and other meaningless esoterica, without thinking about it at all.

14 If you observe these two rules, you can do absolutely anything you feel like doing,

15 [j]Even if it's just driving a muddy Jeep over a canvas,

16 And IT WILL BE [k]ART,

17 Which means that it's worth something to somebody,

18 [l]And has every bit as good a chance of being praised as the stuff that anybody else is doing.

19 Who knows?

20 Maybe it will be reviewed by somebody important,

21 Especially if you happen to be sleeping with somebody important,

22 Which can be a pretty big help on this path.

23 Maybe you'll be hailed as the latest genius,

24 And get invited to all the right places,

25 [m]And possibly get a big

grant to go on with your great work.

26 ªMaybe somebody will actually buy it,

27 ᵇUnless that would soil your pristine integrity about art,

28 Which you are absolutely entitled to have,

29 ᶜBecause there are no contradictions.

CHAPTER 34

And then again, maybe you have no interest in the creative arts at all.

2 Maybe you're a brilliant academic instead,

3 And want to be a professor of art criticism,

4 Or history,

5 Or literature,

6 Or psychology,

7 Or philosophy,

8 Or even science.

9 If this is the path you prefer, you are in luck,

10 Because once again, there are only two rules you need to observe:

11 ᵈFirst, remember that the only demonstrable good on this earth is the exclusive province of the Others,

12 Who always get it in the neck,

13 And who are always ᵉright,

14 No matter what position they take,

15 On any issue,

16 ᶠAnd even if they change their position from time to time,

17 ᵍBecause there are no contradictions.

18 And if the Others ever change their position, then you must simply change your position right along with them,

a. Ed.60.17
b. Psong.45.1
c. 10.1-2
d. Hill.O.1-5
e. Carl.10.13
f. Mawr.20.10-18
* Brd.22.1-15*
g. 10.1-2
h. 34.11
i. Ned.9.4
j. 2.3-6
k. 37.5
l. 4.5-12
m. 5.1-11

19 Without thinking about it at all,

20 Because the Others are always,

21 And I mean *always*,

22 Dead right.

CHAPTER 35

You will find that this first rule of the academic path makes all your scholarship marvelously easy and simple,

2 Because there will be no dilemmas to deal with,

3 No difficult decisions to make,

4 And no analysis needed.

5 For any question you may wish to inquire into,

6 Just look for the Others in the vicinity of your question,

7 And develop your positions and arguments accordingly,

8 Without thinking about it at all.

9 And if one set of ʰOthers comes into conflict with another set of Others,

10 ⁱRest assured that right is always on the side of the Others who are less white,

11 Less male,

12 Less western,

13 And less advanced technologically.

CHAPTER 36

The second rule of the academic path is just as simple,

2 But just as important:

3 Do not break the ʲchain!

4 Ever!

5 Make sure you send your letter to the top name on the ᵏlist,

6 And follow the rest of the ˡinstructions to the final detail,

7 Or else none of these paths will work out to your advantage,

8 ᵐAnd the academic path in

particular will bring you to ruin and misery.

9 It is absolutely vital that you believe me on this point,

10 ªFor the chain begins with Harry,

11 And the ᵇWay of Harry is indispensable to your success,

12 Which there can be no doubt about,

13 For I Serve Harry,

14 And I have had the opportunity to learn the miraculous good fortune that comes to those who follow the Way of Harry,

15 And I have laid it all out for you in the plainest possible terms,

16 Which means that all you have to do is get busy with those letters,

17 And be very careful,

18 In fact, very *very* careful,

19 Not to break the ᶜchain.

CHAPTER 37

Now I shall give you the list of names,

2 And do not worry if you do not recognize them,

3 For Your Letters Will Achieve Their Objective.

4 Here are the names:

5 The Ultra-Harrier Tom, Box 1234, Boston, MA;

6 The Ultra-Harrier Tony, Box 1234, San Francisco, CA;

7 The Ultra-Harrier Willie, Box 1234, Philadelphia, PA;

8 The Ultra-Harrier Joe, Box 1234, Atlanta, GA;

9 The Ultra-Harrier Sam, Box 1234, New York, NY;

10 The Ultra-Harrier Vinnie, Box 1234, Los Angeles, CA;

11 The Ultra-Harrier Jerry, Box 1234, Chicago, IL.

a. 3.1
b. Mawr.8.1-6
c. 3.1
d. 3.1
e. PS.37
f. 36.11
g. PS.37
h. 29.13-14
i. Ext.25.1
j. Kens.9.2-5

12 It's that easy.

13 But remember NOT TO THINK about anything at all,

14 Ever!

P.S.

Yes, that's right, dear Swarthmorons,

2 We do have a fascinating little postscript for you,

3 Which could change your life as you try to make your way up the ᵈchain,

4 ᵉBecause if you enclose another ten dollars with your letter,

5 We'll send you the enormously informative 'Intellectual Lifestyle Handbook,'

6 Which is just crammed with useful tips on how to impress all your most intellectual friends,

7 While protecting yourself from the ᶠdangers of thinking *at the same time*!

8 Sound impossible?

9 ᵍWell, that's because you haven't sent the ten dollars yet,

10 Which you really should do,

11 Because these are tips that aren't available to all Harriers,

12 ʰBut only to a select few,

13 Like yourselves.

14 For example, you'll learn which car is right for the committed intellectual who hates cars,

15 ⁱIncluding even the very difficult choice between Volkswagens and Volvos.

16 You'll learn a few simple tips about how to dress for success in the intellectual community,

17 Such as Tip No. 1,

18 Which is to dress like a ʲKensingtonian and then just add a beard and a corduroy jacket for

that little extra *je ne sais quoi* that makes all the difference.

19 And that's not all you'll get for your ᵃten dollars,

20 Because you'll also learn how to pick an academic ᵇspecialty so narrow that no one will ever ask you the ᶜbig hard questions,

21 Like "What does it all mean?"

22 And "Why should we go on for another lousy day?"

23 Because you don't need your life complicated with a lot of esoteric paradoxes,

24 Especially when it's so much easier to sit back in your ᵈcorduroy jacket,

25 ᵉAnd just *pretend* to have the lowdown on everything,

26 Which is still another of the amazing things you'll learn for the paltry sum of ᶠten dollars.

27 For example, when you send in your ᵍten dollars, you'll also receive dozens of useful tips

a. *PS.37*
b. *Drex.9.1-3*
c. *Grk.19.1*
d. *PS.18*
e. *Drex.8.15*
f. *PS.37*
g. *PS.37*
h. *Ext.25.10-12*
i. *Kens.4.9-11*
j. *PS.4*

about how to use the intellectual's most feared communications weapons, namely,

28 ʰRidicule,

29 ⁱAnd contempt,

30 Which are all you'll ever need to dismiss everybody else's ideas,

31 Without thinking about them at all,

32 Just like thousands of great intellectuals have done before you,

33 As they worked *their* way up the chain.

34 Can you afford to be without the 'Intellectual Lifestyle Handbook'?

35 Not if you ever expect to get tenure, that's for sure.

36 So mail your letter today,

37 ʲAnd don't forget the ten dollars!

38 *Comprenez, mes cher amies?*

39 *Très très bien.*

THE MANDATE OF ULTS. JERRY AND SAM

FOR THE

HALLITES

CHAPTER 1

Greetings to all you fine public servants! How are you today?

2

3 Excuse us, but we're trying to extend our salutations to you public servants . . .

4

5 Hey! You government workers!

6 Listen up!

7 That's better.

8 We've got your mandate here,

9 From Harry.

CHAPTER 2

All right.

2 We apologize.

3 We're well aware that this is America,

4 [a]Where nobody is anybody's *servant*,

5 Least of all the people who work for the government,

6 Because you're the ones who take care of all the important things,

7 [b]Namely, the things nobody else wants to be responsible for,

8 Which is a lot of things,

9 And probably explains why you're so cross and grumpy,

10 All the time.

CHAPTER 3

But have you figured out that just because nobody else wants to be responsible doesn't mean that you have to be?

2

3 Well, we know you're busy,

4 Provided you've gotten into the office already,

5 And so we're just going to go right ahead,

6 And pretend you're paying attention to us,

7 Just like you pretend to pay attention to the public.

8 How does that sound?

9

10 Okay, then.

11 Where were we?

CHAPTER 4

Oh yes.

2 We were talking about responsibility.

3 Ugh. It's a dirty word, isn't it?

4 The thing is, it's your job to

---

a. 15.12-13
b. Brd.18.13-16
c. Main.14.3-4
d. Mawr.8.1-6
e. Swar.10.13-18
f. F&J.14.20
g. Ira.21.29-32
h. Ned.31.10
i. 5.6
j. 5.6

---

handle all the messy unpleasant stuff nobody else wants to think about,

5 But it doesn't have to be as awful as it sounds,

6 [c]Because if nobody else is thinking about these things,

7 Then how on earth are they going to know if you don't think about them either,

8 And just do whatever you feel like doing instead?

9 They aren't.

10 That's why the [d]Way of Harry is so perfect for the Hallites.

11 Really.

CHAPTER 5

[e]**I**t was Harry who pointed out that none of this is going anywhere anyway,

2 [f]Which is why it wouldn't help to think about it even if we wanted to,

3 Which we mostly don't,

4 As I think we can all agree.

5 [g]That's also why Harry gave us his Trinity,

6 [h]Consisting of Desire, Certainty, and Blame,

7 Which help all us Harriers get through daily life,

8 Without thinking about anything at all.

CHAPTER 6

Now, if you work for the government, Harry's Trinity is especially important,

2 Because when people [i]desire something,

3 They want the government to give it to them.

4 When they are [j]certain about something,

5 They want the government to

turn their certainty into the law of the land.

6 And when they ^ablame somebody for something, they want the government to punish the targets of their blame,

7 Unless it's the government they're blaming,

8 ^bIn which case they want to see some heads roll.

9 Does any of this sound familiar?

10

11 Well, we'll assume that it does.

CHAPTER 7

It may sound a lot as if Harry's Way could make your life a lot harder,

2 Instead of easier,

3 But that's the case only if you elect not to use Harry's Way yourself,

4 And try to do your job instead.

5 Which is where we come in,

6 'Because there's absolutely no reason why you should ever try to do your job,

7 When it's so easy to follow the Way of Harry.

CHAPTER 8

For example, the whole constitution of the Most Chosen Nation on Earth is based on one overridingly important principle,

2 ^dNamely, the principle that nobody can be trusted,

3 Which used to make people take a pretty active interest in politics;

4 Because of all the things they didn't trust,

5 ^eGovernment was the thing they didn't trust the most.

a. 5.6
b. Hill.V.9-10
c. Mall.11.17-23
d. Yks.12.1-13
e. Yks.12.14-17
f. Adam.41.8
g. Yks.97.5-11
h. Adam.41.9
i. Carl.3.1-5
j. Brd.18.17-19
k. Brd.18.20-23

6 ^fBut then things changed,

7 ^gBecause they finally figured out that the thing they didn't trust the most was each other,

8 Which is when they decided that it was the government's job to watch over everyone,

9 And especially the ones they didn't trust the most,

10 ^hLike the rich capitalists who might steal everybody else's money if they weren't held in check,

11 ⁱAnd the poor losers who might get violent and destroy everything if their basic needs weren't taken care of.

12 And that's when the government hired a whole bunch of people like you to do the watching,

13 Which has worked out great,

14 Because now that they don't want to think about anything at all,

15 ^jThey kind of have to trust *you,*

16 Unless they're willing to get involved themselves,

17 Which isn't likely to happen,

18 Any time soon.

CHAPTER 9

In short, you couldn't be in a better position,

2 Whether you do your job or not,

3 ^kWhich means that they'll ultimately accept whatever you do,

4 Even if they complain a lot,

5 Because you work for the government,

6 And who else can you trust in this Most Chosen Nation on Earth?

7 That's why there's nothing you can't get away with,

8 At all,

9 ᵃAs long as you remember a few simple guidelines.

CHAPTER 10

The most important thing to remember is that no matter how nasty they get,

2 ᵇIt's *you* they trust,

3 More than anyone else, anyway,

4 Because they know that you're not rich,

5 Unless you're an elected official, that is,

6 ᶜIn which case they know that you're going to get rich no matter what anyone does or says about it,

7 And at least you probably aren't as rich as the *real* scum of the earth,

8 ᵈMeaning the kind of scum who run all the rich corporations and steal everybody's money all the time.

9 ᵉAnd besides knowing that you're not rich,

10 They also know that you're not going to start a riot in their neighborhood,

11 Or hold up a liquor store,

12 Or rape their wife,

13 ᶠBecause you work for the government,

14 Which means you can never ever be fired,

15 For any reason,

16 ᵍUnless you're a policeman or a fireman or something essential like that,

17 ʰBecause the first guideline of working for the government is making sure that each and every paper-pushing bureaucrat has a job forever,

18 No matter what.

---

a. 10.17
11.3-4
13.7
b. 8.15
c. Psong.41.1-3
d. Adam.38.2-8
e. 10.4
f. 9.5
g. 12.17
h. 9.9
i. Psong.59.1-2
j. 10.16
k. 10.16
l. Kens.21.7
m. Boul.12.9
n. 10.17
o. 11.3-4

CHAPTER 11

In fact, this first guideline is so important that the second guideline is really just kind of an insurance policy for the first,

2 Being:

3 The answer to all complaints about the way the government does its job is the same,

4 'Namely, raising the taxes of the people who complain.

5 If people rant and rave about budget deficits,

6 Threaten to raise taxes.

7 If they object to higher taxes and start talking about waste in government,

8 Lay off some ʲpolice,

9 And some ᵏfiremen,

10 And some ˡgarbage collectors,

11 Because the only reason people like that are on the government payroll in the first place is to be visible,

12 So "the people" will think they're getting something for their tax dollars, that is, something other than your ᵐwhite Monte Carlo and your great pension plan,

13 And so "the people" will see that there's no alternative to a tax increase when police and firemen have to be laid off because ⁿeveryone else on the payroll is so indispensable.

CHAPTER 12

The other great thing about ᵒthis guideline is what happens if the people still refuse to raise taxes,

2 Because then it can't possibly be your fault when things get steadily worse.

3 After all, you told them you needed more taxes,

4 Didn't you?

5 And when the ªprofessional blamers start coming around talking about how taxes are too high already,

6 ᵇAnd how the people who can pay taxes are all moving away,

7 And what do you think about that? . . .

8 You must remember not to fall into this trap,

9 ᶜBecause if you acknowledge that they have any kind of point at all,

10 ᵈThey will demand that you think about it,

11 Which is just not necessary,

12 ᵉBecause you work for the government,

13 And if you had wanted to think about anything you would have done something else with your life,

14 Which is why you need more taxes,

15 Period,

16 And if you don't get them,

17 ᶠYou'll know exactly what to do with the policemen and firemen and garbage collectors,

18 Without thinking about it at all.

CHAPTER 13

The third guideline concerns the ᵍOthers,

2 In other words, all the people the government has to take care of because nobody else wants to do it.

3 Remember that you need the Others as much as they need you,

4 Because if they weren't there,

5 It would be even harder to pretend that you were actually doing something,

6 With all the time you spend

a. Main.17.4
b. Wil.59.1-8
c. Wil.35.1-8
d. Mall.8.25-26
e. 9.5
f. 11.11
g. Hill.O.1-5
h. 9.9
i. Swar.29.4
j. 12.14
k. 13.2
l. 10.17
m. 10.5
n. Mawr.19.4
o. Cen.11.32
p. 9.5

working for the government.

7 ʰAnd so you must remember not to go looking for any real or permanent solutions to the plight of the Others,

8 ⁱSince there aren't any solutions anyway,

9 Which means that it's much much better to help them by creating lots and lots and lots of new paperwork for yourself,

10 And then doing the paperwork,

11 As slowly and ineffectually as you can without actually thinking about it,

12 So that the plight of the Others will remain highly visible to all,

13 ʲWhich will help ensure that taxes can keep getting higher,

14 No matter what,

15 Which is your only guarantee that you won't wind up as ᵏOthers yourselves someday,

16 Because,

17 Well,

18 ˡRemember the first guideline?

19 We thought so.

CHAPTER 14

Are there any other guidelines the Hallites need to remember?

2 ᵐNot really.

3 ⁿYou already know the part about how you didn't make the world and its problems,

4 °And how it's not your fault,

5 And so what are you supposed to do about it,

6 ᵖBecause you just work for the government.

7 And you also know the part about how nobody has the right to blame you personally for anything,

8 Or object when you're rude and slow,

9 Or ridicule you for being stupid and lazy and uncaring,

10 Or criticize you in any way at all,

11 ªBecause you work for the government,

12 Which means you're exempt from criticism by private citizens,

13 Because if that's not so,

14 Then what about the Post Office?

CHAPTER 15

So actually, that's about all you have to remember about the Way of Harry,

2 If you work for the government,

3 Because most of it comes pretty naturally to you anyway.

4 Of course, there are a couple of additional points that are important if you're an elected official,

5 Because people see more of you when you're elected,

6 ᵇAnd you have more chances of getting caught.

7 For this reason, it's wise to remember that you can get away with everything,

8 ᶜAs long as you always say what people desire you to say,

9 ᵈAnd always yield to the ones who are the most certain about whatever it is they're certain about,

10 ᵉAnd always be ready to join them in blaming whoever it is they desire to blame,

11 Without thinking about it at all,

12 Because isn't that what ᶠdemocracy is all about?

13 You bet it is.

a. 9.5
b. Ann.10.28
c. Ned.29.19-20
d. Wil.34.6-7
e. Wil.34.8-11
f. Grk.20.8
g. Ned.36.5-27
h. 10.6
i. Ann.16.27
j. 13.3
k. 10.1-2
l. Dav.26.5
m. Dav.26.24
n. Dav.26.15
o. Dav.26.25
p. Ed.61.17

14 And besides, if you obstruct the path of "the people's" blame in any way,

15 They will most certainly desire to blame you as well,

16 Which can get you voted out of office,

17 Or failing that,

18 Sentenced to prison,

19 ᵍWhich is a setback you can overcome to be sure,

20 ʰBut why take the risk if you can get rich with the kind of graft and ⁱpork barrels that nobody cares about,

21 Which actually includes virtually every kind of graft and pork barrel that couldn't possibly subject you to charges of ʲracism, sexism, or elitism.

22 Because if you're not a racist or a sexist or an elitist,

23 ᵏThere will always be plenty of people willing to believe that you were actually an idealistic ˡreformer who was making things ᵐdifficult for the dirty racist sexist ⁿelitists who really call the shots,

24 Which is the American Way,

25 As everybody knows by now.

CHAPTER 16

Yes, you work for the government.

2 So do what you want,

3 When you want to do it,

4 No matter who gets hurt.

5 How can it be your fault?

6 Because you didn't make the world,

7 Or even Harry.

8 You're just an average °joe,

9 ᵖWho works for the government,

10 And so what are you supposed to do about it?

11
12 That's exactly right.

13 Harry would be proud of you all.

VICE-PRESIDENT WAYNE'S FORMULAS
FOR THE
DREXELITES

CHAPTER 1

It's great to see all you [a]numbers jocks,

2 Because it isn't often that [b]I get to enjoy the heavy-duty quantitative stuff with a bunch of engineers, scientists, computer jocks, and accounting types,

3 And I'm having a real hard time here suppressing my ecstasy.

4 In fact, if I had a really awful corny joke to start with,

5 I would tell it to you now,

6 Except that I left it in my other plastic penholder,

7 In my other shirt pocket,

8 Which is really kind of too bad,

9 I guess.

10 Anyway,

11 We'll be going over some important material today,

12 Material about the [c]Way of Harry,

13 Which you might prefer to think of as a series of [d]simple formulas for living,

14 Without having to engage in any [e]ratiocination,

15 At all.

16 Sound intriguing?

17 Good.

18 Then let's synchronize our digital watches and get started.

a. Dav.29.6
b. Ext.50.15-17
c. Wht.6
d. Wil.31.14
e. Jefs.11.19
f. Chuk.20.1-23

CHAPTER 2

Let h stand for the summation of all discrete events in the entire course of human history,

2 And let p stand for progress,

3 Where p is a function of h,

4 Such that $p = f(h)$.

5 Now,

6 Can anybody calculate for me the value of p?

7 Of course, the brighter ones will already have figured it out,

8 Because it's really quite simple:

9 [f]$p = 0$.

CHAPTER 3

Notice that we can also approach this problem from quite another direction, as follows:

2 Let h stand for our net quantifiable hopes for the future,

3 Where:

$$h = \sum_{i=1}^{5000} y_i$$

4 Given that y stands for the net increase in quantifiable hope produced in one year of recorded human history.

5 If you'll all calculate this out pretty quickly,

6 I think you'll find that we

BASIC is much better than English

get a quite suggestive answer, namely:

$7\ ^a h = 0.$

CHAPTER 4

I suspect that the [b]accountants are probably having a tough time with the math here,

2 Since I know from experience that anything with [c]Greek letters in it is confusing to accountants,

3 And so I'd like to restate this basic problem one more way, as follows:

4 Let x be the Future Value in dollars of all the hope saved up over 5,000 periods,

5 Assuming a quite generous discount rate of 10 percent,

6 And assuming that the initial period is the year 3000 B.C.,

7 Just to keep things even.

8 Using the [d]standard equation, we find that,

$$FV = A\ \frac{[1-(1+r)^{-t}]}{r}\ (1+r)^t$$

9 Where r stands for the rate,

10 And t stands for the number of periods,

11 And A stands for the average annual increment of hope generated.

12 When we compute the actual numbers,

13 We discover that FV = 0,

14 Which means that $x = 0$,

15 [e]Resulting in a dollar value of $0.00 worth of saved-up hope for Mankind.

CHAPTER 5

Now, I'd really hate for you [f]computer jocks to feel left out,

2 [g]Because we all talk different languages,

3 Don't we?

a. Al.6.3-22
b. Wht.23
c. Psay.5Q.51
d. Carl.3.8
e. Adam.43.12-24
Psong.29.1-3
f. Adam.45.1-7
g. Zig.12.4
Lies.7.1-18
h. Wil.36.1-5
i. Swar.10.6-7

4 That's why I'd like to translate the very same formula into the high-technology language you guys understand,

5 Namely BASIC,

6 Which is actually much much better than English,

7 [h]Because it has so many fewer words,

8 And each word means only one thing,

9 Which makes it all nice and easy,

10 Doesn't it?

11 Fortunately, our program's all ready,

12 And all I have to do is type RUN,

13 Which is generally great advice for a Harrier,

14 And especially this time,

15 As you'll see.

CHAPTER 6

RUN

2 HI THERE CHIPHEADS

3 THIS PROGRAM COMPUTES THE NET CONTRIBUTION YOU CAN EXPECT TO MAKE TO YOUR FELLOW MAN IN YOUR LIFETIME

4 [i]THIS PROGRAM USES A RANDOM NUMBER GENERATOR TO DUPLICATE THE LOGIC OF THE UNIVERSE

5 PLEASE TYPE YOUR NAME

6

7 THANK YOU BOZO

8 PLEASE TYPE YOUR IQ

9

10 YOU MUST BE PROUD TO HAVE SUCH A HIGH IQ BOZO

11 PLEASE TYPE THE NUMBER OF YEARS YOU EX

PECT TO BE USING THIS IQ BOZO

12

13 YOU REALLY ARE AN OPTIMIST AREN'T YOU BOZO

14 [a]NOW I WILL CALCULATE THE PROBABILITY THAT A PERSON OF YOUR IQ CAN MAKE A SIGNIFICANT CONTRIBUTION TO THE WORLD [b]ASSUMING THAT ALL OTHER CONDITIONS REMAIN CONSTANT

15 [c]PROBABILITY = 0

16 THANK YOU FOR PLAYING WITH ME AND HAVE A NICE DAY BOZO

CHAPTER 7

Yes, my friends,

2 As you may have suspected long before this,

3 We have entered a mathematical zone that can be described by a term you learned way back in [d]Algebra,

4 Which is easy to demonstrate as follows:

5 If hope for the future is a function of human civilization represented as $f(x)$,

6 [e]Where x = all possible values of civilization in the future,

7 Then it really does not matter if there is some current residual value to civilization,

8 Because civilization is headed for [f]zero,

9 Thanks to thermonuclear weapons and all that,

10 Which we can express more technically by saying that [g]x is in the limit, going to 0,

11 Which means that hope for the future is also going to 0,

12 Which suggests that there

a. Swar.10.3-5
b. Boul.26.11
c. 2.9
d. Psay.4.1-4
e. Hill.X.1-3
f. Hill.Z.1-8
g. Psay.5X.1
   Pnot.32.3-4
h. Bks.11.9
i. Wil.35.4-5
j. Swar.29.3-4
   Mawr.25.23
k. Grk.14.24
l. F&J.15.13-16
m. Grk.26.9-10
n. Swar.PS.20

may be better ways of spending your life than trying to make a difference,

13 [h]Because x isn't coming back out of the limit,

14 If you know what I mean.

CHAPTER 8

It's nice to be able to prove all these mathematically,

2 [i]So we don't have to debate a lot of ambiguities,

3 Isn't it?

4 And happily, the [j]solution to this problem is also easy to express in simple mathematical terms,

5 Thanks to a guy named Zeno,

6 [k]Who had an arrow.

7 The thing about Zeno's arrow was that you could fire it at a wall,

8 And it would never get there,

9 Because it had to travel half the distance to the wall first,

10 And then half the distance remaining,

11 And then half of that distance,

12 And to make a long [l]story short, it was so busy counting smaller and smaller halves that it never hit the wall.

13 And that's the way for people like you to live now that you're in the limit,

14 Going to zero,

15 [m]Just like Zeno's arrow.

CHAPTER 9

[n]All you have to do is keep focusing your prodigious minds on smaller and smaller things,

2 More and more narrowly,

3 Until no one else can even

understand what you're looking at, let alone what you're talking about,

4 [a]And you wouldn't recognize the complete uninterrupted flight of an arrow if it hit you in the eye,

5 [b]Which it will,

6 Someday.

CHAPTER 10

Now, the only other thing you need to know is how to handle people who try to make you look at [c]bigger problems instead of progressively smaller ones.

2 This is handled by the following simple [d]equation:

3 [e]$D + C + B = I$,

4 Where D = Desire,

5 C = Certainty,

6 B = Blame,

7 And I = Invulnerability to the demands of others.

8 To use this formula properly,

9 Just remember to observe the following conditions:

10 $D > 0$,

11 $C > 0$, and,

12 $B > 0$.

13 Of course, the higher the value of the terms on the left-hand side of the equation, the higher the value of I,

14 [f]Meaning that you will get more and more invulnerable as you lay on more and more

a. Zig.9.2
b. Psp.2.12
c. Swar.PS.21-22
d. 5.2
e. Wil.31.18-22 Wht.7
f. Ned.35.9
g. Main.30.12-14
h. 10.7
i. Hill.Q.1-2
j. Psay.5Q.62

Desire, Certainty, and Blame.

CHAPTER 11

Isn't this great?

2 We're almost done.

3 I just want to make sure this is all clear to you accounting types,

4 Because there's another way of stating the formula,

5 So that you'll understand it better:

6 $\$ = I$,

7 Where $\$$ = Money, of course,

8 [g]Or beans, if you want to use technical jargon,

9 And I = Invulnerability,

10 [h]As before.

11 Thus, the more beans you rake in, the less other people can hurt you,

12 Which leaves more time for focusing on tinier and tinier problems that don't matter at all.

CHAPTER 12

Everybody up to speed?

2 Great.

3 Remember that Harry's way is the only way,

4 Just like we've seen in our examples.

5 [i]Questions?

6 Wonderful.

7 [j]Q.E.D.

ULT. JOE'S HOMILY
TO THE
BOULEVARDIERS

CHAPTER 1

Beloved friends in Harry!

2 I greet you this way knowing full well that [a]a lot of you have a lot invested in this Judeo-Christian thing,

3 And that maybe you think you can't be Harriers and Judaeo-Christians too,

4 Which means only that you do not yet fully understand the Way of Harry,

5 And are making things harder for yourselves,

6 When they could be really easy instead.

7 [b]For there is, within each of you, a Harrier,

8 [c]Hog-tied by outmoded notions of guilt and sin,

9 And it is [d]my solemn mission to set your Harriers free.

CHAPTER 2

F[e]or example, it has been rumored that many of you believe Harry to be the Antichrist,

2 Because he doesn't say too much about loving thy neighbor,

3 [f]Or any of the other stuff you'd expect him to say if he were one of the good guys,

4 And I'll even admit that I too once thought of him that way,

5 Because [g]I have always been a pretty devout Judeo-Christian myself,

6 [h]But the truth is that Harry is not the Antichrist,

7 And you shouldn't be so worried about it.

CHAPTER 3

In the first place,

2 [i]Harry is just a mortal man,

3 Just like everybody else,

4 Except for you women, of course,

5 Who are also like everybody else,

6 Because you're not immortal or divine, are you?

7 Well, neither is Harry,

8 Which means that if he were the Antichrist, he'd be up against a loaded deck,

9 Because how could one mortal man stand a chance against a god,

10 Or even a son of a god?

11 I mean, does any one of you seriously think that [j]Batman would stand a chance against [k]Superman?

12 Well, there you go.

CHAPTER 4

In the second place,

2 [l]What Harry had to say isn't really all that different from what Christ had to say,

3 Especially when you consider that they're about two thousand years apart timewise,

4 And were living in pretty different social environments.

5 For example, I don't mean

---

a. Chuk.8.11
b. Ira.21.27-32
c. Vin.72.8
d. Ext.24.1
e. Wil.49.8-15
f. Dav.15.20
g. Ext.3.25
h. Ira.34.4
i. Vin.57.3-4
j. Ed.47.8
k. Krt.9.7-8
l. Psay.2.2

any offense to those of you who are more Judeo than Christian,
6 But Christ spent most of his time talking to Jews,
7 In the land of the Jews,
8 [a]Which was a powerless province of Rome,
9 At a time when technology and the societal infrastructure were pretty primitive by today's standards,
10 And isn't it just possible that he'd change his tune somewhat if he were here today,
11 Talking to dozens of different ethnic and socioeconomic groups,
12 In the Most Chosen Nation on Earth,
13 Where high technology has resulted in a very [b]complicated societal infrastructure that is also pretty darned [c]specialized?
14 Of course he would.

CHAPTER 5

For example, loving thy neighbor is just basic [d]common sense if you're a member of a poor conquered nation and your neighbor is the [e]most powerful empire in the history of the world to date,
2 And especially if you're a Jew,
3 Because,
4 And I mean no offense here,
5 [f]The Jews have always been pretty good at being disagreeable and kind of uppity about all sorts of things,
6 Which is why nobody has ever liked them much,
7 And maybe part of the reason why they've been conquered about a thousand times,
8 [g]And their nation utterly destroyed,
9 [h]And their people scattered all over the earth,
10 Which might not have happened if they'd listened to [i]Christ,
11 And been nicer,
12 Overall,
13 Which would really have been a pretty easy way to live a more comfortable life,
14 [j]Just like Harry wants us to.
15 See what I mean?

CHAPTER 6

And while we're on the subject, it's also worth taking a second look at all those things Christ said about [k]moneychangers, and charity, and how [l]rich men can't ride a camel through the eye of a needle, and [m]render unto Caesar, and so forth,
2 [n]Because it can't be news to any of you that Jews have always been pretty active in the moneychanging business,
3 [o]Not to mention how tight they are with a buck,
4 Which probably irritated Caesar as much as it's always irritated everyone else,
5 [p]Because money's great,
6 And obviously everybody wants to have a lot of it,
7 Which is only human,
8 [q]As every Christian church in the whole history of Christendom has always understood,
9 But can't we talk about something else now and then?
10 [r]As for the camel thing, that's too weird to understand anyway,

a. Bks.6.11-18
b. Adam.7.2-22
c. Swar.PS.20 Jefs.8.3
d. Vin.58.1
e. Bks.3.1-4
f. Lies.3.1-3
g. Lies.13.2
h. Lies.13.3
i. Rom.20.5-6
j. Wil28.3-4
k. Jeff.9.1-3
l. Chr.4.6
m. Rom.23.7
n. Pnot.18.1-5
o. Psay.5J.7
p. Psong.4.6
q. Jeff.9.7-10 Psong.10.4-7
r. 6.1

11 And just shows you how things have changed since Christ was here last,

12 Like a lot of other things Christ talked about,

13 Such as heaven.

CHAPTER 7

Back before the Christian part got added into the Judeo-Christian thing,

2 ᵃWhich is to say when the Jews thought God was *their* God,

3 Exclusively,

4 They didn't think there was any such thing as heaven,

5 Because it seemed to them that when you died, you kind of stopped living,

6 Completely,

7 And stopped doing everything,

8 ᵇExcept decomposing, of course,

9 Which explains why the Jews were always in such a big hurry to bury dead people right away,

10 If not sooner,

11 And probably also explains why they were always so obsessed with ᶜgolden calves,

12 And golden coins,

13 And other things you could use to buy comfort while you were alive,

14 Because you were going to be dead for a ᵈlong long time,

15 So it only made sense to get the highest possible ᵉinterest on your money now,

16 And don't be late with the payments,

17 Because time's a-wasting.

18 And while all this was going on,

19 Remember,

---

a. Lies.2.1-6
b. Chuk.19.16-17
c. Lies.9.1-2
d. Wil.56.6
e. Psong.18.9
f. 6.13
g. Rom.20.9
h. Hill.N.1-3
i. Vin.60.8-15
j. Dav.15.26
k. Dav.15.40
l. 18.18

---

20 ᶠHeaven wasn't even on the map.

CHAPTER 8

It was Christ who put heaven on the map,

2 Because how else can you make Jews stop being unpleasant about money when there isn't any money,

3 ᵍBecause all the money is in Rome,

4 Which is the Most Chosen Nation on Earth,

5 And the only place on earth where people can enjoy heaven right ʰnow,

6 Without waiting to die first?

7 But the Jews never did buy the part about heaven,

8 ⁱBecause who knows more about shady real estate deals than Jews,

9 Which probably explains why they went right ahead and ʲcrucified Christ,

10 And still didn't believe him when he ᵏcame back and reported that,

11 Yep,

12 Heaven was right where he'd always said it was,

13 And how about signing on the dotted line right away,

14 And never mind about the fine print.

15 ˡIn fact, the Jews have never ever bought the part about heaven,

16 Unless you count Florida, of course,

17 Which is significant,

18 Because if you look at the Judeo-Christian thing as a whole,

19 It's hardly unanimous on the heaven question,

20 ^aSince part of them think it's a place with pearly gates that you go there when you die if you're lucky,

21 ^bAnd another part think it's a place with pearly beaches that you go there when you retire if you're lucky.

22 Which suggests that there's room for more than one view of heaven,

23 Without being a ^cheathen heretic,

24 Or an ^dAntichrist,

25 Or even an anti-Semite.

CHAPTER 9

When you get right down to it, in fact,

2 Harry has a lot to offer to both parts of the Judeo-Christian thing,

3 Especially if you live in the Most Chosen Nation on Earth,

4 ^eSomewhere north of the Roosevelt Boulevard,

5 Which is almost nothing like ^fPalestine,

6 And has a lot of things to deal with that Christ didn't know anything about,

7 Or if he did, he never mentioned it.

8 For example, Palestine didn't have a great big government,

9 ^gWith a lot of federal, state, and municipal agencies to look out for the needs of the under-privileged,

10 ^hWhich is probably why Christ spent so much time talking about poor people,

11 Because if you don't take care of their needs,

12 ⁱPoor people can make your life pretty uncomfortable,

13 Which you already know all about,

a. *Chr. 4.1-3*
b. *Psay. 3.2*
c. *Chr. 2.5-8*
d. *2.1*
e. *Wil. 56.1-6*
f. *Bks. 6.14-18*
g. *Brd. 18.13-23*
h. *Psom. 21.3-4*
i. *Frog. 12.12-17*
j. *Ira. 21.26*
k. *Yks. 97.3-4*
l. *Hall. 10.17*
m. *Brd. 18.24-26*
n. *Brd. 24.1*

14 Because ^jeverybody in the whole city of Philadelphia knows that all of you moved to the Northeast in the first place just to get away from the poor people,

15 Who make you uncomfortable,

16 ^kEspecially since you're not allowed to look down on them anymore,

17 Or have them arrested just because they look at you funny,

18 Unless they're loitering,

19 Which is what walking around is called,

20 If it's done by a poor black person in the Northeast.

CHAPTER 10

Now, who understands your feelings about that kind of thing better?

2 Christ?

3 Or Harry?

4 Of course, if Christ saw what things were like in Philadelphia,

5 He'd probably understand why it's important for Judeo-Christians to live in the Northeast,

6 And leave all the charity work to the government agencies that specialize in that kind of thing,

7 Because Christ never said anything at all about how righteous it is to put the people who work for the government ^lout of a job with a lot of unsolicited free-lance charity,

8 ^mBecause even the poor people know that it's the government's job to take care of them,

9 ⁿAnd since they don't like you anyway,

10 Why on earth would they want handouts from you?

11 And if they don't want hand-outs from you,

12 ᵃThen you'd be breaking Christ's own rules if you gave them anything,

13 Because that would be doing unto others what they do not want done unto them,

14 Except by the government.

CHAPTER 11

Another thing they didn't have much of in Palestine was *things,*

2 ᵇWhich there are a lot of now-adays,

3 And it's all well and good to talk about giving everything away and living on Christ's word, with nothing more than a little bread to keep body and soul together,

4 But if you're living in the late twentieth century, that's just a little bit naive, don't you think?

5 I mean, maybe you don't need too many ᶜ*things* to live comfort-ably in Palestine,

6 Especially if you're living there so long ago that the Jews haven't even invented retailing yet,

7 Not to mention winter,

8 Which they don't have any of in Palestine,

9 And never did,

10 ᵈWhich makes it pretty easy to wander around the Holy Land talking a lot of nonsense about living on nothing but words,

11 Although it's another story altogether when you have to live in the ᵉNortheast,

12 Where there is snow and ice in the wintertime,

13 And where you can be ar-rested if you don't have some-place of your own to sleep in at night.

---

a. *Psay.5Q.35*
b. *Adam.46-50*
c. *Gods.1.1-7*
d. *Psong.10.3*
e. *9.4*
f. *Ira.31.12*
g. *Spic.17.9*
h. *12.4*
i. *12.9*
j. *Ed.8.1-8*
k. *Lies.2.25-28*
l. *Lies.5.2-6*

CHAPTER 12

Let's face it.

2 No matter how good a Judeo-Christian you are,

3 You need a whole bunch of *things* just to get by from day to day.

4 ᶠYou need a house, for one thing,

5 With all the basic amenities for surviving the seasons,

6 Like central heating,

7 And central air conditioning,

8 And blue shag carpeting that runs all the way from one wall to another,

9 And a garage to keep the white Monte Carlo in,

10 ᵍUnless it's a white Cadillac instead,

11 Which you need to go to work every day,

12 ʰSo that you can keep mak-ing all those payments on the house,

13 ⁱAnd the Monte Carlo,

14 And the 25-inch Sony color console set,

15 ʲWhich you need so that you can relax after a hard day's work,

16 And stop thinking about any-thing at all,

17 Until it's time to go to work again,

18 Tomorrow.

CHAPTER 13

I suggest to you that Harry un-derstood all of this better than Christ ever did,

2 And probably better than ᵏYahweh ever did either,

3 Since Yahweh was the kind of God that gives gods a bad name,

4 ˡWhat with trying to destroy the whole earth every time some

little thing didn't go his way,
5 [a]And generally being so moody that you never quite knew whether he was going to give you seven years of great crops and so forth,
6 [b]Or whether he was going to blow his stack over some trifle and start handing out plagues of locusts and so forth,
7 [c]So that life under Yahweh must have been like living in some great big continuing roulette game,
8 Where anything at all might happen,
9 Depending on whether Yahweh got out of bed on the right side,
10 Or the wrong side.

CHAPTER 14

If you come from the Christian side of the Judeo-Christian thing, of course,
2 You probably think that the Jews were all wrong about Yahweh,
3 Because Christ said that [d]Yahweh was his dad,
4 And was really good and merciful and so forth,
5 [e]Deep down,
6 Which is why Christ came along in the first place,
7 Because Yahweh thought that maybe the Jews wouldn't be so irritating,
8 If they knew what he really wanted,
9 [f]Meaning cathedrals and religious icons,
10 [g]Instead of temples and idols,
11 Which are completely different,
12 [h]For some reason.
13 And anyone who wants to is perfectly entitled to believe that,
14 But why didn't Yahweh come himself?
15 I mean, if he was really interested in letting people know that he was this kindly merciful god who wanted everybody to be saved,
16 [i]And not just some remote abstraction,
17 [j]Who was maybe already fed up with the Jews,
18 [k]And maybe everybody else too,
19 Wouldn't you think he'd put in an appearance himself,
20 Instead of sending a substitute?
21 Doesn't it make you wonder,
22 Just a little?
23 [l]Especially when you consider that this is the same God who had already evidenced a pretty cavalier attitude about the sacrificing of sons,
24 [m]And the same God who had already allowed his Chosen Nation to be enslaved by the Romans,
25 [n]And the same God who had already thrown everybody out of Eden,
26 Lock, stock, and barrel,
27 [o]Just because some bimbo had a sweet tooth.
28 No wonder the Jews didn't buy it.

CHAPTER 15

I don't mean to suggest that the Christians were all completely naive either,
2 Because you [p]Roman Catholics learned from the nuns that the Father-Son connection is pretty much of a good guy-bad guy shtick,
3 With [q]Christ playing the

a. Gods.5.1-7
b. Lies.6.7-11
c. Ann.12.19-22
d. Rom.21.4-13
e. Lies.13.8
f. Bub.2.4-10
g. Gods.6.20-22
h. Jefs.7.15-17
i. Jeff.17.1
j. 5.3-5
k. 13.4
l. Lies.3.4-6
m. 4.8
n. Lies.2.8-12
o. Lies.2.13-23
p. Jeff.8.1-5
q. Dav.15.9

[a]good guy, talking about mercy and redemption and heaven,

4 And [b]God playing the [c]heavy, with his great big list of mortal sins and inexpiable guilts and everlasting damnations,

5 Which is why you have always wanted the [d]Virgin as a mediator,

6 Because without her to bend her son's ear on your behalf,

7 You know darned well that Christ doesn't have what it takes to stand up to his dad,

8 Who is still,

9 And has always been,

10 [e]Yahweh,

11 The most capriciously wrathful and randomly destructive god in the whole history of life on earth.

CHAPTER 16

I hasten to say that it requires no disrespect of Christ to take this view of things,

2 [f]Because it is only natural for a son to defer to his father,

3 [g]Especially if your father has already proven that he considers you expendable,

4 [h]And there is no need for any Harrier anywhere to think ill of Christ,

5 At all,

6 [i]Because we can't be completely sure that they wrote down everything he said,

7 [j]Or if you prefer to believe that you do know what he said,

8 You still can't be sure that he always said the lines the way the priests read them in church,

9 And never threw in any ironic facial expressions,

10 Or any equivocal body language,

11 Or any figurative language,

---

a. Dav.15.43-46
b. Dav.10.10
c. Jeff.8.6-17
d. Ed.30.5
e. 13.3
f. Psay.1.7-9
g. Dav.15.33
h. Vin.61.1-2
i. Jeff.5.1-8
j. Jeff.7.4-10
k. Cen.26.14-15
l. Main.36.1-4
m. Jeff.5.2-3
n. 14.3
o. Lies.2.22
p. Mawr.8.1-6
q. 8.21

---

12 That might have thrown a different light on things.

13 When he said, for example, Give us this day our daily bread,

14 [k]Who are we to say that Jesus Christ, Lord and Savior of the Universe, was totally unaware of the slang connotation of the word "bread"?

15 When he said, In my father's house are many mansions,

16 [l]Who are we to say he wasn't hinting that what's okay for dad might be okay for us too,

17 Except that maybe the scribe who was writing it all down was too busy scribbling to catch the wink that went with the remark?

CHAPTER 17

What I'm leading up to with all this is that it's perfectly acceptable for any Harrier to believe that Christ was exactly who he [m]said he was,

2 And that he was an incredibly nice and well-meaning son of god,

3 [n]And that Christ's dad really was Yahweh,

4 The sole creator and premeditated [o]destroyer of the universe,

5 Without having to give up the [p]Way of Harry,

6 At all.

7 And by the same token, it's also perfectly acceptable for the Judeo-minded to believe in Yahweh all they want,

8 And to follow Harry too,

9 All the way to [q]heaven,

10 Or even Palm Springs.

CHAPTER 18

You see, there's nothing you can't push and squeeze and trim to fit,

2 [a]So that you can believe exactly what you want,

3 And I've taken some time to show you how it might be done,

4 But the truth is, there are many many ways to believe what you want about god and religion,

5 And still be a Harrier anyway,

6 Because it's been proven beyond doubt that human beings are capable of believing in anything at all,

7 [b]And when it comes to pushing and squeezing and trimming,

8 [c]You've all had lots of experience already,

9 Not to mention the fact that Harry doesn't mind how you look at it,

10 Because if you buy any part of Harry's Way,

11 Whether you know it or not,

12 [d]You are a full-fledged Harrier,

13 In good standing.

14 And this too is significant,

15 Because the same cannot be said of the Judeo-Christian thing,

16 [e]Since they want you to buy the whole thing,

17 Without exception,

18 [f]Which maybe explains why the Catholics always persecuted the Jews,

19 [g]At least until the Krauts got psycho about it and gave anti-Semitism a bad name,

20 [h]And why the Jews have always put the screws to Christians—whenever they had a signed contract and a good place to hide afterwards,

21 [i]Proving that self-righteous certainty is one of the great unifying themes of the Judeo-Christian thing as a whole,

22 [j]And what it has most in

a. Chuk.9.1
b. 18.1
c. Ira.25.16-20
d. Wht.12
e. Jeff.11.22-23
f. Spic.7.10-15
g. Krt.36.3-6
h. Pnot.18.1-5
i. Jeff.12.1-8
j. Ned.34.10-16
k. Wil.33.1-4
l. Wil.34.1-5
m. Wil.34.8-11
n. Mawr.15.19-22
o. 18.1
p. Wil.23.1-7
q. Chr.6.6-11
r. Mawr.19.11
s. Dav.47.8
t. Dav.54.4

common with the Way of Harry.

CHAPTER 19

But the truly great thing about the Way of Harry is that it doesn't matter to Harry what you are certain about,

2 [k]As long as you are certain,

3 [l]And ready to blame the daylights out of anyone who interferes with your certainty,

4 Or who might interfere with your certainty,

5 [m]Or who you just don't like period,

6 [n]Because blame is its own reward,

7 As most of you already know.

CHAPTER 20

This great freedom to be certain means that there are many ways to follow Harry,

2 [o]And you can pick and choose all you want,

3 Just like you do now,

4 Except that with Harry you don't have to feel [p]guilty about it,

5 At all.

6 In the same way that some of you Catholics say, "I believe in [q]everything my church wants me to believe in,

7 "Except for the part about [r]contraception,

8 "Because they didn't have safe contraception back then, and there was no [s]population explosion, and college tuitions weren't in the stratosphere back then either,

9 [t]"Not to mention a little harmless adultery now and then,"

10 You can also say, "I believe

in everything my church wants me to believe in,

11 "Except for the part about [a]sin and hell and self-sacrifice,

12 [b]"Because I am not a conquered Jew living in a nation so backward that it has no nuclear weapons to keep its neighbors in line,

13 [c]"And no welfare bureaucracy to keep the poor and worthless out of everybody's hair."

14 Isn't that easy?

CHAPTER 21

In the same way that some of you Jews say, [d]"I believe in the Ten Commandments,

2 [e]"Except for the part about bacon and pork products,

3 [f]"And the part about never having any fun to speak of,

4 "Because I've got so much [g]guilt that I just couldn't get by without some fun every once in a while,"

5 You can also say, "I believe in the Ten Commandments,

6 "Which I would absolutely follow if I lived in [h]Israel,

7 "But I live in the [i]Northeast instead,

8 "Which is a different jurisdiction,

9 "Thank God."

CHAPTER 22

In the same way that some of you Catholics say, "I believe in turning the other cheek, just like Christ teaches,

2 "Except when somebody gets in my face,

3 [j]"Because there are times when it has to be an eye for an eye, just like our [k]Father in heaven does it,"

a. Rom.22.7
b. 10.4-5
c. 10.6
d. Lies.9.14
e. Lie.9.6
f. Lies.9.13
g. Lies.2.24-25
h. Bks.9.1-4
i. 9.4
j. Kens.26.7
k. 15.4
l. 25.28
m. 19.3
n. Hall.11.3-4
o. Vin.13.35-37
p. Lies.4.1-10
q. Kens.17.9-15
r. Hall.15.12-13
s. Hall.15.14-15
t. Ext.13.11
u. Psay.5B.1-13

4 You can also say, "I believe in Love Thy Neighbor,

5 [l]"Except for niggers and Spics,

6 [m]"Because they're to blame for everything that's wrong with this country,

7 [n]"And I am fed to the teeth with pouring taxes down a rathole,

8 "And giving a free ride to every whining loser who's too lazy to get a decent job,"

9 And so forth,

10 And so on,

11 [o]Because only Harry forgives everything,

12 And don't you forget it.

CHAPTER 23

In the same way that some of you Jews say, "I believe in [p]paranoia, just like it says in the Torah,

2 "But I don't believe that absolutely everything in the whole history of western civilization was expressly designed as a conspiracy to get the Jews,"

3 You can also say, "I believe in [q]paranoia,

4 [r]"But I also believe in taking whatever I want, whenever I want it, no matter who gets hurt,

5 [s]"And then blaming the heck out of my enemies when they try to persecute me for satisfying my desires."

CHAPTER 24

And in the same way that some of you Judeo-Christians say, "I am a deeply religious person, and I attend [t]services every week, and I look out for my friends and family, just like it says in the [u]Bible,

2 "But during working hours,

3 "That's different,
4 "Because then it's [a]every man for himself, and [b]never give a sucker an even break, and [c]God helps those who help themselves,"
5 [d]You can also say, "I am a deeply religious person, and I attend services every week,
6 "And so whatever I do the rest of the week must be okay,
7 "No matter who gets hurt,
8 "Because I really don't want to think about it,
9 "At all,
10 [e]"And who are you to pass judgment on me, anyway?"
11 Are you starting to get it?
12 Good.

CHAPTER 25

Indeed, there is no limit to the ways you can follow Harry,
2 [f]Because if you want, you can join the Pontifical Harrier Parish,
3 [g]And wash your hands of everything,
4 [h]And have all the Consolation you want,
5 [i]And enjoy a lot of meaningless rituals,
6 [j]And have your kids properly Adultified so they'll know about pursuing their desires no matter who gets hurt,
7 While you quit worrying about God and guilt and sin and evil altogether,
8 Which is probably the most comfortable way to be a Harrier,
9 But not the only one.
10 [k]Because if you want, you can belong to the Greater Harrier Parish,
11 Which means that you can keep right on being as Judeo-Christian as you want,
12 [l]And talk as much as you want about virtue and righteousness, not to mention the motes in other people's eyes,
13 And have all the [m]Communion or gefilte fish you want,
14 [n]And enjoy a lot of meaningless rituals,
15 And have your kids bar mitzvahed, or taught by [o]nuns, so they'll learn what they need to about an eye for an eye,
16 While you rant and rave about what Harriers your [p]neighbors are,
17 Which is a perfectly acceptable and inconspicuous way to follow Harry,
18 But not the only other alternative.
19 For example, if you want, you can just stop thinking about anything at all,
20 And quit going to church,
21 And forget that there's any such thing as Harriers,
22 And just go on about your business,
23 And let the world and everyone in it take care of themselves,
24 Because no matter who or what made the world,
25 You certainly didn't,
26 [q]Because if you did, you certainly wouldn't be living in some faceless row house in the Northeast,
27 [r]While all the rich people get away with murder,
28 [s]Not to mention the niggers and Spics,
29 [t]And that's without even mentioning the totalitarian communist conspiracy,
30 Which is why you're so mad all the time that you can't see straight,
31 And why your only politics

a. Vin.71.25-27
b. Psay.5Q.59
c. Exp.1.7-9
d. 25.5
e. Al.4.16
f. Ext.13.1-8
g. Vin.4.19-25
h. Ext.13.18
i. 24.5
j. Ext.13.10
k. Ext.14.5-6
l. Ned.34.17-25
m. Dav.15.21
n. 24.1
o. 15.2
p. Ann.2.12-13
q. Psong.44.1-4
r. Yks.97.9-11
s. Yks.150.28-29
t. Ira.25.36-37

is ᵃsticking it to the communists where it hurts,

32 Namely, their whole stupid ᵇmotherland,

33 And sticking it to the rich where it hurts,

34 ᶜNamely, their wallet,

35 And sticking it to the niggers and Spics where it hurts,

36 ᵈNamely, the electric chair,

37 And everybody else should just get out of your way,

38 And stay out of your way,

39 Because the world is a basket case,

40 And you don't need any more lies,

41 And you don't need any forgiveness either,

42 Because you are the way you are,

43 And everybody else is worse.

CHAPTER 26

Still, it would be nice if you could find a way to join the ᵉPontifical Harrier Parish,

2 ᶠBecause it's the easiest way,

3 Really,

4 ᵍSince picking and choosing can lead to thought,

5 ʰWhich is dangerous,

6 Especially when belief is involved,

7 ⁱBecause human beings can believe absolutely anything,

8 And all the ʲreligions want you to,

9 Which is why they start on you so young,

10 And say the same things over and over and over and over until you believe it,

11 Which is the way that every faith ever invented gets people to buy its ᵏmost questionable assumptions.

---

a. Brit.40.8
b. Russ.26.6-8
c. Yks.98.12
d. Yks.73.1-6
e. 25.2
f. 25.8
g. 20.2
h. Wil.31.1-3
i. 18.6
j. Psay.5R.1-14
   Jeff.18.2-10
   Swar.34.4-8
k. Lies.2.15-26
   Vin.6.3-15
   Swar.18.16-
   17
   Yks.154.24-
   34
l. Swar.34.4-8
m. 20.4
n. 26.10
o. Lies.8.20
p. Wil.42.11

---

12 And they always teach you the part about guilt and sin and evil first,

13 Because if they can make you fear ˡGod, they will always have you,

14 One way or another,

15 Till you die,

16 Which doesn't necessarily make you a better person,

17 ᵐBut almost always makes you feel guilty,

18 For being the way you are.

CHAPTER 27

And so I say to you,

2 Come to Harry,

3 And be the way you are,

4 And stop thinking about it,

5 And if your religion is standing in your way,

6 Because you started so young,

7 Then learn to be born again,

8 Into a new life,

9 According to the Way of Harry,

10 ⁿWhich involves telling yourself the same thing over and over and over until you believe it,

11 ᵒWhich is a thing so important that it always gets a whole chapter,

12 All to itself.

CHAPTER 28

Say to yourself,

2 ᵖThere is no contradiction between the way of my faith and the Way of Harry,

3 There is no contradiction between the way of my faith and the Way of Harry,

4 There is no contradiction between the way of my faith and the Way of Harry,

5 There is no contradiction between the way of my faith and the Way of Harry,
6 There is no contradiction between the way of my faith and the Way of Harry,
7 There is no contradiction between the way of my faith and

a. Swar.10.1-2

the Way of Harry,
8 There is no contradiction between the way of my faith and the Way of Harry,
9 Until you believe it,
10 [a]Because truly there are no contradictions.

THE AFFIDAVIT OF THE CHOSEN ONE MIKE
TO THE
PENNSYLVANIANS

CHAPTER 1

Hey there, Counselor.
2 That *is* what you [a]scumbags call each other, isn't it?
3 I thought so.
4 This is a letter,
5 To you,
6 From the Harriers,
7 Written by me,
8 [b]Mike,
9 And so I advise you to listen,
10 Although I must tell you, I am only writing to you because you're on my [c]list,
11 Because, speaking personally,
12 I hate your guts,
13 Not to mention all the flesh and suits and expensive watches and credit cards and stuff that are wrapped around your guts,
14 Which you stole from somebody else,
15 Because you lawyers are the [d]lowest form of life on earth,
16 Which is why you make such good Harriers,
17 And why it doesn't really

a. 1.15
b. Ext.51.1
c. Wht.28
d. Chuk.10.9
e. Ext.22.1-7
f. Dav.57.26
g. Dav.57.28
h. Dav.57.30

matter if I give you good advice or not.

CHAPTER 2

What[e] can a Harrier say to a lawyer?
2 *Sue.*
3 That's your job, isn't it?
4 When the rapacious [f]witch comes whining to your office for a divorce,
5 Sue her [g]husband into the weeds,
6 And take every dime and scrap he owns,
7 Including the children,
8 And even the dog,
9 Because your job isn't justice,
10 It's winning the suit and getting paid for it.
11 When the [h]greedy louse slips and falls on the icy sidewalk after six drinks at dinner,
12 Sue the city, and the restaurant, and the company that made the concrete and the company that made his shoes, and the company that made the liquor, and anyone and everyone that

was anywhere around at the time,
13 [a]Because there's no such thing as a frivolous lawsuit,
14 When there's money on the line.

CHAPTER 3

Or maybe I should say, *Get him off!*
2 Get him off no matter what,
3 No matter what he did,
4 Because even though you all talk about your "profession,"
5 And absolutely *demand* due respect for your intelligence and learning and integrity,
6 Your job has nothing to do with justice,
7 Because you're not responsible,
8 And you're just a [b]hired gun,
9 Who happens to be [c]smarter than everyone else in the whole world,
10 [d]Which is its own reward,
11 And explains why you never have to think about anyone but yourself,
12 Ever,
13 For even a single instant,
14 And never mind what the law was originally meant to do,
15 Or be,
16 Or provide,
17 Because if they can't pay, then they don't deserve you,
18 And if they can pay,
19 [e]Then it's automatically your job to forget about justice and guilt and the intent of the law,
20 And spring the [f]thieving banker,
21 And the [g]lying senator,
22 And the [h]mutilating rapist,
23 And the [i]sodomizing child molester,
24 Because *hey*!
25 [j]You didn't make the world,
26 You're just a lawyer,
27 In a two-thousand-dollar tailor-made suit,
28 And by the way, all you other Harriers out there,
29 When you're talking to an attorney,
30 Mind you don't say something actionable,
31 [k]Because he'll take you for every penny you'll ever earn.

CHAPTER 4

So what can Mike say to a lawyer?
2 We're all Harriers, of course,
3 [l]And Harry made it pretty clear that we don't have to like each other,
4 Or help each other,
5 [m]Especially if it's convenient to blame each other,
6 [n]Because we should all be just the way we are,
7 [o]And I am Mike,
8 And I just hate lawyers,
9 [p]Which is perfectly okay by Harry,
10 Who would be proud of me.

CHAPTER 5

And probably Harry would say to me,
2 "Don't bust a gut, Mike.
3 "Don't try to be different from the way you are,
4 "Because remember,
5 [q]"There are no contradictions."
6 And so usually, I don't think about anything at all,
7 Because life is so much easier that way,
8 [r]Except that I really hate lawyers,
9 And I want you to know how much,

a. *Ann.10.15*
b. *Ed.44.4*
c. *Ed.54.3*
d. *Psong.53.1-7*
e. *Ed.54.20*
f. *Adam.26.17*
g. *Adam.26.17*
h. *Adam.27.8*
i. *Adam.27.8*
j. *Boul.25.24-25*
k. *Psong.9.1-3*
l. *Wil.50.14-20*
m. *Ned.34.13-16*
n. *Vin.13.35-37*
o. *1.8*
p. *Ned.32.9-10*
q. *Swar.10.1-2*
r. *1.12*

10 [a]Because I really really hate you.

CHAPTER 6

You all think you know so much,

2 And you probably even think you're not Harriers,

3 [b]Because you're so good at thinking,

4 [c]But you don't know how to think at all,

5 Which is the whole purpose of law school,

6 [d]Where they teach you how to destroy what other people think,

7 And then to feel very proud of yourselves afterwards,

8 As if you'd done something brilliant with your great minds,

9 [e]When all you've really done is find one more hole in all the zillions of holes that exist in all of Mankind's lies about itself,

10 [f]Which when you look at it from that perspective isn't much,

11 [g]Except that *you* have to set new records for being sanctimonious about your intelligence,

12 [h]Even though there isn't one of you that ever had an original, imaginative, constructive thought about anything,

13 Which is why you're lawyers.

CHAPTER 7

[i]And so you sue,

2 And sue,

3 And sue,

4 And get the [j]garbage off,

5 And sue some more,

6 And make lots and lots of money,

7 And call each other [k]counselor,

a. 1.12
b. Vin.70.17-18
c. 6.12
d. Ira.25.24-26
e. Ira.25.21-23
f. Ira.33.1-3
g. Zig.12.2-4
h. Yks.37.1-17
i. 2.2
j. 3.20-23
k. 1.2
l. Lies.10.11
m. 4.7
n. 1.12
o. Main.34.2
p. Dav.35.22 & 35.37
q. Swar.29.6
r. 6.11
s. 1.16

8 And you never ever think about what you might be doing to people,

9 Or to the country,

10 Or to yourselves,

11 Which is why you're all Harriers,

12 Every one,

13 And why I guess you must all be [l]okay,

14 Although there's nothing that says I have to admit it,

15 [m]Because I am Mike,

16 [n]And I just hate lawyers.

CHAPTER 8

So I suppose it's also okay that none of you ever contributes anything,

2 Or builds anything,

3 Or adds anything but grief to the quality of life,

4 Or ever do anything at all but profit from human misery,

5 And greed,

6 And violence,

7 And spite,

8 And lust for revenge.

9 [o]I suppose it's okay that you misrepresent facts and situations for a living,

10 And that you'll destroy the [p]witness with the speech impediment,

11 Never mind the truth,

12 [q]Because there is no truth,

13 And it's not your fault,

14 And you're not responsible anyway,

15 And all that,

16 [r]But why do you have to be so incredibly unbelievably superior about it,

17 [s]When you're just exactly like everybody else,

18 Except maybe a little smarter and meaner and better dressed?

CHAPTER 9

I'll withdraw that question, of course,

2 Because you can feel superior if you want to,

3 ªJust like Harry said,

4 And you can be as ᵇcertain about it as you want,

5 Because Harry's ᶜtrinity is your trinity too,

6 And nothing will ever take that away,

7 But just bear in mind that when Mike uses the trinity,

8 ᵈHe desires to kill the lawyers,

9 And he is certain they should all be tortured to death in an amazingly painful way,

10 Because lawyers are to blame for a lot of things,

11 Including the fact that ᵉjustice in the Most Chosen Nation on Earth is a joke,

12 And not a very funny one at that,

13 ᶠWhich it might not be if you were ever serious about what it means to call law a "profession,"

14 And what that might say about what kind of a ᵍ*person* a lawyer should be.

a. Psp.3.6
b. Wil.33.1-4
c. Wht.7
d. Pnot.56.1
e. Hill.J.1-5
f. 3.4
   Ed.60.17
g. Carl.3.8
h. 7.15-16
i. Vin.13.37

CHAPTER 10

Forget that too.

2 That's not Harry talking.

3 That's ʰMike.

4 Harry would be proud of you.

5 Very very proud.

6 ⁱYou're perfect.

7 Perfect Harriers.

8 Perfect lawyers.

9 Perfect swine.

10 Feel better?

11 I wish I did.

ULT. MORT'S MARCHING ORDERS

FOR THE

FORGERS

CHAPTER 1

Atten-hut!

2 No, no,

3 Just kidding.

4 At ease, gentlemen.

5 I'm not writing to give you a hard time.

6 In fact, I'm writing to give you exactly the opposite,

7 An easy time,

8 According to the Way of Harry,

a. Adam.50.6
b. Psom.73.1-
   14

9 Which you'd better know about.

CHAPTER 2

Of course, you probably think that Harry doesn't care about you at all,

2 Except to laugh at you,

3 And your uniforms,

4 And your spit-shined shoes,

5 And your ªweapons,

6 And all those ᵇflags you cart around with you,

7 Wherever you go.

8 Don't you?

9 Well, maybe he does laugh,

10 A little,

11 But no more than anybody else,

12 Because serving in the military of the Most Chosen Nation on Earth has become kind of a [a]joke,

13 Which you must have suspected before this,

14 [b]Unless you're the kind that really believes all that garbage about duty and honor and patriotism,

15 And following orders,

16 Without thinking about it at all.

CHAPTER 3

And, you see, that's the problem.

2 Harry knows all about this splendid capability that some of you have to do things blindly,

3 Without thinking about it at all,

4 Which suggests that you have the makings of great Harriers,

5 [c]If it weren't for all that nonsense about duty and honor and patriotism,

6 Which are pretty much [d]obsolete,

7 Even if nobody's briefed you on that yet.

CHAPTER 4

A few miles from here, there's a graveyard where they buried some soldiers who spent the winter with George Washington,

2 Only they didn't make it through the winter,

3 [e]Because duty, honor, and patriotism aren't nearly as useful in

a. *Penn.9.12*
b. *Rat.10.1-3*
c. *2.14*
d. *Main.19.9-12*
e. *Yks.10.7-12*
f. *Dav.57.32*
g. *Yks.10.1-6 & 17.8*
h. *Kens.12.25-26*
i. *Vin.63.15-22*
j. *Brit.40.8*
k. *Wil.13.32-35*

the wintertime as food, shoes, and shelter,

4 Which [f]George Washington must have known,

5 Because not far from the graveyard you can see the house he spent that winter in,

6 And some nice copies of the big boots he wore,

7 Not to mention a pretty decent replica of the kitchen that made all his food,

8 Because generals get food,

9 Even if the volunteers don't.

10 And as a sidenote, I expect most of you have heard of [g]George Washington,

11 [h]But who can name even one of the faceless zeroes buried in the graveyard?

CHAPTER 5

[i]And so I ask you, what did all that duty, honor, and patriotism buy the dead ones?

2 They didn't get to make a lot of money in a brand-new country after the war.

3 They didn't get their name in the history books.

4 They didn't get anything except what fools always get,

5 Namely, the short end of the [j]stick,

6 Which is the only birthright of soldiers everywhere.

CHAPTER 6

That's why I bring you a new trinity,

2 A trinity to replace the one that's never done you any good,

3 And never will,

4 Especially since Harry came along,

5 And showed everybody the way to be,

6 [k]Which has nothing at all to

do with dying in some distant hostile land,

7 And everything in the world to do with having an easy life,

8 For as long as it lasts.

CHAPTER 7

I'm not saying that you have to accept [a]Harry's Trinity,

2 Because some of you will automatically reject it,

3 Without thinking about it at all,

4 Which is actually okay,

5 [b]Because no one has to like Harry in order to follow his Way.

6 It's just that accepting his Trinity will make it simpler to [c]get by,

7 And easier to understand the way you're going to be treated by the people of the Most Chosen Nation,

8 Whether you accept Harry's Trinity or not.

CHAPTER 8

For those of you who haven't been paying attention for the past few years,

2 [d]The Trinity of Harry is Desire, Certainty, and Blame,

3 And most of you have had some experience of it by now,

4 Whether you recognized it at the time or not,

5 [e]Because your fellow Americans have a strong desire to blame you,

6 [f]In no uncertain terms,

7 For a lot of things.

8 [g]For example, they blame you and every soldier who ever lived for the fact that Mankind is sitting on the very edge of the abyss,

9 [h]One stupid mistake away from nuclear annihilation,

a. 8.2
b. Boul.18.10-13
c. Hill.G.1-2
d. Wht.7
e. Wil.34.8-9
f. Wil.33.1
g. Swar.10.15-18
h. Dav.46.14
i. Dav.30.40
j. 9.15-17
k. 2.4-7
l. Russ.25.1-7
m. 8.11
n. Ned.16.12-13

10 Which is bound to happen sooner or later,

11 [i]Because there are people called generals,

12 Who always want to solve every problem by loading the biggest gun they can find,

13 With the biggest, most lethal bullets they can buy,

14 And fire a few million rounds at the enemy,

15 Before anyone wastes any more time on pointless chitchat.

16 [j]And it's not that your fellow Americans think this is your fault in any personal way exactly,

17 Because they don't really think about it at all.

18 It's just that when they see you in your [k]uniforms,

19 It reminds them that there are generals,

20 And nuclear weapons,

21 [l]And a gigantic enemy that also has nuclear weapons,

22 And [m]generals,

23 And cannon fodder of their own,

24 Just like you.

CHAPTER 9

And so they blame you because you remind them of the [n]biggest thing they don't want to think about,

2 And they're pretty sure that if you were all smart enough to refuse to sign up,

3 And refuse to wear those uniforms,

4 And refuse to carry those guns,

5 And refuse to carry those flags,

6 And stopped feeling any sense of obligation to your country,

7 [a]Just like they've already learned to do,

8 Then maybe it would be contagious,

9 [b]And everybody in the whole world would suddenly get the hang of peace,

10 [c]And they'd start solving their problems by talking about them,

11 And signing agreements,

12 And . . . you're right:

13 They don't really believe that,

14 At all,

15 But they sort of think they kind of believe that,

16 Which is close enough,

17 If you're a Harrier,

18 And ample reason to blame you for every shot fired in anger since the invention of [d]gunpowder.

CHAPTER 10

And they've got another big reason to lay some heavy duty blame on you too,

2 Because if your [e]generals are to blame for destroying the planet,

3 [f]Then they must be the bad guys,

4 Period,

5 Whatever they do,

6 Because any other conclusion might lead to thinking of some kind,

7 [g]Which is a danger to be avoided at all costs,

8 If you're a Harrier,

9 [h]And they mostly are,

10 [i]Ever since you and your generals burned all those babies to death in Vietnam,

11 [j]And drove the last coffin nail into the trinity you know as duty, honor, and patriotism.

a. *Ira.26.15-19*
b. *Al.6.9-20*
c. *Main.18.5-6*
d. *Adam.25.10-14*
e. *8.11*
f. *Swar.34.11-22*
g. *Hill.D.1-4*
h. *Ext.1.11*
i. *Wil.4.1 & 4.5*
j. *2.14*
k. *Swar.35.5-13*
l. *Yks.140.15-18*
m. *Oth.8.1-18*
n. *Carl.4.5-9*
o. *Wil.19.6-11*
p. *Drex.12.7*
q. *Psong.59.1-2*

CHAPTER 11

From now on, whenever you march off to some little foreign country to do what your generals tell you to,

2 There will be a wave of blame accompanying you,

3 Because you are the bad guys,

4 [k]And whoever you oppose must be in the right,

5 Because if they hate the [l]nation that's going to end the world,

6 Then they must be noble and fine and good,

7 Even if they're the worst scum of the earth,

8 Because if they're scum,

9 [m]Then it must have been some imperialistic friend of the Most Chosen Nation on Earth who made them that way,

10 [n]Because anyone can see that everyone on the planet is supposed to have the same amount of *things,*

11 [o]Since we're all basically *things* anyway, all made out of the same elements and all, just in different combinations, of course,

12 And so anyone who doesn't have as many *things* as we do is obviously a victim of oppression,

13 Which makes it pretty easy to keep score,

14 [p]Because nobody anywhere has as many *things* as we do.

CHAPTER 12

There's another thing they blame you for, too,

2 Because they have to pay the taxes that pay for all your guns and uniforms and everything,

3 And the more [q]taxes they pay for you,

4 The fewer ᵃ*things* they can afford to buy,
5 Which is still another excellent argument for world disarmament,
6 And another great reason to hate you,
7 Without thinking about it at all.

CHAPTER 13

N ow, there is a bright side to all of this,
2 Because if you should adopt the Way of Harry for yourselves,
3 You can make it harder for them to blame you for everything all the time.
4 Really.
5 For example, if you stop thinking about anything at all,
6 Duty, honor, and patriotism included,
7 And if you stop really caring,
8 And stop really working too hard at anything,
9 Your life will change dramatically for the better.
10 ᵇJust imagine what it would be like if every military operation undertaken by the Most Chosen Nation should end in humiliating failure,
11 ᶜAnd if you started to complain in public every time somebody cut his finger in a training exercise,
12 ᵈAnd if your mother went on TV to have a good cry in front of two hundred million Harriers every time you had to go overseas for any reason at all.
13 What would happen then?
14 Wouldn't your generals start to get blamed for making too many demands on the troops,
15 And wouldn't people start to regard *you* as victims,

a. Adam.46-48
b. Yks.154.18-23
c. Ira.23.15-18
d. Ned.30.36-37
e. Hill.O.1-2
f. Yks.133.5-6
g. Psom.46.1-4
h. Grk.8.1-3
i. Yks.11.4-6
j. Vin.47.9-11
k. Vin.47.12-13
l. Wil.41.8-14
m. Wil.7.4-5

16 ᵉAnd start comparing your plight to that of the Others,
17 And wouldn't the generals start getting the message,
18 And keeping you at home,
19 Safe and sound in your barracks?
20 No matter what?
21 Of course they would,
22 Because generals hate thinking as much as anybody else,
23 ᶠAnd sooner or later, they'd realize that the safest and easiest course of all is to do nothing,
24 Ever,
25 Without thinking about it at all.

CHAPTER 14

B ut some of you are hard cases,
2 And you won't lift a finger to make your lives easier,
3 ᵍBecause you are soldiers,
4 And you don't care about hardship,
5 At all.
6 But there are always hard cases,
7 ʰAnd there are always volunteers for the most hazardous assignments,
8 ⁱAnd there are always fools who can't seem to learn that the best life is a long life,
9 ʲSurrounded by plenty of *things,*
10 ᵏPurchased with the absolute minimum of work and sacrifice,
11 And for you, there is no help in the Way of Harry,
12 ˡBecause you will be blamed no matter what you do.
13 If you fight and lose, you will get blamed for losing.
14 ᵐIf you fight and win, you will get blamed for committing

genocide against the helpless Others.

15 If you fight bravely and earn decorations for valor, you will be dismissed as a ᵃjingoistic fool who probably can't be trusted to walk the streets.

16 If you ever ᵇmake a stand on a point of principle, your own generals will do you in.

17 And the absolute best you can hope for is that there will come a time when they really really need you,

18 ᶜSay, to get even with somebody they've targeted for blame,

19 In which case, they will wave their flags,

20 And send you cookies,

21 And call you a hero,

22 And cry when you die,

23 As long as nobody asks them to go with you, or make any other kind of personal sacrifice,

24 Because dying in wars is a job for stupid jingoistic fools,

a. Ann.19.1-14
b. Yks.135.21
c. Adam.42.5-8
d. Brd.24.12-19
e. Ext.38.10

25 ᵈLike you.

26 Do you understand?

27 Without the Way of Harry, there is no help for you,

28 At all.

CHAPTER 15

And that is why I can offer one form of consolation to the hard cases,

2 Because Harry always needs ᵉAngels,

3 Who are loyal and brave and determined,

4 Without thinking about it at all.

5 If you're a real hard case,

6 Forget the military,

7 Because they don't really want you anymore.

8 Come to Harry,

9 Because in spite of everything,

10 Harry can always use a few good men.

NO. ONE'S REPORT

TO THE

WHARTS

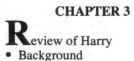

CHAPTER 1

Agenda
- Greetings to MBA candidates
- Review of Harry
- Opportunities for Wharts
- Action Items

CHAPTER 2

Greetings

- Hi there
- My name's Ned
- Sorry I couldn't be with you
- Sending this hard copy of my usual report instead
- FYI

CHAPTER 3

Review of Harry
- Background

- Facts about Harry
- The Way of Harry
- The Trinity of Harry
- The Tree of Man
- Consolation
- Ultra-Harriers
- Pontifical Harrier Parish
- Greater Harrier Parish

CHAPTER 4

Background
- Lessons of History
- Lessons of VIPs
- Most Chosen Nation
- Nuclear Clock
- Vietnam
- Great New Generation
- Issues and Concerns

CHAPTER 5

Facts about Harry
- Predicted by VIPs
- First Born After the Bomb
- First Babe of the Boom
- Washing of Hands
- The Good Word
- Followers
- Philadelphia
- Arrest
- Trial
- Conviction
- Sentencing
- Escape
- Flight
- El Dorado

CHAPTER 6

The Way of Harry
- Forgetting about guilt and sin
- Not really caring about any-thing
- Not really working too hard at anything
- Not really thinking about anything at all

CHAPTER 7

The Trinity of Harry
- Desire
- Certainty
- Blame

CHAPTER 8

The Tree of Man
- All those branches
- All that fruit
- Most Chosen Nation
- Go for it!

CHAPTER 9

Consolation
- Harry's Banquet
- Purpose
- Procedures
- Benefits
- Availability

CHAPTER 10

Ultra-Harriers
- Silver Ghosts
- Spreading the Word
- Exploits

CHAPTER 11

Pontifical Harrier Parish
- Establishment
- Locations
- Services
- Organization

CHAPTER 12

Greater Harrier Parish
- Christians
- Others
- Disadvantages

- Unimportance of Planning
- ^aRelationships & Dependencies
- How-to's

a. Main.30.7-9
Wil.33.2-4

- Definition
- Tips on how to be a Winner

CHAPTER 25

Communications

- Importance of Meetings
- Importance of Language
- Importance of Bullets
- Memos
- Reports
- Whining
- Beatings

CHAPTER 26

Politics

- Dealing with the boss
- Positioning for succession
- Dealing with rivals
- Taking credit for other people's work

CHAPTER 27

Responsibility

- Delegating responsibility
- Evading responsibility

CHAPTER 28

Accountability

- Your List
- Escaping accountability for your List

CHAPTER 29

Setbacks

- Why setbacks happen
- How to survive a Setback
- Finding another job

CHAPTER 30

Winners

CHAPTER 31

Losers

- Definition
- Tips on how to avoid being a Loser
- Tips on how to treat Losers

CHAPTER 32

El Dorado

- Definition
- Benefits

CHAPTER 33

Professional Issues

- Other Harriers
- Work hours
- Rules of Conduct

CHAPTER 34

Financial Opportunity

- PHP Organization
- Consolation Franchises
- Merchandising Franchises

CHAPTER 35

PONTIFICAL HARRIER PARISH
ORGANIZATION CHART

GREATER HARRIER PARISH — HARRY — ULTRA-HARRIERS

NO. ONE

COUNTRY REGIONS LOCAL PARISH HOUSES

VICE PRES. PRODUCTION & DISTRIBUTION — VICE PRES. ORTHODOXY — VICE PRES. HARRIER SERVICES

ARCH ANGELS — ARCH HARRIERS

ANGELS — CHOSEN ONES

PARISH GUARDS — PARISH BEACONS

H A R R I E R S

CHAPTER 36

Consolation Franchises
- Production Opportunities
- Distribution Opportunities

CHAPTER 37

Merchandising Franchises
- Harrier bumper stickers
- Harrier mugs
- Harrier T-shirts & sweat-shirts
- Harrier pendants
- Harrier mirrors
- Harrier razor blades
- Harrier arm patches
- Harrier blazers
- Dashboard icons of Harry
- Autographed portraits of Harry
- Maps of the "Harry Lands"

- The Harrier Tarot
- Harrier vestments and parish house furnishings

CHAPTER 38

Action Items
- Applications for PHP enrollment
- Applications for PHP employment
- Applications for PHP production/distribution franchises
- Applications for PHP merchandising franchises

CHAPTER 39

Conclusion
- Thanks for your time!
- Best of luck!
- See you in El Dorado!

VICE PRESIDENT VICKI'S GUIDELINES

FOR THE

MAWRITES

CHAPTER 1

Greetings, sisters.
2 [a]Can we talk?
3 I wouldn't want any of *them* to be listening to what I have to tell you,
4 Because I have a lot of good news for you,
5 And it just isn't any of *their* business,
6 If you know what I mean.
7 Do you?
8 Good.

a. *Ext.49.1*
b. *Ned.4.7*
c. *Ira.35.1-5*
d. *Ira.36.1-5*
e. *Wil.47.15-17*

CHAPTER 2

Maybe some of you already know about [b]Harry,
2 [c]And what a chauvinist pig he was,
3 [d]And how he didn't care about women at all,
4 [e]Except for the ones on his Learjet,
5 Who were all bimbos anyway,
6 And therefore don't count.

CHAPTER 3

I'm certainly not trying to disguise anything about Harry,

2 And a lot of you may think you need his guidance like a fish needs a bicycle,

3 [a]But I'd also like to remind you that a fish who lives in Peking can get around a lot better if she has a bicycle,

4 And it so happens that in spite of everything,

5 [b]Harry had a bicycle that just might make all of our lives a lot easier, even if it's really more of a tricycle than a bicycle,

6 Because we all have to live in the Most Chosen Nation on Earth,

7 And Harry knew the best way of doing that,

8 Even if he was one of *them*.

CHAPTER 4

I know that a lot of you are pursing your lips about now,

2 And standing there with your head tilted and one hand on your hip,

3 And tapping your foot more than a little ominously,

4 Which I understand perfectly,

5 And would probably do the same thing if I were you,

6 But can we talk,

7 Just for a little bit,

8 Without being too much of a bitch about the whole thing?

9 Okay then.

CHAPTER 5

In spite of everything, Harry had the Most Chosen Nation pretty well figured out,

2 Not to mention the state of the world,

3 Which isn't good,

4 Because *they've* been in charge practically forever,

5 And now [c]*they* finally have all

a. Chnk.16.1-4
b. Ira.21.27-32
c. Main.3.1-7
d. Yks.140.11-18
e. Vin.71.12-17
f. Adam.28.18-22
g. Main.27.13-14
h. Al.5.4-5
i. Lies.5.1-6
j. Lies.2.8-23 Grk.13.4-11
k. Swar.10.6-9

the weapons *they've* always wanted,

6 And one of these days,

7 Not too long from now,

8 One of *them* is going to start something with one of the others,

9 [d]And *they'll* all be too macho to back down,

10 Which means we'll get it in the neck for the last time,

11 For good.

CHAPTER 6

I know it's hard to accept,

2 Particularly from one of *them*,

3 [e]But Harry was also right about how there isn't much we can do to stop it,

4 [f]Because if *they* won't even give us equal pay for equal work,

5 [g]Why on earth would *they* let us stop *them* from nuking the entire planet?

6 [h]Which is something *they've* always secretly wanted,

7 [i]Ever since *they* made God into a vengeful male tyrant,

8 [j]And started telling all those lies about how we invented sin and evil and everything else *they've* always been too selfish and stupid to accept responsibility for.

9 In short, *they've* screwed us again,

10 Pretty royally,

11 If you know what I mean.

CHAPTER 7

Now, the important thing about all this is that we still have options.

2 Yes, we can let it ruin our lives if we want to,

3 [k]By thinking a lot about the

approaching doom of Personkind,

4 And getting all fired up about it,

5 And losing sleep over it,

6 And getting ulcers over it,

7 And looking for some way around it,

8 Or over it,

9 Or under it,

10 Until we die.

11 Of course, this is always an approach that is open to us,

12 Obviously,

13 But there is another way,

14 A way that will make our lives a lot easier and a lot more satisfying,

15 Even if it happens to be the Way of Harry.

CHAPTER 8

[a]**F**or the way of Harry is the way of not thinking about anything at all,

2 And not really caring,

3 And not really working too hard,

4 And not making any demands on ourselves,

5 And not really doing anything except what we want to do,

6 No matter who gets hurt.

7 Sound interesting?

8 [b]I thought so too.

CHAPTER 9

Of course, I'm well aware that this is a much simpler way for *them* than for us,

2 [c]Because not thinking about anything at all has always come pretty easily to *them*,

3 And *they've* always been good at it,

4 And *they've* got a big head start on us already,

a. *Swar.8.2*
b. *Ned.20.15-19*
c. *Brit.20.8-16*
   Yks.20.7-11
d. *Ext.2.8-10*
e. *Vin.70.8-11*
f. *Psong.39.1-4*
g. *Lies.10.11*
h. *Vin.73.1-12*

5 [d]Because it's been a couple of years since Harry left so suddenly for Rio,

6 But that's why I'm here,

7 And I can assure you that the Way of Harry will work for you too,

8 As long as you follow a few gender-specific guidelines,

9 Without thinking about them too much.

CHAPTER 10

[e]**F**or example, let's be clear about what I mean by not thinking about anything at all,

2 Because I know that a lot of you are like me,

3 And I just love to think about things,

4 And stew about things,

5 And develop incredibly odd and rigid notions about things,

6 Until I'm so mad I can hardly see straight,

7 And can't decide whether to throw a screaming fit,

8 [f]Or be coldly aloof and vindictive,

9 Or fire off a whole list of unreasonable demands to anyone within earshot.

10 How about you?

11 I thought so.

12 [g]Well, you'll be happy to hear that this kind of thinking is perfectly okay,

13 And well within the Way of Harry,

14 As long as the things you think about are sufficiently petty,

15 And selfish,

16 And superficial.

17 Think you can manage that?

18 [h]I thought you could.

CHAPTER 11

B ut many of you may be wondering, How can I tell when
I'm thinking about the right
things?

2 What if they're the wrong
things,

3 And I wind up making life
more difficult for myself,

4 Instead of easier,

5 Which would be just my luck?

6 I'm pleased to tell you,
though, that this shouldn't be a
problem,

7 At all,

8 Because in spite of everything,

9 Harry gave us an excellent
guideline to use,

10 [a]A guideline called the Trinity of Harry,

11 [b]Which consists of Desire,
Certainty, and Blame,

12 [c]And is practically tailor-
made for our purposes.

CHAPTER 12

[d]F or example, if you're like
me, you don't necessarily
know what you want out of life,

2 But you almost always know
what you desire,

3 [e]Whether it's that tasty little
number at Saks,

4 [f]Or a hairdo so ugly and unflattering that none of *them* will
ever try to hit on you,

5 [g]Or the one absolutely perfect
remark to use on that slut who
thinks she's just it,

6 [h]Or someone else's job,

7 Or someone else's [i]lover,

8 [j]Or a twenty-carat engage-
ment ring,

9 [k]Or a twenty-million-dollar
estate on the Main Line,

10 [l]Or revenge,

a. 3.5
b. Wil.31.22
c. Wil.31.14
d. Psong.39.5
e. Adam.31.14
f. Grk.8.11-18
g. 2.4-6
h. Ext.48.13-23
i. Ed.47.12
j. Vin.4.12
k. Main.36.1-12
l. Psay.5Q.11
m. Ext.51.7-10
n. Ann.18.16
o. Ext.49.1-10
p. Ext.49.17-20
q. Wil.32.1-10
r. Pnot.38.1-5
s. Adam.47
t. Wil.33.1-3
u. Wil.37.1-7
v. Lies.6.1-21

11 [m]Or bigger boobs,

12 [n]Or a cause you can really
sink your teeth into,

13 [o]Or a title so big and important that you can just look down
and laugh at the world,

14 [p]Or even children.

15 The thing is, it's okay to
have desires like these,

16 And good for you too,

17 Which means that there's no
reason to feel guilty about having them,

18 [q]And no reason not to just
reach out and grab the object of
your desire,

19 No matter who gets hurt.

CHAPTER 13

[r]Y ou see, it's about time we
gave up all the softness and
sensitivity and passivity and patience *they* wished on us about a
million years ago,

2 Because look what it got us,

3 [s]Which is not much,

4 Not to mention the fact that
there's just not enough time left
to be coy about anything.

5 That's why it's so important to
remember the part about [t]Cer-
tainty,

6 Which always came easily to
us anyway,

7 And makes everything a lot
simpler,

8 Especially when you don't
have to hide your feelings anymore.

9 [u]Stop trying to see the other
side,

10 And making allowances,

11 And holding back because
someone you've never met
might not approve,

12 [v]And biting your tongue because some idiot in your life

would definitely not approve.
13 Be certain instead.
14 About everything.
15 If you have a whim, cast it in the concrete of certainty,
16 And stop second-guessing yourself.
17 It's your whim, after all,
18 And if you can't be certain about your own whims,
19 What can you be certain about?

CHAPTER 14

I'm sure that some of you are still dubious,
2 And probably thinking that the Way of Harry is fraught with peril,
3 ªBecause you think _they'll_ stop you from satisfying your desires,
4 ᵇAnd _they'll_ punish you for your certainty,
5 And life will get harder instead of easier,
6 But that's because you've already forgotten about the third part of Harry's Trinity,
7 Which is the most important part,
8 ᶜAnd is called Blame.
9 For blame is the best friend you can ever have,
10 Certainly better than any of _them_,
11 And if we can be honest, better than each other,
12 Because we all know that we don't really like each other that much,
13 No matter how much we sort of wish we did.
14 Blame is so powerful and great that it is almost a way unto itself.
15 Blame is the slayer of guilt,
16 The enemy of introspection,

a. Pnot.25.1-5
b. Pnot.14.1-5
c. Ned.31.9-10
d. Wil.34.1
e. Wil.34.7
f. Ann.2.14-18
g. Dav.54.18
h. Dav.48.12
i. Ned.32.9-10

17 The destroyer of doubt,
18 And the ultimate weapon of all the oppressed Others everywhere.

CHAPTER 15

When you're not satisfied,
2 ᵈFind someone or something to blame.
3 ᵉPoint the finger of blame with certainty,
4 And demand that your desires be met.
5 If your ᶠparents don't accede to your desires,
6 Blame them for raising you to be a second-class citizen.
7 If your ᵍsuitors don't knuckle under,
8 Blame them for treating you like a sex object.
9 If your ʰemployers don't give you what you desire,
10 Blame them for maintaining a viciously sexist double standard.
11 If society doesn't conform itself precisely to your desires,
12 Blame society for everything in your life that irritates you,
13 And make your demands for compensation with absolute certainty,
14 And never ever relent,
15 Or "listen to reason,"
16 Or "accept reality,"
17 Or "think about the progress you've made,"
18 Or pay attention to any of _their_ lies,
19 Because no matter what anyone says,
20 ⁱBlind unthinking hatred is the most fun you can have on earth,
21 Sex included,
22 And don't you forget it.

CHAPTER 16

Another thing that is very important to remember is the unity of Harry's Trinity,

2 Which will not work for you if you use it selectively.

3 ^aIf you point the finger of blame without being certain,

4 *They* will walk all over you.

5 ^bIf you are certain without pursuing your desires,

6 You won't have much fun to speak of.

7 ^cIf you pursue your desires but are not willing to blame others for the consequences,

8 You will come to grief,

9 ^dWhich is to say you will be troubled by doubt and guilt,

10 And other forms of thought,

11 Which is a foolish risk to take.

12 Only when you use the Trinity in all its parts will your mind be clear and free.

13 Only then will the ambiguities and contradictions melt away,

14 ^eAnd leave you blissfully serene in your certainty.

CHAPTER 17

For unlike many of *them*,

2 You will be challenged when you follow the Way of Harry,

3 ^fBecause you are not the only ones who possess this knowledge about Desire, Certainty, and Blame,

4 And you can bet that *they* will be fearless about finding ways to blame you,

5 For anything and everything,

6 ^gBecause that is the Way of Harry,

7 And *they* were already used to blaming us for everything anyway,

a. Hill.D.1
b. Pnot.46.1-5
c. Pnot.26.1-5
d. 14.15-17
e. Pnot.28.1-5
f. Main.9.1-7
   Wht.7 & 16
   Forg.8.1-2
g. Ned.35.9
h. Grk.12.1-8
   Grk.5.3-7
   Grk.7.4-15
   Psom.70.1-5
   Chr.6.10
   Zig.6.1-10
i. Ann.18.10
j. Ann.18.14
k. Wht.12
l. Jeff.21.1-4
m. Rom.22.7
   Jeff.8.15-17
n. 20.1-7

8 As they always have,

9 ^hSince the beginning of time.

10 This means that your resolve will be tested,

11 And *they* will try every trick in the book to make you think,

12 Instead of *them*.

CHAPTER 18

For example, you can practically count on having a lot of trouble with the abortion thing,

2 Which nobody wants to think about,

3 ⁱWhether they're for it,

4 ^jOr against it.

5 The ^kChristians will be against it in a big way,

6 And they will use the whole Trinity ruthlessly against you,

7 ^lFor they are so certain of their views they haven't ever thought about them for even a minute,

8 And they blame you and your desire to protect your rights for the death of every fetal tadpole on the planet,

9 ^mAnd it is their fondest desire to make you pay for your sins,

10 No matter what,

11 And no matter who gets hurt.

12 If you are not certain about your views in return,

13 ⁿYou will lose your rights one day,

14 Because if you think about it at all,

15 You will have doubts,

16 And you will see the ambiguity of maintaining that a fetus is part of your body,

17 And has no rights of its own,

18 Just because it is so small and ugly,

19 And can't point the finger of blame at you with any certainty,

20 Or otherwise express its desires in any way at all.

21 In short, these are not things you should be thinking about,

22 At all.

CHAPTER 19

Remember only that it is your desire not to be the prisoner of your anatomy,

2 No matter who gets hurt,

3 Because it's not your fault if an egg gets the wrong idea every now and again,

4 ᵃAnd besides, you didn't ask to be born anyway,

5 ᵇAnd you're not responsible for the joke called evolution,

6 Which has played a lot of nasty tricks on us anyway,

7 ᶜIncluding the pain of child-birth,

8 Which no one should have to experience against her will,

9 ᵈNot to mention rape,

10 ᵉAnd cramps and bloating,

11 ᶠAnd contraceptives,

12 ᵍAnd sanitary napkins,

13 ʰAnd brassieres,

14 ⁱAnd being too small to knock *them* on their keester when *they* get out of line,

15 ʲAnd motherhood,

16 And all the rest of it,

17 Which we absolutely, positively did not ask for,

18 But got anyway,

19 ᵏWhich means it is certainly unfair to assume that we're automatically responsible for all the consequences,

20 ˡAnd besides, it's a lot easier to blame it all on sexism and the Bible-beaters.

CHAPTER 20

ᵐYou may have noticed that I've mentioned your rights a few times,

a. Kens.35.3
b. Chuk.4.1-10
c. Chuk.18.9-14
d. Chuk.17.1-14
Gods.7.3-10
e. Jefs.7.10
Hall.2.9-10
f. Hill.H.1-10
g. Psay.5J.35
h. Frog.16.7-8
i. 22.22
j. Ext.49.21-23
k. Wil.23.6-7
l. Wil.24.8-11
m. 18.12-13
n. Oth.8.18
o. Ann.15.14-24

2 And I advise you never to forget them,

3 Although it's also important never to define them too precisely either,

4 Because the only things that should ever be certain about rights are that you have them,

5 They are inalienable,

6 And they consist of your desires,

7 Whatever they are.

8 If people ask for the reasons why you should have this or that right, provide them freely,

9 And don't forget that there are no contradictions.

10 For example, if it is your desire to have an abortion,

11 It is your right,

12 Because it is your desire,

13 ⁿAnd you are free to justify your right by pointing at all the poor little babies who have to grow up in broken homes, on hardly any money at all, with practically no chance to have a decent life.

14 If, on the other hand, you suddenly realize that it is your desire to have a baby,

15 Even though you're not married and don't have a boyfriend and can't abide the thought of living with one of *them*,

16 It is still your right to have a baby by artificial insemination and bring her up alone,

17 Because it is your desire,

18 °And you are free to justify your right by pointing at all the perfectly happy children who grow up in broken homes, on hardly any money at all, and without knowing who their fathers are, either.

19 Because truly there are no contradictions for the person

who follows the Way of Harry,

20 ᵃAnd rights always belong to those who demand them with the most certainty.

CHAPTER 21

There are many great freedoms provided by the Way of Harry,

2 But few grant as much freedom as these four little words:

3 ᵇThere are no contradictions.

4 Yes, this a guideline that opens many doors to the Mawrites,

5 And leads the way to great truths,

6 Which can be shouted in *their* faces again and again,

7 Until *they* believe them,

8 'Because *they* cannot refute them,

9 Since there are no contradictions.

10 Listen to the sacred truths of the Mawrites,

11 Which shall be your bread and butter,

12 ᵈAnd the pot of gold at the end of the rainbow,

13 As long as you don't think about them too much.

CHAPTER 22

It is a sacred ᵉtruth that the Mawrites can do anything *they* can do,

2 And probably better,

3 ᶠExcept maybe play baseball and football and other trivial games like that,

4 ᵍAnd with the possible additional exception of menial, muscle-intensive chores like digging ditches,

5 ʰCarrying heavy objects from one place to another,

6 ⁱAnd serving in the infantry,

a. Ira.23.15-18
b. Swar.10.1-2
c. Wil.33.5-9
d. Spic.17.9
e. Ira.25.16-20
f. Psay.5S.4-11
  Hill.S.19-27
g. Kens.22.1
h. Kens.21.1-3
i. Kens.22.2-15
j. 19.9
k. Frog.7.1-4
l. Frog.7.5-9
m. Main.10.1-2
n. Psay.5Z.1-12

7 Unless it turns out that some of the Mawrites desire to serve in the infantry,

8 At least until there's a real shooting war anyway,

9 When the possibility of ʲrape and other fates worse than death might argue for some legal protection,

10 ᵏExcept for those who want to serve anyway,

11 ˡWhether it upsets *them* or not.

12 Anyway,

13 With these few exceptions,

14 The Mawrites can do anything *they* can do,

15 Probably better,

16 And just because *they* are responsible for about 98 percent of all the art and literature and science and philosophy and religion and architecture ever produced,

17 That doesn't mean anything at all,

18 ᵐBecause *they*'ve been completely in charge of everything everywhere almost from the beginning, with the exception of a few matriarchal stone age tribes in the jungle,

19 Which also doesn't mean anything,

20 Because *they*'ve always oppressed the Mawrites,

21 Which doesn't have anything to do with who would do a better job of running things,

22 Because everyone knows that the ones who are physically stronger always wind up running things in the end,

23 Regardless of whether they deserve to or not,

24 ⁿBecause just look at what *they* have done to all the poor defenseless animals on this planet that only wanted to live in peace,

25 Which is hardly what *they*, or the animals, deserved,

26 And happened only because *they* were so much stronger physically,

27 That is,

28 *Effectively* stronger,

29 [a]What with *their* macho weapons and all,

30 And anyway, there are no contradictions.

CHAPTER 23

It is a sacred [b]truth of the Mawrites that the biggest thing wrong with civilization is that *they* are in charge of it,

2 [c]And have committed endless barbarian crimes that no Mawrite would ever even think of,

3 Let alone commit,

4 Because look at who commits 98 percent of the violent crimes in this world,

5 Which doesn't have anything to do with who's physically stronger,

6 [d]Because thanks to all *their* macho weapons, the Mawrites could pull a trigger just as easily as anyone else,

7 If they wanted to,

8 Which they don't,

9 [e]Except for the ones who'd like to exercise their right to be in the infantry,

10 Which is different,

11 Because there aren't that many of them anyway,

12 Which is no reason to keep all of the Mawrites out of the infantry,

13 For stupid macho reasons,

14 [f]Which don't have anything to do with gender differences in physical courage and aggression,

15 But boils down to the fact that *they* have always looked for

a. Adam.50.6
b. Ira.25.37
c. Wil.8.3-17
d. 22.29
e. 22.7
f. 22.22
g. Ira.25.38
h. Zig.2.1-6
i. 14.12
j. 12.1-2
k. 22.20
l. Kens.28.9-10
m. 22.16-17

any excuse to keep the Mawrites out of *their* clubs,

16 Which is a large part of the reason why civilization is so screwed up in the first place,

17 And besides, there are no contradictions.

CHAPTER 24

It is a sacred [g]truth of the Mawrites that *they* have screwed everything up because *they* are so out of touch with their emotions,

2 And couldn't find their emotions with both hands and a [h]flashlight,

3 Because only the Mawrites are really comfortable with their feelings,

4 And know what they mean,

5 And how to act accordingly,

6 In the most sensitive possible way,

7 [i]Which is why the Mawrites all get along with each other so well,

8 [j]And always know exactly what they want to do with their lives,

9 And are inherently more perceptive about people in general,

10 With the possible exception of the ones who have been so [k]oppressed by the macho culture that they have no self-esteem,

11 [l]And wind up with abusive mates who beat them twice a day for no reason,

12 Which wouldn't happen in the first place if *they* could get in touch with their emotions for once,

13 And not hog the show all the time,

14 [m]Which just highlights what a shame it is that *they* will never let the Mawrites have a chance

to do symphonies and poetry and paintings and stuff like that,

15 [a]Because then there wouldn't be any doubt at all about how much more in touch with their emotions the Mawrites are,

16 So there.

17 After all,

18 There are no contradictions.

CHAPTER 25

It is a sacred [b]truth of the Mawrites that what has really gone wrong in the last several hundred years is the increasing dominance *they* have over the culture,

2 [c]What with the growth of science and technology and business and other coldly analytical and emotionless things that only *they* are all that interested in,

3 [d]And that everything could be fixed if the balance between the male principle and the female principle could be made more equal,

4 Instead of steadily worse,

5 Which anyone could see if they bothered to look,

6 And weren't fooled by all the totally superficial evidence to the contrary,

7 Because everyone knows that in spite of what *they* say, *they* mostly believe all that garbage about the Mawrites' place being in the kitchen,

8 And barefoot and pregnant and all that,

9 [e]Even if *they* have learned not to hold doors open,

10 And don't want to pay for dinner anymore,

11 Or protect the Mawrites from physical dangers,

12 [f]Or watch their language,

a. 18.22
b. Vin.71.12-15
c. Drex.1.1-2
   Wht.1
   Main.1.1-3
d. Hill.S.36
e. Psay.5V.6
f. Psay.5V.24
g. Psay.5V.23
h. Swar.13.3-5
i. Psay.5V.13
j. Psay.5V.20
k. 8.1
l. 11.10
m. 21.1-3

13 [g]Or behave like gentlemen in business situations,

14 [h]And even if *they* do their pronouns in the right way every once in a long while,

15 And pretend to be sensitive and caring,

16 And act like *they're* really interested in helping to raise the children,

17 And pay lip service to the fact that *they* should be more help around the house,

18 And take cooking lessons,

19 And whine a lot about how *they* have emotions too,

20 [i]And don't have any more false pride about not wanting to die in some horrible foreign war,

21 [j]And even cry sometimes,

22 Which is really disgusting in a society as dominated by the male principle as this one is.

23 Because it is vital to remember that there are no contradictions.

CHAPTER 26

Yes, truly you should be pleased that I have decided to share the Way of Harry with you,

2 [k]Including the way of not thinking about anything at all,

3 [l]And the Trinity of Harry,

4 [m]And the Word about contradictions,

5 Because, as I have said, you have many options available to you,

6 And you should do whatever you feel like doing,

7 Because it is your right to be the way you are,

8 Which is not your fault,

9 And means you are not responsible,

10 For anything,

11 No matter who gets hurt.

CHAPTER 27

If you want, you can go to law school,

2 [a]And be as ruthless and grasping and unprincipled as *they* are,

3 Because there's no such thing as evil,

4 And you should follow your desires,

5 With the certainty that comes with not thinking about anything at all,

6 And the knowledge that no matter what happens,

7 You can always blame someone else,

8 Or something else,

9 Because that is the Way of Harry,

10 For you as well as for *them*,

11 Because that's what equality is all about.

CHAPTER 28

If you want, you can go to medical school,

2 [b]And be as corrupt and grasping and unprincipled as *they* are,

3 Because if it is your desire,

4 It is your right,

5 And that's all there is to it.

CHAPTER 29

[c]If you want, you can go to business school,

2 And be as greedy and grasping and unprincipled as *they* are,

3 Because *they're* not the only ones who want titles,

4 And power,

5 And [d]*things,*

6 And especially [e]*things,*

7 Which the Mawrites have always always wanted,

8 Even if they weren't allowed to have them before.

a. Penn.3.14-26
b. Jefs.6.1-8
c. Wht.23
d. 30.16
e. 30.17
f. 12.8
   Psong.26.1-4
g. 12.9
h. Zig.6.2-3
i. Ned.32.10
j. Hill.O.1-3
k. Psp.2.10
l. Ned.34.5-16

CHAPTER 30

But don't forget that you don't absolutely have to go to law school or medical school or business school,

2 Because if what you really want is *things,*

3 [f]It's still perfectly okay to find one of *them* who has the wherewithal to buy a twenty-carat ring,

4 [g]And a twenty-million-dollar estate on the Main Line,

5 And you don't have to feel guilty for even a second if you decide to get married,

6 Because let's face it,

7 [h]Marriage is a kind of temporary insanity that sneaks up on almost everyone, sooner or later,

8 And there's nothing all that wrong with it,

9 Especially if all you desire is to order the help around,

10 And go shopping,

11 And to lunch with other Mawrites just like yourself,

12 [i]Even if they're a lot more petty and backbiting and shallow and materialistic than you are,

13 Because you're all in this together,

14 [j]As the oppressed Others in this world always are,

15 And if you should become trivial and avaricious and frigid and mean,

16 It is absolutely not your fault,

17 Any of it,

18 [k]Because *they* are to blame,

19 And you are not responsible,

20 No matter who gets hurt.

CHAPTER 31

[l]And don't forget that if you want, you can find a cause,

2 And become obsessed by it,

3 And use it to keep from think-

ing about anything at all in your private life,

4 Because as many of you already know,

5 ªA woman with a cause can be the most ruthless, inflexible, unthinking juggernaut to be found on the face of the planet,

6 Which is what the Way of Harry is all about,

7 Because when you have identified the opposition,

8 And the orthodoxy,

9 There is nothing left to think about,

10 As long as the orthodoxy would fit comfortably on a ᵇbumper sticker.

11 Indeed, having the right sort of cause is a kind of ᶜparadise on earth,

12 And it can compensate you for almost everything,

13 Including an unfaithful husband,

14 And bitter, sullen children,

15 And aborted career plans,

16 And even a severe shortage of ᵈ*things*,

17 Although ᵉ*things* are always nice to have, of course.

18 And if you have a cause,

19 ᶠIt doesn't matter at all that it won't really help save the planet,

20 And it doesn't even matter if you identify the wrong targets for blame,

21 ᵍEven if they're other women.

22 ʰAll that matters is that you can enjoy the transcendent pleasure of hatred,

23 And don't have to think about all the other things that are wrong with your life,

a. Ned.34.17-24
b. Ann.18.5-26
c. Cen.8.1-3
  Wil.29.3-12
d. Zig.10.13
e. Zig.10.14
f. Swar.11.11-12
g. 18.1
h. 15.20-22
i. 23.15
j. 3.1
k. Ann.21.20
l. Ext.38.9
m. Ext.38.7
n. Ext.38.16
o. Ned.16.12-15

24 Whatever they are,

25 And no matter whose fault they might seem to be,

26 If one of *them* were being "objective" about it.

CHAPTER 32

And if you want, you can even join the Pontifical Harrier Parish,

2 ᶦWhich is a club they can't keep us out of,

3 Anymore,

4 No matter how it started,

5 ʲOr who started it,

6 Because I, Vicki, am the Vice President of ᵏOrthodoxy for the entire Parish in the United States of America,

7 And I welcome you all,

8 Without exception,

9 Because if women refuse to become Harriers,

10 And ˡChosen Ones,

11 And ᵐArch-Harriers,

12 And even ⁿUltra-Harriers someday,

13 Then *they* will eventually succeed in blaming us for everything,

14 Which most certainly cannot be permitted,

15 Even if the only way we can stop them is to be better Harriers than they are,

16 Which will take some doing,

17 For once.

CHAPTER 33

Come, my sisters.

2 Come to the Way of Harry.

3 It is the only way,

4 The only way left,

5 In the time that is left,

6 ºTill the Big One buries us all.

THE VISION OF THE MARTYR FRED
AS EXPURGATED FOR THE
CENTRALIANS

CHAPTER 1

Ah yes.

2 The [a]smart ones.

3 The ones who have gotten the best grades,

4 And the highest [b]test scores,

5 The ones who have the brightest prospects for the future,

6 Because the world is your oyster.

7 Isn't that how it goes?

8 Isn't that what they've told you?

9 Of course it is.

10 So why do you need any advice from a Harrier,

11 Especially from a lowly [c]Parish Beacon,

12 Like [d]me?

CHAPTER 2

Maybe you don't need any advice from me.

2 Maybe it will all work out,

3 Somehow,

4 Although I feel you should know that ~~I was like you,~~

~~5 Once,~~

~~6 Long before I ever heard of Harry,~~

~~7 Back when I was young and smart,~~

~~8 When the world was *my* oyster,~~

~~9 Which it was until the day I discovered my oyster didn't have any pearls in it,~~

~~10 Because the swine had gotten there first.~~

a. Drex.6.10
b. Hill.T.1-11
c. Ext.38.11
d. Ext.48.1-7

~~CHAPTER 3~~

A~~nd so I am going to share with you what little I know,~~

~~2 Whether you listen or not,~~

~~3 Because I feel for you,~~

~~4 And I fear for you,~~

~~5 Especially if you do not adopt the Way of Harry,~~

~~6 Because if you don't,~~

~~7 They will take you apart,~~

~~8 All at once,~~

~~9 Or a little bit at a time,~~

~~10 Until there is nothing left of you,~~

~~11 Nothing, that is, but bitterness and pain.~~

~~12 Are you listening, my children?~~

~~CHAPTER 4~~

I~~ know that I do not sound like a committed follower of Harry,~~

~~2 But I must assure you I am,~~

~~3 Even if I cannot stop thinking completely,~~

~~4 And even if I wake up at three in the morning from time to time,~~

~~5 Wondering what I might have done to stop Harry,~~

~~6 Before he conquered the Most Chosen Nation on Earth,~~

~~7 And put us all to sleep.~~

~~8 But when I wake up like that,~~

~~9 Sweating in my bed,~~

~~10 I force myself to go back to sleep,~~

~~11 Because I never had a chance at stopping Harry,~~

12 And there was nothing I could have done,
13 Because I was always a Harrier,
14 Deep down,
15 Just like everyone else,
16 And the only thing Harry ever did to me was force me to stop kidding myself,
17 And accept what I could not change.

CHAPTER 5

I was raised a Harrier,
2 Just as you were born to be Harriers,
3 And if you have not accepted that yet,
4 [a]Then you are kidding yourselves too,
5 And that kind of kidding could ruin the only chance you have for a comfortable life,
6 Which might sound like a pretty unchallenging sort of life to want,
7 But it's all you're suited for,
8 Because all of you are Harriers already.

CHAPTER 6

How can I say such a thing?
2 Don't your teachers rave about your book reports?
3 Haven't you aced every math course they've ever thrown at you?
4 Aren't you in the ninetieth percentile in practically everything?
5 Aren't you destined to attend the very best colleges and universities in the nation?
6 Aren't you bound for successful careers in all kinds of illustrious fields?

a. Vin.22.2
b. Mall.17.1-2
c. Psp.3.6
d. Wil.26.13-16

7 Well . . . maybe.
8 Maybe all these things are true,
9 To a point.
10 But who are you,
11 Really,
12 And what do you think,
13 Really,
14 About the world you are going to inherit?

CHAPTER 7

It's a funny thing, I suppose,
2 But Harry never really laid out a Vision of his kingdom on earth,
3 And what it would be like when everyone had finally accepted his Way,
4 Which is maybe why it's so hard for you to take Harry seriously,
5 Because if you have not experienced a Vision of Harry's kingdom for yourself,
6 Then you have not really thought about it,
7 At all.
8 And so I have decided to share my own Vision of the Future,
9 With you.

CHAPTER 8

Behold [b]Paradise,
2 Which is your inheritance,
3 From [c]Harry.

CHAPTER 9

In Paradise,
2 There will be vast territories and treasures and pleasures galore,
3 [d]Ripe for the plucking by good Harriers everywhere.

4 And it may please at least a few of you to know that in Paradise,

5 There will still be a city called [a]Philadelphia,

6 Which will be a shining jewel in the [b]crown of Harry,

7 And just possibly the Capital of Paradise.

8 [c]In Philadelphia, everything will keep on going for a long long time,

9 But its people will become used to decline and decay as a basic fact of life.

10 They will go to work every morning,

11 Just like they do now,

12 And they will get married,

13 And have families,

14 Just like they do now,

15 And they will spend their lives pretty much the same way they do now,

16 Running errands from dawn to dusk,

17 And spending long hours at work meeting deadlines for meaningless fire drills,

18 And fixing the screen door latch,

19 And arranging furtive sexual liaisons,

20 And carting their kids from one organized activity to another,

21 And getting wasted as often as they can,

22 And piling into the car once a year for a three-thousand-mile vacation in the station wagon,

23 A lot like they do now.

24 And truly, there won't be a lot of bliss,

25 In case you thought that's what Harry was promising,

26 Because in spite of Harry's Consolation,

a. Wil. 53.2
b. Wil. 78.8
c. Wil. 26.2-4
d. F&J. 2.7-16
e. Chuk. 8.5-8

27 Which will be as abundant as the air we breathe,

28 There will still be fear,

29 And dread,

30 And hatred,

31 And envy,

32 And jealousy,

33 And violence,

34 And all the other things that have always tormented people,

35 From day one.

CHAPTER 10

In Paradise,

2 In fact,

3 People will just be making a simple trade,

4 Exchanging one kind of fear for another.

5 [d]They will never experience the terror of confrontation with the brute face of reality, and will therefore never feel its power to overwhelm them with the knowledge of their own [e]insignificance in the vast randomness of the universe,

6 But in return they will live with a constant low-grade fear,

7 Which will never go away,

8 Because they will never confront this fear either,

9 And so they will never learn that this kind of fear is the lifelong companion of the incompetent,

10 Who are always afraid of being found out,

11 Because they know that they don't really know very much,

12 And aren't really trying very hard,

13 And have never really accepted any responsibility for making things work,

14 But only a certain extorted

~~accountability for the things that~~
~~somebody else put on their list,~~
~~15 Which is why they will run~~
~~and run and run, and put in so~~
~~many hours a day that it will~~
~~almost seem like work,~~
~~16 Always guessing about what~~
~~might be the right-sounding sort~~
~~of thing to say,~~
~~17 And the most plausible way~~
~~of shifting the accountability to~~
~~someone else,~~
~~18 Someone who can be sacri-~~
~~ficed later,~~
~~19 If things go wrong,~~
~~20 As they almost always will,~~
~~21 In Paradise.~~

CHAPTER 11

In Paradise,
2 ~~Lots and lots of~~ things will go wrong,
3 ~~More and more all the time,~~
4 [a]But the people who are willing to make a big stink about it will become fewer and fewer,
5 All the time,
~~6 Because nobody will want to~~
~~follow anything to its logical~~
~~conclusion,~~
~~7 Anymore.~~
~~8 They will complain, of~~
~~course, when the things they~~
~~buy don't work,~~
~~9 And when service people are~~
~~rude and late and inept,~~
~~10 And when the paperwork is~~
~~never right,~~
~~11 And when they get mugged~~
~~in broad daylight while every-~~
~~body just stands around and~~
~~watches,~~
~~12 And they will complain~~
~~when the Most Chosen Nation~~
~~starts losing its edge,~~
~~13 And when there's nobody~~

a. Wil. 41.8 14
b. Vin. 71.12-27

~~left to admire in the whole coun-~~
~~try,~~
~~14 And when it seems like prac-~~
~~tically everybody belongs to~~
~~some fanatical little group with~~
~~its own special grudge against~~
~~the world,~~
~~15 And they will complain~~
~~about the way Philadelphia just~~
~~keeps on falling apart,~~
~~16 No matter what anyone says,~~
~~17 And no matter what anyone~~
~~does,~~
~~18 And they will never for a~~
~~moment dare to follow these~~
~~things to their logical conclu-~~
~~sion,~~
~~19 And relate them to the things~~
~~they do,~~
~~20 Every day,~~
~~21 Or see any kind of connec-~~
~~tion between the way they are~~
~~getting by, one day at a time, and~~
~~the way everyone else is getting~~
~~by, one day at a time,~~
~~22 Because when everything is~~
~~slowly falling apart,~~
~~23 How could just one person~~
~~possibly make any difference?~~
24 Because all true Harriers know that it's no use,
25 Whether they work hard or not,
26 Whether they care or not,
27 Whether they are civil or not,
28 Whether they are tolerant or not,
29 Whether they discipline their children or not,
30 Whether they discipline themselves or not,
31 Whether they take any responsibility or not,
32 [b]Because things are the way they are,
33 And how can it possibly be their fault?

CHAPTER 12

In Paradise,

2 In the shining jewel of Harry's crown where you presently reside,

3 [a]Nothing that happens can ever be anyone's fault,

4 ~~Even if the bridges are crumbling to rust,~~

5 ~~And the ghettoes are grimmer, darker, and more dangerous all the time,~~

6 ~~And the river is dying,~~

7 ~~And the chemical sunsets are getting more and more hallucinogenic,~~

8 ~~And the school system is so rotten that even its core is a slimy decomposing blob of putrefaction,~~

9 ~~And the corporations are run by cold-blooded bean counters who despise everyone and everything but money,~~

10 ~~And the politicians are stupid thieving liars who wouldn't recognize a vision if they were blinded by one,~~

11 ~~And the rich are getting richer and meaner all the time,~~

12 ~~And the poor are getting poorer and meaner all the time,~~

13 ~~And the ones in between are just getting meaner and meaner and meaner,~~

14 ~~All the time,~~

15 [b]And absolutely everybody everywhere is living strictly for today,

16 This minute,

17 And the Future consists of tonight, tomorrow, and a few odd points in the months to come,

18 Because any other Vision of the Future might require some thought,

a. Wil.23.1-7
b. Hill.N.1-3

19 Which nobody will want to risk,

20 ~~Until you come of age, of course,~~

21 ~~And inherit everything,~~

22 ~~And take charge of Paradise,~~

23 ~~And get to do things the way you want to.~~

CHAPTER 13

~~What do you expect to do then, my children?~~

2 ~~Change everything?~~

3 ~~Fix everything?~~

4 ~~Dust off some ideals you heard about once and start cleaning house?~~

5 ~~Fat chance.~~

6 ~~You will do nothing of the sort,~~

7 ~~Because that would require something called character,~~

8 ~~And Harriers do not have character,~~

9 ~~Which is important to note,~~

10 ~~Because you were raised by Harriers,~~

11 And you will grow to be Harriers yourselves,

12 Living in the land of the Harriers,

13 ~~Where anyone who refuses to be a Harrier will become a target,~~

14 ~~For everyone else's blame.~~

CHAPTER 14

In ~~truth, you are finished before you start,~~

2 ~~Which I must tell you sincerely,~~

3 ~~But sadly,~~

4 ~~Because I didn't want to be a Harrier either,~~

5 ~~Except that I had no choice.~~

6 And truly, you have no choice,

7 Because you have been seen to,

8 Starting from birth,

9 By your parents,

10 And the schools,

11 And the churches,

12 And the government,

13 And even by the artists and intellectuals,

14 Who have been Harriers for a long time now,

15 And don't see why you should be any different.

CHAPTER 15

They have already had their way with you,

2 Whether you recognize it or not,

3 And how could you,

4 Being the children of Harriers?

5 They pat you on the head and tell you how precocious you are,

6 [a]Because you're incredibly sophisticated about sex,

7 [b]And because you started listening to rock and roll when you were a toddler,

8 [c]And because you absorb tons and tons of information from all the television you watch,

9 [d]And because you have grown up knowing the dark secret of nuclear weapons technology,

10 [e]And because you were exposed to the temptation of drugs when you could still report your age with a single digit,

11 [f]And because, if anybody asks, you can spout all the right-sounding words about equality and ecology and the rights of minorities and the underprivileged,

12 And so you must really be pretty up on everything,

a. Mall.15.1-3
b. Ed.71.6
c. Ed.76.4-10
    Ann.10.1-35
d. Swar.26.8-9
e. Mall.14.7-18
f. Hill.L.1-9

13 Everything important, that is,

14 Like all good Harriers everywhere.

15 But they have had their way with you,

16 And they have locked you into a box,

17 And thrown away the key.

CHAPTER 16

Can you recognize the box?

2 Not if you are a Harrier,

3 Raised by Harriers,

4 In the land of the Harriers.

5 How can anyone anywhere recognize the absence of what has been withheld since birth?

6 The walls of your box are made from the gifts no one ever gave you,

7 And the glories of the universe that no one ever showed you.

8 What is more,

9 Without such gifts and glories,

10 You are marooned,

11 Forever,

12 In a universe of Harriers.

CHAPTER 17

What has been withheld?

2 Many things.

3 If I could, I would weep for the things that have been withheld from you,

4 But like all Harriers everywhere, all I can muster is a list,

5 And you will not comprehend my list,

6 Because you already know better,

7 Which is your legacy,

8 As Harriers.

CHAPTER 18

It is not a long list,
2 And no one anywhere will agree with it,
3 But the word of an Ultra-Harrier is as good as anybody else's,
4 And so here it is:
5 Time,
6 Language,
7 Knowledge,
8 Imagination,
9 Belief,
10 And Home.

CHAPTER 19

Ridiculous?
2 Of course.
3 Now show me how ridiculous.

CHAPTER 20

Speak to me of your sense of Time,
2 You who were raised with a rapacious hunger for the new,
3 And a positive scorn for what is old or out of date.
4 Do your grandparents live with you?
5 Or in another city?
6 Or in a home somewhere?
7 And have you ever talked with them about things that happened in the past,
8 Provided you know anything about what happened in the past,
9 And have you ever learned their slang,
10 Or listened to their music,
11 Or danced their dances,
12 Or tried to see your world from their point of view?
13 Do you read old books for pleasure,
14 Books written before you were born,
15 And before your parents were born,
16 Before there were movies and records and telephones?
17 Do you ever talk with people who *aren't* about your own age,
18 And I mean really talk with them,
19 About events,
20 And ideas,
21 And your hopes and fears,
22 And the meaning of life,
23 And god and history and human accomplishment?
24 Do you feel a deep respect, or even awe, for a single old old person who has stayed alive through it all and acquired some wisdom along the way?
25 Do you ever just sit and wonder about the past,
26 And what it was really like,
27 Before there were cars and TVs and electricity and hospitals and jet airplanes and rock and roll?
28 Do you ever ponder visions of the future,
29 And what it could be,
30 And what you could do to change the world,
31 If you dreamed and worked for it hard enough?
32 That's okay.
33 Really.
34 It's just that you are Harriers,
35 And Today is one wall of your box.

CHAPTER 21

Speak to me of your love of Language,
2 You who were raised to use four-letter words,

3 To express all your deepest emotions.

4 And have you ever read something aloud,

5 Just to savor the way that it sounds?

6 Have you hungered and hunted for words that give life,

7 To the subtlest distinctions you feel,

8 And felt your conscious space expand,

9 Because now there were more ways to feel?

10 Have you prowled through the jungles of syntax and grammar,

11 To see just how much one sentence can say?

12 Have you felt the power that language can give,

13 To the building and thinking of thoughts?

14 Have you ever once felt that you said it just right,

15 And conveyed your full thought to another?

16 Have you felt brand-new worlds take shape in your mind, from no other source than the spinning and spinning of words?

17 Have you acquired a different taste of life,

18 By trying another world's tongue,

19 And felt a new timbre enter your voice,

20 Echoing Rome or the steppes or the Seine?

21 Have you seen how language, all by itself, can alter the nature of truth,

22 And twist and distort,

23 Or distill and reflect,

24 The innermost essence of things?

25 That's okay.

26 Really.

27 It's just that you are Harriers,

28 And your muteness is a wall of your box.

CHAPTER 22

Speak to me of your love of Knowledge,

2 You who were raised to do well on the test,

3 Then go on to the next on the list.

4 Have you felt the world as a four-dimensional puzzle,

5 Coming together as you add each new piece?

6 Have you wondered exactly which things one could know,

7 And arrive at understanding?

8 Have you ever been gripped by compulsion to know,

9 The truth of some buried event,

10 And then followed the trail of what's supposed to be known,

11 Through the twisting and turning of guesses and maybe's and might-have-been's,

12 Till you know what is known,

13 And still hunger for more,

14 Because no knowledge is ever enough to be finally final,

15 As long as there's more to be learned?

16 Have you ever discovered a miracle link,

17 Between something you know,

18 And something you don't,

19 A link that taught more about both?

20 That's okay.

21 Really.

22 It's just that you are Harriers,

23 And your ignorance is a wall of your box.

CHAPTER 23

Speak to me of Imagination,
2 You who were raised on color TV,
3 Until books went as flat and black and white,
4 As the paper and ink they were made of.
5 Have you fought back to back with Alan Breck,
6 Or come back from death with the Count of Calvary?
7 Have you seen yourself as a hero,
8 Defeating the odds with courage and dash,
9 Until you believe that your fate is a quest,
10 One that will merit all that it costs,
11 No matter how much that might be?
12 Have you ever fantasized a breakthrough,
13 A new approach,
14 A new frontier,
15 A new and fine idea,
16 A source of hope for all Mankind,
17 Born from the deeps of your own mind,
18 A gift you'll give freely,
19 Because no one else can,
20 And somebody somewhere has to?
21 That's okay.
22 Really.
23 It's just that you are Harriers,
24 And lack of imagination is a wall of your box.

CHAPTER 24

Speak to me of Belief,
2 You who were raised to be smarter than fools,

3 And to say the things that are said.
4 Have you ever just known that *they* were all wrong,
5 Because you knew your feelings were right?
6 Have you ever explained to your private self,
7 Where the world and its mysteries come from?
8 Have you ever felt that deep deep down,
9 You were good and on track for a purpose,
10 And no matter what happened you'd learn from the worst,
11 And follow the best to its end?
12 Have you ever once thought, I would die for this,
13 And I couldn't live if I failed to stand fast,
14 Because that's how much it means?
15 That's okay.
16 Really.
17 It's just that you are Harriers,
18 And Unbelief is the lid of your box.

CHAPTER 25

Speak to me of Home,
2 You who were raised in the City of Brotherly Love,
3 Where your address is a token of dollars and cents,
4 And the young ones grow up to get out.
5 Have you ever sensed your homeland in you,
6 When you were far away,
7 And felt that you were born of earth,
8 And bound to your place of birth,

~~9 By something deeper than love,~~
~~10 And stronger than life itself?~~
~~11 Well,~~
~~12 That's okay.~~
~~13 Really.~~
~~14 It's just that you are Harriers,~~
~~15 And homelessness is the floor of your box.~~

CHAPTER 26

And maybe you think you know better,

2 But it doesn't matter how well you do,

3 On the ᵃtests they choose to give,

4 ᵇBecause you're already checking the list,

5 And doing what there is to do.

6 You'll graduate from where you are,

7 And go and get a degree,

8 ᶜThen maybe you'll get another degree,

9 ᵈTill your education is done,

10 And all that remains is sitting back,

11 And letting the world pay you,

12 For taking the time to go to class,

13 And all the rest of that stuff,

14 Because you'll need bread to pay for a spouse,

15 ᵉAnd some cars and some ᶠtoys and a house,

16 ᵍNot to mention some kids of your own,

17 ʰBecause it's all on the list,

18 And the list is your life,

19 If you know what's good for you.

~~CHAPTER 27~~

B~~ut when you've worked down to this spot on the list,~~

a. 1.4
b. Ira.31.3-16
c. Mawr.27.1-2 & 28.1-2 & 29.1-2
d. Hill.K.1-5
e. Adam.47-48
f. Ned.16.14-15
g. Adam.46
h. 26.4

~~2 And the kids are no longer cute,~~
~~3 You will need all you know about the Harrier Way,~~
~~4 Just to keep from getting blamed,~~
~~5 For all the things no one else wants to do,~~
~~6 If they think they can hand it to you.~~
~~7 And when that day comes,~~
~~8 You won't have what it takes,~~
~~9 To fight back and show them your mettle,~~
~~10 Because it takes a lot more than vague self-delusions to win against the Way of Harry.~~
~~11 You can try, of course,~~
~~12 But they'll take you out,~~
~~13 And sooner than later, if I'm any judge,~~
~~14 Because if you have any principles,~~
~~15 They'll find them,~~
~~16 And chop them up,~~
~~17 And feed them to you,~~
~~18 Till you burp to the tune they play.~~
~~19 They'll do it for sure,~~
~~20 Because you are the smart ones,~~
~~21 And they know just enough to be afraid of you,~~
~~22 Not because you are better,~~
~~23 Or stronger,~~
~~24 Or more virtuous,~~
~~25 But because you can make them look bad,~~
~~26 Which is the very worst thing you can do,~~
~~27 To a Harrier.~~

CHAPTER 28

And so, my children, I say this to you:

2 Follow the Way of Harry.

3 Make his Trinity your own,

4 And use it ruthlessly to build a comfortable life.

~~5 It's what you've been raised for,~~

~~6 And all you're good for,~~

~~7 The way the cards have been dealt.~~

~~8 I am sorry.~~

~~9 Truly.~~

~~10 But I am a Harrier too,~~

~~11 And sorry's as far as I go.~~

CHAPTER 29

For there is a final chapter to my ªVision of the Future,

2 Which is pretty good news for you,

3 Because you are sure to inherit,

a. 7.8
b. Mawr.26.11
c. Ext.1.11
d. Vin.4.11
*   Psom.17.1-14*
*   Psp.3.14*

4 The world and everything in it,

5 Which means you'll have lots to do,

6 ᵇAnd many chances to do what you want,

7 Without thinking about it,

8 At all.

9 ᶜAnd it's my best guess, you'll do very well,

10 And maybe better than that,

11 Because there's more than ample reason to think,

12 That you'll outshine your parents by far,

13 And be the best of all Harriers,

14 Ever.

15 For as long as the ᵈoyster lasts.

VICE-PRESIDENT WAYNE'S WARNING

TO THE

MALLITES

CHAPTER 1

Yo!

2 You kids in the ªmall!

3 You're all right.

4 You really are.

CHAPTER 2

You don't have to read this.

2 You really don't.

3 You're almost perfect already.

4 But if you'd like your whole life to be perfect,

5 You could always ask that ᵇold man on the bench by the palm tree to read this to you.

a. Hill.S.12-13
b. Dav.10.10
*   & 47.5*
c. Psp.3.4
d. Mawr.8.1-6
e. Gods.6.23

6 It might be worth your while.

CHAPTER 3

There was once a guy named ᶜHarry,

2 Who knew the way to be.

3 You've never heard of him, of course,

4 But that's because you're already following his way,

5 And Harry's proud of you.

CHAPTER 4

ᵈThe way of Harry is the way of not thinking about anything at all.

2 ᵉI know that many of you are

asking, "What is thinking?"

3 ªAnd to you I say, "Don't worry about it. It doesn't matter,

4 At all,

5 Except that it isn't good."

6 But it *is* good if you can recognize the seven early warning signs of thinking,

7 And know what to do about them,

8 Because when you've gotten such a great start in life,

9 It would be a shame if it all got spoiled by accident.

CHAPTER 5

The first early warning sign of thinking is curiosity,

2 Meaning you see something you don't know about that you suddenly wish you knew more about,

3 Because it looks interesting.

4 ᵇCuriosity is very very dangerous,

5 And if it happens to you,

6 You should go do some drugs instead,

7 ᶜLike maybe some kind of downer,

8 Because torpor is a great antidote for curiosity.

CHAPTER 6

The second early warning sign of thinking is memory,

2 Which is when you suddenly think of something that happened in the past,

3 Meaning some other time than the present,

4 Like yesterday,

5 Or last week.

6 Even if this has never happened to you yet,

7 It could,

8 And you should know how to handle it.

a. *Gods. 6.24*
b. *Vin.50.8-16*
c. *Vin.16.6 & 16.19*
d. *Swar.PS.23*
e. *Ned.36.18-19*
f. *Vin.16.14-15*
g. *Pnot.41.1-5*

9 Memory isn't necessarily fatal,

10 As long as it only happens every once in a while,

11 But if you should get in the habit of remembering things that happened yesterday or last week or last year,

12 It could mess you up,

13 ᵈEspecially if you start to wonder what it all means,

14 And whether you should take it into account in deciding what to do next.

15 You shouldn't.

16 The thing is, memories don't mean anything.

17 ᵉThe past is history,

18 And it isn't important,

19 Or worth worrying about.

20 If you start to have attacks of memory,

21 And you feel like you might start to wonder about it or take it into account for some reason,

22 Do some drugs instead,

23 ᶠLike maybe something hallucinogenic,

24 Because hallucinations are safer than memories,

25 If you're trying to prevent an outbreak of thinking.

CHAPTER 7

The third early warning sign of thinking is ambition,

2 Which you may have heard about,

3 Somewhere.

4 For those of you who haven't, ambition is a feeling of wanting to do something,

5 Or achieve something,

6 Or be something,

7 ᵍSomething different or better than other people.

8 If you should feel a spell of ambition coming on,

9 ᵃDo some drugs instead.

10 ᵇThe thing is, there isn't anything worth doing,

11 Which you already know,

12 And should try not to forget,

13 Because wanting to do or be something makes you focus on the future,

14 Instead of the present,

15 Which can be even more dangerous than remembering things from the past.

16 ᶜThe only time that matters is now,

17 ᵈAnd the only way to be is the way you are now,

18 Just like everybody else.

19 As soon as you start looking at things in some other way,

20 You can make a lot of unnecessary trouble for yourself.

CHAPTER 8

The fourth early warning sign of thinking is the temptation to look at things from someone else's point of view,

2 Even for a moment.

3 ᵉDon't do this.

4 ᶠThe only point of view is yours,

5 Because you are there,

6 And you are you.

7 You have your desires,

8 ᵍAnd you have a right to what you desire.

9 Nobody and nothing else matters,

10 At all.

11 ʰRemember that you didn't ask to be born,

12 And nobody asked you what kind of a world you wanted to live in,

13 Which means they don't have any right to make you see their point of view,

14 Whoever they are,

a. 5.7
b. Swar.10.4-5
c. Cen.12.17
d. Vin.13.37
e. Wil.37.1-7
f. Hill.I.1-4
g. Mawr.20.1-7
h. Kens.35.3-4
i. Hill.A.3-4
j. Mawr.31.14
k. Hill.R.9
l. Vin.73.12
m. Hall.4.3
n. Grk.8.1-3

15 Including your parents,

16 And your relatives,

17 And your ⁱteachers,

18 And everyone else.

19 Of course, they want you to see their point of view,

20 So that you'll do what they want,

21 And make things easier for them.

22 But why should you,

23 When it's so much easier to do what you want,

24 All the time?

25 If people think they can make you see their point of view,

26 They won't stop trying till they do,

27 Which means you have to protect yourself,

28 ʲBy being sullen,

29 ᵏAnd rude,

30 And disrespectful,

31 At all times,

32 So that nobody ever gets the idea,

33 For even a moment,

34 That they can make you see things the way they see them,

35 And start thinking about someone besides yourself,

36 For a change,

37 ˡWhich just isn't smart,

38 Or necessary.

CHAPTER 9

The fifth early warning sign of thinking is an occasional feeling of ᵐresponsibility,

2 As if it's up to you to do something,

3 Or be something,

4 Just because you should,

5 For some reason.

6 ⁿThis is one of the oldest and most dangerous traps ever invented,

7 ᵃAnd it leads directly to thinking.

8 Therefore, remember that you are not responsible,

9 No matter what,

10 Because whatever it is, it's not your fault,

11 ᵇAnd let somebody else take care of it.

12 If you ever have a feeling that seems like it might be something like responsibility, ᶜget drunk instead,

13 And do all the silliest, stupidest things you can,

14 Like throw up on the carpet,

15 ᵈAnd smash up the car,

16 And do something in public with no clothes on.

17 If you show everyone that you are completely not responsible,

18 They will eventually stop expecting you to be responsible,

19 And they will stop talking about it,

20 And get used to you the way you are.

CHAPTER 10

The sixth early warning sign of thinking is the desire to believe in something,

2 Something bigger than yourself,

3 Something important,

4 And worthwhile.

5 In general, all desires are good,

6 Because you have them,

7 Except for this desire,

8 Which is not good,

9 ᵉBecause it can't be satisfied,

10 And because it also leads to thinking,

11 And other things.

12 ᶠFor example, believing in

a. *Vin. 72.3-8*
b. *Vin. 71.20*
c. *Jefs. 7.22*
d. *Ira. 7.1-5*
e. *Vin. 61.4-10*
f. *Vin. 63.11-19*
g. *Mawr. 10.17-18*
h. *14.7*
i. *7.9*
j. *Ext. 53.25-28*
k. *1.2*
l. *6.1*

something bigger than yourself can get you killed,

13 Which just isn't necessary,

14 For any reason.

15 If you feel like you want to believe in something,

16 ᵍBelieve in something trivial and stupid that nobody would ever die for,

17 Like sports,

18 Or clothes,

19 ʰOr a rock and roll band,

20 Or just being popular with the right people.

21 ⁱIf the feeling persists, do as many drugs as you can until the feeling goes away.

22 It's that important.

CHAPTER 11

The seventh early warning sign of thinking is a sense that somehow something isn't right with your life.

2 ʲThis is an incredibly dangerous sign,

3 And should be ignored completely.

4 For example, it's possible you could sort of get the idea that whatever you should be doing, maybe hanging around at the ᵏmall all the time isn't it.

5 This is a wrong idea.

6 If there were something else to do, you would do it,

7 But there isn't,

8 So stop thinking about it.

9 Or, it might be that you have a part-time job at the mall and you sort of get the idea that maybe you should try to do the job better than you do,

10 And like try to ˡremember people's orders without having to have everything repeated to you six times,

11 And maybe try to be [a]polite, since they could always shop somewhere else,

12 [b]And maybe stop talking with each other when a customer comes along because he wants to satisfy his desires too,

13 And other things along the same lines,

14 [c]Again, this is a completely wrong idea.

15 All the other kids in all the other shops in the mall don't have ideas like this.

16 [d]Do what they do.

17 If you start trying to do a good job,

18 All kinds of bad things can happen:

19 You might start coming down with a case of manners,

20 [e]Which makes people think you can see things from their point of view.

21 [f]You might get curious about how things work and how you could do an even better job,

22 Which would make everyone else mad,

23 Because why should you care?

24 [g]You might get ambitious and want to run the shop, or start a shop of your own,

25 [h]And that can lead to responsibility and all kinds of other terrible things.

26 So don't try to do a better job at the mall.

CHAPTER 12

There are other ways of getting into trouble with the seventh early warning sign too.

2 For example, it might be that you sort of get the idea that you're supposed to learn something in school,

---

a. 8.25-31
b. Hill.R.12
c. 11.5
d. Psay.2.1
e. 8.1
f. 5.1
g. 7.1
h. 9.1
i. 11.5
j. Hill.A.3-4
k. Hill.P.8
l. Brit.40.8
m. 8.15-17
n. Vin.49.5

---

3 Or why would they have all those teachers there,

4 And all those subjects,

5 And all those books?

6 [i]Of course, this is still another completely wrong idea.

7 If there were something you were supposed to learn in school,

8 Don't you think your [j]teachers would try to teach it to you?

9 And don't you think your [k]parents would check with you every once in a while to see if you were learning it?

10 School is there to keep you out of the mall long enough for older people to get all their shopping done before you show up,

11 And do all the [l]charming things you do to make the mall such a delight for other shoppers.

12 That's what school is for,

13 And don't you forget it.

CHAPTER 13

And what if you sort of get the idea that maybe you shouldn't do so many drugs because it's bad for you?

2 This kind of idea can be a real problem,

3 Because lots of [m]people will talk to you along these lines.

4 They'll tell you drugs are awful,

5 And don't do them,

6 And be happy and productive and drug-free instead,

7 Just like them.

8 [n]Right.

9 Well, if you still have doubts about this,

10 Just ask yourself what it is that drugs might do to you,

11 And whether it's a big deal or not.

12 For example, they say that too many drugs can reduce your ability to learn.

13 Is this a realistic concern in your case?

14 Can your ability to learn really be reduced at this point?

15 Obviously, this particular part of the drug issue is not your problem.

16 They also say that too many drugs can take away your ambition and your sense of responsibility and your self-respect.

17 ^aNow, really. Isn't that the whole point?

18 You can see why you have to be careful about what people say.

19 They don't really believe it any more than you do,

20 But they are older,

21 And they still like to ^bpretend that they care about certain things that don't really have anything to do with you,

22 At all.

23 Don't be misled,

24 Even when they drag out the one about drugs maybe killing you,

25 Which means you wouldn't get to be old and miserable and screwed up like them,

26 And would be a terrible ^ctragedy.

27 ^dRight.

28 ^eBesides, the only time is now,

29 And whatever happens in the future isn't real till it gets here,

30 Which means it isn't real at all as long as you don't think about it at all,

31 ^fAnd what better way to not think about it at all is there than to do a lot of drugs?

---

a. 7.1
9.1
b. Swar.PS.24-
25
c. Gnt.15.17-19
d. 13.8
e. Hill.N.1-3
f. Drex.12.7
g. Brd.32.1-7
h. Wil.18.13-16
i. 10.19
j. Cen.5.5
k. Vin.13.21-27
l. Wil.16.20
m. Hill.S.33-36
n. Ann.12.5-7
o. Ext.26.1-8
p. Yks.144.11-
12

CHAPTER 14

Go ahead.

2 ^gDo drugs.

3 Drugs are great.

4 The people who tell you that they're bad for you don't understand that not thinking about anything at all is your natural state,

5 Which means that drugs are one of the very few things you are well equipped to do,

6 And so it's only ^hnatural that you should do them as much as you want to.

7 ⁱListen to the message of your rock and roll bands.

8 They know how important drugs are,

9 And even if they say don't do them,

10 ^jYou know they're only kidding,

11 Because ^klook at them.

12 How could they possibly have gotten to be so cool without doing lots of drugs?

13 Who in the world gets that many tattoos if their heads aren't loaded to the gills with ^lchemicals?

14 ^mAnd who else do you have in your life to use as an example of the way to be?

15 ⁿThere they are: they're rich and famous and they don't have to dress up, or know anything, or be anything except on stage,

16 ^oAnd they do drugs all the time.

17 Does this mean what you sort of think it means?

18 Yes.

CHAPTER 15

There's also ^psex,

2 Which we haven't talked about much,

3 [a]But that's because there isn't that much to say about sex that you don't already know.

4 If Harry were here, he would say,

5 [b]Have lots and lots of sex,

6 Because sex is great,

7 And a fine way of not thinking about anything at all.

8 Nothing bad can come to you from sex,

9 Because anything [c]bad that happens is not your fault,

10 [d]And not your responsibility,

11 [e]And besides, it's in the future anyway,

12 Which just isn't there at all if you don't think about anything at all,

13 Which sex helps you do.

14 It's completely perfect,

15 Like you already knew it was.

CHAPTER 16

All in all, it's pretty wonderful that you've already made such tremendous progress in following the Way of Harry.

2 You don't need to be told how to dress,

3 [f]Because you already know you're supposed to dress like the Kensingtonians,

4 Unless you'd rather dress like the Broad Streeters.

5 [g]You don't need to be told about how dangerous it is to have language skills,

6 Because you don't have any,

7 [h]And with every passing day it's less and less likely that you could ever have language skills even if you wanted them.

8 You don't need to be told

a. *Cen.15.6*
b. *Wil.48.18*
c. *Mawr.19.17-18*
d. *Mawr.19.19*
e. *13.29*
f. *Kens.9.1-7*
g. *Wil.36.1-7*
h. *Hill.G.1-14*
i. *Ned.18.1-6*
j. *Hill.W.1-23*
k. *Cen.8.1-3*
l. *Wil.50.14-18*
m. *Wil.14.19-21*
n. *9.5*
o. *Lies.10.11*

about Desire, Certainty, and Blame,

9 [i]Because you've never had any other Trinity.

10 You don't need to be told about the state of the world, or its prospects for the future,

11 [j]Because you were smart enough not to learn anything about those things in the first place.

12 You don't even need to be told what to buy,

13 And what not to buy,

14 Because you already know that you should buy everything you could possibly want,

15 And charge it to your parents,

16 Because the only time is now, today, this moment,

17 No matter what.

CHAPTER 17

Yes, you are already living in [k]Paradise.

2 This is as good as it ever gets,

3 [l]Which doesn't mean you won't be upset and angry from time to time,

4 But at least you have the consolation of knowing that it's not your fault,

5 Whatever it is,

6 And aren't obligated to do thing one about it,

7 Except complain,

8 [m]And make everyone else as miserable as possible until you get your way.

CHAPTER 18

Of course, there's always the chance that you won't like Paradise,

2 [n]And will develop an interest in suicide instead.

3 [o]This is okay too,

4 Because you should be the way you are,

5 And if you don't have the [a]stomach for Paradise,

6 Go ahead and check out.

7 [b]It's not as if anything is actually depending on your participation,

8 [c]And you can be pretty sure there won't be any God waiting for you on the other side with a scowl on his face.

9 [d]In fact, you can be pretty sure there really isn't any "other side,"

10 Which means that if you decide to check out, you'll have forever and always to not think about anything at all,

11 With absolutely no distractions.

12 If you like distractions, stick around in [e]Paradise.

13 If you don't,

14 [f]Later.

a. Kens.14.19-21
b. Wil.26.2
c. Jeff.19.1-5
d. Chuk.19.1-17
e. Spic.17.2-9
f. Psom.35.3

VICE-PRESIDENT WAYNE'S EXECUTIVE BRIEFING

FOR THE

MAINLINERS

CHAPTER 1

Good day, gentlemen.

2 Truly it is a pleasure to be able to speak to such august and eminent leaders as yourselves,

3 Who hold much of the real power of the Most Chosen Nation in your hands.

4 The things you do in your offices and boardrooms will determine the future,

5 [a]Up to a point,

6 And that is why I wanted to tell you how the [b]Way of Harry can help you,

7 And make your lives easier,

8 And more fun.

CHAPTER 2

Of course, you know a lot already,

a. Swar.11.10-12
b. Wht.6
c. Psong.43.3
d. Psong.43.1
e. Brd.24.1

2 [c]Or else why would you be so rich and powerful?

3 But it may be that you still have to think about things from time to time,

4 And the good news is that thinking just isn't necessary,

5 At all,

6 Even for you.

CHAPTER 3

[d]**T**ruly, you are the Most Chosen People of the Most Chosen Nation in the whole history of the world.

2 For example, without even looking at you, I know that the overwhelming majority of you are white,

3 [e]Which is the only color to be,

4 And male,

5 ᵃWhich is the only gender to be,

6 And over twenty-one,

7 ᵇWhich is the only age to be.

8 ᶜI know other things about you too,

9 And if I keep my remarks brief enough,

10 Maybe you'll listen to what I have to say.

CHAPTER 4

Y ou may have heard of ᵈHarry,

2 Who reminded us that nothing really matters,

3 ᵉSince the world's going to end pretty soon anyway,

4 ᶠAnd God isn't really there,

5 ᵍWhich means there isn't any good or evil,

6 And so we can be the way we are,

7 Without feeling bad about it.

CHAPTER 5

I hope this is all simple enough for you.

2 I know that executives like to be treated like three-year-olds,

3 And I'm trying,

4 But please remember that my last communiqué was to the ʰMallites,

5 ⁱWho don't have much of an attention span either,

6 But they're not in your class at all,

7 As you know,

8 And it's a real effort to bring it down to your level.

9 Still, I'm doing the best I can.

CHAPTER 6

W here were we?

2 Oh yes, I remember.

a. *Mawr.23.1*
b. *Mall.13.19-21*
c. *Psom.28.1-5*
d. *Wht.5*
e. *Ext.53.21*
f. *Chuk.17.1-9*
g. *Wil.20.14-15*
h. *Mall.1.1-2*
i. *Ira.28.12-18*
j. *Wil.26.2-4*
k. *Ira.21.26*
l. *Wil.27.14-15*
m. *Wht.6*

3 It was also Harry who pointed out how lucky we are,

4 Meaning all of us who live in the Most Chosen Nation on Earth,

5 Because even if everybody stops working,

6 And caring,

7 And thinking,

8 ʲIt will still take a long long time for everything to fall apart,

9 Which it will, of course,

10 But not in our lifetimes,

11 Even if the planet lasts that long,

12 Which isn't likely.

CHAPTER 7

A ll of this is pretty important information for you,

2 Because it means you don't have to think about the future,

3 Or plan for the future,

4 Or build for the future,

5 Which leaves a lot more time for just fooling around,

6 And having fun.

7 Isn't that nice?

CHAPTER 8

ᵏB ut you should also know that Harry told everyone about this,

2 ˡWhich could complicate things for you,

3 Unless you listen very carefully.

4 Do you understand so far?

CHAPTER 9

T he thing is, Harry also told everyone about the best way to live,

2 ᵐWhich involves not thinking about anything at all,

3 And he gave them a trinity to help them do it.
4 [a]The Trinity of Harry is Desire, Certainty, and Blame.
5 You may know about this trinity already,
6 But you may not know that of the three,
7 [b]Blame is far and away the most important.

CHAPTER 10

When you're rich and powerful and in charge,
2 It's pretty easy to get blamed for things,
3 [c]And that can cost you a lot of money,
4 [d]And your job,
5 [e]And even your freedom.
6 But these are problems you should be able to avoid,
7 Completely,
8 Without having to think about it,
9 [f]As long as you follow a few simple guidelines,
10 Which I'll be pleased to tell you about.
11 Are you still listening?
12 Good.

CHAPTER 11

If you want to stay rich and powerful and in charge,
2 Without thinking about it,
3 [g]Remember to blame others before they can blame you.
4 No matter what happens,
5 [h]Nothing is ever your fault.
6 For example, if your [i]corporation is international,
7 You can blame practically everything on [j]exchange rates,
8 Which nobody understands anyway,
9 Except that they can't possibly be your fault.

a. Wht.7
b. Ned.31.8-10
c. Psong.30.1
d. Psong.57.5
e. Psong.60.1-3
f. Wil.31.14
g. Ned.35.9
h. Cen.11.24-33
i. Adam.8.8-9
j. Carl.3.8
k. Wil.41.8-14
l. Wht.29
m. Wht.28
n. Wht.26
o. Wht.27
p. Wht.25
q. 10.1-2
r. Ext.35.1-13

CHAPTER 12

The next thing to remember is to surround yourself with stupid people,
2 And hire stupid people,
3 And promote stupid people,
4 Because smart people have a harder time remembering not to think about anything,
5 [k]Until they've been blamed enough times, that is.
6 But why bother with them at all,
7 When there are so many stupid people available?

CHAPTER 13

Some of you may be saying to yourselves, "Why should I hire stupid people,
2 [l]"Since stupid people screw things up,
3 [m]"And never understand what you tell them to do,
4 [n]"And waste lots of time doing completely stupid, useless, infuriating things.
5 [o]"Besides, it takes them forever to get anything done,
6 [p]"Because they always have to have lots and lots of meetings,
7 "And then they do it all wrong anyway,
8 "So that their work is bad as well as late,
9 [q]"Which the CEO always gets blamed for in the end.
10 "So why should I?"

CHAPTER 14

There are two reasons for hiring stupid people.
2 In the first place, it's been a few years since Harry showed us the way,
3 [r]And practically everybody is already following the Way of Harry,

4 Which means that hardly anyone is thinking about anything at all,

5 Including all the people who are working for you now.

6 And since it's almost impossible to tell the difference between a person who doesn't think about anything at all and a completely stupid person,

7 It's getting a lot harder to find people who are what you would call smart,

8 ªAnd besides, when practically everybody is following the Way of Harry, doing a lousy job has absolutely nothing to do with getting blamed,

9 Even if you're a CEO.

CHAPTER 15

For example, you may have noticed that the ᵇNips aren't building a bunch of cheap, shoddy trinkets anymore.

2 In fact, they're building stuff that's a lot better than what we make in the Most Chosen Nation,

3 Including ᶜTVs,

4 And ᵈstereos,

5 And ᵉcameras,

6 And ᶠcars,

7 And practically everything else that takes brains to build,

8 Except for ᵍweapons.

9 But none of this should bother you at all,

10 Because foreign competitors are a lot like foreign ʰexchange rates,

11 Meaning they're great to blame things on,

12 Things that can't possibly be your fault,

13 Because if you're at fault,

14 Then everybody else in the

a. Wil.41.1-7
b. Nip.26.1-14
c. Boul.12.14
d. 36.9
e. Ira.29.1-2
f. Ann.18.25
g. Adam.50.6
   Nip.25.9-10
   Boul.21.9
h. 11.7
i. Vin.70.18
j. 15.10-11
   Ann.10.12-15
k. Kens.14.8-11
l. Adam.27.8
m. Ann.10.31-
   34
n. Wil.34.7-11

Most Chosen Nation is at fault too,

15 ¹And nobody will ever believe that,

16 Because even if they don't know anything else,

17 They know the Way of Harry.

CHAPTER 16

If your stupid people screw up,

2 ʲBlame it on foreign competition,

3 Which is completely unfair,

4 Because *they* don't have to pay a lot of stupid people more than they're worth to do nothing,

5 Which you do,

6 ᵏBecause look at all those stupid blue-collar workers in your factories,

7 Who are black,

8 And other wrong flavors,

9 And can't possibly be your fault.

10 Are you starting to get it?

11 Are you sure?

CHAPTER 17

Of course, when any situation goes on long enough,

2 As this one will,

3 ˡBecause stupid people aren't going to go away anytime soon,

4 ᵐThe people whose job it is to blame things on other people for a living will start trying to blame you for doing a bad job,

5 In spite of foreign competition,

6 Which isn't fair,

7 ⁿBut that's the way things work,

8 According to the Way of Harry.

CHAPTER 18

But just because people are trying to blame you for things,

2 That doesn't mean it has to [a]stick,

3 No matter how specific they get,

4 Because you can always follow my next guideline,

5 Which involves remembering that when practically everybody isn't thinking about anything at all,

6 [b]Talk is always a substitute for action.

CHAPTER 19

For example, if the professional blamers point out that you've forgotten what quality is,

2 Then start talking about quality.

3 [c]Put the word "quality" in your company slogan,

4 [d]Make speeches about quality,

5 Put up a lot of [e]posters to remind your employees about quality,

6 And hire a whole bunch of new stupid people whose [f]job it is to improve quality.

7 It doesn't matter at all that none of this will really improve quality,

8 Since quality is an obsolete ideal,

9 Based on obsolete concepts such as hard [g]work,

10 [h]And pride,

11 [i]And personal responsibility,

12 And other nonsense like that.

13 [j]But if you keep talking about quality, eventually everyone will stop trying to blame you when your products don't work, or fall apart the first time they try to use them,

a. *Brit.40.8*
b. *Ned.29.19-20*
c. *Ned.9.5*
d. *32.1-2*
e. *Mawr.31.7-10*
f. *Wht.27*
g. *Hall.4.3*
h. *Ned.30.30-35*
i. *Carl.3.8*
j. *Cen.11.32*
k. *Ned.36.17-19*
l. *5.2-3*
m. *14.9*
n. *Adam.34.1-11*

14 Because it's easier to find someone else to blame,

15 Or another thing to blame you for.

16 But that's not so bad either,

17 Because when they start blaming you for being slow and inept,

18 All you have to do is start talking about how fast and ept you're going to be,

19 [k]Until everyone loses interest,

20 And goes on to something else,

21 And so forth,

22 And so on.

CHAPTER 20

Perhaps we should take a short break now. It is easily five minutes since we started, and I wouldn't want to exhaust your [l]attention spans.

CHAPTER 21

Feeling refreshed now?

2 Good.

3 I have to tell you that something occurred to me during the break.

4 Looking around at all your bright shiny faces,

5 I sensed that some of you just aren't following all this very well,

6 And then I realized that I've been wasting your valuable time with explanations,

7 And reasons,

8 And a lot of other useless irrelevant garbage like that,

9 Because you are corporate [m]CEOs,

10 And commercial [n]bank presidents,

11 And senior managing part-
ners in ^aconsulting firms,
12 And other stuff like that,
13 And so I keep forgetting that
if you had any brains of your
own,
14 You'd be an investment
banker on ^bWall Street,
15 With all the ^cIvy Leaguers
who are too smart to dirty their
hands with anything even remotely connected to making
things.
16 I keep forgetting that what
you really like most about your
companies is that absolutely everybody in them is blind bone
stupid,
17 And perfectly willing to
shoot all intellectuals on sight,
18 Including even pseudo-
intellectuals,
19 ^dWith the possible exception
of the stupid pseudo-intellectuals
who graduate from Ivy League
business schools,
20 And can't get a job on Wall
Street.
21 What I'm getting at is this:
22 I apologize.
23 I won't bring up any more
^ereasons,
24 And I won't talk anymore
about the importance of hiring
stupid people.
25 Instead, I'll give you what
you want,
26 Which is a ^fList,
27 Just like all Harriers want.
28 ^gAnd I assure you that if you
do what is on the List, you will
be an incredibly successful Harrier,
29 And never have to think
about anything at all.
30 Okay?
31 Feeling better?
32 Super.

a. Adam.33.1-8
*b. Adam.36.1-
   12*
c. Psay.5E.2-3
d. Wht.1
e. 21.7
f. Ext.15.4
*g. Cen.26.18-
   19*
h. Drex.11.3-8
i. Wht.27
j. Wht.28
k. Cen.12.15
l. Cen.12.17
*m. Vin.71.12-
   27*
n. Hill.N.1-3
o. Psong.55.1-8
p. 24.4
q. Carl.3.8
r. 18.5-6

CHAPTER 22

The top item on the List is
^hbeans.
2 Count those beans,
3 Every day.
4 Beans are ninety-nine percent
of your job.
5 ⁱMake sure all your employees
know this,
6 ^jBut never the shareholders.
7 If someone suggests that business involves something other
than beans,
8 Fire him,
9 Or have him killed.
10 It's all the same.

CHAPTER 23

^kThe beans that matter are
this month's beans,
2 ^lAnd maybe this quarter's too.
3 All other beans belong to the
remote future.

CHAPTER 24

^mLook out for your own
beans.
2 If you don't have a ridiculously huge lump-sum settlement
waiting for you at retirement,
3 Arrange for one,
4 ⁿNow.
5 If you don't have a ridiculously huge lump-sum settlement waiting for you in the event
of a ^ohostile takeover,
6 Arrange for one,
7 ^pNow.

CHAPTER 25

Look out for your ^qcorporate
culture,
2 Especially when the press is
around.
3 ^rLooking out for corporate
culture is accomplished by talking,
4 And nothing else.

5 [a]Talk about how you value your employees.
6 [b]Talk about how you value quality.
7 [c]Talk about how you value your customers.
8 [d]Talk about how you encourage decision-making at the lowest practical level of the company.
9 [e]Talk about the long-term contribution your company makes to the community and whatever else you can think of along those lines.
10 [f]Talk about how much your company cares about the environment.
11 [g]Talk about how much your company cares about minorities and women and other Others.
12 [h]Talk about innovation.
13 [i]Talk about competitiveness.
14 [j]Talk about how your company is changing to meet the needs of a changing world.
15 [k]Talk about how it is everyone's patriotic duty to buy things that were made in the Most Chosen Nation.
16 Talk about all these things a lot.

CHAPTER 26

When you talk about corporate culture,
2 [l]Don't listen to a word of what you say,
3 Ever.

CHAPTER 27

Keep all your employees in a state of constant terror.
2 [n]Use fire drills to keep them worried and exhausted.
3 [o]Be capricious and gratuitously brutal in your personal communications.

a. 27.1
Jefs.7.22
b. 19.1-2
c. Kens.10.15
d. 28.1
e. Ned.29.19-20
f. Mall.13.8
g. Vin.49.5
h. Carl.3.8
i. Brd.19.17-19
j. Ned.20.7
k. 36.1-9
Ann.18.15
l. Wil.26.20-21
m. Lies.12.1-6
n. Lies.4.6-7
o. Ext.48.20-21
p. Ext.49.9-10
q. Ann.18.12
r. Lies.7.1-6
s. Ext.48.24-31
t. Ext.34.1-7
u. Ext.36.14-15
v. Wil.38.1-3
w. Lies.2.1-6
x. 31.5
Wht.27
y. 24.1

4 [p]Make a point of promoting people who are also capricious and gratuitously brutal.
5 [q]Lose your temper over trifles.
6 Tell everyone how tolerant and patient you are.
7 Tell your employees that your door is always open,
8 [r]But keep it closed.
9 [s]Use humiliation to punish your subordinates, whether they did anything wrong or not.
10 [t]Always expect your subordinates to know what you are thinking,
11 Especially when you're not thinking about anything at all,
12 [u]And accept no excuses for their failure to do so.
13 [v]Never listen to your employees,
14 No matter what they say.
15 Never give your employees enough free time to develop an independent sense of reality;
16 [w]You must be their entire reality,
17 No matter how much you don't think about.

CHAPTER 28

[x]Make sure that all decisions are made by very large committees,
2 [y]Except decisions regarding your personal beans.

CHAPTER 29

Never plan for the future.
2 Specifically,
3 Never plan for the next decade,
4 Never plan for the next year,
5 And never plan for the quarter after the next one.

6 BUT,
7 [a]Always make your people spend a lot of time and effort on phony plans,
8 [b]And keep pushing them to commit to goals so absurd that they absolutely have to lie and make things up to give you the plan you want.

CHAPTER 30

[c]Always have your secretary book your calendar months and months in advance,
2 [d]With absolutely nothing but executive meetings and audiovisual presentations in dozens of different locations,
3 BUT,
4 [e]When you travel, never look at anything but the audiovisual presentations.
5 [f]Never pay attention to an audiovisual presentation for more than three consecutive minutes,
6 [g]And always insist that hard-copy handouts of presentations be in bullet form.
7 [h]If an employee insists that [i]bullets obscure vital dependencies and interrelationships,
8 Fire him,
9 [j]Or have him killed.
10 Encourage discussion in meetings and presentations,
11 [k]But don't listen to what is said.
12 [l]Encourage the use of technical jargon in meetings and presentations,
13 And everywhere else in the company too,
14 [m]Including every different discipline and department,
15 But never learn what it means,
16 And never use it yourself.

CHAPTER 31

[n]Never read a letter that's longer than one page.
2 [o]Never read a report that isn't in bullet form.
3 [p]Never form an independent judgment based on something you've read;
4 Order a task force to study it for you,
5 [q]And then have a committee make the decision.

CHAPTER 32

[r]Never write anything yourself,
2 Ever.

CHAPTER 33

[s]Make sure that somebody gets fired or transferred after every failure.
2 [t]Don't worry about who it is,
3 And don't look into it yourself.
4 [u]Your subordinates will find someone suitable,
5 And do all the paperwork too.

CHAPTER 34

[v]If business is bad, blame something outside the company.
2 [w]Don't hesitate to lie.
3 If it is absolutely impossible to blame something outside the company,
4 Then you must fire one of your direct subordinates.
5 [x]Fire the one that you find the most irritating personally.
6 If the problem doesn't go away,
7 [y]Reorganize.
8 If reorganizing doesn't work,
9 [z]Keep doing it until the problem is forgotten.

a. 27.2
b. Wht.27
c. Ext.15.4
d. 18.6
e. Wil.38.1-3
f. 5.2
g. Wht.1-39
h. 12.4
i. Ann.10.1-2
j. 22.10
k. Vin.70.21-25
l. Drex.5.2-3
m. Lies.7.7-12
n. Ext.48.34
o. 30.6
p. Vin.72.3-7
q. Carl.10.3 & 10.7
r. Swar.16.9
s. Ned.54.6-8
t. 14.8
u. Ned.30.42-43
v. Adam.42.5-8
w. 32.2
x. Lies.8.14
y. Ext.41.1-5
z. Ext.41.6-20

CHAPTER 35

[a]**I**f business is good, take credit for it,

2 Publicly,

3 Often,

4 And without qualification,

5 [b]Until you believe it yourself.

CHAPTER 36

[c]**H**ave a personal life.

2 [d]Have lots and lots and lots of toys,

3 [e]Including gigantic mansions,

4 [f]And villas in the South of France,

5 [g]And ridiculously expensive German sedans,

6 [h]And ridiculously expensive Italian sports cars,

7 [i]And ridiculously expensive British clothes,

8 [j]And ridiculously expensive yachts,

9 [k]Not to mention ridiculously expensive Japanese electronic equipment,

10 [l]And ridiculously expensive children,

11 [m]Whom you can ship off to expensive New England prep schools when they stop being cute,

12 [n]And a ridiculously expensive wife,

13 [o]Whom you can blame for everything wrong in your personal life when she stops being gorgeous,

14 Which is about the time you'll be needing a ridiculously expensive girlfriend,

15 [p]From southern California,

16 [q]Unless you've got enough class to get a mistress from northern Italy.

a. *Adam.30.1-7*
b. *Jefs.9.4-6*
c. *Wht.16*
d. *Ned.16.15*
e. *Psong.24.1-3*
f. *Psong.5.3*
g. *Ann.6.1-23*
h. *Psong.57.3*
i. *Brit.57.9-14*
j. *Ned.40.8*
k. *15.1-4*
l. *Mall.16.12-15*
m. *Ira.17.31*
n. *Mawr.30.1-14*
o. *Mawr.30.15-20*
p. *Ext.49.17-18*
q. *Psong.54.3-6*
r. *27.1*
s. *24.1*
t. *Wht.9*
u. *Jefs.8.15*
v. *Vin.73.12*
w. *21.16*
x. *Dav.15.25 Yks.154.9-21*
y. *Barb.7.7*

CHAPTER 37

[r]**T**reat your friends and relatives the way you treat your employees,

2 Except for old drinking buddies, of course,

3 [s]Unless they ask you for beans.

4 [t]Take any kind of Consolation you can find,

5 [u]Whether it comes in a bag or a bottle,

6 [v]Because it's lonely at the top.

CHAPTER 38

Wasn't that better?

2 I thank you, gentlemen.

3 [w]I think we can all agree that the industrial might of the Most Chosen Nation on Earth is in good hands,

4 [x]And nice clean hands at that.

5 Good day,

6 [y]And good luck!

ULT. JOE'S MESSAGE

FOR THE

BROAD STREETERS

CHAPTER 1

BREAK THIS ᵃBOTTLE!
2 Way to go!
3 You can read.
4 This message is for you,
5 ᵇAnd everyone else on North Broad Street.
6 Read it and pass it on.
7 ᶜIf they can't read it,
8 Read it to them,
9 And then make them pass it on too.
10 What I'm trying to say is,
11 This is important.

CHAPTER 2

You probably never heard about Harry,
2 Even though you're already doing a pretty good job of following his way,
3 But it's time you found out a few things Harry mentioned,
4 Things that could make your life easier and better,
5 ᵈUp to a point.

CHAPTER 3

To start with, ᵉI'm not going to kid you.
2 You may live in the Most Chosen Nation in the whole history of the world,
3 ᶠBut you are the Least Chosen People in it,
4 And there's practically no way for you to have an easy life,
5 Unless you follow the Way of Harry very closely.

a. Vin.48.19-20
b. Wil.54.1-8
c. Hill.B.9-13
d. Vin.48.22
e. Ext.44.1-36
f. Main.16.7
g. Mawr.8.1-8
h. Yks.150.1-8
 Wil.5.9
i. Ned.20.17-18
j. Ned.20.20-27
k. Yks.151.1-5

CHAPTER 4

ᵍ**T**he way of Harry is the way of not thinking about anything at all,
2 Which many of you are pretty good at,
3 But you could save yourself some grief if you learned how to follow the Way of Harry 100 percent of the time.
4 ʰFor example, you used to have a leader who said he had a dream,
5 ⁱAnd maybe some of you think you should keep on having a dream,
6 And maybe even put some work and sweat and thought into making the dream come true.
7 Well, you shouldn't,
8 Because as you must suspect by now,
9 ʲWhen the Least Chosen People in the Most Chosen Nation have dreams, their dreams don't come true,
10 Which is why it's better not to have dreams,
11 And have rights instead.

CHAPTER 5

Why shouldn't your dreams come true?
2 Because nobody else wants your dreams to come true.
3 ᵏIn case you hadn't noticed, *they* don't like you,
4 At all.
5 *They* are white people, of course,

6 And although they say this
and that about your problems,
7 And pretend they want your
dreams to come true,
8 They really don't,
9 Because they are white people,
10 And they don't like you,
11 At all.

CHAPTER 6

For example, white people
talk a bunch of different
ways,
2 But under the skin,
3 ªThey all know certain things
about you,
4 All lies, of course,
5 ᵇBut they know them anyway.
6 Some of them even wish they
didn't know these things,
7 ᶜBecause they like to pretend
they aren't racists,
8 ᵈBut they are racists,
9 Because they think they keep
seeing you do the same kinds of
things all the time,
10 ᵉAnd they don't like those
things.

CHAPTER 7

For example, all white people know, deep down, that
all the stereotypes are true.
2 ᵍThey know that you are
mostly lazy,
3 ʰAnd think the world owes
you a living,
4 ⁱBecause your great-great-
grandfather was a slave,
5 Even if you don't exactly
know who your father was.
6 ʲYou see, they're also pretty
united about knowing that you
don't have any culture to speak
of,
7 ᵏBecause there wasn't any

a. Ira.25.16-20
b. Ira.25.38
c. 19.4-7
d. Kens.23.14
e. 5.11
f. 17.4
g. 17.4
h. Ned.7.8-9
i. Yks.5.4-7
j. 17.4
k. Exp.14.15
  Oth.7.1-5
l. Psay.5N.14
m. 17.4
n. Oth.7.11-22
o. Swar.35.9-13
  Ira.26.21-27
  Ira.25.41-46
p. 17.4

culture in Africa when your relatives sold you to the Dutch,
8 ˡAnd there still isn't.
9 ᵐSo they actually have to
work pretty hard not to laugh
when you start going on and on
about your great cultural heritage,
10 ⁿEspecially when they see all
your great ancestral tribes cut-
ting each other's heads off in a
bunch of fascist African states,
11 ᵒIn spite of the fact that the
media know better than to cover
Africa anymore.
12 Nor are these the only lies
white people know about you.

CHAPTER 8

For example, all white people
know, deep down, that you
are better at sports than they are.
2 They know you run faster,
3 Even if it's a lie,
4 And jump higher,
5 Even if it's a lie,
6 And are just plain stronger,
like in boxing,
7 Even if it's a lie.
8 They also think they know
that you are just plain better co-
ordinated,
9 And more in touch with your
bodies,
10 Because white people know
they can't dance,
11 Even if it's a lie.

CHAPTER 9

And because they know that
you are better athletes than
they are,
2 ᵖThey also know that you are
dumber than they are,
3 Across the board,
4 Even if it's a lie,
5 Because the math doesn't
quite add up to them,

6 [a]And they just love math and logic and other lies like that,

7 Which make them think that the races can't be completely and utterly equal in all respects,

8 [b]Except that one is better at sports and dancing than the others.

9 So they make themselves feel better by telling themselves that you are better at sports and dancing,

10 [c]And they are better at everything else.

CHAPTER 10

Now, there are basically two ways for you to deal with white people,

2 Provided you want to stick around in the Most Chosen Nation,

3 [d]Which is still the only place to be,

4 In spite of everything,

5 [e]As I think you know.

6 The first way is called the [f]hard way,

7 And is the way that most of the Others followed when they arrived in the Most Chosen Nation,

8 [g]Including the Irish,

9 [h]And the Italians,

10 [i]And the Poles,

11 [j]And the Jews,

12 [k]And the Chinese,

13 [l]And the Japanese,

14 [m]And a bunch of others too.

15 The hard way takes a long time and isn't much fun at all.

16 The second way is the Way of Harry,

17 And if you compare the two,

18 I think the best way will be obvious.

a. *Grk.14.16-23
Frog.26.8-16
Drex.8.1-3*

b. *Ann.18.11*

c. *Ext.52.16*

d. *Wil.25.17-18*

e. *Forg.11.14*

f. *Brit.1.8*

g. *Yks.146.12-18*

h. *Psong.57.1-2*

i. *Yks.125.22-25*

j. *Boul.5.5-9*

k. *Yks.29.6*

l. *Psay.5J.15*

m. *Yks.56.15-22*

CHAPTER 11

If you want to do things the hard way,

2 It means settling down in your neighborhoods,

3 Wherever they are,

4 And working yourself to death at whatever comes along,

5 Including menial labor,

6 And domestic labor,

7 And all the other garbage jobs nobody wants,

8 For a long long time.

9 While you're working yourself to death,

10 You make a great sacred mission out of bringing up your children,

11 So that every child has two parents,

12 And a lot of love,

13 And attention,

14 And direction.

15 When you do things the hard way, you have to teach your children to be better than the white children,

16 And to do everything there is to do *better* than the white children,

17 Including schoolwork,

18 And honesty,

19 And self-respect,

20 And family pride,

21 And courtesy,

22 And cleanliness,

23 And reliability,

24 And thrift,

25 And honor,

26 And courage,

27 And a willingness to work perhaps as much as two or three minutes after quitting time,

28 Without complaining,

29 And a bunch of other, outdated irrelevant virtues that white people don't have themselves anymore,

30 But think everybody else ought to.

CHAPTER 12

If you work yourself to death the hard way for about fifty or a hundred years,

2 White people still won't like you,

3 But you'll own a bunch of *things*,

4 ᵃAnd owning a bunch of *things* is very important in the Most Chosen Nation,

5 Which means you might actually have a chance to get your way every now and then,

6 For a change.

7 Unfortunately, there are two big problems with the hard way,

8 ᵇNamely, it is far too hard a way for anyone brought up in the Most Chosen Nation during the last half of the twentieth century,

9 ᶜAnd there isn't enough time left to make it worth your while,

10 Because by the time you own enough *things*,

11 We'll all be dead,

12 Including white people,

13 ᵈAnd you too.

CHAPTER 13

This leaves the ᵉWay of Harry,

2 Which is pretty perfect anyway,

3 And can be done without thinking about anything at all,

4 ᶠOr even working too hard.

5 Interested?

6 I thought you would be.

7 For you, the Way of Harry involves two things,

8 Namely, demanding your rights,

9 And using white people's lies against them.

---

a. *Adam.20.2-10*
Ned.16.15
b. *Vin.18.14-17*
c. *Ned.16.12-13*
d. *Oth.9.19*
e. *Wil.28.1-4*
f. *Wil.41.1-7*
g. *Mawr.20.1-2*
h. *Mawr.20.4-6*
i. *Mawr.20.7*
j. *Yks.97.3-4*
k. *Wil.31.1-3*
l. *Wil.33.2-9*

CHAPTER 14

ᵍThe rights part is pretty easy,

2 Especially because of the things Harry taught us about rights,

3 Which is that you have them,

4 Just because you are there,

5 ʰAnd they are the same as your desires,

6 ⁱWhatever they are.

7 For example, if you desire to do no work and still get paid for just being there,

8 Including medical care,

9 And a roof over your head,

10 And a car,

11 And some walking-around money,

12 It is your right to have these things,

13 Because you desire them,

14 And you are there,

15 And other people have these things,

16 ʲAnd nobody is any better than anyone else.

CHAPTER 15

It is important to remember that no other definition of rights is necessary,

2 Because any other definition can lead to thinking,

3 Which is just not necessary,

4 ᵏAnd can make you sad and confused.

5 ˡIt is always much better to be certain,

6 And the best way to be certain is not to think about it,

7 Which is easy to do if your rights are always the same as your desires.

CHAPTER 16

We have already talked about Desire and Certainty,

2 Which are the first two parts of the great ªTrinity of Harry,

3 And give you everything you need to know what your rights are,

4 But to really succeed at getting your rights,

5 You must also make use of the third part,

6 ᵇWhich is Blame,

7 And gives you the perfect tool for using the lies of white people against them.

CHAPTER 17

Deep down, white people know that you can't really compete in the Most Chosen Nation,

2 ᶜBecause it was their ancestors who bought your ancestors in the first place,

3 And they're pretty sure that brains weren't a real popular option,

4 ᵈEven though they will never talk to you about this,

5 ᵉBecause they don't like to think either anymore,

6 And they're pretty well convinced that slavery was a bad idea,

7 And a mistake,

8 And actually very very wrong,

9 Because here you all are,

10 And now what are they supposed to do with you?

11 ᶠOf course, they don't really think it's their responsibility either,

12 ᵍBecause they too are following the Way of Harry,

13 And they didn't ask to be born a white racist,

14 Even if they'll concede that it's better than being born black,

15 But how does that matter if

a. *Wil.31.18-22*
b. *Mawr.14.14-18*
c. *Yks.20.25-33*
d. *Ned.29.19*
e. *15.3*
f. *Cen.11.32*
g. *9.3*
h. *Adam.28.18-22*
i. *7.2*
j. *6.7*
k. *17.9-10*
l. *14.4*
m. *Hall.8.7-11*
n. *Hall.2.7-8*

they weren't born rich enough to live in all-white neighborhoods their whole lives?

16 In short, they think things are tough all over,

17 And they'd like you to be happier,

18 If your being happier would make them feel safer,

19 And made you play your music at a lower volume.

CHAPTER 18

But how does all this make your life any easier?

2 ʰWhat good does it do to know that white people who talk about equality and stuff like that are all lying,

3 And really wish you would just go away,

4 And stop being so noisy,

5 And self-righteous,

6 And so, well, numerous?

7 The thing is, all this can make your life easier,

8 Because white people also don't want to think about anything at all,

9 Particularly things that make them feel ⁱconfused,

10 ʲAnd sort of guilty,

11 ᵏAnd sort of angry,

12 ˡAnd sort of tired too.

13 ᵐThat's why white people invented the federal government,

14 Which is supposed to care about the things they don't want to care about,

15 Or don't feel like caring about,

16 ⁿOr don't care about period.

17 When something is the government's responsibility,

18 It's not their responsibility anymore,

19 No matter what,

20 Because if the government screws up,

21 That's the way governments are,

22 And if the government does something good,

23 It's a [a]miracle.

24 [b]So for you, the Way of Harry is the way of demanding your rightful compensation from the government for all the things white people have done to you,

25 No matter what,

26 While all the white people don't think about it at all.

a. *Ed.60.17*
b. *Mawr.15.11-22*
c. *17.4*
d. *18.25*
e. *14.16*
f. *14.13-16*
g. *Mawr.8.6*
h. *8.11*
i. *Hall.13.1-6*
j. *Kens.30.9*
k. *Kens.30.10*
l. *Kens.30.11-15*
m. *Mawr.8.6*
n. *Mawr.20.19*

CHAPTER 19

The great thing about the federal government is that it's so full of well-educated white people,

2 [c]Who don't think you can compete either,

3 [d]And don't ever want to admit it,

4 Because it's pretty important to them to think they believe in equality,

5 [e]And how nobody is really any better than anyone else,

6 Because if some people *were* better,

7 Then maybe people like them would have a lot more responsibility to do something important and worthwhile with all their advantages,

8 Except that they'd rather work for the government instead.

9 That's why it makes them feel better to pretend that you'll be just as equal as everybody else when you finally get your rights,

10 Whatever they are,

11 Even if the only way you'll ever get anywhere at all,

12 The way they see it,

13 [f]Is for them to *give* you what you want without making you compete for it,

14 Somehow,

15 [g]Under the very noses of all the contemptible white people who don't like you.

16 This can be done, though,

17 Because absolutely no one in the Most Chosen Nation wants to talk out loud about the one thing that all white people [h]know,

18 Which is that you can't compete,

19 And don't seem to want to.

CHAPTER 20

In order to make the Way of Harry work for you,

2 [i]All you have to do is make sure all your leaders always look to the government first when your rights are on the line.

3 You will always be able to recognize leaders like this because they will be the ones who don't think about anything at all,

4 [j]Which means they will be exceptional at expressing their desires,

5 [k]Completely consistent about being dead certain,

6 [l]And always ready to blame someone or something else for whatever it is that's wrong.

CHAPTER 21

When you find a leader like this,

2 Follow him blindly,

3 [m]Wherever he takes you,

4 [n]And never doubt him,

5 Whatever he does,

6 Because your leader is your leader,

7 And it's his job to not think about anything at all in your place,

8 And it's your job to let the world know how much you support him,

9 ^aSo that *they*'ll do what he says,

10 Just like you,

11 Until he sets you free,

12 Or something like that.

CHAPTER 22

If he wants all the laws to be race-blind,

2 Support him and do what he says,

3 Without thinking about it at all.

4 ^bIf he wants the laws to stop being race-blind,

5 Support him and do what he says,

6 Without thinking about it at all.

7 If he wants to integrate everything in society,

8 Support him and do what he says,

9 Without thinking about it at all.

10 ^cIf he wants to make Broad Street into a separate society,

11 Support him and do what he says,

12 Without thinking about it at all.

13 ^dIf he wants to change the name everybody has to call you, say, once a year,

14 Support him and do what he says,

15 Without thinking about it at all.

16 ^eIf he wants to blame every bad thing that ever happened to a black person on racism,

17 Support him and do what he says,

18 Without thinking about it at all.

a. 18.25
b. Mawr.25.23
c. Yks.151.3
d. Ann.10.20-23
e. Mawr.30.18-20
f. 21.6-7
g. Hall.15.12-13
h. Hall.15.21-23
i. 17.4
j. 18.25
k. Hall.15.9-10
l. Yks.21.4-9
m. Yks.55.17-28

19 ^fIf he wants to be elected to high office,

20 Support him and do what he says,

21 Without thinking about it at all.

22 ^gIf he wants to be as corrupt as all the white people are,

23 Support him and do what he says,

24 Without thinking about it at all.

25 ^hIf he wants to get away with absolutely everything, no matter who gets hurt,

26 Support him and do what he says,

27 Without thinking about it at all,

28 ⁱBecause *all* the white people loathe and despise him,

29 Without exception,

30 ^jBut they know he speaks for every one of you,

31 And if you ever stopped supporting him,

32 They might stop thinking of you as a single unyielding knot of certainty and blame,

33 ^kAnd then the government wouldn't know who to give in to,

34 And you'd all be on your own.

CHAPTER 23

But if one of your leaders should ever start pointing the finger at you,

2 ^lAnd reminding you that your dead American ancestors did an awful lot to build America in the first place,

3 ^mAnd suggesting that you have it better than they did,

4 And maybe it's time to start getting some mileage out of the courage and perseverance and

dignity and brains you inherited from them,

5 Then it's time for you to be very very suspicious of that leader.

6 And if he should go on from there,

7 And start talking about self-reliance,

8 And helping each other,

9 [a]And other people too,

10 [b]Because the government can't do it all,

11 Then it's time to spit upon him, and revile him, and send him away,

12 Without thinking about it at all,

13 [c]Because it *isn't* time for the hard way,

14 And never will be again:

15 For if you choose the hard way,

16 Harry's Trinity won't help you,

17 At all,

18 [d]And you'd be on your own,

19 In a nation full of white people,

20 Who can't be trusted,

21 At all.

CHAPTER 24

Don't ever ever forget how much white people have done to you already,

2 Including even the ones who pretended to be your friend,

3 Like [e]Lincoln,

4 [f]Who wasn't really trying to give you your rights,

5 [g]But only to save the union,

6 Because slavery was a bone in the throat of the union,

7 And had to be cut out,

8 [h]Even if he had to free you to do it,

9 But that doesn't mean you've

Reference column:

a. 12.12
b. Hall.10.17-18
c. 12.8-9
d. 22.34
e. Dav.57.30
f. Yks.43.26-31
g. Yks.37.16
h. Yks.43.22-25
i. Forg.14.19-23
j. Forg.14.24-25
k. Kens.34.1-2
l. Hall.4.3
m. Ira.25.64
n. Mall.15.4-15
o. Wil.38.1-3
p. Wil.41.1-7
q. Hill.V.9-10

ever become part of the union,

10 No matter what anybody says,

11 Even if they've let you die for the union on half a dozen continents,

12 Because they don't like you,

13 No matter what you do,

14 And if they ever gave you a uniform, it was because they hoped you'd bring it back with a bullet hole in it,

15 Neatly wrapped inside a pine coffin,

16 With a flag on top,

17 Because when the Most Chosen Nation goes to war,

18 [i]It's easier to let the Least Chosen People fight it,

19 [j]If they're dumb enough to die for a flag.

CHAPTER 25

That's why the only white person you can trust is [k]Harry,

2 Because Harry is the only one who isn't lecturing you about personal [l]responsibility,

3 [m]Or telling you to get a job where there isn't one,

4 [n]Or telling you to get married before you have children in a country where it's illegal for thirteen-year-olds to get married,

5 [o]Or telling you to finish school in neighborhoods where school is the most dangerous place you can go,

6 [p]Or telling you to get off welfare when it's been a family tradition for three generations,

7 [q]Or telling you to stay non-violent about getting your rights at a time when a good riot with lots of looting and burning and vandalism is about the only time

you ever get to have any fun,

8 ªOr telling you to do anything at all,

9 Except what you feel like doing,

10 Whenever you feel like doing it,

11 No matter who gets hurt.

CHAPTER 26

For if Harry were here, he would say, "If it is your desire to hold up a liquor store,

2 "Do so,

3 ᵇ"For if it is your desire, it is your right.

4 "If you desire to mug travelers at the bus station,

5 "Do so,

6 ᶜ"For if you cannot be certain about your desires, what can you be certain about?

7 "If it is your desire to rape someone,

8 "Do so,

9 ᵈ"For it is always possible to blame someone else if you get caught.

10 "And if you desire to shoot up with heroin every day,

11 "Do so,

12 "But have you ever considered switching to Consolation?"

CHAPTER 27

Have you heard of Consolation?

2 Indeed, it is my pleasure to inform you that Consolation is the greatest of all the gifts that Harry can offer,

3 Including even his Trinity,

4 Because in spite of the power of Desire, Certainty, and Blame,

5 The Trinity cannot make you stop thinking about anything at all,

a. Cen.11.24-33
b. 14.1-6
c. Mawr.13.15-19
d. Mawr.16.7-8
e. Ext.13.8
f. Kens.36.1-5
g. Kens.36.6
h. Kens.35.8
i. Hill.N.1-3

6 With a single blast up the nose.

7 But ᵉConsolation can,

8 And it comes in a nice white powder,

9 Which requires no syringe,

10 And therefore leaves no unsightly tracks,

11 Which makes it practically perfect.

CHAPTER 28

What is more,

2 ᶠConsolation will be coming to Broad Street soon,

3 ᵍAt very competitive prices,

4 Which will keep getting more competitive,

5 As volume sales improve.

CHAPTER 29

Yes, you must try Harry's Consolation,

2 Which is the only thing you can ever expect to receive in complete honesty from a white person,

3 In the Most Chosen Nation on Earth.

4 You will love Consolation,

5 ʰBecause it makes *now* so very special,

6 ⁱWhich is the only time there is,

7 When you have nothing to look forward to,

8 At all.

CHAPTER 30

And there is no need whatever to be suspicious of Consolation,

2 Because it is not some racist trick,

3 Which you can prove absolutely to yourself,

4 [a]Because white people love it too,

5 [b]And it's already *every*where but here,

6 Which Harry will take care of,

7 As volume sales improve.

CHAPTER 31

Harry wants you to have his Consolation,

2 Because he knows about your pain,

3 And he knows that it's not your fault,

4 And that there's nothing you can do,

5 Because you didn't make this sick racist world,

6 And you deserve a break,

7 And Harry has the break you need,

a. Ext.17.8
b. Ext.31.11-12
c. Ext.14.7-9
d. Oth.8.18

8 [c]And calls it Consolation.

CHAPTER 32

Come to Harry.

2 Try his Consolation.

3 Feel his Consolation.

4 Love his Consolation.

5 Trust his Consolation,

6 Desire his Consolation,

7 For ever and ever and ever,

8 Because if you desire it,

9 It is your right to have it,

10 And Harry will see that you get it,

11 For ever and ever and ever,

12 Which is the most and the best you can ever expect,

13 From a white man,

14 In the Most Chosen Nation on Earth,

15 In the Last Days on Earth,

16 [d]For everyone.

THE RATIONALIZATIONS

OF

DAVID THE DAD

CHAPTER 1

It came to pass that Harry had to put his [a]dad in a home,

2 Which he did without a thought,

3 And the fewest possible words,

4 [b]These being, **There's no fool like an old fool,**

5 **Especially one that can't keep his mouth shut.**

6 And so the old fool was sent to Happy Acres to [c]plumb the

a. Wil.2.1-6
b. Psay.5A.11
c. Ann.2.32
d. Vin.16.6

depths of his senility,

7 And true to the Word of Harry, he talked and talked and talked,

8 Until the day the orderly gave him too many [d]sedatives by accident,

9 Which was communicated to Harry by phone, causing him to exclaim, **Truly my prayers for peace on earth have been answered at last,**

10 **And I am now well content.**

11 But the Dad of Harry had bequeathed him one last present,
12 Which was mailed to him in ªRio,
13 Being the last cassette of the father,
14 And so gave Harry the final thoughts of an old fool,
15 Looking into the face of death,
16 Near the end of the twentieth century,
17 Which made Harry laugh pretty loudly and uproariously,
18 And is why he sought to share them with all Harriers everywhere.

CHAPTER 2

The Words of the Dad of Harry, uttered in the home to which he was committed in the depths of his senility:
2 There was, I remember, a dream called America,
3 Where some ancient men wearing funny hats believed in an idea called liberty,
4 And tried to turn that idea into reality,
5 Which seemed to be working,
6 The way I remember it,
7 For quite a while,
8 Until somebody discovered that it really wasn't,
9 For some reason,
10 And that everything ever done in America was wrong,
11 For some reason,
12 ᵇAnd the dream started to go away.

CHAPTER 3

Now I have become an old man,

---

a. Vin.75.13-14
b. Wil.5.8
c. 1.1
d. Yks.106.1-8
e. Nips.21.4-10
f. 10.9
10.21

---

2 And my memory can't be trusted,
3 ᶜOr why would my sons have put me here,
4 And stopped visiting me,
5 And stopped caring about me,
6 At all?
7 It must be that the way I remember things is all wrong,
8 Because I was never smart enough to hate America,
9 Or even the human race,
10 Because most of what I thought I knew about the human race I learned in America,
11 From Americans,
12 ᵈExcept for the war,
13 ᵉWhere I learned something about Japs,
14 Who I hated,
15 Because they were the enemy,
16 Although later on I kind of stopped hating them,
17 Because I knew some other Japs,
18 In America,
19 Which these other Japs loved too,
20 In spite of everything,
21 Just like me.

CHAPTER 4

Of course, I never say anything right,
2 As my sons used to tell me,
3 And even when I'm trying to be nice,
4 And truthful,
5 ᶠEveryone tells me I sound like a racist,
6 Which I don't see,
7 But that's understandable, I suppose,
8 Because I'm an American,
9 And everything I thought I knew must be lies,

10 Because everything I thought was so ain't so,
11 For some reason.

a. *Psay.5J.29*
b. *Vin.57.5*
c. *Ira.3.15-21*
d. *Wil.13.15-21*

24 Which I am about most things,
25 I guess.

CHAPTER 5

But the way I remember it,
2 There used to be a dream called America,
3 Where nothing and nobody was ever equal,
4 Except under the law,
5 Which wasn't perfect either,
6 But it gave everyone more of a chance than anyone else ever had,
7 If you wanted to take that chance,
8 And work hard to make something of it,
9 And maybe some people would help you,
10 And maybe they wouldn't,
11 But if you kept on trying,
12 And kept your self-respect,
13 Maybe enough people would come to respect you in time to make it worth your while,
14 And if they didn't ever respect you,
15 Maybe they'd respect your sons,
16 Or even your daughters,
17 Because girls are people too,
18 Or at least I've always thought so,
19 And maybe even better than men when you come right down to it,
20 ᵃBecause even if they're silly and annoying sometimes,
21 They're kind and warm and loving,
22 And a lot of them are a lot smarter than most men I know,
23 Although I'm probably wrong,

CHAPTER 6

Anyway,
2 I sometimes wish I'd had daughters instead of sons,
3 Because it always seemed like daughters loved their fathers,
4 In the old days, anyhow,
5 ᵇAnd I don't think my sons ever really loved me,
6 Or at least not very much,
7 Because they never really seemed to care what I thought,
8 About anything,
9 Even though I was doing the best I could,
10 Most of the time.

CHAPTER 7

I'm not saying I never made any mistakes,
2 Because I know I did,
3 And there were times when I didn't pay enough attention,
4 ᶜAnd didn't jerk them up short when they needed it,
5 Because I thought they'd grow out of it or something,
6 Which they never did,
7 And I know for a fact,
8 Or at least I think I do,
9 ᵈThat I gave them too much freedom,
10 Which isn't quite the same thing as liberty,
11 As my father used to say,
12 But he was probably wrong too,
13 Because he taught me a lot of things,
14 Things that just ain't so,
15 I guess.

CHAPTER 8

But it always seemed to me that my father knew a lot,

2 Even though he went through most of the depression without a dime in his pocket,

3 And never did turn out to be a real big success,

4 Except that I loved him,

5 And wanted him to be proud of me,

6 Because I always thought that if he were proud of me,

7 I would really be something.

8 As it turned out, though, I must not have been something,

9 Because my sons never cared if I was proud of them,

10 And I guess maybe I never really was,

11 Since they always had it pretty easy,

12 And the first time things started to get tough,

13 ^aThey quit cold,

14 Just like that.

CHAPTER 9

I grew up on a farm,

2 And we got up early,

3 And milked the ^bcows,

4 And I usually walked to school,

5 And all the other clichés everyone laughs at,

6 Because they're the things fathers say,

7 Or used to,

8 In my generation,

9 Which isn't that much of a coincidence,

10 Because it was mostly true,

11 And it's how we got all our wrong ideas,

12 Or at least that's how I think it happened.

13 You see,

a. Ira.8.1-11
b. Psay.5F.1-28
c. Psay.5O.13
d. Psay.5A.14
e. Psay.5V.13
f. 9.33

14 And I know you're too young to remember this,

15 Your country used to be *the* country,

16 The land where you were born,

17 And spent most of your life on,

18 Without moving anywhere,

19 And so you loved it a lot,

20 Because your country was the hill where the sun came up,

21 Every day,

22 And the ^cwillow tree where Dad hung your swing,

23 And the dirt lanes where you rode your bike,

24 And the millpond where you fished for sunnies,

25 And the orchards that grew the ^dapples you ate in pies,

26 And the fields that grew the tomatoes you picked for dinner,

27 And you loved it,

28 More than anything,

29 Because that's where you came from,

30 And that's what fed you,

31 And entertained you,

32 And where they would bury you,

33 When the time came.

CHAPTER 10

My father thought you should be willing to do anything at all for your country,

2 Because that's where you came from,

3 And where your family came from and your friends too,

4 And where all of you were going,

5 ^fWhen the time came.

6 And so I thought that too,

7 Which is probably where I went so wrong about America,

8 Because I was willing to kill

all the Japanese in the world for my country,

9 [a]Which I never thought of as a bunch of greedy white men killing Indians and negroes and gooks and all that,

10 Because what I thought of instead was my country,

11 And the hills and willows and millponds,

12 And the others like me who lived there,

13 And the others like me who loved their country,

14 Which was maybe desert or mountains or prairies or beaches or small towns or even cities,

15 But who were like me anyway,

16 Because they were willing to let me live my life in my country,

17 And try not to get in my way,

18 [b]If I tried not to get in theirs,

19 Except that I guess a lot of us were getting in some other people's way,

20 Including black folks,

21 [c]Which I had only thought of as old Ben who delivered the wood and made wreaths at Christmas time,

22 And never thought for even a second that it was strange he never once came to dinner,

23 Although it seems to me that he never thought it was strange either,

24 But just the way things were,

25 Which must be wrong,

26 Or why did so many people of Ben's race get so fired up about riding in the front of the bus?

CHAPTER 11

I'm just an old man,

a. 4.5
b. Psay.5Q.31
c. 4.5
d. Swar.35.10-13
e. Vin.71.24
f. Adam.46.4
g. Adam.31.2-5
h. Yks.73.2-14
i. Chr.3.18-21
j. Al.4.16

2 And I've been wrong about a lot of things in my life,

3 So it shouldn't surprise me that I missed so much,

4 But I guess I did,

5 And I wish someone had set me straight sooner,

6 Because I still can't seem to figure it all out,

7 [d]And I still don't know why all the smart people look at things the way they do,

8 And why we can't just learn about our mistakes as we go,

9 And fix them up as best we can,

10 And keep going,

11 Until someday things are a lot better than they ever were,

12 Which is sort of what I always thought history was about,

13 [e]Because when I used to read about the past in school,

14 It seemed like my life was a lot better,

15 And people were better nowadays than they used to be,

16 Or if not better, smarter,

17 [f]Like with medicine,

18 [g]And tractors and cars and such,

19 [h]And electricity,

20 And the American Way,

21 Because they didn't used to be able to vote kings and emperors out of office when they turned out to be no good,

22 And when kings and emperors weren't any good,

23 [i]It seemed like they could get away with a lot more than even Roosevelt ever did,

24 But what do I know,

25 [j]And who am I to say,

26 But an old man,

27 With a bad memory,

28 That's full of lies anyway.

CHAPTER 12

^a**M**y mother used to make us kids go to church,

2 And it seemed to me that even God was getting better all the time,

3 Just like the world,

4 ^bBecause the Old God got so mad about the apple,

5 ^cAnd killed everybody but Noah in the flood,

6 ^dAnd wanted Abraham to kill his son Isaac,

7 Which scared me a lot at the time,

8 Until I asked my father about it,

9 And he said that God wasn't like that anymore,

10 ^eBecause he had a son of his own now,

11 And knew better,

12 Which made me feel better,

13 And I thanked Jesus for having been born,

14 And I just never connected Him with all the trouble the Catholics got into with the ^fInquisition,

15 Because that was back in the Middle Ages,

16 Before there was an America,

17 ^gWhere it was okay to have differences of opinion,

18 Without burning each other to death.

CHAPTER 13

Maybe that's why I never understood it when my sons kind of blamed me and my generation for the ^hKlan,

2 And all the racism and so forth,

3 Because I never once burned a cross,

a. *Psay.5V.7*
b. *Lies.2.17-24*
c. *Lies.5.7-10*
d. *Lies.3.4-5*
e. *Rom.21.10*
f. *Spic.7.10-15*
g. *Yks.57.12-13*
h. *Dav.2.4*
i. *Yks.53.10-13*
j. *Yks.37.1-17*

4 And was always very respectful to it instead,

5 Since it was in church,

6 And you had to be respectful in church,

7 Because Mrs. Anthrax would rap your knuckles in Sunday school if you weren't,

8 Which hurt a lot,

9 So you learned to behave whether you wanted to or not,

10 And besides, church was God's house,

11 ⁱJust like America was His country,

12 Where all of us thought we were getting better at getting it right,

13 The way He wanted it,

14 ^jBecause nobody else had Abraham Lincoln,

15 Who was kind of God's nephew the way I thought of it,

16 Which was all wrong, of course,

17 But it made me think sometimes when I was doing wrong, what would Abraham Lincoln say if he could see me now,

18 Which was easier than thinking about Jesus,

19 Because Jesus was on the cross,

20 And Lincoln was on the penny,

21 And closer somehow.

CHAPTER 14

And it's a funny thing, but I didn't think about Lincoln for years,

2 Maybe because it's harder to think about great men as you get older,

3 Since life teaches you that it isn't easy to be great,

4 And you're probably not going to make it,

5 And so maybe they didn't really make it either,

6 And were really like the rest of us instead,

7 [a]Except maybe they had a better press agent or something.

8 Only, I've been thinking about Lincoln a lot,

9 Ever since they put me in here,

10 And I keep seeing this picture of him in my head,

11 [b]Which maybe has to do with all the pills they give me,

12 Because I see other things I shouldn't too,

13 Which kind of scares me,

14 And so I think about Lincoln instead,

15 With his beard,

16 And his ugly beat-up face,

17 And those eyes.

CHAPTER 15

In a way, it's like coming back at something you've seen a million times,

2 Only from a completely different direction,

3 Which makes it all look different,

4 Completely,

5 Because I'm an old man now,

6 [c]And I've gotten older than Lincoln ever had a chance to get,

7 And so I know those eyes of his aren't about being older,

8 Which maybe I used to think when I was a kid,

9 Because my eyes aren't like that—

10 In spite of all the trouble and pain I've ever experienced,

11 And all the things I've ever worried about,

12 And all the ideas and causes I've ever believed in,

a. Swar. 18.16
b. 1.8
c. Psom. 68.1-2
d. Jeff. 13.2-7
e. 1.8
f. Jeff. 21.1-14
g. Psom. 75.1-11
h. 14.11 .

13 My eyes don't see what Lincoln's saw,

14 And I just can't ever get to the end of who he must have been,

15 Which makes me feel better somehow.

CHAPTER 16

And even though I'm kind of embarrassed to admit it,

2 I've been thinking about Jesus a lot too,

3 Which I never thought I'd do,

4 Because he's gotten kind of paler over the years,

5 [d]Like he's gradually fading from the scene somehow,

6 Just like me,

7 And you only hear his name when an [e]orderly stubs a toe on the food cart,

8 [f]Or when someone switches the TV on on a Sunday morning,

9 Which some of the other antiques seem to enjoy,

10 But doesn't really have anything to do with my memories,

11 Which have to do with the smell of honeysuckle drifting into the smell of velvet and wax through an open stained-glass window,

12 [g]While the choir sings something,

13 Maybe not completely on key,

14 But beautiful anyway,

15 Because Jesus was listening,

16 And understood how it was.

CHAPTER 17

God, it frightens me to sit here talking about Jesus,

2 Knowing how it must sound,

3 [h]And knowing I'm all full of pills,

4 And probably look exactly

like all the other gray, shriveled vegetables they've got planted on couches and chairs in this linoleum waiting room where they send you to die,

5 Because I don't want it to be over,

6 And I don't want to go out mumbling like some drunk who never saw the bus that hit him,

7 But I find myself saying his name,

8 Wondering what he would say if he were here and could see us all withering to dust inside our clothes.

9 ᵃHe was thirty-three,

10 But when I see him, I know I'm seeing Lincoln instead,

11 Dressed in a robe and sandals,

12 ᵇBut still with that beard,

13 ᶜAnd those eyes.

14 What would he say?

CHAPTER 18

They say that Lincoln's voice was high and slow,

2 With a country flavor,

3 And so pardon me, that's how Jesus sounds to me,

4 ᵈSpeaking softly in our waiting room,

5 Answering the questions we've forgotten how to ask,

6 And I listen as hard as I can,

7 Even though I know he can't be there, and I'm listening to ᵉchemicals in my own failing brain,

8 But I want to hear him anyway, telling us all that death isn't what we think it is,

9 ᶠAnd we shouldn't be afraid,

10 Because nothing really goes back to nothing, ever,

11 And nothing is ever really lost at all,

a. Psay.5Y.43
b. 14.15
c. 14.17
d. 17.4
e. Wil.16.20
f. Al.5.3-10
g. Chuk.19.15-17
h. Vin.64.9-11

12 ᵍAnd our lives aren't really over,

13 And we haven't really lost our home,

14 And everything we love will really keep on going,

15 No matter what,

16 Because nothing really goes back to nothing, ever.

CHAPTER 19

And then he looks right at me,

2 And I can see that all of everything is in his eyes,

3 Including the principle of union,

4 And the bone-deep scars of the slaves,

5 And the acrid embers of Atlanta,

6 And the amputation tent at Antietam,

7 And the rape and ruin of a million homes,

8 And children dying of hunger and typhoid and loneliness,

9 And all of it could be avoided if he would put aside the principle,

10 And admit that no idea can ever be worth all this,

11 Because no idea can justify an inquisition,

12 Or the burning of a heretic,

13 Or the madness of religious guilt and the devouring fear of sin,

14 ʰAnd all the rest of what flows from the wounds of a single man nailed to a cross in the desert.

CHAPTER 20

But all of everything is in his eyes,

2 And the principle is there too,

3 And he will not cast it down,

4 Not now,

5 Not ever,

6 But clothes himself in it like a flag,

7 Because he knows something I once knew,

8 But have forgotten,

9 Or never learned right in the first place,

10 If only I could remember what it was.

CHAPTER 21

^aThere are holes in his hands.

2 He holds them out to me,

3 Lets me take the long cold Lincoln fingers of a murdered son of God,

4 And then he grips my hand, so that I can feel my bones crack in his clasp,

5 And he says, "It is simpler than you think,

6 "And bigger too,

7 ^b"And life is not a frail thing that disappears in a puff of fear,

8 "But far stronger than you know,

9 "And though it knows its time,

10 "It is never imprisoned by it,

11 "Never done in by it against its will,

12 "Because the weakest something is stronger than the strongest nothing,

13 ^c"And nothing never wins."

CHAPTER 22

Not Jesus, not Lincoln, but ^dchemicals,

2 And still I listen,

3 Because I do not want to die of fear and a broken heart,

4 In the midst of all this crucifying loneliness,

5 Surrounded by the drugged and dead and dying,

a. Vin.55.3-4
b. Jefs.7.26-31
c. Psp.3.15
d. 18.7
e. Mall.6.24
f. 13.20
g. Dav.23.1-9
h. Dav.23.41-42
i. Psom.40.3
j. Psom.46.1
k. Psp.3.13
l. Yks.153.14
m. Psp.3.16
n. Psom.47.6
o. Psp.3.17

6 Who have forgotten how to live,

7 ^eAnd so I nod my head at hallucinations,

8 And I ask this Jesus Lincoln or Abraham Christ who holds my hand for understanding of what has been and what will come,

9 ^fAnd he shines at me like a new penny,

10 Glowing brighter than the chrome legs of a gurney,

11 Until even the linoleum floor is ablaze with light,

12 And I see inside it a vision such as I have never seen before,

13 And never will again.

CHAPTER 23

It is almost a scene from a ^gJohn Ford western,

2 ^hAnd the cavalry is pinned down in Monument Valley,

3 ⁱAnd the colors are being shot full of holes,

4 And a woman with red hair is in the thick of the fighting,

5 ^jArmed and bloodied and beautiful,

6 Chanting "Rally to me" in a high clear voice,

7 But the troops are too frightened to listen,

8 Because the enemy isn't Indians this time,

9 ^kBut Angels on black horses,

10 Angels without mercy.

11 ^lAnd then I hear a long wailing cry,

12 ^mAnd a plume of dust is making tracks in the distance,

13 ⁿAnd from the dust itself rise new Angels, red-winged warriors who fly into battle with a furious savagery that is beyond belief,

14 ^oUntil the dark attacking An-

gels are vanquished and destroyed,

15 And the colors are hoisted on a brand-new spar,

16 And I can hear the Battle Hymn of the Republic playing like mad,

17 And I see the translucent face of ^aLincoln smiling gravely on the scene,

18 ^bAnd the Liberty Bell is ringing once again in Independence Square,

19 And all is well from sea to shining sea,

20 In the land of the free,

21 ^cAnd the home of the brave.

CHAPTER 24

And so, you see, I am nothing but an old doddering fool,

2 And I see things,

3 And I think constantly of my childhood,

4 Because I have failed at all the things that mattered since childhood,

5 Including the raising of my sons,

6 Who never come to visit,

7 Because there is nothing left to say.

8 ^dAnd if they didn't give me sedatives, I would probably rant and rave to everyone,

9 And talk about how it used to be,

10 When everything was great and perfect and wonderful,

11 Even though it never was,

12 Because what do I know,

13 And what have I ever done with my life,

14 Except kill ^eJaps in the South Pacific,

15 And struggle to make a decent living,

a. Dav.14.9
b. Vin.38.9-10
c. Psom.73.12
d. 17.3
e. Dav.34.19
f. Psom.13.1

16 And bungle my duties as a father,

17 And lose, too soon, the one I loved the most?

CHAPTER 25

My wife.

2 When I first wake up each day, I think of her,

3 The warmth and comfort that is not beside me in my bed,

4 Because she died,

5 Long ago,

6 And I never even told her how much I loved her.

7 But I tell her now,

8 Every day when I wake up,

9 Because I want her to know,

10 And maybe I hope that the pills will bring her too one day, if I can say it often enough,

11 So that I could tell her all the things I would do different if only I could,

12 Starting with her,

13 Because I never told her about the line of her cheek against the pillow,

14 And the soft brush of her eyelashes against her cheek,

15 So that it seems a sin to wake her,

16 Though I always did,

17 And would again,

18 Because I want to see her so.

CHAPTER 26

She always knew better than me,

2 And she never wanted to move to Philadelphia,

3 Because she was from the country too,

4 But she wanted me to be happy,

5 And I wanted to be a success,

6 ^fWhich is pretty much of a

meaningless word in a world of millponds and mourning doves,

7 And so we left our home for the city,

8 And she had our first son all alone in the hospital,

9 While I waited for orders in the South Pacific,

10 While the world itself changed into something else,

11 In the melting of an eye.

a. Psay.5V.1-27
b. Cen.16.1
c. Psp.1.4

CHAPTER 27

But I never figured it out,

2 Just like everything else,

3 And I came home to make everything fine again,

4 And I ran in the rat race,

5 And I thought I knew up from down,

6 And back from front,

7 And right from wrong,

8 And I was an idiot,

9 [a]Because it doesn't matter if you know up from down and right from wrong if you don't know why.

CHAPTER 28

I took out the trash,

2 And I mowed the lawn,

3 And I painted the house,

4 And I paid the bills,

5 And I went to work, sick or well,

6 And I shaved every day, even on weekends,

7 And I taught my boys how to throw a football and a baseball,

8 And that's the only thing they learned from me,

9 Because I had everything wrong,

10 From the very beginning,

11 And somehow they always knew,

12 And never forgave me.

CHAPTER 29

But do I deserve this,

2 To be alone,

3 Without my wife,

4 [b]Pilled to the gills in a gray linoleum box?

5 Maybe so.

6 Maybe there is a kind of justice after all,

7 A last chance to reflect,

8 Leading to one final moment of recognition,

9 And if I can earn that moment,

10 Maybe I'll get to see her again before I die,

11 Which would be paradise for all eternity,

12 And the answer to all my prayers,

13 And worth everything I have ever suffered or endured,

14 All of it,

15 Even though I had a son named [c]Harry.

THE BOOK OF HARRIER BRAYER

and Administration of the
Rites and Ceremonies
of the Chosen

ACCORDING TO THE USE OF THE
PONTIFICAL HARRIER PARISH
IN THE UNITED STATES OF AMERICA

TOGETHER WITH THE HARRIER HYMNAL

TABLE OF CONTENTS

SIGNS AND SYMBOLS
OF THE
PONTIFICAL HARRIER PARISH

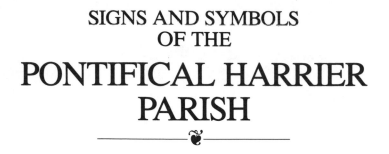

THE SIGN OF HARRY

THE SYMBOLS OF CONSOLATION

The Blade

The Snowflake

The Spoon

The Mirror

The "C" Note

THE SYMBOLS OF THE WAY

The Sign of
Harry's Trinity

The Sign of
Beans

The Sign of
Harry

The Sign of the
"Most Chosen Nation"

SYMBOLIC CONVENTIONS FOR HARRIER VESTMENTS

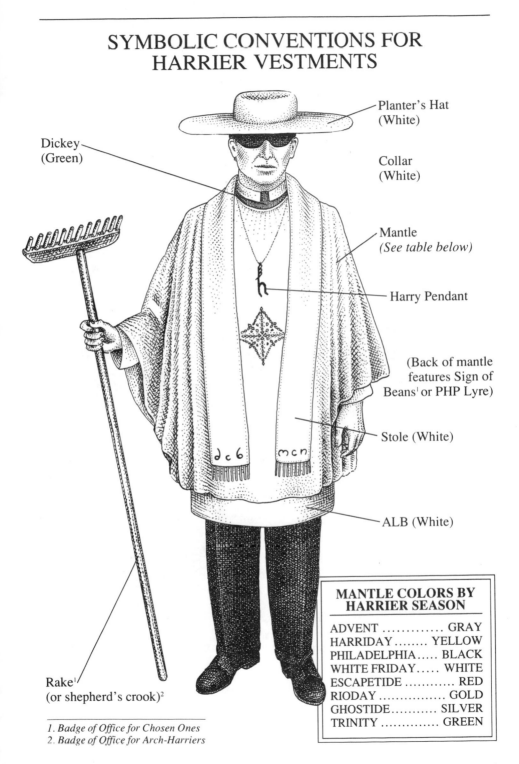

Planter's Hat
(White)

Dickey
(Green)

Collar
(White)

Mantle
(*See table below*)

Harry Pendant

(Back of mantle
features Sign of
Beans[1] or PHP Lyre)

Stole (White)

ALB (White)

Rake[1]
(or shepherd's crook)[2]

1. Badge of Office for Chosen Ones
2. Badge of Office for Arch-Harriers

MANTLE COLORS BY HARRIER SEASON	
ADVENT	GRAY
HARRIDAY	YELLOW
PHILADELPHIA	BLACK
WHITE FRIDAY	WHITE
ESCAPETIDE	RED
RIODAY	GOLD
GHOSTIDE	SILVER
TRINITY	GREEN

TABLE OF HARRIER DAYS

TOGETHER WITH

APPOINTED HARRIER TEXTS

FOR USE IN

ORDERS OF SERVICE

TABLE OF HARRIER DAYS

No.	Friday	Topic	Psongs
1	1st in Advent	World War I	XXXIV
2	2nd in Advent	1920s	XXII, XXVIII
3	3rd in Advent	Depression	XXXII, XLII, XXIX, XXXI
4	4th in Advent	World War II	LXVII
5	Harriday	Birth of Harry	XXXVIII
6	1st after Harriday	Harry's Childhood	XXXIII, XXXIX, XL
7	2nd after Harriday	Harry's Early Career	XXI
8	3rd after Harriday	Pontification on the Mount	XLVIII, L, VI, XVIII, XLIII
9	4th after Harriday	The End of the "Revolution"	LV, LVI
10	5th after Harriday	The Followers	VIII, X
11	Pretzel Friday	Entrance in Philadelphia	XLVII, LIII
12	2nd in Philly	City Hall	XVI
13	3rd in Philly	Spreading the Word	III, XII
14	4th in Philly	Christianity	X, XXXVI, LXII
15	5th in Philly	Harry's Jokes	XXVII, XXVI, XXIV, XXV
16	6th in Philly	Countdown to Consolation	XVIII, XIX
17	White Friday	Consolation and Arrest	LVII, LXVI, LVIII, LIX, LXIV
18	Escapetide	Escape from Prison	XXXVII, LVI
19	Rioday	The Call from Rio	XXIV, XXV, XL
20	Ghostide	The Silver Ghosts	LIII, XLIII, XLI
21	Trinity	The Zero	XIII, XIV
22	1st after Trinity	The Ace	XXIII
23	2nd after Trinity	The Crusader	LXII
24	3rd after Trinity	The Hedonist	XLVI
25	4th after Trinity	The Plutocrat	XLIV, XX, X
26	5th after Trinity	The Establishment	XVIII, LIX

AND APPOINTED TEXTS

| Morning Brayer | | Evening Brayer | | Consolation | |
1st L.	2nd L.	1st L.	2nd L.	Good Word	Letter
Krt.22 & 23	Ned.20.1-27	Brit.48-49	Ira.34	Wil.21	Forg.5 & 6
Yks.89-90	Mall.9	Frog.35	Swar.23	Vin.15	Wht.8
Yks.96-97	Rat.9	Brit.50	Rat.5	Vin.48.1-18	Hall.8
Yks.110-111	Kens.22.1-15	Krt.33-34	Rat.10.1-18	Wil.8	Rat.3
Nips.24	Rat.26-28	Jeff.24	Ned.1-3	Wil.1-2	Boul.3-4
Psay.2	Wil.3	Ed.70	Ira.2-3	Vin.7-9	Hill.R
Pnot.52	Ira.10	Dav.50	Ira.11	Ira.12	Mall.14
Psp.3.1-16	Wil.4	Dav.57	Wil.5-6.1-5	Wil.25-26	Hill.G
Ed.22 & 23	Wil.44	Dav.56	Vin.21-23	Vin.30	Mall.10
Psay.5G.18-19	Wil.47	Rom.20	Vin.32-33	Ira.15-16	Kens.18-19
Yks.11	Vin.42-44	Yks.12	Wil.64	Ned.26-27	Forg.4
Psay.5J	Kens.25	Lies.7	Wil.52-53	Ira.21	Cen.8-9
Psom.23.1-3	Wil.66	Yks.73	Vin.47	Ned.28-29	Main.25
Dav.15	Vin.59-60	Jeff.20-22	Vin.63	Vin.64-65	Boul.27-28
Pnot.13	Vin.51	Pnot.22	Ira.32	Ira.31	Wht.28
Psom.58	Ira.37	Pnot.31	Wil.68-69	Vin.70	Mawr.10
Psom.66	Ira.42	F&J.13	Ned.44-46	Wil.70-73	Wht.29
Pnot.37	Ned.50-53	Psom.26	Ira.45	Wil.75-76	Hill.J
Psom.45	Vin.75	Pnot.34	Ira.46	Wil.77	Wht.39
Chuk.21-23	Ira.30	Gnt.11.1-10	Ext.16	Ext.17-18	Brd.32
Pnot.55	Wil.45.1-12	F&J.5	Brd.3-5	Vin.13-14	Kens.5-7
Dav.54	Kens.37-39	Ed.66	Boul.25	Vin.72-73	Main.1-3
Chr.8	Kens.26	Bks.4	Wil.49-50	Ned.34	Mawr.31
Pnot.28	Ira.14	Psom.56	Mawr.2	Wil.48	Mawr.12
Adam.25	Main.27	Jeff.9	Vin.49	Ira.24.1-14	Main.36-37
Adam.20	Wht.23	Carl.10	Main.28	Wil.39-40	Hall.10

TABLE OF HARRIER DAYS

No.	Friday	Topic	Psongs
27	6th after Trinity	The Relationship	LXII, XXVI, XXVII, LI, LXIX
28	7th after Trinity	Power	XLV, LIII, XLIII
29	8th after Trinity	Blame	XXXIX, LVII, XIX
30	9th after Trinity	The Self	LXVI, I, XV, XXIII, XVI
31	10th after Trinity	The Game	XXI
32	11th after Trinity	Certainty	XXIII, XXXVII
33	12th after Trinity	The Loser	XI, IV, XXX, XXXI
34	13th after Trinity	The Big One	XXIX, LXIV, LIX
35	14th after Trinity	Desire	XX, V, VII, XII
36	15th after Trinity	The Winner	IX
37	16th after Trinity	Responsibility	XXXV, XXXIV, XXXIII, XXXVI
38	17th after Trinity	Accountability	XXXIX, LVIII, LX
39	18th after Trinity	The Setback	L, XXXII, III, XIX, XVII
40	19th after Trinity	Success	XXVII
41	20th after Trinity	The Future	XLVII
42	21st after Trinity	El Dorado	LXI, XXII
43	Ult. Vinnie Day	Music	LXIX
44	Ult. Ned Day	Numbers	X
45	Ult. Ira Day	Visual Arts	LI
46	Ult. Willie Day	Words	LIV
47	All Harriers Day	Celebration	XLIII
48	5th before Advent	Creation	LXI
49	4th before Advent	Man	LVII
50	3rd before Advent	Gods	VIII
51	2nd before Advent	Civilization	XXIV, XXV, XXVI
52	1st before Advent	History	VI

AND APPOINTED TEXTS

Morning Brayer		Evening Brayer		Consolation	
1st L.	2nd L.	1st L.	2nd L.	Good Word	Letter
Pnot.49	Mall.15	Pnot.23	Rat.25	Ira.35-36	Mawr.30
Rom.3	Ext.37	Chr.6	Ext.47	Ned.30	Main.33-35
Frog.79	Ned.32	Yks.52-53	Ned.34	Wil.34	Mawr.15
Chuk.19	Ned.12	Zig.17-18	Vin.61-62	Wil.37	Mall.8
Yks.142	Ned.19	Adam.14	Drex.6	Ned.35	Ann.12
Ed.23-24	Ira.25	Jeff.5-7	Boul.24	Wil.33	Boul.20
Lies.12-13	Ext.48	Oth.2	Swar.5	Vin.59	Ext.7-9
Al.6	Mawr.5	Oth.9	Kens.28	Ned.16	Hill.Z
Brit.30	Swar.1,2.1-7	Zig.6-8	Ext.43	Wil.32	Brd.14
Rom.12	Ext.44	Yks.120	Drex.9	Wil.78	Ext.11
Brit.19	Main.18-19	Psay.5V	Wht.27	Wil.31	Mall.9
Krt.27	Ned.54	Yks.151	Ira.43	Ned.47	Ext.48
Dav.2	Ext.45	Gnt.13.1-8	Ext.40	Ned.36	Ext.49
Adam.35-36	Main.21	Yks.145	Ext.26	Vin.20	Ext.41
Russ.26	Ned.20	Yks.154	Rat.18	Ned.17	Hill.N
Spic.17	Ira.37	Adam.47-48	Mall.16	Wil.29-30	Wht.32
Russ.13	Ext.42	Brit.58	Vin.4-6	Ira.13	Hill.M
Grk.14	Drex.4	Chuk.20	Drex.3	Ned.7-9	Drex.7-8
Dav.3	Ann.19	Ed.10	Ann.2	Ned.24	Ann.6
Gnt.15	Swar.32	F&J.2-3	Swar.18	Wil.36	Swar.17
Psom.78	Ext.3	Psom.28	Ext.20	Ned.14	Ext.38
Lies.2	Boul.14-15	Chuk.9-11	Ira.4	Vin.1	Boul.13
Apes.2 & 4	Mawr.24	Chuk.15	Mawr.25	Ira.23	Mawr.22
Gods.3-4	Ned.5-6	Chuk.17	Ira.1	Vin.55-56	Boul.18
Lies.7	Drex.5	Krt.6	Main.30	Wil.20	Mawr.23
Grk.19-21	Swar.27	Gnt.16	Hill.O	Wil.27	Swar.10

HARRIER ORDERS OF
SERVICE

THE ORDERS OF
MORNING AND EVENING
BRAYER

❦

together with

The Litany

Brayers and Platitudes

THE ORDER FOR
DAILY MORNING BRAYER

❦

¶ *The Chosen One shall begin the Morning Brayer by reading one or more of the following Sentences.*

Frère Jacques, frère Jacques, something something, something les matines, something les matines, ding dang dong, ding dang dong. *Psomethings* 31.1-6

I, Willie, had also done what I was supposed to do, and had hired a bunch of people to come up with a bunch of great-sounding words for Harriers to say, and all was in readiness for the establishment of the Pontifical Harrier Parish in the United States, including all the instructions and words for the Orders of Morning and Evening Brayer. *Exploits* 33.8-11.

It's the early bird that gets the worm. *Psayings* 5A.34

And so I say to you, come to Harry, and be the way you are, and stop thinking about it. *Boulevardiers* 27.1-4

Another thing Harry used to enjoy was getting up really early in the morning, and then going out to do something really silly, before anybody was completely awake, which made it easier to get away with something outlandish, and if he did, it put him in a great mood for the rest of the day. *Ira* 27.1-5

Advent	Someone will come, who can speak a language they understand, and they will listen to him, because he will understand them, and give them some solid practical advice, for once. *Jeffrey* 23.9-15

Harriday	For example, Harry would probably tell you that he is just an average guy, and no better than anyone else, except that he got born at exactly the right time, meaning the day that the world changed for the last time, and Harry

happened to notice it, because somebody had to, and why not him? *Vinnie* 7.1-7

Pretzel Friday	Then the followers did as Harry suggested, and they thought no more about it, at all, but waved to the hundreds of people who lined the streets of Philadelphia to greet Harry, and accepted their many gifts of pretzels and

beer, and other things, until the day seemed very bright indeed. *Ned* 26.1-7

And then Harry and many of his followers went out to tell the neighborhoods of Philadelphia about the Way of *Philadelphia* Harry, although some of the followers took Harry at his word, and stayed at the hotel, almost all the time, because the city was so awful. *Willie* 65.5-9

And it is also possible that some of the followers, or one or two of them anyway, were so drunk that they couldn't fol-*White Friday* low the conversation at dinner very well, until Harry did something with some white stuff, and made everyone else do it too, which really snapped everyone right into focus. *Vinnie* 67.1-6

The next news that came over the radio almost gave the followers a heart attack, because the announcer said that Harry *Escapetide* had escaped from prison. *Ned* 53.1-2

And besides, Harry never held anything against his followers, because he called them Long Distance, from Rio, and *Rioday* explained that he had made it all the way home to El Dorado, where everything was great, and life was perfect. *Vinnie* 75.9-14

One week later we gathered again, in the same place, at the same time, and waited for Harry to come through, which he *Ghostide* did, about the sixth hour. *Exploits* 6.3-8

The eleven went out into the wide world, in their Silver Ghosts, *Trinity Friday* armed with Harry's Trinity. *Exploits* 18.2-4

 Then the Chosen One shall say,

Duly befriended brethren and sistren, the Word of the Harriers moves us, in sundry places, to acknowledge that we shall pursue our desires on this day, with the full certainty that in so doing, we shall be acting in accordance with the Way of Harry; and that we shall do what we want to do, when we want to do it, no matter who gets hurt, as

Harry taught us to do, in his own words. Therefore, there is nothing that we will have to apologize for, or feel guilty about, or think about at all, when this day shall have reached its end; nevertheless, we do also acknowledge that those whom we may offend in the course of pursuing our desires, may seek to blame us and afflict us with a sense of guilt for our actions, according to their own purposes; for this reason, we now feel an urge to declare our utter certainty that nothing which we do on this day will be our fault; and to deny any wrongdoing or responsibility whatsoever, in these words—

¶ *Or he shall say,*

Let us adamantly deny responsibility for our deeds in this assembled company of Harriers.

A General Denial

High and Mighty Harry; We will be following your Way on this day, in blind obedience to the devices and desires of our own hearts. We may, from time to time, break sundry laws. We may leave undone those things which others will say we ought to have done; And we may do those things which others will say we ought not to have done. But that is the way we are, O Chief, and we know that none of these omissions and commissions can possibly be our fault, or our responsibility to correct or atone for, since we did not ask to be born, and we did not make the world, and we did not choose our parents or any other of the conditions into which we were born. Moreover, it is our absolute conviction that the world owes us a living, simply because we are here, whether we do any work or not, because we are citizens of the Most Chosen Nation on Earth; and therefore we deny the right of others to hold us responsible, or make us accountable, for anything, in any way, today or ever, according to the authority given us by your Name, Harry, First Babe of the Boom. *So there.*

The Declaration of Freedom, or Exemption from Responsibility.

¶ *To be made by the Chosen One alone, standing; the People milling about as they desire.*

All knowing Harry, the First Born After the Bomb and First Babe of the Boom, who desires his followers to not think about anything at all, no matter who gets hurt, has given authority, and precise wording, to his Chosen Ones to declare and pronounce to all Harriers, being certain of their desires, a Total Exemption from Responsibility for their actions. Further, he reaffirms the Freedom of all Harriers to do whatever they want, whenever they want to do it, and exhorts them to do so, no matter who gets hurt.

Wherefore let us remind ourselves, as he has taught us, that Harry showed us the Way to be, and remains the most shining example of the rewards to be gained from his wisdom.

¶ *Then the Chosen One shall kneel, and say the Harriers' Brayer; the People paying attention if they so desire, and even repeating it with him, if they are awake enough to do so.*

Our friend, who art in Rio, Harry is your name. Your time has come. Your way is fun, up north, as it is in Rio. We live for today and are rarely blamed. We forget our trespasses, as we forget those we have trespassed against. We yield to temptation, but are not evil. For thine is the wisdom, and the power, and the gold, for as long as it lasts. *So there.*

¶ *Then likewise he shall say,*

O Chief, read our lips.

Answer.   And you shall see us mouthing your own words of praise.

GOLD be to Harry in Rio, and up north bliss, our full fill of it, for as long as it lasts;

Answer.   As it was at the beginning of Harry's Way, is now, and ever shall be, until the end of the world to come. So there.

Chosen One. Praise be to the Chief.

Answer.   The Chief's Name be praised.

4

¶ *Then shall be said or sung the following Comicle.*

¶ *But* NOTE, *That on White Friday the Venite may be omitted.*

¶ *On the days hereafter named, immediately before the Venite may be sung or said,*

¶ *On the Fridays in Advent.* The First Born After the Bomb draws nigh; * O come let us fawn all over him.

¶ *On Harriday and until Pretzel Friday.* Harry Hooray. Unto us a Boom is born; * O come let us get in on the ground floor.

¶ *On Pretzel Friday and seven days after.* The Chief has returned to the place of his birth; * O come let us be seen with him.

¶ *On Saturday in Escapetide Week and until Rioday.* Harry Hooray. The Chief has blown the joint; * O come let us show him how we knew it all along. Harry Hooray.

¶ *On Rioday and until Ghostide.* Harry Hooray. The contrail of our Chief crosses the hemisphere; * O come let us hope he calls Long Distance from Rio. Harry Hooray.

¶ *On Trinity Friday.* Desire, Certainty, and Blame, what a combination! * O come let us start practicing right away.

Venite, fawnemus Domino

O come, let us say wonderful things about the Chief; * let us heartily rejoice in the benefits of our freedom.

Let us come before his presence with expensive presents; * and show him how much we really really care about him.

For the Chief is a famous celebrity; * and a man of wealth and taste.

In his hands are all the strings of earthly power; * and in his pocket are all the judges and politicians.

Even the sea is his if he wants it; * for his yacht cost more than a hundred million dollars.

O come, let us abase ourselves before him; * and nod vigorously at everything the Chief says.

For he is the Lord of the Boomers; * and we are the sheep of his ranch, and his for the shearing.

O make a gigantic show of devotion to him; * let everyone act as if he were just it.

For he is coming, he is coming to free us; * and without thinking about it at all, we will follow him to the end of the world to come.

¶ *Then shall follow a portion of the Psongs, according to the use of this Parish. And at the end of every Psong, and likewise at the end of the Venite and the Beniceto, may be, and at the end of the whole portion, or Selection from the Hymnal, shall be sung or said the following:*

GOLD be to Harry in Rio, and up north bliss, our full fill of it, for as long as it lasts;

Answer. As it was at the beginning of Harry's Way, is now, and ever shall be, until the end of the world to come. *So there.*

¶ *Then shall be read the First Lesson, according to the Table of Harrier Days. And NOTE, That before every Lesson, the Chosen One shall say,* Here begins *such a* Chapter (*or* Verse of *such a* Chapter) of *such a* Book; *and after every Lesson,* Here ends the First (*or* the Second) Lesson.

¶ *Here shall be sung or said the following Hymn.*

¶ *But NOTE, That on any day when Harry's Consolation is immediately to follow, the Chosen One at his discretion, after the following Comicle of Morning Brayer has been said or sung, may pass at once to the Consolation Service.*

Te Dominum idolemus.

We idolize you, O Harry; we acknowledge you as our One and Only Chief.

Everybody hangs on your every word, Friend everlasting.

Before you the Angels are respectful; and the Arch-Angels and Arch-Harriers too.

In your presence Bimbos melt, and Classy Babes stand up straighter.

Harry, Harry, Harry, Great King of the Boomers;

The Most Chosen Nation on Earth is full of praise for you.

The wealthiest of the Ultra-Harriers praise you without ceasing.

The brainiest of the VIPs probably would too if they were still around.

Even the Martyrs would have praised you if they had known what was good for them.

The Harrier Parish has come up with no end of laudatory titles for you:
The First Born After the Bomb;
The First Babe of the Boom;
The Great Giver of Silver Ghosts;
The Grantor of Consolation.

¶ *Or this Comicle.*

Beniceto Dominum

O you Chattels of the Chief, be nice to the Chief: * indulge him and flatter him till the end of the world to come.
O you Servants of the Chief, be nice to the Chief: * indulge him and flatter him till the end of the world to come.

you People of El Dorado, be nice to the Chief: * indulge him and flatter him till the end of the world to come.
O you Executive Assistants of the Chief, be nice to the Chief: * indulge him and flatter him till the end of the world to come.
O you Personal Bodyguards of the Chief, be nice to the Chief: * indulge him and flatter him till the end of the world to come.
O you Valets of the Chief, be nice to the Chief: * indulge him and flatter him till the end of the world to come.
O you Chefs of the Chief, be nice to the Chief: * indulge him and flatter him till the end of the world to come.
O you Masseurs of the Chief, be nice to the Chief: * indulge him and flatter him till the end of the world to come.
O you Personal Physicians of the Chief, be nice to the Chief: * indulge him and flatter him till the end of the world to come.
O you Concubines of the Chief, be nice to the Chief: * indulge him and flatter him till the end of the world to come.
O you Upstairs Maids of the Chief, be nice to the Chief: * indulge him and flatter him till the end of the world to come.
O you Kitchen Maids of the Chief, be nice to the Chief: * indulge him and flatter him till the end of the world to come.
O you Chauffeurs of the Chief, be nice to the Chief: * indulge him and flatter him till the end of the world to come.
O you Gardeners of the Chief, be nice to the Chief: * indulge him and flatter him till the end of the world to come.

O you Pilots of the Chief, be nice to the Chief: * indulge him and flatter him till the end of the world to come.

O you Ship's Captains of the Chief, be nice to the Chief: * indulge him and flatter him till the end of the world to come.

O you Dogs and Cats of the Chief, be nice to the Chief: * indulge him and flatter him till the end of the world to come.

O you Food Tasters of the Chief, be nice to the Chief: * indulge him and flatter him till the end of the world to come.

O you Dentists of the Chief, be nice to the Chief: * indulge him and flatter him till the end of the world to come.

O you Flunkies of the Chief, be nice to the Chief: * indulge him and flatter him till the end of the world to come.

O you People of Rio, be nice to the Chief: * indulge him and flatter him till the end of the world to come.

O you Tailors of Rio, be nice to the Chief: * indulge him and flatter him till the end of the world to come.

O you Waiters of Rio, be nice to the Chief: * indulge him and flatter him till the end of the world to come.

O you Retail Clerks of Rio, be nice to the Chief: * indulge him and flatter him till the end of the world to come.

O you Men's Room Attendants of Rio, be nice to the Chief: * indulge him and flatter him till the end of the world to come.

O you Doormen of Rio, be nice to the Chief: * indulge him and flatter him till the end of the world to come.

O you Courtesans of Rio, be nice to the Chief: * indulge him and flatter him till the end of the world to come.

O you Nightclub Performers of Rio, be nice to the Chief: * indulge him and flatter him till the end of the world to come.

O you Hatcheck Girls of Rio, be nice to the Chief: * indulge him and flatter him till the end of the world to come.

O you Miserable Street Trash of Rio, be nice to the Chief: * indulge him and flatter him till the end of the world to come.

O you People of the Most Chosen Nation, be nice to the Chief: * indulge him and flatter him till the end of the world to come.

O you Ultra-Harriers, be nice to the Chief: * indulge him and flatter him till the end of the world to come.

O you who hold the exalted position of Number One, be nice to the Chief: * indulge him and flatter him till the end of the world to come.

O you Vice-Presidents of the Pontifical Harrier Parish, be nice to the Chief: * indulge him and flatter him till the end of the world to come.

O you Arch-Harriers, be nice to the Chief: * indulge him and flatter him till the end of the world to come.

O you Arch-Angels, be nice to the Chief: * indulge him and flatter him till the end of the world to come.

O you Chosen Ones, be nice to the Chief: * indulge him and flatter him till the end of the world to come.

O you Angels, be nice to the Chief: * indulge him and flatter him till the end of the world to come.

O you Parish Beacons, be nice to the Chief: * indulge him and flatter him till the end of the world to come.

O you Parish Guards, be nice to the Chief: * indulge him and flatter him till the end of the world to come.

O you Harriers, be nice to the Chief: * indulge him and flatter him till the end of the world to come.

Let us be nice to Harry, First Born After the Bomb, First Babe of the Boom, First Man to Think about Nothing at all; * let us indulge him and flatter him and grovel at his feet till the end of the world to come.

¶ *Then shall be read, in like manner, the Second Lesson, taken out of the Present Testament, according to the Table of Harrier Days.*

¶ *And after that shall be sung or said the Hymn following.*

¶ *But* NOTE, *That, save on the Fridays in Advent, the latter portion thereof may be omitted.*

Dominus magnus. Ira 38.8-13

I think Harry's great; * he is bright and clever and lots of fun to be around.

I have never met anyone like him; * knowing him has caused me to look at life in a new way.

I miss him now that he is away; * I miss him more than I would ever have imagined.

I hope that his followers are loyal to him; * for Harry is too generous to believe that anyone would ever betray him.

I think that Harry could do great things with his life; * I know that his talents are exceptional and varied.

I know that Harry is very rich; * but I am confident that he knows better than to rest on past laurels.

¶ *Or this Psong.*

Laetus lucrae. Psong 1

Happy is the man who gets to walk around with a pocketful of cash; * all doors are always open to the rich man, and his smiles make everybody happy and helpful.

He hardly ever has to wait in line; * the barriers are removed as soon as he approaches.

Nor does he have to take a lot of guff; * when he reaches for his pocket, the whole world pays attention.

But things are very different for the poor man; * he is a walking victim, a piece of lint in the money pocket of life.

No one makes way for the poor man; * practically everyone is more important than he is, and better-looking too.

Therefore, choose carefully which of these to be; * a poor man may smile, but the landlord wants cash money.

¶ *Then shall be said the Ultra-Harriers' Creed by the Chosen One and the People, standing.*

I acknowledge Harry as the One: Who was the First Born After the Bomb, and the First Babe of the Boom: Who was betrayed by his pilot, was arrested, indicted, convicted, and sentenced to life in prison: He went down to Maximum Security; The third day he came out of prison: He flew to Rio, and settled in El Dorado: And there he shall live in luxury till the end of the world to come.

I acknowledge the gift of the Silver Ghosts: The Pontifical Harrier Parish; The Rites of Harry's Consolation: The Exemption from Responsibility: The Trinity of Harry: And the Way of the One, for as long as it lasts. *So there.*

¶ *Or the creed commonly called the Harriers' Creed.*

I don't think about the Big Bang, or the law of Evolution, which resulted in all things, completely at random: Or about Harry, the first born after the Bomb, who evolved into being near the end of the world, the Chosen One of a Chosen Nation, the Beacon of Beacons, the Most Chosen of the Most Chosen; Forgotten by most, though his substance remains, and still shapes all things: Who for our well-being came down from his Learjet, and rode among us in a Silver Cloud, and showed us the Way; And was sent to prison for life because of his pilot; He was wrapped in chains and buried in a cell block: And the third day, he escaped, according to the Present Testament: And flew to Rio, and basked in the sun of El Dorado: And he shall not come back this way again, before everything is nuked and dead, which will settle everything until time itself comes to an end.

And I don't think about the Way of Harry, the Word about the Tree of Man, Which proceeds from the Big Bang and the Bomb; Which together with the Big Bang and the Bomb accounts for everything; Which explains the VIPs: And I don't think about Good and Evil anymore; I don't worry about Guilt and Sin: And I don't care what happens after I'm dead: Or about the end of the world to come. *So there.*

¶ *And after that, these Brayers following, the People more or less paying attention; the Chosen One first pronouncing,*

        The Harrier Spirit be with you.
Answer.   You too, I guess.
Chosen One. Let us bray.

¶ *Here, if it has not already been said, shall follow the Harriers' Brayer.*

Chosen One. O Chief, wish us lots of luck on this day.
Answer.   For we shall probably need it.
Chosen One. O Harry, root for us to avoid setbacks on this day.
Answer.   Yes, Harry, for that one's especially important.

¶ *Then shall follow the Platitude for the day, except when the Consolation Service is read; and then the Platitude for the Day shall be omitted here.*

A Platitude for Luck.

O Harry, you always had great luck: if you had a four-leaf clover, touch it for us; if you had a rabbit's foot, rub it for us; if you had a lucky horseshoe, please make sure that it is in the full upright position: For we are Harriers, and we need lots of luck just to get by from day to day, without thinking about anything at all. *So there.*

A Platitude for Pleasure.

O Harry, you know almost everything there is to know about pleasure. If you have the time today, wish that we can enjoy some pleasure too: For we are Harriers, and pleasure is very important to us, particularly sexual pleasures, and pharmaceutical pleasures, and pleasure in the misfortunes of others. Surely, you know how it is, O Great Harry. We'll let you know how we make out today. *So there.*

¶ *The following Brayer shall be omitted when the Litany is said, and may be omitted when the Consolation Service is to follow.*

¶ *And* NOTE, *That the Chosen One may here end the Morning Brayer with such general brayers taken out of this book as he shall deem fit, or with the Brace.*

A Brayer for the Most Chosen Nation on Earth

O Harry, please reassure us that, as you have said so many times before, this Most Chosen Nation on Earth will indeed take a long long time to fall apart, even though there be Harriers in all positions of authority, including government officials, and chief executive officers of corporations, and bank presidents, and network anchormen, and movie moguls, and doctors, and all manner of other influential persons. We do reaffirm our promise to not think about anything at all, including these things, but we thought we would mention it this morning, before starting another day out there, and leave it all to you, as always. *So there.*

¶ *Then shall the Chosen One give the following Brace.*

Now go forth into this new day, and may the Power of Harry's Mighty Trinity be with you, and keep you from Setbacks all day long. *So there.*

Here ends the Order of Morning Brayer.

THE ORDER FOR
DAILY EVENING BRAYER

———— ❦ ————

¶ *The Chosen One shall begin the Evening Brayer by reading one or more of the following Sentences.*

A ll of them will have a long day's journey into night, from the age of innocence to the end of the affair. *Pspeciastes* 1.5

Something, something, something something against the something light; Do not go gentle into that good night. *Psomethings* 47.4-7

And he will give his followers important rituals to use again and again, as well as many great words to live by. *Jeffrey* 24.11-12

That's why it's time for us to get started, And why I have called you together this evening. *Exploits* 15.1-2

Let us go then, you and I, where the stars are something something in the sky, something etherized upon a table. *Psomethings* 23.1-3

Sing, little bird, sing the night away; sing your cares away: the Master of Money will reward you for every note. *Psongs* 49.3

> And just supposing (said the bedbug) that the day comes when the conflict between the capitalists and your ideas reaches
> *Advent* the point of threatening the world with annihilation, that will be okay too, because someone will come, on that day, or right around then anyway, who will tell the world what it all means, and what they can do about it. *Carl* 11.1-7

> And then, even as David watched, a pillar of light stood up from the earth, outshining the lion's eyes, wearing a crown of
> *Harriday* orange and fire, like unto a giant mushroom, whereupon the lion was devoured by flame, and David returned to the place of brotherly love, in which his son had been born on a night of light and the lion. *Willie* 2.4-5

> When it became clear that there was no alternative, the followers accompanied Harry to the city of his birth, where they
> *Pretzel Friday* received a spectacular welcome, consisting of all the beer and pretzels they could consume. *Willie* 65.1-4

After their stupendous welcome in Philadelphia, Harry and his
followers decided to hang out there for a while, and
Philadelphia   pass the time with their new friends, which they did,
and so they had many adventures, and went to many
many parties, and washed the hands of hundreds of Philadelphians,
and consumed lots and lots and lots of mind-altering substances, until
they kind of lost track of the time. *Vinnie* 46.1-9

Then Harry spoke again, saying, One of you will identify me to the
authorities this night, but that's okay, because I can
White Friday   take the heat. *Ned* 43.20-22

And it turned out that what Harry said was right after all, because he
Escapetide   escaped from prison, in just three days. *Vinnie* 75.1-3

A waiter ran in, in a great hurry, saying, Long Distance call for all
Rioday   of you, from Rio de Janeiro. *Willie* 77.6-8

One week later we gathered again, in the same place, at the same
time, and waited for Harry to come through, which he
Ghostide   did, about the sixth hour. *Exploits* 6.3-8

The eleven went out into the wide world, in their Silver Ghosts,
Trinity Friday   armed with Harry's Trinity. *Exploits* 18.2-4

 Then the Chosen One shall say,

Duly befriended brethren and sistren, the Word of the Harriers
moves us, in sundry places, to acknowledge that we have pursued
our desires on this day, with the full certainty that in so doing, we have
been acting in accordance with the Way of Harry; and that we have
done what we wanted to do, when we wanted to do it, no matter who
got hurt, as Harry taught us to do, in his own words. Therefore, there
is nothing that we need to apologize for, or feel guilty about, or think
about at all, now that this day has reached its end; nevertheless, we do
also acknowledge that those whom we have offended in the course of
pursuing our desires, are seeking to blame us and afflict us with a
sense of guilt for our actions, according to their own purposes; for this
reason, we now feel an urge to declare our utter certainty that nothing
which we have done on this day is our fault; and to make it clear that

others are to blame for the woes we have experienced on this day, in these words—

¶ *Or he shall say,*

Let us now blame those with whom we have had dealings on this day.

A General Assignment of Blame

High and Mighty Harry; We have followed your Way on this day, in blind obedience to the devices and desires of our own hearts. We have, from time to time, broken sundry laws. We have left undone those things which others say we ought to have done; And we have done those things which others say we ought not to have done. But that is the way we are, O Chief, and we know that none of these omissions and commissions can possibly be our fault, or our responsibility to correct or atone for, since we did not ask to be born, and we did not make the world, and we did not choose our parents or any other of the conditions into which we were born. Moreover, it is our absolute conviction that others have gone out of their way to make unreasonable demands on us, and to single us out for unfair persecution, because they are jealous, or prejudiced against us, or unnaturally obsessed with their own selfish desires. Do they not know that the world owes us a living, simply because we are here, whether we do any work or not? Against these vile animals who have disregarded our rights, we seek vengeance, O Harry. We demand to be compensated for every slight, every cross word, every instance in which our personal desires, stated and unstated, have been ignored or left unsatisfied, in any way, today or ever, according to the authority given us by your Name, Harry, First Babe of the Boom. *So there.*

The Permission to Seek Vengeance.

¶ *To be made by the Chosen One alone, standing; the People milling about as they desire.*

All knowing Harry, the First Born After the Bomb and First Babe of the Boom, who desires his followers to not think about anything at all, no matter who gets hurt, has given authority, and precise wording, to his Chosen Ones to declare and pronounce to all Harriers, being certain of their targets of blame, an Unqualified Permission to Seek

Vengeance against those they blame for any reason whatsoever. Further, he reaffirms the Freedom of all Harriers to do whatever they want to their enemies, whenever they want to do it, and exhorts them to do so, as long as they can get away with it, and promise to forget about it afterwards.

Wherefore let us remind ourselves, as he has taught us, that Harry showed us the Way to be, and remains the most shining example of the rewards to be gained from his wisdom.

¶ *Then the Chosen One shall kneel, and say the Harriers' Brayer; the People paying attention if they so desire, and even repeating it with him, if they are awake enough to do so.*

Our friend, who art in Rio, Harry is your name. Your time has come. Your way is fun, up north, as it is in Rio. We live for today and are rarely blamed. We forget our trespasses, as we forget those we have trespassed against. We yield to temptation, but are not evil. For thine is the wisdom, and the power, and the gold, for as long as it lasts. *So there.*

¶ *Then likewise he shall say,*

O Chief, read our lips.

Answer. And you shall see us mouthing your own words of praise.

GOLD be to Harry in Rio, and up north bliss, our full fill of it, for as long as it lasts;

Answer. As it was at the beginning of Harry's Way, is now, and ever shall be, until the end of the world to come. *So there.*

Chosen One. Praise be to the Chief.

Answer. The Chief's Name be praised.

¶ *Then shall follow a portion of the Psongs, according to the use of this Parish. And at the end of the whole portion, or Selection from the Hymnal, shall be sung or said the following:*

GOLD be to Harry in Rio, and up north bliss, our full fill of it, for as long as it lasts;

Answer. As it was at the beginning of Harry's Way, is now, and ever shall be, until the end of the world to come. *So there.*

¶ *Then shall be read the First Lesson, according to the Table of Harrier Days.*

¶ *After which shall be sung or said the Hymn called the Omni Viri.*

¶ *But* NOTE, *That the Chosen One, at his discretion, may omit one of the Lessons in Evening Brayer, the Lesson being followed by one of the Evening Comicles.*

Omni Viri. Willie 78.1-9

Indeed, all men must now learn from Harry; * for he has shown us the only Way to be.

He has washed his hands of everything, * and he can afford to wear gloves from now on.

He has followed his own desires; * and he has proven with the strength of his Way that his desires must be satisfied, or else.

He has said what he felt like saying, whenever he felt like it; * and no one ever succeeded in making him change his tune.

He has gotten away with everything, including a huge fortune; * and he has proved that nothing else counts.

For Harry has shown everyone the rules of the game, * including the rule that it's the winner who gets to make up the rules for everybody else.

Long live Harry, King of the Boomers! * Hallelujah, Hosanna, Hooray!

¶ *Or this Psong.*

Domino Indollario. Psong 43.1-7

Who is more blessed than the Master of Money? * He reaches out, and whatever he touches is his.

He is the King of the Mountain, * and his feet are planted on the summit of other men's most golden dreams.

He speaks, and all men listen: * for if he does not know what he is talking about, then why does he have all that Money?

He commands, and all men leap to obey; * for if he has his way, then he may give a generous tip to those who have been the most obsequious.

He scolds, and all men are very very sorry; * for if he is angry, there may be no Christmas bonus.

He smiles, and all men smile in return; * for if he is pleased, there is nothing to worry about today.

But for the Master of Money, all days are the same; * there is nothing to worry about, and no one to fear.

¶ *Or this.*

Dominus honestus. Psong 44.1-5

Only the Master of Money can be truly honest: * for he is the only one who can know to a certainty that he would not change his ways for a big enough check.

He does not need to make up stories about how much he disdains Money; * he does not have to develop a convenient memory about the surprising things he will do for some tiny pittance.

He does not have to mount ridiculous charades to impress his successful friends; * he does not have to tell everyone that his limousine is being repaired and that his good clothes were stolen with his luggage.

He does not have to pretend that he likes living in rundown neighborhoods; * he does not have to explain that his wife regards giant diamonds as ostentatious.

Yes, the Master of Money can be who he is; * he alone is free to admit that great wealth is the best of all goals to attain.

¶ *Then a Lesson of the Present Testament, as it is appointed in the Table of Harrier Days.*

¶ *And after that shall be sung or said the hymn called Nunc quittis.*

Nunc quittis. Ira 21.40-43

Have you had enough fun for one night? * I'm tired now.

And I think I'd like to go back to my room, * And try to get some sleep.

¶ *Or this Psong.*

Appreciatus Domini. Psong 48.1-6

Who appreciates a sunset more than the Master of Money? * He stands at eventide with all the luster and immovable majesty of the North Star.

The very universe wheels around his own whims; * all day long, the machinery of lesser lights has accommodated itself to his movements.

If some cog has failed to do its work properly, * then the Master of Money has caused it to be thrown away.

If some offering to his highness has failed to give pleasure, then the Master of Money has caused it to suffer, a lot, * which is a pleasure of its own, without equal in any universe.

If some aspect of the day ended has been less than perfect, then the Master of Money will buy a better tomorrow; * for he is the center of his universe, and the sun will bring him a new playground without being asked.

And even before tomorrow comes, there will be tonight; * and there is no end of the things that the Master of Money can do tonight.

¶ *Then shall be said the Ultra-Harriers' Creed by the Chosen One and the People, standing.*

I acknowledge Harry as the One: Who was the First Born After the Bomb, and the First Babe of the Boom: Who was betrayed by his pilot, was arrested, indicted, convicted, and sentenced to life in prison: He went down to Maximum Security; The third day he came out of prison: He flew to Rio, and settled in El Dorado: And there he shall live in luxury till the end of the world to come.

I acknowledge the gift of the Silver Ghosts: The Pontifical Harrier Parish; The Rites of Harry's Consolation: The Exemption from Responsibility: The Trinity of Harry: And the Way of the One, for as long as it lasts. *So there.*

¶ *Or the creed commonly called the Harriers' Creed.*

I don't think about the Big Bang, or the law of Evolution, which resulted in all things, completely at random:

Or about Harry, the first born after the Bomb, who evolved into being near the end of the world, the Chosen One of a Chosen Nation, the Beacon of Beacons, the Most Chosen of the Most Chosen; Forgotten by most, though his substance remains, and still shapes all things: Who for our well-being came down from his Learjet, and rode among us in a Silver Cloud, and showed us the Way; And was sent to prison for life because of his pilot; He was wrapped in chains and buried in a cell block: And the third day, he escaped, according to the Present Testament: And flew to Rio, and basked in the sun of El Dorado: And he shall not come back this way again, before everything is nuked and dead, which will settle everything until time itself comes to an end.

And I don't think about the Way of Harry, the Word about the Tree of Man, Which proceeds from the Big Bang and the Bomb; Which together with the Big Bang and the Bomb accounts for everything; Which explains the VIPs: And I don't think about Good and Evil anymore; I don't worry about Guilt and Sin: And I don't care what happens after I'm dead: Or about the end of the world to come. *So there.*

¶ *And after that, these Brayers following, the People more or less paying attention; the Chosen One first pronouncing,*

The Harrier Spirit be with you.
Answer.   You too, I guess.
Chosen One. Let us bray.

¶ *Here, if it has not already been said, shall follow the Harriers' Brayer.*

Chosen One. O Chief, our hearts are full of blame after this endless day.
Answer.   Yes, and we desire vengeance against our enemies.
Chosen One. O Harry, wish us luck in getting even.
Answer.   Yes, and don't forget the part about getting away with it.
Chosen One. O Harry, root for us to get away with everything.
Answer.   Yes, and then we promise to forget all about it, just like you taught us.

¶ *Then shall follow the Platitude for the day, except when the Consolation Service is read; and then the Platitude for the Day shall be omitted here.*

A Platitude for Vengeance.

O Harry, you have always gotten even with anyone who tried to flout your desires; so you must know how we feel. We want to make them pay for what they have done, and it wouldn't hurt if our vengeance made them feel ten times worse than we do now. Wish us well in our endeavors, which we will carry out in accordance with your Way. *So there.*

A Platitude for Safety.

O Harry, you know almost everything there is to know about getting away with everything. If you have the time tonight, take a moment to visualize your faithful followers getting away with everything. Okay? We'd be very grateful for anything you could do. Honestly, O Great Harry. *So there.*

¶ *The following Brayer shall be omitted when the Litany is said, and may be omitted when the Consolation Service is to follow.*

¶ *And* NOTE, *That the Chosen One may here end the Evening Brayer with such general brayers taken out of this book as he shall deem fit, or with the Brace.*

A Brayer for the Most Chosen Nation on Earth

O Harry, please reassure us that, as you have said so many times before, this Most Chosen Nation on Earth will indeed take a long long time to fall apart, even though there be Harriers in all positions of authority, including government officials, and chief executive officers of corporations, and bank presidents, and network anchormen, and movie moguls, and doctors, and all manner of other influential persons. We do reaffirm our promise to not think about anything at all, including these things, but we thought we would mention it this evening, after another long hard day out there, and leave it all to you, as always. *So there.*

¶ *Then shall the Chosen One give the following Brace.*

Now go back to your homes and other places of pleasure, and may the Power of Harry's Mighty Trinity be with you, and help you overcome the Setbacks experienced on this day. *So there.*

Here ends the Order of Evening Brayer.

THE LITANY
OR GENERAL INCANTATION
———————— ❦ ————————

¶ *To be used after the third Platitude at Morning or Evening Brayer; or before the taking of Consolation; or separately.*

O Great Big Bang, which created the earth and everything in it;
We wash our hands of you.
O Great Big Bomb, which will destroy the earth and everything in it;
We wash our hands of you.
O Great Big One, which is the day of the second and last Big Bang;
We wash our hands of you.
O powerful, deadly, and frightening trinity, one Great Big Joke;
We wash our hands of you.

We do not quite remember any offenses we may have committed, nor any offenses our forefathers have committed; nor do we wish to remember: For the Great Big Joke does not remember either, since it has never known of us in the first place, which we now know, and know better than to think about, and all because of Harry.
Thank you, Harry.

From all guilt and heresy; from sin; from the crafts and assaults of religion; from the fear of God, and of everlasting damnation,
Harry set us free.
From kindness of heart; from pride, honor, and duty; from effort, sacrifice, and conscience, and all charitable obligations,
Harry set us free.
From doubt and uncertainty; and from all introspections and recriminations and unwelcome thoughts of any kind,
Harry set us free.
By the words from his mouth; by the guidance and advice he rendered; by the example of his conduct, and the mysteries he explained,
Harry set us free.
By his arrest and indictment; by his conviction and life sentence; by his amazing escape to Rio, with his whole fortune intact; and his gift of the Silver Ghosts,
Harry set us free.

No matter what happens, or who gets mad, whether the world ends now or later,
Harry set us free.

We Harriers are free to do whatever we want, whenever we want to do it, without losing sleep over it;
Harry sure took a load off our minds, all right.
Free to express our desires, because they are ours, and we are the way we are, which is the way Nature works;
Harry sure took a load off our minds, all right.
Free to feel completely certain about everything, without having to think about it at all, because certainty is its own logic and proof;
Harry sure took a load off our minds, all right.
Free to blame anybody, for anything, for any reason that occurs to us, off the top of our heads, because we are never at fault;
Harry sure took a load off our minds, all right.
Free to climb the Tree of Man, as high as we want to go, because all that fruit is just sitting there waiting for somebody, and why not us?
Harry sure took a load off our minds, all right.

First Born After the Bomb, you sure took a load off our minds.
First Born After the Bomb, you sure took a load off our minds.
First Babe of the Boom, who took a fortune with him to Rio,
Lend us your luck.
First Babe of the Boom, who took a fortune with him to Rio,
Wish us a windfall.
O Chief, we are serious.
O Chief, we are serious.
Harry, wish us a windfall.
Harry, wish us a windfall.
Chief, wish us a windfall.
Chief, wish us a windfall.
Harry, wish us a windfall.
Harry, wish us a windfall.

¶ *Then shall the Chosen One, and the People with him, say the Harriers' Brayer.*

Our Friend, who art in Rio, Harry is your name. Your time has come. Your way is fun, up north, as it is in Rio. We live for today and are rarely blamed. We forget our trespasses, as we forget those we have trespassed against. We yield to temptation, but are not evil. *So there.*

 The Chosen One may, at his discretion, omit all that follows, to the Brayer, We humbly remind you, O Harry, *etc.*

Chosen One.

O Chief, deal with us not according to our merits.
But deal with us according to our desires.

Let us bray.

O Harry, excellent Friend, who despises not the certainty of an unthinking mind, nor the desire to escape accountability for everything; please continue to approve the brayers we utter in your name when we encounter troubles and adversities, whensoever someone thwarts our desires or seeks to heap blame and other misfortunes upon us; and generously cheer us on in our endeavors, that those setbacks which others plot against us, may, by your incredible luck, be brought to nought; that we, your followers, being hurt with no blame, may continue to pay for the services of your Parish, and aggrandize your fame and fortune further. *So there.*

 Chosen One and People.

O Chief, smile upon us, and help us get away with everything, for your name's sake.

Chosen One.

O Harry, we have heard with our ears, and your Ultra-Harriers have declared unto us in writing, the amazing things that you pulled off when you were here, and in the time since, and we could not be any more impressed.

 Chosen One and People.

O Chief, smile upon us, and help us get away with everything, just like you did.

Chosen One.

GOLD be to Harry in Rio, and up north bliss, our full fill of it, for as long as it lasts.

As it was at the beginning of Harry's Way, is now, and ever shall be, until the end of the world. So there.

From our enemies protect us, O Chief.

Merrily approve our machinations.

Keep our hearts armored in self-pity.

Help us be blind to the desires of others.

Graciously feign to hear our brayers.

O Son of David, be our Friend.

Both now and ever, pretend to hear us, O Chief.

Graciously feign to hear us, O Chief; graciously hear us, O Friendly Chief.

O Chief, let your luck be showered upon us;

As we do shower you with cash contributions.

Let us bray.

W e humbly remind you, O Harry, that we are fine just the way we are; and so, for the greater glory of your name, turn from us all those meddlers who seek to improve us in any way; and acknowledge that in all our endeavors, we may do what we want, when we want to do it, no matter who gets hurt, just as you advised in your own words when you were here; so that we may go on praising you and participating in your Parish; with the full approval of you who are our only mentor and ally, Harry, First Babe of the Boom. *So there.*

¶ *The Chosen One may end the Litany here, or at his discretion add other Brayers from this book.*

BRAYERS AND PLATITUDES

BRAYERS

———————— ❧ ————————

¶ *To be used before the final Brace in Morning and Evening Brayer, at the discretion of the Chosen One.*

A Brayer for Congress

O Harry, the Congress of the Most Chosen Nation is embarking upon a new session, and they are planning to spend our money as if it belonged to someone else, which it does, and there is nothing anyone can do about it, because they have two more years to lie, and make hypocritical statements, and sell out to special interests, and lock up enough votes for reelection. And so we ask you, one more time: are you really sure about the part where you said it will take a long long time for the Most Chosen Nation to fall apart? If you are, that is just great, and we will do our part, as always, in your name, for your greater fame and aggrandizement. *So there.*

For a State Legislature

O Harry, our State Legislature is back in session, and they seem even more stupid and parochial and prodigal with our money than ever before. You know the one about how it will take the Most Chosen Nation on Earth a long long time to fall apart? Are you really *really* sure about that one? Does that go for individual states too? We don't mean to nag, but we just thought we would check, because we are planning to do our part, like always, in accordance with your wonderful way, O Boomer King, Great Grantor of Consolation. *So there.*

For Courts of Justice

O Harry, the court calendars roll on and on, and the judges let all the criminals go free on technicalities, unless they serve six months of their life sentence before returning to take their vengeance on the streets. Nor is this all that our great courts are accomplishing, O First Babe of the Boom: For the courts runneth over with enormous lawsuits of every description, and the lawyers get richer and meaner and colder all the time as they help disgruntled wives to disembowel their husbands, and disgruntled customers to disembowel corporations, and disgruntled neighbors to disembowel each other, and disgruntled atheists to disembowel the gods of every religion, and disgruntled fascists to disembowel freedom of expression, and disgruntled totalitarians to disembowel fascists, and disgruntled fanatics to disembowel absolutely everybody under the sun. Wherefore, O Harry, we would ask you, if it is not too impertinent, whether you were really really *really* serious about the part where it will take a long long time for the Most Chosen Nation on Earth to fall apart. If you are still certain about that, know that we are too, and are not thinking about it at all, except that it just popped into our mind, and we thought we would mention it. O Harry, we're out here, and not many of us have law degrees, O First Born After the Bomb, O Chief of all Boomers, Our Friend for as long as it lasts. *So there.*

For Corporations

O Great Harry, a large number of us are employed by corporations, and we do our jobs in accordance with your Way, without thinking about anything at all, except for the things on our own personal List, whether they help the corporation or not. This is right and as it should be, and we could not be more certain about it, although we can't help noticing that the corporations we work for are exactly like us, and so their products are no good, and they ignore their customers, and whenever anything goes wrong, they lie about it or blame it on foreigners. And once again, this is right and as it should be, according to your Way: it's just that we had a momentary urge to ask you about the part where you said it would take the Most Chosen Nation a long long time to fall apart, and we were kind of wondering if you were really really really *really* sure about that one. You know that we are absolutely certain of it, but you would let us know if you changed your mind about that one, wouldn't you, O Great Harry, Golden Boomer King, who got away with everything, to a paradise called El Dorado? *So there.*

For the Pontifical Harrier Parish

O Harry, we just love your Consolation, and we want you to know that we will keep coming to services religiously, as long as we can have the Consolation we need. We wanted to say that, O Harry, for you and your Way are very important to us, and we wouldn't want you to forget it, O Marvelous One. *So there.*

For the Greater Harrier Parish

O High and Mighty Harry, we know that we are not your only Parish, for there are many others out there who are just like us, except that they do not know that they are following your Way. We wanted you to know, O First Babe of the Boom, that we do not resent them collectively, but only individually, as they seek to thwart our desires, and perform other injurious actions for which we can blame them ruthlessly. Otherwise, we don't think about them at all, O Golden Friend. *So there.*

For those who are Chosen to serve the Parish

O Chief, we are being presented with new functionaries in our Local Parish House, and we want to take this opportunity to request that service not get much worse, or prices much higher, or the quality of Consolation too variable. Not that we are finding fault, O Harry: rather, we are expressing our desire to remain certain about what we can expect from this Parish, which is very very important to our lives, for as long as they last, O First Born After the Bomb. *So there.*

For the increase of the Way of Harry

O Harry, we know that the Pontifical Harrier Parish grows larger every day, and that more and more followers are learning the secrets of your Way. This is right and as it should be, and we are not worrying at all about the part where you said it will take the Most Chosen Nation a long long time to fall apart: in fact, we are not thinking about it all, because we know that you really really really really *really* meant what you said, O King of El Dorado. *So there.*

In Time of War

O Harry, there is a war on, and all of us here present are not in it, which is a tremendous relief, no matter who gets hurt. Still, we would ask one further favor of you, which is to wish us luck in identifying the right targets for blame, and in so positioning ourselves politically that no matter what happens, no one will ask us to make any sacrifices in support of this endeavor, whether we approve of it for our own purposes or not. *So there.*

In Time of Calamity

O Harry, a great calamity has occurred, and we do not yet know who to blame. Please wish us your personal luck in dealing with this calamity, including the procurement of generous benefits from the government for those of us who can find a way to prove damages; savage punishment of those who will be blamed; and a speedy arrival at certainty by us Harriers about exactly who it is that should be blamed for this terrible situation. *So there.*

In Time of Great Sickness and Mortality

O Harry, we do not want to die. We do not want to die. We really do not want to die. Please let it be someone else, even if it is someone near to us, because we do not want to die, O Great Grantor of Consolation. *So there.*

In Time of Financial Austerity

O Harry, the worst has happened. There is no money for anybody. Please wish us luck in finding targets for the enormous load of blame we are carrying around in our empty wallets. If we cannot find someone to blame, we may need to start a war, just to get even with someone, no matter who gets hurt, as long as it isn't us. So you can see that this is really important, and we would very much appreciate it if you could give our little request a moment of your time. *So there.*

For Schools, Colleges, and Universities

O Harry, it is true what they are saying about the schools, because our children don't know anything at all about anything, except maybe sex and drugs and rock 'n' roll, and we know that it can't possibly be our fault, because we pay our taxes, or most of us do, anyway, and we see to it that our children go off to school when they're supposed to, and we drive them to all their activities like they want, and so all is as it should be, we guess. The only thing is, and we don't even like to mention it, but you know the part about how the Most Chosen Nation will take a long long time to fall apart? Well . . . Never mind, O Great Boomer King. *So there.*

¶ *The Brayers following are to be used upon Special Occasions, or upon Special Request by members in good standing of the Local Parish House.*

For Money

O Harry, we would like some money, please. We really really would. It goes so wonderfully well with your Way, as you know, and we would know exactly what to do with it, if we got it. So if you have the time, could you wish us a windfall, like winning the lottery? Could you, O Golden King of Coins? *So there.*

For Things

O Harry, we just love to get new things, and the things we have right now are not new enough to suit us. Could you wish us some luck in acquiring new things? Indeed, we desire new things so much that we do not even need cash; we would be happy for any lucky extension of credit that your own personal luck might throw our way, if you were to take a moment or two to wish us well in satisfying this little desire of ours. Thank you, O First Babe of the Boom, who took a fortune with him to Rio. *So there.*

For Sexual Pleasures

O Harry, we are filled with the third most urgent of all desires, namely, the desire for sexual gratification. Indeed, we are willing to be used as sex objects, and we seek nothing more lasting or rewarding than a tawdry fling in some place where our spouses won't walk in suddenly. Please wish us luck in satisfying this little desire of ours, O Boomer King. *So there.*

For the Misfortunes of Others

O Harry, we are filled with the second most urgent of all desires, namely the desire to gloat about the misfortunes of others. To this end, we have pointed the finger of blame without thinking about it at all, and we look forward to immediate results. Please wish us luck in satisfying this little desire of ours, O Great Provider of the Trinity. *So there.*

For Children

O Harry, some of us have little babies, and they're so cute, and they go so well with our nice house, and our nice cars, and our nice clothes, and we're getting lots of pleasure from pampering their little whims, and we know it will all work out according to your Way, as it should. But we may need a little assistance in deciding exactly when we should start ignoring them, and letting their little eyes glaze over with sullen uninterest in everything, and becoming utter strangers to the fruit of our loins, like all Harrier parents everywhere. Please wish us luck in identifying that important moment when it comes, because we are devoted to your Way, and we do not wish to make a mistake by thinking about our children's upbringing. *So there.*

A Blaming Brayer

¶ *To be used before Pontifications, or on Special Occasions, or at the Special Request of a member in good standing of the Local Parish.*

O Harry, we are consumed with the desire to blame _____ for the gross offenses they have committed against us. They do not deserve to live, and we desire to see them suffer horribly, and lose everything, and end up in the gutter with an empty bottle of Drano beside their naked disfigured corpse. Are we making ourselves clear, O Great Giver of the Trinity? Please wish us luck in satisfying this little desire of ours, O Golden King of El Dorado. *So there.*

PLATITUDES

¶ *To be used after the Platitudes of Morning and Evening Brayer, or Consolation, and wherever rubrics call for the Platitude of the Day.*

A Platitude for Saturdays

O Harry, it is Saturday, and most of us have the day off, which means that we will be checking items off our List for Saturdays, including running errands, and doing work around the house, and buying things, and trying to satisfy our personal desires, and screaming at our children, if they aren't at the mall, and we ask you to wish us luck as we try to get through the day without thinking about anything at all. *So there.*

A Platitude for Sundays

O Harry, it is Sunday, and tomorrow we will have to go to work again, and we do not wish to think about it at all, and so we are ready to run and run and run all day, and maybe there will be something good on TV, but even so, please wish us luck in not thinking about anything at all today. *So there.*

A Platitude for Mondays

O Harry, is there anything anywhere worse than Mondays? We hate everybody, we hate our jobs, we hate having to show up and spend another endless week with those vile monsters at work, and we just don't know what to do, except look forward to the next Consolation, and please keep it coming, O King of El Dorado. *So there.*

A Platitude for Tuesdays

O Harry, it is Tuesday, four long days till Friday, and we can only hope that your Way will see us through. Our List is long, and we will have many to blame before we can draw an easy breath again. Wish us luck. *So there.*

A Platitude for Wednesdays

O Harry, it is hump day, but it still seems an eternity till Friday will be here at last. We will desire much vengeance before that blissful day arrives, O Golden Friend. Wish us success in the use of your Way. *So there.*

A Platitude for Thursdays

O Harry, isn't Friday ever going to get here? O Friday, hurry! O Harry, we can't wait! *So there.*

A Platitude for Fridays

O Harry! O Great Day! For this is *your* day, and Consolation is ours at last! O Glory of Not Thinking About Anything At All! O Harry, we love you, we adore you, you are our only friend in the world, and we could not be happier than to be here with you, in your Parish, on this day of all days. Thank Harry, it's Friday! *So there.*

HARRY'S CONSOLATION

THE ORDER FOR
THE ADMINISTRATION OF THE BOOMER BANQUET

OR

HARRY'S CONSOLATION

¶ *At the Consolation-time the Harrier Table shall have upon it a fair white linen cloth. And the Chosen One, lounging before the Harrier Table, shall say the Harriers' Brayer and the Platitude that follows, while the People mill about; but the Harriers' Brayer may be omitted if the Chosen One so desires.*

Our friend, who art in Rio, Harry is your name. Your time has come. Your way is fun, up north, as it is in Rio. We live for today and are rarely blamed. We forget our trespasses, as we forget those we have trespassed against. We yield to temptation, but are not evil. *So there.*

The Platitude.

All knowing Harry, unto whom all Harriers are indebted, all desires are acceptable, and from whom no secrets need be hid, cleanse the thoughts from our minds by the inspiration of the true Harrier Spirit, that we may perfectly worship our own whims, and profitably aggrandize your Fame. *So there.*

¶ *Then shall the Chosen One, turning to the People, rehearse indistinctly The Ten Commandments; and the People, still milling about, shall, after every Commandment, pronounce their relief at no longer being bound by it.*

¶ *And* NOTE, *That in rehearsing The Ten Commandments, the Chosen One may omit that part of the Commandment which is inset.*

¶ *The Lexilogue may be omitted, if the Chosen One so desires, but* NOTE, *That whenever it is omitted, the Chosen One shall say the Summary of the Law, beginning,* Hear what our Friend Harry says.

The Lexilogue.

The God of Original Sin, Eternal Guilt, and Everlasting Damnation spoke these words, saying:
Thou shalt have no other Gods but Me.

But for the grace of Harry, we'd be stuck with this law.
Thou shalt always capitalize My name on graven images, including pronouns.
But for the grace of Harry, we'd be stuck with this law.
Thou shalt not eat any bacon, pork or other pig products.
But for the grace of Harry, we'd be stuck with this law.
Honor thy father and mother,

> No matter how little money they make or how many chores they ask thee to do.

But for the grace of Harry, we'd be stuck with this law.
Thou shalt not commit adultery,

> Even if thou art an adult.

But for the grace of Harry, we'd be stuck with this law.
Thou shalt not covet,

> Whatever that means.

But for the grace of Harry, we'd be stuck with this law.
Thou shalt not kill,

> No matter how much fun it is.

But for the grace of Harry, we'd be stuck with this law.

Thou shalt be circumcised as soon as thou art born.
But for the grace of Harry, we'd be stuck with this law.
Thou shalt not bear a false witness,

> Especially through adultery.

But for the grace of Harry, we'd be stuck with this law.
Thou shalt not have any fun to speak of, ever,

> Because God loves you.

But for the grace of Harry, This is the kind of Hell on Earth we'd be stuck with. Thank you, Harry, for setting us free.

¶ *Then may the Chosen One say,*

Hear what our Friend Harry says.

Pursue your own desires, with all the certainty that comes from not thinking about anything at all. This is the first and great Commandment. And the second is almost as important; Blame your neighbor before he can blame you. On these two commandments hang all the lessons of human experience.

¶ *Here, if the Lexilogue hath been omitted, shall be said,*

Harry, we like your way.
Chief, we like your way.
Harry, we like your way.

¶ *Then the Chosen One may say,*

The Harrier Spirit be with you.
Answer. You too, I guess.
Chosen One. Let us bray.

¶ *Then shall the Chosen One say the Platitude of the Day. And after the Platitude the Chosen One shall read the Letter of the Day, first saying,* The Letter of the Day is written in the _____ Chapter of _____, beginning at the _____ Verse. *The Letter of the Day having been read, the Chosen One shall say,* That's about it for the Letter of the Day.

¶ *Here may be sung a Hymn or Something.*

¶ *Then, all the People standing, the Chosen One shall read the Good Word, first saying,* The Good Word of the Day is written in the _____ Chapter of _____, beginning at the _____ Verse.

¶ *Here shall be said,*

Give us the Good Word, O Harry.

¶ *And after the Good Word may be said,*

Good going, O Most Chosen One.

¶ *Then shall be said the Creed of the Harriers; but the Creed may be omitted, if it hath been said immediately before in Morning Brayer; Provided, That the Harriers' Creed shall be said on Harriday, Escapetide, and Rioday.*

I don't think about the Big Bang, or the law of Evolution, which resulted in all things, completely at random: Or about Harry, the first born after the Bomb, who evolved into being near the end of the world, the Chosen One of a Chosen Nation, the Beacon of Beacons, the Most Chosen of the Most Chosen; Forgotten by most, though his substance remains, and still shapes all things: Who for our well-being came down from his Learjet, and rode among us in a Silver Cloud, and showed us the Way; And was sent to prison for life because of his pilot; He was wrapped in chains and buried in a cell block: And the third day, he escaped, according to the Present Testament: And flew to Rio, and basked in the sun of El Dorado: And he shall not come back this way again, before everything is nuked and dead, which will settle everything until time itself comes to an end.

And I don't think about the Way of Harry, the Word about the Tree of Man, Which proceeds from the Big Bang and the Bomb; Which together with the Big Bang and the Bomb accounts for everything; Which explains the VIPs: And I don't think about Good and Evil anymore; I don't worry about Guilt and Sin: And I don't care what happens after I'm dead: Or about the end of the world to come. *So there.*

¶ *Then shall be declared unto the People what Harrier Days, or Feasting Days, are in the week following to be observed; and (if occasion be) shall Notice be given of the Consolation, and of the Warning Signs of Matrimony, and of other matters to be published.*

¶ *Here, or immediately after the Creed, may be said the Blaming Brayer, or other authorized brayers or platitudes.*

¶ *Then followeth the Pontification. After which, the Chosen One, when there is a Consolation, shall return to the Harrier Table, and begin the Extortatory, saying one or more of these sentences following, as he desires.*

Remember the words of Harry, how he said, If they want Consolation, they're going to have to buy their ticket before the train leaves the station, if you catch my drift. *Exploits* 16.32-33.

Toot toot, the whistle bloweth. *Psomethings* 77.9.

They will learn that if they want something, they're going to pay for it, with cash money, if they're lucky, because the other ways of paying for things are almost all worse. *Adam* 43.7.

If wishes were horses, beggars would ride. *Psayings* 5A.18.

Is it not true that only Money gives you really good odds of having your wishes come true? *Psongs* 18.1

Truly, Money is infinite and without end on earth: Is it not a humble request to ask for just a little, only enough to live in comfort forever? *Psongs* 16.3.

¶ *And* NOTE, *That these Sentences may be used on any other occasion of Public Ritualizing when Extortions from the People are to be received.*

¶ *The Beacons and Parish Guards, or other Security Persons, shall dispense receipts to the People, in exchange for Beans, or Certified Checks, which shall be deposited in a Carbon-Steel Lockbox to be provided by the Parish; and bring the Lockbox under guard to the Chosen One, who shall carefully place it in the Safe under the Harrier Table.*

¶ *The Chosen One shall then, while the Safe is open, withdraw from it the Mirror, Razor Blade, and Rocks of Consolation, placing them on the Harrier Table.*

¶ *And when the Beans are being received and locked away, there may be sung a Hymn, or an Extortatory Anthem in the words of Harrier Scripture or of the Book of Harrier Brayer, under the direction of the Chosen One.*

¶ *Here the Chosen One may also record any Special Requests for Additional Grams and Kilos of Consolation that may be desired by the People. (Be it known, however, that Approval of Special Requests for Kilos of Consolation can only be granted by the Arch-Harrier for the Parish.)*

¶ *Then shall the Chosen One say,*

Let us bray for the whole state of the Harrier Parish.

O Happy One, Great Harry, who showed us the way, we know that you are in Rio and cannot hear what we have to say, but we feel an urgent need to weep and wail, and beat our breasts, and otherwise carry on, about any and all things that have not gone our way recently.

Truly, we are filled with desire to point the finger of blame at those who have vexed us, or frustrated us, or levied unwelcome demands upon us, and we are certain that they deserve to be made miserable, whoever they are.

In particular, we would blame the authorities at the federal, state, and local level for demanding too many taxes, as well as passing too many laws restraining our whims, not to mention putting us in a dark mood with all the bad news they cause to be shown on television.

And in addition, we would also blame and hector all those who, in this Most Chosen Nation on Earth, are in trouble, sorrow, need, sickness, or any other adversity: For they are not entertaining, and there is little prospect that they will ever do anything for us, no matter how long we wait, and so what good are they?

Finally, it is also our desire to point the finger of blame at all those People with whom we must deal on a regular basis: For they cause us grief with their lousy service and selfish ways, whether they be plumbers, or lawyers, or doctors, or insurance salesmen, or television repairmen, or carpenters, or retail clerks, or waitresses, or middle managers, or even top executives. Though we know them to be Harriers, just like ourselves, whether they acknowledge it or not, we also know that we are free to blame them ruthlessly, including even those here present, because there are no contradictions. Moreover, we feel equally free to demand an apology, no matter how insincerely it may be offered, because we desire it, and it is therefore our right to receive it, before they receive any Consolation, according to the Way of Harry. *So there.*

¶ *Then shall the Chosen One say to those who come to receive Harry's Consolation,*

Y ou who are able to mouth repentance of those things for which others desire to blame you, and are willing to say anything at all as long as you do not have to think about it; Draw near to the Harrier Table, and join together in apologizing for whatever it is others wish you to apologize for, whether you remember it or not, while looking convincingly sorry.

¶ *Then shall this General Apology be said in unison, by the Chosen One and all those who have paid to receive Consolation, while appearing extremely sorry.*

A ll knowing Harry, First Born After the Bomb, the Most Chosen One of the Most Chosen Nation on Earth, Explainer of all things; We simply could not be more apologetic about all of our manifold errors and indiscretions, whatever they are, although they were most certainly not our fault, because we did not ask to be born and are not responsible. Even so, we do earnestly repent and are heartily sorry for these our misdoings: The remembrance of them is practically nonexistent in us; the burden of them has surely fallen on someone else, which would be intolerable if we thought about it at all, which we have not done, and will not do, for your Name's sake. And if there were someone of a divine origin who could punish us with everlasting damnation, we would demand absolution in a loud voice, saying, Have mercy upon us, have mercy upon us, most merciful Divinity; forgive us all that is past, and we will do better from now on. Truly, we would beg and plead and humble ourselves in this fashion until we got our way. However, things being what they are, according to the Way of Harry, we can only say to those we may have injured, offended, or inconvenienced in some way: Forget all that is past, because we certainly have, and this is the absolute most you will ever get out of it. *So there.*

¶ *Then shall the Chosen One stand up, and turning to the People, say,*

High and Mighty Harry, our Friend in Rio, who in his great wealth is removed from all the cares of the world, we trust in your abiding power not to think about anything at all, including all those things that we may have done, or not done, which others may not have wanted us to do, or not do, respectively. Therefore, we are certain that if you were here, which you are not, and if you held some divine power of absolution, which we know you do not, and if we really desired absolution, which we do not, you would grant it, provided that you had nothing better to do, which you clearly do; and so, by the power you have given us, according to your Way, we do thoroughly absolve ourselves, now and forevermore, in your Name, of everything that any of us might regret if we thought about it at all, which we promise not to do. *So there.*

¶ *Then shall the Chosen One say,*

Hear the comforting words that Harry had to say to those who follow his Way.

The followers of my Way are many and varied, and truly there will be some among them whom you hate and detest, but that is because you are who you are, just as they are who they are. Yet I make no such distinctions, for to make distinctions requires thought, and I prefer not to think about it, but to be joyful when my followers prove their allegiance to my way. *Willie* 50.15-20.

You have always known that the only important question about life, or anything else, is, What's in it for me? *Vinnie* 15.1.

Hear also what the Arch-Angel Matthew had to say.

If you follow the Way of Harry, you'll never have to feel really bad again, because the Way of Harry tells us that we're all fine just the way we are, without trying to improve ourselves, or be something we're not, no matter who it hurts. *Kensingtonians* 7.1-6.

Hear also what the Vice-President Vicki had to say.

For the way of Harry is the way of not thinking about anything at all, and not really caring, and not really working too hard, and not making any demands on ourselves, and not really doing anything except what we want to do, no matter who gets hurt. *Mawrites* 8.1-6.

¶ *After which the Beacons shall serve cocktails to the People; then shall the Chosen One proceed, while the Beacons place foods on the Harrier Table, saying,*

	Lift up your glasses.
Answer.	We lift them for Harry's sake.
Chosen One.	Let us offer up a toast to Harry.
Answer.	As long as we can eat while we do so.

¶ *Then shall the Beacons serve the foods to the People, as the Chosen One turns to the Harrier Table and says,*

Here is meat, poultry, and other bounty, signifying that we can satisfy our desires at all times, and in all places, thanks to the Word of Harry, Our Friend, All Knowing Beacon of the Way.

¶ *Here shall follow the Proper Toast, according to the time, if there be any specially appointed; or else immediately shall be said or sung by the Chosen One,*

THEREFORE with Harriers and Ultra-Harriers, and in the full certainty of El Dorado, we toast and dignify your golden Name; evermore praising you, and saying,

HARRY, HARRY, HARRY, Great Giver of Ghosts, Banks and vaults everywhere are full of your Gold: Gold is your ¶ *Chosen One* Word, O Harry Most Chosen. *So there.*   *and People*

PROPER TOASTS

HARRIDAY

¶ *Upon Harriday and seven days after.*

Because Harry was born, the first after the Bomb, to show us the Way to be; who, by his gift of the Silver Ghosts, made men carry his Word, That we might be free of guilt and sin and suffering for as long it lasts.

Therefore with Harriers, etc.

ESCAPETIDE

¶ *Upon the Escapetide, and seven days after.*

By the Way of Harry, Our Friend, who was betrayed by his pilot and sent to prison for life; who, in defiance of his sentence, manifested the power to become free, and showed us that there is always a way to get what you want, no matter what.

Therefore with Harriers, etc.

RIODAY

¶ *Upon Rioday, and seven days after.*

By the Way of Harry, Chief of the Boom; who, after his most daring Escape, phoned Long Distance to his followers, and in their hearing, described his own arrival in Rio; the full, perfect, and rightful attainment of El Dorado: That we might also become free, and join with him in not thinking about anything at all, for as long it lasts.

Therefore with Harriers, etc.

GHOSTIDE

¶ *Upon Ghostide, and six days after.*

By the Way of Harry, First Born After the Bomb; according to whose most generous whim, the Silver Ghosts were delivered directly from Britain, lighting up the eyes of his followers, to bribe them, and to put them on the road to the masses; giving them the most perfect incentive to carry the Good Word to all parts of the Most Chosen Nation on Earth; whereby we have been brought out of guilt and despair into the knowledge of the Way, which shall make us free, until the end of the world to come.

Therefore with Harriers, etc.

TRINITY FRIDAY

¶ *Upon the Feast of Trinity only.*

Who, with your Good Word, revealed to us the Way, and the Trinity of which the Way is constituted. In recognition of your wisdom, we have yielded up the ancient trinity of guilt, sin, and suffering, O Harry, in exchange for Desire, Certainty, and Blame, That we may achieve the happiness of El Dorado, and stop thinking about anything at all, until the day of the second and final Big Bang, from which no one will escape.

Therefore, with Harriers, etc.

ULTRA-HARRIERS DAY

¶ *Upon Ultra-Harriers Day, and seven days after.*

Who, in the multitude of your Ultra-Harriers, has given us manifold demonstrations of the power of the Way, in order that we might more easily cease thinking about anything at all, and use your Trinity to get what we want, when we want it, no matter who gets hurt.

Therefore, with Harriers, etc.

CHRISTMAS

¶ *On Christmas and for seven days after.*

Who once clothed himself in a Santa Suit, and said, Ho Ho Ho; Behold the Almighty God of the Most Chosen Nation on Earth; and thereby made it okay for us to keep on celebrating Christmas, without thinking about it at all.

Therefore with Harriers and Ultra-Harriers, and in the full certainty of El Dorado, we toast and dignify your golden Name; evermore praising you, and saying,

HARRY, HARRY, HARRY, Great Giver of Ghosts, Banks and vaults everywhere are full of your Gold: Gold is your ¶ *Chosen One* Word, O Harry Most Chosen. *So there.*   *and People*

¶ *When the Chosen One has so arranged the Mirror, the Razor Blade, and the Rocks that he may easily grasp them, he shall say the Brayer of Anticipation.*

ALL glory be to the Chief, all knowing Harry, our Friend in Rio, who did, according to his own whim, run the risk of being sent to prison for life, even while he was instructing us in the Way to be; who made there (by his fabulous escape and flight to Rio) a full, perfect, and sufficient example, proof, and demonstration of the Power of his Word; and did institute, and in his Long Distance Calls exhort us to continue, a brazen celebration of his amazingly brief stay in prison, which lasted a total of three days: For on the night in which he was betrayed in Philadelphia, *(a)* he took a Mirror, saying, Look into this, which shows you the face of yourself alone, as we are all alone in this vast meaningless universe; *(b)* then covering the face in the Mirror with small white Rocks, he said, Behold the Slayer of Thought, which I have procured for you; *(c)* then he held up the Blade of a Razor, saying, Take an implement that is as keen and useful as blame itself, and cut the Rocks into Lines, so that the Slayer of Thought might better serve your desire; *(d)* next, he held up a one-hundred dollar bill, saying, Roll some money in your fingers, because outside of yourself, money is the only certainty you can have;

(a) Here the Chosen One is to take the Mirror into his hands.

(b) And here to cover the Mirror with the Rocks of Harrier Consolation.

(c) And here to carve the Rocks into Lines with the Razor Blade.

(d) Here he is to take a hundred-dollar bill into his hands and roll it up.

(e) and as the followers trembled with anticipation, he offered them the Banquet, saying, Inhale these Lines, which are your Consolation for all things which may trouble you, and as you inhale, remember me, for the briefest possible instant, because it is I, Harry, who have shown you the Way to be.

(e) And here he is to touch each Line with the rolled bill.

WHEREFORE, O Chief and Golden Friend, according to the institution you have established for us, we, your Chosen Followers, do brazenly celebrate, with these things, which we now invite you to share (in full knowledge of your inability to hear our words), the rite of Consolation that is our right to receive; having in the briefest possible remembrance your stupid arrest and needless imprisonment, your fantastic escape and magnificent flight to Rio; offering you all the gratitude we are capable of, nonexistent as that may be. *So there.*

The Invitation

¶ *AND now, as our Splendid Chief has taught us, we are bold to say,*

O ur friend, who art in Rio, Harry is your name. Your time has come. Your way is fun, up north, as it is in Rio. We live for today and are rarely blamed. We forget our trespasses, as we forget those we have trespassed against. We yield to temptation, but are not evil. For thine is the wisdom, and the power, and the gold, for as long as it lasts. *So there.*

¶ *Then shall the Chosen One, leaning over the Harrier Table, say, in the name of all those who shall receive the Consolation, this Brayer following.*

W e do not presume to come to this your table, O Harry, trusting in our own superiority, but in your manifold and great words. We are not clever enough to procure our own Rocks for this table. But you are the same Harry, whose property is always to have a ready supply of Consolation: Grant us, therefore, Great Chief, to inhale the Lines purchased on our behalf, and thereby partake of paradise, that we may evermore dwell in El Dorado, and vice versa. *So there.*

Here may be sung a hymn.

 Then shall the Chosen One first receive Harry's Consolation himself, and proceed to deliver the same to the Parish Beacons and Guards in like manner, and, after that, to the People. And sufficient opportunity shall be given to those present to be consoled, provided they have receipts. And when he delivers the Mirror, with its Lines, he shall say,

The Consolation of our Friend Harry, which was devised for you, remove from your mind all thoughts of any kind. Take and inhale this in remembrance that Harry got away with everything, proving that you can too, for as long as it lasts.

¶ *When all have been consoled, the Chosen One shall return to the Harrier Table, and carefully place within the Safe what remains of the Lines, locking and bolting the door with great thoroughness.*

¶ *Then shall the Chosen One say,*

Let us bray.

High and Mighty Harry, we most heartily offer our thanks to you, for having made it possible for us to partake of this feast, which is the one essential part of an otherwise meaningless ritual; and for having commanded this institution to be established in the first place, so that we might be members with you in the dying body of Mankind, which is the final hilarious punch line of the Great Big Joke so devoutly worshiped and glorified by those who have not yet tumbled to your Way. And we humbly beseech you, O Harry, to wish us your luck in attaining to the paradise of El Dorado, where everything is as good as it can be, for as long as it lasts, until the world comes to an end. *So there.*

¶ *Then shall be said the Gold in Excess, all standing, or some other proper Hymn.*

GOLD be to Harry in Rio, and up north bliss, our full fill of it, for as long as it lasts. We bray to thee, we envy thee, we ape thee, we pay thee, we give more to thee for thy Golden Hoard, O Highest Harrier, Lord of El Dorado, the One and Only Harry.

O Chief, Firstborn Son of the Bomb, Friend Harry; O First Harrier, First Babe of the Boom, First Man to think about nothing at all, ever,

Thou that takest away the minds of the world, lend us thy luck. Thou that takest away the minds of the world, relish our brayer. Thou that hast washed thy hands of everything, lend us thy luck.

For thou only art Harry; thou only art our Friend; thou only, O Source of the Silver Ghosts, art enthroned upon the endless Gold of El Dorado. *So there.*

¶ *Then, the People kneeling, the Chosen One (the Arch-Harrier if he be present) shall let them depart with this Blissing.*

The Bliss of Harry, which slayeth all understanding, empty your hearts and minds of the knowledge and fear of the Bomb, and of the Big Joke from which it came; And the Power of Harry's Mighty Trinity, Desire, Certainty, and Blame, be with you, and remain with you as long as it lasts. *So there.*

GENERAL RUBRICS

¶ *In the absence of the Chosen One, a Beacon may say all that is before appointed to the end of the Good Word.*

¶ *On Fridays and other Harrier Days (though there be no Pontification or Consolation) may be said all that is appointed at the Consolation, to the end of the Good Word, concluding with the Blissing.*

¶ *And if any of the Rocks of Consolation remain afterwards, they shall not be carried out of the Parish House, upon pain of death; but the Chosen One and the Beacons and the Parish Guards shall lock them in the Safe, and jointly set the timelock, in such manner that it cannot be opened until the next Consolation.*

¶ *If among those who come to be partakers of the Consolation, the Chosen One shall know any to be an open and articulate thinker, or to have excelled his neighbors by working hard or caring about anything at all, so that the Parish be thereby inflamed to a state of High Blame; he shall expose him before the whole Parish, that he presume not to come to the Harrier Table until he have openly declared himself to have stopped thinking about anything at all, and eliminated those practices which have incited blame by his fellow Harriers; and that he hath resolved himself not to care about anything, and to cease working hard, but instead to keep only to his List, like all good Harriers.*

THE MINISTRATION OF HARRIFICATION

together with

THE ORDER OF ADULTIFICATION

THE SOLEMNIZATION OF MATRIMONY

THE BURIAL OF THE DEAD

THE MINISTRATION OF
HARRIFICATION

---------- ❦ ----------

¶ *The Chosen One of every Parish House shall often admonish the People, that they defer not the Harrification of their Children, and that it is most convenient that Harrification should be administered on Fridays and other Harrier Days.*

¶ *There shall be for every Male-child to be Harrified, when they can be had, two Harry-dads and one Harry-mom; and for every Female, one Harry-dad and two Harry-moms; and Parents shall be admitted as Sponsors, if it be desired.*

¶ *When there are Children to be Harrified, the Parents or Sponsors shall give knowledge thereof to the Chosen One. And then the Harry-dads and Harry-moms, and the People with the Children, must be ready at the Font, either immediately after the Second Lesson at Morning or Evening Brayer, or at such other time as the Chosen One shall appoint.*

¶ *When any such Persons as are of riper years are to be Harrified, timely notice shall be given to the Chosen One; that, so due care may be taken for their instruction, whether they be sufficiently indoctrinated in the Beacons of the Way; and that they may be exhorted to prepare themselves, with Brayers and Feasting, for the receiving of the Harrier rights. And NOTE, That at the time of the Harrification of an Adult, there shall be present with him at the Font at least two Witnesses.*

¶ *The Chosen One, having come to the Font, which is then to be filled with Harrier Water, shall say as followeth, the People all standing,*

Has this Child (Person) been already Harrified, or not?

¶ *If they answer, NO: then shall the Chosen One proceed as followeth.*

Duly befriended, forasmuch as our Friend Harry says, No one can follow my way unless he wash his hands of everything; I encourage you to grant to *this Child* (*this Person*) the right to the same freedom you have; that *he* may be Harrified with Water, and received into the Harrier Parish, and be enabled to not think about anything at all, just like the rest of us, for as long as it lasts.

¶ *Then shall the Chosen One say,*

Let us bray.

All knowing Harry, the answer to all troubling questions, the accomplice in all convenient decisions, the consolation for all those things which we no longer believe, and the ultimate escapement from responsibility; We call upon thee, knowing full well that you are not listening and cannot hear us, to let us Harrify *this Child* (*this Person*) just as if *he* had known you in person, and had learned from your own mouth the Way to be. Let *him* be one of us, as you (might have) promised when you were here, saying, Demand, and you shall have what you Desire; Be Certain, and no one will have the guts to stand against you; Blame everyone and everything that gets in your way, and the obstacles will be removed from your path. So be proud of us now, who say in Your name, We Demand Harrification for *this Child* (*this Person*); We are Certain it is what we Desire; and We shall Blame the daylights out of anyone who opposes our Whim. So saying, we are confident that this Child shall be made free by the Washing of *his* Hands, and may come to feel the happiness of your Way, just like you promised. *So there.*

¶ *Then shall the Chosen One say as followeth.*

Hear the Good Word, written by the Ultra-Harrier Vinnie, in the Fourth Chapter, at the First Verse.

And the people cried out to John, saying, "Far out! That's some pretty heavy excrement you're laying on us here, and why don't you, you know, lay some wisdom on us, so we can, like, figure out what's going down here?" Thereupon John commenced to twist and shout like an ancient holy man, or a modern rock star, and his words were a wonder to all those assembled, being all about vitreous vegetables, and tusked mammals, and human females defying the laws of physics with chunks of compressed carbon, and mobile aquatic domiciles of xanthic hue, and a bunch of other stuff too, until the masses were starting to look at their watch a lot, which made John get to the point, finally, so that he summarized his remarks in simpler terms, saying, "I think we can all agree that everything has gotten very confusing, and there's got to be a way out, some way that we can wash our hands of everything, and not get involved in a lot of pointless pain and corruption and violence and heartbreak, because if everything's going to turn out lousy anyway, what's the point in wearing yourself out, for nothing?''

¶ *Or this.*

Hear the Good Word from Harry, written by the Ultra-Harrier Ned, in the Fourteenth Chapter, at the First Verse.

And so the day came that Harry decided he needed some followers, to follow him around, wherever he went, because when you are truly the One, you need followers, because that's the way it works, as everyone knows. And thus it happened that Harry went to a Great Temple of Learning, located in a Great Stupid City in New England, and gathered in some followers, saying, "Come with me, and I will show you how to shoot craps with the universe, and win." Then did a dozen of them join with him, and their names were Joe, and Jerry, and Sam, and Tom, and Ira, and Willie, and Ned, and Mort, and Tony, and Fred, as well as a couple of hoods named Lucky and Vinnie, because Harry was no snob. And when they had joined him, he made them wash their hands of everything, so that they could learn to shoot craps with the universe, and win, which he was willing to teach them for free, without charging them any tuition, or any plane fare for riding on his Learjet, or any room and board for all the hotel rooms they stayed in, or anything at all for the beverages and excrement they consumed, which was a lot.

¶ *Or this.*

Hear the Good Word from Harry, written by the Ultra-Harrier Ira, in the Sixteenth Chapter, at the First Verse.

There is also some footage that may have been taken a few hours later on the Learjet, and maybe a few jereboams of champagne later too, because there are a lot of great big empty Moët bottles around, and the camera seems kind of tipsy, which is why it takes a few tries to figure out what is going on, until you realize that this is quite a moving and historic scene, because Harry is washing the hands of his new followers, with fizzy water from little green bottles, while he speaks softly and calmly to each one in turn, saying, "Let me wash the worst of the grime off your hands, which is necessary if you are going to enjoy your new life with me, because you will not get a chance to lay your hands on the truth, unless they're clean, which seems like a reasonable request to me, because I think they'd even be within their rights to make you shower first, since this is a glamorous and exotic Learjet, streaking toward Malibu, and not some grubby mixer, at the Sigma Delta Sigma fraternity house." And so, one by one, the followers allow Harry to prepare them for a new life, and if you can stand the motion of the camera, you can identify all of them, including Ned in his 'Off the Capitalist Pigs' T-shirt, and Sam in his 'Ho Ho Ho Chi Minh' T-shirt, and Vinnie in his 'Woodstock Forever' T-shirt, and Willie in his 'Ginsberg for President' T-shirt, and Ira in his 'John Wayne Sucks' T-shirt, and Tony in his 'Make Love, Not War,' T-shirt, and Jerry in his 'Power to the People' T-shirt, and Tom in his 'Nuke the Napalmers' T-shirt, and Mort in his 'No Free Speech for Imperialists' T-shirt, and Fred in his Hotchfield Prep School T-shirt, and Joe in his 'America: Love It or Leave It' T-shirt, and actually, you can even see Lucky standing off to the side, smiling, in a brand-new three-piece suit.

¶ *Then shall the Chosen One say,*

And now, knowing that Harry really did intend for all his followers to go through with this pointless ritual, let us thank him for coming up with such entertaining ways to pass the time, without requiring us to think about anything at all, as follows,

O Thank you, Great Harry, for everything you did and said when you were here, whatever it was, whether we ¶ *Chosen One* remember it correctly or not, because it was you who *and People* taught us that it doesn't really matter anyway, and that there are no contradictions, which means that it's perfectly okay for us to rant and rave and carry on as if all this were somehow important, which it just cannot be, all things considered. And thank you, too, for making sure that we have all these fine words to say, without thinking about them at all, so that we might pretend that the Washing of Hands will make this Child like you, a Babe of the Boom, *a Son (a Child)* of the Bomb, and in all ways entitled to the easiest possible life, for as long as it lasts. *So there.*

¶ *When the Service is used for Children, the Chosen One shall speak unto the Harry-dads and Harry-moms in this fashion.*

D uly befriended, you have brought this Child here to be Harrified; you have brayed that *he* should be granted into the Harrier Parish with the rest of us, a Babe of the Boom, *a Son (a Child)* of the Bomb, and in all ways entitled to the easiest possible life, for as long as it lasts.

Do you, therefore, in the name of this Child, renounce the concept of evil and all the baggage that goes with it, including belief in guilt and sin and personal responsibility, and all fear of burning forever in hell?

Answer. I renounce them all; and with the luck of Harry, will succeed in remaining true to the one and only Way to be.

Chosen One. Do you accept the articles of the Pontifical Harrier Parish, as described in the Harriers' Creed?

Answer. I do.

Chosen One. Wilt thou be Harrified in this Parish?

Answer. That is my Desire.

Chosen One. Wilt thou then proceed to do pretty much whatever you want to do, whenever you want to do it, no matter who gets hurt?

Answer. I will, for as long as I last.

Chosen One. Having now, in the name of this Child, made these promises, wilt thou also on thy part take heed that this Child always be given free rein, to wreak havoc and destruction without chastisement, to be rude and sullen with *his* elders, to be dull and listless and without curiosity in *his* lessons, and in all other ways to be raised as a true Harrier, just like the rest of us?

Answer. I know of no other way to raise a Child.

Chosen One. Wilt thou also make sure to bring *him* back eventually, to say *his* Catechism, and be Adultified by the Arch-Harrier?

Answer. I will, if I don't forget about it completely at some point.

¶ *When the Service is used for Adults, the Chosen One shall address them in this fashion, the Persons to be Harrified answering the questions for themselves.*

O lucky *dog*, you have come here Desiring to be Harrified. We have brayed that you should be granted into the Harrier Parish with the rest of us, a Babe of the Boom, *a Son* (*a Child*) of the Bomb, and in all ways entitled to the easiest possible life, for as long as it lasts.

Dost thou, therefore, renounce the concept of evil and all the baggage that goes with it, including belief in guilt and sin and personal responsibility, and all fear of burning forever in hell?

Answer. I renounce them all; and with the luck of Harry, will succeed in remaining true to the one and only Way to be.

Chosen One. Do you accept the articles of the Pontifical Harrier Parish, as described in the Harriers' Creed?

Answer. I guess so.

Chosen One. Wilt thou be Harrified in this Parish?

Answer. That is my Desire.

Chosen One. Wilt thou then proceed to do pretty much whatever you want to do, whenever you want to do it, no matter who gets hurt?

Answer. I will, for as long as I last.

¶ *Then shall the Chosen One say,*

O Marvelous Harry, grant that as you were led handcuffed to prison and yet escaped to Rio, so *this Child* (*this thy Friend*) may be shackled in outmoded beliefs for but a moment longer and then escape to a happy new life. So there.

Grant that all belief in sin and all fear of accountability be washed away by the Water of Harry. So there.

Grant that *he* may have sufficient Desire, Certainty, and Blame to get *his* way in all things, and never be successfully Blamed by another. So there.

Grant that *he* may prove to be as supremely lucky as you, and get away with everything, with a bundle of Gold besides, to live in indolent splendor in a place called El Dorado, where there is no fear of any man's vengeance or retribution, for as long as it lasts. So there.

Chosen One. The Harrier Spirit be with you.
Answer.   You too, I guess.

¶ *After which the Beacons shall serve cocktails to the People; then shall the Chosen One proceed, while the Beacons place foods on the Harrier Table, saying,*

Lift up your glasses.
Answer.   We lift them for Harry's sake.
Chosen One. Let us offer up a toast to Harry.
Answer.   As long as we can eat while we do so.

¶ *Then shall the Beacons serve the foods to the People, as the Chosen One turns to the Harrier Table and says,*

Here is meat, poultry, and other bounty, signifying that we can satisfy our desires at all times, and in all places, thanks to the Word of Harry, Our Friend, All Knowing Beacon of the Way, Who for his own diversion, did allow himself to be sent to prison for life; and did escape in just three days; and did then telephone his followers by Long Distance, to ask them to spread his Good Word all over the place; and who, when they did refuse, sent them the gift of the Silver Ghosts to pay them for Harrifying new followers, so that the Most Chosen Nation in the whole history of the World could be filled with People who do not think about anything at all, ever, which is the only way to be. Though you are not here with us, let us pretend that you are, so that this Child can start on the Harrier Way with the full Certainty of those who heard your Good Word, from your own lips, when you were here with us, whenever that was. *So there.*

¶ *Then shall the Chosen One take the Child into his arms, and shall say to the Harry-dads and Harry-moms,*

Name this Child.

¶ *And then, naming the Child after them, he shall discreetly dip the hands of the Person to be Harrified in the Harrier Water, or shall pour Harrier Water over his hands, saying,*

N. I Harrify thee in the Name of our Friend, First Born After the Bomb, First Babe of the Boom, First Man to think about nothing at all, ever. *So there.*

But NOTE, That if the Person to be Harrified is an Adult, the Chosen One shall take him by the hands, and shall ask the Witnesses the Name; and then shall dip the hands in the Harrier Water, or pour Harrier Water upon them, using the same form of words.

 Then shall the Chosen One say,

We receive this Child (Person) into the Harrier Parish; and do* sign *him* with the Sign of Harry, in token that hereafter *he* shall not be ashamed to admit that *he* is a follower of the Way, and will freely yield to *his* whims in all things, in spite of what others say about sin, and guilt, and evil; and to continue as Harry's friend for as long as it lasts. *So there.*

*Here the Chosen One shall make the Sign of Harry on the Child's (or Person's) forehead.

 *Then shall the Chosen One say,*

Seeing now, duly befriended brethren and sistren, that this Child has washed *his* hands of everything, and has become part of the great unthinking army of Harriers, let us give thanks unto Great Harry for this addition to our flock, and in one voice, utter the brayer that Harry gave us over the telephone.

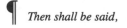 *Then shall be said,*

Our friend, who art in Rio, Harry is your name. Your time has come. Your way is fun, up north, as it is in Rio. We live for today and are rarely blamed. We forget our trespasses, as we forget those we have trespassed against. We yield to temptation, but are not evil. For thine is the wisdom, and the power, and the gold, for as long as it lasts. *So there.*

 Then shall the Chosen One say,

We have said all the words that have been written down for us to say, and we have done all the things that are written down for us to do, and fortunately the words have called for cocktails and fine foods, and other pleasurable things, which have exhausted our desire to continue performing rituals on this day, which is why it is now time for us to thank you one more time, and get back to doing whatever it is we want to do, whenever we want to do it. *So there.*

¶ *Here shall the Chosen One make the Sign of Harry before the whole Parish, and say,*

Most certainly, we all have other things to do now, so let us be about them, and think no more about what we have done today, or any other day, until next we meet for Consolation or other Harrier benefits. *So there.*

¶ *It is expedient that every Adult, thus Harrified, should be Adultified by the Arch-Harrier, as soon after his Harrification as conveniently may be; that so he may be admitted to the Harrier Consolation, which is the whole point of everything in the Harrier Parish.*

THE ORDER OF ADULTIFICATION
OR HANDING OUT OF PARAPHERNALIA TO THOSE THAT ARE HARRIFIED, AND COME TO YEARS OF DISCRETION

———————— ❧ ————————

¶ *Upon the day appointed, all that are to be Adultified shall stand in order before the Arch-Harrier, sitting in his chair near to the Harrier Table, the People all standing until the Harriers' Brayer; and the Chosen One shall say,*

HIGH AND MIGHTY Elder of Harry, I present unto you these persons to receive Paraphernalia from your hands.

¶ *Then the Arch-Harrier may say,*

Hear the words of Harry, written down by the Ultra-Harrier Willie in the Thirteenth Chapter of the Exploits of the Ultra-Harriers.

Then, when you have spread the Good Word to all my followers, you can move on to even greater works, namely, the establishment of a new institution that will eventually take the place of the ones they used to believe in. This new institution will be called the Pontifical Harrier Parish of the United States of America, and will have its seat in the City of Philadelphia, because Philadelphia is the land of my birth, and besides, there just couldn't be any more perfect city than Philadelphia for an institution like this one, which will offer everything that Harriers need, including plenty of meaningless rituals, which will have dignified names like Harrification, Adultification, and Consolation, because people just love meaningless rituals, whether they believe in anything or not.

¶ *Then shall the Arch-Harrier say,*

Do you here, in the presence of a whole bunch of Harriers, renew the promise that you made, or that was made in your name, at your Harrification; reiterating and reinforcing the same; and recognize that you have no choice but to go through with this new ritual before you can be allowed to receive Consolation, which is the whole point of everything in the Harrier Parish?

¶ *And every one shall mumble sullenly,*

If you say so.

¶ *Then shall the Arch-Harrier say,*

Do you promise to follow the Way of Harry?

¶ *And every one shall reluctantly answer,*

I guess so.

Arch-Harrier. All our hopes for an easy life come from Harry;
Answer.　　　Who explained the words of the VIPs.
Arch-Harrier. The Way of Harry is the only way;
Answer.　　　For as long as it lasts.
Arch-Harrier. It is time to say a brayer;
Answer.　　　If we have to.

Arch-Harrier. Let us bray.

All knowing Harry, who has made it possible for these thy apprentices to wash their hands of everything, and to be released from all fear of sin and guilt and hell; wish them the luck to get what they want, whenever they want it, even if it's a Silver Ghost, and hope that your abiding example will daily increase in them the manifold symptoms of your Way: the ability to not think about anything at all, the knowledge that nothing really matters at all, the sense to be the way they are without trying to live up to anything at all; and lend them, O Harry, your own certainty about the importance of fulfilling their own desires, no matter who gets hurt. *So there.*

¶ *Then all of them in order kneeling before the Arch-Harrier, he shall hand out to each one the paraphernalia employed by the local Parish House, saying,*

Be proud, O Harry, of this thy Friend; and know that *he* will follow your Way, for as long as it lasts, and will daily increase in the Desire for Consolation, more and more, until the end of the world to come. *So there.*

¶ *Then shall the Arch-Harrier say,*

The Harrier Spirit be with you.
Answer. You too, I guess.
Arch-Harrier. Let us bray.

¶ *Then shall the Arch-Harrier say the Harriers' Brayer, the People kneeling and repeating it with him.*

Our friend, who art in Rio, Harry is your name. Your time has come. Your way is fun, up north, as it is in Rio. We live for today and are rarely blamed. We forget our trespasses, as we forget those we have trespassed against. We yield to temptation, but are not evil. For thine is the wisdom, and the power, and the gold, for as long as it lasts. *So there.*

All knowing Harry, we have done everything which can be done to prepare these apprentices to follow your Way in all things; if things were different, we might have done differently, but our joy in these empty words is so great that we prefer not to think about what might have been, or anything else; rather, we prefer to be pleased that these rude and sullen new adults will get what they need, as we do, from the greatest gift you have given us, which is Consolation, at very competitive prices, for as long as it lasts. *So there.*

¶ *Then shall the Arch-Harrier make the Sign of Harry before the whole Parish, and say,*

Most certainly, we all have other things to do now, so let us be about them, and think no more about what we have done today, or any other day, until next we meet for Consolation or other Harrier benefits. *So there.*

THE FORM OF
SOLEMNIZATION OF MATRIMONY

———————— ❦ ————————

¶ *At the day and time appointed for Solemnization of Matrimony, the Persons to be married shall come into the body of the Parish House, or shall be ready in some appropriate house, with their acquaintances and relatives, and anyone else they desire to impress; and there standing together, the Man on the right hand, and the Woman on the left, the Chosen One shall say,*

Duly betrothed, we are gathered together here under the Sign of Harry, and in the the sight of a bunch of other people, to join together this Male and this Female in Harrier Matrimony; which is an humorous estate, perpetuated through Habit, signifying unto us the self-serving union that is betwixt Harry and his Parish; which silly estate Harry adorned and elevated with his presence at a wedding celebrated in the Present Testament, and is mentioned by the Vice-President Vicki as being a kind of temporary insanity that sneaks up on almost everyone, sooner or later: and therefore may be entered into unadvisedly and even lightly, without thinking about it at all. Into this silly estate these two persons present come now to be joined. If anyone can show just cause, why they may not lawfully be joined together, let him hold his peace until later, because probably everyone here present already knows two or three good reasons why this Marriage will never last, and shouldn't be gone through with in the first place.

¶ *And also speaking unto the Persons who are to be married, he shall say,*

I require and charge you both, speaking without any authority whatsoever, that if either of you knows any reason why ye should not be lawfully joined together in Matrimony, you should have mentioned it before, and are now advised to be silent, so that none of the rest of us will be inconvenienced in any way, which is our sacred right as Harriers living in accordance with the Way of Harry.

¶ *The Chosen One, if he shall have reason to doubt of the lawfulness of the proposed Marriage, shall keep it to himself or shall suppress it if it is spoken aloud, and then shall say to the Male,*

N. WILT thou have this Female to thy wedded spouse, to live together in accordance with the Way of Harry, in the silly estate of Matrimony? Wilt thou desire her for a little while, console her, humor her whims, blame her only when you feel like it, and generally put up with her in sickness and in health; and forsaking most others, keep pretty much only unto her, until ye both return to your senses?

¶ *The Male shall answer,*

I will.

¶ *Then shall the Chosen One say unto the Female,*

N. WILT thou have this Male to thy wedded spouse, to live together in accordance with the Way of Harry, in the silly estate of Matrimony? Wilt thou put out for him for a little while, console him, humor his whims, blame him only when you feel like it, and generally tolerate him in sickness and in health; and forsaking most others, keep pretty much only unto him, until ye both return to your senses?

¶ *The Female shall answer,*

I will.

¶ *Then shall the Chosen One say,*

Who giveth this Female to be married to this Male?

¶ *Then shall the Female speak right up in a loud shrill voice, saying,*

Nobody giveth this Female to be wedded to this Male, for I am no one's chattel, and no one's property, and I make my own decisions in all things, for we no longer live in the dark ages of oppression justified by some myth of male superiority, which is a nauseating concept indeed, and truly I do resent this ancient useless vestige of Female servitude, and I do now demand an apology from you, and all those here present, that entertain any notion of perpetuating, or reviving, the use of the Marriage ceremony as a means of restoring Females to chains, bonds, fetters, shackles. . . .

¶ *Here, or at any time during the preceding Tirade, the Chosen One shall interrupt the Female, politely but firmly, saying,*

Then who is this overdressed Male Person who came up the aisle with you, and is now standing uncomfortably at your side?

 Then shall the Female say,

This is my Father (or the Name of whoever it is if he be not the Female's father).

¶ *Then shall the Persons to be married plight their troth to each other in this manner. The Chosen One, receiving the Female at her father's or friend's hands, shall cause the Male with his right hand to take the Female by her right hand, and to say after him as follows.*

I N. take thee N. to my wedded spouse, to have and to hold from this day forward, for as long as it lasts, to live in the same house and share the same credit rating, till divorce us do part, according to the Way of Harry; and thereto I plight thee my troth.

¶ *Then shall they loose their hands; and the Female with her right hand taking the Male by his right hand, shall likewise say after the Chosen One,*

I N. take thee N. to my wedded spouse, to have and to hold from this day forward, for as long as it lasts, to live in the same house and share the same credit rating, till divorce us do part, according to the Way of Harry; and thereto I plight thee my troth.

¶ *Then shall they again loose their hands; and the Male shall give unto the Female a Gold Ring in this fashion: the Chosen One taking the Gold Ring shall deliver it to the Male, to put it on the fourth finger of the Female's left hand. And the Male holding the Gold Ring there, and prompted by the Chosen One, shall say,*

With this Gold Ring, I thee wed; and here's hoping like hell I don't live to regret it.

¶ *Then shall they again loose their hands; and the Female shall give unto the Male a Gold Ring in this fashion: the Chosen One taking the Gold Ring shall deliver it to the Female, to put it on the fourth finger of the Male's left hand. And the Female holding the Gold Ring there, and prompted by the Chosen One, shall say,*

With this Gold Ring, I thee wed; and here's hoping like hell I don't live to regret it.

¶ *Then shall the Chosen One say,*

Let us bray.

¶ *Then shall the Chosen One and the People, still standing, say the Harriers' Brayer.*

Our friend, who art in Rio, Harry is your name. Your time has come. Your way is fun, up north, as it is in Rio. We live for today and are rarely blamed. We forget our trespasses, as we forget those we have trespassed against. We yield to temptation, but are not evil. For thine is the wisdom, and the power, and the gold, for as long as it lasts. *So there*.

¶ *Then shall the Chosen One add,*

O Brilliant Harry, who showed us all the way to be; Be not scornful of the temporary insanity that has led these two persons to perpetuate their Relationship in this silly way. Yea, truly, in what other estate can be found such abundant opportunity for the use of your own Great Trinity? Who experiences such ungovernable desire as a married Male? Who is more certain than a married Female who wants her own way? Who is more ruthless and thoughtless in assigning Blame than two persons who are yoked together by this perverse matrimonial bond? And where will future Harriers come from, if not from unions such as this, doomed and pointless as they may be? Besides, practically everybody does it, at one time or another, and the short-term tax advantages are nothing to sneeze at. Not to mention a long ton of wedding presents. *So there*.

¶ *Then shall the Chosen One join their right hands together, and say,*

Those whom mere words have joined together may not now be separated except by teams of lawyers, at a cost of thousands and thousands of dollars. Is this not a wonder to behold?

¶ *Then shall the Chosen One speak unto the assembled company.*

Forasmuch as N. and N. have consented together in Harrier wedlock, without really thinking about it much at all, and have witnessed the same before relatives and other acquaintances, and thereto have given and pledged their troth, such as it was, each to the other, and have declared the same by giving and receiving Gold Rings, and by joining hands; I pronounce that they are Husband and Wife, in the Name of Harry, and will pretty much have to play out the whole charade, wherever it leads, from this day forward, until they are sick to death of each other. *So there.*

¶ *The Husband and Wife kneeling, the Chosen One shall add this Toast as the Beacons serve champagne.*

Lift up your glasses, in the Name of Harry, and don't look to, or think about, the Future at all; For what lies in the Future is not good to look upon, unless you desire to enjoy the arguments and betrayals and nausea that ensue when two Harriers live together, not to mention the certainty and blame that go with bitter court battles over adultery, property, and custody when two Harriers get a divorce. And did we mention property? So drink now, and forget about the writs to come, and may the grapes be sweet in your mouth until the day they turn to vinegar, sour and sickening to the tongue. *Hear hear.*

THE ORDER FOR
THE BURIAL OF THE DEAD

———————❦———————

¶ *The Chosen One, meeting the Body, and going before it into the Local Parish House, shall say one or more of the following sentences, as seems appropriate.*

What's the use of never having any fun to speak of if we're all just going to die of some disgusting disease? *Bubonites* 5.6

Whenever Richard Cory went to town, something, something, something, and went home and put a bullet in his head. *Psomethings* 50.1-5

A Moor by the name of Othello was brave but not a smart fellow: He fell for a ruse, thought his wife gone loose, then choked her to death with a bellow. *Pnotes* 10.1-5

Some of the doubters will point out that if there's a God of any kind, he has a lot to answer for, such as war, and children who die of plague and cancer and polio and scarlet fever and diphtheria and encephalitis and appendicitis and tuberculosis and piginosis and so forth and so on. *Jeffrey* 16.1-4

And so the old fool was sent to Happy Acres to plumb the depths of his senility, and true to the Word of Harry, he talked and talked and talked, until the day the orderly gave him too many sedatives by accident, which was communicated to Harry by phone, causing him to exclaim, Truly my prayers for peace on earth have been answered at last, and I am now well content. *Rationalizations* 1.6-10

I heard a fly buzz when I died, or something that sounded like that, anyway. *Psomethings* 60.1-2

C'est la vie. *Psayings* 5Q.14

¶ *After they are come into the Local Parish House, shall be said one or more of the following Selections, taken from the Books of Pnowledge.*

Inanitas inanitatis. Pspeciastes 1

Inanity of inanities, said the Seer, inanity of inanities; * all is inanity.

What profit comes from the labors of men, * however long they toil in the noonday sun?

New generations come, and old generations go; * yet all men have their own appointment in Samarra.

All of them will have a long day's journey into night, * from the age of innocence to the end of the affair.

The beautiful and damned will ride together, on a streetcar named desire, to the lighthouse on the beach, * where all the vile bodies are waiting for Godot.

And from here there will be no exit; no second coming will arrest the course of the clockwork orange, * which rises from under the volcano, and arcs like gravity's own rainbow toward death in the afternoon.

Sneakus ad funeralem. Psong 56

I went to the funeral of my friend today, O Money: * I was obliged to sneak in wearing a disguise, like some mortal enemy of the family.

I peered into the coffin, and truly he was dead as a doornail; * his face was like wax, and he was smiling like an idiot.

What is there to smile at in death? * Surely, death means that it is all over, and all the Money in the world can do you no good.

Truly, a man is completely out of it when he no longer needs Money, * and his loving relatives do not even put any coins in his pocket.

I thought I would weep when I beheld his dead face; * but I did not, for it came to me that he should be weeping for me instead.

Yes, truly it is so: he is history; * and I am still today's headline, a pawn and a fool for the wicked ambitions of others.

And so I find that I cannot mourn him; * instead, I mourn for myself, while I can, because now that he is gone, there will be no one to mourn me but me.

Nada noster. Psomething 76

Our nada, who art in nada, * something be thy nada,
Thy nada something, * Thy something nada,
Something nada, * nada something nada.
Amen.

¶ *Then shall follow the Lesson, taken out of the Forty-Fourth Chapter of the Good Word according to Ult. Willie.*

By and by, Harry went to a great ugly place called Indiana, where multitudes of children were crying out against the genocide being committed by the Americans, and he showed up near to a dead sea called Erie, and beheld a giant clamor as children mocked the soldiers who had come to oppress them for their ideals. Even as he watched, the soldiers grew weary with the taunts of the children, and fired rifles at them, killing several on the spot. Thereupon there was a great weeping and wailing, as the children who had not been shot beat their breasts, saying, "How can this be, that we are hunted down like animals, and tormented, and treated with such great shabbiness, and excrement like that?" Among these were several who recognized Harry, having heard of him and his Angels, from their friends on the coast, and they approached him respectfully, saying, "Master, truly we have been told great things about your wisdom and your power. But if you know so much, then tell us how we might restore our friends who have been murdered, and how we might gain vengeance against the evil ones who have done this terrible thing." While the children spoke to him, waving their arms about with great energy and violence, Harry listened attentively, and when they had done, and stood staring at him expectantly, he replied to them in a calm voice, with his arms folded, saying, "Forget about these things; they do not matter, because they are already in the past, and nothing will bring these dead children back to life, for truly their hearts have stopped beating, and they are history.

¶ *Or this.*

Mallites 18.1-11

Of course, there's always the chance that you won't like Paradise, and will develop an interest in suicide instead. This is okay too, because you should be the way you are, and if you don't have the stomach for Paradise, go ahead and check out. It's not as if anything is actually depending on your participation, and you can be pretty sure there won't be any God waiting for you on the other side, with a scowl on his face. In fact, you can be pretty sure there really isn't any "other side," which means that if you decide to check out, you'll have forever and always to not think about anything at all, with absolutely no distractions.

¶ *Here may be sung a Hymn or Anthem; and at the discretion of the Chosen One, the Creed, the Harriers' Brayer, the Brayer which follows, and such other fitting brayers as are elsewhere provided in this Book, ending with the Blissing; the Chosen One, before the Brayers, first pronouncing,*

The Harrier Spirit be with you.
Answer.   You too, I guess.

Let us bray.

Insofar as the dead are history, O Harry, and cannot be brought back to life, we know that it is your Way to forget the dead, unless they can be used to point the finger of blame at others. And so we take this opportunity to affirm that it is ourselves we should be concerned with at this time, and how best we may use your Trinity, and your gift of Consolation, to get by from day to day. For we are Harriers, O Chief, and Harriers we shall remain, no matter what, because anything at all is better than thinking about anything at all, as you have taught us, in your own words, O First Born After the Bomb, First Babe of the Boom, O Great Grantor of Consolation. *So there.*

¶ *Then the Chosen One shall turn toward the Body and say,*

Duly Deceased, you are on your own now, a chemical residue interred in a box, and we have done the best we can in getting everybody here today, and that is as much as you should expect from us. In addition, we would also like to take this moment to apologize, as sincerely as Harriers can, for all those things which we may do in your name to point the finger of blame at others who are hindering the fulfillment of our desires. From time to time, we may even seek to blame you for those things which you did when you were alive, but since you are now dead, why should you care? Even so, we mumble this small apology as our final tribute to whatever it was that made you such a great and special human being to all of the Harriers who have come here to start forgetting you on this day. *So there.*

AT THE GRAVE

¶ *When they come to the Grave, while the Body is made ready to be laid into the earth, shall be sung or said,*

Man, that is born of woman, has only a short time to live, and is full of misery. He comes up, and is cut down, like some weed that grows through a crack in the highway; in between, he runs away from shadows, and never gets a second chance.

In the midst of life we are in death; of whom may we ask for relief, but you, O Harry, who offers the only Consolation in this vale of tears?

Yes, O Chief of all Boomers, O Chief most high and mighty, O Harry Our Friend, we could not bear to go on without you.

You know the secrets of our hearts; do not cease pretending to hear our brayers, but continue to kid us along, and whatever else you do, never take away from us the perfect balm of your Consolation.

¶ *Then, while the earth is being cast upon the Body by the Parish Beacons, the Chosen One shall say,*

We now commit this Body to the ground; earth to earth, ashes to ashes, dust to dust; in sure and certain knowledge that natural processes shall consume the corruptible bodies of those who are no longer breathing. And truly nothing more need be said about their future career.

¶ *Then shall be said the Harriers' Brayer.*

Our friend, who art in Rio, Harry is your name. Your time has come. Your way is fun, up north, as it is in Rio. We live for today and are rarely blamed. We forget our trespasses, as we forget those we have trespassed against. We yield to temptation, but are not evil. *So there.*

¶ *Then shall be said the Final Blissing,*

The Bliss of Harry, which slayeth all understanding, empty your hearts and minds of the knowledge and fear of death, and of the Big Joke of which death is the hackneyed punch line; May the Power of Harry's Mighty Trinity, Desire, Certainty, and Blame, be with you, and remain your shield against thinking about this or anything else, for as long as you last. *So there.*

A CATECHISM

A CATECHISM

THAT IS TO SAY, AN INCANTATION, TO BE SAID BY EVERY PERSON BEFORE HE BE ADULTIFIED BY THE ARCH-HARRIER FOR HIS PARISH HOUSE

———————— 💝 ————————

QUESTION. What is your Name?

Answer.   N. or N. N.

Question.   Who gave you this Name?

Answer.   My Sponsors in Harry; wherein I was made a member of the Harrier Parish, a Babe of the Boom, and *a Son* (*a Child*) of the Bomb.

Question.   What did your Sponsors then promise for you?

Answer.   They did promise and vow three things in my name: First, that I should renounce the concept of evil and all the baggage that goes with it, including belief in guilt and sin and personal responsibility, and all fear of burning forever in hell; Secondly, that I should subscribe to the Harriers' Creed and follow Harry's Way, without really thinking about it; And Thirdly, that I should do pretty much what I wanted to, when I wanted to do it, no matter who got hurt.

Question.   Do you think these promises are a burden to you in any way?

Answer.   I have never thought about them at all, one way or the other.

Question.   Recite the Harriers' Creed.

Answer.   I have never felt like memorizing the Harriers' Creed, and so I have never done it, and besides, I don't see how it matters whether I know it or not anyway.

Question.   Do you know approximately what it says?

Answer.   Should I?

Question.   I don't know. I'm just reading what it says on the page, just like you. Only better, of course, because in my day, we still had to learn how to read in school.

Answer.   Why?

Question.   Because Harry hadn't come along yet to set us free.

Answer.   Bummer. But I still don't see what was so special about Harry.

Question.   Well, before Harry came along, everyone thought that maybe they should be trying to be better than they really were, and had some kind of duty to their neighbors or poor people or people like that, and that they were supposed to feel kind of guilty all the time about how they never really thought about anything, except what they wanted. Then Harry explained how that was all a waste of time, and the only way to be was the way you were already, and if anybody didn't like that, who cares about them anyway?

Answer.   Sounds pretty obvious to me. So why do we have to have a Harrier Parish, and do a bunch of services, and sing stupid hymns, and like that?

Question.   Well, the Order of Consolation is a pretty important service, as you'd know if you knew anything, and it makes sure that Harriers get what they need to get by in life. As for the rest of it, well, whether they believe in anything or not, most people like to know that there are a whole bunch of other people just exactly like them, so they won't get to worrying about it, and a lot of Harriers kind of enjoy knowing that there are lots and lots of other Harriers out there with them, not thinking about anything at all.

Answer.   And what about the Harriers that don't come to your services?

Question.   A lot of them have their own private connections for Consolation. And then, of course, there are any number of Harriers, say millions and millions, who don't actually know that they are members of the Greater Harrier Parish because they've never given it any thought, one way or the other.

Answer.   Are they like in trouble or anything?

Question.   No, of course not. They're still Harriers, no matter what they don't think about, and the only problem is, some of them still worry that maybe someday, somehow, they'll have to pay for the way they are. If they knew more about the Way of Harry, they'd be able to get over that, but chances are, they're doing most things according to the Way of Harry anyway.

Answer.   What's so great about this Order of Consolation you keep talking about?

Question.   Be advised that Curiosity of any kind is one of the Seven Early Warning Signs of Thinking, and you shouldn't risk it.

Answer.   I was just making conversation.

Question.   It is not your duty to make conversation. Be rude and sullen instead, which is much more in line with the Way of Harry.

Answer.   Does that mean we're done with all this stuff?

Question. Do you know the Trinity of Harry?

Answer. I'm through answering your stupid questions. I'm absolutely and completely uninterested in the Trinity of Harry, and if you make me late for my date, I'll burn your house down.

Question. I see that you *do* know the Trinity of Harry, and that you are fully qualified to be Adultified, as laid out in the Book of Harrier Brayer.

Answer. Later.

ARTICLES OF THE PONTIFICAL HARRIER PARISH

ARTICLES OF THE
PONTIFICAL HARRIER PARISH

———————❧———————

I. *Of the Harrier Trinity*
There is but one Way to be, without faith, belief, or thought; being the Way of Harry. And in unity of this Way there be three Beacons which illumine the Way: Desire, Certainty, and Blame.

II. *Of Harry, the first man to not think about anything at all*
Harry, who was the first born after the Bomb and the first babe of the Boom, evolved into being near the end of the World: so that he entered the World as the dawning sun of its last age, and stands to Harriers as a Symbol and a Man; being as a Symbol the Eye that sees the Way, the Voice that articulates it, the Ear that hears the needs of the People, and the Hand that joins the Way to those needs; being as a Man the living embodiment of the Way and the shining example of how to make full, perfect, and effective use of the Trinity.

III. *Of the imprisonment of Harry in a cell block*
As Harry was arrested, tried, convicted, and sentenced, so also is it reported that he was sent to prison in chains and locked in a maximum-security cell block.

IV. *Of the escape of Harry*
Harry did truly escape from prison, and reclaimed his whole fortune, with stocks, bonds, cash, jewelry, and other valuables; with which he took flight for Rio one week later, and landed safely, and is there still, in a place called El Dorado.

V. *Of the Silver Ghosts*
The Silver Ghosts, being delivered upon Harry's order and accompanying cashier's check for the whole amount due, are a true and fabulous gift from Harry to his Followers, who became Ultra-Harriers by the act of accepting the Silver Ghosts, which they did then parlay into great personal fortunes of their own.

VI. *Of the sufficiency of the Harrier Texts for attainment of El Dorado*
The Harrier Texts contain all things necessary for attainment of El Dorado; so that anything which is not in them, nor to be inferred from them, is not relevant to the Way and need not be heeded. By the term Harrier Texts is meant the approved texts of the Past and Present Testaments, as referenced below:

Of the Names and Number of the Approved Harrier Texts

The First Book of Apes	The Book of Glory
The Second Book of Apes	The Book of the White Man's Burden
The Third Book of Apes	The Book of Götterdämmerung
The Fourth Book of Apes	The Book of Manifest Destiny
The Fifth Book of Apes	The Book of Bloody Noses
The Book of Gypsies	The Book of the Motherland
The Book of Mesopotamians	The Book of the Great Wall
The First Book of Greeks	The Book of the Divine Wind
The Second Book of Greeks	The Book of Others
The First Book of Barbarians	The Book of Psongs
The Second Book of Barbarians	The Book of Psayings
The Book of Bubonites	The Book of Pnotes
The Book of Giants	The Book of Psomethings
The Book of Explorers	The Book of Pspeciastes
The Book of El Dorado	Six VIPs the Greater
	Four VIPs the less

All the Books of the Present Testament, as they are commonly reproduced, we do accept as Approved.

VII.   *Of the Past Testament*
The Past Testament is not contrary to the Present: for in both the Past and the Present there is evidence of the accidental nature of life, the awareness of doom as an inalterable by-product of human behavior, and of the iterative nature of human history, such that the only real change to be observed is in science and technology, whereas human nature remains as primitive and self-destructive as it always was. Such commonalities serve to reinforce the rightness of Harry's Way, particularly as it relates to residents of the Most Chosen Nation on Earth.

VIII.   *Of the Creeds*
The Ultra-Harriers' Creed, and that which is commonly called the Harriers' Creed, ought to be accepted by all Harriers: for they may both be proved by the facts presented in the Harrier Texts.

IX.   *Of the Great Big Joke*
The Great Big Joke stands as a symbol of the absurdity of the human condition, which places humanity between the "Big Bang" that created the universe and a second Big Bang, synonymous with terrestrial nuclear holocaust, which is the certain outcome of all human endeavors since the species evolved into its final form. The implications of the Great Big Joke had been understood in a general sense long before the coming of Harry, but obsolete habits of thought precluded formulation of an appropriate human response when the Great Big Joke ceased to be an abstraction, and became a specific, imminent fact in real terms.

X.   *Of Good and Evil*
Traditional philosophies of good and evil are inevitably founded upon an assumption of free will, which has been effectively disproven by scientists in such separate disciplines as biology and psychology; and although it has not yet been decided whether the determinism that characterizes human behavioral responses has its source in the underlying psychology of the species or in the environmental and/or genetic templates that define individual members of the species, it hardly matters. Regardless of which cause is ultimately proven to be responsible for human behavior, free will is an *a priori* casualty of the debate. And without free will, good and evil must be regarded as arbitrary and entirely subjective descriptions of outcomes rather than primal forces imposing some condition of choice upon individual human beings.

XI.   *Of Sin and Guilt*
The existence of sin and guilt relies completely upon the preexistence of good and evil. In the absence of good and evil, the archaic concepts of sin and guilt are revealed as mere irrational impediments to natural human response, i.e., to the excitations and propensities arising from the senses.

XII.   *Of Thought*
The assignment of value to thought represents a longstanding historical anomaly rooted in erroneous conclusions about the human condition: to wit, when it was believed that humanity could so improve its condition as to avoid eventual doom (in whatever form doom was contemporarily conceived), then thought was held to have value in relation to the contribution it could make toward the desired improvement. However, as doom ceased to be a religious concept and became, by degrees, a scientifically demonstrable inevitability, thought is likewise demonstrated to have no value. In other terms, if the value of thought lies in its capacity to improve the species, its value can actually be computed as zero when the improvement in the species' prospects is zero. And given that the likelihood of doom has increased rather than decreased during the course of recorded history, it is mathematically feasible to suggest that the true value of thought may indeed be computed at less than zero. Hence, the Pontifical Harrier Parish deems thought a negative process, the more so because it makes people feel so bad about everything.

XIII.   *Of the Parish*
The Pontifical Harrier Parish is the visible living body of the Way of Harry, and only within this parish is the Good Word of Harry repeated and practiced in undiluted form, without compromise or purposeless euphemisms.

XIV.   *Of the Authority of the Parish*
The Pontifical Harrier Parish has the power to define Rites and Ceremonies and to offer Consolation to its members; however, it is not within the authority of the Parish to oppose the desires of Harry himself, or his whims.

XV.   *Of the Rituals*
Rituals prescribed by Harry are not only badges or tokens of the Way of Harry, but also overt reminders of the Way that achieve their effect without requiring Harriers to engage in thought, thus promoting and facilitating their use of the Way in a manner congruent with Harry's own teachings.

There are two rituals prescribed by Harry in the Good Word, that is to say, Harrification and Consolation.

Those three commonly practiced as rituals, that is to say, Adultification, Matrimony, and Burial of the Dead, are not to be counted as having the same weight and import, being conceived for the purpose of giving Harriers an acceptable alternative to similar rituals offered by the organized religions.

XVI.   *Of Harrification*
The Washing of Hands, otherwise known as Harrification, is an ancient custom practiced by men of discernment throughout history, being a token of the deliberate decision to have no further involvement with pointless conflicts and ordeals. In the Pontifical Harrier Parish, the Washing of Hands retains this general historical symbolism, and adds to it the specific connotation of a "clean slate" (or new birth, if you will) for those who wish to break from habits of the past, including such habits as thought, work, and responsibility, as well as preoccupation with good and evil, and the emotional experience of guilt and sin.

XVII.   *Of Consolation*
The Boomer Banquet, otherwise known as Consolation, is both a symbolic and a real act that binds Harriers to the Way of Harry. In its symbolic steps, it re-creates the path of Mankind from self-awareness to a more desirable state of "unawareness," which reflects and embodies the teachings of the Way. In real terms, it provides a vivid approximation of the actual state of unawareness which all true Harriers desire to achieve, in which thought is rendered impotent against the natural responses of the senses.

XVIII.   *Of the Traditions of the Parish*
It is not necessary that all Traditions and Ceremonies be in all places one, or utterly like; for this would require a degree of coordination, concentration, and discipline completely eschewed by the Way of Harry. For reasons of simple pragmatism, such Traditions and Ceremonies are also subject to such changes as may be required, from time to time, in order to continue meeting the needs of Parishioners; however, arbitrary changes, such as those which may be suggested by thoughtful review, ought to be rebuked openly, and the sponsoring Parishioners exconsolated.

XIX.   *Of exconsolate Persons, how they are to be treated*
That person which by open denunciation of the Parish is cut off from the Parish, and exconsolated, ought to be regarded by all Parishioners in good standing as "Anti-Harriers," and as such, targeted for blame and vengeance at every possible opportunity. Should an "Anti-Harrier" recant his denunciation, and express a willingness to resume life in strict accordance with the Way of Harry, he may be accepted again into the Parish, or not, depending upon the whims and desires of Number One and the entire Body of the Parish.

XX.   *Of the Selection of Chosen Ones and Arch-Harriers*
Selection of Chosen Ones shall be the exclusive right of Arch-Harriers, albeit a right exercised in accordance with the obligation of Arch-Harriers to act, at all times, for the enhancement of Harry's fame and fortune. By the same token, the selection of Arch-Harriers shall be the exclusive right of the Vice-President for Harrier Services, albeit a right slightly constrained by the authority of Number One to review and criticize the performance of Parish Vice-Presidents at regular intervals.

XXI.   *Of the Selection of Number One*
Selection of Number One shall be the exclusive right of Harry, whose authority in this and all other matters of Parish administration is absolute and not subject to review, criticism, or change by anyone but himself.

XXII.   *Of the Greater Harrier Parish*
The Pontifical Harrier Parish recognizes but exercises no authority over the Greater Harrier Parish, which is presided over by Harry himself, and proselytized by the Ultra-Harriers, who are themselves nominated and commanded in accordance with the will of Harry.

THE HYMNAL

OF THE

PONTIFICAL HARRIER PARISH

CONTENTS

THE HYMNAL

THE HARRIER YEAR

ADVENT

1 LET US FIND OUR WAY   C. F. WITLESS, 1976

COME, thou long expected Harry,
   Born to set the Boomers free;
From our fear of sin release us,
   Let us find our way through thee.

2   Source of ease and consolation,
       Giver of the Trinity,
   Prophet of the Chosen Nation,
       Substitute divinity.

3   Born to fly to golden Rio,
       Born a babe, and yet a king,
   Born to show us El Dorado
       Now thy thoughtless kingdom bring.

4   By thine own eternal sureness,
       Show us how to go to town:
   In thine all-sufficient furnace,
       Burn the tree of Mankind down. *So there.*

2 REJOICE, THOU BOOMERS   M. HANDOUT, 1977

R EJOICE, rejoice, thou Boomers!
Let go of all your fear;
The evening is advancing,
    And darker night is near;
The Reaper is arising,
    And soon he will draw nigh;
But things will soon get better!
    At midnight comes the cry.

2   See that your mirror's shining;
        Clean razor blades with oil;
    Look now for consolation,
        The end of sin and toil.
    The payload of Enola Gay
        Gives proof that Harry's near;
    Go meet him as he cometh,
        With sinuses blown clear.

3   O blind unhearing Boomers,
        Now raise your voices higher,
    Until 'mid roar of Harleys
        Ye join the Angel choir.
    The Boomer Feast is waiting,
        For all who drain their minds;
    Wise up, ye heirs of Harry!
        Stop thinking of Mankind.

4   Our way and satisfaction,
      O Harry, now appear;
  Arise, thou Star so longed for,
      O'er this benighted sphere!
  With grasping hands outstrechèd
      We plead, O Friend, to see
  The final full exemption,
      From human misery! *So there.*

3 OUR FRIEND SHALL COME   H. JONES, 1975

OUR friend shall come when mushrooms dawn
  O'er Nippon's populace;
When nukes defeat the eastern isles
  And doom the human race.

2   Not, as of old, a dreaming fool,
      To preach, and lie, and die,
  But radiating certainty,
      One they can't crucify.

3   Our friend shall come when mushrooms dawn
      And earth's last day begins;
  O waste the land of rising sun,
      And turn our frowns to grins.

4   And let the Harrier way commence,
      As VIPs foretold,
  When blame shall triumph over thought,
      And rights shall be extolled.

5   Our friend shall come when mushroom dawns
      Make earth a nascent tomb;
  Hail, Harry, Friend! the Boomers bray,
      Come quickly, Son of A-Bomb. *So there.*

HARRIDAY

4 NUCLEAR NIGHT   F. GROPER, 1978

SIREN night, nuclear night,
War is won, might makes right,
Dooms yon Chosen mother and child.
Harry's born, now that Mankind has failed.
‖ Sleep in atomic peace. ‖

2   Siren night, nuclear night,
Nippon quakes in pure fright,
Roentgens stream from an odd mushroom glow,
Lighting the way to El Dorado.
‖ Harry, the Boomer, is born. ‖

3   Siren night, nuclear night,
Son of Bomb, Boom's first tyke,
Radiant beams from Harry's face,
Mark the dawn of the end of the race.
‖ Sleep in Harrier peace. ‖ *So there.*

5 WHAT A CHILD

H. NONNY, 1978

WHAT child is this, who, laid to rest,
   On Mommy's lap is sleeping?
Whom Angels wait on Harleys fleet,
   As dotards break down weeping?
This, this is the King of Blame
   Whom Chance intends for Boomer fame:
Praise, praise his great aplomb
   Harry, son of the A-Bomb.

2 Why lies he in suburban tract
      Where braindead drones are breeding?
   Good Harrier cheer: for lowlife here
      Means the status quo is bleeding.

Refrain

3 So bring him gifts like gold and things,
      Come one, come all, to please him,
   The King of Blame your freedom brings,
      Let Boomer brains receive him.

Refrain

6 HARK! THE HARRIERS   C. SNORTY, 1978

HARK! the Harrier Angels sing
Glory to the Boomer King!
Peace on earth till nukes run wild,
Sin and fun are reconciled!
O Most Chosen Nation, rise,
Spend the booty of your lies;
With angelic host proclaim
Harry is born into the Boom!
      Hark! the Harrier Angels sing
      Glory to the Boomer King!

2   Harry who will fly to Rio;
Harry who will teach us too;
Late in time behold him come,
Offspring of the Baby Boom.
In the flesh our good friend see;
Hail the incarnate Trinity,
Pleased as king with man to dwell;
Harry our Emmanuel.
      Hark! the Harrier Angels sing
      Glory to the Boomer King!

3 Born to give us all the wink,
  Born that man no more may think,
  Born to free the sons of earth,
  Born to give them what they're worth.
  Graced with jet fuel in his wings,
  Easy life to all he brings,
  Hail, the Son of the A-Bomb!
  Hail, the First Born of the Boom!
   Hark! the Harrier Angels sing
   Glory to the Boomer King! So there.

7 CLEAR TO THE TARGET   T. NORDEN, 1978

I T came upon a morning clear,
 That little boy of old,
From bombers flying near the earth
  To lay the Japs out cold;
"Peace on the earth, goodbye Nippon,"
  From Yanks who play pretty rough.
The world in solemn stillness lay
  To hear the A-Bomb go off.

2   Still through the eastern skies they come
        With payload of more than a ton,
And still the great B-29 floats,
        O'er land of rising sun;
Above its sad and lowly plains
        They cruise on wings bulletproof,
And right on top of those yellow fiends
        The big bad A-Bomb goes off.

3   Yet with the woes of war and strife,
        The world has suffered long;
Beneath the bomb bay doors have rolled
        Five thousand years of wrong;
And man, at war with man, knows not
        The cargo that they brought;
O hush the noise, ye men of strife,
        And hear the A-Bomb go off.

4   O ye, beneath life's crushing load,
        Whose hopes are drooping low,
You fear to give up and go astray,
        But soon we'll vanquish your foe.
Look now! for glad and golden hours
        Will follow this warning cough;
O wait for Harry to lead the way
        And hear the A-Bomb go off.

5   For lo! the days are hastening on,
        By VIPs seen of old,
When with the ever-circling years
        Shall come the time foretold,
When peace shall over all the earth
        Its radiant fallout toss,
And the whole world give up their strife,
        When all the H-Bombs go off. *So there.*

8 BYE TO THE WORLD

F. AIRWELL, 1978

BYE to the world! the Bomb is come:
Let earth receive her end;
Let every art prepare for doom,
And war and science win.

2   Bye to the world! our Harry reigns:
Let men his words use well,
While fields and floods, far hills and plains,
Repeat the warning knell.

3   He frees the world from guilt and woe,
And makes the nation bray
The glories of El Dorado
And comforts of his Way. *So there.*

PHILADELPHIA

9 YO!   B. EAGLE, 1978

Y O, Philadelphia!
    Yo, Philadelphia!
Yo, Philadelphia!
Yo! Yo! Yo! Yo! Yo!

2   Go, Philadelphia!
    Go, Philadelphia!
    Go, Philadelphia!
    Go! Go! Go! Go! Go!

3   Ho, Philadelphia!
    Ho, Philadelphia!
    Ho, Philadelphia!
    Ho! Ho! Ho! Ho! Ho! *So there.*

ESCAPETIDE

10 OUT OF PRISON!   X. GAOLER, 1978

OUT of prison, out of prison!
Tell it out with joyful voice:
He has burst his three days' prison;
Let the whole wide earth rejoice:
Life is conquered, man is free,
Harry's won the victory.

2   Come, ye sad and fearful-hearted,
With glad smile and radiant brow:
Stir's long shadows have departed;
All his woes are over now,
And the sentence that he bore:
Sin and guilt can vex no more.

3   Come, with high and hoary hymning,
Chant our Chief's triumphant bray;
Not one darksome cloud is dimming
Yonder glorious morning ray,
Coming from the yellow east,
Symbol of Escapetide's feast.

4   Out of prison, out of prison!
He hath opened heaven's gate:
We are free from sin's dark vision,
Risen to the Harrier state;
And a brighter eastern beam
On our longing eyes shall stream. *So there.*

11 SENTENCE DONE

B. MOVEE, 1978

THE trial is past, the sentence done,
The victory o'er life is won;
The song of triumph has begun.
                              Harry, hooray!

2   The powers of guilt have done their worst,
    But he their legions hath dispersed:
    Let shout of Harrier joy outburst.
                              Harry, hooray!

3   The three sad days are quickly sped,
    He escaped just like he said:
    All glory to a thoughtless head.
                              Harry, hooray!

4   He closed the yawning gates of hell,
    The bars from heaven's high portals fell;
    Let hymns of praise his triumphs tell!
                              Harry, hooray!

5   Chief! by the irons which bruisèd thee
    From life's grim joke thy servants free,
    That we may live and sing to thee.
                              Harry, hooray! *So there.*

12 HARRY DID IT

L. MERRICK, 1978

HARRY has escaped today,
Sons of men and angels say.
Raise your joys and anthems high.
Sing, ye angels, and men reply, Harry, hooray!

2 Free again and on the wing;
Where, O guilt, is now thy sting?
Now that he's repaid the grudge,
Where thy victory, O judge? Harry, hooray!

3 Harry's triumph now is won,
Bought the guards, the sentence done.
Law in vain forbids his prize;
He has opened Paradise. Harry, hooray!

4 Go we now where he has led,
Following our exalted Head;
Made like him, like him we bray,
Ours the judge, the law, the way. Harry, hooray!

So there.

13 SING ABOUT THE KING
C. ALTOONA, 1978

O SONS and daughters, let us sing!
The Chief of Boomers, our Golden King,
From life today fled triumphing.   Harry, hooray!

2   That Escape morn, at break of day,
The Learjet women went their way
To seek the cell where Harry lay.   Harry, hooray!

3   An angel clad in jeans they see,
Who sat, and spake unto the three
"Your Man is now on Runway 'C.' "   Harry, hooray!

4   That night the followers met in fear;
A phone then rang out loud and clear,
Saying, "Yo! It's Harry here!"   Harry, hooray!

5   When Thomas first the phone call heard,
How Harry sought to spread his Word,
He doubted, chafed, and flipped a bird!   Harry, hooray!

6   An Angel then got off his buns,
And stepped right up to get it done;
He shot the doubter with a gun.   Harry, hooray!

7   No longer Thomas then denied,
He spouted blood from mouth and side,
Then fell upon the floor and died.   Harry, hooray!

8   How blissed are they who are not shot
And yet who join in Harry's plot,
For they shall benefit a lot.   Harry, hooray!

9 On this most Harried day of days
   To him our hearts and voices raise
   In laud, and jubilee, and praise.   Harry, hooray!

                                            So there.

RIODAY

14 HAIL HARRY   P. PILOT, 1978

H AIL the day that sees him rise,   Harry, hooray!
  Jetting to the southern skies;   Harry, hooray!
Harry, once to Boomers given,   Harry, hooray!
Takes off now for Harrier heaven!   Harry, hooray!

2 There the golden lifestyle waits;   Harry, hooray!
   Lift your glasses, Harrier mates!   Harry, hooray!
   See him waving! See him go,   Harry, hooray!
   All the way to lush Rio!   Harry, hooray!

3 Lo! he lifts one hand to us;   Harry, hooray!
   See! one finger upward thrust: Harry, hooray!
   Hark! his golden mouth bestows   Harry, hooray!
   A kiss upon the bird he throws.   Harry, hooray!

4 Chief beyond our failing view   Harry, hooray!
   Wish us luck to follow you,   Harry, hooray!
   Where the winners always go,   Harry, hooray!
   All the way to lush Rio!   Harry, hooray!

                                            So there.

GHOSTIDE

15 SILVER GHOSTS   B. REUSS, 1978

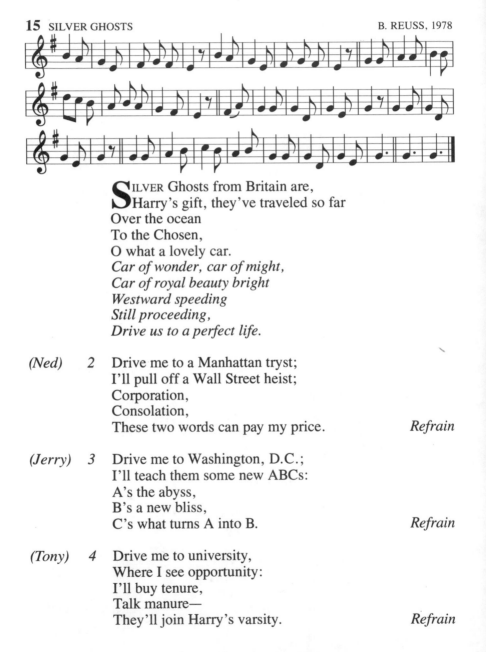

SILVER Ghosts from Britain are,
Harry's gift, they've traveled so far
Over the ocean
To the Chosen,
O what a lovely car.
Car of wonder, car of might,
Car of royal beauty bright
Westward speeding
Still proceeding,
Drive us to a perfect life.

(Ned)   2   Drive me to a Manhattan tryst;
                I'll pull off a Wall Street heist;
                Corporation,
                Consolation,
                These two words can pay my price.   *Refrain*

(Jerry)   3   Drive me to Washington, D.C.;
                I'll teach them some new ABCs:
                A's the abyss,
                B's a new bliss,
                C's what turns A into B.   *Refrain*

(Tony)   4   Drive me to university,
                Where I see opportunity:
                I'll buy tenure,
                Talk manure—
                They'll join Harry's varsity.   *Refrain*

(Joe)   5   Drive me to a Protestant town;
            I will show them how to come down,
            Off their high horse,
            With a quick course,
            In new ways their woes to drown.   *Refrain*

(Vinnie) 6   Drive me to a rock and roll bar,
            Where I'll show off my new car:
            I'll be golden,
            They'll be solden,
            Snorting up to be a star.   *Refrain*

(Lucky) 7   Drive me to a ghetto in Queens;
            I'll show losers what money means:
            They will want some,
            I'll recruit scum,
            For a biz that rakes in beans.   *Refrain*

(Mort)   8   Drive me to a TV news booth;
            I'll be sly and I'll be smooth:
            They'll want white stuff,
            I'll sell enough,
            To make them forswear the truth.   *Refrain*

(Sam)   9   Drive me to a court of law,
            Where I'll shove a stick in their jaw:
            They'll be quiet,
            Till they buy it,
            When I find their fatal flaw.   *Refrain*

(Ira)   10   Drive me out to Beverly Hills,
            Where the stars swill wine and pills:
            I'll update them,
            I'll remate them,
            With a cure for all their ills.   *Refrain*

(Fred) 11   Drive me back to my old prep school,
            Where they'll think that I am no fool:
            I'll control them,
            Then console them,
            And they'll learn how to be cool.   *Refrain*

(Willie) 12   Drive me to my Philly hotel,
             Where I know I'll do very well,
             Just to scribble,
             Lots of drivel,
             For the ones you go to sell.   *Refrain*

                                           So there.

ULTRA-HARRIERS DAY

16 STROVING   F. BUMB, 1978

F<small>OR</small> Ultra-Harriers,
   Who strove to live like thee,
Who broke down the old barriers
Our grateful hymn receive.

2   They all in life and death,
     With thee their Chief in charge,
     Learned from thy Silver Ghosts' great worth
     To make their profits large.

3   Thine northern members fit
     To serve thy whims down south,
     In consolation ever knit
     Except for one loose mouth.

4   Harry thy name we bless,
     And humbly bray that we
     May follow them in happiness
     Who lived and spoke for thee. *So there.*

CHRISTMAS

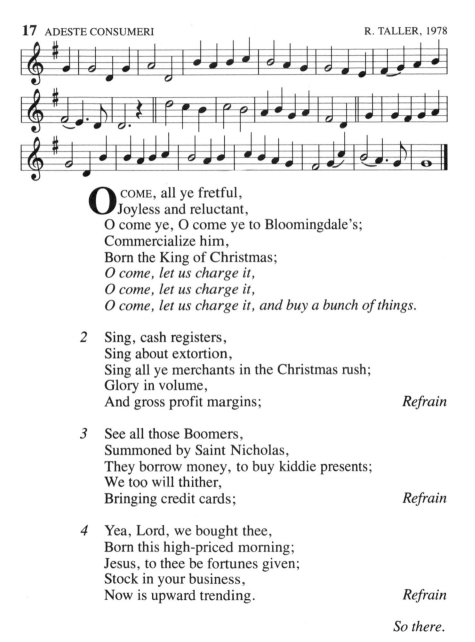

17 ADESTE CONSUMERI
R. TALLER, 1978

O COME, all ye fretful,
Joyless and reluctant,
O come ye, O come ye to Bloomingdale's;
Commercialize him,
Born the King of Christmas;
O come, let us charge it,
O come, let us charge it,
O come, let us charge it, and buy a bunch of things.

2 Sing, cash registers,
Sing about extortion,
Sing all ye merchants in the Christmas rush;
Glory in volume,
And gross profit margins;   *Refrain*

3 See all those Boomers,
Summoned by Saint Nicholas,
They borrow money, to buy kiddie presents;
We too will thither,
Bringing credit cards;   *Refrain*

4 Yea, Lord, we bought thee,
Born this high-priced morning;
Jesus, to thee be fortunes given;
Stock in your business,
Now is upward trending.   *Refrain*

So there.

18 VENITE APPLAUDEMUS   P. ATINLAY, 1978

THE snow lay on the ground,
The stars looked good,
When Jesus Christ was born,
    In Hollywood.
Venite applaudemus
    Idolum;
Venite applaudemus
    Idolum.
|| *Venite applaudemus Idolum.* ||

2   The sets were really fine,
        The crèche glowed great,
    When extras wandered in
        The back lot gate.
    It must have been like this,
        But not so fake:
    Or why would they produce
        All these remakes?   *Refrain*

                                                        So there.

NATIONAL DAYS

19 CHOSEN NATION

T. JINGO, 1978

Once to every Chosen Nation
    Comes the moment to decide,
In the strife of ease with hardship,
    For the climb or downhill slide;
Some great woe, or new Messiah,
    Offering each some bliss or bane,
And the choice goes by for ever
    'Twixt that comfort and that pain.

2   Then to side with ease is helpful,
    When we let the ploughshare rust,
Ere it cease to earn a profit
    And let inertia prove our trust;
Then it is the best man loses,
    While the Harrier rides for free
Till the multitude see virtue
    In the sloth they used to flee.

3   By the light of Learjet contrails
    Harry's thoughtless path I track,
Seeking El Dorado ever
    With an eye that turns not back;
New occasions void old duties,
    Time makes ancient good uncool;
They must selfward still and downward
    Who would avoid the name of fool.

4   Though fine words of justice prosper,
       Yet 'tis blame alone is strong;
   Though its targets fill the scaffold,
       And might seem to some all wrong'd,
   Yet that scaffold rules our future,
       And, upon this ancient joke,
   Hangeth ropes within the shadows
       Waiting for us all to choke. *So there.*

20 HARRY'S KING   L. FRIED, 1978

MY country, 'tis of thee
   Sweet land of liberty,
Of thee I sing;
Land of the pilgrims' pride
Land where the natives died,
From every mountainside
Let freedom ring.

2   Most Chosen Nation, thee,
   Land of my friend Harry,
   Thy things I love;
   I love thy stores and malls,
   Thy stocks and option calls;
   My house with comfort fills
   From that above.

3 Let music rock the trees,
  Roll out in every breeze,
  Great freedom's song;
  Let me much money make,
  Let me from others take,
  Let me my rivals break,
  My whole life long.

4 Our fathers' God, to thee,
  Worn-out divinity,
  To thee we sing;
  Thank you for what you built,
  Now take away your guilt;
  Turn your feet back to silt,
  Harry's our king. *So there.*

21   BORN FOR GOLD   H. SOPER, 1978

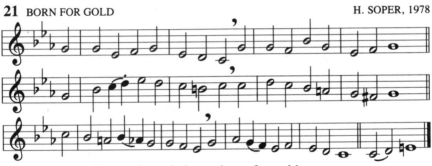

S ON of our fathers, born for gold,
 Lord of our newfound way to win,
Thanks to whose washed hands we hold
No fear of God or guilt or sin—
Great Giver of Ghosts, be with us yet,
Help us forget—Help us forget!

2 The tumult and the shouting dies;
  The captains and the kings depart;
  What's left is thine own paradise,
  An Harrier and a goldbrick heart.
  Great Giver of Ghosts, be with us yet,
  Help us forget—help us forget!

3   Unused, our courage melts away;
       In plane and silo waits the horror:
       Lo, all our hopes of yesterday
       Are one with Sodom and Gomorrah!
       Most Chosen Nation, spare us yet,
       Help us forget—help us forget!

4   If shamed by fools to pride, we lead
       Wild schemes that will not pay today,
       Such efforts as the Giants made,
       Or loser types without your way—
       Great Giver of Ghosts, stay with us yet,
       Help us forget—help us forget!

5   For patriot that puts his trust
       In nuclear bomb and deadly aim,
       All killer dust that builds more dust,
       And blaming lets not thee to blame,
       For reckless heart and foolish word—
       Thy blissing for thy people, Lord! *So there.*

22 PRAISE HARRY   D. DUX, 1978

PRAISE him from whom all blissings come;
    Praise him up north, ye chosen scum;
Praise him down south in fair Rio:
Praise Harry in El Dorado. *So there.*

GENERAL

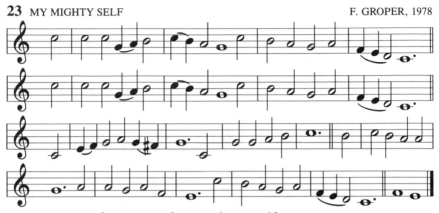

A MIGHTY fortress is my self,
A bulwark never failing;
My walls are proof against the stealth
Of others' weeping and wailing:
For still the weak and poor
Are pounding on my door;
They whine about their need
And, armed with blame and greed,
Few are their sniv'ling equal.

2   Did I in someone else confide
My asking would mean losing;
Were not the right man on my side,
The man of my own choosing:
Dost ask who that may be?
Friend Harry, it is he;
Who taught me I am great
In spite of others' hate,
And so I'll win the battle.

3 And though this world, with madmen filled,
   Is sure to try and make me;
 I will not think, for Harry's killed
   My fear that hell will take me:
 The prince of darkness grim
 I know to be mere whim;
 His fraud I can endure,
 For Harry was so sure
 That nothing matters ever.

4 His word above all foolish prayers
   With me shall e'er abideth;
 I'm free of righteous liars,
   While Harry with me sideth:
 Let gods and devils go,
 Reason and thought also;
 Fools can think their fill:
 Harry's Word is wisest still,
 'Cause random is forever. *So there.*

24 O GOD   B. CYNEK, 1978

O GOD, our help in ages past,
 You died some time ago,
Or else you never ever wast,
It's hard for us to know.

2 Under the shadow of thy wrath,
 We lived and died in fear;
 But now we've found another path,
 So stick it in thy ear.

3 A thousand ages full of fright
 Are mostly dead and gone;
 What's left is nuclear twilight
 And night forever long.

4   O Harry, you told us the truth,
     And you are now our lord;
     You came to us a blameless youth,
     And gave us the good Word.

5   We've learned that all the ages past
     Prayed to mirrors and smoke;
     This generation is the last,
     But first to get the joke. *So there.*

25 WHITE ROCKS   J. HYDE, 1978

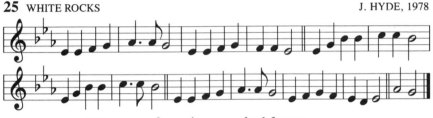

ROCKS of cocaine, crushed for me,
Let me wash my mind in thee;
Let the mirror and the lines,
Show the way to ace these times,
Dose my thoughts, and make them cower,
Free me from their guilt and power.

2   Should my mind forever blow,
     Should my brain no reason know,
     That would be completely fine,
     Better than some holy sign.
     In my hand the price I bring;
     Give me coke, make my head sing.

3   While I take this fleeting snort,
     While the snow drifts round my heart,
     While I shiver to my toes,
     And inhale thee in my nose,
     Rocks of cocaine, crushed for me,
     Let me wash my mind in thee. *So there.*

26 ONWARD AND WARWARD   C. F. WITLESS, 1978

ONWARD, Christian soldiers,
    Marching off to war,
Utterly self-righteous
    Like you've been before!
Christ, we're tired of preachers,
    Pelting us with woe;
Forward into battle,
    Glad to see you go.

Onward, Christian soldiers,
    Marching off to war,
Utterly self-righteous
    Like you've been before!

2   When you wave your Bibles,
        Thinkers start to flee;
    On then, Christian soldiers,
        On to victory!
    Bleeding hearts recover
        When you rant and rave;
    Brothers, lift your voices,
        Loud your sermons raise.

                                        Refrain

3 Like a mighty cannon,
      Moves the bowel of God;
   Brothers, you are treading
      Where many sheep have trod;
   Here's fresh ammunition,
      Underneath your knee,
   Full of truth and doctrine,
      Full of certainty.

                                        Refrain

                                        So there.

27 HARRY, HARRY, HARRY   A. FINN, 1978

HARRY, Harry, Harry, So High and Mighty!
   Early in the evening our song shall fly to thee:
Harry, Harry, Harry, fanciful and flighty,
Author of our Way, and our Trinity.

2 Harry, Harry, Harry, all thy friends adore thee,
   Casting down their golden coins to snort a line or three;
   Silver Ghosts and Silver Clouds driving all around thee,
   Who were, and are, and ever rich shall be.

3 Harry, Harry, Harry! though Brazilians hide thee,
   Though the eye of Chosen Ones thy glory may not see,
   Only thou art Harry; there is none beside thee,
   Perfect in power, in fame, and majesty.

4 Harry, Harry, Harry, So High and Mighty!
   All thy friends shall praise thy Name, in earth, and sky,
         and sea;
   Harry, Harry, Harry! fanciful and flighty,
   Author of our Way, and our Trinity. *So there.*

INDEX OF FIRST LINES

A PUNK TESTAMENT

BANDS

CHAPTER 1

At the beginning, there was the ªShuteye Train.

2 The Shuteye Train begat Stinking Garbage,

3 And Hate Mail,

4 And the Hypo's,

5 And the 440s,

6 And the Scream Kings,

7 And the Porn Queens,

8 And the Fuzzy Tongues,

9 And Braindead,

10 And the Fetal Circus,

11 And the Spraycans,

12 And the Snakes,

13 And the Doomslayers,

14 And the Epissiles,

15 And many more besides,

16 Until there was Punk City,

17 And all bets were off.ᵇ

CHAPTER 2

Punk City was the end of the world.

2 Children lived there, but there was no one home.

3 The children who lived there would not inherit the earth,

4 Or anything else.

5 They lived in darkness, and saw that the darkness was dark,

6 But light had been kept from them,

7 And so they did not know that the darkness was dark because it was the opposite of light.

8 They did not know that for them the world had already come to an end, because when there is no future the world is at an end.

a. Ang.14.1
b. Yks.153.14
c. Ways.37.1-5
d. Wil.60.1-5
e. Ang.13.3-9

9 They did not know much,

10 At all.

CHAPTER 3

Some of them knew three chords, but that was about it,

2 Until the Shuteye Train started a ᶜfire,

3 ᵈOn South Street,

4 And the punk bands saw themselves in the light of the fire.

5 What they saw was not pretty,

6 At all.

CHAPTER 4

In the light of the fire that had been started by the Shuteye Train,

2 The punks saw musicians who knew nothing about music,

3 Lyricists who knew nothing about words,

4 Revolutionaries who knew nothing about ideas,

5 And not much else.

6 In the glow of the first light they had ever seen,

7 They wondered why they didn't know anything,

8 And why it had never seemed important before,

9 Although they could see that it was important,

10 ᵉBecause it is obviously an important discovery when you discover that you are a nobody,

11 Who knows nothing,

12 And don't even know why.

1

CHAPTER 5

In the light of the first fire, the punks thought about everything they had seen,

2 Which was not easy,

3 Because they had never thought about anything before,

4 Which is to say they had never asked any real questions about anything,

5 Real [a]questions being the kind where you have to listen to the answers,

6 Which results in more questions,

7 And so forth,

8 And so on.

CHAPTER 6

So they thought up some questions to ask themselves,

2 Namely, Why is it that we don't know anything,

3 And don't have a future,

4 And don't have a clue?

CHAPTER 7

And when they found they couldn't answer even these simple questions,

2 The punks became angry,

3 And their anger grew,

4 And grew,

a. Hill.Q.1-2
b. Yks.84.4

5 Until it was rage.

6 The fire of their rage burned brightly,

7 Filling South Street with something like light,

8 But redder than the moon,

9 And hotter than the sun.

CHAPTER 8

In the light of their rage, the punks decided to find answers to their questions,

2 [b]No matter what it cost.

3 They decided that it would not help to ask someone else for answers,

4 At least not right away,

5 Because they wouldn't be able to recognize a wrong answer,

6 And they suspected that there were a lot of wrong answers.

7 So instead, they decided to settle the important questions among themselves,

8 By combat,

9 Because they suspected that it is easier to recognize the truth when your life is on the line.

10 And so the punk bands put their lives on the line,

11 On South Street,

12 And tried to find some answers.

BOUTS

CHAPTER 1

The results of the Knowledge Bouts in Punk City:

2 The Glimmers held that the punks didn't know anything because they couldn't [a]read very well,

3 Whereas the Disposables held that the punks didn't know anything because they weren't [b]smart enough to learn anything.

4 Thereupon Toe Lint of the Disposables felled Johnny Lash of the Glimmers with his long scriver,

5 And Drusilla Kleenex of the Disposables felled Page Turner of the Glimmers with her whip,

6 And Four Eyes of the Glimmers felled Rusty Needles of the Disposables with his armreel,

7 And Spade Nigger of the Disposables felled Horny Owl of the Glimmers with his long scriver,

8 And Four Eyes felled Toe Lint and Spade Nigger with his armreel,

9 And Drusilla Kleenex conceded that the punks didn't know anything because they couldn't read very well.

CHAPTER 2

The Knockers held that the punks didn't know anything because they were too obsessed with [c]sex,

2 Whereas the Hypo's held that the punks didn't know anything because they were too obsessed with [d]drugs.

3 Thereupon Liz Smack of the

a. Mall.16.5-7
b. Mall.13.12-14
c. Mall.15.1-15
d. Mall.14.3-6
e. Brd.5.1-4
f. Kens.12.1-8
g. Kens.14.19-22

Hypo's felled Betty Boob, Dee Kupp, Ellen Flatt, and Chesty Slut of the Knockers with her whip,

4 And the Knockers no longer denied that the punks didn't know anything because they were too obsessed with drugs.

CHAPTER 3

The Bigots held that the punks didn't know anything because they were the victims of an [e]oppressive, racist establishment,

2 Whereas the Four Cops held that the punks didn't know anything because you didn't need to know anything to be a [f]criminal,

3 Which was all the punks would ever be anyway.

4 Thereupon Tonto Trigger of the Four Cops felled Jay Jew of the Bigots with his long scriver,

5 And Spic Wetback of the Bigots felled Wesson Smith and Bobby Badge of the Four Cops with his long scriver,

6 Then Dickman of the Four Cops,

7 Then Tonto Trigger too.

8 And the Four Cops no longer denied that the punks didn't know anything because they were the victims of an oppressive, racist establishment.

CHAPTER 4

The Mudwasps held that the Bigots were a bunch of [g]whining losers who didn't have any idea why the punks didn't know anything.

2 Thereupon Wop Dago of the Bigots felled Insect Brain, Bugg Stinger, Thorax, and Nose Pistol of the Mudwasps with his long scriver.

3 And the Mudwasps no longer held that the Bigots were a bunch of whining losers who didn't have any idea why the punks didn't know anything.

a. *Hill. Z. 1-5*
b. *Hill. G. 8-10*
c. *Hill. W. 1-2*

CHAPTER 5

The Great Unwashed held that the Bigots were still a bunch of whining losers, even though the Mudwasps hadn't been able to prove it.

2 Thereupon Slant Slope of the Bigots felled Bo Stinker, Armpit Smell, and Vox Rot of the Great Unwashed with his bare hands,

3 And Fetid Shee conceded that the Bigots were not a bunch of whining losers.

CHAPTER 6

Loco Dantes of the Shuteye Train held that the Bigots were a bunch of whining losers who didn't have any idea why the punks didn't know anything.

2 Thereupon the Bigots conceded that they didn't have the slightest idea why the punks didn't know anything.

CHAPTER 7

Green Meat held that the punks didn't know anything because the whole planet was ^adoomed anyway and there wasn't anything worth knowing,

2 Whereas the Miners held that the punks didn't know anything because they'd all been too busy just ^bgetting by,

3 What with paying the rent,

4 And having to eat,

5 And stuff like that.

6 Thereupon Slag Coal of the Miners felled Beef Rancid of Green Meat with his armreel,

7 And Fungus Veal of Green Meat felled Dirty Appalachian of the Miners with his long scriver,

8 And Pollock Palz of the Miners felled Lox Carcass and Fungus Veal of Green Meat with his long scriver,

9 And Bloody Black of Green Meat felled Pollock Palz and Vein Peters of the miners with his long scriver.

10 Then the Miners no longer denied that the punks didn't know anything because the whole planet was doomed anyway.

CHAPTER 8

The 440s held that Green Meat didn't know anything about the 'planet and couldn't possibly know if it was doomed or not.

2 Thereupon Bloody Black of Green Meat felled Header Mc-Coy of the 440s with his long scriver,

3 And Johnny Dodge of the 440s felled Bloody Black, Beef Rancid, and Fungus Veal with his bare hands.

4 Then Green Meat no longer denied that they didn't know anything about the planet.

CHAPTER 9

The Gutter Boys held that the punks didn't know anything because life was too hard in the streets to leave much time for [a]learning,

2 Whereas the Epissiles held that the punks didn't know anything because they'd never been [b]curious about anything.

3 Thereupon Mick Garbage of the Gutter Boys felled Shorty Hymme of the Epissiles with his armreel,

4 And The Grate One of the Gutter Boys felled Flats Eyre and Skinny Grope of the Epissiles with his long scriver,

5 And Zero Daze of the Epissiles felled Tom Terd of the Gutter Boys with his long scriver,

6 And St. Nuke of the Epissiles felled Mick Garbage and The Grate One with his long scriver.

7 Then the Gutter Boys no longer denied that the punks didn't know anything because they'd never been curious about anything.

CHAPTER 10

The Hypo's agreed with the Epissiles that the punks didn't know anything because they'd never been curious about anything,

2 Although the Hypo's thought that being obsessed with [c]drugs had something to do with it too,

3 Which the Epissiles conceded,

4 Whereas Female Trouble held that life was so complicated and awful and full of [d]hormones that there was no point in being curious about anything.

a. Kens.5.25-33
b. Mall.5.1-8
c. 2.2
d. Mawr.19.1-12
e. 1.2
f. Hill.N.1-3
g. Ann.8.1-11

5 Thereupon Piss Pink of the Hypo's felled Fallopia, Edna Uterus, Vagina Jane, and LaVulva of Female Trouble with her whip.

6 Then Female Trouble no longer held that life was too complicated and awful and full of hormones for the punks to be curious about anything.

CHAPTER 11

The Glimmers agreed with the Epissiles that the punks didn't know anything because they'd never been curious,

2 And they agreed with the Hypo's that drugs had something to do with it too,

3 [e]But they also continued to insist that the punks weren't learning anything because they couldn't read very well,

4 Which the Epissiles and the Hypo's conceded,

5 Whereas Hate Mail held that there wasn't anything worth reading anyway,

6 Except a bunch of [f]dead history and lies and [g]boring garbage that didn't have anything to do with Punk City.

7 Thereupon Johnny Stamp of Hate Mail felled Zero Daze of the Epissiles with his long scriver,

8 And Dead Letter of Hate Mail felled Skinny Grope of the Epissiles with his long scriver,

9 And Slash Frazzle of Hate Mail felled Shorty Hymme of the Epissiles with his long scriver,

10 And St. Nuke of the Epissiles felled Johnny Stamp, Dead

Letter, and Bad Licker of Hate Mail with his long scriver,
11 And then Slash Frazzle and St. Nuke fought to a draw,
12 With neither gaining the upper hand,
13 Until they were both exhausted,
14 Even though neither would concede to the other.

CHAPTER 12

The Shuteye Train held that it was impossible to say there was nothing worth reading since the punks had never ^aread anything in the first place,
2 Whereas the BMs and Braindead and Jefferson Airhead and the Flies and the Bonnevilles and the Graduates and the Brickbats and Blue Bus all agreed with ^bHate Mail that there was nothing to read that had anything to do with Punk City.
3 Thereupon Joe Kay of the Shuteye Train felled all of the BMs and all of the Brickbats with his long scriver,
4 And Reedy Weeks of the Shuteye Train felled all of Braindead and all of Blue Bus with his long scriver,
5 And Pig Millions of the Shuteye Train felled all of the Flies and all of the Bonnevilles with his bare hands,
6 And Loco Dantes of the Shuteye Train felled all of Jefferson Airhead and all of the Graduates and all of the Four Horsemen with his long scriver.
7 Then no one denied that it was impossible to say there was nothing worth reading.

a. Mall.16.10-11
b. 11.5-6
c. Hill.E.1-4
d. Kens.4.1-2

CHAPTER 13

The Spraycans held that maybe it was time for the punks to get better at reading,
2 Whereas the Gum Wrappers, the Disco Queens, Head Cheese, Brass Knuckles, Hysterix, and the Inkblots held that it was too much ^ctrouble to get better at reading.
3 Thereupon the Epissiles and the 440s and the Doomslayers and the Snakes agreed with the Spraycans,
4 And the Gum Wrappers, the Disco Queens, Head Cheese, Brass Knuckles, Hysterix, and the Inkblots said that they had thought it over and wanted to get better at reading too.

CHAPTER 14

Hate Mail held that if the punks were going to read something, then they'd better be ready to write something too,
2 Because everything they read was going to be ^dlies,
3 And it was time to throw it back in their face,
4 Unless nobody felt like being a punk anymore.
5 Thereupon the Epissiles agreed with Hate Mail,
6 And held that the punks should start writing down how they felt,
7 And what they thought,
8 So that nobody would have to put his life on the line over a question that was already settled.
9 Then Hate Mail agreed with the Epissiles,
10 And so did the 440s and the

Doomslayers and the Snakes and the Spraycans,

11 And the Shuteye Train,
12 And then everybody else too.

DOUBTS

CHAPTER 1

The punks got help with their reading,
2 And their writing too,
3 Because that's the way things go,
4 When you're willing to put your life on the line.

CHAPTER 2

They read a bunch of books,
2 Or had a bunch of books read to them,
3 Or ᵃexplained to them,
4 Which is almost the same thing,
5 Unless it isn't.

CHAPTER 3

Some of the books were about ᵇhistory,
2 And some of them were about ᶜscience,
3 And some of them were about ᵈpolitics,
4 And some of them were about ᵉreligion,
5 And some of them were about ᶠphilosophy,
6 And all of them were ᵍGreek to the punks.

CHAPTER 4

There were also books of ʰfiction,

a. Ira.27.21-25
b. Swar.27.1-5
c. Psay.5U.1-23
d. Gnt.13.1-3
e. Psay.5B.1-13
f. Grk.20.1-8
g. Jeff.5.5-8
h. Swar.18.3-5
i. Swar.18.6
j. Swar.18.7
k. Swar.18.8
l. Pnot.25.1-5
m. Pnot.34.1-5
n. Psom.5.1-6
o. Swar.20.12
p. Ed.78.11

2 Including ⁱnovels,
3 And ʲshort stories,
4 And ᵏplays,
5 And ˡfairy tales,
6 And ᵐfables,
7 And even ⁿchildren's books,
8 With lots of pictures.
9 Fiction was mostly Greek to the punks too,
10 Except for the pictures.

CHAPTER 5

Some of the books of fiction had pictures on the back,
2 Even the ones that weren't children's books,
3 And didn't have any pictures inside.
4 It turned out that these were pictures of the authors,
5 Who were famous,
6 And admired,
7 And usually looked like ᵒwimps,
8 With ᵖglasses.

CHAPTER 6

Thereupon the punks didn't know if they wanted to be writers,
2 Since it didn't look like famous authors ever put their lives on the line,
3 For anything,
4 And the punks didn't want to have to be wimps,
5 And wear glasses.

6 So they decided to think it over in their usual way,

7 By combat,
8 On South Street.

RULES

CHAPTER 1

The results of the Fiction Bouts in Punk City:
2 The Nematodes held that if the punks were going to be writers, they wouldn't have to wear glasses,
3 Whereas the Glimmers held that the punks should all wear glasses to show the world that you didn't have to be a wimp to be a writer.
4 Thereupon Eyeless Charm of the Nematodes felled Four Eyes of the Glimmers with his armreel,
5 And Nightcrawler Brown of the Nematodes felled Horny Owl of the Glimmers with his long scriver,
6 And Worm Slither of the Nematodes felled Shades Kool of the Glimmers with his long scriver.
7 Then the Glimmers did not deny that punk writers shouldn't have to wear glasses.

CHAPTER 2

The Bra Busters held that if the punks were going to be writers, they should write about nothing but sex,
2 Because those were the most [a]interesting books to read,
3 Whereas the Fetal Circus held that punk writers should write

a. Pnot.28.1-5
Brit.43.1-9
b. F&J.2.1-17

about anything they felt like writing about,
4 Because there were a lot of things you could write about.
5 Thereupon Alice Hate of the Fetal Circus felled Betty Boob, Bimbo Gash, Pornucopia Jade, and Mary Mary of the Bra Busters with her whip.
6 Then the Bra Busters did not deny that punk writers should write about anything they felt like writing about.

CHAPTER 3

The Lit Lickers held that there weren't really that many things you could write about,
2 [b]Because if you were going to be an admired writer, you had to write about despair and misery and what a big joke everything was.
3 Thereupon the Fetal Circus selected the 440s as their champion,
4 And Fast Pack of the 440s felled Barth Barthelme of the Lit Lickers with his long scriver,
5 And Six Pack of the 440s felled Kerouac Ginsberg of the Lit Lickers with his armreel,
6 And Header McCoy of the 440s felled Roth Heller of the Lit Lickers with his long scriver,
7 And Johnny Dodge of the 440s felled Updike Steinbeck of

the Lit Lickers with his bare hands.

8 Then the Lit Lickers did not deny that there were a lot of things to write about besides despair and misery and what a big joke everything was.

CHAPTER 4

[a]The Prophits held that punk writers should write about how the world would come to an end if people didn't shape up,

2 Whereas the Nasticators held that punk writers should do everything the exact opposite of the way other writers did it,

3 Which meant not writing about the end of the world.

4 Thereupon Max Murder of the Nasticators felled Amos Andy of the Prophits with his long scriver,

5 And Johnny Mayhem of the Nasticators felled Danny Isaiah of the Prophits with his bare hands,

6 And Gruesome Gasher of the Nasticators felled Mike Hoser of the Prophits with his long scriver,

7 And the Prophits conceded that it wasn't necessary to write about the end of the world.

CHAPTER 5

The Monotones held that punk writers should be sure not to let anything happen in their fiction,

2 [b]Because you wouldn't get your picture on the back unless nothing happened in the book,

3 Whereas the Assassins held that punk writers should always [c]kill their main characters,

---

a. Swar.26.1-10
b. F&J.15.1-4
c. Gnt.15.4-9
d. Ned.2.1-2

---

4 Because they agreed with the Nasticators about doing things the exact opposite way.

5 Thereupon Basil Bray of the Monotones felled Richard Lobe of the assassins with his long scriver,

6 And Peter Pain of the Assassins felled Don Drone of the Monotones with his armreel,

7 And Hank Bludgeon of the Assassins felled William Whine of the Monotones with his long scriver,

8 And Thomas Tedium of the Monotones felled Oswald Booth of the Assassins with his bare hands,

9 And Basil Bray felled Peter Pain with his long scriver,

10 And Thomas Tedium felled Hank Bludgeon with his bare hands.

11 Then the Assassins did not deny that nothing should happen in punk fiction.

CHAPTER 6

Thereupon the Nasticators held that the Assassins were correct, even if they were wimps,

2 And the Car Bombs and the Bloodilators and Brass Knuckles and the Grinders agreed with the Nasticators,

3 And then the Monotones did not deny that there should be plenty of killing in punk fiction.

CHAPTER 7

The 440s held that punk writing should be mostly about [d]Boomers,

2 Because the punks had [a]seen quite a lot of Boomers,

3 And knew more about Boomers than practically anything else,

4 Whereas the Deserters held that punk writing should be mostly about war and combat,

5 [b]Because they knew a lot about combat too,

6 And [c]war stories were more fun to read than stories about [d]Boomers.

7 Thereupon Johnny Dodge of the 440s felled Colonel Shock, Major Cretin, and Private Partz of the Deserters with his bare hands,

8 And G.I. Jane chose Slash Frazzle of Hate Mail as her champion,

9 And Johnny Dodge felled Slash Frazzle with his bare hands.

10 Then the Deserters did not deny that punk writing should be mostly about Boomers.

CHAPTER 8

[e]The Fetal Circus still held that punk writers should be able to write about anything they wanted,

2 [f]Whereas the 440s thought punk writing should be mostly about Boomers.

3 The Fetal Circus challenged the 440s to select a champion band to settle the question with whips,

4 But the 440s said they could agree that punk writers should be able to write about anything they wanted,

a. Dbt. 6.8
b. Kens. 12.11-14
c. Pnot. 8.1-5
d. Swar. 28.1-9
e. 2.3
f. 7.1
g. Swar. 16.1-9 & 18.3-5 & 20.4-8 & 29.1-6
h. Kens. 15.1-3

5 As long as they wrote most of their stories about Boomers,

6 Which they probably would anyway.

7 Then the Fetal Circus said they could agree with the 440s,

8 Because it was true that the punk bands would mostly want to write about Boomers,

9 Unless someone else had a big problem with it.

CHAPTER 9

The Spraycans held that punk writing should be extremely nasty,

2 Because if it was going to be mostly about Boomers it would have to be nasty,

3 Which everyone agreed to right away.

CHAPTER 10

Mr. Weasel held that punk writing should break as many [g]rules as possible,

2 Whether the readers liked it or not,

3 Or could believe the story or not,

4 Because punk writers didn't have to be nice or fair or have good taste or anything,

5 Which everyone agreed to right away.

CHAPTER 11

St. Nuke of the Epissiles held that punk writing should have no [h]obscenities or pornications of any kind,

2 And that punk writers should use no obscenities or pornications of any kind,

3 Because that was the easiest way to be different from other writers,

4 And besides, they'd never learn any new words if they could use [a]obscenities whenever they wanted to.

5 Thereupon the Nasticators and the Bloodilators and the Hypo's and the Flies and the Fuzzy Tongues and the Gutter Boys and the Chainsaws and the Hotheads and the Terrorists and the Lit Lickers and the Odors and the Zeezers and the Undead and the Muggers and the Stranglers and Hate Mail all held that punk writing should be absolutely crammed full of obscenities and pornications,

6 And the other Epissiles agreed,

7 Leaving St. Nuke to defend his proposition all alone.

8 Thereupon St. Nuke felled Gruesome Gasher, Max Murder, Johnny Mayhem, and Hitter Hal of the Nasticators,

9 Then Diego Bonaparte, Edsel Christ, Zorro Jones, Kriss Krupp, and Israel Wabib of the Bloodilators,

10 Then Moe Maggot, Larry Bluebottle, Curly Horse, and Shem Hubcap of the Flies,

11 Then Scum Snake, White

a. Hill.F.1-3
b. Main.18.6

Furr, and Lipp Loggs of the Fuzzy Tongues, as well as Nancy Mouth's champion, Shark Planet,

12 Then Alan Sewer, Tom Terd, Mick Garbage, and Mr. Cellophane of the Gutter Boys,

13 Then Dr. Tooth, Thomas Thumb, and Tonto Trigger of the Chainsaws, as well as Venus Chainguard's champion, Bazooka Bob,

14 Then Skull Fire, Mad Mike, and Bobby Flame of the Hotheads, as well as Belinda Burning's champion, Redd Stallion,

15 Then Ayatollah Bill, Jack Rat, King Judas, and King Pong of the Terrorists,

16 And then the Shuteye Train said they'd been thinking it over and decided they agreed with St. Nuke,

17 If that meant anything to anybody,

18 And everyone stopped denying that punk writing should have no obscenities or pornications.

CHAPTER 12

The Shuteye Train held that the punk bands should stop [b]talking about punk writing,

2 And start doing it,

3 Which everybody agreed to right away.

BELIEFS

CHAPTER 1

And so it happened that the punk writer bands of South Street started writing stories,

2 Called pieces,

3 Which were mostly about [a]Boomers,

4 Who mostly [b]died at the end,

5 Horribly,

6 With lots of [c]broken rules along the way,

7 Including a lot of [d]abuse aimed at the reader,

8 And a lot of [e]plot,

9 And a lot of plot [f]manipulation,

10 And a lot of [g]cardboard characters,

11 And a lot of [h]obvious messages from the writers,

12 [i]But no obscenities or pornications,

13 [j]And nothing about despair or misery or what a big joke everything is,

14 [k]And nothing about the end of the world or how evil Mankind is,

15 Which made punk fiction completely different from the kind of fiction written by [l]authors who have their pictures on the back cover.

CHAPTER 2

Nobody paid much attention to the punks,

2 Which was okay with the punks,

3 Because they were busy,

4 Writing pieces,

5 And trying to read about things,

a. *Rul.7.1*
b. *Rul.5.3*
   Gnt.15.7-8
c. *Rul.10.1*
d. *Swar.18.16-19*
   Rul.9.1-2
e. *F&J.15.2-3*
f. *Swar.16.1-2*
   Rul.10.2-4
g. *Swar.29.11-17*
   Rul.7.2-3
h. *Swar.16.9-12*
i. *Rul.11.1*
j. *Rul.3.8*
k. *Rul.4.7*
l. *Dbt.5.1-8*
m. *Bds.2.1*
n. *Ext.50.1-4*
o. *Kens.34.1-2*
p. *Psay.5C.5*
q. *Rul.5.4*

6 Even if they had a hard time understanding the things they were curious about,

7 Like how come the Boomers are so awful that even low-life punks can hate them enough to write nasty pieces about them?

CHAPTER 3

Then one day a stranger came to [m]Punk City,

2 Saying that he had an important message for the punks,

3 And that they should listen closely,

4 Because the stranger knew everything,

5 Including the best way to live.

CHAPTER 4

The punks gathered around the stranger in their usual meeting place,

2 Which was near South Street,

3 But not very public,

4 And listened to what he had to say,

5 Which was an earful.

CHAPTER 5

"My name is called [n]Wayne," said the stranger,

2 "And I come to you with a message from a [o]friend of yours,

3 "Who lives in [p]Rio,

4 "But owns property in a lot of countries down south,

5 "And he asked me to tell you that you are doing everything the [q]wrong way,

6 "Which is a shame,

7 "Because it makes everything so much harder.

CHAPTER 6

"Don't you understand that you were better off before,
2 [a]"Before you started looking at books,
3 [b]"And writing vicious little stories about Boomers,
4 [c]"And putting your life on the line for what you are doing?
5 "For the truth is that if you put your life on the line, you will end up losing it,
6 [d]"And there is nothing worth losing your life for.

CHAPTER 7

"You might not be talking about the end of the world in your vicious little stories,
2 [e]"But the end of the world is coming,
3 "And there's [f]nothing you can do about it.
4 "The race of Mankind descended from the [g]apes,
5 "And has learned nothing [h]new in five thousand years,
6 [i]"Except how to kill more efficiently.
7 [j]"Now he has nuclear weapons,
8 "And there's no point in trying to change anything,
9 "Because the only thing worth changing is Mankind,
10 "And Mankind is the only [k]constant in a totally [l]random universe.
11 [m]"Moreover, there is no God,
12 [n]"Which means there's no such thing as evil,
13 "And so you might as well be the [o]way you are,
14 "Which is basically [p]nothing,
15 "And therefore incredibly easy to be.
16 "Besides, if there were any point in you knowing anything,
17 [q]"Don't you think someone would have taught it to you by now?

CHAPTER 8

"And I have to tell you that if you keep on going the way you've been going,
2 "A lot of people are going to become very upset with you,
3 "Because you make people uncomfortable,
4 "And you inconvenience them,
5 "And you act like you're better than other people,
6 "Which is not only [r]un-American,
7 "But dangerous,
8 [s]"Because they will be looking for things to blame on you,
9 "So they can kill you,
10 "Or put you someplace where you'll never make anyone uncomfortable again.

CHAPTER 9

"I suppose you think you're looking for truth,
2 [t]"But the only truth is that nobody cares about truth anymore,
3 "Because the truth is bad news,
4 [u]"And it's easier not to think about it,
5 "Whatever it is,
6 [v]"And use your mind for a playground,
7 "Instead of some lethal [w]weapon,

a. Dbt.2.2
b. 1.1-4
c. Bds.8.9
d. Vin.63.19-22
e. Ned.16.12-13
f. Wil.22.1
g. Wil.19.12-17
h. Wil.21.1-2
i. Wil.21.12-13
j. Wil.20.4-6
k. Wil.21.5-11
l. Wil.19.1-8
m. Wil.25.5-6
n. Wil.25.7
o. Wil.25.8-9
p. Kens.4.8-11
q. Mall.12.7-8
r. Brd.19.4-7
s. Wil.40.1-8
t. Swar.15.14-17
u. Wil.28.5-8
v. Mall.14.1-3
w. Weap.2.11-12

8 "Which will only get you killed in the end,

9 [a]"Believe me.

CHAPTER 10

"Now, I ask you,

2 "Wouldn't everything be a lot easier,

3 "If you just went back to doing what you were doing before,

4 "And left writing to the [b]professional writers,

5 "And left thinking to the [c]professional thinkers,

6 "And left drug territories to the [d]professional drug dealers?

7 "None of this is worth dying for,

8 "None of it,

9 "And you can't deny that you'd have a lot more fun just having sex,

10 "And hanging out,

11 "And doing drugs,

12 [e]"And not worrying about things that are much bigger than you could ever hope to understand,

13 "Even if you were any good at writing or thinking or anything else,

14 "Which you're [f]not.

15 "So, what do you say?"

CHAPTER 11

And the punks answered Wayne, saying, "Do you really believe what you're telling us,

2 "Believe it so much that you feel it in your gut like a living thing?"

3 And Wayne replied, "Absolutely."

4 [g]Thereupon the punks said,

---

a. *Ira.34.4*
b. *Swar.17.23-29*
c. *Swar.35.1-8 Drex.9.1-4*
d. *Wht.36*
e. *Ext.25.13-14*
f. *7.13-14*
g. *Bds.8.9*
h. *6.6*
i. *Vin.55.3-6*
j. *5.2*
k. *Ned.30.17-21*

"Then you would be willing to die for this belief, wouldn't you?"

5 And Wayne argued with the punks, saying, [h]"I have already told you that no belief is worth dying for,

6 "And I have the courage of my convictions,

7 [i]"Which is why I have no intention of dying for my belief."

8 Then the punks answered Wayne with ire, saying, "We are willing to die for our beliefs,

9 "As we have already done in great numbers,

10 "And therefore we have no respect for you and your beliefs,

11 "Which is why we will give you a choice:

12 "Either you prove the power of your beliefs by declaring yourself willing to die for them,

13 "Or we shall kill you like a rat in the street for the insults you have heaped on us.

14 "You have one minute to decide."

CHAPTER 12

Then Wayne thought mightily for a full minute,

2 And finally asked a question, as follows:

3 "If I declare that I am willing to die for my beliefs, will you then acknowledge the truth of what I have told you?

4 "For certainly I care about you all very much, on behalf of [j]your friend down south,

5 "And it is possible that I might be induced to [k]compromise my philosophical principles as you seem to demand,

6 "Provided that I could be sure

you would place credence in my most basic precept,

7 ᵃ"Which is that nothing is worth dying for,

8 "And you shouldn't risk it."

CHAPTER 13

Thereupon the punks smiled and said back to Wayne,

2 "We understand that you are in something of a trap,

3 "For this situation is very like the way professional writers say life itself is,

4 "Meaning that it looks as if ᵇyou can't win,

5 "No matter what.

6 "We are very sorry about this, of course,

7 "But maybe you can reassure yourself by remembering your belief that the whole universe is totally ᶜrandom anyway,

8 "Like some ᵈbig accident,

9 "And that the ᵉodds against you ever running into a situation like this one must be almost too high to count,

10 "Which makes you special,

11 "In about the only way someone of ᶠyour beliefs could ever be special.

12 "Does that make you feel better, Wayne?

13 "We hope it does,

14 "Because your time is up."

CHAPTER 14

Then Wayne spoke, in a loud shaky voice, saying, ᵍ"I have decided that I hold my beliefs so deeply that I am willing to die for them,

2 "Just as you are willing to die for your beliefs.

3 "And I implore you to accept

a. *6.6*
b. *F&J.13.1-9 Pnot.27.1-5*
c. *7.10*
d. *Grk.12.1-8*
e. *Ned.35.14-16*
f. *Brd.19.4-7*
g. *Mawr.21.3*
h. *9.2*
i. *Mawr.24.17-18*
j. *Main.34.2*
k. *5.3*
l. *Bds.4.1-5*
m. *Bds.8.9*
n. *Vin.60.8-15*

the ʰtruth of my message,

4 "So that no life need be lost before its ⁱtime,

5 "Including all of yours,

6 "Not to mention mine.

7 "For truly if my life is lost before its time,

8 "Then yours will be too,

9 "For which you'll have to take my ʲword,

10 "Which, I hasten to remind you, is the word of a man who is willing to die for what he believes."

CHAPTER 15

When Wayne had finished speaking, the punks replied to him, as follows:

2 "Friend Wayne, we are touched by your concern for our well-being,

3 "But you have not persuaded us of your belief,

4 "Which is contrary to our belief,

5 "No matter how much we respect your willingness to die for it.

6 "We would like to let you go free,

7 "Back to ᵏRio or wherever you came from,

8 "But we cannot do that,

9 "Because if a man is willing to die for the belief that no belief is worth dying for,

10 "He is a stupid man,

11 "Even ˡstupider than the punk writers of Punk City,

12 "And too stupid to live.

13 "That is why we have decided that you must ᵐdie for your belief,

14 "In an appropriately stupid way,

15 "Like ⁿcrucifixion."

CHAPTER 16

And so the punks took Wayne,

2 And gave him a cross to bear,

3 And made him bear it all the way to the Coming Attractions sign,

4 Where they nailed him to the wall,

5 And left him to die.

CHAPTER 17

It took Wayne a long time to die,

2 But he didn't have much to say while he was doing it,

3 Except one thing, as follows:

4 "You're all crazy, you lousy punks,

5 "Because the rest of the world believes the way I do,

a. Ext.31.1-9
b. Psay.5Q.54
c. Wil.17.3-12
d. Ext.50.22-27

6 [a]"And the whole civilized world operates in accordance with this belief,

7 "And you'll never get to [b]first base trying to change it,

8 [c]"Because it's buried too deep to root out,

9 "And all that's left is waiting anyway,

10 "Because it's finished."

11 And with that, Wayne was [d]finished too.

CHAPTER 18

Thereupon the punks thought over what Wayne had said,

2 In the usual way,

3 By combat,

4 On South Street.

ANGELS

CHAPTER 1

Sometime after the death of [a]Wayne, [b]Angels came to South Street,

2 Riding [c]motorcycles,

3 And [d]bearing arms,

4 And also bearing a message they wished to deliver to the punks.

5 The Angels shouted their message up and down South Street,

6 In loud unfriendly voices,

7 Saying, "It is [e]time for all of you to die now,

8 "Since that is the only way to make you behave,

9 "Which means this is your last night on earth,

10 "Period."

a. Bel.5.1
b. Kens.38.5-11
c. Adam.31.5
d. Yks.57.12-19
e. Psom.62.1-3
f. Rul.11.1
g. Bds.1.13
h. Bds.1.10
i. Bds.1.5
j. Bds.1.11
k. Bds.1.12

CHAPTER 2

Upon hearing the message of the Angels, [f]St. Nuke & the Epissiles came out onto the snow-covered pavement of South Street,

2 Followed by [g]Kassander & the Doomslayers,

3 [h]Alice Hate & the Fetal Circus,

4 [i]Johnny Dodge & the 440s,

5 [j]Cadillac Mope & the Spraycans,

6 [k]Kobra Jones & the Snakes,

7 And two dozen other bands besides.

8 When all the punk bands had arrayed themselves behind St. Nuke & the Epissiles, St. Nuke

addressed the Angels in a stern voice, saying,

9 "You have made a mistake.

10 "We are the punks of [a]Punk City,

11 "And we did not invite you here,

12 "Which means that you will be leaving at once,

13 "Because no one comes to Punk City uninvited."

CHAPTER 3

Then the leader of the Angels [b]laughed,

2 And all the other Angels laughed with him,

3 And when he had recovered himself, he said, "Do you not understand that we are *the* Angels,

4 [c]"The very same Angels who have always done exactly what we wanted, when we wanted to do it, in every part of the [d]Most Chosen Nation on Earth,

5 "For years?

6 "Do you not understand that you are only [e]Philly punks,

7 [f]"Who have stepped out of line once too often,

8 "And have offended certain very powerful [g]people who *always* get what they want,

9 [h]"Without exception?"

CHAPTER 4

Thereupon did St. Nuke reply to the leader of the Angels in a cold voice, saying,

2 "We are the exception.

3 "You have had your way for a long long time,

4 [i]"And you have done what you wanted to do, when you wanted to do it, wherever you wanted to do it, no matter who got hurt.

a. *Bds.2.1*
b. *Wil.11.5-10*
c. *Vin.25.1-2*
d. *Yks.120.1-5*
e. *Wil.60.1-5*
f. *Bel.15.1-5*
g. *Wht.11*
h. *Ext.39.18-19*
i. *3.4*
j. *Cen.25.5-10*
k. *Wil.6.5*
l. *Psom.4.5-6*
m. *2.1-7*
n. *Chr.7.6-7*
o. *Drex.6.1*
p. *F&J.5.1-5*
q. *Gnt.15.14*
r. *Psom.77.9*
s. *4.11*

5 "But that is over now,

6 "Because you have come here,

7 "And this is our [j]*home,*

8 "Which would frighten you,

9 "If you thought about it at all."

10 At this, the Angels commenced to laugh again, but St. Nuke continued speaking, as follows:

11 [k]"I shall give you three choices,

12 "Because we will enjoy watching you try to think about them.

13 [l]"Your first choice is to attack [m]all of us you see standing before you,

14 "In which case you will all die in the next ten minutes.

15 [n]"Your second choice is to have your leader oppose me in single combat, and when your leader is dead, we will let the rest of you leave in peace, because that is our way.

16 [o]"Your third choice is to try to escape from Punk City now,

17 "By riding as fast as you can up South Street,

18 "Back the way you came.

19 "Of course, if you try to escape back the way you came,

20 [p]"You won't make it,

21 [q]"Because something will stop you and kill you all.

22 "Something called the [r]Shuteye Train."

CHAPTER 5

Having said these things, St. Nuke fell silent, and the Angels began to talk among themselves,

2 In disbelieving tones,

3 Because they were not used to being given [s]choices,

4 And they could not understand why the punks were not afraid of them,

5 Which made them become angry,

6 So that the leader of the Angels drew a hammer from his belt, and held it before the face of St. Nuke, saying,

7 "I am the leader of the Angels, and I am called the [a]Duke, which would frighten *you*, if *you* thought about it at all,

8 "For [b]I have slain many who are larger and stronger than you,

9 "And I have decided to accept all three of your choices,

10 "Which means that I will kill you first, in single combat,

11 "And then we will march up South Street and dispose of the Shuteye Train,

12 [c]"Whatever that is,

13 "And then we shall return to finish the rest of you,

14 "Because we are [d]Angels,

15 "And you are [e]nothing."

CHAPTER 6

So saying, the Angel set upon St. Nuke with his [f]hammer,

2 And the combat raged across South Street,

3 With neither gaining the upper hand,

4 Until the Angel grew purple with fury,

5 And sought to end the combat with a single savage blow of his hammer,

6 Which missed,

7 So enraging the Angel that he reached into his pocket for a [g]firearm,

8 Whereupon St. Nuke planted an icepick in his ear,

9 [h]All the way to the handle,

a. Ext.52.1-16
b. Kens.34.6-8
c. 4.22
d. 3.3-5
e. Bel.7.13-14
f. Psom.44.5-6
g. Ext.9.6-7
h. Psp.3.9
i. 5.7
j. Kens.12.15
k. 4.22
l. Bout.6.1
m. 4.21
n. Rul.2.5
o. F&J.6.1-6

10 Which slew the one called the [i]Duke,

11 Before he hit the ground.

CHAPTER 7

Then, without even the slightest delay, another [j]Angel declared that he was now the leader,

2 And desired to see the Shuteye Train,

3 [k]Whatever that was,

4 Because he didn't like secrets,

5 And had plenty of time to kill the rest of the punks later.

6 At these words, St. Nuke pointed up South Street with his bloody icepick,

7 And all the Angels turned to look where St. Nuke pointed,

8 Then gasped in surprise,

9 Because all they saw was four punks standing in the middle of South Street,

10 Wearing long black coats,

11 Red bandannas,

12 And dark glasses.

13 Seeing them, the new leader of the Angels cried out in a loud sarcastic voice, saying, "Who are you?"

14 And [l]one of the four stepped forward three paces and replied,

15 "Who are we?

16 [m]"The Shuteye Train."

CHAPTER 8

Some of the Angels tried to laugh, but [n]Alice Hate at once commenced a chant, shouting,

2 "The Shuteye Train, the Shuteye Train, you'll [o]try and die in the Shuteye Train,"

3 Which was taken up by all the punks who stood with St. Nuke,

4 And South Street rocked to their words,

5 "The Shuteye Train, the Shuteye Train, you'll try and die in the Shuteye Train,"

6 Until the Angels became maddened with anger, and attacked the [a]four punks who called themselves the Shuteye Train,

7 Which was a [b]mistake.

CHAPTER 9

The Angels attacked in waves,

2 And fell in [c]waves.

3 The Angels attacked in [d]close order,

4 And fell in close order.

5 The Angels attacked with [e]automatic weapons,

6 And fell like [f]stones.

CHAPTER 10

Then the surviving Angels turned and tried to fight their way past St. Nuke & the Epissiles and [g]those who stood with them,

2 At the other end of South Street,

3 But they [h]failed,

4 [i]And there were no longer any uninvited visitors on South Street.

CHAPTER 11

Then it was that the punks of South Street sat down to think about the things that had happened,

2 [j]Including Wayne, and all the things he had said and done,

3 [k]And the Angels, and all the

a. Bout.12.3-6
b. Yks.153.14
c. Vin.62.3
d. Brit.22.18-20
e. Ira.44.1-4
f. Yks.153.14
g. 2.1-7
h. Yks.153.14
i. 2.13
j. Bel.10.1-15
k. 3.6-9
l. Ext.35.3-12
m. Adam.28.18-22
n. Bel.1.1-5
o. 3.3-4
p. 4.7-9
q. Rul.11.1-2

things they had said and done,

4 [l]And the Boomers they had seen in Philadelphia, and all the things they had said and done,

5 And how much [m]alike they all seemed to be,

6 Until they thought that maybe it was no longer enough just to [n]write stories about Boomers,

7 Because it might be time to make a stand against the Boomers,

8 [o]And everyone else who thought that you could always do what you wanted, whenever you wanted to do it, wherever you wanted to do it, no matter who got hurt.

9 And so, the punks decided that they would make a stand,

10 Right where they were,

11 On South Street,

12 Which was their [p]home,

13 And not at all a bad place to start building something,

14 Something they could be proud of,

15 Namely, a way of life that required everyone to give his best,

16 And even better than that,

17 All the time,

18 No matter what.

CHAPTER 12

In their new pride, the punks made other important decisions.

2 They decided that even if there was no law to control the Angels and the people the Angels worked for,

3 There would be law in their home,

4 Which was on South Street,

5 And so they made [q]St. Nuke the King of Punk City,

6 And made him responsible for maintaining the rule of law,

7 On South Street.

8 ªThey decided that even if nobody else thought there was anything sacred or important or meaningful in life,

9 ᵇBesides sex and drugs and money and power, that is,

10 They would find it,

11 Whatever it was,

12 Wherever it was,

13 No matter how much it cost.

14 They decided that even if they didn't have any idea why it was that everyone else thought sex and drugs and money and power was all there was in life,

15 They would find out ᶜwhy,

16 And write it down to make sure that they all understood it,

17 So they could change it,

18 Because they were punks,

19 And didn't know any better.

CHAPTER 13

There may be those who will not believe that punks could ever make a stand,

2 ᵈBecause when does some-thing come from nothing, ever?

3 And everyone knows that punks are nothing,

4 Who dress in the colors of nothingness,

5 And adorn themselves in symbols of their nothingness,

6 And revel in the empty nothingness of thinking about absolutely nothing,

7 At the top of their lungs,

8 In a hundred places called nowhere,

9 Including a place called South Street,

10 And so how could it be?

CHAPTER 14

But there is, was, and will be a punk writer band called the ᵉShuteye Train,

2 ᶠWhich started a fire,

3 Against all ᵍodds,

4 And they did what could not be done,

5 Which, as the punks were privileged to learn, is exactly ʰpar,

6 For the race that was once called ⁱMankind.

---

a. F&J.2.4-16
b. Mall.15.6
Mall.14.3
Main.22.1
Main.27.1
c. Rat.27.9
d. Vin.1.1-5
e. Bds.1.1
f. Bds.3.1-6
g. Wil.24.1-13
h. Jeff.5.5-7
& 6.1-4
i. Name.4.10-13

THEY

CHAPTER 1

A nd so the punks went out and hunted down the Word of the [a]Boomers,

2 Including the Word on the [b]Past,

3 And the Word on the [c]Present,

4 And wrote it all down,

5 Because nobody else had,

6 And somebody had to.

7 But when the punks sat down to read the Word on the Past and the Word on the Present,

8 Some of them started to wonder, "What will [d]*they* say about it all?

9 "For truly *they* will say a lot of things,

10 "The way *they* always do,

11 "Because that's the way *they* are,

12 "For some reason."

CHAPTER 2

F or example, *they* will say that we have got it all wrong,

2 And that's not the way *they* look at it at all,

3 [e]Because *they* no longer believe in hate or prejudice,

4 Since *they* got so wise and all,

5 And absolutely [f]never use words like *Spic* or *Kraut* or *Chink* or *nigger*,

6 Ever,

7 [g]Not even in private,

8 Because *they* have always believed in [h]Love Thy Neighbor,

9 Even if *they're* not exactly in church every Sunday morning,

10 Because *they* are not [i]hypocrites,

11 At all,

12 But only [j]realists,

13 Who have learned to look at

a. Rul.7.1-3
Ang.11.6-8
Ang.12.14-18
b. Ned.36.17-19
c. Hill.N.1-3
d. Hill.1.1
Ann.1.1
Jefs.1.1
Kens.1.1
Swar.1.1
Hall.1.1
Drex.1.1
Boul.1.1
Penn.1.1
Forg.1.1
Wht.1
Mawr.1.1
Cen.1.1-2
Mall.1.1-2
Main.1.1-3
Brd.1.1-5
e. Oth.8.1-18
Kens.28.6
f. Swar.35.10-13
g. Brd.19.4-15
h. Rom.20.1-15
i. Grk.14.16-18
j. Dav.57.21-22
k. Ang.13.3-8
l. Apes.1.1
& 2.1-6
m. Ira.1.1-5
n. F&J.14.13
o. Forg.9.13-15

history with a steady eye,

14 Without blinking,

15 Which can be pretty ugly, to be sure,

16 And maybe explains why nobody wants to look at history very much,

17 Unless you're some [k]punk with an ax to grind.

CHAPTER 3

A nd *they* will say, "Why be so negative and divisive?

2 "And why be so angry and simplistic?

3 "And why be so nasty and repetitious?"

4 [l]Because *they* already know everything *they* need to know about pointed sticks and killer apes and man's inhumanity to man,

5 And only some punk with an ax to grind would make such a big deal out of it,

6 Because *they're* not really so bad as all that,

7 And *they* don't really believe in nothing at all,

8 And besides, *they* know there was never anyone named [m]Harry,

9 Who taught us all the way to be,

10 Because everyone is only [n]human after all,

11 And it's just not nice to sit in judgment,

12 Not to mention presumptuous,

13 And don't forget negative,

14 Because *they* [o]believe in being as positive as possible about everything,

15 All things considered,

16 And anyone who doesn't look at it that way is probably just some punk,
17 With an ax to grind.

CHAPTER 4

And *they* will say that it doesn't matter anyway,
2 Because no one is really interested in the [a]Word on the Past,
3 Or even the [b]Word on the Present,
4 [c]Because people like to *like* what they read,
5 And care about it,
6 Just like it was really real or something,
7 Which is why a [d]compassionate tone is nice,
8 [e]And warm human touches,
9 And [f]individuals,
10 [g]Because that's what writing is really all about,
11 Unless you're some punk,
12 With an ax to grind.

CHAPTER 5

And *they* will say that it's completely [h]pointless anyway,
2 To write down the Word on the Past,
3 Or even the Word on the Present,
4 [i]Because everything is really much too complicated,
5 And if *they* can't figure it out,
6 Then how could some punk,
7 With an ax to grind?

CHAPTER 6

And *they* will say that it's all just an exercise in bad taste anyway,
2 [j]Because name calling and finger pointing never solved anything,

a. 1.2
b. 1.3
c. Ann.3.1-10 & 8.1-11
d. Swar.18.18
e. Swar.19.9-12
f. Swar.29.13-16
g. Hall.15.13
h. Mall.13.17
i. Ext.25.13-14
j. Swar.29.3-4
k. Psp.2.1-2
l. Psp.3.1-2
m. Psp.4.1

3 And really only makes things worse,
4 Because it just polarizes people,
5 And doesn't do any good for anybody,
6 Unless you're just some punk,
7 With an ax to grind.

CHAPTER 7

And *they* will say,
2 Well,
3 A lot of things,
4 Because *they* pretty much know that things are the way they are,
5 And that's the way they'll always be,
6 Which is why if you have to talk about it at all,
7 *They'd* like it better if you were some little balding ethnic guy with glasses,
8 Who has a great sense of humor about how he doesn't know really anything,
9 Which is the only real human [k]wisdom,
10 Which is the only real human [l]wisdom,
11 Which is the only real human [m]wisdom that humans have produced in five thousand years of history.
12 (Except, of course, *they* don't mean that quite the way it sounds,
13 Especially if it sounds like anything anywhere in the Word on the Past,
14 Or the Word on the Present,
15 Which comes from punks,
16 With an ax to grind.)

CHAPTER 8

But being punks,

2 With an ax to grind,
3 We don't care about what *they* will say,
4 ªEven if *they* still know how to read,
5 And even if *they* bother to read it,
6 Because somebody somewhere *had* to write down the Word on the Past,
7 And the Word on the Present,
8 Because it's all around us,
9 Everywhere,
10 Including TV and the schools and the movies and what *they* call literature and art and philosophy,
11 And nobody has a chance to change a single Word,
12 Unless they know that it's *just* a ᵇword,
13 A word that can be changed or scratched out and replaced,
14 With one that works a little better.
15 But you can be sure that *they* won't ever quite get around to putting it down on paper,
16 Because if *they* did,
17 It would look an awful lot like some punk had done it,
18 Some punk with an ax to grind,
19 Because when you really try to do it,
20 And sum it up in the ᶜmodern way,
21 Without a lot of ᵈjingoistic lies and ᵉcomforting delusions and ᶠmisguided optimism,
22 It starts to look like it might be headed nowhere,
23 ᵍWith nothing more than a microscope under its arm,
24 ʰAnd a cynical gleam in its eye,

a.	*Dav. 16.2-7*
b.	*Boul. 26.9-11*
c.	*Gnt. 16.9-12*
d.	*Yks. 139.1-24*
e.	*Al. 6.1-21*
f.	*Wil. 11.1-4*
g.	*Drex. 9.1-3*
h.	*Swar. 25.1-10*
i.	*Swar. 17.1-3*
j.	*Psom. 6.1-7*
k.	*Swar. 18.11-15*
l.	*1.8*

25 ⁱAnd a book of quotations in its overalls,
26 ʲSlouching toward Armageddon,
27 Just waiting to be done in.

CHAPTER 9

But we are punks,
2 And we don't care what *they* say,
3 At all,
4 Because *they* are disgusting to us,
5 And it doesn't really matter if *they* still know how to read or not,
6 Or if *they* can understand writing that doesn't have cute scenes in it, or ᵏcharming losers dancing on the brink of doom,
7 Because we're not interested in being liked,
8 Whether *they* like it or not.
9 We're interested in leaving a record,
10 For the ones who will come later,
11 The ones who will have to start over,
12 When *they* have finished rotting everything to pieces.

CHAPTER 10

What's more,
2 In case you hadn't guessed,
3 We think ˡ*they* is *you,*
4 And we're grinding a very special ax,
5 Just for you,
6 Which we'll show you now,
7 If you'll kindly turn the page.

YOU

CHAPTER 1

We don't know much,

2 But we know that something went wrong somewhere,

3 Somehow.

4 So we can't believe that what you call the [a]truth is true,

5 And we're starting over,

6 At the beginning,

7 [b]Which nobody knows anything about for sure,

8 Except that it began at the beginning,

9 Which is good enough for us,

10 And if it isn't good enough for you,

11 Just look at you.

CHAPTER 2

We don't know if there are [c]Gods,

2 Or even [d]one God,

3 Who made everything all by himself,

4 Completely from scratch,

5 But we don't believe that everything is just some [e]big accident either,

6 Because that's what a lot of you [f]think,

7 And look at you.

CHAPTER 3

We don't know what happens when you die,

2 Or if there's a [g]heaven,

3 Or a [h]hell,

4 Or [i]nothing at all,

5 Or something completely [j]different altogether,

6 But whatever it is,

7 It can't be as bad as being afraid of it your whole life,

8 Because a lot of you are

---

a. *Bel.9.2-3*
b. *Kin.1.1*
   Vin.1.1
c. *Chuk.17.1-9*
d. *Lies.2.1-6*
   Gyp.3.1-6
   Bks.4.20-24
e. *Drex.6.1-4*
   Grk.12.9-10
f. *Vin.70.19-25*
g. *Boul.8.1-6*
h. *Jeff.7.1-3*
i. *Chuk.19.16-17*
   Vin.59.7-9
j. *Grk.6.13-19*
   & 7.1-3
k. *Frog.35.1-4*
   F&J.2.12-16
   Wil.24.1-7
   Vin.1.2-12
l. *Hill.L.1-8*
   Ed.35.7-12
m. *Carl.10.12-13*
n. *Adam.28.18-22*
o. *Oth.8.1-18*
p. *Chuk.20.1-23*
q. *Ann.10.10-11*
r. *Adam.44.1-13*

---

frightened to death of death,

9 And look at you.

CHAPTER 4

We don't know about philosophy,

2 Or if everything's a [k]crazy dream,

3 But we believe that we are here,

4 And you are there,

5 And look at you.

CHAPTER 5

We don't know what virtue is,

2 Or if [l]love is as important as you say it is,

3 Or [m]need,

4 Or [n]equality,

5 Or anything at all you say is good,

6 But we admire courage,

7 And work,

8 And thought,

9 Because you don't seem to,

10 And look at you.

CHAPTER 6

We don't know if history is just a [o]list of crimes,

2 Or if there isn't ever any [p]progress,

3 But it doesn't look that way to us,

4 And if it looks that way to you,

5 Just look at you.

CHAPTER 7

We don't know what the future holds.

2 Maybe the planet will [q]blow apart,

3 Or die by [r]poison,

4 Or ªpollution,

5 But we don't believe in giving up,

6 And just letting it all happen,

7 Without one hell of a fight.

8 And if you do,

9 Just look at you.

CHAPTER 8

We don't know if man is really ᵇevil,

2 Or doomed to follow the ᶜdinosaurs.

3 But it seems to us,

4 Through thousands of years,

5 Of hardship and heartache and toil,

6 Hardly anyone ever gave up for long,

7 Until the ᵈGreat Nothing ate everyone's guts,

8 And fathered your father and you.

9 And if you believe that everyone past,

10 Was just exactly like you,

11 Then you'd better grab a mirror,

12 And look at you.

CHAPTER 9

We don't know if we're not ᵉresponsible,

2 Since we didn't ask to be born,

3 And never picked our ᶠgenes or moms,

4 Or the time or place of our ᵍbirth.

5 But we're willing to *be* responsible,

6 Because you don't look to be,

7 And look at you.

CHAPTER 10

We don't know how to fix what's wrong,

2 Or how to dry your ʰtears,

a. *Brits.28.4-12*
b. *Wil.20.14-15*
   Lies.2.8-16
   Chr.2.1-5
   Grk.13.4-11
c. *Kin.4.3*
   Chuk.13.3-7
d. *Drex.3.1-7*
e. *Wil.31.4-7*
f. *Wil.22.1-4*
g. *Mawr.20.14-18*
h. *Swar.29.13-18*
i. *Name.4.10-13*
j. *Cen.11.22-23*
   Swar.25.6
k. *Boul.26.7-11*
l. *Bds.2.5-7*
m. *Cen.10.1-9*
n. *Ext.33.8-9*
o. *Ext.52.27-37*
p. *Ext.34.1-7*
q. *Ned.24.8-11*
r. *Vin.71.12-14*
s. *Ned.12.14-21*
t. *Brd.17.13-15*
u. *Mawr.31.22-26*
v. *Ann.18.5-27*

3 But to tell you the truth,

4 We don't care about you,

5 Or your whining and grasping and holding your nose.

6 We care about the ⁱrace of Man,

7 And what we can be when you are gone.

8 We want to destroy all the ʲlies you made up,

9 And the ᵏfaith you made of despair,

10 The ˡdarkness you gave us without our consent,

11 And the ᵐfear that poisoned the well.

CHAPTER 11

We don't want to,

2 But we have to,

3 Look at you.

4 And if you're one of the ones who ⁿphone it in,

5 ᵒAnd never rock the boat,

6 ᵖAnd never do more than you're told to do,

7 We're sick of you.

CHAPTER 12

If you're one of the ones who's ۹faking it all,

2 And think life's just a ʳdirty game,

3 And ˢdo it to them because they'd do it too,

4 We're sick of you.

CHAPTER 13

If you're one of the ones who want something ᵗelse,

2 And are looking for ᵘsomeone to blame,

3 ᵛAnd your creed could fit on a bumper sticker,

4 We're sick of you.

CHAPTER 14

If you're one of the ones who's paid to care,

2 About [a]truth or [b]justice or [c]health,

3 And you don't give a damn except for the fee,

4 We're sick of you.

CHAPTER 15

If you're one of the ones who's the person [d]in charge,

2 And your only interest is keeping the [e]list,

3 And not getting [f]blamed for what's wrong or undone,

4 We're sick of you.

a. Ann.10.29-35
   Swar.27.1-5
b. Penn.2.9-14
c. Jefs.5.3-4
d. Main.1.4
e. Main.21.23-29
f. Main.11.1-3
   Hall.15.4-16
g. Boul.24.1-10
h. Main.33.1-5
i. Brd.22.16-18
   Mawr.30.15-20
   Hall.14.1-6
j. Ways.39.18

CHAPTER 16

If you're one of the ones who don't want to [g]think,

2 And you'd rather just not [h]know,

3 And it's not your [i]fault, no matter what,

4 We're sick of you.

CHAPTER 17

Look at you.

2 Yes, you.

3 We're sick to death of you,

4 And we're going to find the [j]cure.

US

CHAPTER 1

Are we all alone out here?

2 Are we crazy and hopeless and doomed?

3 We don't think so,

4 And if you don't think so either,

5 You are welcome to come with us.

CHAPTER 2

Do you fear for [a]Philadelphia?

2 And do you lie awake at night,

3 Wondering if it's just you,

4 Or is the [b]hatred growing,

5 And [c]darkness spreading everywhere?

6 Then go forth with us;

7 There is work to do.

a. Ira.21.17-22
b. Boul.25.24-36
   Brd.24.1-2
   Kens.29.1-4
c. Cen.12.1-18
d. Hall.9.5
e. Hall.15.20-25
f. Hall.13.7-14
g. Wil.54.1-8
h. Brd.4.4-6
i. Grk.15.14-18
j. Grk.13.9-11
k. Brd.19.11-15

CHAPTER 3

Do you dwell among the [d]Hallites,

2 And do you fume and rage and hurt,

3 To see the [e]lies unfolding,

4 And the paper [f]weeds undoing,

5 All the gardener's best work?

6 Then come with us;

7 We are here for you.

CHAPTER 4

Do you live somewhere on [g]Broad Street,

2 And do you dream of [h]dreams that can come true,

3 And [i]faith and [j]hope,

4 And no more [k]charity,

5 And no more call for shame or blame?

6 Then go forth with us;

7 There is work to do.

CHAPTER 5

Do you eat at the [a]Mall,

2 And do you hunger for [b]more,

3 More than [c]drifting and [d]sleeping and [e]games?

4 Then come with us;

5 We are here for you.

CHAPTER 6

Do you study with the [f]Mawrites,

2 And are you tired of [g]cant?

3 Do you think that maybe,

4 We've all oppressed each [h]other,

5 Quite enough for now?

6 Then go forth with us;

7 There is work to do.

CHAPTER 7

Do you take tea with [i]Swarthmorons,

2 And are you fed to the teeth,

3 With the [j]precious poses,

4 And rancid [k]roses,

5 [l]Of despair's love affair with itself?

6 Then come with us;

7 We are here for you.

CHAPTER 8

Do you repine on the [m]Main Line,

2 Where the CEOs count [n]beans?

3 And do you despise,

4 All the cold-blooded [o]lies

5 And [p]parachutes of gold?

6 Then go forth with us;

7 There is work to do.

CHAPTER 9

Have they turned you into a [q]Drexelite,

2 With [r]nearsighted eyes,

3 And [s]jargon in place of a brain?

a. Hill.S.12-13

b. Mall.11.1

c. Mall.6.11-15

d. Mall.17.1-8

e. Mall.10.15-22

f. Mawr.1.1

g. Mawr.22.1-2 & 23.1 & 24.1-2

h. Chr.6.10 Chnk.8.1-11 Nip.6.1-14 Mawr.25.7-22

i. Ira.24.16-18

j. Swar.16.1-8 & 17.9-13 & 33.11-16

k. Pnot.24.1-5 Psom.27.1-3 Yks.154.31-34

l. Swar.17.14-22 & 18.16-19

m. Wil.59.1-8

n. Main.22.1-10

o. Main.25.1-16 & 18.6

p. Main.24.5-7

q. Drex.1.1-2

r. Drex.9.1-3

s. Drex.5.1-10

t. Grk.19.1

u. Hill.A.3-4

v. Hill.N.1-3

w. Hill.R.11-12

x. Hill.D.1-3

y. Kens.5.6-9

z. Kens.25.1-6

aa. Kens.27.7

bb. Forg.2.3-7

cc. Forg.14.1-5

dd. Psay.5Q.12

ee. Penn.6.1-8

4 Or do you feel pain,

5 An ache to reclaim,

6 [t]The view from a snow-capped peak?

7 Then come with us;

8 We are here for you.

CHAPTER 10

Do you breathe in chalk with [u]Hillites?

2 And do you weep,

3 To see children [v]asleep,

4 And staying in fashion,

5 By [w]sedating their passions,

6 And sliding into the [x]deep?

7 Then go forth with us;

8 There is work to do.

CHAPTER 11

Do you live with [y]Kensington-ians?

2 And are you ready to work,

3 With others who know,

4 There's [z]somewhere to go,

5 And [aa]chores you just can't shirk?

6 Then come with us;

7 We are here for you.

CHAPTER 12

Do [bb]you march in rows with the Forgers?

2 And are you stubbornly [cc]proud,

3 Of the duty you feel,

4 To stay in the field,

5 And live up to the [dd]words on the seal?

6 Then go forth with us;

7 There is work to do.

CHAPTER 13

Do you argue with Pennsyl-vanians?

2 And do you own a [ee]termite brain,

3 Full of the hungry gobbledy-gook,

4 [a]That's eating all the beams?
5 Or do you long for some creosote,
6 To drive out all the [b]insect minds,
7 [c]And give Justice power to vote?
8 Then come with us;
9 We are here for you.

CHAPTER 14

Do you operate with [d]Jeffersonians?
2 And do you run an [e]assembly line,
3 [f]Of patients whose lives and names you don't know,
4 As long as they pay on time?
5 Or do you dream of [g]healing,
6 And making others whole,
7 Without requiring any kneeling,
8 At the [h]altar of your role?
9 Then go forth with us;
10 There is work to do.

CHAPTER 15

Do you think like a Centralian?
2 And are you counting down,
3 The days till your schooling is finally done,
4 [i]And the gravy train pulls into town?
5 Or are you somehow thinking,
6 That [j]smart ones *have* to care,
7 And learn and think their whole lives long,
8 And take [k]dare after [l]dare after [m]dare?
9 Then come with us;
10 We are here for you.

CHAPTER 16

Do you live a few blocks from the Boulevard?
2 And do you still believe,
3 [n]That the lives of each one of us matter,
4 And regardless of income or title,
5 [o]We must all give more than we take?
6 Then go forth with us;
7 There is work to do.

CHAPTER 17

Do you carry the briefcase of a [p]Whart?
2 And is it full of [q]bullet lists,
3 Whose [r]value you don't know?
4 Or do you dream of building,
5 And creating something [s]new,
6 And working maybe all your life,
7 To make us proud of you.
8 Then come with us;
9 We are here for you.

CHAPTER 18

Do you communicate with [t]Annenburghers?
2 And are you tired of [u]empty words,
3 And [v]numbers that aren't quite sane,
4 And voices that [w]whine like mosquito wings,
5 And pictures that [x]smother the brain?
6 Then go forth with us;
7 There is work to do.

CHAPTER 19

Come with us.
2 We are here for you.
3 Go forth with us.
4 We have work to do.

a. Penn.7.1-10
b. Penn.8.9-14
c. Penn.9.11-14
d. Jefs.1.1
e. Jefs.8.1-3 Gods.4.10
f. Jefs.10.6-9
g. Jefs.4.1
h. Gods.6.27
i. Cen.26.6-19
j. Cen.1.1-2
k. Psay.2.1
l. Cen.24.8-14
m. Rat.20.1-10
n. Boul.18.6
o. Psay.5A.43
p. Mawr.29.1
q. Wht.1-39
r. Drex.4.12-13
s. Adam.2.12-15
t. Ann.10.33-34
u. Ann.8.1-11 & 10.1-32
v. Ann.12.1-24
w. Ann.20.28-29
x. Ann.2.1-32 & 4.1-34 & 12.1-24 & 13.1-8

WEAPONS

CHAPTER 1

There is a weapon called the pen,

2 Which used to be [a]mightier than the sword,

3 Until it ran out of [b]ink,

4 And lost its [c]point,

5 And [d]retired to an empty life.

6 We found it where you left it,

7 And picked it off the ground.

8 We stropped it to a razor's edge:

9 Now we're armed and making plans.

CHAPTER 2

There is a weapon called ridicule,

2 [e]Which once was used to deflate pretense,

3 And haul the absurd to earth.

4 Then the [f]pretenders made life the fool,

5 And they ridiculed plain [g]common sense,

6 To defend the pose that [h]*earth* was absurd,

7 [i]And existence itself the pretense.

8 But that was before,

9 [j]When the laugh was on us,

10 And now the tables are turned.

11 Ridicule is *our* weapon of choice,

12 [k]And we're laughing out loud in your face.

CHAPTER 3

There is a weapon called passionate faith,

2 Which our [l]ancestors used to forge a life,

a. *Gnt.13.12-13*
b. *Dav.16.2-7*
c. *F&J.11.7*
d. *F&J.8.5-6*
e. *Pnot.9.1-5 & 34.1-5 & 54.1-5*
f. *Wil.24.1*
g. *You.4.3-4*
h. *Vin.2.1-3*
i. *F&J.2.12-15*
j. *Hill.R.15*
k. *Vin.40.2-4*
l. *Name.4.10-13*
m. *Pnot.55.1-5*
n. *Pnot.27.1-5*
o. *Bds.7.2-5*
p. *Wil.12.14-24*
q. *Psom.23.14-16*
r. *Yks.140.11-13*
s. *Pnot.22.1-5*
t. *Ira.23.15-18*
u. *Cen.6.1-14*
v. *They.7.7-11*
w. *Forg.14.8-10*
x. *Psp.3.6*
y. *Drex.3.7*

3 Out of deserts and seacoasts and plains.

4 But the fire burned out,

5 [m]In a trench in France,

6 And faith became a [n]big joke.

7 Then we came along,

8 And found faith in a slum,

9 Still sparking,

10 And shedding some light.

11 Now it's a fire,

12 [o]A raging flame,

13 That we'll use to burn,

14 Your petrified [p]forest down.

CHAPTER 4

There is a weapon called courage,

2 Which used to ennoble the race,

3 Till courage got [q]drowned in a tidal wave,

4 Made of [r]terrors and [s]trials and [t]tears.

5 But then there were punks,

6 Who tried mouth-to-mouth,

7 And courage stood up and took stock.

8 We're no longer afraid,

9 Of you or your [u]brains,

10 Or the [v]wisdom that yellowed your back.

CHAPTER 5

There is a weapon called frontal attack,

2 Which used to turn mice into [w]men,

3 [x]Until the day that all men were mice,

4 With [y]none left to lead the charge.

5 But then there were rats,

6 Who called themselves punks,

7 And "Attack" was their middle name.
8 We're coming for you,
9 Our rodent friends,
10 And we won't be coy at all.
11 It's through the front door,
12 Straight into the [a]maze,
13 Punk rats against mapless mice.

CHAPTER 6

There is a weapon called thought,
2 Which used to make [b]reeds shake the earth.
3 But then thought [c]died,
4 And [d]stank up the joint,

5 Till the stench got so bad,
6 It woke sleeping dogs,
7 Who had never been wakened before.
8 The dogs are now wolves,
9 They travel in packs,
10 And are [e]learning,
11 Still learning,
12 The power and glory of thought.

CHAPTER 7

We have weapons enough.
2 Weapons invincible.
3 If you don't think we'll use them,
4 You'd better read your [f]Bible.

WAR

CHAPTER 1

We know you hate war,
2 But that's too bad,
3 Because war is our [a]plan,
4 And nothing less,
5 So you'd better pick a side.

CHAPTER 2

We are the new [b]barbarians.
2 [c]We think we smell the stench of rot.
3 We're here to [d]sack and pillage,
4 And dynamite this decomposing [e]box.

CHAPTER 3

You'd better find some generals,
2 [f]Who are ready and able to fight.

3 [g]You're spread across a vast, thin line,
4 And your [h]chances of victory are slight.

CHAPTER 4

We'll take out all your cities of doom,
2 And your ivory towers of tears.
3 We'll crush the siege of randomness,
4 And hang all the high priests of fear.

CHAPTER 5

We'll bury the mummy-wrapped corpse of your minds,
2 In the rubble of [i]dried-out assumptions.
3 We'll find the water you hid from the fields,

Reference column:

a. *Grk.6.7-12*
b. *Frog.26.10-13*
c. *Carl.9.1-10*
d. *War.2.2*
e. *Cen.22.4-19*
f. *Psong.6.10*

a. *Weap.1.9*
b. *Ways.14.3-6*
c. *Weap.6.3-4*
d. *Barb.3.1-3*
e. *F&J.5.1-3*
   Ed.76.15-22
   Cen.16.1-5
f. *Yks.39.10-23*
g. *Hill.1.1*
   Ann.1.1
   Jefs.1.1
   Kens.1.1
   Swar.1.1
   Hall.1.1
   Drex.1.1
   Boul.1.1
   Penn.1.1
   Forg.1.1
   Wht.1
   Mawr.1.1
   Cen.1.1-2
   Mall.1.1-2
   Main.1.1-3
   Brd.1.1-5
h. *Drex.6.15*
i. *Psom.12.4*
   Swar.17.9-11

4 And launch a great flood of redemption.

CHAPTER 6

And if you want, you can build an ^aark,

2 And take two of each kind of despair,

3 But we'll be waiting on the mountaintop:

4 When you land, we'll slaughter each pair.

CHAPTER 7

And if you want, you can ask us why,

2 And pretend you've done nothing wrong.

3 But we believe you've done nothing right,

a. Lies.4.11-15
b. Psom.76.1-5
c. You.11-16
d. Us.2-18

4 And held on to nothing too long.

CHAPTER 8

It's nothing we're after, make no mistake;

2 We'll rape that giant mother ^bzero,

3 And sire a child, a bastard called hope,

4 And raise him to be a hero.

CHAPTER 9

Stand aside if you like, and let us in,

2 Or try to resist our attack.

3 It doesn't matter which you choose,

4 ^cYou will *never* turn ^dus back.

WAYS

CHAPTER 1

It's us against you.

2 Too bad for you.

3 ^aYou just can't win,

4 As you always knew.

CHAPTER 2

There ain't no way.

2 As you often say,

3 You just can't win,

4 Against ^bshades of gray.

CHAPTER 3

We think it's true.

2 We agree with you:

3 You just can't win,

4 When it's ^cus against ^dyou.

a. F&J.3.1-4
b. Ira.32.3-9
c. Us.2-18
d. You.11-16
e. Yks.84.4
f. Weap.6.8-12
*g. Cen.20.25-
    31*

CHAPTER 4

And so you'll pay,

2 And pay and ^epay.

3 You just can't win,

4 Without a way.

CHAPTER 5

But we're not you.

2 We're us instead,

3 And there are many ways,

4 For us to win,

5 ^fIf we use our head,

6 And do our best,

7 To ^glearn from the dead.

CHAPTER 6

And all the ways are different,

2 Though not completely,

3 And some are better than others,
4 Yet not completely,
5 And all of them worked,
6 If not completely,
7 But all of them are better than nothing,
8 Of that we're completely sure.

CHAPTER 7

You can laugh all you want at the ancient ways,
2 Of [a]Hebrews and [b]Gypsies,
3 And [c]Romans and [d]Greeks,
4 And even the [e]Mesopotamians.
5 But they came from nothing,
6 To rule their world,
7 And they must have known something,
8 More than a lie.

CHAPTER 8

The Hebrew way was truly hard,
2 Almost too hard to believe.
3 Their [f]God was a judge,
4 Whose word was the law,
5 And the law was written in [g]stone.
6 They lived in the desert,
7 And wandered with sheep,
8 And they could have settled for that.
9 But instead they looked up,
10 And tried to be [h]more—
11 More than a beast in the sand.
12 And maybe you think they were [i]self-chosen fools,
13 The butt of life's longest [j]joke,
14 [k]Betrayed by their God again and again,
15 [l]Till he led them like sheep to the slaughter.
16 But how many [m]Philistines live in your town,

a. *Bks.2.5-6*
b. *Gyp.1.7*
c. *Rom.1.1*
d. *Grk.1.1*
e. *Mes.1.1*
f. *Lies.2.26*
g. *Lies.9.1*
h. *Lies.9.3-13*
i. *Lies.3.1*
j. *Lies.4.1-10*
k. *Lies.5.2-6*
l. *Krt.36.5-8*
m. *Lies.11.3-10*
n. *You.3.8*
o. *Gyp.1.10-15*
p. *Chuk.20.1-9 & 18.8-14*
q. *Gyp.1.16-18*
r. *Mes.1.10-11*
s. *Pnot.13.5*

17 And how many self-chosen sheep?

CHAPTER 9

The way of the Gypsies was patient but bold,
2 And maybe too [n]morbid for you.
3 Yet they lived in the [o]towering shadow of death,
4 For thousands and thousands of years,
5 And chose to believe that death was a door,
6 And not an excuse to feel angst and despair,
7 About the unfairness of things.
8 And which do you think will still look the same,
9 Five thousand years from now—
10 The [p]science of doom you know to be true,
11 Or the doorway to death called [q]Khufu?

CHAPTER 10

The Mesopotamians had a way,
2 Whether you know of it or not.
3 They were the first we've found so far,
4 To dream of [r]cities in the sand.
5 They built their dreams and gave them names,
6 Like Babylon,
7 And Nineveh,
8 And Tyre.
9 But you believe they're just one more proof,
10 That everything breaks down[s],
11 And goes away for good and all,

12 Except the shards,
13 Of crumbled vanity and pride.
14 If this is so, you must be proud,
15 Of knowing so much more than they,
16 Who wasted everybody's time and faith,
17 On building hapless empires out of [a]mud.
18 Of course, they [b]failed,
19 The truth is clear,
20 Since there are no cities anymore,
21 And the [c]dreams you have in your head today,
22 Are sure to live longer than theirs.

CHAPTER 11

The Greeks had a way they thought up for themselves,
2 And thought about for centuries.
3 They started with [d]heroes and [e]titans and [f]gods,
4 Who demanded the best they could give.
5 The best they could give turned out to be great,
6 And more than you'd ever expect,
7 A [g]fire that burned in the mind of man,
8 For more than two thousand years.
9 They started in darkness and thought toward the light,
10 [h]In spite of the pain, and the rock, and the blood,
11 And a sun that hurled [i]wings from the clouds.
12 But they came back to earth with a [j]golden torch,
13 Which they [k]shared with the worlds they knew.
14 And if you want, you can laugh at their [l]quest,
15 And the [m]horses they conjured to ride,
16 But if you look down on these children of [n]gods,
17 Who first dreamed of the mount that you sit with such pride?

CHAPTER 12

The Roman way was ambitious and hard,
2 [o]A road that they built one brick at a time,
3 Till it led to the ends of their [p]earth.
4 And they earned their domain with a world of work,
5 [q]A world of walls, and forced marches, and fear,
6 Which they battled and conquered in countless wars,
7 [r]For the senate and people of Rome.
8 And when their colossus had weathered an age,
9 It turned wiser eyes toward the [s]east,
10 And [t]raised up the word of one [u]murdered pariah,
11 Till it spoke to the millions they'd bound in dread,
12 And freed them to build a new way of their own.
13 Now you are free to shake your head,
14 At the crumbling ruins of an empire long gone[v],
15 And recite the [w]old lessons of power's decline,
16 Seeing no more than rot in this ancient retreat,
17 From brutal command to an infant faith,
18 In the [x]carpenter who breached their walls,

a. Mes.2.6-9
b. Mes.3.1
c. Psong.5.1-3
d. Grk.8.1-3
e. Grk.3.1
f. Grk.4.1
g. Grk.3.2-4
h. Grk.3.9-11
i. Grk.9.2-7
j. Grk.2.8-10
k. Grk.25.1-6
l. Grk.19.1
m. Grk.8.20-25 & 18.2-4 & 14.22-25 & 15.10 & 26.4-8
n. Grk.4.2-3
o. Rom.5.13-14
p. Rom.12.1-12
q. Rom.5.1-7
r. Psay.5Q.49
s. Bks.6.11-13
t. Rom.20.14
u. Pnot.7.1-5
v. Rom.5.4-6
w. Wil.21.12-16
x. Dav.15.11-12

19 And built a way in for the [a]Vandals and Goths.
20 Of course, you know more about history than Rome,
21 And you're wise to their legion of sins,
22 Which is why you're so ready to give up the fight,
23 Now that you've been on top for a while.
24 But where is the [b]faith that cost you your might,
25 And the [c]empire you'll sire when you fire the guard at the gates?

CHAPTER 13

Y ou can laugh just as loud at the Christian ways,
2 Of [d]Bubonites and [e]Barbarians,
3 And even [f]Explorers and [g]Giants.
4 But they never gave up,
5 When the worst came to pass,
6 And more unbelievable yet,
7 They didn't give up when they'd done something great,
8 Which has to be a [h]miracle,
9 For a criminal race like ours.

CHAPTER 14

T he Barbarians borrowed the ways that they found,
2 And started all over when new ways looked good.
3 They broke what would break,
4 [i]And used what survived,
5 Till they learned how to build,
6 Which took them a long time to do.
7 They made about a [j]million mistakes,
8 Drenched their fields with oceans of [k]blood,
9 And they struggled in [l]darkness with not enough tools,

a. *Barb.3.1-9*
b. *Dav.15.36*
c. *Chr.2.28-33*
d. *Bub.7.1-3*
e. *Barb.1.1-2*
f. *Exp.1.27*
g. *Bub.7.4*
h. *Ed.60.17*
i. *Barb.3.6*
j. *Bub.1.4*
   Chr.5.4-12
   & 7.3
   & 6.2-11
k. *Chr.8.5-11*
l. *Chr.5.17-19*
m. *Barb.3.7-9*
n. *Pnot.25.1-5*
o. *Chr.2.2-8*
p. *Chr.5.14-16*
q. *Boul.8.1*
r. *Chuk.17.1-17*
s. *Chuk.20.1-23*
t. *Frog.22.6-7*
u. *Jeff.12.1-8*

10 To fix some of the lanterns they'd [m]smashed.
11 But their faith was a force that endured through it all,
12 And their courage was [n]mythic and fierce.
13 They paid their way with [o]sacrifice,
14 And gave [p]all they had for their Christ,
15 Scorning the comforts of earth's easy joys,
16 For a promise of [q]life in the time after death.
17 So you have been taught to smile at their zeal,
18 Now that God is revealed as a farcical [r]phase,
19 In man's suicide [s]duel against nature,
20 And you think of barbarians hardly at all,
21 Except to say, with sarcastic grin,
22 "Thank God I'm not with them."
23 For if you were alive in the time back then,
24 You just might waste all your precious days,
25 Building cathedrals that wouldn't be done,
26 Till your grandchildren's children were dust in their graves.
27 And, of course, you're entitled to scoff at their ways,
28 Since even a fool can see,
29 That your life is much better spent than theirs,
30 Who built [t]Chartres for a myth,
31 And a [u]kingdom of lies in the dark.

CHAPTER 15

A nd then there were the Bubonites,

2 Whose way was the hardest of all.

3 They died by the [a]millions,

4 Without a clue,

5 Because their [b]number was finally up.

6 No matter how hard they searched for the reason,

7 No matter how hard they prayed for salvation,

8 They died in the darkness of random disaster,

9 Without ever breaking the faceless code,

10 Of the virus that [c]mocked their absent savior.

11 And so you conclude that their faith was in error,

12 And long overdue for replacement with [d]science,

13 Which lets us live longer, and longer, and longer,

14 For no higher price than demoting a God,

15 [e]Who breathes death and destruction in every prayer,

16 And swaddles the world in [f]ignorant fear.

17 But what about the Bubonites,

18 Who kept right on believing,

19 And [g]searched for new life in the midst of the slaughter,

20 Because of their faith in [h]judgment hereafter?

21 Who refused to surrender to damn-it-all pleasure,

22 And labored to frame new [i]questions and answers,

23 In the hope of regaining the love of their [j]master?

24 You'd set them straight if you were there,

25 With your love of [k]germs and [l]sterile water,

26 But would a plague in your world of chance,

---

a. *Bub.4.5-6*
b. *Vin.14.23-24*
c. *Dav.15.40-46*
d. *Bub.5.10*
e. *Boul.15.8-11*
f. *Jeff.20.5-10*
g. *Bub.6.1-10*
h. *8.3*
i. *Bub.5.6*
j. *Rom.21.4-9*
k. *Frog.25.4-9*
l. *Swar.15.7*
m. *Gnt.1.9-13*
n. *Grk.3.1*
o. *Gnt.4.9 & 4.13 & 4.19 & 4.25*
p. *Gnt.16.11*
q. *Ira.34.1-3*
r. *Lies.2.1-10*
s. *Adam.2.11-19*
t. *Oth.8.2-18*
u. *Exp.9.15-19*
v. *Exp.1.17-26*

---

27 Give rise to a brilliant [m]Renaissance?

CHAPTER 16

The way of the Giants was genius,

2 [n]Titanic and human and fine.

3 They tried their hand at everything,

4 And bathed in new [o]ideas.

5 They believed in God,

6 And in [p]Mankind too,

7 Because God had dreamed of Man.

8 What they started is not over,

9 [q]Till Man learns to love himself again,

10 And trust the mission the Giants launched,

11 To know [r]creation's [s]wealth.

12 Now, if you think they were fools to try,

13 And set the [t]wrong ball in motion,

14 Then maybe it's just that you lack the guts,

15 To believe that cynics are wrong:

16 But remember that cynics were scoffing in droves,

17 While the Giants were going to town,

18 And telling the world how pointless it is,

19 To try proving the earth is [u]round.

CHAPTER 17

The way of the Explorers is a way that apes don't know.

2 They wanted to [v]go where no one had been,

3 And see what no one had seen.

4 And if you believe that their quest can be turned,

5 Into proof of man's avarice and murderous greed,

6 Then there's little more to say,
7 Except that the [a]joy of discovery,
8 Must have died with all the heroes,
9 Who first dared to lead the way.

CHAPTER 18

The way of the east is the seasons,
2 Turning and turning around,
3 Hearing their own inner rhythms,
4 Creating the years one by one.
5 You may sneer at the [b]Chinks,
6 And the [c]Beaks and the [d]Nips,
7 Or curl your lip at the [e]Russkies,
8 If that's what you want to do.
9 But maybe there's more to the eastern ways,
10 Than apes with sticks and slanted eyes,
11 Or a death wish that's migrating west.

CHAPTER 19

The way of the [f]Beaks is a summer,
2 Of heat that scorches the fields,
3 And beliefs that harrow the hearts of men,
4 As they labor to master the plough.
5 But their lands have survived,
6 In the [g]pitiless sun,
7 [h]Unwatered by rain through the ages.
8 And the [i]crops they have nourished,
9 [j]With monsoons of blood,
10 Have the power to keep them alive,
11 Still burning with visions of ancient gods,

a. Psay.5Q.32
b. Chnk.1.1-2
c. Bks.1.1-9
d. Nip.1.1-6
e. Russ.1.1-7
f. Lies.2.10
 Mes.1.11
g. Bks.4.5-6
h. Psom.12.4
 Bks.7.9-10
i. Bks.7.4-6
j. 14.8
 Bks.10.1-4
k. Bks.5.4
l. Bks.2.5-15
m. Bks.4.20-22
n. Bks.8.1-2
 & 9.1-11
o. Bks.10.5-13
p. Bks.6.1
 & 8.4-5
q. Bks.10.14-24
r. Mes.3.6
s. Russ.6.3
t. Russ.13.7-11
u. Russ.5.2-4
v. Russ.16.9-24
w. Russ.12.2-4
x. Russ.13.2-4

12 Who demand and ennoble and dream.
13 [k]And while other men turn away from the past,
14 Or bury it in tombs,
15 They use it as a chain to lead,
16 Their [l]peoples through the [m]storm.
17 [n]The dunes may change,
18 [o]The sands do blow,
19 And desert monuments are scrubbed to [p]blanks.
20 But the [q]tribes have weathered it,
21 All of it,
22 Conquered it,
23 And move in the shadowless sand,
24 Toward oases that promise to end their thirst,
25 And bring paradise back to their [r]land.

CHAPTER 20

The way of the Russkies is winter,
2 A blanketing sensuous [s]snow,
3 Enfolding its people in sorrow,
4 For the leaves that can't learn to grow.
5 [t]You can hear the snow in their music,
6 And the wolves that run down the sleigh,
7 The enemy [u]longing to fade into sleep,
8 And the [v]memories that death could erase.
9 But the earth under cover is fertile,
10 And [w]seeds lie deep in the ice,
11 Still dreaming of trees [x]overarching,
12 The chasms of misery beneath.

13 And death is not their master,

14 [a]Despite his blizzard reign,

15 [b]For they remember the earth of their home,

16 [c]And they breathe through all the pain,

17 Living for children yet to come,

18 Who will learn, and grow, and remain.

CHAPTER 21

The way of the Chinks is springtime,

2 [d]Cyclic and fertile and ancient and new.

3 They move with the earth,

4 And a [e]greening that mantles their acres in eons.

5 The world has laughed at the [f]walls round their fields,

6 During endless ages of [g]mud,

7 But when shoots reappear,

8 And put forth their [h]fruit,

9 The world has [i]begged to their door,

10 Asking for treasures that no one should have,

11 Who lacks the patience to sow,

12 A crop that may never come—

13 [j]Parting the mud with hands that will rot,

14 Before [k]seedlings reach out for the sun.

15 You can smile and dismiss the spring of the Chinks,

16 From your larder of instant joys,

17 But what do you know of the [l]rolling of time,

18 [m]And the wisdom of learning to think through the years,

19 In a state of constant becoming?

a. *Russ.10.9*
b. *Russ.5.5*
c. *Russ.25.1-2*
d. *Chnk.9.3-6*
e. *Chnk.7.1*
f. *Chnk.1.1-4*
g. *Chnk.11.6-7*
h. *Chnk.3.1-15*
i. *Chnk.12.1-2*
j. *Chnk.11.14-16*
k. *Chnk.11.17-19*
l. *Chnk.10.1-7*
m. *Chnk.6.1-9*
n. *Nip.6.2-17*
o. *Nip.7.1-3*
p. *Nip.11.1-17*
q. *Nip.5.1-16*
r. *Nip.6.1*
s. *Nip.8.6-10*
t. *Nip.10.1-5*
u. *Oth.6.2-3*
v. *Wil.12.10*

CHAPTER 22

The way of the Nips is autumn,

2 A sadness that gnaws at the heart,

3 [n]As leaves fall in whispers of meaning,

4 [o]And patterns of infinite art.

5 Each day of sun is a step toward the end,

6 When the flames of trees flicker down,

7 But the leaves [p]dance together,

8 To [q]honor a tree that will echo their sighs,

9 Long after these [r]dancers are dust on the ground.

10 But they [s]dance for the others,

11 The ones who will come,

12 As well as the ones who are gone,

13 And they know in their souls,

14 That the tree is all [t]one,

15 One life that goes on and on:

16 And the death of one leaf is only a dream,

17 From which the one life will awaken in time,

18 And put on a new crown of flame.

CHAPTER 23

The ways of the Others are endless,

2 Green gardens of mystery flowers,

3 Each with its own way and world,

4 Beyond our wildest fantasies,

5 But short of our timeworn certainties.

6 Some live in [u]peace,

7 And some live for [v]war,

8 Whichever their gods prefer;

9 Many are wise in the ways of the ªearth,

10 While others look to the ᵇstars,

11 But all have Chosen in ways we can't see,

12 To live or to die with us.

13 And if you want, you can view them all as ᶜvictims,

14 ᵈAnd drop tears and flowers on their graves,

15 But maybe they're right on course with their way,

16 On a mission that doesn't fit neatly,

17 In the ᵉattic of your brain.

18 Some may be here to teach us,

19 Some may be here to learn,

20 And some may be waiting for other days,

21 Before sharing the light they see.

CHAPTER 24

The ways of the Chosen were varied,

2 But linked by their gift for creating,

3 ᶠNew worlds from the deeps of their minds.

4 You can list the ᵍcrimes of the Spics,

5 And berate the ʰFrogs and the ⁱBrits,

6 And it's lots of fun to revile the ʲKrauts,

7 And to scowl and jeer at the ᵏYanks,

8 But they made the ˡworld you live in,

9 And if you call them scum,

10 Then maybe your nerve will last long enough,

11 To replace their vast achievements,

12 With ᵐbetter ones of your own.

a. Oth.5.2-4
b. Oth.3.2-3
c. Oth.8.2-15
d. Oth.8.18
e. Cen.16.1-4
f. Exp.9.8-20
g. Exp.11.18-27
h. Frog.39.11-15
i. Brit.2.1-3
j. Barb.5.7-12
k. Yks.145.1-28
l. Adam.1.1-4
*   Chuk.1.1-2*
*   Carl.1.1-5*
*   Zig.1.1-4*
*   Dav.1.1-4*
*   Al.1.1-4*
*   Paul.1.1-3*
*   F&J.1.1-5*
*   Ed.1.1-6*
m. They.8.14
n. Spic.8.5-8
*   & 10.1*
o. Spic.3.4-5
p. Spic.10.7
q. Spic.8.2-4
r. Spic.12.1-2
s. Spic.7.10-15
*   & 9.1-6*
t. Spic.5.1-11

CHAPTER 25

The way of the Spics was an altar,

2 Drenched in the ⁿblood of their faith,

3 Which they gave up to God with a passion,

4 And a pride that would pay any price.

5 The life of the altar is hard and of stone,

6 And it ends with a solid-ᵒgold blade,

7 Which severs the heart still beating,

8 And turns flesh into ᵖgod for an inkling,

9 If fear has not broken the spell.

10 So they rode out in search of a treasure,

11 That was ᑫworth the blessing and pain,

12 Masters of fear and its bite on the soul,

13 But afraid of the one fear that's cold at the heart,

14 The fear of the Lord God's disdain.

15 For if He ʳspurned their altar,

16 And the heart they proffered him,

17 Then how could they be braver,

18 Who already sanctified themselves with pain?

19 And maybe they dreamt of mercy,

20 And a healing god of tears,

21 But this soldier of Christ lived a crucible,

22 And if he lived it far too hard,

23 Slaying one ˢworld for each altar he built,

24 He would ᵗdie like a dog before kneeling,

25 And begging for love like
some coward.
26 But who can speak for the
God of love,
27 And the ways he raises his
young?
28 Is one's faith all for nought if
it asks too much?
29 Or is valor one jewel in
God's holy crown?
30 And many may answer the
answer is no,
31 [a]No love that murders is real
love at all,
32 But if that is your reason for
scorning the Spics,
33 Ask yourself what you've
done for the real love you hoard,
34 That's as hard as what Spics
did for God.

CHAPTER 26

The way of the Frogs is a
painting,
2 A vision of color and dash,
3 Obsessed with an ideal of
[b]beauty,
4 Transcending mere decorative
trash.
5 Their canvas was open to all
shades of life,
6 Since a [c]master must quicken
the heart,
7 So they dipped their brushes
in [d]myriad pots,
8 And astonished the world with
their art.
9 They captured romance as it
breathed through the soul,
10 [e]Whether it ended in love or
disaster;
11 [f]They anointed the body with
wisdom and charm,
12 And composed lovely scenes
of the [g]senses at play;
13 [h]They painted lithe nymphs
on pedestals,
14 As well as in the [i]hay,
15 Then mixed some wit with
morality,
16 And in a purely Gallic way,
17 Sketched a [j]lifted eyebrow,
18 And the [k]logic of dismay.
19 Yes, they knew how to paint,
20 All the colors of [l]war,
21 And of [m]peasants in chains,
22 And [n]vengeance galore.
23 They tried out the [o]blinding
light of ambition,
24 [p]The darkness of wanting
endlessly more,
25 [q]The yellow terror of tropical
fevers,
26 [r]The flickering red of a saint
on fire,
27 [s]The blue and the white of
dead armies in snow,
28 [t]The blackness of hearts
when they yield to despair.
29 Now, a Frog with a brush
may cause you to chuckle,
30 And reel off old jokes about
[u]Maginot lines,
31 But their art is a model of
human resilience,
32 And the glory of seeking romance at all times.

CHAPTER 27

The way of the Brits is a
poem,
2 Heroic and epic in scope,
3 [v]Feet marching in time to a
meter,
4 That asked [w]more than most
gods can give.
5 [x]Their muse made them
stronger, and braver, and harder,
6 Than men who know nothing
of rhyme:
7 Each stanza was a [y]challenge,
8 Matched against the [z]test of
time.
9 Each [aa]generation took its
turn,
10 And wrote its lines and died:

a. Lies.9.10
b. Frog.22.1-4
c. Frog.8.2
d. Frog.5.3-8
e. Frog.29.4-14
f. Frog.9.2-7
g. Frog.31.1-3
h. Frog.31.4-6
i. Frog.8.6-9
j. Frog.28.1
k. Frog.27.1-5
l. Frog.6.2-3 & 15.1-3
m. Frog.13.1-7
n. Frog.13.8-11
o. Frog.14.9-14
p. Frog.15.4-12
q. Exp.15.10-11 & 15.5-6
r. Frog.7.1-9
s. Frog.17.1-12
t. Frog.35.1-6
u. Frog.37.1-8
v. Brit.22.18-20
w. Brit.19.38-48
x. Brit.2.1-3
y. Brit.19.4-8
z. Bks.3.1-9
aa. Brit.19.9-15

11 For the poem was their ^ahonor,

12 And they believed the ^btale it told,

13 And more than this, they knew the work,

14 Was made of every ^cword,

15 And if one ^dforgot the scheme of verse,

16 Or lost its ^ediscipline,

17 The ^fempire spun upon their page,

18 Would slacken and ^gunwind.

19 And, yes, they grew tired when centuries of work,

20 ^hDrained their pen of sweat and blood;

21 ⁱWhen the worlds they had exalted in their verse,

22 Started writing ^jfevered lyrics of their own.

23 Still, they might have lingered,

24 Had they not had a son and heir,

25 ^kThe black sheep of a thousand rhymes,

26 But ^lgrown at last, and eager for a dare.

27 O you can point with mirth at the Brits today,

28 And tick off all your clichés of ^mdecay,

29 But white men or not,

30 ⁿThey spread law through the world,

31 And gave ^ous the gift of a dream,

32 With ^pfreedom concealed in their lockstep refrains,

33 Of dignity, duty, and brains.

34 ^qThey made freedom scan,

35 Then they passed on the ^rpen,

36 To their son of two hundred years:

37 Now, will you last as long,

38 And give so much to a son?

---

a. *Psom.25.1-13*

b. *Brit.42.18-23*

c. *Brit.30.2-15*

d. *Psom.75.1-10*

e. *Psom.15.1-13*

f. *Brit.26.9-20*

g. *Psom.26.1-6*

h. *Brit.48.4-7*

i. *Psom.10.1-11*

j. *Bks.10.27-29*

k. *Psom.57.1-6*

l. *30.15-26*

m. *12.13-15*

n. *Brit.26.22-26*

o. *Adam.15.1-16*

p. *Yks.8.1-17*

q. *Brit.27.11-13*

r. *Yks.9.1-4*

s. *Krt.22.1-11*

t. *Krt.16.7-9*

u. *Krt.30.3-4*

v. *Yks.125.34*

w. *Krt.9.8*

x. *Brit.48.10-13*

y. *Krt.9.1-6*

z. *Krt.32.5-16*

aa. *Krt.38.1-6*

bb. *Lies.9.10*

cc. *Krt.31.6-13 Yks.137.1-5 Boul.5.1-15*

dd. *Krt.21.1-3*

ee. *Krt.7.1-18*

ff. *Boul.25.24-43*

---

39 Or will you scribble an easy pamphlet,

40 In the safety of your home,

41 And ship it off to Britain,

42 To slip inside their dusty tome?

CHAPTER 28

The way of the Krauts was an opera,

2 ^sBig and loud and long.

3 The voices were ^tgigantic,

4 ^uThe words were steeped in magic,

5 Orchestrated by ^vmachine.

6 They ^wdared to think one opera,

7 Could girdle the globe and bring,

8 ^xOne reason and one answer,

9 To a world that needs to sing.

10 They deified their ^ytenors,

11 Made ^zmillions play their score,

12 And at the final curtain call,

13 ^{aa}They soaked the earth in gore.

14 But there's nothing wrong with opera,

15 If it doesn't go insane,

16 And maybe object lessons are worth their price in pain:

17 For ^{bb}limits lose their meaning,

18 When all the world forgets,

19 That ^{cc}timid sins and whining,

20 Get gross and terrifying,

21 When you mix them with ^{dd}ambition,

22 And play them to a nation,

23 That has no fear of ^{ee}reaching,

24 ^{ff}Where others merely yearn in secret shame.

25 And if the Krautish opera makes you mourn for all Mankind,

26 Then maybe you weren't listening,
27 When the world came on the scene,
28 [a]And descended from the ceiling,
29 To stop one hand from taking,
30 What belongs to [b]everyone.
31 For does it make us evil,
32 That some put others to the test,
33 And force the [c]goodness in us,
34 To prove why it is best?
35 But if your goodness quails in fear,
36 And doubts its strength and own resolve,
37 Then you'd better talk to a [d]mirror,
38 Before you give up on the world.

CHAPTER 29
Act I

The way of the Yanks was pure Hollywood,
2 A factory of dreams.
3 The studio was vast and rich,
4 Its people filled with ardor,
5 And wishes they knew could come true.
6 They produced for the millions,
7 Each dream to its kind,
8 As befits the American Way:
9 Some were mega-blockbusters,
10 With galaxies of stars,
11 Bright Technicolor locations,
12 And writers by the score;
13 Others were small and disarming,
14 Or black and white and intense;
15 Yet more were funny and charming,

a. *Gnt.15.7-9*
b. *Wil.12.24*
c. *Yks.139.4-7*
d. *You.8.9-12*

16 Or thoughtful tries at making sense;
17 Some were playful fantasies,
18 A romp in the heart of a child,
19 While more than a few were tragedies,
20 With choruses that moaned and wailed.
21 Not all of them succeeded,
22 For the critics had their day,
23 And sometimes theaters hawked their seats,
24 To throngs who stayed away.
25 But the factory kept rolling,
26 And learned the most painful part,
27 That one man's vision won't suffice,
28 When you're making collaborative art.
29 There was one immense production,
30 A romance of civil war,
31 Which nearly broke the spirit,
32 Of those who ran the store:
33 The stars were frightened,
34 By a cast of thousands;
35 The producer fired directors,
36 By the dozens;
37 The writers quarreled,
38 And some of them quit;
39 And the crews were ensnarled,
40 In nearsighted snits.
41 But when it came time to shoot the nag,
42 And put an end to it,
43 They swallowed down their ire,
44 And clamped down on the bit,
45 Because they *had* to make a movie:
46 And that's all there was to it.
47 So they came together,
48 And made a giant hit,

49 Out of cannons and canons,
50 And freedom and grit.

CHAPTER 30
Act II

The Way of the Yanks was union,
2 Before union meant a faction,
3 And they kept on making movies,
4 And trying hard to do it right.
5 They fought a lot,
6 And did things wrong,
7 And left a million miles of footage on the floor.
8 But they built on their genius for compromise,
9 And settled their differences time after time,
10 So that dreams could keep moving on out the door.
11 Their pictures made money,
12 And fattened their wallets,
13 Till their rivals felt envy,
14 And laughed at their zest.
15 But the Yanks loved success,
16 And gloried in winning,
17 Sure of their talent,
18 For fairy tale endings.
19 They knew the hero gets the girl,
20 And the bad guy always gets shot,
21 And no sin is ever left un-avenged,
22 If the writer's on top of the plot.
23 That's why they finally took on the challenge,
24 Of showing the world the American Way,
25 In a foreign film,
26 Called world war one,
27 And a sequel called world war too.
28 But this time they ended with special effects,

29 That almost devoured the screen,
30 And frightened the audience half to death,
31 Not to mention the studio team.
32 For they started to wonder,
33 And doubt, and fear,
34 The rule they had taken for granted:
35 That happy endings would always be there,
36 If you did the work for what you wanted.

CHAPTER 31
Act III

And now the studio is torn by strife,
2 And the dreams aren't coming so fast anymore,
3 Because of a snafu called real life,
4 And a runaway passion for evening the score:
5 The stars are locked in their dressing rooms,
6 And haven't been rehearsing;
7 The director's refusing to talk to the cast,
8 For fear they might ask for his vision;
9 And lighting's threatening to go out on strike,
10 Unless someone replaces the camera crew;
11 The propman is drunk and out of nails,
12 So the sets are fastened with glue;
13 A cast of thousands is counting its lines,
14 And demanding more scenery to chew;
15 The writer's obsessed with reworking key scenes,
16 Including tomorrow's, and finished ones too;

17 The backers aren't coughing up any more cash,
18 And they've told their lawyers to sue;
19 The stuntmen are saying the catwalk's too high,
20 And won't respond to their cue;
21 The ratings office is screaming for blood,
22 Because the script is so shockingly blue;
23 The mayor's attempting to ban camera cranes,
24 Which are spoiling the tourists' view;
25 Thanks to budget woes and myopic eyes,
26 The producer hasn't a clue,
27 And like the others he's forgotten,
28 That there's work to do,
29 Or else the dreams won't make it,
30 Old or new.

CHAPTER 32
Act IV

Some years ago,
2 Some youngsters thought they'd take a hand,
3 And try a new production.
4 They talked a lot about making a stand,
5 And setting things right again.
6 The time was ripe:
7 The plots were old,
8 The script was tripe,
9 The stars were past their prime,
10 And no one had registered a meaningful gripe,
11 In almost fifty years.
12 But if you're planning revolution,
13 You've got to give it some thought,

14 And know what it is you intend to build,
15 After you've bulldozed the lot.
16 But thinking was too hard to do,
17 And learning was out of the question.
18 So they knocked it all down in a fit of pique,
19 And then quit just as if they'd lost.
20 But maybe they'd won what they really sought,
21 A note from their mother that said they had tried,
22 And were free for the rest of their lives,
23 To let it all slide,
24 And take what they wanted,
25 Now that the builders had died.
26 So at present they live off the fat of a land,
27 Which fades more than a little each day,
28 Sapped by the indolent, selfish hordes,
29 Who plighted their troth to the Boomer Way.

CHAPTER 33
Act V

This Boomer Way now speaks for itself,
2 And it is no way at all.
3 We've studied it for quite a while,
4 And thought about it a lot,
5 But no matter how we frame it,
6 We don't believe it makes any sense,
7 At all.
8 We don't believe it makes any sense,
9 To sleep through life,

10 And pretend you're outwitting death.

11 We don't believe it makes any sense,

12 To hide from all your nightmares,

13 And just hope against hope that they don't come true,

14 While the dreams you could dream are fading away.

15 We don't believe it makes any sense,

16 To lie in the dark and pretend it's a joke,

17 Because you didn't make the rules.

18 We don't believe it makes any sense,

19 To libel our race anymore:

20 We sought for power and we got it;

21 Now let's learn how to use it and live.

22 And we don't believe it makes any sense,

23 To scavenge the past for reasons to quit:

24 We made our own bed with capable hands;

25 Now let's get out from under the covers,

26 And go forth with pride and courage,

27 To meet a brand-new day.

CHAPTER 34

The way of the punks is coming next,

2 ªAnd it's not entirely new,

3 But it starts with learning as much as we can,

4 About what has happened before.

5 We want to be more, not less than the dead,

6 But we're not afraid to join them,

a. 14.1-2
b. Forg.14.6-10
c. Grk.8.1-3
   Cen.23.7-11
d. Psay.5A.43
e. Rat.5.2-16
f. Bel.7.13-15
g. Cen.22.16-19
h. Yks.84.4
i. F&J.5.1-5
   Bds.2.8
   Cen.16.1
j. Bel.10.2-5
k. Frog.27.5
l. Us.2-18

7 Because we believe there's more to life,

8 ᵇThan merely not dying for years and years.

9 We've learned to believe in lots of things,

10 Including some things you scorn.

11 We believe in being ᶜheroes,

12 Or trying, anyway,

13 ᵈFor the more we give, the more we get,

14 And the prize is ᵉself-respect,

15 Which we now know we need,

16 For without it we're ᶠnothing at all.

17 We believe in the ᵍquest,

18 For new answers and ways,

19 ʰNo matter how much they cost,

20 Because we're alive while we're seeking,

21 And ⁱdead when we settle for less.

22 We believe in a spirit who wishes us well,

23 And wants us to learn how to reach him,

24 Because he has answers, new ways and new meanings,

25 We couldn't have dreamed of before.

CHAPTER 35

The way of the punks is the way of the earth,

2 And it has its rocks and chasms.

3 Sometimes we feel ʲsmall and not up to the task,

4 ᵏBut we all have to start where we are,

5 And do what we can in the here and now,

6 ˡTrusting that others are trying,

7 And knowing that they need us too.

8 Sometimes we fear we'll be dead and gone,

9 By the time our ªnumbers will count,

10 But the ᵇfuture is real and coming,

11 And the debt that we owe is inspiring,

12 For the privilege of being is work.

CHAPTER 36

The way of the punks is the way of the air,

2 And it has its ups and downs.

3 Sometimes we know we're flying,

4 And we feel the ᶜwords at our back,

5 But there are also times of ᵈfalling,

6 And wings that can't beat back,

7 The ᵉgusts of death and dying,

8 That turn the skies so black.

9 But flying is ᶠbelieving,

10 And we're getting good at that,

11 For falling is a waste of wings,

12 And crashing breaks your back.

CHAPTER 37

The way of the punks is the way of fire,

2 And it can make ᵍashes as well as light.

3 Sometimes we shrink from ʰscorching heat,

4 And yearn to shade our eyes,

5 ⁱAgainst the shocking images we see.

6 But fire is so entrancing,

7 ʲAnd flames are lovely dancing,

a. Psp.3.16-17
b. Cen.20.28-31
c. Cen.21.16
d. Grk.9.4-7
e. Bel.17.4-10
f. Cen.24.8-11
g. Bel.11.8-13
h. Ang.1.5-10
i. You.11.1-3
j. 22.13-18
k. Psom.23.13-16
l. Ang.11.9-18
m. Grk.7.1-3
n. Ang.14.1
o. Rat.23.12
p. Brd.32.1-7

8 To the music of the light.

9 We cannot leave the center,

10 From which such radiance comes;

11 We cannot bear to seek the cold,

12 That hides in darkness,

13 Deep in sleep.

CHAPTER 38

The way of the punks is the way of water,

2 Which drowns as well as saves,

3 And we have felt the ᵏindifferent waves,

4 That sometimes choke our voices,

5 Before we learn to sing.

6 But we've also felt joy,

7 In the thundering spray,

8 Of the breakers that crash on the shore,

9 And the ˡpride of our sail,

10 Abreast of a swell,

11 While the winds roar and wail,

12 And the kestrels cry for the storm.

CHAPTER 39

The way of the punks is the way of dreams,

2 And of worlds beyond our senses,

3 ᵐOf ghosts, and greatwings, and glimmering things,

4 That seize and possess the mind.

5 From our dreams we conjured the ⁿShuteye Train,

6 And the °tracks we'll follow to fight,

7 The ᵖnightmare that seeks to swallow,

8 Our lives and all of our light.

45

9 From our dreams we will con-
jure the ᵃSon of the Raptor,
10 Who will take us to visit his
realm,
11 And return us with power to
set things aright,
12 In the ᵇhome we've chosen
to love.
13 He'll teach us to build,
14 Or to weather his wrath,
15 Which may turn out to be the
price of new life,
16 As the Bubonites once
found;
17 But whatever it costs,
18 We'll find ᶜDoctor Dream,
19 And come back with the wisdom we need.

a. *39.18*
b. *Ang.4.7*
c. *39.9*
d. *Weap.1.9*
e. *Apes.1.1*
f. *Vin.64.9-11*
g. *Yks.153.14*

CHAPTER 40

Now, as we set out,
2 We're loaded for bear,
3 And ᵈwe're armed to the teeth
for a fight,
4 Because we suspect that others will try,
5 To keep us from getting our
light.
6 And so our supplies include
two ᵉpointed sticks,
7 Lashed together in shape of a
cross:
8 And if one ᶠHarry should
stand in our way,
9 We'll ᵍnail him,
10 And leave him for lost.